GETTYSBURG JULY 1

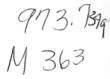

GETTYSBURG JULY 1

Completely Revised Edition

David G. Martin

COMBINED BOOKS
Pennsylvania

PUBLISHER'S NOTE

Combined Books, Inc., is dedicated to publishing books of distinction in history and military history. We are proud of the quality of writing and the quantity of information found in our books. Our books are manufactured with style and durability and are printed on acid-free paper. We like to think of our books as soldiers: not infantry grunts, but well dressed and well equipped avant garde. Our logo reflects our commitment to the modern and yet historic art of bookmaking.

We call ourselves Combined Books because we view the publishing enterprise as a "combined" effort of authors, publishers and readers. And we promise to bridge the gap between us—a gap which is all too seldom closed in contemporary publishing.

We would like to hear from our readers and invite you to write to us at our offices in Pennsylvania with your reactions, queries, comments, even complaints. All of our correspondence will be answered directly by a member of the Editorial Board or by the author.

We encourage all of our readers to purchase our books from their local booksellers, and we hope that you let us know of booksellers in your area that might be interested in carrying our books. If you are unable to find a book in your area, please write us.

First published in the USA in 1995 by Combined Books and completely revised in 1996. Combined Books publications are distributed internationally by Greenhill Books, Lionel Leventhal Ltd., 1 Russel Gardens, London NW11 9NN

Maps by Paul Dangel
Printed in the United States of America.

Dedicated to my mother and father, who fostered and nourished my passion for history from the beginning.

Acknowledgments

I wish to thank Robert Pigeon of Combined Books for encouraging me to write this book, which I have been longing to do all my adult life. Thanks are also due to my editor, Ken Gallagher, for his patience and skill, and to cartographer Paul Dangel for his excellently done maps.

Much of this work's detail and accuracy is due to the research help and editorial criticism of my friend Jim Clouse of Gettysburg. I am also grateful to Edward G. Longacre for research help and advice on the role of Buford's cavalry in the battle, and to Benedict Maryniak and Tim Smith for similar help at interpreting the fighting on Oak Hill.

Additional research assistance was provided by Joseph G. Bilby, Scott Hartwig, Robert K. Krick, and Seward Osborne. I am also grateful to the helpful staffs at the Princeton University library and the War Library and Museum in Philadelphia.

Thanks are owed to the following for permission to quote from their copyrighted material:

New Hampshire Historical Society (John B. Bachelder papers).

Alderman Library, University of Virginia (John W. Daniel Papers #158, Manuscripts Division, Special Collections Department, University of Virginia Library).

Yale University Library (William H. Warren Diaries, Civil War Manuscripts Collection, Manuscripts and Archives, Yale University Library).

Contents

I.	The Confederate Tide Crests	11
II.	The Army of the Potomac Moves North	33
III.	Opening Shots	59
IV.	Reynolds to the Rescue	89
V.	Noontime Lull	167
VI.	The Fight on Oak Hill	203
VII.	Collapse of the XI Corps	257
VIII.	Climax on Seminary Ridge	337
IX.	Cemetery Hill	467
	Appendices	570
	Notes	595
	Abbreviations	699
	Bibliography	700
	Index	719

Maps

1. Evening, 30 June 1863   30

2. Night, 30 June, Troop Positions   44

3. 0900, 1 July 1863   78

4. 1015, 1 July 1863   103

5. The Railroad Cut, 1100, 1 July 1863   124

6. Iron Brigade's Attack, 1045, 1 July 1863   150

7. 1230, 1 July 1863   179

8. Iverson's Attack, 1430   225

9. Arrival of XI Corps, 1300, 1 July 1863   266

10. Early's Attack, 1515, 1 July 1863   285

11. Early's Attack, 1530, 1 July 1863   300

12. Coster's Last Stand, 1545, 1 July 1863   312

13. 1430, 1 July 1863   348

14. Heth's Attack, 1445, 1 July 1863   355

15. Ramseur's Attack, 1545, 1 July 1863   388

16. 1600, 1 July 1863   400

17. Pender's Attack, 1600, 1 July 1863   421

18. Town of Gettysburg   455

19. Detail of Union Positions, 1800, 1 July 1863   494

20. 1800, 1 July, Troop Positions   537

Preface

Gettysburg is without doubt the most studied battle in the history of America. Even before the fighting was over it was viewed as the most decisive battle of the Civil War, and a legion of writers have since recorded their narratives and offered their interpretations of the battle. All too often, however, historians have downplayed the fighting on the first day in favor of the more familiar scenes at Devil's Den, the Peach Orchard, the Wheatfield, Little Round Top, Cemetery Hill, Culp's Hill, and Pickett's Charge. The fierce fighting on the first day at McPherson's Woods, the Railroad Cut, Oak Ridge, and Barlow's Knoll are mentioned only in passing and as a precursor to the greater conflict that followed.

The first day at Gettysburg was more than a simple prelude to the second and third days. The day's conflict involved one-quarter of Meade's army (about 22,000 men) and over one-third of Lee's army (about 27,000 men) and the proportions would be even higher if they included troops that arrived late in the day but were not actually engaged (Anderson's and Johnson's Confederate divisions and the Union III and XII Corps). By the number of troops engaged, the first day at Gettysburg alone ranks as the 23rd biggest battle of the war, according to the numbers compiled by statistician Thomas L. Livermore.

The first day at Gettysburg, then, is a major battle deserving a detailed history on its own merit. The bloody encounter of the first day was a classic battle engagement closely contested from dawn until sunset. It was filled with incidents of heroism and error, with heroes and scapegoats, every bit as much as the more famous episodes on the second and third days of the battle. The stand of the 16th Maine on Oak Ridge was as heroic as the more famous stand of the 20th Maine on Little Round Top, and Pender's charge against the I Corps line on Seminary Ridge was as brave and bloody as Pickett's Charge (and more successful). The conflict between the 26th North Carolina and the 24th Michigan of the Iron Brigade in Herbst Woods was perhaps the single bloodiest and most stubborn regimental duel of the war, and John Burns was as much a local hero as Jennie Wade.

All these stories and more are told in this narrative. *Gettysburg July 1* is based almost entirely on primary sources and is by far the most detailed account of the first day's battle yet written. Many histories of the battle, especially more recent studies, have relied on the same limited set of sources and so tell the same story with the same conclusions. The late Edwin B. Coddington did a great service to history by opening up the Bachelder papers and their exciting comments by the battle's participants. The present study goes even deeper to employ still more primary sources in the retelling of the first day's fight, some of them only seldom, or even never, cited before. In addition, this study makes use of conclusions reached by a number of very good recent brigade and regimental level monographs, in order to produce a much more complete view of the entire day's action than was ever possible before. For instance, Buford's five-hour-long fight against Heth's infantry at the beginning of the day is recounted here with a thoroughness not approached elsewhere.

The first day's fighting features more than its share of controversies; all of which are fully investigated here. Who fired the first shot on each side? Who were the first casualties on each side? Who killed General Reynolds? Who collapsed first, the Union I or XI Corps? And why didn't the Confederates make one last sweeping attack against Cemetery Hill at the end of the day? The book also examines why it was that additional troops on each side near the battlefield did not join in the fighting; each army could have doubled its strength on the field had all its troops in the battlefield area been committed to action.

I have taken great pains to explain how and why the battle came to be fought at Gettysburg. Some historians believe that the battle was certain to occur there, while others claim that it happened at Gettysburg entirely by accident. It is the conclusion of this study that the decisive battle between Lee and Meade could have occurred anywhere between York, Pa., and Frederick, Md. That it began near the town of Gettysburg on 1 July was the result of a series of specific decisions made by Lee and Meade on 28 and 29 June and by Hill and Heth on the one side and Buford and Reynolds on the other side on 30 June and early on 1 July. These are explained clearly in the text as a prelude to the fighting. Likewise, the results of the first day's battle and the dispositions made then dictated the course of the rest of the battle on 2 and 3 July.

CHAPTER I

The Confederate Tide Crests

On 28 June 1863 Confederate General Robert E. Lee's summer offensive into Pennsylvania was in its twenty-sixth day and had met nothing but success since the army had started moving north from its camps at Fredericksburg on 3 June. Lieutenant General Richard Ewell's Second Corps had smashed Brigadier General Robert H. Milroy's Union command at Winchester on 14-15 June, and now stood poised to move against the invasion's next goal, the Pennsylvania state capital at Harrisburg.[1] Rodes' division, supported by Johnson's, was at Carlisle, 16 miles west of Harrisburg, and Early's division was occupying the rich town of York, 24 miles southeast of Carlisle. Ewell's cavalry under Brigadier General Albert Jenkins was already probing Harrisburg's western defenses, and Brigadier General John B. Gordon's brigade of Major General Jubal A. Early's division was attempting to seize the Susquehanna River Bridge at Wrightsville.[2]

Most of the remainder of Lee's army was encamped at or near Chambersburg, about 22 miles southwest of Carlisle, guarding the army's supply lines to Virginia. A primary purpose of Lee's invasion of Pennsylvania was to give some respite to the ravaged fields of northern and eastern Virginia, and in the process live off the fatted farms of Pennsylvania. The Confederates found the Cumberland Valley and adjacent plains of south central Pennsylvania to be filled with animals, foodstuffs and supplies beyond their imagination. York alone provided Early with 1200 pairs of shoes, 1000 pairs of socks, 1000 hats, and a levy of $28,000 in exchange for a promise that the town would not be looted.[3] Food and supplies were bought or appropriated in every town and county through which the army passed. Ewell noted that, "At Carlisle, Chambersburg, and Shippensburg requisitions were made for supplies, and the shops were searched, many valuable stores being secured. At Chambersburg, a train was loaded with ordnance and medical stores and sent back. Near 3000 head of cattle were collected and sent back by my corps, and my chief commissary of substance, Major Hawks, notified Colonel Cole of the location of 5000 barrels of flour along the route traveled by my command."[4]

Early Passes Through Gettysburg
26 June

It is interesting to note that part of Early's command passed through Gettysburg on 26 June while on the way to York, and found only a limited amount of civilian supplies there. Early had been encamped at Greenwood for two days (the 24th and 25th) when he received instructions from Ewell "to cross the South Mountain to Gettysburg, and then proceed to York, and cut the Northern Central Railroad, running from Baltimore to Harrisburg, and also destroy the bridge across the Susquehanna at Wrightsville and Columbia, on the branch road from York toward Philadelphia, if I could, and rejoin him at Carlisle by the way of Dillsburg."[5]

Before leaving for Gettysburg on the morning of 26 June, Early sent most of his trains to Chambersburg. The only wagons he allowed to accompany his columns were his ambulances, four medical wagons (one for each brigade), the ordnance wagons, one cook wagon per regiment, and "fifteen extra wagons to gather supplies with."[6] The expedition had marched only two miles when it reached Thaddeus Stevens' ironworking complex at Caledonia Furnace, which Early ordered to be robbed and burned in flagrant violation of Lee's General Orders No 72 (issued on 21 June) concerning respect for private property.[7] By Stevens' own account, Early's men burned his iron furnace, sawmill, two forges, a rolling mill, and 8 tons of grass (fodder), and took with them $4000 worth of bar iron, 4000 pounds of bacon, $1000 worth of other grain, plus the remaining contents of his company store, as well as all his horses and mules and their equipage.[8]

Not long after leaving Stevens' permanently ruined ironworks, Early learned that there was a Union force of unknown size at or near Gettysburg. He at once determined to send part of his force directly towards Gettysburg on the Chambersburg Pike "to skirmish with and amuse the enemy in front" while he took most of his command along a by road that ran through Hilltown to Mummasburg, from where he would swoop down into the enemy's rear and "cut off the retreat of such force as might be at Gettysburg." He selected Gordon's brigade to take the Cashtown Road, preceded by the 35th Virginia Cavalry Battalion ("White's Comanches"), which had just been assigned to his command. Early took the remainder of his division, along withColonel W.H. French's 17th Virginia Cavalry.[9]

Gordon's column was at first hindered by a few trees felled across the road, and then made good time marching along the macadamized pike in spite of a drizzling rain that began to fall. By early afternoon the column, preceded by about 40 men of White's Comanches, was nearing the bridge over Marsh Creek, about three miles west of Gettysburg. Here it ran into vedettes of Captain Robert Bell's militia company of Adams County Cavalry, which were screening the nearby encampment of the 26th Pennsylvania Militia. The militia unit, which had just been mustered on 18 June, consisted of 743 totally green troops under the command of Colonel William C. Jennings. Jennings had been ordered to watch the road to Cashtown, and had just that morning moved his men out from Gettysburg to a camp east of Marsh Creek.

Jennings had no interest in holding his position once he learned the size of Gordon's column. He at once ordered his men to break camp as quickly as they could, and then led them off in haste to the northeast. Their retreat quickly degenerated into a confused rout with no semblance of order. Most of the militia fled to the northeast towards Bailey's Hill, located three miles due north of Gettysburg. Bell's cavalry company, plus a cavalry troop from Philadelphia and a company of the 26th that had been posted as a provost guard in Gettysburg, took a different route, and fled to the east to Hanover and then on to York and Wrightsville.[10]

White's cavalrymen were thoroughly amused at the scared militiamen who either fled precipitously or "threw down their bright, new muskets, and begged frantically for quarter." Nobody actually got hurt in the very brief engagement "if we except one fat militia captain, who, in his exertion to be first to surrender, managed to get himself run over by one of Company E's horses, and bruised somewhat."[11]

Most of the Comanches, who were known to be a somewhat disorderly lot, did not make it a priority to try to pursue and catch the fleeing militiamen, but instead stopped to plunder the enemy's hastily deserted camp or poke around in Gettysburg. By the time the Confederates could organize a pursuit, the enemy was "too far gone to overtake." According to Frank Myers, historian of the Comanches, the Union cavalry managed to get away largely because of the quality of their fine mounts.[12]

Even so, the onset of the Comanches made quite an impression on the citizens of the town.[13] Professor Jacobs of Gettysburg College observed that "The advance guard of the enemy, consisting of 180 to 200 cavalry, rode in Gettysburg yelling and shouting like so many savages from the wilds of the Rocky Mountains; firing their pistols, not caring whether they killed or maimed man, woman or child; and rushing from stable to stable in search of horses, the most of which, however, had fortunately a few hours before been sent forward to Hanover and York."[14] The wildness of the Comanches was exacerbated by the fact that a fair number obtained liquor from the citizens: "in a little while all who ever did indulge in the ardent were in a half-horse, half wild-cat condition, and each man imagined himself to be the greatest hero of the war; in fact, some were heard recounting to the horrified citizens of Gettysburg the immense execution they had done with the sabre in a hundred battles."[15]

General Early arrived at about 1700 and must have been both disgusted and amused at the inebriated confusion of the Comanches. He ordered the battalion "to go on up the railroad and catch some Yankees," but they had little success in doing so and returned "after a long chase" with no more "boys in blue."[16]

French's cavalry enjoyed somewhat more success in its pursuit of Jenning's disordered command. Early had sent French in pursuit of the enemy before he departed Mummasburg for Gettysburg, and later sent two of Hays' infantry regiments as reinforcements once he reached Gettysburg and saw the disarray of White's command. French captured a number of militiamen at first, but then met increasing difficulty as the enemy scattered through the fields in their flight. Towards evening he ran into a Yankee rearguard of sorts at the Witmer farm on Bailey's Hill. A half hearted volley by some nervous militia men persuaded French to form a skirmish line and send out scouts to determine the strength of the enemy line. His delay enabled most of Jennings' force to escape, and French decided to turn back when it started to get dark.[17]

Altogether Early's troops managed to capture only about 175 of the routed Yankee militiamen. Early did not think much of the militia's poor performance, and wrote in his memoirs, "it was well that the regiment took to its heels so quickly, or some of its members might have been hurt, and all would have been captured."[18] He formed them up in the Gettysburg town square and lectured them that they would have been safer to stay home with their mothers. They were then paroled and told to march north. The embarrassed troops reached Carlisle three days later, only to run into more Confederate troops, to be captured and paroled a second time.[19]

Early's main concern that evening, though, was not the capture of the additional running militia. Instead, he was much more concerned with securing supplies and provisions. Soon after he arrived in Gettysburg, he met with the leaders of the town council and made a hefty demand for $10,000 cash or the following list of supplies: 1000 pairs of shoes, 500 hats, 1200 pounds of salt, 7000 pounds of bacon, 10 barrels of onions, and 10 barrels of whiskey.[20] When he was told that the townsmen were poor and could furnish no supplies, Early "caused the town to be searched and succeeded in finding only a small quantity of articles suited for commissary supplies, which were taken."[21] Apparently the town's tradesmen had sent most of their money and best goods to Lancaster and other points east for safekeeping, and then did a good job of concealing what remained. Since it was by then late in the day, Early "had no opportunity of compelling a compliance with my demands in this town, or ascertaining its resources, which, I think, however, were very limited."[22]

The best find of the day was a train of 10 or 12 railroad cars containing 2000 rations stored up for Jennings' militiamen. Early eagerly confiscated the rations and then set the cars afire. The food was issued to Gordon's infantry, which encamped along the York Pike just east of Rock Creek, about a mile east of town. Some of Brigadier General Harry Hays' men, who encamped with French's cavalry along the Mummasburg Road a mile northwest of town (on Oak Hill near the present day Peace Memorial) received a more palatable issue—a generous portion of liquor apportioned from local taverns.[23]

The Confederates marched out early the next morning (27 June) and reached Hanover by noon. After driving a portion of the 20th Pennsylvania Militia away from Hanover Junction, they burned the station and headed towards York, where the division would be reunited on the 28th. York was clearly a more prosperous town than Gettysburg, and so received a much heavier requisition: 2000 pairs of shoes, 1000 hats, 1000 pairs of socks, $100,000 in cash, and three days' rations, comprising 165 barrels of flour, 28,000 pounds of bread, 1650 pounds of coffee, 300 gallons of molasses, 1200 pounds of salt, and 32,000 pounds of fresh beef or 21,000 pounds of pork. The townsmen were unable to collect all these supplies by the appointed hour of 1600, but did manage to get together enough to please Early—$28,000 cash, 1200 to 1500 pairs of shoes, and all the hats, socks and rations requested.[24]

It is difficult today to tally the large amount of supplies gathered in Pennsylvania by Early's command, which was just one prong of Lee's widespread invasion force. By 28 June the supply gathering phase of the invasion had been largely fulfilled, and most of the thousands of animals and thousands of pounds of foodstuffs and other goods were safely on their way back to Virginia via the Cumberland Valley and Chambersburg.

It was now time for Lee to begin concentrating on his next goal, the location and defeat of the Army of the Potomac. The occupation of York and Carlisle by Ewell's Corps had also been intended to throw a scare into Northern officials, particularly with the all too real threat of movement against Harrisburg, Baltimore, or even Philadelphia. Lee had been concerned that Hooker might move south against Richmond or west against the Confederate line of communications at Winchester, instead of marching north to cover Washington and meet the invading column. The widespread and well publicized plundering expedition by Ewell's men, which was safely conducted with only occasional token opposition from local militia, was actually a lure to entice Hooker to move north. Meanwhile Lee concentrated the bulk of his army at Chambersburg for two purposes. One was to guard the army's retreat route should Hooker attempt to break through the barrier of South Mountain, as McClellan did at the height of the Antietam campaign; this retreat route was also the line by which the captured supplies were being funneled back to Virginia. The second purpose was to be able to move eastward across the screen of South Mountain to confront or even pounce on Hooker's columns as they marched north to deal with Early.

Lee's thinking at the time can be understood from the following conversation he had in Chambersburg before 28 June with Major General Isaac Trimble. Trimble had just recovered from a severe wound he received at Second Bull Run, and was accompanying the army though he had not been reassigned to a command. Trimble relates that Lee spread out a map of Pennsylvania and asked him his opinion of the topography in front of the army. Lee then observed, "When they hear where we are, they will throw themselves by forced marches between us and Washington, Baltimore or Philadelphia but strung out on a long line, fatigued, hungry and somewhat demoralized by surprise and apprehension of danger. Our forces have marched at leisure, are well rested and in fine spirits, and can be concentrated on any point east of the South Mountain in forty-eight hours or less—my plan is to throw an overwhelming force against the enemy's advance, as soon as I learn the road they take, crush them, and following up then sweep beat them in detail, and in a few hours throw the whole army into disorder and probably create a panic by separated sweepers, and joining them to concentrate in large forces."[25]

It is also clear from other accounts that Lee had no intention of fighting a pitched battle as the aggressor. In his final campaign report, Lee observed that "It had not been intended to deliver a pitched battle so far from our base unless attacked."[26] Likewise he told Colonel William Allan in spring 1868, "he did not intend to give battle in Pennsylvania if he could avoid it."[27] Lee felt that the campaign would be a success even without a culminating battle, provided that he could transfer the summer's field of operations from Virginia, gather in a large amount of supplies from the countryside, and disturb the enemy's "plan for the summer campaign as to prevent its execution during the season of active operations."[28] But if the opportunity arose to overwhelm a portion of Hooker's army, he would take it. Colonel Allan in the 1868 conversation just cited, recalled that Lee "did not want to fight unless he could get a good opportunity to hit them in detail," and he expected "to move about, manoeuvre, and alarm the enemy, threaten their cities, hit any blows he might be able to deliver without using a general battle, and then, towards Fall, return and recover his base."[29]

Lieutenant General James Longstreet, Lee's senior corps commander, understood the military strategy of the campaign to be a bit different. At the beginning of June, before the campaign commenced, Longstreet and Lee had several long discussions about the prospects of the campaign. Longstreet strongly felt that "after piercing Pennsylvania and menacing Washington, we should choose a strong position, and force the Federals to attack us, observing that the popular clamor throughout the North would speedily force the Federal general to attempt to drive us out." In short, the campaign would be "one of offensive strategy, but defensive tactics."[30]

Longstreet explained his understanding of the campaign's strategy in more detail in a letter he wrote to his former division commander Lafayette McLaws in 1873: "under no circumstances were we to give battle, but exhaust our skill in trying to force the enemy to do so in a position of our own choosing... The First Corps to receive this attack and fight the battle. The other corps to fall upon and try to destroy the Army of the Potomac."[31] This last statement would seem to indicate that Longstreet's defensively based strategy was too focused. Most other accounts agree that Lee was not going to hesitate to attack a portion of the enemy's army if an advantageous situation arose; all agree that Lee had no intention of initiating a pitched offensive battle with the enemy.[32]

Lee's major difficulty by 28 June, then, was to determine the location of the Army of the Potomac, specifically whether it was moving en masse or in separate columns. As already discussed, one purpose of Ewell's foray towards the Susquehanna was to draw Hooker out of Virginia and into Pennsylvania. The absence of cavalry commander Jeb Stuart at this critical time was a particular concern to Lee. Everyone at headquarters noted his anxiety, and General Trimble remembered Lee saying, "I am hourly expecting to hear from Gen. Stuart and our cavalry, and to learn where the enemy crosses the Potomac and the route they take, in order to concentrate our forces and make their attack."[33]

It was now a critical point of the campaign. Lee felt that he could not remain where he was, since some of his troops had been at Chambersburg for four days and the supply of forage there would not last indefinitely, and he did not feel he had enough troops to guard his line of communications if he advanced the main body of his army any farther into Pennsylvania. On 25 June he had written President Jefferson Davis that he would have to abandon his communications,[34] and late on the 28th he decided to make that critical step. In order to force the enemy to come to face him in southern Pennsylvania, Lee decided to shift all of his troops east of the mountains. Major Charles Marshall, one of Lee's staff officers, recalled, "On the night of the 28th of June I was directed be General Lee to order General Ewell to move directly upon Harrisburg, and to inform him that General Longstreet would move the next morning (the 29th) to his support. General A. P. Hill was directed to move eastward to the Susquehanna, and, crossing the river below Harrisburg, seize the railroad between Harrisburg and Philadelphia, it being supposed that all reinforcements that might be coming from the North would be diverted to the defence of that city, and that there would be such alarm created by these movements that the federal Government would be obliged to withdraw its army from Virginia and abandon any plan that it might have for an attack upon Richmond."[35]

Marshall had just dispatched these orders at about 2200 when the course of the campaign took another critical turn. A "dirt stained, travel worn, and very much broken down" civilian had been taken in by Longstreet's pickets and brought to the First Corps Headquarters. Colonel Moxley Sorrell, Longstreet's Chief of Staff, learned that the mysterious stranger was actually Longstreet's favorite scout, Harrison, whom the General had sent out to watch the enemy before the army left Culpeper. Sorrell at once woke Longstreet, who was surprised to learn "that the enemy had crossed the Potomac, marched northwest, and that the head of his column was at Frederick City, on our right."[36]

Longstreet immediately forwarded Harrison to Lee, whose headquarters were close by. Major Marshall was just returning to his tent when he was sent for by his commander. "I found him sitting in his tent with a man in citizen's dress, whom I did not know to be a soldier, but who, General Lee informed me, was a scout of General Longstreet's, who had just been brought to him. He told me that this scout had left Frederickstown that morning, and had brought information that the Federal army had crossed the Potomac, and that its advance had reached Frederickstown and was moving thence westward towards the mountains."[37]

J.E.B. Stuart's Mission

Harrison's report, which Lee had no choice but to give serious credence to, was especially disconcerting because Lee had been waiting for days to hear news of the Federal advance from Stuart. In his official campaign report, Lee commented, "It was expected that as soon as the Federal army should cross the Potomac, General Stuart should give notice of its movements, and nothing having been heard from him since our entrance into Maryland, it was inferred that the enemy had not yet left Virginia."[38] Oddly enough, it cannot be shown from surviving evidence that Lee actually specifically ordered Stuart to let him know when the enemy began crossing the Potomac. Lee's orders of 22 or 23 June do not give this command in so many words;[39] Lee's assumption that Stuart would report such a key happening was indeed a dangerous one, as events showed.

Lee's handling of Stuart's cavalry during the entire campaign has, of course, long been a matter of controversy. Lee wanted Stuart to guard Ewell's right (southern and eastern) flank in Pennsylvania, but gave him two options as to his route. If the enemy were not moving, Lee thought it would be best for Stuart to cross the Potomac at Shepherdstown and proceed to Frederick. If the enemy were moving north and Stuart thought he were able, he had permission to "pass around their army without hindrance, doing them all the damage you can, and cross the river east of the mountains," in essence riding around the Federal army on his way to join Ewell; this was to be attempted only if two brigades were left behind to guard the mountain passes and Lee's supply line.[40]

Stuart chose the second option, and departed at 0100 on 25 June for the rear of the Union army. He apparently did not let Lee know of his intended route, and would be out of communication with his commander for the most critical week of the campaign.[41] He took with him his three best brigades (Hampton's, Fitzhugh Lee's, and Chambliss') and left two brigades of lesser quality (Robertson's and Jones') to guard the mountain passes.

Stuart has been roundly criticized through the years for misinterpreting Lee's orders as to the route he should take. Any fault in this case more properly lies with Lee, who issued Stuart unclear orders with an option as to which general route he might take to join Ewell. Nor was Lee left entirely bereft of cavalry for scouting purposes, as he laments several times in his reports.[42] He allowed Robertson and Jones to remain inactive at Ashby's and Snicker's Gaps in Virginia's Blue Ridge Mountains, and also had available Jenkins' brigade, White's Comanches (35th Virginia Battalion), and the 1st Maryland Cavalry, all of which he assigned to Ewell's command. As events would soon clearly show, it would have been wiser for him to have kept at least one cavalry regiment with him at headquarters for his own security and reconnaissance use.[43]

Nor should Lee have been as surprised as he claimed to be to learn that Hooker had crossed the Potomac. He knew before he crossed the Potomac himself that Hooker had been shifting his troops towards Leesburg, and on the 23rd he found out that the enemy was preparing a pontoon bridge at Edwards' Ferry.[44] It was not at all likely that Hooker was going to sit still on the south side of the river. At the least, he might be expected to move north to cover Washington, as McClellan had done during the early stages of the Antietam campaign. Lee certainly was right to be wary of a possible Union move against the mountain passes, or even against Richmond. All he had to do was to order Robertson or Jones to be a little more aggressive on their front to determine Hooker's whereabouts.

Lee Recalls Ewell

Lee's initial reaction to the news that Hooker was at Frederick was to recall Ewell's corps. As Longstreet wryly noted in his memoirs, "the march of Ewell's east wing had failed of execution and of the effect designed"[45] by not drawing Hooker farther to the northeast, and Lee wanted to have all his troops on hand in case a battle developed. The ensuing sequence of events would be critical to the course of the battle on 1 July, as will be understood later.

Late on the night of the 28th, or very early on the 29th, Lee sent orders to Ewell at Carlisle to countermarch his corps to Chambersburg.[46] The directive arrived somewhat before 0900,[47] and made Ewell greatly upset, because he had already finalized his plans to attack Harrisburg. Jed Hotchkiss of Ewell's staff observed that "the General was quite testy and hard to please, because disappointed, and had everyone flying around."[48] Ewell dutifully sent Johnson's division off first, since Johnson was encamped on the west side of Carlisle and so was closest to his appointed destination of Chambersburg. It was late morning, though, before Johnson got underway. He was accompanied on his march by the corps trains and both battalions of Ewell's reserve artillery, which began moving at 1300.[49] Doubtless all of Johnson's men shared the disappointment of Major W. W. Goldsborough of the 1st Maryland, who wrote, "Great was the surprise of the officers and men of the division when they found themselves countermarching."[50]

Early, who was at York, did not receive his countermarch orders until the evening of the 29th, when Captain Elliot Johnston of Ewell's staff arrived with a copy of Lee's note and verbal instructions from Ewell "to move back, so as to rejoin the rest of the corps on the western side of South Mountain."[51] Because of the lateness of the hour, and the need to recall Gordon from Wrightsville, Early would be unable to set out until dawn of the 30th. Rodes claimed that he did not receive his withdrawal order until the morning of the 30th, when he was already on the march towards Harrisburg.[52] Perhaps faulty staff work was to blame for the delay in transmission of the order.

Sometime during the night of 28-29 June, Lee changed his mind and decided it would be better to have Ewell reunite his divisions at a point east of the mountains. This change was tied to his decision to move Longstreet and Hill eastward to Cashtown in an effort to force Hooker to stay east of the mountains. As Major Marshall understood this situation, Lee was not so much concerned with guarding his communications as he was in keeping up his ammunition supply line to Virginia. The best way to accomplish this was not to withdraw to the south or advance against Frederick, but "to move his own army to the east side of the Blue Ridge so as to threaten Washington and Baltimore, and detain the Federal force on that side of the mountains to protect those cities."[53] Cashtown offered a perfect point at which to gather his forces and await the enemy's next move—from there he could maneuver to the east, withdraw his supply lines at Chambersburg, or take the tactical defensive in the gap if the enemy came up and chose to attack.

Lee accordingly sent a new set of orders to Ewell at 0700 on 29 June, with directions to march via Heidlersburg "to Cashtown, near Gettysburg."[54] The change in orders did not affect Early and Rodes, who were not yet in motion in response to Lee's first set of instructions. It did affect Johnson, though, who was already in motion towards Chambersburg. Ewell elected not to recall Johnson, but directed him to continue on past Shippensburg on the road to Chambersburg; when he reached Greenville, he was to turn southeast towards Scotland and then reach the Chambersburg Pike at Greenwood, 10 miles west of Cashtown.[55] This seemingly slight change in route would unintentionally be the cause of a huge traffic jam on the Chambersburg Pike on the afternoon of 1 July that would delay the advance of not one, but two other infantry divisions, and so profoundly change the entire course of the battle.

Ewell made a more culpable error on the 29th by his inattentiveness to Brigadier General Albert Jenkins' cavalry brigade. Jenkins' men would have proved useful for leading Ewell's march and protecting his flanks, but instead, the general left them behind at Mechanicsburg for a day. Historian Edwin B. Coddington suggests that Ewell may have wanted Jenkins to screen Major General Darius Couch's infantry at Harrisburg from reaching the rear of the withdrawing infantry.[56] This is possible, but there was no need for Jenkins' whole brigade to do the job. It seems more likely that Ewell may have neglected to notify Jenkins of his change in orders.[57] Jenkins had been operating under Ewell's direction for the previous week, but Ewell may have figured that Lee would send the cavalryman orders directly. Whatever was the cause, Jenkins did not receive orders to withdraw from Mechanicsburg until 1400 on 30 June. He gathered his somewhat scattered troops at Carlisle, which he departed about midnight. The column encamped at Petersburg, PA, at about 0200 on 1 July, but got little rest out of fear of an enemy attack. Thus most of the brigade was not in optimum shape when it arrived at Gettysburg at midafternoon on 1 July.[58]

A.P. Hill must have received Lee's revised orders early on the 29th to move to Cashtown, but he oddly did not mention the fact in his battle report.[59] During the next day he advanced Heth's division to Cashtown, which was located on the eastern side of Cashtown Gap, some eight miles west of Gettysburg. The rest of the corps remained in its camps at Fayetteville, 12 miles west of Cashtown. Major General Dorsey Pender was sent to Cashtown early on the 30th, and Hill intended to bring up R. H. Anderson on 1 July.[60] Had he sent Anderson to Cashtown with Pender on 30 June, the battle on 1 July would surely have progressed differently, as will be seen.

Longstreet advanced most of his corps from Chambersburg to Greenwood (located almost two miles east of Fayetteville) on 30 June. Two significant units were left behind. Major General George Pickett's command, the smallest division in the army, was detained at Chambersburg until it could be relieved by Brigadier General John Imboden's cavalry brigade. It would not reach the battlefield until the afternoon of 2 July. Longstreet also left behind Brigadier General Evander Law's brigade of Major General John B. Hood's division, which was guarding a pass at New Guilford, about three miles south of Fayetteville. Law would not rejoin his division until midafternoon on July 2; his late arrival would be one of the contributing causes of Longstreet's delayed attack that afternoon.

Ewell's corps also had a relatively easy day on 30 June. Major General Robert E. Rodes, accompanied by Ewell, marched south from Carlisle through Petersburg (now York Springs), and encamped at Heidlersburg, which was located about 10 miles north-northeast of Gettysburg.[61] Early came up that afternoon from York and went into camp about three miles to the east of Heidlersburg.[62] Johnson and the corps artillery continued on their independent march and camped near Shippensburg.[63]

Lee on 30 June was still not certain exactly where the enemy army was located, though several minor clashes during the day gave evidence that the enemy, or at least his advance force, was not too far away. Sometime during the morning a detachment of Heth's command had a brief skirmish with some Union cavalry at Fairfield, located ten miles south of Cashtown and eight miles southwest of Gettysburg.[64]

Pettigrew's March to Gettysburg
30 June

Later in the morning Brigadier General J. J. Pettigrew's brigade had a brief encounter with Union cavalry just west of Gettysburg. Soon after arriving at Cashtown on 29 June, Harry Heth heard that there were "army supplies (particularly shoes)" located in Gettysburg, just eight miles up the Pike, and he determined to investigate the report.[65] It is interesting to note that his September 1863 battle report, just quoted, places emphasis on the army supplies over the shoes. When he wrote up his memoirs after the war, however, he mentioned only his interest in the shoes: "My men were sadly in want of shoes. I heard that a large supply of shoes was stored in Gettysburg. On the morning of the 30th of June, I ordered General Pettigrew to march to Gettysburg and secure these shoes."[66]

We do not know today how Heth heard the rumor that there were shoes available in Gettysburg. Perhaps the report was brought in by some of the Confederate foragers who were combing the countryside east of Cashtown.[67] Historian Wilbur Nye believes that Early had noticed a shoe factory in Gettysburg when he occupied the town on June, and had reported this to the troops in Chambersburg, but he gives no evidence for this.[68] We cannot even be certain that Heth was aware that Early had passed through the town on 26 June. If he were not aware of Early's stay in the town four days earlier, there would be stronger cause for him to anticipate that military supplies and shoes might be available there. And if he did know of Early's route, he would have had less reason to expect that any large quantity of shoes might still be available there. Whichever was the case, Heth decided a large scale foraging party was worth the gamble. This decision was totally consistent with his impulsive nature, especially if it also might help determine what, if any, enemy forces were in his front.[69]

Heth gave Pettigrew very specific instructions for his expedition. Lieutenant Louis G. Young, who was serving as an aide-de-camp to Pettigrew, later recalled, "General Early had levied on Carlisle, Chambersburg, and Shippensburg, and had found no difficulty in having his requisitions filled. It was supposed that it would be the same at

Gettysburg. It was told to General Pettigrew that he might find the town in possession of a home guard, which he would have no difficulty in driving away; but if, contrary to expectations, he should find any organized troops capable of making resistance, or any portion of the Army of the Potomac, he should not attack it. The orders to him were peremptory, not to precipitate a fight. General Lee with his columns scattered, and lacking the information of his adversary, which he should have had from his cavalry, was not ready for battle—hence the orders."[70]

Young also relates that Pettigrew was directed to take with him "three of his four regiments present, three pieces of the Donaldsonville Artillery of Louisiana, and a number of wagons, for the purpose of collecting quartermaster stores for the use of the army."[71] The regiments Pettigrew brought with him were the 11th, 26th, and 47th North Carolina. His 52nd North Carolina remained behind near Cashtown.[72] Company B of that regiment had been sent five miles down the Emmitsburg Road from Cashtown to picket Millerstown (Fairfield), where it had a skirmish with some Union cavalry during the night of 29-30 June.[73]

We do not know why Heth chose Pettigrew for this mission. Perhaps it was simply because Pettigrew may have been encamped on the eastern edge of the division encampment, and so was the closest brigade to Gettysburg. Or it may have been because Pettigrew's brigade, even lacking one regiment, was the largest single command Heth had. Brigadier General James Archer had about 1200 men, Brockenbrough had only about 1000, and part of Brigadier General Joe Davis' brigade had been detached to Fairfield, leaving him with only about 1200 men on hand.[74] Even without the 52nd North Carolina, Pettigrew still had over 2000 men in his other three regiments.[75]

Pettigrew's men broke camp soon after dawn on 30 June and shook off their gear that was wet from a rain during the night. After completing their monthly pay muster, they were ordered to leave behind their knapsacks and any men not able to make a forced march, and were on the road at 0630. Those who stayed behind stowed the rest of their regiment's gear, including the officers' tents, and sent the equipment back to the wagon camp at Cashtown, one quarter mile distant.[76]

Pettigrew's column had marched out only a mile and a half when it reached the picket line of Colonel W.S. Christian's 55th Virginia of Brockenbrough's brigade. Christian had been posted there at sunset the night before with careful instructions "not to mistake friends for foes" because he "might meet some of Ewell's command or Stuart's." Christian had been somewhat confused by these orders, and went to Brockenbrough for specific instructions on where to go. When Brockenbrough said that he did not know and he was just relaying an order from Heth, Christian rode to Heth, who said that he was relaying an order he received from Hill. Since it was by then getting dark, Christian decided he could "waste no more time getting specific instructions" and marched his men out about a mile and a half to the intersection of a broad crossroad. He posted his men there, some in a fair sized cemetery, and sent out scouts and pickets.[77]

Christian had just spent a sleepless but uneventful night and was breakfasting on some "confiscated chicken," when he saw Pettigrew's column approaching from the west. Pettigrew told him he was making a reconnaissance in the direction of Gettysburg, "and asked me to attend to him with my regiment. I reminded him that we had spent a sleepless night out there, and that I had heard nothing from my Brigade Commander. He then said that he had no right to command my presence, but that his troops, while splendidly drilled and equipped, were comparatively new men, and that he wished to have a veteran Regiment go with him. Upon these grounds I readily consented to go."[78]

Somewhere farther down the road Pettigrew's command ran into "General Longstreet's spy" (probably Harrison), who passed the column and quickly returned with the report that 3000 Union cavalry under Buford had just arrived and were holding Gettysburg. This information was soon confirmed by a "Knight of the Golden Circle" who came out to furnish a warning. Pettigrew, of course, was gravely concerned, and he at once sent the news on to Heth with a request for further instruction. Lieutenant Young noted, that "The message received in reply, was simply a repetition of the orders previously given coupled with an expression of disbelief as to the presence of any portion of the Army of the Potomac."[79]

Pettigrew's 47th North Carolina was almost at its destination when its men were shot at by some unseen force—whether civilians, cavalry or stray militia we do not know—from a woods along their line of march. Captain John A. Thorp of Company A of the 47th wrote later that, "a person in citizen's dress, on a farm horse, rode leisurely from the adjacent woods up to the fence, on the other side of which we were moving, inquired for our commander, and paced up to the head of the column. On his arrival there the command 'Halt!' rang down our line." It is unclear whether this man was a spy, or someone who came to warn the Confederates of a possible ambush. Whichever was the case, the 47th's commander, Colonel G.H. Faribault, ordered his men to retire quickly. Thorp continues his brief account of the episode: "'About face—quick time, march!' and back we went but not without several shots at long range being fired at us from both sides of the road. So we escaped the ambuscade that had been set for us."[80]

Pettigrew proceeded on until the head of his column reached Seminary Ridge, just three quarters of a mile west of the town, between 0930 and 1000.[81] Instead of entering the town at once, Pettigrew decided to halt and send forward some skirmishers to determine if and where enemy troops might be. One source relates that about two dozen infantry pickets advanced "as far down as Mr. Sheads' house," located next to the Pike about 300 yards east of the ridge. While the skirmishers advanced towards town, Confederate officers were seen "contenting themselves with examining it through field glasses and conversing with such citizens as they could find." Some Gettysburg residents feared that the Confederates might open fire at any minute; Sarah Broadhead remembered that "we had a good view of them from our house, and every moment expected to hear the booming of cannon, and thought they might shell the town."[82]

Pettigrew's skirmishers had not reported back when the Confederates at about 1030 saw the lead elements of Brigadier General John Buford's cavalry approaching the town from the southwest via the Emmitsburg Road.[83] Since he had orders not to fight "any organized troops," Pettigrew thought it best to retire. He was also concerned that "some of his men reported the beat of drums (indicating infantry) on the further side of town."[84] Lieutenant Young later insisted that Pettigrew was more than willing to fight Buford's cavalry, "supported no doubt by a home guard," had his orders not forbidden it.[85] Colonel Christian of the 55th Virginia noted that he was "in sight of Gettysburg" while Buford was "retiring before us" when he received orders to retire to Cashtown.[86] Several Union accounts are clear that the Confederates withdrew "without showing fight,"[87] and one claimed the capture of a few Rebels in the town.[88]

When Pettigrew began his countermarch, he found that he was being tailed by some of the enemy's cavalry. Lieutenant Young relates that, "Buford's cavalry followed us at some distance, and Lieutenant Walter H. Robertson and I, of Pettigrew's staff, remained in the rear to watch it. This we easily did, for the country is rolling, and from behind the ridges we could see without being seen and we had a perfect view of the movements of the approaching column. Whenever it would come within three or four hundred yards of us we would make our appearance, mounted, when the column would halt until we retired. This was repeated several times. It was purely an affair of observation on both sides and the cavalry made no effort to molest us."[89]

After Pettigrew reached Marsh Creek, he formed three of his regiments as a rear guard to face a possible Union pursuit and allow his artillery and wagons time to retire to Cashtown. He posted one regiment on each side of the road "under cover of a hill," with a third regiment astride the road slightly in their front. One Union source thought the front regiment was a decoy "to induce pursuit by our men." The Confederates held this line for a little under two hours without being molested, whereupon the force retired farther up the Pike toward Cashtown.[90]

When Pettigrew retired, he left behind Colonel Henry Burgwyn's 26th North Carolina as pickets on the west side of Marsh Creek. Surgeon George Underwood's historical sketch of the 26th notes that the regiment "later in the afternoon proceeded to within about three and one-half miles of Gettysburg, just this side of little creek, crossed by a stone bridge, where we filed to the right and bivouacked in a beautiful grove."[91] Before dark the unit received provisions from supply wagons sent from Cashtown.[92] At dark Lieutenant Colonel J.R. Lane took charge of the picket lines. Soon after the picket line was established, two ladies came up who were much agitated because they were cut off from their houses. Lane assured them that "the Confederate soldier did not make war upon women and children, but ever esteemed it his duty and privilege to protect them." He accordingly advanced his picket line to include the ladies' houses, which were close by.[93]

Pettigrew did not march his 11th and 47th regiments back to their previous night's camp near Cashtown, but instead camped somewhere between McKnightstown and Seven Stars, in ready supporting distance of the 26th.[94] The 55th Virginia,[95] and probably the artillery and wagons, were sent back to Cashtown. It is not clear if the 52nd North Carolina rejoined the brigade at this time. Company B of that unit had been recalled from Millerstown during the day and "reported at camp," which, accordingly to one source, was not moved from the time the regiment first reached Cashtown until it left for Gettysburg on the morning of 1 July.[96] At least part of the brigade's picket line that night was manned by a portion of the 47th North Carolina.[97]

The news of Pettigrew's "scrape" caused considerable excitement in the Confederate camps. Julius Lineback wrote that he was aware by 1400 that "General Pettigrew, who had been making a reconnaissance in force, had taken some prisoners, who said that Hooker had been reinforced by Meade... Our troops, in coming in contact with the enemy, had quite a little brush, but being under orders not to bring a general engagement fell back, followed by the enemy."[98]

Later in the afternoon Pettigrew rode back to Cashtown to report the results of his expedition to his immediate superior, Harry Heth. Heth summarized Pettigrew's words as follows: "He reported that he had not gone to Gettysburg; that there was evidently a cavalry force occupying the town, the strength of which he could not tell; that some of his men reported the beat of drums (indicating infantry) on the further side of the town; that if he entered the town his men when searching for shoes would have become scattered, and if there was a large force there, it might have proved disastrous to his command. Under these circumstances, he deemed it prudent to return and not carry out my orders."[99]

Heth could not believe that there was any large Union force at Gettysburg, and was still speaking with Pettigrew when A. P. Hill rode up from his headquarters at Fayetteville. Heth directed Pettigrew to repeat his report to their corps commander, who replied, "The only force at Gettysburg is cavalry, probably a detachment of observation. I am just from General Lee, and the information he has from his scouts corroborates that I have received from mine— that the enemy are still at Middleburg, and have not yet struck their tents."[100]

In the discussion that followed both Hill and Heth continued to disbelieve Pettigrew's insistence that there might be Union infantry in Gettysburg, so Pettigrew called on his aide, Lieutenant Louis G. Young, for support. He figured Young's evidence might have some weight with Hill because the lieutenant was well known to him from having served as a staff officer in Pender's brigade of Hill's division during most of 1862. Hill asked Young what was the character of the column he saw, and Young replied that "their movements were undoubtedly those of well trained troops, not a home guard." Hill "still could not believe that any portion of the Army of the Potomac was up, expressed the hope that it was, as this was the place he wanted it to be."[101]

Heth, still believing that there was only a small cavalry force and perhaps a little militia in Gettysburg, requested permission from Hill to go and search for the shoes he had not had time to look for that afternoon: "If there is no objection, I will take my division tomorrow and go to Gettysburg and get those shoes." Hill approved and responded, "None in the world."[102]

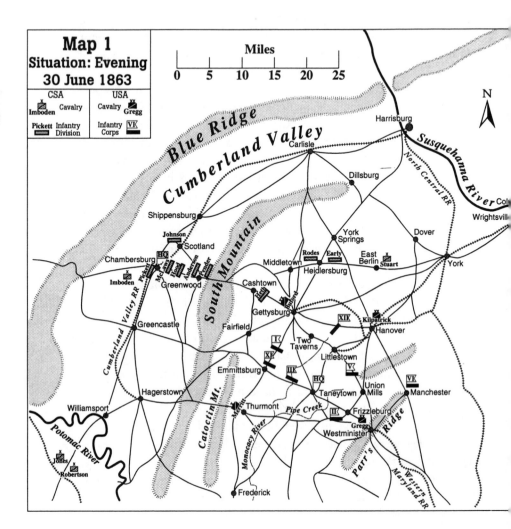

Hill had other interests than obtaining shoes when he gave Heth permission to march back to Gettysburg the next morning. He claimed in his battle report that he wanted to "discover what was on my front,"[103] but he may actually have been looking to start a fight. Hill could be impetuous at times (as he was in attacking prematurely at Mechanicsville and Gaines' Mill during the Seven Days' battles), and he may have been jealous of the fact that Ewell's troops had already won glory at the battle of Second Winchester two weeks earlier, while his own newly formed Third Corps had yet to win any such honors.

Hill did not plan his advance without first consulting Lee. He had informed Lee of Pettigrew's report as soon as he had received it,[104] and may have met with his commander again that evening;[105] if not, the two were definitely in communication by courier. Lee, like Hill and Heth "could not believe" that the Federal army was at Gettysburg.[106] Since he had no cavalry with him at Cashtown, he did not object to Hill sending Heth to reconnoiter at Gettysburg again, provided that he did not start a big fight; Lee did not want to begin a battle before Ewell's corps rejoined the army. Lee accordingly sent orders to direct Heth "to ascertain what force was at Gettysburg, and, if he found infantry opposed to him, to report the fact immediately, without forcing an engagement."[107]

Having received authorization for his expedition, Hill decided to beef it up by sending Pender's division plus his two battalions of corps reserve artillery to support Heth. He clearly did not want Heth to be turned back like Pettigrew had been, and also wanted to be ready to fight if anything did develop. As an extra precaution, Hill directed Anderson to bring his division up to Cashtown. He also sent a note to Ewell that he was going to make a reconnaissance in force to Gettysburg.[108]

Before returning to his troops, Pettigrew described the nature of the road to Gettysburg to Brigadier General James J. Archer, whom Heth had selected to lead the division's advance on the morrow. Lieutenant Young relates that Pettigrew "described to him minutely the topography of the country between Cashtown and Gettysburg, and suggested that he look out for a road that ran at right angles to the one we were on, and which might be used by the enemy to break into his line of march." He also told Archer "the configuration of the ground in the vicinity of the town" and mentioned "a ridge on which he would probably find the enemy, as this position was favorable for defense."[109] Pettigrew then headed back to his command, which was encamped about two miles east of Cashtown.

CHAPTER II

The Army of the Potomac Moves North

*P*resident Abraham Lincoln was unhappy with Major General Joe Hooker, commander of the Army of the Potomac since 26 January 1863, as soon as he heard of the retreat from Chancellorsville on 6 May. In his opinion, he felt that "both the attack at Chancellorsville and the retreat were inexcusable, and that Hooker must not be intrusted with the conduct of the battle."[1] This opinion was shared by a number of the army's leading officers, including Major General Darius N. Couch, commander of II Corps, who had so much disgust for Hooker that he asked for a transfer on 22 May rather than serve under him any longer.[2]

Lincoln was still trying to decide whom to appoint to replace Hooker when Lee began moving northward in early June. Hooker was aware of the President's distrust of him, and on 5 June wrote for instructions. Interestingly, one of his suggestions was to "protect his rear" once most of Lee's army had left Fredericksburg, which was specifically what Lee did not want to happen. Lincoln, who had already seen his army defeated twice in that area, vetoed the idea, adding the comment, "I would not take any risk of being entangled upon the river, like an ox jumped half over a fence, and liable to be torn by dogs in front and rear without a chance to gore one way or kick the other."[3]

Hooker's orders were to stay on the same side of the Rappahannock as Lee, and he did so skillful a job of shielding Washington as Lee moved toward the Potomac that some parties in Washington began to overlook his recent failure and returned "to the hopeful state they were in before the late battle."[4] It soon became clear that Lee was going to cross into Maryland, and Hooker for a time toyed with the idea of striking the enemy while Lee's forces were separated by the Potomac. He soon thought better of the idea, and informed Major General Henry W. Halleck that he would begin to cross the river as soon as he confirmed that Lee was doing so. When such confirmation arrived on the afternoon of 24 June, he ordered his troops north to the river, which they crossed on 25 and 26 June.[5]

Hooker gathered his corps on a line from Middletown to Frederick and let his men rest on 27 June. It is not totally clear what his plans were going to be from there; his position served his primary purpose of guarding the approaches to Washington, while it also gave him the opportunity to strike across South Mountain at Lee's communications, or to move to the northeast to confront Lee in Pennsylvania or northern Maryland. It will be recalled that Lee at this time had more than half of his army concentrated at Chambersburg, about 40 miles north northwest of Frederick, and that the Confederate commander still did not know that Hooker had crossed the Potomac.

Meade Takes Command

Hooker's advance, though, had not been as speedy as it might have been, and Ewell's open depredations in south central Pennsylvania as far east as York and Carlisle were causing grave concern, even hysteria, in the north. In Washington, Secretary of War Edwin Stanton and others held hopes that Hooker would resign before fighting another battle, and were dismayed to see him "so full of hope and energy." Accordingly to Charles F. Benjamin, Lincoln also became alarmed "at the last moment."[6] The opportunity to remove Hooker surfaced suddenly on 27 June, in the context of a disagreement Hooker was having with Halleck over the use of the Harpers Ferry garrison. Hooker wanted to take control of the troops posted there and use them to reinforce his army, but Halleck refused to allow him to do so. At 1300 on 27 June Hooker asked to be relieved if he could not get his way, probably in the belief that the administration would not accept his resignation because a fight with the enemy was so imminent. In this he was dead wrong.[7]

Halleck acknowledged receipt of Hooker's request at 2000, with a simple note that he had referred the matter to the President; he explained "as you were appointed to this command by the President, I have no power to relieve you."[8] Hooker's unexpected request to be relieved certainly removed the President from the awkwardness of firing him and the uneasiness of seeing him fight another battle. Lincoln did not take the time to call his full cabinet together, but appears to have discussed the matter only with Halleck and Stanton, and probably Secretaries Salmon P. Chase and William H. Seward.[9] Their consensus was that Hooker should be removed. They decided not to entrust so important an order to the telegraph office, and instead thought to send it via a personal emissary familiar to Hooker, James A. Hardie, Chief of Staff of the Secretary of War.

The next question, clearly, was whom to appoint to replace Hooker. Fortunately, everyone was in agreement, particularly since there was no time to bring in anyone from the west, and one of the leading candidates, Major General John F. Reynolds of I Corps, had declined interest on the somewhat restrictive terms Lincoln had proposed to him on 2 June.[10] The new commander would be Major General George G. Meade of V Corps, whom Couch had openly recommended before he left the army, and whom Stanton and Halleck clearly favored. Meade was a loyal and efficient officer with a good combat record, but was not as flamboyant as any of his predecessors. It was perhaps these very characteristics that recommended Meade to Lincoln. The President was also swayed by the fact that Meade made his home in Philadelphia, and as a Pennsylvanian would "fight well on his own dunghill."[11]

For the sake of secrecy as well as speed and expediency, Colonel Hardie was imposed on to deliver Meade's appointment in person before informing Hooker of his removal. Hardie was not at all eager to carry out the task, but was persuaded by both Stanton and Lincoln that it was his duty to do so. Elaborate precautions were taken to insure that Hardie would be able to complete his important mission—he was given proper orders and passes, along with money to buy his way through any delays or obstructions; if he ran into Stuart's cavalry, he was instructed to destroy his papers and deliver his orders verbally.[12]

Hardie, wearing civilian dress, left Washington by special train bound for Frederick, where most of the army was known to be encamped. At the station he managed to hire a buggy and driver (at no small fee), and began a difficult search in the darkness for Meade's headquarters. At length he found his way to Meade's tent at about 0300. The general was asleep, and his staff st first refused entry to Hardie. But the envoy insisted on waking Meade, and at length entered the tent to do so. At first Meade groggily thought he was being arrested. When he learned he was to replace Hooker as army commander, he demurred in favor of Reynolds. Stanton had anticipated such protests (which included no defense of Hooker), and had steeled Hardie to stick by his guns. Meade at length acquiesced, being persuaded most by Hardie's opinion "as a professional soldier, that he had no lawful discretion, to vary from the orders given."[13]

Meade reluctantly agreed to accompany Hardie on his mission to tell Hooker of the change of command. The scene was embarrassing for everyone, particularly since Hooker had begun to believe that the delay in the response to his offer to resign meant that he was secure in his post. Things became even more tense when Meade learned the disposition of the army, and expressed shock that it was so widely scattered. As Mr. Benjamin aptly noted, "Hooker's chagrin and Meade's overstrung nerves made the lengthy but indispensable conference rather trying to the whole party." The two generals met again that afternoon to formalize and finalize the change in command, and Hooker left camp that evening.[14]

It is interesting to note that Reynolds went to greet his new commander as soon as he heard what had happened. Meade reportedly told him "how surprisingly, imperative and unwelcome were the orders he received; how much he would have preferred the choice to have fallen on Reynolds; how anxious he had been to see Reynolds and tell him these things." Reynolds replied that "the command had fallen where it belonged, that he was glad such a weight of responsibility had not come upon him, and that Meade might count upon the best support he could give him."[15]

The change in command was not a complete surprise to the officers and men of the army, though some would have preferred the return of Major General George McClellan as their commander.[16] When Lee heard the news (probably on 30 June rather than the 28th, see Chapter I, note 37), he expressed surprise that Lincoln would change commanders "at that critical stage of affairs." The change was a good one for the Union army, he felt, because "he had always held Meade in much higher estimation than Hooker."[17] At some point he observed that "General Meade will commit no blunder on my front, and if I make one, he will make haste to take advantage of it."[18] However, the timing of the change and the fact that Meade would need time to become accustomed to his new command "would more than counter balance his superiority as a general over the previous commander." Lee was therefore "rather satisfied than otherwise by the change." Nor did the fact that the enemy's army had a new commander much concern the Confederate troops; "They had known the same thing to happen in several previous occasions with rather loss than gain to the Federal cause, and the news tended to add to their hopes of success."[19]

Meade was a bit discomforted by the army's location and the fact that Hooker had no campaign plan, and would not share his intentions. Meade's immediate guidelines were laid out by Halleck in an explanatory letter that was sent along with his orders to take command. Here Meade was charged with the twofold task of being "the covering army of Washington as well as the army of operation against the invading forces of the rebels." He was directed specifically to "maneuver and fight in such a manner as to cover the capital and also Baltimore, as far as circumstances will admit. Should General Lee move upon either of these places, it is expected that you will either anticipate him or arrive with him so as to give him battle." Two additional significant clauses gave Meade control of the troops at Harpers Ferry (authority which had previously been denied to Hooker), and authorized him to remove or appoint any officers he deemed proper.[20]

Meade responded to Halleck at 0700 on the 28th, by acknowledging his appointment and acknowledging that, as a soldier, he would obey the order. Since he did not know exactly where the enemy was, he could only promise that he would move toward the Susquehanna, "keeping Washington and Baltimore well covered, and if the enemy is checked in his attempt to cross the Susquehanna, or if he turns to Baltimore, to give him battle."[21] This line of action was approved by Halleck in a return telegram sent at 1300.[22]

Meade persuaded Major General Dan Butterfield, Hooker's Chief of Staff, to stay on and help provide continuity of command, even though Butterfield was a much better friend of Hooker than of the new commander. He then took strong steps to reorganize and reinvigorate his cavalry. Brigadier General Julius Stahel's newly arrived division was assigned to the aggressive Judson Kilpatrick, and was sent off with Brigadier General David M. Gregg's veteran 2nd Division to guard the army's trains and chase after Stuart, who was last reported near Rockville, Maryland. Brigadier General John Buford's 1st Division, strengthened by the

Reserve Brigade of U. S. Regulars, was sent north to look for Lee. In an unprecedented move, Meade promoted three promising cavalry captains, Elon Farnsworth of the 8th Illinois, George A. Custer of the 5th U. S., and Wesley Merritt of the 2nd U. S., to be brigadier generals, and gave them each a brigade (Merritt took the Reserve brigade, while Custer and Farnsworth served under Kilpatrick).[23] These moves were designed to make the Union cavalry more aggressive during the campaign, and would succeed at doing so.

As previously noted, Meade did not much care for Hooker's troop dispositions. One of his first orders was to concentrate his army at Frederick by bringing in the I, III and XI Corps from Knoxville, MD, and the II Corps from Barnesville; the VI Corps was directed to swing farther to the east, from Poolesville to New Market, MD, 10 miles east of Frederick.

It was a long day's march—over 20 miles for much of the army—but it was well worth it to Meade, who by the end of the day had his army disposed on a 25 mile arc from Emmitsburg to near Westminster, facing Carlisle and York. He intended to shift even more to the right to cover Baltimore better, in the process switching his supply base from Frederick to Westminster. If Lee were attempting to cross the Susquehanna, he hoped that Couch's militia would delay the enemy long enough for him "to fall upon his rear and give him battle." The rear of the Confederate army, as he understood it, had passed beyond Hagerstown towards Chambersburg, and his main objective was "to hold my force well together, with the hope of falling upon some portion of Lee's army in detail." Stuart's cavalry raid seemed at worse to be only an annoyance that he was ready "to submit to win some measure."[24]

Meade's next goal was to push his corps forward quickly up to the Maryland-Pennsylvania boundary in an effort to locate Lee and bring the enemy to battle. The army was to advance on a broad front in order to achieve more speed, and was grouped into three wings, each within supporting distance of its neighbor. Reynolds led the I and XI Corps to Emmitsburg on 29 June; his advance was covered by Buford's cavalry division, since the enemy was thought to be nearby beyond South Mountain. The III Corps marched that evening to Taneytown, which was 10 miles east of Emmitsburg. The army's center, the XII and V Corps, reached Middleburg and Libertytown, respectively, on the 29th, while on the right, the II and VI corps, marched to within 5 miles of Westminster. Army headquarters was set up for the moment at Middleburg.

Thus Meade was intending to move towards York on 30 June,[25] when news from his left wing caused him to shift his attention farther to the west. On 29th June Brigadier General Alfred Pleasonton had directed Buford to take two brigades and a battery north from Middletown (MD) to Emmitsburg, and "from thence to Gettysburg by tomorrow night." Their purpose was to "cover and protect the front, and communicate all information rapidly and surely."[26] Buford was a veteran officer, well suited to the task, and had already seen valuable service earlier in the campaign in the Middleburg (VA) area before crossing the Potomac on 27 June. The troops he took with him to Gettysburg were the two experienced brigades commanded by Colonel William Gamble and Colonel Thomas C. Devin, along with the six 3-inch rifled guns of Lieutenant John Calef's Battery A, 2nd U. S. Artillery. The force mustered 3038 officers and men present when it was mustered for pay on the morning of the 30th.[27] Buford's third brigade, Brigadier General Wesley Merritt's 2500 man Reserve Brigade, was detached to Mechanicstown, MD, to guard the army's rear and bring up stragglers, and so would not be with Buford on 30 June and 1 July.[28]

Buford left Middletown at 0900 on 29 June and headed north through Boonesboro and Cavetown.[29] The march was uneventful until the column crossed into Pennsylvania at about 1600, when the troops' enthusiasm was kindled at the sight of a trooper of Company G, 17th Pennsylvania, "who stood with streaming guidon, on the boundary line of the state, indicating our exit from doubtful Maryland into loyal Pennsylvania." Many of the troops broke out in "responsive and ringing cheers," while several of the captains gave "short but eloquent speeches."[30]

The column crossed South Mountain at Monterey Springs and encamped for the night at 2200 at Fountaindale, located near the eastern end of the pass.[31] The troops were pleased to see that the region was "abounding in forage and water for our jaded horses."[32] The men of Company G, 17th Pennsylvania, enjoyed a special treat that night, which was their first back in the state since they had enlisted. Most of them came from Waynesboro, just over 10 miles west of Fairfield. Their captain, L.B. Kurtz, sought and received permission from regimental commander Colonel Josiah H. Kellogg to return home for the night, on condition that they all be back in time for roll call the next morning. The men all kept their pledge of honor and returned promptly as promised.[33]

Buford had his men up between 0200 and 0300 on 30 June in order to be able to depart camp at dawn.[34] As they were preparing their horses, some of Devin's troops were pleased to see an old Pennsylvania farmer and his daughter drive into camp in a one horse wagon full of bread and cakes . He said that his family had stayed up all night baking for the soldiers, and gladly handed out the fresh victuals free of charge.[35]

Skirmish at Fairfield
30 June

The Union cavalry broke camp at dawn and headed northeast toward Fairfield, some four miles distant. The morning was so foggy that the lead skirmishers, a detachment of Gamble's 8th Illinois, were unable to see very far in front of them. About half a mile from Fairfield they quite unexpectedly encountered fire from Confederate skirmishers.[36] The Confederate troops consisted of a detachment of Heth's division—the 42nd Mississippi of Davis' brigade and Company B of the 52nd North Carolina of Pettigrew's brigade, plus a two gun detachment of artillery. They had been in Fairfield (Millerstown) since the previous evening, under orders to protect the road from Cashtown to Emmitsburg.[37]

Gamble's skirmishers promptly returned fire and began driving the enemy back. Buford waited "to feel it and drive it, if possible," but was unable to do so easily after additional Confederate troops joined the fray. He felt that he would now need artillery help to push the enemy back, but he did not wish to disturb the enemy "for fear cannonading from that quarter might disarrange the plans of the general commanding." His line of march was four or five miles west of his assigned route up the Emmitsburg Road, and he "did not wish to bring on an engagement so far from the road I was expected to be following." He accordingly disengaged and headed south towards Emmitsburg.[38]

Buford in his battle report expressed considerable disgust and dismay that the natives of Fairfield had not informed him of the enemy's presence in the town: "The inhabitants knew of my arrival and the position of the enemy's camp, yet none of them gave me a particle of information, not even mentioned the fact of the enemy's presence.The whole community seemed stampeded, and afraid to speak or act, often offering as excuses for not showing some little enterprise, 'The rebels will destroy our houses if we tell anything.' Had anyone given me timely information, and acted as guide that night, I could have surprised and captured or destroyed this force."[39]

Private Thomas Withrow of Company C, 8th Illinois, had quite a close call during the brief engagement. He was struck early on by a ball that hit his stomach but did not penetrate because it hit his buckle or something else hard. The blow, though, did knock him off his horse, and he continued to fight, dismounted, from behind a nearby barn. He sadly found himself isolated when Buford disengaged and withdrew; he was unable to follow because his horse had gone with the rest of the column. Withrow nevertheless kept on firing until a Confederate officer came up and ordered his men to search the barn. He hid himself in the hay and luckily escaped detection. Before long the Confederates began bringing their wounded into the very same barn, and Withrow heard that the enemy had lost one man killed and three wounded. He claimed he had the opportunity to shoot a Rebel colonel dead, but did not wish to reveal his hiding place. Towards evening the Confederates withdrew from the town. "As a citizen entered the barn, Tom inquired if there was a chance of escape. The man was at first frightened, and answered, 'I don't know,' but soon learning that Tom was a Union soldier, took him to the house and gave him a good dinner, being highly pleased with the adventure of the brave fellow." Withrow then proceeded to Gettysburg, where he rejoined his regiment.[40]

Buford Encounters Pettigrew at Gettysburg
30 June

Buford reached Emmitsburg at midmorning,[41] and passed through the lines of I Corps, which was already in position north of town. He doubtless informed Reynolds of his skirmish at Fairfield before heading eight miles to the east to Gettysburg. On his march he kept his eyes open for more Confederates as well as for elements of Kilpatrick's cavalry, which he expected to be in the area.[42]

As Buford's advance rode up the Emmitsburg Road and neared the southern edge of town, they spotted some of Pettigrew's Confederate troops on Seminary Ridge, as related in Chapter I.[43] Colonel Gamble, whose brigade led the column, at once sent a squadron of the 8th Illinois (Companies D and F, under Captain Hotopp) "to ascertain who they were."[44] Pettigrew withdrew his men without firing a shot because he was under orders not to start a fight, and Hotopp's small force remained at a respectful distance once they determined they were facing regular Confederate infantry. The Confederates were completely gone by the time Buford's main column turned off the Emmitsburg Road onto Washington Street and entered the town.[45]

Buford's advance was led by a portion of Company C, 3rd Indiana Cavalry, under command of Captain Harry B. Sparks. The Hoosiers rode into town at full gallop and captured three or four Confederate soldiers who "seemed to be straggling through the streets and mingling with the citizens."[46] Historian Glenn Tucker suggests that these prisoners were probably not some of Pettigrew's skirmishers, but were more likely to have been stragglers from Early's division, part of which passed through town on 26 June.[47] This seems likely because none of the sources for Pettigrew's units mention the loss of any men on the 30th.

The first full regiment to enter the town was the 8th Illinois, followed by the 8th New York and the rest of Gamble's brigade. The 17th Pennsylvania or 9th New York then led Devin's column.[48] Both brigades turned left when they struck the intersection of Washington Street and Chambersburg Pike, and proceeded westward in the direction the enemy had gone.[49]

The citizens of the town were overjoyed to be rescued by the cavalry, and expressed their pleasure with hearty cheers that were responded to in kind by the troopers. Some townspeople waved flags or threw flowers to the troops, while others brought forward fresh victuals such as bread and butter, fresh meat, pies, cakes, and many other kinds of goodies. Some boys tried to set off a quantity of fireworks they had originally obtained to use to celebrate the 4th of July.[50]

The troops particularly remembered all the patriotic songs they were serenaded with as they passed through the town, especially those sung by groups of young ladies. These included the "Star Spangled Banner," and the "Red, White, and Blue," which was sung "most loyally and charmingly." Some of the men of the 9th New York heard a new tune called "Rally Round the Flag Boys" for the first time and thought it was "wonderfully inspiring." Lieutenant John Calef, commander of Buford's horse battery, recalled hearing "Battle Cry of Freedom" and "Cheer Boys Cheer" sung by school children who were dressed in white and assembled on the street corners, carrying wreaths of flowers. At one point a diffident "little miss" came out into the middle of the street to present him with an immense bouquet as he rode through town at the head of his battery.[51]

Fifteen year old Matilda (Tillie) Pierce, who resided at 301-303 Baltimore Street, went to see the cavalrymen and was greatly impressed by their numbers: "It was to me a novel and grand sight. I had never seen so many soldiers at one time. They were Union soldiers and that was enough for me, for I knew we had protection, and I felt they were our dearest friends." She then joined a group of "us girls" at the corner of Washington and High Streets. As the girls were waving at the troopers, Tillie's older sister Margaret began singing the old patriotic song "Our Union Forever." The other girls joined in, and "as some of us did not know the whole of the piece, we kept repeating the chorus." Afterwards they were a bit embarrassed to hear that a few of the cavalrymen thought that the girls' song sounded a bit repetitive: "Some of these soldiers told us that the singing was very good, but that they would have liked to have heard more than the chorus."[52]

Buford Deploys His Pickets

Buford's cavalrymen had no time to stop and enjoy the hospitality of the Gettysburgians at the moment. Buford was assigned to hold the town, and he at once understood that the best way to do so was to occupy one of the ridges west of town, facing the greatest immediate threat, the large body of troops known to be near Cashtown. Accordingly, he sent Gamble west on the Chambersburg Pike with orders to "select the most eligible line of battle beyond the Seminary that could be found, encamp the Brigade, and send one or two squadrons to find the enemy and remain in front on picket to watch the movements of the enemy."[53] Pursuant to these orders, Gamble rode west past Seminary Ridge and decided he would set up a line on McPherson's Ridge, less than one half mile to the west. He set up camp in the vale between the two ridges, with the 8th Illinois in front, south of the Pike, and the 8th New York to its rear. The 12th Illinois and 3rd Indiana encamped north of the Pike.[54] Calef bivouacked on eastern McPherson Ridge near the Chambersburg Pike. By standard practice, he unlimbered his six guns in order to be ready for action if the enemy should renew his advance from Cashtown, but none of his artillerymen were "imbued with the idea that a great battle was pending."[55]

As soon as Gamble began to set up camp, he sent two squadrons of the 8th Illinois to monitor Pettigrew's withdrawal. Some of this detachment, perhaps Hotopp's squadron already mentioned, followed the Confederates at a distance, and were careful not to provoke a fight themselves; for this reason they stopped every time the apparent

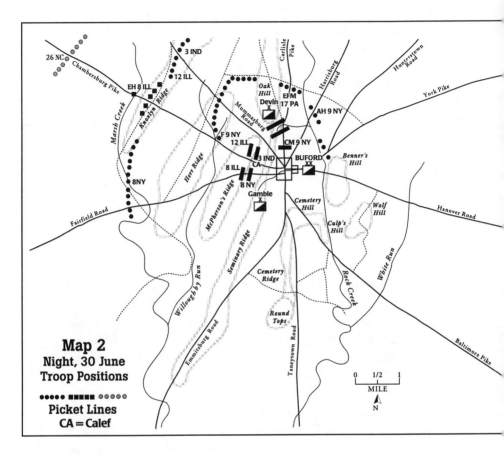

Map 2
Night, 30 June
Troop Positions

●●●●● ■■■■■ ⊙⊙⊙⊙⊙
Picket Lines
CA = Calef

Confederate rearguard halted. They also managed to avoid an ambush near Marsh Creek, as already noted in Chapter I.

After he learned that Pettigrew had withdrawn across Marsh Creek towards Cashtown, Major John L. Beveridge of the 8th Illinois sent Captain Daniel W. Buck's squadron (Companies E and H) to picket the main pike in the direction of Cashtown. Buck rode out a mile to the Herr Tavern, which he made his headquarters. He then sent Lieutenant Marcellus E. Jones with 35 men out as his forward picket. Jones proceeded out another mile to the west and established his picket reserve "under cover of the ridge east of Marsh Creek and about three miles from town." His main picket line was set up 500 yards farther west on the west of the ridge, with an advanced post "on the pike at a blacksmith's shop near the bridge over Marsh Creek."[56]

Captain Buck set up six picket posts in rear of Jones' advanced outpost—three south of the road, one on the road, and two to the north.[57] The brigade picket line to his left was manned by a squadron of the 8th New York, which may have been covering the ground along Marsh Creek from Buck's left past Fairfield Road all the way south to Marsh Creek's confluence with Willoughby Run.[58] The 12th Illinois and 3rd Indiana picketed Knoxlyn Ridge to Buck's right, north of the Pike.[59] Curiously, no sources mention any contact with the Confederate skirmishers of Pettigrew's 26th North Carolina, which later in the afternoon were stationed west of the creek.

While Gamble was setting up camp west of the Seminary, Devin led his brigade through town and out the Mummasburg Road about one half mile, where it encamped in an open field on the right of the road. Companies C and M of the 9th New York were directed to occupy the nearby grounds of Pennsylvania College.[60] Once camp was set up, squads of men were permitted to go into town to seek what provisions they could from the grateful population. James Bell noted that when he rode into town that evening, "Every one wanted to talk and at every house they would ask me in to eat supper. It done me lots of good to go there."[61] In addition townspeople came out to the camps to offer "soft bread, biscuits, pies, cakes, meats, jellies, preserves, fruits, and all kinds of delicacies."[62]

Devin's brigade picket line that night was in charge of Colonel William Sackett of the 9th New York, the brigade officer of the day. The line consisted of detachments from each of the brigade's four regiments, and covered a broad arc about three miles long stretching from where Chambersburg Pike crosses Willoughby Run north to Oak Ridge and then east to the York Pike.[63]

The left of Devin's picket line ran on the east side of Willoughby Run between the Chambersburg Pike and Mummasburg Road, with a strong picket reserve on Seminary Ridge. The farthest left post was stationed on the Chambersburg Pike and was manned by a detachment of Company F, 9th New York, under the command of Corporal Alphonse Hodges. This post consisted of a corporal and three men, and was relieved every two hours. Its men were instructed "not to fire on anyone approaching from the front, but to notify the pickets in each direction and the reserve." Post vedettes of an unnamed unit were advanced on the Mummasburg Road as far as the Forney residences.[64]

The right of Devin's picket line ran across the plain north of Gettysburg, covering all the principal roads. The identity and location of all the posts is not known except for the following. Companies E, F and M of the 17th Pennsylvania, under the command of Major J. O. Anderson, covered the Newville and Carlisle Roads, and Companies A and H of the 9th New York were posted east of Rock Creek in the Hunterstown and Harrisburg Roads.[65] One of the posts was manned by a squadron of the 8th New York. Devin's vedettes east of Gettysburg apparently extended only as far as Rock Creek on the York Pike, and Benner's Hill on the Hanover Road.[66]

General Buford first set up his headquarters in town at the Eagle Hotel, located on the northeast corner of the intersection of Chambersburg and Washington Streets.[67] Soon after his arrival he sent an informative dispatch to Pleasonton stating that he had arrived at Gettysburg at 1100 and "found everyone in a terrible state of excitement on account of the enemy's advance upon this place." The enemy troops, which he felt were the same that he had encountered that morning at Fairfield, had turned back about one half mile from the town, and withdrew towards Cashtown. Even though his men and horses were "fagged out," he had patrols operating towards Cashtown, Mummasburg, Hunterstown and Harrisburg. He was unable to locate any grain, and the lazy locals were not much help. Nor could he find any horse shoes or nails, since "Early's people" had seized all they could find.[68]

Buford's active scouting parties did an excellent job at locating and identifying the positions of Lee's widespread divisions that afternoon. One detachment north of Gettysburg managed to intercept a Confederate courier who was carrying a dispatch ordering Ewell to march to Cashtown. At about 1700 a patrol of 18 men from the 9th New York rode out the Hunterstown Road to Hunterstown and returned via the Harrisburg Road. On the way back they were cut off by some enemy cavalry (probably part of French's 17th Virginia) and turned about and charged, capturing one man. During the night Devin's scouts captured a number of additional prisoners. One who was taken on the road to Oxford bore the following order from General Early, probably intended for Colonel W.H. French of the 17th Virginia: "Get between Gettysburg and Heidlersberg, and picket at Mummasburg and Hunterstown. Send in the direction of Gettysburg and see what is there, and report to General Ewell at Heidlersberg. A small body of Yankee cavalry has made its appearance between Gettysburg and Heidlersberg. See what it is." The patrols on the Mummasburg Road and the Carlisle Pike ran into the pickets of White's Comanches, who were screening Rodes' advance.[69]

Sometime during the afternoon or evening Buford moved his headquarters from the Eagle Hotel to the Seminary so as to be closer to his most threatened front.[70] It was there that he had a lengthy conference with Colonel Devin that was later remembered in some detail by Lieutenant Aaron B. Jerome, who was serving as a signal officer on Buford's staff: "On the night of the 30th, General Buford spent some hours with Colonel Tom Devin, and while commenting upon the information brought in by Devin's scouts remarked that 'the battle would be fought at that point,' and that 'he was afraid it would be commenced in the morning before the infantry would get up.' These are his own words. Devin did not believe in so early an advance of the enemy, and remarked that he would 'take care of all that would attack his front during the ensuing twenty-four hours.' Buford answered:'No, you won't. They will attack you in the morning and they will come booming— skirmishers three deep. You will have to fight like the devil to hold your own until supports arrive. The enemy must know the importance of this position and will strain every nerve to secure it, and if we are able to hold it we will do well.' Upon his return, he ordered me, then first lieutenant and signal officer of the division, to seek out the most prominent points and watch everything; to be careful to look out for camp-fires, and in the morning for dust. He seemed anxious, more so than I ever saw him."[71]

Buford had good cause to be anxious about his position. By evening he was well aware from the reports of his active scouts that there was much Confederate activity to the west, north and northeast of Gettysburg. He clearly explained the situation in lengthy dispatches he sent to Reynolds and Pleasonton at 2230 and 2240 respectively—Hill was massed at Cashtown, with advanced pickets only four miles from Gettysburg, and Ewell's corps was crossing the mountains south of Carlisle.[72]

Buford has often been praised for his bold and brave decision to shield Gettysburg while in the face of the enemy, and so preserve the important hills south of town for Meade's use later in the battle. These hills, however, were not much on his mind on 30 June, when Buford was simply securing Gettysburg as he had been ordered by Pleasonton two days earlier. Holding the town necessitated picketing all the major roads to the north and west, and there certainly were a lot of them. This task was not particularly difficult in the plain north and northeast of town, but was more challenging to the west, where several successive ridge lines dominated the landscape. Buford could not hold Gettysburg without occupying one of these ridge lines, so he formed his main line in that sector on McPherson's Ridge, with Seminary Ridge as a secondary line. At no point, though, was Buford's command in any great danger on 30 June. There were only a few scattered Confederate cavalry patrols facing him north of Gettysburg, and the closest Confederate force, Pettigrew's troops west of Marsh Creek, were definitely known to have no cavalry with them. Buford knew that if any strong enemy forces began to threaten him, he could simply mount up and quickly reach supporting infantry by riding out the Emmitsburg, Taneytown or Baltimore Roads. His primary purpose on the 30th was to locate Lee's scattered units and deny the enemy use of the important road hub at Gettysburg. He succeeded most admirably at both. He doubtless was aware of Cemetery Hill, Culp's Hill, and the Round Tops, but there is no evidence he ever visited them or considered them as potential defensive positions for his own troops or Meade's.

It is interesting to note that Pleasonton did not give particular credence to Buford's report that the bulk of Lee's army was between Chambersburg and Cashtown, and instead intended to believe Kilpatrick's report that Lee was with a heavy infantry force at Berlin, 10 miles east of Heidlersburg.[73] Pleasonton was having a difficult time interpreting reconnaissance information during this stage of the campaign, particularly because of the uncertainty caused by Stuart's passage around the rear of the army. His gravest error came on the 29th, when he mistook Gregg's position and discounted citizens' reports that Stuart was at Westminster, thereby missing a chance to crush Stuart's command between Kilpatrick's division and II Corps.[74]

Reynolds' Plans

Reynolds, who had been receiving all of Buford's reports, interpreted them properly and became even more concerned about his exposed position on the left wing of the army. He was not as much afraid of a surprise attack from the direction of Cashtown and Gettysburg, because Buford's well placed force would surely give him advance warning, as he was, of a large and overwhelming advance from that quarter. He had with him about 12,000 men in his I Corps and slightly fewer in XI Corps, which was within easy supporting distance and under his control as wing commander. The rest of the army was stretched out to the east and southeast, towards Taneytown and Westminster, and Reynolds was not sure they could reach him in time if Lee suddenly moved to the attack with both Hill's and Longstreet's Corps. Reynolds was particularly concerned that the enemy might march against him from Cashtown via Fairfield, which he mistakenly thought to be held by one of Buford's regiments.[75] He would have been still more disturbed to know that Buford had left no men in Fairfield, but had taken his entire command to Gettysburg.[76]

Meade's marching orders sent out on 29 June directed Reynolds to move forward from Emmitsburg to Marsh Creek, "halfway to Gettysburg," on 30 June, and Reynolds dutifully obeyed them.[77] At midmorning he advanced about three miles on the Gettysburg Road and posted Brigadier General Samuel Wadsworth's division with Hall's battery to cover the bridge over Marsh Creek, while Brigadier General Abner Doubleday's division with Cooper's battery guarded the road to Fairfield, which met the Gettysburg Road just south of the creek at the hamlet of Fairplay. Brigadier General John Robinson's division and the remaining three corps batteries were held in reserve a couple of miles to the rear, behind Middle Creek.[78]

When he moved forward, Reynolds sent word to Major General Oliver O. Howard to bring up the XI Corps from its camps a mile south of Emmitsburg and occupy the heights immediately north of the town, an order that was confirmed through army headquarters. Reynolds was particularly concerned about an enemy advance through Fairfield, and directed Howard to be alert in that quarter.[79] Howard accordingly moved one division to Reynolds' old camp on the heights north of Emmitsburg, and placed another near the Gettysburg Road, on the right of the town. Brigadier General Carl Schurz's third division encamped on the grounds of St. Joseph's College, on the south side of town. He then sent out reconnaissance parties toward Cashtown and Fairfield, and a party of 103 men from the 75th Ohio was sent towards Greencastle.[80]

Howard at first understood that his mission was to support Reynolds if I Corps were attacked. He reported to Reynolds that his men were prepared to move at short notice and asked if he wanted the XI Corps to join him on the Gettysburg Road. Later in the day, though, he received word that the I Corps would fall back to Emmitsburg if attacked.[81] This was also Doubleday's understanding of the situation. He wrote of Reynolds' advance to Marsh Creek, "It was Reynolds' intention to dispute the enemy's advance at this point, falling back, however, in case of serious attack, to the ground already chosen at Emmitsburg."[82]

Reynolds felt that the heights above Emmitsburg were a strong place to fight a defensive battle should the enemy advance from Gettysburg, and urged Meade to send an engineer officer to reconnoiter the position. Earlier in the day he was uncertain whether Lee was advancing from out of the Cumberland Valley in order to move on York or to initiate a battle. Now he felt more strongly that Lee would advance in front of the mountains by way of Fairfield in order to turn the army's left between Emmitsburg and Frederick.[83] In this way he would be able to defeat an advance portion of the Union army, and still have the security of the South Mountain passes nearby if all did not go well.

Meade understood Reynolds' concern, and gave him permission to fall back from Marsh Creek to Emmitsburg if attacked. He explained that he had advanced I Corps to Marsh Creek "more with a view to an advance on Gettysburg, than a defensive point." In order to bolster his threatened left wing, Meade at 1445 directed Major General Dan Sickles to march his III Corps from Taneytown to Emmitsburg. He also formally ordered Reynolds to take charge of the army's expanded left wing, consisting now of I, III, and XI Corps, about one-third of the army.[84]

Sickles' men broke camp by 1500 and were well under way when he received conflicting orders from Reynolds and Meade. Apparently Reynolds had also sent orders for Sickles to proceed to Emmitsburg, and directed him to encamp on Cattail Branch (about three miles east of the town), "to face towards Gettysburg, and cover the roads towards Gettysburg." These instructions were at odds with some unrecorded verbal orders he received from Meade, and also conflicted with Meade's 1445 orders to "throw out strong pickets on the roads from Emmitsburg to Greencastle and Chambersburg." Since he was uncertain what to do (and perhaps resented being placed under Reynolds' command), Sickles stopped his column at Bridgeport and asked Meade to clarify his situation and his orders.[85] He must have received another verbal communication from Meade, for at 1945, he wrote to Reynolds that "By direction of the general commanding, I have gone into camp here, countermanding a previous order to go to Emmitsburg, and I am to await here further orders from headquarters Army of the Potomac." He did do Reynolds the courtesy of telling him that Brigadier General David B. Birney's division with two batteries was across Middle Creek (less than two miles from Emmitsburg).[86]

This snafu concerning Sickles' march on the 30th was indeed unfortunate. Had he carried out his original orders from Meade, or the set he received from Reynolds, he would have been in close support of the I and XI Corps, and so might have arrived at Gettysburg in time to participate in the fighting on 1 July. The confusion seems to have been due to faulty staff work at Meade's headquarters, and perhaps a bit of petulance by Sickles. Historian Edwin Coddington suggests that Meade just could not resist the temptation to give commands directly to Sickles in order to make sure his own wishes were being carried out.[87] He was new as army commander, and also could not resist sending orders to Howard, also bypassing Reynolds.[88] It would have been much more appropriate for Meade to have directed Sickles to report to Reynolds at Emmitsburg, and then send Reynolds directions on where to post him.

There is no evidence that Sickles made any effort to meet with Reynolds, who was only a few miles away on a direct road between Bridgeport and Fairplay. At least Howard and Reynolds were in tune with each other. They had been in constant communication all day,[89] and at sunset Reynolds requested the XI Corps commander to come to see him at his headquarters in the Moritz Tavern, located on the right side of the Gettysburg Road near Marsh Creek. Howard, accompanied by Major Charles Howard and Lieutenant F.W. Galbreath of his own staff, arrived just as Reynolds and his staff were sitting down to supper in the front room of the tavern. All were at ease, and their dinner talk included "a cheerful conversation on ordnance tactics;" Howard had served as an instructor of mathematics at West Point while Reynolds was the Commandant of Cadets.[90]

After supper, the two generals retired to a back room, where Reynolds showed Howard the order placing him in command of the army's left wing, as well as several circulars from the commander, and a confidential communication from Meade. One circular asked that "Corps and other commanding officers address their troops, explaining to them briefly the immense issues involved in the struggle." Clearly, a battle was near, and the two officers "consulted together, comparing notes and information, until a late hour." They were in hopes of receiving orders for the next day, but when these did not arrive by 2300, Howard returned to Emmitsburg.[91]

Meade's Plans for 1 July

It is not known why Meade was so late getting out his marching orders for 1 July. During the day he had transferred his headquarters from Middleburg to Taneytown in order to keep at the center of his army's front, and he had certainly found enough time to write quite a number of circulars and dispatches. It is most likely that he was waiting until the last minute in order to have all the latest reconnaissance information at hand. Besides, all his corps were already in camp, and no night marches were planned. But by midnight he had to make his decision, in order for the corps commanders to receive their commands in time to be on the road at daybreak if necessary.

Meade's thinking was still controlled by the goals he had written to Halleck soon after he assumed command on the morning of the 28th —to cover Washington and Baltimore, and to offer battle if the enemy were turned back from the Susquehanna or advanced on Baltimore.[92] He was certainly gratified that all reports seemed to indicate that Ewell had turned back from Harrisburg and the Susquehanna, so signalling that the Confederate invasion had crested in that direction. As historian Edwin B. Coddington points out, Meade's confidence was increased by the belief that his movements had compelled Lee to pull Ewell back, whereas Lee had already ordered the movement upon learning that the Union army was across the Potomac at Frederick.[93]

As already shown, Meade was concerned about Lee's concentration near Cashtown, and so had sent III Corps to reinforce Reynolds' left wing at Emmitsburg. Yet he was also concerned that Lee might be planning to pass through the Cashtown Gap to join Ewell somewhere south of Carlisle.[94] Reynolds' report that Anderson's division was marching through Mummasburg toward Berlin was particularly disconcerting in this regard, as was Gregg's report of an infantry concentration at Berlin.[95] In order to meet this threat and keep Baltimore covered, Meade decided to push on to Hanover on 1 July. This would enable him to meet and turn back the lead elements of Lee's invasion, and would also allow him to set up a new rail supply line to Baltimore from a base at Hanover Junction, which he hoped to have secure by 2 July. Meade shared these thoughts with Halleck in a confidential telegram he sent at 1630 on 30 June. In it he also expressed the concern that, "I fear I shall break down the troops by pushing on much faster, and may have to rest a day."[96]

Meade must have finished drafting his marching orders close to midnight, for they still bore the dateline 30 June. In the context of a seven paragraph directive, he stated his belief that the invasion had crested and it was time to fight the decisive battle: "The general believes he has relieved Harrisburg and Philadelphia, and now desires to look to his own army, and assume position for offensive or defensive, as occasion desires, or rest the troops." In preparation for the coming fight, the corps commanders were instructed to send their empty wagons, surplus baggage, and other impedimenta to Union Mills (3 miles from Middleburg), where a new supply base would soon be set up. He also instructed everyone to be "ready to move to the attack at any moment," and cautioned his commanders not to "wear the troops down by excessive fatigue and marches and thus render them unfit for the work they will be called upon to perform."[97] An accompanying circular directed the troops to be provided with three days' rations and 60 rounds of ammunition each, a sure sign that battle was near; ammunition wagons and ambulances were to keep close to the camps.[98] Yet another circular authorized corps and other commanders to order the "instant death of any soldier who fails in his duty at this hour."[99]

Meade's specific marching orders for 1 July were as follows. On the right, the V Corps was to proceed from Union Mills to Hanover, to be supported by VI Corps, which was to march through Westminster to Manchester, 10 miles south of Hanover. On the left, Reynolds was directed to move his I Corps to Gettysburg, followed closely by XI Corps, with the III Corps in supporting distance at Emmitsburg. In the center, XII Corps was to march from Littlestown to Two Taverns, while II Corps would serve as a reserve at Taneytown, where army headquarters would remain. The cavalry was to watch "the front and flanks, well out in all directions, giving timely notice of positions and movements of the enemy."[100]

Meade's greatest fear was that the Confederates might get by his army on either flank. In a separate communique he told Pleasonton that "He looks to you to keep him informed of their movements, and especially that no force concentrates on his right, in the vicinity of York, to get between him and the Susquehanna, and also that no force moves on to his left toward Hagerstown and the passes below Cashtown." In the same message Meade shared his intentions more openly with Pleasonton than he had with his other corps commanders: "His projected movement is toward the line of the Baltimore and Harrisburg road. His instructions require him to cover Baltimore and Washington, while his objective point is the army under Lee. To be able to find if this army is divided, and to concentrate upon any detached portion of it, without departing from the instructions which govern him, would be a great object."[101]

Study of Meade's planned dispositions for 1 July show that he was sending most of the army to the left, towards Gettysburg, rather than to the right at Hanover, as he had indicated to Halleck that he would be doing. Half his command was committed to the front—the I and XI Corps were to join Buford at Gettysburg, with III Corps at Emmitsburg supporting their left and XII Corps at Two Taverns supporting their right. Meade was certainly well aware of the recent Confederate probes to Fairfield and Gettysburg, and may well have been trying to provoke Lee into initiating a fight at or near Gettysburg. If Lee elected to do battle there before Ewell arrived from Carlisle and York, Meade was ready to meet him with half of his army in hand. If Lee did not chose to do battle, Meade could then shift his left more towards Hanover, as he had told Halleck he would do.

Meade made this bold opening move on the supposition that Ewell's troops were still at Carlisle and York, and that Hill's troops were no closer to Gettysburg than Cashtown. Buford's detailed report sent at 2230 on the 30th outlined the true situation much more accurately, but Meade did not receive it until late the next morning.[102] Had he received this or other related dispatches that came in during the morning of 1 July, at an earlier time, he might not have chosen to order Reynolds forward into such a precarious situation.

Meade apparently was not aware of Ewell's movement to the west until the early hours of 1 July, after he had composed and sent out his marching orders for the day. At 0700 he acknowledged receipt of several telegrams concerning Ewell that had been sent by Halleck and by General Couch, the militia commander at Harrisburg.[103] He should then have altered his orders to Reynolds, whose ordered move to Gettysburg might put him in a vise between Hill's troops at Cashtown and Ewell's coming from York. Instead, he chose to send Reynolds forward in order to develop the situation. In a carefully worded note that would be the last he would send to Reynolds, Meade warned his lieutenant that the enemy was concentrating "either at Chambersburg or at a point situated somewhere on a line drawn between Chambersburg and York, through Mummasburg and to the north of Gettysburg." Meade frankly admitted that he could not decide "whether it is his best policy to move to attack until he learns something more definite of the point at which the enemy is concentrating." If the Confederates were concentrating east of Gettysburg, "that point would not at first glance seem to be a proper strategic point of concentration for this army." If the enemy were concentrating in front of Gettysburg or to the west of the town, Meade was not "sufficiently well informed of the nature of the country to judge of its character for either an offensive or defensive position." He flatly stated that he wanted to have Reynolds' first hand view of the situation and suggestions as to what course to follow, particularly since "you know more of the condition of the troops in your vicinity and the country than he does." In short, Reynolds was being trusted to make a decision whether to fight, offensively or defensively, at Gettysburg - a decision he would not hesitate to take on 1 July. In closing, Meade stated, almost apologetically, that "The movement of your corps to Gettysburg was ordered before the positive knowledge of the enemy's withdrawal from Harrisburg and concentration was received."[104]

Remarkable to say, Meade was also planning a third strategy that night, besides the move towards Hanover and preparation for a possible fight at Gettysburg. If he were not able to meet the enemy on favorable terms in southern Pennsylvania, he would withdraw the army to northern Maryland and form behind Pipe Creek on the heights of Parr Ridge. There he could set up a strong 20 mile long line from Middleburg to Manchester that would shield both Washington and Baltimore and force the Confederates to attack in a "Fredericksburg in reverse" scenario.

Meade's famous "Pipe Creek Circular" was completed sometime after midnight on 30 June/1 July, not long after his 1 July marching orders were sent out, and was forwarded to his corps commanders later that morning. It contained detailed marching orders that called for Reynolds, when ordered, to pull the left wing back to Middleburg while Major General John Sedgwick occupied Manchester. Major General Henry Slocum was to take command of the center (XII and V Corps) and take positions behind Pipe Creek south of Union Mills. II Corps would serve as a reserve between Uniontown and Frizzleburg, where the artillery reserve would also concentrate. The army's trains, which had already been ordered to proceed to Union Mills, would be sent farther east to Westminster, located at the center of Parr Ridge.[105]

The circular began with a carefully worded preface that summarized the General's thinking: "From information received, the commanding general is satisfied that the object of the movement of the army in this direction has been accomplished, viz., the relief of Harrisburg, and the prevention of the enemy's invasion of Philadelphia, etc., beyond the Susquehanna. It is no longer his intention to assume the offensive until the enemy's movements or position should render such an operation certain of success. If the enemy assume the offensive, and attack, it is his intention, after holding them in check sufficiently long... to withdraw the army from its present position, and form line of battle with the left resting in the neighborhood of Middleburg and the right near Manchester... The time for falling back can only be developed by circumstance. Whenever such circumstances arise as would seem to indicate the necessity of falling back and assuming this general line indicated, notice of such movement will at once be communicated to these headquarters and all adjoining corps commanders."[106]

Interpretation of this circular has long been controversial. Meade's enemies after the battle used it as evidence that he was planning to retreat from the battle and never planned to fight at Gettysburg.[107] Historian Kenneth Williams felt that it showed intense uncertainty and a lack of "moral courage" in Meade.[108] Confederate Artillery Commander E. P. Alexander wrote after the war that he thought Meade ordered Reynolds forward to Gettysburg for the express purpose of delaying Lee long enough for preparations to be completed on the Pipe Creek line.[109]

These interpretations do not hold because Meade made it clear in the 1 July circular that the Pipe Creek plan was a conditional order that would be enacted only when and if conditions warranted: "This order is communicated, that a general plan, perfectly understood by all, may be had for receiving attack, if made in strong force, upon any portion of our present position." The fact that he was not committed to a defensive posture in Maryland is shown by the note, "Developments may cause the commanding general to assume the offensive from its present position.[110]

Meade's strategy that night, then, was fluid. He had confidence that Lee's invasion had crested, and that the enemy was no longer aiming to cross the Susquehanna. Whether the enemy was planning to advance against York, Baltimore, or Frederick, or was going to take a defensive position behind South Mountain, was not yet determined. Meade still saw his primary mission as the shielding of Baltimore and Washington, so he was beginning to shift his troops towards Hanover, a move that he was prepared to complete on 2 July if nothing developed on the 1st. He would defeat any isolated portion of Lee's army he could find, and was ready to challenge the Confederate troops known to be near Gettysburg. If Lee took up the challenge, that was fine, because Meade knew he had half his army nearby and most of the rest less than a day's march away. If nothing transpired at Gettysburg, he would complete his shift to Hanover the next day. And if Lee did attack in force or get around either of the army's flanks, the Pipe Creek plan would provide a prepared defense with which to meet the threat.

It was certainly a late night for Meade's headquarters staff, who had to transcribe and dispatch separate copies of marching orders and the Pipe Creek circular to all eight corps commanders and additional mentioned parties. The marching orders went out first. Howard, who was only 10 miles away at Emmitsburg, received his copy at 0330,[111] and Reynolds'copy arrived at his headquarters a few miles to the north at 0400.[112] The Pipe Creek circular was dispatched somewhat later than the marching orders, so much so that Reynolds had not received his copy before he departed for Gettysburg at about 0800.[113]

CHAPTER III

Opening Shots

*H*eth's troops were up before dawn (which came at 0436)[1] on the morning of 1 July, and were on the road at 0500.[2] The marching orders came unexpectedly, so much so that Archer's brigade did not have time to call in all its pickets. Colonel John A. Fite of the 7th Tennessee had decided to have breakfast with a picket detachment of his unit that was stationed about a mile east from the brigade's camps near Cashtown. They were still eating when "a courier came forward and ordered all of my pickets in and when I got back to where they were, they were getting ready to go into battle."[3] Privates W. H. Bird and Sam Biekly of Company C, 13th Alabama, who had gone out early to forage, were not so lucky, and did not get back to camp before their brigade moved out. The two had gone out with a number of canteens and haversacks, and were having their fill of cherries—they had located some cherry wine, and were up a cherry tree "eating the finest cherries I ever saw" when they heard the long roll beating the fall in for the march. By the time they returned to camp, the brigade was gone, but their friends had left the men's guns and knapsacks behind. The two wayward soldiers picked up their gear and soon rejoined their command.[4]

Lieutenant A. M. Moore of Company B, 7th Tennessee, had a different adventure that also caused him to miss the brigade's departure. On the morning of 30 June he had been sent out with 40 men to set up a picket on the Gettysburg Road outside of Cashtown, as noted in Chapter I. Soon after daybreak on 1 July he saw some Union cavalry appear on the same ridge where he had seen a few Union scouts the previous day. He was still observing them when he received orders to rejoin his regiment, which was forming to march to Gettysburg. The detachment arrived after their regiment departed, and they, too, had to hurry to rejoin their command.[5]

Heth had no cavalry to lead his command, so he chose to send Pegram's artillery battalion up the road first. Captain Edward A. Marye's Fredericksburg Artillery led the way, followed by the remaining four batteries of the battalion. Archer's brigade came next, with the 13th Alabama in the lead. Two regiments of Davis' brigade followed Archer. Davis initially had only two regiments, the 42nd Mississippi and 55th North Carolina, ready to move out.[6] The 2nd Mississippi was on guard duty at Cashtown and would march out a little while later to join the brigade by midmorning.[7] The 11th Mississippi was left behind as division train guard, and would not rejoin its brigade until evening.[8] There was an interval in Heth's column between Davis' regiments and the rest of the division that followed.[9]

Some sources state that Pettigrew's brigade led the second half of Heth's column, but most of this command had encamped the previous night between Mechanicstown and Marsh Creek (as shown in Chapter I). Perhaps the unit referred to was Pettigrew's 52nd North Carolina, which appears to have remained in Cashtown when the rest of the brigade advanced towards Gettysburg the previous day.[10] Brockenbrough's Virginia brigade, the smallest in the division, marched last in the column.[11] Heth's divisional artillery battalion, led by Lieutenant Colonel John J. Garnett, did not accompany the division, but remained in camp on the other side of Cashtown, near Anderson's division.[12]

Pender's division, accompanied by McIntosh's battalion of reserve artillery, followed Heth's division down the Chambersburg Pike at 0800. The division had reached the Cashtown Gap the previous afternoon, and encamped on the north side of the road on the west side of Cashtown. Pender was directed to leave his divisional artillery battalion behind at Cashtown, commanded by Major William T. Poague. He also left behind the 1st South Carolina Rifles of Colonel Abner Perrin's brigade as a wagon guard.[13]

In retrospect, it seems odd that Hill would have led his advance with Heth's command, which was a makeshift division pieced together after Chancellorsville under a new division commander. When Lee reorganized his army after the death of Stonewall Jackson and created three corps out of two, he promoted A.P. Hill to command of the new Third Corps, which was formed around the nucleus of Hill's famous "Light Division." The light division's four best brigades, Scales', Lane's, Thomas' and Pender's, were given to Dorsey Pender as new division commander, and Heth was given a totally new division composed of the Light Division's two smallest brigades, Archer's and his own Virginia brigades, plus two relatively inexperienced brigades (Davis' and Pettigrew's) from the defenses of Richmond. Heth was a friendly and competent commander but not particularly inspiring or aggressive, and so made a strange choice to lead the Third Corps down the road to Gettysburg.[14] Hill might have done better to have sent Pender to carry out the task, but Heth had specifically asked for the job, and his men were encamped closer to the objective than were Pender's.

It was awkward, even dangerous, for Heth to send his artillery first, particularly since he had no cavalry to scout and clear the road ahead of him. Heth later admitted that he was careless to march with his batteries in advance. He had done so out of overconfidence because he did not know that any of Meade's army was north of the Potomac, and believed all he would face would be local militia, who would run as soon as he appeared.[15]

It would have seemed more appropriate for Heth to have Pettigrew lead his column. His was the largest brigade in the division, and its men had become familiar with the road to Gettysburg the day before. In addition, Pettigrew was by far the most dynamic, if not the most experienced, of Heth's brigade commanders.

Heth's order of march was also strangely chosen. Archer and his five commands from Alabama and Tennessese were all veterans, but the brigade's regiments were all badly depleted and averaged only 240 men each.[16] Davis' brigade was the second largest in the division, but not all its units were present when the brigade marched out, as previously noted. The brigade's only two veteran regiments, the 2nd and 11th Mississippi, were absent for the moment, and the two regiments that were present, the 42nd Mississippi and the 55th North Carolina, had never been in battle before.[17] To make matters worse, the brigade's commander, Joseph R. Davis, owed his position solely to the fact that he was the nephew of the Confederate President. He had been a politician and lawyer before the war, and had only minimal military experience. In fact, his nomination as brigadier general had been initially rejected by the Confederate Senate amidst widespread cries of nepotism.

His confirmation as brigadier general on 15 September 1862 and subsequent placement as a brigade commander in the field generated additional controversy around him.[18]

Heth's column proceeded pleasantly along without any special concern for any Union troops being nearby, in spite of the warnings that Pettigrew had given to Archer and Heth the previous evening. Captain Marye of the Fredericksburg Artillery noted that, "The morning was lovely. A soft, fresh breeze rippled over ripe wheat fields stretching on either side of us. We moved forward leisurely smoking and chatting as we rode along, not dreaming of the proximity of the enemy."[19]

Between 0600 and 0700 the Confederate column passed by the camp of Pettigrew's brigade near McKnightstown; Private E. T. Boland of the 13th Alabama mistook the command for Anderson's division.[20] Someone in Pettigrew's camp incorrectly told Davis' men as they passed that they would only have Pennsylvania militia to fight.[21]

Boland notes that he next passed through a small village "of a few brick houses," probably Seven Stars. A half mile farther on the road descended to the thick, wet woodland along Marsh Creek. The command halted there under a misty rain that had begun to fall. Union pickets had been spotted on the other side of the stream, and Colonel B. D. Fry of the 13th Alabama wanted the regiment's color guard to come forward and uncase their colors before entering action. Boland continues his account: "We discovered about this time a squad of Federal cavalry up to our right in an open field, holding their horses. We were then ordered to file to the right into an apple orchard and to load our guns at will. Companies B, C and G of the 13th Alabama, and the 5th Alabama Battalion were ordered out and deployed on the skirmish line."[22]

Major Pegram had also noticed the Union cavalry across the creek, and ordered his artillery column to halt. Captain Marye relates, that "Somewhere between the hours of seven and eight o'clock, Colonel Pegram's attention was suddenly called to what in the distance seemed to be a line of men on a hill to the right of us, but too far ahead to discern the color of their uniforms. Colonel Pegram deemed it prudent to halt his column. Most of us argued that the men we saw must be some of Longstreet's corps. It being generally understood that he was advancing along a road to the right of us. That idea was dispelled by one of our sergeants who, having been left behind in Virginia and who had overtaken us on the night before, rode forward and informed Colonel Pegram that he had passed Longstreet's corps and that it was two days march in our rear. That decided the question, and at a word from Colonel Pegram the leading gun, a three-inch rifle piece of accuracy and long range, was at once unlimbered and swung around."[23]

First Shots by 8th Illinois Cavalry

The Union cavalry squadron spotted by Marye and Pegram was the advance vedettes of the 8th Illinois Cavalry. As already noted, Gamble had posted a squadron of this unit on the Chambersburg Pike near Marsh Creek late on the afternoon of the previous day. At 0600 the regiment's vedette post no. 1, located about ¾ mile east of the bridge over Marsh Creek near the intersection of the Knoxlyn Road with Chambersburg Pike, was relieved by Privates Thomas B. Kelley and James O. Hall of Company E. Ten minutes later the two noticed a cloud of dust rising on the horizon some three miles distant. The cloud soon broadened and deepened as it grew closer on the line of Chambersburg Pike.[24]

At about 0700 Kelley and Hall saw the head of the Confederate column with "the old Rebel Flag" in front. The two anxious troopers could not see their sergeant, Levi S. Shafer, nearby, so Kelley rode quickly to alert the picket reserve, located some 48 rods to the rear.[25] He must have given the alarm to Private George Heim, who in turn passed it on to the picket commander, Lieutenant Marcellus E. Jones. Jones had just toured the picket line, but got hungry, and rode back toward the reserve in order to purchase some bread and butter for himself and some oats for his horse from a farm house. Jones had just arrived and given his victuals to his servant, when Heim rode up in haste and reported that Sergeant Shafer wanted him at once on the picket line. Jones at once lept on his horse, not waiting for his servant to saddle a fresh one, and shouted, "Get the entire command to the outpost."[26]

Jones rode quickly to the front and lept from his horse, handing the reins to Private Hall. He at once saw the cloud of dust rising from Heth's marching column, and tore a leaf from his memoranda book to report this to his regimental commander, Major Beveridge. Jones ordered his men to dismount and sent their horses to the rear with their horse holders. He then met Sergeant Shafer, who had returned to the post, and asked to borrow the sergeant's carbine. Jones placed the gun in the fork of a nearby rail fence and at about 0730 fired at a man riding on a gray horse to the left of the enemy colors that were advancing up the road.[27] The distance was at least one-half mile, so Jones had little likelihood of actually hitting his target. The shot was clearly heard by Private Boland of the 13th Alabama, who noted, "After the line of the brigade was formed, the command 'Forward March' was given. As soon as the skirmish line entered the swamp a shot rang out, it being the first gun fired in the great battle of Gettysburg."[28]

In 1886, some 23 years after the battle, Jones and two of his comrades erected a small marker commemorating their role in starting the battle. The stone, which was quarried and cut in Napiersville, Illinois, is 5 feet high and tapers from 18 inches square at the base to 9 inches square at the top. It was erected on ground purchased in the yard of a private home located on a rise on the north side of Chambersburg Pike near its intersection with the Knoxlyn Road, and is still preserved today, though far from the boundaries of the Gettysburg National Military Park. The four sides of the stone read as follows: "First shot at Gettysburg, July 1, 1863, 7:30 A. M.;" "Fired by Captain M. E. Jones with Sergeant Shafer's carbine, Co. E, Eighth Regiment Illinois Cavalry;" "Erected by Captain Jones, Lieutenant Riddler, and Sergeant Shafer"; "Erected 1886."[29]

Other Claims for the First Shot

It should be noted that Jones' shot was not the first of the day, though it was often claimed to be so by a number of zealous sources.[30] The actual first shots of the battle were fired at dawn between vedettes of the 17th Pennsylvania Cavalry posted on the Carlisle Pike and some Confederate troops under Ewell's direction, probably a detachment of the 1st Maryland Cavalry or possibly of French's 17th Virginia Cavalry.[31]

The second skirmish of the day took place sometime between 0500 and 0600 on the Hunterstown Road. Soon after dawn Privates Thomas Smith and Marcus Hall of Company E, 9th New York, were sent out to picket the road to Hunterstown. They proceeded out as far as the town and spotted four mounted Confederates near the town's hotel. Hall rode to a house and asked some men on the porch how many rebels were in the area. Upon hearing there were "about 300," the two troopers immediately rode out of town. They were spotted by the Confederates, who began to pursue them. Smith and Hall rode as fast as they could back towards Gettysburg. As they passed over a hill, they luckily ran into another patrol from their regiment, which charged and captured all four of the surprised enemy riders as they came up.[32]

The most insistent rival to Jones' claim for firing the first shot was put forward in favor of Corporal Alphonse Hodges of Company F, 9th New York Cavalry of Devin's brigade. The unit's regimental history claims that, "At daylight on the morning of July 1, Corporal Alphonse Hodges, of Co. F, 9th N. Y., with three men were on duty at this post [on the Chambersburg Pike near Willoughby Run]. Men were seen approaching on the road beyond Willoughby Run and nearly a mile away. Acting on his orders, Hodges sent his men to notify the line and the reserve while he advanced across the stream, stopping to water his horse. He then rode to the higher ground beyond far enough to see that the men approaching were Confederates. He then turned back and as he did so they fired on him. Hodge retired to the bridge where, from behind its stone abutments, he fired several shots at the advancing enemy. These are supposed to be the first shots fired from our side on the morning of July 1st at Gettysburg, and occurred about 0530, as near as Hodges can remember."[33]

The most serious argument against Hodges case for firing the "first shot" is the simple fact that it is unlikely any Confederates made it past Gamble's forward picket line to Hodge's post on the Chambersburg Pike near Willoughby Run, especially since the enemy had no cavalry. It is possible that Hodges was mistaken about the time, and actually meant to refer to Heth's advance at about 0800; the remainder of the 9th New York account refers to Devin forming his brigade in battle line soon after Hodge fired, as will be noted shortly. Major Beveridge is less kind, and suggests that Hodges fired at "some imaginary foe" or was alarmed by "the champing of the bit, the clink of the saber, or the clattering of the hoof."[34] He may even have shot at some of Gamble's pickets returning down the pike to their brigade camp.

Another Union claimant for the honor of firing the first shot was Private F.W. Whitney of Company B, 17th Pennsylvania. He asserted that he was on duty on the Chambersburg Pike when he fired at the advancing enemy at about 0600. This story is not credible, since the 17th Pennsylvania was not picketing the Chambersburg Pike. However, Whitney may have confused his road names, and actually may have instead meant one of the roads north of town picketed by Devin's brigade. If so, his case would be stronger.[35]

A last claimant for this honor has an even weaker case. An unnamed cavalryman of the 6th New York Cavalry claimed to have fired the first shot at dawn. The 6th New York's vedettes were posted along Willoughby Run north of the Chambersburg Pike, but no Confederates are known to have been in that area at the time. This man may simply have been nervously firing at a stray noise.[36]

The Confederates also have their claimant for the first shot in the battle. As already noted, when the Union vedettes were first observed east of Marsh Creek, Major Pegram ordered a 3-inch rifled gun of the Fredericksburg artillery to unlimber and prepare to fire. The gun was deployed near a house with a porch on front, and when the command "Load with shrapnel shell" was given, a man in shirt sleeves rushed onto the porch and exclaimed, "My God, you are not going to fire here, are you?" He then ran off with his hands up in the air, as the gun blasted forth its first shell, which "burst high above the line of the men on the hill. Thus was fired the first shot in one of the greatest battles of modern times," wrote Lieutenant John Marye. It may well have been the first gun fired by the Confederate side, since Archer's skirmishers were probably not in position yet. But it seems likely that Lieutenant Jones' carbine shot came first, though not by much, since it was aimed at Archer's lead troops as they were moving towards Marsh Creek.[37] It is unlikely that Marye's artillerymen heard or noticed Shafer's shot; the Union sources would probably have mentioned the Confederates' artillery shot if it had come first.

The first Confederate shots of the day were actually fired "just after daylight" on Gamble's picket line southwest of Gettysburg. Two soldiers of the 8th New York Cavalry, Alfred W. Davies and William Rollinson, took their horses to a stream to drink, and were fired at by two shots. They at once fled for cover, and Davies came upon the Confederate soldiers who were reloading their weapons. He commanded them to surrender, and they did. It is not recorded what unit they were from.[38]

Shortly after Jones fired his famous first shot, Archer's skirmishers crossed Marsh Creek and began to return fire. By now the initial skirmish line of the 5th Alabama Battalion and three companies of the 13th Alabama was probably reinforced by a body of sharpshooters from the 1st Tennessee under the command of Major Buchanan.[39] These sharp-shooters and skirmishers were apparently backed up by the remainder of the 5th Alabama Battalion, and were probably deployed on the south side of Chambersburg Pike. The remainder of Archer's brigade proceeded in column up the road, apparently still preceded by Pegram's artillery. At the same time Davis deployed skirmishers on the north side of the road, consisting of at least a detachment of the 55th North Carolina.[40]

He apparently kept the remainder of his brigade in column formation on the Pike.

Jones' small Union force dismounted and covered what ground they could, and fell back slowly under the pressure of Heth's more numerous skirmishers. Before 0800 Captain A.E. Dana, commander of Jones' Company E, 8th Illinois, arrived to support Jones with the "larger portion" of his company, which had been posted as the picket reserve about a mile west of Gettysburg, near the Chambersburg Pike. When he arrived at the outpost, Dana "could see the enemy's skirmish line advancing slowly, and reaching from right to left across the Cashtown Road, as we thought, for a distance of a mile and a half, concealed at intervals by timber, a continuous line formed for advancing; a short distance in the rear of this skirmish line, in the open road, were columns of infantry deploying in the woods, evidently forming their line of battle."[41]

Dana sent a hasty report to Colonel Gamble, and prepared his men for action by ordering them to dismount and send their horses to the rear with every fourth man as a horse holder. He then called in all the pickets and formed a line of 20 men across the pike and railroad bed "a few hundred yards in rear of the picket line held during the night." He scattered his men in a thin skirmish line at intervals of 30 feet and stationed them behind post and rail fences at the edge of a large open field. The men were specifically directed to rest their carbines on the top rail of the fence and set their sights for 800 yards.[42]

Dana noted that the Confederates at this point began an artillery barrage, probably more rounds from Marye's gun already mentioned. Most of the artillery rounds, however, overshot the Union skirmishers, and endangered only "the orderlies carrying our reports to and from the front."[43]

Dana's force, by now reinforced by other elements of Gamble's forward skirmish line, was pushed back slowly towards Herr Ridge by the much longer and stronger Confederate line. Dana noted that "The true character and length of our line soon became known to the enemy, and they promptly moved upon our front and flanks. We retired, and continued to take new positions, and usually held out as long as we could without imminent risk of capture."[44]

First Casualties

The first casualties of the battle may have been canines, not humans. W. F. Fulton of Company A, 5th Alabama Battalion, recorded that he and his comrades took their mascot, a little dog, into action with them, and the poor creature was wounded by the first round of shots from the Union cavalry. Fulton related, "He was an innocent bystander, a harmless onlooker, so to speak, with no concern either way as to which side should whip, yet he was the first struck in the shower of lead and his life surrendered in the good cause of States Rights and Home Rule."[45]

Fulton and his friends exacted some revenge for the loss of their mascot after they passed through the wheatfield on the western slope of Herr Ridge. They were dodging Union carbine shots and ran for cover to a house beyond the field, only to be confronted by a fierce barking dog. This racket roused the dog's owner to come out from his cellar hiding place. He asked, "What are you looking for?" and the soldiers bemusedly responded that a big battle was starting. The amazed farmer asked, "By whom?" and the Confederates responded, "By General Lee and the Yankees." The man, who may have thought that only militia were on hand, asked the Alabamians to "Tell Lee to hold on just a little until I get my cow out of the pasture." The farmer ran to get his cow, and Fulton's Company A pushed on.[46] Soon afterwards two companies of the 13th Alabama approached the house. Once again the farmer's dog began barking. This time the farmer was not right there to quiet him, and some of the Confederates shot the animal dead. The noise of their shots brought out the farmer's wife, who sharply berated the slayers of her dog. Private W. H. Bird of Company C, 13th Alabama, wrote that "Then the old lady got stirred up; some of the boys had knocked down her ash hopper, so that, with the death of her dog, gave her room to believe that the Rebels were terrible fellows."[47]

It took less than an hour for Heth's skirmishers and sharpshooters to push back Gamble's skirmish line to the western slopes of Herr Ridge, which was about a mile east of the spot where Jones fired his first shot. The ground west of Herr Ridge was almost entirely open, but the dismounted Union troopers skillfully took advantage of "every stone, stump, tree and fence" to retard the Confederate advance.[48]

The balance of the fight changed noticeably a little after 800 when Dana's company received heavy reinforcements in the form of another squadron from the 8th Illinois and three squadrons of the 8th New York that had been sent forward from Gamble's camp near Seminary Ridge.[49] These reinforcements, which added about 300 men to the Union skirmish line,[50] must have slowed Heth's advance to a crawl. It was probably at this time that two Parrott guns of the Fredericksburg Artillery were run forward, unlimbered in the road, and opened on a piece of woods to the left of the pike in order to give support to Heth's skirmishers.[51]

The first human casualty of the battle appears to have occurred when Gamble's four fresh squadrons reached Dana's skirmish line. Up until this point all the Union troopers had been fighting dismounted. At approximately this point in the battle, an unnamed Union trooper rode his white horse in advance of the Union line and was promptly felled by Confederate fire.[52] The felled trooper may have been one of Gamble's reinforcements, part of which were sent forward mounted—Buford related in his battle report that "three squadrons, part dismounted, were ordered to the front, and deployed as skirmishers to support the squadron on picket, now being driven back by the enemy's artillery and skirmishers."[53]

Not long afterwards Private John E. Weaver of Company A, 3rd Indiana Cavalry, was badly wounded in the left thigh by Confederate artillery fire. He had to endure an amputation, but could not recover, and died on 3 August in Camp Letterman.[54]

The Confederates had also began to suffer their first casualties by this point. The first Confederate wounded in the battle was Private C. L. F. Worley of Company A, 5th Alabama Battalion. He suffered an ugly wound in the thigh and was carried back to the division's field hospital. One of the doctors there told him his leg had to come off and prepared to give him a dose of chloroform. Worley stoutly refused, saying "cut off the leg, Doc, but leave off the chloroform, if you can stand it, I can." The 5th Alabama Battalion lost two additional men wounded during this early stage of the battle, Private J. T. Barnes of Company A and Private E. H. Griffin of Company B.[55]

Heth Deploys

The fighting became more intense as the Union troopers pulled back over the crest of Herr Ridge.[56] There was a large woods south of the Chambersburg Pike on the eastern slope of the ridge, and this slowed the advance of Archer's skirmishers considerably. As a result, Heth decided to deploy the remaining infantry of his two front brigades along the crest of Herr Ridge as soon as that height was secured. Since Pegram's artillery was still at the front of the column on the road, Heth directed Pegram to place "a couple of batteries in position" and "fire at the woods to his front for half an hour and see if he could get a response."[57] The two Parrott guns already mentioned, which had just fired 8 or 10 rounds at the Yankees as they passed over Herr Ridge, were brought up first. Pegram also brought up an additional 10 Napoleons and 5 rifled pieces ready for action. He chose not to deploy two howitzers of one battery because of their limited range. In addition, one rifled piece of the Pee Dee Artillery was not deployed because "it was disabled while being brought rapidly into action."[58]

Heth's motive in posting Pegram's batteries was as much to feel out the enemy's position as it was to allow his infantry to come up and form. During his march that morning he had received a dispatch from Lee "ordering me to get the shoes even if I encountered some resistance."[59] He felt that these directions overrode the orders he had received the previous evening not to force an engagement if he met Union infantry.[60] He remained convinced that there was no regular infantry in his front, just militia,[61] and felt that Pegram's shells might send them packing just as Early had scattered the 26th Pennsylvania Militia on much the same ground 5 days earlier.

Archer's brigade was deployed on the south side of the Chambersburg Pike, the general line its skirmishers had held since their advance first began. The 7th Tennessee was posted with its left on the road itself. To its right, in order, were the 14th Tennessee, 1st Tennessee, and 13th Alabama;[62] the brigade skirmish line, composed of the 5th Alabama Battalion and two companies of the 13th, was sent out about 100 yards to the front.[63] W. H. Moon of Company I of the 13th noted later that his regiment first formed up near a two story dwelling behind some woods on Herr Ridge, a mile west of Herbst Woods.[64] This was probably the B. Herr house, located 3/8 mile southwest of the Herr Tavern and Chambersburg Pike. Moon also observed that a "Confederate battery of three guns came up and took position on the right front of my regiment, the 13th Alabama, in the edge of an open field which extended down to and across Willoughby Run."[65]

At the same time Davis deployed his brigade on the north side of the Pike, with his right resting on the road itself. He posted the 42nd Mississippi on the right, the experienced 2nd Mississippi (which had just arrived from Cashtown) in the center, and the 55th North Carolina on the left. As already noted, Davis' fourth regiment, the 11th Mississippi, had been left at Cashtown to guard wagon trains and would not be engaged on 1 July.[66]

Heth's front line was about ⅝ of a mile long. Davis' line extended about ¼ mile north of the Pike, and ran across Willoughby Run, perhaps as far as the Bender east-west farm lane.[67] Due to the threat of Devin's cavalry skirmish line that extended farther to the north, a company of the 55th North Carolina was thrown out to protect the brigade's left flank. Archer's line extended about ⅜ mile to the south, with at least the far right regiment, the 13th Alabama, posted in a heavy woods. When they came up, Pettigrew's and then Brockenbrough's brigades were stationed in reserve on the western slope of the ridge, just south of the Pike, across the lane from Herr Tavern.[68]

Pettigrew's advance towards Gettysburg had not been a smooth one that morning. After marching some distance from its camp near Seven Stars, the 47th North Carolina, which led the brigade's column, was fired on from ambush by dismounted Union cavalry on both sides of the road; who these Union troopers were cannot be determined exactly, but they were surely from Gamble's brigade. Colonel G.H. Faribault of the 47th at once halted the column and ordered Captain Cameron Iredell of Company C to take five men from each company to charge the enemy on the right, and Lieutenant Westray of Company A was to take the same number of men to the left. One historian of the 47th describes the action that followed: "Faribault then gave the order for our regiment to march in column to the right by fours, thus heading our column directly towards the attacking party, who were on the right of the road. Colonel Marshall, who was just in rear of the Forty-seventh Regiment with the Fifty-second, made the same movement with his gallant regiment, to the left of the road, thus the brigade faced three ways. The main line composed of the Forty-seventh and Fifty-second, faced in the direction of Gettysburg, while the two skirmish lines faced the enemy on our right and left respectively. As soon as the rear and left of the Forty-seventh reached the cleared ground on the right of the road and the rear and right of the Fifty-second had reached the cleared ground on the left, both regiments were ordered to halt. The Forty-seventh was ordered to face about and march on its side of the road, and passed the Fifty-second some distance. Then it was halted and the Fifty-second faced about and marched the same distance beyond the Forty-seventh, thus constantly keeping one regiment facing the enemy who was in our font trying to advance from that direction, while the skirmishers of the Forty-seventh were hotly engaged with them on the right and left of the road, respectively. This movement and fight was kept up then until the Forty-seventh was enabled to strike the enemy's line on the right of the road and the Fifty-second to strike the enemy's line, which was on the left of the road. This being done, a forward movement by the Forty-seventh and Fifty-second was again ordered, one on the right and one on the left, which was gallantly done without any loss except four or five slightly wounded. The enemy broke and fled towards Gettysburg at the second volley from the two regiments. The Eleventh and Twenty-sixth were not engaged in this skirmish. Marching in the rear, they did not have room to form in line in time, for the Forty-seventh and Fifty-second had about 1,300 men in line in both regiments. After repulsing the attack at this point we again marched back to the road, called in our skirmishers and took up our march, which was continued about one mile, when we were subjected to a severe cannonading from batteries in our front and here we commenced to get into position and form line of battle for the great struggle which was about to take place on 1 July, 1863."[69]

Buford Deploys

At about the time Heth was beginning his dispositions on Herr Ridge, Buford was completing the formation of his two brigades on McPherson's Ridge, a mile to the east of Heth's line. The morning had started calmly enough for the Union cavalry encamped near Seminary Ridge, despite the numerous reports received during the night that strong Confederate columns were nearing Gettysburg from the direction of Hunterstown, Carlisle and Cashtown. Buford's men apparently were up at dawn, and a number of officers and men headed to town for refreshment or other personal needs. Trooper A.R. Mix of the 9th New York secured permission from General Buford to go to town to get a pair of boots. Lieutenant John Calef, commander of Buford's battery, made plans after breakfast to "make a hasty inspection of Gettysburg, there to make some purchases for our mess."[70] There were also a number of Gettysburg civilians who ventured out to Buford's camp soon after dawn. Young Leander Warren was even permitted to help lead horses to drink at a stream.[71]

Early morning skirmishes involving Devin's troopers north of town have already been described. At about 0700 Colonel Devin sent Companies C and M of the 9th New York out the Harrisburg Road past Rock Creek to relieve Companies A and H, which had been posted there and on Hunterstown Road the previous afternoon. Once they arrived, twelve men of Company M were sent to picket the Hunterstown Road half a mile to the east. The forward vedettes on both the Hunterstown and Harrisburg Roads were within sight of Confederate vedettes a half mile to the north.[72]

At about 0700 Buford was informed of Heth's approach by Lieutenant Aaron B. Jerome, a signal officer attached to his staff. Jerome had been directed "to look out for a prominent position and watch the movements of the enemy." He climbed to the "steeple" (cupola) of the Seminary and noted Heth's advance down the Chambersburg Pike, which he at once reported to Buford.[73]

Buford, however, did not take action until an hour later, when he received positive news that Heth's skirmishers were pressuring his forward vedettes. It seems that in the meanwhile he may have gone into town for some reason. General Doubleday later related a story that Lieutenant Colonel John A. Kress of General Wadsworth's staff entered Gettysburg just before the fighting grew heavy and found General Buford surrounded by his staff in front of a tavern. When Buford asked, "What are you doing here, sir?" Kress replied that he came to get some shoes for Wadsworth's division. Buford said that the officer ought to return at once to his command, to which Kress replied, "Why what is the matter, General?" Just then the voice of a single gun was heard, and Buford mounted his horse to ride to his men after saying "That's the matter."[74]

Buford was not at his headquarters at 0800 when a courier arrived from Captain Daniel Buck, commander of the 8th Illinois' forward picket line on the Chambersburg Pike near Marsh Creek, and reported to the 8th's commander, Major John L. Beveridge, that "The enemy was advancing in force in two columns." Beveridge was unable to locate his superior officers, so he took it upon himself to send another squadron of the 8th Illinois to support Buck. He sent orderlies "uptown" to give the alarm to whatever troops were in Gettysburg, and soon afterwards Colonel Gamble and General Buford rode up. Gamble's camp was soon in an uproar as "boots and saddles" was sounded, then the order "to horse!"[75]

Gamble, who claimed in his battle report that he received Buck's warning directly from the front, says that he communicated the news directly to Buford, "who ordered my command to be in immediate readiness to fight the enemy." He sent three squadrons to reinforce Buck, as already noted (probably including the one mentioned by Beveridge), and then posted his brigade in battle line, on McPherson's Ridge astride the Chambersburg Pike. He placed the 3rd Indiana on the right, north of the railroad cut, and the 12th Illinois between the cut and the Pike; both were under command of Colonel George H. Chapman of the 3rd Indiana. The 8th Illinois formed south of the Pike near the McPherson farm and orchard, while the 8th New York was stationed one quarter mile to the left, to the left and rear of Herbst Woods.[76] He then sent 900 dismounted skirmishers of the 8th Illinois, 8th New York and 3rd Indiana to the base of McPherson's Ridge at Willoughby Run with orders "to keep back the enemy as long as possible till our infantry came up to our support."[77] If Gamble's figure is correct, he committed over half his men with the pickets or on the skirmish line.[78] However, the letter containing this information contains other errors, and may not be totally accurate.[79] When Buford drew up his men, he "seemed to sense the hard work before him" and sent all "poorly mounted" men to the rear. Asa Hardman was one of five men from his company of the 3rd Indiana who were sent to the rear. They turned their horses in at a corral in the rear, and three of the party returned to the front.[80] The detaching of those "poorly mounted" men was in addition to the loss of horse holders from the front lines; when troopers were dismounted, one man out of every four went to the rear to hold the party's horses.

Gamble also ordered Lieutenant Calef to advance his battery to the battle line. As already noted, Calef was preparing to go into Gettysburg when the fight on the skirmish line began to heat up. As he was waiting for his horse, one of Buford's orderlies galloped up and directed him to prepare for action at once because the enemy was advancing. As a result Calef never did make it to town, and he did not get a chance to make his contemplated visit to Gettysburg until thirty-one years later.[81]

Calef's men broke camp "in an incredibly short time" and sent their baggage and caissons to the Seminary building, located in the rear near their camp. Gamble gave Calef latitude to select his own battle position, so Calef prepared to form on the Pike at the center of Gamble's line "on a crest in front of the one he had occupied during the night." He sent out a detachment to knock down the fences between his camp and the proposed battle position, and also knocked down the fences in front of the new position in order to clear a field of fire.[82]

Calef had just moved his guns forward when he saw Buford ride up nearby. He reported to him for further instructions and received orders to spread his battery out by posting four of his guns along the Pike and two on the brigade's left flank. Calef accordingly placed Lieutenant John W. Roder's right section on the right of the Pike and Sergeant Joseph Newman's left section on the left of the road. Sergeant Charles Pergel's center section was sent 600 yards to the left and formed behind a north-south fence in the area southeast of Herbst Woods, near the position of the 8th New York.[83] The battery was split up in this manner in order "to cover as large a front as possible with my battery (his only artillery) for the purpose of deceiving the enemy as to his strength."[84]

As soon as his guns were in position, Calef directed Lieutenant Roder to fire "on the head of a column of rebel cavalry advancing on the right of the road."[85] Who this cavalry was cannot be determined, since the Confederates are not known to have had any organized cavalry units available on this front; perhaps Calef saw some of Pegram's mounted artillerymen or a body of officers on reconnaissance.[86] Calef recognized the import of this first Union artillery shot of the battle, and recorded the gun's serial number. The tube was identified after the war, and now rests at the foot of Buford's statue on the battlefield, at the site where the shot was fired.[87]

Amelia Harmon, who lived just southwest of Herbst woods, heard Calef's first shot and then was surprised to see the 8th New York and Pergel's two cannons come dashing by her house. "At nine a.m. came the boom of a cannon to the west of us. We rushed to the window, to behold hundreds of galloping horses coming up the road, through the field and even past our door. Boom! again spoke the cannon, and more galloping horses, their excited riders shouting and yelling to each other and pushing westward in hot haste, past the house and barn, seeking shelter of a strip of woods on the ridge beyond."[88]

When Calef's guns began firing in long range support of Buford's skirmishers, they attracted the attention of Pegram's batteries, which had just ceased their half hour bombardment ordered by Heth because they had received no reply from Buford's line. Calef in his battle report noted that he became engaged in a brisk contest with two Confederate batteries of four guns each, one on each side of the Pike on Herr Ridge.[89] When more Confederate batteries soon joined the fight, Calef became concerned and "directed the firing to be made slowly and deliberately and reported to Buford what was in my front."[90]

Buford also ordered Devin's brigade to deploy when he sent Gamble's troopers into line on McPherson's Ridge. Because of the immediate threat from the west, Devin was instructed "to prepare for action and form on the crest of the hill on the right of the First Brigade."[91]

The first troopers that Devin sent forward were the men of the 9th New York Cavalry, who were already horsed because they happened to be watering their horses by squadron in "Rock Creek" at about 0800.[92] Some of the 9th's men had already seen a few of Davis' skirmishers deploying northward and toward the Mummasburg Road. The regiment's unit history describes in detail the New Yorkers' movement to the front: "As soon as each squadron returned it was ordered out on the Mummasburg Road to support the pickets. Frapier, the bugler, blew the calls 'Boots and Saddles,' 'Double Quick,' 'Prepare to Mount' in quick succession, the men promptly responding, companies F and K having watered their horses were the first to saddle up and reach the picket line. Lieutenant A. C. Robertson with 20 men of Company F, by Captain Harley's order, rode out the Mummasburg Road to near the Hoffman House and found the enemy approaching in considerable force through the woods south of the road. Robertson was driven back to the open field east of the Forney House. Here Hanley's squadron held its position, his line extending across the Mummasburg Road, until the enemy's skirmishers reached the Forney buildings when some men of the squadron dismounted and drove the enemy from behind these buildings. In this skirmish, W. A. Scranton of Company F, was wounded."[93]

After this brief skirmish, Hanley's squadron of the 9th retired towards Seminary Ridge, which was located 100 rods to the east of the Forney House. By this time the other regiments of the brigade had come up and deployed, apparently still mounted, to connect the 9th New York's line with the Mummasburg Road on the right and Buford's line north of the railroad cut on the left. Evidence is contradictory, but it appears that the 17th Pennsylvania was on the right of the 9th New York, with its right on the Mummasburg Road, while the 6th New York and the squadron of the 3rd West Virginia formed between the left of the 9th New York and the right of Gamble's 3rd Indiana.[94]

Devin continued to maintain his skirmish line after he brought up his brigade, and sent a squadron on the 6th New York to his front and left to support Gamble's pressured line near the Chambersburg Pike. The remainder of his skirmish line ran north along Willoughby Run to the point where it had been bent back by Davis' skirmishers who had advanced toward the Hoffman and Forney Farms.[95] Devin was also called upon to send a squadron of the 17th Pennsylvania (Companies

E and L) to the left to support Calef's four guns on the Pike.[96] The brigade's vedettes and outposts established the previous evening on the roads north and northeast of Gettysburg were left in place, due to increasing pressure from the advance elements of Early's and Rodes' divisions.[97]

As already noted, some of Davis' skirmishers struck Devin's skirmish line near the Hoffman farm and readily pushed the Union troopers there back towards Seminary Ridge. The remainder of Davis' skirmish line to the south made good progress because of their advantage in numbers and the open lay of the land. During the opening part of the engagement Devin had kept most of the troops in his main line mounted in the open fields where they had formed on Gamble's right. As such they posed a fine target for Pegram's guns, which shelled them vigorously.[98] Shortly before 0900 Devin thought it wise to pull back and take advantage of the woods and stone walls on the top of Seminary Ridge in his rear.[99] Devin noted in his battle report, "I was ordered to retire gradually, as they (the enemy) succeeded in getting the range of my position. This I affected in successive formations in line to the rear by regiment."[100]

When they completed their withdrawal, Devin's troopers took up a position in front of Wills Woods, which ran along much of northern Seminary Ridge. Some of the men were mounted and some dismounted. The historian of the 9th New York noted that Hanley's battalion of that unit "formed dismounted behind a stone wall along the crest of the ridge supported by the other companies of the regiment mounted."[101] The right end of the line, held by the 17th Pennsylvania, did not have cover from the woods, which receded to their rear. Devin's dispositions on the new line were complete by 0900.[102] At about this time General Buford rode up to Colonel Devin, who was near the position of the 9th New York, and urged him, "Devin, this is the key to the army position. We must hold this if it cost every man in your command."[103] Another version of the story has Buford saying that Seminary Ridge must be held, and "You now have to fight like the devil to do it."[104]

After Devin's line was reformed on the ridge, some of his men saw Confederate skirmishers creeping forward on their hands and knees through the wheatfield in their front. Daniel Cornish of Company F, 9th New York, spotted one Confederate close by, and shot him dead. "The regiment cheered, and the enemy, evidently thinking that our men would charge on them, hastily withdrew out of the wheatfield." As the Confederates pulled back, Perry Nichols of Company F of the 9th ran

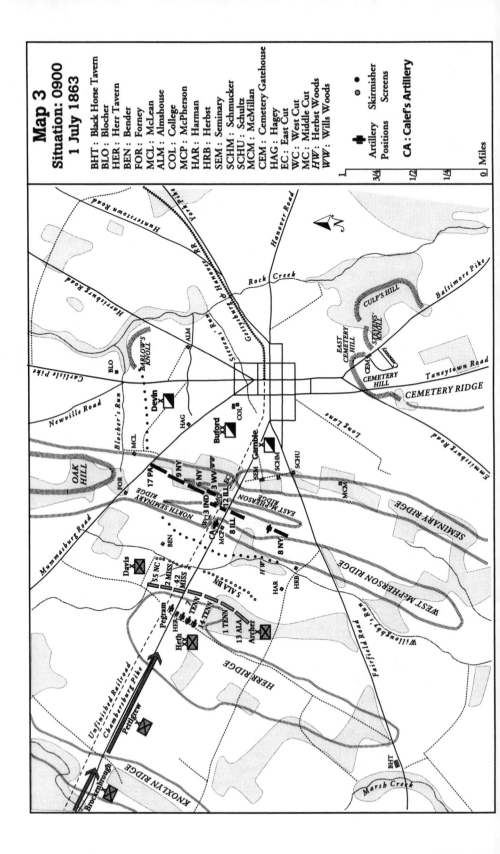

Map 3
Situation: 0900
1 July 1863

BHT : Black Horse Tavern
BLO : Blocher
HER : Herr Tavern
BEN : Bender
FOR : Forney
MCL : McLean
ALM : Almshouse
COL : College
MCP : McPherson
HAR : Harman
HRB : Herbst
SEM : Seminary
SCHM : Schmucker
SCHU : Schultz
MCM : McMillan
CEM : Cemetery Gatehouse
HAG : Hagey
EC : East Cut
WC : West Cut
MC : Middle Cut
HW : Herbst Woods
WW : Wills Woods

Artillery   Skirmisher
Positions   Screens

CA : Calef's Artillery

1   3/4   1/2   1/4   0   Miles

out and captured one man who had stopped behind a tree in the field near the road. This man was said to be the first Confederate prisoner captured in the battle. "He was immediately taken to Buford's headquarters, and gave the first information we received from the enemy's side."[105]

It may have been at this time that Devin was requested to send some men to help close the gap between his left and Gamble's right. He elected to send a portion of Company G, 9th New York, under Sergeant Holcomb. While Holcomb's command was advancing into position, "some of the enemy rose from behind a fence in front and fired at the detachment, killing Corporal Cyrus W. James." The historian of the regiment believed that James was the first Union man killed on the battlefield but "this honor belonged to another."[106]

Gamble also became concerned about the intensity of Pegram's artillery fire and the number of enemy troops advancing towards him. As soon as he had heard that his pickets were being pressured at 0800, he went forward and observed Heth's men "cautiously approaching in column on the road, with three extended lines on each flank." A quick skirmish followed as Heth's men took control of Herr Ridge, whereupon Heth began deploying his artillery and infantry, as already noted. At this point "our artillery opened on the enemy's column, doing some good execution. The enemy moved forward [deployed]; two batteries opened on us, and a sharp engagement of artillery took place." It was then that Gamble thought it best to move his line back two hundred yards to the next ridge, "and there make a stand."[107] His next line was on eastern McPherson Ridge, the rise east of Herbst Woods where the brigade's regimental markers are now located. Since Gamble did not recall his skirmishers, and Calef's battery remained where it was first posted, the slight withdrawal was most likely intended to protect the troopers and horses from the Confederate artillery fire that was concentrating on Calef's four guns posted on the Pike immediately west of the McPherson farm buildings.

Major Beveridge of the 8th Illinois also noted the same sequence of events seen by Gamble: when Gamble formed his line and Calef fired a few shots, Davis' brigade was seen to advance in column "through the depression of hills to the northwest, three-fourths of a mile away, beyond Willoughby Run." Calef then turned his fire to the head of the Confederate column as they began to come over Herr Ridge. Beveridge clearly saw Gamble's skirmishers being driven back: "Presently the boys of the 8th Illinois with the led horses were seen coming over the ridge west of Willoughby Run, in our immediate front; then a line of smoke along and beyond the crest of the hill; then our pickets; then another line of smoke, then the (Confederate) skirmishers; then twelve guns wheeled into line, unlimbered, and opened fire." Major Beveridge then saw Gamble's pickets retire slowly down the eastern slope of Herr Ridge, followed by Heth's skirmishers.[108]

The only Union account of the fighting on Herr Ridge is the post war journal of Lieutenant Marcellus E. Jones, the man who had opened the fighting in this sector at 0730. Jones reported that the Confederates had taken an hour to drive him and his company back the mile from School House Ridge to Herr Ridge. "The smoke of our carbines was visible along our entire line...Now we were determined to hold the crest of [Herr] Ridge. At last we yielded to superior numbers and slowly retired down the hill, keeping up a hot fire. Now as the enemy skirmishers came in full view of them, [Calef's] four guns echoed along the hills, to show the enemy we had support at hand. Soon however the enemy ran up to their skirmish line sixteen pieces of artillery and opened fire." Faced with this heavy fire, Jones' men and Gamble's other pickets fell back to Willoughby Run "pursued by their skirmishers."[109]

Buford's Strategy and Weapons

A great deal has been made over the years of the claim that Buford's dismounted skirmishers boldly and bravely delayed the advance of Heth's skirmishers for two hours or more and so saved the course of the battle.[110] It cannot be denied that the experience of Buford's men forced the Confederates to deploy and then advance slowly towards their goal. Yet it should be noted that Heth at first did not press the issue—he kept most of his infantry in column formation while eight companies of Archer's brigade formed as skirmishers and easily pushed Gamble's pickets back about 1½ miles from Marsh Creek to Herr Ridge. It was not until then that the fighting became really serious, as Gamble's picket line was reinforced by three fresh squadrons, and additional skirmishers from Archer's and Davis' commands, supported by two of Pegram's rifled cannons, joined the fray. Even so, the Confederates carried the ridge without difficulty and forced Gamble's skirmishers to retire to the woods along Willoughby Run. The light intensity of the fighting to this point is shown by the fact that the Union cavalry units involved did not bear any heavy losses before 0930, and few names or anecdotes of casualties of any kind are preserved for this period. Colonel B.D. Fry's 13th Alabama, which was on the Confederate skirmish line from 0730 to 0930, lost only 7 men wounded during this time. After the war Fry explained to historian John B. Bachelder, "As to the resistance made by the cavalry to the advance of our brigade on the morning of the 1st, I remember that it was inconsiderable, and did not delay us. Only small parties appeared in our front, and though I observed some instances of individual gallantry they did us no damage."[111]

Buford's greatest service was not so much in the bravery of his men as in his decision to stand and fight on McPherson's Ridge. By keeping most of his men in column during their advance, Heth showed that he expected the Union cavalry to continue to withdraw. Buford had been in contact with Reynolds and he expected to be reinforced momentarily, so he determined to hold on to McPherson's Ridge, or fall back to Seminary Ridge if necessary, in order to keep control of the town of Gettysburg and its important road net. As previously noted, Buford would have been able to mount his men at a moment's notice and escape readily if seriously threatened, particularly so since he was aware that Heth had no cavalry with him.

Heth, for his part, was in no particular hurry to get to Gettysburg. He had clearly been opposed only by cavalry pickets for the first 90 minutes after the initial contact was made with Gamble's vedettes near Marsh Creek. After he secured Herr Ridge and saw Buford's line formed ready for battle on McPherson's Ridge, he had no choice but to form a line himself and bring up Pettigrew's and Brockenbrough's brigades from the rear of his column. By all accounts it took him from 0900 to 0930 to accomplish this, during which time he directed Pegram to give his men a covering fire. It is highly probable that he deliberately held his skirmishers back until his main infantry line was formed on the ridge. There would have been little purpose in pushing his tired skirmishers into the woods along Willoughby Run, which were known to be full of Union troops.[112] Thus it is reasonable to assume that Gamble's pickets were permitted to retire into the Willoughby Run thicket without much opposition, and that Heth did not send his skirmishers forward again in earnest (except for Davis' probe against Devin's right) until he was ready to begin his major attack at 0930.

One of the great legends of the battle is that Heth's advance was slowed down principally because of the heavy carbine fire that he encountered from Buford's men. The Union troopers that day carried a mixture of Sharps, Burnside, Gallagher, Merrill and Smith carbines.[113]

These guns were all single shot weapons loaded mechanically through the breech, not through the multistep process by which the longer muzzle loaders were loaded. As a result, they could be fired faster than a muzzle loader—perhaps 5-8 times per minute, as opposed to 2-3 for a muzzle loader.[114] This would enable the cavalrymen to fire at about twice the rate of Heth's infantryman, with the added advantage that the troopers could load while prone or behind cover, whereas Heth's men had to load while standing and so exposing their arms while ramming or drawing their ramrods. These weapons were certainly an advantage to the Union cavalrymen, but not a spectacular one. Popular misconception is that Buford's men carried seven shot Spencer repeaters or other repeating rifles, which simply was not the case.[115] This misconception led to the often repeated but demonstrably out of place anecdote: "Seven charges in the magazine and one in the chamber gave birth to the expression from our first prisoners taken in action: 'What do you do—load on Sundays and fire all week!'"[116] Heth's advance, therefore, was not delayed by rapid fire from Spencer repeaters but by a combination of factors—Heth's decision to keep most of his infantry in column from 0730 to 0900, his decision to stop and form his division on Herr Ridge from 0900 to 0930, and the somewhat increased firepower furnished by Buford's single shot carbines.

Heth Renews His Advance

Heth now gave his brigade commanders orders to advance, "the object being to feel the enemy; to make a forced reconnaissance, and determine in what force the enemy were—whether or not he was massing his forces on Gettysburg."[117] Archer ordered his skirmishers forward in greater force, and those Union pickets who were still on the west side of Willoughby Run rapidly crossed to the safer side. Marcellus Jones noted that he and his men splashed through the run "with the exception of 25 or 30 men who in crossing the run used an old railroad bed for protection" and then rejoined their brigade.[118]

Pegram's cannons held their fire as Heth's infantry passed through them.[119] The two regiments on Archer's right, the 13th Alabama and 1st Tennessee, had their initial advance down Herr Ridge sheltered by a heavy woods that covered above half the distance to Willoughby Run. When they cleared the woods, they at once came under an effective fire from Pergel's two guns southeast of Herbst Woods, whose firing was being directed by Lieutenant Calef.

Calef had just ridden to the left from the battery's primary position along Chambersburg Pike. On the way he had run into General Buford, who was accompanied by only a bugler and was calmly smoking his pipe. Buford had just reviewed the cavalry's line and observed to Calef, "Our men are in a pretty hot pocket, but, my boy, we must hold this position until the infantry come up; then you withdraw your guns in each section piece by piece, fill up your limber chests from the caissons and await my orders." The two officers' brief conference was terminated by a Confederate shell that burst so near that both their horses reared up in fright.[120]

When Calef reached Pergel's position he saw "a double line of battle in gray, and not over a thousand yards distant," advance down the slopes of Herr Ridge; "their battle flags looked redder and bloodier in the strong July sun than I had ever seen them before." Calef directed Pergel's men to aim at the enemy flags, and their shells quickly threw the Confederate lines "into some confusion."[121] In order to escape this rain of shot and shell, the two regiments were ordered to double quick towards the woods along Willoughby Run.[122] They moved just fast enough to keep ahead of Calef's shells, most of which were falling behind them.[123] Major A. S. van de Graaff, commander of the 5th Alabama Battalion, was startled to see a shell explode at his feet and cover him with dirt that got into his eyes. He had been relieved of his duty as Provost Marshal in order to enter the battle, and was lucky not to be killed by the shot.[124]

W. H. Moon of Company I, 13th Alabama, gives a detailed account of the initial stages of Archer's attack: "We had been in battle but a short time after our battery took position until the order was given: 'Forward!' As we debouched into the open field, a Federal battery located about one hundred yards south of where the Reynolds monument now stands [Pergel's section of Calef's battery] saluted us with a shower of shells. Our line of advance placed the 13th on a direct line between the Federal and Confederate batteries. The descent to Willoughby Run is a gradual slope with a dip about one hundred and fifty yards from the Run, so our battery could not engage the Federal guns until we had gone about a half mile down the slope. As soon as we were below the range of our guns, they fired a volley at the Federal battery, and I thought it the sweetest music I had ever heard as the balls went whizzing just above our heads. At the second volley from our battery, I saw one of the Federal guns topple and fall to the ground. This raised a terrible Rebel yell all along the line."[125]

Moon was the color guard on the left of the 13th Alabama's color bearer, Tom Grant. "He was a big, double jointed six-footer, and having that morning imbibed freely of Pennsylvania rye or apple juice, he was waving the flag and hollowing at the top of his voice, making a fine target while the shells were flying thick around us. I said, 'Tom, if you don't stop that I will use my bayonet on you.' Just then a fusillade of rifle balls from the Federals greeted us, and Tom needed no further admonition from me."[126]

The 13th Alabama now reached and passed through its skirmish line, which had been stymied by the Union fire from the east side of the Run.[127] Private Moon observed that the Federals kept up their fire and held their ground, but did not counterattack. Soon they were being slowly driven back by the superior weight of Archer's line.[128] Moon relates, "we continued to advance, but at a walk, loading and firing as we went, until we reached a strip of low land along the Run. There we were protected from the fire of the enemy by the abrupt rise across the Run in our front."[129]

A number of reasons caused the 13th Alabama and 1st Tennessee to shift to the right during their attack and so become separated from the left two regiments of their brigade. Their advance had been initially slowed, as already noted, by the woods through which they had to pass on upper Herr Ridge. They then quickened their pace in order to reach the protective shelter of the trees at the base of the ridge and escape the shells of Pergel's two guns southeast of Herbst Woods; some historians suggest that the two regiments may even have been interested in pushing forward to capture the two Union guns in their front. The 13th Alabama and 1st Tennessee, who apparently were accompanied by General Archer during this stage of their attack, also found themselves ahead of the rest of their brigade because Willoughby Run swung to the east in their front. In moving up to the Run, the two regiments found themselves 100 or more yards east of the 7th and 14th Tennessee regiments, which were being slowed by the trees of Herbst Woods.[130]

Archer was concerned about this break in his line and the fact that he had out distanced his supports on Herr Ridge. He ordered the two regiments to halt and reform, an order that the winded men gladly obeyed. Private Moon noted that they took the opportunity to reload, catch their breath, and cool off a little; by then the morning had become "hot, hotter, hottest."[131]

At this point General Heth came up and ordered Archer forward to determine the "strength and battle line of the enemy." Archer was not eager to do so, and "suggested that his brigade was too light to risk so far in advance of support."[132] Heth was not persuaded and repeated his order. Archer complied and sent the 1st Tennessee forward into the southwest corner of Herbst Woods. At the same time the 13th Alabama began climbing the bluff in its front; Captain B.A. Bower of Company C was sent out with 15 or 20 men to cover the brigade's open right flank.[133] The Run was not easy to cross because its banks were thick underbrush and briars, but the Confederates made it across with minimal enemy interference.

As the two regiments moved up McPherson's Ridge they began encountering the full fire of Pergel's two guns and the 8th New York Cavalry. Lieutenant Calef, who was still on this flank, was very concerned for the safety of these guns: "Having but a small cavalry support, and the woods occupied by the enemy extending up within 200 yards of the right of the section, I thought it unadvisable to wait till they arrived within canister range, and therefore withdrew the section."[134]

The left wing of Archer's brigade, the 7th and 14th Tennessee regiments, had to face continuous fire from Calef's four guns on the Chambersburg Pike as they advanced eastward over the open fields between the Pike on their left and the woods on their right through which the right wing of the regiment was passing. Sergeant G. W. Lambertson of Company A, 7th Tennessee, received a canister round that tore the breach off of his musket and spun him around.[135] It was perhaps at this time that Corporal Henry C. Rison of Company B, 7th Tennessee, fell casualty. Some sources cite him as the first Confederate killed at the battle.[136] He was actually wounded in the left thigh by a musket shot, and was badly wounded enough to be left behind when Lee's army retreated after the battle. He was taken prisoner by Union troops on 5 July, and was eventually taken to a hospital in Chester, PA, where he died on 1 August 1863.[137]

The historian of the 8th Illinois described the action as Heth's infantry pressed forward: "The long line of the enemy came in full view, and their batteries rained upon our men showers of shot and shell, but our brave boys stood firm and fell back only when ordered. The 8th New York, on our left, was wavering some, but the Third Indiana, on the right, never flinched. About this time it began to be warm work. Sgt. Goodspeed, of Company M, was wounded and taken to the depot, where a temporary hospital had been established, and soon after

Williams of Company M had his arm shattered by a ball, which required amputation."[138]

The troopers deployed near Calef's battery suffered heavily, even though they were dismounted, because the terrain here offered them no cover from Heth's guns. Gabriel B. Durham of Co. I, 12th Illinois, suffered seriously when both his "nates" were carried away by a solid shot (he died on 23 July) and W.M. Redman of the same regiment reported that his company lost four casualties—one killed by a shell, one wounded, badly, another wounded in the hip, and one wounded and taken prisoner.[139]

As the 7th and 14th Tennessee regiments neared Willoughby Run, they slid to the right in an effort to avoid the fire of Calef's guns and also keep contact with the brigade's right two regiments. When they approached the line of woods along Willoughby Run, they drove back the Union cavalry skirmishers, who withdrew up the ridge or into nearby Herbst Woods. Some of the men turned their attention to the Union cannons near the Pike some 400 yards ahead on their left. R.T. Mockbee of the 14th Tennessee noted that his regiment "raised a yell and charged across Willoughby Run."[140] It is not clear exactly where they crossed the Run. Evidence would seem to suggest that they crossed it and entered Herbst Woods; some if not all of the left of the 7th Tennessee may have been just north of the woods in a swale at the edge of the Run.[141] Private Moon of the 13th Alabama noted that at this point "the Tennesseans on our right advanced through a copse which ran up a ravine, spreading out into a fan shape as it neared the top of the Ridge."[142] This observation doubtlessly refers to the 14th Tennessee crossing Willoughby Run and entering Herbst Woods.

Davis' brigade was able to advance faster on the north side of the Chambersburg Pike than Archer's because it encountered no large woods there to impede its advance. As already noted, Davis had formed at 0900 with the 55th North Carolina on the left, 2nd Mississippi in the center and 42nd Mississippi on the right. The 2nd Mississippi was probably placed in the center because it was Davis' most veteran unit, even though its men were very tired from having been on picket duty all the previous night. The brigade's line of 1700 men stretched about 400 yards from the Chambersburg Pike on the left to the westward bend of Willoughly Run on the right.[143]

Davis sent forward his skirmishers and then commenced his attack at 0930.[144] Colonel John M. Stone of the 2nd Mississippi, which was at the center of the line, experienced difficulty at first when his regiment encountered a strong post and rail fence along both sides of a lane leading to the Grist farmhouse; it divided the regiment into two unequal halves, the larger part passing to the right and the smaller to the left.[145] The 42nd Mississippi also encountered a little difficulty at the beginning of its advance. Its commander, Colonel H.R. Miller, ordered Companies C and D to deploy as skirmishers. Before they could advance, two brothers who had just been transferred to Company C that morning, Mitch and Jack Scott, were shot down.[146]

Davis sent his skirmishers forward with his main line of battle close behind. The greater weight of his line readily pushed Devin's skirmishers back under a continuous fire. The 55th North Carolina crossed Willoughby Run first because of a westward bend of the stream. It then headed northeastward past the Bender house and orchard. The brigade's other two regiments also drifted to the left during their advance, probably in order to avoid the fire of Calef's battery. This line of advance dangerously extended Davis' frontage to 2000 feet and helped draw the brigade still farther to the left. The brigade's front also encountered increasingly heavy fire from Devin's skirmishers the closer the Confederates approached to the main Union line.[147]

The left wing of the 55th North Carolina's skirmish line swung still farther to the left and began advancing through a wheatfield south of the Forney house.[148] Their movement caused great concern to Colonel William L. Heermance, commander of the 6th New York's portion of the brigade skirmish line. Since the enemy was well beyond his right, Heermance's men had to return on foot under a severe fire down the Mummasburg Road. They were then dismayed to learn that their horses were not there, but had been taken farther to the rear: "Seeing that the enemy had gotten so far in rear of our flank, the men in charge supposed we had been gobbled up, and had gone back to the Seminary grounds with them, and exhausted as we were we had to double quick another mile before we reached them."[149]

Davis' other two regiments also shifted to the left after crossing Willoughby Run. Their movement was probably initiated as an effort to bypass the fire of Calef's four guns on the Chambersburg Pike, but the two regiments were also aiming to hit Cutler's infantry regiments that were formed in their front (see next chapter). Before long the right of the 42nd Mississippi was advancing north of the unfinished railroad line. From here the right of the unit was able to pour a flanking fire into Calef's four guns on the Pike.

Davis' shift to the left managed to give him a temporary tactical advantage against the troops in his front, but his movement, combined with Archer's unplanned shift to the right, created a one quarter mile gap in Heth's center around the Chambersburg Pike. This gap would force the two brigades to fight separate actions when the Union infantry came forward. When added to the fact that the two Southern brigades had outdistanced their supports, as Archer feared, the situation spelled disaster for the Confederates.

The threat of being taken in the rear became so great that Calef found it necessary to withdraw his guns piece by piece, as Buford had previously suggested. This was accomplished only with some difficulty. Just as Calef was giving the order to Sergeant Newman, an enemy shell burst under the horse team of one of his guns and killed or disabled four of the six animals. Calef sent for a spare limber from one of the caissons in reserve at the Seminary, but Newman was able to bring off the gun with another team. By then the Confederate infantry were so close that the Union cannoneers were unable to cut the harnesses off their fallen horses before they pulled back. [150]

Despite the growing intensity of Heth's attack along the Chambersburg Pike, Buford was also concerned with the approach of Ewell's corps from the north. His pickets during the night had made him well aware of heavy enemy activity along the road from Mummasburg to Hunterstown,[151] and his pickets had been having minor clashes with both Rodes' and Early's advance detachments since dawn. He had been in steady contact with General Reynolds at Emmitsburg, and his expectation of the coming of the I Corps infantry is what convinced him to hold on to McPherson's and Seminary Ridges until their arrival. At 1010 or earlier Buford sent the following concise and disturbing report to Meade, carried by Lieutenant Colonel W.G. Bentley of the 9th New York:[152] "The enemy's force (A.P. Hill's) are advancing on me at this point, and driving my pickets and skirmishers very rapidly. There is also a large force at Heidlersburg that is driving my pickets at that point from that direction. General Reynolds is advancing, and is within three miles of this point with his leading division. I am positive that the whole of A.P. Hill's force is advancing."[153]

CHAPTER IV

Reynolds to the Rescue

M ajor General John F. Reynolds, commander of the
left wing of the Union army, went to sleep near midnight on 30 June
not knowing what the next day would bring. He had formed his I Corps
on the Gettysburg Road near Marsh Creek, two miles north of
Emmitsburg, in what he understood to be a jumpoff position for a
movement to Gettysburg, some six miles distant. Yet precise marching
orders had not yet arrived from Meade, and Reynolds did not know
whether he would be directed to advance, hold his position, or retire.
He was anxious that Lee might move against his left from Cashtown
or some point farther down the Cumberland Valley, and expressed this
concern to Meade in a message he sent earlier in the evening via his
aide, Major William Riddle.[1] Just before retiring for the night he received
a message from Buford in Gettysburg at 2230 that the Confederates
were active in the direction of Heidlersburg and had pickets within four
miles of Gettysburg on the Chambersburg Pike.[2] If the enemy attacked
via Gettysburg and no new orders arrived from Meade, Reynolds would
have to fall back to Emmitsburg pursuant to an order he had received
from Meade during the afternoon.[3]

Since the next day promised to be an active one and would probably
require him to awaken early, Reynolds did not bother to undress. He
simply wrapped himself in a blanket and went to sleep on the floor of
his headquarters at the Moritz Tavern.[4] As he anticipated, he was not

able to sleep until dawn. At 0400 Major Riddle returned from Taneytown with Meade's orders for Reynolds to march to Gettysburg.[5] Riddle hated to wake his commander up from his sound sleep, so he opened the dispatch to see if it was important enough to require his being awakened. When he found that they were Meade's anxiously awaited orders for the day, Riddle woke Reynolds up. The general was understandably groggy, and asked Riddle to read the dispatch to him three times as he lay on the floor resting his head on his hand.[6]

Reynolds had no reason to rush to Gettysburg, and allowed his men their usual early morning routine. Within a short time the sun rose red, clear and warm,[7] and the troops of I Corps were astir in their camps. The men of the 6th Wisconsin enjoyed a "hearty breakfast of coffee and hardtack" before they began packing up their gear.[8] The 19th Indiana had "plenty of good butter and bread from good citizens" before they were mustered for pay.[9] Some officers of the 150th Pennsylvania wanted to supplement their frugal fare and sought permission to send out and buy a sheep because they had been without their commissary wagons for two days, but permission was denied because "there was prospect of an early movement."[10] Some members of the 147th New York managed to obtain fresh bread and coffee from some farmhouses near their camp. Lieutenant J.V. Pierce of the 147th breakfasted on two hard tacks and a cup of black coffee, and would not enjoy another meal until three days later.[11] Even so, he was one of the lucky ones—hundreds of his companions would not live to see another meal.

The men knew for sure that a battle was coming when they saw ordnance wagons come up into the camps. Meade had ordered that each man be issued 60 rounds of ammunition,[12] so each soldier picked up six packs that contained ten rounds each. Two of the packs were inserted in the tins in their cartridge belts, and others were broken open and laid loose on top of the tins. Each man then put the remaining rounds in his pockets as best he could. Some of the men of the 24th Michigan received their hardtack and ammunition issue while they were kneeling in a prayer led by Chaplain William C. Way.[13]

The men of the 76th New York found they had extra work to do while their comrades stowed their gear and prepared to break camp. They had been ordered to load their guns before stacking them for the night, so that they might be able to fight at a moment's notice if the enemy made a sudden attack. A shower that fell during the night wet their cartridges, and so forced the men to tend to their weapons in order to make them serviceable again.[14]

While his troops were making their preparations for the day's march, Reynolds sent out orders to the three corps under his command. He directed Sickles, who had been already ordered by Meade to march to Emmitsburg,[15] to take position on the high ground to the left of the town when he arrived. Sickles was to post most of his corps to the left of the Gettysburg Road, and was to pay particular attention to the road that led from Fairfield along the mountain to his left. Reynolds also reminded Sickles that Howard's troops would be leaving Emmitsburg to march to Gettysburg.[16]

By 0700 Reynolds received a message Major General O.O. Howard had sent at 0600 from his camp below Emmitsburg reporting that he had been ordered by Meade to "move within supporting distance of you at Gettysburg." Unless he heard otherwise from Reynolds, Howard said he would march his command the crossroads near "J. Wintz's (Wentz's) place" and encamp there for the night; this intersection of the Emmitsburg Road would become famous the next day because of the nearby Peach Orchard. The XI Corps would march with one division (Barlow's) and a battery (Dilger's) following the I Corps up the Gettysburg Road, while the rest of the corps and its trains would take the route by Horner's Mill. In this manner, Howard suggested, the I Corps trains on the Gettysburg Road would not delay all the XI Corps infantry, and he would have his own trains more readily at hand.[17] Reynolds did not approve of this arrangement and wrote back immediately that "the movements of the trains are to be subordinate to those of the troops." Howard was told to bring all his troops up the Gettysburg Road. The trains of both I and XI Corps would then be brought up, hopefully by evening. Meanwhile all empty wagons, useless horses, etc., were to be sent to Union Bridge in accordance with Meade's directions.[18]

Reynolds also sent a directive to Major General Abner Doubleday to prepare the I Corps to move. Doubleday, the I Corps' senior division commander, had been given command of I Corps when Reynolds took active command of the army's left wing the previous evening; Doubleday in turn had given command of his 3rd Division to Brig. Gen. Thomas A. Rowley, and command of Rowley's 1st Brigade devolved on Col. Chapman Biddle of the 121st Pennsylvania. Doubleday then issued orders for his old 3rd Division to march out first; Wadsworth's 1st Division had led the march into Emmitsburg the previous day, and it was the custom for the divisions to rotate that favored position, which had the advantage of fresh roads and avoidance of all the dust (or mud) stirred up by so large a column. Next would come the corps' artillery brigade, commanded by Colonel Charles S. Wainwright, followed by Robinson's 2nd Division and then Wadsworth's 1st Division. One brigade of Rowley's division, accompanied by a battery, was to march as an advance guard a mile and a half in advance of the column. The corps' rearguard would consist of two Vermont regiments from Stannard's green Vermont brigade, which had just joined the corps.[19]

Reynolds, however, had his own plans for the I Corps' line of march that day. He had already met with Wadsworth and instructed him to take his division up the road first.[20] As previously noted, it was the custom for the division which led the previous day's march to relinquish that post the next day. The reason why Reynolds chose to do this is not known. He may have wanted to save some time by having Wadsworth lead the day's march, since the 1st Division had encamped closest to Gettysburg the previous afternoon.[21] But it is also possible that Reynolds felt that Wadsworth's was his best division, and sent it out first in case there was any immediate trouble at Gettysburg.

This difference in plans became apparent when Reynolds called Doubleday to his headquarters before leaving for Gettysburg.[22] Reynolds read to Doubleday the latest dispatches he had received from Meade and Buford, and explained to him "the movements of the rebels and the latest positions of our troops." He then told Doubleday that he had already given orders for Wadsworth's division and Hall's battery to lead the way, and that he himself would accompany the vanguard. Doubleday was directed to draw in the corps' pickets and follow with the balance of the corps. Doubleday, of course, had no choice but to acquiesce and amend the marching orders he had just sent out.[23] It would take him at least an hour to ready the 2nd and 3rd Divisions; if the 1st Division met any trouble it would have to stand alone for at least that long.

This change in marching orders was no particular cause for alarm to Colonel Wainwright, commander of the I Corps' artillery brigade. He had breakfasted soon after sunrise and felt that the day promised to be a quiet one. Doubleday's first order arrived just as he was finishing up his 30 June monthly return and muster reports. He promptly formed his command to move out, and then had to wait for Rowley's division to come up so that he could assume his assigned place in the corps line of march. During this delay Wainwright rode on ahead towards Reynolds' headquarters "to learn what I could as to the prospects of a fight." He saw General Reynolds, who "said that he did not expect any; that we were only moving up so as to be within supporting distance to Buford, who was to push out farther." Reynolds then told Wainwright that he was going to send Wadsworth out first, with Hall's battery, and that he would accompany the advance guard. Wainwright would stay behind and come up with Doubleday and the rest of the corps' infantry.[24]

It was shortly before 0700 when Wadsworth sent out the command for his regiments to fall in and be ready to march. The historian of the 14th Brooklyn of Cutler's brigade notes that "at 7 AM an aid galloped up to Col. Fowler's tent with orders. A moment later came the clear command of the bugles to pack up."[25] Cutler's brigade was formed up and ready to move between 0730 and 0800.[26] The command marched out of its camp immediately south of Marsh Creek and crossed the creek by the main bridge on the Emmitsburg-Gettysburg road. Cutler's men then marched past Wadsworth's other brigade, led by Brigadier General Solomon Meredith, which was still forming up in its camp.[27] The two brigades took turns leading the division's line of march, and this day it was Cutler's turn to have the honor.[28]

General Cutler and his staff led the brigade's line of march, accompanied by General Wadsworth and his staff, and a headquarters guard composed of Sergeant H. H. Hubbard and 18 men of the 147th New York. The brigade's regiments marched in the following order: 76th New York, 56th Pennsylvania, 147th New York, 95th New York, and 14th Brooklyn.[29] Captain James H. Hall brought up the six 3 inch rifled guns of his 2nd Maine battery at the rear of the infantry column.[30] Cutler's sixth infantry regiment, the 7th Indiana, had to be left behind for the moment because it had not yet been relieved of its guard assignment. The regiment had been assigned to guard the corps train and cattle herd since 26 June, and was supposed to be relieved on the morning of 1 July by one of Stannard's new Vermont regiments. The regiment formed up in marching order soon after dawn, and waited impatiently for five hours with no sign of the Vermonters. At length the order, "Fall in, forward march!" was given. Whether or not this was in obedience to orders, "your historian sayeth not."[31]

Meredith probably received his marching orders shortly before 0700, the same time as Cutler did. Colonel Rufus Dawes of the 6th Wisconsin was writing his wife when he received orders to "pack up, be ready to march immediately."[32] It appears that either Wadsworth or Meredith directed the brigade to move out at 0800. Colonel Samuel J. Williams of the 19th Indiana, which was on picket duty a little farther up the road that morning, reported that he had been ordered to "fall into its proper place in the column as it came marching by."[33] For these reasons the Iron Brigade was still forming up in its camp 200 yards north of

Marsh Creek when Cutler's brigade came marching past. However, by the time Meredith's men began their march, there was a gap of at least a mile between their head unit and the rear of Hall's battery.[34] One of Wadsworth's aides, Clayton Rogers, believed that the gap was caused by a "delay in giving orders" on Meredith's part.[35] The gap more likely was caused by a combination of factors that included the difference in scheduled departure times for the two brigades and a fast march rate by Cutler's men. It is also possible that Reynolds or Wadsworth got Cutler moving slightly ahead of schedule, under the belief that Meredith would eventually catch up.

Meredith's order of march was as follows: 2nd Wisconsin, 7th Wisconsin, 19th Indiana (which had been on picket duty), 24th Michigan, and 6th Wisconsin.[36] The column was closed up by a 102-man brigade guard composed of 20 men from each of the brigade's five regiments, plus two officers, Lieutenant Lloyd G. Harris of the 6th Wisconsin and Lieutenant Levi Showalter of the 2nd Wisconsin.[37]

The cannoneers of Stewart's battery (B, 4th United States) were inspired as they saw Meredith's men cross part of Marsh Creek. "The little creek made a depression in the road, with a gentle ascent on each side, so that from our point of view the column as it came down one slope and up the other, had the effect of huge blue billows of smoke topped with a spray of shining steel, and the whole spectacle was calculated to give nerve to a man who had none before." Some of the artillerymen joked with the foot soldiers as they passed by saying "Tell the Johnnies we will be right along." To which came the reply, "All right. Better stay here till we send for you."[38]

Most of the men in the Iron Brigade remained in high spirits as they marched up the road. The troops of the 6th Wisconsin were particularly jolly as some of the Germans in Company F sang a stirring song in their native language. Then some members of Company K who had "about as much melody as the company mule" began to sing a ditty about a cow on the plains. Before long much of the column was ringing with the chorus, "On the distant prairie, hoop de dooden do." Reportedly the din alarmed animals in the fields as well as some civilians who came out to see the troops march by. When this silly song finally disintegrated into a fit of laughter, Private Thomas Flynn quieted everyone by belting out the song "Paddy's Wedding." When he was done the men finally quieted down. James P. Sullivan of Company K thought it was "odd for men to march toward their death singing, shouting, and laughing as if it were parade or holiday."[39]

Most of the troops of Cutler's brigade were equally unconcerned that they might be marching to one of the greatest battles of the war. Part way to Gettysburg the column stopped on a hill, probably to rest the troops for a moment and allow Meredith's brigade to catch up somewhat.[40] The 76th New York happened to halt near a "long row of cherry trees loaded with ripe fruit." As they looked longingly at the luscious cherries, Major Andrew J. Grover rode up and at once analyzed the situation. In a loud voice clear to all he stated, "Boys, the General charges you to be very particular to keep strictly within the rules, and not meddle with these cherry trees. Be sure you don't break the trees down!" When he turned his back to ride away, the men caught his hint and rushed the orchard, being careful as they could not to harm the trees as they feasted on their fruit.[41]

While the troops were halted a small group of citizens passed by from the direction of Gettysburg, "gray haired old men tottering along; women carrying their children, and children leading each other, while on the faces of all were depicted the indices of the terror and despair which had taken possession of them."[42] What was the cause of this dismay could not at once be determined.

While the column was halted a number of high ranking officers gathered on the brow of the hill to examine maps and study the lay of the land in the direction of Gettysburg. The center of the group was General Reynolds, who had ridden forward to be at the head of the column as soon as Cutler broke camp. Also present were generals Wadsworth and Cutler, and a great number of staff officers. A number of scouts came in to report their findings.[43]

After the column had renewed its march and proceeded a little farther, Reynolds decided to ride on ahead. Some of his staff thought that he was even more silent than usual.[44] A little more than halfway to Gettysburg the general met one of Buford's staff officers who was "riding in great haste with the information that the enemy was advancing on Gettysburg by the Cashtown or Chambersburg Pike, and that General Buford was then sharply engaged." Reynolds dismounted at once and sent staff officers to tell Doubleday and Howard to hurry forward. He also sent an aide to tell Wadsworth "to close up his division and come on." Another officer was given a note for General Meade "giving him the information," i.e. that Buford was under attack and Reynolds was marching to his aid.[45] Captain Stephen M. Weld, who carried the note to Meade, says that he left Reynold's side at about 1000.[46] Reynolds also must also have sent a note to Buford to announce his coming and the fact that his leading troops were nearby; Buford at 1010 or earlier wrote Meade that "General Reynolds is advancing, and is within 3 miles of this place with his leading division."[47]

When Reynolds resumed his ride towards Gettysburg, he began to hear cannon blasts and note puffs of smoke rising above Buford's position west of the town. About one half mile south of Gettysburg he ran into a frightened civilian on horseback, and asked him "what the trouble was." He was told simply that "our cavalry was fighting." Reynolds' party next halted at "Mr. Giorgi's house" to inquire the way to the front.[48] He found "considerable excitement" as he entered town and then rode west towards Seminary Ridge.[49] One tradition relates that he met a local citizen named Peter Culp in front of the Eagle Hotel in town, and Culp gave him directions to Buford's headquarters at the Seminary.[50]

Reynolds Meets Buford

Reynolds' meeting with Buford is one of the great sagas of the battle. As we have already seen, Lieutenant A. B. Jerome, the signal officer attached to Buford's staff, had taken up a post in the Seminary cupola at 0700. Apparently Buford came up to the cupola more than once to get a better view of the fighting on his front. It must have been about 0915 when Jerome looked in the direction of Emmitsburg and "called the attention of the General to an army corps advancing some two miles distant, and shortly distinguished it as the first on account of their corps flag."[51] Buford, whom Jerome thought was planning a possible withdrawal to Cemetery Hill, was relieved, and responded, "Now we can hold this place."[52]

Buford then left the Seminary building while Jerome continued his watch. After about 20 minutes or so he saw Reynolds and his staff approaching on horseback, and sent a messenger to Buford "that Reynolds himself will be here in about five minutes, his corps is about a mile behind."[53]

Buford promptly returned to the Seminary, and was in the cupola when Reynolds rode up at about 0945 and called out to him.[54] Lt. Jerome continues his account: "Gen. Reynolds and a few of his staff rode up on a gallop and hailed the Gen. who was with me in the steeple, our lines being but shortly advanced. In a familiar manner General

Reynolds asked Buford 'how things were going on' and received the characteristic answer 'let's go and see.'"[55]

Buford then began climbing down the ladder from the cupola, and Reynolds met him partway down with the question, "What's the matter, John?" Buford replied, "the devil's to pay."[56] Reynolds responded with the assurance that he would bring his men up as fast as he could, and added that "he hoped Buford could hold out until his corps came up." Buford in his characteristic brevity answered, "I reckon I can."[57]

It is probable that Reynolds during his conference with Buford climbed into the actual cupola himself in order to view the terrain to the west. Abner Doubleday related that he heard that an aide of Howard's (he presumed that it was Major Hall) "soon after Reynolds descended from the belfry, came up to ask if he had any instructions regarding the Eleventh Corps." Reynolds then sent orders for Howard to "bring his corps forward at once and form them on Cemetery Hill as a reserve."[58]

This meeting between Buford and Reynolds at the Seminary cupola has been brought into question, most notably by Edwin B. Coddington. Coddington points out that there are some inconsistencies in Jerome's entire account, which forms the basis of the saga, and that it is more likely that Buford would have been at the front with his troops when Reynolds arrived than at the cupola.[59] It is indeed strange that Sergeant Charles H. Veil, who was at Reynolds' side all morning, makes no mention of the Seminary building or of the conversation recorded by Jerome. Veil simply states that Reynolds and his staff "found Gen'l Buford engaged on ridge in front of Seminary (McPherson's farm I think). Just as we arrived the enemy opened a Battery from a position in the road in front of a house."[60] This statement does not expressly declare where Buford and Reynolds met; his word "there" could as well refer to the Seminary as to McPherson's Ridge. Since both Jerome and Doubleday expressly place Reynolds at the Seminary building, and Veil's account does not definitely contradict them, the incident is best accepted rather that rejected.[61]

When the officers came down from the cupola, Reynolds suggested to Buford that they ride out to McPherson's Ridge to inspect the lines there.[62] As they rode forward Buford warned Reynolds not to expose himself excessively. According to Lieutenant Jerome, Reynolds just laughed and moved even closer to the fighting.[63]

During his conference with Buford, Reynolds told the cavalryman to "hold on as long as he could and that he would hurry his men forward to his assistance."[64] This decision certainly reaffirmed Buford's choice the previous day to position his troops as a shield to the town. Reynolds, too, was preoccupied with keeping control of Gettysburg. Veil quotes him as telling Buford "to hold the enemy in check as long as possible to keep them from getting into town."[65] Reynolds knew that it would be difficult to dislodge the Confederates from the town if they managed to occupy it, and also wanted to keep the enemy from using the important road junctions there. But he was also well aware of the strength of the hills south of Gettysburg, which he noted as he rode northward into town; almost every Union general who saw them that day commented what a fine position they offered.[66] Indeed, Captain Joseph G. Rosengarten of Reynolds' staff stated soon after the battle that Reynolds ordered up all his troops for the express purpose of holding the town and Cemetery Hill.[67]

Reynolds' determination to keep the Confederates from gaining possession of Cemetery Hill and the other heights south of Gettysburg can be seen in the following message he sent to Meade via his aide, Captain Stephen M. Weld. Reynolds deemed the message, which was oral and not written, to be so important that he directed Weld to ride his horse into the ground if necessary. It ran, "The enemy are advancing in strong force... I fear they will get to the heights beyond the town before I can. I will fight them inch by inch, and if driven into the town, I will barricade the streets and hold them back as long as possible." Meade received this terse report at Taneytown, 14 miles from Gettysburg, at 1120. He asked Weld to repeat the message and then exclaimed, "Good! That is just like Reynolds, he will hold on to the bitter end!"[68]

Meade clearly supported Reynold's decision to fight the enemy at Gettysburg even though Reynolds had not received any explicit orders to do so. Meade was looking to locate and engage a portion of Lee's army, and hopefully defeat it. Now that Buford and Reynolds had come to grips with Hill's Corps, Meade could rush his remaining troops to their aid. Howard, Sickles, and Slocum were all in ready supporting distance of Reynolds, which could put half of the Union army at Gettysburg that day. He also prepared to bring up the rest of his army and directed Couch at Harrisburg to threaten Ewell's rear at Carlisle and try to delay his march westward.[69]

No sources mention it, but Reynolds also may have been thinking of overwhelming Hill's advance, if the enemy were not present in any great force. His messages to Meade and Howard only show what he was prepared to do in the worst case scenario—should there be a large number of Confederate troops coming from Cashtown or should Ewell's troops appear from the north.

The remaining question is when exactly did Reynolds decide to fight and support Buford in the ridges west of town. He probably did not do so before he rode past Cemetery Hill on his way into Gettysburg and then saw for himself the advantageous nature of the ground both south and west of town. While at the Seminary he promised to come to Buford's support, but he was still not entirely sure he would do so on Seminary Ridge - nor was he even sure his troops would arrive before Buford was driven out of his position. The final decision to try to push Wadsworth's men forward to the ridges west of town apparently was not made until he left Buford and rode back south to a short but important meeting with Wadsworth. The two briefly discussed whether Wadsworth's division should form in the town or at Buford's position. It was then that Reynolds decided that it would be better to fight on the ridges where Buford was formed, since they were not a bad defensive position—Herbst Woods offered cover for the center of the line, and the troops there, thanks to Buford's wise decision the previous day, could still fall back to Seminary Ridge is they were pressed hard. To be certain, the position was vulnerable to being flanked by Confederate troops coming from the north, but no enemy forces were yet advancing from that quarter. A deciding factor that influenced Reynolds to fight west of town rather than in it was his concern that Confederate shells might injure the town and harm civilians.[70]

As soon as he was finished speaking with Buford, Reynolds sent directives to Sickles and Howard to come forward as fast as possible.[71] Captain Rosengarten of Reynolds' staff says that the General directed Howard "to bring his corps forward at once and form them on Cemetery Hill as a reserve."[72] He also sent instructions to Wadsworth to turn the head of his column across country from the Emmitsburg Road and head towards the Seminary.[73] At about this time, Captain E.P. Halstead of Doubleday's staff arrived with a message, and was instructed "to hurry forward the other two divisions of the troops as fast as possible."[74]

Reynolds then rode back to town and took a side street that ran by John Burns' house to the Emmitsburg Road; one account relates that it was John Burns himself who gave Reynolds directions at this time.[75] After riding south for one-half mile he stopped near the Codori house and "ordered his escort tear down all the fences and make way for the troops to get across the fields to the Seminary."[76] It was probably then, or during his ride south from town, that he stopped to have the conference with Wadsworth already mentioned, where it was decided to form his division west of town rather than in it.

It was not long before the head of Cutler's column appeared. Cutler's men had seen the whitish colored puffs of smoke west of town and heard the sound of artillery firing, so they quickened their pace. As the historian of the 14th Brooklyn put it, "It looked like serious work ahead, and every man's veins swelled and pushed with the thought of what he was going into."[77] News began to filter through the ranks that Buford was being bested by a great number of Confederates. One orderly who dashed by said "The Rebs were thicker than blackberries beyond the hill."[78] The chaplain of the 147th New York noted that "We were being hurried at the utmost speed along the road on that hot July morning, sweltering from every pore, as for me, my clothes could not have been wetter if I had fallen into a pond of water."[79]

Before long the head of Cutler's column reached the Codori farm and saw Reynolds waiting at the point where he wanted the troops to leave the road and head north directly toward the Seminary. At once pioneers were sent forward to tear down fences on the line already begun by Reynolds' staff members. There were so many fences to be knocked down that members of Cutler's lead regiment, the 76th New York, were obliged to pitch in "as they led the army through fields, gardens and yards."[80] When the main body of the column began passing through Codori's field, the men heard a sharp escalation in the artillery fire just two miles distant. This was the key for the officers to order, "Forward, double quick! Load at will!" There was no straggling as the "wild rattle of jingling ramrods" ran down the line of moving men.[81] Not all the regiments, however, were ordered to load at the same time. The "Red Legged Devils" of the 14th Brooklyn did not do so until they reached the area of the Seminary.[82]

As the men of the 147th New York were crossing the rocky bed of Stevens' Run, they saw the six 3-inch rifles of Hall's battery go dashing by. The battery, though, had to halt its progress temporarily when it reached the post and board fence along both sides of the Fairfield Road. While Hall's cannoneers knocked the fences down, some of the foot soldiers of the 147th simply clambered over them. Lieutenant J. V. Pierce of the 147th observed that pioneers were ordered to the front to help tear the fences down and chop off the posts.[83]

When the 147th passed by the Schmucker house, immediately to the south of the Seminary, a few soldiers stopped to receive cool drinks of water being dispersed by two women at a gate. Their officers got annoyed with them for leaving the ranks at such a crisis and kicked over the water pails.[84] As the column passed by the Seminary it came under shell fire from the Confederate cannons on Herr Ridge.[85] Their advance was an object of enthusiastic admiration to a number of spectators who gathered in the Seminary cupola and "other adjacent elevated positions" to view the spectacle.[86]

Meredith's Iron Brigade was not far behind when Cutler's Brigade turned off the Emmitsburg Road at the N. Codori farm. One source estimates that Meredith's advance unit, the 2nd Wisconsin, had by then closed the gap between it and Cutler's rear unit to only one quarter mile.[87] At the rear of Meredith's column, Colonel Rufus Dawes of the 6th Wisconsin decided to unfurl his colors and bring his drum corps to the front of his unit. The regimental drum major, R. N. Smith, had begun to play "The Campbells Are Coming," and Dawes wanted "to make a show in the streets of Gettysburg." The tune also helped the regiment to close ranks and move with a quicker step.[88]

Dawes' band had not played long when the noise of cannon fire was detected to the north. The colonel noted that for some reason the sound was very dull and "did not attract our attention as indicating any serious engagement."[89] Lieutenant L. G. Harris, who was serving with the brigade guard at the rear of the 6th Wisconsin, commented that "The Pennsylvanians have made a mistake and are celebrating the 4th three days ahead of time." Soon, though, the sound became clear that this was artillery being fired in action.[90] Somehow word passed through the column that Buford had "found the Johnnies over at York or Harrisburg."[91] Colonel Dawes knew better, and when he saw the troops ahead (Cutler's brigade) turn to cross the fields towards the Seminary, he directed his regimental band to stop playing and "turned to engage in the sterner duties involved in war."[92]

At about this time an even odder rumor spread down the ranks of the 6th Wisconsin. The brigade adjutant, James D. Wood of the 2nd Wisconsin, rode madly by shouting to each unit, "Boys, little Mac is in command of the Army of the Potomac!" Even though most were aware that Meade was now the army's new commander, everyone "cheered like mad, glad to be rid of such vain glorious fools as... drunken Joe (Hooker)."[93] George H. Otis of the 2nd Wisconsin noted that, "There was immediately a lighter and more elastic step. Our hearts were full of gratitude....The announcement of McClellan in command was sufficient to create the greatest enthusiasm."[94] The origin of the rumor has never been identified.[95]

When the Iron Brigade reached the broken fence line near the Codori house, it headed north across the fields, behind Cutler's men. The brigade band, which had been playing "Red, White and Blue," turned to the more familiar "Yankee Doodle" in double quick time. Soon the 2nd Wisconsin, then the other regiments, broke into a run. The increasing din of musketry and artillery quickened their pace.[96] Most everyone now was panting from the heat as the column began to pass knapsacks and other gear tossed aside by Cutler's men. At this time the units of the Iron Brigade also began to drop off their non-combatants and useless baggage.[97] The officers of the 2nd and 7th Wisconsin regiments dismounted and sent their horses to the rear as they neared the Seminary and artillery shells began to land nearby.[98]

Cutler vs. Davis

Reynolds had by now returned to the front and was waiting anxiously to deploy Wadsworth's troops as they came up. Colonel Gamble was equally anxious and rode up to the general crying out, "Hurry up, General, hurry up! They are breaking our line! They are breaking our line."[99] Reynolds was well aware that Buford's front was in a critical condition all up and down the line—Devin's troopers on the right were suffering from Davis' fire; Calef's battery had already been forced to withdraw in the center, and the 8th New York on Gamble's left was in bad trouble. In addition, Gamble's skirmishers were being pushed back into Herbst Woods by Archer's infantry, who had momentarily stopped to reform along Willoughby Run.

Reynolds' first concern was to stabilize the center of his line, and give cover to his infantry as it came up and formed. For this he needed fresh artillery, so he sent for Hall's battery to come forward at once. Captain Hall recalled that he was just coming up the hill slope east and south of the Seminary when Colonel James M. Sanderson of Reynolds' staff "came to me stating that Gen. Reynolds desired to see me in person as soon as possible, and for my battery to come forward at a trot." Hall rode quickly forward and found Reynolds on the Chambersburg Pike near the McPherson Barn. Reynolds directed Hall to "Put your battery on this ridge to engage the guns of the enemy." Hall was also told "to hold the attention of the enemy until the infantry got into position."[100] In another version of this encounter, Hall quotes Reynolds as saying, "I desire you to damage the artillery to the greatest possible extent, and

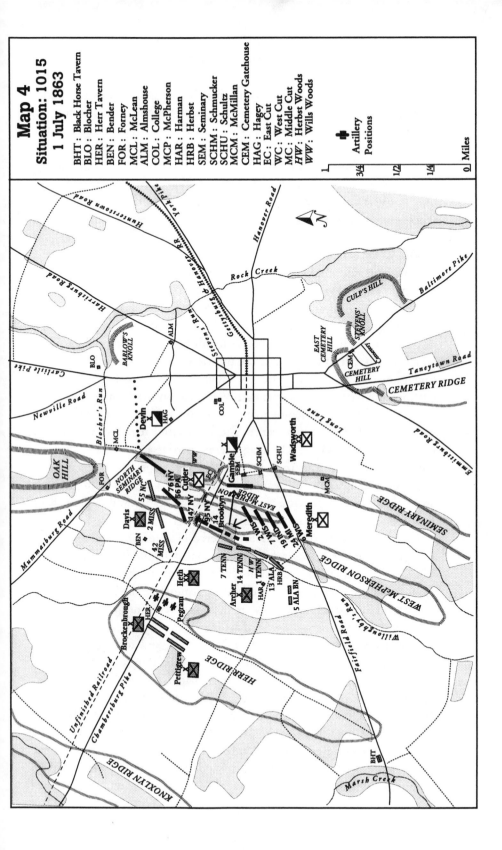

Map 4
Situation: 1015
1 July 1863

BHT : Black Horse Tavern
BLO : Blocher
HER : Herr Tavern
BEN : Bender
FOR : Forney
MCL : McLean
ALM : Almshouse
COL : College
MCP : McPherson
HAR : Harman
HRB : Herbst
SEM : Seminary
SCHM : Schmucker
SCHU : Schultz
MCM : McMillan
CEM : Cemetery Gatehouse
HAG : Hagey
EC : East Cut
WC : West Cut
MC : Middle Cut
HW : Herbst Woods
WW : Wills Woods

Artillery
Positions

0 Miles

keep their fire from our infantry until they are deployed, when I will retire you somewhat as you are too advanced for the general line." At the same time Reynolds directed Wadsworth, who was also present with Hall, "General, move a strong infantry support immediately to Hall's right for he is my defender until I can get the troops now coming up into line."[101] It is uncertain if Reynolds could see Archer's men at this time because they may have been all concealed by Herbst Woods and the trees along Willoughby Run. Davis' troops to the north of the railroad cut posed no immediate threat to the center of Buford's line on the Chambersburg Pike.

Hall returned quickly to his battery, which was coming up from the Seminary at a gallop and had already begun attracting fire from Pegram's guns on Herr Ridge. Hall turned the head of the column to the right and moved by the flank under cover of the crest of McPherson's Ridge until it reached the rear of the position pointed out to him by Reynolds, which was north of the pike at the position earlier occupied by Calef's four guns. He then moved his six rifled guns forward formed "to the left into the battery," and opened fire at once on the Confederate guns in his front.[102] Hall's deployment was seen by a member of the 14th Tennessee, which was in advance, and the second regiment but one to the left of Archer's line. The Confederate private noted that "a federal battery dashed out and took position on the ridge and opened fire." Hall's sudden appearance, unsupported, urged the men of both the 14th and 7th Tennessee to raise a yell and charge across Willoughby Run into the woods on the other side.[103]

At the same time that Reynolds ordered Hall forward, he personally directed Wadsworth to send a strong support to the battery's right.[104] Wadsworth at once rode to Cutler, who was just then approaching the Chambersburg Pike with his two leading regiments, the 76th New York and 56th Pennsylvania, which were moving in columns of fours up the swale west of the Seminary. Wadsworth directed Cutler to take these two lead regiments, plus the 147th New York, and form on the right of the road beyond the railroad line. They were then to advance westward to support Hall.[105] Doubleday suggests that Wadsworth had not seen Davis' troops advancing, so he sent Cutler into position without first conducting a reconnaissance; the time was between 1020 and 1030.[106]

Cutler led the 76th New York and the 56th Pennsylvania across the Pike and formed them into a battle line over 100 yards north of the railroad bed.[107] Meanwhile Wadsworth commandeered Cutler's rear two regiments, the 14th Brooklyn and the 95th New York, and directed them to proceed forward to protect the left of Hall's battery. Wadsworth directed Colonel Edward Fowler of the 14th Brooklyln to take charge of the two units, which moved briskly forward about 400 yards to their assigned position. As they did so, a number of Gamble's dismounted skirmishers pulled back through the advancing infantry. Some of the exhausted troopers called out in encouragement, "We have got them now" and "Go in and give them hell!"[108] At the same time the main body of the 3rd Indiana and 12th Illinois withdrew from their exposed position toward Seminary Ridge.[109]

While Fowler was advancing, General Reynolds came forward with his staff to give him specific directions where to deploy. Fowler then led his command of some 559 men "up into the orchard toward the crest of the ridge where the cavalry were skirmishing." Fowler formed on the western edge of the McPherson orchard with the left of the 14th Brooklyn next to Herbst Woods, and the right of the 95th New York near the McPherson house and garden.[110] He was on a line with Hall's battery, but there was a gap of about 100 yards between Fowler's right and Hall's left above the Chambersburg Pike.

Fowler's troops had barely formed when they encountered fire from Archer's skirmishers. The colonel related later that month that the enemy "Immediately opened fire on us from a strong line of skirmishers in the woods on our left and front, which we replied to and soon drove them back." His command suffered a few casualties, and Fowler and his staff made fine targets while mounted on their horses—he was struck on the thigh by a spent ball that passed through his coat and caused a severe contusion, and his own horse and that of his adjutant were hit in the head. The Confederate fire also wounded Colonel George H. Biddle of the 95th, who was succeeded by Major Edward Pye.[111] At this time Archer's main battle line had not yet reached Willoughby Run, but was advancing about halfway down Herr Ridge.[112]

During these maneuvers the 147th New York became separated from the 76th New York and 56th Pennsylvania, which it was supposed to follow to the north side of the Pike.[113] Historian James McLean believes that Hall's battery had cut off the 147th from the rest of its column when the guns were pushing forward to their assigned position.[114] The regimental account in New York at Gettysburg, however, claims that Lieutenant Colonel Miller of the 147th had received no orders to follow Cutler, so he instead drifted westward towards Fowler's line.[115] Lieutenant J.V. Pierce of the 147th states simply that the regiment was following the 56th Pennsylvania when "the command was given 'front' facing us towards the enemy."[116]

As the 147th moved westward, its men saw Fowler's two regiments move "up beyond the farmhouse in our front."[117] Miller's men moved forward until they reached the orchard behind the McPherson farm buildings, and stopped there in line.[118] Their commander directed them to lie down in order to escape the enemy shells that were bursting overhead.[119] Private John Bartlett obtained even more secure safety from the enemy cannons when he entered the stone basement of the McPherson barn.[120]

The 147th was only at this position about five minutes when it received orders to move to the right.[121] Accounts vary as to whether Lieutenant Colonel Miller rode to Wadsworth to seek orders, or a staff officer came to ask him to move. Captain Charles Parker of Company C reported that a staff officer came and told Miller that Hall's battery would be flanked if he did not move at once to the battery's right.[122] Whichever was the case, Miller directed the regiment to "right face" and marched it across the Pike and past the railroad bed in between the two cuts on the north end of McPherson's Ridge. During this brief march the command passed by the caissons in rear of Hall's battery. The unit was then ordered to march by the left flank, and came into battle line facing west, about 100 yards behind the line of Hall's guns.[123] It was an awkward position to say the least, since a rail fence perpendicular to the line separated the right companies from the rest of the unit, and the chasm of the western railroad cut prevented direct linking up with Hall's battery. To make matters worse, the regiment's right wing was totally up in the air and was some 300 yards in advance of the 76th New York and 56th Pennsylvania.[124]

The Confederate troops that concerned Hall were the three regiments of Davis' brigade, as already discussed. Davis' advance on the north side of the Pike had not been much hindered by the open terrain or Devin's cavalry skirmishers; the greatest opposition to his attack had been posed by Calef's four guns on the Pike, which had forced Davis' units to slide slightly to their left in order to avoid the Union artillery blasts coming straight up the Chambersburg Pike. Calef's withdrawal, though, permitted the Confederate brigade to advance more securely, and Hall, when he did come up and form, directed his first shots against Pegram's artillery on Herr Ridge rather than at Davis' infantry, which in the smoke of the battle he "had no idea" was so near.[125]

Davis' left regiment, the 55th North Carolina, did not keep contact with the rest of the brigade as it advanced, perhaps out of its commander's eagerness to support the regiment's skirmish line, which had extended all the way to the Mummasburg Road. The main line of the 55th passed by the Bender farm[126] and moved through the large orchard behind it, heading up the ridge west that rose south of the J. Forney house. In their front they saw what Davis noted in his battle report: "a commanding hill in the wood, the intervening space being enclosed fields of grass, and grain, and was very broken. On our right was the turnpike and a railroad, with deep cuts and heavy embankments, diverging from the turnpike as it approached the town."[127]

Colonel J. K. Connally of the 55th North Carolina was not at all concerned with the cavalry in his front, which was apparently mounting up and withdrawing from Oak Ridge. Instead, his attention was caught by Cutler's two regiments (76th New York and the 56th Pennsylvania) marching north across the railroad line in the field in front of the woods on Oak Ridge. Connally formed his men in line in the tall grass on the brow of the ridge, and awaited Cutler's approach.[128]

Meanwhile Davis' other two regiments had not been able to keep in line with each other. While the 55th North Carolina was forming on the Forney ridge, the 2nd Mississippi was some 300 yards to the southwest, at the eastern edge of the Bender orchard. The 42nd Mississippi was slightly to the 2nd's right, astride the railroad line. All three regiments had skirmishers out, and were ready for action.[129]

General Cutler was concerned about the possible nearness of the Confederate advance, and directed Colonel J. William Hofmann of the 56th Pennsylvania to form his regiment into battle line; the unit was then about 100 yards or more north of the railroad cut and the "gentle elevation" where its monument now stands.[130] Since Cutler was with the 56th Pennsylvania when he gave the order, that unit was already forming before the 76th New York received its orders to do so.

After he formed his regiment, Hofmann advanced it slightly until he saw Connally's 55th North Carolina on his right "just rising to the crest of the swell west of the one we were on."[131] General Cutler, who was still with the 56th, also saw Connally's line, and directed Hofmann to fire a volley in that direction, the first infantry shots on this part of the field, and probably of the battle.[132] Cutler described the scene in a letter he wrote to Pennsylvania's Governor Andrew Curtin on 5 November 1863: "It was my fortune to be in the advance on the morning of July 1st. We came upon the ground in front of the enemy, Colonel Hoffman's regiment (being the second in the column) got into position a moment sooner than the others, the enemy now advancing in line of battle within easy musket range. The atmosphere being a little thick, I took out my glass to examine the enemy. Being a few paces in the rear of Colonel Hofmann, he turned to me and inquired, 'Is that the enemy?' My reply was 'Yes.' Turning to his men, he commanded, 'Ready, right oblique, aim fire' and the battle of Gettysburg was opened."[133] The time was about 1020.[134]

Hofmann's volley was fired too early, since it only wounded two members of the 55th North Carolina's color guard.[135] It sparked a return fire that caused heavy damage in the 56th, all the more so because the Carolinians outnumbered Hofmann's men about 640 to 282.[136] General Cutler noted that, "When Colonel Hoffman gave the command, 'aim,' I doubted whether the enemy was near enough to have the fire be effective, and asked him if he was in range; but not hearing my question, he fired, and I received my reply in a shower of rebel bullets, by which many of the colonel's men were killed or wounded. My own horse, and those of two of my staff, were wounded at the same time."[137]

Hofmann's volley spurred the 2nd Mississippi to enter the fight, and the Confederate regiment all at once let loose a terrible fire on the 76th New York, some 156 yards to the southeast. The 76th was still "marching by the flank" and had not yet formed into line when they were fired upon; therefore the unit's compact marching formation was much more vulnerable to the Confederate fire. Nor did the New Yorkers initially see their foe, who were "lying down concealed from view in a wheatfield." Apparently Major Grover of the 76th thought that the fire from his front might be coming from friendly units, so he cautioned his men "to hold their fire until the enemy appeared." During several minutes that must have seemed like an eternity to the New Yorkers in line, they had to endure at least three Confederate volleys before they were permitted to return fire.[138] The 76th also found itself under enemy artillery fire; Captain Robert Story of Company B was almost severely injured by a cannonball that passed safely between his legs.[139]

The 55th North Carolina enjoyed a superiority over the 76th New York in both numbers and position, and Colonel Connally was determined to press his advantage. Since his line greatly overlapped the Federal right, Connally had his men perform a wheel to the right that brought him squarely on the 76th's flank. He then ordered his men to charge with bayonets, and they pushed forward with a yell. Connally himself "seized the battle flag and waving it aloft rushed out several paces in front of the regiment. This drew upon him and the color guard the fire of the enemy and he fell badly wounded in arm and hip." Major A. H. Belo rushed up to the colonel and asked him if he were badly wounded, to which Connally replied, "yes, but the litter bearers are here; go on, and don't let the Mississippians get ahead of you."[140] Connally's left arm would be amputated, and he would be taken prisoner near Cashtown after the battle. When the 55th's Lieutenant Colonel, Maurice T. Smith, was mortally wounded not long afterwards, Major Belo took over command of the regiment.[141]

The Confederates suffered additional officer casualties at this time. Colonel John M. Stone had experienced difficulty getting the men of his 2nd Mississippi to advance across a fence into the field where the 55th North Carolina was engaged. Since he could not find an opening to take his horse through, he had to dismount and climb over it. Just as he was going over the top rail, he was hit by an enemy bullet (he does not say where) and had to leave the field. Command of the 2nd devolved on Major J.A. Blair. Stone admittedly was more of a politician than a field officer. After the war he wrote to General Davis, "I was very much like the French soldier of whom you sometimes told us who never saw anything while the battle was going on except the rump of his fat file leader. In battle I rarely knew anything that occurred beyond the immediate vicinity of my own command. In battle when I commanded a company it engaged my whole attention, when a regiment, I knew little of any other command, and so on." He would be elected Governor of Mississippi after the war.[142]

The two Union regiments held on valiantly for almost 30 minutes despite heavy losses. As the line weakened, some Confederates were able to close in for hand to hand combat. Lieutenant A.K. Roberts of the 2nd Mississippi made a dash into the line of the 56th Pennsylvania and managed to temporarily capture a flag, only to be killed moments later.[143] Finally General Wadsworth directed the two Union regiments to withdraw rather than be destroyed.[144] Cutler later reported their heavy battle casualties (169 out of 375 in the 76th New York and 173 out of 252 in the 56th Pennsylvania), but failed to mention the number of men captured. The 42nd Mississippi claimed to take 150, and the 55th North Carolina may have taken equally as many.[145]

One of the Union men wounded early in this fight was orderly Sergeant Henry Cliff of Company F of the 76th New York. He was badly wounded in the left leg and had to be left behind when his command was forced to withdraw. Cliff had no cover from the noonday heat of the sun and requested a passing Confederate to carry him to the shade of a nearby tree. The soldier replied, "I shan't do it, get some of your damned Yankee horde to help you. If you had been at home, where you belonged, you would not have needed help." As a result Cliff had to lie in the open field for five days "with broken limb, unable to stir, almost dying from thirst and hunger, and nearly roasting, while day after day he watched the cool shade in its slow journey around the tree, never quite reaching him, but advancing and then retreating, as though tantalizing him for his loyalty!" Cliff was found, barely alive, after the Confederates retreated from the field. He lost his leg to amputation, but lived to tell the story of his ordeal.[146]

General Davis noted that the two Union units made a stubborn resistance until his line was up on them, at which point they "fled in much confusion."[147] Part of the 76th New York appears to have withdrawn in good order to the railroad cut near the Seminary,[148] but most of the surviving Yankees headed for the nearby Wills Woods on northern Seminary Ridge. W. B. Murphy of the 2nd Mississippi claimed that he saw some cavalry form up and begin to charge his line from the timber on the ridge. He called out to his comrades, who fired a volley into the timber, whereupon the horsemen disappeared. Murphy later was led to believe that the group was General Cutler and his staff, and claimed that "he and several of his staff were killed and wounded by our deadly fire." The group may have been Cutler and his staff, though the general was not struck during the battle. The horsemen may also have been some of Devin's troopers.[149]

Colonel Dawes of the 6th Wisconsin saw Cutler's men "running back in disorder," while Captain John Cook of the 76th New York claimed that the withdrawal "was done in good order."[150] The truth may have been more in the modicum. General Cutler himself admitted that the two battered units withdrew first to the line of woods on Oak Ridge and then moved "further back."[151] Captain John A. Kellogg, who was serving as acting assistant adjutant general for the brigade that day, later reported that Cutler "received an order to fall back to the town and barricade the streets." The two regiments had passed the ridge and were on the plain before the town when this order was countermanded and the troops recalled to northern Seminary Ridge.[152]

Stand of the 147th New York

While the 76th New York and the 56th Pennsylvania were engaging

Davis' left, the 147th New York was taking on the right of the 2nd Mississippi. As the 147th was moving into position north of the railroad line, Lieutenant J.V. Pierce noticed "innumerable heads of rebels bobbing up and down" on the north side of a field of wheat at the top of the ridge to his right.[153] Private Francis Pease saw the Rebels "not more than 30 or 40 rods off and their colors flying."[154] Lieutenant Pierce recounted, "The firing from the rebels commenced as we were advancing. Men began to fall on all sides before we fired a shot."[155] The first to be killed in the unit were corporal Fred Rife and his file closer, Hiram Stowell.[156]

The 147th moved forward under increasing enemy fire until its left was even with Hall's battery. There the regiment's commander, Lieutenant Colonel Francis C. Miller, directed the men to "Lie down! fire through the wheat close to the ground."[157] The effect of this first volley was recorded by Captain Leander Woollard of Company B, 42nd Mississippi, who wrote, "Just as we were charging them we came to the top of a hill in a wheat field and beheld a regiment of the blue bellies immediately in front and not over 100 yards from me and just as they leveled their guns I gave the command to 'lay down' and a shower of balls passed over our heads, wounding a few of my men."[158] The intensity of the fire fight that followed was recorded by officers from both sides. Captain James Coey of the 147th recalled: "The line of the 147th New York was lying in a field at and below the ridge, a wheatfield ready for harvest. The fire of the enemy, the zipping of their bullets cut the grain completely covering the men, who would reach over the ridge, take deliberate aim, fire, and then slide back under the canopy or covering of straw, reload and then continue their firing. Those of the regiment wounded here were wounded in the head or upper part of the body, consequently more fatal."[159] The troops of the 42nd Mississippi did not have the advantage of any such cover. It was the regiment's first fight, and a few began to waver. Captain Woollard found it necessary to take a post at the rear of his regiment along with one of his lieutenants, where he threatened to use his sword to kill anyone who tried to run away. After that, "not a man showed a willingness to go back but an anxiety to go ahead."[160]

The next 15 minutes saw intense fighting as the 147th New York blasted away at the 42nd Mississippi in its front and the 2nd Mississippi on its right. In places the opposing lines were only 100 feet apart, and the 147th began to take heavier casualties. Captain Delos Gary fell to one knee after being struck in the head, and Private Franklin Halsey was also shot through the head.[161] In all the mayhem, Lieutenant J.V. Pierce noticed that Captain Nathan Wright of Company K was pounding the ground and yelling at the top of his voice, "give them hell."[162] During this crisis Lieutenant Colonel Miller received an order from General Wadsworth to withdraw his regiment, which was now isolated by the withdrawal of the 76th New York and 56th Pennsylvania. Before he could execute the command, Miller was severely wounded in the head, and his frightened mount carried him off to the rear. Command of the 147th devolved on Major George Harney, who was unaware of Wadsworth's withdrawal order and maintained the unit in its exposed position.[163]

The attack of the 42nd Mississippi was also putting great pressure on Hall's battery at this time. As already noted, Hall had not paid attention to Davis' advance when he first deployed, but concentrated his fire on the Confederate cannons on Herr Ridge. The captain related in his battle report that his first six shots had been so well aimed that the enemy had to redeploy two of their pieces and put them behind the cover of a barn.[164] He "had no idea of the enemy's infantry being so near, till they rose up on my front and right, at a distance of not more than 50 yards."[165] Hall apparently had not been aware of the railroad cut, which the skirmishers of the 42nd Mississippi were using as a conduit to infiltrate in between the 147th New York and Hall's right guns. The heavy Confederate skirmish fire soon began to take a toll on Hall's men and horses.

Lieutenant Pierce of the 147th New York discovered that the enemy's skirmishers were giving Hall's battery a rough time when he advanced his Company G and Company C to the ridge crest on his left front, overlooking the railroad cut. There he "discovered a line of Confederate skirmishers on our front, advancing from the valley up a slope towards a rail fence, firing as they advanced into Hall's battery, which was fighting for dear life." Pierce saw a group of the enemy gather in a fence corner not far from the cut, and diverted his command to "Left oblique, fire!" After several rounds the Confederates withdrew down the hill "with several of their number stretched on the hillside."[166]

The Confederates, though, did not give up on their attempt to capture Hall's battery, which seemed vulnerable in its exposed position and was deemed quite a prize. Hall noted that "a column of the enemy's infantry charged up a ravine on our right flank within 60 yards of my right piece, when they commenced shooting down my horses and wounding my men." Hall directed his center and right sections to load with canister and fire on this infantry column, while the left section continued to engage Pegram's guns. The canister fire achieved its desired effect and broke up the Confederate attack.[167] Yet the pieces continued to suffer against the loose formation of the Confederate skirmishers; as Lieutenant Pierce put it, "artillery against the skirmishers is like shooting mosquitoes with a rifle."[168]

The exposed position of both the 147th and Hall's battery became even more tenuous as Davis' left two regiments, the 55th North Carolina and 2nd Mississippi, began to swing southward following their defeat of the 76th New York and 56th Pennsylvania. The left end of the long Confederate line was headed for the right rear of the 147th when some of the New Yorkers called out, "They are flanking us on the right." Major Harney wisely swung his right companies back to face this threat and formed them behind a fence line that ran parallel to the railroad line. This maneuver bent the regiment's line into an "L," just as the 76th New York had been forced to form a few minutes earlier.[169] The disadvantage of this position, though, was that it subjected the angle of the line to a cross fire from all portions of the Confederate line.

Awkward as the 147th's position was, the men enjoyed a temporary respite while Davis' left swung forward and his right regiment turned most of its attention to Hall's battery, as already noted.[170] Major Harney quickly gathered some of his few remaining officers and asked if they thought they should continue to defend their position, or should follow the 76th New York and 56th Pennsylvania in retreat.[171] Unknown to Major Harney, at that very moment Lieutenant Pierce, who was still at the left of the regimental line, saw "an officer ride down from Oak Hill in our rear, and wave his cap in retreat." The officer, whom he thought was I.C. Cluseman of Cutler's staff, did not dare to "venture into this maelstrom between the railroad cut and that fence," and the withdrawal order, if such it was, was never properly delivered or understood.[172]

The dangerous position of the 147th New York became even worse when Captain Hall began withdrawing his battery. Hall had seen Cutler's 76th New York and 56th Pennsylvania withdraw on his right, and saw no reason to remain in his exposed position under the heavy fire he was receiving from Davis' skirmishers. He stated in his report that, "Feeling that if the position was too advanced for infantry it was equally so for artillery, I ordered the battery to retire by sections, although having no order to do so."[173] Hall in fact was quite annoyed with Wadsworth for apparently abandoning his guns in their exposed position, and he told him so in clear words a few minutes later. At a later date Wadsworth explained to Hall that he thought Reynolds was looking out for the battery, since it had been Reynolds who first posted it. Hall did not much care for Wadsworth's excuse, but did respect him as a man of glory and good fame in the rest of the war.[174]

Hall clearly had no idea that he was abandoning the 147th New York, whose position he could not see through all the smoke. He first directed Lieutenant William Ulmer to take the two guns of his right section and withdraw to the next crest some 75 yards to the rear, where he could hopefully put up fire to cover the withdrawal of the rest of the battery. Ulmer, though, had to withdraw right across the front of the advancing 55th North Carolina. By the time he unlimbered his guns he had lost all the horses belonging to one, and the raking musketry fire that swept in his position from the right was so great that he could not fire a shot. It was only with difficulty that he managed to extricate the guns safely, pulling the one piece by hand that had lost all its horses.[175]

When Hall realized he would get no aid from Ulmer, who had his own hands full trying to withdraw his two guns, he decided to pull back his remaining four guns the only way he could—directly to the rear. Since a high fence along the Chambersburg Pike, and enfilading Confederate fire that came right up the Pike, made it impossible to use that avenue for retreat, Hall had no choice but to move back through the fields between the Pike and the railroad line. The Captain directed his guns to continue firing while he went in person to the limbers still parked at the foot of the ridge. He ordered the limbers to "reverse" where they were and then had the guns withdrawn by hand to their limbers under cover of the smoke. The guns were then limbered up and driven eastward toward Seminary Ridge, "passing into the Cashtown Road just after crossing the next ridge to our rear."[176]

Major Blair of the 2nd Mississippi saw Hall's guns retiring and turned his attention from Cutler's fleeing infantry to the capture of the cannons. W.B. Murphy of Company A noted "We were ordered right in line and first company to capture that piece of artillery. We poured such a deadly fire into them that they left their gun and ran for life."[177]

Hall recalled, "From where we limbered up to point of going into the Cashtown Road, it was hellish. The scattering rebels along the railroad cut that had been firing upon me, the moment they saw we were getting away, rushed forward and fired as rapidly as they could. My own horse was shot through the rump under me while getting the guns over the fence, but one gun being able to pass at the same time, and the enemy got so thick it was hard to say which outnumbered, gray or blue, and the horses on the last gun were all bayonetted, and fell dead over the fence." Hall was loath to abandon his gun, but left in hopes that some infantry would help him secure it, since the Confederates then appeared no stronger than a skirmish line.[178]

One of Hall's gunners managed to bring off his gun at the cost of his life. The following account of this unnamed hero was recounted in the regimental history of the 76th New York: "In another instance, the rebels had killed nearly all the gunners of one piece of our artillery, and were advancing to capture it. Observing their movement, one of the gunners hastily attached the horses to the gun, and was just preparing to mount and ride off, as the rebel lieutenant placed his hand upon the piece and ordered him to surrender. Instead of obeying the order, he put spurs to the horses and dashed off. But, as he started, the lieutenant, who had reached the horses' side, presented a cocked pistol at the head of the gunner. Determined to save the gun, regardless of the danger ahead, when the lieutenant fired, the ball entering the body of the gunner; he, however, managed to stay upon his horse until the gun was safe within our lines, and then fell to the ground dead!"[179]

When Hall reached Seminary Ridge, a full half mile behind his original position, he ran into General Wadsworth and exclaimed how cowardly it was for the infantry to abandon him, as already mentioned. Wadsworth did not have time to discuss the point and directed Hall to "Get your guns back, to some point to cover the retiring of these troops." Hall objected, arguing that the Seminary Ridge line was a good one to hold, but Wadsworth replied, "Oh no, go beyond the town for we cannot hold this line."[180]

Hall made one last plea to be allowed to save his abandoned gun, but Wadsworth "snappishly" replied, "lose no time in getting your guns into position to cover the retreat." Even so, Hall sent a sergeant and five men to try to retrieve the gun. All were wounded or captured.[181]

Hall was dismayed to see what a shambles his command was in after he retired through the town and arrived at Cemetery Hill "to the left of the enclosure." Of his 119 men engaged, 2 had been killed and 18 wounded, which were unusually high losses for a battery. In addition, 28 horses had been killed. Only three of the unit's guns were still serviceable—one had been lost on the field, a second had been dragged back on one wheel after a Confederate solid shot knocked the other wheel from its carriage, and Ulmer's gun that had lost all its horses had been hitched to a caisson and sent to the rear in search of a fresh limber.[182] It is probable that most or even all of the battery would have been captured had the 147th not held its ground and shielded it from the full onslaught of Davis' brigade.

Amazingly, the 147th New York was still holding its position as Hall's five cannons were heading to the rear. Lieutenant Pierce noted that "the smoke of carnage rose as an incense, and wrapped the folds of the flag defended within its shortened lines. Not a man flinched, none left the field except the wounded; the untouched living and dead remained."[183] By now the 55th North Carolina had crossed the rail fence and was moving towards the 147th's right rear as it pressed forward and fired volleys into Hall's retreating artillery men. Pierce noted: "The colors drooped to the front. An officer in front of the center corrected the alignment as if passing in review. It was the finest exhibition of discipline I ever saw, before or since, on the battlefield."[184] At the same time the 42nd Mississippi was preparing a change, after some of its officers discounted a claim from Captain H. Gaston of Company B that there was an order to retreat. The troops held on "nobly" and would soon launch a charge "with a shout such as Southern enthusiasm alone can give."[185]

The 147th Regiment would surely have been swallowed up by Davis' men had not General Wadsworth at length taken note of their continued presence in their exposed position. Archer's brigade had just been routed, as will be discussed in a moment, and the 147th was the only unit still fighting on the battle line. Wadsworth noticed their line, and wondered what the regiment was doing there, since he had 15 or more minutes earlier directed all the infantry north of the Pike to retire. Divisional assistant adjutant general Captain T. E. Ellsworth wrote to H.H. Lyman of the 147th in 1888 that, "Rolling back towards the rear with General Wadsworth, the position of your regiment was observed by him, apparently the only command remaining on that third ridge and seemingly under heavy fire. He asked me what that regiment was doing up there; said he had given orders sometime ago for those troops to be withdrawn, and directed me to go and withdraw them unless there was some special occasion, which was not apparent to him for their remaining."[186]

Ellsworth bravely rode up the valley between the two crests of McPherson's Ridge, passing between Hall's withdrawing artillerymen and their abandoned gun. He then went "directly up the hill" to the center of the 147th's line. He at once found Major Harney and asked him what he was doing there. When Harney said he had no orders to withdraw, Ellsworth gave the needed command to fall back, and then "got out myself as rapidly as I conveniently could."[187]

Harney knew that his situation was desperate, since the 55th North Carolina was threatening to cut off the Chambersburg Pike to the rear and the 42nd Mississippi was behind his regiment on the left; had it not been for the protection the railroad gave to the unit's left rear, the 147th would probably have been captured already. Harney knew that his men would have to run for their lives, so he ordered them to drop all their gear except their rifles and cartridge boxes. Captain James Coey regretted leaving his haversack: "Thus went our rations, and until July 4, only two crackers from a passing regiment sustained us."[188]

Harney now gave the unmilitary but effective order, "In retreat, double quick, run." Just as the men rose, Color Sergeant Hinchcliff was riddled by bullets and fell with his flag, drenching the colors with his blood. The flag was not missed until part of the unit reached Chambersburg Pike. It was then that Sergeant William A. Wybourn, "a brave Irish lad," returned to the regiment's original line, unrolled the dead color bearer from the folds of the flag, tore the standard from its broken staff, and raced again to the rear. Wybourn had crossed the Pike and was in a small peach orchard when he was struck by an enemy shot and fell to the earth on the flag. Lieutenant Pierce saw him fall and went up to him to recover the flag. "I tried to remove the colors, but he held to them with true Irish grit. I commanded him to let go, and to my surprise he answered, 'Hold on, I will be up in a minute,' rolled over and staggered to his feet, and carried them all through the fight, and was commissioned for his courage."[189]

It was indeed difficult for the 147th to leave so many of its dead and wounded on the field as it retired. Private Pease noted, "We got no orders to retreat until the Rebs got up very close. We was [sic] ordered to retreat, which we did at a fast rate. We left awful sight [sic] of dead and wounded on the field as we retreated."[190] Lieutenant Pierce endured an especially painful moment as he pulled back. When he first started to the rear he found Edwin Aylesworth painfully wounded by a shot in the right thigh. Aylesworth begged not to be left behind, so Pierce and Sergeant Peter Shultz helped him to his feet and tried to carry him. When they could not do so, they had to lay him down. His piteous appeal, "Don't leave me, boys" rang in Pierce's ears and lived in his memory ever after. This delay caused Pierce and Shultz to be among the last to leave the field; Shultz would be mortally wounded a few minutes later.[191]

The men of the 147th retreated in small groups as best they could. Their line was at once overrun by elements of all three of Davis' regiments. Major Belo of the 55th North Carolina noted that the Federal line "was well marked by their dead and wounded. The first wounded man I asked replied; 'We are all Joe Hooker's men, and have marched five miles this morning;' so I told one of my officers that we had struck the regular army, and not the militia."[192] Major J.A. Blair of the 2nd Mississippi was also struck by the orderly line of the 147th's casualties: "I could, I recollect, distinctly trace the line of the Union forces by the dead and wounded lying on the ground."[193]

The majority of the men of the 147th stayed with Major Harney and withdrew on the north side of the railroad line, literally in the teeth of the advancing 55th North Carolina. Captain Coey recounted: "Fresh from lying down, with the enemy winded by their quick thrust forward, we made progress to the rear. As soon as our guns were loaded the line halted, faced about, the volley given, then the march continued, men falling at every step. Many of the enemy, in their excitement and haste to capture us failed to draw their ramrods after loading their guns, shooting them at us...The enemy was now so near, even their camp hatchets were hurled among us, with vile and opprobrious taunts as bitter as their bile, calling us to surrender.[194] Even so, Harney managed to bring most of his command to safety on Seminary Ridge, where he eventually rejoined the remnants of the 76th New York and 56th Pennsylvania.

About 40 men of the 147th on the left end of the line climbed into the eastern railroad cut to escape the enemy's fire. Lieutenant J.V. Pierce related that they "went into the R.R. cut where it was about two feet deep. I was no sooner in the cut than I found it was death trap [sic]; for the rebels had penetrated the lower end (north) of the cut and the moment we got off in there to avoid the charge of the enemy on our right they opened on us with a score of rifles. How we climbed out I can barely realize, but I know I climbed up the steep sides and got out."[195] Lieutenant Pierce and his men quickly headed southeast across the meadow between the railroad line and the Pike. They then entered a small peach orchard when Pierce saw Sergeant Wybourn with Sergeant Hinchcliff's flag, as already noted. They retired to Seminary Ridge, and eventually rejoined the rest of their regiment on the north side of the Pike.[196]

Not all the members of the 147th, however, were able to find a good escape route. A fair number of them chose to retreat through the middle railroad cut, the same one that would be equally alluring to much of Davis' brigade a few minutes later. Private Pease related, "We got into an old railroad ravine, and was going along as fast as we could, but not very, for the road was crowded. Besides, there was a good many wounded men that had hobbled along and got into the ravine. The Rebel balls whistled over the ravine like hail. Soon the Rebels came up each side of the bank in large numbers, and we had to throw down our arms and surrender ourselves to them as their prisoners."[197] The regiment lost during the morning's conflict some 126 dead and missing, plus 163 wounded, a total of 289 casualties out of 380 engaged.[198]

The stand of the 147th New York was truly one of the great heroic episodes of the battle. Had the regiment not held its position so bravely, Davis would have turned back Hall's battery sooner and then might well have proceeded across the Chambersburg Pike to deal with Fowler's two small regiments and possibly outflank the Iron Brigade. Even so, the regiment's accomplishment has been largely overlooked by historians, some of whom, even recently, have claimed that the regiment had followed the 76th New York and 56th Pennsylvania and was defeated with them.[199] Because of this misconception the members of the regiment had to wage a long campaign in order to prove where they actually fought, and were unsuccessful at getting permission to have their regimental monument erected at the site of their heroic stand on Hall's right, north of the western railroad cut.[200]

The Bloody Railroad Cut

The fighting just described on the north side of the Chambersburg Pike lasted at least 45 minutes, and there was still more to come. Davis' troops were disorganized by their success as they congregated around the middle railroad cut gathering in prisoners from the 147th New York. Major J.A. Blair of the 2nd Mississippi noted that "all the men were jumbled together without regard to regiment or company."[201] Command control was made very difficult by the fact that all three regiments had lost heavily in officers, including Colonel J.M. Stone of the 2nd Mississippi and Colonel Connally and Lieutenant Colonel M.T. Smith of the 55th North Carolina. No accounts mention where General Davis was at this stage of the fighting, so it is at least apparent that he was not having a direct impact on the action; likewise the whereabouts of Colonel H.R. Miller of the 42nd Mississippi at this time is not known.[202]

Major Blair of the 2nd Mississippi noted, "When the line confronting retired, we pursued for awhile and then halted for a moment. I was the only field officer left. After a few words with some of the men, we determined to move forward and capture Gettysburg."[203] Blair's men had not moved far, however, when they began to receive fire from south of the Pike, which they had to turn and face.

The new firing encountered by Blair and the rest of Davis' brigade came principally from Fowler's two regiments, the 14th Brooklyn and 95th New York, which had been posted south of the Chambersburg Pike since after 1000. As already noted, Fowler had been detached from the rear of Cutler's column and had been directed to move to support the left flank of Hall's battery. He had encountered only a brief period of fire from Archer's skirmishers as he formed on the western edge of the McPherson orchard with his left at the northern boundary of the Herbst Woods and his right near the McPherson barn; his line did not reach all the way to the Chambersburg Pike, and there was a gap of about 100 yards between his right and the left of Hall's battery on the north side of the Pike.[204]

Fowler's fire persuaded the skirmishers opposed to him to slide to their right and seek the protection offered by Herbst Woods. The colonel then saw the main body of Archer's brigade advancing "about six hundred yards to our front and left;"[205] one if not both of the regiments on his immediate front, the 7th and 14th Tennessee veered to the right in order to avoid his fire and also gain shelter from Herbst Woods. Curiously, Archer's troops did not seek to use the woods to their advantage in order to work around Fowler's left flank. Instead, their full attention was devoted to the Iron Brigade's counterattack, as will be shown shortly.

Fowler's line enjoyed perhaps half an hour of relative quiet as the battle raged in the woods to his left and across the Pike to his right. Since there was little Confederate infantry in his immediate front, the principal fire he was exposed to was some long range artillery fire from Pegram's guns of Herr Ridge. This interlude ended about 1040 when Fowler noticed Hall's battery retiring; "At this time, looking to our right and rear, I discovered to my surprise and consternation, the enemies' line of battle advancing steadily, one of our guns was in front, deserted except by one man, a brave fellow who fired the piece when the enemy were upon him and ran."[206]

Fowler sized up the situation quickly, and then swung his whole line back 90 degrees, using his extreme left company as a point. This complicated maneuver is described as follows in the 14th Brooklyn's regimental history: "Colonel Fowler ordered his command, the Ninety-fifth and the Fourteenth, to change front on Tenth Company. This difficult maneuver the command executed coolly, although the men were already beginning to drop. The command retreated until on line with the enemy, and then, changing front forward on the right, faced the Confederates in the railroad cut."[207]

Fowler's new line was on the north side of the rear half of Herbst Woods. Once formed there, the two regiments calmly advanced to a point closer to the Chambersburg Pike, and lay down there for a few minutes.[208] Fowler's movements for the moment stabilized the Union center and relieved his command of the jeopardy of being taken on the flank.

It was the timely arrival of the 6th Wisconsin, however, that changed the course of the action in this sector. As already noted, the 6th was the last regiment in the division's line of march that morning, followed only by the 102-man brigade guard. When the head of the Iron Brigade was passing in front of the Seminary at about 1020, the other four regiments of the brigade were sent at once into action against Archer's brigade in Herbst Woods. While the 6th was passing the crest of the ridge south of the Seminary, Colonel Rufus R. Dawes received the following order from Lieutenant Gilbert M. Woodward, an aide of General Meredith: "Colonel, form your line and prepare for action." The experienced regiment quickly changed from column to line formation and hurried forward at the double quick, loading as they ran.[209]

At this point the 102 men of the brigade guard reported to Colonel Dawes, following a command just issued by Captain Clayton Rogers of Wadsworth's staff. The men of the guard were tired from running to catch up with Dawes' column, but they had loaded on the run and were ready for action. Lieutenant Lloyd Harris, commander of the detachment, remembered that he was heartened at the moment by the strains of "Hail Columbia" being played by the regimental band on a little knoll "as we turned to the left into a field."[210]

Dawes directed Lieutenant Harris to divide his command into two provisional companies and position one on each end of his battle line. Harris accordingly took charge of 50 men and formed them on the 6th's left flank, while 2nd Lieutenant Levi Showalter of the 2nd Wisconsin took the other 50 men of the brigade guard to the right flank of the 6th.[211] Harris felt uneasy about leading his mixed command into combat, men "who no doubt felt a novel sensation in fighting under a strange officer, and away from their companies and regiments." To reassure his men, he told them, "I know how much you would like to be with your own commands, and I am just as anxious to join company C over there on the right of the 6th, but it cannot be so; do the best you can and I will do my duty towards you."[212]

It was not long before Dawes received an order from Meredith to advance and set up a line on the left flank of the Iron Brigade. He had hardly begun to move forward, however, when he received another order from Doubleday to halt; Doubleday rightly foresaw that the regiment would be more useful as a division reserve than it would be on the far left of the Iron Brigade line. When Dawes stopped his troops, their left rested on the Fairfield Road, and there were no Confederate troops on his immediate front.[213]

Dawes headed toward the extreme left of the brigade, south of Herbst Woods. As he advanced, Dawes heard heavy firing to his right, and saw a line of rebel skirmishers running back across his front.[214] The regiment had just reached the bottom of the swale between Seminary and McPherson Ridges when Lieutenant Benjamin T. Marten of Doubleday's staff galloped up and said, "Colonel, General Doubleday is now in command of the first corps, and he directs that you halt your regiment." Dawes stopped his line as ordered, and directed his men to lie down for cover.[215] Private Albert Young of Company E noted that the field where they lay was planted with "fast ripening wheat."[216] As the firing intensified in the woods to the right, Frank King of Company E spoke to his corporal, Lyman White, with the sad premonition, "Lime, this finishes my fighting."[217]

The rapid deterioration of Cutler's line on the right prompted Doubleday to call for his only reserve, Dawes' regiment. He sent his orderly, Lieutenant Meredith Jones, to Dawes with orders to "move your regiment to the right." The colonel promptly gave the command; "Right Face!" and "Double Quick March," and headed his column through the open fields towards the rear of Herbst Woods. On the way he met Captain J.D. Wood of Meredith's staff, who repeated the command with the exhortation to "Go like hell! It looks like they are driving Cutler's men."[218] Within a few minutes, Lieutenant Clayton Rogers of Wadsworth's staff arrived with the same orders.[219] The situation was indeed serious, to receive the same command from corps, brigade and division commanders at nearly the same time.

The men of the 6th Wisconsin rushed forward by the right flank for about 400 yards, panting under the weight of their packs. Dawes then ordered them to file by the right and rear to form a battle line facing north about 100 yards south of the Pike. Here they could see Hall's battery withdrawing, and all the general confusion of the 147th's retreat.[220] Sergeant George Fairfield of Company C saw Union infantry "with knapsacks on" flying before the enemy."[221] To him they were "scattering like sheep, leaving the artillery and out running the enemy."[222] The beleaguered infantrymen of the 147th New York, however, had a quite different perspective. To them the 6th Wisconsin's sudden appearance came as a salvation that saved them from being made prisoners.[223] Some of the men of the 6th noted a few officers pass solemnly by carrying a body in a blanket; they later learned that this was their fallen commander, General Reynolds.[224]

As his column neared the Chambersburg Pike, Dawes saw "a long line of rebels coming over the ridge beyond the railroad cut;" they were generally facing east and had their right flank open to attack. Without hesitation, he gave the command to "File right, March," and led his column to the right until it was on a line with the open flank of Davis' "strong but scattered line of battle."[225] He then formed his regiment into battle line by a complicated maneuver: "I saw at once the necessity of changing front, and ordered my men to file right on toward the Seminary. Extending battalion length in that direction, I moved by the left flank in line of battle. This threw my line parallel to the turnpike and railroad cut, and almost directly upon the flank of the enemy."[226]

Dawes now led his line north towards the Pike into "leaden rain and iron hail." One of the first casualties was Dawes' own horse. Dawes had ridden out ahead of his unit, and formed an obvious target to the enemy. When his mount slowed and began to lunge, Dawes began spurring her on, unaware that she had been struck. In a moment she fell heavily on her haunches. Dawes felt lucky not to be trapped under the animal; instead he was thrown sprawling in front of his men, who gave him a hearty cheer.[227] He scrambled up and shouted, "I am all right boys," and had to fight the rest of the day on foot. This was actually a stroke of luck for him, considering the rate at which mounted officers were being felled.[228]

The line of the 6th opened up to pass Dawes' fallen horse, then closed up as it moved forward. As he looked back, the colonel saw his valiant mount hobbling to the rear on three legs. Somehow she made it safely to the brigade's wagons, and survived the war for a number of years, despite a bullet wound that penetrated seventeen inches into her breast. Dawes related that "for years she carried the bullet, which could be felt

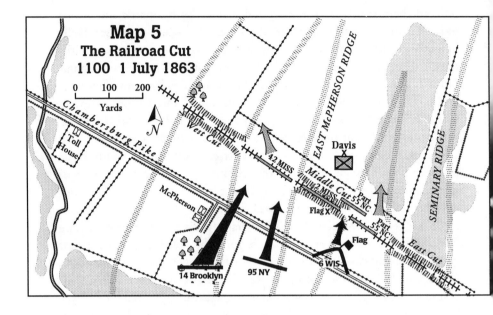

Map 5
The Railroad Cut
1100 1 July 1863

under the skin behind the left shoulder blade, but woe to the man who felt it, as her temper had been spoiled."[229]

Dawes halted his line when it reached the post and rail fence on the south side of the Chambersburg Pike. Here he gave an order to "fire by file" at Davis' troops, who were only 40 yards distant. This fire took the enemy by enfilade, and at once turned the enemy's attention away from the pursuit of Cutler's troops. Dawes noted that "the fire of our carefully aimed muskets, resting in the fence rails, soon checked their headlong pursuit. The rebel line swayed and bent, and suddenly stopped firing."[230] Private Young of the 6th noted that "The Johnnies were so intent upon following up their advantage that they did not for sometime discover what was going on their right."[231] The 6th's timely arrival saved the remnants of the 147th New York from destruction, a deed for which the New Yorkers were grateful ever after.[232]

Major A. H. Belo of the 55th North Carolina, however, had seen the danger presented by the 6th Wisconsin as it marched at right angles towards his right flank. While Dawes' men were forming, he suggested to Major Blair, now commander of the 2nd Mississippi to his right, that they should conduct a charge before the enemy completed their formation; he strongly believed "that the side charging first would hold the field."[233]

Blair agreed with Belo, but before they could act, they received orders "to form a new alignment." Someone—and it could have only been General Davis—directed Blair's and Belo's regiments to stop their pursuit of the 147th New York and form parallel to the Pike, facing the threat posed by the 6th Wisconsin. As the two regiments "swung around by the right wheel," they came under such a heavy fire from Dawes' men that some of the Confederates began to seek shelter in the depression of the middle railroad cut.[234]

The middle railroad cut, however, had disadvantages as well as advantages. It provided a ready made defensive trench for the troops that held either end of the 600 foot long cut, but its center was so deep and steep (approximately 10 to 15 feet) that the troops that went there could not even see to fire out.[235] Sergeant Vairin of the 55th North Carolina observed that, "our men thought [it] would prove a good breastwork, but it was too steep and in changing front the men were all tangled up and confused."[236] Major Blair of the 2nd Mississippi noted that "when we got into the railroad cut, the Second and Forty Second and the Fifty Fifth North Carolina were one mass of men."[237] W. B. Murphy of the 2nd Mississippi was near the eastern mouth of the cut and noted that "the ditch was not more than two feet deep where I passed over the railroad."[238] Captain Leander Guy Woollard of Company B, 42nd Mississippi, sized up the situation well when he wrote, "We were feeling the day at that point at least was ours—lo, a cloud of blue coats, fresh and eager for the fray, confronted us. An order came down the line from whom I cannot tell, to lay down in a cut for a railroad nearby. Well we obeyed—and in obeying sacrificed our freedom for a time at least, for the cut was too deep to fire over except at the extreme left and the 2nd Mississippi and 55 North Carolina having passed over my company were too thick to either fight or escape."[239]

The Confederate commands, then, were very much disordered and jumbled, particularly at the center of the cut, which already contained dead and wounded from both sides who had fallen during the 147th New York's retreat. However, several companies, particularly at the ends of the cut, must have retained their cohesion, since Dawes and Fowler both spoke of the fire that their charging troops met after crossing the pike. These organized companies would have been in the same relative positions their regiments had held during their advance—42nd Mississippi on the right, 2nd Mississippi in the center, and 55th North Carolina on the left. It is clear that at least half of the 55th North

Carolina extended in line east of the cut, to a distance of about 100 yards.[240] W.B. Murphy and the color guard of the 2nd Mississippi somehow found themselves "fifty spaces East of the cut" and "ten spaces south of the Railroad." Since he notes that his regiment stopped at the railroad for protection, Murphy's color guard may have actually been slightly in advance of the regimental line.[241]

The two lines now engaged in a sharp fire fight in which the fresh muskets of the 6th Wisconsin made a telling fire on the Confederate line. The weight of Dawes' regiment of about 400 effective men was probably increased at this time by 550+ men of Fowler's command, who most likely joined the fight from the position they had taken along the Chambersburg Pike fence line, slightly to the left of where Dawes came up. The riflemen of Company A of the 6th Wisconsin noted that the Confederates returned a "terrific fire,"[242] but the Confederate line was not as cohesive as Dawes' and Fowler's, and a number of Davis' men within the cut were unable to see out to fire. When the 6th Wisconsin advanced, the color guard of the 2nd Mississippi was, as already noted, in the open a little to the southeast of the cut. Within five minutes of the 6th Wisconsin's arrival at the Pike fence, every man in the 2nd Mississippi's color guard fell as a casualty. In addition, their flag was pierced by more than a dozen bullets, and the flag staff was splintered, all by the concentrated Federal fire.[243]

To many of Dawes' men it seemed as if much of the Confederate line had simply disappeared into the earth. Colonel Dawes himself had not been aware of the cut, "and at first mistook the maneuver of the enemy for retreat."[244] Lieutenant Lloyd Harris, on the left end of Dawes' line, noted that when "the enemy discovered us coming, they gave up the pursuit of Cutler's men and wheeled to the right to meet [us]. I could not help thinking, now, for once, we will have a square 'stand up and knock down fight': No trees, nor walls to protect either, when presto! their whole line disappeared as if swallowed up by the earth."[245] Mickey Sullivan of Company K observed "it seemed as if the ground had opened and swallowed them up; but we soon found that they were still on top of it—as they opened a tremendous fire on us, from an old railroad cut."[246] Augustus Klein of Company E thought that the Confederates were "Kowardly [sic] sons of bitches" for taking cover in the cut.[247]

Davis' difficulty was increased when portions of Cutler's 76th New York, 56th Pennsylvania and 147th New York reformed in the woods north of the railroad cut on Seminary Ridge, and reentered the fight.

W.B. Murphy of the 2nd Mississippi saw General Cutler and his staff riding along the ridge line, and before long Union fire from that sector began to enfilade Davis' line. At the same time Lieutenant Calef began returning his replenished battery to action, and his first piece was unlimbered on Seminary Ridge just north of the Pike, where it also joined the fight.[248]

Davis became concerned by this enfilading fire and the strength of the three regiments on his front, so he decided to order a retreat. The decision was not a bad one; his three regiments were of approximately equal strength with the units opposed to him, but they were tired and disorganized, and had lost a fair number of officers. In addition, his east-west line was out of position, and he had no supports nearby, particularly since Archer's brigade had just been routed. In his battle report Davis complained of the "greatly superior numbers of the enemy," though he did admit that "our men gave way under the first shock of his attack." What also concerned him was the fact that Fowler's men overlapped his line to the west, though they had not "opened a heavy fire on our right flank and rear," as he complained in his report.[249]

Davis ordered the 2nd and 42nd Mississippi to withdraw through the road cut, covered by the 55th North Carolina.[250] Major Blair of the 2nd Mississippi believed that the 2nd and the 42nd were greatly intermingled even though he had been endeavoring to reform his regiment for a forward movement.[251] Davis later complained in his report that the retreat "was done in good order, leaving some officers and men in the railroad cut, who were captured, although every effort was made to withdraw the commands."[252] Such was far from the case, as will now be shown.

Colonel Dawes saw the Confederate fire slacken as Davis' men prepared to pull out, and boldly ordered an attack. His advance was made doubly difficult by the fences on both sides of the Pike. Some of the men climbed the first fence, so exposing themselves even more to enemy fire, while others knocked down sections of what one private called a "high rail fence."[253] Mickey Sullivan noted that, "In the road our fellows straightened up their lines and waited for all hands to get over the fence."[254] The second fence, of Virginia rail construction, proved more of an obstacle because it was closer to the Confederate line. Captain John Ticknor was killed while climbing over it, and Private Albert V. Young observed that "Several of our poor boys are left dangling on the fence." Colonel Dawes later wrote to John Bachelder that "to climb that fence in face of such a fire was a clear test of mettle and discipline."[255]

It was not until he crossed the second fence that Dawes was aware of the presence of the 95th New York "coming gallantly into line upon our left." He did not know where they came from, but was certainly glad to see them.[256] Apparently it was at this time that Major Edward Pye of the 95th ordered his troops to rise from the line they had been holding and move forward to support the 6th Wisconsin. Dawes had not been able to see Pye's men previously because of all the smoke and the lay of the land.

Dawes at once ran over to Pye, who "appeared to be in command" of the regiment, and shouted out through the noise of battle, "we must charge." Pye responded, "Charge it is," and both officers sent their troops forward.[257]

Dawes insists that he was not aware at this time of the presence of Fowler's regiment farther down on Pye's left. He had 500 fresh men in his command, and was confident in them, especially with the added support of Pye's men.[258] His claim seems reasonable, in view of the topography and the fact he was not aware of Pye's presence until the 95th New York reached the Pike.

Colonel Fowler, on the other hand, was well aware of Dawes' approach, and independently ordered his command to charge, probably for the same reasons that induced Dawes to attack. Fowler also apparently sent an aide to direct Dawes to attack along with him;[259] for this reason he later tried to claim credit for organizing the entire attack by the three regiments.[260] Dawes violently objected to Fowler's claims, and flatly states that he was not aware of Fowler's presence until the charge was over.[261] The accumulated evidence seems to indicate that Fowler's line, though it had advanced to the fence near the Pike, was primarily in a defensive posture until the attack was ordered, whereas Dawes' entire advance was offensive in purpose, and separately orchestrated.

All accounts agree that the Confederate fire facing the 6th Wisconsin was a perfect rain of hail; Cornelius W. Okey of Company C noted that the only way he could see the Confederate line "in front of us was by their flag which was planted on the edge of the excavation, and by the smoke from their muskets as they gave us volley after volley."[262] The Wisconsin men were being felled by the scores; altogether the regiment would lose 180 men in this charge that would cover a mere 175 paces.

Dawes observed, "We were receiving a fearfully destructive fire from the enemy. Men who had been shot were leaving the ranks in crowds."[263]

Due to the heavy losses and noise of battle, the surviving men of the 6th tended to bunch on their colors at the center of the line. Their instinct was encouraged by Dawes, who kept repeating orders to "Align on the colors! Close up on the colors!" As a result, the center of the line advanced more resolutely than the rest, with the color guard forming the point of an inverted "V" heading towards the enemy.[264] Dawes later stated that he gave this command because "the regiment was being so broken up that this order alone could hold the body together."[265]

The horrible extent of the unit's casualties can be appreciated in part from this brief passage written by Earl Rogers: "Andy Miller of Co F falls dead, near him Gottlieb Schriebster wounded, but a few yards more and Broughton is killed, then Sweet falls wounded. Then Jim McLane and Alf. Thompson are wounded. Now Sutton falls dead. Goodwin and Charlie Jones are wounded. They reach the cut and Levi Steadman drops dead and Ed Lind is wounded."[266]

Private Mickey Sullivan had several interesting experiences during the charge. For some reason he initially stayed behind at the fence near the Pike. He noticed that his gun would not fire, and then discovered it was double loaded, so he turned to the regimental adjutant, Edward Brooks, who gave him a weapon he had just picked up off the ground. Sullivan tried to fire the piece, only to find that his percussion caps were bad. So he ran over to Captain John Ticknor with his problem and Ticknor told him to take what gear he needed from Corporal Charles Crawford, who had just got down with a bad wound. Ticknor helped Sullivan roll Crawford over, and Sullivan undid the corporal's cartridge box and put it on. When he finished and looked up, he saw Ticknor stagger to the rear and then keel over, where he soon expired.[267]

The regiment's national flag formed an obvious target at the point of the attack, and went down at least three times during the charge, only to be raised up each time. At one point Dawes himself took up the fallen flag, only to have it seized from him by a corporal of the color guard.[268]

As the Union line neared the Confederates, any cohesion that remained simply broke down as everyone rushed up toward the enemy. Sergeant George Fairfield of Company C, which was in the right portion of the 6th's line, was about 30 feet from the enemy line when he observed their fire to slacken. He sensed that a volley was coming, and sure enough one erupted when he advanced another 10 feet. It struck to the left of his position and seemed to fell half of the regiment. On the far right of the line Lieutenant Showalter of the improvised brigade guard company fell wounded. At the other end of the line, Lieutenant Harris, commander of the other brigade guard company, saw his command "hold their own with the 6th....The fire was the worst I ever experienced, yet not a man failed to move promptly forward and closed in to the right as the men fell before the murderous fire of the rebels in the railroad cut."[269]

As the 6th's line came up almost to that of Davis' troops, some of the bolder Union troops were attracted by the alluring prize of the flag of the 2nd Mississippi, which was only a few feet distant. Lieutenant William Pennington of Company I, which was near the left end of the 6th's line, felt that he could take the Confederate ensign, and moved behind his own men to the right towards the apex of the regiment's advance before attempting a mad dash at his prize. He was wounded in the neck and right shoulder, and had to return to his own lines. There he "spoke to Major Hauser, got d——d for going after the flag, and started for the rear on my best run. Flag taking was pretty well knocked out of me." Despite his lack of success, Pennington later still felt that he could have taken the flag.[270]

Pennington did not know that at least three other members of his unit rushed the Confederate flag right behind him. Cornelius C. Okey of Company C saw Pennington go down in front of him, but pressed on because it was simply too late to turn back. He reached the flagstaff first and grabbed it down low, only to find it firmly planted in the ground. As soon as he stood up he was wounded by a rebel corporal he had seen nearby with a bayonet on his musket. Drummer Lewis Eggleston reached the flag at the same time as Okey and grabbed the staff higher up, only to be felled by a shot through both arms. Private John Johnson of Company H rushed forward to try to save Eggleston, who was one of his messmates, but found that his gun would not fire because the ramrod was jammed in the barrel. He raised his gun to use it as a club, and was wounded in the right arm.[271]

This episode was clearly remembered by Corporal W.B. Murphy of Company A, 2nd Mississippi, who was carrying the flag that day because Color Sergeant Christopher Columbus Davis was sick. "Just about that time a squad of soldiers made a rush for the colors with one of the most deadly struggles that was ever witnessed during the war. They still kept on rushing for my flag and there were over a dozen shot down like sheep in their madly rush on the colors." Murphy, however, denied that any

Confederates were killed by clubbed muskets, and after the war contested several other details of Dawes' account of the charge.[272]

The fighting now reached a crisis as the left flank of the 6th reached the railroad cut proper. Vicious hand to hand and bayonet fighting broke out, and a cry arose from some of the Wisconsin men, "Throw down your muskets!" Dawes heard the commotion and made his way to the front of the center of his line, which had struck near the eastern end of the cut. He wrote later, "Running forward and through our line of men, I found myself face to face with hundreds of rebels, whom I looked down upon in the railroad cut, which was, where I stood, four feet deep."[273]

It was much to Dawes' good fortune that regimental adjutant Edward Brooks had taken about twenty men and moved across a low worm fence to block the eastern exit of the cut. Fire from here was able to enfilade the mass of Confederate troops in the cut, as Davis' men understood all too well.[274] Had Brooks not done so, the outcome of the fighting along the cut might have turned out quite differently. Lieutenant Lloyd Harris, who was at the left end of the regimental line at the spot where the cut was the deepest, noted that it was "an even question of who should surrender" to whom at this point of the line. The line of Wisconsin men here was painfully thin, but the Mississippi men packed into the cut could not see beyond the line of blue troops along the rim of the cut in order to ascertain this.[275]

Colonel Dawes boldly seized control of the situation by shouting, "Where is the colonel of this regiment?" Major John Blair of the 2nd stood up and responded, "Who are you?" Dawes sternly replied, "I command this regiment. Surrender or I will fire." Dawes later described the scene, "The officer replied not a word, but promptly handed me his sword, and his men, who still held them, threw down their muskets. The coolness, self possession, and discipline which held back our men from pouring a general volley saved a hundred lives of the enemy, and as my mind goes back to the fearful excitement of the moment, I marvel at it."[276]

Dawes at once accepted Blair's sword, though he later regretted that he did not chivalrously offer to return it; he was, after all, new to this business of receiving captured enemy regiments. In a moment six other officers of the regiment also handed over their swords, and Dawes held an awkward armful of cutlery until adjutant Brooks relieved him of his bundle.[277] There was such a crush of soldiers on both sides that Corporal Isaiah Kelly of Company B and a few of his mates kept a special lookout to make sure none of the enemy took a shot at the Colonel. As he was being led away Major Blair asked what troops had captured him, and upon learning that they were the 6th Wisconsin, replied "Thank God, I thought it was a New York Regiment."[278]

At this point Corporal Frank Wallar (also spelled "Waller") and his brother Sam made a dash for the flag of the 2nd Mississippi. One Confederate aimed his gun at Frank, but Sam pushed it aside and bashed his opponent with the butt of his own musket. While his brother protected him, Frank took possession of the flag and its bearer, Corporal W.B. Murphy. Murphy later wrote, "Over a dozen men fell killed or wounded, and then a large man made a rush for me and the flag. As I tore the flag from the staff he took hold of me and the color. The firing was still going on, and was kept up for several minutes after the flag was taken from me."[279]

The fighting, though, was not over by any means along the 6th's front. The Mississippians were loath to give up their colors, and the conflict had never really ceased following Lieutenant Pennington's initial foray mentioned earlier. Private "Rocky Mountain" Anderson swung his musket and crushed the skull of the Confederate who had just killed Lewis Eggleston. Private Bradley Jones of Company A managed to grab the flag but was shot dead.[280] John Harland of Company I moved toward the flag, only to be felled, and his body rolled into the cut to the feet of the soldier who killed him. Harland's comrade Levi Tongue angrily raised his gun on the rebel, who shouted, "Don't shoot, don't kill me!" But Tongue would not listen and shot him through the body, and he fell on Harland's lifeless form.[281]

The "burly man" whom Murphy referred to was Frank Wallar, who would later be given a Medal of Honor for his deed.[282] Wallar relates, "Soon after I got the flag, there were men from all the companies there. I did take the flag out of the color bearer's hand...My first thought was to go to the rear with it for fear it might be retaken, and then thought I would stay, and I threw it down and loaded and fired twice standing on it."[283] W.B. Murphy, color bearer of the 2nd Mississippi, noted that before Colonel Dawes and Major Blair "could cease hostilities there was three or four men killed or wounded before they got the colors from me."[284]

Dawes now directed Major Blair "to have his men fall in without arms" before being marched to the rear.[285] Not all the Confederates came peaceably, however. One captain refused to turn his sword over to Lyman White of Company A, and White was about to bayonet him when Captain John Marston intervened to save the officer's life.[286] Another lieutenant refused to surrender, and drew his revolver and began firing; he was killed on the spot by John Killmartin of Company G.[287]

Quite a number of Confederates, though, managed to escape by various means. Many simply broke to the rear rather than surrender, while others climbed out of the cut where they could during all the confusion.[288] Lieutenant P.W. Humphrey successfully led a large contingent of the 2nd Mississippi to the rear when the 6th Wisconsin attack was striking home.[289] Private D.J. Kell of the 2nd Mississippi wrote later that he "was disgusted with the idea of surrendering and in fact became very much demoralized. I saw a bloody, muddy blanket lying on the ground, also two wounded men lying near me. I tumbled down by them and covered myself with that blanket, I then went to practicing all maneuvers and moaning that I thought would become a badly wounded and suffering man."[290]

After so thoroughly defeating the 2nd Mississippi, some of Dawes' men encountered troops of the 55th North Carolina, which Davis had formed near the cut in order to cover the withdrawal of the rest of his brigade. Major A.M. Belo, commander of the 55th, related that, "One officer, seeing me, threw his sword at me and said: 'Kill that officer, and we will capture that command.' One of my men, however, picked him off and we were able to get out of the railroad cut after a severe struggle."[291]

The Yankee soldier whom Belo encountered was Mickey Sullivan of Company K, 6th Wisconsin, who left his own curious account of the incident. It seems that Sullivan had been passing through the cut in order to reach the other side, when a rebel captain handed him his sword. Sullivan continued on, and just as he climbed to the top of the cut he saw "a big rebel break for the rear and I called on him to halt, to which he paid no attention, and I flung the rebel sword at him with all my might, but I never knew whether I hit him or not, for just as I turned to throw the sword, a bullet hit me on the left shoulder and knocked me down as quick as if I had been hit with a sledge hammer."[292]

Colonel Dawes directed Major John Hauser to march Major Blair and the other prisoners to the rear. He then called for volunteers to man a skirmish line on the edge of the cut to guard against a counterattack, and 10 or 15 men under Lieutenant William Goltermann of Company F volunteered to do so. At this time, there was still sporadic firing going on. Private Enoch Jones saw one Confederate soldier start to run up the ridge, and shot him in the leg. Dawes directed Corporal

I.F. Kelly of Company B to climb the railroad embankment and "look around." Kelly did so, even though he had a slight leg wound, and saw no Confederates, but when he returned, "two shots were fired from the old stone fence from which I had just returned. One shot struck Corporal Mead in the head and killed him and the other went through the rim of my hat so close to my head that it almost burned a blister. Mead was the last one of the brave color guard who went into the fight." When Mead went down, Captain John Hyatt of Company B picked up his fallen national flag and asked several of his men to hold it. When they for some reason refused, Corporal Kelly volunteered to take the flag and, despite his wound, carried it proudly for the rest of the day.[293]

One of the men who volunteered to join Dawes' skirmish line was none other than Frank Wallar, the captor of the 2nd Mississippi's flag. Wallar still had the flag, and asked Dawes what he should do with it. The colonel said, "Give it to me," and in turn passed it on to Sergeant William Evans of Company H, who was at that moment hobbling to the rear with the aid of two muskets as crutches because he had been badly wounded through the upper leg. Dawes did not want to spare an able bodied man to take the flag to the rear, so he directed Evans to wrap the colors around his body and take it from the field. At the same time Dawes sent six of the captured swords to the rear with another wounded man. (The swords were turned over to the regiment's chief surgeon, Dr. A. W. Preston, but were lost to the enemy when Preston's hospital was captured later in the day.)[294]

Fowler's two regiments enjoyed equal success in their attack on Davis' center and right, though their victory was not as spectacular as Dawes'. As already noted, the impetus of Dawes' advance gave him a head start in the three regiments' impromptu charge. When Dawes' troops moved forward to cross the Pike, Lieutenant Lloyd Harris, commanding the impromptu brigade guard company on the left of Dawes' line, was dismayed not to see the 95th New York moving, as its commander had promised Colonel Dawes. He at once ran over to the 95th's right wing and yelled to the first field officer he saw, "For God's sake, why don't you move forward and join our left."[295] W. B. Murphy of the 2nd Mississippi also noted Fowler's delay in advancing. He had seen Fowler's line before he reached the railroad cut and before the 6th Wisconsin made its charge. Murphy remembered that the regiment on his front (Fowler's command) halted at the Pike fence and "remained there some time before they attempted to charge us at the railroad."[296]

The men of the 95th New York did move forward a few minutes

later, and crossed the fences along the Pike in the face of the same heavy fire that decimated the regiment on each flank. They then rushed up to the western end of the cut occupied by the 2nd Mississippi, which they reached about three minutes after the 6th Wisconsin arrived there, according to one of Cutler's staff officers who witnessed the entire attack from the woods on Seminary Ridge north of the Pike. [297] The regiment apparently exchanged a few volleys with the 55th North Carolina as it withdrew up the slope behind the cut, and then opened fire on all the fleeing Confederates before helping to gather up prisoners all along the front.[298]

There is more evidence, some of it controversial, for the role of Fowler's 14th Brooklyn in the attack. According to the account just cited, Fowler's demi-brigade moved forward a few minutes after Dawes started the final stage of his attack. It is probable, as historian Scott Hartwig suggests, that the 14th had not yet completed its right wheel when the 6th charged, and so needed time to orient facing Davis' line. The 14th Brooklyn rushed forward with a cheer, mounted the fence south of the Pike, and climbed a three foot high ascent that led up to the roadway. Colonel Fowler noted that "All this time we were exposed to a very heavy fire from the enemy, who seeing us advancing had fallen back to a railroad cut in which they took cover, showering bullets at us like hail, and our brave boys were dropping at every step, but although their ranks were fast tiring, they continued steadily to advance while crossing the Pike. The 14th reclaimed Hall's lost cannon, which lay in their line of advance.[299]

The 14th's line met a "murderous hail of musket bullets" when it was crossing the Pike. "The balls came so thick and fast that the whirring noise they made sounded like the steady rhythm of machinery. For just an instant, as the full force of this terrible fire broke along their front, the line wavered. But it was only for an instant, and then, with another cheer, louder and more determined, the men rushed on."[300]

Fowler saw the Confederates before him waver for a moment, then stiffen. He knew that a halt would be fatal, so he urged his men on over the last hotly contested yards to the line of the railroad. By now some Confederates were fleeing to the west, while others sought shelter in the western end of the cut. Here the regiment encountered its hottest fighting, some of it hand to hand or with clubbed muskets.[301]

It was just before reaching the cut that Fowler sent his adjutant to order the 6th Wisconsin to advance its right and seal off the eastern end of the cut. Because of this command Fowler claimed most of the credit for the success of the affair at the railroad cut on behalf of himself and his regiment. The 14th's regimental history mentions capturing Davis' brigade "with the help of the 6th Wisconsin" and Fowler in his battle report makes it clear that he had directed the 6th Wisconsin to move to flank the enemy.[302] Dawes and the members of his command denied Fowler's claim, even to the point of denigrating the 14th's role in the attack.[303] In 1878 Lieutenant Colonel William Dudley of the 19th Indiana, who was not exactly a neutral and unbiased commentator wrote, "It is but just to say that Major Pye with his regiment, the 95th New York volunteers, seeing the attack and charge of the 6th Wisconsin, while retreating turned and joined with the Sixth on its left, and participated in the capture of the Rebels in the railroad cut above referred to. The 14th Brooklyn, under Colonel Fowler seeing the change in affairs, also turned and came up rapidly upon the left of the 95th New York, but too late to materially assist in the capture of Davis' Rebel troops. To them the firm and dauntless bearing of the Iron Brigade was an inspiration, and they assisted manfully in turning defeat into victory."[304]

It now seems clear that Dawes received neither of Fowler's orders, neither the one to initiate the attack nor the one to block the eastern end of the cut. He made the decision to attack on his own, and adjutant Brooke also moved on his own to block the eastern end of the cut. Dawes emphatically stated that he was confident in the attack because of the size and freshness of his unit; it is interesting to speculate whether Fowler would have attacked had he not seen Dawes go in first. Thus Fowler's claims that he masterminded the attack are exaggerated, though he had intended to do so. The 6th Wisconsin certainly bore the brunt of the charge, as the extent of its casualty list shows, but the help of the 95th and the 14th should not be down played as much as Dawes and Dudley at times asserted.

As Fowler's men helped gather in Davis' prisoners, Fowler noted that he saw many of the Confederates withdrawing to the west, some through the western railroad cut behind the 147th New York's earlier battle line. The extent to which the Confederate regiments were intermingled at this time can be seen by Frank Wallar's statement about what happened after he secured the 2nd Mississippi's flag near the eastern end of the cut: "While standing on it there was a 14th Brooklyn man took hold of it and tried to get it, and I had threatened to shoot him before he would stop. By this time we had cleaned them out."[305]

Near the close of the action General Buford sent up one of Calef's guns to help turn back Davis' troops from the railroad cut. As previously noted, Calef had withdrawn his six guns from their position on the western ridge at about 1000, when their primary position astride the Chambersburg Pike was relieved by Hall's battery. Calef withdrew his guns to the Seminary and was about to replenish his ammunition chests when Buford directed him to send a piece "to enfilade a ditch occupied by the enemy." Calef sent Lieutenant Roder with his right piece, and Roder moved forward quickly to a position from which he could strike the left of Davis' line in the railroad cut. As he came up, some of Davis' men saw him coming and cried out, "There is a piece, let's take it!" Calef relates, "as soon as the piece was unlimbered, Corporal [Robert] Watrous, Chief of Piece, in bringing up a round of canister, was shot in the leg by a minie bullet and dropped. Private Slattery, with commendable presence of mind, took the round from his hands and carried it to the piece." The effect of this round saved the gun, since some of the enemy were by then so close that some of them were literally blown away from the muzzle when it was discharged.[306]

Colonel Fowler of the 14th Brooklyn saw Roder's gun deploy and fire its first shot. He rode up to Roder and directed him to move to the position occupied by the 6th Wisconsin and set up so he could enfilade the cut and "give a dose of canister to the flying rebs." But before the gun could change its position, Fowler was ordered to retire and join the rest of his brigade, "then far to the rear."[307] W.B. Murphy of the 2nd Mississippi apparently saw Roder's gun come up and form, though he did not see it fire. He stated, "The battery [sic] did not have time to fire a shot. If they had they could have killed all of us as we were not more than 200 yards from them when they unlimbered their piece."[308]

Fowler was recalled by General Wadsworth, who had been anxiously watching the fighting at the cut. When he had heard the firing dwindle, and then saw the Union colors flying over the cut, he reportedly exclaimed, "My God the 6th has conquered them."[309] By the time he rode forward, Fowler's men were beginning to receive heavy flank fire from Pegram's cannons on Herr Ridge, so they were ordered to retire to the shelter of the woods on Seminary Ridge where the rest of Cutler's brigade was reforming.[310] One of the most vivid tragedies of the day occurred just as the 14th began to pull back. It seems that Corporal George W. Forrester of Company C had been wounded in the regiment's first advance to the McPherson farm, and still lay wounded among several of the regiment's slain. Four of his comrades did not wish to leave him behind, and volunteered to bring him in, "although a veritable storm of shot and shell was sweeping the exposed situation in which he lay." They took a piece of tent canvas, and rolled the wounded corporal onto it. Each man then took a corner of the canvas, but just as they raised it up they were struck by an exploding Confederate shell. Three of the would-be rescuers were killed instantly, and the fourth man had his leg torn off; "his scream of agony was heard even above the vast pulsating roar of the battle." Corporal Forrester died of his compound wounds the next day.[311]

Wadsworth also ordered Dawes' decimated regiment to withdraw in order to regroup and reorganize. Before moving back to the woods north of the Seminary, some members of Company I, under Captain Levi P. Converse, dragged Hall's abandoned gun back to the Chambersburg Pike so that its artilleryman could recover it, an act for which Hall's men thanked them a "thousand times."[312] Apparently some men of the 14th Brooklyn also dragged the piece for a distance up the Pike, where it was later reclaimed by a detachment of Hall's men sent to fetch it.[313]

As the 6th withdrew, Dawes sent the prisoners captured during the attack to the rear under the guard of Major John F. Hauser, who had instructions to turn them over to the provost guard. The total captured by all three regiments was 7 officers and 225 enlisted men, including 87 men of the 2nd Mississippi.[314] This did not include all the Confederates captured, since Corporal Isaiah Kelly of Company B of the 6th Wisconsin later stated that a number of the enemy on his part of the line were captured and turned over to some Union cavalry to be taken to the rear.[315] W. B. Murphy of the 2nd Mississippi, pointed out "that there were prisoners of the 42nd and 11th Mississippi volunteers taken at the railroad and not in the cut as had been reported time and again by some men that were not on the ground at the time the desperate struggle was going on."[316] Murphy's impassioned claim, however, does not seem accurate in view of other evidence. Interestingly, General Davis even years after the war would still admit only to losing a major and 80 or 90 men at the cut.[317]

Captain Leander Woollard of Company B, 42nd Mississippi, was made a prisoner at the railroad and left an interesting account of his capture and departure from the field: "The Brigade of the enemy in our front had but to come up and take us in, which they did after killing a number of men all around me. Several of my own company. I tried to make my way out and escape but the press was very great and just as I was trying to squeeze through, a big Wisconsin man thrust his bayonet at me and said, 'Give me that sword and stop your men from shooting here or we will kill the last damned one of you.' I will never forget and yet I can never describe my feelings and thoughts, when I found I was a prisoner. Well, as minnie balls and shells were still falling thick around us our captors hurried us off out of danger. Our captors, both officers and men being soldiers, knew how to treat soldiers (though they were enemies), who had been unfortunate enough to fall into their hands, but as we passed through town, Gettysburg, some of the citizens, a few miserable cravens too cowardly to engage in honest warfare against us, jeered and laughed at us from their doors, tops of houses and other places of safety....Through town and out of danger we were halted in an old field and we sat down to rest. A surgeon came and dressed the wounds of our men with care. We had not been here more than an hour when we saw a mighty rushing of wagons, ambulances and artillery towards us which was from the battle ground, then the roar of our guns came nearer, and we knew the enemy were falling back - our boys forcing them back through town - then our captors' cavalry partaking of the spirit of the rear movement, started us at almost a double quick towards Baltimore."[318]

Many of the Confederates captured at Gettysburg ended up being incarcerated at Fort Delaware, located in the Delaware River below Wilmington. Corporal W.B. Murphy, the color bearer of the 2nd Mississippi who was captured near the railroad cut, had a quite different route to prison than did Captain Woollard. He and his party were marched back through Gettysburg to Cemetery Hill where one of the guards punched Murphy in the side and took his fine pair of field glasses. At about nightfall they were marched south and took a train to West Chester, Pennsylvania, which they reached at 1100 the next day. From here he was transferred to Fort McHenry in Baltimore, and then to Fort Delaware on 6 July. Murphy was fortunate enough to escape on 28 July, and managed to rejoin his command on 10 August. He then secured a furlough to go home, only to be captured by the 5th Ohio cavalry near Corinth. He was returned to Fort Delaware, where he remained imprisoned until he took the oath of allegiance on 13 June 1865.[319]

When Dawes brought his men back to Seminary Ridge, he dissolved the brigade guard and sent its men back to their regiments. He also sent some men back to help bring in the unit's wounded from the railroad cut and nearby field. Next "a sad half hour was spent calling the dead roll and reorganizing the companies."[320] Altogether his brave regiment lost 165 in the brief action—2 officers killed, 105 wounded, and 25 men missing. Casualties in the 102-man brigade guard, which had fought alongside the 6th, were between 30 and 35, including both of its officers.[321]

Casualties were also high in the two New York regiments. The 14th Brooklyn lost about 125-150 of its 318 officers and men engaged, while the 95th New York lost perhaps 70-90 of its 241 men.[322] Thus the three Union regiments involved in the attack on the railroad cut lost from 390-440 of their approximately 1184 men engaged.[323] Their sacrifice was well worth the effort, though, as they not only blunted Davis' attack and prevented him from striking the rear of the Iron Brigade, but they also so overwhelmed Davis' brigade that the unit was unable to participate significantly in the fighting for the rest of the day, after losing about 500 killed and wounded and over 200 prisoners out of 1707 engaged.[324] The 6th Wisconsin and Fowler's two regiments, on the other hand, would have still more fighting to face that afternoon. However, when considering the heavy losses suffered by the 56th Pennsylvania and 76th New York at the beginning of the fight—including numerous captured—the casualties for both sides were approximately equal during this portion of the engagement.

Death of General Reynolds

The fighting waged by Cutler's men and the 6th Wisconsin against Davis' brigade on the north side of the Chambersburg Pike lasted continuously from about 1020 to at least 1115. During this same time period an equally fierce fight was fought south of the Pike between the rest of the Iron Brigade and Archer's Confederate troops.

As already noted, it was about 1000 when General Reynolds met Cutler's advancing brigade and directed its placement so as to support both flanks of Hall's battery. When he had done so, an aide arrived from General Doubleday to report that he had ridden ahead of his troops and would be soon on the field.[325] Reynolds, who apparently believed that the Confederates were advancing on both the Fairfield and Cashtown Roads, responded, "Tell Doubleday I will hold on to this road, and he must hold on to that one."[326]

After sending those directions to Doubleday, Reynolds rode to his left in order to examine conditions there and determine the best place to post Meredith's regiments as they came up. He rode into the eastern edge of the Herbst Woods, some 200 yards south of the McPherson

Barn, and was dismayed to learn that Archer's Confederates were working their way through the woods in force, driving Buford's skirmishers before them. He must have been alarmed that the enemy was so close to turning the left flank of the position he had just designated for Cutler, so he at once turned and rode back towards the Seminary in order to intercept Meredith's lead regiment and rush it forward.[327]

Meredith's leading regiment, the 2nd Wisconsin, was then passing in front of the Seminary, and Reynolds gave word for it to move forward into line at the double quick.[328] As the regiment's experienced men formed by battalion into line, its mounted officers dismounted and took their "proper positions in line." The movement was made in such haste that the 2nd did not wait for the rest of the brigade to come up and support their left. Nor did the men even stop to load, but did so as they advanced.[329]

The regiment passed through the swale west of Seminary Ridge and proceeded up the gentle slope beyond to the crest of eastern McPherson's Ridge. They now came into the full view of Archer's 14th Tennessee, and as the 2nd neared the rail fence near the eastern edge of Herbst Woods, a tremendous volley erupted from the Confederate line that felled a large part of the unit. Among the casualties was Lieutenant Colonel George H. Stevens, who was painfully struck in the left side and bowels. He was taken to the division hospital and died four days later.[330] Some of the men of the 2nd began to return fire, so laying the foundation to a controversy that would rage for years after the war that they, not the 56th Pennsylvania, fired the first Union infantry volley of the battle.[331]

Reynolds saw the 2nd shudder under the impact of this volley, and rode forward to encourage them with the words, "Forward men, forward, for God's sake, and drive those fellows out of those woods."[332] The regiment then realigned and continued its advance, but obliqued slightly to the right because of the intensity of the enemy fire. They soon entered the edge of Herbst Woods, and proceeded another 50 yards under continued heavy enemy fire. Casualties continued to mount, and Colonel Lucius Fairchild was struck in the left arm at the elbow. He had to leave the field and relinquish command to Major John Mansfield.[333]

Reynolds accompanied the 2nd into the edge of the woods, and was apparently behind the regiment's right flank.[334] Sergeant Veil of the General's staff stated in 1864 that Reynolds was "leading the charge in person,"[335] but did not make clear whether he was in front of the line or behind. Veil's postwar memoir, however, claims that he was "leading in person, and riding considerably in advance of his troops."[336] It also declares that when the 2nd was obliqued to the right, it left "the General and myself alone in front of the Confederate line." This dramatic account does not seem to be supported by the topography of the woods, and the latter statement is contradicted by Veil's 1864 letter to McConaughy, where he says that Captains Mitchell and Baird were also with the General when he was shot. Lastly, it does not seem logical that a major general and wing commander would have proceeded ahead of his troops into a woods known to be filled by the enemy.

Reynolds, then, was probably behind the right wing of the 2nd Wisconsin when he turned to look back to see if any reinforcements were coming up. Sergeant Veil recounted in 1864, "The enemy still pushed on, and was not much more than 60 paces from where the Gen'l was. Minnie balls were flying thick. The Gen'l turned to look towards the Seminary (I suppose to see if the other troops were coming on). As he did so, a minnie ball struck him in the back of the neck, and he fell from his horse dead."[337] Major Rosengarten of Reynolds' staff added a few more details to the scene. Reynolds' horse moved a slight distance towards the point of the woods. The General at first "sat for a moment or two still in his saddle, then swayed and fell to the ground" near a group of trees at the edge of the wood.[338] Sergeant Veil later marked the spot where the General fell by carving an "R" into a large oak tree at the site. The tree survived until it was felled by a wind storm on 30 June 1987. The time Reynolds was shot was around 1030.[339]

Captain George Otis of Company I, 2nd Wisconsin, claimed he saw Reynolds fall, and wrote the following account after the war: "The story has it that General Reynolds was killed at the opening of the battle, which is quite true, and he was killed directly in the rear of the right of the Second Wisconsin Regiment, and not more than 100 feet distant. He was struck by a stray ball immediately after the volley the Second Wisconsin received as it charged over the top of the ridge where Archer's brigade was lying. The writer was at that time on the right of the regiment, and as the line came to a temporary halt when it reached the top of the ridge, he turned to look for those of his company who had fallen, and glancing down the slope to the rear saw General Reynolds fall from his horse."[340]

Veil and Captains Robert W. Mitchell and Edward C. Baird at once jumped from their horses as they saw the General fall off the left side of his horse onto his face. A few of the General's orderlies were hit at the same time Reynolds was, and Veil's horse was killed right after he dismounted. Veil turned Reynolds on his back and could see no wound except a bruise over his left eye, which he had received when he fell off his horse.[341] Everyone thought the general had merely been stunned by a spent ball. Veil reached Reynolds first and cradled his head in his lap. They all agreed that the fallen commander had to be carried to the rear. Veil wrote, "I caught the Gen'l under the arms, while each of the Capt's took hold of his legs, and we commenced to carry him out of the woods towards the Seminary."[342]

It is interesting to see how much Veil's postwar memoir differs at this point: "My next impression was to save him from falling into the hands of the enemy. Not having any assistance, no one of our men being near, I picked him up by taking hold under his arms and commenced pulling him backwards towards our line in the direction in which we had come from. As I did so the Confederates called to me: 'Drop him, drop him,' but I kept on backing off as fast as I could and finally got over the brow of the rise, where I found some men, and where we were out of range of the enemy's fire."[343] Here again, Veil's earlier account is to be preferred where details differ, especially since the encounter with the Confederate troops is not mentioned by any other accounts of the scene.

Veil in his 1864 account continues, "When we got outside of the woods the Capt's left me to carry word to the next officers in command of his death. I in the meantime got some help from some of the orderlies who came up about this time, and we carried the body towards the Seminary, really not knowing where to take it to, as the enemy appeared to be coming in on our right and left."[344] Apparently Veil and the orderlies carried the body in a blanket, since Colonel Dawes of the 6th Wisconsin remembered passing "some officers carrying in a blanket the body of our corps commander" as he rushed in front of the Seminary towards the railroad cut.[345] While crossing to the Seminary, Veil noticed that the General was gasping, and thought that he was coming to his senses: "we stopped a moment and I gave him a drop of water from a canteen but he would not drink."[346]

After reaching the Seminary, Veil had the body carried back to the Emmitsburg Road. He took it to Mr. George's stone house (still standing, with a marker to that effect) and "laid it on the floor in the little sitting room." It was now that Veil discovered the wound in the back of his neck. "I then saw that the Gen'l was dead...I have often wondered why it was that the wound did not bleed. I think now that he must have bled internally."[347] He explained in his postwar memoir, "The wound did not bleed externally, and, as he fell, his coat collar had covered up the wound, which accounted for my not discovering it at first."[348]

After reaching George's house, Veil sent for an ambulance, and he and Captain Rosengarten of the general's staff rode into town to try to get a coffin. In his 1864 letter Veil says they were unable to locate a coffin, so they got a box from the marble cutter's; since it was too short, they knocked one end out of it to lay the body in. His postwar memoirs says that "The best we could do was to get a case that caskets are shipped in, and one end was knocked out of it." Captain Rosengarten states only that the body was "hastily confined."[349]

The sad entourage left Gettysburg at midafternoon, when "the Rebel advance threatened the safety of the place."[350] Captain Rosengarten rode in the ambulance with the driver, while Veil went mounted on Reynolds' horse, "he having run into our lines after the General fell." Veil's own horse, as already noted, had been killed right after the General fell.[351] The party went over to the Taneytown Road and then headed south. On the way it passed Generals Winfield Hancock and John Newton, who were on their way to the front. At Taneytown the escort members gave a personal report on the morning's battle to General Meade. Late at night they moved on to Union Bridge.[352] Here they had a box made for a coffin, and laid some ice in with the body. Early the next morning the party entrained for Baltimore, where Major William Riddle joined the entourage. After the body was embalmed, it was moved by train to Philadelphia, and then to Lancaster, where the general was buried in his family's plot in simple ceremonies held on 4 July. The only soldiers present were the orderlies and staff officers who had accompanied the body. Veil remembered that Reynolds' family was very much grateful to him that he had prevented the general's body from falling into the hands of the enemy.[353]

A sad epilogue to the Reynolds story is that he at the time had a favorite lady friend who was unknown to his family. When the General's body was being removed from the field, Major Riddle found a Catholic medal around his neck, and on the same chain was a gold ring with the inscription, "Dear Kate."[354] In addition, the General's West Point ring was missing. Reynolds had never mentioned having a special friend, but such was apparently the case. The identity of his lady friend became apparent on the morning of 3 July, when Miss Kate Hewitt came to the Reynolds family home in Lancaster and asked to pay her respects to his body. The two had met while coming back from California in 1860, and she had made a promise to enter a convent if anything ever happened to him. Records show that she actually did send an application on 12 July 1863 to enter St. Joseph's Central House of the Sisters of Charity in Emmitsburg, Maryland. Whether or not she actually did so is not known, although it is clear that she spent several years at St. Joseph's School in Albany, New York.[355]

It was indeed unfortunate for the Army of the Potomac that Reynolds was felled at the battle. He was one of the army's best generals, and was well thought of by all. His decision to press the fight on the ridges west of Gettysburg was the correct one, as the events of the next two days would show, but it was this very aggressiveness that led him to be with his troops in the front lines and so expose himself to such deadly danger. The General's biographer, Edward J. Nichols, believes that Reynolds went to the front in order to set an example for his volunteer troops. He also suggests that the General was especially eager to defend his home state and to force the battle that would drive the enemy from it.[356] Whatever were his motives, there was certainly no need for him as a wing commander to be at the very front posting Hall's battery, Cutler's troops, and then the 2nd Wisconsin. This was more properly the duty of General Wadsworth, and Reynolds could have just as well —and certainly with more safety— have directed the fighting from a more secure position at or near the Seminary. His decision to fight on McPherson's Ridge was certainly a critical one, but his presence on the front lines did not affect the fighting, except negatively by his death.

It is interesting to conjecture what would have happened had Reynolds not fallen at this early stage of the fighting. Command in the field devolved on Major General Abner Doubleday, who was an experienced officer but did not inspire confidence in anyone. He later as much as admitted to being overwhelmed by the "great responsibilities" of the moment.[357] Though he and his corps fought well for the rest of the day, one cannot help but think that Reynolds might have handled his left flank better, and might have posted Howard's troops more advantageously later in the day. But such remains speculation.[358]

There has been much discussion over the years as to where the shot came from that killed General Reynolds. Confederate Major General Harry Heth thought that he was killed by a shot from one of Pegram's batteries, and Captain E.B. Brunson of Pegram's battalion suggested that the Fredericksburg (VA) artillery may have been responsible for Reynolds' death.[359]

After the war Charles B. Fleet of Marye's battery made the same claim, and cannoneers Henry A. Strode (who later became the first president of Clemson University) and Henry G. Chesley of the same unit claimed they had aimed the fatal shot.[360] However, this could not have the been the case since all the Federal sources agree that Reynolds was slain by a musket ball.

The most persistent accounts over the years are that Reynolds was killed by a sharpshooter.[361] One claimant to the deed was sharpshooter Frank Wood from Surry County, North Carolina. According to a 1947 account, a Pennsylvanian was visiting North Carolina after the war and happened to go to the quarries at Mount Airy, NC, where the Pennsylvania Monument at Gettysburg was being made. There he was told that one of the blacksmiths working on the project had been the soldier who shot Reynolds, whose statue was one of those being made for the memorial. The Pennsylvanian went to visit the blacksmith, and heard the following story: "Sharpshooter Frank Wood and Private Cox, it developed, were in the thick of the fight at Gettysburg. In some way they became separated from their company and found themselves in a railroad cut, right in the line of fire. Nearby, they saw a rail fence and ducked to it for protection. From this cover they surveyed the scene. A few hundred yards away they saw on a big horse, a man, gold braids on his hat, epaulets on his shoulders, scabbard and boots with spurs and other accoutrements speaking of high rank. He was standing up in his stirrups, waving his sword and shouting to his men, 'Give them hell boys. Give them the grape. Give them hell. Give them the grape.' Private Cox asked Sharpshooter Wood if he couldn't pick that man off at that distance. Wood wasn't sure, but thought he could. He estimated the distance, raised the sights on his musket, and fired. The man fell from his horse." Wood always assumed that the officer he shot was General Reynolds, and had no reason to think otherwise.[362]

This account is an interesting one, but raises the question on several accounts. Firstly, there is no Frank Wood listed as a member of the 55th North Carolina, the only North Carolina unit engaged at this time, in Jordan's exhaustive roster.[363] Secondly, Reynolds was not with an artillery battery when he was shot. Thirdly, Davis' troops did not reach the fence along the railroad cut until the battle had been going on for at least 45 minutes, at which time it probably would have been too smoky to see Reynolds, particularly if he were inside the eastern edge of Herbst Woods, as all accounts agree.

A more detailed sharpshooter claim surfaced in 1902 and gained much exposure when it was recirculated in 1952.[364] The basis of it is that after the war a Mr. Leander T. Hensel of Quarryville, Lancaster

County, was on a business trip to North Carolina, and happened to run into Private Benjamin C. Thorp, who had fought at Gettysburg as a sergeant and "first" sharpshooter in Company K, 55th North Carolina. Thorp related that his company at the opening of the battle had been sent out on the skirmish line, and that he "had been posted a short distance off the Cashtown Road, at the edge of an ancient orchard, several hundred yards to the rear of the intermittent firing along the skirmish line." There was an old stone house nearby, and Thorp climbed a cherry tree to begin firing at the artillery crew that were unlimbering their guns. Before long Captain Henry Webb, who was standing at the base of the tree, saw an important officer through his field glasses and called to Thorp, "Look at your right, at the battery on the hill there. There's a general, try him." Thorp continued: "The battery, and the general seemed to be about 400 yards beyond the skirmish firing on our front, and I asked Captain Webb to judge the range for me. This was about 10 o'clock in the morning, I guessed. The captain looked closely again through his glasses, then told me the range was 1100 yards. I raised my sight to that elevation and fired. 'I am too high' I told Captain Webb, and lowered my sight to 900 yards. Fired again 'You are yet too high' said Captain Webb. 'Bring it down a trifle.' I then reset the sight for 800 yards, aimed carefully and fired the third time. Captain Webb shouted, 'Well done Thorp, you got him.' Watching, I saw the officer reel and fall from his horse, into the arms of a soldier nearby. That evening, we had collected a lot of prisoners and they told us that a sharpshooter had killed General Reynolds of the First Corps, in a shot apparently fired at extreme range." Thorp carried his heavy sharpshooter rifle through the rest of the battle, only to be captured at Falling Waters, Maryland, on 14 July 1863. He did not fight again, but was imprisoned at Point Lookout, Maryland, and then Elmira, New York, until he was paroled for exchange on 10 March 1865.[365]

Thorp's account has been greatly studied over the years, and a number of objections have been raised. Chief among these is the fact that Reynolds was not posting artillery when he was shot. Also, it is unlikely that Thorp could have seen Reynolds when the general was in Herbst Woods and the sharpshooter was 800 yards to the west northwest on the other side of the woods. In addition, as was the case with Wood's claim, it is unlikely that Thorp could have seen Reynolds at that distance through all the smoke, particularly with Hall's guns firing away on the Pike.[366] Most significantly, Thorp himself in 1903 backed off from his claim that he shot Reynolds, though he did insist that he knocked some officer off his horse at a distance of 900 yards.[367]

Yet another, more persistent sharpshooter account was penned by Reynolds' aide, Captain Joseph G. Rosengarten. After stating that the general was "a shining mark to the enemy's sharpshooters," Rosengarten declared "he was struck by a minnie ball, fired by a sharpshooter hidden in the branches of a tree almost overhead, and killed at once; his horse bore him to a little clump of trees, where a cairn of stones and a rude mark on the bank, now almost overgrown, still tells the fatal spot."[368]

Though Rosengarten gives no source for his assertion, it has been accepted by no less an authority than historian Edwin B. Coddington.[369] Coddington was heavily influenced by a statement from the General's sister Jennie that the fatal bullet struck Reynolds behind the right ear and traveled around his skull before lodging in his chest.[370] It is difficult to believe, however, that any of Archer's men were posted in the trees as sharpshooters when their line was proceeding steadily through the woods. There is also the question of how a sharpshooter could sight in on Reynolds' head when he was mounted and riding near the woods, with the line of the 2nd Wisconsin between him and the enemy.

It does not seem likely, then, that Reynolds was felled by a Confederate sharpshooter. What seems more reasonable is that he may have fallen from a shot fired by one of Archer's men. Captain Rosengarten wrote in 1871: "He was moving toward the point of the woods, when there was a sharp fire from the Rebels, who lay in the edge, and it was drawn upon Reynolds by his little escort." The likelihood that Reynolds was struck by fire from a line of troops is increased by the evidence that several of his orderlies were hit at the same time, and that Sergeant Veil's horse was killed as soon as he had dismounted.[371]

Two separate claimants from Archer's brigade, both from the 13th Alabama, have emerged as the possible source of the shot that killed Reynolds. One claim was made by Private John Hendrix of the 13th. His friend Private E.T. Boland asserts that during their attack on the 7th Wisconsin the two noticed a Union officer with some infantry about 80 to 100 yards to their left front. Hendrix aimed and shot the officer, and asked Boland if he saw him hit his target. The two later claimed that the officer that Hendrix had shot was General Reynolds, but he was more probably aiming at Lieutenant Colonel John R. Callis of the 7th Wisconsin.[372]

Callis may also have been the target of an unnamed member of Company F of the 13th Alabama who also reportedly felled a mounted

Union officer that morning. After the war Captain Simpson of that unit related that his command was on the left of its regiment's line, adjoining the 1st Tennessee. When Simpson saw a mounted officer only 30 yards to the front, he directed one of his men to "shoot the man on the horse," which was promptly done. The officer who was struck might well have been Reynolds, but the soldier might also have been shooting at Lieutenant Colonel Callis who lost his horse and was himself wounded in the side and hip at about this time.[373]

Captain George H. Otis of the 2nd Wisconsin believed that General Reynolds was shot by one of Archer's men during Archer's retreat before the Iron Brigade counterattacked.[374] This, however, was too late in the action by all other accounts.

There is also the possibility that the fire that felled Reynolds came not from Archer's troops to the west, but from Davis' troops to the north. Corporal W. B. Murphy of the 2nd Mississippi claimed that after his unit defeated the 14th Brooklyn, "Genl. Reynolds and staff rode up in about 100 yards to our right just over the hill in some timber to our right and Reg. 2nd Miss gave him one volley from our rifles and I was told that Genl Reynolds was killed and nearly all of his staff killed and wounded."[375] This account is plausible, but would place the General's death at about 1100, later than all other accounts. It would also have been difficult, but not impossible, for a volley by the 2nd Mississippi to strike the General's party at a distance of 300 yards.

The accumulated evidence, particularly the fact that Sergeant Veil's horse and some of the general's orderlies were struck at about the same time that Reynolds was hit, would appear to suggest that he was not killed by a sharpshooter or by a solitary stray shot. Instead he was probably felled by directed fire from Archer's line, either by troops aiming directly at the General's party, or by shots fired by Archer's infantry at and over the line of the 2nd Wisconsin.[376] No one can or will know exactly who it was who fired the fatal shot.

The Iron Brigade Captures General Archer

When Reynolds' body was being removed from the field, the action in Herbst Woods was rapidly reaching a climax. As already noted, Reynolds had rushed the 2nd Wisconsin forward so quickly that not all its men had a chance to load their muskets before they received the enemy's first deadly volley. As the 2nd pushed into the woods, they did

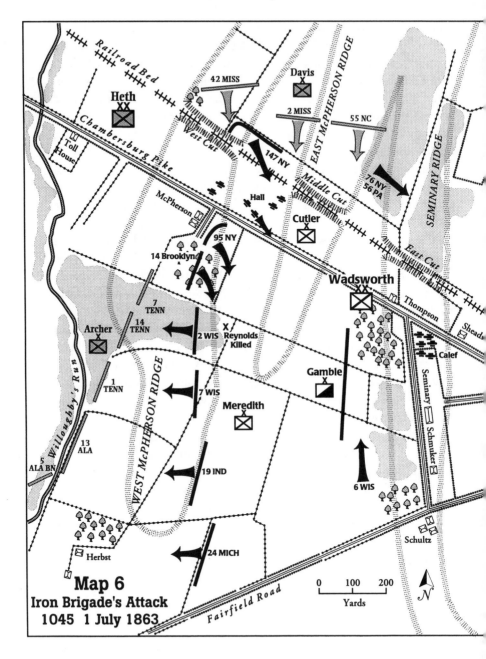

Map 6
Iron Brigade's Attack
1045 1 July 1863

150

not receive immediate support from the next regiment in the column, Colonel William Robinson's 7th Wisconsin. Robinson reported that he had seen Gamble's cavalry line in position on the eastern branch of McPherson's Ridge, and then received orders "to take position on the ridge in front of the cavalry as quickly as possible." He at once formed his companies into line and advanced at the double quick to the top of the ridge where the cavalry line was. There he decided to wait for the regiments behind him to come up on his left, and for this reason did not move immediately to the support of the 2nd Wisconsin. No one was expecting to be engaged at once, so orders had not been received for the men to load. Robinson nevertheless took it on his own initiative and "gave the order to load during the movement, which was executed by the men while on the double quick, so that no time was lost by this omission."[377]

Robinson thus held his troops in line for a few minutes while the 19th Indiana, the next regiment in the column, moved up on his left. While he waited he watched the regiment ahead of him, the 2nd Wisconsin, form into line and advance into Herbst Woods. In no time heavy fire and dense smoke arose from the woods, with the firing extending all the way to the ravine on Robinson's front south of the woods. Robinson was at first uncertain whether the fire on his front was coming from the enemy or from the left wing of the 2nd. At that point Captain Craig W. Wadsworth of the division staff rode up, and Robinson asked him "Could he tell what troops those were firing in the ravine." Wadsworth pointed to a rebel battle flag a little farther to the left up the ravine and said it was the enemy, "and that the general directed that we should drive them out." Robinson accordingly advanced his line to the crest of the ridge and ordered a volley fired. The men advanced with a shout into the heavy enemy fire.[378] The regiment's first casualty was Captain L.E. Pond of Company E, whom one source falsely claimed was "the first infantry soldier wounded on the Union side."[379]

Lieutenant Colonel Callis of the 7th Wisconsin remembered a slightly different course of events when his regiment entered the fight. He recalled that a number of officers and men in the 7th were killed and wounded by the enemy's first volley, which hit the regiment while it was "marching by the flank, right in front." Callis says he formed his men into line at once, and was concerned about their "perilous condition" because their guns were not loaded. Since he did not feel like "standing under that gallant fire to load," he ordered his men to fix bayonets and charge. Just then Captain Craig Wadsworth of General Wadsworth's staff came up behind Callis and ordered "Halt Halt!" Callis called out for his men to stop, but it was too late to stop their rushing charge. [380]

The 19th Indiana had barely formed in line on Robinson's left when the 7th charged. The 19th had marched up the eastern side of Seminary Ridge after leaving the Emmitsburg Road until it was directly in the rear of the Seminary. From there it moved to the left, and while crossing the ridge, its men noticed "a battery and some cavalry on high ground west of the Seminary, and General Reynolds and staff near the Seminary."[381] While the 2nd Wisconsin at the head of the brigade opened the action, Colonel Samuel J. Williams advanced his 19th Indiana forward over the eastern branch of McPherson's Ridge and saw Archer's line only 75 yards distant, partly hidden in the low shrubbery along Willoughby Run.[382] Abraham Cunningham, of the 19th's color bearers, hurried to uncase his flag, but was told by a staff officer not to. Cunningham's friend A.J. Buckles urged him with the words, "Abe, pull the shuck." Cunningham did so, and as his flag unfurled, it was struck by a flurry of bullets that also felled its bearer. Buckles then took up the flag, the second of eight color bearers in the 19th Indiana this day.[383]

Private M.C. Barnes of the 19th noted the "while crossing a fence on the ridge we received the fire of some Tennessee troops in the hollow. I was in Company H and under the flag, which was new, I remember that more than a dozen balls went through it, the first round." Fortunately for the men, they did not need to stop to load their weapons—theirs were already loaded because the unit had been on guard duty the previous night, and the 19th was the only regiment of the brigade to enter the action that day with its weapons ready to fire.[384] Williams proudly noted that his men did not "stand upon the order of their firing, but fired at once" as soon as they saw the enemy.[385]

The 24th Michigan on Dudley's left apparently had not completed its formation into battle line when the 7th Wisconsin and 19th Indiana attacked, so it lagged somewhat behind, giving the advance an "en echelon" form. Nor had these troops been allowed time to load their weapons. Colonel Henry A. Morrow observed in his report that "the brigade were ordered to advance at once, no order being given or time allowed for loading our guns. I halted my regiment for this purpose, but was directed by a staff officer—I think he belonged to the staff of General Wadsworth—to move forward immediately without loading, which I did."[386] Color Sergeant Abel G. Peck was the first man killed during the charge; his flag was taken up by Color Corporal Charles Bellore of Company E before it touched the ground. Private William

B. Smith of Company B was the first man of the regiment wounded. Lieutenant William R. Dodsley of Company H was the first officer wounded, and Lieutenant Gilbert A. Dickey of Company G was the first officer killed.[387]

After the 24th Michigan moved to the attack, Major General Abner Doubleday "rode over to the left to see if the enemy's line extended beyond ours." As already noted, Doubleday had ridden on ahead of his own troops; he claims that he reached the field during the initial fight between Davis and Cutler. He at once sent to ask Reynolds for instructions, and received this reply, "I will hold on to this road and he must hold on to that one"; by this Doubleday understood that he was to watch the Fairfield Road while Reynolds supervised the forces along the Chambersburg Pike.[388] After he rode ahead of the Iron Brigade and saw the importance of holding Herbst Woods, he urged Meredith's rear regiments "to hold it to the last extremity." They replied proudly, "If we can't hold it, where will you find men who can?"[389]

It was in response to Reynolds' instruction, then, that Doubleday rode to investigate the corps' southern flank along the Fairfield Road. He saw only a few Confederate skirmishers there, and returned to set up a reserve: "I knew there was fighting going on between Cutler's brigade and the rebels in his front, but as General Reynolds was there in person, I only attended to my own part of the line, and halted the Sixth Wisconsin regiment as it was going into line, together with a hundred men of the Brigade Guard...in the open space between the Seminary and the woods."[390] It was a bold move that would have deep ramifications on the course of the battle. Dawes' command would soon see timely service in helping to repulse Davis' troops at the railroad cut. But had Doubleday sent the 6th Wisconsin into action on the left of the 24th Michigan he might have captured almost all of Archer's troops on his front. If this had happened, it is interesting to conjecture if Fowler's men could have held Davis in check along the Pike without Dawes' aid, long enough for Cutler to rally his three defeated regiments (56th Pennsylvania, 76th and 147th New York) on Seminary Ridge and turn back Davis' men.

Gamble's weary cavalrymen were greatly relieved to see Meredith's brigade come up to their support. As discussed previously, some elements of Gamble's command had been in action since dawn. The rest of the command had been formed into line about 0800, taking position on the western crest of McPherson's Ridge. Gamble's skirmishers engaged Archer's troops for a full two hours, and had been forced steadily back to Herbst Woods and the line of trees along Willoughby Run. By 1000 the weight of Archer's advance was pushing the skirmishers back, and Gamble had been forced to withdraw his main line of battle. Gamble's line was in particular trouble at this time on the left flank of the position, where the 8th New York was under heavy fire from Archer's troops.

Gamble had already withdrawn the right portion of his skirmish line before the Iron Brigade came up. The units posted north of Chambersburg Pike, the 3rd Indiana and 12th Illinois, were in open ground and had suffered from the Confederate artillery fire ever since Pegram's guns opened up. The cavalrymen nevertheless held their lines until Heth's division began its advance. It was a critical time for the troopers, who were uneasy about the fact that they were dismounted and some of their horses in the rear had been killed by the artillery fire, so they could not all mount up and ride off like they usually did in tight situations. The men looked anxiously over their shoulders for the arrival of the infantry they were told was coming, but when none appeared, they had to begin falling back towards the town. The men of the 3rd Indiana had just passed over the brow of the "1st hill" when they saw Reynolds rushing up with the 2nd Wisconsin. They gave the infantrymen a cheer, and rallied long enough to allow the infantry to form.[391]

The 8th Illinois, which had been posted between the Pike and Herbst Woods, had been withdrawn when Fowler's troops came up on that front. The unit's commander, Major John L. Beveridge, was also concerned about the progress of Archer's strong infantry line against his relatively unprotected left. He later wrote, "To uncover Cutler's front, the Eighth Illinois filed to the left, in rear of the Iron Brigade, and took position to the left and rear of the Eighth New York, near Seminary Ridge."[392]

The troopers of the 3rd Indiana and 12th Illinois at this time probably formed on the eastern branch of McPherson's Ridge, where Colonel Robinson of the 7th Wisconsin saw cavalry when he came up to form his men into line. Major Mansfield of the 2nd Wisconsin also saw this line, and formed his command in their front. These troops were probably only partially engaged at this time, and may have been partially mounted, since Robinson specifically mentions they had "skirmishers dismounted and thrown forward of the ridge."[393] The only skirmishers still engaged at this time, however, were those in the woods, where they had protection from the trees, and those of the 8th New York on the left, who were exposed on the open ridge and under pressure from Archer's main line at or near the Run.[394]

Gamble recalled his skirmishers once the infantry came up to relieve his line. Not all the tired cavalrymen were eager to pull back. General Buford saw one plucky skirmisher of the 8th Illinois who refused to withdraw, whether because he had not heard the order or because he refused to yield. Buford noted that he "at first stood his ground, then lay down in the grass until the enemy's line was nearly upon him, when he arose and cried out at the top of his voice, 'Come on, we have them.' Whether the rebels were astonished at his madness, or thought he was an officer leading a host, we know not, but their line faltered."[395] A few brave members of the 3rd Indiana even found horse holders, borrowed muskets, and went into the woods to fight with the Wisconsin regiment that relieved them. Two of these brave Hoosiers were troopers Matt Glenber and Will Rhea, who later admitted that he had stayed behind for the selfish reason of hoping to capture a Confederate horse or gear. Whatever their reasons, the Indiana troopers must have felt more at home with the Iron Brigade's infantry, since all were wearing black Hardee hats.[396]

Gamble held his command in position on the eastern branch of McPherson's Ridge while the fighting intensified to his front. However, he was exposed to Confederate artillery fire there, and after a while withdrew farther back to Seminary Ridge. When they reached the Seminary, they heard "a band of ladies from the female college" in the cupola singing (quite appropriately) "Rally Around the Flag Boys" amidst the shrieking shells.[397]

Gamble's men had indeed fought well that morning. Their experience enabled them to resist Heth's advance for an extended time, though they were not actually pressed seriously until the last half hour or so before the infantry came up. Trooper William H. Redman of the 12th Illinois, who was posted north of the Pike, wrote his family two days later that he had fired his weapon only 10 or 12 times; this does not attest to any heavy fighting.[398] Still, they had suffered fairly heavily for cavalry, certainly enough to belie the old quip, "Who ever saw a dead cavalryman?" The 8th New York, which had suffered badly on the brigade's left flank, lost during the day some 40 men, while the 3rd Indiana lost 32 (including Major Charles Lemon, who was badly wounded and died the next day), and the 12th Illinois 20. Curiously, the large 8th Illinois, whose troops had opened the battle on the Pike, had only 7 casualties during the day.[399]

Archer's troops were definitely not expecting a vicious counterattack by experienced Union infantry after they reached the protective banks of Willoughby Run.[400] They had made slow but steady progress against Gamble's outnumbered skirmishers, and confidently expected to resume their advance successfully. As already noted, the two regiments on the left (7th and 14th Tennessee) had crossed the stream first, and so became separated from the rest of the brigade to their right. The two regiments were attracted by the firing of Hall's battery, and may also have taken a few shots at Fowler's men, if indeed they saw them. Opinions vary as to whether the entire 7th Tennessee was in the woods, or a portion extended to the left.[401] Whichever was the case, it was the men of the 14th who probably delivered the critical volley that stunned the 2nd Wisconsin.

The 7th Tennessee was only 40 to 50 yards from the 2nd Wisconsin when it opened fire "with terrible effect," as Lieutenant Colonel S. G. Shepard learned when he visited the ground the next day.[402] Before long the 2nd Wisconsin began to push the two Tennessee regiments back, and it penetrated some 50 yards into the woods.[403] The woods and all the smoke made it difficult for the men of the 7th and 14th Tennessee to determine the size of the force that had so suddenly appeared to confront them, and made it impossible to see that they actually outnumbered their attackers. The lore of the battle says when Archer's troops saw the distinctive Hardee hats worn by the men of the Iron Brigade, they exclaimed, "There are those damned black-hatted fellows again. 'Taint no militia. Its the Army of the Potomac." The original source of this quote, though, is never identified.[404]

By now Archer's right wing, the 1st Tennessee and 13th Alabama, had emerged out of the Willoughby Run ravine and was advancing to the west of the ridge. It was perhaps the 13th's flag that Colonel Robinson of the 7th Wisconsin saw before he decided to open fire on the troops in his front.[405] At this point Lieutenant Colonel Newton George of the 1st Tennessee (the only officer of the brigade to make the attack on horseback) rode to Lieutenant Colonel James Aikin of the 13th and requested him to wheel his unit to the left in order to put a crossfire on the 7th Wisconsin. Dr. W. H. Moon of the 13th noted that "this move placed the right of our regiment on or near the crest of the ridge and about seventy-five yards from the bluecoats, into whom we were pouring volley after volley as fast as we could."[406]

It was perhaps now that Private John Hendrix of the 13th Alabama, and maybe also an unnamed private of Company F, fired at a mounted officer on their front whom they later thought was General John F. Reynolds.[407]

While Private Moon and his friends on the left of the 13th Alabama line were "rather enjoying the fray,"[408] the regiment's open right flank was encountering serious difficulty. Private Bird noticed the 24th Michigan coming up on his flank: "We seen a line of skirmishers some one hundred yards in front; the field officers were cheering their men and urging them forward." But the 13th had a much more immediate problem to deal with. All at once the 19th Indiana came over the crest of the ridge and poured a devastating volley into Bird's unsuspecting line: "all of a sudden a heavy line of battle rose up out of the wheat, and poured a volley into our ranks."[409] The 19th Indiana did not pause to form, but charged forward and hit the 13th's line while it was still wavering from the impact of the 19th's initial volley. Instinctively the Alabamians fell back to the ravine for cover.[410]

When the right wing of the 13th Alabama fell back, an order was sent for the left wing to do likewise. Private Moon noted that "we could see no reason for the order, as the Tennesseans were keeping the 'blue boys' busy, and things seemed going pretty well for us, as we had only a skirmish line to our right, to which we gave little attention."[411] But soon the import of the order became apparent - those who did not retire promptly toward the Run were quickly cut off by the 19th Indiana. As E.T. Boland put it, "All who had not grasped time by the forelock and left when they realized what a deadly trap they were in, surrendered."[412] Those who could flee ran back to Willoughby Run, or to the left towards the 1st Tennessee and the apparent safety of Herbst Woods.

The Confederates who fled to the ravine in their rear soon found themselves overwhelmed by pressure from the 19th Indiana on their front and the 24th Michigan in their rear. Because his line overlapped the left of Archer's position, Colonel Morrow of the 24th was able to brush aside the skirmishers on his front, cross the Run below Archer's line, and swing right into the rear of the Confederate troops who had withdrawn into the ravine along the Run. Private Moon of the 13th thought that it was Union cavalry that had gotten into Archer's rear, and perhaps a few members of the 8th New York did accompany Morrow's attack.[413] Moon wrote, "I suppose the order to fall back to Willoughby Run was prompted by Buford's cavalry driving our skirmishers back and forming a line of battle in the open field to our rear, through which we had passed. When we reached the Run, order was given to 'lie down.' The blue coats soon covered the hillside in our front, ordering us to surrender. Our only hope now was that a supporting line would come up, drive the cavalry from our rear, fall in line with us, and drive the Federals from Seminary Ridge. But, alas, our support did not materialize, so we were forced to surrender."[414] Some of the Confederates in the ravine did not surrender peacefully, though, and there were some sharp scuffles in places.[415] Private Bird of the 13th wrote "it seemed to me there were 20,000 Yanks down in among us hallowing surrender." Two officers and some privates came up to Lieutenant H. H. Pond of Company C urging him to surrender, and he looked to Bird for advice asking, "What the hell shall I do?" Bird replied that there was little to do but surrender, and Pond threw down his sword. Bird then surrendered also, since he had just discharged his gun and could not reload it.[416]

The collapse of the 13th Alabama exposed the right flank of the 1st Tennessee, which was already experiencing trouble on its left. At the height of the fighting, Private Moon of the 13th Alabama observed that the men of the 1st Tennessee "were hotly engaged at close quarters, the Yanks charging them in column, the Tennesseans lying on their backs to load and whirling over to fire."[417] The smoke was so thick that for a time no one could see the movements of the enemy. When the firing ceased for a moment, Captain J.B. Turney of Company K, 1st Tennessee, dropped to his knees and looked under the smoke, only to see "the feet and legs of the enemy moving to our left." He was dismayed that the 7th Wisconsin was moving into the gap in Archer's center and at once reported his observation to Archer. The General refused to believe it, saying, "I guess not, Captain, since Gen. Joe Davis is to occupy that timber to our left." By the time Turney returned to his command, the 13th Alabama was in shambles and the 19th Indiana was on his flank. He succeeded in escaping with the greater part of his company by falling back some two hundred yards to a skirt of timber.[418]

As the 1st Tennessee fell back, the 19th Indiana and 7th Wisconsin both rushed towards Willoughby Run and began gathering up prisoners. Colonel Robinson of the 7th noted that all the Union regiments "rushed into the ravine with a yell. The enemy—what was left of them able to walk—threw down their guns, ducked between our files, and passed to the rear."[419] Many of Archer's men, though, managed to escape simply by running for their lines. Private Moon of the 13th Alabama noted that, "Quite a number of the 13th Alabama made their escape as we fell back to the Run by remembering the old adage, 'He who fights and runs away may live to fight another day.' Those who escaped were mostly from the left of the regiment and near the woods, occupied by the

Tennesseans, which afforded considerable protection from the Federal rifles."[420]

The slugfest between the 7th and 14th Tennessee on one side and the 2nd Wisconsin on the other had continued unabated while the rest of Archer's line disintegrated. Slowly, though, Meredith's men were gaining the upper hand as the 2nd Wisconsin continued its push deeper into the woods. In addition, the 7th Wisconsin was able to turn more and more of its fire on to the 14th Tennessee's right flank. The intense fire caused the flag of the 14th Tennessee to be felled twice, and each time it was raised up by fresh hands. R.E. McCullough of the 14th felt that his line was surrounded by the enemy, and others were concerned about the rush of friendly troops fleeing across their rear from the right.[421]

Lieutenant Colonel John Callis of the 7th Wisconsin personally captured one Confederate officer at this time at some danger to himself. It seems that the Confederate was running at him shouting, "I surrender," but had his saber drawn and pointing right at him. Callis shouted, "That is no way to surrender," and swung his own sword at the Confederate's saber. The blow struck the officer's weapon from his hand, whereupon Callis took a swipe at his foe's neck but missed. By now the Confederate officer was too close to strike at, so Callis told him, "If you surrender, order your men to cease firing, pick up your saber and order your men to go to the rear as prisoners." The officer complied, and Callis saw that "we had more prisoners than men of our own."[422]

Major John Mansfield of the 2nd Wisconsin sensed the Confederate fire slacken and ordered his men to advance to close quarters. This pressure caused the enemy line to break. Some of the Confederates fled to the rear, joining the large crowd that had been driven into the northwest corner of the woods by the events to the south. Others sought cover in a deep depression near the Run from which they were soon driven out or captured by the advancing 2nd Wisconsin. A number of the Confederates retired from tree to tree, firing as they went.[423] Some attempted to reform their broken lines at a slight elevation, but Major Mansfield ordered the 2nd Wisconsin to charge at the double quick, a move that forced the enemy to break "in confusion to the rear, escaping into the open fields beyond."[424]

The men of the 2nd pushed on through the woods to Willoughby Run and crossed over the stream to the slope beyond, as did the troops to their left. Here they encountered the same dense undergrowth that had impeded the 7th Tennessee in its initial advance to the stream. At the edge of the undergrowth was a fence, and beyond an open field. A number of the Confederates were delayed in crossing the fence, including General Archer, who was much exhausted with heat and fatigue.[425] Private Patrick Maloney of Company G, 2nd Wisconsin, saw the General in a clump of willows about 30 paces from the stream and rushed forward to seize him.[426] Lieutenant D.B. Bailey of Company B, 2nd Wisconsin, was on the right of the regiment's line and personally witnessed Maloney's capture: "Patrick Maloney, the brave young patriotic and fervent young Irishman, doubly risked his life for the capture of Archer, by going in advance of his comrades and among the fleeing Confederates, for the sake of his prize. Archer at first resisted arrest, but soon Maloney had help and the sullen General was subdued. When I arrived on the spot, Gen. Archer appealed to me for protection from Maloney."[427] Maloney would be killed in action later in the day.

There is a variety of stories concerning what happened to Archer's sword after he surrendered. The General, of course, could not offer it to Maloney, who was only a private, so he approached the first officer he saw, Captain Charles Dow. Dow, however, refused it, saying, "Keep your sword General, and go to the rear; one sword is all I need on this line." Maloney then escorted Archer to his commander, Major John Mansfield, and the General offered up his sword to him. Mansfield claims he passed it on to Lt D.B. Dailey, as he was gathering up prisoners to be taken to the rear.[428] Dailey gives a slightly different account, and says he was at the front with Maloney and Archer when "I then requested him to give me his sword and belt, which he did with great reluctance, saying that courtesy permitted him to retain his side arms." After Archer was taken to the rear, Dailey took off his own sword and put on the General's, "Archer's sword being much lighter than my own."[429]

A quite different story of the fate of Archer's sword was told by W. A. Castleberry of the 13th Alabama. Castleberry says that he was the color bearer of the 13th, and when he was cornered and captured, Archer directed him to drop his flag. At the same time, "he broke his sword in the ground, so that the enemy not get either." This dramatic story obviously does not correlate with the Mansfield-Dailey-Harries account, and should be discounted because of other inaccuracies contained in Castleberry's full account. It is interesting, though, that Castleberry twice makes mention that the 13th had run out of ammunition and so was unable to continue the fight.[430]

One often repeated account describes how Archer was brought before General Doubleday on his way to the rear. The story goes as follows:

"A guard brought him back to General Doubleday, who, in a very cordial manner, they having been cadets at West Point together, said, 'Good morning, Archer! How are you? I am glad to see you!' General Archer replied 'Well, I am not glad to see you by a damn sight!'"[431] This incident and meeting may well have happened, though Doubleday himself did not mention it.[432] However, the two could never have met at West Point, since Archer never attended there (he graduated from Princeton). Historian Roger Long suggests that they may have met in the "old army" before the war.[433]

After capturing General Archer and at least 75 of his men, the men of the 2nd Wisconsin pushed on into the open field beyond the brush and formed in line with the 7th Wisconsin and 19th Indiana on the left.[434] The 24th Michigan appears to have advanced somewhat farther up Herr Ridge. Colonel Morrow in his battle report indicated that he advanced "to the crest of the hill beyond the run, where we halted and threw out skirmishers to the front and also to the left, near a brick house."[435] The crest Morrow mentions was probably on the Harman farm, and the brick house was probably Harman's.[436]

Before long General Meredith was ordered to recall his brigade from its advanced line, perhaps because the remainder of Heth's division was seen forming on Herr Ridge. Colonel Robinson of the 7th Wisconsin reported that "we had occupied our new position but a few minutes when Captain Richardson of the brigade staff brought an order to change front to the rear on the left battalion." Colonel Morrow also reported that "the brigade changed front forward in the first battalion and marched into the woods known as McPherson's Woods, and formed in line of battle."[437] During this movement the 24th Michigan lost two officers to enemy fire. Lieutenant Colonel Mark Flannigan was severely wounded in the leg (which had to be amputated) and adjutant William H. Rexford was struck in the groin.[438] Colonel Williams of the 19th Indiana reported that he lost two or three men wounded during this "dash" across the creek. One of the wounded, James Stickley of Company C, refused to leave the field, and would be killed in the afternoon's fighting.[439]

The Iron Brigade had certainly accomplished a great deal in just over an hour of fighting. Four of its regiments, the 2nd Wisconsin, 7th Wisconsin, 19th Indiana and 24th Michigan, succeeded at overwhelming Archer's brigade and inflicting heavy casualties on it. To be certain, these four regiments had a slight numerical superiority over Archer, about 1450 to 1200,[440] and they were fresh while Archer's men were not. In addition, General Meredith and his regimental commanders performed much better than Archer's commanders, in spite of reasonably heavy losses in men and officers. The 2nd Wisconsin lost particularly heavily—over 30% of its strength—and three of the brigade's field officers were felled (the colonel and lieutenant colonel of the 2nd, and the lieutenant colonel of the 24th). Besides defeating Archer, the Iron Brigade was able to send the 6th Wisconsin to the right to relieve the pressure on Cutler's brigade, where it was primarily responsible for the victory over Davis' brigade at the Railroad Cut. It was a grand morning indeed for the Iron Brigade, but there was still much more fighting to come.

Casualties in Archer's brigade are difficult to determine because of incomplete reports and the heavy losses sustained in the assault of 3 July. Historians Marc and Beth Storch have analyzed the brigade's losses during the battle and estimate the following casualties for units. The brigade's largest unit, the 13th Alabama lost 168 of its 308 men, principally because it bore the brunt of the attack of the Iron Brigade's left wing. The 1st Tennessee, which was also on Archer's right, experienced heavy losses, 109 out of 281 engaged. The 7th and 14th Tennessee lost less heavily because they enjoyed the protection of Herbst Woods, and were not initially outflanked by the Iron Brigade's attack. The 14th lost 62 of its 220 men, and the 7th lost 30 of its 249. The brigade's lightest casualties were in the 5th Alabama Battalion, which apparently lost only 4 of its 135 men due to the fact that it was engaged mostly as skirmishers against Buford's cavalry; these figures suggest that the battalion was probably not with Archer's main line when the Iron Brigade attack struck.[441] Likewise Companies B and G of the 13th only lost one man on July 1st, because they also were principally engaged on the skirmish line.[442] The number of Archer's men who were captured cannot be precisely determined. Lieutenant Colonel S.G. Shepard of the 7th Tennessee claims that only about 75 were lost as prisoners, while General Doubleday claims it was as many as 1000.[443] The actual number lost clearly lies somewhere in between these two extremes. Historian Robert K. Krick has determined that the brigade lost 432 prisoners and missing during the entire battle. If the brigade's losses were approximately equal on each day, as Marc and Beth Storch suggest, the brigade may have lost about 216 men prisoners and missing on 1 July.[444]

The most noted of the brigade's prisoners, General Archer himself, was captured on the west bank of Willoughby Run along with Lieutenant Colonel Aikin of the 13th Alabama and several men of W. H. Moon's

Company I of that regiment. Moon noted that the firing on this front ceased soon after he was captured. He and his more important fellow prisoners were taken to Gettysburg along the Chambersburg Pike, where they passed Hall's gun that had been disabled during the fighting; a solid shot had struck its axle and cut it completely in two. The prisoners were held on the battlefield until about 1600, when they were sent southward because of the looming Confederate success on the field. They were marched all night and reached Taneytown at about dawn on 2 July. Here they were officially enrolled as prisoners of war, and rested for about three hours.[445]

At midmorning on 2 July General Archer and his party were marched to Westminster, where they were entrained for Baltimore, which they reached before dark. By the time of Longstreet's climactic assault on 3 July, Archer was confined safely in secured quarters at Fort McHenry in Baltimore Harbor. A fellow prisoner noted that all were well "except Archer, who has been complaining all week." The General was soon transferred to Fort Delaware, and was from there sent to Johnson's Island Prison in Ohio. His imprisonment was stressful on his health, though he apparently had the means to buy supplies for more than one party. In December 1863 he bribed a guard at Johnson's Island and attempted unsuccessfully to cross the ice to safety. In the summer of 1864 he was one of 50 Confederate officer prisoners selected to be exposed to the guns of Fort Sumter in possible retaliation for a Confederate threat to expose 50 Union officers to the Union guns there. The awkward situation developed into a stalemate, and neither side carried out their threat. The end result was fortunate for Archer—he was exchanged in early August. He returned to duty at Petersburg, but died of simple exhaustion on 24 October 1864.[446]

Private W. A. Castleberry of Company F, 13th Alabama, was initially captured by the Iron Brigade but managed to escape. As already related, he was with Archer when the General was captured, and claimed to see Archer break his sword rather than give it up. He was serving as regimental color bearer, and had dropped his flag to the ground, as Archer suggested. But when Archer and some other officers were being marched off, Castleberry had second thoughts about giving up his flag: "I thought of what my Colonel, Aiken, had told me when he gave me the colors at Chancellorsville. He said: 'Don't let the Yankees have them.' So, in order to keep the Yankees from getting them, I tore the flag from the staff and put it in my bosom. As I started off a Yankee struck me with his sword and cursed me, telling me to come back. I told him I would die if I did not get a drink of water soon, for I claimed to be very sick."[447]

Castleberry's ruse worked, and he crawled off into the wheatfield beyond the Run. Before long some skirmishers of Pettigrew's brigade came forward (he mistakenly thought they were Longstreet's), and thought Castleberry was dead. After they passed over him and began to drive the enemy back, Castleberry crawled behind a cord of wood to watch the action. He was spotted there by a mounted officer, who asked what unit he belonged to. He answered, but really "didn't want to be bothered just then." A few minutes later the officer returned and told Castleberry that General Lee wanted to see him. "Of course I felt very strange, because I thought I would be put under guard." When questioned, he told Lee what had happened in the woods, and claimed that Lee seemed to be relieved to learn that Archer had been captured, not killed. "General Lee then said to me, 'We are forming a hospital near some springs a mile from here, so you go there and get all your men you can together, and don't let anyone put you in battle today.' I took the colors from my breast and showed them to him. He rubbed the tears from his eyes and said 'Go on.'"[448]

As Castleberry noted, the Iron Brigade was turned back by the sight of Heth's second line, composed of Pettigrew's and Brockenbrough's fresh brigades, which were belatedly being sent to the support of Davis and Archer. Heth certainly had not handled his troops well that morning. He readily admitted that at 0900, "I was ignorant of what force was at or rear Gettysburg, and supposed it consisted of cavalry, most probably supported by a brigade or two of infantry." Before he launched Davis and Archer, he was aware that "there were infantry, cavalry and artillery in and about the town."[449] Even so, he did not push his second line forward promptly to support Archer and Davis. Nor did he make any attempt to control the advance of these two brigades, which drifted apart during their advance to the point that they could not offer mutual support. Thus Heth's "forced reconnaissance" was disastrously defeated and both brigades were soundly thrashed.

Heth, Davis and Archer were all deceived by the delaying tactics of Buford's skirmishers. They all had plenty of evidence that there was a strong force of regular cavalry at Gettysburg, though they did not know whether the infantry that came up was regular or militia. Collective evidence would seem to support John S. Mosby's observation that both Hill and Heth "evidently expected to bag a few thousand Yankees, return to Cashtown, and present them to General Lee that evening. But...'they bit off more than they could chew.'"[450]

Confederate brigade leadership did not help their cause in the initial infantry confrontation. Davis won initial success against Cutler's awkwardly deployed regiments, but failed to maintain control of them after Cutler's line collapsed and so fell victim to the flank attack made by Dawes and Fowler. On the right flank, Archer was not able to keep his brigade line together, and did not send skirmishers across Willoughby Run to screen his front and alert him to the full strength of his opposition. He also should have made more of an effort to watch his right flank. In the last analysis, though, Archer's defeat and personal capture was due not so much to any poor leadership as to the fact that he was counterattacked by a larger brigade. Davis, at least at the railroad cut, did not have this excuse.[451]

CHAPTER V

Noontime Lull

Wadsworth's victory over Davis' and Archer's brigades was clearly a sound one, but it still left the Union line battered and somewhat disorganized. The conclusion of the combat at about 1130 found Wadsworth's infantry spread out over the distance of a mile in three separate clusters. Most of the Iron Brigade (19th Indiana, 24th Michigan, 2nd and 7th Wisconsin) was about 100 yards west of Willoughby Run, at the point where they halted their pursuit of the remnants of Archer's defeated brigade. In the center, Dawes' 6th Wisconsin and Fowler's two regiments (14th Brooklyn and 95th New York) had taken the railroad cut alongside the Chambersburg Pike, but lacked an overall commander and were certainly in no position to deal with Heth's artillery, which was still advantageously posted on Herr Ridge. On the right, Cutler was attempting to rally three of his battered regiments (56th Pennsylvania, 76th New York, 147th New York) in Wills Woods on northern Seminary Ridge. Buford's two cavalry brigades were still on hand to guard Wadsworth's flanks, but there was a distinct shortage of artillery. Hall's battery had suffered so much that it had been sent to the rear at Cemetery Hill, and Calef's six guns, which had already seen heavy action, were the only cannons on hand.

The greatest problem facing the victorious Union troops was one of command. Reynolds' guiding hand was gone, and command on the field had for the moment fallen on the I Corps' senior officer, Major

General Abner Doubleday. Doubleday was a competent officer, but never had held corps command, and he paled in almost every quality when compared with Reynolds' confidence and aggressiveness. He was unsure of Reynolds' intentions because his superior had not outlined them to him before his death at about 1030, and the language of his battle report seems to indicate that he was at first overwhelmed by his situation and its responsibilities. It appears that he may have considered retiring from the field, despite the victory of his troops. However, he decided to stay, probably because he knew that the rest of his own corps would soon reach the field, and that Howard was within supporting distance, as Reynolds had told him that morning at Emmitsburg. He also felt that "to fall back without orders from the commanding general might have inflicted lasting disgrace upon the corps, and as General Reynolds, who was in confidence of General Meade, had formed his lines to resist the entrance of the enemy into Gettysburg, I naturally supposed that it was the intention to defend the place."[1]

Doubleday's immediate task was to reform his separated commands in case the enemy might renew their attack. He determined to retain the Iron Brigade on McPherson's Ridge, with Cutler's brigade in support on the right on Seminary Ridge. Doubleday, like Reynolds and Buford before him, saw the advantage of a defense in depth on the ridges west in town. If the Iron Brigade ran into trouble on McPherson's Ridge, it would withdraw to Seminary Ridge, and the line on Seminary Ridge could be withdrawn to Cemetery Hill if necessary. This position, though, was not without its shortcomings, as Colonel Charles Wainwright noted when he arrived at the Seminary at about 1115. He noted that the "position was not a bad one at which to resist a frontal attack, though it lacked depth and was vulnerable to being outflanked." On more consideration, however, he decided, "that he did not like this advanced position at all because its right flank was exposed to a high ridge on the north, that afforded good cover for an enemy attack."[2]

Though Doubleday was not much respected by some officers of the corps (Wainwright called him "a weak reed to lean on"),[3] he did a good job rearranging his lines with the forces at hand. Meredith's four regiments were recalled from their foray across Willoughby Run. They were not in immediate danger there, but their line was not a particularly strong one, and Doubleday did not want to provoke Heth into making a counterattack. The withdrawal was not made without incident. As already noted, the 24th Michigan lost both its lieutenant colonel and adjutant at this time.[4]

When Meredith reformed his line in Herbst Woods, he had the 19th Indiana and 24th Michigan exchange places; the reason for this is not understood today. In this new configuration, the 19th held the left of the line, the 24th the center, and the 7th Wisconsin the right, all facing west across the Run. Mansfield's 2nd Wisconsin, which had suffered by far the greatest number of casualties in the morning's engagement, was placed in a second line "about midway through the timber."[5] Dawes' 6th Wisconsin did not rejoin the brigade, but was permitted to fall back and reform on Seminary Ridge north of the Seminary.[6] All of the regiments posted along Willoughby Run sent forward skirmishers, which at once became engaged with those of the enemy.[7]

The Iron Brigade's position was a good one, but had weaknesses, particularly since it had no artillery support or fresh reserves. The trees in the woods offered a degree of protection from the enemy but the ridge here was markedly lower than Herr Ridge to the west, where the Confederates were establishing an even stronger artillery line. The lay of the ground forced the 24th Michigan to form at an awkward angle, with its right bent back to link up with the 7th Wisconsin and its left bent back towards a deep hollow; because of the trees it was not possible for one end of the 200 yard long regimental line to see the other.[8] In addition, both ends of the brigade line were vulnerable. The 7th Wisconsin had to angle its line back to the right in order to guard against a flank attack, and its right rested on the open field near the McPherson buildings.[9] The 19th Indiana was in an even more vulnerable position on the left of the brigade line. It was first formed in the open fields of the eastern branch of McPherson's Ridge, along Willoughby Run.[10]

While the Iron Brigade regrouped in Herbst Woods, Cutler was reforming his used up brigade at the woods north of the eastern railroad cut. As already noted, his command was well scattered at the close of the fighting that morning—Fowler's two regiments were reasonably intact along the middle railroad cut, but the 147th New York was broken up in several detachments along Seminary Ridge, and elements of the 76th New York and 56th Pennsylvania were scattered about between the ridge and the town. Cutler rode towards the town, gathered in the remnants of his brigade that had rallied on its outskirts, and led them back to Wills Woods, just north of the railroad cut on Seminary Ridge.[11] When Major Harney arrived with a portion of the 147th New York, Cutler lashed out at him for losing his flag. He was stopped in the middle of his tirade when Sergeant William Wybourn, wounded, came staggering up with the flag.[12] Before long Fowler arrived with the 14th Brooklyn and 95th New York, and formed a second line behind the brigade's other three regiments. It was then that Colonel Biddle of the 95th, who had been wounded earlier in the day, at last decided to leave the field, so formally leaving its command to Major Edwin Pye.[13]

When the fighting drew to a close, Brigadier General John Buford reassigned his cavalry units as he deemed best. He, too, did not much care for Doubleday,[14] and apparently made his dispositions without consulting Reynolds' replacement. Since Gamble's men were pretty played out and needed to reorganize, he directed them to withdraw from the field west of the Seminary (where they had continued to suffer from Confederate artillery fire during the fighting in Herbst Woods) and move "to the south side of the town." A short while later the 8th Illinois was sent out to watch the Iron Brigade's flank near the Fairfield Road.[15]

While Cutler's brigade was reforming on Oak Ridge, Devin's cavalry was shifted eastward in order to watch for the coming of Ewell's troops, which were known to be approaching Gettysburg from the north. Devin's line extended all the way across Carlisle Pike to Rock Creek and beyond. The sources are sketchy for this time period, but it appears that at least part of the 17th Pennsylvania was posted along the York Pike, and portions of the 6th and 9th New York were on the Heidlersburg (Harrisburg) Road.[16]

Oddly enough there was apparently no Union artillery deployed during this interlude, except perhaps one of Calef's guns near the middle railroad cut. As already noted, Hall's 2nd Maine battery had been withdrawn by 1045, and was so shot up that it was sent to regroup on Cemetery Hill. Calef's battery was available at this time on Seminary Ridge, where it had just replenished its ammunition. However, it was not brought into play (except for Roder's gun sent to the railroad cut), perhaps for fear it would be overwhelmed by all the Confederate guns gathering on the Ridge.

It was not until after the Iron Brigade had reformed that Doubleday learned of Reynolds' death an hour or so earlier. The message was probably brought by Captain John Carson, commander of Reynolds' headquarters guard, who had been assigned the task of informing Doubleday.[17]

Arrival of the Remainder of I Corps

Fortunately for Doubleday, numerous reinforcements were at hand. The first to arrive were three batteries of the I Corps artillery, under the command of Colonel Charles Wainwright. Wainwright was supposed to be third in line in the corps line of march that day, behind Wadsworth's and Rowley's divisions, and ahead of Robinson's command. Rowley's command, however, had taken another road, so putting Wainwright at the head of the column that was moving up the Emmitsburg Road towards Gettysburg about an hour behind Wadsworth.[18] Wainwright's other two batteries were serving with specific divisions this day. Cooper's was with Rowley's, and Hall's, as we have already seen, was with Wadsworth's.

Wainwright had received his marching orders at 0800 and had left Emmitsburg about 0900. He had no idea that there would be any fighting that day, and "moved quietly along without dreaming of a fight, and fully expecting to be comfortably in camp by noon." So at ease was the colonel that he for the first time threw his saddlebags (with his supply of chocolate, tobacco, and other sundries) into a wagon. In addition, when his horse "Billy" threw two shoes, he stopped at a farmhouse to have one of his farriers replace them, and stayed 15 minutes longer until a heavy shower passed by.[19]

After his pit stop, Wainwright rode to the head of his column, where he fell in with General Doubleday. The two discussed Meade's promotion, and Doubleday complained that he should have been given command of a corps, since he was senior to George Sykes, who had been given Meade's V Corps. Before long they heard cannon fire to the north. When they reached the area of the Peach Orchard, an officer (Wainwright did not remember whom) rode up from the front with orders for everyone to hurry forward at once. Doubleday left immediately to find Reynolds, with whom he claims to have communicated just before the latter was killed.[20]

Wainwright put his column in motion again, and rode on ahead of his troops in order to study the field before they arrived. When he reached the Codori farm, he took the same cross field short cut that Wadsworth's men had cleared earlier in the day. Halfway to Seminary Ridge, he met Captain Craig Wadsworth of General Wadsworth's staff, who sadly informed him, "The General is killed, Reynolds is dead." A short time later he passed the General's body as it was being brought off. He halted and uncovered briefly in respect for his fallen commander, since that was all there was time for.[21]

It is not clear at what time Wainwright reached the Seminary area. Since he makes no mention of any fighting going on, he must have arrived at 1115 or shortly thereafter, just after the infantry completed their attacks. The first thing he did was to survey the field by riding along Seminary Ridge and "the one beyond" (east McPherson Ridge). He was not much impressed by what he saw, as already noted.[22]

Wainwright's cannoneers also proceeded at a leisurely pace during the first half of their approach to Gettysburg. Augustus Buell wrote that Stewart's battery "was marching at a walk, most of us were walking with the guns instead of riding on the limbers."[23] Their attention perked up when they were "probably halfway up from Marsh Creek" and began to hear the noise of the fighting on Reynolds' front. John Holland, a volunteer infantryman from the 2nd Wisconsin on detached service with the battery, properly deduced that the Iron Brigade had entered the action, and cried out, "Hear that, my son! That's the talk! The old slouch hats have got there, you bet!"[24]

The three batteries also took Wadsworth's by now well worn short cut across the fields past the Codori farm. They were halted southwest of the Seminary, between the ridge and the town, and formed in a field. Lieutenant George Breck of Reynolds' battery noted "clouds of cavalry skirmishers, which having been relieved by the infantry, were falling back down the hillsides."[25] These were probably Gamble's troopers retiring to their reforming area near the town; many would have been walking because they had lost their mounts during the morning's fight.

While the batteries were parked, Wainwright sent word for them to send their battery wagons to the rear and prepare for action. It should be noted that it is not clear whether Wainwright halted his batteries here on Doubleday's orders, as he stated in his battle report,[26] or because he found disarray on the field and could get orders from no one, as he claims in his journal.[27] His journal adds the caustic comment, "all I could do then was to put my batteries in position where they could be got at easily...and wait in condition to start at a trot the instant orders came."[28]

The next Union reinforcements to arrive were the two brigades of Rowley's division of the I Corps, which came up after 1130 by slightly different routes. Due to the fact that Rowley's division had been posted on the left of the I Corps in order to watch for a possible enemy approach from the direction of Fairfield, Rowley's men did not follow the rest of the corps on its march up the Emmitsburg Road to Gettysburg, as is commonly believed. Rowley's two brigades instead took a series of back roads to reach the field, as will be described.

Since Colonel Roy Stone's 2nd Brigade of Rowley's division reached the field first, its journey will be described first. Stone's command consisted of about 1300 men in the 143rd, 149th and 150th Pennsylvania Regiments. All three units had been raised in 1862 and had seen limited service at Fredericksburg and Chancellorsville, but they were now about to enter their first real combat. The brigade left its camp at the Brown farm on the north side of Marsh Creek at 0900 or a little after. Stone headed north on the Red Rock Road until its junction with the Millerstown Road, where he probably met up with Biddle's 1st Brigade, which had been marching north on the Bull Frog Road. The two brigades traveled together as far as the fork in the road at the Pitzer School. There they separated as Biddle turned to the left towards Black Horse Tavern and Stone continued eastward on the Millerstown Road towards its juncture with the Emmittsburg Road.[29]

The weather was "intensely sultry, the air being charged with moisture, and the men quickly felt the weight of their campaigning outfit, and perspired as they had rarely perspired before." After about an hour of marching the troops had begun to hear the sounds of cannons booming to the north. More evidence of the closeness of the enemy was met once the command reached the Emmitsburg Road and turned left towards Gettysburg. The column met several groups of civilians who were heading south, some driving their cattle and horses ahead of them. Some of the men were particularly affected by the sight of a boy and girl who were riding one horse together and "crying as if their little hearts would break."[30]

As the brigade was passing the Sherfy Peach Orchard, a staff officer rode up with orders to "hasten the march." Stone gave the command to double quick, and soon more than a few weary men began to fall out and drop by the wayside. Among the latter was Captain William P. Dougal of Company D, 150th Pennsylvania, who was "the largest and most corpulent officer in the regiment." Dougal asked permission to fall behind, and was allowed to do so on condition that he would gather up all the stragglers he met and bring them up on his return. He did as ordered, and would fall wounded during the afternoon's fighting.[31]

Stone's brigade had hustled northward on the Emmitsburg Road for a little less than a mile when it received orders to leave the road near the Codori house and take the now well worn short cut that Wadsworth's men had laid out from the Emmitsburg Road to the Seminary area.[32]

The brigade halted to catch its breath in the fields southeast of the Seminary, where it was formed into column of regiments. Generals Doubleday and Rowley then came up to address them with standard words of patriotic fervor, "reminding them that they were upon their own soil, that the eye of the Commonwealth was upon them, and that there was every reason to believe they would do their duty to the uttermost in defense of their State." Whatever encouraging effects these brief speeches might have engendered was undermined by the effects of the Confederate shells exploding nearby, and the news that spread like wildfire from the officers through the ranks that General Reynolds had just been killed.[33] Even so, a number of the men cried out to their commanders, "We have come to stay!" and stay they would.[34]

Rowley issued orders for his men to unsling their knapsacks and load their muskets.[35] He then sent them on the double quick towards the ridge near the Seminary. It seems that Colonel Langhorne Wister of the 150th in all the excitement forgot to order his command to load, and a dozen voices called out for him to do so. Wister responded with an order to stop and load, which was done with much merriment.[36]

Colonel Stone pushed his men forward to support the exposed right of the Iron Brigade, on the line between Herbst Woods and the Chambersburg Pike that had been held for a time by Fowler's two regiments earlier that morning. The 150th went forward into battalion front with flags uncased and took up the left of the line, between the woods on their left and the McPherson barn. The 143rd, under Colonel Edmund L. Dana, formed in the center near the farm buildings, and the 149th, under Lieutenant Colonel Walton Dwight, formed between the McPherson house and the Chambersburg Pike.[37]

Major J. F. Slagle of the 149th Pennsylvania claimed that his unit had to drive back some Confederate skirmishers in order to take its assigned position,[38] and all three units encountered enemy artillery and long range skirmish fire as they moved up.[39] Once in line, Stone ordered each regiment to send out a company as skirmishers. Accordingly, Company B of the 150th, Company A of the 143rd, and Company K of the 149th were deployed and sent forward.[40] Captain G. W. Jones of the 150th's company asked Colonel Wister how far he should go, and Wister responded "Go forward until you feel the enemy and engage him."[41] Colonel Stone proudly reported that all his skirmishers dashed forward and without firing a shot drove the enemy's skirmishers from a fence beyond an open field towards the base of the hill.[42] They then occupied the woods along the course of Willoughby Run, a line they would continue to hold for several more hours.[43] Colonel Stone also asked Lieutenant Colonel Dwight of the 149th to send forward a company to watch his right, which was totally unsupported. In response Dwight sent Captain Zarah C. McCullough's Company E forward 100 paces to a fence along the Pike.[44]

Stone's advance had caught the attention of the enemy, who turned a number of their cannons on his line. The only response Stone could make was to direct his men to lie down and shelter themselves from the fire of the enemy.[45] Most had to lie still for the next hour under increasingly heavy Confederate shelling. The enemy artillery fire tended to unnerve the men much more than the occasional skirmisher who came limply back from the forward line. Perhaps the first man of the brigade to be killed was Jacob Yale of Company I of the 143rd Pennsylvania, who was struck in the forehead by a musket ball.[46] John S. Weber of Company F, 150th Pennsylvania, tried to relieve the tension by standing up and yelling, "Come boys, choose your partners! The ball is about to open! Don't you hear the music?" Before the day was over he would receive a bad wound in his arm that would send him home and out of the war.[47]

While Stone's brigade was forming to support the right flank of the Iron Brigade, Biddle's brigade of Rowley's division was moving up to support Meredith's left. Biddle's command consisted of four regiments: the 121st, 142nd, and 151st Pennsylvania and the 20th New York State Militia, with Cooper's Pennsylvania battery of four guns attached. The three Pennsylvania regiments had not yet seen much combat, though they had been present at Fredericksburg and Chancellorsville; the 151st or "School Teacher's Regiment" was a nine months unit, and its survivors would be mustered out at the end of the month. The brigade's fourth regiment, the 20th New York State Militia,[48] had seen extended service since 1861, but did not join the brigade until the afternoon before the battle. It had been on guard duty at Aquia Creek since Fredericksburg, and was recalled to Alexandria in mid June to help meet the threat of Lee's invasion. On 26 June Reynolds directed the 20th to join him in the I Corps, and the footsore regiment finally caught up with him at the Moritz Tavern north of Emmitsburg late in the morning of 30 June. Reynolds assigned it to Doubleday's division, and the regiment reported to its new commander for duty at 1600. Doubleday assigned it to Rowley's first brigade. Soon after the regiment joined Rowley, there was a large scale shakeup in the corps' command structure. When Reynolds assumed active command of the army's left wing, Doubleday took over the I Corps and Brigadier General Thomas A. Rowley assumed command of the 3rd Division. These changes elevated Colonel Chapman Biddle of the 121st Pennsylvania to command of Rowley's old brigade on the eve of the battle.[49]

The 20th New York State Militia reported to its new brigade at the command's outpost position on the Bull Frog Road about 2½ miles west of the Moritz Tavern, where it had been assigned to watch the approaches from Fairfield.[50] Because of this advanced position, the brigade did not march to Gettysburg on the Emmitsburg Road, as already noted. Instead it advanced via back roads and actually approached Gettysburg from the west. Its purpose may have been to serve as a flank guard against Confederate troops that were feared to be approaching from the Fairfield area.

Biddle's troops were up soon after dawn on the damp morning of 1 July. They had received orders the previous night to prepare three days' rations, which signified a march was impending, but not all the men were in a rush to get ready. Corporal John Owendorf and Private Enos Vail of the 20th New York State Militia decided that they needed to clean their clothes, so they proceeded to nearby Marsh Creek and began to do their washing. No sooner had they done so when "The bugle sounded the assembly." The two had to wring out their clothes as best they could before running back to camp.[51]

Biddle's camp was astir because at about 0730 Lieutenant Harrison Lambdin of Doubleday's staff had brought orders for the command to march to Gettysburg.[52] Captain John Cook of the 20th remembered that, "A hundred rumors circulated through the camps as to what was going on or going to happen."[53] Within half an hour most of the brigade was ready to march. Corporal Owendof and Private Vail decided it was best to fix their bayonets and so hang their heavy wash out to dry; Vail noted that "Thus decorated we were a fine looking pair."[54]

Biddle was anxious to get going, and started his lead regiment out at 0800[55] before the 121st Pennsylvania, which had been on picket, was able to come in and form up. The 121st then quickly fell into the column, with two companies deployed as flankers;[56] the brigade had orders "to promptly engage the enemy wherever met."[57] The 20th New York, perhaps because it was so new to the brigade, marched at the rear of the column.[58]

Biddle's march began at an intersection at the center of his line of camps called Ross White Crossroads, where Bull Frog Road met the Millerstown Road. His course took him northeastward through the rich countryside that appeared even more lush in comparison to the war-ravaged fields of Northern Virginia. On the way a number of farmers came out with their families to greet them, "the first time since we had crossed the Potomac a year and a half before. The people on our line of march gave us friendly greeting." In addition, some of the women offered fresh baked bread, pails of milk and crocks of sweet fresh butter for the delight of the men "who one after another stopped by long enough to receive the treat." But not all of Gates' New Yorkers were able to enjoy these treats. Captain Cook relates, "This feeling was somewhat disturbed when some of our regiment came cursing back from an application for their bounty and said that it had been refused because they were New Yorkers and not Pennsylvanians. I do not know that all made that distinction but some of these people certainly did, and as we were then to repel a hostile invasion of Pennsylvania, we thought it hardly fair to us." But Cook's men were not to be deterred from obtaining refreshment: "It was easy enough to say they were Pennsylvanians and a little thing like that hardly troubled the conscience of an old campaigner, however much he might resent the subtlety of subterfuge. Our boys got their portion all right."[59]

The column, which by now had met up with Stone's brigade, had covered almost three miles when it took a sharp turn to the right and then crossed Sach's Mill Bridge over Marsh Creek, a covered bridge that is still standing. It then crossed Willoughby Run, and swung left (north) along the Black Horse Tavern Road, while Stone's brigade continued eastward on the Millerstown Road. Biddle's command marched north for about a mile, and then it turned right along Willoughby Run Road, on the west bank of the stream.[60]

The men by now could clearly hear the booming of Heth's cannons just over a mile to their front.[61] When the column reached the broader Fairfield Road at a point about two miles west of Gettysburg, Colonel Biddle cautiously formed the brigade in line of battle facing north, with its regiments still in their relative line of march, the 20th New York State Militia being on the left of the line.[62] After the dusty morning's march, Captain Cook of the 20th appreciated the "cool shade and quiet" of this position, located in "a woods pasture, a beautiful grove of large trees with a carpet of springy sod."[63]

But Cook and his men would not be allowed to rest long. Biddle decided to send out skirmishers and began advancing his line northward.

They had proceeded no more than 2-300 yards when "the occasional crackling of musket fire" broke out.[64] The Confederate troops Biddle encountered were probably a detachment of skirmishers stationed on the David Finnefrock farm, perhaps from Archer's 5th Alabama Battalion. Biddle's line of march had accidentally brought him on to the right of Heth's line stationed at Herr Ridge. Had he continued northward, he would have encountered some of Meredith's men as they completed the rout of Archer's command. But he also would have run into Pettigrew's and Brockenbrough's fresh brigades, which were then advancing their skirmishers down the eastern slope of Herr Ridge to come to Archer's aid. Biddle, however, was unaware of all the Confederate infantry in his front. What caught his attention was all the Confederate artillery in that sector, so he wisely chose to slide to his right and seek the location of the rest of his corps.[65] Had he been more aggressive, or had a responsible division commander been with the column (Rowley had traveled with Stone's brigade), Biddle might have continued to push northward from his Fairfield Road line, and so changed the course of this part of the battle.

The brigade sustained its first casualty as it changed from line to column and started marching eastward. Captain Cook noted, "As we moved out of the woods toward our new position one of the men fell suddenly, stricken down by a stray bullet from the forest. Our surgeon leaped from his horse and ran to help the wounded man, and as we swept past in hurrying march we had an impressive intimation of what was to come. The incident thrilled everyone with a sense of danger as great perhaps as that felt during the battle itself."[66]

The brigade marched by the right flank about ½ mile to the east, and crossed Willoughby Run between the Fairfield Road and the John Herbst farm.[67] Enroute it passed by elements of Gamble's 8th Illinois Cavalry, which had just been sent out to patrol this approach.[68] Biddle must have been relieved to at last locate the corps' line. Upon his approach he was directed by Doubleday to form in front of the Seminary, as a support to the left rear of the Iron Brigade.[69] Biddle took up position along a fence line in the swale between the Seminary and eastern McPherson Ridge.[70] Captain Cook of the 20th New York State Militia did not much care for this position because the "left of the line thus terminated in an open field without any support or anything on which to rest. The line was as long as the numbers of the force would permit, but its left extremity was technically 'up in the air.'"[71]

While Biddle's men were filing into position, Colonel Wainwright

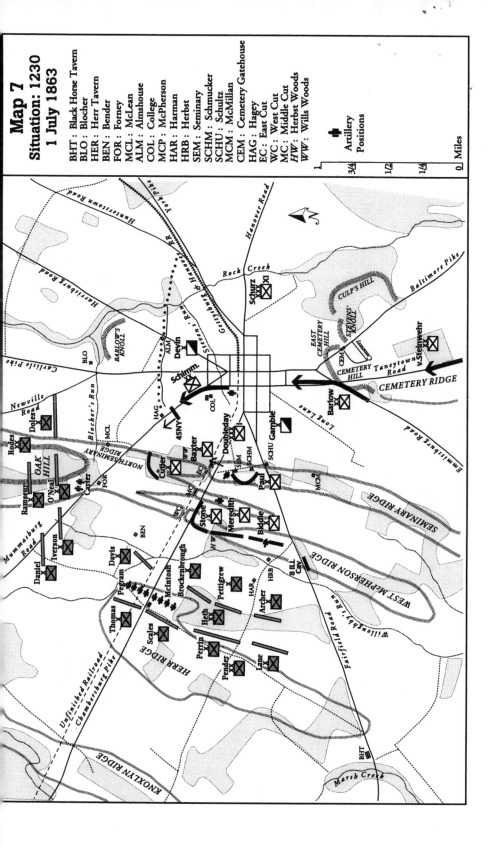

Map 7
Situation: 1230
1 July 1863

BHT : Black Horse Tavern
BLO : Blocher
HER : Herr Tavern
BEN : Bender
FOR : Forney
MCL : McLean
ALM : Almshouse
COL : College
MCP : McPherson
HAR : Harman
HRB : Herbst
SEM : Seminary
SCHM : Schmucker
SCHU : Schultz
MCM : McMillan
CEM : Cemetery Gatehouse
HAG : Hagey
EC : East Cut
WC : West Cut
MC : Middle Cut
HW : Herbst Woods
WW : Wills Woods

Artillery
Positions

Miles
0   1/4   1/2   3/4   1

rode up to meet them and "placed Cooper's battery in position on the open ridge about where I thought the left of the division would rest, and ordered him to await events."[72] Cooper's deployment attracted the attention of Heth's artillery, which opened fire on him and caused Biddle's men to lie even closer to the ground behind the ridge as they "listened with acute interest to the roar of artillery on our right and to the shriek of shells that passed overhead."[73] Soon after Cooper began to return fire, one of his four 3-inch rifled guns broke its axle and so was out of action for the rest of the day.[74]

Once they were formed, Biddle's men were directed to unsling their packs and ready for action. At this point "the men abandoned their former hilarity, and, becoming more seriously disposed, mechanically set themselves to work with the seeming determination of annihilating any obstacle that should present itself."[75]

Biddle's men had been in line barely ten minutes when they received an order to advance to the ravine of Willoughby Run, in order to connect directly with Meredith's line in Herbst Woods.[76] Their new position was not a good one. The open ground to the west rose to a crest, along which was a fence that afforded excellent to the enemy's skirmishers. Colonel Gates observed, "The field was alive with them. In this ravine the brigade found itself under a hot infantry fire, and was unable to see the enemy from whom the fire came, and did not attempt to reply to it." In fact, no one was quite sure "just why the brigade was sent down into that valley."[77]

Biddle's order to advance probably came from General Rowley, whom Doubleday had specifically charged with handling this end of the line.[78] Rowley was not having a good day. Formerly a colonel of the 10th Pennsylvania, Rowley had been promoted to brigadier general on 29 November 1862.[79] He had an undistinguished battle record, and had succeeded to division command only the evening before the battle, when Doubleday took over as corps commander. Apparently none of the other officers in the corps cared for him much,[80] and the fact that his two brigades were deployed on separate fronts made it harder for him to control them. His placement of Biddle's troops upon their arrival, and strange behavior later in the day, appear to have been caused by drunkenness. He appeared to Wainwright to be inebriated later in the day.[81] The stern Colonel Gates noted aptly that "During the fighting on the first day the General commanding the division was hardly competent to judge correctly the conditions of things, or to know what transpired on the field."[82] Rowley's behavior later in the day was so erratic that he had to be arrested and escorted from the battlefield.[83]

Biddle's men were not in their exposed position along Willoughby Run very long before they received orders to withdraw back towards the Seminary. The command was about faced and marched under enemy fire "back over the position from which it last marched."[84] This time, though, they were posted along the crest of eastern McPherson's Ridge, in front of Cooper's battery and not in the protection of the reverse slope and swale. The brigade's line was not quite long enough to cover all the ground between the Fairfield Road and the area to the rear of Herbst Woods, and its regiments had to be strung out as best they could. They were as follows from left to right: 121st Pennsylvania, 20th New York State Militia, 142nd and 151st Pennsylvania.[85] Their presence on the ridge crest made them much more obvious to the enemy, and soon "a swarm of artillery missiles showed that we were seen by the enemy."[86]

Biddle's somewhat exposed position had not been ordered, it appears, by Rowley or Doubleday, but by Wadsworth, commander of the corps' 1st Division. Wadsworth was an active and familiar figure on the corps line following Reynolds' death, and did not hesitate to give orders to troops not belonging to his own division. Wadsworth was apparently concerned that Heth might try to move against Meredith's left flank if it appeared to be unguarded, so he posted Biddle's men on the ridge in the plain view of the enemy. It was unfortunate for Biddle's men that all the ground there was open and offered no cover to the Confederate artillery fire. Captain Cook recorded, "As usual some of the men began to grumble at what seemed needless exposure. But it was reported that it was necessary to occupy the ground; that General Wadsworth, who had been our first brigade commander and was then with the next division of the corps, had recommended us for the duty; that he knew our regiment would go where it was sent and stay where it was put. This story spread quickly all along the line and whether true or not, I know it helped to console us for the exposure to which we were subjected."[87]

Besides being harassed by Confederate artillery fire, Biddle's line soon came under annoying musketry fire from a strong body of skirmishers (probably from Archer's command) based at the Emmanuel Harman Farm, ½ mile to the west, on the other side of Willoughby Run. The farm consisted of a well built two story brick house with accompanying barn and outbuildings, all located on a rise above the Keystone Mill Road.[88] Their position was a strong one, and the snipers based there began to fell so many of Cooper's gunners that the 20th New York State Militia had to send infantry volunteers to help with the guns.[89]

About 10 minutes after the brigade line was formed, General Wadsworth rode up to Colonel Gates and requested him to send a company out to drive off the enemy's skirmishers and seize the Harman Farm.[90] This locale should not have been a direct concern of Wadsworth's, unless the enemy skirmishers there were also striking the left flank of the Iron Brigade troops near the Herbst Woods. Wadsworth may have wished to put up a show of force on the left of his division's front, but he lacked spare troops to carry it out. Whatever were his reasons, he probably approached Gates for the job because of their previous familiarity; Gates at once complied.

The unit Gates chose for the job was Captain Ambrose Baldwin's Company K. Since Baldwin had less than 40 men under his command, he solicited a few additional volunteers, including Alexander Tice, a friend of Enos Vail. Tice had told his buddy earlier in the day, "You know that I have never been in battle, and I have a presentiment of being killed." Tice's foreboding turned out to be true enough. After Baldwin's command had rushed to the cover of the ravine along Willoughby Run, they charged up the hill towards the Harman farm buildings. Tice was struck in the chest and died instantly.[91]

Baldwin's men succeeded at driving the Confederates away from the Harman buildings, and then proceeded to break into the house to make sure no enemies lurked there. The house was indeed occupied, but not by Confederate soldiers. Amelia Harman and her aunt had decided to remain in the house when the fighting started. They had locked the door and were hiding in an upstairs room, when "a sudden violent commotion and uproar below made us fly in quick haste to the lower floor. There was a tumultuous pounding with fists and guns on the kitchen door." The frightened women unlocked the door and gladly let in some of Baldwin's powder blackened but friendly troops. They persuaded the ladies to take safer refuge in the basement, and then sent marksmen to occupy the building's windows. Before long Private Addison Hayes was wounded in the right arm, and left for the rear to have the appendage amputated at a field hospital.[92]

Baldwin's bold attack annoyed the Confederates, who sent back more men to recapture the Harman farm. Baldwin sent his lieutenant, Jake Young, back to the regiment for reinforcements. Apparently Young was quite excitable, especially after he had had a drink or two for stimulant. As he ran along Gates' line, where the men had been lying down nervously for some time in order to escape the enemy's shells, he began singing as loud as he could a verse from his favorite bawdy ballad. He then raised his cap, wiped his brow, and reported to Gates, "Colonel, its damned hot out there." This behavior caused a whole section of the line to break out in laughter, so relieving "the mental strain which the long waiting under fire had caused."[93]

Colonel Gates, with the consent of Colonel Biddle, sent out Captain William H. Cunningham's Company H as reinforcements for Baldwin. Cunningham's men fought their way through to the Harman house, and the two companies succeeded at holding their position under increasing enemy pressure for the next two hours.[94] It is likely that the strength and determination of their stand played a large role in deterring Heth and Pender from making a firm attack on Doubleday's left flank. Thus the two companies played a key, but generally overlooked, role in aiding the defense of the overextended Union line that afternoon.

Apparently some of the Confederates on Biddle's front still thought they were facing raw militia, even after the Union success against Davis and Archer during the morning. During the skirmishing on Gates' front a Confederate officer was somehow captured, who commented that "some surprise was expressed that raw troops would persevere so good an alignment in advancing and be so steady, especially as shot and shell were dropping rather plentifully amongst them." One of the soldiers took a field glass, and after examining the regimental colors for a few minutes, exclaimed "Twentieth NYSM, Army of the Potomac, by God, I have seen that damned color too often not to know whom it belongs to."[95]

While Biddle's line was being advanced, withdrawn, and readjusted on Meredith's left, still more Union reinforcements were arriving, in the form of Brigadier General John C. Robinson's 2nd Division of I Corps. Robinson had ordered his men to be under arms at an early hour, and at least one of his regiments, the 12th Massachusetts of Baxter's brigade, was ready to move out at 0400.[96] A number of the regiments started marching between 0600 and 0800, but only got as far as their jump off points.[97] Robinson had been assigned the rear position in the corps' line of march, and so had to wait for all the other units in the corps to form up and move out. As already related, Wadsworth's 1st Division was in no hurry to break camp, and did not begin marching towards Gettysburg until around 0730. His last troops cleared out by 0800, but Rowley's division and Wainwright's three batteries did not move out until 0900. Thus Robinson's men could not begin their march until after 0900.[98] Brigadier General Gabriel R. Paul's 1st Brigade marched first, followed by Brigadier General Henry Baxter's 2nd Brigade. Baxter's 11th Pennsylvania was the last unit in the column because it had been on picket duty. It was recalled at 0700, and reached camp about 0900 just after the rest of the division had pulled out.[99]

By now the day was getting warm, and the dust of the Emmitsburg Road was well churned up by the passage of the rest of the corps ahead of Robinson's men. John Vautier of the 88th Pennsylvania was at the very end of the corps column, and remembered, "The morning was blistering hot, and the stifling clouds of yellow dust, settling on the ranks like a blanket, filled the eyes, mouth, nostrils and entire person of the soldier with an impalpable powder, while perspiration, running down the skin, ploughed furrows through the dirt."[100] Abner Small of the 16th Maine recalled, "The road was hazy with the dust of the marching column, and the farm lands, drifting by, were dry and shimmering in the sultry heat."[101]

As the brigade headed northward, some of the men could not help breaking out into song in order to ease the tedium of their march. The men of the 88th Pennsylvania enjoyed several versions of "John Brown's Body" and during the rousing "Glory Hallelujah" chorus kept "time with their feet to the words and notes of that inspiring song."[102] Before long the rumor began to circulate, perhaps passed on from troops farther ahead in the column, that General McClellan had returned to command the army. Isaac Hall of the 97th New York noted "This was generally believed by the men and many of the officers, till the close of the day, and added not a little to the spirited resistance to the Confederate attack in that first day's encounter."[103]

As they neared Gettysburg, Baxter's men also met citizen refugees headed south to avoid the fighting and the advancing Confederates. One soldier noted that some families were "stowed away in the front of their wagons, with what goods and chattels they could pack in a big bundle to the rear." When the 90th Pennsylvania passed by the Peter Rogers house, ½ mile north of the Peach Orchard, Private Rufus Northrop saw an old man supported by a young girl who "exhorted us in beseeching, tremulous tones. 'Whip 'em, boys, this time. If you don't whip 'em now, you'll never whip 'em.' The boys replied with a 'Bully the old man' and a 'hip-hip for the girl' and quickened their pace towards Gettysburg."[104]

By now Robinson's men were able to clearly hear the artillery fire from the combat on McPherson's Ridge, which caused them to accelerate their pace. One of the General's aides passed down the column with an order to keep closed up. When the division reached the Codori farm, it, too, headed northward at the double quick across the fields on the most direct route to the scene of the fighting.[105] As they approached the Seminary, some of the men could see Confederate artillery shells exploding over the trees nearby. Private John Vautier of the 88th Pennsylvania remembered "hearing the crackle of rifles mingled with the manly cheers of the Union soldiers and occasionally the shrill yelp of the rebels."[106] But there were other more painful evidences of the battle being fought. Vautier also observed that "the wounded, dripping with blood, began to appear, limping slowly and painfully to the rear in search of field hospitals."[107] Lieutenant Francis Wiggin of the 16th Maine and numerous of his comrades were saddened to hear the news conveyed by an orderly that General Reynolds had been killed by a sharpshooter.[108]

Robinson's troops began to arrive at the Seminary after 1130. Since the corps line along McPherson's Ridge was adequately defended for the moment, General Doubleday decided to hold Robinson in reserve. Devin's active troopers had made it clear that Ewell's troops might be approaching from the north at any moment, and Doubleday wanted to have troops available to meet them if needed. And if Ewell's men did not appear, Robinson could be used to help face Hill's troops if the Confederates should renew their attack from the west.

Paul's Brigade, which arrived first, apparently halted for some time to the east of Seminary Ridge before its six regiments were sent around to the western face of the building. Here they were ordered by General Doubleday "to throw up some slight entrenchments, to aid me in holding that point in case I should be driven back."[109] While Paul's men were catching their breath, one member of the 13th Massachusetts saw a strange and tragic scene transpire in the fields west of the Seminary. It seems that a spent solid shot from one of the Confederate batteries on Herr Ridge was rolling slowly towards the Seminary, and a soldier from one of Meredith's Wisconsin regiments playfully stuck out his foot to try to stop it. This was a tragic mistake, since the cannonball had enough impetus to sever the poor soldier's leg. He wept briefly, not so much for the loss of his limb as for the careless way in which he lost it; he would have much preferred to have lost it in combat with the enemy.[110]

Baxter's brigade arrived about one half hour after Paul's and proceeded directly to the woods on the west side of the Seminary. The members of the 88th Pennsylvania were glad to be able to stop and make coffee, since they had missed having breakfast that morning.[111] Some members of the 83rd New York took up a more serious task and began gathering fence rails to erect a "crescent shaped" barricade on the western side of the Seminary.[112]

Formation of Heth's Division

The Confederates were also bringing up reinforcements and rear-ranging their lines in the hour following the defeat of Archer and Davis. As already discussed, Heth erred greatly by not ordering Brockenbrough and Pettigrew to advance in close support of Archer and Davis in the attack launched at 0930. Their presence would have markedly changed the outcome of Heth's initial clash with Wadsworth's division; they would certainly have prevented the disasters that befell Archer and Davis, and would probably have helped drive Doubleday and Buford off McPherson's and Seminary Ridges. As it was, Heth chose to retain Brockenbrough and Pettigrew in reserve as supports to the artillery line posted on Herr Ridge. Here their only contribution to the battle was a number of casualties lost to Union artillery fire directed at Pegram's cannons.[113]

By the time Heth advanced supports to help Archer and Davis, the fighting had already been decided on the front. Colonel R.M. Mayo of Brockenbrough's 47th Virginia related that his brigade was formed on the south side of the Chambersburg Pike and then was moved forward to support Archer. When Mayo arrived in the woods on the eastern slope of Herr Ridge, he heard the firing on Archer's front, but by the time he neared Willoughby Run, he saw Archer's men falling back, "having been outflanked and overpowered by numbers." When Brockenbrough saw that "the enemy's force outflanked us at least half a mile on each side," he withdrew 150 yards to the woods on Herr Ridge.[114]

When Brockenbrough retired, Pettigrew came up and formed farther to his right in the same woods, with his regiments in the following order from right to left: 52nd, 47th, 11th, and 26th North Carolina.[115] Both brigades sent forward skirmishers in sufficient quantity to persuade Meredith's units to fall back to Herbst Woods from the advanced position west of Willoughby Run that they had occupied following Archer's defeat. The rival skirmishers then began an intense competition that would continue for over two hours. During this time Stone's less protected front between Herbst Woods and the Chambersburg Pike suffered more severely from Confederate fire than the Iron Brigade troops in Herbst Woods to Stone's left.

Heth took advantage of the lull in fighting towards noon to reform Archer's and Davis' shattered commands and post them on the flanks of his new line on Herr Ridge. Davis' command, which Heth felt was too shattered to bring back into action, was "kept on the left of the road, in order that it might collect its stragglers," and probably formed between the Pike and the railroad, in the light woods west of Willoughby Run. Archer's brigade, now under the command of Colonel B.D. Fry of the 13th Alabama, was placed in the woods on Pettigrew's right, facing the Harman and Finnefrock farms, as well as the skirmishers of Gamble's 8th Illinois Cavalry, which had just been posted along the Fairfield Road. In the early afternoon Colonel William Marshall, commander of Pettigrew's right wing regiment, the 52nd North Carolina, formed his men in square in order to resist a threatened mounted attack by some of the Illinois cavalrymen. Marshall's adjutant later wrote proudly that "This maneuver was executed as promptly and accurately as if it had been upon its drill grounds."[116]

Arrival of Pender's Division

Pender's fresh division of 6500 men was in supporting distance of Heth's embattled front line during the height of the morning's fighting, but was not called upon to enter the conflict. Pender's men had been up early that morning, but did not break their camp on the north side of South Mountain, near Chambersburg, until 0800.[117] Even so, preparations to march were made in haste and with a certain tenseness that portended a battle at hand.[118] Colonel Perrin concluded "from the hurried and confused manner of our getting out of camp that the enemy was not far off."[119]

Perrin's South Carolina brigade was assigned to lead the division's column that morning, and the 12th South Carolina led Perrin's brigade.[120] Perrin did not bring all his troops with him, but left the 1st South Carolina Rifles behind at Cashtown to guard the division's wagon train.[121] Perrin was followed by Scales', Lane's, and Thomas' brigades, in that order. The division's artillery battalion under Major William Poague was left behind at Cashtown, and instead Pender's men were accompanied by Major David McIntosh's better armed battalion from the corps' reserve artillery.[122]

Pender's line of march took him along a mountain trail for a distance until he could reach the Chambersburg Pike, which one South Carolinian called "a fine road" that ran through much better country, with some pretty houses and orchards along the way. The regiments did not move along particularly quickly, but they were not allowed time to rest, either.[123]

After the column had been in motion for about an hour, the men began to hear the booming of Pegram's guns on Herr Ridge. Couriers began to hurry back and forth on the road, and the soldiers nervously began to prepare for battle by filling their canteens or throwing their playing cards by the side of the road.[124] At some point the column halted for awhile, then proceeded on over the Marsh Creek bridge. The sound of small arms could now be heard distinctively as Davis' and Archer's brigades moved to their attack 1½ miles closer to Gettysburg.[125]

It was thus about 0930 when the head of Perrin's command reached the first hill past Marsh Creek, the very spot from which Sergeant Levi Shafer had first fired on Heth's advancing troops just two hours earlier. Pender decided to stop here and form a battle line before advancing to the support of Heth's troops, who had just begun their attack from Herr Ridge, one mile to the east. Perrin's brigade was sent to the right down the Knoxlyn Road, with orders to leave "sufficient room between my left and the Gettysburg Road for General Scales' brigade, and to throw out skirmishers to cover my right" between Perrin's left and the Pike, while Lane and then Thomas continued the line in the fields north of the road on Knoxlyn Ridge. Altogether the line ran for about a mile, perpendicular to the road at its center.[126]

Once the division's line was formed and skirmishers were sent forward, Pender ordered an advance toward Herr Ridge. He was in no particular hurry and halted his line after he had advanced ½ mile through the fields. It was now about 1030, at the height of the morning's action, and the presence of Pender's troops on Herr Ridge might have had a significant effect on their course of the morning's combat. Indeed, had Pender and Heth been in better contact, Pender could have marched his troops in column directly to Herr Ridge instead of taking the time to deploy in a divisional battle line on Knoxlyn Ridge.

After a lengthy wait east of Knoxlyn Ridge—J.F.J. Caldwell of Perrin's 1st South Carolina felt it to be an hour—Pender's line resumed its advance toward Herr Ridge. All the while they heard intense musketry firing and the boom of Pegram's cannons, yet they did not see any enemy troops. Lieutenant Caldwell could only note that "These advances in line of battle are the most fatiguing exercise I had in the army. The perspiration poured from our bodies."[127]

Pender's line reached Herr Ridge at about 1100,[128] just as the tide was turning against Archer's command in Herbst Woods. Instead of being rushed forward into action, the division was halted in support of Pegram's guns. Pender's reasons for not being more aggressive will never be understood, since he was mortally wounded in action late on 2 July and so never could file a battle report. Perhaps he was hesitant to enter the fight without specific orders from Hill or Lee, and was honoring Lee's orders not to bring on a general engagement much more carefully than Heth was.

Because of the westward bend of Willoughby Run north of Herr Ridge, Pender posted only one brigade, Thomas', on the left of the road in support of Pegram's batteries posted there. Scales' brigade was put into line on Thomas' right, to the south of the road; both units were on the reverse slope of the ridge. Perrin's brigade was placed in Scales' front on the forward slope of the ridge, behind the woods where Brockenbrough and Pettigrew were stationed. Lane's brigade was shifted from the left center of the line to Perrin's right.[129] Though Pettigrew and Archer were in his front, Lane was concerned about the security of his right flank, particularly in view of the Union cavalry that he saw in the area. To guard against them, he positioned the 7th North Carolina as skirmishers on his right, at right angles to his main line.[130]

Midday Artillery Duel

While Pender was deploying his command behind Herr Ridge, Major David McIntosh brought up his artillery battalion and formed it where needed along the front. He found Pegram's battalion, which had already been in action for almost two hours, had deployed along the crest of the ridge with its center on the Pike. Eleven guns (six Napoleons and five rifles) of McGraw's, Zimmerman's and Brander's batteries were on the left of the Pike, and six guns (four Napoleons and two rifles) of Marye's and Johnson's batteries were on the right of the road.[131] McIntosh placed 10 of his guns (six Napoleons and two rifles from Rice's and Wallace's batteries, plus the two Whitworth rifles from Hurt's battery) on Pegram's right along the ridge crest, and after a while sent six rifles from Johnson's and Hurt's batteries $\frac{5}{8}$ mile to the right to support Pettigrew's and Archer's brigades in the first line. These six guns formed on what McIntosh termed a "commanding hill" near the Fairfield Road; they were actually posted on the edge of a woods ¼ mile west of the Harman farm.[132]

The concentration of Confederate artillery—some 33 guns in all—caused considerable discomfort to the Union lines arrayed just over ½ mile to the east. They conducted a slow shelling of the Union lines throughout the midday lull, and increased their fire whenever they saw Union units moving or fresh batteries coming up. McIntosh directed his longer range Whitworths "to shell the woods on the right of the town," probably the woods on Seminary Ridge north of Chambersburg Pike where Cutler's brigade had reformed. The six guns moved to the right of the line were not actually engaged, but Pegram managed to create an effective flanking fire from the left by moving Brander's battery forward to a hill ¼ mile north of the Bender farm house. Though Brander's unit was in an exposed position here and was supported by only a few skirmishers from Davis' brigade, he succeeded at enfilading Stone's regiments posted north of Herbst Woods, and forced them to realign in order to seek shelter from his fire. During this stage of the fight, or slightly earlier, Lieutenant John Morris, ordnance officer for Pegram's battalion, was mortally wounded "while riding in rear of our guns across the line of fire."[133]

Stone's 149th Pennsylvania suffered particularly heavily from this artillery barrage. Shells came in so accurately that some of the men at first thought they were being mistakenly hit by their own cannons. One shell that struck in the midst of Company B killed 3 men and wounded 5 more, 2 mortally. John Bessler was hit, and remembered "how one of the wounded came hopping down along the line on hands and feet crying out, 'I am killed, I am killed,' followed by the unfeeling utterance of Colonel Dwight, 'The hell you are killed, go back to your place'—and how the poor fellow stretched himself on the opposite bank and died." One soldier in Company G, probably James Logan, was struck by a solid shot that took off his head and left blood spurting all over. A shell struck in Company A and instantly killed Captain Alfred Sofield along with Private Edwin Dimmick and Corporal Nathan Wilcox; Sofield was literally cut in two, "leaving his heels in contact with his head."[134]

Doubleday had a great deal of difficulty trying to counter such effective and concentrated Confederate artillery fire. He did not have enough guns or a satisfactory position from which to reply to the enemy, and experienced difficulty trying to concentrate even a few batteries to meet the Confederate fire. As already noted, Calef had done a good job against Pegram's guns during the opening of the fight, but he had to withdraw at around 1000 because of heavy pressure from Heth's infantry. He was soon replaced at the Chambersburg Pike by Hall's battery, which lost heavily to Confederate infantry and artillery fire before it was forced to withdraw at the height of Davis' attack after only half an hour's combat. As we have seen, Hall had only three usable guns when he withdrew to Cemetery Hill, and Calef needed to resupply his ammunition before he could reenter the fight. As a result, there were no Union guns in action along Doubleday's front for about half an hour, from 1100 to 1130, except possibly one of Calef's guns that was brought into action at the middle railroad cut. This forced the Union infantry to seek whatever shelter they could find behind woods or terrain features after they reformed their lines following the defeat of Davis and Archer.

Doubleday was pleased to see the remaining four batteries of the I Corps artillery arrive sometime after 1100, but was disappointed to find that their commander, Colonel Charles Wainwright, was not in a very cooperative mood. Soon after Wainwright arrived, one of Doubleday's staff officers rode up to him on Seminary Ridge and requested that a battery be posted on McPherson's Ridge, if possible. The colonel directed Captain Gilbert H. Reynolds to prepare to move his New York battery forward, and rode out himself to inspect the position. When Wainwright found that the battery would be without support in an exposed position, he exercised his discretion and recalled Reynolds before he reached the front lines.[135] Reynolds, who had left his caissons behind Seminary Ridge, was perhaps halted on the ridge near the Schmucker house.[136]

A short while later General Wadsworth requested Wainwright to send a battery to occupy the position held earlier in the fight by Calef and Hall. Once again, Wainwright declined to respond, claiming that it was not a safe position because there was no infantry in place to protect its right flank there.[137] The only one of Wainwright's fresh batteries that was even slightly engaged by noon was Cooper's, which had been deployed on the left of the corps line with Biddle's brigade. Cooper fired about 25 rounds at one Confederate battery in his front, and when that quit firing he shifted his attention to another posted farther to his right.[138]

Doubleday and Wadsworth must have been exasperated with Wainwright by now, though they did not express themselves openly in their battle reports.[139] Wainwright's private journals, however, though, were more blunt. He recorded that Wadsworth "was much provoked at my not allowing Hall to bring his battery back at once." When Wadsworth tried to send Calef's horse battery forward to its former position on the Chambersburg Pike, Calef refused "on the ground that it was not a proper place for a battery." Wadsworth angrily ordered Calef to be sent to the rear in arrest, and then sent four of the horse battery's guns forward.[140] It is not clear if Calef actually left his command at this time; he states in his battle report that "the left and center sections of my battery were then ordered up again by General Wadsworth to reoccupy the ground just abandoned by Captain Hall."[141]

Calef's four guns, which had just replenished their ammunition near the Seminary, moved forward "under a heavy fire of musketry." Roder's right section of the battery was perhaps left behind because one of its guns may still have been in position near the eastern end of the middle railroad cut. Calef's description of this advance by his command is evocative enough to be quoted in full: "It would be impossible to forget the appearance of that field. The ridge we were to occupy was the one my guns had so peacefully peeped over the afternoon before. Now how changed was my camping ground, over which the men from Wisconsin and New York had charged Davis' brigade. Crossing the Cashtown Pike, the guns in 'column of pieces' threaded their way through the dead and dying and came into battery on the crest. It was one of those momentous lulls in the storm when scarcely a shot could be heard, and it seemed as though both sides had retired to their corner, awaiting the call of 'time.' The field, however, presented a true battle picture, such as one sees occasionally portrayed on canvas, but which, seen in all the horrors of reality, can never be effaced from memory. Here was one gun of Hall's with the horses all lying dead in harness. Another unlimbered and pointing toward our own line, left in that position by the cannoneers, who lay dead or dying beside it. Still another with the cannoneers making Herculean efforts to get it off the field...the wounded begged us not to drive over them, and I cautioned my men to drive carefully."[142]

Calef's men were greeted by a shower of enemy bullets when they reached the crest of McPherson's Ridge, and Calef was astounded to find his battery "without supports of any kind and not a skirmisher between the guns and the enemy." Wadsworth's infantry units were still reforming to the rear on Seminary Ridge,[143] but eventually infantry support was sent forward in the form of Dawes' 6th Wisconsin, which was soon afterwards joined by the 14th Brooklyn. Dawes advanced carefully to the eastern crest of McPherson's Ridge, and on the way lost a number of men to enemy artillery fire.[144] He then moved up to Calef's position on the ridge's western crest, where he met fire from "a heavy line of rebel skirmishers, upon whom we opened fire, and drove them into Willoughby Run." By now Dawes' men had attracted the attention of the Confederate artillery, and enemy projectiles came flying so thick and fast that the unit had to lie upon the ground under the brow of the ridge for protection.[145]

Despite Dawes' help, Calef still had to endure heavy enemy musketry fire, and lost a number of men to Confederate minié balls. He also had to endure fire from more numerous enemy cannons, whose fire became even more destructive about 15 minutes later when Brander's battery shifted farther to the Union right and began to enfilade his position. Calef held his line as long as he could, but the Confederate crossfire soon forced him to withdraw about 400 yards to the southeast, where the corner of Herbst Woods offered a shield against the Confederate cannons on central and southern Herr Ridge.[146] During the height of the fighting, Calef was surprised to see some of his horses calmly munching their oats. It seems that Hall's battery had left a quantity of oats on this line earlier in the day. Some of Calef's men fed these to their horses, "who ate them with as much relish and as little concern as though they were at the picket-rope, merely raising their heads if a shell burst near, some of them being killed while munching their grain."[147] During this part of the engagement, Calef lost 12 men wounded, and 13 horses killed.[148]

Calef's battery was having such a tough time that Buford insistently requested Doubleday to have it relieved. Wainwright, who had just completed his tour of the corps' line, rode up to Doubleday as the latter was conferring with Buford in front of the Seminary. It was at this time that Wainwright learned how annoyed Wadsworth was at him for not recalling Hall's battery, as already noted. Wainwright agreed to send Gilbert Reynolds' battery to support Calef's, on condition that "the Battery might not be required to report to General Wadsworth." Doubleday granted the request, on condition that Wainright accompany Reynolds' battery himself.[149]

Wainwright was anxious about this movement, since Calef's position appeared to be in an "ugly place." Reynolds' arrival in support of Calef's four guns only brought on an increase in enemy fire. Reynolds scarcely had enough time to deploy his first section when the Confederates "in addition to the galling fire in front" opened up an enfilading fire on the right, which completely swept the position. Reynolds attempted to steady his men, only to be struck in the left eye and side by a case shot. He for a time gallantly refused to leave the field, but was soon persuaded to do so. Wainwright himself almost lost his left leg to an enemy shot that went through his pantleg and grazed his ankle but did not break his boot. Wainwright soon found it necessary to order the two batteries to withdraw to the left so they could at least secure some shelter from Hill's guns on Herr Ridge. Wainwright was chagrined that Calef's battery managed to pull out quicker than Reynolds, though "it could not be expected that the crack battery of the army should have been outdone." Calef withdrew to "a position nearly on a line with my former one, but better covered by a cover of woods from the batteries in front." Lieutenant George Breck, who succeeded Reynolds, withdrew some 500 yards to the southeast and formed facing north, directly behind the broadest part of Herbst Woods.[150]

Wainwright still had two fresh batteries in reserve south of the Seminary (Stewart's and Stevens'), but chose not to deploy them, probably because of the intensity of Confederate fire that had ravaged Calef's, Hall's, and Reynolds' batteries. Wadsworth, however, did not hesitate to bring forward additional infantry support on the right. Towards noon he directed Cutler to advance his regiments from the woods on northern Seminary Ridge where they had reformed and move to the support of the artillery posted one half mile to the west.[151]

Cutler's regiments, which had lost half their strength in the morning's engagement, apparently did not advance in unison. Surviving accounts state that the 56th Pennsylvania and 76th New York marched westward along the railroad grading for a short distance before heading north along the western edge of the woods in which they had reformed. The 95th New York apparently followed along, and the three units formed facing west on the ridge where they had first met Davis' brigade three hours earlier. The 147th New York, ever independent minded, moved forward by a different route and formed on the right of the brigade line, next to the 56th Pennsylvania.'"[152] The 14th Brooklyn apparently formed in a second line, before it was sent forward and to the left to help the 6th Wisconsin support Calef's battery.[153]

Cutler had to order his men to lie down so as not to become targets for the Confederate artillery, since the ridge on which he was posted offered no natural protection. He had been in this position from 30 to 45 minutes when he saw Confederate troops coming up on the right, and shifted to meet them, as will be discussed in the next chapter.[154]

Arrival of Howard and XI Corps

While Doubleday was waging his unequal battle with the Confederate artillery on Herr Ridge, still more Union reinforcements arrived in the form of Major General Oliver O. Howard's XI Corps. Howard had been at Reynolds' headquarters at the Moritz Tavern until almost 2300 the previous night, and had to leave for his camps near Emmitsburg without receiving his marching orders for 1 July. He retired to a comfortable bed at St. Mary's College, but enjoyed only an hour's sleep before he was awakened by an orderly with orders from Meade's headquarters. Though the orders were addressed to Reynolds as wing commander, Howard opened and read them, and noted that they directed the I Corps to move to Gettysburg and the XI Corps to move to supporting distance of Gettysburg. Howard then added a note and sent the orders on to Reynolds.[155]

Howard was up at dawn, but could not begin moving his troops until he received direct orders from Reynolds, his immediate superior. Since he knew from Meade's message what his corps' goal for the day would be, he took the initiative for preplanning his line of march. He anticipated that I Corps would occupy the direct road from Emmitsburg to Gettysburg for a considerable time as it advanced, so he assigned just one of his own divisions (Barlow's, plus Wilkeson's battery) to march on that road. The corps' other two divisions and four remaining batteries would take the side road through Horner's Mill and cross over to the Taneytown-Gettysburg Road, where their advance would be unimpeded.[156] Howard outlined his line of march, and the reasons for it, in a letter he sent to Reynolds at 0600. In the same note he stated that he would encamp "near J. Wintz's (Wentz's) place, near the crossroads about 2 miles this side of Gettysburg" unless Reynolds desired otherwise.[157]

Howard at length received his orders from Reynolds at 0800, and had his troops moving towards Gettysburg by 0830. Once his troops were in motion, he rode on ahead with his staff and a detachment of his cavalry headquarters escort. He rode quickly, keeping to the fields along the road in order to avoid all the congestion caused by the I Corps and trains on the highway.

At about 1030, when he was about two miles short of Gettysburg, Howard met one of Reynold's staff officers bringing him instructions. The officer told him about the beginning of the battle, and told him that Reynolds wanted him to "come quick up to Gettysburg." Howard did not quite understand these instructions, since the orders he had received earlier in the day from Meade via Reynolds directed him to move in supporting distance of the I Corps at Gettysburg—an interval that he had judged to be four or five miles "when neither corps was in action." For this reason Howard asked the aide to state specifically "where the general wished to place me," to which the aide replied, "Stop anywhere about here, according to your judgement, at present." The location was the Sherfy Peach Orchard on the Emmitsburg Road.[158]

Howard was still concerned about where he should place his troops, and sent Captain Daniel Hall, and possibly another staff officer or two, "to find Reynolds and bring me word that I might go to him." Meanwhile, he decided to scout the terrain south of town, "as was my habit when coming to a new field...with the view of obtaining the best locations in that vicinity for our troops." He first visited a section of southern Seminary Ridge, and then turned eastward to Cemetery Ridge. His tour then took him a mile northward to Cemetery Hill, where he was struck by the broad view "which embraced the town, the Seminary, the college, and all the undulating valley of open country spread out between the ridges." Offhandedly he remarked to his adjutant general, Colonel T.A. Meysenberg, "This seems to be a good position," and Meysenberg replied, "It is the only position, general."[159]

The conversation just cited may or may not be apocryphal. Howard had much at stake after the battle, and desperately wanted to prove that it was he, not Buford, Reynolds or Doubleday, who saw Cemetery Hill as the key to the field. He certainly was the first high ranking Union officer to actually set foot on Cemetery Hill, though all the other Union generals on the field had probably noted its location and strength. However, Howard had no reason to expect at the time that there would be occasion for any fighting at that location.

Howard's action in riding to Cemetery Hill, though, seems a bit odd in view of his expressed concern "to find General Reynolds, in order to report to him in person."[160] Only an hour earlier Reynolds had experienced no difficulty in locating Buford by sending staff officers forward and then riding to the sound of the guns. Howard, on the other hand, did not push forward himself, but instead went riding about the countryside, so making it more difficult for his staff officers to locate him once they established contact with Reynolds. His failure to establish direct personal contact with I Corps might have affected the course of the battle much more severely had Heth and Pender renewed the fighting immediately after the repulse of Davis and Archer.

From Cemetery Hill Howard rode forward into Gettysburg; it is uncertain whether he was trying to find Reynolds or was still reconnoitering. Just below the Cemetery he ran into his aide, Captain Daniel Hall, whom he had sent to find Reynolds when he had reached the Peach Orchard about half an hour earlier. Hall reported that he had found Reynolds and told him the XI Corps was coming up: "In reply he told me to inform you that he had encountered the enemy in force, and to direct you to bring your corps forward as rapidly as possible to the assistance of the first." Howard's mission was now much clearer than before: he was to bring his troops all the way up to Gettysburg instead of stopping at the Sherfy Peach Orchard. He sent an aide to convey this order to Schurz and Barlow, and continued his ride into Gettysburg.[161]

Strange to say, Howard did not ride out to Seminary Ridge to discuss with Reynolds in person where he ought to deploy the XI Corps when it arrived, but he instead decided to stop in town to try to find a tall building from which he might observe the field and the fighting. After trying in vain to gain access to the Adams County Court House and its belfry, located at the southwest corner of Middle and Baltimore Streets, a citizen of the town named Daniel Skelly called his attention to the observatory on the Fahnestock building across the street. Howard climbed to the observatory and was delighted at the prospect, and began comparing the routes of the roads with those on his maps. He also used his field glasses to study the battle, and took particular note of a large body of Buford's cavalry drawn up between the town and Seminary. He was also pleased to note that "Confederate prisoners were just then being sent to the rear in large groups from the Seminary Ridge down the street past my post of observation."[162]

Howard had not been on the roof of the Fahnestock building long when he saw Sergeant George Guinn (Quinn) of Cole's Maryland Cavalry ride up the street, stop, salute him, and call out "General Reynolds is wounded, sir." Howard responded to him, "I am very sorry; I hope he will be able to keep to the field." It is indeed odd that Howard did not ride out to the I Corps line at that point. If Reynolds were indeed incapacitated, Howard would now be the senior officer on the field, in charge of his own XI Corps as well as I Corps. Instead, he remained where he was until a short while later, when Captain Hall stood in the street below and called out, "General Reynolds is dead, and you are the senior officer on the field." Only then did Howard realize the situation and the weight of his responsibility. He judged the time to be 1130—a full hour after Reynolds had been killed.[163] A short while later Major Charles H. Howard arrived with the same message Hall had brought. Both Hall and Howard had been sent by Doubleday to ensure that the news about Reynolds would reach Howard.

Howard admitted in his autobiography that his heart was heavy at the grave situation. In view of Meade's orders for the day, he did not feel authorized to withdraw any of the troops on the field; he instead stated, "God helping us, we will stay here till the army comes." He did not hesitate to take over Reynolds' role as wing commander, and sent Captain Hall of his staff to tell Schurz to take over the XI Corps and hurry forward. Howard also sent Captain Edward P. Pearson with orders for Barlow to hurry forward on the Emmitsburg Road. Other couriers were sent to order Sickles to bring the III Corps up from Gettysburg, and to urge Slocum to come up from Two Taverns on the Baltimore Pike.[164]

For some reason Howard did not attempt to establish contact with Doubleday, but instead rode back to Cemetery Hill in order to set up his headquarters there near the cemetery.[165] In Howard's defense, the general situation and intermittent artillery fire west of town indicated that Doubleday's line was in no immediate danger. Nevertheless, Howard should have made much more of an effort to get in touch with Doubleday in order to get a better appraisal of the entire situation. As things developed, it was Doubleday who initiated contact with Howard. Shortly before noon he sent a messenger to inform Howard that "his left was safe and pushing the enemy back," but his right was hard pressed.[166] At about the same time General Wadsworth sent a dispatch reporting that "the forces before him were apparently not very strong, and that he thought, although he had no clear evidence of it, that the enemy was making a movement to his right."[167] It was not until about 1400 that Howard would find time to go out and meet with Doubleday personally.[168]

The first XI Corps unit to arrive was Schurz's 3rd Division, now under the command of General Alexander Schimmelfennig. Schurz's men had spent the previous night encamped on the grounds of St. Joseph's College (a young ladies' Catholic school) in Emmitsburg. The college's Lady Superior had hosted the troops very graciously, and Schurz was pleased to note in his memoirs that "the conduct of my troops camped around the institution was exemplary." He had received a personal tour of the school that evening under the guidance of the college's chaplain, Father Borlando, and one of his officers had even been permitted to play on the chapel organ, "which he did to the edification of all who heard him."[169]

Major General Carl Schurz slept peacefully that night until he was awakened at daybreak by a marching order from Howard directing him to move towards Gettysburg. Schurz and his officers had no idea a battle was pending; all they were told from various sources was that the I Corps was ahead of them, and that there were "some rebel troops moving towards Gettysburg."[170]

After breaking camp,[171] Schurz headed north for the Gettysburg Road until about ½ mile past the Moritz Tavern, where he reached the crossroad that ran to Horner's Mills; his orders were to cross over to the road from Taneytown to Gettysburg in order to avoid all the congestion on the Emmitsburg Road. He did not have all of his 3100 man division with him, since most of the 58th New York of Krzyzanowski's brigade had been left behind at Emmitsburg. During the night of 30 June/1 July Captain Emil Koenig had been directed to take 100 men of the 58th and make a reconnaissance towards Creager-stown to investigate a report of rebel cavalry being seen there. Koenig marched about five miles but saw no signs of the enemy, so he permitted his men to stop and get some sleep. They had not rested long when orders arrived to return quickly to camp, since the corps had already departed for Gettysburg. He reached the now deserted camp at 0900, and soon linked up with a detachment of pickets from his regiment who had also been left behind. When Koenig pushed on, he was ordered to slow down and help guard the corps' wagons. He stayed with them until his column was within about four miles of the town, when the sound of heavy cannonading persuaded him to leave the wagons and rush to the front. He reached Gettysburg at about 1530 and "after some delay in finding the Corps," rejoined his brigade on Cemetery Hill. As a result only two companies of the 58th marched out with their division in the day's battle.[172]

Schurz's column passed Horner's Mills at 1030 and then received orders from Howard to come forward as quickly as possible because the I Corps "was engaged with the enemy in the neighborhood of Gettys-burg." This news came as a surprise, "for we did not hear the slightest indication of artillery firing from that direction." Schurz ordered his men to double quick, and then rode on ahead to meet with Howard.[173] The troops hurried on as best they could over rough roads that were muddied by a heavy shower. Private Bernard Domschke of the 26th Wisconsin called this "the most difficult and exhausting march" he made in the war.[174]

As Schurz rode on ahead of his troops, he passed in the road civilian fugitives of all ages and sizes who seemed to be in great terror. He particularly remembered one middle aged woman who was leading a small child and carrying a large bundle on her back. She tried to stop the general and cried out, "Hard times at Gettysburg! They are shooting and killing! What will become of us?" When Schurz reached Gettysburg and heard nothing beyond occasional musketry and cannon fire, he judged the fight to be only a "small affair."[175]

Schurz reached Cemetery Hill between 1130 and noon, and found Howard there just as he was setting up his headquarters. To the front he saw Doubleday's troops rearranging their lines on McPherson's Ridge. A short while later he watched Reynolds' body being somberly carried southward on Emmitsburg Road by his staff. Messages from Doubleday and Wadsworth expressed concern for the I Corps' right flank, so Howard directed Schurz to take his division and Barlow's when it came up and form to support Doubleday's right.[176]

Schurz's troops began to arrive between 1200 and 1230.[177] Since the weather was sultry, the men were "streaming with perspiration and panting for breath" after marching several miles at a rapid pace. Because of the speed of the march, the division's regiments had large intervals between them and did not arrive all at once.[178] The 45th New York of the first brigade arrived first, and was directed to march through the town on Washington Street. Behind it came Dilger's Ohio battery, the only artillery with the division. Dilger's men had not gotten off to a very good start that day because someone had neglected to issue them their marching orders, and they were not aware the corps was moving out until they heard nearby infantry buglers giving the call to pack up.[179] The rest of the first brigade came up after Dilger, and then Colonel Wladimir Krzyzanowski's second brigade.

After the Third Division was sent forward through town, Schurz awaited the rest of the corps at the intersection of the Taneytown and Emmitsburg Roads. The next troops to arrive were Barlow's 1st Division. As already noted Barlow had a shorter and more direct route to travel to Gettysburg (11 miles versus 13 by Schurz), but his advance had been delayed by all the I Corps troops and wagons in front of him. As a result his troops did not begin reaching the Cemetery Hill area until half an hour after the third division (about 1300).[180] Barlow had one battery with him. the six Napoleons of Wilkeson's Battery G 4th United States. Wilkeson had directed his men to advance their horses at a trot the final two miles, and must have arrived near the head of the division.[181]

Barlow's command left almost ¼ of its strength behind in Maryland for various reasons and reached the field with only about 2200 men.[182] A large detachment of 100 men and 4 officers of the 75th Ohio were left behind because they had been sent to scout the Greencastle Road from Emmitsburg and did not return before the Corps marched out.[183] In addition, the entire 41st New York of Von Gilsa's brigade was left behind when the corps left camp. At 0200 on 1 July Captain Clemens Knipschild of Company A of the 41st had been directed to take 200 men and arrest all the farmers and civilians he found on the roads near Emmitsburg; the purpose of this was probably to prevent news of the army's movements from being conveyed by civilians to the enemy. Because Knipschild had not returned by the time the corps left camp, the remainder of the 41st was ordered to stay in camp and wait for it. The entire regiment was then to proceed to Gettysburg as guards for an ammunition train. Lieutenant Colonel Detleo Von Einsiedel, commander of the 41st, waited in vain most of the day for Knipschild's detachment to return. When it did not do so, he left for Gettysburg late in the afternoon with 14 officers, 187 men, and 17 musicians, and arrived after dark.[184]

After Barlow's men were sent northwards through Gettysburg, the next XI Corps units to arrive were the remaining three batteries of the corps artillery. They had been traveling with Von Steinwehr's division, which was trailing Schurz's on the Taneytown Road. When the batteries were about five miles from Gettysburg, they had been ordered to hurry forward, so they broke into a trot and pulled ahead of von Steinwehr's infantry. Captain William Wheeler of the 13th New York Battery reported that he proceeded so quickly that his unit lost a large amount of forage "from the roughness of the road." In addition, two of his caissons broke down as he passed through Gettysburg.[185] Heckman's and Wiedrich's batteries were detained on Cemetery Hill when they came up, in order to serve as reserves.[186]

The last XI Corps division to reach the field was Von Steinwehr's 2nd Division, which had followed Schurz's division on the march via Horner's Mills to the Taneytown Road. They received orders to hasten their march when they were about five miles from Gettysburg, and arrived tired and thirsty. Colonel Orland Smith, commander of the 2nd Brigade, noted that many of his men were weary from marching due to their previous inactivity in camp, and reported that the shoes of some were worn out, "thus leaving many men to march barefooted sometimes over very rough roads."[187]

Von Steinwehr's men did not begin to arrive in the Cemetery Hill area until 1400. They were then ordered by General Howard and Schurz to halt on Cemetery Hill to serve as a general reserve. Von Steinwehr placed Colonel Charles Coster's 1st Brigade on the northeast end of the hill, in support of Weidrich's battery, while Colonel Orland Smith's 2nd Brigade was initially formed "in line of battle in battalions in mass in rear of Cemetery Hill."[188] The decision to hold Von Steinwehr in reserve on Cemetery Hill was a significant one, since it established fresh troops at a rallying point that would prove critical later in the afternoon.

CHAPTER VI

The Fight on Oak Hill

The arrival of the XI Corps gave Howard and Doubleday what appeared to be a numerical majority, about 21,000 to about 15,000 in Heth's and Pender's Divisions with their supporting artillery. Indeed, had additional Confederate troops not been headed for the battle area, it is highly likely that Lee would have recalled Heth and Pender early in the afternoon, being satisfied with Heth's report that "The enemy had now been felt and found to be in heavy force in and around Gettysburg."[1] The brief morning engagement near Gettysburg on 1 July would have been recorded as a quick and clear Union victory, and the decisive battle of the campaign would probably have been fought somewhere between Cashtown and Frederick.

The battle, however, was already taking a different course because of the approach of two of Ewell's divisions from the north. As noted in Chapter I, Lee had sent orders on 29 June to recall Ewell's lead divisions from their advanced positions at Carlisle and near Harrisburg. Rodes' division, accompanied by Ewell, marched from Carlisle to Heidlersburg on the 30th, and Early marched from the direction of Harrisburg to within three miles of Heidlersburg, which is located 10 miles northeast of Gettysburg on the Harrisburg Road.[2]

After reaching Heidlersburg, Ewell received orders from Lee "to proceed to Cashtown or Gettysburg, as circumstances might dictate." A message also arrived from Hill saying that he was at Cashtown.[3] After dark Ewell had a conference to discuss his plans for the next day with Rodes, Early (who had ridden in from his camp three miles away on the road to Berlin), and Major General Isaac Trimble, who was accompanying Ewell in an advisory capacity since he had not yet been reassigned to command after recovering from a bad wound he had received the previous summer at the battle of Groveton.

In an account written after the war, Trimble stated that Ewell told the assembled officers about Lee's orders and a fresh report that the Federal XI Corps had arrived at Gettysburg. This situation made him undecided about what to do under Lee's order, "which was read over repeatedly and variously commented on, General E. especially commenting in severe terms on its ambiguity with reference to Cashtown or Gettysburg as the objective point." Trimble expressed the opinion, based on his conversation with Lee a few days earlier, that Ewell should march straight on Gettysburg, since he understood Lee's objective was "to attack the advance of the enemy, wherever found, with a superior force and turn it back in confusion." When no decision was reached that night, Trimble the next morning urged Ewell to send a messenger to Lee for instructions, and in the meanwhile march to Middletown, which was indirectly on the route to both Cashtown and Gettysburg.[4]

Trimble's account is an interesting one, and if true, would give him a key role in setting the stage for Ewell's critical and timely arrival on the Gettysburg battlefield on 1 July. However, his presentation of the situation is not substantiated by any of the other principals who were present at Ewell's conference on the evening of 30 June. Neither Early, Rodes nor Ewell mentioned any indecision or lengthy discussion of the import of Lee's command, and Early specifically stated that "the object was to concentrate the corps at or near Cashtown."[5] Since Trimble wrote his account after the war, it would seem that he either did not remember the events clearly, or he wished to exaggerate his role in contributing to the success of the first day's battle.

Ewell, however, did employ some latitude in arranging his line of march for 1 July. He directed Rodes to take the main road westward from Heidlersburg to Cashtown, which passed through Middletown (Biglersville) and Arendtsville and reached South Mountain at the northern branch of the Cashtown Gap. Early was not ordered to follow Rodes, but was directed to swing southward to Hunterstown and then march westward to Cashtown via the road through Mummasburg.[6] Ewell's purpose in assigning Early a different route was to allow him to avoid the possibility of being delayed by Rodes' troops, which might well have occurred had both divisions used the same route. As a result, Early would be marching westward on a route roughly parallel to, and three miles south of, that being used by Rodes. Because he had to travel southward in order to pick up the road through Mummasburg, Early's westward progress would be proceeding an hour or two behind Rodes'. This timing and placement would have a critical effect on the day's battle, as will soon be seen.

Arrival of Rodes' Division

Rodes had his troops on the march by sunrise on 1 July.[7] Ewell, who was accompanying the rear of Rodes' column, had not quite reached Middletown when he received notice from Hill sometime before 0900 that the Third Corps was advancing on Gettysburg. Once again, Ewell used his initiative, and ordered Rodes to turn his march towards Gettysburg once he reached Middletown. He also ordered Early to march directly to Gettysburg on the Heidlersburg (Harrisburg) Road.[8] His decision was based on the discretion Lee offered him "to proceed to Cashtown or Gettysburg, as circumstances might dictate." Also, if he were eager for a fight, he would be more likely to find one at the moment at Gettysburg than at Cashtown.

Ewell sent a staff officer, Major G. Campbell Brown, to inform Lee of his change of direction,[9] and continued on with Rodes' division. The column proceeded south on the Carlisle (Newville) Road for just over an hour until, about four miles from Gettysburg, the "sound of a sharp cannonade" was heard. Rodes at once made preparation for battle by deploying the regiments of his lead brigade (Iverson's) in line; the others remained in column on the road.[10]

By around 1100 Rodes' advance skirmishers made contact with Devin's cavalry vedettes posted on Keckler's Hill, about five miles north and a little west of Gettysburg. At this point Iverson sent out a force of sharpshooters under Captain Ben Robinson of the 5th North Carolina. Robinson's men pushed the Union vedettes back slowly down the Carlisle Pike until they reached Devin's main skirmish line at the Samuel Cobean farm. The increased Union resistance compelled Rodes to reinforce his skirmish line with Major Eugene Blackford's sharpshooters from O'Neal's 5th Alabama. Blackford reported that, "After receiving instructions from General Rodes to keep connected with those on my right, and feel for General Early's advance on the left, I moved steadily forward upon the town, driving in the cavalry vedettes, posted in the road and on commanding hills. About half a mile from the suburbs, a large force of cavalry was observed in line, with a heavy line of men dismounted as skirmishers. The former charged us twice, but were easily repulsed." After skirmishing with the cavalry for an hour, O'Neal saw a "cloud of skirmishes" advance as the XI Corps infantry began advancing into position north of Gettysburg, as will be discussed in Chapter VII.[11]

As Rodes drew nearer to Gettysburg, he heard more artillery fire, then infantry fire at about 1130. The general noted that all the fighting was taking place on the ridges west of town, to his right. Instead of proceeding directly southward into the town, he thought it would be better to swing to the right and advance down the high wooded ridge there (Keckler's Hill, the northern extension of Oak Hill) in order to strike the Union lines on the flank. He explained his thinking in his battle report by saying he thought he could "strike the force of the enemy with which General Hill's troops were engaged upon the flank, and that, besides moving under cover, whenever we struck the enemy we could engage him with the advantage in ground."[12]

Rodes' decision to march to Keckler's Hill was the first of several ill-advised moves he would make that day. Had he marched directly into Gettysburg, or even cut across the fields towards the rear of Doubleday's line near the Seminary, he might have reached the Union rear before Rowley's and Robinson's divisions came up, and certainly would have changed the course of the battle. More significantly, his move to Keckler's Hill greatly slowed down his advance, both by the height of the ridge there and the denseness of its woods. As a result, he was not ready to enter the battle until after noon, whereas he might have been ready for action an hour or more earlier had he stayed on the plain north of Gettysburg. There can be no doubt that the imposing heights of Oak Ridge/Keckler's Hill looked alluring to Rodes from the plain below. The position, though, would prove to be geographically awkward, even though it placed him (at least initially) in a perpendicular position to Doubleday's right.

Rodes advanced to the crest of Keckler's Ridge, and then moved southward, with Iverson's brigade still deployed in advance. The rest of the division followed in column. As the ridge widened out, Iverson was shifted to the right, and O'Neal was formed to his left, with Doles on O'Neal's left. The division proceeded south in this formation along the ridge for about a mile until it reached the crest of Oak Hill "whence the whole of that portion of the force opposing General Hill's troops could be seen." During his advance, Rodes' skirmishers engaged some vedettes of the 9th New York Cavalry, which were still picketing the Oak Hill area. Rodes noted that the enemy lines were about a half mile distant, and in order "to get at these troops properly...it was necessary to move the whole of my command by the right flank, and to change direction to the right."[13]

This decision was the second ill-advised command Rodes would issue this day. Due to the lay of the land and the woods on northern Seminary Ridge south of Oak Hill, Rodes was unable to see Cutler's brigade in its position in the woods just north of the eastern railroad cut. Instead, all he saw was the Union troops on McPherson's Ridge, approximately a mile southwest of Oak Hill. Had he seen Cutler's troops, he probably would have advanced against them at once and readily overwhelmed their battle depleted ranks. Even so, Rodes still had a golden opportunity to advance and crush the center of Doubleday's line, which was thrust forward at an awkward angle between Herbst Woods and the Chambersburg Pike (Stone's portion of the line). However, he decided he needed time to deploy all his troops first, and so forfeited the momentary advantage he had been offered.

While he shifted his infantry to the right and brought up Daniel's and Ramseur's brigades in his second line, Rodes brought forward two of Colonel Thomas H. Carter's batteries and posted them in front of the woods on the crest of Oak Hill, approximately 1/4 mile in advance of his first infantry line.[14] W.P. Carter's King William (VA) artillery had two Napoleons and two 10-lb Parrott guns, and Fry's Richmond "Orange" artillery was armed with two 3-inch rifles and two 10-lb Parrotts. These were the first pieces of Confederate divisional artillery to be deployed in the battle. They opened fire on the enemy sometime soon after 12 noon.[15]

The fire of Rodes' two batteries was particularly effective at achieving an enfilade fire on Calef's and then Reynolds' batteries posted near the Chambersburg Pike.[16] In addition, the opening of Carter's guns caused McIntosh and Pegram to increase their rate of fire from their position on Herr Ridge, so catching the Union guns in a wicked crossfire. As already noted, Reynolds' battery was particularly devastated and had to be repositioned behind Herbst Woods; Calef's battery was pulled back and then withdrawn to join Gamble's cavalry. Even Cooper's battery on Doubleday's left was also repositioned to fire north at the threat posed by Carter's guns.[17]

The fire of Carter's guns also forced a realignment of the Union infantry lines in Doubleday's center. The 6th Wisconsin and 14th Brooklyn, which had been supporting Calef's guns, were pulled back to the eastern railroad cut. Here they formed to support Stewart's battery of regular artillery, which was called up from its reserve position near the Seminary. Stewart formed with three of his guns on each side of the railroad cut through Seminary Ridge. Lieutenant Davidson commanded the left-half battery, which covered about half the space between the pike and the railroad near the Thompson house. The right-half battery extended from the railroad cut to the edge of the grove in which Cutler's brigade had reformed earlier. Stewart's men were glad to have good infantry support here, although one of the battery's wags commented that the infantry "were put there to shoot the recruits if they flinched." Corporal Packard took offense to the remark and retorted that the wag should "see that he himself behaved as well as the recruits."[18]

Stone's infantry, which were posted in the open ground between Herbst Woods and the Pike, suffered especially from the fire of Carter's guns. Stone had seen Carter advance and deploy, and had shifted his lines somewhat to meet the threat of an advance from that quarter—he bent the right wing of his right regiment, the 149th Pennsylvania, back along the line of the Pike at a 90 angle to its left wing. When Carter's guns began firing, Stone thought it best to deploy the entire 149th along the Pike, and ordered its men to seek shelter in a ditch along the south side of the road. This positioning, however, only made the 149th more vulnerable to a flanking fire from the Confederate guns on Herr Ridge, which increased their fire when they saw Stone's men begin moving.[19]

Colonel Langhorne Wister of the 150th Pennsylvania noted that "the range of the enemy's guns was so exact" that he had to move his unit to the shelter provided by the McPherson Barn. Just as the regiment began to withdraw, a Confederate shell exploded in the midst of Company C, killing four men and dangerously wounding several others.[20] Another shell felled seven members of Company B, 149th Pennsylvania, and yet another shot tore off the head of a private standing next to Francis B. Jones of Company G, 149th Pennsylvania.[21]

Before long, Colonel Stone thought up a clever way to try to deceive the enemy and draw the heavy Confederate fire away from the 149th. He sent an orderly to instruct Color Sergeant Henry G. Brehm of the 149th to advance his colors to a slight breastwork of rails that had been erected earlier by some of Buford's cavalrymen at a position some fifty yards north of the Pike and a little to the left front of the regiment. J.

M. Bassler of the 149th noted that, "In this position, our flags were plainly visible over the standing wheat, to the battery to the west of us, but the rail piles and the men lying behind them were hid from their view, and, evidently thinking that the regiment had changed front, they now directed their fire in that direction. Stone's ruse had succeeded."[22]

General Wadsworth was not about to let the heavy Confederate fire from Herr Ridge go unopposed, so he appealed again to Wainwright for some artillery support at the front. Wainwright responded by sending only two guns of Battery L, 1st New York (Gilbert Reynolds' battery, now under the command of Lieutenant George Breck) under Lieutenant B. W. Wilber. Wilber deployed between Herbst Woods and the McPherson farm buildings, which offered some protection against Carter's guns on Oak Hill. But his two 3-inch rifled pieces were no match for the massed Confederate firepower on Herr Ridge, and soon had to be withdrawn.[23]

Lieutenant Colonel Tom Carter's two batteries, however, did not carry out their fire unmolested. As the Union batteries on McPherson's Ridge realigned, they concentrated more and more of their fire on Carter's eight guns, which were exposed and open to view on the bare crest of the hill. Though the enemy's fire was slow and deliberate, W. P. Carter's battery soon lost four men killed outright and seven wounded, over 10% of its strength.[25] General Ewell personally witnessed the effectiveness of the Union fire when he came to Captain Carter's position. The body of horsemen may have caught the attention of an alert Union gunner. A shell struck Ewell's horse in the head, and several men were wounded nearby. Ewell was thrown from his horse, but was undaunted and mounted another at once.[26] One Union shell that overshot Carter's two batteries landed in the midst of Daniel's brigade. It nearly hit General Daniel, and killed or wounded nine of his men.[27]

Rodes stated in his battle report that he was particularly pleased that Carter's fire appeared to catch the enemy by surprise. He noted that the enemy at that moment "as far as I could see, had no troops facing me at all."[28] Apparently Rodes did not stop to think that the opening of his artillery before his infantry was fully formed served only to formally announce his presence to the enemy, so allowing Doubleday time to react before Rodes' infantry could attack.

Soon after Carter's guns started firing, Major Brown returned from Lee's headquarters with further instructions for Ewell. Brown, as we have already seen, had been sent from Middletown about 0900 to tell Lee that Ewell was heading his two divisions towards Gettysburg instead of Cashtown. Brown met Lee on the Chambersburg Pike a couple miles east of Cashtown, and conveyed his message as ordered. Lee, anxious about the location and safety of Stuart's command, asked Brown if he had any news of his missing cavalry, but the Major had none. "Lee then expressed approval of Ewell's line of march, but warned him in strong terms not to bring on a general engagement until the rest of the army could come up."[29] Ewell, however, felt the circumstances were forcing him to ignore his commander's wishes: "By the time this message reached me, General A.P. Hill had already been warmly engaged with a large body of the enemy in his front, and Carter's artillery battalion, of Rodes' division, had opened with fine effect on the flank of the same body, which was rapidly preparing to attack me...It was too late to avoid an engagement without abandoning the position already taken up, and I determined to push the attack vigorously."[30] In this way Lee had the battle thrust upon him by the aggressiveness of his subordinates, first by Heth and Hill, then by Rodes and Ewell.

Ewell's decision to fight contrary to Lee's orders was no doubt influenced heavily by the fact that he knew that Early's division was close by in ready and supporting distance of Rodes. After giving Rodes orders to pursue his attack, Ewell sent two of his staff officers, Captain Thomas T. Turner and Major Campbell Brown (who must have been tired after just riding to Lee's headquarters and back) to Early "to hurry to him and tell him to attack at once."[31]

Stuart and the Cavalry

Oddly enough, not long after Ewell received Campbell Brown's directive from Lee to try to find Stuart, Major Andrew R. Venable of Stuart's staff arrived with direct information on Stuart's location. It seems that Stuart, who had been encamped the previous night at Dover (30 miles northeast of Gettysburg), had sent Venable that morning with orders to locate Ewell. Stuart's instructions from Lee before crossing the Potomac had been to place himself on Ewell's flank, and Stuart was having difficulty doing so because he could not locate Ewell's troops where he expected them to be in the vicinity of Harrisburg. Since he understood that Early had just turned westward towards Shippensburg, he sent Venable in that direction to find him or Ewell. Ewell had little use for Stuart's officer, except to learn from him that he had seen no Federals between Dover and Gettysburg. The General simply told

Venable where to find Lee and sent him to the army commander for instructions.[32]

After sending Venable to locate Ewell, Stuart marched his weary command to Dillsburg and then to Carlisle, which he understood had recently been held by some of Ewell's men. He arrived at Carlisle the afternoon of 1 July, only to find that Rodes' division had left the town the previous morning and headed to the southwest. Stuart's men were low on rations, so he desired to make a levy on the town, but would not do so because he learned that Union militia was concealed in its buildings. He sent a message for the militia to surrender or be subject to a bombardment, and set up his artillery to do so. When the militia refused to surrender, he began his shelling and set fire to the large cavalry barracks there (which Ewell had deliberately not burned, on orders from Lee).[33]

Stuart let his weary men encamp near Carlisle, and during the night of 1-2 July received a dispatch from Lee ("in answer to one sent by Major Venable from Dover, on Early's trail") that "the army was at Gettysburg and had been engaged on this day with the enemy's advance." He then sent Hampton orders to march at once 10 miles towards Gettysburg early on the next day. Stuart himself set out for Gettysburg that night, and as his command came up formed it on the left of the army on the York and Heidlersburg Roads.[34]

It has often been discussed how differently the battle would have gone on 1 July if Stuart had crossed the Potomac with the army's infantry and headed north with Ewell's corps rather than conducting his ride around the Union army in order to meet Ewell's advance somewhere in central Pennsylvania. Had Stuart been with Ewell all the while, his patrols probably would have controlled all the roadways between Cashtown and York, perhaps as far south as Gettysburg and Hanover. This would have made Meade much more concerned about Lee's advance wing (Ewell) and would not have enabled Meade to receive such concise information about the location of Ewell's divisions on 28-30 June. As a result, Meade (given his concern for covering Philadelphia and Baltimore) would probably have shifted his advance more to the east, and the decisive battle of the campaign might have occurred on the line of York and Hanover rather than at Gettysburg.

Thus it is likely that there would have been no meeting engagement at Gettysburg had Stuart been with Ewell's advance, since the primary attention of both commanders would have focused more to the east. This is not to say, however, that Lee would have had had any more cavalry with him than he did accompanying Hill's and Longstreet's corps at Chambersburg. Stuart's presence with Ewell's advance would have permitted Ewell to employ Jenkins' command more on Rodes' front, in the direction of Gettysburg and Hanover, and these might have given Ewell more information as to Union movements in that sector.

Ewell did not make effective use of the cavalry he had. On 30 June he left most of Jenkins' cavalry behind near Harrisburg,[35] and only the 17th Virginia was used to screen Early's advance to Gettysburg.[36] Captain Bond's Company A of the 1st Maryland was put to better use. Bond, who had been stationed near Carlisle, was sent towards Gettysburg by Ewell on the afternoon of 30 June. Bond reached "the immediate vicinity of Gettysburg without encountering the enemy." Bond left Sergeant Hammond Dorsey behind with a picket of six men and returned to report to Ewell that there were "no enemy near." During the night Dorsey captured three Pennsylvania artillerymen "who, having been refused leave to go to their homes, had taken horses and slipped away, thinking they could return before daylight without being missed." These men, according to one historian, "gave General Ewell the first information he had of the whereabouts of Meade's army."[37] Bond's command or some of White's Comanches may have been the Confederate troopers encountered by some of Devin's vedettes early on 1 July.[38] It is unlikely that Rodes had any usable cavalry with him to scout the Union position or screen his advance. If he did, he might have been able to break through Devin's screen on the Carlisle Pike and then push into the town of Gettysburg late in the morning, before the XI Corps began to arrive.

Even with the absence of Stuart, Lee had sufficient cavalry available to screen his infantry in Chambersburg, if he had used it properly. Stuart took the army's three best cavalry brigades with him, but left Lee with four serviceable brigades—Albert Jenkins' Virginia brigade of about 1100 men, Beverly Robertson's North Carolina brigade of nearly 1000 men, Grumble Jones' Virginia brigade of about 1500 men (not counting White's Commanches, serving with Ewell), and John Imboden's command of cavalry, mounted infantry and artillery, about 2100 men.[39] Once Lee sent Jenkins (and White's Comanches) to Ewell, he still had three brigades available, but he used them to guard his rear rather than his front and flank.

Before crossing the Potomac, Lee stationed Robertson in Ashby's Gap and Jones in Snicker's Gap in Virginia's Blue Ridge, both with orders to screen the army and keep an eye on Hooker's army. Both carried out their screening function status satisfactorily, but neither proved particularly aggressive, and they failed to keep Lee properly informed when Hooker began crossing the Potomac on 24 June. Even so, Lee left the two brigades in Virginia long after the last of his infantry crossed the Potomac on 26 June, and did not even bring them north to cover the passes in South Mountain, a fact that surprised Hooker. Had he done so, they would have been able to observe Hooker's concentration at Frederick, and the decisive battle of the campaign might well have occurred near Emmitsburg. Imboden's command, on the other hand, was employed on the left flank of the army's advance on North Mountain in the direction of Mercersburg, and none if his men were used to scout eastward for the infantry gathered at Chambersburg. Lee did recall Imboden on 30 June, but the cavalryman did not advance quickly, and for this reason Lee had to leave Pickett's division behind to patrol the town until Imboden came up. That is the reason Pickett was not available for action on 2 July.[40]

These are the reasons why Hill had no cavalry to send with Heth's advance on 30 June or 1 July, and why Rodes did not have a cavalry screen with him when he advanced on Gettysburg from Middletown on the morning of 1 July. This Confederate shortcoming was all the more glaring in view of the effective way in which Hooker and Meade used their cavalry. In the absence of any mounted Confederate opposition, Buford (who was skilled and aggressive to begin with) was able to totally dominate the front on the Union left and play such a decisive role in the origin and early stages of the battle.

As previously noted, Rodes had encountered a few Union cavalrymen from the 9th New York during his advance over Keckler's Hill. They were driven steadily southwards towards Oak Hill by a force of about 150 sharpshooters under the command of Captain Benjamin Robinson.[41] Rodes' approach was reported to Buford and Doubleday by Lieutenant A.C. Robertson of the 9th New York, so the Union command was able to anticipate Rodes' arrival.[42] This is the principal reason why Robinson's division was not deployed on McPherson's Ridge when it arrived, but was held in reserve at the Seminary in order to await developments on northern Seminary Ridge.

When the fire from Carter's two batteries prematurely announced Rodes' arrival on the field, Doubleday at once began shifting troops to meet him. The first unit to be deployed on Rodes' front was Cutler's brigade, which formed the right of the I Corps line. At the time that Carter's guns opened fire, Cutler's brigade (less the 14th Brooklyn, which was supporting the batteries near the Chambersburg Pike along with the 6th Wisconsin) was deployed facing west of the northern branch of McPherson's Ridge. The fire from Carter's guns enfiladed Cutler's line so badly that Cutler was forced to reform so as "to face this dangerous battery."[43]

Cutler reported that he "changed front to right" in order to face the direction of Rodes' advance, but the details of his movement are not known.[44] Some sources argue that he pulled back to the woods or northern Seminary Ridge before turning to face north. Historian James McLean, though, interprets the evidence to show that Cutler swung his four regiments to the right and formed along an east-west fence line that roughly paralleled the Mummasburg Road. Initially only the two right regiments (147th New York and 56th Pennsylvania) were under the cover of the woods, while the two left regiments (76th New York and 95th New York) were not. A short while later, McLean suggests, Cutler refused his left regiments to the woods, with the result that his line formed a right angle along the north and west edge of the woods.[45]

After forming their new line, Cutler's men at once set to work constructing a slight breastwork made of rails and possibly some bales of hay.[46] They were even allowed to stack their arms, since no threat of a Confederate infantry attack seemed imminent![47]

After a short while, the Union batteries along the Chambersburg Pike were withdrawn, and Colonel Fowler rode back to fetch the 14th Brooklyn and reunite it with its brigade.[48] The 14th was placed in the woods on the left of the 95th New York. Apparently the 6th Wisconsin, which had been stationed with the 14th, followed the 14th to its new position. After reforming ranks, the 6th marched to the woods on the right of the 14th Brooklyn.[49]

Baxter Moves to the Right

Cutler would not have to face Rodes' division alone. Soon after Robinson's division arrived at the Seminary, Doubleday directed Robinson to send one of his brigades to meet the threat posed by Rodes.[50] Since Paul's brigade had already been posted and Baxter's brigade was still arriving, Robinson ordered Baxter to move up the ridge to his right. Baxter sent two of his regiments (11th Pennsylvania and 97th New York, both under command of Colonel Leonard Coulter of the 11th) ahead, with the remainder of his command to follow. When Robinson sent

Baxter forward, he directed Paul's command "to entrench the ridge on which it is situated."[51]

The 11th Pennsylvania and the 97th New York initially moved across the Chambersburg Pike to the line of the railroad bed, whereupon Baxter sent forward a skirmish line composed of companies A and F of the 97th New York, under the command of Captain Delos Hall of Company A. The two regiments moved along the easterly slope of Seminary Ridge, in Cutler's right rear, until they came near a strip of woods next to the Mummasburg Road. At this point, "a puff or two of smoke, and bullets" announced the presence of Confederate skirmishers of Iverson's 12th North Carolina at the far end of the strip of woods.[52] The 97th's skirmishers struck a Confederate detachment posted behind a stone wall and embankment near the Mummasburg Road, and initially drove them back.[53]

Meanwhile the main body of Coulter's command advanced and formed on the west ridge crest "at the northerly edge of a piece of woods on the westerly slope." Coulter placed the 97th New York on his right and the 11th Pennsylvania on the left, connecting with the 147th New York of Cutler's brigade. To Coulter's front was a meadow "covered with a rank growth of timothy." Before long, Hall's two companies of skirmishers fell back and rejoined the line of the 97th New York.[54] As they formed, Coutler's men were greeted by one of Devin's troopers who rode by and shouted, "There are no troops behind you! You stand alone between the Rebel army and your homes. Fight like hell!"[55] The Union trooper, however, was incorrect because he did not know that Baxter was bringing up the rest of his brigade to the right of Coulter's position.

While Baxter's remaining four regiments were coming up, Coulter advanced his two units a few yards into the meadow in his front in order to try to develop the Confederate position. Hall's two companies of the 97th were sent ahead as skirmishers, as before. They were directed to move forward to a high rail fence that ran parallel to Coulter's lines about 200 yards distant. Once again Confederate skirmishers were encountered, and several men fell casualty, including one man of Company F killed, before the fence was reached and held.[56]

At about the time that Hall's skirmishers achieved their objective, the 12th Massachusetts came up along the eastern slope of the ridge and proceeded up to the edge of the Mummasburg Road. The 12th's advance was resisted by a number of Confederate skirmishers, who "were handsomely disloged (sic) by Company K, Capt. Hazel, who, deployed his company, moved forward at a double quick, and drove them at the point of the bayonet." The rest of the regiment then came up and formed facing north at an angle to the Mummasburg Road.[57] Adjutant C.C. Wehrum of the 12th later claimed that it was his suggestion that persuaded Colonel Bates to move his right forward as the regiment formed. When Bates gave the order to advance, Wehrum called for the left and right regimental guards (guides), but the colonel laughingly said that they would not be needed "on this occasion." One of the regiment's first casualties was Lieutenant Charles G. Russell, from Boston, who was shot in the brain and killed in this, his first battle. Earlier in the day he had welcomed the coming battle as "an opportunity to show the men that I am no coward."[58]

When the 12th Massachusetts was formed at what was for now the extreme right flank of the I Corps, the 97th New York "flanked to the right" and moved along the east crest of the ridge to form in the left rear of the 12th. The line the 97th took was facing west behind a stone wall on the east of J.S. Forney's field, and was at roughly a right angle to the 12th Massachusetts on the right. At the same time Colonel Coulter moved his 11th Pennsylvania to the right and formed on Wheelock's left, continuing the 97th New York's line to the south. During this movement Colonel Wheelock once again recalled Hall's skirmishers to rejoin his command. Hall's withdrawal permitted the Confederate skirmishers who had just been driven back from the Mummasburg Road to the west, to return to their former position. Some even advanced into the first field south of the road, where they began a harassing fire on Baxter's line.[59]

When Baxter's remaining three regiments came up, they were formed along the Mummasburg Road to the right of the 12th Massachusetts. The 90th Pennsylvania came first, and formed along a stone wall that fronted the road. The 83rd New York came up next, and formed on the 90th's right; both units were exposed to Confederate artillery and infantry fire as they came up.[60] Last to arrive was the 88th Pennsylvania, which had loaded its guns when it left the Seminary area. During its march to the north some of the regiment's men began singing "John Brown's Body," and soon the whole regiment was joining in its familiar refrain. The unit reached the Mummasburg Road "after some preliminary skirmishing by the advance" and formed on the right of the 83rd New York, facing to the northeast. Major Benezet Faust then sent skirmishers into the woods north of the road "to ascertain what the rebs were about."[61]

Baxter's line, which was formed about 1300, was not a strong one by any means. His six under strength regiments, totaling some 1300 men, were bent back in a "U" shape with the 12th Massachusetts at the base; the left flank of the brigade swung to the south while its right flank ran southeast along the Mummasburg Road. Only one regiment, the 12th Massachusetts, directly faced the 8000 men of Rodes' division. In addition, Baxter's line had no artillery support, and its only infantry support was Cutler's battered brigade, which was itself unsupported. Lastly, there was a 400 yard gap between Baxter's right and the left wing of the XI Corps, which had just formed on the McLean farm in the plain east of Oak Hill.[62]

Doubleday might have been better advised not to post Baxter so far to the right; Baxter might have been more securely placed on Cutler's right, where the 11th Pennsylvania and 97th New York had initially deployed. General Robinson was aware of this problem once Baxter formed in his advanced position, and was attempting "to change front forward on his left battalion, and to close this interval" when Rodes began his attack.[63] In Doubleday's defense, he did receive assurance from Howard that Schimmelfennig's and Barlow's divisions were being sent to support Baxter's right.[64] It was beyond his control that this juncture never was carried out, and that Howard turned most of the promised troops to meet the threat posed by Early's arrival from the northeast. Lastly, there was actually not much that Doubleday could do to counter Rodes' timely arrival squarely on his flank.

Rodes had his infantry dispositions nearly completed by 1330.[65] His front line ran on an east-west course for about a full mile from the Carlisle Pike to the Mummasburg Road, with three brigades in front and two in reserve. Doles' Georgia brigade held the left of the line, astride the Newville Road in the plain north of Gettysburg; his action against the XI Corps will be described in the next chapter. O'Neal's Alabama brigade held the center of the line, from the foot of Oak Ridge to the wooded crest of the hill, and Iverson's North Carolina brigade held to the right of the line from the crest of Oak Ridge to the Mummasburg Road. The division's second (reserve) line consisted of two brigades. Daniel's large but green North Carolina command was placed in line of regiments on the west of the hill behind O'Neal's right.[66] Ramseur's veteran brigade, which had been marching at the rear of the column behind the divisional trains, was ordered to form as a reserve behind O'Neal's left; he was still coming up into position at 1300.[67]

The men of O'Neal's 5th Alabama particularly enjoyed the brief rest they were allowed while the rest of the division deployed. The 5th formed the extreme left of its brigade, and had to move rapidly—frequently at a run—as the division made a right wheel from the Newville Road to Oak Ridge. Once the regiment reached the ridge, its men found that "The ground was very rough. In places the regiment moved through orchards, gardens, over wood and stone fences, which, with the rapidity of the march, fatigued the men, causing many of them to faint from exhaustion."[68]

Rodes' entire line enjoyed cover and protection from the woods on Oak Hill, except for Doles' Brigade and part of O'Neal's. Even so, a number of O'Neal's Alabamians were lost to Union artillery fire, as will be detailed shortly. The line's greatest weakness was the fact that O'Neal did not connect with Doles' line on the open slope below Oak Ridge. This was because of a combination of factors—the steepness of the open slope, increasing fire from Dilger's and Wheeler's XI Corps batteries, and Rodes' decision to push the thrust of his attack to the right. As already noted, W.P. Carter's and Fry's batteries were formed in advance of Rodes' line while the infantry was forming, and placed an effective fire on the Union center. A short time later, Page's and Reese's batteries were placed on the eastern slope of the ridge to deal with Schurz's artillery.[69]

Both Ewell and Rodes showed concern over the two different Union forces being moved forward against the Second Corps' line. Rodes noted that "the enemy began to show large bodies of men in front of the town, most of which were directed upon the position which I held, and almost at the same time a portion of the force opposed to General Hill changed position so as to occupy the woods on the summit of the same ridge I occupied."[70] The ongoing skirmish fight with Baxter's men along the Mummasburg Road and on the Forney farm, combined with the determined advance of Von Amsberg's XI Corps brigade, convinced Rodes that he had to act quickly. He continues, "Being thus threatened from two directions, I determined to attack with my center and right, holding at bay still another force, then emerging from the town (apparently with the intent of turning my left), with Doles' brigade, which was moved somewhat to the left for this purpose, and trusting to this gallant brigade thus holding them until General Early's division arrived, which I knew would be soon, and which would strike this portion of the enemy's force on the flank before it could overpower Doles."[71]

While Rodes was making his plans for the attack, he grew concerned over the effect of the Union artillery fire on the exposed portion of his line, particularly on O'Neal's brigade. One Union shell killed a captain of the 12th Alabama, and another shot badly wounded two men.[72] Another felled Captain T. R. Lightfoot of the 6th Alabama and several of his men.[73] To Colonel O'Neal and Colonel S.B. Pickens of the 12th Alabama, the annoying Union artillery fire seemed to last more than an hour.[74]

Rodes soon came to the conclusion that O'Neal's line needed to be shifted so as to avoid the "annoying" Federal artillery fire. Therefore he directed O'Neal to fall back from the line he occupied to a new position in the rear, "so as to obtain some little shelter for the troops." Rodes sent a direct order to the commander of O'Neal's right regiment, Colonel C. A. Battle of the 3rd Alabama, to form on a line with Daniel's brigade, and instructed Colonel O'Neal "to form the balance of the brigade upon it."[75]

Rodes' plan of attack was not fully thought out, but was designed entirely to meet the enemy, "who was rash enough to come out from the woods to attack me." His attention was apparently focused on the aggressiveness of the skirmishers of the 97th New York and Robinson's other regiments, and he determined to meet the Union advance "as soon as he got to the foot of the hill I occupied." At the appropriate moment he would order O'Neal and Iverson to attack straight forward. Daniel was instructed "to advance to support Iverson, if necessary, if not, to attack on his right as soon as possible."[76] Ramseur, who was still coming up, would serve as a general reserve to the attack.

Rodes' plan of attack was not by any means the best that could have been devised in that situation. He had a number of advantages in his favor—he was squarely on the Union flank, had a superiority in artillery (Baxter and Cutler had no guns facing north), and outnumbered the opposition 2 to 1. His failure to place any artillery fire on the apex of Baxter's line (its sharp angle at the Mummasburg Road) or to move to exploit Baxter's unsupported right can only be explained by inadequate reconnaissance of the length and position of the Union line opposed to him. This oversight would prove to be particularly detrimental to Iverson's brigade, as will be seen shortly.

Rodes has also been criticized for leading his attack with his least experienced brigade commander. Forty-four year old Colonel Edward Asbury O'Neal was an experienced lawyer and politician, who succeeded to command of Rodes' old Alabama brigade simply because he was the brigade's senior colonel when Rodes was elevated to command of D. H. Hill's old division. Rodes was not in favor of O'Neal's elevation, but could not win his way before Gettysburg was fought. Rodes' fears about O'Neal's skills were unfortunately fulfilled at Gettysburg, and Lee would subsequently block O'Neal's advancement to brigadier general and permanent brigade command.[77]

At least one recent historian has argued that Rodes might have done better to have Ramseur participate in the division's opening attack rather than O'Neal or even Iverson. Twenty-six year old Ramseur was certainly one of the most promising brigadiers in the army, and almost any brigade commander would have led the coming attack better than Iverson did. But Ramseur's was the last brigade in the division's line of march that day, and he was still forming his men when Rodes' attack began; there was not enough time to bring him up to the front line and displace one of the other brigades there. All too often a command's line of march would place the wrong unit in the wrong place at the wrong time.[78]

O'Neal's First Attack

Rodes' haste to move to the attack may also have been influenced by overconfidence generated by the perceived weaknesses of the Union line before him. One account related that a "Colonel Swallow" of Early's division reached Rodes' position about 1300, and noted the gaps between the various Union divisions, especially between the I and XI Corps. He felt that this is what led Rodes to send a message to Early that, "Heth and Pender are in Reynolds' front. I can burst through the enemy in an hour." Swallow relates that when Rodes was told that it was the Union XI corps forming north of Gettysburg, the general exclaimed, "Why, those are the very same chaps that our fellows routed at Chancellorsville."[79]

The exact order of events during Rodes' initial assault is not entirely clear. Some sources indicate that O'Neal attacked first,[80] while others seem to indicate that Iverson moved to the attack first.[81] Since O'Neal's attack was defeated in about 30 minutes (and perhaps as few as 15)[82] and was followed up by subsequent attacks, it is difficult to determine what was the exact sequence of events. The balance of the evidence appears to indicate that O'Neal attacked first, then Iverson, then Daniel. The time at which these attacks began is also unclear. The best evidence seems to indicate that they began at about 1400.[83]

Rodes in his battle report states that he gave Iverson his order to advance and "at the same moment gave in person to O'Neal the order to attack, indicating to him precisely the point to which he was to direct the left of his four regiments."[84] O'Neal actually had five regiments in his brigade, but Rodes had directed that Colonel J. M. Hall's 5th Alabama be held in reserve on the brigade's left in order to guard the gap between O'Neal's left and Dole's right.[85]

O'Neal's right regiment, the 3rd Alabama, also did not participate in the brigade's attack. As previously noted, Rodes had aligned the 3rd with Daniel's left when he pulled O'Neal's command back slightly in order to find cover from the Union artillery fire coming from McPherson's Ridge. When O'Neal advanced, he declined to send orders to the 3rd regiment, believing it to be under Daniel's or Rodes' command.[86] A more experienced brigade commander would have sent for the 3rd, but O'Neal chose not to do so. His lack of control of the situation can be seen in his battle report, dated 24 July, where he states, "Why my brigade was thus deprived of two regiments, I have never been informed."[87]

Thus O'Neal stepped off to his attack with only three of his five regiments, about 1000 of his 1700 men.[88] These were about the same strength as Baxter's four regiments lined up along the Mummasburg Road, from left to right: 12th Massachusetts, 90th Pennsylvania, 83rd New York, 88th Pennsylvania.[89] Since Baxter's right had the advantage of an established defensive line along the fence bordering the south side of the road, the advantage in the coming confrontation would seem to lie with the defense, unless O'Neal contrived to concentrate his force on the projecting left of Baxter's position.

Rodes noted in his report that O'Neal's men attacked with alacrity but a fair degree of confusion. He also states that they were not moving "in accordance with my orders as to direction."[90] Unfortunately, he does not specify where it was that he had personally directed the brigade to attack. Since he indicated to O'Neal where to guide the left of his advance,[91] it is more likely that he wanted the Alabamians to concentrate on the apex of Baxter's line (held by the 12th Massachusetts) rather than swing to the left or right of Baxter's position.[92]

O'Neal advanced behind a strong line of skirmishers who soon struck the skirmishers that had just been sent out by the 88th Pennsylvania, which occupied the right of Baxter's line. The 88th's historian notes that, "After alignment, skirmishers were sent into the woods to ascertain what the rebs were about; but no extended investigation was necessary, as the boys from the other side were coming right along, supported by O'Neal's Alabama brigade in line of battle, cocked and primed for a fight."[93]

Baxter's skirmishers engaged O'Neal's advance briskly, and then fell back as the Confederates approached the roadway. A soldier from the 88th relates that his line waited behind their fence until O'Neal's units were "in easy range, the order was given, 'Commence firing.' With the sharp crack of the muskets a fleecy cloud of smoke rolled down the front of the brigade and the minnie balls zipped and buzzed with a merry chorus toward the Southern line, which halted, and after a brief contest, retired to the shelter of the woods."[94] Lieutenant George Grant of the 88th Pennsylvania thought that O'Neal's advance was so handily defeated because the Confederates had not been able to see Baxter's right regiments come up and form, and so were taken by surprise because they were not expecting any resistance.[95]

O'Neal's attack scarcely advanced to within 200 yards of Baxter's line before it was turned back. On O'Neal's right, Robert E. Park of the 12th Alabama lay flat on the ground and urged the men near him to do the same in order to escape the heavy enemy fire: "Balls were falling thick and fast around us, and whizzing past and often striking some one near." Before long he was struck in the hip. Park commented, "It was a wonder, a miracle, I was not shot a half dozen times."[96]

The left of O'Neal's attack faced a more difficult time than the rest of its brigade because of the added opposition on Von Amsberg's troops of the XI Corps. Here O'Neal's left unit, the 6th Alabama, began the attack confidently enough, due to the shelter offered by the big red McLean barn. The adjutant of the 12th Massachusetts noted that O'Neal's left advanced from "behind this and under its cover the enemy... deployed in several columns to the right (our left), we firing upon them as best we could."[97]

O'Neal's advance had been observed by Colonel Adolphus Dobke, commander of the 45th New York, which was deployed in skirmish formation south of the McLean buildings, on the left flank of the XI Corps. Dobke saw a long line of enemy moving on the extreme flank of the I Corps, passing directly in his front and offering their flank to his command: "The left wing of our regiment at once gave fire at very short distance (50 or 100 yards) with such terrible effect that, in result with the combination of the fire from the extreme right of the First Corps, the whole of the enemy's line halted, gradually disappeared on the same spot where they stood, and the remainder, finding they could not retrace their steps surrendered, partly to the First Corps, and a great number to the Forty-Fifth Regiment."[98]

Since O'Neal's men, particularly on the left, "were making no impression" on the Yankee line, Rodes committed his reserve regiment, the 5th Alabama. Colonel Hall of the 5th was not particularly eager to assault the enemy position, which was composed "of two heavy lines of infantry in front and a line of sharpshooters, supported by infantry and artillery, on my left flank." Hall found it necessary to form his command into a "V," the left wing facing the XI Corps troops and the right wing facing Baxter's line.[99]

Despite the advance of the 5th Alabama, O'Neal's attack continued to unravel from the left, where the 6th Alabama was turned back by Von Dobke. Colonel O'Neal reported, "We were compelled to fall back, as the regiment on the extreme left, being flanked by a superior force of the enemy; gave way. It was impossible to hold the position we had gained, as the enemy had the advantage in numbers and position."[100] O'Neal judged that the "desperate fight" had lasted about half an hour. Colonel S. B. Pickens, commander of the 12th Alabama on the right flank of the attack, thought that the climax of the assault was briefer: "We attacked them in a strong position. After a desperate fight of about fifteen minutes, we were compelled to fall back, as the regiment on our left gave way, being flanked by a large force. I rallied my regiment about 300 yards in the rear, and formed a line."[101] In this Colonel Pickens was aided by the 12th's major, Adolph Proskauer, who was an able officer as well as the "best dressed man in the regiment." Captain Robert Park was amazed how "our gallant Jew major smoked his cigars calmly and cooly in the thickest of the fight."[102]

Hall's 5th Alabama fought on until their commander was informed that the rest of the brigade was falling back, whereupon the unit withdrew to the position it had previously occupied. Hall noted that "This was done all the more conscientiously because the odds opposed were very great, and my command was under a front and enfilading fire, with no support, and suffering a very severe loss."[103]

O'Neal's advance and defeat were watched with dismay by Colonel Cullen A. Battle of the 3rd Alabama, who had been left behind in his position adjacent to Daniel's command. Battle kept in line with Daniel until the latter moved to support Iverson. At this point, Battle sent an officer to Daniel for orders, to whom Daniel replied that he had none and Battle must act on his own responsibility. Battle then offered his services to Ramseur, who was preparing to move forward. Ramseur accepted the offer, and Battle's unit would serve with Ramseur's brigade for the rest of the afternoon.[104]

Responsibility for the poor tactical management of O'Neal's attack rests solely on O'Neal himself. He misunderstood the objective pointed out to him by Rodes himself, and did not maintain good control of his troops as they advanced. Nor did he make any particular effort to time his advance with that of Iverson on his right. To make matters worse, O'Neal did not advance with the main body of his command, but stayed behind with his reserve regiment (5th Alabama) on his extreme left. Rodes was greatly surprised to find O'Neal there when he rode to the 5th to order it to enter the fight. Even more incredibly, O'Neal entered the action on foot, and none of his staff officers were mounted, either. This made it extremely difficult for him to communicate with his officers during the attack, and left each regiment to fight pretty much on its own.[105]

The Devastation of Iverson's Brigade

O'Neal's badly supervised attack left Iverson's left flank wide open and invited disaster to the latter's attack. Rodes had intended for both brigades to attack at the same time and along the same axis, but their movement did not come off as planned. O'Neal must bear much of the fault here, since he advanced without making an effort to coordinate with Iverson on his right. If he had kept contact with Iverson, he would have learned that the North Carolinians were not yet ready to advance. Iverson reported that he had received instructions from Rodes "to advance gradually to the support of a battery he intended placing in front." Iverson did not understand "the exact time which the advance was to take place," so he sent a staff officer to Rodes to find out when he should move forward. He received the unclear reply "not to move forward until my skirmishers became hotly engaged." Iverson was still contemplating these instructions when he received more concise orders a short while later. He was to advance to meet the enemy, who seemed to be approaching in order to take W.P. Carter's battery. In addition, Rodes directed him "to call up Brigadier General Daniel for support; that Colonel O'Neal's (Alabama) brigade would advance on my left, and the batteries would cease firing as I passed them."[106]

Upon receipt of Rodes' orders, Iverson sent a staff officer to notify Daniel of his advance, and sent another to observe when O'Neal should

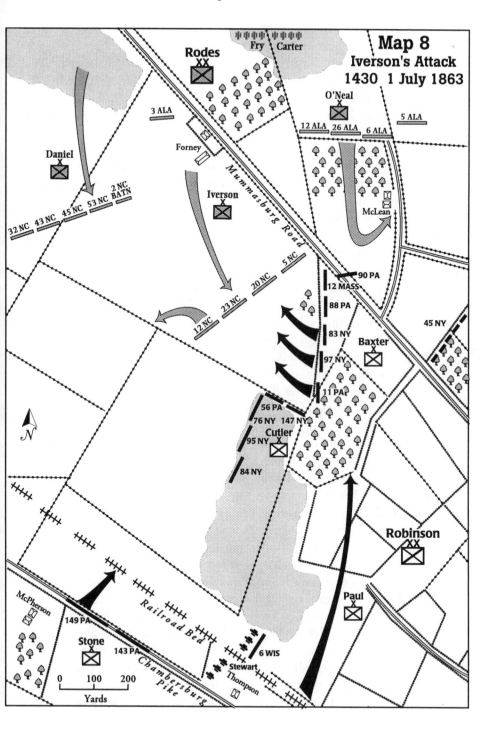

Map 8
Iverson's Attack
1430 1 July 1863

begin to move. To his astonishment, he learned that O'Neal was already moving, so he began his own advance at once.[107]

For some reason, Iverson chose not to advance with his troops, but stayed behind near their jump off point.[108] His absence from the front line meant the brigade had no guiding hand to direct it. Rodes had perhaps intended the unit to attack straight down the Mummasburg Road into the center of Baxter's line. Instead, it drifted to the right. The reason for this is not understood today. Perhaps Iverson's regimental commanders did not see Baxter's line, and headed towards Cutler's men in the far woods, to their right, whom they could see. Another interpretation according to some sources is that Iverson directed his regiments to head towards the gap between Baxter's and Cutler's commands.[109] Iverson's men may also have been concerned about the lack of support on their left, where O'Neal's troops had been so quickly turned back.

Iverson's brigade was formed on a 600 yard wide line astride the Mummasburg Road with its regiments in the following order from left to right: 5th, 20th, 23rd and 12th North Carolina. Just before the brigade advanced, General Rodes rode up to the 12th North Carolina on the right of the brigade and encouraged its men, "Boys, they are advancing on us; go ahead and meet them." This anecdote confirms Rodes' preoccupation with the heavy skirmishers of the 97th New York and fellow Union regiments in the Forney field. It may well be true that he mistook the realigning of Baxter's regiments as a preparation to advance on his division (and T.H. Carter's two batteries), as Walter Montgomery of the 12th North Carolina has suggested.[110]

Iverson's advance began sometime between 1400 and 1430, probably closer to the later terminus. Its line of advance was through the open fields of the Forney farm with "not a bush nor a tree between the place where Iverson formed and the Federal line, a distance of nearly half a mile."[111] The field was all open meadow, covered with timothy.[112] It was traversed by a wooden east-west fence (no longer extant) some 700 feet south of the Mummasburg Road and by a second east-west fence (which survives) another 500 feet further south.[113]

Iverson's men "bounded forward" at the beginning of the attack, and then "advanced under artillery fire through the grass in gallant style, as evenly as if on parade." General Iverson exhorted them forward with the cry to "give them hell," but did not accompany the brigade's advance, and instead stayed in the rear.[114] Some other troops in the division thought he stayed behind because he was a drunk, a coward in hiding, or both.[115] The historian of the 12th North Carolina blames Iverson's absence for the fact that the brigade made a partial wheel once it passed the Forney house and so "was put in a false alignment, in a northeast and southwest line."[116]

It appears from Iverson's battle report, however, that he simply chose to lead his brigade from the rear. He was aware of the brigade's line of advance, and may have ordered the partial wheel himself. If his men proceeded directly south from their original position on Oak Hill, they would have struck Cutler's brigade and left their eastern flank exposed to the troops who engaged O'Neal; a shift of some sort was necessary in order to move to a southwesterly line of advance and strike the Union troops on northern Seminary Ridge above Cutler's position.[117] From his position in the rear of his command, Iverson was aware of the gap on his left, but from what he had been told by Rodes, he "presumed that it would soon be filled by the advancing Alabama brigade, under Colonel O'Neal." He also met personally with Daniel to request "immediate support, as I was attacking a strong position." Daniel promised to send a strong regiment, which satisfied O'Neal. Iverson then requested Daniel to take care of "a large force of the enemy who were about to outflank my right," and Daniel began moving off in that direction.[118]

Iverson's gravest error was not in staying behind his troops during their attack, but in failing to reconnoiter their line of advance before the attack began. His regiments apparently proceeded in perfect parade ground order, with no skirmishers in their front. Had any skirmishers been sent out, they surely would have encountered Baxter's line just beyond the crest of Oak Ridge on Iverson's left.

If Iverson's men did not see Baxter's line, Baxter's men surely saw Iverson's line approaching. General Robinson arrived on northern Seminary Ridge just as Iverson was beginning his advance, and became concerned about the gap between Baxter's left and Cutler's line. For this reason, he directed Baxter "to change front forward on his left battalion, and to close this interval, toward which the enemy was making his way."[119] Baxter complied by shifting his left two regiments, the 11th Pennsylvania and 97th New York, to their left so as to connect with Cutler's line.[120] They formed behind a rock fence that ran near the crest of the ridge to the west, but it was the ridge crest, not the fence, that offered real shelter to the new line. Isaac Hall of the 97th New York later wrote that he had to step forward up slope "and stretch my neck" in order to get a view of Iverson's advance."[121] The regiment's line at this time was some 16 yards east of the site of its monument.[122]

Since the leftward shift of the 11th Pennsylvania and 97th New York left a gap between the right of the 97th and the 12th Massachusetts line at the Mummasburg Road, Baxter pulled the 83rd New York and 88th Pennsylvania from his right in order to fill the void.[123] These units were available to face Iverson because O'Neal was not at the moment posing a threat from the north. Captain Edmund Patterson of the 88th Pennsylvania reported that his regiment "changed our position by the left flank, file left, which brought us up a slight hill."[124] This movement brought the regiment to the top of the hill, where it formed behind a stone wall nearly perpendicular to the road.[125] John Vautier of the 88th Pennsylvania wrote that he was able to see Iverson's advance while kneeling behind the stone fence;[126] thus the fence was closer to the west of the hill at this point than it was farther to the left, where the 97th New York was posted.

While the left of the brigade was being realigned, the 12th Massachusetts shifted its line to the left to face Iverson. It formed along the same rock fence occupied by the rest of the brigade to the left, except here the fence was offset to the west some 20 yards.[127] The movement of the 12th Massachusetts permitted the 90th Pennsylvania, which now formed the right of the brigade line, to slide to its left. The left wing of the 90th formed facing westward, while its right wing formed along the Mummasburg Road, facing north.[128]

During this movement the 90th Pennsylvania found itself exposed to a heavy fire from O'Neal's skirmishers to the north,[129] and the 12th Massachusetts encountered fire from another advancing enemy line, perhaps the 3rd Alabama.[130] Robinson could not afford to leave his right unsupported, so he called forward Paul's brigade from its reserve position in front of the Seminary. Doubleday was able to spare Paul's men because there was not at the moment any other Confederate pressure along his line. Doubleday directed Robinson to accompany Paul's advance in person.[131] Paul's command, however, would not arrive in time to meet the height of Iverson's attack.

Baxter's men reformed their line facing Iverson very carefully so they would not be seen by the enemy. As already noted, the left part of the line was hidden from Iverson's view by the crest of the ridge, while the right portion lay behind a stone wall. V.E. Turner of the 12th North Carolina remarked that Iverson's men were "not knowing certainly where the enemy was, for his whole line, with every flag, was concealed behind the rock wall on their right and the drop in the ground on their left. Not one of them was to be seen."[132]

Baxter also apparently kept his position concealed by not sending out skirmishers; none are mentioned in the accounts of this portion of the engagement by either Union or Confederate sources. Besides, there was no need for skirmishers, since the line of Iverson's advance was in plain view across the Forney field. The Confederates advanced in perfect alignment, with their colors to the front. The veteran troops of Baxter's brigade held their fire and "quietly awaited their command to open." Word was quietly spread to aim low when the time came.[133] John Vautier of the 88th Pennsylvania commented that: "Iverson's men, with arms at a right shoulder, came on in splendid array, keeping step with an almost perfect line. They reached and descended a little gully or depression in the ground, and moving on ascended the opposite slope as if on brigade drill, while behind the stone wall the Union soldiers, with rifles cocked and fingers in the triggers, waited and bided their time, feeling confident that they could throw back these regiments coming against them."[134]

When Iverson's line was about 100 yards from Baxter's concealed fire, the Yankees rose up and delivered a mighty blast of musketry into the unsuspecting Confederate line.[135] The historian of the 88th Pennsylvania observed that "at the command a sheet of flame and smoke burst forth from the wall with the simultaneous crash of the rifles, flaring full in the faces of the advancing troops, the ground being quickly covered with their killed and wounded as the balls hissed and cut through their exposed line."[136] V.E. Turner of the 23rd North Carolina wrote that "when we were in point blank range the dense line of the enemy rose from its protected lair and poured into us a withering fire from the front and both flanks."[137]

The Union fire particularly devastated the 5th and 20th North Carolina regiments, which were on Iverson's left and therefore closer to the Union line. Baxter's two right regiments, the 90th Pennsylvania and 12th Massachusetts, were able to get a raking and cross fire on Iverson's left that was "fatal all along the line."[138] The surprised Confederate line suffered such heavy loses that its dead lay in a distinctly marked line of battle.[139] Many of the slain Confederates did not even have the opportunity to fire a shot in their defense. Those who could still fight attempted to do so, but Lieutenant Oliver Williams of the 20th believed that "every man who stood up was either killed or wounded." These two regiments were already short on officers (the 5th entered action under the command of a Captain Speight B. West), and heavy officer losses restricted the units' ability to react. Lieutenant Williams of the 20th was wounded early in the fight, as were the regiment's senior officers, Lieutenant Colonel N. Slough and Major J.S. Brooks. In the 20th North Carolina, all four captains present were wounded, and three lieutenants were killed.[140]

At the right center of Iverson's line, the 23rd North Carolina was rocked by Baxter's fire but managed to stagger forward with heavy loss under deadly fire for about 20 yards to an irregular hollow at the center of Forney's field. Here the regiment was subject to continued "pitiless rifle fire" from the front, "as well as from the more distant corner of the field in our front." The 20th, along with the survivors of the 5th and 12th who were still able to fight, "lay down in this hollow or depression in the field and fought as best it could" since it was "unable to advance , unwilling to retreat." The 23rd also suffered heavily in officers as well as men. Major C.C. Blacknall was shot through the mouth and neck in the initial Union volley. After reaching the hollow, Lieutenant Colonel R.D. Johnson was badly wounded, and Colonel D.H. Christie was mortally stricken. Altogether, the regiment would lose all its commissioned field officers but one in the action.[141]

Iverson's right regiment, the 12th North Carolina, did not suffer as severely as the rest of the brigade because of the lay of the land and the fact that it was farthest (about 200 yards) from Baxter's line. One account states that Baxter's initial volley affected only the two left companies of the regiment. The regiment was able to hold its ground because most of it was protected by a slight rise of ground in its front. Even so, the regiment's two left companies continued to lose severely to enemy fire.[142]

The 12th North Carolina had more than Baxter's line to deal with. Cutler saw Iverson's attack coming and opened up a long range fire on his left, which the Confederates apparently did not at first stop to answer. He then advanced his command out of the woods and proceeded by right oblique a short distance to a good position from which he could fire on Iverson's left.[143] Lieutenant Colonel W.S. Davis of the 12th North Carolina found that the best way to deal with Cutler's advance and ensuing enfilade fire was to withdraw about 100 yards to the west to a little bottom in a wheatfield.[144]

W.S. Davis' withdrawal left the rest of Iverson's brigade to even further devastation at Union hands. On the far left, the surviving elements of the 5th and 20th regiments had withdrawn, leaving the ground covered with their dead and wounded, and rallied in the same swale already occupied by the 23rd North Carolina. Here they "rallied and opened a sharp fire on the Union line." A few even attempted to renew their attack, only to be "again driven back to the ditch."[145]

Baxter's men replied to Iverson's fire and kept up a "steady, death dealing fire." Lieutenant George W. Grant of the 88th Pennsylvania recalled "our men loading in comparative safety, and then resting rifle on boulders before them, would fire coolly and with unerring aim."[146] Sergeant Sam Boone of the same regiment saw that his men were all behaving splendidly and all his officers were present, so he left his post in the rear of the line and "picked up the musket of a wounded soldier, took cartridges from the cartridge boxes of the man and done some wicked firing into the mess of Confederate soldiers lying down in the field within short musket range."[147]

The Confederates in the gully, though, did manage to return an effective fire in the face of all this opposition. Private Jacob Menges of Company D, 11th Pennsylvania, was shooting from a prone position and recalled that the enemy fire was fierce enough to "cut off the timothy heads above our own backs."[148] In the 88th Pennsylvania, Sergeant Henry Evans of Company B was maintaining a steady fire along with Private John Witmoyer of Company H. When he saw a Confederate color bearer defiantly flaunting his colors, Evans aimed his gun and said to his companion, "John, I will give these colors a whick." Just then Witmoyer heard the dull thud of a bullet, and turned quickly to ask if the Sergeant were hit. Evans gave no reply, but slowly brought his musket down, and fell over dead with a bullet wound in his heart.[149]

By now many of Iverson's men had had enough, and began waving hats and handkerchiefs in token of surrender. Some of the Union officers, though, feared a trap, and held an impromptu conference to consider what to do.[150] Just then General Baxter rode up and gave the order, "up boys, and give them steel!"[151] His decision to conduct a bayonet counterattack may have been influenced by the fact that some of his men were beginning to run out of ammunition.[152]

Privates Joseph Trainor and George Renair of Company D, 88th Pennsylvania, took up Baxter's order and jumped over the fence in their front in order to charge the Confederate line.[153] They were followed at once by other members of their own unit and by men from the three regiments on their left, the 83rd New York, 97th New York and 11th Pennsylvania.[154]

The regimental historian of the 97th New York gives a different version of the beginning of this counterattack that emphasizes the role of his own regiment. He relates that the 97th's lieutenant colonel, John P. Spofford, was riding his horse near the left flank of the regiment when he saw the Confederates in the gully raise tokens of surrender. He says that Spofford, "taking in the situation at a glance and without waiting for orders, said 'Boys of the 97th, let us go over and capture them'." The regiment promptly sprang over the wall towards the gully, supported by the 11th Pennsylvania on its left and part of the regiment on its right; the entire regiment on the right "was shut out from this rapid movement by the aforementioned high rail fence, which from the wall, towards the west, intervened between it and the charging force." Colonel Wheelock of the 97th happened to be dismounted in the rear of the regiment when Spofford ordered the attack. He was "surprised at the action of this officer," but "took in the situation and went forward with his regiment without interfering with the order." Spofford later admitted, "I knew I was liable to a dismissal from the service for giving the order to charge without the authority of Colonel Wheelock, and if the movement had met disaster I should have been; but to be successful I knew action must be taken before the Confederates recovered from their panic and the moment was critical; so I could not help it."[155]

Apparently a few men from the 12th Massachusetts, which was posted to the right of the 88th Pennsylvania, also participated in Baxter's counterattack. Adjutant C.C. Wehrum of the 12th noted that, "our fire must have taken terrible effect, for soon they laid down and a number of them tied handkerchiefs to their guns in token of surrender, it was a surprising spectacle to us for I could easily see they were in much stronger force than we were."[156]

As the Confederate attack began to break up, Wehrum heard "a great deal of hollering, some to cease firing, others to charge bayonets." Wehrum asked a comrade "what is the order," and was told "forward!" So he cried out, "forward, boys!" and charged forward with "a number of our regiment and a number of the regiment on our left" (88th Pennsylvania). They "ran right up to the rebel lines and several hundred of the rebs left their arms on the ground and rushed through our lines and they were directed to run out of range as quick as possible which they did without urging."[157] Not all the members of the 12th, though, took part in the charge. The right end of the regiment's line may have been held back by fire from O'Neal's troops to the north.[158] This fire also bothered the counterattacking troops of the 97th New York, who "suffered from a flank and near fire in the adjoining field on the right" that came from O'Neal's troops.[159]

During this attack Colonel James L. Bates of the 12th Massachusetts was wounded in the neck. Adjutant Wehrum saw that his commander was bleeding badly, and tied his handkerchief around the colonel's neck. He feared that Bates might bleed to death and urged him to go to the rear. A lieutenant offered to escort the colonel, but he refused to go, stating that "we need every available officer at the post." Bates stayed with his men until he received a second wound within the hour, and had no choice but to retire.[160]

General Baxter, who selflessly joined in the counterattack himself, was apparently unaware that some men of the 12th Massachusetts participated in the charge. However, he did acknowledge that the regiment aided in repulsing Iverson by making "a galling fire on the flank of this brigade, which I think had a great influence on its surrender."[161] Cutler's regiments to the left also succeeded at achieving an enfilade fire, on the right of the advancing Confederate line.[162]

The men of the 88th Pennsylvania, who led Baxter's counterattack, headed for the largest body of enemy troops in their front, the 23rd North Carolina. The Confederates surrendered in droves, and were at once hurried to the rear. First Sergeant Edward L. Gilligan of Company E secured the capture of the 23rd's flag, and for this deed was later awarded the Medal of Honor. He later related, "Captain Joseph H. Richard of my company singled out the color bearer of the Twenty-third and had a hand-to-hand fight with him. The Confederate pluckily held on to the colors and only gave them up when I reasoned with him with the butt on my musket."[163]

At the same time Lieutenant Eldridge Levans of Company I, 88th Pennsylvania, captured a flag whose identity is not clear from the sources. After securing the colors, Levans presented it to General Robinson with "an impromptu speech." Lieutenant Grant of the 88th believed the flag had been lost by one of O'Neal's Alabama regiments that was serving with Iverson, but none of O'Neal's units are otherwise known to have done so.[164] Captain Edmund Y. Patterson of the 88th thought it belonged to the 16th Alabama, but this unit was not at Gettysburg.[165] Some sources suggest that Patterson may have meant O'Neal's 26th Alabama, even though this unit was serving on the eastern crest of Oak Ridge.[166]

A third Confederate flag was captured by the 97th New York. The 97th's attack was led by Company C, under the command of Lieutenant Ebenezer B. Harrison. Company C reached the Confederates in the "ditch" first, and Sergeant Sylvester Riley grabbed the flag of the 20th

North Carolina. He at once handed it to Lieutenant Ebenezer Harrington, who in turn passed it on to Colonel Wheelock. Colonel Wheelock in his battle report noted that his command "brought out as prisoners 213 officers and men of the 20th North Carolina with their colors, ... more prisoners than we had men in our regiment."[167]

A fourth flag, that of the 5th North Carolina, was captured by Captain Erastus Clark of Company A, 12th Massachusetts. Clark for some reason never turned in his captured prize, but kept it with him until the end of his days. The flag was actually found on his body when he died in a strange knife duel in Louisiana in 1911.[168]

Yet another stand of colors was reportedly captured by some of Cutler's troops. As already noted, Cutler had advanced his brigade a short distance north of the woods where it had been posted to a fence line from where it was able to lay down an effective fire on the enemy "who lay behind a fence in a hollow."[169] While here, the 76th New York shot down a set of colors, the third time that day they did so. When Baxter's troops made their charge, part of the 76th also attacked along with the 94th New York of Paul's brigade, which had just come up. Together they captured a large body of the enemy, along with a stand of colors.[170] The identity of this flag has not been established.

All accounts agree that Iverson's line was in total disarray when Baxter's attack struck. The historian of the 83rd New York observed that the Confederates were "huddled up in great confusion."[171] Sergeant Boone of the 88th Pennsylvania remembered that the enemy troops "rose singly and in groups, holding their hands in a token of surrender."[172] Boone later felt badly that he had pushed one laggard prisoner to hurry faster to the rear: "One Confederate soldier came toward me in a stooping position, with his piece at trail arms. Thinking that he meant mischief, I struck him across the back with the side of my sword and ordered: 'Drop your arms; hasten to the rear.' The blow fell lightly on him but as he was passing me I noticed blood trickling from beneath his accoutrements. The poor fellow had evidently been wounded, but in his pain, misery and excitement had forgotten to drop his musket."[173]

While their comrades were busy gathering up prisoners by the score, a few plucky members of the 88th Pennsylvania pushed forward past the Confederate line and up the west slope of the gully which had been held by Iverson's men. Here they ran into a heavy fire on their front and both flanks from a variety of sources—O'Neal's skirmishers on the right, Ramseur's troops and the 3rd Alabama in their front, and the 12th North Carolina and Daniel's brigade on the left. This "galling fire" made their position "too hot to hold," so they withdrew to the stone wall from where they had initiated the attack.[174] John Vautier of the 88th Pennsylvania observed that "rifle balls were cutting the grass with a switching sound, taking effect among the Confederate prisoners as well as in our own ranks." The regiment then, "quickly realizing that their usefulness at this point was over, that pressing engagements called them to the stone wall, fell back without unnecessary delay, driving their willing captives before them.[175] The farthest point of the 88th Pennsylvania's advance was later marked by a stone erected in Forney field about 80 yards west of the regiment's monument on the crest of the ridge.

Isaac Hall of the 97th New York remembered that his unit was struck by fire from the north as it withdrew, and that several Confederate prisoners were wounded by this fire.[176] A member of the 23rd North Carolina who survived the attack noted that the Federals left their wounded behind when they withdrew but used bayonets and clubbed muskets to drive off their prisoners. They also "carried our flag with them."[177]

General Iverson did not at first understand the enormity of the disaster that was befalling his brigade. As already noted, he had sent to Daniel for a "large regiment" as support before the attack began. When he saw that his movement was in trouble, he sent his assistant adjutant general, Captain D. P. Halsey, to ask Daniel again for help. Halsey enroute met one of Daniel's staff officers and was told that a regiment had been sent, and none more could be spared. Much to Iverson's dismay, he discovered that the regiment that Daniel sent had formed on the right of O'Neal's 3rd Alabama, which was standing firm somewhere to the immediate west of the Forney farm buildings.[178] Iverson then tried to organize a charge by the 3rd Alabama and 12th North Carolina in order to take advantage of "the confusion among the enemy incident to the charge and capture of my men." However, he was unable to mount the attack, "because in the noise and excitement I presume my voice could not be heard."[179] This is certainly no example of strong and decisive leadership on Iverson's part. The crux of the matter, however, was that Iverson's men were overwhelmed so quickly—in 15 to 30 minutes—that there was no time to bring up any assistance from any of the three brigades in immediate supporting distance.[180]

Iverson appears to have panicked when he saw white handkerchiefs being raised by his troops. At one point he reported to Rodes that his battle line was lying down in position, and that a whole regiment had gone over to the enemy.[181] After the action, though, he realized that his troops had not lain down to escape combat, but had been felled where they stood by the initial Union volley; he found "that 500 of my men were left lying dead and wounded on a line as straight as a dress parade."[182]

The disaster that befell Iverson's brigade was one of the most severe of the war, as costly as that suffered by Pickett's brigades two days later. Altogether the brigade lost over 65% of its strength, 71% if the less engaged 12th regiment is excluded. The 5th North Carolina on the left flank lost 289 of its 473 men (61%), while the adjacent 20th North Carolina lost 253 of 372 (68%). The 23rd North Carolina, which was struck hardest by Baxter's charge lost a whopping 89% (282 of 316). Casualties in the 12th regiment, which did not see heavy action from its position on the right of the line, were a much lighter 36% (79 of 219). Altogether the brigade's reported losses (which were clearly understated) amounted to 182 killed, 399 wounded, and 322 captured or missing.[183] Some Union accounts claim that as many as 1000 of Iverson's men were captured, but this was not possible since the brigade had only about 1384 engaged.[184] Confederate sources admit to from 250 to 300 captured; but the number was clearly higher than that. Lieutenant Walter Montgomery of the 12th North Carolina estimated that the brigade numbered only 350 or 400 men right after the battle. If this is true, the brigade must have lost closer to 900 men on the first day.[185]

Those who saw the field of Iverson's defeat after the fight were appalled at the sight. One poor Confederate was found with five bullets in his head, still clutching his musket.[186] Everyone commented on how perfectly dressed the line of dead was. Henry Berkeley of the Confederate artillery observed 79 North Carolinians laying dead in a straight line within a few feet. Their line "was perfectly dressed. Three had fallen to the front, the rest had fallen backward; yet the feet of these dead were in a perfectly straight line."[187] John Vautier of the 88th Pennsylvania wrote that, "Hundreds of the Confederates fell at the first volley, plainly marking their line with a ghastly row of dead and wounded men, whose blood trailed the course of their line with a crimson stain clearly discernable for several days after the battle, until the rain washed the gory record away."[188] Lieutenant George Bullock of Company I, 23rd North Carolina, confirmed Vautier's grisly description: he said "that it was the only battle and he was in all in which his command was engaged from Williamsburg to Appomattox—where the blood ran like a branch. And that, too, on the hot, parched ground."[189]

Iverson's men were soon buried in trenches near where they fell. The brigade's pioneers dug four shallow pits "in the lowest part of the depression, in the rear of the battleground of Iverson's Brigade." The surface of the pits could easily be discerned by the more luxuriant growth of grass and crops over them. Even at the turn of the century, 30 years after the bodies of Iverson's dead had been disinterred and conveyed South, it was possible to find "flattened bullets which had evidently fallen from the disinterred skeletons," and other relics of war, in the Forney field. "Iverson's Pits" were held in dread for years. Mr. Forney, owner of the field, related that "after the battle there was a superstitious terror in regard to the field, and that it was with difficulty that laborers could be kept at work there on the approach of night on that account."[190]

Many of Iverson's troops justly blamed their commander for the disaster that befell them at Gettysburg. Some believed that their commander "not only remained in the rear but that a big chestnut log intervened between him and the battle and that more than once he reminded his staff that for more than one at a time to look over was an unnecessary exposure of person."[191] Private J. D. Hufham Jr. of the 20th North Carolina of Ramseur's brigade heard that "General Irison (sic), who was a drunk, I think, and a coward besides, was off hiding somewhere."[192] Colonel Daniel H. Christie of the 23rd told some of his men as he lay dying from a mortal wound that he would make sure that "The imbecile Iverson" should never lead them into battle again.[193] Colonel Thomas F. Toon of the 20th North Carolina wrote in his postwar sketch that the regiment was "sacrificed at Gettysburg,"[194] and the historian of the 23rd North Carolina wrote plaintively: "Unwarned, unled as a brigade, went forward Iverson's deserted band to its doom. Deep and long must the desolate homes and orphan children of North Carolina rue the rashness of that hour."[195]

Iverson certainly deserved the criticism heaped upon him. Despite the promise he had shown at Gaines' Mill and the experience gained at South Mountain, Antietam, Fredericksburg, and Chancellorsville, Iverson appears to have done nothing right at Gettysburg.[196] He did not properly coordinate his attack with O'Neal (who was not having a good day himself), did not reconnoiter the ground over which he was to attack, and let his men go forward without a covering force of skirmishers. He also was not clear about the axis of his attack, and failed to bring up reinforcements that were readily available. Most significantly, he, like Pickett, did not advance with his men.

Thus it is no wonder some of his officers and men refused to serve under him after the battle. He reportedly "went to pieces and became unfit for further command" during the rest of the battle, though he did a reasonable job during the retreat to Virginia. Lee declined to have him serve longer in his army, and Iverson was shipped off to command Georgia state troops at Rome, Georgia. He was given a chance to redeem himself in early 1864 when he was given command of a brigade of cavalry in Joe Johnston's army, and won acclaim for capturing Union cavalry General George Stoneman near Macon in July. Iverson managed orange groves in Florida after the war, and died in Atlanta in 1911 at the age of 63.[197]

As already noted, the 12th North Carolina on Iverson's right managed to survive the attack relatively intact because of the lay of the ground and the fact that it was farther from Baxter's line than was the rest of the brigade. Its commander, Lieutenant Colonel W.S. Davis, withdrew to a swale some 200 yards southwest of the Forney farm buildings, and managed to fight off the enemy by refusing both his wings.[198] After the rest of the brigade was repulsed, Davis noted, "On my left there was a gap made as far as I would see. On the right there was a considerable gap between us and Daniel's brigade. I was left alone without any orders (our general in the rear, and never coming up), with no communication on right or left, and with only one hundred and seventy five men confronting several thousand." He felt fortunate that the Union troops in the woods to his right front did not counterattack; all he saw was an occasional vedette run out to the margin and run back.[199] Eventually Davis' position was reinforced by the remnants of the brigade's other regiments, which had been rallied by Captain D.P. Halsey.[200]

Daniel Attacks Stone

The collapse of Iverson's attack also jeopardized Daniel's attack to his right. Before the division's attack began, Daniel was ordered to support Iverson's right and guard the right flank of the division. He began moving at the same time that Iverson did, with his green regiments in the following order from left to right: 2nd North Carolina Batallion, 45th North Carolina, 43rd North Carolina, 53rd North Carolina and 32nd North Carolina.[201] His direction of advance was directly to the south; he apparently understood that the entire division was advancing on one line, and that his objective was to be Stone's regiments along the Chambersburg Pike, rather than Cutler's or Baxter's troops to his left.

Daniel's line had started from a woods about 200 yards in the rear of Iverson, and advanced at a corresponding distance behind Iverson's right regiment, the 12th North Carolina. After the line proceeded a short distance, Daniel rode forward to reconnoiter and was astounded to discover that Iverson had changed direction considerably to the left, and had sent him no notification of doing so. Iverson's change of front forced him "to execute a corresponding change to the left," so he directed two of his regiments to switch front to the southeast and move to the support of Iverson's beleaguered command.[202]

Daniel's 53rd North Carolina moved to Iverson's support first, apparently in response to Iverson's appeal that Daniel send a large regiment to his support.[203] Colonel William A. Owens of the 53rd led his command by the left flank and formed on the left of the 3rd Alabama, which was then on Iverson's right. Since the 3rd Alabama was not moving to attack, Owens shifted around to the right of the Alabamians and then "moved forward through a wheatfield to within 50 yards of some woods in front."[204]

The Union troops that the 53rd faced at this point were from the right flank of Cutler's brigade, which had advanced from Wills Woods to fire at Iverson's exposed flank. The threat posed by the 53rd North Carolina (along with the 3rd Alabama, 12th North Carolina, and remainder of Daniel's command) quickly persuaded Cutler to swing his command back to the woods, where he formed on Baxter's left, facing westward towards the 53rd North Carolina and the other Confederate regiments nearby.[205] At one point the 147th New York mistook movement on its right to be a counterattack by part of Robinson's division, so it advanced, going nearly all the way through the woods before the mistake was discovered. During this maneuver Major George Harvey of the 147th was wounded in the hand.[206]

Colonel Owens felt exposed at his forward position even after Cutler pulled back into the woods. It seems that the regiment to its right, the 43rd North Carolina, had not moved up to support the 53rd, but had halted in a lane on the south side of the Forney field. When the 43rd finally did move, it proceeded "by the left flank to a position between the 2nd Battalion and Fifty Third Regiment, with orders to support either on the right or the left, as necessity dictated."[207] As a result, the 43rd never really gave any substantial support to either the 53rd or the 2nd Battalion. The 53rd remained in this position for some time, subject to a crossfire from Cutler's troops to the left and Stone's men to the right. After a while it was ordered to move to support the 2nd Battalion. In obeying this command, the regiment's right lost heavily to a crossfire from the front and flank, and lost several men, including Captain W. C. Ousby killed. The 43rd supported the 2nd for only a short time before it was withdrawn to the cover of the hill from where it had started its attack.[208]

Since Colonel Owens of the 53rd had no close support on his right, he felt obliged to pull back when he saw the 3rd Alabama on his left retire. As he fell back by the left to a new position some 50 yards to the rear, he was subjected to a severe fire from both flanks. He then decided it was best to follow the 3rd Alabama, "which was then going off to the left." After a short distance he fronted, and formed on the left of Iverson's 12th North Carolina.[209]

Despite sending a large portion of his command to support Iverson, Daniel directed the remainder of his brigade to continue moving due south towards Stone's line along the Chambersburg Pike, some ¼ mile distant. This attack was spearheaded by the 45th North Carolina and 2nd North Carolina Battalion, which had originally been on the brigade's left flank before the 45th and 43rd were moved to the left.[210]

The 45th and 2nd Battalion suffered severely during their lengthy advance from the fire of Union guns of Cooper's and Reynolds' batteries to their front, and Stewart's battery on the ridge to their left.[211] One source claims that two units "when halfway between our starting point and their line, were ordered to lie down whilst the guns in the rear" played upon the Union ranks.[212] At length they reached the fence 75 yards north of the railroad line, from which they had to drive off the skirmishers of Company E, 149th Pennsylvania, before continuing on against Stone's main line.[213]

Colonel Stone had seen Rodes' attack developing to the north, and about 1330 shifted the 143rd Pennsylvania from his left (where the Confederates on Herr Ridge were not posing any immediate threat) to his right, where it formed along the Chambersburg Pike to the right of the 149th Pennsylvania. This maneuver left only one of his regiments, the 150th Pennsylvania, and three companies of skirmishers, to face the Confederates on the other side of Willoughby Run.[214] From his position along the Pike, Stone was able "to trace their formation for at least two miles. It appeared to be a nearly continuous line of deployed battalions, with other battalions in mass or reserve." Stone carefully watched the Confederate advance break up as its components shifted obliquely to the Confederate left in order to engage Baxter and Cutler. This movement created breaks in the enemy line, and exposed their flank to his two regiments formed along the Pike. He ordered his men to open fire on the exposed Confederate right, and even "though at the longest range of our pieces, we poured a most destructive fire on their flanks."[215]

After witnessing the defeat of Iverson's brigade at long range, Stone saw Daniel's brigade begin moving in his direction. Initially he was able to oppose Daniel's advance only by the skirmishers of Company E of the 149th Pennsylvania, which had been sent forward about 100 paces to the fence on the north side of the railroad line. In order to protect his skirmishers, Colonel Dwight of the 149th directed his command to fire over their heads at the enemy line, then some ⅓ mile distant. They continued to do so until Daniel's three remaining regiments approached the fence line, whereupon the skirmishers who were driven in formed on the right of the regiment.[216]

Stone directed his main line to hold their fire until he gave the order, and then to continue shooting "as long as a man was seen moving in that field in front of us."[217] The critical moment came when Daniel's men began climbing the fence that the 149th's skirmishers had just abandoned. The brisk Union fire stopped Daniel's first line in its traces. Some of the Confederate officers noted that this was the most destructive fire they ever witnessed.[218]

A number of Daniel's men rushed to the railroad cut to their front, and scrambled down its steep bank. When they were unable to scale the opposing bank, they found themselves in quite a fix because of the terrible effect of Stewart's enfilading fire from the left; Union canister was sweeping through the cut with terrible effect. At this point Lieutenant Colonel Wharton J. Green of Daniel's staff suggested to Colonel E.C. Brabble that he should order his men in the cut "to face to the left and clear the gap." Before Brabble responded, Green "scrambled to the top and got one shot at the advancing foe with a musket taken from a sick boy at the start, with whom my horse was left. Believe it was with effect, as it caused a pause in the line behind and delayed a down pouring fire until we got out of that horrible hole."[219]

Green, Brabble and their men barely managed to escape out of the cut in the face of a determined counterattack by the 149th Pennsylvania. Colonel Stone had seen the Confederates waver under the effects of his musketry fire and Stewart's enfilading canister, and directed Colonel Walton Dwight to lead the 149th forward. Dwight readily chased the Confederates out of the cut, and then advanced beyond it to the rise that had been held so valiantly by the 147th New

York earlier in the day.[220] Captain J. C. Johnson of the 149th recalled, "Our men delivered a volley, then crossed the cut, loading as they went, and having delivered another volley, charged, driving the enemy over the fence in confusion."[221] Captain John Bassler of Dwight's Company C noted that it was easy for the Colonel and the right companies of the regiment to cross the shallow eastern end of the cut, "but the further to the left the deeper the cut, and the more difficult to cross."[222] General Doubleday had witnessed Dwight's counterattack and thought it to be a bold move. He was certainly pleased to see its results were satisfactory.[223]

After repulsing Daniel's first attack, Dwight formed his men in single file on the edge of the cut, "their arms resting on the bank, with orders to take deliberate aim at the knees of the front rank of the enemy as he came up." His account clearly states that his line was "in the cut," and Captain John Irwin suggested the same when he reported, "our regiment went into this (cut) and lay along the opposite side, pouring a sharp fire over the top of the bank."[224] If these accounts are true, and the regiment was indeed on the inside rim of the cut, rather than on the rise previously held by the 147th New York, just north of the cut, there must have been an unmanned stretch of the 149th's line for 10-20 yards, at the center of the cut, where the slope was too steep for anyone to stand on. Dwight at the same time also placed his colors some 20 paces from the left flank of his command, at Colonel Stone's orders, in order to draw enemy fire from the regimental line.[225]

Daniel was not about to let his suddenly demoralized men break for the rear, as they wished to do. Lieutenant Colonel Green of Daniel's staff was quite impressed with the way that Daniel took charge of the situation and "plucked the flower safely out of the nettle danger...." In his stentorian tones audible in command a quarter of a mile or more away, he ordered the men to halt and reform on him. This they did without regard to company or regimental formation almost to a man.[226] After rallying the 2nd Battalion and 45th North Carolina, Daniel directed the 43rd and 53rd to cover his right, and brought up the 32nd to support his left.[227] Colonel E. C. Brabble of the 32nd had advanced on the brigade's right flank during Daniel's first assault, but did not push forward very aggressively and withdrew "for want of support" when he saw that "the cut in front of the other regiments was too difficult for them to cross."[228] Daniel also sent a staff officer to request Archer's command to support his right. He had seen these troops "lying down in the line of battle" only a short distance to his right, and was disappointed when they "for some cause failed to comply."[229]

Daniel's second assault advanced confidently until it reached the by now bullet ridded fence north of the railroad line. It was not until then that the Confederates noticed Dwight's regiment along the northern rim of the cut. The first Confederate volley was aimed at the regimental flags on the 149th's left, and so did not cause a great deal of harm. Dwight responded by ordering his men to fire by battalion at the Confederate line, only 22 paces in their front: "Its effect on the enemy was terrible, he being at the time brigade 'en masse;' a 9-pace interval." Dwight's initial fire staggered Daniel's advance, but the Confederates recovered and proceeded over the fence. By now Dwight's men had reloaded. Dwight directed them to hold their fire "until we could almost reach him with the muzzles of our pieces." The Union volley once again devastated Daniel's ranks, and Dwight reported that the enemy's dead and wounded completely covered the ground in his front.[230]

Despite this success, Dwight soon found that his advanced position was becoming untenable. The Confederate troops on his front maintained a steady fire on his line, and his left flank was threatened by a Confederate regiment (the 32nd North Carolina) that was charging past the railroad line towards the Chambersburg Pike. In addition, his line began to receive heavy fire from "three or four pieces of artillery [Brander's battery] in an orchard on our left, about half a mile distant, commanding the cut I occupied."[231] Dwight's order to retreat came just in the nick of time. Companies A and F on the right end of the line managed to escape the cut easily because its banks were only a few feet high. The troops on the left had a much more difficult time "because of the deepness of the cut." Some lost their hold when near the top and slid back again; some ran to the right to get out, and numbers on the left never got out, except as prisoners, for the enemy was upon them before they could clear the cut."[232] Needless to say, the rest of the men of the regiment withdrew in some disorder. Not having their flags to rally on, those who could gathered around the tall form of their commander.[233]

Dwight was much embarrassed that he had to leave his command's colors behind when he withdrew. As already noted, he had placed them some 50 yards to the left front of his left flank in order to deceive the enemy as to the true location of his line. During the Confederate counterattack, Dwight did not have time to recall his color guard from their exposed position. He later reported, quite apologetically, "To have saved my colors would have been to advance between two forces of the enemy, both my superiors in numbers; also to have put my command under an enfilade battery fire. It would have been certain surrender or destruction. I saved the regiment and lost the colors."[234] Luckily for the abandoned color guard, the railroad cut in their front for the moment shielded them from attack in the quarter. In addition, the Confederates were cautious to approach the flags, because they believed the entire regiment that belonged to the flags was there lying in the wheat.

The men of the 45th North Carolina would have liked to pursue Dwight's scattered and disordered command, but their advance was blocked by the unexpected appearance of the cut in their front. About a quarter of the regiment nevertheless slid down the embankment, soon to emerge with "several squads of prisoners, some 20 or 30 in number." By then Lieutenant Colonel Boyd decided to withdraw about 50 paces in order to reform. It proved not to be a good move, for the regiment now found itself exposed without cover to a flanking fire from Stewart's battery on the ridge to their left. Captain J.A. Hopkins of the 45th reported that "During the reformation of this line, the regiment suffered more than it ever did in the same length of time." Officer losses were particularly heavy at this time—Lieutenant Colonel S.H. Boyd was wounded, as was Lieutenant Samuel F. Adams Jr.; Captain P.P. Scales was mortally wounded, and Lieutenants George F. Boyd and W.E. Harris were killed.[235]

The 2nd North Carolina Battalion had attacked on the left of the 45th North Carolina, and was able to cross the railroad line where its cut was shallow in the swale between East and West McPherson Ridges. Its men were eager to get at Dwight's fleeing regiment, but they ran directly into the fire of Colonel Edmund Dana's 143rd Pennsylvania, which had held its position along the Chambersburg Pike when the 149th Pennsylvania advanced to its left. This fire "checked their impetuosity, and sent them back in 'Double Quick Time' without regard to order and lossing heavy (sic) all the way."[236] The 2nd lost heavily in officers during this attack; Lieutenant Colonel H.L. Andrews was killed and Major John M. Hancock was wounded. Command of the battalion for the rest of the battle devolved on Captain Van Brown of Company H.[237] Elements of the shattered 2nd withdrew to the shelter of the railroad cut to their right, but Daniel withdrew most of the unit about 40 more paces to the reverse crest of the ridge, where the 45th North Carolina was attempting to secure shelter from Stewart's cannons on Seminary Ridge.[238]

While Daniel's 45th and 2nd Battalion were facing the 149th and 143rd Pennsylvania, the 32nd North Carolina on the right wing of the attack was moving straight towards the McPherson farm buildings in the rear of Stone's line. Colonel Langhorne Wister of the 150th Pennsylvania, which was found facing west on McPherson's ridge at a right angle to the Pike, saw the 32nd coming and was aware of the great gap of over 200 yards between his right near the McPherson house and the forward position of the 149th Pennsylvania at the western railroad cut. He accordingly divided his command into two wings in order to meet the crisis. Major Thomas Chamberlin was directed to hold the regiment's original line on McPherson's Ridge with four companies, while Lt. Colonel Henry S. Huidekoper took charge of Companies A, F, and D and swung them to the right to face the advance of the 32nd North Carolina. The maneuver succeeded "in good order, though under a severe musketry fire."[239] The 32nd was for the moment checked, and its commander decided to fall back for want of support on the left and the right.[240]

Union officer casualties were also heavy at this time, and continued to mount, as did those of the men. Colonel Roy Stone was badly wounded in the hip and arm when he went forward to reconnoiter, and had to be taken to the McPherson barn; command of the brigade was passed on to Colonel Langhorne Wister of the 150th.[241] Lieutenant Colonel Walton Dwight of the 149th was wounded in the thigh at the railroad cut, and his acting Major, Captain John Irvin, was wounded in the head early in the action and had to leave the field. Captain John M. Bassler was wounded early in the fight, and Captain A. J. Scofield of Company A was killed during the second charge to the railroad cut. Captain Brice Blair of Company I stayed on the field after losing his arm until compelled by loss of blood to retire. Captains Soult and Jones of Companies H and G were also both wounded severely. Loss of regimental officers was so severe that command of the 149th at the end of the day was turned over to Captain James Glenn, who had commanded the division's provost guard during the day and so missed the hard fighting at the railroad cut.[242]

Colonel Wister, now elevated to brigade command, surveyed the situation along the Pike and was concerned by the strength of the Confederate "sharpshooters" (a portion of the 2nd North Carolina Battalion) located in the western railroad cut. Since Huidekoper's detachment of the 150th Pennsylvania was occupied with the 32nd North Carolina on its front, Wister directed the 149th Pennsylvania to charge the cut yet another time. The 149th had barely regrouped after its rapid retreat from the cut a few minutes earlier, but bravely stepped forward to the task. Captain Bassler of the 149th sadly noted that "this charge cost us dearer than the enemy."[243] Nevertheless, the attack achieved its objective and cleared the enemy out of the cut. This time the regiment did not stop to form along the cut. It was receiving such heavy fire from the 45th North Carolina to its front and the 32nd to the left that it soon had to fall back to the road.[244]

The 149th's withdrawal from the railroad cut encouraged Colonel E.C. Brabble of the 32nd North Carolina to renew his advance toward the McPherson farm buildings. The regiment was now advancing on the front occupied by Huidekoper's three companies of the 150th Pennsylvania, but the Confederates apparently did not see the Yankee line as it crouched behind the fence adjoining the road. Huidekoper directed his men to hold their fire until the enemy was within 50 yards. They then poured forth a devastating volley "Which staggered them so completely that a second one was fired before an attempt was made to advance or retreat."[245]

Colonel Wister now boldly decided to counterattack in order to follow up his advantage and attempt to relieve pressure on the 149th Pennsylvania. He at once directed Huidekoper's men to fix bayonets, and led the attack in person by drawing his sword and hopping over the fence, calling upon the regiment to follow. Huidekoper wheeled his three companies to the left, and advanced them until they were "within pistol-shot of the rebel line, which, after delivering a destructive fire, gave way and fled in confusion."[246] It appears that Wister at this time may have temporarily swung the left wing of his regiment to the right and the Chambersburg Pike. Their line extended too far west along the Pike, downhill towards Willoughby Run. As a result, they did not hear Wister's order to charge, and stayed on the Pike, being at the time "busily engaged in breaking up a force which had gathered in the corner of a field beyond the railroad bed." They succeeded at scattering this force, which was either the right of the 32nd North Carolina or part of Davis' command.[247]

One source claims that Wister's attack succeeded at reclaiming the colors of the 149th Pennsylvania, which could be seen "still planted in the wheatfield in front of the right of the 150th."[248] This account is not correct, as will be seen in Chapter VII.

Wister's command suffered additional heavy losses, particularly in officers, in this attack. Colonel Wister himself was shot through the mouth and face while returning towards the McPherson barn. He was "not actually disabled," but found he was unable to speak because of the excessive flow of blood, and reluctantly had to yield brigade command to Colonel Edmund L. Dana of the 143rd Pennsylvania.[249] At about the same time, Major Thomas Chamberlin, and adjutant Richard I. Ashurst of the 150th Pennsylvania were wounded.[250] All these accumulated casualties placed captains in charge of both the 149th Pennsylvania and 150th Pennsylvania.

Paul's Brigade Joins the Front

While Stone and Daniel were slugging it out in attacks and counterattacks, the rest of Rodes' division was continuing to maintain position against Robinson's line on Oak Ridge. Iverson's 12th North Carolina maintained a fire against Baxter's left, and O'Neal's brigade mounted another attack against the right center of the line where it was bent back to the Mummasburg Road. O'Neal was unable to force the main body of the 90th Pennsylvania back, but some of his skirmishers did succeed at occupying the northern edge of the stone wall that ran up the ridge crest to the road.[251] In addition, Ramseur's veteran brigade of just over 1000 men was at last moving to the attack in belated support of Iverson.

Baxter's line was more than a little disorganized when the troops who had counterattacked Iverson's line returned to Seminary Ridge along with all the prisoners they had captured. A number of able bodied men had to be detached to guard these prisoners and escort them to the rear.[252] One member of the 83rd New York remembered seeing Ramseur advancing to the attack, and Lieutenant George W. Grant of the 88th Pennsylvania felt that the lull on his immediate front following the defeat of Iverson was "only the calm preceding the storm."[253]

Baxter's tired but exhilarated men must have been glad to see Paul's fresh brigade of 1500 men arriving to assist them just after the repulse of Iverson, so doubling the number of Union defenders on this stretch of Seminary Ridge.[254] As already noted, Paul's brigade had initially been posted in front of the Seminary, where they had engaged in constructing breastworks of rails.[255] When they were ordered to the right, they advanced by the right flank around the northern end of the Seminary, across the rear of Stevens' battery, and across the railroad line. They then marched through the Wills Woods to the rear of Baxter's line.[256]

The 13th Massachusetts arrived first, and was pushed across an open field east of the ridge in order to protect the right rear of Baxter's line. The regiment pushed back some of O'Neal's men as it advanced, even capturing a few, and then formed facing northeast along the Mummasburg Road, facing the Confederate troops in the plain below. Colonel Leonard was wounded during this early part of the action, and Lieutenant Colonel N.W. Batchelder took command of the regiment.[257] Another early casualty in the 13th was private John Flye of Company K. He had to be left on the field at the end of the day's fighting, and at some point a Confederate soldier exchanged his own worn out gray pants for Flye's Union blue pair. When the Confederates left him behind after the battle, Union doctors at first refused to believe he was a Federal soldier because of his gray pants. He was eventually identified properly, but died on 26 July, and is now buried in the Gettysburg National Cemetery.[258]

Leonard's regiment was followed by the 104th New York, commanded by Colonel Gilbert G. Prey. As the regiment neared the front, General Robinson ordered Prey to form on the right of the 13th Massachusetts. A short while later, while Prey was moving to his appointed station, Robinson changed his mind and shouted down from the crest of the ridge in a loud voice, "Colonel Prey, god damm you, where are you going? Form on the left!" Robinson was known for his temper, so Prey obediently shifted his march without making objection. He also remembered that the guns were not yet loaded, so he gave the command to "March! Load at will!" as the regiment advanced.[259]

As Prey moved forward, the left of his line fell under heavy fire from some of O'Neal's men, who were "strongly posted behind a stone wall with thick underbrush." He directed his three left companies to charge the wall and dislodge the enemy, which they did "in gallant style." Prey was then able to advance his entire command to the line of the roadway. In the process the regiment captured some 35-40 prisoners, who were forwarded to the rear to join others just captured by the 13th Massachusetts, since Prey had "neither officers nor men to spare to take charge of them." In the next few minutes another 15 to 20 Confederates were captured and likewise sent to the rear.[260]

Paul's next regiment to arrive was the 16th Maine, commanded by Colonel Charles W. Tilden. The 16th had to clamber over a field of stones and thick bushes in order to reach the crest of the ridge, where it wheeled to the right and moved through some trees to a rail fence to face O'Neal's Confederates. During this movement they began receiving enemy fire, and Captain Stephen C. Whitehouse was killed. Once the regiment was formed at the fence, Confederate fire intensified, and Corporal Yeaton of the color guard was killed. In addition, Captain William H. Waldron was struck in the neck; he stubbornly stood by a tree, and urged his men on, refusing to be taken to the surgeons. At the same time Colonel Charles W. Tilden's horse was shot dead, and fell heavily with its rider. The Colonel, though, was unhurt and at once jumped to his feet. As the Confederates withdrew, Tilden ordered the regiment to counterattack. They crossed the fence in front of them with a shout, but soon had to be recalled when they ran into heavy artillery fire.[261]

Paul's remaining two regiments, the 107th Pennsylvania and 94th New York, were not sent to Baxter's right, but were ordered to support his left along the crest of the ridge. The men of the 107th had just cleaned their guns that morning, and its men had arrived on the field with empty weapons. When the unit was sent to the right from the Seminary in order to reinforce Baxter, the 107th's Major, H. J. Schaefer, reminded his commander, Lieutenant Colonel James McThompson, that the men ought to be ordered to load. McThompson declined to do so without orders from General Paul. Schaefer then took matters into his own hands by riding ahead of the unit, and ordering each company as it crossed the railroad line to load, which they did on the run.[262]

The 107th Pennsylvania was formed by left into line, and was rushed up to the top of the ridge to the portion of Baxter's line that the 88th Pennsylvania and its neighbors to the left had just vacated in order to counterattack Iverson's men.[263] The 94th moved up on the 107th's left, and may have fallen in with a portion on Cutler's command when it reached the ridge crest.[264] The two regiments arrived in time to be able to lay claim to helping to repulse Iverson's attack, and the 107th Pennsylvania even claimed to have helped capture some of the North Carolinians.[265]

The men of Baxter's 97th New York were not particularly pleased with the behavior of the 107th Pennsylvania when they returned to the ridge crest after defeating Iverson. The historian of the 97th relates that, "When the regiment reached the position from which it had started, a large regiment of fresh troops had formed on the easterly slope fronting north, where the 97th had rested. As our regiments came over the wall with the prisoners, and bringing off their wounded, this regiment became unsteady; though, as yet only under fire of a skirmish line, some began to go to the rear, when Colonel Wheelock immediately ordered his regiment to their rear to rally them." When this was done, the 97th turned back to recross the wall and face Ramseur's approaching attack.[266]

Captain Hall of Company A, 97th New York, however, did not see the rest of his regiment return to action. His command, which was the regiment's right company, did not hear the order to move "in the noise and confusion incident to rallying a regiment." Hall supposed the regiment had retired, and when he saw a large group of prisoners being escorted by a regiment some 300 yards off, he assumed this was the 97th and at once took after it at the double-quick. It took a while for him and his men to catch up to the prisoner guards. When he learned of his error, Hall directed his command to return to try to find the regiment, but was unable to do so before the I Corps line collapsed.[267]

When the men of the 88th Pennsylvania retired to their original line on the ridge crest, they commenced returning a steady fire against the Confederate troops in their front. Ammunition began to run short, so they emptied the cartridge boxes of the dead and wounded in order to maintain their fire.[268] Some members of the regiment even began ransacking the knapsacks of the fallen for more ammunition.[269] William Henry Locke of the 11th Pennsylvania recalled that "when the ammunition began to fail, wounded men, carried from the field, passed their cartridge boxes to the front."[270]

Sharpshooters were active on both sides during this brief lull before Ramseur's first attack struck home. Lieutenant George W. Grant of the 88th Pennsylvania noted that anyone who carelessly exposed himself was likely to be hit: "A head or body shown above the wall became a target, and many fell dead or wounded."[271]

At this time Colonel Charles Wheelock of the 97th New York was also attracting the fire of Blackford's Alabama sharpshooters deployed north east of the Seminary Ridge. It seems that he for some reason was defiantly waving the captured flag of the 20th North Carolina in order to taunt the foe. General Baxter did not approve of this and ordered Wheelock to send the flag to the rear for safe keeping. Wheelock refused to do so, saying, "My regiment captured these colors and will keep them." Baxter ordered Wheelock to be placed under arrest for this behavior, whereupon Wheelock called up one of his captains and gave him the flag. Wheelock then ran his sword through the flag, tearing it from the staff; whereupon he resumed waving the torn banner while the captain brandished the staff. The captain at once paid for the taunting when he was shot dead by a sharpshooter ball that struck him in the forehead.[272]

At about this time, O'Neal's brigade began its third attack on Baxter's right. One member of the 88th Pennsylvania heard "yelling from the timber on the right," followed by increased firing from that direction. It seemed to him that the line was about to be flanked, and his fellows began to grow uneasy.[273] To meet this new threat, Baxter had the 90th Pennsylvania shift front to the right. The maneuver was successfully executed under fire by Major Alfred J. Sellers, who "rushed to the front, superintended the movement, and quickly established the line in its new advantageous position." Because he was not the regiment's commander at the time, Sellers was later awarded the Medal of Honor for his deed. Lieutenant George A. Deering, of the 16th Maine, helped in his own way to drive back this attack by picking up the musket of a fallen soldier to use against the enemy. However, he forgot to remove the gun's rammer before he fired, "and the rammer went hurtling away with a crazy whizz that set the boys of his company laughing. It was strange to hear laughter there, with dead men by."[274]

At this time (about 1500), General Ramseur was at length bringing his fresh brigade into the fray. Ramseur had earlier been instructed by Rodes to send two of his regiments to support O'Neal and the other two to support Iverson. He accordingly sent the 2nd and 4th regiments to his left, and the 14th and 30th to the right. During this advance, the right wing met O'Neal's orphaned 3rd Alabama heading in the same direction, so Ramseur requested its commander, Colonel C. A. Battle, to join him, which he cheerfully did.[275]

Paul's right wing regiments, the 13th Massachusetts and 104th New York, had a clear view of Ramseur's left as it approached, and faced a little more to the north in order to meet the attack. During this maneuver General Paul rode up behind the 104th and received a terrible wound through the face that penetrated one eye and came out under the other, blinding him for life. At the same time, Colonel Prey's horse was felled. Prey later remembered that General Robinson expressed regret for the wounding of Prey's horse, since he wanted all his regimental commanders to be mounted. Even so, Prey did not remember seeing any other regimental commanders mounted during that fight.[276]

Prey now felt that his troops were becoming demoralized with no commander. He commented about this to General Robinson who was in command of the brigade. Robinson asked "Where is Colonel Root?" Prey replied that he did not know. "Where's Colonel Leonard?" Prey replied, "Not with his brigade." Robinson then told him, "You are the next in rank, take the brigade!"[277]

In actuality, command of the brigade when Paul was wounded first fell to Colonel Samuel H. Leonard of the 13th Massachusetts. He, however, was soon wounded, and the command fell next to Colonel Adrian R. Root of the 94th New York. Because of all this command confusion, Robinson at this point of the action gave Prey temporary command of the brigade. Later in the day, when the division had retired to Cemetery Hill, Robinson transferred the 11th Pennsylvania to Paul's brigade in order to make its commander, Colonel Richard Coulter, the acting brigade commander. Coulter was wounded on 3 July, and command passed to Colonel Peter Lyle, who was transferred from Baxter's brigade for this purpose. Lyle was the brigade's sixth commander during the battle.[278]

After being temporarily promoted, Prey led his regiment to the left, where a tremendous fire was coming from the angle of the road and the stone wall. Already seven color bearers had been struck down. Prey judged that he would soon have no men left if he did not drive the enemy back, so he ordered the left wing of the regiment to charge on the wall "or they would be dead men." For the only time during the war, the regiment hesitated. Prey stepped forward and shouted, "I'll lead you boys," and his men responded as he hoped they would. The wall was captured and the enemy driven back. Prey then returned to the right wing of the 104th and ordered a charge towards the Mummasburg Road. It, too, succeeded, and captured about 60 prisoners.[279]

Lieutenant Colonel N.W. Batchelder of the 13th Massachusetts also encountered heavy opposition as he shifted to the left to meet Ramseur's attack.His regiment had kept up a steady fire for an hour after they were first deployed along the Mummasburg Road. During this time they were "seriously annoyed by the fire of a regiment sheltered behind the banks of the Chambersburg Pike [Mummasburg Road]." When the enemy tried to charge across the road, "we let them have it in good shape as they ascended the bank nearest us. They tried to get back to the other side of the road, and we had them at our mercy. 'Give it to em for Fredericksburg!' shouted someone, whereupon they threw up their hats to stop the firing." A bayonet charge ordered by Batchelder then captured 7 officers and 125 of the enemy.[280]

Lieutenant Colonel Batchelder, however, neglected to mention that his regiment's successful counterattack took it too far from its supports. Sergeant Austin Stearns of the 13th remembered that his regiment was concentrating so much on the enemy in front that its men did not see a Confederate line advance towards a gap on the 13th's left and then let loose a devastating enfilade fire.[281] By now Ramseur and O'Neal had mounted a full counterattack of their own, and the 13th, "being almost surrounded, lost three quarters of its men before it got clear."[282]

Confederate accounts do not give us much detail of their first attack by Ramseur's left. Colonel Bryan Grimes of the 4th North Carolina reported that his unit and the 2nd North Carolina had moved to the attack earlier, but were recalled after proceeding only a few hundred yards and placed on a hill (Oak Hill) to repel an anticipated attack from the southeast. When this attack did not materialize, but the enemy instead shifted a regiment (104th New York) on the oblique to the left, the two North Carolina units were again ordered to advance. "After getting from under the cover of the hill, we were exposed to a severe, galling fire from a woods to our right, which compelled me to change front toward the right."[283] The 2nd North Carolina lost its commander, Major D. W. Hurtt, wounded early in the action.[284] Since neither the 2nd nor 4th North Carolina mentioned any men captured at this point, most of the prisoners taken by the 104th New York and 13th Massachusetts must have come from O'Neal's command.

The right wing of Ramseur's brigade likewise made little progress in its initial attack. Confederate accounts chose to gloss over it, emphasizing instead his much more successful second attack. Union recollections, however, make it clear that Robinson's line stopped this attack, and that several units even conducted limited counterattacks.[285] The 97th New York and a portion of the 107th Pennsylvania charged into the meadow near the edge of the woods on the left, and managed to capture some 80 members of Ramseur's command before being compelled to fall back to their line at the wall.[286]

Many of Baxter's men watched Ramseur's pending attack with extra anxiety because they were exhausted and almost out of ammunition. John Vautier of the 88th Pennsylvania remembered that the men of his regiment were totally worn out from fighting for three hours in the harsh sun, especially since they were without water, their lips parched and smeared with powder. Some were already beginning to drop out one by one "as the weary hours wore on." As Ramseur's attack neared, "it became evident to the exhausted soldiers that they had no further business being there."[287] Nevertheless, the units bravely held their positions. The men of the 12th Massachusetts had no cartridges left and boldly held their line for some time with empty guns and fixed bayonets; this fact is commemorated by the empty cartridge box depicted on the base of their regimental monument on the field.[288] This regiment, as well as Vautier's 88th, was relieved that the severest part of Ramseur's attack struck farther to the right and did not approach their lines.

Baxter's depleted regiments were now at last given leave to withdraw. Lieutenant George Grant of the 88th Pennsylvania remarked that "Tardy orders came to fall back." The regiments withdrew slowly to the southeast, subject to a "withering fire on front and flanks" that knocked men down at every step. Lt. Grant proudly stated, though, that the withdrawal was not hastily done: "We halted, fired, and checked the enemy, again and again, loading while retreating to make a stand and deliver another volley."[289]

Before reaching the railroad cut, the regiments of the brigade were rallied by General Robinson and moved to the support of Stewart's battery, which was deployed astride the deep eastern railroad cut in Seminary Ridge. Here they joined the 6th Wisconsin, and were soon reinforced by three of Cutler's regiments, the 14th Brooklyn, 76th New York and 147th New York.[290]

Cutler's likewise exhausted regiments had earlier pulled back to Baxter's right in order to escape the pressure of Daniel's troops on the left of their position in the Wills Woods. They had then been permitted to pull back to the eastern side of northern Seminary Ridge, shortly before Baxter was withdrawn. They rested there for at least half an hour, as Cutler waited for some much needed fresh ammunition to be brought up. Since they were subject to occasional shells from one of Rodes' batteries on Oak Hill, Cutler withdrew his regiments farther to the south to try to get some shelter from the railroad cut. While there he received an order through Colonel Henry C. Bankhead (I Corps inspector general) to send three regiments "to aid in repelling the enemy near the Seminary." He at once dispatched the three New York regiments already mentioned, and they were assigned to support Stewart's battery.[291] The aide who brought this order to the 14th Brooklyn had the misfortune of having his hand torn off by a Confederate shell as he was standing in his stirrups and pointing out the way the regiment was to go.[292]

The withdrawal of Cutler's and Baxter's brigades to the center of the I Corps line left Paul's brigade to hold the northern end of Seminary Ridge all alone. This certainly did not bode well for Paul's regiments, who had already lost heavily, particularly in officers. Though Rodes' initial attacks on Baxter's, Paul's, Cutler's, and Stone's brigades had been disjointed and sometimes even disastrous, they were repetitive and showed no signs of stopping. Since the Confederates had the superior force on the field and Doubleday was almost out of reserves, there was little doubt that Rodes' men would ultimately carry their portion of the field, particularly in view of what was happening to the XI Corps to the east. The only question was when and how they would break Paul's line.

CHAPTER VII

Collapse of the XI
Corps

*T*he ultimate outcome of the fighting between Rodes and Robinson on the northern end of Seminary Ridge was also greatly influenced by the events that transpired at the same time on the plain north of Gettysburg and east of Oak Hill, as noted in Chapter VI. Major General O.O. Howard had initially intended to support and extend Robinson's right with the first two XI Corps divisions that arrived on the field, Schimmelfennig's (recently Schurz's) and Barlow's. These troops at first successfully countered Rodes' left (Doles' brigade), but the timely arrival of Early's division on the Harrisburg Road totally changed the complexion of the battle, as Lieutenant General Richard Ewell had originally anticipated when he made the decision to escalate the battle at about 1300, contrary to Lee's instructions.

Major General Carl Schurz received his orders on where to post Schimmelfennig's and Barlow's divisions when he rode on ahead of his troops and met with Howard on Cemetery Hill shortly after 1200. Schurz understood that he was to push these two divisions on through the town "and to endeavor to gain possession of the ridge then partly held by the First Corps." In compliance with this command, he directed Schimmelfennig, whose division reached Gettysburg slightly ahead of Barlow's, "to advance briskly though the town, and deploy on the right of the First Corps in two lines." Howard's original intentions, it should be understood, were to prolong Robinson's line to the north, not to form in Robinson's rear as a support, as some historians have interpreted.[1]

Schimmelfennig's lead brigade was his own former command, now led by Colonel George Von Amsberg of the 45th New York, who in turn passed command of his regiment over to Lieutenant Colonel Adolphus Dobke. The 45th happened to be heading the brigade's column when it arrived at Gettysburg about 1230.[2] Since its men were exhausted and breathless from covering the last four miles at quickened pace after the thundering of the Confederate artillery was first heard, Colonel Von Amsberg directed Captain Francis Irsch to take the four right companies of the regiment and advance them as skirmishers up the Mummasburg Road. The colonel promised that he would bring up the rest of the regiment "as soon as they had gained breath and closed up."[3] Thus it can be seen that the Union commanders were not in any special hurry to rush to support Robinson, who was just then completing the formation of Baxter's brigade on northern Seminary Ridge.

Irsch's exact instructions were to advance out the Mummasburg Road, past the college, "taking McLean's red barn on Oak Hill for his objective point," and deploy to the right of the road as far as he could. Irsch's men met no opposition until they began deploying about ¾ mile from the town in a field of wheat or rye. Here they first fell under the fire of the four Napoleons of R.C.M. Page's Virginia battery of T. Carter's battalion, which Rodes had ordered placed on the eastern slope of Oak Hill in order to deal with the Union infantry that he saw approaching.[4]

When Irsch's line began advancing, "fronting Oak Hill," it ran into Major Eugene Blackford's skirmishers from the 5th Alabama. Blackford had been sent out by Rodes when he first began deploying his division two miles north of Gettysburg, under orders "to keep connected with those on my right, and feel for General Early's advance on the left." He moved steadily forward, brushing back Devin's vedettes, until he was within a mile of the town and came upon one of Devin's regiments drawn up in line, fronted by a heavy line of dismounted skirmishers. The cavalrymen charged him twice, but were readily repulsed. After about an hour of steady skirmishing, he encountered Von Amsberg's infantry advancing from the town.[5]

Irsch's men pushed their Confederate opponents back through the wheat/rye field for about 400 yards, making good use of their long-range Remington rifles. They suffered steady casualties, and at length sought shelter behind a fence running northwestward from the Hagy apple orchard.[6] Major Blackford reported that his skirmishers did a fine job at blocking Irsch's advance, which he judged to be the vanguard of a movement to seize Rodes' batteries on Oak Hill. His right company gave particular annoyance to the enemy until Doles' infantry brigade began to come up after 1300.[7] Doles' brigade had been assigned the left of Rodes' front line when Rodes began forming his command for action on Keckler's hill around noon. His portion of the line was on the open eastern slope of the hill, while Iverson and Daniel to his right enjoyed protection from both the height of the hill and the woods that covered it. When Rodes became aware a short while later of the approach of the XI Corps from Gettysburg, he moved Doles' command still farther to the left, for the twofold purpose of guarding the division's left, and providing a link with Early's division, which was expected to arrive soon on the Harrisburg Road. Doles met some resistance from Devin's cavalry skirmishers as he advanced, particularly on his left flank. After he dispatched some skirmishers of his own to dislodge them, Doles formed astride the Pike with three regiments left of the roadway (12th, 4th and 44th Georgia, left to right) and the 21st Georgia on the right.[8]

Due to his movement to the left, Doles' command no longer connected with O'Neal's brigade to his right. The open interval was screened in front by Blackford's skirmishers. Doles' command held a defensive posture for over an hour after it came up, being sensitive to its unsupported left as well as its weakly supported right. Doles was genuinely concerned that the XI Corps might try to make an advance against Rodes' batteries on Oak Hill, and he was pleased to prevent this from happening, as he held his ground and anxiously waited for Early to come up.

Arrival and Deployment of XI Corps

When Schurz and Schimmelfennig surveyed the Confederate dispositions north of Gettysburg, they were concerned about enemy strength both on their front and on their proposed objective at Oak Hill. For the moment all they could do was to deploy skirmishers to face Blackford and Doles; no push against Oak Hill could be even attempted until more regiments arrived at the front. For this reason Dobke deployed the rest of the 45th New York in skirmish order to the right of his original line when the fresh companies came up. These reinforcements permitted the unit to advance its line to the next fence, which abutted the McLean farm lane to the right.[9]

Schimmelfennig's next two regiments were formed in skirmish order on the right of the 45th New York when they came up, because of the need to face the rest of Blackford's sharpshooters and the skirmishers of Doles' brigade. The next regiment to arrive, the understrength 61st Ohio (which had only 143 men after leaving 40% of its strength in Maryland),[10] was formed east of the McLean farm lane at an angle to that of the 45th New York.[11] Its commander, Lieutenant Colonel H.H. Brown, reported that his unit was actively engaged with the enemy for the first half hour after it deployed, and succeeded at pushing the Confederates back through an open field into the woods.[12] During this time the 74th Pennsylvania came up and extended the 61st's skirmish line to the Carlisle Pike.[13] It also was sharply engaged, and lost its commander, Colonel Adolph Von Hartung, to wounds. Hartung, who as senior officer present had been commanding the brigade skirmish line, was succeeded as regimental commander by Lieutenant Colonel Alexander Von Mitzel.[14]

When the remaining two regiments of his brigade came up, Colonel Von Amsberg stationed them as supports about ¼ mile to the rear of his ½ mile long skirmish line. The 82nd Illinois was placed on the right, near the Carlisle Pike, and the 157th New York was deployed on the left, near the Hagy apple orchard.[15] From here the brigade gave what support it could to Robinson's men on the left, while keeping a watchful eye on Doles' brigade to the front and right.

It should be noted that Von Amsberg's brigade—and thus the entire XI Corps—at no time actually linked up with Robinson's lines on Oak Hill. To do so, Von Amsberg would have had to push some 400 yards to his left, across the Mummasburg Road, to link up with the right of Baxter's brigade, which was then just arriving on the northern end of Seminary Ridge. Such a move would have been in the teeth of Page's Confederate battery, something that Von Amsberg did not want to face, and since nobody ordered the move, he never attempted it.

Schurz noted simply that he "connected with the first corps' left as well as he could under the circumstances."[16] Thus Howard's troops never gave direct physical support to Robinson's soon-to-be-beleaguered troops on northern Seminary Ridge. As it turned out, this did not make a difference because of Rodes' poor handling of his initial attacks. However had Rodes coordinated his attacks and directed them better, Howard's failure to support Robinson more closely would have been much more significant. What actually did happen was that Howard ended up forming the XI Corps at right angles to the I Corps, a situation that would not benefit either. Their lines were awkwardly placed, particularly at their open juncture, and neither corps used the advantage of the Union army's interior lines to reinforce the other.

Von Amsberg was fortunate to have ample artillery support under a skilled and energetic officer, Captain Hubert Dilger, of Battery I, 1st Ohio Light Artillery. Dilger, whose six Napoleons had accompanied the 3rd Division's column on the march to Gettysburg, reached Gettysburg at about the same time as the 45th New York. He was then ordered by Schimmelfennig "to take a position between the Taneytown [Carlisle] and Baltimore [Mummasburg] road, wherever I might find it necessary," in order to support the corps' intended advance to Oak Hill. Dilger decided to deploy only Lieutenant Clark Scripture's section at first, and held the rest of the battery for the moment on Cemetery Hill.[17]

Scripture moved out at once past Pennsylvania College and formed his two guns on what high ground he could find midway between the Hagy orchard and the Carlisle Pike. From here, he offered much needed relief to the skirmishers of the 45th New York on his left and front, who were receiving an effective fire from Page's four Napoleons located on the eastern slope of Oak Hill some $\frac{1}{2}$ mile distant. Scripture's arrival at once caught the notice of Page's pieces, and the two units began an artillery duel at the distance of about 1400 yards.[18]

Soon Rodes sent his last available battery, Reese's Alabama battery, to Page's support. Reese's four 3-inch rifles, which had a longer range than Page's Napoleons, went into action on the eastern slope of Oak Hill about 400 yards north of Page's position.[19] This disparity in guns, eight Confederate against Scripture's two, persuaded Dilger to bring the rest of his command to Scripture's aid. Dilger's four guns found Gettysburg full of infantry troops as they moved to battle, but the cannoneers did not slow down, and the wary infantrymen did well to step aside in order to avoid being trampled or bruised by the artillery horses and guns. The men of the 157th New York, though, were glad to see more artillery coming forward to support their brigade, and gave the artillerymen rousing cheers when they came rushing by.[20]

Dilger brought his four guns up to Scripture's position and then opened fire with uncanny accuracy: "The first shot from the Ohio Battery flew over the Confederate (Page's) Battery. At this the rebels yelled in derision. Captain Dilger now sighted the gun himself and fired it. The shot dismounted a rebel gun and killed the horses. Captain

Dilger tried it a second time, sighting and firing the gun. No effect being visible with the naked eye, Colonel [Philip] Brown [of the 157th New York], who was near, asked, 'What effect, Capt. Dilger?' Captain Dilger, after looking through his glass, replied, 'I have spiked a gun for them plugging it at the muzzle. After the battle a wounded soldier from the 17th Connecticut saw this cannon with its muzzle plugged by an artillery shot.[21]

The artillery duel, now on more even grounds, quickly intensified. Many of the Confederate shells overshot their mark and caused a number of casualties in the ranks of the 157th New York, which was nearby within supporting distance of Dilger's guns.[22] Page tried to gain an advantage by advancing two of his guns to within 1000 yards of Dilger's command, but the move proved to be ill advised. Dilger's accurate fire battered Page's entire battery so much that the Confederate unit had to be withdrawn after suffering heavy losses of two men killed, two mortally wounded, and 26 wounded. Page's total loss of 39 men in the entire battle would be the highest numerical total of any Confederate battery in the engagement. Page also lost 17 horses at this time, and so had to temporarily leave five of his caissons behind, which were retrieved later. During this action Dilger's battery lost only two men wounded.[23]

After Page withdrew, he reopened his fire on Dilger, but it was now the fire of Reese's rifled pieces that began disturbing Dilger more. After about half an hour of trying to combat the longer ranged Confederate guns Dilger appealed to his battalion commander, Major Thomas W. Osborn, for help. Osborn responded by directing Lieutenant William Wheeler to take his four 3-inch guns and report to Dilger. Wheeler had recently arrived with Von Steinwehr's division and had taken up his initial position on Cemetery Hill.[24]

Wheeler advanced so briskly through the town that the rear body of two of his caissons broke down; one was later recovered, but the other was too badly shattered to be repaired. He pushed his guns forward and took up a position on a slight rise to Dilger's right. Wheeler's four pieces soon neutralized Reese's guns, so much so that Dilger decided to redeploy part of his command to his right front in order to get a better angle on the Confederate cannons. He boldly sent Lieutenant Wiedman's two-gun section about 600 yards and placed it on the right of the Carlisle Pike, supported by the skirmishers of the 61st Ohio.[25]

After posting Wiedman, Dilger returned to the rest of his battery and began to advance it to the right also, under the covering fire of Wheeler's guns. During their advance the four guns unexpectedly ran into a field ditch about five feet wide and four feet deep. Since he could not go around it, Dilger ordered his cannoneers to dismount and fill enough of it with fence rails so that his guns could pass in column by pieces. This was successfully accomplished in spite of a very heavy enemy fire. Dilger then advanced the guns about 400 yards into a wheatfield on the left side of the Carlisle Pike.[26]

As soon as Dilger was deployed in his new position, he sent for Wheeler to come up and form on his right. Wheeler's advance was delayed for a time by a strong fence that blocked his route; he could not proceed until axes were brought up from his caissons to chop down a section. Wheeler's rifled guns then redeployed and began an effective shelling of the Confederate guns on Oak Hill, which by now had inceased to 12. Rodes had become concerned about the efficacy of Dilger's fire and sent W. Carter's battery "to the foot of the high ridge" to help support Doles along with Page's and Reese's commands, which left only Fry's battery of the division's artillery on the western side of Oak Hill to fight the cannons of the I Corps. The opposing batteries kept up such a heavy fire upon each other that Dilger had to employ three caissons to bring forward fresh ammunition; even so, he almost ran out of ammunition twice.[27]

While Dilger and then Wheeler were engaging Rodes' artillery, the 45th New York on Von Amsberg's left had become engaged with the troops of O'Neal's Alabama brigade, which at about 1400 advanced south from their pre-attack position on the central and eastern portion of Oak Ridge. As already noted in Chapter VI, O'Neal advanced with only three of his five units, the 6th, 12th, and 26th Alabama (left to right); Rodes had detached the 5th Alabama to cover the gap between Oak Hill and Doles' brigade, and the 3rd Alabama through a misunderstanding of its orders attached itself to Daniel's brigade for awhile. Several sources from O'Neal's brigade mention the intensity of the artillery duel on their left that preceeded their attacks; their casualties included Captain T.R. Lightfoot and several privates of the 6th Alabama, wounded by Union shells.[28]

The men of the 45th New York were able to see O'Neal's left flank advance along the McLean farm lane at the base of Oak Ridge, "stealthily moving towards our left, where a gap between the right flank of the First Corps and our left seemed their objective point." The Confederates advanced steadily to their own right "without heeding our fire much" as they strove to strike the flank of Baxter's recently arrived troops on northern Seminary Ridge. At this point Captain Irsch of the 45th asked

Dilger to fire canister or shrapnel on the Confederates, which he did while the troops of the 45th lay down for cover. This fire made the massed enemy halt and waver. They nevertheless continued on "in a wavering and half resolute manner," past the front of the 45th.[29]

Captain Irsch decided to take advantage of the situation and advanced his four companies obliquely to the left, so as to be able to set up a flank and rear fire on O'Neal's line. When he was less than 100 yards distant, he ordered a terrible fire that, coupled with Dilger's canister and the resolute defense of Baxter's troops from behind a stone wall along the Mummasburg Road, caused the enemy line to halt and then melt away. O'Neal's men then "began to break and run up the slope of Oak Hill toward McLean's barn, and the Virginia battery (Page's) limbered up and lastly retired." A number of the Confederates, though, "finding they could not retrace their steps," surrendered to troops of the I Corps or to the 45th New York. In addition, Irsch's four companies charged the flank and rear of the retreating enemy, "capturing many prisoners, and finally took McLean's red barn, with many more prisoners." All told, the 45th claimed to take about 300 prisoners; the commander of the 26th Alabama complained that "some 40 were taken by the enemy, but it is my opinion that every man could have escaped being captured had they done their duty." This success did not come cheaply for the 45th. Colonel Dobke at one point saw eight comrades killed, "one after another, and some shattered to pieces." Thus O'Neal's first attack was defeated in the space of about 15 minutes.[30]

Just after O'Neal was repulsed, the men of the 45th saw a second Confederate attack moving southward from Oak Hill against Baxter's troops. This was Iverson's attack, which has been discussed in Chapter VI. Irsch's four companies opened on Iverson's left flank from their temporarily advanced position at the McLean barn, while the remaining six companies of the regiment also fired at the North Carolinian's flank from long range. The effect of this fire could not have been substantial, especially in view of the devastating volleys Iverson's lines received from Baxter's and Cutler's men on northern Seminary Ridge. One regimental sketch of the 45th claims that Von Dobke's six companies helped capture many of Iverson's men, with "our four companies of skirmishers in the rear picking up about three hundred prisoners more," who were sent back to Pennsylvania College.[31] There is physically no way that the 45th captured any of Iverson's men; the prisoners referred to must have belonged to O'Neal's command, though this brigade could not have lost 600 prisoners to the 45th New York alone. O'Neal's brigade had only 1688 men in the battle, and reported just 184 casualties missing or captured.[32]

While Iverson's attack was being repulsed, Schimmelfennig's second brigade, about 1200 men under the command of Colonel Wladimir Krzyzanowksi, began to arrive on the field.[33] As already noted, this brigade also was not at full strength, having left most of the 58th New York and 50 men of the 75th Pennsylvania in Maryland on various duties.[34] Schimmelfennig ordered the brigade to form north of Pennsylvania College in an orchard on the right side of the Mummasburg Road. The command was not moved forward to the front line because it was serving as support to Dilger's batteries and also as a counter to whatever movement Doles might make from his position astride the Carlisle Pike. For this reason the brigade's regiments were deployed in double column of companies[35] in the following order from east to west: 26th Wisconsin, 119th New York, 75th Pennsylvania, 82nd Ohio.[36] The assignment of the two companies present from the 58th New York is not certain. Colonel Krzyzanowski deployed one company (H) of the 119th New York as skirmishers "in order to prevent Doles' skirmishers from advancing to a large barn and several adjacent buildings to our right" (probably the Almshouse complex between the Carlisle and Harrisburg Roads).[37]

The mass of men in Krzyzanowski's command formed an inviting target for the Confederate cannons on Oak Hill that were already engaged in their duel with Dilger's guns. Corporal Alfred Lee of Company E, 82nd Ohio, observed: "The return fire of the rebel guns was lively, and their shot and shell ricochetted splendidly over the open fields. While the regiment was taking its position, a corporal of my company (23-year-old Corporal Isaiah Mahan) was struck by one of these missiles and thrown prostrate. Directly another soldier was struck, and the regiment, being unable to return fire, slightly shifted its position. Then the rolls were called, and the men quietly responded to their names amid the boom of cannon and the screech of exploding shells."[38] The 75th Pennsylvania suffered particularly from the Confederate shelling as it moved up. The regiment's colonel, Francis Mahler, was mortally wounded (he died on 5 July) before the regiment formed, and soon afterwards another officer was killed and two men wounded. This officer was none other that Lieutenant Henry Hauschild, a former resident of Gettysburg who a few minutes before had received "while marching with his regiment through the town, the salutations of his friends and former fellow citizens."[39]

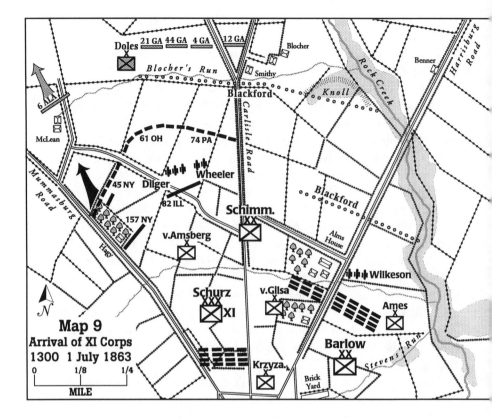

Map 9
Arrival of XI Corps
1300 1 July 1863

0 1/8 1/4

MILE

Schurz arranged Schimmelfennig's troops in such a way that be could begin a push as ordered to occupy Oak Hill, once Barlow's division came up and formed. However, he had sincere doubts about his ability to do so because of the number of Confederate troops (Doles' and Blackford's) on his immediate front, let alone the even greater number of enemy troops and cannons seen to be on Oak Hill. This is why he did not begin an immediate movement towards Oak Hill once the 45th New York and Dilger's guns began to meet heavy opposition on the Hagy and McLean farms.

Meanwhile General Howard had come to the same conclusion. He had originally intended for Schurz to "push out a strong force from his front and seize a wooded height [Oak Hill] situated some distance north of Robinson's position." Since he did not have time to reconnoiter the ground north of Gettysburg in person, he sent Major Charles H. Howard to do so at the same time that Schurz began deploying his troops. The younger Howard returned about an hour later with the unwelcome news of Early's approach from the northeast, a fact that was confirmed soon afterwards by dispatches from Schurz and Buford.[40]

This "alarming intelligence" persuaded Howard to direct Schurz to halt his command "to prevent his right flank from being turned." Even so, Howard cherished hopes of occupying Oak Hill, and directed Schurz "to push forward a thick line of skirmishers" to seize Oak Hill.[41] Howard's logic was clearly faulty, since there was no way that any line of skirmishers was going to wrest control of Oak Hill from most of Rodes' division. Apparently Howard was unable to see all of Rodes' men from his vantage point on Cemetery Hill because of the heavy woods on the crest of Oak Hill.

In accordance with Howard's orders, Schurz directed Barlow to form to the right of Schimmelfennig's division, where he could counter any Confederate units approaching from the northeast. Schurz's plan was for Barlow's first brigade to connect with Krzyzanowski's line, while the second brigade would be "held in echelon behind the right of the first brigade east of the Mummasburg Road."[42]

These dispositions gave Schurz's two divisions a frontage of about ¾ mile from the Hagy farm on the left to the Almshouse on the right. This force of about 5200 men was certainly strong enough to deal with the 1600 men opposing them in Doles' brigade and the 5th Alabama. Indeed, had Early not come on the scene, Schurz would have been able to advance on Oak Hill as Howard was still wanting to do.

Early's pending arrival, though, completely changed the situation. Schurz realized the import of what was occurring when he rode to his left and climbed up to a rooftop (probably the Hagy house) in order to see the progress of the fight against O'Neal.[43] From there he witnessed the severe struggle in which the I Corps was engaged, but he was more concerned with "the advance of the enemy on my line, especially the right. The enemy was evidently stronger than he had been at the commencement of the battle, and the probability was the reinforcements were still arriving." He felt particularly anxious about his far right, "which was liable to be turned if any one of the enemy's forces were advancing by the Heidlersburg Road." For this reason he sent one of his aides to Howard to request that one of the brigades of the 2nd Division, then being held in reserve on Cemetery Hill, be "placed upon the north side of the town, near the railroad depot, as an echelon to the First Division. My intention was to have that brigade in readiness to charge upon any force the enemy might move around my right."[44]

From the timing of events, it appears that Schurz sent Howard his request for reinforcements at about 1400. Howard in his battle report, though, implies that he did not receive Schurz's request until after 1500. By that time his right was heavily engaged against Early, and he replied to Schurz that no troops could be spared from his reserve of only "two small brigades."[45]

Howard's thinking at this time (1400 to 1500) is difficult to understand. It must have been clear to him by then that the Confederate position on Oak Hill was too strong to attack. Nevertheless he did not cancel or modify the orders he had just sent for Schurz to advance his skirmishers towards Oak Hill. The information that a large enemy force of unknown size was approaching from the northeast made it necessary for the XI Corps to go on a defensive posture rather than an offensive one. In spite of this change in circumstances, he insisted on keeping one-third of his troops in reserve rather than reinforcing his soon to be threatened right.

Howard must have been aware of the relatively weak line Schurz held in the plain north of Gettysburg, especially in view of the advantageous position the Confederate batteries held on the heights of Oak Hill. The awkward angle at which Schurz's line met Doubleday's should also have caused Howard concern. Nevertheless, he chose to hold both the I and XI Corps in position in spite of the increasing Confederate build-up on all fronts. His primary reason for doing so was probably the absence of a direct order from Meade to withdraw. Howard, or at least his corps, had been roundly critized for its behavior during the defeat at Chancellorsville two months earlier, and Howard was not about to abandon the field to the enemy at this point, particularly since the Union forces under his command had already achieved a number of significant successes against Davis, Archer, Iverson and O'Neal.

Howard's decision to maintain his position was also probably influenced by the knowledge that a large number of possible reinforcements was within just a few miles' march of the battlefield. Major General Daniel E. Sickles and the III Corps were known to be at Emmitsburg at 1300, and Major General Henry W. Slocum with the XII Corps was near Two Taverns, less than five miles to the southeast of Gettysburg. These two corps together contained about 20,000 men, slightly more than the number that Howard had on the field (including Buford's cavalry).[46]

At 1300 Howard sent a brief message to Slocum, with a duplicate to Sickles, to inform them that "Ewell's corps is advancing from York. The left wing of the Army of the Potomac is engaged with Hill's Corps."[47]

Half an hour later he sent another message with a staff officer to Sickles informing him that Reynolds had been killed and requesting him to come to support him at Gettysburg.[48] These orders placed Sickles in somewhat of a dilemma, since he had orders from Meade to hold Emmitsburg. He decided to resolve the situation by leaving two brigades and a battery at or near Emmitsburg, and to advance the rest of the corps to Gettysburg by two parallel roads. Howard's 1330 dispatch reached Sickles at 1515, and he at once replied that he would move on Gettysburg immediately.[49] In the next few minutes he forwarded Howard's dispatch on to Meade, as requested, and sent Meade two dispatches outlining his movements.[50] Since he had a two hour march to reach the field, however, Sickles would not arrive in time to participate in the battle. His prompt response to Howard's 1330 request shows that he could have marched out quickly at an earlier hour, and so reached the field much sooner in the day.

Howard apparently also sent Slocum at least one request (not extant) for help, which reached the XII Corps commander at about 1530. Slocum responded at 1535 that he was advancing the XII Corps "so as to come in about 1 mile to the right of Gettysburg."[51] His delay in reaching the field, and the impact had he marched sooner to aid Howard, will be discussed in Chapter IX.

At 1400 Howard sent the following terse note to Meade directly: "The First Corps came in position in front of the town; two divisions of the Eleventh Corps on the right of the town; one division of the Eleventh Corps in reserve. Enemy reported to be advancing from York (Ewell's Corps). The First and Eleventh Corps are engaged with Hill's forces. Have ordered General Sickles to push forward."[52]

Curiously, Howard in this dispatch did not ask Meade for reinforcements or further instructions. Perhaps these or other messages were conveyed verbally by the officer who carried the dispatch to Meade.

Shortly after 1400 Howard decided that it was about time that he personally inspected the lines of both corps under his command. It was a good time to do so, because no serious fighting had yet erupted on the XI Corps front and there was only limited action (an artillery duel and Daniel's attack on Stone's line) along the I Corps line. Leaving his chief of staff in charge at his headquarters on Cemetery Hill, Howard rode north into Gettysburg along with a part of Barlow's division.[53] He then rode along the corps line towards Seminary Ridge.[54] There was not really much to review, since Schimmelfennig's front consisted only of a reinforced skirmish line supported by Dilger's guns. The most significant information Howard gathered at this point of his tour was about the lay of the land on Schurz's front, which offered no advantageous posts to speak of. Most significantly, Howard did not meet with Schurz or seek to find him (historian Scott Hartwig suggests that Schurz may have been on top of the Hagy house roof at the time).[55] Such a meeting would have been most beneficial for both parties to discuss lines of defense and general strategy.

After sending Major C.H. Howard to see Buford, General Howard went to inspect the position of the I Corps. He later wrote that he "rode off to the left, passing in the rear of Robinson."[56] Since Baxter's brigade of Robinson's division was stationed on the northern end of Seminary Ridge (Paul was not yet deployed), and there was a large woods (Wills Woods) behind Baxter's left, it is likely that Howard simply rode south along the eastern edge of Seminary Ridge until he reached the railroad line, and so would not have reviewed Paul's actual line on the western crest of the edge; nor would he have seen Cutler's line deployed in the Wills Woods.

Howard next rode to Wadsworth's line (which he much later remembered as being entirely to the right of the railroad) and "had a few words" with that general.[57] Howard told Wadsworth "to hold Seminary Ridge as long as possible"[58] and then "stopped a short time with Doubleday farther to the west."[59] Since he conferred with Doubleday "about a quarter mile beyond the Seminary,"[60] it would appear that he saw Wadsworth near the position of Stewart's battery at the eastern railroad cut, and met Doubleday behind Herbst Woods.

The full extent of Howard's conversation with Doubleday was not recorded. Doubleday much later wrote simply that Howard "also examined my position and gave orders, in case I was forced to retreat, to fall back to Cemetery Hill."[61] These orders, and the directions he gave to Wadsworth, show that Howard, even after reviewing the strengths and weaknesses of the lines of the I and XI Corps, was still determined to hold on to their advanced positions. He apparently did not linger to discuss strategy with Doubleday, but simply left him in tactical command of that part of the field as before. Howard concludes his brief account of their meeting simply by stating, "After inspecting the position of the First Corps, and examining that part of the field, I returned to my former position at the Cemetery."[62]

It is clear that Doubleday would have had a lot more to say to Howard if he had been given the chance. In his battle report, written on 14 December 1863, he commented that he had hoped that Howard would have connected directly with his right instead of leaving "a wide interval between the two corps." He suggested that "this gap might have been filled by my falling back to the Seminary Ridge, but unfortunately that ridge is open ground" that could be enfiladed by the enemy batteries. As a result, he had to send Robinson's division from his reserve in order to man the northern extension of Seminary Ridge.[63] In his book *Chancellorsville and Gettysburg*, Doubleday extended his critique by complaining that the gap between Robinson and Schurz might have been avoided by placing Schurz and Barlow on a bit broader front: "This was a serious thing to me, for the attempt to fill this interval and prevent the enemy from penetrating there, lengthened and weakened my line, and used up my reserves." Lastly, he judged that the XI Corps line, as approved by Howard, was too far out, and should have been "echeloned in rear of the right of the First Corps."[64]

Barlow's Move to Blocher's Knoll

While Howard was reviewing the I Corps line and meeting with Doubleday, Barlow was deploying his division on the right of Schimmelfennig's. Barlow's command had begun arriving in Gettysburg at 1300,[65] about one half hour after Schimmelfennig's. Though it had advanced by the more direct road straight from Emmitsburg, its progress had been delayed by all the I Corps troops ahead of it. Howard later reported that "Barlow that day, always vigorous and pushing, owing to the heat of the weather, a road full of ruts and stones, and still obstructed by the supply wagons of the preceeding corps, made an average of but two and one-half miles per hour."[66]

As already noted, General Howard accompanied Barlow through Gettysburg before riding to the left to survey that portion of the corps line that was already formed. After debouching from Washington Street, Barlow moved his command across the fields north of Gettysburg, in the rear of Krzyzanowski's brigade, in order to carry out Schurz's orders to form on Schimmelfennig's right. He struck the Harrisburg Road between Crawford's farm and the town,[67] and formed his men astride the road at the top of Stevens' Run, a small tributary of Rock Creek that ran on an east-west course between the Crawford farm on the south and the Almshouse complex to the north. Von Gilsa's brigade was placed on the left of the road, and Ames' brigade formed on the right side of the road, "in a meadow by the road close column in mass for a rest."[68]

Barlow was accompanied by Lieutenant Bayard Wilkeson's regular battery of six Napoleon guns, which was serving with his division that day.[69]

The movement of Barlow's division attracted the attention of some of Rodes' gunners on Oak Hill, who began shelling his columns at the same time that they were targeting Krzyzanowski's men just to their left. Reuben Ruch of the 153rd Pennsylvania observed that "The shells were coming pretty thick before we reached the barn;" one shell caused almost the whole regiment to dodge it, though no one got hit.[70]

Barlow surveyed the terrain on his front while his division was massing, and did not like his position very much. The ground was open and the slight rise along Stevens' Run did not offer much advantage to a defensive live. Worst of all, there was a fair-sized knoll some mile to his front from which the enemy might dominate his front—and the entire flank of the corps—if they secured its possession. After some deliberation, Barlow decided to push his line forward and seize the 400 foot high knoll, then called Blocher's Knoll, but now known to history as Barlow's Knoll.[71]

Barlow's decision to advance was clearly not in line with Schurz's intent, but did technically follow the wording of Schurz's orders. What Schurz had directed was for Barlow to form his 1st Brigade on Schimmelfennig's right, with the 2nd in echelon in the rear as a support to the 1st's right.[72] Schurz clearly envisioned Barlow as forming on Krzyzanowski's right, near the Almshouse, but Barlow took license with his instructions to form on the right of Schimmelfennig's advance skirmish line. He may also have been influenced in his decision by the advanced position of Dilger's cannons, particularly the section on the east side of the Carlisle Pike 200 yards in advance of the rest of the battery. Another attraction might have been the apparent opportunity to deal with Doles' brigade, which could be more easily dealt with—or even attacked—from the knoll.[73]

Barlow did not send notice to Schurz of his intentions, but simply directed Colonel Leopold Von Gilsa to advance his 1st Brigade and occupy the knoll. Von Gilsa had only 900 men with him in three regiments, since the 41st New York had been left behind on guard duty in Maryland.[74] As the brigade passed through the field near the Almshouse the men were ordered to halt and unsling their knapsacks.[75] Most units did this before entering action; they usually left a guard for them, but were not always able to recover them later.

After this stop, Von Gilsa sent just over half his men (54th and 68th

New York, plus two companies of the 153rd Pennsylvania) forward as skirmishers to deal with the numerous Confederate sharpshooters known to be on the knoll. Since the 153rd was a nine months' unit that was due to be mustered out soon, Von Gilsa kept most of it (8 companies) en masse in the rear as a reserve.[76]

As often happened with short term units, their officers and men scarcely had time to master the complexities of military maneuver before it was time to be discharged. So it was with the 153rd Pennsylvania. It seems that the regiment's companies had become jumbled in their order when the regiment had formed in double column of companies near the Harrisburg Road before its advance. Somehow its two skirmish companies (A and F) found themselves at the rear of the regiment, while the color company was at the front. When the unit's commander, Major John F. Frueauff, directed the "1st division" to go forward as skirmishers, the color guard thought they were included, and began to move forward, even though it was unheard of to post colors on the skirmish line. Colonel Von Gilsa noticed the faux pas and sternly asked Frueauff, "What in hell that color division was deploying for." Fortunately for Frueauff, 2nd Lieutenant J. Clyde Miller of Company A corrected the situation by alertly ordering companies A and F to skirt the flanks of the regiment and rush forward at the double quick by the right and left oblique to take position on the skirmish line.[77]

Miller carried out this movement so quickly and skillfully that 1st Lieutenant Benjamin Shaum remarked to him how splendidly it was done. No sooner had Shaum spoken than he was wounded in the knee cap. This was ironic because Shaum had just the day before returned to the regiment and had not yet been paroled. When the 153rd had stopped near the Almshouse to drop its packs, Miller requested Shaum not to enter the fight. Shaum replied "that he would go in with the boys anyhow, parole or no parole." Since Shaum outranked him and had no sidearms, Miller offered him his own sword as well as command of the company (A). Shaum refused, and was wounded as noted just a few minutes later.[78]

The 153rd took a number of additional casualties as it advanced to action in what would be its last battle. 2nd Lieutenant William M. Beaver of Company D was shot in the chest near the heart just as he gave his men the order to advance, and would die later that day. 2nd Lieutenant Miller, who had just brought his skirmishers forward, saw a shell fly by so close to his face that he could feel its rotating fuse brush his skin.[79] In order to steady his skirmishers, Von Gilsa rode behind them and ahead of the main column of the 153rd Pennsylvania. Reuben Ruch of Company F, 153rd, heard the fiery colonel urging his skirmishers not to "shoot unless they saw something to shoot at, as ammunition was worth money, and they must not waste it."[80]

Von Gilsa's skirmishers pushed their opponents from Blackford's and Doles' commands back readily, forcing the Confederates to retire tree by tree on the right. Miller's command from the 153rd Pennsylvania pushed on over the brow of the hill and passed over and down its side, there forming the center of the brigade's line in Blocher's woods. A large portion of the 68th New York that had advanced through the wheatfield west of the knoll deployed between there and the Carlisle Pike to the left. The remainder of 68th New York was then posted in the woods along Rock Creek to the right of Miller's command, along the northeastern face of the knoll. The 54th New York continued this line southeastward to the bridge over Rock Creek.[81] The main body of the 153th Pennsylvania was not massed in one spot as a reserve, but was stretched out in one long thin line behind the center of the brigade's front for as far as its 400 men could reach. Its men then lay down in the grass to try to get some rest and try to avoid the bullets that were flying overhead from the continuing action on the skirmish line.[82]

Von Gilsa's line was certainly an awkward one, to say the least. It was not straight, but bent forward to an apex at the northern point of the knoll. Each wing of the line was about ¼ mile long. With only 500 men to cover this front, there was only about one man every yard. This line then, was actually little more than a reinforced skirmish line. His left was posted in open fields, but at least had the advantage of higher terrain above the channel of another east-west stream on this front. The troops on the right enjoyed no particular advantage from being posted in the woods along Rock Creek; all they could see was more woods to their front. Worst of all, the brigade at first had no support to its right or left. Nor was it in any position to attack Doles' larger command to its left front; in fact, Von Gilsa's unit as deployed was vulnerable to attack, as Doles soon noted. The only thing that Von Gilsa's advance accomplished, then, was a preemptive move to prevent the Confederate infantry from occupying the knoll.

While Von Gilsa was deploying on the knoll, Barlow also advanced Ames' brigade, but only as far as the rise on which the Almshouse was located. He had Ames form three of his regiments in double column of companies on the right (east) side of the Harrisburg Road, in the following order from east to west: 107th Ohio, 25th Ohio, 17th

Connecticut. The 75th Ohio was formed across their rear as support.[83] Wilkeson's battery was apparently formed in front of the brigade "near the poor house."[84]

It is difficult to see why Barlow formed Ames' brigade at this location, which was some ¼ mile to Von Gilsa's rear. The most likely explanation is that he was simply following Schurz's orders to form Ames "en echelon behind the right of the first brigade."[85] But it would have been much better to form Ames closer to Von Gilsa's line, especially since Von Gilsa's men were so thinly spread out.

Once his brigade was formed, Ames directed Lieutenant Colonel Douglas Fowler, commander of the 17th Connecticut, to send forward four companies as skirmishers to cover the brigade's front. Specifically, he was "to throw out two companies as skirmishers, the other two to be held as a reserve, and to take and hold the brick (Benner) house to the left and beyond the bridge" over Rock Creek.[86] This move, if successful, would certainly secure the wooden bridge of the Harrisburg Road over Rock Creek, which was located on the right flank of Ames' brigade. But it would do little to secure the rest of the ground in front (northeast) of Ames' position near the Almshouse. He should have sent out additional skirmishers in that direction.

Lieutenant Colonel Fowler requested volunteers to serve as a skir-mishers, and Major Allen G. Brady requested to lead them. Then Captain Henry Allen of Company F stepped forward and saluted, saying, "Colonel Fowler, Company F is ready." Soon the commanders of companies A, B and K did likewise, and Brady had his complement filled. He advanced his command forward and over the bridge, and then quickly deployed two of his companies as skirmishers along the creek to the right of the bridge. "The other two, held as reserve, were advanced in line, loading and firing as rapidly as possible, making at the same time a left wheel, so as to swing our right around the house, the reserve keeping near and conforming to the movements of the skirmishers."[87]

Brady's advancing skirmishers, who were the only organized Union infantry to fight east of Rock Creek on 1 July, were approaching the Benner house when all at once "the enemy opened upon us with shot, shell, grape, and canister" from a large number of cannons about half a mile to the northeast. These cannons, which comprised Jones' battalion, announced the arrival of Early's fresh Confederate division, which was then deploying to attack Barlow's unsuspecting flank. Clearly, Barlow would not have formed his troops where he did if he had anticipated Early's arrival. Since both Howard and Schurz were aware of this, having been kept informed of Early's approach by Devin and his cavalry patrols, they must be assigned the responsibility for not briefing Barlow. It is particularly strange that Howard did not explain the dangers of the situation to Barlow when he accompanied Barlow though Gettysburg just before the division was first deployed near the Crawford farm.

Schurz also must bear much of the blame for Barlow's predicament, since he had not been paying much attention to how and where Barlow was positioning his men on the corps' right flank. Schurz knew that Barlow was coming up right after Schimmelfennig's men arrived—indeed he had met the head of Barlow's division at the junction of Taneytown and Emmitsburg Roads at about 1300—but he did not take the time to personally supervise his deployment. Instead, he rode to his left to view O'Neal's attack on Baxter's brigade, and while he was there missed having a potentially significant meeting with Howard at about 1400, perhaps because he was watching the fighting from the roof top of the Hagy house.

Needless to say, Schurz was quite dismayed when he discovered that Barlow had pushed his line forward to the knoll. In his battle report, he stated, "After having taken the necessary observations on my extreme left, I returned to the Mummasburg Road, where I discovered that General Barlow had moved forward his whole line, thus losing contact with the Third Division; moreover, the Second Brigade, of the First Division, had been taken out of its position en echelon behind the right of the First Brigade."[88] He was also concerned, as he expressed in his memoirs, that Barlow had "instead of refusing, pushed forward his right brigade, so that it formed a projecting angle with the rest of the line." Schurz was never quite sure why Barlow had advanced to this exposed position. At one point he conjectured that "he had misunderstood my order, or that he was carried away by the ardor of the conflict."[89] Barlow himself never did explain his action fully. He was severely wounded in the battle, and so did not file a battle report, and did not write any memoirs in order to defend himself.[90]

Schurz took decisive action to try to make the best of the bad situation, since he expected Early's arrival at any moment: "I immediately gave orders to the Third Division to reestablish connection with the First, although this made still thinner a line already too thin and hurried one staff officer after another to General Howard with the urgent request for one of his two reserve brigades to protect my right against the impending flank attack by the enemy."[91] However, "before the forward movement of the First Division could be arrested by my orders" and Barlow could be withdrawn, Early's artillery had opened and there was no chance to do so.[92]

The best thing that Schurz could do at the moment was to send Krzyzanowski's brigade to support Barlow. This could be done because Schimmelfennig was under no threat at the moment, while Barlow certainly was in his exposed position, particularly if Doles should move to support Early.

Barlow also sensed the danger, and began rushing supports to Von Gilsa's aid. He sent four of Wilkeson's guns to the crest of the knoll in order to oppose Jones' battalion, leaving the left section under 2nd Lieutenant C.F. Merkle in position "on the south side of the York Road, near the poor house."[93] The 25th Ohio was sent to the center of Von Gilsa's line, and formed along the creek with two companies (A and F) sent out as skirmishers. The 107th Ohio deployed on the left of the 25th, at the apex of the division's line, and faced northwestward towards Dole's command. The 75th Ohio and six companies of the 17th Connecticut that had not been sent to the skirmish line formed as a reserve behind the crest of the knoll.[94] Brady's companies of the 17th, which had been ambushed by Jones' artillery, valiantly held their ground, even though the enemy's shelling set the Benner house on fire. Benner family tradition relates that "the house was struck by eight shells, one passing through, setting fire to the building, but for the continuing efforts of Mr. Benner the house would have been burnt."[95]

Barlow's decision to reinforce Von Gilsa's command on the knoll meant that he was ready to fight there, which seems a strange decision under the circumstances. Apparently Barlow genuinely felt that the knoll was an "admirable position "to hold.[96] He was also probably influenced by the fact that he had no good defensive position to fall back to. Whatever were the reasons for this decision to defend the knoll, this—and his original decision to advance to the knoll—would spell disaster for himself, his command, and the army.

Early Launches His Assault

Early's timely arrival on the right flank of the XI Corps was one of those rare strokes of good luck that sometimes benefited an army in action. His approach on the Harrisburg Road was set up, as has been shown, by his decision to advance towards Cashtown on a more southerly route than Rodes; this route through Hunterstown actually brought him closer to Gettysburg, though at about a two hour delay behind Rodes. It is interesting to speculate what the course of the battle might have been had Early arrived sooner. He had not been in any special hurry that morning, and did not break camp until 0800. Had he started out even two hours earlier, he would have reached the field while Schimmelfennig was just forming Von Amsberg's brigade near the McLean farm. Barlow's division was not yet up at that time, and Early would have been able to advance directly through the town towards Cemetery Hill. Howard surely would have held the hill, at least until additional Confederate troops could come up, with Barlow's and Von Steinwehr's divisions. But Early would have forced Doubleday to abandon Seminary Ridge, so exposing Doubleday's flank to an attack by Rodes, and setting up a mid-afternoon confrontation between Doubleday and Hill on western Cemetery Hill or northern Cemetery Ridge.

As already noted, it was late morning when Early received orders from Ewell to direct his march directly to Gettysburg. He does not seem to have have been in any particular haste to advance; none of the Confederate accounts mention the urgency cited by almost all the approaching Union units after they heard the cannons booming on the field. When he received Ewell's report that Rodes had made contact with the enemy northwest of Gettysburg, Ewell sent some of Lieutenant Colonel Elijah White's cavalry forward to scout his advance.[97]

Early's advance, as well as Rodes', was closely monitored by cavalry patrols from Devin's brigade, which had positioned itself to cover the roads entering Gettysburg from the northwest after it was relieved by the arrival of the I Corps west of town shortly after 1000. One source reports that Devin's troops formed a continuous skirmish line from the Carlisle Pike east to Rock Creek.[98] After his outposts on the left were pushed back by the advance of Rodes' troops soon after 1200, Devin concentrated his efforts on delaying Early's advance from the direction of Heidlersburg. Devin, "knowing the importance of holding that point until the infantry could arrive and be placed in position," sent the carbineers of the 9th New York to support his skirmishers along the Heidlersburg Road, and dismounted much of the rest of the brigade behind the 9th New York. Then, as White's Confederate troopers began to push his vedettes back, Devin directed his troops to retire "to the rear by successive formations in line by the regiment." In this way be "succeeded in holding the rebel line in check for two hours, until relieved by the arrival of the Eleventh Corps."[99]

One of Devin's outposts was manned by companies C and M of the 9th New York Cavalry, which were stationed on high ground across Rock Creek, along the Harrisburg Road. When Captain James R. Dinnin, commander of the post, saw the Confederate advance approaching, he sent a trooper to report this to Devin. A short while later he sent a second man with the same message. When neither of these men returned from Devin, Dinnin himself rode back to find his superior and receive orders.[100]

The 9th New York's regimental history continues the story: "Before Dinnin returned, the near approach of the enemy's line made the picket post untenable. The vedettes were called in and the squadron moved back rapidly toward the village and the flying bullets of the enemy's advancing line emerging from the woods along Rock Creek. While crossing Rock Creek, two of the men crossed below the bridge and one, Asa Comstock, had his horse shot and came back afoot through the fields, bringing his saddle and bridle. On the way back the squadron met Dinnin waving his saber for the men to come on. The captain's colored boy Jim had been to a house near the picket post to get some washing done for the officers of the company. When the vedettes were being called in, Jim hurried to the house for the washing, hastily placed the pieces in the nosebag strapped to the saddle of the Captain's favorite horse, mounted and galloped back toward the village ahead of the squadron. The enemy's bullets began tossing about him, he lay flat to his horse. The nosebag was flying and shirts, collars, drawers and stockings were scattered along the road and, no doubt, these garments afterward did service for the Southern Confederacy."[101]

After this somewhat hasty retreat, Dinnin's squadron halted on the road toward the village and immediately found itself within range of a Confederate battery that was replying to a battery (probably Dilger's) of the XI Corps that had just come up. "One shell struck the top rail of the road fence tumbling a man who was sitting there. Another shell came directly through a brick house near and the family rushed out in a panic." Since this position was not tenable, the squadron moved to the right, and soon located the rest of its regiment deployed in an open field near Rock Creek on the right of the York Pike.[102]

After the XI Corps began to arrive, Devin had been ordered "to mass my command on the right of the York Road and hold that approach." His function was to guard the right flank of the XI Corps and prevent it from being turned. To do so, he faced his command to the front and advanced his pickets some ¾ mile out the York Pike.[103]

While in this position, Devin unexpectedly began receiving a heavy fire from Cemetery Hill in his rear. "The fire becoming very hot and persistent, and many of the shells bursting among us, I was led to suppose for a moment that the enemy had succeeded in gaining that position, and I immediately removed my command into the town, the column being shelled the whole distance. After I retired, the battery turned its attention to my pickets on the road, and shelled them out."[104]

Devin later discovered that the source of this artillery fire was not the enemy, but Wiedrich's New York battery, which had been stationed on Cemetery Hill since it first reached the field in the early afternoon.

Sergeant Frederick Smith of Wiedrich's battery relates this incident as follows: "When the battery took position on East Cemetery Hill, General Howard was there, and addressing himself to the men said, 'Boys, I want you to hold this position at all hazards. Can you do it?' When a chorus responded, 'Yes, sir!' Just then a shell from a Rebel battery came screeching over the hill, and, as was natural, and from force of habit, some of the men ducked their heads. General Howard, noticing it, exclaimed, 'Don't be alarmed, boys, that was an elevated shot, fired at random.' That Rebel battery was soon silenced, and then the firing was directed at some masses of troops in the distance, towards the York Road, which were evidently part of Ewell's corps, when a man on horseback, who appeared to be a courier or staff officer, rode up to the officers of the battery, and ordered them to cease firing, that the troops in the distance were our own men, and that the shells were doing much execution. The order came, 'cease firing,' but was resumed in a few minutes. It looked very suspicious to the men of the battery, and a good deal of grumbling was done, for it was thought that the rider was a Rebel who came through the lines."[105]

Wiedrich stated in his battle report that "During the afternoon we had some skirmishing with a rebel battery which was posted near the road leading from Gettysburg to York," but he later admitted that "he supposed Devin's brigade to be a force of the enemy's cavalry."[106]

Devin's troopers lost a few horses but no men to this authenticated case of "friendly fire." The real significance of Wiedrich's mistake, however was that he forced Devin to fall back and leave Barlow's right flank unguarded just at the critical moment when Early was preparing to assault the same position. Had Devin been able to hold his position near Rock Creek, he might have forced Early to deploy additional men on the Confederate left, and so could have slowed down the enemy attack. He also could have countered or even prevented the several flanking attacks that Early would make against the withdrawing XI Corps troops as they attempted several times to make a stand.

When Early drew near the battlefield not long after 1400, he was well aware from the noise of the artillery that there was "an engagement in progress on the Cashtown and Harrisburg Roads, the enemy's troops being advanced out from that town on both roads for a mile." He could see Union artillery on Cemetery Hill, but could not make out if there were any infantry supports there. It was clear that he was squarely on the right flank of the troops opposing him, but his immediate concern was that Rodes' command seemed to be overlapped by a large force (Barlow) that seemed to be pressing back that flank. He at once called for his brigade commanders "to double quick to the front and open the lines of infantry for the artillery to pass." Early's veterans obediently piled their knapsacks and packs, and began hurrying forward towards the sounds of battle.[107]

In order to relieve some of the pressure on Doles, Early ordered Lieutenant Colonel H.P. Jones "to put the batteries into position so as to open fire" until his infantry could be formed to attack. Jones formed 12 of his 16 guns on a rise east of the Harrisburg Road about ½ mile northeast of Barlow's Knoll (now in the midst of a housing development).[108] From here he had a clear view of the field and was able to strike Von Gilsa's line as well as enfilade Wheeler's and Wiedrich's guns along the Carlisle Pike. Lieutenant Colonel Jones reported that he "opened fire with considerable effect on the enemy's artillery, and upon the flank of a column of troops that were being massed upon our right."[109] The effect of this sudden outburst of fire on the skirmishers of the 17th Connecticut near the Benner house has already been noted. The hour was about 1500.[110]

It was to counter Jones' guns that Barlow brought four pieces of Wilkeson's regular battery up to the knoll. Wilkeson's guns, which had been briefly stationed near the Almshouse (where the battery's third section was left for the moment) succeeded all too well at getting Jones' attention, and at once began drawing a terrible fire from the Confederate cannons. One gun was disabled, 12 horses were killed, 4 men were wounded, and Private Charles F. Hoefer was killed by a shell.[111] The enemy fire was so heavy that it began to unnerve some of the men of the 17th Connecticut, which was posted to the rear of Wilkeson's guns. Lieutenant Colonel Fowler tried to steady his men by calling out,

"Dodge the big ones, boys."[112] Wilkeson and Barlow, both of whom would soon fall casualty, quickly realized that they needed more guns to counteract Jones' numerical superiority. Wilkeson sent for Lieutenant Christopher F. Merkel to bring up the remaining two guns of the battery from their post near the Almshouse. Merkel formed on the western crest of the knoll and began firing solid shot at one of Rodes' batteries.[113] At the same time Barlow appealed in vain to Colonel Osborn for another battery to be sent up from the reserve on Cemetery Hill.[114]

Mounted officers in the thick of combat were always ready targets to the enemy, and it was not long after the battery was deployed that Lieutenant Wilkeson was struck by a shell that killed his horse and all but tore off his right leg. The shot that felled Wilkeson was witnessed by Major Campbell Brown of Early's staff: "I saw a knot of horsemen gallop up near their battery, having with them one of the large white flags used to designate a corps commander, and just as they got up, a shell from our guns dispersed (sic) the party, killing at least one, whom I saw them carry off. From the consternation plainly caused by his fall and the fact that their battery limbered up without firing another shot, I concluded he was an officer of high rank—but never knew whom."[114]

According to one source, Lieutenant Wilkeson bravely used his own pen knife to cut the few remaining sinews that still held his mangled leg. After the fighting ended he was taken by the Confederates to a hospital set up at the Almshouse. His wound was severe and he was suffering gravely from loss of blood. At some point during the night he asked for some water to relieve his thirst. He was given a canteen, but passed it on untouched to a wounded soldier lying next to him who begged, "For God's sake give me some." Wilkeson did not complain as the other soldier drank every drop. He just smiled on the man, turned slightly, and expired. He was only 19 years old. His father, Samuel Wilkeson, was a correspondent with the *New York Times* and was present at Meade's headquarters later in the fight.[115]

Though Jones' command had a clear superiority in numbers over Wilkeson's guns on Barlow's Knoll, it did not emerge from this action unscathed. One Napoleon of Garber's Virginia battery was permanently disabled "by being struck on the face of the muzzle and bent by a solid shot from the enemy."[116] Early in the action, one of Captain C.A. Green's two 10-pounder Parrott rifles was disabled "by a shot too large lodging itself halfway down the bore, which we found impossible to force home."[117] During the engagement Jones also had two other guns disabled by oversize ammunition, reflecting a difficulty encountered by Confederate artillerymen throughout the war.[118] His casualties amounted to only one man killed (Private Louis Tebault of Green's Louisiana Guard artillery), one man of the Staunton artillery wounded, and at least two horses wounded.[119]

During this artillery duel of about ½ hour,[120] Early completed the forming of his four infantry brigades. Brigadier General John B. Gordon sent one of his regiments, the 26th Georgia, to support Jones' guns, and formed his remaining five regiments of 1500 men on a line with the division's artillery on the western side of the Harrisburg Road; his line reached almost all the way to Rock Creek on the right.[121] Gunner Robert Stiles of Carrington's battery thought that "Gordon was the most glorious and inspiring thing I ever looked on. He was riding a beautiful coal-black stallion, captured at Winchester, that had belonged to one of the Federal generals in Milroy's army—a majestic animal whose 'neck was clothed with thunder.' From his grand joy in battle, he must have been a direct descendant of Job's horse, or Bucephalus, or Black Auster. I never saw a horse's neck so arched, his eye so fierce, his nostril so dilated. He followed in a trot, close upon the heels of the battle line, his head right in among the slanting barrels and bayonets, the reins loose upon his neck, his rider standing in his stirrups, bareheaded, hat in hand, arms extended, and, in a voice like a trumpet, exhorting his men. It was superb, absolutely thrilling." Stiles was disappointed to learn later that Gordon rode this horse in action only at Gettysburg: "He behaved well at first under artillery fire, but later, encountering a fierce fire of musketry, he turned tail and bolted to the rear a hundred yards or more."[122]

Early's second line consisted of Avery's North Carolina brigade of 1200 men, and Hays' Louisiana brigade of 1300 men. Colonel Isaac Avery, who was still holding temporary command of Hoke's brigade after Hoke had been badly wounded at Chancellorsville, formed his three regiments east of the Harrisburg Road, behind Jones' guns; his fourth regiment, the 54th North Carolina, had been left behind at Winchester.[123] Brigadier General Harry Hays, whose brigade had been marching in the rear of the division's column, was brought forward and formed his five regiments on Avery's right, astride the road.[124] Early held Brigadier General "Extra Billy's" Virginia brigade in reserve about ½ mile to the rear, along with Carrington's Virginia battery. Smith formed his three regiments on the east side of the road. He had only 800 men on the field, since two of his commands (13th and 58th Virginia) had also been left near Winchester.[125]

While Early was forming his division, he observed that Doles' brigade of Rodes' division was encountering some difficulty about ½ mile to his right. As already noted, Doles had been sent by Rodes at about 1300 to occupy the Carlisle Pike and guard the division's left flank from being turned. His very presence there had dissuaded Shurz from advancing all of Von Amsberg's brigade against O'Neal's left, and his skirmishers, along with Blackford's of O'Neal's 5th Alabama, had done a good job of dislodging Devin's cavalry pickets and securing control of the plain from the McLean farm to Barlow's Knoll and beyond. The arrival of the XI Corps had pushed these skirmishers back, particularly on the right, and Barlow's advance to the Knoll forced the skirmishers there to retire. Doles became concerned that Barlow might attempt to attack his left and rear, so he pulled his command back by the left flank.[126]

Generals Early and Gordon had seen Doles pull back, and seeing Ames' brigade moving in Doles' direction, became concerned for Doles' safety. Gordon noted in his battle report, "The enemy had succeeded in gaining a position upon the left flank of Doles' brigade, and in causing these troops to retreat."[127] Early was more dramatic about the situation, and wrote that a part of the enemy was "in line moving against the left of Rodes' division held by Doles' brigade," and that "Doles' brigade was getting in a critical condition."[128] Years after the battle Gordon turned most dramatic of all when he wrote his memoirs: "The Union forces...were again advancing and pressing back Lee's left and threatening to envelop it. The Confederates were stubbornly contesting every foot of ground, but the Southern left was slowly yielding. A few moments more and that day's battle might have been ended by the complete turning of Lee's flank."[129]

This was overstating the situation, since Barlow was not about to launch an assault on Doles with Early's command perched on his right flank.[130]

Nevertheless, the perceived danger to Doles persuaded Early to lead his attack with his right wing rather than his left. It might have been more effective for Early to put his weight on his left in order to turn and smash Barlow's right, which was not supported at all after Devin's cavalry withdrew into the town. Attacking Barlow's center with Gordon's brigade would surely be costly, but it would be the quickest way to get relief to Doles.

It was between 1500 and 1530 when Gordon received his orders to launch his attack.[131] His regiments at the time were deployed in the following order from left to right, about ½ mile northeast of Barlow's

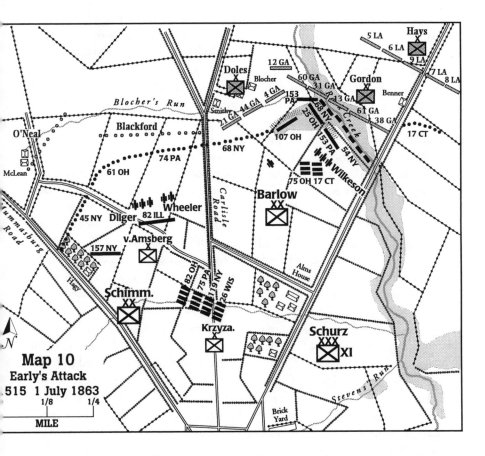

Map 10
Early's Attack
515 1 July 1863

1/8   1/4

MILE

position on the Knoll: 38th, 61st, 13th, 31st and 60st Georgia.[132] Because his men were "much fatigued" from making what was already a full day's march of about 12 miles, he let then move forward slowly until they were within 300 yards of the Union line, "when the advance was as rapid as the nature of the ground and a proper regard for the preservation of my line would permit."[133]

The first Union troops that Gordon encountered were the heavy skirmishers of the 54th New York and much of the 68th New York, which were posted in the woods along the western side of Rock Creek. Captain Miller's two skirmish companies of the 153rd Pennsylvania, posted farther to the left, were not yet engaged, but began suffering casualties from fire coming in from the right and rear. Miller got annoyed at what he thought was carelessness on behalf of the rest of the 153rd posted to his rear (more "friendly fire"), and sent a corporal back to the regiment to put an end to it.[134] Because of the cover provided by the trees in their front, Gordon's men were not subject to fire from Bancroft's battery during the last leg of their attack; Bancroft's guns instead turned their muzzles towards Doles' regiments to the west.[135]

Gordon was extremely proud of the way his brigade charged in what was to be one of the best executed attacks of the war: "Moving forward under heavy fire over rail and plank fences, and crossing a creek whose banks were so abrupt as to prevent a passage excepting at certain points, this brigade rushed upon the enemy with a resolution and spirit, in my opinion, rarely excelled. The enemy made a most obstinate resistance until the colors on portions of the two lines were separated by a space of less than 50 paces, when his line was broken and driven back."[136] Private G.W. Nichols of the 61st Georgia spoke of the initial obstinacy of the Union defense: "We had a hard time moving them. We advanced with our accustomed yell, but they stood firm until we got near them. They then began to retreat in fire order, shooting at us as they retreated. They were harder to drive than we had ever known them before. Men were being mown down in great numbers on both sides."[137]

As the 54th and 68th New York fell back, Gordon's men fell upon the nine months' soldiers of the 153rd Pennsylvania. Private Reuben Ruch of Company F, 153rd, was in the midst of the confused fighting as he withdrew from the skirmish line at the northern base of the hill. He saw Corporal Peter Smith strike the musket of a man next to him who seemed to be aiming at one of the retiring Union skirmishers. Ruch fired at the enemy line splashing across the creek, and as he reached for another cartridge the man to his rear was hit and fell forward "his face towards me." Then the man on his left was killed. Ruch fired a few more rounds and then heard an order to fall back. He at first hesitated to do so, and aimed his musket at a Confederate color bearer who was jumping through the creek and "yelling like an Indian." For some reason he decided to change his target, and instead felled a Georgian who was coming over the top rail of a fence just a few yards away.[138]

The 153rd was now in deep trouble as Gordon's men overlapped both its flanks. The corporal whom Lieutenant Miller had sent back to complain of the friendly fire in the back in the 153rd's skirmishers, returned to report "the rebels coming in our rear and right of our right flank, and that part of the regiment was gone." Miller pulled back to the brow of the hill and fell in with a party of the regiment that was being held together by 2nd Lieutenant Reisinger. Captain Reeder then came up and ordered him to turn around and return to his proper position on the left of the New York skirmishers. As he was doing so, Miller saw the entire line collapse and headed for the rear.[139]

The men of the 153rd suffered under a vicious crossfire as they fell back. Private Ruch remembered seeing his dead comades "piled in every shape, some on their backs, some on their faces, and others turned and twisted in every imaginable shape." Several members of the 153rd turned to flee rather than fight. Private Ruch remembered "an old fellow in the company by the name of John Snyder, whom nobody supposed could be moved to go faster than a walk. He was hard of hearing, and being too slow for drill, he was used for doing the chores about camp. But he always carried a gun. He was good enough to go into battle, for he could stop a bullet as good as anybody. Just as I came out of the woods I looked toward where the battery had been posted on the hill and I saw John Snyder in full retreat, his head drawn behind his knapsack and his heels flying. He was the only man in our company that I saw running at Gettysburg."[140]

Ruch himself was then hit twice in the legs. As he lay on the ground he saw Private John Trumbauer load his musket beside a big tree and say, "Come, boys, let us give them what they deserve." Trumbauer was then wounded in the right shoulder, and his gun fell to the ground. Undaunted, he raised it to his good left shoulder and squeezed off his last shot. Captain Howard Reeder of Company G emptied his pistol into the onrushing enemy troops, and then managed to escape when he turned to run away. John Ruch of Company K was hit in the left arm and then took another wound in the right collarbone. As he staggered to the rear, a lieutenant tried to rally him, and then told him to break his weapon in order to keep it from being used by the enemy. When Ruch said he could not move his arms, the lieutenant told him to pass him caps and cartridges while he fired Ruch's musket. The lieutenant did so for a short time until the Confederates drew too near, whereupon he left for the rear, allowing Ruch to be captured.[141]

The collapse of Von Gilsa's three regiments left Gordon's men a clear path to the five working guns of Battery G 4th US Artillery. Lieutenant Eugene A. Bancroft had withdrawn his three pieces a short distance after Lieutenant Wilkeson was wounded, and then aimed them to the left against Doles' troops, "firing spherical case and canister, until our infantry giving way in disorder, the want of support compelled me to withdraw the guns."[142] Lieutenant Merkle, whose two guns were deployed a little bit farther to the left of Bancroft, did the same. He had used shell and spherical case shot against Doles' lines, "and as the line of the enemy came closer, and I ran out of shot, shell, and case shot, I used canister; the enemy was there within canister range. At the same time, our infantry fell back rapidly, and left me almost without support," so he limbered to the rear and retired to the town.[143]

Doles' Georgians were greatly relieved to see the Union artillery retire from the knoll. Though he had no orders to so, Doles had moved his command to the attack when he saw Gordon advance. He did so even before he had reformed all his sharpshooters who had been driven back from Barlow's Knoll, or the ones who had been deployed east of the Knoll and had been displaced by Early's arriving troops.[144] Doles commented in his battle report that "we suffered severely from the enemy's batteries and musketry in this attack."[145] His regiments received one volley from the defenders that did "considerable execution" and then charged before the Yankees could reload, driving them from behind their line behind a rock fence. Lieutenant Colonel D.R.E. Winn of the 4th Georgia was killed in this first attack, leaving his regiment to Major W.H. Willis.[146] Though the Union defense was "a little stubborn," it soon gave way "with considerable loss."[147] The success of the Confederate attack was greatly aided by the fact that Doles' line outflanked the left of the 107th Ohio to the right (west), where the small detachment of the 68th New York deployed in skirmish order was the only Union force between Barlow's left and the Carlisle Pike. Barlow would have been better advised to have posted one of his two reserve regiments (75th Ohio or 17th Connecticut) on this line in order to prevent his position on the knoll from being outflanked on the left.

During this attack a strange incident befell General Doles that could have had a deleterious effect on both him and his brigade. "Gen. Doles was riding a very powerful sorrel horse, and before he could realize it the horse had seized the bit between his teeth and made straight for the Federal line as a bullet, and going at full speed. We thought the General was gone, but when in about fifty yards of the line he fell off in the wheat. The Federals, being in wavering condition, did not seem to pay any attention to him. The horse ran apparently to within ten or fifteen feet of the Federal line, wheeled, and came back to our brigade; and strange to say, he had no sign of a wound about him."[148]

The 450 men of the 107th Ohio which was opposing Doles did not give way solely because of the ferocity of Doles' attack. The 107th was receiving an enfilade fire from Gordon's advancing troops to the east, just as the regiment to its right was also receiving enfilade fire from Doles' troops to the west. Such was the disadvantage of holding the apex of Barlow's angled line. No battle report was filed for the 107th Ohio, which closed the battle under the command of a captain, John M. Lutz, after its colonel, Seraphim Meyer, was wounded. Lieutenant Colonel Jeremiah Williams of the 25th Ohio was captured on 1 July, and heavy loss of other officers left command of the unit to Lieutenant Israel White. He wrote in his battle report simply that "The regiment engaged the enemy, and maintained its position until compelled to retire before the superior force of the enemy."[149]

Colonel Andrew L. Harris of the 75th Ohio gives the best account of this portion of the action: "It was not long after the line was formed, until the whole division was hotly engaged. Gordon's brigade of Early's division was pressing Colonel Von Gilsa's brigade, and O'Neal's sharp-shooters, and Doles' brigade of the enemy were pressing Ames' brigade very hard. The sharpshooters were formed and advanced in very close skirmish line supported by Doles' brigade. The pressure soon became so great and the fire of the enemy so hot and deadly that it was evident our brigade and in fact the division could not long hold."[150]

At this point Ames ordered Harris to have his men "fix bayonets, pass to the front between the 107th and 25th Ohio, and if possible check the advance of the enemy." The 75th moved forward, passing over the high ground where the line had first been formed, and entered the thin woods on the forward slope of the hill. "It was a fearful advance and made at a dreadful cost of life." Harris had to halt and start firing because he could advance no farther. He was able to check the enemy for a moment in his front, but could not stop them on his flanks. As time passed, his situation became "perilous in the extreme." The 75th could not advance, and the regiment was losing men fast—4 of its 12 officers who made the charge were dead or dying, and half of the enlisted men were down. He kept expecting "orders to fall back on assistance to hold on," but none came. At last, Harris began to fall back without orders, and as he did so he found the whole division retiring.[151]

The 17th Connecticut had been ordered to counterattack at the same time that Harris was, and met the same difficulties as the 75th Ohio. The 17th, which had been stationed to the right of the 75th on the back slope of the knoll, still had only six of its companies in line, since four had been sent earlier on skirmish duty to the east side of Rock Creek. When the 17th's commander, Lieutenant Colonel Douglas Fowler, received his orders to attack, he "at once rode to the front and gave the command to deploy columns, and swinging his sword said:

'Seventeenth, do your duty! Forward, double quick! Charge bayonets! and with a yell, which the boys knew how to give, they charged.'"[152]

The 17th, though, had its advance impeded by some of Von Gilsa's retreating troops who broke though Fowler's line as the regiment advanced. When the 17th reached the top of the hill, they fired a good volley, and then had to fall back ten feet in order to avoid being surrounded. The regiment's men fell in droves. Among the first to be killed was Lieutenant Colonel Fowler, who was conspicuously mounted on a white horse. Private Williams H. Warren was the witness to the grisly scene when his commander was struck by an artillery shell: "Lieut. Colonel Fowler was killed, and his head shot off and his brains flew on the Adjutant." At the same time Captain James E. Moore was killed, and Captain Wilson French and Lieutenant Henry Quien were wounded.[153] One Confederate volley wounded Private J. Henry Blakeman of Company D and killed his good friend Stephen Crofut. Three days later Blakeman described the scene in an emotional letter to his mother: "Stephen was killed by the same volly [sic] that wounded me. He was within three feet of me was shot through the head and killed instantly. Stephen was liked by the whole co. and will be much mourned. I know it will almost kill his mother but reality is better than suspense and what I tell you, you can depend on."[154]

The fighting now grew fierce as Gordon's troops closed in. At one point a color bearer of the 17th was banging his flagstaff against the flagstaff of one of the Georgia regiments, an episode rare enough to be specifically commented on afterwards.[155] The 17th's men were being pushed back all along that line, and soon had no choice but to retreat, as the 75th Ohio was doing to their left. Despite the maelstrom, Sergeant Major C. Frederick Betts was not about to leave the body of his commander behind. He and another soldier tried to lift Lieutenant Colonel Fowler's body onto Adjutant M. Whitney Chatfield's horse, but "found it impossible to do so, as his weight was beyond our strength, and after several attempts we reluctantly left him." By then the enemy was close all around, and was "more rigorous than polite," ordering Betts to surrender. He chose instead to try to flee "by scaling a fence in front of us towards the stone wall of the poor house."[156]

The men of the 17th sincerely regretted that they could never recover the body of their brave lieutenant colonel. Lieutenant Doty and some companions returned to the scene of the fighting on 4 July, after the Confederates had withdrawn to Seminary Ridge, in order to find Fowler's body. They were disgusted to find that the Union dead on the knoll had been "stripped of all but underclothing by the rebels and thrown into a ditch and covered over...so it was impossible to recognize them." In 1889 the survivors of the regiment would erect a flagpole on the crest of the knoll to mark the spot were Fowler was killed.[157]

Private William H. Warren also barely escaped from the knoll with his life: "I partly loaded with my back to the enemy, then they commenced to run again so I run—a little ways farther & Rufus Warren fell, he was about a rod ahead of me, he fell the opposite way he was running then throwed up his hands and hollowed 'O Dear, help me, help me.' It was not a time for me to stop so I kept on before I had hard gone a rod farther a bullet cut a hole out of my pants...but did not touch me...bullets were coming in a shower I thought I was spoke for, still kept moving on and shortly I expect it was a piece of spent shell struck my right shoulder blade and almost knocked me over...I ran across the field and everything before me looked as white as a sheet."[158]

The Barlow-Gordon Saga

Twenty-nine-year-old Brigadier General Francis C. Barlow tried valiantly to check the retreat of his men as his line crumbled under the attack by Doles and Gordon. At one point he rode to the top of the knoll and turned back to appeal to some of Von Gilsa's men to rally and "form another line to the rear." Before he could turn his horse back to the front, he was shot in the left side about halfway between the armpit and the head of the thigh bone. He dismounted and attempted to walk to the rear, while around him "every one was then running to the rear and the enemy was approaching rapidly." Two of his men came up and offered to help him, one supporting each side, but one was soon wounded and fell to the ground. The other erstwhile helper apparently left for safer ground. The general, now alone, was hit a second time by a spent ball that struck his back and "made quite a bruise." He tried to go on but became faint and had to lie down. He lay there for about five minutes in the midst of some heavy fighting as the Confederates pushed back the last remnants of his line. One bullet went through his hat and another grazed a finger on his right hand.[159]

The general did not expect to survive, when the fighting suddenly passed by and a group of Confederates led by Lieutenant A.L. Pitzer of General Early's staff came up and offered him help. They had him removed to the woods at the base of the hill, placed him on a bed of leaves, and gave him some water before they had to return to the fight. Barlow was still not out of danger, however. Before long, a Union battery began to shell the hill, and he was unable to move himself to safety. Fortunately some of his own troops who had been captured recognized him and saw his predicament. They placed him in a blanket and carried him to a house farther off on the Blocher farm. By now his clothes were saturated with blood. They placed him in a bed, and at about dark three Confederate surgeons came to tend him. They gave him chloroform and probed the wound. When he revived, he was told that the bullet had lodged in the cavity of the pelvis and "there was very little chance for my life."[160]

Barlow, though, did not die. The next day he was moved to a house on the northern outskirts of the town, where he was kindly cared for by an elderly lady and her daughter. They even found him some books with which to while away his time when his mind was clear enough from the morphine he was being given.[161] Because of the serious nature of his wound, the Confederates soon exchanged him. Barlow had to spend ten months in the hospital before he was well enough to return to command a division of the II Corps during Grant's 1864 overland campaign against Richmond. He had to go on extended leave of absence that winter because of his health, but returned to the army in time for the Appomattox campaign. He was promoted to Major General on 25 May and briefly commanded II Corps in the closing stages of the war. After the war he was a lawyer and maintained an active life until his death in 1896, 33 years after his severe wounding at Gettysburg.[162]

Barlow's wife, Arabella, was a nurse with the U.S. Sanitary Commission. She was working at a hospital in Maryland when she heard that her husband had been wounded, so she at once hurried to Gettysburg in order to nurse him back to health, as she had done after he had been wounded at the the battle of Antietam the previous September. When she reached the field, probably on 3 July, she sought out General Howard and asked his aid in getting within the enemy's lines. Howard directed her in the right direction, and deliberately did not ask her if she possessed a pass from General Meade authorizing her to go through the Union lines to those of the enemy. The brave woman walked down Baltimore Pike from Cemetery Hill, only to be turned back by sniper fire. She eventually did manage to enter the town, because at dusk a Gettysburg lad named Daniel Skelly saw her on Chambersburg Street being escorted by two Confederate soldiers as she searched for the house where the general was being cared for. It is not clear from surviving accounts when or if she finally did locate him. Barlow's brave wife continued her service as a nurse until she died in July 1864 from typhus she contracted in one of the army hospitals.[163]

After the war Confederate General John B. Gordon gave a quite different version of Barlow's treatment after he was wounded: "In the midst of the wild disorder in his ranks, and through a storm of bullets, a Union officer was seeking to rally his men to a final stand. He, too, went down, pierced by a minie ball. Riding forward with my rapidly advancing lines, I discovered that brave officer lying upon his back, with the July sun pouring its rays into his pale face. He was surrounded by the Union dead, and his own life seemed to be rapidly ebbing out. Quickly dismounting and lifting his head, I gave him water from my canteen, asked his name and the character of his wounds. He was Major General Francis C. Barlow, of New York, and of Howard's Corps. The ball had entered his body in front and passed out near the spinal cord, paralyzing him in the arms and legs. Neither of us had the remotest thought that he could possibly survive many hours. I summoned several soldiers who were looking after the wounded and directed them to place him upon a litter, and carry him to the shade in the rear."[164]

Gordon continues his story: "Before parting, he asked me take from his pocket a package of letters and destroy them. They were from his wife. He had but one request to make of me. That request was that if I should live to the end of the war and should ever meet Mrs. Barlow, I would tell her of our meeting on the field of Gettysburg and of his thoughts of her in his last moments. He wished me to assure her that he died doing his duty at the front, that he was willing to give his life for his country, and that his deepest regret was that he must die without looking upon her face again. I learned that Mrs. Barlow was with the Union army, and near the battlefield.... Passing through the day's battle unhurt, I despatched at its close, under flag of truce, the promised message to Mrs. Barlow. I assured her that if she wished to come through the lines she should have safe escort to her husband's side. In the desperate encounters of the two succeeding days, and the retreating Lee's army, I thought no more of Barlow, except to number him with the noble dead of the two armies who had so gloriously met their fate."[165]

There is still more to Gordon's story. Years later, when Gordon was serving his second term as U.S. Senator from Georgia, Congressman Clarkson Potter of New York invited him to a dinner and introduced him to a former Union general named Barlow. Gordon, who never knew that Barlow had recovered, asked "General, are you related to the Barlow who was killed at Gettysburg?" Barlow, who had heard that Gordon's cousin with the same initials, General J.B. Gordon of North Carolina, had been killed near Richmond in 1864, replied, "Why, I am the man, sir. Are you related to the Gordon who killed me?" Gordon responded, "I am the man, sir." He concluded his narrative with the observation, "Nothing short of an actual resurrection from the dead could have amazed either of us more. Thence forward, until his untimely death in 1896, the friendship between us which was born amidst the thunders of Gettysburg was greatly cherished by both."[166]

These episodes have become part of the great epic of the battle, and have long been accepted at full value. Recent scholarship, however, has called Gordon's entire account into question.[167] The most striking evidence against Gordon is the fact that Barlow never mentioned meeting the general on the battlefield. The detailed letter Barlow wrote to his mother on 7 July mentions being aided by a Lieutenant Pitzer (whom Barlow called "Major Pitzera") and several other men, but does not include a meeting with Gordon. To be certain, Barlow was in great pain at the time, but the wealth of other detail he told his mother shows that he was lucid enough to have remembered having a personal conversation with Gordon, a Confederate general, had he indeed done so.[168]

Gordon's alleged help to Barlow's wife also seems to be more dramatic than accurate. In an earlier 1901 version of the story, Gordon claims that Mrs. Barlow received his note about her husband that very night: "Late that night, as I lay in the open field upon my saddle, a picket from my front announced a lady on the line. She was Mrs. Barlow. She had received my note and was struggling, under the guidance of officers of the Union army, to penetrate my lines and reach her husband's side. She was guided to his side by staff during the night."[169] This account is questionable because it was highly unlikely that Arabella could have heard of her husband's wound and been able to reach the field before nightfall. Even more significant is that fact that Barlow would surely have mentioned his wife's arrival at that time in his 7 July letter to his mother, if she had indeed arrived with Gordon's help on the night of 1 July.

Lastly, the exact words of the 1893 conversation in Washington between Barlow and Gordon are difficult to accept without confirming evidence from Barlow or another party. It also seems unlikely that Gordon, who was one of Lee's leading officers at the close of the war, would have been unaware that the Barlow of Gettysburg was one of Grant's lieutenants in 1864-65. It is more believable, though, that Barlow might have confused our General John Brown Gordon with cavalry commander James Byron Gordon, though the former's military exploits in 1864-65 and political successes after the war would have been hard to escape notice.

The bulk of the evidence, then, suggests that Gordon greatly embellished, or even fabricated, his story about his acquaintance with Barlow. But for what purpose? The answer to this question can perhaps be seen in the fact that he was an accomplished lecturer who toured the country and spoke before countless audiences at the turn of the century. One of his favorite themes was the reunification of the country after the war, and his favorite vehicle for conveying this theme was his Barlow speech, which grew to be so popular that it was quoted in full in a volume of "Famous Lectures" published by the Modern Eloquence Corporation in New York in 1923. Witness, for example, the closing lines of one version of the speech: "Such were the circumstances under which was born the friendship between Barlow and myself, and which I believe is more sincere because of its remarkable birth and which has strengthened and depended with the passing years. For the sake of our reunited and glorious Republic may we not hope that similarities will bind together all the soldiers of the two armies—indeed all Americans— in perpetual unity until the last bugle call shall have summoned us to the eternal camping grounds beyond the stars?"[170]

Lastly, it should be noted that the full blown version of the speech about Barlow was not fully developed until after Barlow had died in 1896, and was no longer able to contest its facts. The other principal in the story, Arabella, had died in 1864, and could not comment on the story either. This is probably why Gordon was able to elaborate his story for his own purposes on the lecture circuit and in his wartime reminiscences, which were published in 1903, shortly before he died in January 1904.[171] We may never know for sure if Gordon ever even saw the wounded General Barlow on Barlow's Knoll on the afternoon of 1 July 1863. His battle report of 10 August 1863, does, however, show that he was aware that among the Union casualties on the day "was a division commander (General Barlow) who was severely wounded."[172] It should be pointed out, though, that Barlow's wounding was known to quite a few members of Gordon's brigade, including Private Nichols of the 61st Georgia, who wrote that, "The gallant General Barlow, the enemy's commander, fell into our hands, severely wounded. He was treated kindly."[173]

Collapse of Krzyzanowski's Brigade

We now return to the battlefield. While Gordon and the left wing of Doles' brigade were driving Barlow's men in disorder from Barlow's Knoll, Doles' right was encountering pressure from Krzyzanowski's brigade of Schimmelfennig's division. As already noted, Schimmelfennig had originally posted Krzyzanowski in massed columns at the right of his line, just west of the Carlisle Pike, ½ mile southwest of Barlow's Knoll. When Schurz saw that Barlow had unexpectedly advanced to the knoll, and was about to be attacked by Early, he sent Krzyzanowski to his support. However, because of the time needed to relay the orders and the quickness with which Gordon and Doles overwhelmed Barlow, Krzyzanowski was not able to reach the knoll area before Barlow's line was broken.

Krzyzanowski did not advance in battle line, but in column of divisions, so that he might move his units more quickly to Barlow's support. His regiments were deployed in the following order from left to right as the brigade moved to the northwest in one giant blue clad mass: 82nd Ohio, 75th Pennsylvania, 119th New York, 58th New York detachment, and 26th Wisconsin. On their way they encountered a number of fences "which had to be taken down under a heavy fire of the enemy." The moving brigade quickly attracted the attention of Rodes' guns on Oak Hill as well as Early's cannons to the northeast of Barlow's Knoll. Captain Alfred Lee of Company E, 82nd Ohio, noted that his command received artillery fire from at least two or three different directions "and their shells plunged through our solid squares making terrible havoc."[174]

Colonel John T. Mercer of Doles' right flank regiment, the 21st Georgia, saw Krzyzanowski's advance, and wheeled to the right to meet it alone; the rest of Doles' command was still advancing obliquely to the left and front against Barlow's command.[175] Captain Alfred Lee of the 82nd Ohio admired Mercer's advance: "Their movements were firm and steady, as usual, and their banners, bearing the blue Southern cross, flaunted impudently and seemed to challenge combat."[176] Mercer advanced into a wheatfield and began to fire on the enemy line, which halted and returned the favor. Mercer soon realized how outnumbered his command was, and directed his unit to fall back to the Blocher farm lane: "Having attracted their fire, and finding their force too strong for the exposed position we then occupied, we fell back some 40 yards to a lane, where we awaited their approach."[177] Major August Ledig of the 75th Pennsylvania had a different view of Mercer's withdrawal, and reported, "When within 100 yards of them, in a wheatfield, we charged upon them and drove them back."[178] The left of Krzyzanowski's line then advanced on the 21st Georgia, whose men lay on the ground until their opponents were "within a few yards," whereupon they rose and commenced firing. At this the Union troops halted and returned the fire.[179]

Doles reacted to this threat on his right by wheeling his remaining three regiments to the right to face Krzyzanowski's advance. They were able to do this because Barlow's troops had just been driven off the knoll and Gordon was successfully pursing them southwards towards the Almshouse. During his wheel to the right Doles shifted his far left regiment, the 12th Georgia, to his far right, to assist the 21st Georgia. This left the 4th and 44th as the left flank units of the brigade.[180]

According to one account, it was not General Doles, but the experience of his men that caused most of his brigade to shift to the right to meet the threat posed by Krzyzanowski's advance: "After we had driven the Federal right into the town, a Federal brigade was discovered in the little valley made by the creek, on our right flank, making an effort to get to our rear. Gen. Doles was without his horse, and, all the field officers being near the left of our brigade, did not see the Federal brigade, but word came up the line, 'By the right flank.' The men did not wait to learn who gave the order, but instantly obeyed, and almost as quickly the yell came from the right, and without any command from anyone the men instinctively changed front forward on the right into line by regiment."[181]

General Ewell was excited to see Doles' change in front from his vantage point on Oak Hill: "Gen. Ewell afterward, at Front Royal, on our way back from Pennsylvania, in speaking of the incident to the writer and some other comrades, stated that he did not believe that over twenty-five escaped unhurt; but this, of course, was an exaggerated opinion, for the General at times became very much excited in battle, and that day at the moment our men discovered the movement, he was dismounted and standing by his horse; and having but one leg, he could not mount, having no staff officers or couriers with him at the time. Seeing the movement of the Federals so nearly accomplished, he was almost in despair because he could not get notice to Gen. Doles of the danger his brigade was in. His joy knew no bounds when he saw Doles' brigade change front, whereby it almost annihilated the Federal brigade. It was a pleasure to watch the play of the General's countenance when he was relating the incident. The wonderful sparkle and flash of those great brown eyes was enchanting."[182]

The 21st and 44th Georgia struck Krzyzanowski's command head on, and the two sides halted their lines in order to blast volleys at each other from a distance of about 75 yards. One Union soldier thought that the enemy's colors were so close that "the names of battles printed on the Confederate flags might have been read had there been time to read them." The intensity of the Confederate fire was so great that Major Benjamin A. Willis of the 119th New York was convinced that he was facing "an enemy more than twofold our number."[183]

Doles' frontal attack stopped Krzyzanowski's advance, but was not enough to turn all the northern regiments back by itself. Here the decisive blow was once again registered by Gordon's brigade. As most of his regiments were pursuing Barlow's troops towards the Almshouse, the right portion of Gordon's line (31st and 60th Georgia) turned to the right in order to face Krzyzanowski's troops. Their enfilading fire struck the brigade's right wing regiment, the 26th Wisconsin, with a devastating effect. Some of the Badgers were also felled by the fire of Early's artillery on the other side of Rock Creek. Over 100 members of the regiment fell casualty, including the commander, Lieutenant Colonel Hans Boebel, who lost a leg, and Major Henry Batz, who was severely wounded. Other casualties included Captain William Smith, Lieutenant Martin Young, Corporal George Chalupka, and Privates Frank Benda and Frank Suchara killed.[184] The Confederate fire from the front and flank was so severe that Colonel William K. Jacobs of the 26th wrote in his battle report that the regiment was being "furiously assaulted by vastly superior numbers."[185] The regiment's next in command, Captain John Fuchs, was barely able to rally the regiment and keep them in line. The disorganization of the 26th was a severe blow to the rest of the brigade, since the regiment's opening strength of 443 men made it the largest regiment by far in the brigade.[186]

Gordon's flank fire also had a deleterious effect on the next regiment to the left of the 26th Wisconsin, the 119th New York. Colonel John T. Lockman fell wounded, and his adjutant, Theodore A. Dodge, lost a leg and would never play his beloved game of cricket again. Captains Otto Trumpelman and August Volkhausen were wounded, and Lieutenants Matthias Rasemann and Emil Frost were killed. Sergeant Louis Morell was raising his ramrod to load his musket and was struck at the same time by two bullets. One destroyed his left eye and the other passed through his body. When he fell to the ground he was hit in the left thigh by yet a third bullet. The unit also lost over 100 men in just a few minutes, but Lieutenant Colonel Edward F. Lloyd and Lieutenant Leopold Biela managed to hold the unit together for the moment.[187]

Meanwhile Krzyzanowski's left flank regiment, the 82nd Ohio, was having difficulty of its own because it was being outflanked to the left by the fire of the 44th Georgia. The intense Confederate flanking fire caused heavy casualties—particularly among the regiment's officers— and in the first few minutes no less than two captains (John Costen and William Mitchell) and four lieutenants (Stowell Burnham, George McGreary, Philander Meredith, and Meredith Jacoby) were killed. About 50% of the regiment's strength was felled, and the unit began to waver and give way.[188]

Captain Alfred Lee of the 82nd tried to do his part to stop the enemy's advance by picking up a stray musket to fire at the enemy. As he was loading it, a soldier fell at his side and pitifully cried out, "Oh help me." He reached for Lee's hand but found that he was unable to rise and told Lee, "Oh I'm gone. Just leave me here." An instant later Lee "felt the sting of a bullet, and fell, benumbered with pain. It was an instantaneous metamorphosis from strength and vigor to utter helplessness." He called to a nearby soldier for help, but that man, too, was struck, and headed for the rear.[189]

As the 82nd Ohio was giving way, Colonel Francis Mahler ran to the left flank of his 75th Pennsylvania in order to keep it from being outflanked and crushed. His unit, too, had suffered severely from the initial Confederate volleys. The colonel's brother, Lieutenant Louis Mahler, had been killed, and Lieutenant William Sill, Sergeant Major Kahl, and numerous privates were wounded.[190] Mahler was on foot because he had just had his horse shot out from under him. The line of the 44th Georgia was just 40 yards away, and let loose another devastating volley. Colonel Mahler was severely wounded, and was carried to the rear by Lieutenant T. Albert Steiger. He would die from his wound four days later. Command of the regiment devolved on Major August Ledig, who ordered the unit to fire by the left oblique at the 44th Georgia before the enemy could cut off his retreat. Ledig then began moving his unit to the left so as to face the 44th and also gain access to an opening in a sturdy fence that was blocking a more direct

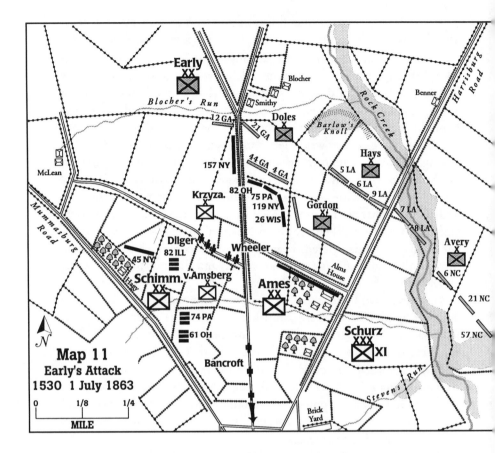

Map 11
Early's Attack
1530 1 July 1863

withdrawal. In just 15 minutes of fighting, the 75th Pennsylvania had lost 111 men killed and wounded, over half of its strength.[191]

Both Schurz and Krzyzanowski realized how desperate the situation was. Schurz stopped to say a last farewell to Colonel Mahler, whom he had known in Germany, and then lost his horse to a bullet in the neck as soon as he remounted.[192] Krzyzanowski observed that "the troops were sweaty, blackened by the gunpowder, and they looked more like animals than human beings." They had bloodshot eyes, and the whole scene was like a "portrait of hell."[193] Krzyzanowski also had his horse shot from under him, and he fell painfully to the ground. He had such difficulty breathing that Schurz urged him to leave the field. However, the colonel refused to go, and remained with his men after receiving aid from surgeon Charles Stein of the 58th New York.[194] By then the two officers decided that they had no choice but to pull Krzyzanowski's men back towards the college and the town.

The defeat of Krzyzanowski's command in just over 15 minutes is difficult to explain. Krzyzanowski had just over 1200 men in his command, about the same number that faced him in Doles' left two regiments (4th and 44th Georgia) and Gordon's right two regiments (60th and 31st Georgia). Since the lay of the ground did not give an advantage to either side, the action on paper should have gone in favor of the defensive troops, particularly since the attackers had just lost a number of men while defeating Barlow. Krzyzanowski's men also had an advantage in artillery support, since Dilger's guns were able to turn to the right and blast at Doles' right just 100 yards away.[195] Jones' artillery pieces were not able to support this attack once it drew near to Krzyzanowski's line, for fear of striking their own men, though they did cause some casualties in the 26th Wisconsin before the Confederate attack struck. The Union sources do not mention it, but Krzyzanowski's units may not have been entirely deployed into line when they encountered the first Confederate fire. Their denser formation would help account for their heavy rate of casualties. What is clear is that the Confederates held a distinct advantage by overlapping both ends of Krzyzanowski's line. In addition, the Confederate units that faced Krzyzanowski simply had better fire control and better cohesion than the Union troops, who had trouble holding up and returned a less effective fire than their opponents.[196]

The disaster that befell Krzyzanowski's brigade would have been still worse if Schimmelfennig had not sent one of Von Amsberg's regiments, the 157th New York, to support his advance. This was the only unit he had available for the job, since three of his regiments (45th New York, 61st Ohio and 74th Pennsylvania) were already committed to the brigade's skirmish line, and his fifth regiment, the 82nd Illinois, was busy supporting Dilger's and Wheeler's batteries.

Colonel Philip B. Brown led his 409 men forward, unsupported, to their date with destiny. His goal was to strike the right flank of Doles' advance, and to this end he marched his command up to, and parallel with, the Carlisle Pike just south of its fork.[197] From here he succeeded at establishing a fire on the flank of the 44th Georgia, but he did not see the 21st Georgia lying in a lane on his left front, or the 12th Georgia coming to the support of the 21st.

The situation was already spelling disaster for the 157th when Major W.M. Peebles turned his 44th Georgia to face the 157th. Peebles described his maneuver as follows: "The right of our regiment just reached the road. The enemy came up to within 30 or 40 yards of us.

As soon as it was discovered that we were flanked, we made a wheel to right, faced the new fire, and began to fire upon him. Thus checked in his movement, he faced us, and opened a severe fire upon us. The Fourth Georgia soon came to our assistance, it being on our immediate left."[198]

The attack of the 44th and 4th Georgia regiments on Brown's front and right flank might alone have been enough to defeat the 157th New York and send its survivors scurrying to the rear. At just the right moment the troops of the 21st Georgia rose up from the concealment and fired a crushing fire on the left wing of the unsuspecting soldiers of the 157th. Some Confederates of the 44th Georgia were eyewitnesses to what transpired: "The Twenty-first Georgia was a little in front of our line, at exactly the right place, and lay on the ground until the Federals had advanced to within a short distance of them, when at the command of their colonel, they sprang to their knees and poured such a volley into the enemy that they were not only checked but stampeded."[199]

The devastating Confederate fire from the left, front and right literally decimated the 157th. To make matters even worse, one of Rodes' batteries on Oak Hill began firing shells into the unit's rear. Colonel Brown was shot in the head, and over 200 members of the regiment fell as casualties. Brown later remembered that "The men were falling rapidly and the enemy's line was taking the form of a giant semi-circle... concentrating the fire of their whole brigade upon my rapidly diminishing numbers." Brown kept looking to the rear for support or an order to withdraw. At one point he saw one of Schimmelfennig's aides remove his saddle from his dead horse and then head for the rear. Later he learned that the officer had "hallooed to me to retreat" but was not brave enough to come and deliver the order face-to-face. As a result, Brown held his ground until the regiment was all but exterminated, and then ordered a retreat.[200] The 157th's losses during this brief fight amounted to 27 killed, 166 wounded, and 114 captured or missing, some 75% of the 409 men engaged, the sixth greatest percentage loss of any Union regiment in the entire battle.[201]

Doles' troops lost a number of men in this attack, including Lieutenant Colonel S.P. Lumpkin, commander of the 44th Georgia, who was mortally wounded just as his regiment was charging across the Pike into the wheatfield where the 157th was formed. He was succeeded in command by Major Peebles. As the 44th drove the remnants of the 157th back, Captain T.H. Connolly of Company E halted long enough to give his canteen to Lieutenant Frank Gates of the 157th, who was badly wounded and "suffering for water as he lay in the wheatfield."[202]

While Doles' right flank was dealing with the 157th New York, his left two regiments were assisting Gordon's right in pursing Krzyzanowski's troops back to the northern edge of the town. The converging Confederate attack enabled the victors to take prisoners by the score, both wounded and unwounded. It is difficult to say how orderly was the retreat of Krzyzanowski's units. Major Ledig of the 75th Pennsylvania says that after the Confederate attack, "I began now to retreat about 200 yards to an orchard. The one hundred and nineteenth New York, on my right, suffered also heavily from the flank attack, and moved backward also to the garden." Once they arrived at the orchard on the north edge of town, the regiments attempted to reform to face the enemy. They apparently were not being hard pressed, since the officers of the 119th New York found time to conduct a roll call, to which only 130 men answered.[203] Krzyzanowski's battered regiments were apparently allowed a brief respite because the bulk of Doles' command was moving to the left to meet some of Von Amsberg's troops, and most of Gordon's men were heading to the right to deal with a line that Ames was attempting to form at the Almshouse.

The collapse of Krzyzanowski's brigade and the 157th New York exposed Dilger's cannons, which all the while had maintained their post near the Carlisle Pike, engaging the Confederate cannons on Oak Hill. Due to the lay of the land and the closeness of the Union troops, Dilger had not been able to lend much support to Barlow's defense on the knoll. Once Barlow's men began to fall back and the Confederate troops passed over the knoll, Lieutenant William Wheeler was able to change the direction of his right section and begin firing canister into Doles' left flank. He held this position until the enemy was almost in his rear, whereupon he began to retire by prolonge toward the town, firing as he went.[204] His withdrawal was conducted under great pressure because of the closeness of the enemy infantry and the increasing fire of the Confederate cannons on the left and right. This fire caused him to lose one of his pieces: "While moving across the field to this point, a shot struck the axle of one of my pieces and broke it, dismounting the piece. I slung the piece under the limber with the prolonge, and carried it for some distance until the prolonge broke, when I was obliged to abandon the gun, but recovered it on the 5th, and it is now in serviceable condition."[205]

Dilger's battery, which was posted to the left of Wheeler's, likewise had difficulty retreating. Dilger maintained his position west of the Carlisle Pike until it was exposed by the collapse of Krzyzanowski's counterattack. As Krzyzanowski withdrew, Jones' cannons directed their fire on Dilger's guns, "enfilading our line completely, causing great damage to men and horses, and disabling one piece of mine and one of Wheeler's battery."[206] Dilger shifted the direction of his guns so as to face Jones, but soon found a heavy force of enemy infantry massing some 100 yards to his right. At this point Dilger took his left section to the right to help cover Wheeler's withdrawal, and directed Lieutenant Clark Scripture to retire down the Carlisle Pike. Dilger blasted away at the advancing Confederate infantry with his two guns, and directed Lieutenant Wheeler to leave him two of his guns to help. Wheeler's two guns were rifled, though, so Dilger soon sent them to the rear "because I would not expose them too much at this short range, at which they commenced to be useless." Dilger's two guns were then the last of the XI Corps artillery to leave the field.[207] Bancroft's (formerly Wilkeson's) battery had already retired from Barlow's Knoll and was reforming on the northern edge of the town, where its sections reunited and the cannoneers even found time to refill the ammuntion chests of the gun limbers.[208]

The retreat of Barlow's command from Barlow's Knoll was apparently more disorganized than Krzyzanowski's withdrawal. An account of exactly what happened is not possible because so many officers were lost during this retreat and afterwards that few of the division's regiments were able to turn in detailed battle reports. The general situation during the division's initial retreat was a hectic one. Adelbert Ames, who had been thrust into command of the division after Barlow was wounded, reported simply that "The whole division was falling back with little or no regularity, regimental organizations having become destroyed."[209] One of the few units that retained its integrity at this time was Colonel Andrew L. Harris' 75th Ohio. Harris' command was evidently the last to withdraw from Barlow's Knoll. Harris later recalled that "My regiment being in the rear drew much of the enemy's fire, but as we retired in skirmish line our loss on the retreat was slight." As he was falling back, and walking alongside his color bearer, Harris was notified by Ames to take command of the brigade because Barlow was wounded and Ames was taking up the division.[210]

The retreat of Barlow's men, however, did not seem too disorganized to Private G.W. Nichols of the 61st Georgia.: "They began to retreat in line order, shooting at us as they retreated. They were harder to drive than we had ever known before. Men were being mown down in great numbers on both sides. We drove them across a fence, where they stopped and fought us for awhile. We advanced and drove them into and out of a deep road cut and on to the Almshouse, where the Yankees stopped and made a desperate stand."[211]

Ames' men might not have stopped to try to reform at the Almshouse had it not the been for the heroic efforts of Colonel Leopold Von Gilsa, and several other officers. Von Gilsa, like Krzyzanowski and Schurz, had lost his horse during the initial Confederate attack, but he soon managed to obtain another. The Almshouse area provided some shelter for the retiring troops because it was located on a rise west of the Harrisburg Road and had a number of buildings with an orchard nearby. Von Gilsa rode into the troops that were passing by and encouraged them to stop and reform. One soldier of the 153rd Pennsylvania saw him ride "up and down through that line through a regular storm of lead, meantime using the German epithets so common to him."[212] Von Gilsa and his lieutenants were seen by Private Nichols of the 61st Georgia, who saw that "Their officers were cheering their men on and behaving like heroes and commanders of the 'first water.'"[213]

Von Gilsa's makeshift line, unsupported by artillery or fresh troops, was no match for Gordon's victorious veterans. General Gordon observed that "an effort was made here by the enemy to change his front and check our advance, but the effort failed, and this line, too, was driven back in the greatest confusion, and with immense loss in killed, wounded and prisoners."[214] As Ames' troops fell back in disorder, losing prisoners at every step, he received an order "from General Schurz, or one of his staff," to occupy the outskirts of the town. Due to the division's disarray, this command was soon cancelled, and Ames was directed to fall back through the town. Barlow's division was essentially done for the day.[215]

Gordon did not proceed far after driving Ames away from the Almshouse line. His command was somewhat disordered from its success and the loss of over 25% of its strength in half an hour of hard fighting; three of his regiments at the center of his line that had born the brunt of the fighting had suffered at our near 40% losses (13th, 38th, 61st Georgia).[216] Because of this, Early decided to let Gordon's men rest, and ordered his second line (Hays and Avery) to enter the action. Gordon stopped his line in the "hollow" between the Crawford farm and the Almshouse.

In the elation of the moment of victory, Robert Stiles of Carrington's battery called out to Gordon "in a momentary pause," "General, where are your dead men?" Gordon, replied, "I haven't gotten any, sir; the

Almighty has covered my men with his shield and buckler!"[217] Such was certainly not the case—Gordon's brigade during the battle suffered losses of 112 killed, 297 wounded and 128 missing, a total of 537 men, almost all on the first day.[218] Even so, his brigade's accomplishment in this action was one of the most successful charges of the war. According to gunner Robert Stiles, General Ewell believed that "Gordon's brigade that evening put hors de combat a greater number of the enemy in proportion to its own numbers than any other command on either side ever did, from the beginning to the end of the war."[219]

The Brickyard Fight

What also influenced Early to bring up his second line was the fact that he saw a line of fresh Union troops moving through the western end of the town to support Barlow's division. This line was composed of four regiments of Colonel Charles R. Coster's brigade of the 2nd Division, which Howard had been holding in reserve on Cemetery Hill for just such an emergency. Indeed, Schurz had been appealing since soon after 1300 for reinforcements to be sent to his right flank, but Howard had not decided to answer his calls for help. Had he done so earlier, Coster might have been able to help stabilize Ames' line for long enough to allow Krzyzanowski to come up, and so give the whole wing a chance to make a fighting withdrawal in better shape than it did. As affairs developed, however, Coster was sent forward too late to assist Barlow, and, being unsupported himself, was outflanked and overrun.

Coster's men had left their camps at Emmitsburg at 0800, and had not been in a particular hurry to head northward, Lieutenant Colonel D.B. Allen of the 154th New York suspected there might be trouble and directed his men to leave their knapsacks and baggage behind.[220] The brigade, with its division, marched via the Horner's Mill Road to the Gettysburg-Taneytown Road. A rain shower turned the road to mud, and as a result it took two hours just to reach the Pennsylvania line. Their spirits were perked up when they came to within five miles of town and heard "the rattle of musketry and roar of cannon" [that] "told us that our long race after the enemy was ended."[221]

The division reached Cemetery Hill sometime after 1400, and was told by Howard to wait in reserve. Its commander, Brigadier General Adolph Von Steinwehr, could see Barlow's and Schimmelfennig's divisions deploying and going into action in the fields north of town. He placed Coster's 1st Brigade on the northeast end of the hill, supporting Wiedrich's battery, which had come up at the same time. His 2nd Brigade, commanded by Colonel Orland Smith, was placed at the northwestern crest of the hill in support of Heckman's battery.[222]

Coster sent half of his command forward to secure the lower approaches of East Cemetery Hill and keep the enemy from placing sharpshooters on the edge of the town, if they should come up. One regiment was formed as skirmishers, while another was stationed in "a large stone church and the surrounding houses in town."[223] The men were then allowed to rest. Most grabbed a quick lunch of hardtack and whatever else they had in their haversacks; some cleaned their guns; the noise of artillery firing to the north and west of the town made the situation too tense for sleeping. During this interlude a number of stragglers came up who had fallen behind during the day's march for various reasons. Private Newell Burch of the 154th New York came up late, being sick with diarrhea, while Sergeant Horace Smith and Private Benjamin Bently of Company D, 154th, were late for another reason. They had "flanked out and got a lot of bread, butter, milk and eggs for our company—but had no chance to eat it."[224]

Coster's men had rested for just an hour when they were ordered to move north through the town. Schurz, as has been noted, had been anxious to have a brigade sent to reinforce his right, and then requested that one brigade be sent out on a "reconnaissance upon the York Road, whence Ewell's Corps was expected to debouch." He became so annoyed when Howard refused his requests that he sent his assistant adjutant general, Captain Fred Winkler, with another plea. This time Howard acquiesced. Winkler noted that he "urged haste impetuously, and set it in motion at once."[225]

The brigade moved into action with about 1100 men in its ranks; a detachment of 50 men from each regiment had been left "as an observing party" in Maryland that morning. The details from the 154th New York and 73rd Pennsylvania had been sent out at dawn on a reconnaissance to Sabillasville under Major Louis Warner of the 154th, and did not return in time to join the column's march to Gettysburg.[226] The brigade headed down Baltimore Street with the 134th New York in the lead, followed by the 154th New York and the Pennsylvania regiments, the 73rd and 27th.[227]

If Coster's men did not already know a battle was going on in their front, they would surely have learned so from the number of wounded and refugees they passed in the town. Sergeant John F. Wellman of

Company F, 154th New York, noted that "The sidewalks are lined with wounded." Charles McKay saw that "all around was confusion and disaster" from the retreating troops that were headed the ther direc- tion.[228] As the column pushed through town, Captain Lewis Heckman's battery rushed past them from its reserve position on Cemetery Hill. Heckman proceeded north through the town square and deployed on the northern edge of town, between the Carlisle and Harrisburg Roads. Confederate infantry was already in sight as he deployed, and his guns commenced firing as soon as possible after they were unlimbered.[229]

Soon after Coster passed through the town square, he decided to drop off one of his regiments, the 73rd Pennsylvania, near the train station, located two blocks north of the square.[230] His reason for doing so is not understood. He may have wanted to secure the main artery through the town, or simply to post the regiment as a guard to the station and nearby buildings, which were being used as makeshift hospitals. Whatever were his reasons for doing so, the decision would weaken his command by ¼ in his coming fight.[231]

Coster sent Captain Winkler ahead to locate Schurz and find out where he should deploy. Winkler passed by fugitives from the corps who were "in a retreat less orderly than it should have been, crowding the sidewalks on both sides." He was ashamed for his corps, particularly since "it was a northern village."[232] Winkler found Schurz at the northern edge of town and told him of Coster's approach. The general then headed back through town to meet Coster and led his brigade in person to the spot where he wanted to deploy it on the eastern edge of town. Wrote Schurz, "I led it out of the town, and ordered it to deploy, on the right of the junction of the roads near the railroad depot, which the enemy was fast approaching." The ever aggressive Schurz had hoped to lead this brigade in a counterattack against the enemy's left flank, something he felt he could have executed had the command arrived just ten minutes sooner. Now it was too late for that, and all he could do was deploy Coster's men as a rear guard to assist the withdrawal of the rest of the corps.[233]

Coster's three regiments marched up Stratton Street towards the northern edge of the town. Once they emerged into the open, the column caught the attention of Early's advanced artillery. Sergeant John F. Wellman of Company B, 154th New York, recalled, "as they uncovered from the town, the shells... came shrieking closer to their heads, and every shot a little closer.... I looked for disorder, but I swear to you today, not one man broke step from the head of the column to the rear.

I said they were brave. I wanted to take off my hat and cheer them right then."[234]

Schurz led Coster's three regiments further up Stratton Street, and had them turn right at a carriage gateway at John Kuhn's house (221 North Stratton Street) and proceed into the grounds of the large Kuhn brickyard. When the rear of the 27th Pennsylvania, the last regiment in the column, had entered the brickyard, Colonel Coster gave the order to "Halt! Front! Right dress!" The length of the column caused the brigade's lead regiment, the 134th New York, to deploy in a wheatfield to the east of the brickyard. Lieutenant Colonel Allan H. Jackson deployed his 430 men facing north in a line even with the sturdy post and rail fence that bordered the brickyard. To his left was a small run on the edge of the brickyard that caused a slight gap to exist between his line and the center regiment, the 154th New York. Lieutenant Colonel D.B. Allen directed the 220 men of the 154th to advance to the rail fence and kneel; they were to hold their fire until the enemy "came close enough to make our volley effective."[235] Colonel Lorenz Cantador also led his regiment, the 280 men of the 27th Pennsylvania, forward to the fence.

The brigade's position was far from ideal. The ground to the left of the 27th Pennsylvania rose up abruptly, so much so that no one could see what motions the enemy might be making on the other side. The same rise ran, but not so sharply, across the front of the 154th New York. Private McKay of that unit recalled that, "The ground in our front was higher than at our position, gently rising until, 40 rods away, it was perhaps 20 feet above us and covered with wheat just ready for the sickle."[236] This meant that the men of the 154th would not be able to see the enemy approaching, and would be lucky to get off more than a few volleys once the enemy did come into view. Coster would have moved his men forward to occupy the rise on their front, had the Confederate attack not already been upon him.[237]

General Early was in his prime in this battle, and was in masterful control of his troops from the time that he first reached the field. He had used his artillery to soften up Barlow's defense first, and then took a calculated risk by sending Gordon to the attack first on the right rather than by trying to maneuver his way around the Union right. If Gordon's attack faltered, Early was certainly able to send his second line to his immediate support. As things turned out, his gamble paid off twice—Gordon broke Barlow's line (with Doles' help) with unexpected ease, and the rest of the division was now primed and ready to follow up on his success. To be certain, Early's troops entered the battle in a most advantageous position. But Early had the skill this day to take full advantage of the opportunity that was offered, unlike Rodes, who failed to exploit the advantageous situation he had found when he came up on Doubleday's right at noon.

Gunner Robert Stiles ever after remembered Early's earnestness as he gave the order to advance: "his glossy black ostrich feather, in beautiful condition, seeming to glisten and tremble upon the wide brim of his gray-brown felt hat, like a thing of life." Early's martial majesty, Stiles thought, contrasted markedly with another figure he saw at the same time: "a dwarfish, dumpy little fellow, of the division pioneer corps, who at this moment came running up to his command, just as I was leaving it to take my place with the artillery, carrying under each arm a great, round, Dutch loaf of bread about the size of a cart wheel, giving him, upon a side view, such as I had of him, the appearance of rolling in on wheels."[238]

After Gordon and Doles carried Barlow's Knoll, Early ordered his second line, Hays' and Avery's brigades, to enter the action. Both units advanced southwestward from their positions behind Jones' guns, which had to cease firing while the infantry passed by. Avery's three regiments were in the following order from left to right: 57th, 21st, and 6th North Carolina, and Hays' were in the following order in the same fashion: 8th Louisiana, 7th Louisiana, 9th Louisiana (astride the Harrisburg Road), 6th Louisiana, 5th Louisiana.[239]

The advance of Hays and Avery initially met no opposition except for the four companies of skirmishers from the 17th Connecticut that had been sent east across Rock Creek even before Early's men came up. Avery's men had been skirmishing with the Connecticut skirmishers for some time, and must have been glad to be able to push them back at last. Major Allen Brady, commander of the Union detachment, had been lucky to hold his position so long. Gordon's advance had struck only the far right end of his line, which he simply pulled back in order to continue facing the left portion of Early's line. He continued sparring with the Confederate skirmishers for another half an hour or more, when he received an order from General Ames "to draw in his skirmishers and return to town as rapidly as possible, and take command of his regiment." Ames' order came just as Early's second line began to move forward. Brady had some difficulty in drawing off Captain McCartney's Company K "as they were so earnestly engaged and making such havoc among the rebels," but he finally did get his command safely across the creek. His losses on the east side of Rock Creek had totalled 3 men killed, 1 captain and 1 lieutenant wounded, and 1 sergeant and 3 men prisoners. Ironically, the loss in these four companies would surely have been many times greater had they been fighting along with the rest of their regiment on Barlow's Knoll.[240]

The resistance put up by Brady's men made an impression on General Hays, who noted that "pressing steadily on, I met with no other opposition than that presented by the enemy's skirmishers and the firing of his artillery until I came up to the line of Gordon's brigade." Hays then advanced and helped deal with the last Union troops still in the Almshouse area, whereupon he continued on, "driving before me all the force opposed until I arrived at the railroad...just striking the edge of the city of Gettysburg."[241] Hays' speedy advance cut off Brady's command from marching directly to join the rest of their brigade, part of which was forming behind the batteries that were reforming on the northern edge of the town. Brady felt that the enemy was deliberately trying to "cut us off and capture us before we got to the town, but we foiled them in this attempt by making a circuit and entering the town near the upper end, and soon rejoined the remainder of the regiment, which we found near the lower end of the town."[242]

Hays and Avery were just crossing Rock Creek when Early saw that Gordon's troops had encountered a second line just outside of the town in a strong position behind some houses, and halted his brigade behind the crest of a low ridge in an open field. Early rode up to speak with Gordon, and noticed Coster's men forming with their right extending beyond Gordon's left, so he directed Gordon to "remain stationary" while Hays and Avery advanced on his left.[243]

Hays' advance was delayed somewhat by his advance through the woods near the Almshouse and then the passage over Gordon's halted brigade. His center and right then ran straight into blasts of canister from Heckman's battery, but the Louisianians still pressed on. By this time, Hays' left was overlapped in front by the right half of Avery's brigade. Avery had not encountered any obstacles during his advance other than Brady's skrimishers and the creek. For this reason, the North Carolinians got slightly in front of Hays' left, and had the honor of striking Coster's line first.

Avery's line also came under the fire of Heckman's guns as it advanced. Colonel A.C. Godwin of the 57th North Carolina described his attack as follows: "The enemy had formed a line of battle on the hillside in ground of the town, under cover of a strong fence, portions of which

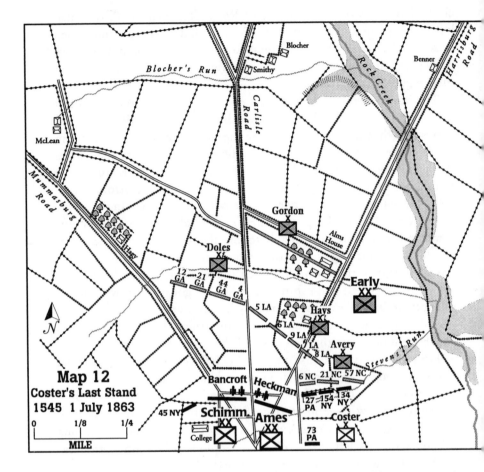

Map 12
Coster's Last Stand
1545 1 July 1863

0   1/8   1/4
MILE

were made of stone. Our advance was made with great deliberation until we approached a sluggish stream [Stevens' Run], or slough, about 200 yards in front of the enemy's lines, when the batteries opened upon us with grape and canister, seconded by a very destructive fire from the infantry."[244]

Avery's advance furnished quite a spectacle to Coster's defenders when the Confederate line came over the rise some 200 yards to their front. Sergeant Charles McKay of Company C, 154th New York, remembered that "It seemed as though they had a battle flag every few rods, which would indicate the formation was in solid column."[245] The whole Union line at once erupted into a blaze of fire. The 6th North Carolina was halted with a large number of casualties, and the advance of the 21st North Carolina was also checked.[246]

The issue on this line, though, was quickly decided because Avery's left regiment, the 57th North Carolina, overlapped the right of the 134th New York so much that the Confederate unit was able to swing around almost into the rear of the 134th. The resulting rear and enfilade fire all but destroyed the unfortunate Union regiment, and even caused numerous casualties farther down Coster's line. In just a few minutes, the 134th lost 42 killed and 151 wounded, almost half its strength.[247] The 134th was decimated so quickly that its survivors were in full retreat before any help could be sent. Colonel Cantador of the 27th Pennsylvania had become aware of the gap between the 134th and the 154th and had called for his second battalion to move at the double-quick to the right and plug the hole. In the noise of the battle, only 50 men answered his call under the command of 1st Lieutenant Adolphus F. Vogelbach. By the time Vogelbach reached Jackson's unit, he found that the line of the 134th had disintegrated.[248]

The collapse of the 134th opened up the right flank of the 154th to Avery's 57th North Carolina, and Lieutenant Colonel Allen quickly had no choice but to order his command to withdraw. Adjutant Alanson Crosby was well aware that "The enemy was gradually closing in upon us, and to remain was certain capture."[249] Most of the men of the 154th had had time to fire only 6 to 9 shots apiece before the order came to withdraw.[250] Janus Quilliam had just fired twice and was aiming to shoot again "when a spent ball hit me on the bone under the left eye, then dropped on the ground. It made me dizzy for a spell. I then fell on the ground to [see] if I would find the ball, and there it was."[251]

Since Allen had received no orders to withdraw, he directed his men to fall back by the only route that was open, the left rear: "When I reached a position in rear of where the twenty-seventh had formed, I found that they had withdrawn without my knowledge." He later learned that Colonel Coster had given an order for the entire brigade to retreat. Colonel Cantador of the 27th Pennsylvania had received the order, but Allen never did, much to the devastation of his regiment. He now knew that "the enemy had outbalanced us to a much greater extent upon our left than on the right; that their line had advanced unopposed down the road and across the open field beyond. The ground directly in the rear of the position which we had occupied was cut up into village lots surrounded by board fences, so that retreat was greatly impeded in that direction. The men being almost surrounded by the enemy, who outnumbered them more than five to one were right in their midst, many of the men were compelled to surrender."[252]

The scene in the brickyard was total bedlam. Fierce hand-to-hand fighting broke out, especially among those who had no interest in surrendering. Adjutant Crosby remembered, "The men had no idea of giving themselves away, for they fought after being surrounded and a few escaped by cutting through."[253] Only those who were fast and lucky made it to safety, since the Confederates did not hesitate to fire into the backs of all those who tried to flee.

Several sources speak of Union prisoners being gobbled up by the score.[254] Private Quilliam, who had been wounded in the face a short time before, tried to head for the rear but did not get far before the regiment was overwhelmed: "I got up and went as fast as any of them, but when we got to the road, it was full of rebels and they were coming up behind us, so there we had to stay, and but few got away."[255] Corporal Newell Burch of the 154th was among the last of his unit to be captured, and "was greatly surprised to find so many of the regiment" in enemy hands.[256] Lieutenant Vogelbach, commander of the detachment of the 27th Pennsylvania that had been sent to plug the gap between the 134th and 154th, was caught up in the maelstrom and invited to surrender. He refused to do so and was shot down, whereupon his men gave up in dismay.[257]

1st Lieutenant John Mitchell of Company C, 154th New York, did not pull out immediately when be heard the order to withdraw. Instead, he held on a brief while longer, until he saw the rest of the regimental line giving way. He then led his men to the gateway where they had come in. Mitchell spotted two mounted horsemen on the edge of Stratton Street, but they were not whom he thought they were: "I ran towards them and found myself in the midst of Company B, who, with Capt. [Simeon V.] Paul, were sitting down with their guns on the ground. I thought this is a strange proceeding." Private Charles McKay did not realize the import of what was happening until one of his fellows, Private Addison Scott, came up and one of the horseman called upon him to surrender. When Scott did not do so promptly, the horseman banged him on the head with his sword. In the ensuing confusion, Scott, McKay and Private Albert E. Hall all managed to escape by running the other direction. They skipped through Stevens' Run and then dove behind its embankment on their way to safety.[258]

There was particularly heavy fighting around the regimental flags of the 134th and 154th, which were always considered a prize capture. Miraculously, both flags were carried to safety, but at a cost of many lives and much heroism. Sergeant Lewis Bishop was hit while bearing one flag of the 154th, as were several others who took up the colors from him. Corporal Albert Mericle carried the unit's state flag as far as where Stratton Street crosses Stevens' Run before he fell wounded. 2nd Lieutenant James W. Bird of Company B picked up the flag and carried it to safety while a comrade on either side was shot down.[259] The 154th's national flag was found on the ground and rescued by a member of the 134th New York, who was wounded in the process.[260] Meanwhile, one color bearer of the 134th had to hold both his unit's flags when the rest of the color guard was felled. He saw that he was being surrounded, and ripped the state colors from their staff and hid them beneath his uniform; he even managed to keep them concealed while he was held a prisoner for four days. The national colors of the 134th were rescued by Captain Matthew B. Cheney of Company G, 154th who thought they belonged to his command. Cheney was badly wounded as he crossed the railroad, but still managed to bear his prize to safety.[261]

When the Confederates tallied up their prisoners from this one short segment of the battle, they found that they had 178 members of the 154th New York, 59 of the 134th New York and 78 from the 27th Pennsylvania (most from Lieutenant Vogelbach's detachment). In addition, the 154th New York lost 1 man killed and 21 wounded, a total of 200 out of 239 engaged, the highest percentage casualty rate of any Union unit in the battle (83.7%). In comparison, the 134th lost "only" 63% and the 27th Pennsylvania 39%.[263] When the survivors of the 154th reached Cemetery Hill, Lieutenant Colonel Allen was able to count only 17 men besides himself—Captain Matthew Cheney (who was wounded), Lieutenant James Bird, and 15 privates, of whom at least two were wounded.[264] Today the brigade's brief stand is commemorated on the field by a monument to each of the three regiments, a brigade tablet, and a most interesting 80 foot long mural of the height of the Confederate attack. It was painted on the side wall of a warehouse by Rhode Island artist Johan Bjurman in 1988.[265]

The many prisoners from Coster's brigade were marched back about two miles from the battlefield to join the hundreds and hundreds of other unfortunate Yankees captured this day. Their captors were kind enough to drop off most of their wounded charges before they exited the town. Coster's men saw death and destruction everywhere as they trekked back over the battlefield. John Wellman of the 154th observed, "The ground over which we passed to reach the rear was thickly strewn with the dead and dying, showing that the first day's fight at Gettysburg was no idle play."[266]

Captain Harrison Cheney of Company D, 154th New York, years later told a story that is quite interesting, if it is not apocryphal. He claimed that he came upon General Lee as he was walking down the road (probably the Chambersburg Pike). The General stopped him and asked, "Captain, how many men do you have on that hill?" Cheney, knowing that there was only one fresh brigade in reserve on Cemetery Hill, quickly responded: "Not less than 10,000 or 15,000 men." Cheney later claimed this interview helped dissuade Lee from assaulting the hill and crowning his day's victory.[267]

The Confederates apparently tried to persuade their prisoners to sign paroles even before they were transported off the battlefield, which was not the proper way of doing things, and only a few of Coster's men accepted the offer. Most thought that they would soon be paroled on a legal basis, but in this they were mistaken. They and hundreds of their fellows captured at Gettysburg were taken to Southern prisons. Survival rates there are not all known, but records show that over ⅓ of the captives from the 154th New York (60 of 172) perished in Southern prisons; 39 perished at Belle Isle in Richmond and another 20 at Andersonville in Georgia. At least 6 lucky members of the 154th managed to escape their captors, most in their original march to Richmond. These included Adjutant Alonson Crosby and Lieutenant John Mitchell, Captain Harrison Cheney, Sergeants William Clark and Frederick West and Corporal Marshall McShannon.[268]

In the days after the battle, one fallen soldier of the 154th New York became perhaps the most celebrated enlisted man to have fallen in the engagement. As the Union burial details were conducting their gruesome task, one detachment found the body of an unidentified Union sergeant near the corner of Stratton and York Streets, several blocks south of where Coster's brigade had fought in the Kuhn brickyard. In his hands was a picture of three young children, two boys and a girl. A Philadelphia doctor named John Francis Bournes hoped he could identify the soldier with the help of the picture, and had it copied and published in newspapers throughout the north. Four months after the battle Mrs. Phylinda Humiston of Portville, New York, saw the picture and recognized the children as her own offspring, Franklin, Alice and Frederick. The slain soldier was her husband Sergeant Amos Humiston of Company C, 154th New York, who now lies buried in Plot B-14 of the New York section of the Gettysburg National Cemetery. The publicity surrounding the photograph and the plight of the families of fallen soldiers led to the writing of a number of patriotic and sentimental essays, poems, and songs, and ultimately resulted in the establishment of the soldiers' orphans' home, established on Cemetery Hill next to Baltimore Street in Gettysburg. Among its first residents was the family of Sergeant Amos Humiston.[269]

While the men of Avery's 21st and 57th North Carolina regiments were "gobbling up" Coster's troops, his 6th North Carolina swung to the right through the empty line vacated by the early retreat of the 27th Pennsylvania. The 6th, which had lost heavily during its initial attack on the 27th, then charged the guns of Heckman's Ohio Battery, which already had their hands full facing Hays' command to their front. Before Heckman could pull his guns back, Avery's men were upon him, and he had to leave two of his Napoleons in the possession of the enemy. Heckman had been in action just 30 minutes, during which time he fired 113 rounds of ammunition, mostly canister. His combat losses amounted to two men and nine horses killed, ten men and one officer wounded.[270]

Heckman's guns might have been saved if any of the withdrawing Union infantry had stopped to aid him. Major Winkler of the 26th Wisconsin came upon a force of over 100 men of Krzyzanowski's brigade who had been rallied and were trying to face Hays' advancing brigade: "It was useless, of course, to try to resist the long rebel forces that were approaching, but we could delay them and thus ensure a safe retreat to the rest of the troops." But when Hays' line drew nearer, all of the Yankee force fled except 32 men of Winkler's regiment. He directed them to kneel, and watched Coster's command get overrun on his right. He ordered the small band to fire a volley into Hays' right, and then ordered them to withdraw into town rather than be overrun themselves. "It seemed so awful to march back through those same streets whipped and beaten. It was the most humiliating step I ever took," the Captain later lamented.[271]

Somewhere near Heckman's battery, another brave Union officer tried to get his men to stand and face the advancing Confederates: "A little to the left of Hays, a tattered Federal regiment faced about and tried to make a stand, led by a mounted officer, who, riding among them, waved his hat and sword, shouting, 'Don't run, men, none but cowards run.' Some of the Confederates, admiring his pluck, cried out, 'Don't shoot that man'; but a volley brought him down, and his heroic command was scattered by the advancing battalions of Hays and Avery."[272]

Lieutenant Eugene Bancroft and Captain Hubert Dilger were as frustrated as Captain Heckman in their efforts to stop Early's advance with just their own guns. Dilger, as we have already seen, had previously sent all his guns to the rear except for one section, which be posted on "market road" in order to bang away at the advancing Confederate infantry. He was soon afterwards relieved by a section of Bancroft's battery (probably Merkle's two guns), and attempted to retire up the Carlisle Pike. However, he found that "The main road was completely blocked by artillery, infantry, and ambulances," so he took the "first road to the left" (Washington Street) and "marched around the town, and rejoined my command on Cemetery Hill, having lost on this day 14 men, 24 horses, and 1 piece disabled."[273]

Bancroft's battery did not remain in position long after Dilger departed. His guns, which were deployed west of the Carlisle Pike near Heckman's line, were soon threatened by Hays' long advancing line. Lieutenant Merkle reported that "The enemy came rather close at the time, so I fired two double rounds of canister, with prolonge fixed at their line at the end of the town; then limbered up and retired." Bancroft admitted simply that he "retired slowly through Gettysburg" after refilling his ammunition chests; neither apparently stayed around long enough to close with Hays' troops. The last Union artillery shots fired during the withdrawal were apparently discharged by Lieutenant Scripture of Dilger's battery, who unlimbered two guns near the town square long enough to clear the streets with canister and allow the retreating infantry a few more precious minutes to escape.[274] One of the units that had tried to support Dilger's guns for a few moments was the remains of the 119th New York, which for a short while "made a plucky stand at the foot of Washington Street, holding the enemy in check for a while and then retreating in good order to the hill."[275]

Another of the few organized infantry units to try to help the Union batteries on the north edge of the town was the 17th Connecticut of Ames' brigade. Major Allen Brady, who had managed to rejoin his regiment after his withdrawal from the east side of Rock Creek, observed: "The enemy were at this time advancing rapidly through the town. The regiment was immediately deployed through the streets, and fired several volleys into the ranks of the enemy, much thinned their ranks and retarded their advance. We kept the enemy from advancing through the town until ordered to clear the street of our men for the purpose of planting a battery. The battery not being placed in position as intended, and the regiment being in line on the sidewalk, the enemy took advantage of this, and with a superior force rushed through the main street, which compelled us to fall back, which we did reluctantly, but not without contesting the ground inch by inch."[276]

Bancroft's battery also had to withdraw from the north edge of town at this time because his supporting infantry, composed of assorted units of Schimmelfennig's division (mostly Krzyzanowski's men) had withdrawn. General Schurz, supported by his staff officers, had done his best "to rally and reform what was in my reach of the First Division, for the purpose of checking the enemy's advance round my right, and to hold the edge of town, but was soon ordered by Howard to withdraw to the south side of the town and to occupy a position on and near Cemetery." After he led Coster's brigade forward to its unsuccessful rearguard action at the northeastern edge of town, he rode to the left to assist the 3rd Division (Schimmelfennig's) which was engaged in a "very difficult and delicate fight at very close quarters." These troops were attempting to support Bancroft near the Carlisle Pike, but soon they too were ordered to fall back. General Schurz stopped to say a sad farewell to his old friend from Germany, Colonel Francis Mahler of the 75th Pennsylvania. Schurz felt lucky to emerge from the day's conflict unscathed, though his horse "had a bullet hole clean through the fatty ridge of the neck just under the mane."[277]

The last XI Corps infantry to fight north of Gettysburg were the troops of Von Amsberg's brigade, which was posted on the far left of the Corps' line. As we have already seen, Von Amsberg sent his only spare regiment, the 157th New York, to try and relieve the pressure on Krzyzanowski's brigade, only to see the brave regiment torn to pieces near the forks of the Carlisle Pike. The defeat of the 157th, along with the withdrawal of Krzyzanowski's command and Dilger's cannons, left Von Amsberg's flank wide open to Doles' advancing brigade. Von Amsberg sent the 82nd Illinois to try to assist Krzyzanowski, but it too was overrun, losing 35% casualties, including 89 missing.[278] The 45th New York was more fortunate. It had been sent, too late, to help the 147th New York, and managed to withdraw at a "leisurely" pace to the college.[279] Their withdrawal was perhaps covered by a rear guard composed of the 61st Ohio (which lost 22% casualties in the battle) and the 74th Pennsylvania (which lost 33%, including 60 missing).[280]

Doles' troops remembered well their triumphal sweep of the fields northwest of Gettysburg in this closing stage of the day's action. These Georgians had already done more than their fair share of the fighting for the day, yet they nonetheless continued pressing on after their defeat of the 157th New York and Krzyzanowski's brigade. Because of the angle at which Avery and Hays were advancing, Doles directed his advance to the southwest, towards Von Amsberg's scattered regiments. Major William Peebles of the 44th Georgia reported that, following the repulse of Krzyzanowski, "we soon had nothing in our front, and we removed toward our right, where a heavy column was pressing some brigade near the hills on our right [Rodes attacking Robinson]. The enemy, discovering our move, began to retreat. Had our men not been so nearly exhausted, we should doubtless have captured the greater portion of the artillery and men; but only a few who could not flee as rapidly as the main body fell into our hands."[281]

By this time (1600), the Union I Corps was being forced back from Seminary Ridge and Doles pushed his troops rapidly forward by the left flank in order to try to cut the Yankees off from the town. This effort did not succeed because the enemy "retired faster than we advanced."[282] During this movement, Doles' advance was hindered for a few moments by a "severe fire" from one of the Rodes batteries, a two-gun section of brass pieces "stationed on the side of the hill where General Rodes' headquarters were at the opening of the engagement." Doles complained about the accident in a specific memorandum he sent to General Rodes on 19 July 1863.[283]

Though Doles was not able to cut the main Union retreat artery along the Chambersburg Pike, he did succeed at attacking their rear and hurrying them on into town. C.D. Grace of Doles' command recalled that "Doles' brigade reached the railroad hill just in time to catch the federals as they fell back along the railroad, closely pressed by A.P. Hill and the balance of Rodes' division. We charged and drove them from the railroad track through south of town to the cemetery ridge, part of the brigade going through the town."[284] Another account notes that, "our brigade then marched rapidly by the left flank in an attempt to cut the enemy off from the town, but was unable to do so. We continued the pursuit through the town, and had a sharp engagement in the streets, killing, wounding and capturing a good many men, with small loss to ourselves."[285]

Doles' detour in pursuit of the retiring I Corps enabled Von Amsberg's brigade a brief respite as it reformed near the northwest corner of the town. As the brigade was retiring, the 45th New York proceeded unmolested to the grounds of the college, where it was joined by some of the rest of the brigade (classes at the college had begun as usual that morning, but had been promptly cancelled as soon as the cannons began booming). The units then prepared to make a stand against the enemy to their front (Doles' brigade), who "pressed very feebly forward." At the same time, the Yankees looked to their left and saw "the left of the First Corps broken to pieces and pursued by overwhelming numbers of the enemy making for the left of the town."[286]

The 45th New York and its brigade remained unchallenged at the college for some 15 to 20 minutes before the division bugler sounded the retreat and then the double quick. The intrepid Captain Francis Irsch, though, was not about to retreat, and called out to his men: "Kameraden, zum schnellen Retiriren ist's zu spät; hier giebt's hur trotziges Kämpfen, Gefangenschaft oder Tod!" His men agreed and all cried out in reply, "So wollen wir hier stehen und Kämpfend sterben, oder in Gefangenschaft untergehen!"[287]

As the enemy drew closer, Colonel Von Amsberg decided that the college grounds were not the best place to to make a stand after all, and he ordered his brigade to begin a withdrawal. The Union troops "retreated slowly, left in front, into the town, cautiously followed by the enemy in the rear." The column proceeded cautiously down Washington Street, until it reached the Eagle Hotel (corner of Chambersburg Street), where they were fired on by enemy troops to the west.[288]

The 45th was now in for trouble as it got lost in the town and was impeded by the traffic of other retreating troops. The regiment marched another block south to Middle Street, where it met an enemy fire that felled Major Charles Koch and a number of others in the unit. Lieutenant Colonel Aldolphus Dobke then led it back to Chambersburg Street and headed for the town square, only to be struck by Confederate fire from the east. At this point the head of the regiment, led by Captain Andrew B. Searles and the color guard, retreated to mid-block and then decided to head south via the alleys on each side of the Lutheran Church. About 100 in number, they ran to safety by cutting through the town and climbing several fences in order to reach the security of Cemetery Hill.[289]

While the lead companies of the 45th fled to safety, the four rear companies covered for them by splitting up to face the Confederates coming from the west and from the town square to the east. As one regimental history described it, they "rear faced against the enemy each way, holding them at bay." They then made a fateful and fatal decision. Lieutenant Henry Ahlert had taken possession of some houses near the Eagle Hotel, so the rear guard of the 45th headed northward, away from their beacon of safety. Most entered an "alley that led into a spacious yard surrounded by large buildings, which only offered an entrance, but no way to pass out, excepting a very narrow doorway, to freedom and heaven; but the enemy's sharpshooters had already piled a barricade of dead Union soldiers in front of this doorway."[290] The stranded detachment of the 45th was soon joined by other stray elements of the I and XI Corps, and began to engage in some real urban fighting.[291]

One regimental history of the 45th tells their story: "We broke down the fences of the yards, and Captain Dietz gained more houses up to an alley near the market place, occupying windows, barns and alleyways from which the enemy was continually harassed, and several attempts of the enemy to dislodge us were repelled successfully. Repeated demands to surrender were refused until towards sundown, when Captain Irsch was invited, after a parley, to come out under a safe conduct and see the hopelessness of further defence, which being accepted, he was taken to the market place where a brigade of infantry and a battery were drawn up. Baltimore Street, up to the base of Cemetery Hill, was filled with Confederate troops; the eastern and western outskirts were full of the enemy, and the fields in front of the town were massed with infantry and artillery, and no federals were in sight, excepting such as having taken refuge in cellars and houses were brought out as prisoners. Upon returning and reporting what he saw, Captain Irsch, with other officers, ordered their men to destroy their arms and ammunition and throw them into the wells, and then all formally surrendered. While being taken to the rear past the college we saw many of our former prisoners set free [hundreds of troops captured from O'Neal's command, who had been left at the college without a guard, were liberated by Doles' advance]. As we passed the lane near the Mummasburg Road, where we fought during the day, we saw a great many of the enemy's dead and wounded, and some of ours."[292]

Captain Francis Irsch would be awarded a Medal of Honor for his brave conduct this day, both in the attack on the McLean barn and for his handling of his troops when they were surrounded near the Eagle Hotel. The 45th New York was indeed a hardy outfit. The unit's regimental monument in the field notes that all its prisoners refused to be paroled, hoping "to encumber the enemy, believing that the Union army would capture the cripple foe and thereby effect their release."

As the prisoners of the 45th were halted near the Mummasburg Road, "a remarkable incident happened, brought to our knowledge as we talked with some of our former prisoners. One of the Confederates, named Schwarz, asked whether his brother, who belonged to our Company 'B' was among us. This brought out the fact that the interrogator was among the prisoners taken from McLean's red barn, and as companies A and B, under Captain Korn and Lieutenant Lindemeyer, took most of the prisoners at and in the barn, he recognized his brother of Company B, and they embraced there and then, not having seen each other since they left Germany many years previous. The brother, of Company B (Corporal Rudolph J. Schwarz), was killed while his Confederate brother was being marched to the rear as our prisoner."[293]

Captures and Escapes

Affairs were equally chaotic on the other side of town from where Irsch's band was captured. General Early wanted to shell the retreating Union troops and sent for Carrington's fresh Virginia battery to come forward and do so by following Gordon's advance. Carrington was more than eager to do so. His men had grown quite impatient during their inaction, and just fifteen minutes previously he had impertinently asked Early when his unit would be sent into action. The general had replied to him good naturedly "that I need not be impatient, that there would be plenty to do in awhile."[294]

Upon receipt of his orders to advance, Carrington limbered up and headed towards the Harrisburg Road bridge over Rock Creek. All at once the narrow wooden bridge gave him pause. It seemed to him to be hazardous to try to cross; the enemy's artillery was still shelling the area and the bridge would be blocked "if any of the horses had been knocked down." He hesitated over the best way to approach the problem, until someone—he remembered that it might have been Early himself—suggested that he should cross one piece at a time. After crossing the bridge in this manner, Carrington turned to the right and proceeded across the field behind Gordon's troops. At this time General Early came up and rode with him for awhile. The general was quiet, deep in thought, for sometime. Then "he stated to me very briefly in substance, that if anything happened to Gordon's brigade, he wanted me to unlimber my battery immediately; I suppose, as a rallying point."[295]

A very short while later, Early sharply instructed Carrington to put his guns into position, which he did. While he was waiting to see what would happen next, one of his sergeants came up and reported that there was a wounded Federal lieutenant colonel nearby who wanted to see him. Carrington had the officer removed to a safer spot, as he requested. In return for the favor, the lieutenant colonel offered

Carrington his "handsome pair" of field glasses. The captain at first refused to accept out of respect for Lee's order to respect the Northerners' private property, but he acquiesced when the Federal expressed a concern that "they would be a temptation on account of their value for some Federal or Confederate who might pass by, to knock him in the head." Carrington after the war learned from the battle's early great historian, John B. Bachelder, that the lieutenant colonel he had helped was named Lee and later became the lieutenant governor of Ohio.[296]

Carrington figured that he spent about ten minutes dealing wth the Union officer. About fifteen minutes later, Hays' and Avery's infantry came up on the left and routed Coster's line. "Much to my delight, and that of my company, an order came to me to advance into the town. I had not advanced perhaps over four hundred yards into the main street, I think, of Gettysburg, when I received, an order to halt. I did so, of course, and seeing the confusion ahead of me in the street, and not knowing what would turn up, I unlimbered three of my pieces and ordered my men to get several rounds of canister from the caissons and place them near the muzzle of the guns." Carrington was very proud to be the commander of the only Confederate battery to actually deploy in the streets of Gettysburg that day.[297]

Early's other three batteries stayed behind during this advance. This was certainly not because they were low on ammunition—during the battle Garber fired only 106 rounds, Green 161, and Tanner 595.[298] Early probably just thought that they were a little played out from their half hour of intense fire before Gordon's attack. Besides, they did not have a clear field of fire at the retreating Union troops. Once Gordon began his assault, Jones had to direct his fire farther to the left in order to avoid hitting the Georgians. He kept up this fire on the disordered masses of the enemy that were rapidly retreating before the Confederate troops "until the advance of Hays and Avery rendered it dangerous to continue firing from that position."[299] In short, the infantry attack succeeded so well and so quickly that Early did not have the time, or the need, to bring all of Jones' battalion and deploy it on Barlow's Knoll or elsewhere in order to soften up a second Union line.

A young lieutenant named Robert Stiles had command of one of Carrington's guns during his battery's advance, and he had a quite different view of what was happening than did his captain. He later enthusiastically wrote, "We drove the enemy pell-mell over rolling wheat fields, through a grove, across a creek, up a little slope, and into the town itself. The pursuit was so close and hot that, though my gun came into battery several times, yet I could not get in a shot." After the battery was moved into the town, Stiles remembered well how he loaded his gun and had "several rounds of canister taken from the ammunition chest and put down hard by the gaping muzzle, ready to sweep the street in case they should come upon us."[300]

At this moment Stiles saw young George Greer, a favorite clerk of General Early, come riding by. Greer was "a chubby boy of sixteen...more fond of riding courier for him and of driving spurs into the flanks of a horse than of driving pen across paper." Stiles called to him to be careful as he disappeared into the smoke and dust ahead. Much to Stiles' amazement, "In a few moments a cloud of blue coats appeared in the street in front of us, coming on, too, at a run. I was about to order the detachment to fire, when beyond and back of the men in blue I noticed Greer, leaning forward over the neck of his horse, towering above the Federals, who were on foot; and with violent gesticulations and in tones not the gentlest ordering the "blue devils" to "double quick to the rear of the piece, which they did in the shortest time imaginable. There must have been over fifty of them. I am aware this statement sounds incredible, but the men had thrown away their arms and were cowering in abject terror in the streets and alleys. Upon no other occasion did I see any large body of troops, on either side, so completely routed and demoralized as were the two Federal corps who were beaten at Gettysburg on the evening of July 1st."[301]

Stiles then witnessed the following incident involving an Irishman from Hays' brigade and a captured son of the Emerald Isle: "There was an Irishman named Burgoyne in the Ninth Louisiana,—Harry Hayes' brigade,—a typical son of the Emerald Isle, over six feet high in his stockings (when he had any), broad-shouldered and muscular, slightly bow-legged, and springy as a cat; as full of fire and fight and fun as he could hold; indeed, often a little fuller than he could hold, and never having been known to get his fill of noise and scrimmage. Whenever the Ninth supported Hilary Jones, if the musketry fire slackened while the artillery was in action, Burgoyne would slip over to the nearest gun and take someone's place at the piece. Seeing us unlimber in the street, as above related, he had come over now for this purpose, seized the sponge-staff and rammed home the charge and was giving vent to his enthusiasm in screams and bounds that would have done credit to a catamount.

"Standing on the other side of the gun, with his arms folded, was a Federal Irishman, a prisoner just captured—a man even taller than

Burgoyne and somewhat heavier in frame, altogether a magnificent fellow. Catching Burgoyne's brogue, he broke out, 'Hey, ye spalpane! say, what are yez doing in the Ribil army?'

"Quick as a flash, Burogoyne retorted:'Be-dad, ain't an Irishman a freeman? Haven't I as good right to fight for the Ribs as ye have to fight for the _____ Yanks?'

"'O, yes!' sang out the Federal Irishman, 'I know ye, now you've turned your ougly mug to me. I had the plizure of kicking yez out from behind Marye's wall, that time Sedgwick lammed yer brigade out o'there!'

"'Yer a _____ liar,' shouted our Pat, 'and I'll just knock yer teeth down yer ougly throat for that same lie,' and suiting the action to the word, he vaulted lightly over the gun, and before we had time to realize the extreme absurdity of the thing, the two had squared off against each other in the most approved style and first blow had passed, for the Federal Irishman was as good grit as ours. Just as the two giants were about to rush to close quarters, but before any blood had been drawn in the round, I noticed that the right fist of the Federal gladiator was gory, and the next movement revealed the stumps of two shattered fingers, which he was about to drive full into Burgoyne's face.

"'Hold!' I cried; 'your man's wounded!' On the instant Burgoyne's fist fell.

"'You're a trump, Pat; give me your well hand,' said he. 'We'll fight this out some other time. I didn't see ye were hurt.'"[302]

Just as this fist fight was adjourned, one of Early's staff rode up and ordered Stiles to limber up and head to the rear. Stiles questioned the order, only to hear it repeated. He said to himself, "I reckon the town's barricaded, and we'll just pass round it to the front." But that is not what would happen. The battery pulled back at least a mile, and went into position on a hill far from the action. Stiles never did quite figure out why, and he could not have been more disappointed.[303] By this time at least one other battery of the battalion, Tanner's, had advanced toward the town. It did not deploy, but was returned for the night to a position near where it had been engaged earlier.[304]

Major Henry Gilmor of the 1st Maryland Cavalry Battalion (CSA) was also eager to get into the action and capture some Federal prisoners. The 1st Maryland had been detached from Jeb Stuart's Cavalry division and was assigned to accompany Ewell's infantry during the invasion of Maryland and Pennsylvania. Ewell assigned Company A of the battalion to serve with his vanguard, and directed Companies B, C, and D, under the temporary command of Major Gilmor in the absence of Major Ridgely Brown, to accompany Stewart's brigade of Johnson's division on a large scale foraging expedition to McConnellsburg. After completing this assignment, Gilmor led his command westward to Chambersburg, and rejoined Stewart at Shippensburg, on the road to Carlisle. From there he received directions to return to Chambersburg and then report to Ewell.[305]

Gilmor and his command proceeded to Chambersburg and then rode on to Gettysburg, reaching the field on the early afternoon of 1 July. The battle was already well in progress, and he was ordered to ride to the left and support Jones' artillery.[306] When he saw the XI Corps begin to retreat, Gilmor left his command in charge of Captain George M. Emack and rushed after the flying enemy, accompanied by Captain Warner Welsh and Lieutenant William H.B. Dorsey. The three rode past Hays' and Avery's infantry and into the town; to Gilmor it seemed that he and his friends were the first Confederates to enter Gettysburg. As they rode along, a dismounted Union cavalryman appeared and took a shot at them, which barely missed Gilmor's ear. Gilmor impulsively stopped to pick up a loaded musket from the ground and fired at the Yankee. He hit his mark, and appropriated the man's pistol and saber before he continued on.[307]

Gilmor's cavalry could certainly have been better used scouting the roads off to Early's left, as historian Harry Pfanz suggests.[308] Early had twice ordered Smith to bring up his Virginia brigade and join the pursuit of Schurz's men, but Smith declined because of reports from his scouts and skirmishers that a large body of the enemy (Slocum's XII Corps) was approaching from the east. Proper use of Gilmor's cavalrymen, or any of the other various mounted units that Ewell had on hand, would have given Ewell, Early and Smith a better idea of what was happening on their left (see Chapter IX).

The Union cavalryman who fired at Gilmor was probably a member of the 9th New York Cavalry. At about noon Sergeant E.A. Holcomb of the 9th had been sent with a detachment of Company G to watch the Hanover Road bridge over Rock Creek. Holcomb held his position even after Devin pulled the rest of his brigade back from its position east of the town in order to escape Wiedrich's "friendly fire" into his rear. The retreat of Barlow's division and advance of Avery's brigade, though, threatened to cut him off from the town, so Holcomb ordered his command to retire: "Calling in his videttes, he moved back and found the village streets too full of troops for him to pass. The enemy's bullets were becoming quite annoying when someone called out, 'They're going to shell the street.' Immediately the troops vanished, the streets became clear, and Holcomb and his men rode back without any further trouble and joined the regiment."[309]

By this time Devin had retired to the fields west of Cemetery Hill, near the Emmitsburg Road. Soon after Holcomb's detachment rejoined its regiment, Confederate skirmishers (probably from Doles' brigade) began to make their appearance known at the southern edge of the town. They halted there, and using the cover of the buildings and garden fences, began firing at Devin's cavalrymen, especially the officers. Devin reacted promptly by dispatching companies I and G of the 9th New York, which was deployed closest to the town, to deal with them. The troopers dismounted and charged the enemy skirmish line back through the village. In this action Corporal Landrus A. Godfrey of Company G was killed and Frank C. Cave of Company I was wounded.[310]

The 9th's regimental historian was proud of how Devin described this action in his battle report: "The enemy, having gained the York Road, entered the town immediately after my pickets retired, and, passing through with their sharpshooters, attacked the flank of the brigade, killing and wounding several men and horses. I immediately dismounted one squadron of the Ninth New York, who, with their carbines drove them some distance into the town, punishing them severely."[311]

Hays' Louisianians were the only Confederate infantry to enter the eastern half of the town of Gettysburg. Avery's brigade had advanced toward the town after overrunning Coster's command, "but, while still in the outskirts, was wheeled to the left and reformed on the railroad."[312] Gordon, as already noted, had stopped his command between the Almshouse and the Crawford Farm, and Smith was heading towards the York Road far to the east of town.

Hays in his initial charge had met the enemy "in considerable strength" near the Almshouse. He had no difficult in pushing these troops aside, however, and succeeding in driving all the opposition before him until he reached the line of the railroad. Here "the fire to which my command was subjected from the enemy's batteries, posted upon well-selected rises of the ground, was unusually galling. But so rapid and impetuous was the movement of my troops in this advance, that my skirmishers, keeping well to the front, captured two pieces of artillery."[313]

Hays barely had time to pause at the railroad after chasing off Ames' and Coster's commands, when he saw the remains of Schimmelfennig's division coming into the town "advancing rapidly, threatening my right. Perceiving that a forward movement on my part would expose my flank to an attack from this force, exceeding in numbers that under my command, I immediately changed front forward on the first company, First Battalion, of a portion of my brigade—the Fifth, Sixth, and the right wing of the Ninth Regiments. With this line, after several well-directed volleys, I succeeded in breaking this column on my right, dispersing its men in full flight through the streets of the city."[314]

Hays was certain he could have captured the rest of Heckman's battery and more if Ames' troops and Schimmelfennig's troops had not threatened his right in their onrushing tide: "But for this movement on my flank, I should have captured several pieces of artillery opposite the left of my line, upon which the Seventh Regiment was advancing in front and the Eighth by a side street by the time I halted."[315]

Hays then reformed his line of battle and advanced through the town, "clearing it of the enemy and taking prisoners at every turn. During this time, as well as in my progress to the city, a great number of prisoners was captured by my command, but, unwilling to decrease my force by detailing a guard, I simply ordered them to the rear as they were taken. Many of these following the road to the left, fell into the possession of Major General Rodes' troops."[316] One of Hays' lieutenants, Joseph Jackson, remembered that "we shot them down, bayoneted them, and captured more prisoners than we had men."[317] General Hays in his battle report estimated that the Union troops that afternoon lost at least six times as many casualties as the Confederate attackers. The casualties in his own brigade were reported as only 1 officer and 6 men killed, 4 officers and 37 wounded, and 15 men missing.[318]

Conditions in the town were certainly disorganized during the Union withdrawal that went on for about two hours from 1600 to near 1800.[319] At the height of the retreat the roads were jammed with troops, wagons, artillery, and wounded. It is significant that few sources mention Union troops literally running to the rear. Most were simply tired and dejected, and moved through the town in small groups or regimental clusters that congregated around key officers or unit flags.[320] The XI Corps troops were more fortunate in their retreat than those of the I Corps because they at least had passed through the town and so were slighty familiar with its layout and main thoroughfares. They also had at least seen Cemetery Hill, which is where most of the troops seemed to be headed. Even so, large groups of troops, as in the case of the 45th New York, readily found themselves cut off by the advancing Confederates, particularly when the Southerners came upon them via cross streets.

General Schurz wrote a fair description of the corps' retreat, though he was a little optimistic about the troops' degree of organization once they reached Cemetery Hill: "It has been represented by some writers, Southerners, that the Union forces on the first day of the battle of Gettysburg were utterly routed and fled pell-mell into the town. This is far from the truth. That there were a good many stragglers hurrying to the rear in a disorderly fashion, as is always the case during and after a hot fight, will not be denied. Neither will it be denied that it was a retreat after a lost battle with the enemy in hot pursuit. But there was no element of dissolution in it. The retreat through the town was of course more or less disorderly, the streets being crowded with vehicles of every description, which offered to the passing troops exceedingly troublesome obstructions. It is also true that Eleventh Corps men complained that when they entered the town, it was already full of First Corpsmen, and vice versa, which really meant that the two corps became more or less mixed in passing through. It is likewise true that many officers and men, among others General Schimmelfennig, became entangled in cross streets, and alleys without throughfare, and were captured by the enemy pressing after them. But, after all, the fact remains that in whatever shape the troops issued from the town, they were promptly reorganized, each was under the colors of his regiment, and in as good a fighting trim as before, save that their ranks were fearfully thinned by the enormous losses suffered during the day."[321]

A number of Union troops, though, were brave enough or lucky enough to escape when caught in a tight situation that might have otherwise landed them in a prison camp. Captain Friedrich Von Fritsch, one of Von Gilsa's staff members, was riding through town with Von Gilsa's rear guard. For some reason he stopped to explain to a surgeon what be ought to do if he were captured. Just then he was suddenly surrounded by a group of Confederates. One shouted, "Surrender! Get down, you damn Yank!" Von Fritsch yelled out, "You be damned," and sliced the man's hand with his sword. Then he raced his horse into a yard, only to find it surrounded by a fence. More Confederates yelled at him to surrender and fired a few shots at him as he jumped his horse over the fence. In this way he barely escaped—though he was wounded in the left leg, his shoulder strap was shot away, his saddle was hit by a bullet, and he wrenched his knee and tore off a stirrup while going over the fence.[322]

Captain Edward C. Culp of the 25th Ohio had an ever more exciting escape from his would-be captors. He found himself trapped at the center of the block by a mass of disorganized Union troops at one end of the street and some Confederate troops moving up from the other end. Without stopping to think, he turned and rode his horse up on to the porch of a house. After quickly pushing the front door open, he rode his mount into the house's parlor and asked the frightened family that was congregated there how to get to the back alley. A girl led him into the back yard, which was fenced in. She offered to remove some slats to let him out, but the officer quickly had his horse jump the fence, and rode to safety.[323]

The most famous Union escape story is that of Brigadier General Alexander Schimmelfennig, commander of the XI Corps' 3rd Division during the battle. During the retreat, the general was heading down Washington Street and for some reason turned off into an alley. To his misfortune, the alley ended at a barn and had no outlet except another alley that headed north towards Breckinridge Street and the Confederates. The barn belonged to the family of an 18-year-old young woman named Anna Garlach. She tells the story of Schimmelfennig's ordeal and escape: "The Rebels were at his heels and when he reached our barn his horse was shot from under him. He jumped over the alley fence into our yard and ran toward Baltimore Street, but the Rebels were in possession of that street and he realized that he must be captured. There was an old water course in our yard at the time, now converted into a sewer, and for twelve feet from the street it was covered with a wooden culvert and General Schimmelfennig hurriedly crawled out of sight under this culvert. He remained there until after dark. It was night when my mother went out of the house, following the path to the stables, for purpose of feeding our hogs. Along the pathway was the woodshed and against the shed and running some distance from it was several ranks of wood and in front of the wood two swill barrels. We had been using the barrels and there was a space between barrel and next rank of wood being enough to hold a man. As mother went up the barrel the General said: 'Be quiet and do not say anything.' He had taken off the wood and built a shelter overhead to better hide himself. It was remarkable that he was not captured. The Rebels had torn down fences from Breckenridge street southward through the yards and there were Rebels on all sides of us and any movement of his in daytime might have been seen from a number of points. On the second day mother made a pretense of going to the swill barrel to empty a bucket.

In the bucket however was water and a piece of bread and instead of these going into barrel they went to the General in hiding. Mother was so afraid that she had been seen and the General would be found that she did not repeat this. General Schimmelfennig was in hiding between the barrel and rank of wood from the evening of the first day to the morning of the July 4th. That last night everything grew so quiet and as soon as there was light we got up and mother hurried down and out, anxious to know what had become of the man. He was already out of his hiding place before she reached him. When I first saw him he was moving across our yard toward the Benner property. He was walking stiff and cramped like. At the fence was a number of Union men and they proved to be some of his own men. They thought he had been killed and when they saw him they went wild with delight. I saw them crowd around him and some kissed his hand and they seemed beside themselves with joy. That was the last we saw of Gen. Schimmelfennig at that time. Some years later some of his relatives came to see us and we showed them the culvert and wood shed and they got pictures of the same. The two days he was there were hot days and his thirst must have been something awful for in the two days and three nights he did not have anything to drink or eat, that we knew of, except what mother gave him on that one occasion."[324]

It was none other than General Carl Schurz who found Schimmelfennig after the battle. When the Confederates evacuated Gettysburg before dawn on 4 July, Schimmelfennig crawled out of his hiding spot and was standing in a doorway when Schurz rode by on a reconnaisance. Schimmelfennig called out to him, and even cooked a hearty breakfast for them both from a few eggs he found in an abandoned house. During the meal he told Schurz the account of his ordeal. Some of its details differ from Anna Garlach's version just cited. Schurz's account says that when Schimmelfennig reached the fence at the end of the blind lane, he dismounted from his horse in order to cross it: "While he was on the top rail, his pursuers came up to him, and one of them knocked him on the head with the butt of his gun. The blow did not hurt him much, but he let himself drop on the other side of the fence as if he were dead, or at least stunned. Fortunately, he wore an ordinary cavalry overcoat over his general's uniform, so that no sign of his rank was visable. The rebel soldiers, thus taking him for a mere private, then passed by him." The general then sought shelter in Anna Garlach's garden. Schurz concludes, "a happy moment it was to me when I could telegraph to Mrs. Schimmelfennig, who was with my family at Bethlehem, Pa., that her husband, who had been reported missing after the first day's battle, had been found, sound and safe!"[325]

Altogether, the Confederates would capture over 1400 men of the XI Corps, about $\frac{1}{4}$ of its engaged strength. Total losses in the XI Corps would amount to about 3200 this day (about 300 killed and 1200 wounded), about 60% of its strength.[326] Losses were spread fairly evenly through all the brigades engaged. The Confederates, on the other hand, quite amazingly suffered only about 1000 casualties. Gordon's brigade did the lion's share of the fighting, and suffered about 400 casualties (27%) in the process. Doles' brigade, for all the fighting it did, lost only about 200 men (16%) of its strength, while Hays and Avery lost perhaps 200 and 100 men respectively.[327] This disparity in losses, and the fact that the attacking Confederates had less than 6000 men in four brigades (Gordon, Avery, Hays and Doles) attacking over 8000 Union troops in 5 brigades, rightly brings into question the fighting qualities of the Union troops, and the abilities of its leaders that day.

The fighting qualities of the XI Corps were already in question before the battle because of the way in which the corps had been defeated and broken by Stonewall Jackson's famous flank attack at Chancellorsville on the evening of 2 May, 1863. Prejudice was also easy to raise against the corps because so many of its troops were foreign born (particularly German and Polish). But close study of what happened at Chancellorsville shows that most of the troops fought well, or at least as well as most other troops could have under those conditions. Most of the blame for the rout of the corps at Chancellorsville should instead rest with General Howard, the corps' commander, and Gen. Charles Devens, a division commander, both of whom failed to guard the corps' right flank adequately and failed to properly interpret all the reports they received about Jackson's advance.[328]

The situation appears to have been much the same at Gettysburg. Individual officers (Irsch, Dilger, Wilkeson, and Ames, for example) and units (154th New York, 157th New York, 45th New York, 17th Connecticut, 25th Ohio, and almost all the XI Corps batteries) fought bravely and with distinction. Their efforts as brigades, however, were not coordinated by their upper level commanders, and as a result the corps' brigades were chewed up one by one by the Confederate attack. Barlow made a gross error by advancing to the knoll that bears his name, where he was unsupported on both flanks. Schurz did not keep a close enough eye on Barlow, and once he did see his subordinate's error, he sent Krzyzanowski's brigade and also the 157th New York as unsupported fodder to resist the Confederate attack. Likewise Howard sent Coster into action too late, and he, too, was quickly overrun. The only really weak combat performance exhibited was by Krzyzanowski's brigade, which was for some reason not able to withstand the fire from the four Georgia regiments facing it.

The ultimate blame for the Union disaster on the field north of Gettysburg may well rest at Howard's feet. Howard was well informed by Buford's active cavalry that two strong Confederate columns were approaching Gettysburg, on the XI Corps' front—one from the north-west (Rodes) and one from the northeast (Early). Even so, he persisted in trying to push his 3rd Division to take Oak Hill. He also did not acknowledge how weak and thinly spread out his line was on the plain north of Gettysburg, even though he personally inspected it at about 1400. There was simply too much ground for four understrength brigades to cover; none of his brigades were very strong to begin with, and all were weakened by leaving various detachments for different reasons in Maryland. It also should be noted that Howard did not particularly instill confidence in his men or his troops. Schurz had difficulty in communicating with him when he kept asking for rein-forcements in vain, and he did not share with Barlow his intelligence about Early's pending arrival. There can be no question that Reynolds' untimely death and Howard's assumption of wing command had a negative effect on the XI Corps. Howard chose to lead his new command from the rear, and the reshuffling of the corps' command structure put two officers (Schurz and Schimmelfennig) in important posts they may not have been ready to handle.

This is not to say that there were not other elements at play that put the XI Corps at a disadvantage. Howard had to keep a watchful eye on Rodes' troops on Oak Hill, though Schimmelfennig's presence northwest of town certainly was a concern to Rodes during the Confederate advance and had a direct effect on the defeat of O'Neal and Iverson. And there is no question that Early's timely arrival on Schurz's right flank was a stroke of luck. But more than that, Early took advantage of his luck to take full control of the battle by carefully staging the placement and timing of his attack. His troops were all veterans, and his experienced brigade commanders all cooperated with each other and performed almost faultlessly. In addition, Early's attack was aided by an artillery superiority that also had the advantage of converging fire from Jones' position and Carter's on Oak Hill. These factors, plus the fact that

Confederate generalship was so superior to that of their XI Corps counterparts, spelled disaster for Schurz's troops this day, regardless of the reputation or fighting qualities of the so-called "Flying Dutchmen."

CHAPTER VIII

Climax on Seminary
Ridge

*I*t is one of the great ironies of the battle that neither
army commander was on the field for the entire first day of the battle
of Gettysburg. Major General George G. Meade, the newly appointed
commander of the Union's Army of the Potomac, was not anywhere
near the field when the fighting started, and then chose to remain in
the army's rear at Taneytown, some 12 miles to the south of Gettysburg,
in order to hurry his troops forward to the battleground. In his absence,
he trusted the management of the field to his experienced left wing
commander, Major General John F. Reynolds, and when he heard that
Reynolds had been killed early in the fighting, he sent Major General
Winfield S. Hancock of the II Corps to supervise the Union forces on
the field, as will be shown in Chapter IX.

General Robert E. Lee, commander of the Army of Northern Virginia,
spent the night of 30 June/1 July at his headquarters in a grove of woods
on the outskirts of Chambersburg, some 25 miles west of Gettysburg.
As we have seen, he had one if not two conferences with Lieutenant
General A.P. Hill, commander of the Third Corps, concerning Hill's
desire to make an armed reconnaissance into Gettysburg to locate a
supply of shoes said to be there and to determine what Union troops
were in the town. Lee greatly desired to determine the location of the

advancing Union army so that he might defeat its segments in detail as they came up,[1] but he did not wish to begin an engagement before his widespread army was concentrated, a premise he told Hill on the evening of the 30th and would repeat several times the next day. Longstreet's First Corps and Hill's Third Corps were already well in hand between Chambersburg and Cashtown, located in the key gap in the Cumberland Mountains only eight miles from Gettysburg. But Ewell's far-flung divisions, elements of which had penetrated Pennsylvania as far as the Susquehanna River, would need at least another full day to reach the Cashtown/Gettysburg area. In addition, Lee was gravely concerned about the safety and location of Stuart's cavalry, which was believed to be somewhere in Maryland or Pennsylvania on the far side of the Union Army.

Lee determined to move his headquarters from Chambersburg to Cashtown on the morning of 1 July. Just as he was mounting to leave he greeted Rev. James P. Smith, a member of the late Stonewall Jackson's staff who had ridden all night to join the army. The two talked briefly of Jackson's passing and the welfare of Stonewall's wife and baby. Then the commander asked Smith if he had any news of General Jeb Stuart, who was supposed to be bringing three brigades of his cavalry up to join the army's vanguard in Pennsylvania. Smith replied that he had spoken with two of Stuart's couriers on the afternoon of the 29th, who told him that the cavalry commander was then east of the Blue Ridge and south of the Potomac.

At Lee's request, Smith accompanied the general's staff on his ride to the east. While on the way Lieutenant Colonel Walter M. Taylor also asked him about Stuart. Smith repeated his news, and Taylor acted greatly surprised: "He said it was a great disappointment to General Lee, who had expected Stuart would have reported to him in Pennsylvania, and that he was troubled that his cavalry forces were not between him and the enemy, as he had expected them to be."[2]

Before leaving his Chambersburg headquarters, Lee invited Lieutenant General James Longstreet, commander of his First Corps and the army's senior officer after Lee, to ride with him. Longstreet recalled that his commander was in his "usual good spirits" as they rode forward.[3] Lee had sent Anderson's division of Hill's corps on ahead to join the rest of its corps at Cashtown, and Longstreet's veterans, led by McLaws' division, marched jauntily forward. Hood's division (less Law's brigade, which was on picket duty at New Guilford) followed next, trailed by the corps' two battalions of reserve artillery. Longstreet's third division, under Major General George E. Pickett, was for the moment left in Chambersburg to guard the army's wagons and trains.[4] He would march to rejoin the corps as soon as he was relieved by Imboden's cavalry brigade.

Longstreet's vanguard had not made much progress when it came upon Major General Edward Johnson's division of Ewell's corps coming into the main Chambersburg Pike at Greenwood from a side road to the left. Johnson was proceeding to a rendezvous with Ewell's other two divisions just to the east of Cashtown, and happened to be traveling this rather circuitous route from Carlisle for the reasons cited in Chapter I. As historian Douglas Southall Freeman observed, Lee must have been pleased to see all his army begin to concentrate at Cashtown, which he judged to be a necessary preliminary to advancing against the Union army.[5]

But Johnson's presence on the road boded a major problem, one whose significance no one yet appreciated. His column, including supply wagons, stretched for 14 miles, and Lee let the entire column have the right of way ahead of Longstreet's command. The length of Johnson's column would delay Longstreet's march so long that it would not reach Cashtown until midafternoon; the rear of Longstreet's column did not even leave Chambersburg until noon. There was only one road available through the mountains between Chambersburg and Gettysburg, and six of Lee's nine divisions needed to use it. The resulting traffic jam was so great that McLaws' division would not reach Marsh Creek, 4 miles west of Gettysburg, until after sunset, too late to be of use in the battle that day, and Hood would not arrive there until midnight.[6] Had Johnson marched to Cashtown on the east side of South Mountain, his men and Longstreet's divisions would all have arrived at Gettysburg several hours earlier, in plenty of time to change the outcome of the battle drastically.

Lee did not wish to wait for Johnson's troops to clear Longstreet's front, so he rode on ahead towards Cashtown, still accompanied by Longstreet. Before long they heard the thunder of cannons from the other side of Cashtown, and Lee left Longstreet's side to go ahead and see what was happening. He was particularly anxious because Stuart's absence had left him uninformed about the location of the Union army. He at first thought that the cannon firing was just a minor affair. However, by the time he reached Cashtown at about 1100, the noise was so heavy and ongoing that he knew from long experience that a big fight was going on. This anxiety and impatience caused him to openly regret the absence of his cavalry. One of his staff officers, Colonel E.B.

Long, heard Lee say that "he had been kept in the dark ever since crossing the Potomac, and intimated that Stuart's disappearance had materially hampered the movements and disorganized the plans of the campaign."[7]

Lee's apprehension was not assuaged when he came upon Hill, who that day was admittedly feeling very unwell or "delicate."[8] All that Hill could tell him was that Heth's division had encountered some Union cavalry near Gettysburg. Hill reassured Lee that he was following his orders not to precipitate a battle, and had sent Heth instructions "to ascertain what force was at Gettysburg, and, if he found infantry opposed to him, to report the fact immediately, without forcing an engagement." Then, as the sound of the artillery increased, Hill left to hasten to the front himself.[9]

Lee did not follow at once, but sent for R.H. Anderson to see what he knew of the fighting. Anderson, though, could not tell his commander much because he had just arrived at Cashtown from Chambersburg about 1000. After the battle Anderson shared the course of this meeting with Longstreet: "About twelve o'clock I received a message notifying me that Lee desired to see me. I found General Lee intently listening to the fire of the guns and very much disturbed and depressed. At length he said, more to himself than to me, 'I cannot think what has become of Stuart. I ought to have heard from him long before now. He may have met with disaster, but I hope not. In the absence of reports from him, I am in ignorance as to what we have in front of us here. It may be the whole Federal army, or it may be only a detachment. If it is the whole Federal force, we must fight a battle here. If we do not gain a victory, those defiles and gorges which we passed this morning will shelter us from disaster.'"[10]

Lee now felt that he had no choice but to ride forward to the field and find out for himself what was occurring. He directed Anderson to move forward to Gettysburg,[11] and then rode eastward with his staff, still nervous as the sound of the artillery continued. A couple miles to the east of Cashtown he was met by Major Campbell Brown, who came from Ewell to report that Ewell was marching from Middletown towards Gettysburg instead of Cashtown. As noted in Chapter VI, Lee vainly asked Brown if he had any news of Stuart, and then gave his approval to Ewell's line of march. He sternly cautioned Ewell, though, not to bring on a general engagement until the rest of the army came up.[12]

Not long after Brown left to return to Ewell, Lee began to hear the crackle of musketry fire. This caused him surprise and regret[13] because it meant that the action ahead was more than a minor skirmish. He rode on, and sometime after 1300 stopped on the heights of the Knoxlyn Ridge in order to survey the scene in front of him; Hill's guns on the next ridge (Herr's) were banging away at a line of Union troops between them and the town, and another body of Confederate troops was charging the flank of the Union line off to the left.[14]

Soon A.P. Hill came up to confer with Lee, and at about 1330 Harry Heth rode up to ask for instructions: "Rodes is very heavily engaged, had I not better attack?" Lee promptly replied, "No, I am not prepared to bring on a general engagement today—Longstreet is not up."[15] Lee was still not certain about the number and nature of the Union force in his front, and still did not wish to join in a general engagement until he had most of his army together.

In the next few minutes Lee must have continued to confer with Hill. He probably learned now of the repulse of Archer and Davis, and the fact that Heth probably faced all of the Union I Corps, plus some cavalry. But there was also good news—Rodes' division was already attacking the Union left (contrary to Lee's orders, see Chapter VI), Pender was on the field and Johnson would soon be up. Since Longstreet's two divisions were not far behind, Lee decided it would be proper to support Rodes' attack; enough of the army was on hand to engage the I Corps and whatever other Union troops might be on hand. It is unlikely that Lee at this time knew of Early's approach to the battlefield, or even of the presence of Howard's corps on the field; it was not possible for him to see the plain north of Gettysburg from his vantage point on Knoxlyn Ridge.

The deciding factor in persuading Lee to make the engagement a general one was probably the fact that he could see Doubleday shifting Biddle's troops from Hill's front to face Daniel along the Chambersburg Pike. He was also no doubt influenced by the fact that Pender's division was then in position to support Heth.[16] Around 1415 Heth came back to Lee to point out this fact, and again requested permission to attack. This time the General responded more favorably: "Wait awhile and I will send you word when to go in." Heth returned to his troops, and about 1430 received his long awaited orders to attack.[17] He was also told that Pender's division would be in support.[18]

Heth's Assault on McPherson's Ridge

Heth planned to launch his assault using his two fresh brigades, Brockenbrough's and Pettigrew's, which had been posted in the woods on the eastern slope of Herr Ridge since Archer had been repulsed late that morning. These brigades were both posted on the south side of the Chambersburg Pike, and could attack directly eastward towards the Union line posted in nearby Herbst Woods and on McPherson's Ridge to the south. Heth did not expect much from the battered remains of Davis' brigade, which had taken up a position along Willoughby Run on the north side of the Pike. In this he was right, since Davis' troops were at that moment declining to assist Daniel's right during that commander's attack on Stone's line along the Chambersburg Pike. Heth's fourth brigade, Archer's, had also suffered heavily that morning. Its remnants were now led by Colonel B.D. Fry of the 13th Alabama, and were posted in the woods to the right of Pettigrew and Brockenbrough, supported by six guns of McIntosh's battalion.

Union General Abner Doubleday, commander of I Corps, had only three brigades with about 4000 men with which to oppose the six fresh brigades, some 10,000 men total, that Heth and Pender were preparing for the attack. The strong point of Doubleday's position, Herbst Woods, was held by his best unit, the Iron Brigade. Meredith's command had not been engaged particularly heavily in its morning attack, except for the 2nd Wisconsin, which had suffered about 30% casualties. For this reason Meredith had shifted the 7th Wisconsin to the right of his line, and put the 2nd to its left, followed by the 24th Michigan and 19th Indiana. The Iron Brigade's fifth regiment, the 6th Wisconsin, had been detached that morning before its attack on Davis' troops at the middle railroad cut, and was still absent, supporting Stewart's battery at the eastern railroad cut, some 1600 yards east and somewhat north of Herbst Woods.

The Iron Brigade had troops supporting each of its flanks, but neither wing was very strongly posted. Stone's brigade of only three regiments occupied an awkward angle that ran from the northern edge of Herbst Woods past the McPherson farm buildings to the Chambersburg Pike, and then turned at a right angle to the east along the road. Stone's troops, as has already been shown, had suffered severely from the crossfire of Confederate artillery posted to the west on Herr Ridge and to the northeast on Oak Hill. Calef's and Reynolds' (now Breck's) batteries had been hit so hard by this fire that both batteries had to be withdrawn and repositioned, as will be shown in a moment.

The weakest portion of Doubleday's line was its left wing, where Biddle's brigade was assigned to hold the open fields along Seminary Ridge as far as the Fairfield Road. Biddle, however, did not like the flanking fire he was receiving from Carter's batteries on Oak Hill, and during the afternoon shifted the position of his command several times in a effort to find them better cover. At the time the Confederate attack began (1430) Biddle's troops were actually facing north near the Fairfield Road, almost perpendicular to their earlier position, so leaving a quarter mile gap on the Iron Brigade's flank that was guarded only by the two companies of the 20th New York State Militia that were west of Willoughby Run at the Harman farm, and by the artillery posted near the Seminary! Even when Biddle quickly corrected his line and reoccupied the north-south crest of McPherson's ridge, he did not connect with Meredith's left. Due to the lay of the land and the Iron Brigade's forward position in Herbst Woods, the right of Biddle's command would be some 200 or more yards to the rear of the left of the 19th Indiana, the Iron Brigade's left regiment. In addition, Doubleday had no more infantry with which to secure Biddle's left. That task was being served for the moment by the 8th Illinois of Gamble's cavalry brigade, which had deployed at and near the Fairfield Road, on Biddle's left. The rest of Gamble's cavalry was being held in reserve at the moment in the fields southwest of Gettysburg.

This section of Doubleday's line was also made awkward by the fact that there was no effective division commander with the troops to coordinate their movements. The Iron Brigade belonged to Wadsworth's 1st Division, and Wadsworth seemed to be spending his time with his second brigade, Cutler's, which was posted on Seminary Ridge to the north of the eastern railroad cut.[19] Stone's and Biddle's brigades belonged to the 3rd Division, nominally under the command of Brigadier General Thomas A. Rowley. Rowley was not having a good day, and was thought by several of his fellow officers to be drunk during the battle.[20] The void in divisional leadership on this part of the corps line was apparently filled by Doubleday himself.[21]

Doubleday's line was also in trouble because it had no reserves to speak of. Rodes' pressure on Baxter's brigade, which was posted on northern Seminary Ridge soon after noon, had just forced Doubleday to send his last large reserve, Paul's brigade, to support his far right.

When Paul was moved north from his reserve position near the Seminary, Doubleday "borrowed" Biddle's largest regiment, the 467 men of the 151st Pennsylvania, and set it up in reserve behind the provisional breastwork of rails set up by Paul's troops just west of the Seminary.[22] It was a necessary measure, but one that further weakened the left of the corps line.

The only real advantage of Doubleday's position, other than the Iron Brigade's strongly posted line in Herbst Woods, was the fact that there was a good second line already formed just ¼ mile to the rear along Seminary Ridge. This secondary position already had some rudimentary defensive works (the rail breastworks started by Baxter's command and added to by Paul's) and a good backing of artillery (9 guns of Wainwright's battalion in Stevens' and Cooper's batteries). This second line and its artillery core were certainly an advantage lacking to Robinson's division on Doubleday's right.

Doubleday appealed to Howard more than once for more troops to help him hold his position. Late in the morning he had requested Howard to send him help to protect the right of his corps from the advance of Ewell's corps. In reply he was told "to hold Seminary [sic] Hill at all hazards, if driven back."[23] In the early afternoon he sent an aide, Lieutenant Jacob F. Slagle, to Howard to ask for reinforcements, but received no response.[24] At last he sent his adjutant general, Captain E.P. Halstead, to Howard "to represent that further resistance could only end in the sacrifice of the entire command, to request that I be relieved by Steinwehr's division or receive orders to retreat to Cemetery Hill while I was still able to do so in good order."[25] Howard, however, declined to send any, preferring to keep Von Steinwehr in reserve for the moment.

It was not as if Howard were unaware of what Doubleday was facing. At about 1415 Howard finally made a much delayed tour of Doubleday's lines after also surveying Schurz's position north of town. As already noted, Howard visited Wadsworth and encouraged the division com-mader to hold on to the last. He then met Doubleday and approved of his position, though in parting he did give the I Corps commander directions to fall back to Cemetery Hill if forced to withdraw. But there were no promises of reinforcements. As already discussed, Howard was probably reluctant to abandon the field where the I Corps had seen such success that morning, and he certainly did not want to pull back without positive orders to do so from Meade (particularly in view of the criticism he and his XI Corps had received for their role at

Chancellorsville). But Doubleday appears to have made no strong objection to Howard's decision to hold the I Corps where it was, at least at that time. Later he would write, "upon taking a retrospect of the field, it might seem, in view of the fact that we were finally forced to retreat, that this would have been a proper time to retire; but to fall back without orders from the commanding general might have inflicted lasting disgrace upon the corps, and as General Reynolds, who was high in the confidence of General Meade, had formed his lines to resist the entrance of the enemy into Gettysburg, I naturally supposed that it was the intention to defend the place."[26]

The intervening hours between 1130 and 1430 weighed heavily on the troops of both armies posted on each side of Willoughby Run. It was the heat of the day and the constant artillery fire and rattle of the skirmishers gave no rest to anyone. In addition, the dead and wounded from the morning's engagement lay all along both lines, a grim reminder of the day's business at hand. But most disconcerting to the Union troops was the sight and sound of more Confederate troops continually filing on to the field. Major Thomas Chamberlin of the 150th Pennsylvania noted that "during the temporary lull which prevailed on the field, there was abundant opportunity to observe the numbers and dispostion of the enemy to the west, consisting, as we have since learned, of Heth's and Pender's divisions of A.P. Hill's corps—some of the brigades of Pender's command arriving later than our own and defiling in plain view into position south of the Chambersburg Pike. While our own line was but a skeleton, with noticeable gaps between the several brigades, as well as between the regiments, and with no visable reserves, the enemy seemed to be formed in continuous double lines of battle, extending southward as far as the accidents of ground permitted the eye to reach, with ample supports in column in rear. As a spectacle it was striking, but their preponderance in view was so obvious that we might have despaired of the result of the coming engagement, if we had not supposed that additional troops of our own would be up in line to lend us a hand."[27]

The continuous skirmishing along Willoughby Run sent a steady stream of wounded trickling back through the Union lines. In the 150th Pennsylvania, Lieutenant Henry Chancellor Jr. of Company G was so stricken when he saw two of his men, Sergeant Kolb and Corporal Buchanan, return "in a disabled condition," that he begged permission to take his men to join the skirmish line. "This was finally accorded. No sooner had his men risen to their feet to go forward, than one of their number fell dead, pierced by a bullet from beyond the road. Finding the line of the stream sufficiently occupied, and seeing that a further advance would result in unnecessary loss, the lieutenant halted his company midway between the barn and the run, and remained for a time in reserve."[28]

Not all the members of the 150th, however, were as valiant as Chancellor. Soon after Company B had gone into action on the skirmish line, Captain George W. Jones sent Private William Rodearmal to the rear to fill some canteens for his thirsty comrades. Rodearmal, though, was not seen again that day, and in fact did not reappear until the morning of 4 July, "when he presented himself before the captain on Cemetery Ridge with a large collection of freshly filled canteens, and with inimitable assurance said, 'Captain, here's the water. I knew you wanted good water, so I thought I'd go back to Germantown for it, but the provost guard stoped me at Baltimore.' True enough, he had started for home, but was arrested on the way and returned to the army under guard."[29]

The Union sharpshooter fire was particularly annoying from the advanced position at the Harman farm seized late in the morning by a detachment of the 20th New York State Militia. Lieutenant J.A. Lowe of Company G, 26th North Carolina of Pettigrew's brigade, volunteered to take a crack at the Union post. He crept forward along a fence in order to scout their position, and saw several of their sharpshooters positioned behind the chimney on the roof of the old two story Harman house. Lowe soon silenced them all, though the rest of the 20th's detachment continued to hold the lower portion of the house as well as its barn and out buildings.[30]

The Confederate artillery fire from Herr Ridge did not lighten up, but intensified as the afternoon wore on in anticipation of the battle's approaching climax. Hill's troops had the luxury of having more guns available than there was room to deploy them. McIntosh's and Pegram's battalions had some guns in action, and when one of Pegram's batteries began to run out of ammunition, it was readily replaced by six rifled pieces of Maurin's Louisiana battery of Garnett's battalion, which had just reached the field. The remainder of Garnett's command (which was actually a part of Heth's division) remained in reserve, as was Major William T. Poague's 16 gun battalion of Pender's division, which came up at the same time.[31] During the early afternoon the troops in the Union center suffered badly from the weight of the Confederate guns and from the enfilade fire they received from the right. Brander's Virginia battery caused particular problems after it deployed on a hill northwest of the Bender farm, and then advanced even closer to the Union lines.[32]

The fire of Fry's and W. Carter's guns on Oak Hill also caused considerable distress on the Union center and even on Biddle's line on the corps' far left. This pressure was lessened somewhat when Carter moved Fry's battery to the eastern face of Oak Hill in the early afternoon in order to deal with Schurz's batteries.[33]

The Union artillery was not handled nearly as well as the Confederates' during this stage of the battle. As already noted, Wainwright refused to cooperate with Doubleday in trying to establish a counter battery to face the Confederate strength on Herr and Oak Ridges. As a result, the Union batteries that attempted to deploy in the Union center were chewed up individually as they came forward—first Calef's, then Hall's, then Calef's again in the morning, and then G. Reynolds' at noon (when that captain was mortally wounded). The best that the Union batteries could do was to withdraw slightly to their left in order to use the McPherson barn and Herbst Woods as a shield against Pegram's and McIntosh's battalions.

By 1400 there was only one Union battery deployed with Doubleday's front line. Lieutenant John Calef, who had first withdrawn his horse battery to the rear of Herbst Woods, soon afterwards retired to a wheatfield 500 yards to the rear and left. By 1400 he had pulled back entirely to rejoin Gamble's command, which was resting to the southwest of the town.[34] This left Lieutenant George Breck's battery (formerly Captain Gilbert M. Reynold's) as the only battery still in the front. After changing positions a few times, Breck by 1400 had Lieutenant B.W. Wilber's two gun section deployed in Stone's line between the McPherson barn and Herbst Woods, in response to a request from General Wadsworth for artillery support. Colonel Wainwright had personally moved the rest of the battery, four pieces under the direction of Lieutenant William M. Bower, from the center of the line to the left of the line, where Biddle's brigade was posted.[35]

Bower's assignment was to replace Cooper's Pennsylvania battery, which Colonel Wainwright had moved to the rear in one of the stranger episodes of this long day. As already noted, Cooper had been posted soon after noon in Biddle's original line on southern McPherson's Ridge. After being engaged briefly with Pegram's batteries, Cooper's three serviceable guns were withdrawn at the order of Colonel Wainwright to the meadow between McPherson's Ridge and the Seminary and changed front so as to face Carter's newly deployed batteries on Oak

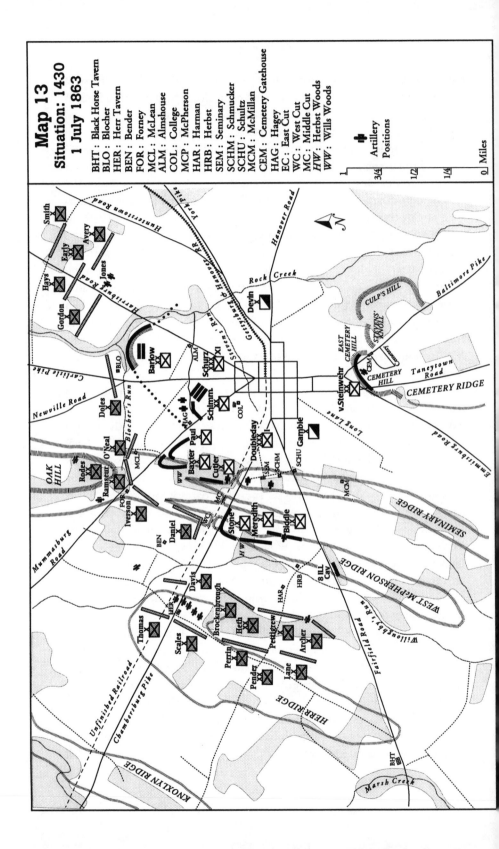

Map 13
Situation: 1430
1 July 1863

BHT : Black Horse Tavern
BLO : Blocher
HER : Herr Tavern
BEN : Bender
FOR : Forney
MCL : McLean
ALM : Almshouse
COL : College
MCP : McPherson
HAR : Harman
HRB : Herbst
SEM : Seminary
SCHM : Schmucker
SCHU : Schulz
MCM : McMillan
CEM : Cemetery Gatehouse
HAG : Hagey
EC : East Cut
WC : West Cut
MC : Middle Cut
HW : Herbst Woods
WW : Wills Woods

Artillery
Positions

0 Miles
1/4
1/2
3/4
1

Hill. From here one battery historian claims that the unit helped turn back Iverson's attack by pouring "a most galling and destructive front and flank fire of case shot" at the enemy attack ¾ mile to the north.[36]

Cooper held this position until shortly before Heth began his final attack,[37] when he was ordered to withdraw to Seminary Ridge. It seems that Colonel Wainwright had overheard one of Howard's German aides tell Doubleday that Cemetery Hill should be held at all hazards. As he later admitted, "What with the aide's broken English and our being on this hill and not knowing that there was a cemetery, I thought it was the Seminary Hill we were to hold." Howard accordingly withdrew Cooper's battery to the front of the "professor's house" on Seminary Ridge, and sent Breck's four guns to the left to replace him in Biddle's line.[38] This move allowed Wainwright to shift Stevens' 5th Maine Battery to the north side of the Seminary to occupy the position held by Stewart's guns before they were moved to the eastern railroad cut. Wainwright's error greatly weakened the strength of Doubleday's front line, but certainly did help beef up the corps' secondary line on Seminary Ridge.

The troops of Pettigrew's brigade were particularly anxious to enter the fight, since most of them had not seen action before. Colonel Henry Burgwyn, the 21 year old commander of the 26th North Carolina, felt that "we were losing precious time" as the afternoon minutes passed. In order to help pass the time, his officers "were keeping our men as quiet as possible, sending details to the rear for water, and watching the movements of the enemy. The enemy's sharpshooters occasionally reminded us that we had better cling close to the bosom of old mother earth." Some of the troops engaged in joke making in order to break tension. Others wanted to hold religious services, as was usually done before entering combat, but this could not be done due to the absence of the chaplains.[39]

Surgeon Louis G. Young of Pettigrew's brigade was pensive as he considered that both sides were "understanding that a conflict of armies was in store for them, we ready to make the attack and they ready to receive it. Only a few hundred yards separated us; they were advantageously posted in three lines on McPherson's Ridge, their right in a wood of large trees, no underbrush, and a wheat field lay between us with no other obstruction than the nearly ripe wheat." Pettigrew's men at last found their waiting brought to an end at 1430, when Heth received his orders to charge. The next 30 minutes would see some of the heaviest fighting of the battle, if not of the war.[40]

The 2500 men of Pettigrew's large brigade by themselves more than outnumbered the troops of Meredith's and Biddle's brigades opposed to them. Pettigrew had formed his regiments "in line by echelon," with the 26th North Carolina (843 men) on the left holding the front of the formation. The 11th North Carolina (617 men) was slightly to its right and rear, the 47th (567 men) to the right and rear of the 11th, and the 52nd (553 men) likewise to the 42nd. This formation of these large regiments made it appear to the Union forces that the Confederates had multiple lines of battle. Pettigrew's plan was to have all the regiments swing into one line as they rose to attack.[41]

Due to the Confederate alignment just described, the 26th North Carolina would lead Pettigrew's attack. The 26th's line of advance would take it straight at the center and left of the Iron Brigade, which was held by the 24th Michigan and 19th Indiana. The right of Pettigrew's command struck Biddle's command on the Union far left. The left wing of Heth's attack, formed by Brockenbrough's under strength brigade, assaulted the 2nd and 7th Wisconsin on the Iron Brigade's right.

At the cry "attention," the men of the 26th North Carolina sprang to their feet. The regiment's officers stepped to their posts, Colonel Burgwyn in the center, Lieutenant Colonel J.R. Lane on the right, and Major J. Jones on the left. The regimental color bearer, J.B. Mansfield, stepped to his usual post, four paces to the front, and the eight other members of the color guard joined him. At the command "Forward, March!" all moved forward in step and in "as pretty and perfect a line as regiment ever made, every man endeavoring to keep dressed on the colors." The Union line began firing as the regiment advanced, but their aim was high, and only a few of the 26th were hit. The regiment then paused to return a volley before continuing.[42]

The 26th managed to maintain its perfect alignment until it reached the ravine of Willoughby Run, where the briars, reeds and underbrush made it difficult to pass. By now the regiment was under heavy fire from the Iron Brigade, which "had massed in heavy force while we were in line of battle in the woods."[43] Colonel Henry A. Morrow of the 24th Michigan had told his men "to hold their fire until the the enemy should come within short range of our guns. This was done, but the nature of the ground was such that I am inclined to think we inflicted but little injury on the enemy at this time."[44] Burgwyn's advance also suffered from an enfilading artillery fire from the right that felled a number of men and forced a crowding towards the center of the line.[45] A shot from one of the first Union volleys knocked the hat off a Confederate officer who was riding in the rear of Burgwyn's line shouting, "give em hell, boys." The officer nonchalantly grabbed it with his hand and continued forward into the battle.[46]

This Union fire and the difficulties of the advance only delayed the 26th's advance for a moment, and the Tarheels soon "came on with rapid strides, yelling like demons."[47] The regiment's historian, Assistant Surgeon George C. Underwood, noted that "our men crossed in good order and immediately were in proper position again, and up the hill we went, firing now with better execution."[48] The engagement was now desperate as the lines blasted away at each other only 20 to 40 yards apart.[49] To Surgeon Underwood "it seemed that the bullets were as thick as hail stones in a storm."[50] Before long the force and strength of the 26th's line forced Morrow to pull his men back to a second line deeper in the woods.[51] When the 26th advanced to encounter the 24th's second line, its dead "marked his line of battle with the accuracy of a line at a dress parade."[52]

Colonel Morrow of the 24th could not have been prouder of the determination with which his men resisted the 26th North Carolina's attack. He thought that the Tarheels were expecting "to meet militia only, and have an easy victory." When the Confederates saw the distinctive headgear of the 24th's men (the stiff broad brimmed, tall black hats, called "Hardee Hats," that were worn by U.S. Regular infantry but by few volunteer units other than the regiments of the Iron Brigade), some of Burgwyn's men were heard by Morrow's wounded to exclaim, "Here are those damned black hat fellows again!"[53]

The color guard of the 26th North Carolina suffered severely during this advance, since the Union troops, as usual, concentrated their fire at the Confederate colors posted in the center of the regiment. The 26th's color guard began to take casualties even before it crossed the run. At least three members of the color company (E) fell before the unit reached Willoughby Run—one man was killed, one wounded, and Sergeant Mansfield was hit in the foot. Sergeant Hiram Johnson of Company G took the colors from Mansfield and was also shot before he could cross the creek. The flag was then taken up by Private John Stamper of Company A. Stamper fell as he entered the underbrush, and Private George Washington Kelly of Company D took up the flag. Kelly lept to the opposite bank of Willoughby Run, only to slip and fall down flat. His friend L.A. Thomas told him to get up, but he could not. He thought his leg was broken, and then saw that he had been hit by a piece of an artillery shell. With the strange humor that sometimes affects men in combat, Kelly asked Lewis to get him the shell fragment so that he could take it home as a souvenir. Thomas carried the colors up the hillside until he, too, fell wounded, whereupon John Vinson of Company G took them. He was wounded and gave them to John R. Marley of Company G, who was promptly killed. Another soldier, unnamed, the last member of the original color guard, now took up his regiment's flag, the tenth man to carry it in the space of about ten minutes.[54]

Both sides agree that the titanic struggle between the 24th Michigan and 26th North Carolina was heaviest at the 24th's second line, which was drawn up in the middle of the woods. Lieutenant Colonel Lane pushed from his post on the right of the regiment to the center to ask Burgwyn how the rest of the unit was doing. Burgwyn replied, "It is all right on the center and on the left: we have broken the first line of the enemy." Lane replied to his commander. "We are in line on the right Colonel."[55] At this point Captain W.A. McCreery, Pettigrew's adjutant general, came up to tell Burgwyn a message from the general, that the 26th "has covered itself with glory today." As soon as he spoke, the most recent color bearer was struck down, and McCreery took up the 26th's flag himself. He waved it in the air a few moments, and was struck dead by a bullet through the heart. He fell, staining the flag with his blood. Next Lieutenant George Wilcox of Company H took up the flag and advanced only a few feet before he was struck by two Union musket balls.[56]

The 24th Michigan and its color guard were also suffering heavily at this time. Color Corporal Charles Bellore, who had carried the regiment's colors since Sergeant Abel G. Peck had been killed in the regiment's attack that morning, was killed near the second line of battle. The regiment's acting major, Captain William J. Speed, of Company D, was killed, as was Lieutenant Gilbert G. Dickey of Company G.[57]

It was now the crisis of the attack as the two regiments continued to take and receive heroic blows like two prize fighters locked in mortal combat. Colonel Burgwyn encouraged his men by yelling out General Pettigrew's words of praise, and took up the regimental colors from the wounded Wilcox. He then stepped forward and gave the orders to dress on the colors. At once Private Frank Honeycutt of Company B broke ranks to run up and request the honor of carrying the flag. Burgwyn turned to hand him the colors, but was hit by a musket ball that entered his left side and pierced both lungs. The force of the blow flung him around, and he was caught in the folds of the flag as he fell. A moment later Honeycutt also fell, shot through the head.[58]

Lieutenant Colonel Lane rushed to the side of his fallen commander and asked, "My dear Colonel, are you severely hurt?" Burgwyn simply nodded towards his left side and squeezed Lane's hand to acknowledge that he was hurt badly. The Lieutenant Colonel could only linger a moment, and then reluctantly rose to leave the fallen Colonel and boldly take charge of the regiment. He quickly went to the right and told Captain J.C. McLaughlin of Company K about General Pettigrew's words of praise; he deftly did not mention that Colonel Burgwyn had been hit. Lane then ordered McLaughlin, "Close your men quickly to the left. I am going to give them the bayonet. " Lane next ran to the left and gave the same order. When he returned to his post at the regiment's center, he found the 26th's flag still lying on the ground between Burgwyn and Honeycutt. Lieutenant Blair of Company K saw it also, and noted, "No man can take those colors and live." Lane agreed, but duty called. He replied, "it is to me to take them now," and advanced with the shout, "twenty-sixth, follow me."[59]

Lane's men gave a yell, pushing the 24th back to yet a third line, on the other side of a slight ravine. No sooner was this line formed than Private August Earnest of the 24th's Company K, who had taken up the colors from Bellore, was killed. His flag then fell at the feet of 1st Sergeant Everard B. Welton of Company H, who picked it up and held it for a moment until Colonel Morrow came over and took it from him. By now Major Edwin B. Wright, the regiment's acting lieutenant colonel, had been wounded by a nasty wound in the eye. His men thought he had been killed when he fell, but he managed to rise up and was taken from the field. Lieutenants Winfield Safford and Lucius Shattuck of Company C and Walter Wallace of Company K were killed at this line, and twelve other officers were wounded.[60]

While most of the 26th North Carolina was attacking the 24th Michigan head on, the far right companies of the regiment helped the 11th North Carolina strike the 19th Indiana, the Iron Brigade's left flank regiment. Colonel S. J. Williams of the 19th had his men ready for action as soon as he saw Pettigrew's troops begin their advance. The strong enemy line easily began pushing back the 19th's skirmishers, Lieutenant Schlagle's Company B. Williams was concerned that the enemy had "three battle lines overlapping me on the left," and also did not like the lower ground on which the 19th was deployed because it was "only sparsely covered with trees." He repeatedly appealed to Colonel William Robinson, the acting brigade commander,[61] for permission to withdraw to "the crest of the hill behind us and throw up rail barricades." But each time the order came back "that we were occupying the line selected by our corps commanders, and that we must hold at all hazards."[62]

Williams directed his men to hold their fire until the Confederate line came within range, and then began blasting away. The 11th North Carolina, though, had the advantage of a much longer line than the 19th Indiana, and the Confederate regiment was able to swing its right in towards the 19th's left because the line of Biddle's supporting brigade was so far to the rear. Williams' command was also hindered by the fact the ground to his left fell away sharply, particularly where the woods ended near the stream.[63]

Williams held his regiment in position as long as he could, even though it was suffering severely from the 11th North Carolina's flank fire. In a few short minutes the 19th Indiana lost 20 dead and over 100 men wounded, some 40% of its strength. Lieutenants Richard Jones of Company B and Crockett T. East of Company K were killed while cheering on their men. When Colonel Williams saw the regimental colors go down for the third time, and all of the color guard were killed or wounded, he directed Sergeant Major Asa W. Blanchard to take charge of them. Blanchard had specifically requested the assignment, and "was put in special charge of the duty of keeping them afloat... as fast as the bearers were felled he detailed others to take them up."[64]

Blanchard would soon fall casualty in the fighting that followed. After a short while, Lieutenant Colonel W.W. Dudley came back to help his sergeant major with the colors, and was wounded badly in the leg. Blanchard was very apologetic about Dudley receiving the wound, and directed two slightly wounded men to move him to a safer spot nearby. Dudley later recounted: "From where I lay I clearly saw him raise the flag. While he was holding it the order came for the line to retire to the top of the hill behind us; this it did slowly, forming a line and frequently facing about to deliver volleys at the advancing enemy until the crest was reached. Here a determined stand was made and I was carried to the Seminary and lost sight of the individuals of the regiment and their actions but could see the line as it gallantly withstood the terrific front and flank fire of the enemy. I was told by others who witnessed it on this line...[that Blanchard] having seen that capture was imminent, had torn the flag from the staff and wrapped it around his body under his sword belt; and that while moving about, cheering and encouraging the men to stand fast, he received a musket ball in his groin severing the artery and causing almost immediate death."[65] Dudley would fall prisoner to the enemy and would lose his leg to amputation,

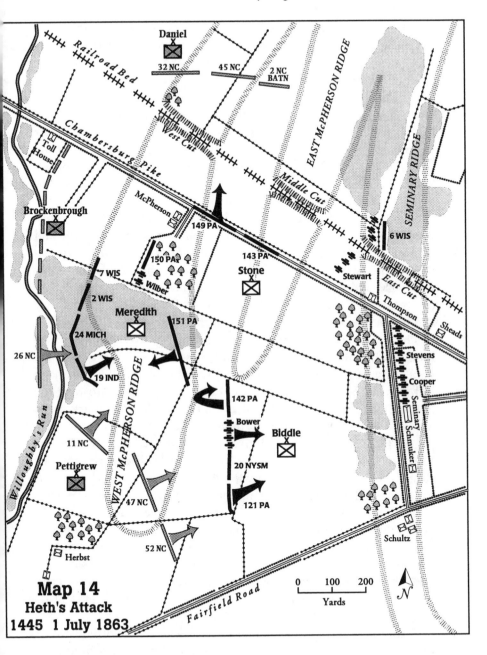

Map 14
Heth's Attack
1445 1 July 1863

0   100   200
Yards

but would be restored to freedom when the Confederates evacuated the town on the night of 3/4 July.[66]

The heavy Confederate pressure from the left forced Colonel Williams to pull back to the east-northeast towards the crest of McPherson's Ridge and the fence that marked the southwestern boundary of Herbst Woods. Here his troops fell in with other elements of the Iron Brigade that were pulling back out of the woods. By now other brave hearts had taken up the regiment's other flag, only to be felled also at this post of honor—Sergeant James Furgason and Andrew Beshears of Company H, Thomas Winset and Thomas J. Daugherty of Company K, Thomas K. Michener of Company E and Allen W. Ogborn of Company B, followed by "many others of less rank who with undaunted courage and true patriotism have taken their lives into their hands and rushed to uphold the honor of the old flag."[67] Confederate casualties were not nearly as heavy as the 19th Indiana's in this attack but the 11th North Carolina did lose both of its top officers—Colonel Collett Leventhorpe was wounded and Major E.A. Ross was killed. One company of the 11th North Carolina started the day with three officers and 35 men, and would have only its captain and four men left afterwards. They would be called on to charge on 3 July, and three of them would fall casualty, leaving only two left in the company at the close of the battle.[68]

The Iron Brigade put up a much sterner fight in Herbst Woods than Biddle's three regiments on lower McPherson's Ridge did against the right wing of Pettigrew's attack. As already noted, Biddle's command had shifted position several times in order to avoid the enfilading fire of Carter's guns on Oak Hill, and at the time that Heth's attack began was actually deployed facing north along the Fairfield Road, perpendicular to its earlier position. However, as soon as General Rowley saw Pettigrew begin his attack from the woods on Herr Ridge, he promptly swung the brigade around to occupy the southern end of McPherson's Ridge as it had done earlier. This movement, Rowley noted, was executed under severe enemy artillery fire. Once back in line facing west, Biddle posted his 142nd Pennsylvania on the right, then the four guns of Breck's battery. The left of the line was formed by the 20th New York State Militia and then the 121st Pennsylvania, the 121st having its left near the Fairfield Road; both regiments formed a provisional "demi-brigade" under the temporary command of Colonel Theodore B. Gates of the 20th New York State Militia.[69]

Pettigrew's two right regiments, the 47th and 52nd North Carolina, together numbered some 1100 men, about 200 more than Biddle had on his line.[70] As a result, the Confederates overlapped Biddle's position considerably on the south. Colonel Gates of the 20th New York State Militia saw them coming in "two very strong lines of infantry."[71] To him one Confederate battle line seemed to extend the front of two full regiments beyond his left flank. Colonel Wainwright, the corps artillery commander, observed Heth's entire advance from his post near the Seminary, and was duly impressed. He saw that the enemy line outflanked Biddle's by half a mile on the left, and felt that. "There was not a shadow of a chance of our holding this ridge."[72]

Pettigrew's advance soon neared the Harman farm and forced Captains Baldwin and Cunningham of the 20th New York State Militia to withdraw their two companies in haste before they were overwhelmed. These brave sharpshooters, who had been in their position on the enemy's very door step for well over two hours, had to head southward along the ravine of Willoughby Run in order to avoid Pettigrew's heavy skirmish line. Fortunately they received cover from some of Gamble's cavalry stationed along the Fairfield Road, and so were able to escape capture. They then moved eastward across the empty fields and rejoined their command that evening on Cemetery Hill. The Confederates were so annoyed at the effective job the 20th's sharpshooters had done that they set fire to the house in order to prevent such an episode from possibly recurring. Amelia Harman and her aunt had just come up from the basement, relieved to have the Yankee soldiers leave their house at last, only to find "the house was filled with Rebels and they were deliberately firing it." The despondent women pleaded in vain to save their home, and then fled to the west for safety as the building went up in flames.[73]

The 47th and 52nd North Carolina regiments halted their advance for several minutes while the Union troops at the Harman farm were driven off. Apparently a large detachment from the 52nd North Carolina followed the retiring Union troops and almost penetrated the position held by the squadron of the 8th New York Cavalry squadron posted in the Meals' orchard. One soldier of the 8th New York wrote that the advancing Confederates were not recognized until they unfurled their flags, whereupon they fired volley after volley at his position. The cavalrymen held their line for about half an hour, losing many horses in the while, until they finally pulled back.[74]

Meanwhile, the remainder of the 52nd North Carolina along with the 47th turned to deal with the heavy fire they were receiving from the main Union infantry line to their front: "As the enemy was keeping up a rather hot fire upon our main line, skirmishers from our regiment (47th North Carolina) were ordered to advance and drive them back out of reach of our line, which was done, but not until several of our regiment were wounded, and our gallant Lieutenant-Colonel, John A. Graves was slightly wounded on the leg, the ball first having hit the iron scabbard of his sword, which was hanging by his side."[75]

Biddle ordered his main line to hold their fire until he gave the order to do so. While the enemy advanced steadily forward, driving the brigade's skirmishers back across Willoughly Run, Color Sergeant Edward Beckett of the 20th New York State Militia bravely advanced his regiment's colors five paces in front of the battle line. The Confederate skirmishers saw this movement and at once peppered the 20th's color guard with shots. One musket ball knocked the eagle off of Beckett's flagstaff, and another struck him in the left hand. Then a shell fragment struck the staff and drove wood fragments into his chest as he fell. The intensity of the Confederate fire was but a forewarning of what was to come.[76]

The men of the 121st Pennsylvania, posted to the left of the 20th New York State Militia, held their fire until they saw the main line of the 52nd North Carolina come to within a few yards of the crest of the ridge immediately on their front. The Pennsylvanians "then rose and delivered their fire directly into their faces, staggering them and bringing them to a stand."[77] The 121st's commander, Major Alexander Biddle, reported that "I saw the line of the enemy slowly approaching up the hill, extending far beyond our left flank, for which we had no defense. As the enemy's faces appeared over the crest of the hill, we fired effectually into them... The immediate attack on our front was destroyed by our first fire."[78] He was pleased that his men had been able to deliver the first fire, and felt that they could have charged up farther but for a fence that would have blocked their advance. After that he ordered the men to fire by file while the guns to their right were being withdrawn.[79]

The troops of the 20th New York State Militia and 142nd Pennsylvania also successfully withstood the first attack of the Confederate regiment on their front, the 47th North Carolina. Lieutenant J. Owen Rogers of Company I of the 47th describes his unit's advance: "It is a grand spectacle. In the line of the Forty-seventh there are over 650 muskets, the men marching steadily to meet the foe, who are on their own soil and strongly posted, with a heavy infantry force and with artillery which at every step rakes through our lines, cutting great gaps, which are quickly filled by the boys closing into the places of those who have just fallen. We cross a stream and then up a hill through a wheat field, and then in our front, not over seventy-five yards off, we see the heavy lines of Yankee soldiers with their guns shining and flags waving; the struggle grows hotter and hotter, men are falling in every direction." Because the day was so hot, some men of the 47th "had difficulty ramming down their cartridges, so slow was the iron ramrod in hands thoroughly wet with perspiration. All expedients were resorted to, but mainly jamming the ramrods against the ground and rocks."[80]

Union losses began to mount as the Confederates renewed their attack. Color Corporal Enos Vail of the 20th New York State Militia was loading just his fifth round when he felt a terrible pain in his back, "as if I had been hit by a club." He tried to stand and finish loading but found that he could not. He had no choice but to leave his gear and head for the rear. He went to the north to the Chambersburg Pike and there came upon a cavalryman who helped him get to the Christ Lutheran Church in town. Vail was lying there when a surgeon of the XI Corps came up to have a look at him. When the surgeon saw Vail's corps badge (a blue circle) and understood that Vail belonged to the I Corps, not the XI, he began to move on to the next patient. Vail complained loudly, and the surgeon agreed to examine him. The brave corporal stood and placed both hands on a pew while the surgeon—without anesthesia—probed his side and removed the bullet that had lodged near his spine.[81]

Private Lambert DuBois of Company C, 20th New York State Militia, remembered the first man to be hit in his company: "I think it was John Boyle, an ugly scalp wound from a bullet striking him just at the top of his forehead, a spattering of blood, a dull thud was all I saw after that."[82] The Confederates' fire was so intense that 1st Sergeant Isaac Buswell of Company B "had five bullets through his haversack, one through his cartridge box, and his rifle was shattered in his hand by a piece of shell."[83] In Company D, Private Reuben Van Leuven saw his good friend Hugh Donihoe struck in the gut by a Confederate shell. Donihoe's face paled as he lay on the ground and whispered to his buddy, "Just break the news to mother." In a moment he was gone. Van Leuven knew that there was nothing he could do for his friend now, so he exchanged his musket with Donihoe's since he knew his friend had always taken exceptionally good care of his musket.[84]

By now Major Alexander Biddle of the 121st Pennsylvania was having increasing difficulty with the long line of the 52nd North Carolina on his front and left. His men "received a crushing fire from their right, under which our ranks were broken and became massed together as we endeavored to change front to the left to meet them...The officers made every possible effort to form their men, and Captains Ashworth and Sterling and Lieutenants Ruth and Funk were all wounded."[85] The 121st's flag, carried by color sergeant William Hardy, was perforated by holes and was splintered in three places.[86]

Colonel Chapman Biddle sensed the 121st wavering and rode over to help encourage the men. His horse was struck and fell heavily with him to the ground. He arose safely, only to receive a slight scalp wound from a musket ball.[87] Some Confederate troops had seen him ride rapidly forward "bearing a large Federal flag. The scattered Federals swarmed around him as bees cover their queen." In an instant "all the guns in front and from right and left turned on the mass and seemingly shot the whole to pieces." The men of the 47th North Carolina were so impressed by Biddle's bravery that they were genuinely and openly pleased to hear that he had not been killed.[88]

By now the 121st was breaking up as the 52nd North Carolina began to get into its rear. Its men headed to the rear, singly and in groups, toward the Seminary, which was about ¼ mile distant. One soldier noted that "the time made by the 121st getting to the cover of the wood was remarkable, probably the best on record."[89]

The retreat of the 121st opened up the left of the 20th New York State Militia, which was now isolated because the artillery and infantry on its right had already begun to pull back. Bower's four guns in the right of Gates' line had only fired a few rounds when Lieutenant Breck received an order to withdraw. It seems that Colonel Wainwright had become concerned about the stability of Biddle's infantry and saw that Breck's firing which "was much hindered by our own infantry moving in front of his pieces." Wainwright had seen Biddle's infantry, and saw that Breck's move to the Fairfield Road and back to the ridge, and had come to the assumption that "we had no regular line of battle on this crest." His hasty decision stripped the backbone out of Biddle's line, but probably saved Bower's four guns from capture. The commanders of the 20th New York State Militia and 142nd Pennsylvania began to withdraw when they saw Bower pull out; Breck himself was glad to get away "as the infantry were falling back close upon the guns."[90]

Gates ordered his men to fire one last good volley at the enemy as they came rushing up the slope in front, and so checked the Confederate advance for a few minutes as it "taught the enemy caution." The Colonel, who was now the only officer of the brigade still mounted, then bravely took up the regimental colors "which had been presented to the regiment by the ladies of Saugerties, and hoisting them over his shoulder, called upon his men to stand by them." Colonel Gates claimed that the men of the brigade "marched slowly and in perfect order, halting as often as they could load, and facing about and delivering their fire with so much coolness and effect that the pursuit was tardy."[91] This may have been how the 20th withdrew, but the account of the 121st Pennsylvania just cited suggests this regiment, at least, retired in a completely different manner.

The 52nd and 47th North Carolina regiments did not advance against Biddle's retreating troops as quickly as they would have liked because they were struck almost simultaneously on their left, right and rear by Union counterattacks. The attack on their right and rear was made by some of the Union cavalry that had been patrolling the Fairfield Road. Some bold cavalry officer whose name is not recorded decided to assist Biddle's men in their retreat by charging into the Confederate infantry. The ploy worked, even though Colonel Marshall of the 52nd North Carolina "was equal to the emergency, for he faced three of his companies about and met this charge, quickly driving the cavalry off with heavy loss to them."[92] These same Union cavalrymen had also stymied the advance of Archer's brigade on Pettigrew's left. Colonel B.D. Fry had advanced this brigade a short distance when the division's attack began at 1440. However, when he saw a large body of cavalry on his right, "he judiciously changed his front, thus protecting the right flank of the division during the engagement."[93]

At the same time that this cavalry detachment charged, the left of the 47th North Carolina received an infantry attack from the 142nd Pennsylvania, Biddle's right wing regiment. Since this unit had no Confederate troops on its immediate front and was still relatively intact as it started retreating following the withdrawal of Breck's four guns, Colonel Chapman Biddle decided to lead the unit into a counterattack to slow down the enemy advance. Biddle bravely took the 142nd's colors and led the unit to the attack. Its numbers, though, were not strong enough to turn the enemy back. The regiment was soon driven in retreat back to Seminary Ridge with the rest of its brigade.[94] In all this confusion, Biddle dropped the regiment's colors, and they remained on the ground until recovered by Lieutenant Colonel George McFarland of the 151st Pennsylvania.[95] Colonel Robert P. Cummins of the 142nd was felled during this counterattack, and several of his devoted men were determined to carry his body from the field even at the cost of their own lives. "Three or four of the remnant of the column...faithful to their old commander, endeavored to carry his lifeless body along;

but the enemy was too close. Several of the boys were shot dead while trying to perform this solemn duty. One was left, and seeing the impossibility to accomplish this purpose himself, he unbuckled the Colonel's belt and came off the field, swinging the colonel's sword, not, however, escaping being wounded, for as he passed me the blood was streaming out of his mouth, and the tears down his cheeks. But with the courage of an infuriated lion, he was swearing eternal vengeance on our enemies."[96]

Lieutenant Rowan Rogers of the 47th North Carolina regiment, remembering that his command had been distracted by the unexpected cavalry charge when the 142nd attacked, noted: "While this was going on the infantry in our front tried hard to rally their somewhat broken lines and regain the ground they lost." He acknowledged that the Union counterattacks succeeded at breaking the momentum of his attack: "The attention of the Forty-seventh was diverted from the enemy in our front and almost before we knew it the enemy had rallied and was attempting to charge our lines. Besides, they had a number of pieces of artillery helping them, wherever the opposing lines were far enough apart for them to use artillery without striking their own men. At this critical moment Captain Cam. Iredell, who commanded Company C, which was the color company of the Forty-seventh, seeing one of his men fall mortally wounded rushes to his side and says, 'My dear boy, I will try to avenge your hurt.' He took his musket and continued to use it until he was struck by a shot from the enemy which caused his death, not, however, until he had seen the enemy turn again and flee. The forty-seventh lost heavily in this fight of July 1."[97]

The collapse of Biddle's brigade, as noted, left the southern flank of the Iron Brigade wide open to the advancing 11th North Carolina. It was now time to commit the I Corps' last reserve, Lieutenant Colonel George McFarland's 151st Pennsylvania, "The School Teachers' Regiment."[98] General Rowley ordered the charge in person, and the regiment at once crossed over its breastworks at the Seminary and headed for the gap on the Iron Brigade's left. Lieutenant Colonel McFarland reported, "The position of the regiment was now such that a little more than one half of its left wing extended beyond the strip of woods on the ridge directly west of the seminary. The enemy greeted me with a volley which brought several of my men down, where I had halted in position. Having previously cautioned the men against excitement and firing at random, and the enemy being partly concealed in the woods on lower ground than we occupied, I did not order them to fire a regular volley, but each man to fire as he saw an enemy on which to take a steady aim. This was strictly observed, and during the next hour's terrific fighting many of the enemy were laid low."[99] The 151st met a "severe and destructive fire," but the unit was big (467 men) and its men were determined to hold their position in this, their one and only great battle. Its officers and men fell fast; General Heth observed afterwards that "the dead of the enemy marked its line of battle with the accuracy of a line at dress parade."[100] But the regiment's counterattack succeeded at winning time for Biddle to withdraw on the left, and for the tattered remains of the Iron Brigade to fall back on the right. As these troops retired to Seminary Ridge, Pettigrew's men concentrated more and more on the line of the 151st. This made the Pennsylvanians suffer terribly, especially under the oblique fire from their left. At length the regiment had no choice but to withdraw, since it was totally unsupported and in danger of being surrounded.[101] Its losses would total 72%, ninth highest of all the Union regiments in the entire battle.[102] The commander of the 151st, Lieutenant Colonel McFarland, was wounded badly in both legs—one would be amputated and the other badly maimed.[103]

The 151st Pennsylvania's counterattack would have been more effective if the 19th Indiana, which was still holding the left wing of the Iron Brigade, had held the field. But Colonel Samuel J. Williams of the 19th mistook the 151st Pennsylvania as coming to his relief, and as the Pennsylvanians came up, he pulled back to the swale between eastern McPherson's Ridge and the Seminary.[104] Williams in his battle report explained that his command by then had been reduced to a mere squad, and he was greatly exposed on the left because of the retreat of Biddle's men: "As the enemy gained the crest of the ridge now in front, they sustained a deadly fire from our guns. But they were three to four to our one and we were now [unable] to avail anything against such odds." He pulled his line back, loading and firing as they could, to the barricades in front of the Seminary.[105]

The early withdrawal of the 19th Indiana forced the 24th Michigan on its right to pull back from the open eastern end of the Herbst Woods to still another line, its fifth of the day, located on the crest of eastern McPherson Ridge. The lack of cover here was a great problem, and one Confederate volley felled both Captain Malachi O'Donnell of Company E and Lieutenant Newell Grace of Company H. Soon afterward Lieutenant Reuben Humphreville of Company K was also killed.[106] The following incident could have happened at this point of the fighting or earlier: "Edward B. Harrison of H was wounded and John Malcho was helping him off the field. John W. Welch of G took Harrison's other arm, and while thus assisting their wounded comrade, a Confederate bullet killed Welch instantly, and at the same moment another bullet instantly killed Harrison, and tore off a part of Malcho's shoe. Harrison and Welch fell side by side. In life they had been friends, and were buried in one grave."[107] So thick were the bullets that the 24th's regimental history speaks of wounded men receiving additional wounds while they were lying on the field waiting for aid.[108]

The regiment continued to fall back towards the Seminary, stopping every several steps to turn and fire another volley. During one of these stops Sergeant Charles M. McConnell of the 24th saw Lieutenant Colonel J.R. Lane of the 26th North Carolina bravely carrying his regiment's colors in advance of the skeleton few of the 26th who remained. McConnell leaned against a tree and waited for Lane to draw closer. At 30 steps, "as Colonel Lane turns to see if his regiment is following him, a ball is fired by this brave and resolute adversary, strikes him in the back of the neck just below the brain, which crashes through his jaw and mouth, and for the fouteenth and last time the colors are down."[109]

The 26th though, would soon have a measure of revenge for the death of its lieutenant colonel. Colonel Henry A. Morrow, who had led the 24th Michigan through all the bloodshed in Herbst Woods and the withdrawal to Seminary Ridge, was himself carrying his regiment's flag to safety. Just before he reached the security of the fence in front of the Seminary, he was wounded in the head. Command of the regiment devolved on Captain Albert M. Edwards of Company F. Edwards found the flag that Morrow was carrying lying on the ground with its fallen bearer just before the retreat to Cemetery Hill, and carried it back to safety himself.[110]

Colonel Morrow's wound was not mortal, and he underwent quite a series of escapades in the next few days. After being wounded he was taken to "a lady of Gettysburg, a true union girl" who dressed the injury and then offered to hide him from the rebels as they took possesion of the town. Morrow refused, feeling certain that he would be found if the Confederates searched her house. He was, indeed, soon taken prisoner, and was ordered out into the street to join other prisoners, wounded or otherwise, who were all marched four miles out on the road to Chambersburg. There he found 54 members of his command. The next day his wound was dresssed by a Confederate surgeon, whom Morrow found to be a master Mason, like himself. This discovery led to him being assigned to a hospital while many of the other prisoners were being marched off to Richmond and prison.

When he returned to Gettysburg, Morrow took advantage of an opportunity to be by himself, and cut off his shoulder straps. He then put on a green sash and "became sort of a surgeon." He had the further good fortune to fall in with Assistant Surgeon Alexander Collar of the 24th, and together the two had the freedom to visit hospitals as they wished. Morrow's disguise was almost revealed when he happened to meet one of the Confederates his men had captured at Fitzburgh Crossing before the battle of Fredericksburg. The Confederate recognized him, but Morrow boldly took charge of the situation and asked if the man had been well treated by him and his men. When the Confederate responded in the affirmative, Morrow asked to receive the same treatment. The fellow then asked him, "Where are your straps?" To which the Colonel turned surgeon replied, "I have lost them for the time being." The Confederate soldier promised not to say a word, and left Morrow secure in his disguise.[112]

During his tour as a surgeon Morrow had still more interesting adventures, two of which will be told here. On 3 July he found time to climb to the "steeple" of his hospital (the cupola of the Seminary) and view Pickett's charge. He eagerly reported the results to the Union men in the hospital, with a warning not to show any exuberance for fear of incurring the displeasure of their guards. Later that day Morrow had the audacity to approach General John B. Gordon and ask, "General, I am informed that our wounded of the first day's battle lie uncared for where they fell and I ask your assistance in having them attended to." Gordon asked a Confederate surgeon if this were true, and was told that no one had time to visit that part of the field in order to tend the wounded. Gordon then approved Morrow's request, and gave him a train of twelve ambulances driven by Confederate drivers to bring in the Union wounded on McPherson's Ridge. "It was a weird sight, that long line of army nurses, as by the fitful light of a half clouded moon, made more obscure by the lanterns they bore, this party threaded its way among the blackened and swollen corpses. The moans and cries for assistance and water were heartrending. Some were delirious and wondered that they had been neglected for so long, while others, in their wild delirium cheered on their comrades as they fought over in imagination the terrible battle."[112]

Colonel Morrow was left behind in his hospital when the Confederates left Gettysburg on 4 July, and simply walked back to his own lines and freedom. He would command his regiment through 1864, be wounded again, and win promotion to brigadier general on 25 January 1865. He served in the regular army after the war, and died in 1891 at the age of 61.[113]

The survivors of the 7th Wisconsin also had a difficult retreat to Seminary Ridge. Lieutenant Colonel John Callis of the 7th was worried that the enemy was outflanking his men on both the left and right, and shared his concern with Captain Henry F. Young; the intrepid captain bravely replied, "Let them flank and be damned, we are giving them hell in front." A short while later Callis received a message from General Meredith saying, "I am hurt and cannot get to you, take command of the brigade and get it out of that little end of a 'V' as best you can." Callis recalled that "I then looked back and saw the large brick seminary on the ridge behind, as I think three fourths of a mile distant. I made that my objective point and gave the order 'by the right of companies to the rear, march.' As soon as I commenced this movement, we commenced to receive an enfilading fire from the right and left and a direct fire from our front then our rear. I then gave the order to 'Halt, right face, right into line, wheel, double quick, march!' This being done, I ordered, 'Ready, aim, fire!, then, by the right of companies to the rear, load while marching!' When loaded we again wheeled into line and fired, and in this way we kept up our march closely followed until what was left of us got back to a point where there was an orchard growing near the Seminary."[114]

By now Pettigrew had been informed that he was acting division commander, since Harry Heth had been wounded during the first attacks on Herbst Woods. Heth was hit between Willoughby Run and the grove, on the front of the 2nd Wisconsin. The general perhaps had his life saved because he had just gotten a new hat. While the army was encamped at Cashtown, he asked his quartermaster to bring him a hat if they captured any, "as mine was in a dilapidated condition." Heth was later brought a box of a dozen or more good felt hats. He tried them on but they were all too large. His clerk solved the problem by doubling up a dozen or more sheets of foolscap paper and placing them between the felt and the hat. Heth wore the hat in this way during the fighting on 1 July. He related later, "I was struck by a minie ball on the head which passed through my hat and the paper my clerk had placed there, broke the outer coating of my skull and cracked the inner coating, and I fell senseless." The hat was indeed a lucky find, Heth felt, "as I am confidently of the belief that my life was saved by this paper in my hat." The general was unconscious for about 24 hours, but recovered and led his division until the end of the war. He died in 1899.[115]

At about 1530 Pettigrew found it necessary to recall his advancing regiments because they were beginning to encounter heavy artillery fire from the Union cannons near the Seminary. He reported that all his regiments pulled back in good order with the exception of the 26th North Carolina, which for some reason had not received his command. Its men, eager for another fight, were busy gathering ammunition from those who had fallen because they had none and wanted to renew the fight.[116]

Once the 26th was given its proper orders and pulled back to rejoin its brigade, its men were able to begin tending to their wounded in a brief respite before the next round of fighting began. Chief among their concerns was their fallen Colonel, Henry K. Burgwyn Jr. He had fallen in Herbst Woods at the height of the fighting, struck by a shot in the chest. Private William Cheek of the 26th helped take this wounded colonel to the rear: "I saw Colonel Burgwyn being carried off the field by two soldiers, named Ellington and Stanton, who were using one of their blankets for the purpose... We carried him some distance toward where our line of battle had been formed, and as we were thus moving him, a lieutenant of some South Carolina regiment came up and took hold of the blanket to help us. Colonel Burgwyn did not seem to suffer much, but asked the lieutenant to pour some water on his wound. He was put down on the ground while the water from the canteens was poured on him. His coat was taken off and I stooped to take his watch, which was hung around his neck by a silken cord. As I did so, the lieutenant from South Carolina seized the watch, broke the cord, put the watch in his pocket and started off with it. I demanded the watch telling the lieutenant that he should not thus take away the watch of my colonel and that I would kill him as sure as powder would burn, with these words cocking my rifle and taking aim at him. I made him come back and give up the watch, at the same time telling him he was nothing but a thief, and then ordering him to leave, which he did. In a few moments, Colonel Burgwyn said to me that he would never forget me, and I shall never forget the look he gave me as he said those words....I left and went in search for one of our litters, in order to place Colonel Burgwyn on it, so as to carry him more comfortably and conveniently.... we found him dying. I sat down and took his hand in my lap. He had very little to say, but I remember that his last words were that he was entirely satisfied with everything and 'The Lord's Will be done.' Thus he died, very quietly and resignedly. I never saw a braver man than he. He was always cool under fire and knew exactly what to do, and his men were devoted to him. He was the youngest colonel I ever saw in all my experience as a soldier."[117]

While Pettigrew's large North Carolina brigade was defeating Biddle's command and the 24th Michigan and 19th Indiana of the Iron Brigade, Brockenbrough's much smaller Virginia brigade was having a much tougher time against the Iron Brigade's two right wing regiments. Brockenbrough's brigade (formerly Heth's) was a veteran one, but battle losses and attrition had lowered the effective strength of its four units to less than 1000.[118] Arranged opposite it were two equally veteran units of the Iron Brigade, the 2nd and 7th Wisconsin, which together had about 550 men after deducting their losses that morning. The two Union regiments were strongly posted in Herbst Woods on the ridge above Willoughby Run, and had ample flank protection on the right from the 150th Pennsylvania and on the left from the rest of Meredith's brigade. This position was not going to be turned but would have to be taken by direct assault.

Brockenbrough began his attack at 1430, the same time as Pettigrew on his right. His regiments were deployed in the following order from right to left in the woods on the eastern slope of Herr Ridge, south of the Chambersburg Pike: 22nd Virginia Battalion, 40th Virginia, 47th Virginia, and 55th Virginia.[119] He advanced with a strong line of skirmishers in his front and soon ran into Stone's skirmish line posted in the woods along Willoughby Run.[120]

The men of the left wing of the 150th Pennsylvania, who were the only troops holding the Union line between the Chambersburg Pike and Herbst Woods after the right wing of the regiment went to help the 149th and 143rd along the Pike, were both impressed and worried when they saw "the troops of Heth's and Pender's division in motion, descending rapidly towards Willoughby Run, regiment upon regiment en echelon, followed by supporting columns, extending southward from the Chambersburg road as far as the eye could reach. Their advance was magnificent, and as mere spectators, or military critics, we might have enjoyed and applauded it, but it boded evil to our scanty force."[121]

The 150th clearly needed to realign in order to meet this grand new threat. The troops on the left wing of the regiment, who had shifted position several times in order to get shelter from the Confederate artillery fire coming in from their front and right, moved forward to a fenceline on the highest ground on their front.[122] The remainder of the regiment "with no undue excitement, and in thoroughly good order, swung back to its original position, facing the west, leaving, however, a large gap between our left and the woods, which it was impossible to fill. The change occupied but a minute or two, but under a scorching fire from our old assailants north of the pike."[123]

Fortunately for the 150th, Brockenbrough's attack took time to develop, and the regiment was able to re-form before the enemy attack struck. Major Thomas Chamberlin noted that "for some unexplained reason the strong force approaching from the west, whose front line was composed of troops of Heth's division, moderated its movements, as if awaiting developments on other portions of the field, and by the time it came within musket reach our regiment was firmly established in its position."[124]

Chamberlin's account continues: "Protected in some measure by a fence, it opened a scattering fire which at once checked the enemy's progress, but failed to scatter or confuse him. The response from vastly superior numbers, equally well armed, was like a hail storm, but our men were as obedient to commands as if they shared the perils of twenty battles. Back and forth, for a few minutes, swept the tempest of bullets, bearing summons of death to many a brave combatant, but in no respect altering the situation. Suddenly, as if elsewhere something decisive, for which they had been waiting, had occured, our antagonists ceased firing, fell back a short distance, and obliquing to their right were soon hidden from view by the woods."[125]

Major John Mansfield of the 2nd Wisconsin, whose unit was located between the 24th Michigan on the left and the 7th Wisconsin to the right, also saw Brockenbrough's advance as soon as it emerged from the timber on Herr Ridge. He saw two lines attacking behind a heavy line of skirmishers. Then, "the front line of the enemy advanced directly to the front, while the second line advanced obliquely to the left."[126] This maneuver seemed strange to the men of the 150th Pennsylvania, whose skirmishers had just withdrawn to the regiment's main line. To them it appeared as if the Confederate line (Brockenbrough's left) was going to advance straight towards them; then the line halted before crossing the stream, changed direction, and crossed the run in front of the Iron Brigade.[127] Brockenbrough doubtless made this course correction on his left in order to link up with Pettigrew's 26th North Carolina on his right. The move made his left flank more secure, and to him it certainly seemed safer to attack through the trees of Herbst Woods rather that the open fields below the position of the 150th Pennsylvania. When he shifted his weight to the left, Brockenbrough left a strong line of troops in the Willoughby Run ravine to occupy the 150th Pennsylvania.[128]

Brockenbrough's advance made little headway against the two Iron Brigade regiments that were so strongly posted in the woods. Major Mansfield reported that "in a short time the enemy's skimishers and our own became actively engaged, which continued with great spirit for a time," but to him it did seem like a major attack.[129] Colonel William Robinson of the 7th Wisconsin noted a similar impression: "In a short time the enemy advanced into the wood on our front, lay down behind the crest of the hill and behind the trees, and opened a galling fire."[130] Captain George W. Jones of the 150th Pennsylvania reported that his men easily repulsed those Confederates from Brockenbrough's line who ventured to attack in their direction: "The enemy's infantry opened fire upon us as soon as we made our appearance, and we became hotly engaged for some time, when the enemy's line was compelled to give way, and they fled in confusion. A second line advanced and met with the same fate."[131]

Confederate accounts do not speak much of this attack, which lasted at least half an hour, except to say that the men fought well and the enemy resisted obstinately. As already noted, it is probable that Brockenbrough left at least his skirmish line, if not a portion of his entire first line, in the woods along Willoughby Run, where they continued to engage the 150th Pennsylvania without success.[132]

This portion of the Iron Brigade line held on firmly until about 1500, when the slow retreat of the 24th Michigan on its left forced Colonel William W. Robinson of the 7th Wisconsin to pull back his left somewhat. As acting brigade commander since Brigadier General Solomon Meredith had been incapacitated that morning,[133] Robinson was also concerned about the lack of support he was receiving on his right from Stone's brigade.[134] Major John Mansfield of the 2nd Wisconsin, who was near to Stone's 150th Pennsylvania, however, was much more concerned with the situation on the brigade's left, where "an attempt was being made to flank our position by the second line."[135]

Since Brockenbrough's men were not pressing their attack very aggressively, Robinson must have felt he could have held on against them indefinitely had it not been for his problem in the left flank. He noted that "the Second and Seventh were keeping up a rapid fire upon the enemy in front, but, I think, without doing much injury, as he was protected by the hill and the timber." He was aware that his 24th and 19th "were being badly cut up by superior numbers," and that a small detachment "from some other division" (151st Pennsylvania) had made an unsuccessful counter attack on that front, but he persisted in holding his line. By now "the Seventh was receiving a galling fire and the Second was being badly cut up" as the enemy was "rapidly gaining ground on our left; still no order came to change our position."[136]

At last Captain Hollon Richardson, acting inspector general of the Iron Brigade, came to Robinson with orders to retire to Seminary Ridge; it is uncertain whether Richardson was sent by Doubleday or Wadsworth. Both the 7th and the 2nd stopped several times during their retreat in order to face the enemy in what might be called a true "fighting withdrawal." Colonel Robinson reported that, "I retired by right of companies to the rear some 150 or 200 yards, halted, and wheeled into line again to support the other regiments in retiring. Then again retired about the same distance, and again wheeled into line, and so on until I reached the foot of Seminary Ridge."[137] Major Mansfield of the 2nd related that "this movement was made in good order, firing as we retired. About half the distance from where we commenced to retire to this new position, I faced the regiment to the front, and again moved to meet the advancing enemy, when I discovered the enemy closing in upon our left. I again faced to the rear, and took up a position on the ridge referred to, on the right of the brigade already in position."[138] Colonel Robinson was also pleased to reach the ridge, where he found a battery already firing on the advancing foe: "Down the slope, some 40 yards in front of this battery, I found a slight breastwork of loose rails, which, I suppose, had been thrown together by some of our troops in the earlier part of the day, behind which I threw the regiment."[139]

Among the numerous casualties that the Iron Brigade left behind during this portion of the battle were two men of particular note. One was Private Patrick Maloney of the 2nd Wisconsin, the plucky soldier who had personally captured General Archer that morning. Maloney was killed at some point in the afternoon fighting, and his body was never recovered; he was probably laid to rest by unfamiliar hands in an unmarked grave sometime on 2 or 3 July.[140]

The Saga of John Burns

Another casualty was a 70 year old citizen of the town who fought alongside the Iron Brigade and would later be made an honorary member. This was the famous John Burns, the legendary former constable of Gettysburg and War of 1812 veteran who came forward to do his part to drive the enemy from his soil.

John Burns stories were in plenty after the battle as he quickly became a national hero, and even met President Lincoln personally at the dedication of the National Cemetery on 19 November 1863. Through the recollections of a number of different soldiers we are able to trace his movements during the day.

According to one account, Burns was first seen on the field at about 1100, between northern Seminary Ridge and Pennsylvania College. At that time "John Burns, an old citizen of the village, since made famous in verse" came walking up and asked a wounded soldier if he were going to use his gun anymore. The soldier replied, "No, you can have it, I can't carry it any further." The soldier also offered Burns his belt and cartridge box. Burns tried on the belt and did not think much of it. He put it down and instead put the cartridges in his pocket, saying that he would carry them best that way. He then headed for the front with the soldier's gun in his hands.[141]

This account does not agree with others that place him west of town, originally equipped with a musket and even a powder horn. Captain E.P. Halstead of General Doubleday's staff says that he saw Burns near the Seminary just about the time Reynolds was killed: "In returning for the second and third divisions I met John Burns in the field east of the Seminary with an old musket on his shoulder and a powder horn in his pocket hurrying to the front looking terribly earnest; when near me he inquired, 'Which way are the rebels? Where are our troops?' I informed him they were just in front, that he would soon overtake them. He then said with much enthusiasm, 'I know how to fight, I have fit before!'"[142]

Burns next appears on the line of the 150th Pennsylvania not long after noon, just before Rodes' cannons began firing from Oak Hill. Major Thomas Chamberlin of the 150th recalled, "An incident which occured about 12 o'clock did much to emphasize the good feeling in our ranks. While we were watching and waiting, our attention was called to a man of rather bony frame and more than average stature, who approached from the direction of the town, moving with a deliberate step carrying in his right hand an Enfield rifle at a 'trail.' At any time his figure would have been noticeable, but it was doubly so at such a moment, from his age—which evidently neared three-score and ten—and from the somewhat startling peculiarity of his dress. The latter consisted of dark trousers and a waistcoat, a blue 'swallow tail' coat with burnished brass buttons, such as used to be affected by well to do gentlemen of the old school about forty years ago, and a high black silk hat, from which most of the original gloss had long departed, of a shape to be found only in the fashion plates of a remote past. The stiff 'stock,' which usually formed a part of such a costume, was wanting—presumably on account of the heat—and no neck cloth of any kind relieved the bluish tint of his clean shaven face and chin. As his course brought him opposite the rear of the left wing, he first met Major Chamberlain and asked 'Can I fight with your regiment?' The major answered affirmatively, but seeing Colonel Wister approaching, said, 'Here is our colonel, speak to him.' 'Well old man, what do you want?' bluntly demanded the Colonel! 'I want a chance to fight with your regiment!' 'You do? Can you shoot?' 'Oh yes,' and a smile crept over the old man's face which seemed to say, 'If you knew that you had before you a soldier of the war of 1812, who fought at Lundy's Lane, you would not ask such a question!' 'I see you have a gun, but where is your ammunition?' Slapping his hand upon his bulging trousers' pockets, he replied 'I have it here.' 'Certainly you can fight with us,' said the colonel, 'and I wish there were many more with you.' He advised him, however, to go into the woods, to the line of the Iron Brigade, where he would be more sheltered from both sun and bullets, with an equal chance of doing effective work. With apparent reluctance, as if he preferred the open field, he moved towards the woods, and history has written the name of John Burns in the roll of the world's heroes, and his brave conduct is imperishably linked with the glories of Gettysburg."[143]

Burns next encountered the 7th Wisconsin, posted in the western portion of Herbst Woods. The author of this account, Rev. E.J. Wolf, mistakenly places this episode in the morning as the 7th was first entering the fight: "'At this time,' says Col. Caddis [Lt. Col. John B. Callis], from whom the particulars have been secured, 'I saw an object approaching from the rear, and I think it the oddest looking person I saw during the war. He wore a bell-crowned hat, a swallow tail coat with rolling collar and brass buttons and a buff vest. He had on his shoulder an old rifle with which he came to a present arms and then said, 'Colonel is this your regiment?' 'Yes,' I said. Then he brought his rifle to an order and said 'Can I fight in your regiment?' I answered, 'Old man, you had better go to the rear or you'll get hurt.' 'And he replied just as a shell burst near him: 'Tut! tut! tut! I've heard this sort of thing before!' These words were spoken in a tremulous voice. I again ordered him to the rear, when he replied, 'No, sir, if you won't let me fight in your regiment I will fight alone.' I asked him where his cartridge box was; he patted his trousers' pocket and said, 'Here's my bullets,' and taking an old-fashioned powder horn from his pocket, 'Here's my powder, and I know how to use them. There are three hundred cowards back in that town who ought to come out of their cellars and fight and I will show you that there is one man in Gettysburg who is not afraid.' The boys made merry over his swallow-tail coat and yellow vest and broad-rimmed hat—an incarnate facsimile of Uncle Sam—but Sergeant Eustis plead with the colonel 'to fix him up, he'll soon get tired of it and go home.'"

The colonel at last relented and the old flintlock was exchanged for a rifle just captured from Archer's sharpshooters. "He was given a cartridge box and belt, but declined to use them new fangled things and instead filled his pockets with fixed ammunition, after which he went into the ranks. He soon grew restless as the general engagement had not begun and advanced to the front towards our skirmishers before he could see a rebel to shoot at. Pretty soon I saw a Confederate officer riding towards their advanced line, mounted on a white horse. Burns drew on him and the horse galloped through our lines without a rider. Whether the officer was killed or not I do not know. The old man loaded and fired away until I called in my skirmishers and ordered my men back to the Seminary.' Sergeant Eustis [Eustice] of the same regiment corroborates Col. Caddis' testimony. He says, 'We boys commenced to poke fun at him, thinking him a fool to come up where there was such danger. He surprised us all when the rebs advanced, by not taking a double-quick to the rear, but he was just as cool as any veteran among us. We soon had orders to move a hundred yards to the right, and were shortly engaged in one of the hottest fights I ever was in.' It was doubtless in this engagement that Burns received his wounds, one in the arm, one in the leg and several minor ones in the breast, and in this disabled condition he was left on the field when our troops were driven past his humble homestead up to Cemetery Hill. Abandoned by those in whose ranks he had fought he realized his peril at being caught as a 'bushwhacker' when the enemy was approaching, and he managed to crawl away from his gun and to bury his ammunition. Questioned by an officer whether he had been in the ranks he stoutly denied having been a combatant, and insisted that he had gone out seeking some help for his invalid wife. The officer gave credit to this piteous story and ordered the wounded non-combatant to be cared for. A rebel surgeon dressed his wounds, and by night-fall he dragged himself to the cellar door of the nearest house, whence he was conveyed to his home in a rickety bone-wagon by a horse too decrepit to be wanted by the enemy, and there, with bullets still crashing over his head he received medical care from the late Dr. Charles Horner, whose widow and daughters are still with us."[144]

The Wolf/Callis account just cited is certainly the fullest narrative of Burns' role in the battle. Sergeant George Eustice's account, cited by Wolf, goes as follows; Eustice was a member of Company F, 7th Wisconsin: "It must have been about noon when I saw a little old man coming up in the rear of Company F. In regard to the peculiarities of his dress. I remember he wore a swallow-tailed coat with smooth brass buttons. He had a rifle on his shoulder. We boys began to poke fun at him as soon as he came amongst us, as we thought no civilian in his senses would show himself in such a place. Finding that he had really come to fight I wanted to put a cartridge-box on him to make him look like a soldier, telling him he could not fight without one. Slapping his pantaloons-pocket, he replied, 'I can get my hands in here quicker than in a box. I'm not used to them new-fangled things.' In answer to the question what possessed him to come out there at such a time, he replied that the rebels had either driven away or milked his cows, and that he was going to be even with them. About this time the enemy began to advance. Bullets were flying thicker and faster, and we hugged the ground about as we could. Burns got behind a tree and surprised us all by not taking a double-quick to the rear. He was as calm and collected as any veteran on the ground. We soon had orders to get up and move about a hundred yards to the right, when we were engaged in one of the most stubborn contests I ever experienced. Foot by foot we were driven back to a point near the seminary, where we made a stand, but were finally driven through the town to Cemetery Ridge. I never saw John Burns after our movement to the right, when we left him behind his tree, and only know that he was true blue and grit to the backbone, and fought until he was three times wounded."[145]

In his offical report, General Doubleday says: "My thanks are specially due to a citizen of Gettysburg named John Burns, who, although over seventy years of age, shouldered his musket and offered his services to Colonel Wister, 150th Pennsylvania Volunteers. Colonel Wister advised him to fight in the woods, as there was more shelter there; but he preferred to join our line of skirmishers in the open fields. When the troops retired, he fought with the Iron Brigade (Meredith's). He was wounded in three places."[146]

O.B. Curtis, historian of the 24th Michigan, adds that Burns received one of his wounds while serving with Morrow's regiment on the eastern edge of Herbst Woods, near the regiment's fourth position as described in the battle marrative. Curtis says that Burns received three wounds that day, and was treated by Assistant Surgeon Collar of the 24th. On 15 July, two weeks later, Chaplain W.C. Way of the 24th visited Burns at his home and found him mending "comfortably." Needless to say, Burns became quite a celebrity after the battle, and was often visited by tourists, veterans and dignitaries. He sold a picture of himself seated in a rocking chair, with his gun and what appeared to be crutches leaning against the wall behind him. The "Hero of Gettysburg" died in 1872 at the age of 78.[147]

Burns, however, was not the only citizen of the town to serve alongside the Union troops that day. At around noon Captain W.G. Bentley of the 9th New York Cavalry was directed to take a squadron (Companies A and H) in order to escort the prisoners captured from Archer's brigade that morning to Washington. Just before he left on his task, "a young man in citizens' clothes, who said his name was James Watson, came to Co. A. and expressed a desire to go into the fight. He had secured a carbine and saber and the men gave him a blouse and he rode along with us."[148]

There was also at least one more civilian who shouldered a gun to help fight the Confederate invaders on 1 July. He was a lad about 15 years old named J.W. (or C.F.) Wheatley who fell in with Company A of the 12th Massachusetts on 30 June when the regiment marched out of Emmitsburg. One historian of the 12th Massachusetts tells his story as follows: "When Baxter's brigade of Robinson's division of the 1st Corps reached Marsh Run on 30 June, it was found that a little boy had followed us from Emmitsburg; and to our great surprise the stripling asked to be enlisted. Col. Bates of the 12th Massachusetts Volunteers— by way of curing his military fever—asked the captain of Company A to take the youngster on trial for a few days; probably with the expectation that a short time would suffice to tire him of this boyish notion. The next morning we hurried into the battle, and when we halted in front of the Seminary to call the roll, behold this young aspirant was on our hands begging to be taken into the fight. As well as we could we dressed our recruit in blue clothes—the result of an impromptu donation—and into the battle we took him. He had been instructed to take the equipments of the first wounded man, and it was not long ere he was briskly loading and firing. Toward afternoon he was wounded on the left hand and left hip, and then all his courage left him. On July 4 I saw him for the last time and then he was in hospital crying bitterly for his mother and sundry other relatives. He was never mustered into the service, therefore he fought as a civilian."[149]

The Union Retreat to Seminary Ridge

While the Iron Brigade was contesting Herbst Woods against Pettigrew's left wing and most of Brockenbrough's Brigade, Stone's small Pennsylvania brigade had its hands full on the right of the woods and along the Chambersburg Pike, where its three Pennsylvania regiments had to deal with Brockenbrough's left, part of Archer's command, and repeated and determined attacks by three of Daniel's regiments. Analysis of the Union defense here is difficult to describe concisely because of the repeated Confederate attacks and the heavy Union officer casualties. The brigade went through three different brigade commanders that afternoon—Colonel Roy Stone was wounded badly in the arm and hip during the brigade's first counterattack against Daniel, and his successor, Colonel Langhorne Wister of the 150th Pennsylvania, was badly wounded in the mouth during a later counterattack, leaving the brigade command to Colonel E.L. Dana of the 143rd Pennsylvania.[150] These changes necessitated other command adjustments in the brigade's three regiments, as did the heavy combat casualties that by the end of the action left the 143rd under command of Lieutenant Colonel John D. Musser, and the 149th and 150th under captains James Glenn and Cornelius C. Widdis, respectively.[151]

The 150th Pennsylvania, as already discussed, readily repulsed Brockenbrough's initial advance against their line when that Confederate officer pulled back in order to shift the center of his attack to his right. This interlude gave the regiment a brief respite that was soon broken by increased activity on the part of the Confederate batteries. At this time the regiment tried to defend as much ground as it could in front of the McPherson buildings, but it simply did not have enough men. Its ranks were depleted by casualties and by the loss of Jones' skirmish company, which had been unable to rejoin the regiment and formed instead near the edge of the woods, adjacent to the right of the 7th Wisconsin. There was a large gap between Jones' right and the left of the 150th, as well as between the right of the 150th and the turnpike.[152]

The Confederates seemed to be aware of the 150th's thinned ranks, and the big McPherson barn offered a clear target for the advancing troops of Brockenbrough's, Davis' and Daniel's Brigades. Another Confederate attack struck the regiment's line at 1445 and was repulsed after managing to drive the Pennsylvanians back several yards. When the line was faltering, Lieutenant Colonel Henry Huidekoper, who felt that all this time his command was facing "one entire brigade," directed the regimental color bearer, Sergeant Samuel Phifer of Company I ("a man of large stature and boundless courage"), to step forward with the colors. "This he did without hesitation, in the face of a galling fire, and the line moved automatically with him."[153]

Phifer's brave act stopped the Confederates for a moment, but they soon returned to the attack. As usual, the Virginians concentrated their fire on the color guard, and the remainder of its original members were now felled. Corporal Reisinger of Company H was hit by three balls, and Sergeant Phifer himself fell mortally wounded, proudly flaunting his colors in the face of the foe "until death releved him of his charge." At the same time Lieutenant Henry Chancellor was mortally wounded in the thigh, and Captain John Sigler, Lieutenant Miles Rose, and Lieutenant Chalkly Sears were all wounded. Lieutenant Colonel Huidekoper, who had already been bruised on the leg, was shot in the right elbow and had to retire to the barn to be treated. He then returned to his men, "but pain and faintness, resulting from shock and loss of blood, soon compelled him to retire."[154] Command of the regiment fell to Captain Cornelius Widdis.[155]

At some point in this part of the engagement, General Wadsworth requested artillery support for the 150th and a section of two guns from Breck's battery was sent forward. The guns formed up in the gap between the left of the regiment and Jones' company. Lieutenant Colonel Huidekoper noted that the arrival of these guns encouraged his men to move forward again, and they fought alongside the artillerymen until the battery wheeled up and moved to the rear.[156]

Matters meanwhile reached a crisis along the Chambersburg Pike, where two of Stone's regiments held a front of over 300 yards in the face of Daniel's growing force. From left to right the Union line consisted of the 149th and 143rd Pennsylvania. The far left of the line suffered from enfilade fire from Brockenbrough's troops and the Confederate artillery on Herr Ridge; likewise the 90 degree turn in the regiment's line compelled the left of the 149th Pennsylvania to fall under an enfilade fire from Daniel's troops. The position Stone's men were asked to hold was never a good one—witness the fact that no battery was long able to hold a position on the Pike at the apex of Stone's angled line. And, to make things worse, the 143rd Pennsylvania had no support on its right other than Stewart's battery some 400 yards to the east. General Daniel, whose troops had been twice repulsed by Stone's men and their counterattacks, had by 1500 at last formed his regiments for a concerted attack. He gave precise orders to the commander of his right wing regiment, Colonel E.C. Brabble of the 32nd North Carolina, "to advance across the cut, keeping his left on the cut and his line perpendicular to it, and to carry the battery at the barn, and drive in the line of infantry between the barn and the hill." He himself took command of the center two regiments, the 45th North Carolina and 2nd North Carolina Battalion, which would face the 149th and 143rd Pennsylvania. He also sent his brigade's assistant adjutant general, Captain W.M. Hammond, to the left to "order all my troops to advance with the center...and also to get all the troops on my left to advance with me, as I intended to carry the hill."[157]

Daniel launched this attack after 1500, encouraged by the noise of Heth's attack on his right front and the approach of Pender's line behind Heth.[158] This time the brigade finally met success. Brabble's 32nd North Carolina was able at last to push the 150th Pennsylvania back and reach the barn, where it halted for a few minutes to allow Brockenbrough's troops to come up to the crest of the hill.[159] At the same time the two regiments directly under Daniel advanced "with a chorus of terrific yelps."[160] They were initially repulsed, but attacked again and at long last began driving Stone's regiments back for good.

It is not clear exactly how much of a fight Stone's center and right actually put up once Brabble's regiment broke through to the McPherson barn. Neither Daniel nor the commanders of his 45th North Carolina and 2nd Battalion mention their final charge on this line, though they described their first two attacks in detail. Colonel Edmund L. Dana of the 143rd Pennsylvania reported that he initially repulsed this final attack "by a well directed fire, but the support both upon the right and left having been withdrawn, his superior numbers enabled the enemy to extend his lines, so as to threaten our flanks and rear."[161] Lieutenant Colonel Walton Dwight of the 149th, who was badly wounded in the leg but refused to leave the field, was also concerned about "the enemy slowly closing up on our rear in large force, also working in rapidly on our flanks."[162] Part at least of the the 149th was driven back from the road line to the barn. In order to escape mass capture Colonel Dana commanded his men to face to the rear and withdraw.[163]

Lieutenant Colonel Huidekoper of the 150th Pennsylvania returned to his regiment just before the unit's line gave way. As already noted, Huidekoper had been wounded in the elbow earlier in the action. He retired to the McPherson barn and had his arm wrapped in a cord that he had taken from his saddlebag "in fear of some such necessity for using it." He bravely returned to his unit, and found that "its right wing had been forced around the colors." In addition, "many men of the 149th Regiment had assembled about our men and were incorporating themselves in the 150th." Since he was now too weak to remain, Huidekoper had to leave the field and retreat slowly to the rear.[164] For his bravery he would be awarded the Medal of Honor in 1905.[165]

Major Chamberlin noted that, "The enemy was pressing in on all sides, even from the woods on our left, and the brigade, already beginning to feel the effects of a cross fire, was in imminent danger of capture. At last Lieutenant Dalgliesh, of the brigade staff, brought an order to withdraw."[166] In spite of the regiment's heavy losses, Lieutenant George Bell of Company H protested the order to retreat, exclaiming, "Adjutant, it is all damned cowardice; we have beaten them and will keep beating them back."[167] Though he was wounded, Adjutant Ashurst assisted Captain Sigler to pull back the left of the regiment's line, since they were the only officers still standing there. Colonel Wister, in spite of the painful wound to his mouth, went to assist Companies A, F, and D in their withdrawal from the neighborhood of the barn, which they held with a portion of the 149th.[168]

At this point there was quite a struggle for the possession of the 149th Pennsylvania's colors, which early in the engagement had been advanced at Colonel Stone's suggestion to a point some 50 yards north of the Pike at the left of the regiment, in order to draw the enemy's fire away from the main regimental line.[169] During the fighting that raged back and forth between 1400 and 1500, the flags, guarded by their faithful color guard, remained stationary, even while the 149th counterattacked to the railroad line, fell back to the roadway, and then counterattacked again.

Sometime after 1400 Major Chamberlin of the 150th Pennsylvania had seen a body of some 250 men suddenly appear in a wheat field near the colors; they had apparently crossed the railroad line much farther to the west, and from the direction of their advance appeared to be a part of Davis' brigade. This presence spurred Lieutenant Colonel Huidekoper to advance the right wing of the 150th. He led the attack in person and stopped the enemy advance, and claimed to rescue the flags of the 149th in the process; however, all other accounts were clear that he did not. Companies A, F, and D, of the 150th suffered heavily in this advance, Company F alone losing one man killed, three mortally wounded, and five or six otherwise wounded. [170]

During all this fighting, the color guard, led by Sergeant Henry G. Brehm, was protected from Daniel's advancing troops by the embankment of the western railroad cut. At about 1500 the flags were threatened from a new direction by a detachment of Davis' troops, who moved forward under the direction of Sergeant Frank Price of the 42nd Mississippi. The Confederate party of about half a dozen men crawled on their hands and knees "till they had nearly reached the desired object, when they suddenly rose, and attacked the color guard."[171]

The details of this short and nasty fight that followed were carefully gathered after the war by J.M. Bassler. Before the Confederate raiding party struck, the members of the color guard had a sharp debate whether or not to retire. Sergeant Brehm, "refused point blank, as his idea of a soldier's duty was to stick to his post as long as he was able unless sooner relieved." Brehm at last agreed to send one of the guard to the rear for orders. Fred Hoffman was selected to go and report "that there was great danger of the colors being captured unless they were ordered back to the regiment at once." Much to his dismay, Hoffman was unable to find either Colonel Stone or Lieutenant Colonel Dwight in the confusion of battle (both had been wounded), so he was unable to deliver his message. He ended up shouldering his musket and doing the best he could to assist to check the enemy in that regard.[172]

Thus there were only five members of the 149th color guard with the two flags when the Mississippians attacked. The course of the fight was recorded in an affidavit from Franklin W. Lehman of the 149th: "We were undisturbed during the progress of the battle until finally a squad of Confederate soldiers made a dash on us out of the wheat field, and that, while being startled to our feet by the rebel yell, I collided with Color Sergeant Brehm and was pushed over on my knees, my flag being tilted over the rail pile, and that it was immediately laid hold of by an enemy on the other side, while another enemy on top of the rails was aiming his gun at me; that I grabbed the barrel of said gun and turned it aside; that my assailant was shot and the flagstaff wrenched from my grasp at the time. When I got to my feet the Confederates were all around us; I saw a rebel stretched on his back and Sergeant

Brehm on top of him; I saw a Confederate striking him with the butt of the gun and another picking up the flag."[173]

At this point Lehman decided to run for help. He took the regimental state flag with him and headed for the Pike, but saw that the Confederates had driven the 149th back. He tried to get by the enemy's left flank, only to fall wounded in the leg. Lehman landed on a rail pile, and a Confederate came up and tried to wrestle the flag from him. H.H. Spayd of the color guard then ran to Lehman's assistance. He found Lehman "on his knees with his colors stretched across the rail pile and a rebel pulling at them on the other side. Frank held on with his right hand and with his left had hold of the barrel of a musket in the hands of an enemy on the top of the rails and was pushing it aside." Spayd shot one of the Confederates and then clubbed his musket and flung it at the other, who had just pulled the flag from Lehman's hands and was drawing it across the rails. The blow stunned the rebel, enabling Spayd to grab the flag. He then ran off, only to be felled by a shot from Sergeant Price, who managed to retrieve Spayd's state flag after losing the national colors that had just been in his grasp.[174]

Sergeant Frank D. Price of the 42nd Mississippi describes his role in the melee: "While at rest the flags in front of us became an interesting topic of conversation. Among the many remarks made in regard to capturing them, foolhardy was often used, by the boys...Being somewhat rested, without permission or orders, I rose upon my feet, waved my hat, and made directly for the flags. When about halfway I discovered I was about to be reinforced by 2 or 3 men from the 42nd and if not mistaken 1 or 2 from the 2nd Mississippi. I did not know Lt. R. of the 2nd, who hastened up and joined me in arms length of the flags. Poor fellow, in the very act of grasping the flag staff he fell...when in a few feet of the rail pile, with 4 bright muskets with bayonets leveled at me I did not look back, but with a super human effort I cleared the points of the bayonets and with the Pa. flag staff in my left hand, and an Enfield rifle in the right, landed in a pile of 4 live Yankees. Now comes the tug of war in earnest. My herculean antagonist [Brehm] bore one flag & all several yards down the slope toward his line of battle. Finally the staff was wrested from his grasp and away I fled back across the brow of the hill passing the rail pole, pressed hard by my heroic enemy. I became entangled in its long silken threads and fell. In an instant my pursuer is in five feet of me... he grasped the proud old flag and was making way with it across the ridge. As soon as I could recover myself, I pursued, when within about ten steps of him...he was shot."[175]

Captain W.R. Bond of Daniel's Brigade witnessed Price's raid, and saw all of his detachment felled except their leader. Price had yet one more travail to pass through before he could bring his prize to safety. A young staff officer of Daniel's brigade, "having carried some message to Heth's people, was returning by a short cut between the lines, and seeing a man with a strange flag, without noticing his uniform, he thought he, too, would get a little glory along with some bunting. Dismounting among the dead and wounded he picked up and fired several muskets at Price; but was fortunate enough to miss him." Price survived the war and lived afterwards in Mississippi.[176]

Brehm, meanwhile, had somehow fended off his attackers. One had laid hold of his flag, the National colors, and said, "this is mine," whereupon Brehm replied, "no by God it isn't." Brehm wrestled his foe to the ground, and then managed to get up and run towards the Union lines, followed by other members of the guard, Friddell and Hammel. They, too were mistaken about the location of their regiment, and in the smoke of the battle ran into a Confederate regiment. Brehm bravely dashed right through the line, only to be shot down with one of his comrades.[177]

James T. Lumpkin of Company C, 55th Virginia, saw Brehm's run for safety as he was fighting just south of the McPherson barn: "Amid the smoke, hurry and confusion of the battle, it appeared to him as if both flags had shot out of the barn. He and his nearest comrades at once directed their fire on Brehm; and when he was shot down, this fleet footed Virginian was the first to reach him." So Lumpkin carried off the 149th's national flag, and as he turned back to his own lines he passed by Bassler, who was lying wounded at the southeast corner of the McPherson barnyard. Lumpkin also brought with him the valiant Sergeant Brehm as his prisoner. Brehm, "though mortally wounded, carried his head held high, his eyes fixed to his beloved flag." He would die of his wound on 9 August in a Philadelphia hospital.[178]

Thus the 149th lost both its regimental flags, the only Union regiment on 1 July to suffer this dishonor. They were certainly not lost ingloriously.[179]

There was considerable confusion during this Union withdrawal around the McPherson house and large barn. Lieutenant Colonel Huidekoper relates that due to the absence of field officers, "all of whom were disabled, the men on the line south of the barn naturally looked for direction. Giving the order to fall back, he assisted Captain Sigler—the only officer left with this part of the command—in holding the remnant of several companies fairly in hand, and moved them through the open field towards the seminary. Sergeant Bell, of Company H, who had just been commissioned second lieutenant, but had not yet been mustered, rendered valuable assistance in the retreat, and distinguished himself by his coolness and courage throughout the day. Companies A, F and D were mostly engaged in the neighborhood of the barn, struggling in connection with the One hundred and forty-ninth against the increasing pressure from the northwest and north, when the order to retire was delivered. Colonel Wister, who had remained on the field, doing what he could by his presence and example to animate the men, although prevented by the lacerated condition of his mouth and face from commanding in person, at once recognized the difficulty of withdrawing this portion of the line, and went himself to assist in the dangerous task. The barn, which had been a protection in the earlier part of the engagement, as well as a convenient shelter for the wounded, now that the enemy had forced their way up to it, became a veritable trap for our own men. Those who were on the outside were started towards the town, but a number had occupied the building, and were firing from every opening looking towards their assailants. Besides these, there were many wounded within, and a sprinkling of stragglers from various brigades and regiments. In his anxiety to bring away all who were able to move, the colonel lingered a moment too long, and found himself, temporarily, a prisoner. The larger number of those engaged at this point, including many of the One hundred and forty-ninth, who, in the final struggle, were a good deal mixed up with our own men, succeeded in getting away, some joining the main group of the regiment as it pushed back through the fied, others uniting with a body of the One hundred and forty-ninth, led by Lieutenant-Colonel Dwight, which took the same direction. Quite a number, however, were cut off at the barn or in passing the farmhous, by the rapid closing in of the rebel lines on both sides. Among these was Captain Gimber, of Company F, who had the misfortune to be headed off in crossing the garden, close to the house."[180]

Colonel W.S. Christian of the 55th Virginia saw what happened when some of the Union troops in the barn began firing: "Pressing the enemy back foot by foot, we swept by a large barn in which many of the Yankees took refuge. Seeing them in the rear we considered that they were our prisoners; but after passing the barn they fired from the windows and the openings into the backs of our men. Whereupon Major [Charles] Lawson of the 55th was ordered to take two companies and attack the barn. An officer standing in the door of the barn, when ordered to surrender by Major Lawson, refused, and fired point blank into Lawson's face, but missed him and shot an officer just behind Lawson. The Federal officer was immediately killed by one of my men, Sergeant Allen, who brought to me his sword and pistol. After some sharp passages, about three hundred and fifty prisoners were gotten out of that barn by Major Lawson."[181]

The troops of Stone's brigade withdrew as best they could under the fire of Brockenbrough's and Daniel's men. Lieutenant Jones of the 150th Pennsylvania, who had fought near the lines of the 7th Wisconsin, led his company back in good order to the Iron Brigade's temporary line at the eastern edge of Herbst Woods. Sergeant McGinley of Company E, "with a handful of men on the left of our line, which had become the right during the retreat, in turning to fire at the pursuing enemy, caught sight of the Iron Brigade still maintaining a firm front, and moving forward with his comrades also threw in his lot with them."[182]

The rest of the 150th and surviors of the 149th Pennsylvania withdrew in groups and clusters rather than one line. The historian of the 150th relates that their men "took advantage of every favorable spot to make a defensive stand, and gave and received severe punishment. At a point nearly midway between the McPherson farm and the Seminary, where the ground swells to the dimensions of a moderate hill, the most determined resistance was made, and here a number of men were killed and wounded. Among the former was First Sergeant Weidensaul, of Company D, a most excellent soldier, whose commission as lieutenant had arrived only the previous day. The adjutant, seeing him bend over and press his hands to his body as if in pain, called out to him: 'Are you wounded?' 'No,' he replied, 'killed,' and half turning, fell dead."[183]

The 143rd Pennsylvania experienced particular difficulty during this retreat because of the pressure from Daniel's troops on its right. After the battle, General A.P. Hill told British observer Lieutenant Colonel A.J. Fremantle that he had seen "a field in the center of which he had seen a man plant the regimental color, round which the regiment had fought for some time with much obstinacy, and when at last it was obliged to retreat, the color bearer retired last of all, turning round every now and then to shake his fist at the advancing rebels. General Hill said he felt quite sorry when he saw this gallant Yankee meet his doom."[184] The name of this valiant color bearer was color Sergeant Ben Crippen of the 143rd Pennsylvania. When the 143rd erected its monument on the field 26 years later, it set the stone up on the spot where Crippen fell, bearing his likeness in marble, "life size, and in that defiant attitude in which he met his death."[185]

As the survivors of Stone's three regiments stumbled back to Seminary Ridge, a sudden calm overtook the battlefield south of the Chambersburg Pike, punctuated only by the salvoes of Wainwright's batteries at any Confederates who ventured too close. Pettigrew stopped his brigades to catch their breath and reorganize, and it would be at least half an hour until Pender's fresh troops could take up the attack.

Rodes Defeats Robinson on northern Seminary Ridge

While both sides reformed their lines in preparation for the final fatal clash south of the Chambersburg Pike, affairs came to a sudden climax on the Corps' right posted on the northern end of Seminary Ridge. As already noted, Baxter's exhausted brigade withdrew from the right around 1500 and moved southward to seek fresh ammunition, eventually deploying in support of Stewart's battery at the eastern railroad cut. This left only Paul's brigade to hold the far Union right. Two of its regiments were deployed on a north-south line along the crest of the ridge—the 94th New York on the left, then the 107th Pennsylvania, extended to a point near the Mummasburg Road, where the 16th Maine deployed at the bend in the brigade line; the 104th New York and 13th Massachusetts extended the brigade's line to the right, along the Mummasburg Road, facing the McLean farm.[186]

The Union position here was a bad one, since it had no artillery support, there were no reserves available, and there were no supports on either flank. Robinson's right had never connected properly with Von Gilsa's left near the McLean farm lane, and the XI Corps on this front was already being pressed back. The brigade's left had recently been patrolled by Cutler's exhausted brigade, but most of these troops had withdrawn farther to their left. Robinson was lucky that for the moment the Wills Woods concealed this weakness from the enemy. A final concern was the fact that Paul's men were running low on ammunition. General Robinson himself helped gather ammunition from the cartridge boxes of the dead and wounded.[187]

Since Daniel's brigade was busy engaged with Stone's Pennsylvanians a mile to the right, and Iverson's command was so decimated that it was essentially useless for further combat (except the 12th North Carolina, which was supporting Daniel's left), Rodes had just two brigades to use against Paul's command. O'Neal's brigade was still posted on the summit and eastern slope of Oak Hill. It had suffered heavily during the day, but still had its five regiments available for duty, though one (the 3rd Alabama) had drifted off to the western side of the hill. This left the weight of the attack to Rodes' last brigade, Ramseur's North Carolina command, which had already attacked and been repulsed once. Altogether Rodes had over 2000 men available to renew his attack, not counting Doles' brigade, which was making its way back towards the division following its successful attack on the XI Corps north of Gettysburg. This was not an overwhelming advantage, but Rodes' men also had the support of W. Carter's artillery battery, and were slightly (at least in Ramseur's command) fresher than Paul's. They also, in theory, had superior leadership because there was no effective brigade commander in Paul's command after their original commander was badly wounded, while Rodes' brigades still had their original leaders (even if O'Neal had been erratic).

Rodes apparently left the attack arrangements up to Ramseur, after advising his brigadier to attack the enemy, "where he had repulsed O'Neal and checked Iverson's advance."[188] Ramseur, though, had learned that it was fruitless to try to hit both wings of the angled Union line, since it was difficult to time the attacks to coincide, and if they did not, the enemy would readily switch units from one wing to the other, as they had already done several times that afternoon. Instead, he would swing his entire command against Robinson's right and rear. He would move his right wing (14th and 30th North Carolina, plus O'Neal's 3rd Alabama) to the left, over Oak Hill, and have them assault Robinson's right en masse along the Mummasburg Road, while his other two regiments (2nd and 4th North Carolina) moved forward from their position on eastern Oak Hill to support the attack. O'Neal's troops would aid the attack as they were able, and he appealed to Iverson's 12th North Carolina to threaten Robinson's left.[189]

Lieutenant Colonel Gilbert G. Prey of the 104th New York saw the Confederates massing on the McLean farm on his front, and reported this fact to General Robinson. He well understood that the enemy would greatly outnumber his troops at the point of contact, and requested reinforcements if he were to hold his position.[190] Robinson had none to give.

It took some time for Ramseur to set the stage for his attack, but it

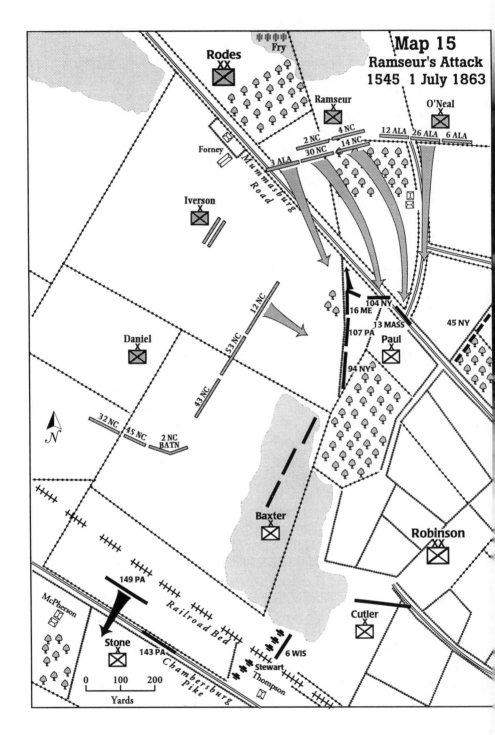

Map 15
Ramseur's Attack
1545 1 July 1863

was time well spent. A detachment of sharpshooters under Lieutenant Frank M. Marney of the 14th North Carolina was sent forward to screen the attack.[191] Colonel R.T. Bennett of the 14th North Carolina, however, did not like the prospect of attacking the Union position behind the stone wall that ran along the Mummasburg Road, and asked Ramseur, "Let me move well to the left and envelop the enemy, and lift him up to the air." Ramseur, who had other plans, replied. "No, let's go directly in on them."[192]

As Bennett anticipated, the attack by the 14th and 30th regiments was closely contested at first because of the strength of the Union position. One soldier noted, "the attack was especially fierce...and for a few minutes the fighting was terrific." Fred Philips of Ramseur's brigade recalled that, "General Ramseur formed the 14th and 30th Regiments at right angles to the rock wall, under cover of some pines on the edge of a hill, and as we reached the open field he wheeled the line to the left and sent us forward in a run to attack the enemy. There was no faltering. Every man was at his post, and some of the gallant men of the 12th North Carolina Regiment of Iverson's Brigade which had been driven back joined us. The attack was especially fierce."[193]

Colonel Francis Parker of the 30th North Carolina was badly wounded in the nose just as his regiment reached the wall. The flags of both units were riddled with bullets, and General Ramseur's fine grey horse was felled just a few yards from the wall. Ramseur was the only mounted officer to enter the charge, and was lucky to emerge unscathed. Ramseur's wounded mount was taken to the rear of the hospital tent, where it keeled over and died that night, in the process knocking the tent over on Colonel Parker.[194]

The pressure on the 14th and 30th was soon relieved by the advance of the rest of the brigade. The 2nd and 4th regiments came up on their right,[195] and Rodes pushed forward Fry's battery to aid the attack.[196] Rodes was also glad to note that "O'Neal's shattered troops, which had assembled without order on the hill, rushed forward, still without order, but with all their usual courage, into the charge."[197] The attack was also supported on the right by the 43rd and 53rd North Carolina regiments of Daniel's brigade, as well as by Iverson's 12th North Carolina.[198] In spite of all these supporting troops, the turning point in the attack did not come until the extreme left of the 14th North Carolina (which extended 100 yards beyond Robinson's right) was able to swing around behind the enemy. This maneuver finally broke the Union line and sent it reeling in confusion.[199]

The men of the 16th Maine held the center of the brigade's line near the Mummasburg Road when Ramseur's attack began. The regiment's Colonel, Charles W. Tilden, was concerned that he had no support around him, so he began to withdraw towards a more favorable position. While doing so, "an aide came from General Robinson with an order for us to advance and hold the ridge as far north as possible." A few moments later Robinson rode up to repeat the order himself. The brigade was badly shaken and needed to be withdrawn, and Robinson was selecting the 16th to be the covering force. Tilden "protested that our regiment without support couldn't hold the ridge; we numbered fewer than two hundred, all told; as well set a corporal's guard to stop the rebel army." Robinson, however, was not about to change his mind, and insisted, "Hold at all costs."[200]

Colonel Tilden sadly told his troops "You know what that means!" and ordered his troops to march back up the ridge toward the Mummasburg Road. Ahead of them was a stone wall that came in from the left and then bent back sharply to the right in order to follow the course of the road. "We got there just as a flag and a line of battle showed up across the way; we heard distinctly the commands of a rebel officer directing his men to fire; and a volley crashed, and we saw some of our men fall. Our line blazed away in reply, and the rebel flag went down, and the officer pitched headlong in the stubble. In the field across the road were dead men and scattered equipments, wreckage of a rebel repulse earlier in the day; and now there were more. But the attacking line came on, and following behind it was another, and we knew that our little regiment could not withstand the onset. With anxious hope we looked again to the rear for support—and saw that the other regiments of our brigade, our division, were falling back rapidly towards the town. The rebels were sweeping in through the fields beyond our right. The ridge could be held no longer. We were sacrificed to steady the retreat. How much time was then passing, I can't say; it was only a matter of moments before the grey lines threatened to crush us. They came on, firing from behind the wall, from fences, from the road," and forced the 16th back.[201]

The rest of Paul's regiments were not interested in aiding the 16th Maine, but retired as best they could. Ramseur noted in his report that the enemy simply "ran off the field in confusion, leaving his killed and wounded and between 800 and 900 prisoners in our hands." Brigadier General George Doles saw Paul's brigade collapse and retreat along the open eastern slope of Seminary Ridge as he was pursuing the left wing of the XI Corps back towards Gettysburg. He changed his course to try and intercept them at the railroad line west of town, but was unable to do so.[202]

Even so, Paul's brigade lost heavily in prisoners to Ramseur's determined pursuit. The brigade's right regiment, the 13th Massachusetts, lost about 100 prisoners. The regiment's historian noted that "so many men had fallen that our line looked ridiculously small to be contending with the large army corps now approaching us. The only thing we would do was to stand still and fire, though the rebel batteries were now getting in their work." At length the unit, now almost out of ammunition, was forced to fall back, "each man for himself, it being impracticale to do otherwise without losing more men....We saw at once that we had stayed at the front a little too long for our safety...over fences, into yards, through gates, anywhere an opening appeared, we rushed with all our speed to escape capture. The streets swarmed with the enemy, who kept up an incessant firing, and yelling, 'Come in here you Yankee ____!' Still we kept on, hoping to find a chance of escape somewhere. The great trouble was to know where to run for every street seemed to be occupied by the rebs and we were in imminent danger of running into their arms before we knew it. There was no time to consider; we must keep moving and take our chances."[203]

The brigade's next regiment, the 104th New York, lost over 90 captured. During the retreat Sergeant Moses of Company E of the 104th had to destroy the regiment's national flag in order to keep it from falling into Confederate hands; Sergeant David E. Curtis saved the unit's state flag, even though he was wounded.[204] The brigade's two left regiments lost even more heavily. The 94th New York was wary of being cut off on the left, and lost its colonel, Adrian R. Root, wounded and captured, as well as 175 men captured or missing, the third highest such total of any Union regiment in the entire battle. The 107th Pennsylvania, which retreated around the south side of the town, had 98 missing.[205]

The 94th New York did not follow the rest of the brigade but withdrew to the nearby woods on its left. It shifted position there on Cutler's right several times until Robinson pulled the unit back to the crest of the hill closer to the eastern railroad cut.[206]

Meanwhile the 16th Maine held on as best it could.[207] The valiant regiment was pushed back from its stone wall, and reformed in a hollow, but could not hold this position either, and fell back to the Wills Woods. It then retreated back, fighting, along the ridge, losing Captain Oliver Lowell and numerous others as well.[208]

The brave men of the 16th Maine held on in the woods, unsupported, as long as they could, until they saw they were again left without support, threatened on the front and flank. Somehow they managed to reach the railroad line by retiring gradually along the ridge until they got to the eastern railroad cut.[209] Just as they thought they might be safe, "we saw grey troops marching in from the west, and they saw us. We were caught between two fires. It was the end. For a few last moments our little regiment defended angrily its hopeless challenge, but it was useless to fight longer. We looked at our colors, and our faces burned. We must not surrender those symbols of our pride and our faith. Our color bearers appealed to the colonel, and with his consent they tore the flags from the staves and ripped the silk into shreds; and our officers and men that were near each took a shred. I have one with a golden star."[210]

Most of the regiment's surviors now found themselves captured. Colonel Tilden was taken by a tall Alabama skirmisher, who spotted him from 100 feet distance and ordered him: "Throw down that sword or I will blow your brains out." Tilden thrust his sword in the ground, and was taken away. He was confined at Libby Prison in Richmond, and managed to escape through a tunnel.[211]

Altogether 92 men and 11 officers besides Tilden were captured during the unit's retreat. Only 4 officers and 31 men managed to reassemble that evening on Cemetery Hill, under the command of Captain Daniel Marsten. During the day's action, the regiment lost 9 killed, 59 wounded, and 164 missing, a total of 78% of its 298 men, the third highest percentage loss of any Union regiment in the entire battle.[212]

Ramseur's 2nd and 4th North Carolina, which had not borne the brunt of the initial attack, led the pursuit of the retiring enemy. One of Ramseur's men remembered that "the retreat of the enemy assumed the character of a rout."[213] An officer of the 2nd North Carolina wrote his mother that, "I was fearful their running troops would crush our little brigade...we had them fairly in a pen, with only one gap open—the turnpike that led into Gettysburg—and hither they fled twenty deep, we all the while popping them as fast as we could fire."[214] Captain Owen Williams of the 2nd North Carolina regretted that his men had not been able to keep up a steady fire on the withdrawing Yankees because of the Confederate sharpshooters who got in front of his command.[215] The advancing Confederates were able to secure prisoners by the handful,[216] but the sharpest recollection Colonel Robert Bennett of the 14th North Carolina had of this advance was the difficulty of getting through the tangled vines and undergrowth, from which he startled a turkey gobbler, which "arose in distracted flight and escaped without hue or cry in his pursuit."[217]

Ramseur's pursuit of the fleeing enemy led him to the northwest corner of the town. The 4th North Carolina claimed to be the first Confederate troops to enter Gettysburg,[218] but this honor would be contested by Hays' men and the 1st and 14th South Carolina of Perrin's Brigade. Once the 2nd North Carolina entered the town, its men "rushed pell mell after them."[219] Private T.M. Gorman reported that "they hid by hundreds in houses and barns, and I had the felicity of capturing any number." Included in his take were three swords and two pistols from officers who surrendered to him.[220] Other skirmishers from the 2nd engaged a Pennsylvania regiment and took its flag.[221]

Ramseur's advance also succeeded at pressuring the Union infantry and artillery who were retreating from the eastern railroad cut, as will be shown later. Some of his troops passed around the west end of town and waited for orders to attack the Union line on Cemetery Hill. When none came, Ramseur reformed his men along Middle Street in the town. Major J.M. Lambeth was happy to see the day end since he was tired from marching 14 miles that morning and fighting all afternoon.[222]

The success of Ramseur's attack and the rapid collapse of Robinson's command encouraged Rodes' right center regiments—Iverson's 12th North Carolina and Daniel's 43rd and 53rd North Carolina—to press their attack, also. Colonel William Owens of the 53rd reported that he fronted, moved forward to the Wills Woods, and there joined the 12th North Carolina for an advance on the eastern railroad cut.[223] This attack readily pushed back the few Union troops there and was soon threatening the right flank of Stewart's battery and its supporting troops posted at the eastern railroad cut. Meanwhile Daniel's 43rd North Carolina, joined by the 2nd North Carolina Battalion and 32nd North Carolina on its right, made a head on assault against the last Union line north of the Chambersburg Pike.[224]

Since the culmination of this attack came at the same time (1615-1630) that Pender's men pushed the remnants of the I Corps' left wing off from their east line on Seminary Ridge, it will be described later in this chapter.

Pender's Climactic Attack on I Corps' Last Line

While Ramseur and his supports were driving Paul's brigade from northern Seminary Ridge, A.P. Hill was preparing Pender's fresh division to enter the action on the Confederate left. Pender had 6400 fresh men in four veteran brigades.[225] As already noted, he had first formed more than a mile west of Herr Ridge when he first arrived on the field late in the morning, with his brigades in the following order from left to right: Thomas', Lane's, Scales' and Perrin's. By noon the division moved forward to Herr Ridge to support Heth's division and the artillery formed there. Not long afterward, Lane's brigade was shifted to the division's far right to help deal with the Union cavalry that was annoying Heth's right near the Fairfield Road.[226]

When Heth sent his division (less Davis' battered brigade) to attack Doubleday's line on McPherson Ridge at 1430, Pender advanced his men (less Thomas' brigade) in close support. His orders were to support Heth if needed, and he sent his adjutant general to Heth to let him know this. Heth, though, declined to ask for assistance, since "he was pressing the enemy from one position to another." As a result, Pender's troops had no choice but to continue their slow advance, "keeping within close supporting distance of the troops in front."[227]

In retrospect, it was most unfortunate for Heth's division that Pender's troops were not called forward to help at the height of its attack. Any one of Pender's fresh brigades could have helped Brockenbrough resolve the half hour stalemate he faced trying to push back the 2nd and 7th Wisconsin regiments. In addition, more support for the 11th and 26th North Carolina could have avoided the heavy casualties these units had to suffer. Lastly, prompt support of Heth's attack and exploitation of his success at driving the Iron Brigade out of Herbst Woods might have enabled the Confederates to overrun Seminary Ridge before the Union infantry could reform there. Of course, the principal reason that Pender's men were not called forward was the fact that Heth had been wounded and knocked unconscious early in the attack on Herbst Woods. It took awhile for Pettigrew to be informed of this and then take up command of the division, and it is unlikely anyone told him of Pender's and Hill's wish that Pender's men be called forward when needed.

Hill, though, must bear some of the blame for not committing

Pender's men earlier or in a more effective manner. He surely must have been aware of the severity of the fighting on Heth's front, yet he did not send Pender promptly to his aid. Nor did he consider moving any or all of Pender's men to the right in an effort to outflank Doubleday's line even farther to the south. There was a handy road available on the reverse slope of Herr Ridge that could safely have led any Confederate troops to the Fairfield Road, but no one in the Confederate high command seems to have seriously considered this option. They were no doubt influenced by three primary factors—the known activity of Gamble's troopers on this flank, an absence of useable cavalry of their own to scout the area, and the stubborn fight put up by the detachment of sharpshooters from the 20th New York State Militia posted at the Harman farm. Hill had no cavalry attached to his command, and Ewell (who was not in very close touch with Hill anyway) had already sent his available cavalry from the Oak Hill area to Early's command on the left.

Pender also must share a little of the blame for not pushing forward sooner to support Heth's men. Since his men were moving forward behind Heth's attack, and did not stay behind on the crest of Herr Ridge after Heth advanced, Pender surely was aware of the difficulty Heth was having against the Union troops in Herbst Woods. Yet he does not appear to have consulted with either Heth (or Pettigrew once Heth was wounded) or Hill about when to join the attack, anytime between 1430 and 1600. A more enterprising commander—and Pender was certainly a good one— might have moved more promptly, and independently if necessary, to aid Pettigrew and Brockenbrough.

It is also strange that Pender did not use his full division when he finally did launch his attack. When he began his advance, he left his far left brigade, Thomas' 1300-man Georgia command, behind as a reserve and support to the artillery batteries. Nor did he even call Thomas forward when some of the artillery on Herr Ridge was advanced to shell the retreating Federals. Pender, though, may have left Thomas behind on specific orders from Hill. Thomas states in his battle report that he was assigned his position on Pender's left specifically by Hill. In addition, Pender's assistant adjutant general, Major Joseph A. Engelhard, states that Thomas "was retained by Lieutenant General Hill to meet a threatened advance from the left."[228] It is not clear exactly what threat Pender felt at that time, particularly since he must have known that Johnson's and Anderson's divisions were approaching the battlefield on the Chambersburg Pike. Pender would never get a chance to write a

Gettysburg report, since he would be mortally wounded on 2 July, and died 15 days later.

Thus Pender would use only three of his brigades in the coming attack on Doubleday's last line: Scales' 1405 North Carolinians would advance on the left, with their left approximately at the Chambersburg Pike; Perrin's 1600 South Carolinians would attack in the center, directly towards the Seminary; and Lane's 1734 North Carolinians would advance on the division's right, where their attention would be diverted by Gamble's cavalry.[229] Pender's attack would also receive support on its left from Daniel's brigade of Rodes' division and some of Archer's men from Heth's.

Doubleday was fortunate that Pettigrew pulled his regiments back to reorganize just before Pender launched his attack at about 1400. This delay gave him a much needed respite of about 15 minutes in which to organize his defensive line on Seminary Ridge. The new line would cover about 600 yards between the Chambersburg Pike on the right and the Fairfield Road on the left. Almost exactly at its center stood the large main building of the Seminary, in front of which Robinson's troops earlier in the day had begun erecting a breastwork of fence rails, little realizing it would be used as a rallying point for other troops that afternoon.[230] The ground to the front and left of the Seminary was also lightly wooded, so offering some cover to the men on the left of the line. Additional cover was provided by fence lines running some 40 or so yards west of and parallel to the road along the crest of the ridge. The ridge at this point was not particularly high, but did rise noticeably enough above the swale between it and eastern McPherson's Ridge. Most significant of all was the fact that the ground west of the Seminary was all open fields as far as the Herbst Woods, ¼ mile away, thereby offering a completely free field of fire to the defenders.

The backbone of Doubleday's line was formed by 15 guns of Wainwright's artillery battalion. As already noted, Stevens' six Napoleons had already been posted north of the Seminary near the Chambersburg Pike; it had been in reserve all day and never left the Seminary Ridge line except to move to this location from its earlier position farther to the left on the ridge at about 1400.[231] Cooper's three 3-inch rifles were posted at the center of the line, on the front and right of the main Seminary building, after they were pulled back from Biddle's line on southern McPherson's Ridge. Lieutenant Wilber's two guns of Breck's battery, which had been briefly posted on Stone's line, pulled back with Wadsworth's troops and formed on the Chambersburg Pike. Breck's other four guns, which fell back after being just a few lines on Biddle's front in order to escape capture, were formed about 100 yards south of the Seminary "in rear of the belt of timber to the left of that building." Doubleday's defensive line near the Seminary was also aided by the six Napoleons of Stewart's battery, which were deployed astride the eastern railroad cut on the northern side of the Chambersburg Pike. As already discussed in Chapter IV, Wainwright's fifth battery, Hall's 2nd Maine battery, had suffered so badly that morning that it had only three serviceable guns, and so was being held in reserve on Cemetery Hill. This line of guns (21 including Stewart's) was by far the most effective concentration of Union artillery yet drawn up that day. The cannons were so closely deployed from the Seminary north to the Pike that they were in places only five yards apart.[232]

Stevens' guns had no infantry support at all for over an hour after Paul's brigade was sent to the right. Nevertheless they were fully prepared for action when the time came. They actively supplied support for the troops retreating from McPherson's Ridge by shooting over the heads of their infantry and by using canister to blast any Confederate units that advanced too close. At this time Captain Stevens even advanced one of his pieces to the front of his main line in order to be better able to fire spherical case and shell at the rapidly advancing enemy.[233]

Cooper's battery, which was stationed in front of the Seminary, was also busy from 1500-1600. It was active in helping to repel the attacks by Archer and Daniel on Stone's line, and engaged in counter battery fire with Brander's battery after the latter moved to a hill east of Willoughby Run and north of the western railroad cut. All the while it was subject to a crossfire from Fry's battery on Oak Hill. The battery then helped drive back Pettigrew's troops after they defeated the Iron Brigade, except the 26th North Carolina, which took shelter in Herbst Woods.[234]

The first Union troops to fall back to the Seminary Ridge line were Biddle's regiments. Since they were on the left of McPherson's Ridge line, Biddle's men reformed to the south of the Seminary when they pulled back. As already noted, the brigade's left flank regiment, the 121st Pennsylvania, was broken first, and retreated in a scattered condition to the rear. Major Alexander Biddle of the 121st reported that his men "retreated to the woods around the hospital and here maintained a scattering fire." Thus, in his case, it was the woods near the Seminary, not Wainwright's artillery line, that persuaded his men to stop and reform. Once they saw other broken regiments also begin to fall back to this line, the men of the 121st prepared to defend "the fence of the hospital with great determination."[235] Their flag had been carried to safety here by Color Sergeant Harvey despite the fact that its staff was shattered in three places.[236]

Colonel Theodore Gates wrote later that Biddle had formed the 142nd and 151st Pennsylvania on Seminary Ridge before his two regiments (121st Pennsylvania and 20th New York State Militia) arrived there, but this does not seem likely to have been the case in view of the 121st's rapid flight and Lieutenant Colonel George McFarland's statement that he held the 151st in place after its costly counterattack until all the troops on his left and right had withdrawn.[237] As already noted, Colonel Gates of the 20th New York State Militia helped steady his men during the retreat by carrying the regimental colors personally. He claimed his men halted as often as they could reload. This may have caused them to reach the new line after the 121st and 142nd Pennsylvania on either flank. Once the line was steadied, Gates returned the flag to his color guard. Among the 20th's last casualties during this withdrawal were Privates Duane Bush, who was killed, and Jessie Kidney, who was wounded and captured.[238] Lieutenant Colonel George F. McFarland was barely able to pull his 151st Pennsylvania back from the line it held to the left rear of Herbst Woods after its desperate counterattack. He reported that he fell back in good order to the temporary breastworks he had occupied before his attack, with the enemy following "closely but cautiously."[239] He took a position with "fragments of Meredith's brigade" on his right and "portions of the twentieth New York State Militia, one hundred and twenty-first Pennsylvania volunteers and one hundred and forty second volunteers" on his left. This makes it likely that Biddle's four regiments formed in front of the Seminary in the same order in which they had been fighting on McPherson's Ridge. As soon as he reached the breastworks, McFarland was met by an unknown mounted officer who was carrying the flag of the 142nd Pennsylvania and wanted to know if it was his. McFarland was aware that the 142nd's Colonel, Robert P. Cummins, had fallen, so he ordered the flag to be placed on his left, where "portions of the regiment rallied around it and fought bravely."[240]

The Iron Brigade occupied the center of the Seminary Ridge line. The 19th Indiana probably arrived first; as previously noted, its lieutenant colonel, W.W. Dudley, had just been felled while waving the unit's flag. The 19th's flag was carried during the withdrawal to Seminary Ridge by Captain Hollon Richardson of Meredith's staff, who bore it "on horseback at the head of the Iron Brigade."[241] Likewise Colonel Henry A. Morrow of the 24th Michigan was wounded just before he reached the Seminary line while carrying one of his regiment's flags.[242] The exhausted men of the Iron Brigade were pleased to find ready made breastworks awaiting them when they reached the Seminary. Colonel S.J. Williams of the 19th Indiana reported that "I placed the remnant of my command behind a barricade of logs and rails, hastily constructed after the commencement of the fight."[243] Colonel William W. Robinson of the 7th Wisconsin noted that "Down the slope, some 40 yards in front of this battery (5th Maine), I found a slight breastwork of loose rails, which, I suppose had been thrown together by some of our troops in the earlier part of the day, behind which I threw the regiment."[244] When Major John Mansfield pulled his 2nd Wisconsin back to the ridge, he formed " on the right of the brigade already in position."[245] This means that the 2nd was the last unit of the Iron Brigade to retire, and that the brigade's regiments formed on this line in the same order in which they had fought on McPherson's Ridge. Some accounts relate that the Iron Brigade's line bowed westward somewhat in front of the Seminary and Cooper's guns.[246] The 2nd Wisconsin was in front of Stevens' battery, and connected with Dana's line farther to the right. The 2nd almost lost its colors during the retreat. Their bearer was shot down, and Corporal J.J. Little had to dash back to retrieve them before they were captured.[247]

Some of the men of the 7th Wisconsin were so close to Wainwright's cannons that they were accidentally hit by their own artillery fire. Lieutenant Colonel John Callis wrote that after he formed his men in the orchard near the Seminary, "here our own batteries that had been firing over our heads from the top of the Seminary Ridge was so near that the grape and cannister began to kill our own men; when I raised my sabre above my head waving it, and at the top of my voice ordering the capt. of the battery to cease firing. But amid the roar of musketry and screeching of shot and shell through the air he seemed not to hear me."[248]

When Stone's three Pennsylvania regiments retired to the rear from McPherson's Ridge, they formed on the right of Doubleday's line, between the Iron Brigade and the railroad cut. The order of the brigade's regiments in this line is not clear; if they formed in the same relative position as they had been fighting earlier, the 150th Pennsylvania would have been on the left, the 149th Pennsylvania in the center, and the 143rd Pennsylvania on the right. Colonel Rufus Dawes of the 6th

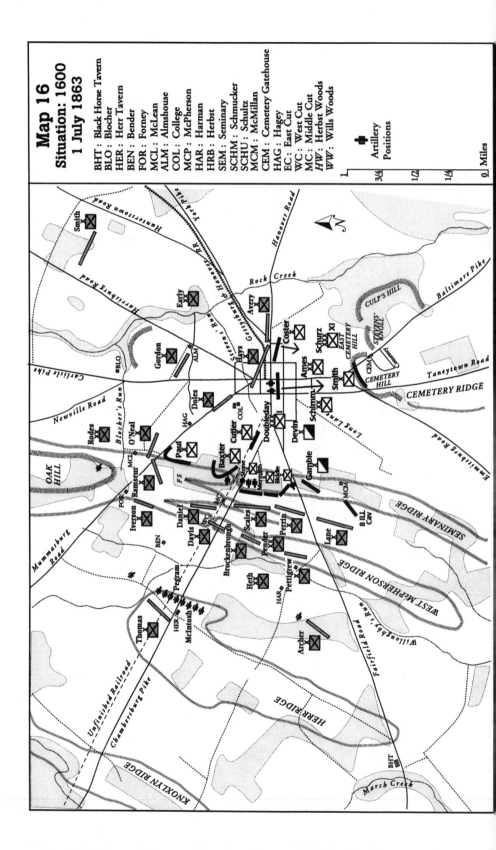

Map 16
Situation: 1600
1 July 1863

BHT : Black Horse Tavern
BLO : Blocher
HER : Herr Tavern
BEN : Bender
FOR : Forney
MCL : McLean
ALM : Almshouse
COL : College
MCP : McPherson
HAR : Harman
HRB : Herbst
SEM : Seminary
SCHM : Schmucker
SCHU : Schultz
MCM : McMillan
CEM : Cemetery Gatehouse
HAG : Hagey
EC : East Cut
WC : West Cut
MC : Middle Cut
HW : Herbst Woods
WW : Wills Woods

Artillery
Positions

Miles
0
1/4
1/2
3/4
1

Wisconsin, however, says that the men of Stone's and Meredith's brigades lay "flat upon their bellies...mixed up together in one line of battle."[249] Stone's regiments apparently formed in front of Stevens' guns, since Stevens mentions how the infantry on his front pulled back and crouched under the muzzles of his cannons in order to avoid their fire.[250]

Several sources agree that it was 1600 when Pender began his attack on Doubleday's Seminary Ridge line.[251] The order must have come to him from Hill, for Pender's assistant adjutant general, Major Joseph A. Engelhard, reported that Pender received instructions "to pass General Heth's division, if found at a halt, and charge the enemy's position."[252] As Pender's men pushed forward, they found Pettigrew's troops exhausted and low in numbers, but not yet willing to give up the fight. Most, though, remained on McPherson's Ridge while Pender's men pushed forward. The significant exception was the casualty ridden 26th North Carolina, which appears to have joined Pender's men in their last attack on Doubleday's new line, along with a few companies of the 11th North Carolina.[253]

Brigadier General A.M. Scales led the left wing of Pender's attack. He advanced with his left flank on the Chambersburg Pike and his five regiments of 1400 men extending to the right in the following order: 38th, 13th, 34th, 22nd and 16th North Carolina; at some point in the attack, probably due to pressure from Perrin's brigade in the center, Scales' units slid slightly to the left, pushing the 38th North Carolina to the northern side of the turnpike.[254] General Scales reported that in his initial advance in support of Heth's division at 1430, his men fell under "a pretty severe artillery fire from the enemy in my front." As he was moving forward, he saw some of Davis' men turned back by Stone's troops along the Chambersburg Pike: "I observed a regiment or two of the enemy about half a mile in our front, marching in line of battle parallel to the turnpike, and directly toward the road. They soon engaged a regiment of our men.... who were advancing on the opposite side of the road. A heavy fight ensued, in which our friends, overpowered by numbers, gave way. Seeing this, the brigade quickened their step, and pressed on with a shout to their assistance. The enemy, with their flank exposed to our charge, immediately gave way, and fled in great confusion to the rear."[255]

After helping break Stone's line, Scales directed his men to continue eastward in close support of Brockenbrough's troops: "We pressed on until coming up upon the line in our unit, which was at a halt and lying down. I received orders to halt, and wait for this line to advance.

This they soon did, and pressed forward again in quick time that I might keep in supporting distance, I again ordered an advance, and after marching one-fourth of a mile or more, again came upon the front line, halted and lying down. The officers on this part of the line informed me that they were without ammunition and would not advance farther."[256]

Scales immediately ordered his own men to take up the advance. His North Carolinians "passed over them, on the ascent, crossed the ridge, and commenced the descent just opposite the theological seminary."[257] Scales would have done better to have stopped to reconnoiter what was in his front before he charged. Had he done so, he would have seen Wainwright's twenty-one cannons lined up directly in his front, ready to sweep the field against any troops who advanced against them—as indeed would happen in a moment. The Confederates had more than enough artillery available, and he could have called for any number of fresh batteries to come up and form on McPherson's Ridge as a counter battery. Scales could then have held back, supporting these guns, while the rest of the division broke or went around Doubleday's left flank.

Such, though, was not to be the case. Scales impetuously led his men forward in a valiant charge that was mowed down with one of the most devastating artillery barrages of the battle, if not the war. Scales continues: "Here the brigade encountered a most terrific fire of grape and shell on our flank, and grape and musketry in front. Every discharge made sad havoc in our line, but we still pressed on at a double-quick until we reached the bottom, a distance of about 75 yards from the ridge we had just crossed, and about the same distance from the college in our front. Here I received a painful wound from a piece of shell, and was disabled. Our line had been broken up, and now only a squad here and there marked the place where regiments had rested."[258]

The following account testifies to the impact of the Union fire on Scales' line: "The whole line of battle from right to left was one continuous blaze of fire. The space between the two ridges was completely filled with the thin blue smoke of the infantry, making it difficult to distinguish friend from foe, while the artillery from their higher position belched forth a tremendous fire of shot and shell, moving their deadly missiles in rapid succession into the ranks of the enemy advancing on our direct front, covering themselves for the moment in dense clouds of white smoke. Our infantry, by the overwhelming numbers of the enemy, five to one were forced back upon a line with the artillery, some of them crouching under the very muzzles of the guns of the Fifth [Maine] Battery to avoid its fire. When our front was clear and within canister range, using double charges, the guns of the Fifth Battery were turned to the right on the columns of the enemy, and when their first line was within about one hundred yards of the Seminary it was brought to a halt by Stewart's, Stevens', Reynolds', and Cooper's batteries—Stevens expending about fifty-seven rounds of canister. But the enemy's second line, supported by a column deployed from the Cashtown or Chambersburg Pike, pushed on, and in the face of the most destructive fire that could be put forth from all the troops in position."[259]

Captain Robert Beecham of the 2nd Wisconsin, which was stationed alongside Stevens' guns, was also overwhelmed by the destruction he saw: "These guns were brimmed with shell or double shotted with canister; they were carefully posted by the best field artillerymen in the army; every man was at his station; and they were awaiting this very opportunity. The charging Confederates were brave men—in fact, no braver ever faced death in any case, and none ever faced a more certain death! Almost at the same moment, as if every lanyard was pulled by the same hand, this line of artillery opened, and Seminary Ridge blazed with a solid sheet of flame, and the missiles of death that swept its western slopes no human beings could endure. After a few moments of the belching of the artillery, the blinding smoke shut out the sun and obstructed the view."[260]

The blasts of Union canister, case shot and shell had totally destroyed Scales' command in just a few minutes. One brigade member sadly reported that this was the "first time in its history" the brigade was repulsed.[261] Every brigade field officer but one was felled, and some companies had no line officers left. The 34th North Carolina lost 150 of the 180 men with which it had entered the fight. One member of the 38th North Carolina wrote of this ill fated charge: "The regiment being on the flank, encountered a most terrific fire of grape and musketry in front. Every discharge made sad loss in the line, but the troops pressed on double quick until the bottom was reached. By this time the line was badly broken. Every officer in Scales' brigade except one, Lieutenant Gardman, upon whom the command devolved, was disabled, 400 men killed, wounded and missing. The loss of the thirty-eighth was 100 in killed, and wounded or captured. General Scales and Adjutant-General Riddick were wounded, and Major Clark killed. Colonel Hoke, Colonel Ashford, Colonel Lowrance, Captain Thoburg, acting Major, were among the wounded."[262] The brigade's casualties were so great that when evening fell only 500 of its men, "depressed, dilipated and almost disorganized," could be mustered.[263]

The bravery of Scales' men in the face of this hailstorm of iron and lead can be seen in the following anecdote related by Brigadier General John B. Gordon of Early's division. In 1897 he had the pleasure of meeting a one armed hero of Gettysburg named W.F. Faucette who was residing in Big Falls, North Carolina. "He was a color bearer of his regiment the Thirteenth North Carolina: In a charge during the first day's battle at Gettysburg, his right arm, with which he bore the colors, was shivered and almost torn from its socket. Without halting or hesitating, he seized the falling flag in his left hand, and, with his blood spouting from the severed arteries and his right arm dangling at his side, he still rushed to the front, shouting to his comrades, 'Forward, forward.'"[264]

The disaster that met Scales' command left the brunt of the division's attack to be carried by Perrin's brigade on Scales' right. Perrin's command had about 1500 men in four regiments available for action, in the following order from left to right: 14th, 1st (Provisional Army), 12th, and 13th South Carolina.[265] The brigade's fifth regiment, the 1st South Carolina Rifles, had been left behind on guard duty.[266] The command formed the center of the division's line when it first reached the field and formed on Knoxlyn Ridge. Before the brigade began its first advance, Colonel Perrin directed the men "to move forward without firing. That they were not to stop under any circumstances, but to close in, press the enemy close, and rout it from its position."[267] As already noted, Perrin's men made a series of advances until they came up behind the Confederate artillery line formed on Herr Ridge. One member of the brigade noted that, "we were advanced some half a mile across the wheat fields, and then rested an hour or more. Now our artillery become more active on the left and in front, and skirmish firing could be heard at some distance before us. The musketry would increase and falter, but, on the whole, became greater. We made a second advance of about the same distance as the first, and halted. These advances in line of battle are the most fatiguing exercise I had in the army. Now the perspiration poured from our bodies. The battle began in earnest. Heth's division, which was on the first line, became regularly engaged. Volleys of musketry ran along his line, accompanied by the shrill rebel cheer. Many of the enemy's balls fell among us who were on the second line, but I recall no farther result than the startling of our nerves by their whistling past our ears and slapping the trees before us."[268]

Perrin reported that he held this position until about 1500, when he moved forward in support of Heth's attack on the Union line along McPherson's Ridge.[269] The line as it advanced passed over an open meadow with a burning house on the right (Harman's), crossed over a "small stream," and then went up the "smooth hill beyond," where it stopped in close support of Heth's division."[270] Thomas Littlejohn recalled seeing a number of women and children scurrying from danger as his line advanced. Near "Willowby Branch" was a particularly sad spectacle of a woman leading a cow, followed by several crying children.[271] Before advancing, the men of the brigade had been reminded "to hold fire, until ordered, press forward, and close in on the enemy."[272]

Perrin held his line here until shortly after 1400, when General Pender rode up to him in person and ordered him "to move forward when I saw Gen. Scales on my left move saying at the same time that his whole line would move, and that if we came upon Heath's division at a halt fighting to move on and engage the enemy closely and manage my brigade according to my own judgement."[273] After the advance was resumed, the brigade "soon came up with and passed Brigadier General Pettigrew's exhausted brigade, the men of which seemed much exhausted by several hours' hard fighting."[274] J.F.J. Caldwell of the 1st South Carolina vividly recalled that "the field was thick with wounded hurrying to the rear, and the ground was grey with dead and disabled. There was a general cheer for South Carolina as we moved past them. They had fought well, but like most new soldiers, had been content to stand and fire instead of charging."[275] Colonel Perrin, however, noted that where he passed Pettigrew's line, "the poor fellows could scarely raise a cheer for us as we passed."[276] Some of the North Carolinians cried out that "we would all be killed if we went forward. The line did not halt for these men, but opened up to let them pass to the rear."[277]

Perrin's men moved bravely forward "with regular steps and a well dressed line" despite the shell and canister that rained from the Union artillery that had "a perfectly clear, unobstructed fire on us" and fired with "fatal accuracy." The brigade lost heavily, especially on its left, but continued on without firing a shot.[278] Thomas Littlejohn, however, remembered that "they began throwing grapeshot at us by the bushel it seems. They shot too high for us as the shots went over our heads. Had they been a little lower, I don't see how any of us could have escaped. As soon as we came in full sight we loaded and continued to advance." Only one man of his company, Tom Willis, was killed in this advance, struck by a grapeshot on the head.[279] J.A. Leach remembered a heavy oblique fire that came from the left, and was almost hit by a can of canister shot that passed just in front of him.[280]

Perrin took advantage of the ravine between east McPherson's Ridge and Seminary Ridge to reform his line, since it offered a bit of shelter from the enemy artillery fire. He then repeated his orders to his regimental commanders "not to allow a gun to be fired at the enemy until they received orders to do so," and renewed his advance "preserving an alignment with General Scales."[281]

Scales' men, however, were unable to pass beyond the ravine because of the intensity of the Union artillery fire already described. Perrin's troops met the same fire, which was not as intense as on Scales' front, and pushed forward into the teeth of the storm. Their commander wrote in his report, "As soon as the brigade commenced ascending the hill in front, we were met by a furious storm of musketry and shells from the enemy's batteries to the left of the road near Gettysburg; but the instructions I had given were scrupulously observed—not a gun was fired."[282]

Colonel Perrin proudly reported that "the brigade received the enemy's fire without faltering," but the view was different from the men in the ranks. J.D.F. Caldwell of the 1st South Carolina noted that "at one time, the line wavered under this murderous fire which we could not return."[283] Perrin privately admitted to Governor Bonham soon after the battle, that the men of the 14th South Carolina for a moment seemed ready to lie down and return the enemy's fire, as Scales' troops were doing, but they soon resumed the charge.[284]

Colonel Perrin must have seen his line falter (though he would not admit it in his report), and boldly rode his horse through the lines of the 1st South Carolina to lead the charge in person. Miraculously, he was not struck down. His troops, "filled with admiration for such courage defied the whole fire of the enemy" followed with a shout "that was itself half a victory."[285] As one soldier put it, "to stop was destruction. To retreat was disaster. To go forward was orders."[286]

Perrin, who did not report his own role in leading this charge, reported that "we continued the charge without opposition, except from artillery, which maintained a constant and most galling fire upon us."[287] This fire came primarily from the three rifled guns of Cooper's battery. Lieutenant James A. Garner of that command later recalled, "Captain Cooper caused our immediate front at the barricade to be cleared of our infantry, and then bearing the guns slightly to the left, poured into Perrin's troops a most disastrous fire of double charges of canister. Our immediate supports and the infantry to our left in the grove...at the same fired deadly volleys of musketry. The severity of this fire staggered and checked Perrin and almost annihilated the left of his brigade, his troops being wholly swept away from the front of our guns. Of all these attacking forces a single color bearer only, with a bravery to be admired, reached the rail barricade in front of us."[288] Perrin acknowledged that, "Here we met the most destructive fire of musketry, grape & canister, I have ever been exposed to during the war. It was, however, but a volley."[289]

There was some Union infantry drawn up in a field to Perrin's front, but they withdrew to their main line "as we got within range of them." About 200 yards from the Union line the brigade crossed a fence line and shuddered as the Yankees fired another destructive volley of musketry.[290] One soldier noted that this fire was "particularly heavy on the two right regiments, for at that point the enemy were protected by a stone fence. The line passed on, many of the men throwing away their knapsacks and blankets to keep up. Struggling and panting, but cheering and closing up, they went, through the shells, through the minie balls, heeding neither the dead who sank down by their sides, nor the fire from the front which killed them, until they threw themselves desperately on the line of the Federals."[291]

As the brigade's line reached the edge of the grove Perrin saw the 14th South Carolina on his left staggered for a moment by the severity of the enemy's musketry: "It looked to us as though the regiment was entirely destroyed." A soldier from the 14th South Carolina later related how difficult and costly this charge was: "At charge bayonets, the enemy were behind a rock fence and we could hear their officers distinctly encourage their fire until the command to fire was given. Thirty-four of our thirty-nine men fell."[292]

The 14th was receiving a deadly enfilade fire, and Perrin now for the first time noted that he was without support on the left or right. The remnants of Scales' battered command, who had been valiantly rallied by their wounded commander and by General Pender and his staff, had advanced to the fence line 200 yards from the enemy, but halted to return the enemy's fire there and proceeded no farther. To the right, Lane's brigade was nowhere in sight.[293] Perrin's men were taking their assault alone.

The Confederate attack might well have been turned back at this point, had Perrin not noticed that the left of the Union line had a weakness where their line of breastworks petered out. "I now directed the First Regiment, under Major McGeary, to oblique to the right, to avoid a breastwork of rails behind, where I discovered the enemy was posted, and then to change front to the left, and attack his flank." The attack succeeded wonderfully at flanking Biddle's exhausted men, and began rolling up the Union left flank. The two regiments, elated in their victory, pushed forward towards the Seminary building, where they met some Union troops "strongly posted behind a stone wall near and to the left of the college." This line, too, was dislodged in a few moments.[294]

J.A. Leach, however, had a different impression of the reason for the 1st South Carolina's change in course. He saw that the regiment's right wing had to contend with a post and board fence "that run obliquely in our front," and was very difficult to cross. It was this fence, Leach thought, that forced his regiment to swing to the left and strike the enemy line in a mass: "There was no artillery on our right that I saw. Now about our obliquing to the left, we did not oblique but was driven in by this board fence, into the grove in one solid body, which of course at this point we were not in good order. But we commenced to fire up behind the breastworks in front of the seminary. The troops remained in breastworks while we fired three or four rounds then retreated down behind the seminary into town."[295]

The success of Perrin's enfilading attack by over 600 relatively fresh troops shattered the hope of Colonel Gates and many other Union officers that they might be able to hold on until the Confederates were driven back or reinforcements came up. When his regiment first formed on this line, Gates was encouraged by the easy repulse of Pettigrew's feeble advance. He wrote that he "rode through the strip of woods at this time, and sat on his horse several minutes watching the right and left of the rebel line, while immediately in front that there was not a Confederate to be seen except dead and wounded."[296] But the Confederates sent in a second line, and no reinforcements came up to help the I Corps.

This was certainly not for want of trying by Doubleday. At 1600 he sent Captain E.P. Halstead to Howard for reinforcements and orders. Halstead found Howard in the cemetery near the gate, and remembered that the general looked "the picture of despair." After hearing that Howard had no reinforcements to send (Howard claimed he had only one regiment in reserve), Halstead "asked if he had any orders to give, and called his attention to the enemy then advancing in line of battle overlapping our left by nearly half a mile. He looked in that direction and replied rather sharply: 'Those are nothing but rail fences, sir.' I said,

'I beg your pardon General, if you will take my glass you will see something besides fences.'" Howard directed a staff officer to look, and he confirmed Halstead. The general next told Halstead, "go to General Buford, give him my compliments, and tell him to go to Doubleday's support." When Halstead asked where to find Buford, Howard replied that he did not know, and thought he was somewhere to the east of the hill.[297]

As Perrin's attack began, Colonel Biddle was struck by a musket ball in the scalp while conversing with Gates. The wound was quite painful, and he had to retire to the rear, but soon returned to action with his head in bandages. Gates was left in temporary command of the brigade while Biddle was absent, and during this time his horse received no less than five wounds. Lieutenant George Brankstone of Company E of the 20th was shot through the head, and drummer Daniel Treat of Company D saw his brother Amos felled by "balls through his breast and head." Before the battle he told his brother "Tell father if I fall, I won't die a coward." He certainly kept his word, for as he breathed out his last, he encouraged his comrades to "stick to the colors, boys."[298]

Major Alexander Biddle of the 121st Pennsylvania saw Perrin's flank attack developing and reported to his brigade commander that "the enemy were moving out on our left flank with the intention of closing in on the only opening in the barricade." Word came back for him to return his troops to the fence barricade. From there he was unable to check the progress of the enemy, and his left flank was soon turned.[299]

The 121st's regimental historian relates how a case of mistaken identity allowed the Confederates to close in on his unit: "Troops moving in a direction parallel with its own line from a point on the right, and not over one hundred and fifty yards in front, were seen marching, as if on parade, toward the left flank. The regiment opened on them without ceremony, but failed to draw their fire, and the officers gave the order to 'stop firing on our own men.' For a short interval, during which the men had an opportunity to take a good look at their new friends, the enemy, everything was quiet, but, suspecting, they were on the alert, with every piece loaded and ready for use. Suddenly their new adversaries halted, and, facing the regiment, deliberately opened their fire, which was returned with promptness, and quite a while the contest raged in the wood alongside the seminary, with determination on both sides. The enemy being in full view and our men having had somewhat of a rest during the lull and partly protected by a slight barricade of rails and boards from fences, felt fully competent to contest the ground, and the thinning out of the rebel ranks soon gave evidence that the calculation was correct. The Confederates, facing the fire without flinching, fell fast, the Union musketry being one continuous rattle, under which no line of troops could long endure. To the dismay of the men holding this position, however, it was ascertained that the rebel forces were marching at this time far beyond and in rear of their flank, and to save themselves from capture they were compelled to 'get up and get' in the most approved fashion, hastening on, without semblance of order, through and beyond the town of Gettysburg, and halting on Cemetery Ridge." [300]

Once his flank was so badly turned, the commander of the 121st felt that he had no choice but to take his regimental colors "with the few men left with them" and pull back through the hospital grounds towards the town.[301] His men saw the urgency of the situation, and hastened back "without semblance of order" to save themselves.[302]

Colonel Chapman Biddle saw that the 121st was driven back, and conferred hastily with Gates. The two concluded that it was impracticable to remain any longer.[303] Gates later explained that "at this time nearly if not quite all our troops were in full retreat upon Gettysburg, and our brigade was exposed to a murderous fire in front and on both flanks. It was impossible to hold the position longer without sacrificing the brigade." The troops moved off in "tolerable order," with the 20th New York State Militia covering the rear under a heavy enemy fire, on its flanks as well as its rear.[304]

Captain John Cook of the 20th's Company I was busy directing fire into Perrin's left and did not hear the order to retreat. All at once he saw the troops around him begin to fall back, and then he spotted the 20th's flag near the Seminary. He realized "that meant an order to retreat," and promptly pulled back in an attempt to avoid capture. As he neared the Seminary he found Captain Daniel McMahon of Company D lying on the ground with a badly wounded thigh. McMahon entreated Cook to help him, and Cook corralled some other soldiers to assist him in carrying the wounded officer to the other side of the Seminary building and "down the walk that sloped from its front across the lawn." By then Cook realized that his weight was delaying his benefactors too much, so he asked them to leave him at a small house on the north side of the lawn. Just at that time some Confederates spotted the group and fired, wounding two of Cook's helpers as they neared a fence. Cook, fearful of being carried off to Libby Prison, made

McMahon as comfortable as he could and then headed northward towards the Chambersburg Pike, and safety.[305]

Lieutenants Alfred Tanner and Edward Ross were not as lucky as Cook. Tanner was wounded in the left leg just below the knee as he retired towards the Seminary. Ross "stopped to help him from the field, not expecting our forces would fall back farther than the hospital." This good Samaritan took Tanner into the Seminary building and tied a wet rag around his wounded leg. When he went to the window "to see where to go to join the regiment," he saw that the hospital was surrounded by Rebels. Ross understood that he could not get out then, so he stayed behind to help the wounded, and so became a prisoner also.[306] Meanwhile most of the remainder of the 20th found their way to the "dirt causeway" (railroad bed) and followed it into the center of Gettysburg. Gates claimed their withdrawal was "deliberate and orderly," but other accounts suggest differently.[307]

The 151st Pennsylvania also enjoyed initial success at repelling Pender's attack, until forced to withdraw by the Confederate troops that oppressed its left and rear. Lieutenant Colonel George F. McFarland noted that "having the advantages of breastworks and woods, our fire was so destructive that the enemy's lines were broken and his first attempt to flank us greeted with such an accurate oblique fire that it failed. But in a second attempt, made soon after, he gained our left flank, moving in single file and at double quick."[308] Up to this time his men had fought as bravely as men could, and no one left their ranks, "even to carry a wounded comrade to the rear."[309]

McFarland saw that the regiments on his left had been driven back and the enemy was going to outflank his line there. He was about to order the regiment back when he saw the Confederate troops in his front "staggering under our galling fire." He cried out, "Give them another volley, boys, which "was done with a will and followed by a hearty cheer as the boys saw the effect of it on the breaking line in front at the edge of the wood."[310] But now that he saw no supports on either flank, McFarland ordered "the shattered remmants of as brave a regiment as ever entered the field" to begin falling back.[311]

McFarland's line had fallen back to within 20 paces of the Seminary when McFarland decided to turn and crouch to examine the position of the enemy: "At this instant, 420pm, I was hit by a flank fire in both legs at the same instant, which caused the amputation of my right leg, and so shattered my left that it is now, at the end of eight and a half months still unhealed and unserviceable." The lieutenant colonel was carried into the Seminary by Private Lyman D. Wilson of Company F, "the only man near me, and who narrowly escaped, a ball carrying away the middle button on my coat sleeve while my arm was around his neck." This regiment meanwhile moved around to the north end of the Seminary, so escaping any additional Confederate flank fire for the moment. It retired to the town to Cemetery Hill, with barely 100 men left of its original 467.[312]

Perrin's defeat of Biddle's brigade spelled the end of Doubleday's Seminary Ridge line. Once the Confederates drove Biddle's infantry back, some quickly proceeded as far as the Seminary, directly at the center of Doubleday's line, as already noted. This penetration forced the Iron Brigade to pull back its left and begin withdrawing, and also easily persuaded Wainwright to start pulling his guns back before they could be captured.

The 24th Michigan on the left of the 19th Indiana was also forced back by the Confederates on the left. Just before withdrawing, Captain A.M. Edwards noticed one of the regiment's flags lying on the ground in the deathlike grip of a young soldier. He picked it up, "and after rallying the men to it amid a shower of bullets, bore it through the town to the cemetery."[313] The 24th, though, did not retreat to the northeast as did the rest of its brigade. For some reason, it proceeded south past the western face of the Seminary and then headed past "the lower branch of the Fairfield Road," where it turned east to the southwest corner of the town.[314] Only 26 men of the regiment were able to follow Captain Edwards and their flag to Cemetery Hill.[315] During the day's fight the flag of the 24th had been borne by no less than ten different soldiers, five of whom were killed and two wounded. In addition, the color guard also lost one killed and three wounded. Altogether nine men of the 24th gave their lives "in the defense of its flag the first day of the great battle, a bloody but most glorious record."[316]

The 19th Indiana was the first regiment of the Iron Brigade to be forced back. During its retreat from McPherson's Ridge it had become disordered, but even so was initially able to face Perrin's attack. Colonel S.J. Williams of the 19th wrote that, "The third line of the rebels in front had become engaged and great gaps in it told of the severity of our fire. We could have held out against the line in front but their maneuvers on the left made the position untenable, and I gave the order to retreat. Men of every division of the Corps had fought side by side, behind this barricade and I found it impossible to form and we retired, each to care for himself, through the town." He explained the reason for his retreat in a letter he wrote later in the month to Governor Morton of Indiana: "The retiring of the 11th Corps exposed us to an uncomfortable fire from the rear. I saw our retreat would soon be entirely cut off, and gave the order to fall back. Many of the men were loth to obey the order, and numerous instances fell under my notice, where men returned again to the barricade to pay the enemy one more compliment."[317]

The 7th and 2nd Wisconsin, on the Iron Brigade's right, were the last of the brigade to withdraw. Colonel Robinson of the 7th was able to turn his men in town to slow down Perrin's advance at least for a moment. He reported that he had stopped the enemy's advance in his front, and then noticed "the brigade which had turned our left flank and was now advancing from that direction in line obliquely to our new position. It was with some difficulty I restrained their men from firing until the enemy got as near as I wanted them. When they were within easy range, the order was given, and their ranks went down like grass before the scythe from the united fire of our regiments and the battery."[318]

Colonel Robinson reported that he held on as long as he could until the battery behind him had retired and so had the troops on both his left and right: "The enemy, in overwhelming numbers, had again turned both our flanks, with a line formed on each perpendicular to ours, and reaching a considerable distance to the rear, forming full sides of a square around us, with the open side to our rear and toward the town." At this point Captain Richardson of the brigade's staff brought an order to retire. Robinson did so, "by the right of companies to the rear, through the orchard over the ridge, and then by the right flank by file left into column, and moved on to the turnpike and through the town to Cemetery Hill, being the rear of the troops from that part of the field."[319]

The 7th Wisconsin's color bearer, Sergeant Daniel McDermott, showed exceptional courage during this retreat when he was badly wounded by a Confederate shell that shattered his flagstaff into a number of pieces. He had carried his flag through all the regiment's battles, and wasn't about to give it up now. Friendly hands lifted him into a passing caisson, "still hanging to the tattered banner, which he waved in defiance at the foe as he rode off."[320]

Among the wounded left behind by the 7th was the regiment's Lieutenant Colonel John R. Callis. He was struck in the breast by a minie ball at the height of the Confederate attack; the bullet penetrated his lung and was never removed. Captain Martin Hobart then "detailed a number of men to take me to the rear, they took me to the Seminary....When I came to my senses I was suffering terribly and thought I was killed, so I begged them to lay me in the shade of the Seminary, and get out of the way as best they could, and get back to the main line and rally. But Capt. Hobart said he could not leave me on the field, and by his order they carried me across an old RR grade into a clover field, where the detail was all killed or wounded, and left me to the mercy of the enemy."[321]

Captain Robert Beecham of the 2nd Wisconsin was stationed some forty yards south of Chambersburg Pike when the Confederate attack began: "We of the infantry fell into line between the artillery sections and assisted with our musketry, keeping up the fire until our pieces grew hot in our hands, and darkness, as if night, had settled upon us. Not a Confederate reached our lines. After we ceased firing and the smoke of battle had been lifted, we looked again, but the charging Confederates were not there. Only the dead and dying remained on the bloody slopes of Seminary Ridge."[322]

Captain Nat Rollins of the color company paused to look at his watch, and said "It is four o'clock," as the smoke cleared more, the men of the 2nd were astonished to see the Chambersburg Pike to their rear filled with Union soldiers in full retreat. Their command had received no such order, but "there was no time to waste; so we stood not on the order of our going, but went at once."[323]

Just as they began pulling back, the 2nd's commander, Major John Mansfield, was felled by a severe gunshot wound in his left leg.[324] His men headed for the rear as best they could, dodging the artillery vehicles that "had the right of way by virtue of their power to possess it, and they drove their horses at a pace that would have surprised Jehu, the mad driver of old."[325]

J.F.J. Caldwell of the 1st South Carolina had respect for the way the defeated Union infantry withdrew from his front: "The enemy, however, did not fly readily. They fought obstinately, every where, and particularly opposite our right. In fact, it was not possible to dislodge them from that point, until, having broken the portion of their line opposed to our left, we threw an enfilade fire along the wall. They then gave back at all points, and the rebel turn came to kill. As the disordered mass fled towards Gettysburg, they suffered a far greater loss than they had previously been able to inflict upon us."[326]

The collapse of the infantry line made it necessary for Wainwright's batteries to withdraw in order to escape capture. General Doubleday was well aware of this and sent Lieutenant Henry T. Lee of his staff to General Wadsworth with orders to withdraw to Cemetery Hill. Lee found Wadsworth with Stevens' battery, "pouring canister into the enemy at short range." He delivered his order, but the general was not yet ready to give up his position and replied, "Tell General Doubleday that I don't know a damned thing about strategy, but we are giving the rebels hell with these guns, and I want to give them a few more shots before we leave."[327]

After a few more minutes of firing, Wadsworth told Stevens to withdraw because "the enemy had driven...our infantry from the woods protecting our left flank." Colonel Charles Wainwright, the corps' artillery chief, however, countermanded this order, and ordered all the batteries to remain in position because he was "still under the false impression as to the importance attached to holding Seminary Hill." The sight of all the retreating Union infantry, though, soon convinced him to order his units to retire.[328]

Lieutenant George Breck's four guns of Battery L, 1st New York Light Artillery had the most difficulty retiring. These were posted at this time "upon the ridge running south from the brick Seminary and in rear of that building." Breck managed to get off a few effectively placed rounds of canister against the advancing Confederate troops before he retired under the cover of some cavalry who came up to "cover the withdrawal of our troops." The battery's right section, commanded by Lieutenant B.W. Wilber and accompanied by Lieutenant Breck, also fired several rounds of canister from its position "near a small house and orchard" on the right of the line, before it was ordered to retire.[329]

Cooper's Pennsylvania battery was lucky to get away in time. Its guns were still actively engaged upon the enemy when Lieutenant Colonel Alfred B. McCalmont of the 142nd Pennsylvania rode up to Cooper and "informed him that the infantry on the left had gone, and unless he immediately withdrew he should be captured." Cooper promptly limbered up his guns, and "passed out on the north side of the Seminary, narrowly escaping capture, the enemy being on both flanks." Just prior to the retreat, Cooper luckily had ordered full limbers for the guns and sent the caisson line to Cemetery Hill.[330]

Needless to say, Perrin's advancing troops were extremely interested in laying their hands upon the Union guns that had so severely tried them: "The men closed upon the guns with all the rapidity their exhausted limbs would permit. The artillerists limbered up with commendable expedition, and applied whip and spur vigorously to their horses. The first regiment was nearest them and therefore most eager. They shot some of the riders and killed a few horses, by which means one piece was effectively stopped. There was now a race for who should first lay hand upon the piece. This was so entirely a matter of legs, that I do not care to discuss the mooted question as to who did reach it first. Suffice it to say, the piece was captured."[331]

The troops of Lieutenant Colonel Joseph N. Brown's 14th South Carolina also had their eyes on capturing some of the Union guns. During their advance the line of the 14th was broken by the Seminary building, and Brown led one portion of the regiment to the left while Major Edward Croft led the other to the right. Both wings then "pushed forward for the possession of a disabled piece of artillery." Troops from the 1st South Carolina got to the gun first. However Croft's detachment arrived next, and the Major took possession of the only uninjured horse left behind by the battery, "which he mounted with the harness still on." When Lieutenant Colonel Brown arrived a few moments later, Croft presented him with a captured sword.[332]

Colonel Wainwright explains the loss of this gun from the Union view point: "All the batteries were at once limbered to the rear, and moved at a walk down the Cashtown Pike until the infantry had all left it and passed under the cover of the railroad embankment. By this time the enemy's skirmishers had lapped our retreating columns and opened a severe fire from behind a paling fence running parallel to within 50 yards of the road. The Pike being clear, the batteries now broke into a trot, but it was too late to save everything. Lieutenant Wilber's [Battery L, 1st New York] last piece had the off wheel horse shot, and just as he had disengaged it, 3 more of the horses were shot down and his own horse killed; so that it was impossible for him to bring it off."[333]

At the same time Stevens' battery almost lost one of its pieces. The battery had lost at least two men while limbering for the rear from its position near the Seminary—Charles M. Bryant was killed and Lieutenant Charles O. Hunt was severely wounded in the thigh. Despite these losses, all the guns were successfully pulled back. But while moving "at a trot march.... near where a brook crosses the Chambersburg Pike, not far from the westerly outskirts of the village," a gun wheel fell off of one of the cannons, and the piece's axle dropped to the road. Despite the proximity of the advancing enemy, the gun's cannoneers managed to halt, raise the gun by hand, and replace the wheel. Captain Stevens even helped out by "springing from his horse and seizing the gunner's pinchers, which he inserted handle first as a lynch-pin, and so saved the gun from capture." This repair work was done with the loss of only one man, Private William Widner, a driver who was killed while on detached duty from the 94th New York.[334]

Stone's three Pennsylvania regiments apparently were not as heavily engaged in the defense of Doubleday's last line. After retreating from McPherson's Ridge, most of the brigade, now under the command of Colonel Edmund L. Dana of the 143rd Pennsylvania, was reformed in a peach orchard north of the Seminary "together with a portion of the battery of artillery [Wilber's] and parties that had become separated from their regiments." The men were almost out of ammunition, and were glad to receive a fresh issue of 60 rounds per man while posted on this line. They fired most of these cartridges at Scales' men, who were already being repulsed by artillery fire.[335]

Dana's command was ordered to withdraw when Wainwright's artillery pulled out, and so did not become engaged with Perrin's infantry or with Scales' troops, who had rallied under the command of Colonel G.T. Gordon and renewed their attack.[336] Lieutenant Colonel John L. Musser of the 143rd Pennsylvania reported that his troops helped save a battery, apparently by forming a screen for it while others pulled it out of range by hand. He noted that "It was with great difficulty that I could get all the men to fall back from this point, which was a good one, and in front of which the enemy fell thick and fast. Still they moved in columns on our right and left, and superior numbers compelled us to fall back to the town, which, I might say, was done in good order, and only when peremptorily ordered to do so."[337] Much of the brigade retired along the railroad embankment to the town, where it fell in with numbers of Wadsworth's men as well as some of the XI Corps, passing through the streets "under a destructive fire."[338]

Adjutant Richard Ashurst of the 150th Pennsylvania managed to escape to Cemtery Hill in a rather unique fashion. He relates, "by the long pause near the Seminary so much time had been lost that the enemy was pouring in on both sides of us, and it was impossible longer to keep much order, particularly as we found ourselves mingled with a crowd of fugitives from another direction.... When I reached the houses the enemy was so close upon us that I found my only chance of escape to climb over fences and cross private grounds, so as to get into another street. Here I found the Second Division retreating up the street, and was fortunate enough to get into an ambulance, which was the last representative of our troops coming from that direction. From the back of the ambulance we could see the rebel skirmishers coming down the streets, firing upon us as they came. One wounded man was killed in the ambulance while I was in it. There was an officer bringing up the retreat, and the ambulance driver kept just behind him, so as to screen him from fire by interposing the white cover of the vehicle."[339]

Captain George W. Jones of Company B took his command to safety by taking a route different than that of the rest of the 150th. Instead of withdrawing along the Chambersburg Pike or the fields nearby, he went south to the Fairfield Road. He kept his men in column formation and reached the edge of the town safely, only to run suddenly into the head of a Confederate regiment that was advancing up an intersecting street. A Southern officer on horseback challenged Jones to halt, but was promptly felled by a well-aimed shot from the gun of Private Terrence O'Connor, who observed, "we take no orders from the likes of you."[340]

Not all the officers of the 150th were as lucky at escaping as Jones and Ashurst. Captain Henry W. Gimber of Company F "unwisely undertook to cross the garden of the Seminary, but before he could clear the second fence, was brought to a stand still by menacing bayonets." Captain Cornelius C. Widdis, and Lieutenants John Q. Carpenter and Joseph Chatburn were taken near the town.[341]

The most lamented loss in the 150th was one of its flags. As in almost all regiments on this awful and bloody day, the 150th's color guard had been almost wiped out during the day's heavy fighting. Color Sergeant Phifer of Company I had held his flag during the entire conflict on McPherson's Ridge, only to be felled by a shot through the head as the regiment pulled back at about 1515. Samuel P. Gilmore of Company C saw him fall, and picked up the flag, even though he himself was wounded in the side. Gilmore bore the flag during the Seminary Ridge fight, and was carrying it on the retreat to the town when Corporal Rodney Conner, who had also been wounded, demanded it because he was one of the few remaining members of the color guard. Gilmore did not wish to do so, but finally was forced to, under protest. Conner took the flag through the town, but was captured opposite Flaharty's Stone Yard at Washington and High Streets: "A column of the rebels came charging down a cross street and cut off about a hundred men with me. A rebel Captain seized the colors from my hand, and the next minute he went down. Another officer went to him, and he gave the colors and told him to present them to President Davis with his compliments." The colors were duly transmitted to Davis with a note from Governor Vance of North Carolina that read "captured from a Pennsylvania regiment, which Lieutenant [unnamed] had put to flight with a handful of sharpshooters." The flag was found among Davis' personal effects when he was captured at the end of the war, and was eventually returned to the state of Pennsylvania by the War Department in 1869.[342]

Perrin's troops were somewhat disordered by their magnificent victory, and were in two separate wings as the Union troops pulled back from Seminary Ridge. The 1st and 14th South Carolina, which had first broken Biddle's left, proceeded northeastward past the Seminary (which temporarily broke the line of the 14th) and then pursued the Union artillery. Their success at capturing a gun and horse from Wilber's section of Breck's battery has already been related. The two regiments then followed the retreating Union troops into town, led by skirmishers of the 1st South Carolina under the command of Captain T. P. Alston, who was now mounted on the battery horse that Major Croft of the 14th had just captured.[343]

The two regiments pushed into the town with their flags unfurled. The 1st South Carolina proceeded on Chambersburg Street, and its men later bragged that theirs was "the first Confederate banner raised in Gettysburg."[344]

J.A. Leach of the 1st South Carolina recalled his unit's moment of glory as follows: "We pushed on to Gettysburg, into the same street, but as we get to the edge of town, Col. Perin ordered a halt so that we might get in order, for all was in confussion (sic) at this time. So while we were just here I saw a line of troops to the north of the town, but had no idea what troops they were, it was so far that I could not tell whether they were federal or Confederate troops. Now when our line was reformed it was long enough to reach across the street with two or three files of men, [it] turned at one end at the command of Col. Perin. We marched on up the street to the 2d and 3d cross street. I am not positive, as we passed the cross streets there were great number of Federal troops on right and left but had no arms at each street, and why we were not all captured has been a mystery to me. It is true we had arms, but I don't think our number exceeded 50 men."[345]

The 14th South Carolina passed to the left and proceeded into town between North Boundary Street and the railroad embankment. After it reached the "Main Street running South through the town" (Carlisle Street), it marched to the right and "was passed by General Pender, at the shade trees on the right, who extended a compliment in passing." A moment later the 1st South Carolina came up to the same point in the town square and was also complimented by General Pender for its gallant conduct. Colonel Brown of the 14th South Carolina saw Colonel Perrin salute his unit's flag and then that of the 1st South Carolina.[346]

The two regiments apparently entered the western part of the town on the heels of the I Corps but just ahead of Schurz's XI Corps troops. Perrin soon became concerned for their safety—the 1st South Carolina had lost one-third of its men and the 14th South Carolina nearly half—and recalled them from the town to await the return of the 12th and 13th regiments from the right. After the 1st and 14th regiments withdrew, Colonel Perrin saw some Confederate troops coming up on the left and asked, "What troops are those?" A nearby staff officer replied, "Rodes' division." Perrin then became "annoyed on account of their going in and taking the place captured by us." As his men fell back, Perrin permitted a small detachment to return into the town "to take such prisoners as the enemy had left in the street."[347] J.D.F. Caldwell of the 1st South Carolina recalled that, "volunteers were called for, to go through Gettysburg and secure such of the enemy as might be lurking there. But so many offered themselves, that details had finally to be made. A few shots were fired at these men, from the windows of the houses, but I am not informed of a single casualty. In consequence a goodly number were brought in."[348]

While Perrin's 1st and 14 South Carolina regiments were breaking up the left of Doubleday's line at the height of their attack, his two right flank units, the 12th and 13th South Carolina, had been shifted to the right in order to deal with the annoying fire of a large force of dismounted cavalry posted behind a stone wall on the edge of the Schultz Woods, just south of the Fairfield Road.[349] It seems that Buford at about 1600, probably in response to a call for help from Doubleday, had sent most of Gamble's brigade to support Doubleday's left. Gamble, who had been resting most of his men is the fields southwest of Gettysburg since late morning, moved forward at a trot and, "deployed in line on the ridge of woods, with the Seminary on our right. Half of the Eighth New York, Third Indiana, and 12th Illinois were dismounted and placed behind a stone wall and under cover of trees." This deployed force of 600-700 men caused continual annoyance to the right of Perrin's brigade as he advanced on the Seminary. Gamble's fourth regiment, the 8th Illinois, as already seen, had been deployed farther west along the Fairfield Road much earlier in the day. Gamble's line was supported at this position by Calef's horse battery, which made some "excellent shots" but was so low on ammunition that it had to fire slowly and deliberately.[350]

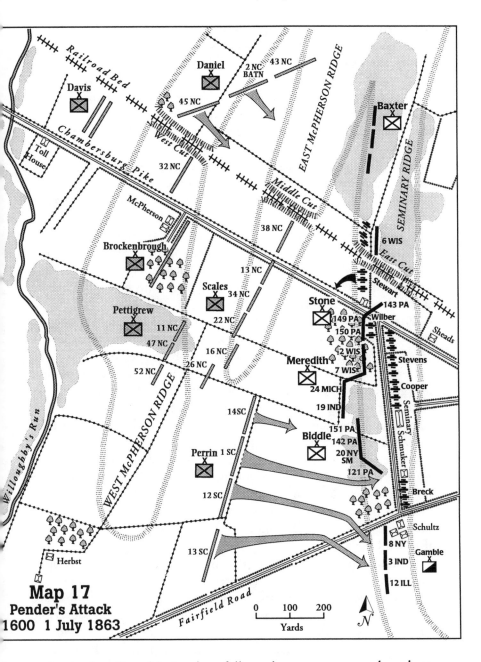

Map 17
Pender's Attack
1600 1 July 1863

Perrin describes this attack as follows; he appears not to have been aware that he was attacking dismounted cavalry: "While the First and Fourteenth regiments were assailing the enemy and driving him from his breastwork near the college, I ordered the Twelfth regiment, under Lieutenant Colonel Brockman, to oblique to the right, and charge the enemy, strongly posted behind a stone fence, to the right of the college, from which position he had kept up a constant and withering fire of musketry upon the right and flank of the brigade. These two regiments had necessarily to change direction to the right somewhat, so as to meet the enemy full in front. This movement was most brilliantly performed by these two regiments, and was most skillfully managed by the officers I have mentioned. They rushed up to the crest of the hill and the stone fence, and pouring an enfilading fire upon the enemy's right flank."[351]

This attack, though, apparently did not go as smoothly as Perrin relates. Surgeon U.R. Brooks of the 13th South Carolina, which held the right wing in this attack, recalled that "when the order was given to charge upon the enemy, who were lying behind some stone fences and in other places of concealment, our men rushed forward with a perfect fury, yelling and driving them, though with great slaughter to themselves as well as to the Yankees."[352]

Private Daniel Pulis of the 8th Illinois was among Gamble's troopers who formed dismounted along the stone wall while their horses were taken to the rear. When he got to the wall, he peeped over it and saw the enemy approaching in a double column. The Union line commenced firing, and as he squeezed off 15 rounds the Confederates began to fall "like rain in the ground." The concentrated fire broke their first line, whose survivors started to run back, but were held in place by their second line, which now came forward with bayonets fixed.[353] At this point Pulis was hit in the forehead by a musket ball that had glanced off a rock in the wall he was crouching behind. He went back to the horse line to look for aid, but could find none and had to ride three miles to the rear to locate an infantry doctor "to take the lead out of my head." The doctor told him the shot would surely have killed him if it had been a direct hit.[354]

Gamble reported that his men caused a large number of casualties before they mounted up and withdrew: "The enemy being close upon us, we opened a sharp and rapid carbine fire which killed and wounded so many of the first line of the enemy that it fell back upon the second line. Our men kept up the fire until the enemy in overpowering numbers approached so near that, in order to save my men and horses from capture, they were ordered to mount and fall back rapidly to the next ridge, on the left of the town, where the artillery was posted."[355] Colonel Chapman thought the line was given up because it was outflanked rather than taken by assault.[356] Gamble's men, who had already served the infantry well by their service that morning, once again rendered valiant service to the I Corps by saving its flank from being turned from 1600 to 1630.[357]

The heavy casualties recorded by the 12th and 13th South Carolina regiments attest to the effectiveness of the fire of the Union troopers. These units, which had already lost heavily in their approach to Seminary Ridge and initial contact with Doubleday's line, each recorded over 100 casualties this day.[358] Lieutenant Colonel Brown of the 14th South Carolina noted that "the 13th was nearest the cavalry with repeating rifles [sic] at the stone fence, and lost more in killed than any other [regiment in the brigade]."[359]

Since the infantry of the 12th and 13th South Carolina had no hope of catching Gamble's mounted cavalrymen, Perrin ordered them recalled as soon as he heard that "the enemy had been routed on the right." General Pender had also been concerned about the progress of these two regiments. He had been watching the battle from the rear (probably from McPherson's Ridge), and watched the brigade as it "appeared from his point to almost mingle with the Union soldiers, and passing the Seminary and the Ridge altogether, he supposed the Brigade was captured." He rode forward anxiously, and met Lieutenant Simmons of the 12th South Carolina, who was wounded, whom he asked if the brigade were captured. Simmons replied, "No, it is over the hill yonder," but the general rode forward to see for himself. He then ordered the 12th and 13th South Carolina to fall back to a point between the town and Seminary in order to protect his right flank, before riding into the town to greet the 1st and 14th South Carolina, as already noted.[360]

During this attack Perrin's right came into contact with Captain James Glenn's Company D, 149th Pennsylvania, which Doubleday had sent to the intersection of the Seminary Road and Fairfield Road to try to delay the Confederate advance. This unit of about 60 men had been serving as the Provost Guard for Doubleday's old division, and was absolutely his last reserve. Glenn's command had not been engaged in the fighting on McPherson's Ridge, but had been initially deployed in a light screen between the Seminary and Fairfield Road, probably to collect stragglers.[361] When Doubleday's troops pulled back from McPherson's to Seminary Ridge, Glenn's company was sent to support the far left of the I Corps' new line near the Fairfield Road, where it helped support Breck's guns near the Schumacher house.[362] When Perrin's attack was approaching, Glenn's men "opened a fire sufficient to induce the enemy to halt, supposing that our forces had made a stand there." One source even claims that some of Glenn's men helped Breck's artillerymen put one of their guns in position, from which three shots were fired.[363]

The truth of the matter was that Perrin's attack had split into two wings—his left to regiments had moved towards the Seminary and his right two regiments were dealing with Gamble's cavalry south of the Fairfield Road. There was actually no direct pressure on Glenn's position until Gamble's men withdrew and the union line at the Seminary was driven back. Captain Glenn gave a more accurate assessment of his company's role in the fighting when he wrote, "up to this time our company had not fired a gun. We opened fire and kept it up but the rebels moved slowly and steadily forwards, and it soon became evident that we could not hold the position.... It now became necessary to run to escape capture and our boys got off that hill in a hurry."[364]

In this short fight, Company D lost one man killed (Joseph H. Baldwin) one man mortally wounded (Alex M. Stewart), and several wounded. Glenn led the survivors of his command down the Fairfield Road and into the town, only to find their way blocked by a Confederate regiment. John W. Nesbit recorded that, "We turned off to the right at the next street we came to and followed the crowd.... We followed this cross street up the hill until we were out of the town and then crossed a corn field and found the reserve division of the Eleventh Corps. We passed through their line over the hill, and completely worn out, dropped down on the grass and rested as best we could."[365]

Colonel Perrin was justifiably proud of what his troops had accomplished—they captured hundreds of the enemy, as well as a cannon, a number of caissons, and at least four flags.[366] A member of the 14th South Carolina captured the "large flag " of the 149th Pennsylvania in the breastworks, after its guard was all slain. Another captured a smaller flag that he kept for himself. It was found still folded in his jacket when he was killed two days later on the picket line in front of Cemetery Hill.[367] The two nicest flags the brigade captured were General Reynolds' I Corps headquarters standard, and "a beautiful flag of the 104th NY Regt. Wadsworth Guards, presented the Regt. by Gen. Wadsworth." Colonel Perrin had intended to send these two flags to Governor Bonham to be displayed in the State House at Columbia, but received orders "to turn them in here, to be sent to Richmond I suppose."[368]

But this success did not come without great cost. All four of his regiments engaged lost at least one-third of their strength, and the 14th

South Carolina lost almost one-half.[369] The brigade's color bearers were hit particularly hard. Every one of the brigade's four color sergeants was killed in advance of their regiments.[370] Four color bearers were killed and two wounded in the 12th South Carolina, and in the 14th the entire color guard but one were slain.[371] Perrin claimed he had only 500 men still in line when Pender directed him to fall back to rest.[372]

Lieutenant Colonel Joseph Brown of the 14th South Carolina noted how devastated the field of his regiment's charge was after the battle: "The nature of the ground was such and the contest so brief that the wounded could not be moved, and were wounded twice, and as many as four times, after being first stricken down. Large numbers died of their wounds... It was the only battlefield in which all avenues of escape for our wounded were closed. There was nothing that the ambulance corps could do. The ground was swept at every point by the deadly minnie balls. The artillery fire is terrible, but the almost silent whine of the minnie ball is the death-dealing missile in battle. Not a foot of ground presented a place of safety. The Union troops fired low, and their balls swept close to the ground on the dishlike field to their front...Men never fell faster in this brigade... On our side the firing was not slack nor wild. The trees in the Seminary grounds where the Union lines ran are still thickly covered with scars, from the ground to the height of a man, made with the bullets of our unerring rifles."[373]

Perrin was understandably upset that his men had not received more support during their advance. He wrote to Governor Bonham, "If we had any support at all we could have taken every piece of artillery they had and thousands of prisoners."[374] The best support he did receive was from Scales' men to his left. Though they suffered terribly from the Union artillery fire in their front, they kept the right wing of Doubleday's line occupied until Perrin was able to break the Union left. In addition, some of Scales' men were rallied and assisted in the mopping up operation on Seminary Ridge and the fields near the town. Perrin also received some help during his attack from Pettigrew's 26th North Carolina, as already noted, as well as Company A, and part of D and F of the 11th North Carolina;[376] at least one member of Company A of the 11th was felled by a grapeshot "the size of an egg."[377] Most of Pettigrew's men, though, did not come up until after the ridge was secured. Captain M.P. Griffith of the 14th South Carolina tells this interesting incident that occurred when he was heading to the rear after being wounded at the edge of the Seminary grove. He passed some of Heth's troops and was asked, "How goes the battle?" He replied, "They are running," to which he was again asked, "Who are running?" "The Yankees," he had to clarify.[378]

What most annoyed Perrin was the lack of support from Lane's large North Carolina brigade on his right. His anger was well justified, since these troops were distracted by one Union cavalry regiment, and so "did not come up until the Yankees were clear out of reach."[379]

As already discussed, Lane's brigade had been formed on the left center of Pender's line when its division first reached the field and deployed on Knoxlyn Ridge. It was then shifted to the right in order to help watch the corps' flank there, and by the time the brigade reached Herr Ridge was deployed with its regiments in the following order from left to right: 33rd, 18th, 28th, 37th and 7th North Carolina. Even before the brigade moved forward to support Heth's front line, Lane was forced to form his right wing regiment, the 7th North Carolina, in skirmish line in order to protect his flank from the fire of Union cavalry.[380]

The cavalry that was opposed to Lane's 7th North Carolina consisted of most if not all of Major John Beveridge's 8th Illinois Cavalry of Buford's Brigade, which at around noon had been "sent well off of the enemy's right flank to watch their movements."[381] Beveridge later wrote that his regiment had "occupied an orchard south of the road, near the timber, and sent a squadron through the timber into the open ground beyond." This orchard was probably Horting's, which was located south of the Fairfield Road and east of Willoughby Run. From here Beveridge sent out mounted and dismounted detachments that harassed the Confederate far right all afternoon. In so doing they virtually neutralized Archer's brigade on Heth's right, and also forced Pender to deploy Lane to check them. This was quite an accomplishment for around 400 Union troopers who had already been heavily engaged that morning.[382]

When Pender's line moved through and out of the woods where Pettigrew had formed for his attack on Herbst Woods, Lane's troops passed over Archer's brigade, who had deployed to the right of the woods to protect Heth's right and also watch the Union cavalry. While Archer's men (who had been badly battered that morning) stayed put, Lane's North Carolinians continued their advance, even though their entire front was now unmasked. As the brigade moved forward, the 7th North Carolina was instructed to "move as skirmishers by the left flank." This formation slowed the unit down so that it could not keep pace with the rest of the brigade and a gap developed between the brigade's right and the left of the trailing skirmish line. In order to fill this gap, Colonel

W. M. Barbour of the 37th North Carolina was ordered to deploy 40 men of Capt. D.L. Hudson's Company G as skirmishers on the line of the 7th.[383]

Lane's main line continued its advance across the open fields unopposed except for some artillery fire on its left front and annoying shots from the Union cavalry on his right.[384] His line of approach brought him across Willoughby Run just south of the Herbst Road ¼ mile south of what had been the far left of Doubleday's line on McPherson's Ridge. For some reason Lane did not keep his line closed up with Perrin's on his left, but he instead drifted slightly to the right, perhaps drawn on by the Union cavalry skirmishers on his right and front. His advance appears also to have been delayed by defensive stances he stopped to form in order to ward off possible mounted charges by the Union cavalry. Major John Beveridge of the 8th Illinois Cavalry observed that, "About this time, Lane's brigade of Pendar's [sic] division, which had formed under cover of the woods skirting Willoughby's Run, emerged from the timber south of McPherson's Woods, in echelon from left to right, his last regiment coming out of the woods near the orchard by the Hagerstown Road, with the Eighth Illinois pickets hanging upon his flank. From our position we saw Doubleday's right falling back, then his centre, and then the Iron Brigade coming out of McPherson's Woods. Biddle's brigade, lying under the ridge, was watching the fight to the north, unconscious of Lane's advance, and unseen by Lane's brigade as it moved steadily forward. Noting Biddle's peril, the officer in command of the Eighth Illinois made a feint for his rescue. He ordered his regiment forward in column of squadrons, and increased its gait to a trot, as if to charge Lane's right. Lane's right regiment halted, changed front, and fired a volley; Biddle's brigade rose to its feet, advanced to the summit of the ridge, fired, and retired across the field to Seminary Ridge."[385]

In this manner the opposition put up by the 8th Illinois cavalry succeeded admirably at delaying Lane's advance and drawing him away from the Union line being posted near the Seminary. Lane in fact continued on until he reached McMillan Woods, a full ¾ mile south of the Seminary. Here he encountered still more fire from the 8th Illinois (supported now by "a few infantry"), so he ordered a charge. His men rushed forward with a yell at the double quick, and compelled the entire enemy force in the woods to beat a "hasty retreat" to Cemetery Hill.[386]

Lane's line now stretched from the McMillan Woods on the right to the Schultz Woods on the left, "a short distance from the Fairfield Road." Since he makes no mention of seeing Perrin's 12th and 13th

South Carolina or the rest of Buford's command fighting in the Schultz Woods, he was either farther to the south than he indicated, or arrived after this brief engagement was completed. After passing beyond the stone fence and into the peach orchard near the McMillan House, Lane received an order from Pender "not to advance farther unless there was another general forward movement." Lane promptly decided that he "could see nothing at that time to indicate such a movement," so he ordered his brigade to withdraw to the stone fence so that it might take cover from one of the Union batteries on Cemetery Hill that was doing us some damage."[387]

Thus Lane did not aid Perrin and Scales in their attack on Doubleday's line beyond dealing with Gamble's cavalrymen, a task that Fry could and should have tended to. Lane's large brigade extended some ¼ mile beyond the Union left, but he clearly became too distracted by the cavalry on his right to move his line of attack to the north side of the Fairfield Road. That was unfortunate for the Confederates, since Perrin and Scales could definitely have used his support. Pender would have done better to order Lane to the left during the attack, or to permit him to advance beyond the McMillan Woods on the line that he did follow. When Lane stopped his brigade there, he had nothing in front of him but Gamble's cavalry and the XI Corps troops and cannons on Cemetery Hill, some ¾ mile to the east. It would have been very easy for him to advance towards Long Lane and the town and thereby cut off the retreat of much of the I Corps. Instead, he stayed near the McMillan house under orders from Pender "not to advance unless there was another general forward movement."[388] Here the 7th North Carolina skirmishers at last rejoined the brigade after being detained in the rear.[389]

Several sources claim that Lane's advance was delayed at this point when one or more of his regiments stopped in order to form squares, a Napoleonic era formation used to defend against cavalry. J.R. Stine writes that Buford "by threatening to charge with Gamble's brigade of cavalry...compelled Lane to form square, which greatly impeded the advance of the enemy's right, which he intended to swing around and thus cut off the retreat of the Iron Brigade....Buford deserves to have a monument erected on the spot where he defied Lane to advance, thereby greatly frustrating the well-conceived designs of the enemy."[390]

At about the same time Colonel Charles Livingston of General Doubleday's staff claimed to see the enemy advancing cautiously towards Seminary Ridge and "also forming against cavalry." Doubleday himself, probably relying on Livingston's account, wrote after the war that "The troops in front of the Seminary were stayed by the firm attitude of Buford's cavalry, and made a bend in their line, apparently with a view to form square."[391]

This incident of the Confederates forming squares should not be confused with the possible episode that may have occurred about an hour earlier. Nor should it be mistaken for the episode described by E.P. Halstead that may have happened still later in the day.[392]

Collapse of Doubleday's Right North of the Pike

The last organized Union unit to stand on Seminary Ridge on 1 July was probably Stewart's Battery B, 4th U.S. artillery, which was posted astride the eastern railroad cut just to the north of the Chambersburg Pike, some 300 yards north of the Seminary. This battery, supported by a smattering of regiments from Wadsworth's and Robinson's divisions, was able to resist frontal attack from Daniel's and Scales' brigades because of the devastating fire it and the batteries to its left were able to pour forth across the open fields. This enabled the battery to hold on until it was forced to retreat by the successful Confederate infantry that advanced on its rear from both flanks at virtually the same time, Ramseur's from the right and Perrin's from the left.

Stewart's veteran command, often called the "Iron Brigade Battery," had arrived on the field in the forenoon and was at first held in a reserve position to the north of the Seminary. After about an hour in this location, it was moved at about noon or shortly thereafter about 300 yards to the right at the orders of Colonel Wainwright.[393] Wainwright was having difficulty maintaining an artillery presence on McPherson's Ridge, where Hall's battery had taken a pounding that morning and Reynolds' battery was soon to do the same. Wainwright hoped that Stewart would at least be able to give defensive covering fire to the right flank of Doubleday's forward line, even if he were not able to engage in counter battery fire against the massive buildup of Confederate artillery on Herr Ridge, a little over a mile to the west. At this new position, Stewart's guns were the farthest north of any I Corps battery this day. The Wills Woods on northern Seminary Ridge prohibited guns from deploying, and Confederate troops to the east, north, and west of the ridge did not allow any guns to be moved north and along the fringe of the woods in order to help Robinson's brigades fight Rodes' division.

When the battery moved to its right, it found its advance impeded by the eastern railroad cut, which was by far the longest and deepest on the field, being some 40 feet deep at the center of Seminary Ridge. The battery's commander, 2nd Lieutenant James Stewart, decided the best way to handle this situation was to deploy astride the shallow western end of the cut, where it was only a few feet deep. There be formed up his guns in a somewhat unusual formation with three to the right of the cut and three to the left; usually batteries functioned in three two-gun sections.

Stewart's formation was described as follows by a member of the battery:[394] "The battery... proceeded at once to form 'by half battery' on both sides of the Railroad cut, on the ridge nearest the town, and abreast of the Thompson house. The formation of the left half battery was open order, and the three guns fronted about half the space between the turnpike and the railroad, the caissons taking cover of the buildings and the rear slope of the ground. Lt. Davison commanded the left half battery, and had with him Ord. Sgt. John Mitchell, Sgts. Thorpe and Moore, Lance Sgt. McDougall, and about 42 corporals, drivers and cannoneers. Our guns pointed due west, taking the Chambersburg Pike en escharpe. The right half battery was in line with us on the north side of the cut. Its right gun rested on the edge of a little grove, which extended some distance farther to the right... As Stewart commanded the right half battery in person, he did not have much to do with us, directly, during the action that followed."[395]

Stewart's guns did not become heavily engaged in the action for over two hours after they were deployed. As already noted, they were out of range of the Confederate cannons on Herr Ridge, and Rodes' guns on Oak Hill apparently could not see Stewart's men because of the intervening woods.[396] All the Confederate guns were concentrating their fire power on Doubleday's forward line posted on McPherson's Ridge, particularly Stone's brigade. The first action Stewart's guns did partake in was to help repel Daniel's first attacks on Stone's line at around 1400.[397] The battery's position was ideally suited for pouring enfilade fire on Daniel's troops who were attacking Stone, and would cause him severe problems for almost two hours. While they waited, Stewart's men saw some 200 or 300 Rebel prisoners (a "tough set") being sent to the rear from the right, no doubt from Iverson's and Daniel's brigades.[398]

Stewart's guns began to play an even more critical role in the battle after about 1515, when the Union troops on McPherson's Ridge were at last pushed back to Seminary Ridge. Since all these units reformed in the Seminary area south of the Chambersburg Pike, the guns of Battery B were given a relatively open field of fire against Heth's advancing troops that were pursuing the retreating Unionists. The only fire that the battery's men were under at this time was stray musketry whose shots "began to zip and whistle around our ears with unpleasant frequency."[399]

The battery's first true test came at about 1600 when Pender's fresh division took up the attack from Heth's by now exhausted command. The left flank of Pender's left brigade, Scales', proceeded directly into Stewart's line of fire. Indeed, Pender's extreme left regiment, the 38th North Carolina, which had its right on the Chambersburg Pike, was heading straight for the battery's position.[400]

The Union cannoneers had a clear view of the launching of this impressive Confederate attack: "This line stretched from the railroad grading across the Cashtown Pike and through the fields south of it halfway to the Fairfield Road nearly a mile in length. First we could see the tips of their color staffs coming up over the little ridge, then the points of their bayonets, and then the Johnnies themselves, coming up with a steady tramp, tramp and with loud yells."[401] There was no question who was going to win the coming conflict between iron and flesh. Stewart's guns opened up with canister, shell and shrapnel and totally decimated the 38th North Carolina on its front. The fire of the Union guns was so devastating that the surviving Confederate infantry had to hug the ground in order to survive.[402]

But the regiments south of the Pike continued to press their attack. Lieutenant Davison (who was suffering from two bad wounds, one of which struck his right ankle and made it impossible for him to stand without aid), saw a perfect occasion to cause even more havoc upon the enemy, and ordered the left half of the battery to swing to the left in order to pour a raking fire on the rest of Scales' command.[403] His exact order was "to form to the left half battery, action left, by wheeling on the left gun as a pivot so as to bring the half-battery on a line with the Cashtown Pike, muzzles facing south." The maneuver succeeded admirably: Davison's fire so swept his new front that "from our second round on a gray squirrel could not have crossed the road alive."[404]

However, this successful change in front brought on a new problem—it exposed the men of the left section to a flank fire themselves, from the Confederates of the 38th North Carolina, who seized the opportunity at that moment to renew their advance: "Then for seven or eight minutes ensued probably the most desperate fight ever waged between artillery and infantry at close range without a particle of cover for either side. They gave us volley after volley in front and flank, and we gave them double canister as fast as we could load." In addition, the battery's infantry supports (primarily from Dawes' 6th Wisconsin of the Iron Brigade) "climbed up over the bank of the cut or behind the rail fence in rear of Stewart's caissons and joined their musketry to our canister."[405]

Stewart's three guns posted north of the railroad cut also did their part to help repulse Scales' assault. Colonel Rufus Dawes, whose 6th Wisconsin was supporting Stewart at this time, was a witness to the magnificent scene: "For a mile up and down the open fields in front, the splendid lines of the veterans of the Army of Northern Virginia swept down upon us. Their bearing was magnificent. They maintained their alignment with great precision. In many cases, the colors of the regiments were advanced several paces in front of the line. Stewart fired shell until they appeared on the ridge east of Willoughby Run; when on this ridge they came forward with a rush. The musketry burst forth from Seminary Ridge, every shot fired with care, and Stewart's men, with the regularity of a machine, worked their guns upon the enemy. The rebels came halfway down the opposite slope, wavered, began to fire, then to scatter and then to run, and how our men did yell, 'come on Johnny, come on....'"[406]

Davison's men held their ground in spite of their growing casualties, and it seemed as if the entire Confederate attack would be turned back: "For a few moments the entire Rebel force, clear down to the Fairfield Road, seemed to waiver, and we thought that maybe we could repulse them, single handed as we were. At any rate, about our fifth or sixth round after changing front made their first line south of the pike halt, and many of them sought cover behind trees in the field or ran back to the rail fence parallel to the pike at that point, from which they resumed their musketry. But this second line came steadily on, and as Davison had now succumbed to his wounds, Ord. Sgt. Mitchell took command of the left half battery."[407]

While Davison's guns were facing Scales' troops, Stewart's half battery was faring less successfully against Daniel's Confederate troops who were now advancing north of the Pike. The regiments advancing straight towards the Union guns (32nd and 45th North Carolina, and 2nd North Carolina Battalion) were kept at a respectful distance by repeated blasts of canister. But farther to the north, Daniel's 43rd and 53rd North

Carolina, aided by O'Neal's 3rd Alabama, entered the woods on Stewart's right and began driving back the few Union troops posted there.

The only Union unit that can be identified with certainty as fighting in the Wills Woods on Stewart's right at this time is the 97th New York of Baxter's brigade. Baxter's troops, as already noted, had been withdrawn from northern Seminary Ridge at around 1500, leaving the defense of the extreme Union right to Paul's brigade. General Baxter reported that his brigade returned to the support of Stewart's battery,[408] where some of the troops that were out of ammunition were resupplied. It is not clear which units were deployed with or behind Stewart's guns, and which were stationed in the Wills Woods. Other evidence to be cited shortly will show that the 11th and 88th Pennsylvania were with the cannons. A passage in the 97th New York's regimental history suggests that it stopped to fight in the woods,[409] and another account says that the 83rd New York "stopped near the position of Stewart's U.S. Battery long enough to prevent its capture."[410] Other sources place some of Cutler's units in the Wills Woods at this time, but Cutler's battle report makes it clear that his brigade was on the eastern side of Seminary Ridge when he sent three regiments (14th Brooklyn, 76th and 147th New York) to aid Stewart's battery.[411]

Stewart's three guns north of the cut held their position until the infantry on their right and supporting infantry in their rear began to melt away. Their most stalwart supporters at the moment were Rufus Dawes' 6th Wisconsin of the Iron Brigade. As already noted, the 6th had been detached from its brigade at the opening of the battle, and after helping capture Davis' men at the middle railroad cut was retained on the north side of the Chambersburg Pike to support the right of the line on McPherson's Ridge. During the early afternoon, the regiment was at several positions between Seminary Ridge and McPherson's Ridge, north of the Pike, fighting off Confederate skirmishers and artillery shells coming from various directions. When Heth attacked at 1430, the 6th was on eastern McPherson's Ridge and, being detached, seemed to be overlooked as Doubleday's front line pulled back to Seminary Ridge. Dawes was aware that the ground to his rear was being swept by fire from Rodes' troops, and that "it would cost many lives to march in line of battle through this fire. I adopted the tactics of the rebels earlier in the day, and ordered my men to run into the railroad cut. Then instructing the men to follow in single file, I led the way, as fast as I could run from this cut to the cut in Seminary Ridge. About a cart load of dirt was ploughed over us by the rebel shells, but otherwise not a man was struck."[412]

After this clever maneuver, Dawes reformed his unit in the strip of woods on Seminary Ridge immediately behind Stewart's three guns. While his men were catching their breath, Dawes went down to stand among Stewart's guns as they began to fire on the advancing Confederate line. He witnessed the repulse of Scales' brigade, as already described, but then saw Daniel's men advance directly on his front. These Confederates advanced cautiously, and from the start poured forth a steady fire of deadly musketry. "This killed Stewart's men and horses in great numbers, but did not seem to check his fire."[413]

Dawes was still with Stewart's guns when he saw Lieutenant Clayton E. Rogers of Wadsworth's staff ride up rapidly. He bore an astonishing message: "The orders, Colonel, are to retreat beyond the town. Hold your men together." Dawes did not understand the purpose of the order, since Stewart's line was holding handsomely, until be looked to his right and rear and saw the XI Corps in full retreat.[414]

Dawes dutifully faced his regiment to the rear by the rear rank, and headed for the town with his right near the railroad embankment. This route took him on a more northerly course than the rest of the Iron Brigade, which retired from Seminary Ridge on a variety of courses between the Chambersburg Pike and Fairfield Road. Dawes knew nothing of Cemetery Hill and was concerned about Ramseur's troops advancing from the left: "If we had desired to attack Ewell's twenty thousand men with our two hundred, we could not have moved more directly toward them... We could see only that the on coming lines of the enemy were encircling us in a horseshoe. But with the flag of the Union and of Wisconsin held aloft, the little regiment marched firmly and steadily. As we approached the town, the buildings of the Pennsylvania College screened us from the view of the enemy."[415]

By now Dawes could clearly see that all the other Union troops of the I Corps were retiring "in a direction at right angles to our line of march." He crossed Washington Street, still heading east, until he ran into some of Ewell's troops, and so turned to the right: "The first cross street was swept by the musketry fire of the enemy. There was a close board fence inclosing a barn-yard on the opposite side of the street. A board or two off from the fence made what the men called a 'hog-hole'. Instructing the regiment to follow in single file on the run, I took a color, ran across the street, and jumped through this opening in the fence. Officers and men followed rapidly. Taking position at the fence, when any man obstructed the passage-way through it, I jerked him away without ceremony or apology, the object being to keep the track clear for those yet to come. Two men were shot in this street crossing. The regiment was reformed in the barn-yard, and I marched back again to the street leading from the Pennsylvania College to the Cemetery Hill. To understand why the street was crossed in the manner described, it should be remembered that men running at full speed, scattered in single file, were safer from the fire of the enemy than if marching in a compact body. By going into the inclosure, the regiment came together, to be at once formed into compact order. It was in compliance with the order, to keep my men together. The weather was sultry. The sweat streamed from the faces of the men. There was not a drop of water in the canteens, and there had been none for hours. The streets were jammed with crowds of retreating soldiers, and with ambulances, artillery, and wagons. The cellars were crowded with men, sound in body, but craven in spirit, who had gone there to surrender. I saw no men wearing badges of the first army corps in this disgraceful company. In one case, these miscreants, mistaking us for the rebels, cried out from the cellar, 'Don't fire, Johnny, we'll surrender.' These surroundings were depressing to my hot and thirsty men. Finding the street blocked, I formed my men in two lines across it. The rebels began to fire on us from houses and cross-lots. Here came to us a friend in need. It was an old citizen with two buckets of fresh water. The inestimable value of this cup of cold water to those true, unyielding soldiers, I would that our old friend could know. After this drink, in response to my call, the men gave three cheers for the good and glorious cause for which we stood in battle. The enemy fired on us sharply, and the men returned their good effect. It cleared the street of stragglers in short order. The way being open I marched again toward the Cemetery Hill. The enemy did not pursue; they had found it dangerous business. We hurried along, not knowing certainly that we might not be marching into the clutches of the enemy. But the colors of the Union, floating over a well ordered line of men in blue, who were arrayed along the slope of Cemetery Hill, became visible. This was the seventy-third Ohio, of Steinwehr's division of the Eleventh Army Corps."[416]

Baxter's troops began pulling out not long after the 6th Wisconsin withdrew. Apparently Doubleday sent a general withdrawal order to all parts of the I Corps to withdraw. Robinson says in his report that he received orders to withdraw "at nearly 5 pm," and that those orders were not received "until all the other troops (except Stewart's battery) had commenced moving to the rear."[417] He then passed on the command and to Baxter, who says "we remained until ordered to retreat by General Robinson, having been outflanked on our right and left."[418]

Robinson reported that his regiments "retired fighting," and conducted frequent charges in route because of "the nature of the enemy's attacks." He and a number of other sources mention the "galling fire" that the retreating troops had to endure from both the left and right.[419] The fact of the matter was that this section of the line was being hotly pressed by both Ramseur's troops coming in from the north and from Perrin's men advancing from the south, and that there was a fair amount of confusion between the ridge and Gettysburg, as the following accounts will show.

John Vautier of the 88th Pennsylvania summarized the difficulties his regiment met during the retreat when he wrote: "The shattered fragments of the regiments comprising Robinson's division fell slowly back, firing as they retreated; but to make an orderly retreat was no easy matter, the advancing enemy pouring a withering fire on front and flanks, knocking down men at every step... Those of the fugitives who cut across lots and avoided the town reached the Cemetery safely, but the unfortunates who tried to pass through the town were nearly all captured."[420]

A good portion of the 88th initially managed to maintain an organized line as they tried to retire to the town. One member reported they "fell back slowly, firing as they retreated;" all the while the enemy was pursuing and firing back.[421] Any attempt to hold cohesion now met frustration when this column reached the town and all the chaos there. John Vautier noted that, "any attempt to make a stand in this bewildered and frantic mob was attended with the greatest difficulty and peril... The crowd was frightful and the men almost prostrated with overexertion."[422]

Several members of the 88th reported their experiences during the confusion of this retreat. Corporal Lewis Bonnin of Company B was wounded in the hip early in the retreat and continued on, carrying the regiment's colors with him. At last he felt he could go no farther, and gave the flag to another to carry. He then "crawled into a building to die." Shortly afterwards he was almost killed by an enraged Confederate who burst into the house claiming that someone from within had tried to shoot him.[423] Sergeant Charles Barber of Company E had a more amicable meeting with the enemy when he was captured. He was lying on the ground with a leg wound when the Confederate line passed over.

He begged the enemy not to shoot him, and the Southern officer responded, "Don't be afraid, my men will not hurt you." He then ordered two of his men to carry Barber to a safer place.[424]

Lieutenant Sylvester Martin of Company K of the 88th Pennsylvania was one of the lucky ones who successfully "ran the gauntlet of the Confederate fire, and though repeatedly shot at and called upon to stop;" he escaped unhurt.[425] Another soldier of the 88th, Lieutenant Robert Beath, gave up his chance to reach freedom when he stopped to aid Private Little, who had been shot through the body. He helped Little to a hospital in town, and stayed with his friend after a surgeon pronounced the wound mortal. Little, however, objected strongly to this diagnosis, and vowed to outlive the surgeon, which he did. Beath decided to make the best of his loss of freedom, and worked actively as a hospital attendant for the rest of the battle.[426]

Samuel Boone of the 88th Pennsylvania tried to retreat toward the Seminary with a "small remnant" of his unit. Finding themselves surrounded, they decided to destroy the flag of Iverson's 23rd North Carolina that they had captured earlier, rather than let the enemy have it back. Captain Joseph M. Richards of Company E cut the flag from its staff, and Boone asked to keep the finial. The group then dispersed and each headed toward the town as the best they could. Boone followed the north side of the railroad line for awhile until he ran into the skirmish line of one of Ramseur's or Doles' regiments. He promptly crossed the railroad line safely, amazed that he was not even shot at by the enemy troops only 60 yards away. He then entered the town on Chambersburg Street, only to meet Confederate fire coming westward from the town square. He was able to make it down Baltimore Street, where he hid for awhile near Jennie Wade's house, only to be discovered and captured by a "Louisiana Tiger" of Hays' Brigade, who sent him to the rear. He soon found himself unguarded for a moment and bolted, but was recaptured and "placed under guard and marched to the diamond, thence with some Eleventh Corps prisoners to a point of Rock Creek, opposite what is now Barlow's Knoll."[427]

George Hussey, later the regimental historian of the 83rd New York, agreed that there was "more or less confusion during the retreat through the town."[428] The 97th New York, a sister regiment of the 83rd in Baxter's brigade, withdrew in fairly good order from Seminary Ridge, only to find itself flanked by a Confederate line from the north and nearly surrounded. Altogether some 70 of its officers and men were captured. At some point during the retreat, the 97th lost the flag of

Iverson's 20th North Carolina that it had captured earlier in the afternoon. Its captor reportedly stayed "too long to show his prize, and when he got ready to go to the town he ran into Daniel's men who kindly and promptly relieved him of any further responsibility for that flag."[429]

Colonel Charles Wheelock of the 97th New York found himself surrounded by the enemy near the Sheads' house, a seminary for girls that is still standing on the north side of Buford Avenue (Chambersburg Pike). The following account is taken from a Washington newspaper: "Among the last to leave the field were the 97th New York infantry, commanded by Colonel Charles Wheelock, who, after fighting hand to hand as long as there was shadow of hope, undertook to lead his broken column through the only opening in the enemy's lines, which were fast closing.... Standing in a vortex of fire, from front, rear and both flanks, encouraged his men to fight with naked bayonets, hoping to force a passage through a wall of steel which surrounded him. Finding all his efforts vain, he ascended the steps of the Seminary, and waved a white pocket handkerchief in token of a surrender. The rebels not seeing it, or taking no notice of it, continued to pour their murderous volleys into the helpless ranks. The colonel then opened the door, and called for a large white cloth. Carrie Sheads stood there, and readily supplied him with one. When the rebels saw his token of surrender, they ceased firing, and the colonel went into the basement to rest himself, for he was thoroughly exhausted. Soon a rebel officer came in with a detail of men, and on entering, declared with an oath, that he would show them 'Southern grit.' He then began taking the officers' side arms. Seeing Colonel Wheelock vainly endeavoring to break his sword, which was of trusty metal and resisted all efforts, the rebel demanded the weapon, but the colonel was of the same temper as his sword, and turning to the rebel soldier, declared he would never surrender his sword to a traitor while he lived. The rebel then drew a revolver, and told him if he did not surrender his sword, he would shoot him. But the colonel was a veteran, and had been in close places before. Drawing himself up proudly, he tore open his uniform, and still grasping his well tried blade, bared his bosom, and bade the rebel 'shoot,' but he would guard his sword with his life. At this moment Elias Sheads, Carrie's father, stepped between the two, and begged them not to be rash, but he was soon pushed aside, and the rebel repeated his threat. Seeing the danger to which the colonel was exposed, Miss Sheads, true to the instincts of her sex, rushed between them, and besought the rebel not to kill a man so completely in his power. There was already enough blood shed, and why add another defenseless victim to the list?... Fortunately at this moment the attention of the rebel officer was drawn away for the time by the entrance of other prisoners, and while he was thus occupied, Miss Sheads, seizing the favorable opportunity, with admirable presence of mind, unclasped the colonel's sword from his belt, and hid it in the folds of her dress.... This artifice suceeded, and the colonel 'fell in' with the other prisoners. Miss Sheads... turned to the rebel officer and told him that there were seventy-two wounded men in the building, and asked if he would not leave some of the prisoners to help take care of them. The officer replied that he had already left three. 'But,' said Miss Sheads, 'three are not sufficient.' 'Then keep five, and select those you want, except commissioned officers,' was the unexpected reply. On the fifth day after the battle, Colonel Wheelock unexpectedly made his appearance, and received his sword from its noble guardian, with those profound emotions which only the soldier can feel and understand, and with sacred blade again in his possession, started at once to the front, where he won for himself new laurels, and was promoted to the rank of brigadier general."[430]

The remains of the 97th New York withdrew from the Sheads house area under command of Major Charles Northrup. In spite of the heavy odds facing the unit, Corporal James Brown insisted on stopping several times to wave the regiment's flag defiantly in the enemy's face. This bravery cost him his life.[431] The men of the 97th, no doubt encouraged by Brown's example, turned several times to form a line and try "to hold the rebels at bay for a few moments." But soon their organization collapsed. Lieutenant W.B. Judd fled for safety, and recalled that it was like "running a gauntlet in the strict sense of the word. The air seemed almost impossible to breathe without inhaling them. Some one fell beside me almost every step. It was here that Serg. Fred Munson fell mortally wounded, and Lieut. James Stiles was killed."[432]

A large group of the 88th Pennsylvania tried unsuccessfully to withdraw to the south to the Seminary, since they knew the ground there from being posted there earlier in the day. They clearly were not aware of Perrin's successful attack on that section of the line. Lieutenant George W. Grant of the 88th recalled, "The avenue of escape was cut off, and we were made prisoners of war, taken by the 12th North Carolina regiment, the same command that barely escaped capture at our hands a few hours before. Such was fate."[433] When Grant was captured, he overheard a southern soldier compliment the Union prisoners on the good fight they had put up: "you-uns fit like hell. The offices told you-uns was melish, but we-uns knowed better."[434] Apparently the Confederate officers of more than one regiment attempted to encourage their troops to fight better by telling them that they were facing militia, not veteran troops.

The 11th Pennsylvania began its retreat when they saw the enemy "gradually extending his line in the left as nearby to touch the Emmitsburg Pike." The unit began its withdrawal by pulling back through the eastern railroad cut. According to the regimental chaplain, William Locke, the 11th retreated in fairly good order: "Shoulder to shoulder they marched, rank after rank. Halting to fire upon the advancing foe, and then closing up again with daring coolness." But they, too, ran into the chaos in the town, which Locke blamed eagerly on the "broken and flying battalions" of the XI Corps: "It was a sight never to be forgotten. Crowding through the streets, and up the alleys, and over fences in utter ignorance of whither they were going, every moment increased the confusion and dismay to add to the terrors of the hour, the enemy gained possession of the town, and firing rapidly into our retreating ranks, shot and shell mingled their horrid sounds with the groans of the dying thus stricken down."[435]

Those of the 11th who could, made their way back to Cemetery Hill. When they arrived there, they sadly found that their beloved mascot, "Sallie the War Dog" was missing. Three days later she was found by an officer of the 12th Massachusetts who was leading a patrol out looking for stragglers. The poor dog had apparently gotten lost or was left behind during her unit's retreat, and returned to the spot where the 11th had fought on northern Seminary Ridge, where she found a few familiar friends in the unit. She remained with them "faithfully licking their wounds or patiently watching their lifeless bodies." Colonel Richard Coulter wrote about her that "During this faithful vigil of three days and nights, she must have been without food, and appeared quite lean fasting."[436] Sallie, who had early birthed at least one batch of puppies while "in the service," rejoined the 11th and stayed with the unit until she was "killed in action" at the battle of Hatcher's Run on 6 Feb. 1865; the regimental adjutant reported that she was in line with the file closers when she was struck by a bullet in the brain. "She was buried where she fell, by some of the boys, even whilst under a murderous fire."[437] Today her bronze image adorns the western face of the 11th's monument on northern Seminary Ridge, where she endured her three days' vigil over the regiment's dead and wounded after the 11th's retreat on 1 July.

The remains of Cutler's battered brigade also withdrew at the same time as Baxter. Cutler reported that "I received orders to move my brigade to the rear in the best order I could." Cutler apparently withdrew with his two regiments that were still posted at or near the railroad embankment east of the ridge (56th Pennsylvania and 95th New York). Captain John Cook of the 76th New York reported that his command had not been engaged with any Confederate infantry before it withdrew.[438] General Cutler stated that "although exposed to the enemy's fire on both flanks, the men marched with perfect steadiness and no excitement. Their steadiness had the effect to bring the enemy to a halt, when he threw out skirmishers, thus relieving us from the fire of the main line on the left." Cutler did not shy from danger during his retreat, and had two horses shot from under him. One was killed on the railroad line and the other was wounded in the town.[439]

The other three of Cutler's regiments (14th Brooklyn, 76th and 147th New York) had been recently sent to support the artillery line near the Chambersburg Pike, as already noted. When he received his orders to retreat, Colonel Fowler of the 14th calmly told his men, "Fall back, boys, but do not make a run of it." When he descended the hill and reached the railroad embankment, Fowler first perceived the extent of the corps' danger: "Our left flank was turned as well as our right. The column moved steadily along the railroad embankment to the town, the artillery moving on a road on the side of the embankment. The enemy's skirmishers were within one hundred yards of us, firing as they advanced, but their desire appeared to be to shoot the artillery horses, and they succeeded in shooting many, but not in capturing any of the guns."[440] Fowler boldy asked permission to throw out skirmishers to face the advancing enemy, but his request was refused.[441]

The historian of the 14th Brooklyn claims that the regiment "moved as steadily as if in parade. As a comrade dropped the ranks moved up." If this were so, the unit's cohesion lasted only until it reached the town, which was full of confusion. "This came about because all the Union troops in retreat attempted to pass through the main street, which was the broadest, utterly disregarding the sidestreets... The enemy had possession of the town ahead of the Union troops and as the 14th advanced they received a severe fire down every cross street. The citizens of the town, caught in the very center of the storm were terrified. Women peered from the windows, or peeped through the cracks of the doors held open only an inch or two, with blanched faces. Many of the inhabitants of the town offered shelter to the Union troops. But numbers of those who accepted it regretted the fact later on, as they were taken prisoners."[442]

Colonel Fowler recalled that "The column of infantry was closely packed and moved without panic." Even so, the enemy pressure from the right and the left made him despair in escaping to safety: "At one time I thought that we would have to disperse, and was on the point of ordering the colors taken from the staffs, but a moment's reflection determined me to carry through. I had a desire to stop and fight them, but their long lines of battle then near the town and advancing rapidly, convinced me that to stop was to lose the regiment."[443]

Fowler greatly faulted the enemy for not bringing up artillery to shell the retreating mass of Union troops. They did not do so until the rear of the Union column (which included the 14th) had entered the town, "and then only for a few shots, as their troops entered the town almost at the same time as ours." One shell struck and knocked down a brick house wall, right where Fowler and his adjutant were riding. Their horses shied across the street, which saved them, though they had been hit by fragments of brick and were covered with mortar.[444] Captain Cook of the 76th New York reported that 8 or 10 of his men were injured by falling bricks or wounded by infantry fire while passing through the streets of the town.[445]

The 14th Brooklyn also lost several men wounded to Confederate skirmishers who had occupied the north end of the town and were firing from behind stoops and windows. The regiment advanced along "main street" until it could proceed no farther because of the many enemy troops that appeared ahead of them. The New Yorkers quickly tore down a fence and cut through a blind alley to another street that led out to the Emmitsburg Road. Fowler, though, saw enemy troops ahead again, and led his command to the point where the Emmitsburg Road entered the town, and led the unit to safety by making a sharp left to Cemetery Hill.[446]

Stewart's battery barely managed to escape as all its supporting infantry began to melt to the rear. Stewart was still holding his own with his three guns on the north side of the eastern railroad cut when an aide from General Robinson rode quickly up. He said that the general had forgotten that the battery had been posted on his left flank, and now ordered Stewart "to fall back to the town as rapidly as possible." Upon inquiry, Stewart was amazed to learn that Robinson's troops were "about a half a mile" away, and that the 6th Wisconsin had been ordered back.[447]

Sergeant Mitchell, who was now commanding the left half of the battery, saw Stewart's guns begin to limber up, so he, too, prepared to withdraw. Since he was closer to the Chambersburg Pike than Stewart's half section, he was able to reach the roadway before the other half of the battery.[448] Lieutenant George Grant of the 88th Pennsylvania noted that the battery's guns during their retreat "dashed through our regiment, separating it."[449]

The battery's historian tells of the narrow escape of Mitchell's guns: "The rebels could have captured or destroyed our left half-battery—and perhaps Stewart's too—if they had made a sharp rush on both sides of the pike as we were limbering up, because as our last gun (the right gun of the left half-battery) moved off their leading men south of the pike were within 50 yards of us! But they contented themselves with file-firing, and did not come on with the cold steel. However, as soon as they saw the limbers coming up the Rebels redoubled their fire both in front and on our left flank, their object apparently being to cripple our teams so we would have to abandon the guns. They hit several horses, three or four of the drivers and two or three more of the remaining cannoneers while we were limbering up. During all this wreck and carnage Serg't Mitchell was perfectly cool, and all the men, following his example, were steady. The driver of our swing team being hit as they wheeled the limber to 'hook on,' Mitchell ordered me to mount his team. Just then the off leader was shot and went down all in a heap. But Mitchell and Thorpe had him cut of the traces sooner that it can be told, and off we went down the pike toward the town, the nearest houses of which were about a third of a mile off."[450]

Meanwhile Stewart was attempting to bring his three guns to safety. The Lieutenant stated that he "moved down through the timber, running a short distance parallel with the railroad cut, and then attempted to cross." He was especially sorry to have to leave his wounded behind, whose beseeching looks quite unnerved him. He was greatly surprised to learn that the cut was full of large rocks, which made it exceedingly difficult for the guns and limbers to pass over the cut. Even so, his men managed to get the first two guns over safely.[451]

The third gun was not so fortunate. Its pintle hook broke, and the tail fell to the ground. To make matters worse, some rebels at that moment came running out of the woods and shouted "Halt that piece!" Stewart was totally taken by surprise, but one of his men boldy made the Confederates stop to think when he shouted back "Don't you see that the piece is halted?" This brief delay enabled Stewart to set up his two lead pieces on the road. They at once opened on the Confederate detachment, who "took cover very quickly."[452]

The damaged gun, though, was still posing a problem: "In the meanwhile, the men were taking the prolonge off the trail and tying up the gun to the limber. When the pintle hook broke, I felt that we would never be able to get the gun out of the cut, as it took us a long time to disengage the prolonge from the trail; then we had to get the limber out of the cut, then the gun; then we had to tie the trail to the rear of the limber; and during all this time the enemy were firing upon us not more than one hundred yards; and just as we got the gun out of the cut, the enemy made a dash, this time getting within fifty or sixty yards, killing one driver (the driver of the swing team), and seriously wounding the wheel driver and two horses, which again caused delay. But the two pieces kept firing at them all the time, and I will say right here if ever men stayed by their guns, it certainly was then."[453]

Once the entire half battery was safely moving along the road, Stewart directed his sergeant to move the guns into town while he went back to see how the left half battery was doing. (Apparently he had never sent these guns a direct order to retire, and he could not believe that Davidson would have left "without informing me of the fact"). He headed for the Thompson house (near Mitchell's left—also the location of Lee's headquarters for the rest of the battle), but when he neared it he saw that it was occupied by the enemy. "On seeing me, they shouted 'Surrender'; but as I had not gone there for that purpose, I wheeled my horse and started him off as fast as he could go."[454] The Confederates fired a volley at him that missed but for two bullets that tore through his blouse.[455]

Stewart continues: "It was my intention to catch up with my sergeant, but I found that I could not reach the road as it was occupied by the enemy—in fact, the enemy was closing in on all sides. On seeing that I could not make my way to where my half battery had gone, I started across the field, when the first thing I observed in front of me was a high fence, and as I could not go either to the right or left without being made a prisoner, I headed my horse for it, and he took the leap in splendid style. As he was making the jump I was struck on the thigh with a piece of shell. The shock was terrible, and I thought at first my leg was broken, but after feeling it I found the bone all right. However, I had scarcely gone any distance before I was so nauseated that I could scarcely keep in the saddle, and seeing some water in a furrow, I dismounted, bathed my face, and drank a mouthful or two of the water, and feeling somewhat relieved of the sickness, I remounted, and, on reaching the other side of the field, I found most of the rails down. A short distance further, I found one of my men bursting the cartridges that were on one of the caissons. The rear axle of that caisson was broken and four of the horses had been killed. I inquired if any one had ordered him to remain and destroy the ammunition, and he said, 'No; but the Rebs are following us up pretty hard, and if the caisson fell into their hands they would use the ammunition upon us.' I remained with him until he had destroyed the last round and then told him to keep with me."[456]

Stewart reached the rest of his battery just inside the town. By then the guns had caught up to Dawes' 6th Wisconsin, which had formed across the street. The regiment opened its line to let the guns pass. One of the men noted that Dawes had an assortment of remnants from other units rallied on his line, and also saw the 6th's adjutant (Brooks) loading and firing a musket with the troops.[457]

Mitchell's lead gun proceeded farther into town, and its men were surprised to see Colonel Lucius Fairchild of the 6th Wisconsin sitting on the porch of a house next to the road. His left arm had just been amputated, but he still had the energy to cry out "Stick to 'em boys! Stay with 'em! You'll fetch 'em finally!" Sergeant Mitchell was reluctant to leave the Colonel behind to be captured, so he "prolonged" his rear gun in the street and prepared to load. But just then Johnny Cook of the battery, came riding up with the news that Lieutenant Stewart would be up with the rest of the battery as soon as he finished destroying the abandoned caisson.[458]

Mitchell rehitched his gun, and continued on down the street. At the next cross roads he found one gun of the 2nd Maine battery drawn up with fixed prolonge. The gun started firing as soon as the 6th Wisconsin passed by and cleared its front. Meanwhile Lieutenant Stewart, riding at the rear of his command, passed by the house where Fairchild was (the colonel was still waving his hat, though well aware he would soon be captured) and caught up to the rest of the battery at the town square.[459] The unit then proceeded calmly to Cemetery Hill, having lost during the day's action two men killed, two mortally wounded, thirteen men badly wounded, and a large number of horses. Its losses in equipment were two guns disabled, three caissons broken down and abandoned in the town, and one caisson destroyed.[460] It would have lost an additional caisson that had broken a wheel unless a few of its men "coolly stopped and in the face of fierce fire jacked up the caisson and replaced the wheel, resuming their march without the loss of a man."[461]

The battery had lost heavily, but was lucky not to have been captured entirely. One battery member was actually astonished at the Confederates' caution in their pursuit: "He seemed to be utterly paralyzed at the punishment he had received from the First Corps, and was literally 'feeling every inch of his way' in his advance on our front. Riding the swing team on our team, I kept looking over my shoulder to see him come on, and wondered why he was so cautious, knowing, as I did, that none of our troops were left in the position that had just been abandoned... without doubt the rebels could have gotten on top of us by a sharp rush while we were limbering up, and we could not comprehend their failure to do so. Everybody expected that we would be taken. But their general [Heth] has told me since the war that they did not understand the situation, not being able to conceive that a battery would hold such a position so long without adequate infantry support, and being convinced that the Railroad cut behind us must have been full of concealed infantry waiting for them to come on."[462]

Colonel Wainwright later noted that the escape of Stewart's guns— and those of all the others but one on the Seminary Ridge line— had been aided by the fact that most of the Union infantry for some reason elected to withdraw along the railroad embankment. This left the Chambersburg Pike momentarily free for the artillery to use. Wainwright shouted "Trot! Gallop!" and the guns from his part of the line took off "in full gallop down the road, which being wide allowed them to go three abreast."[463]

Wainwright watched his guns "at the turn of the road just entering the town" and felt that all was safe, but soon found he was very mistaken. He had to climb over the railroad cut in order to get by his batteries, and so entered the town from another direction (presumably the north). Just then the Confederates pulled up some guns on Seminary Ridge and fired at the rear of the column, wrecking one of Stewart's caissons, as already noted.

Once he entered the town, Wainwright noted, "The streets of the town were full of the troops of the two corps. There was very little order amongst them, save that the Eleventh took one side of the street and we the other; brigades and divisions were pretty well mixed up. The men were not panic stricken; most of them were talking and joking." As he pushed through the crowd, Wainwright came upon General Rowley of the I Corps. Rowley was very talkative, and claimed to be in command of his Corps. The colonel tried in vain to reason with him, pointing out that Wadsworth and several others outranked him. When he could make no headway with this logic, Wainwright concluded that Rowley was drunk, and rode on to Cemetery Hill.[464]

The Confederates Capture the Town

The Union generals on Seminary Ridge certainly did their best to hold out "as long as possible," as Howard had ordered Wadsworth.[465] Doubleday waited in vain for reinforcements from Howard up to the very end; as already noted he had sent at least two messengers to Howard to request help, but none was sent.[466] Doubleday and his aides were very active in the defense of what the General called "Seminary Hill,"[467] and Doubleday himself was seen helping to sight some artillery pieces.[468] Doubleday says that he stayed at the Seminary to supervise the retreat "until thousands of bayonets made their appearance around the sides of the building."[469] This claim is corroborated by an anecdote from another source that says the General "at one time was nearly surrounded by the rebels, and only escaped by reason of their ignorance of his rank."[470]

After leaving Seminary Ridge, Doubleday says, "I then rode back and rejoined my command, nearly all of whom were filing through the town. As we passed through the streets, the pale and frightened inhabitants came out of their houses, offering us food and drink and the expression of their deep sorrow and sympathy."[471] Colonel Rufus Dawes of the 6th Wisconsin also made reference to a citizen who bought water to his men during the retreat.[472] The historian of the 76th New York recounted: "At many of the doors and windows, the ladies, lads and girls stood through that long hot day and passed water and food to the union troops." He even mentions a "nameless heroine" who with a cup in each hand, so busily dealt out water to the thirsty boys, the tears of sympathy running down her lovely cheeks, as the wounded soldiers came hobbling by, until pierced by a rebel ball, she fell dead by the side of her pail!"[473]

As Daniel's troops followed up their success against Stewart's portion the line, they almost ran into a portion of Ramseur's brigade coming in from the left. Fortunately for the Confederates, Ramseur halted his line long enough for Daniel's men to form up and see them. All the while the Union troops were fleeing up the railroad line "like partridges in a nest." Some of Ramseur's men saw their commander and began yelling "Bring us a battery" in order to shell the mass of fleeing Yankees. Ramseur at once screamed at a courier, "Damn it! tell them to send me a battery! I have sent for one a half dozen times!" The general then thought twice about his cursing, and raised up his hands while saying, "God almighty, forgive me for that Oath."[474]

As Ramseur's troops turned towards the town and Daniel's proceeded along the railroad line, Lieutenant Colonel Thomas Carter finally managed to bring some guns up from Oak Hill and commenced firing on the fleeing enemy. He reported later that "my battalion followed, a few pieces unlimbering from time to time to break up the formations of the enemy as they endeavored to rally under cover of the small crest near town."[475] It may have been one of these shots that struck and destroyed a limber from Stewart's battery as it was retiring through the town, as already noted.[476]

One of Ramseur's men thought that Carter's shelling caused a large number of Yankees to surrender quickly to his regiment. One of Carter's last shots hit a Union infantryman who happened just then to jump up on the railroad line. J.D. Hufham saw it strike the man in the breast and cut him right in two. Despite the gory scene, Hufham ran up and grabbed the man's canteen. He was extremely thirsty and had been frustrated all afternoon in his efforts to get a drink. Most of his comrades had filled their canteens with liquor before the battle, and did not want to share. During the brigade's advance he came upon a wounded Yankee with six canteens, but the man wouldn't let him pull any of them away from him. Later he saw a fallen Yankee and went to grab his canteen, only to have the man exclaim "Don't take my water!" Hufham, flustered, simply replied, "Excuse me sir, I thought you were dead." Thus, when he saw the Union soldier killed by the cannon ball he was able to say, "I recken you are dead," as he picked up this man's canteen. He even carried it through the rest of the war and kept it afterwards.[477]

Not long after Doubleday and most of the Union troops left the Seminary, Lieutenant Colonel Charles E. Livingston of his staff returned there carrying a message (perhaps the one telling Robinson to retreat). Livingston must have arrived after most of Perrin's troops had moved on toward the town, and he was lucky to escape safely. In the brief moment he was at the Seminary before he realized his predicament, he saw some of Heth's division advancing towards the Seminary very cautiously, "evidently under the impression there was an ambuscade for them there." He also saw them forming against cavalry, evidently because they had seen more of Buford's cavalry.[478]

There was intense, even bitter, debate after the battle as to which corps retreated first, and so by implication caused the collapse of the entire front. Christian Boehm of the 45th New York says that his regiment was making a stand near Pennsylvania College when he saw "the left of the First Corps broken to pieces and pursued by overwhelming numbers of the enemy making for the left of the town,"[479] and General Carl Schurz asserts that the withdrawal of his men was hindered by "the streets being filled with vehicles of every description and overrun with men of the First Corps."[480]

In reply, the partisans of the I Corps complained that the XI Corps broke first, and so made the I Corps line untenable. Then the troops of Doubleday's command were unable to retreat safely through the town because it was full of frantic "flying Dutchmen." One Union doctor, who was on duty at the railroad station on Carlisle Street, wrote of the XI Corps retreat: "Away went guns and knapsacks, and they fled for dear life, forming a funnel shape tail, extending through the town. The rebels coolly and deliberately shot them down like sheep. I did not see an officer attempt to rally or to check them in their headlong retreat. On came the rebs and occupied the town, winning at that point a cheap victory."[481]

The fact cannot be denied that the XI Corps was driven back first, when Barlow's troops on Barlow's Knoll began to feel the brunt of Early's attack at about 1530. Barlow's defeat endangered Schimmelfennig's division, which in turn was driven back, Von Amsberg's brigade withdrawing last on the left. But the collapse of the XI Corps was not the cause of the defeat of Doubleday's corps. As shown in the text, the I Corps brigades were wearied and outnumbered when they began to be driven back; first Robinson's men on the right, then Wadsworth's and Rowley's on the left. The final defeat of Paul's brigade, the last Union troops to hold northern Seminary Ridge, came solely because of Ramseur's flank attack and not because of any assistance from the troops that had defeated the XI Corps. In fact, Doles' brigade attempted to intercept Doubleday's men after it drove back Schimmelfennig's division, but was unable to reach the Yankees who were retreating along the railroad line from Seminary Ridge to the town in time to stop them.[482]

Numerous commanders in both corps claimed that their regiments withdrew in good order to Cemetery Hill.[483] In actuality, a few units may have done so—particularly of the Union troops posted near the Seminary—but individual accounts and anecdotes make it clear that there was much confusion, particularly in the town, and that there were many individuals and small groups of men who simply ran to safety as best they could.

Historian Harry Pfanz points out that the Union retreat could have been done with much less loss and confusion if someone had posted provost guards (or even cavalry detachments) in the town in order to direct the troops to the rear and their eventual rallying point on Cemetery Hill. But no one thought to do so.[484] General Doubleday thought that the retreat might have been "a very successful one" if Barlow's and Robinson's men (the troops on the right wing of each Corps) had not retreated at the same time and so become entangled in the town.[485] This oversimplifies the matter. Even if the fight on 1 July had been on one front instead of two, the defeated Union troops would have lost heavily during their retreat to and through the town. Such was the nature of battle. What caused all the confusion was not so much the presence of two corps retreating from perpendicular fronts, but the town itself—the Union troops (particularly those on the right of the I Corps) did not know where they were going, and so got lost in the town, only to be captured by the enemy in large and small detachments, especially those who sought shelter in the town itself.

The irony of the situation was that, had Doubleday's line near the Seminary held on just a half hour longer it probably would have had to succumb to the pressure from Ramseur, Doles, and even possibly Hays' troops coming up from the rear. However, as has been shown, Doubleday's decision to withdraw was not based on that pressure, but on the fact that Pender's troops had broken his line south of the Seminary and were outflanking it even farther to the left. He rightly judged that any delay in retreating might result in capture by the enemy troops coming from the left, not the right. The only I Corps troops who were directly attacked by units from the right as well as the left were those posted between the Chambersburg Pike and Wills Woods (Stewart's battery and its supports), who appear to have been the last to withdraw from Doubleday's Seminary Ridge line.

The ultimate irony is that the Confederate victory would probably have been just as complete had Hill's troops not attacked at all in the afternoon—Early's defeat of Schurz would have forced Doubleday to retreat anyway, without the intense loss of life incurred by both sides on McPherson's Ridge, Seminary Ridge, and the swale in between. This scenario would have set up a most interesting confrontation between Hill's six fresh brigades (Pender's four, plus Pettigrew's and Brockenbrough's of Heth's) and Doubleday's somewhat worn out troops on Cemetery Hill and northern Cemetery Ridge—a confrontation the Confederates might well have won.

The extent of the chaos in the town cannot be underestimated. The troops of both Union corps filled the streets, which were already jammed by retreating ambulances, artillery and wagons.[486] Anna Garlach, a resident of Baltimore Street, thought that the roadway was at one time so crowded with troops that she could have crossed the street by walking on their heads.[487]

It should also be pointed out that the Confederate troops were also more than a bit disorganized by their success, and particularly by their efforts to move through the town. The streets were nowhere wide enough to deploy any large units in line, and Union sniper fire from the streets or houses made any hasty advance dangerous. Union cannons deployed in the streets, particularly at the town square, were particularly effective at controlling stretches of roadway with their blasts of canister. Hays' Louisiana troops seemed to have done the best job of advancing through the town in any sort of order, but they passed only through the smaller southwestern part of town.[488] Perrin's 1st and 14th South Carolina entered the town next from the west, and they penetrated as far as the town square, before Colonel Perrin feared they might be cut off, and recalled them. He thought it was more effective to send in squads of volunteers to gather up prisoners, rather than whole regiments, and in this he proved right.[489] Not long after Perrin withdrew the main body of his two regiments, Ramseur's brigade began moving through the western side of town, as also did Doles'.[490] In all this confusion it is a wonder that the Confederate forces did not accidentally begin shooting at each other.[491]

The greatest single capture came late in the afternoon when the troops that had gathered in the buildings around the Eagle Hotel with a large portion of the 45th New York at last surrendered.[492] Another large capture occurred when Coster's brigade was overrun following its brief stand at the tannery.[493] Other captures came singly and in scores throughout the afternoon and evening, particularly of those troops who attempted to hide in the town's houses. Some of Hays' Louisiana Tigers searched the Fahnestock house at Baltimore and Middle Streets and found more than a dozen Union troops hiding there.[494] Three Federal soldiers were captured at the home of Michael Jacobs, located at Washington and Middle Streets. Jacobs' young son Henry was looking out the window from the basement, where the family had taken shelter, and saw a Union soldier go running by. Next came shouts of "Shoot him!" and the crack of a rifle shot knocked the man dead. A few moments later some Pennsylvania troops banged loudly at the door and asked for shelter. Mr. Jacobs accepted one who was wounded and two of his comrades, and sent the rest on their way. Half an hour later a squad of Confederates arrived to search the house. They found all three Yankees, and took the two healthy ones as prisoners, leaving the wounded one for the moment.[495] Someone else later came to take the wounded man prisoner. He may have been Corporal C.L. Burlingame of the 150th Pennsylvania.[496]

Similar captures must have occurred in a great number of other houses in town. Albertus McCreary lived with his family at the southwest corner of Baltimore and High Streets. They, too, had sought refuge in their basement. Mr. McCreary heard a great commotion in the street and looked out a window just in time to see a cannon fire with great noise and a cloud of dust and smoke. A short while later a squad of five Confederate soldiers suddenly threw open the basement's outer doors and everyone thought they were going to be killed. But the Confederates only wanted to search for Union soldiers, of whom they found thirteen. The Confederates got an added bonus when McCreary offered them something to eat from the meal that was laid out in his dining room but had been interrupted by the battle.[497]

Treatment of Casualties

Among the many Union prisoners captured were also the numerous wounded left on the field as well as in various temporary hospitals set up in town. The first aid station in town was actually set up in the railroad depot in Carlisle Street on the afternoon of 30 June to house some six or eight of Buford's men who were ill. Townsman Robert McCreary helped set up the temporary hospital, which was soon equipped with twenty beds.[498] Little did McCreary know that this facility would be teeming with wounded the next day. One of the first battle casualties was Sergeant Goodspeed of Company M, 8th Illinois Cavalry, who was brought to the hospital at the depot. The first amputation there was probably Private Williams of Company M of the 8th Illinois.[499]

By midafternoon Confederate artillery shells began hitting the depot, and it became necessary to move the men being treated there. Dr. Abner Hard of the 8th Illinois recalled that the enemy cannons "opened a torrent of shots upon us, and we soon found that our hospital, at the depot, was in their range; some of the shots striking the buildings and tearing them to pieces." The regiment's wounded were removed from the depot to the Presbyterian Church on Baltimore Street near the center of town. Dr. Hard was helping to amputate the arm of a Confederate soldier "when a messenger announced a dispatch from General Buford that we must fall back hastily arranging for the care of the wounded by leaving surgeons Beck, Rulison, and Vosburg to attend them. We left the church to find the street crowded by the retreating Eleventh Corps; and as we rode up toward the cemetery the rebel bullets fell thick and fast among us."[500]

Interestingly, the doctors of the 19th Indiana took over the vacated depot for their own use a short while after it was vacated. Surgeon Jacob Ebersole was working there when he witnessed the commotion of the XI Corps being driven through the town. When he looked out he saw one frenzied soldier hop on to his horse, which was tethered outside, and "both rider and horse disappeared in an instant." The soldier abandoned the doctor's horse later, and it was identified and returned to the brigade headquarters, where Dr. Ebersole was delighted to recover it on 5 July.[501]

The first hospital for Union wounded directly on the field was apparently located at the Seminary by Dr. George W. New of the 7th Indiana, who was head surgeon of Wadsworth's division. When this began to fill quickly, he "went back into town with other medical officers who took possession of several large rooms, halls, hotels, etc, being the first to open hospitals in the town for the wounded of the battle."[502] Both the Seminary and the large hospital at the McPherson barn were used almost exclusively as Union hospitals after they fell into Confederate hands.[503]

The Christ Lutheran Church on Chambersburg Street was the first of the town's several churches to be used as a hospital. Mary McAllister, who lived just across the street, saw the first Union casualties come into town: "Soon the wounded ones came in so fast, and they took them in different houses and into the church. The first wounded soldier I saw was with John McLean (a civilian). The soldier was on a white horse and John was holding him by the leg. The blood was running down out of the wound over the horse. Our John (Scott) had been sick and was just able to be about and he fainted....They brought him into our house and Martha and I put him on the lounge, and I didn't know what in the world to do."[504]

A citizen of the town named Charles McCurdy lived near the church: "Two doors below our house, the college Lutheran Church was filled with wounded. The auditorium of this church was on the second floor and the wounded had to be carried up a long flight of stairs from the street. Surgeons were at work under very crude conditions....The church yard was strewn with arms and legs that had been amputated and thrown out the windows."[505] Jennie Croll of Gettysburg remembered that forty men were laid out in the lecture room and another 100 in the church proper, where beds were improvised by placing boards over the pews.[506] Melvin Walker of the 13th Massachusetts recalled being treated at the church: "An operating table was placed in an anteroom opening off the main hall and here our surgeon worked with knife and saw without rest or sleep, almost without food, for 36 hours before the first round had been made...After the surgeons' work was done we had no care save such as the few less seriously wounded comrades could give...The first night 23 dead were carried from the room."[507]

Surgeons and chaplains were supposed to be honored as noncombatants, but they, too, occasionally fell victim to the god of battle. The most famous instance of a chaplain being killed was Chaplain Horatio M. Howell of the 90th Pennsylvania, who was killed on the steps of the Lutheran Church during the I Corps' retreat. A tablet erected on the spot states that Howell was "cruelly shot," but Sergeant Archibald B. Snow of the 97th New York saw the scene differently, and believes the chaplain was shot because he was in a dress uniform very similar to that of a Union officer: "Snow was then a sergeant in the Ninety-seventh New York, and knew Chaplain Howell by sight as both belonged to the same brigade. Snow was shot through the jaw, and went to the Lutheran Church Hospital, where his wound was dressed. He then started to leave the hospital, and passed through the front door of the church just behind Chaplain Howell, at the time when the advance skirmishers of the Confederates were coming up the street on a run. Howell, in addition to his shoulder straps and uniform, wore the straight dress sword prescribed in Army Regulations for chaplains, but which was very seldom worn by them. The first skirmisher arrived at the foot of the church steps just as the chaplain and Snow came out. Placing one foot on the first step the soldier called on the chaplain to surrender; but Howell, instead of throwing up his hands promptly and uttering the usual, 'I surrender,' attempted some dignified explanation to the effect that he was a non-combatant, and as such was exempt from capture, when a shot from the skirmisher's rifle ended the controversy. A Confederate

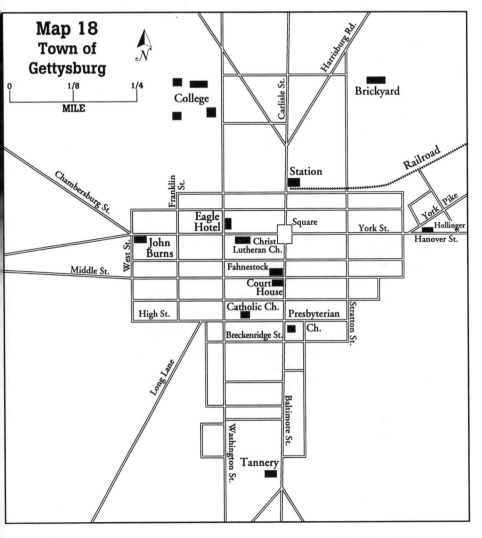

Map 18
Town of
Gettysburg
0   1/8   1/4
MILE

College

Carlisle St.

Harrisburg Rd.

Brickyard

Railroad

Chambersburg St.

Franklin St.

Station

Eagle Hotel

Square

York St.

York Pike

Hollinger

Hanover St.

West St.

John Burns

Christ Lutheran Ch.

Middle St.

Fahnestock

Court House

High St.

Catholic Ch.

Presbyterian Ch.

Stratton St.

Breckenridge St.

Long Lane

Baltimore St.

Washington St.

Tannery

lieutenant, who came up at this time, placed a guard at the church door, and, to the protests of the surgeons against shooting a chaplain, replied that the dead officer was armed, in proof of which he pointed to the chaplain's sash, and light, rapier like sword belted around the chaplain's body. The man who fired the shot stood on the exact spot where the memorial tablet has since been erected, and Chaplain Howell fell upon the landing at the top of the steps."[508]

Private Harry Hunterson of Company B, 88th Pennsylvania, was a witness to Chaplain Howell's death. He had been ordered to escort a wounded Confederate prisoner to a hospital in the rear, and was taking his charge up Chambersburg Street near the Lutheran Church. He saw a Confederate infantryman running along the other side of the street. When the foe raised his musket to fire, Hunterson pushed his prisoner in front of him as a shield. the soldier fired anyway, and the shot, Hunterson claimed, felled Howell. He managed to escape capture by tying a white cloth around his arm to show that he was a nurse. He later saw that someone stole Chaplain Howell's boots from his body.[509]

The most gruesome of the church hospitals might well have been the one established in the basement of St. Francis Xavier Roman Catholic Church on West High Street. Lieutenant Colonel Henry S. Huidekoper was treated at this church after the Union retreat for an arm wound he received near the McPherson farm about 2 ½ hours earlier: "On arrival at the Church (about 5:30 p.m.) I found an operating table placed in the entry, with the double doors open for light during operations....I went into an empty pew on the left hand side of the church, i.e., on the side towards the west and the third or forth pew from the street...asked some men to tear the pew door off its hinges and place it crosswise on the back and front of the pew. On this, I placed my swollen arm....About six o'clock.....I went to the (operating) table and got onto it with my head towards the west. I took some chloroform but not enough, for I distinctly remember having said, 'Oh, don't saw the bone until I have had more chloroform.' What I next remember was my saying, 'You took my arm off, did you, Doctor?' He was Dr. Quinan, Surgeon of my Regiment....I then swung off the table feet first and was told to seek a place in the pulpit to lie down...stepping carefully among the hundreds of soldiers who were lying in the aisles....Spying the gallery at the other end of the church, I worked my way back to the operating table and ascended the stairs to the gallery, which, as I had thought was empty....The night was a horrible one. All night long I heard from downstairs moans, groans, shrieks, and yells from the wounded and suffering soldiers."[510]

Once the churches were full, the numerous Union wounded were taken to private homes. Mrs. Robert Horner lived opposite the Lutheran church, and was surprised by the sudden rush of wounded who were brought into her house: "Before we fully realized there was a battle wounded men were being brought into our houses and laid side by side in our halls and first story rooms until every available place was taken up...In many cases carpets were so saturated with blood as to be unfit for further use, as well as the books that were used for pillows."[511] Jennie

McCreary was helping to tend wounded in a neighbor's house when she returned to find two wounded men in her own home on Chambersburg Street near the square—Colonel Samuel H. Leonard of the 13th Massachusetts, and Dr. Parker of the same regiment. She understood that Dr. Parker had been wounded "whilst coming down the Lutheran Church steps."[512]

Mary McAllister had been helping the wounded at the Lutheran Church, and was also surprised to find her nearby home full of injured when she returned there. "When I came to the door it was standing open and the step was covered with blood....I could hardly get through for the dining room was full of soldiers, some lying, some standing." Among the wounded men was Lieutenant Dennis Burke Dailey of the 2nd Wisconsin. Dailey happened to be carrying the sword of General James I. Archer, which he had received late that morning after the general was captured (see page 160). He asked Miss McAllister to hide it for him, and she did so by putting it in a wood box, "throwing some newspaper and some wood over it." Dailey was captured when the Confederates took possession of the house, but the sword was not found. He escaped on 5 July and went back in order to reclaim his prize and take it home with him.[513]

Dailey continues his story: "Myself and other wounded were taken from the house by a Confederate guard and carried to their rear. During General Pickett's charge, we were under fire of our own artillery, and many of our men being wounded we requested the officer to move us further back. His reply was that he could not do so without orders. On the night of the 4th, while in camp mid-way between Gettysburg and Millertown I made an arrangement with two of the Seventh Virginia Infantry, who were guarding us, to escape, but as soon as the opportune moment approached, the guard was doubled and our plans thwarted. On the night of the 5th, while the enemy was rapidly retreating over the ridge leading to the Hagerstown valley, I eluded the guard, by leaving the road and taking shelter in the dense timber and underbrush. There I remained until the afternoon of the 6th. When the rear of the enemy had entirely passed over into the valley, I made my way slowly, and with great difficulty, back to Gettysburg, and to the house of Miss Mary McAllister, who informed me that Colonel Morrow had taken my sword and belt, with the promise to her, that I should have them on my return."[514]

Dailey caught up to his brigade at South Mountain, and gladly recovered Archer's sword. He then presented it to General Meredith, who kept it until his death in 1881. On the suggestion of General W.W. Dudley, Dailey wrote to Meredith's son and asked to have the sword returned to him, which was done. He later thought several times of returning it to Archer, but decided not to when he heard of some "discourteous" comments Archer made to General Doubleday. After that, he decided to bequeath it to his sons, "with the injunction that it shall never be used against our country and its flag."[515]

Another important captured item was concealed by the Hollinger family, who lived on Hanover Road near its intersection with York Street. It seems that three wounded officers of the 6th Wisconsin (Lieutenant Lloyd G. Harris, Lieutenant W.M. Remington and Lieutenant John Veely) had just been at the temporary hospital in town when they were moved on the advice of their surgeon to the "pleasant quarters" of the Hollingers. Soon afterwards they were joined by Sergeant William Evans of the 6th who was carrying the flag of the 2nd Mississippi that had been captured at the railroad cut that morning. Later in the afternoon Harris heard heavy firing nearby, and went upstairs to see what was happening. He soon saw the XI Corps in retreat, and promptly went downstairs to urge his friends to flee in order to avoid capture. Mrs. Hollinger fainted during all the commotion, and Lieutenant Harris and her husband carried her to the basement. Since the enemy troops were now so near, Harris escaped "by going through houses." After he passed two cross streets, he found his two fellow officers in an ambulance. "Once with them we lead the retreat."[516]

Sergeant Evans was not well enough to run, and had to stay behind. He begged the two Hollinger daughters to help him hide the captured flag. They quickly cut a hole in his bed tick (mattress) and thrust in the flag, and then sewed up the opening. In this way the flag remained hidden as long as the Confederates occupied Gettysburg. When they left early on 4 July, Evans brought his "precious trophy" to Culp's Hill and gave it to Colonel Dawes.[517]

Not all the trophies captured by the 6th Wisconsin were able to be saved during the retreat, however. Colonel Dawes had given six swords captured at the railroad cut to regimental surgeon A.W. Preston to take to the rear. He brought them with him to a hospital site, and lost them when it fell to the Confederates. Dawes had no ill will to the doctor for their loss, "as his hands were full of work with the wounded men."[518]

Among the numerous Union wounded who had to be left behind during the retreat were several high ranking officers. Colonel Roy Stone, commander of one of Doubleday's brigades, was left behind in the

McPherson barn, and Colonel Lucius Fairchild of the 2nd Wisconsin had to remain at a house in town after his arm was amputated.[519] Colonel Samuel H. Leonard was treated at the Smith S. McCreary House on Chambersburg Street, where General Gabriel R. Paul was soon brought. Paul, another of Doubleday's brigade commanders, had been badly wounded in the face, and was not expected to live. His son even arrived in town on 9 July with a coffin and funeral arrangements. But, the general refused to die. Though blind in both eyes, he lived on until 1886, when he was buried in Arlington National Cemetery.[520] Brigadier General Solomon Meredith, commander of the Iron Brigade, was taken from the field by Gilbert M. Woodward of his staff when he was no longer able to stay on the field after his horse was shot and fell on him. He was treated at the Samuel Durboraw Farm, one mile northeast of Two Taverns.[521]

The ordeal of Orderly Sergeant Henry Cliff of Company F of the 76th New York shows how excruciating it could be to be left wounded on the field. He was hit in the left leg early in the fighting and had to be abandoned when his brigade withdrew to Cemetery Hill. The sun grew beastly hot and there was no shade for him. He saw a large tree nearby and appealed to a Confederate soldier to kindly carry him to its shade. The Rebel replied, "I shan't do it, get some of your damned Yankee horde to help you. If you had been at home, where you belonged, instead of fighting for the damned negger, you would not have needed help!" As a result, Cliff lay there for five days, unable to stir because of his broken leg, "almost dying from thrist and hunger, and nearly roasting, while day after day he watched the cool shade in its slow journey around the tree, never quite reaching him, but advancing toward him and then retreating, as though tantalizing him for his loyalty! He was finally found by our men, his limb amputated, and he still lives to tell his story."[522]

Lieutenant Colonel John R. Callis of the 7th Wisconsin also underwent quite an ordeal when he was left on the field. Early in the fighting on McPherson's Ridge he had his horse shot, and then received a slight wound himself. He stayed on the field, only to receive a severe wound in his right side at the height of the fighting on McPherson's Ridge at about 1615. Some of his men took him to a clover field north of the railroad cut, where he spent the next 43 hours with "the burning sun, the flies, and death staring me in the face."

The first Confederate unit to pass Callis was from North Carolina. "Some of them used me pretty rough, a party of one of them pulled off one of my boots. I begged them to unbuckle the leather of my spurs as they were tightly buckled around the instep which made the boots come off hard; they did not heed me but pulled and jerked until one boot came off. They tried it on but could not wear it, so they threw it down and went for my pockets." They found $220 and commenced arguing over it. Meanwhile Callis asked a friendly looking Rebel for some water; he had none but offered some whiskey, which Callis accepted.[523]

Callis then asked to see the colonel of the Confederate regiment, Tom Kenan of the 43rd North Carolina. Kenan came readily when he was told by Lieutenant Henry E. Shepherd that Callis was a native of Fayetteville, which was also Kenan's home town. Kenan took pity on Callis' condition, and had his other boot pulled off to make him comfortable. He also saw to it that Callis' money was returned. He then posted a guard of slightly wounded men over Callis, and left behind his own personal slave when he had to reenter the battle. Callis was forever grateful to Kenan for his kindness, and was upset to learn he had been killed later in the battle. In reality, Kenan had been badly wounded on the morning of 3 July on Culp's Hill.[524]

After dark a Confederate general whom Callis thought was Jubal Early came by and asked what he could do to help. Callis asked for help and a doctor was sent to him, who estimated that Callis only had six hours to live. By then Callis had developed a fever, which was somewhat alleviated by some whiskey that the Confederate general left and cold water brought by his guards.

Callis continues his account: "When the enemy began to retreat over me I begged the guard and a negro to take me over the railroad grade to a little house that stood there, as they said, 'to keep the hosses from stomping me to death.' They dragged me into the house when they dove down into the cellar intending to desert and stayed there until the Rebel army had passed. They then came up and stuck to me until the Union men came up and took me into town." Callis was cared for at the home of David A. Buehler, and then at the house of Dr. John W. E. O'Neal from late July until early September. The bullet that wounded him was never extracted. Thirty years later, in 1893, he was pleased to learn that Kenan had survived the war—he had been captured after Gettysburg and held in prison until August 1865. The two exchanged friendly letters but were not able to meet; Callis died in Lancaster, Wisconsin, on 24 September 1898, and Kenan passed away on 9 January 1912.[525]

The highest ranking Union casualty on 1 July was Major General

John F. Reynolds. As already noted, his body was safely removed for burial after he was killed while leading his troops on the edge of Herbst Woods at 1030. The second highest officer casualty was Brigadier General Francis Barlow. He was taken first to the Josiah Benner House, which was struck by the several artillery shells on the evening of 2 July. "One of these set the house on fire, and only by considerable exertion were the flames extinguished...The other two contented themselves with scattering the plaster;" yet another shell caused the ceiling to collapse on wounded Lieutenant Theodore A. Dodge of the 119th New York, much to his "astonishment, discomfort and pain."[527] Barlow was later moved to the John Crawford House on Harrisburg Road, and then to Hoke's Toll House on the Baltimore Turnpike just past Rock Creek.[528]

The saga of the other Union hospitals—the large ones at Pennsylvania College and Almshouse as well as those at individual houses—is too lengthy to relate here. The reader is encouraged to read Gregory Coco's excellent book on the subject, *A Vast Sea of Misery.*

Most of the Confederate wounded were not treated in the town, since they fell in the fields to the north and west of Gettysburg. Almost all of the farmhouses and barns behind their battle lines were soon full of wounded, and a major temporary aid station for Hill's troops was set up in the woods near the "medicinal springs" just west of Willoughby Run and Herbst Woods.[529] A number of Confederate wounded were also treated at the Herr Tavern and its outbuildings. After the battle some soldiers wondered why the water from the tavern's well tasted so awful. They pumped it dry to find out and "here comes up a little piece of a wrist and thumbs...now that they knew what was the matter, there was alot of gagging done among them."[530]

One of the few houses in town used to house Confederate casualties was the John S. Crawford House, located on the Harrisburg Road at the northwestern edge of town. "About four o'clock in the afternoon, (July 1), the Rebels had possession of us. They made a charge through our hall. We were obliged to open our house for the wounded. Near dark, some of our wounded came staggering into the cellar, covered with blood; the cellar floor was muddy with blood and water, the latter of which had been poured on their wounds...(That evening) the Rebels took their wounded from our house, to the rear of their army; so we went to work and took up carpets, brought down beds, and tried to make our wounded as comfortable as possible...Our troops paid respect to the (hospital) flag that floated over our house...General Ewell wanted to make his quarters with us; but, as we could not, or rather would not put ourselves (to) any trouble to give him two private rooms, he went elsewhere to sleep, but came for breakfast, bringing with him Generals Early and Rhodes."[531]

Despite Samuel Cobean's complaint that the Rebels "stole everything edible about his farm and took all the cured meat and killed the cattle,"[532] the Confederates appear to have behaved quite reasonably in view of the fact that they had just won a major victory on northern soil. J.F.J. Caldwell of Perrin's brigade recalled that "No violence was offered to the citizens by our troops. With the exception of the wheat trampled, and one or two houses fired on the outskirts of the town, by our shells, to dislodge sharpshooters, they were uninjured. They were so badly frightened, that they contributed many articles of food, to pacify us, but there was nothing like a levy made upon them. Some light-fingered persons helped themselves secretly to fowls and other dainties, of course, but even these things were done gently. The bad behavior was in the rear, about the hospitals. There was a general uprooting of gardens and depopulation of henhouses. But there no insult was offered, nor was there any wanton destruction whatever. Servants were more difficult to restrain than soldiers. They insisted on universal pillage. I had one that brought me all conceivable small articles, from a green apple to a prayer book, and was highly disgusted when ordered to return anything."[533]

This is not to say that there was not the usual amount of petty pilfering on the battlefield, where the victors stripped what they could—shoes, clothes and personal possessions—from the fallen dead, and sometimes even the wounded. Nellie Auginbaugh saw a dead Union solder in the street before her house who was checked over by a number of Confederate soldiers who passed by. One took some personal possessions, and tossed a photograph he did not want to the Auginbaughs in case they would like to have it. After he left, Nellie's grandfather went out and rolled the body into a blanket. When another Confederate soldier came by, he saw the body in the blanket, and rolled it out in order to go through the pockets. After he left, Nellie's grandfather wrapped the body up again, and continued to do so each time a Confederate soldier unwrapped it.[534]

Long after the battle Major John W. Daniel, Early's adjutant, remembered how exuberant the Confederate troops were, and how quiet the townsmen were on the evening of 1 July. He noted that all the Southern troops behaved well: "They were tired, but they sought no rest; they were hungry, but they seized no meat; they were in power but they were forbearing." Even so, he was saddened to see all the slain Federals stripped almost to nakedness. Nor, did he admit, was this pilfering limited to the skulkers and non-combatants: "All too often it was done by the soldiers in the front ranks as soon as they overran a Union line."[535]

The losses on both sides west of Gettysburg were much heavier than those north of town, since there were more troops engaged there for a longer period of time. Casualties in the I Corps were so heavy that the famous command would never be the same, and would eventually have to be discontinued. Over 50% of the corps was lost, by far the highest of any Union corps in the entire battle. The XI Corps was second with 41%; the Union army average was 24%.[536] Robinson's and Wadsworth's divisions had the highest percentage loss in the entire battle of all the Union divisions (56.4% and 55.9% respectively) while Wadsworth's and Rowley's had the greatest numerical loss (2155 and 2103, respectively).[537] Likewise the I Corps had the four top brigades in the army by percentage loss, and the top five brigades by numerical loss.[538] It was the same with regimental losses. Of the 19 Union regiments with the highest regimental losses in the entire battle, 13 came from the I Corps in just one day of principal action. In addition, the I Corps furnished 6 of the top 7 regiments with greatest total loss in the battle, as well as 4 of the highest 5 in killed loss, 2 of the top 6 in wounded, and 12 of the top 20 in missing and captured.[539]

Particular note should be made of the losses in several special Union regimemts. Both were fighting in their first major battle. The 24th Michigan of the Iron Brigade carried 496 men into action, and lost 67 killed, 210 wounded, and 86 missing, almost all on the first day. This was the highest number total losses, highest number killed, and second highest number wounded of all the 238 Union infantry commands in the entire battle; its 73.2% loss was eighth highest in the army.[540] The 151st Pennsylvania of Stone's brigade also lost extremely heavily. Almost all its casualties occurred between 1500 and 1530 on 1 July—of 467 men, it lost 51 killed, 211 wounded and 75 missing (72.2%, ninth in the army). This unit was second in total losses and 6th in total killed.[541] The 149th Pennsylvania of the same brigade was right behind the 151st with 336 total losses (third) and 53 killed (fourth).[542] Both the 16th Maine and 147th New York tied for third highest percentage of losses(77.9%) while defending isolated positions—the 147th NY on the right of Hall's battery in the morning and the 16th Maine as a rear guard for Paul's brigade's withdrawal from northern Seminary Ridge.[543]

Confederate losses west of Gettysburg are more difficult to analyze because most of the brigades engaged there also participated actively in the rest of the battle. The significant exception was Iverson's brigade, which lost so heavily in its brief attack on northern Seminary Ridge (903 of 1384 engaged) that it could be only a bystander on Culp's Hill later in the battle. Its losses ranked first percentage wise for all the army's brigades other than Pickett's.[544] Daniel's brigade (750 of 2100 engaged) also lost heavily on 1 July, due to the persistence of its attacks on Stone's and Robinson's commands. Heavy losses were also suffered in Davis' (600 of 2300), Archer's (400 of 1200) and Scales' (400 of 1400) brigades, all of which would be as heavily engaged in Longstreet's great attack on 3 July. Their effectiveness in that assault was, of course, greatly impaired by their heavy losses—particularly in officers—on 1 July.

The heaviest Confederate regimental losses west of town occurred in three of Iverson's regiments (5th, 20th and 23rd North Carolina), two of Pettigrew's (11th and 26th North Carolina), plus Davis's 2nd Mississippi and the 1st and 14th South Carolina of Perrin's brigade. It should be noted that the 26th North Carolina of Pettigrew's brigade suffered a total of 687 losses in the battle—more men lost than any other regiment on either side had present. (The 26th started with 843 men, by far the most of any unit on the field). Altogether the 26th lost 172 killed, and 443 wounded (both the highest in the army by a wide margin) plus 72 missing.[545] About half of these losses occurred on the first day while fighting the 24th Michigan and 151st Pennsylvania, both of which suffered terrible losses themselves. The 26th's color Company F entered action with 3 officers and 88 men, and suffered 100% casualties: 31 were killed or mortally wounded and 60 were wounded; at the end of the day only one private, Robert Hudspeth, was available for duty, and he had been stunned by a shell. The company had three sets of twin brothers, and 5 of the 6 men were killed in the afternoon's fight.[546] One North Carolina clan, the Coffey family, lost 8 men killed or wounded during the day.[547]

James D. Moore of Company F, 26th North Carolina, suffered a unique wound that afternoon—he was shot through the leg by a .44 calibre bullet from a cavalry carbine. He thought that he had been fighting a Union cavalry regiment when he was hit, until he learned differently years later: "After the war Moore went to live in Indiana at a place called Winnamac. There he met a man named Hayes who was a member of the Twenty-Fourth Michigan Regiment and in the battle of Gettysburg. Hayes had lost his Enfield rifle on the forced march of the night before, and as his regiment was going into action on the morning of 1 July, he picked up a carbine dropped by one of Buford's cavalry, and used it during the fight. It was the only carbine in the Twenty-fourth Regiment and just before he retreated, when the colors of one regiment charging him was fifteen or twenty paces distant, he fired in their direction. Moore at the time was alongside the flag and received Hayes' shot. They became good friends and Hayes was of material assistance to Moore so long as the latter lived in the town."[548]

Interestingly, there was actually at least one Union cavalryman in action on northern McPherson's Ridge in the afternoon, though not on the front where the 26th North Carolina fought. General Doubleday in his battle report commended Private Dennis Buckley of Company H of the 6th Michigan Cavalry, who for some reason was on the field. He noted that Buckley, "having had his horse shot under him, also joined the One Hundred and Fiftieth Pennsylvania Volunteers, and fought throughout the day. Shortly after he came up, a shell from a rebel battery exploded in the midst of Company C, killing 2 men and dangerously wounding 3 others. Buckley joined this company, saying, 'This is the company for me'; and remained throughout the entire engagement doing excellent service with his carbine. He escaped unhurt."[549]

Though the Confederate forces west of town outnumbered Doubleday's corps approximately 2-1 (about 20,000 in Heth's, Pender's, and Rodes' divisions to 10,000 Union infantry; these numbers do not include Doles' Confederate brigade or Buford's 1600 cavalry), it took the Confederates almost a full day to drive the I Corps back. This was not because of a substantial difference in the fighting quality of the troops—both sides had veteran units as well as regiments entering their first fight. What basically happened was that Heth's hasty attack negated Hill's advantage on that front, and Rodes' awkward handling of his initial attack negated his advantage of coming in on Robinson's flank. In addition, it is an old military adage that odds of 3-1 or better are needed for an attacker to carry a position, provided the defender makes an adequate defense. It was not until the Union troops began to wear down physically and numerically that the Confederates were able to use their superiority in artillery and men to carry the enemy line—which had the advantage, at least in front of the Seminary, of a defense in depth.

Confederate casualties of about 4800 (4000 killed and wounded) were about 25% of their force, substantially less than the approximately

5900 Union casualties (3600 killed and wounded). Since the Union missing figure of 2200 includes many men who were killed or wounded, the combat loss figures for each side on this front were probably much the same. This means that the harsh combat losses the Confederates suffered as attackers were made up for in the confusion of the Union retreat. Where the Confederates really gained their advantage was in prisoners—they lost only about 800 (and some of Davis' were recaptured), whereas the I Corps lost some 2200, almost 25% of their total engaged.

These figures do not compare at all favorably with the loss comparison on the field north of town. Here the four Confederate brigades engaged (Doles, Gordon, Avery and Hays) lost only about 1000 men out of 5700 engaged, (17.5%), while the XI Corps lost 3000 out of some 5500 engaged (55%). In theory, an attacker should not be able to carry a defensive position at odds of 1-1, let alone inflict three times the number of casualties as suffered. On this front Schurz's men did not have any special defensive advantage from the terrain, nor did they have a defense in depth. Instead, Barlow jeopardized the line by moving forward to an unsupported position, and the corps suffered greatly from a lack of unity when its brigades were defeated one by one as they entered the action.

Thus Reynolds' decision to fight west of Gettysburg was redeemed by the effective defense his troops made throughout the day. With a few more reinforcements he might have held on longer, or at least conducted a better fighting retreat. The real problem this day came on the XI Corps front, where Howard gambled that he could hold on until reinforcements came up. He was fully expecting Slocum's XII Corps, not to mention Sickles' III Corps, to come up at any moment, and their late arrival severely jeopardized the XI Corps' ability to hold its extended line north of Gettysburg, as is shown in Chapters VII and IX.

CHAPTER IX

Cemetery Hill

Major General Oliver O. Howard, overall com-
mander of the Union troops on the field following the death of Major
General John F. Reynolds that morning, was not very happy with the
way events developed after 1500. Less than an hour earlier he had toured
the lines of the XI and I Corps and approved them, even though Schurz's
men were stretched out north of the town without any strong defensive
salients and over half of Doubleday's men had already been heavily
engaged earlier in the day in their position on the ridges west of
Gettysburg. Except for Rodes' attack on Baxter's brigade on northern
Seminary Ridge, the enemy had not been particularly aggressive since
noon in spite of their buildup in strength all across his front. Howard
felt confident that he could hold on until reinforcements arrived, since
he had already sent repeated messages for Sickles to bring his III Corps
up from Emmitsburg, and Slocum was known to be with his XII Corps
at Two Taverns, just 5 miles to the southeast of Gettysburg. In the
meanwhile, his lines appeared to be holding firm, and he had the
advantage of a cavalry brigade posted on each flank of his command
(Gamble's on the left, Devin's on the right), as well as a division (Von
Steinwehr's) and a battery (Wiedrich's) in reserve on Cemetery Hill.

This static situation began to deteriorate rapidly not long after
Howard returned to his headquarters on Cemetery Hill after his tour
of the front. At about 1430 the Confederate troops west of town began

renewing their attacks in earnest, and by 1515 the Union line on McPherson's ridge was in retreat to Seminary Ridge. At the same time, a large new enemy force appeared on Schurz's far right flank and began an artillery bombardment, at about 1300, followed at 1530 by an infantry attack.

This renewed Confederate pressure from all across his front brought appeals for help from all quarters. Schurz sent repeated requests for a brigade to support the far right of his line and even sent orders for Von Steinwehr to send a brigade on reconnaissance to the York Road[1], but Howard refused him in order to nurse his limited reserves. In fact, when Doubleday and Wadsworth requested support in order to deal with Hill, Howard actually directed Schurz "if he could spare one regiment or more," to send it to Wadsworth.[2] Howard's reluctance to release any of his reserves at this time certainly weakened the defensive capacities of Doubleday's and Schurz's lines, which had no local reserves of their own. Yet Howard had little choice—if he sent most or all of his reserves to the front, he could not be assured they would stabilize the situation there, and he would have no final reserves on which to rally the army or form a rear guard if either or both wings were defeated, as actually happened. All he could do was hold on and wait for Sickles or Slocum to arrive. As he wrote in his battle report, "To every application for re-enforcement, I replied, 'Hold out, if possible, longer, for I am expecting General Slocum every moment.'"[3]

In an effort to aid Schurz's right at this time, Howard directed his reserve battery on Cemetery Hill, the six three-inch rifles of Wiedrich's New York battery, to fire on the enemy's flank if they could get the range. Wiedrich's guns, however, by mistake directed their fire on Devin's cavalry brigade posted on Barlow's right, and forced Devin to retire all the way to the town in order to secure cover for his men.[4] Thus this error denied Schurz's far right of essential support just when he would need it most.

By 1530 affairs were going so badly on Schurz's right that Howard belatedly released Coster's brigade in an attempt to try to stabilize Barlow's command. Coster, however, was quickly overrun by Early's command, as we have seen. Howard attempted to ameliorate this bad situation by sending some of Buford's cavalry to slow down Early's advance. Devin's troopers, however, were able to do little more than to slow down Hays' advance through the southwestern quarter of the town.[5]

In the face of the crisis on Schurz's right, Howard also shifted the position of his last remaining brigade, Colonel Orland Smith's, so as to better support the two batteries on Cemetery Hill (Wiedrich's and the three serviceable guns of Hall's) and also be able to oppose the anticipated Confederate attack on the hill from the northeast. Smith had originally deployed his regiments "in line of battle by battalions in mass" in the rear of the hill. He now was ordered to advance over the front of the hill, where he stationed two regiments (136th New York and 73rd Ohio) on the left near the Taneytown Road and sent his other two units (55th Ohio and 33rd Massachusetts) to support the cannons on East Cemetery Hill in the location vacated by Coster's troops. Smith also at this time sent a skirmish line forward to the base of the hill and into the edge of the town.[6]

It soon became clear to Howard that Doubleday's line was also in a bad situation. At about 1600 he sent orders to the I Corps commander directing that "if he could not hold out much longer, he must fall back, fighting, to Cemetery Hill, and on the left of the Baltimore Pike."[7] A few minutes later Captain E.P. Halstead of Doubleday's staff rode up to ask for reinforcements. Howard was by now exasperated, and looked like "the picture of despair" to Halstead. He piquishly responded that he had no reserves but one regiment. Halstead, who as a I Corps partisan perhaps did not care for Howard, says that the General next mistook the troops overlapping Doubleday's line to be fences. Once this error was pointed out and corrected, Howard suggested that Halstead look for help from Buford, whom he mistakenly thought was somewhere to the east of Cemetery Hill.[8]

Within a few minutes it became clear to Howard that neither corps could hold on, and at 1610 he sent "a positive order to the commanders of the First and Eleventh Corps to fall back gradually, disputing every inch of ground, and to form near my position, the Eleventh Corps on the right and the First Corps on the left of the Baltimore Pike."[9] Upon receipt of this directive, Schurz pulled back the remnants of his two divisions that had been attempting to form on the north edge of town, as already shown in Chapter VII. Doubleday, however, insists that he never received either this order or the one sent by Howard ten minutes earlier.[10] As already has been shown, he made an independent decision to pull back his I Corps because of Perrin's breakthrough in Biddle's line.

There was by now a confused mass of troops heading through and around the town in the direction of Cemetery Hill. It is not recorded what troops reached there first. Wounded men and slackers already had been drifting past Cemetery Hill during the day's fighting; there is no record preserved of any cavalry or provost guards posted in or below the town to turn back or channel such traffic. The first combat troops to be driven back to the hill were from Ames' division, followed closely by Von Amsberg's and then Coster's shattered commands. When Ames arrived on Cemetery Hill, he reported to Howard that, "I have no division, it is all cut to pieces." By the time it was rallied, Ames' 25th Ohio could count only 60 men under command of Lieutenant Israel White out of the 220 that had entered the battle. Krzyzanowski, now commanding the 3rd Division, arrived at about 4:55, when the weary units of the I Corps were starting to come up.[11]

The retreating Union troops that made their way to Cemetery Hill consisted of all sorts of detachments from individuals with a buddy or two to fragments of companies to nuclei of regiments clustered around their officers or flags. One ambulance driver from the 107th Ohio who drove through and with the mass of retreating troops to Cemetery Hill did not at first realize that a stand was being organized there. It was only when he saw infantry stopping on each side of the road, and another small line of troops behind the hill turning back the fugitives, that he understood what was happening.[12]

Howard was by all accounts quite active and energetic in his efforts to rally his troops. There is no question that he was not personally courageous, as he had shown when he rallied his troops at Chancellorsville while holding a flag under the stump of the arm he had lost at the battle of Fair Oaks in 1862. Captain Edward C. Culp of the 25th Ohio, who was serving on Ames' staff, spoke glowingly of his brief encounter with Howard at this crisis: "I linger with pride upon that interview, which in two or three minutes taught me what a cool and confident man could do. No hurry, no confusion in his mind. He knew that if he could get his troops in any kind of order back of those stone walls the country was safe."[13]

Howard showed his determination by dismounting with an aide to meet his broken regiments after they emerged from the town into the open ground just north of the cemetery. He relates in his memoirs that "a colonel passed by muttering something in German—his English was not at his command just then; fragments of his regiment were following him." When he saw the regiment's color guard pass by the stone wall at the edge of the city, he called out, "Sergeant, plant your flag down there in that stone wall." The sergeant, who apparently did not recognize Howard, retorted, "All right, if you will go with me, I will." Howard took up the challenge, and took up the flag. Then, accompanied by

Lieutenant Rogers and the sergeant, he set the flag up over the wall. The sergeant's men followed, and Howard was pleased that "That flag served to rally the regiment, always brave and energetic, and other troops."[14]

Major Allen Brady of the 17th Connecticut related a similar incident in his battle report penned just three days later: "About this time Major General Howard, who was in the thickest of the battle, regardless of danger, asked if he had troops brave enough to advance to a stone wall across a lot toward the town, and said he would lead them. We replied 'Yes, the Seventeenth Connecticut will,' and advanced at once to the place indicated, remained a few moments, and again advanced across another lot still nearer the town and behind a rail-fence at the upper end of the town, which position we held until late in the evening, exposed to a galling fire from the enemy's sharpshooters."[15]

Not everyone, though, appreciated Howard's valor that afternoon. His decision to lead the army from his command post on Cemetery Hill instead of being at the front with his troops made it appear that there was "no directing person on the field," as cavalry commander John Buford wrote his superior, Alfred Pleasonton, at 1520.[16] Howard's decision to let Doubleday manage the I Corps' line on his own was probably a good one, since Doubleday did about as well could be expected under the circumstances. Howard's stabilizing influence, though, was sorely missed in the lines of the XI Corps, in spite of his brief tenure as their commander. He also could have made more of an effort to keep in touch with Buford and share his plans with him. Buford greatly appreciated Reynolds' openness and responsiveness in the last hours leading up to the battle, and the two cooperated extremely well. But Howard was not Reynolds, and Buford did not know him at all well; certainly not well enough to trust him to control the field any longer.[17]

Howard took personal charge of posting the XI Corps brigades, and assigned Doubleday to oversee the re-formation of the I Corps.[18] Ames' regiments took up position on the northeastern side of the Baltimore Pike, both on top of East Cemetery Hill and in the fields along its base. Schimmelfennig formed on the southwestern side of Baltimore Pike, "facing the town" on the general site of the modern "Gettysburg Village." Smith's brigade of Steinwehr's division was on Schurz's left, as far as the Taneytown Road; its front covered the northwestern base of Cemetery Hill proper, and the skirmishers of its right flank regiment (55th Ohio) extended to the southern edge of town. The survivors of Coster's battered brigade took up their former position atop East Cemetery Hill, with their advance skirmishers (73rd Pennsylvania) posted in the edge of the town beyond the intersection of the Baltimore Pike and Emmitsburg Roads.[19]

Doubleday arrived on Cemetery Hill at around 1430, and found General Schurz "busily engaged in rallying his men" ordering "all that was possible to encourage them to form line again." He was pleased to see that Howard had made arrangements to secure the Baltimore Pike between the town and the hill. Doubleday found Howard at the gate of the town cemetery with his staff. When he rode up, he was told "to post the First Corps on the left in the cemetery, while he assembled the Eleventh Corps on the right." As he went to do so, Howard rode after him and requested "in case his men (Steinwehr's division) deserted their guns, to be in readiness to defend them." Doubleday was also surprised to hear that Howard's men had been told "that Sigel had arrived and assumed command, a fiction thought justifiable under the circumstances. It seemed to me that the discredit that attached to them after Chancellorsville had in a measure injured their morale and (esprit de corps) for they were rallied with great difficulty."[20]

Doubleday rallied his fragmented regiments as best he could. Most were no larger than companies. The 2nd Wisconsin had only forty-five men under the command of Captain George H. Otis. Its largest company was "I" with nine men. The 24th Michigan reached Cemetery Hill with only twenty-seven men under the command of Captain Albert M. Edwards. He rallied the remains of his unit by taking the regimental flag to the Cemetery, "where he planted it near a battery, and sat down on a grave stone while the remnant of the regiment rallied about its bullet-riddled folds."[21] Compared to these numbers, the 151st Pennsylvania was relatively large with ninety-two men. The 121st Pennsylvania counted eighty men when its remnants reached Cemetery Hill under the command of Captain William W. Dorr of Company K. They were glad to receive fresh ammunition from an ordnance officer of the XI Corps, after which they passed the evening by "singing hymns as they rested on their arms in view of the possibilities of the morrow."[22]

The 13th Massachusetts of Paul's brigade had only 99 ot its 284 men left when it reached Cemetery Hill: "Here we saw the division color bearer standing alone. Some of the men then took the flag, and waving it in turn, shouting and swinging their caps, soon succeeded in establishing the division headquarters." The regiment's men were hungry because they had not eaten since breakfast, so they "munched away on our hardtack." Then many of them fell asleep at once "insensible to the firing that was going on at our right, near Culp's Hill."[23]

Doubleday initially reformed his brigades on the west side of Cemetery Hill. Once this was accomplished, he shifted Robinson's division to the northern edge of Cemetery Ridge, at the left of the cemetery. General Baxter reported that at about 1700 he and the rest of the division moved "from Cemetery Hill to the left and forward, near and parallel with the Emmitsburg Road, where we formed in line of battle and made temporary breastworks."[24] Colonel Edmund L. Dana, commander of the remnants of Stone's brigade, formed his men "near a low wall facing the town," while Biddle's brigade drew up along the Taneytown Road.[25] Wadsworth's men apparently formed up in the hollow on the east side of the cemetery.[26] The men of the 6th Wisconsin, which was among the last units to arrive, were most relieved to at least reach the glorious colors and "well ordered line of men in blue" of Smith's 73rd Ohio, who opened their ranks for Dawes' men to pass through. The weary Badgers then "threw themselves in a state of almost perfect exhaustion on the green grass and graves of the cemetery."[31]

The initial confusion on Cemetery Hill was exacerbated by the strange behavior of Brigadier General Thomas Rowley. As previously noted, Rowley had been elevated from brigade command to command of Doubleday's division when Doubleday took over I Corps on the evening of 30 June after Reynolds assumed active command of the army's left wing. During the afternoon's fighting, Rowley's two brigades (Biddle's and Stone's) were posted on different parts of the I Corps line, but even so Rowley does not seem to have played a very active part in the day's conflict. However, he was seen from time to time riding down his lines while waving his sword and shouting "Here's for the old Keystone State!" At some point after Reynold's death, Rowley mistakenly assumed he was now elevated to acting corps commander, if Doubleday had replaced Reynolds as wing commander; this logic made no sense since both of the corps' other two brigadiers, Henry Wadsworth and John Robinson, were clearly senior to Rowley. During the chaos of the I Corps retreat from Seminary Ridge, Rowley rode about cursing the troops and ordering them to stay and fight; some heard him insist that he was now the I Corps commander, while others could make no sense out of his commands. When he gave up trying to rally his men and headed for the town, he fell off his horse into a ditch and had to be helped up by his staff members.[28]

Colonel Wainwright ran into Rowley in the town, as previously noted, and found him to be "very talkative, claiming that he was command of the corps." After trying to reason with him in vain, Wainwright came to the conclusion that the general was drunk, and continued on to Cemetery Hill.[29] Rowley was still behaving strangely when he reached Cemetery Hill; Colonel Rufus Dawes of the 6th Wisconsin saw that "he was raving and storming, and giving wild and crazy orders," and "had become positively insane," so adding to "the confusion and peril." Lieutenant Clayton E. Rogers, the First Division provost marshal, also saw Rowley acting incoherently. He noted that "General Rowley, in great excitement, had lost his own third division, and was giving General Wadsworth's troops contradictory orders, calling them cowards, and whose conduct was so unbecoming a division commander and unfortunately stimulated with poor commissary [whiskey]." Rogers felt he had no choice but to boldly place the general under arrest; he was unable to find Wadsworth at the time for instructions, so he "called on Col. Dawes to execute the order with the bayonets of the 6th Wisconsin." Dawes dutifully complied, later observing that "this was perhaps the only instance in the war where a First Lieutenant forcibly arrested a Brigadier General on the field of battle."[30] Rowley agreed to leave the field under Dawes' guard, and after the battle found himself assigned to duty at a draft office in Maine. He was eventually brought to trial in April 1864 on charges of being drunk while on duty at the battle of Gettysburg; conduct prejudicial to good order and military discipline; conduct unbecoming an officer and a gentleman; and disobedience of orders. He was convicted on all charges but the last one, but Secretary of War Stanton nevertheless ordered him to be returned to duty. Rowley was then sent to Pittsburgh to command the District of the Monongahela, but he thought it best to resign from the army on 29 December 1864. After the war he was a lawyer, and served as a United States marshal from 1866 to 1870. He died in 1902.[31]

Colonel Charles S. Wainwright, chief of artillery for the I Corps, reached Cemetery Hill at about the same time as his first battery, which was probably Cooper's or Stevens'. Howard was glad to see him, and asked him to take charge of all the artillery on the hill. This was appropriate since Wainwright outranked Major Thomas W. Osborn, chief of artillery for the XI Corps. Howard explained how he was posting the two corps, and informed Wainwright that "this spot must be held until the rest of the army came up." Wainwright at once moved to take charge of the batteries on East Cemetery Hill, where a Confederate attack was expected momentarily. At the same time he directed Osborn to move four of his batteries into the cemetery itself.[32]

Major Osborn, though, gives a different version of the artillery command on Cemetery Hill at this time. In his battle report, he notes that Wainwright took command of the artillery on the northeastern side of Baltimore Pike;[33] by implication he himself retained control of those on the southwest side of the road. This arrangement was explained in more detail in a longer narrative he wrote around 1880, though this contains some errors in detail. There he states that Wainwright "retained command of the First Corps batteries upon Culp's Hill, while I retained command of the Eleventh Corps batteries on Cemetery Hill." This account errs by placing Wainwright on Culp's Hill; there were no guns there at this time, and Osborn must mean East Cemetery Hill instead. In addition, there was no distinct arrangement of batteries by corps, as units of both commanders were intermingled on each front, as will be shown. Osborn also claims that he received instructions on where to place his guns directly from Howard, not from Wainwright.[34]

Wainwright found Wiedrich's New York battery already in place on the northern end of East Cemetery Hill, "at the angle or corner of the hill," where the battery's monument is now located. He left Wiedrich's four guns there, "only throwing his four guns in echelon so that he could fire either to the west of the hill." Cooper's battery when it came up was stationed on Wiedrich's right, "around the corner of the hill and facing north." There was a stone wall between Cooper's three guns and Wiedrich's battery, and the cemetery gate house was across the Baltimore Pike to the rear.[35] After Cooper formed his guns, he "performed staff duty in assisting to establish and strengthen the Union lines" at the request of Doubleday.[36] Next came one section of Stewart's battery, and then the five remaining pieces of Breck's battery, all recessed some 20 yards from Cooper's line "owing to the nature of the ground."[37] Stevens' battery would be deployed still farther to the right when it came up, as will be seen. The remaining three useable guns of Stewart's battery were set up in front of the cemetery gate house, facing northwest in order to "fire directly down the road."[38]

Thus Wainwright by 1500 had an imposing formation of 23 guns formed on East Cemetery Hill, 13 rifles and 10 Napoleons; all but 4 were from his own I Corps. Twenty of the guns faced northeast against the immediate threat of an attack by Early's troops, who could be seen advancing from the eastern edge of the town and the fields beyond. Wiedrich reports that he fired a few rounds of canister at the Confederate troops who advanced past the town, and drove them back. The other batteries may have done the same, after they refilled their caissons. Wainwright then sent his caissons to be parked in the rear of the cemetery.[39] Lieutenant Breck thought his position was "a high and commanding place,"[40] but even so the gunners began digging lunettes to protect their cannons and themselves.[41]

Though his line was by now fairly well formed, Wainwright was still worried about the outcome of a possible Confederate attack. He wrote in his journal that when he had arranged all his units, he gave instructions to his officers not to waste ammunition, and not take orders from any other officer since there was still an hour of daylight left and he felt that there was a good chance the enemy might attack. He was confident that he could hold the angle of his line as long as the enemy did not approach from the town, which offered cover to any attack from that quarter.[42]

While Wainwright drew up these guns on East Cemetery Hill, Osborn was forming the guns assigned to him on the other side of the Baltimore Pike. Hall's three guns of the 2nd Maine battery were already in position, having been posted on the left of the town cemetery (near the Lincoln speech memorial) earlier in the day at Howard's orders. As already has been noted, Hall's command had been badly shot up late in the morning and had lost one gun captured and two disabled.[43] Osborn placed Dilger's and Bancroft's guns behind the wall on the northwestern side of the cemetery, facing the town.

All this commotion and movement of troops certainly made a mess of the cemetery grounds. Lieutenant Breck of Wainwright's command wrote the next day, "a beautiful cemetery it was, but now is trodden down, laid a waste, desecrated. The fences are all down, the many graves have been run over, beautiful lots with iron fences and splendid monuments have been destroyed or soiled, and our infantry and artillery occupy those sacred grounds where the dead are sleeping... It is enough to make one mourn."[44] The historian of the 55th Ohio noted that, "The artillery of the corps was massed on the summit and created havoc in the burial grounds as the teams and heavy guns crashed over the sodded hillocks, or sent gravestones flying, regardless of everything save the necessity of placing the guns to meet the enemy."[45] All this was done in spite of a sign that stood near the entrance to the cemetery stating that, "All persons found using firearms in these grounds will be prosecuted with the utmost rigor of the law."[46]

Osborn reports that Wheeler's and Heckman's depleted batteries came up nearly the last of the XI Corps.[47] Wheeler was stationed on the far left of the corps' line, below the cemetery, where his rifled guns could better reach Hill's troops if the enemy should advance past Seminary Ridge.[48] Sometime later Wainwright sent half of Wiedrich's battery (Lieutenant Christopher Schmidt's section) to reinforce Wheeler's position.[49]

Heckman's battery was in such bad shape after its stand on the north side of the town, where it lost two guns to Hays' troops, that Osborn had to send it to the rear for the rest of the battle.[50] Given the grave crisis at hand, it is odd that Osborn did not find some spot in the line for Heckman to hold.[51]

Altogether, then, Osborn had some 20 guns (eight rifled and twelve Napoleons) to hold the northwest face of Cemetery Hill. Howard came by and approved his dispositions once they were made.[52] Even so, Osborn apparently did not feel totally confident in his position. He had no support to speak of on his left, and the houses that approached the hill from the southern extension of the town would offer shelter and cover to advancing Confederate troops and skirmishers. In addition, Osborn later wrote that Cemetery Hill was only "a low elevation with an extension on the right."[53] This last statement, though, is certainly questionable, since Cemetery Hill—and more so East Cemetery Hill—clearly rose well above the fields to their front.[54]

There can be no question that the situation on Cemetery Hill was very confused, especially at the height of the Union retreat from 1615 to 1645. Colonel Dawes of the 6th Wisconsin felt that, "If fresh troops had attacked us then, we unquestionably would have faired badly. The troops were scattered over the hill in much disorder, while a stream of stragglers and wounded men pushed along the Baltimore Turnpike towards the rear."[55] Major Osborn claims that General Howard was in despair over what might happen if the enemy attacked. The following conversation was not made public until about 1880, many years after Howard received the official thanks of the United States Congress on January 28, 1864, for his role in selecting Cemetery Hill as the rallying point for the army: "While the sun was still up and sufficient time existed for Lee to attack, Howard said to me, 'Evidently, Lee's whole army is on our front, and he will attack yet this evening or early in the morning. I have no support in less than 20 miles. It is impossible for us to successfully withstand Lee, and we shall be wiped out of existence. I have determined to stay and fight to the last, with the view of crippling Lee's army as much as possible so that the remainder of the army, when it arrives, will be able to defeat him.' After making this statement, he said, 'There is no hope of our whipping Lee, but I intend to make the utmost fight I can. Will you stand by me to the end?' Of course, I said that I would do so."[56]

Meade Sends Hancock to Take Charge

Perhaps the greatest steadying influence on the disorganized Union troops on Cemetery Hill was the arrival at 1630 or shortly thereafter of Major General Winfield Scott Hancock, commander of the army's II Corps, who had been sent by Meade to take command of the field. As efficient and determined as Doubleday and Howard were to reform their men and face the enemy yet again, it was by almost all accounts Hancock's dynamic presence that inspired the men of both corps, particularly the officers.

This was certainly not an assignment that Hancock was looking for or expecting that day. The 39-year-old officer was a veteran commander who had only recently risen to corps command. He had arrived at Uniontown, MD, on the evening of June 29, and remained there with his corps until the morning of July 1, when orders came from Meade to march to Taneytown. The II Corps arrived there at 1100, and Hancock proceeded to Meade's headquarters, which were still located there. Meade explained to him his Pipe Creek plan for a defensive line if needed, and Hancock returned to his command to await further orders.[57]

Meade at the time was apparently expecting to activate the Pipe Creek plan. Messages received earlier in the day from Buford strongly suggested that Ewell and Hill might reach Gettysburg ahead of Reynolds. If this happened, Reynolds had been instructed "to hold the enemy in check, and fall slowly back." This is what Meade informed Sedgwick, commander of the army's largest corps, the VI, in an important dispatch that unfortunately bears no time byline. Meade also advised Sedgwick of the possibility of enacting the move to Pipe Creek; but "should circumstances render it necessary for the commanding general to fight the enemy today," Meade outlined the positions of all his corps, and directed Sedgwick to be in readiness to move at a moment's notice.[58]

At the same (unspecified) time, Meade also informed Slocum that the enemy was advancing on Gettysburg, and that he should move to the position indicated by the Pipe Creek Circular if Reynolds should retire and uncover Two Taverns. Meade specifically directed that Slocum should halt his command on receipt of the order, and tell Sykes to halt the V Corps also, and wait there "for a proper compliance with the circular order enclosed in case invitations from General Reynolds render it necessary."[59]

At 1130 Meade began to receive reports that a battle was indeed imminent at Gettysburg. At that hour he received a personal message from Captain Stephen M. Weld of Reynolds' staff, whom Reynolds had sent from Gettysburg at 1000. Weld related that Reynolds told him, "Ride at your utmost speed to General Meade. Tell him the enemy are advancing in strong force, and that I fear they will get to the heights beyond the town before I can. I will fight them inch by inch, and if driven into the town, I will barricade the streets and hold them back as long as possible. Don't spare your horse—never mind if you kill him."[60]

The promise of a battle was confirmed a few minutes later when Meade received Buford's dispatch, bearing the time 1010, that the Confederates were advancing from the north and west, and engaging his pickets on both fronts.[61]

According to Weld, Meade showed agitation at hearing about Reynolds' effort to hold Gettysburg. At one point he exclaimed, "Good God! If the enemy get Gettysburg, we are lost!" Then, since he was easily excited to irritability, he began cursing his chief of staff, Major General Dan Butterfield, "for his slowness in getting out orders" (presumably the Pipe Creek Circular, which would now be needed if Reynolds were defeated or driven back). He also exclaimed upon hearing that Reynolds would barricade the streets if necessary, "Good, that is just like Reynolds; he will hold on to the bitter end!"[62]

Meade seems to have welcomed the news that Lee's army, or at least part of it, had been brought to bay. At noon he wrote Halleck in Washington that his troops were at Emmitsburg, Gettysburg, and Hanover, and that the enemy was known to be at Heidlersburg (Ewell), Cashtown (Hill) and Chambersburg (Longstreet). The rest of this message shows that he was still not certain what step to take next: "This news proves my advance has answered its purpose. I shall not advance any, but prepare to receive an attack in case Lee makes one. A battle field is being selected to the rear, on which the army can be rapidly concentrated, on Pike Creek, between Middleburg and Manchester, covering my depot at Westminster. If I am not attacked, and I can from reliable intelligence have reason to believe I can attack with reasonable degree of success, I will do so, but at present, having relieved the pressure on the Susquehanna, I am now looking to the protection of Washington, and fighting my army to the best advantage."[63]

It is interesting to note that Meade at this time was not ready to push his entire army up to Gettysburg. Slocum and Sykes, as have been shown, had been ordered to halt their troops pending the outcome of the initial fight at Gettysburg, and Sedgwick was likewise holding his troops ready to move whenever circumstances would warrant. Meade was certainly concerned about what would happen when (and if) Reynolds reached Gettysburg, but he was also wary that Lee might swing his army to the left or right, so he for the moment allowed his corps to continue on the line of advance he had ordered that morning. Reynolds had three corps with him, plus Buford's division of cavalry, and Meade probably thought that was enough force to deal with the enemy for the moment. In addition, he apparently did not take Reynolds' word seriously that the advance wing would fight tenaciously to hold Gettysburg. Meade became concerned that Reynolds, if driven back from Gettysburg by Hill and Ewell, might retreat towards Emmitsburg rather than towards Taneytown as the recently issued Pipe Creek Circular directed; Meade was correct in assuming that Reynolds had not received a copy of this order.[64]

Meade's greatest concern, then, was that Reynolds might withdraw towards Emmitsburg, so leaving the center of the army undefended in the area of Taneytown. For this reason he ordered Hancock at 1130 to begin marching on the direct road from Taneytown to Gettysburg. If he met Reynolds' corps withdrawing from Gettysburg, he was to retire to Frizzelburg.[65] If Reynolds went towards Emittsburg, Hancock would be in position to cover the army's center. Lastly, if Reynolds were still engaged or in trouble at Gettysburg, Hancock's men would be able to help him there before the day ended.[66]

Meade at this time did take another step to try to aid Reynolds, though it was not particularly well thought out or effective. At noon he sent a telegram to Major General Darius Couch at Harrisburg to inform him that Hill and Ewell were advancing on Gettysburg. He then asked if Couch would be able to advance on Ewell's rear without endangering his own line of retreat.[67] There was, of course, little Couch could do that day in time to aid the troops at Gettysburg.

Affairs now began to move quickly, but not in a direction to Meade's liking. At 1300 he appended a postscript to the 1200 message sent to Halleck: "The enemy are advancing in force on Gettysburg, and I expect the battle will begin today."[68]

Just after this message was sent to Halleck, the awful news of Reynolds' fall came. Meade reacted quickly, but in an unpredicted manner. Instead of proceeding to the front at once to take charge of affairs, he would send a deputy to do so. It is not totally clear why he did this, and indeed he has fallen under severe criticism for not going to the field at once in person.[69] The most likely explanation is that he wanted to be at Taneytown in order to make the necessary arrangements more easily in case his advance wing had been defeated and was falling back.[70]

Meade's decision not to go to the field himself was also heavily influenced by the nearby presence of the man he apparently trusted most in the army after Reynolds—Hancock.[71] Meade had just spent a considerable length of time explaining his plans and thoughts to Hancock, and he felt the utmost confidence that Hancock would be able to go to the field, assume command of the troops there, and assess the situation.

Instead of summoning Hancock, Meade elected to save time by riding to the II Corps headquarters himself. He told the sad news about Reynolds and explained what he wanted to be done—Hancock should turn over his corps to Brigadier General John Gibbon, and proceed to Gettysburg and take command there. Hancock objected, not on the grounds that he could not handle the job, but because he felt that both Howard and Sickles outranked him, and that Caldwell outranked Gibbon in the II Corps. Meade, though, assured his reluctant subordinate that he had the authority from Stanton to make whatever command changes he felt necessary; indeed that is how he had promoted Custer, Farnsworth, and Merritt from Captain to Brigadier General a few days earlier. He assured Hancock that "at this crisis he must have a man he knew and could trust."[72] By implication he meant that he did not know (or perhaps trust) Howard, and certainly did not trust Sickles.[73]

Hancock at last gave in, perhaps on condition that his authority be expressed in writing. This Meade did in the following directive, a copy of which was sent to Howard:

Headquarters Army of the Potomac
July 1, 1863—1:10 p.m.

Major-General Hancock, Commanding Second Corps:

General: The major-general commanding has just been informed that General Reynolds has been killed or badly wounded. He directs that you turn over the command of your corps to General Gibbon; that you proceed to the front, and, by virtue of this order, in case of the truth of General Reynolds' death, you assume command of the corps there assembled, viz, the Eleventh, First, and Third, at Emmitsburg. If you think the ground and position there a better one to fight a battle under existing circumstances, you will so advise the general, and he will order all the troops up. You know the general's views, and General Warren, who is fully aware of them, has gone out to see General Reynolds.

Later-1.15p.m.

Reynolds has possession of Gettysburg, and the enemy are reported as falling back from the front of Gettysburg. Hold your column ready to move.

Very respectfully, &c.,
Danl. Butterfield,
Major-General, Chief of Staff.
(Copy to Major-General Howard.)[74]

It is interesting to note that this message informed Howard that General Warren was also going to be on the field. Surviving sources do not relate when or with what orders Meade sent his chief engineer to the field. Presumably his orders were to determine if Gettysburg were a good location for a battle, just as Hancock was ordered to do.

Hancock was on his way to Gettysburg by 1330,[75] and Meade would not hear from him until after 1800. For some reason Meade did not report Reynolds' death to Sedgwick, commander of his right wing, until 1630, when he also directed that general to move his VI Corps at once to Taneytown.[76] At 1645 Meade informed Sickles that Hancock was the new commander of the left wing, and directly ordered him to leave a division to hold Emmitsburg, since it was a critical point covering the army's left and rear.[77] Why Meade waited so long to inform his corps commanders of Reynolds' death and Hancock's special assignment, has not been explained.

Meade had yet one more command change to arrange that day. For some reason he did not trust Doubleday to run the I Corps, and late in the afternoon he directed Sedgwick to send Major General John Newton, commander of the VI Corps' 3rd Division, to take charge of the I Corps.[78] Meade may have done this because of a general dislike for Doubleday. When Howard witnessed some of Doubleday's troops pull back late that morning, he "hastened to send a special messenger to General Meade with the baleful intelligence that the First Corps had fled from the field at the first contact with the enemy."[79] Events showed that Doubleday actually did a good job managing his troops that day after Reynolds fell. Thus he justifiably bore a grudge for the rest of his life against both Howard and Meade for being demoted when Newton reached the field soon after midnight, at the point he judged to be the culmination of his military career.

Hancock proceeded to his new command at Gettysburg accompanied by a few aides, his chief of staff, Lieutenant Colonel Morgan, and a signal corps detachment under Captain James S. Hall.[80] He traveled at first in an ambulance so that he might study a "poor little map" of the Gettysburg area. After studying the map, he mounted his horse for the rest of the journey. About four or five miles south of town his party met another ambulance on a quite different mission, carrying Reynolds' body to his home for burial.[81]

Hancock was surprised that he could not hear the noise of the battle until he was within a few miles of the town. He attributed this "to the peculiar formation of the country, or the direction of the wind at the time."[82] It may also be due to the fact that he neared the town after 1620, when most of the artillery fire had died down—Hill's and Ewell's guns had ceased firing for fear of hitting their own advancing troops, and most of Doubleday's and Schurz's cannons were in retreat.

Hancock reached the field at about 1630, and witnessed the height of the retreat of the I and XI Corps.[83] Everywhere there were troops "retreating in disorder and confusion."[84] It certainly was not an encouraging scene, but he was not discouraged in his task. Since he came in on the Taneytown Road, the first organized troops he encountered were those of Smith's brigade drawn up on the hill above the road. Hancock met briefly with Smith and told him, "My corps is on the way, but will not be here in time. This position should be held at all hazards. Now, Colonel, can you hold it?" When Smith replied, "I think I can," Hancock repeated the question until he got the desired response, "I will."[85]

Colonel Smith then saw one of the retreating XI Corps commands pass by his line and continue towards the rear: "The colonel failed to recognize or respond to the order to about face and form line facing the enemy, and was leading his command to the rear. He was arrested and another officer placed over the regiment, which, under a courageous leader, responded with good will. In another case General Howard, noticing some reluctance to halt and form line when the bullets of the enemy began to whistle from the buildings in the town, took the colors from the hand of the color bearer and, carrying them with difficulty under his only arm, started to the front of the new line, where a staff officer placed them in position. The whole brigade saw the incident and came forward with a cheer."[86]

Hancock then proceeded to the top of the hill, where he saw Howard busily rallying his troops. Since Hancock had previously sent a messenger ahead to advise Howard of his pending arrival,[87] Hancock's appearance should not have been a surprise to Howard. It is not certain, however, if Hancock had also forewarned Howard about the change in command and his orders from Meade.

The exact words spoken by Hancock and Howard at this historic meeting were not recorded in full by either of the participants involved. Portions of their conversation, though, were later reported by staff members who happened to be nearby. The most detailed version is that given by Major E.P. Halstead of General Doubleday's staff. Halstead had been sent to request reinforcements from Howard, and was returning to Cemetery Hill because he was unable to locate Buford, as already noted. He saw Hancock ride up at a gallop, "and when near General Howard, who was then alone, saluted, and with great animation, as if there was no time for ceremony, said, General Meade had sent him forward to take command of the three corps. General Howard woke up a little and replied that he was the senior. General Hancock said, 'I am aware of that, General, but I have written orders in my pocket from General Meade which I will show you if you wish to see them.' General Howard said, 'No. I do not doubt your word, General Hancock, but you can give no orders here while I am here.' Hancock replied, 'Very well, General Howard, I will second any order that you have to give, but General Meade has also directed me to select a field on which to fight this battle in rear of Pipe Creek,' then casting one glance from Culp's Hill to Round Top he continued: 'But I think this the strongest position by nature upon which to fight a battle that I ever saw, and if it meets your approbation I will select this as the battlefield.' General Howard responded, 'I think it a very strong position, General Hancock. A very strong position!' 'Very well, sir, I select this as the battlefield.'"[88]

Halstead's account, though certainly dramatic, has several weaknesses. Firstly, it is unlikely that Hancock would have offered to second all of Howard's orders when he had a directive from Meade that put him in sole command. Second, he did not need Howard's "approbation" to select the field as a good one on which to fight. Thirdly, and most significantly, it is highly unlikely that Halstead was close enough to the two generals to hear every word they said.[89]

Two other staff officers also offered their accounts of the meeting of

Hancock and Howard. James S. Wadsworth Jr. of the I Corps recalled that Howard said, "You cannot issue these orders Hancock for I rank you!" To which Hancock replied, "Then I will go back to General Meade." Howard quickly responded, "Don't do that Hancock, but stay here and assist me with your advice."[90] It is hard to accept that Hancock would have volunteered to leave the field, an act which would have left him open to a court martial for disobeying Meade's order.[91]

Colonel Charles H. Morgan of Hancock's staff wrote in an account of the meeting that Hancock said, "General, I have been ordered here to take command of all the troops on the field, until General Slocum arrives." He offered to show Howard his orders, but Howard "waived looking at it and expressed his satisfaction at General Hancock's arrival."[92] This account is somewhat questionable because it does not appear that Meade initially told Hancock to stay on the field until Slocum came up.[93]

Hancock unfortunately left no first hand account of this meeting, though he did at times react to others.[94] Howard later wrote up portions of their conversation, but at a time when he had his reputation to defend. Friction between Hancock and Howard rose in January 1864 when Congress passed a resolution honoring Hooker, Meade and Howard for their roles in winning the battle of Gettysburg. The mere fact that Hooker was cited shows that this resolution was politically motivated. Hancock's supporters took offense and claimed that it was Hancock who restored order on the evening of July, not Howard, and Howard's supporters responded that Hancock did not fully exercise the authority Meade had given him. The two exchanged curt letters on this issue, in one of which Hancock expressed the opinion that Howard had been singled out by the administration in order to make use of his reputation in the next Presidential election.[95]

The issue of who said what on Cemetery Hill was not resolved in 1864. It boiled up again in 1876 when Howard published an article in the *Atlantic Monthly* on the subject. Here he claimed that Hancock greeted him cordially and frankly and said, "General Meade has sent me to represent him on the field." Howard replied, "All right, Hancock, this is no time for talking. You take the left of the pike and I will arrange those to the right." Hancock then rode off to the left.[96] Howard wrote a condensed version of this account in his 1907 autobiography: "When the men were reaching their new position on the heights, and at the time of the greatest confusion between 4 and 5 p.m., General Hancock joined me near the Baltimore pike; he said that General Meade had sent him to represent him on the field. I answered as the bullets rent the air: 'All right, Hancock, you take the left of the Baltimore pike and I will take the right, and we will put these troops in line.' After a few friendly words between us, Hancock did as I suggested."[97]

Hancock responded to Howard's assertions in a lengthy magazine article of his own. Here he claimed that he received command of the field from Howard, who declined to look at Meade's order. However, Hancock here claimed that he reached the field at 1530; it is unclear whether this was an honest error (he claimed in his battle report to have arrived at 1500) or was an effort to buttress his case.[98]

This plethora of accounts makes it extremely difficult to determine exactly what was said when Hancock met Howard. The accounts do agree, however, that Howard did not read Meade's order, and that Howard proceeded to oversee the formation of the troops on East Cemetery Hill. It is very possible, given the strain of the situation, that Hancock did not bluntly state that he was present to replace Howard. This is the line that Howard took in his 1876 *Atlantic* article, where he insists that he did not understand that Hancock was to replace him, until a written order from Meade arrived at 1900.[99]

This state of mind might help explain the last three lines of the following message Howard sent to Meade at 1700:

Hdqrs. Eleventh Corps, Army of the Potomac
July 1, 1863-5p.m.

General: General Reynolds attacked the enemy as soon as he arrived, with one division about 10:45 a.m. He moved to the front of the town, driving in the enemy's advance for about half a mile, when he met with a strong force of A.P. Hill's corps. I pushed on as fast as I could by a parallel road; placed my corps in position on his right. General Reynolds was killed at 11.15 a.m. I assumed command of the two corps, and sent word to Slocum and Sickles to move up. I have fought the enemy from that time till this. The First Corps fell back, when outflanked on its left, to a stronger position, when the Eleventh Corps was ordered back, also to a stronger position.

General Hancock arrived at 4p.m., and communicated his instruction. I am still holding on at this time.

Slocum is near, but will not come up to assume command.

O.O.Howard, Major-General.[100]

Note that Howard here does not admit to a defeat by the XI Corps, but instead blames the army's defeat on the left wing of I Corps. His statement about Slocum infers that there was a definite command confusion on Cemetery Hill, and his assertion "I am still holding on" clearly showed a lack of confidence in the situation.

Later in the evening Howard wrote to Meade that, "General Hancock's order, in writing, to assume command reached here at 7."[101] This short phrase contains the key to the situation. It appears that Hancock actually did explain verbally what his mission was when he arrived on Cemetery Hill, but Howard in the heat of the moment did not acknowledge Hancock's authority until he received written confirmation from Meade at 1900. Fortunately the two did not have a fierce argument over the issue while the fate of the battle hung in the balance between 1630 and 1900. Hancock apparently ordered Howard to tend the line north of Baltimore Pike. This suited Howard fine because almost all the troops there were from the XI Corps, and this was where the enemy was threatening to attack. Hancock then turned his attention to the south side of the road, where Doubleday had already begun to organize the defenses. Thus Hancock and Howard had little if any direct contact with each other after their initial interview.

While Howard rode back to East Cemetery Hill, Hancock actively entered upon the task at hand. He was at once concerned with the weakness of the position's right flank, and determined to send a battery towards Culp's Hill to stop the Confederates from advancing in that direction. At that moment he saw Stevens' and Cooper's I Corps batteries approaching the cemetery gate after their retreat from Seminary Ridge, and called out for the captain of "that brass battery." Captain Stevens, whose 5th Maine battery had six Napoleon cannons, rode up to him and received instructions to "take his battery up to that hill" and "stop the enemy from coming up that ravine." Stevens replied, "By whose order?" and did so promptly when he learned he was being addressed by General Hancock.[102]

Stevens gave the order "Fifth battery, forward!" and moved off to the right just as Cooper's battery began deploying on East Cemetery Hill. He proceeded down the hill on the Baltimore Pike until he found a lane leading towards Culp's Hill. He turned up the lane and soon reached "the summit of a Knoll at the western extremity of Culp's Hill." Since the main summit of Culp's Hill appeared to be too densely wooded to allow him to move there, Stevens deployed his guns on the hillock that now bears his name ("Stevens' Knoll"). From here he had a clear field of fire that controlled "the easterly slope of Cemetery Hill and the ravine to the north." Since the enemy was "sweeping through the village and up across the ravine to our front," Stevens began a vigorous fire that soon arrested their advance. All the time he was nervous about being unsupported by infantry if the enemy should force an attack.[103]

Stevens had not been in position long when Brigadier General Henry Jackson Hunt, chief of the army's artillery, came riding up. Hunt was anxious that Confederate skirmishers might work their way through the woods on Stevens' right, and told the Captain, "I don't like the look of this; send some of your men and tear gaps in the fences between here and the Baltimore Pike, so that you can reach the high land beyond in case you're driven out." This was a wise move, as the historian of Stevens' battery later observed. A battery could deal effectively against massed lines of enemy infantry, but had difficulty with skirmishers who picked off the men and the horses, since "to resist them would be like shooting mosquitoes with musket balls."[104]

Hancock was also concerned about Stevens' exposed position, and went up to General Doubleday to request him to send some troops to the right. Doubleday recalled that Hancock "rode over to me and told me he was in command of the field." Hancock ordered him to send a regiment to Culp's Hill on the right, but Doubleday elected to send the entire Iron Brigade "as my regiments were reduced to the size of companies."[105] These troops were handy for the purpose, since most had rallied in the hollow below (east of) the cemetery.[106] Howard says he became aware of the move, but did not object even though it affected his side of the road, since it was clearly necessary.[107] Doubleday, though, says that "Immediately afterward orders came from Major General Howard, who ranked Hancock, to send the troops in another direction. This occasioned at the time some little delay and confusion."[108]

Hancock clearly triumphed in this conflict of orders, and Colonel W.W. Robinson began moving his men to the right. The battered regiments' route took them right through Stevens' position, and the weary infantrymen marched in between the battery's line of limbers and caissons. They then headed up toward the crest of the hill and began deploying with their right near the hill top, "on the right and a little in advance of the same where it remained during the rest of the battle."[109]

Colonel Rufus Dawes' 6th Wisconsin, which had been detached all day from the Iron Brigade, had rallied in a different area than the rest of its command and so did not move with W.W. Robinson's troops when they departed for Culp's Hill. Dawes recalled that his men had only enjoyed a short breathing spell when Lieutenant Earl N. Rogers of Wadsworth's staff brought him an order to join the rest of the Iron Brigade on Culp's Hill: "As we marched towards the hill, our regimental wagon joined us. In the wagon were a dozen spades and shovels. Taking our place in the right of the line of the brigade, I ordered the regiment to entrench. The men worked with great energy. A man would dig with all his strength till out of breath. When another would seize the spade and push the works. There were no orders to construct these breastworks, but the situation plainly dictated the necessity."[110]

The rest of the Iron Brigade began forming breastworks and entrenchments also, since the terrain of the hill furnished plenty of rocks and trees for building material. Once his command was formed in line on the northern and western slope of Culp's Hill, Wadsworth set up his headquarters on Stevens' Knoll, "planting his headquarters colors near the right gun." He did this in order to be able to have a clearer view of the enemy's movements. Culp's Hill was so wooded that he could not see from there what was happening in his front. Stevens' men were also digging earthworks and emplacements, which would serve them well the next two days.[111]

After sending Stevens' battery and the Iron Brigade to the right, Hancock met Stewart's battery coming up the Pike following its withdrawal from the eastern Railroad cut. Captain Stewart had just reached the cemetery gate when General Hancock called to him and asked how many serviceable guns he had. Stewart replied that he had four. Hancock told him to place three guns on the pike to sweep the approach from the town, and the other at a right angle to them. He then directed Stewart, "I want you to remain in this position until I relieve you in person." After calling up his aide, Captain Mitchell, Hancock "told him to listen to what he was going to say to me: 'I am of the opinion that the enemy will mass in town and make an effort to take this position, but I want you to remain until you are relieved by me or by my written order and take orders from no one.'"[112]

It is unclear where Hancock went next. He is known to have conferred with General Ames and Captain Cooper in front of the cemetery gate house at some point.[113] One of the few high commanding officers whom Hancock did not meet with at this time was Colonel Wainwright of the I Corps artillery.[114]

Hancock also went forward to Wiedrich's battery, located at the far left of Wainwright's line on East Cemetery Hill. After a brief inspection of the position, he told Wiedrich, "Captain, you must hold your position by all means."[115] He then rode along the rest of the lines on Cemetery

Hill with the army's chief topographical engineer, Major General G.K. Warren.[116] With Warren's concurrence, Hancock decided that "if that position could be held until night, it would be the best place for the army to fight on if attacked." He now sent a staff member, Major William G. Mitchell, to report this to Meade.[117]

At some point shortly before 1700, Brigadier General John W. Geary, commander of the 2nd Division of the XII Corps, arrived with two of his brigades (Candy's and Greene's), seeking orders. He had been sent from Two Taverns at 1400 with orders from General Slocum to report to Howard, "whom I should have found at a point some mile and a half east of the town, where an engagement with the right wing [sic] of the enemy's forces was in progress." Why it took him so long to reach the field has never been adequately explained: had Geary arrived earlier he could have prevented the loss of a great number of men in the XI Corps. When Geary was unable to find Howard, he reported instead to Hancock. Hancock told him that "the right could maintain itself," especially since Williams' division was also supposed to be advancing from Two Taverns, but "the immediate need of a division on the left was imperative." Hancock had no authority to give orders to Geary, but he did so in the "crisis of the moment, and Geary consented, due to the threatening emergency."[118]

Geary moved off to the left, and formed a battle line while Buford's cavalry was skirmishing in his front. His line extended from the I Corps left, about one half mile west of the Baltimore Pike, southward towards Little Round Top, in whose front he occupied with two regiments (5th Ohio and 147 Pennsylvania). Geary's other brigade, Kane's, remained in reserve next to the Baltimore Pike some two miles southeast of Gettysburg, along with two guns of Battery K, 5th United States.[119]

Hancock now met General Schurz as the latter came up with the last of his troops, and helped him reform his troops. Once this was done, the two generals sat on a stone fence on the brow of Cemetery Hill to see what the enemy was doing. Schurz recalled, "Through our field-glasses we eagerly watched the movements of the enemy. We saw their batteries and a large portion of their infantry columns distinctly. Some of those columns moved to and fro in a way the purpose of which we did not clearly understand. I was not ashamed to own that I felt nervous, for while our position was a strong one, the infantry line in it appeared, after the losses of the day, woefully thin. It was soothing to my pride, but by no means reassuring as to our situation, when General Hancock admitted that he felt nervous, too. Still he thought that with our artillery so advantageously posted, we might well hold out until the arrival of the Twelfth Corps, which was only a short distance behind us. So we sat watching the enemy and presently observed to our great relief that the movements of the rebel troops looked less and less like a formation for an immediate attack. Our nerves grew more and more tranquil as minute after minute lapsed, for each brought night and reinforcements nearer."[120]

The enemy did not attack, and by 1500 the Union position was stabilized and growing stronger by the minute. This change in affairs was due to a great number of factors—the strength of the hilltop, the steadying presence of Smith's fresh brigade and the growing number of artillery batteries, the valor of the troops, and the efforts of their officers, especially Hancock, Howard, Buford, Schurz, and Warren.[121] Yet it was Hancock's electric presence that everyone remembered most—he helped encourage the defeated troops that were already rallying, and infused them with fresh determination. General Doubleday wrote years later that Hancock, "was our good genius, for he at once brought order out of confusion and made such admirable dispositions that he secured the ridge and held it."[122] General Schurz felt the same: "The appearance of General Hancock at the front was a most fortunate event. It gave the troops a new inspiration. They all knew him by fame, and his stalwart figure, his proud mien, and his superb soldierly bearing seemed to verify all the things that fame had told about him. His mere presence was a reinforcement, and everybody on the field felt stronger for his being there. This new inspiration of self-reliance might have become of immediate importance, had the enemy made another attack—an eventuality for which we had to prepare. And in this preparation Howard, in spite of his heart-sore, cooperated so loyally with Hancock that it would have been hard to tell which of the two was the commander, and which the subordinate."[123]

General Buford did his part to strengthen the army's stance by moving his tired cavalry division to the left of Cemetery Hill and making threatening gestures against the Confederate right. It will be recalled that at about 1615 Doubleday sent Major E.P. Halstead to request reinforcements from Howard, and Howard told Halstead to direct Buford to aid the I Corps. Howard by mistake sent Halstead to the east of Gettysburg to look for Buford, and when Halstead returned to Cemetery Hill he witnessed Hancock's arrival there. He then rode to the west of the hill and in a short time "discovered Buford's cavalry only a little west of the cemetery."[124] These troops were probably Gamble's, which had just been driven out of Schultz Woods.[125]

Halstead delivered his orders, which greatly annoyed Buford, who already had had a very long and taxing day: "The General rose in his stirrups upon his tiptoes and exclaimed. 'What in hell and damnation does he think I can do against those long lines of the enemy out there!" Halstead replied that he didn't know, he was just delivering orders. "Very well," said Buford, "I will see what I can do."[126]

Halstead relates that Buford then "moved his command out in plain view of the enemy and formed for the charge; the enemy, seeing the movement, formed squares in echelon, which delayed them and naturally aided the escape of the First Corps if it did not save a large portion of the remnant from capture. The formation of squares by the enemy that day has been doubted by nearly every one with whom I have conversed upon the subject, and not until the meeting of the survivors of the first corps at Gettysburg, in May 1885, was I able to satisfy Colonel Batchelder, who has made a study of that battle, of the correctness of my statements, and only then after it had been corroborated by two of Buford's officers who were in the engagement."[127]

It is not clear, however, which Confederate units would have formed squares at this time, since no Confederate infantry is known to have proceeded east or southeast of Seminary Ridge below Fairfield Road at the time Halstead mentions. Unfortunately, neither Buford nor any of his subordinates mention Confederate squares in their battle reports.[128] Confederate sources make only one reference to a unit forming squares against cavalry. This was when Colonel Marshall of Pettigrew's brigade formed the 52nd North Carolina "in square" in order to face Gamble's 8th Illinois sometime in the early afternoon.[129] Lieutenant Colonel Charles Livingston of Doubleday's staff saw the enemy "forming against cavalry" at about 1630.[130] This account is also a bit too early to refer to the same episode described by Halstead. It is unclear if these Union "squares" accounts are all conflated recollections of how the 52nd North Carolina faced the 8th Illinois cavalry, or if there were one or possibly two additional episodes of "squares" later in the afternoon—by part of Perrin's or Lane's command at about 1630 as cited by Livingston and/or the incident just cited by Halstead that would have occurred between 1700 and 1730.

After Gamble's brigade helped cover the retreat of the I Corps in this manner, Buford withdrew it to a position closer to Cemetery Hill.[131] He then rode to the hill "for observation." Shortly after he arrived there,

General Hancock came up, "and in a very few moments he made superb disposition to resist any attack that might be made."[132]

Devin's brigade rejoined Gamble's while the latter was drawn up near the Emmitsburg Road; we cannot be certain if this was before or after Buford met Hancock on Cemetery Hill. As has already been shown, Devin spent most of the afternoon facing Ewell's troops to the north and northwest of Gettysburg. After he was forced to withdraw by Early's attack and then some friendly artillery fire from Cemetery Hill, parts of his command contested the Confederate advance through the southern section of the town.[133]

One historian of Devin's 17th Pennsylvania cavalry wrote that, "The retirement of the troops from the first to the second position was rapid, and the difficult task was not executed without confusion. The broken lines of battle were forced in hastily formed columns through narrow streets with artillery, mounted troops and trains. The regiment preserved its formation throughout this trying ordeal, and with the brigade and division went into position on Cemetery Hill, holding the extreme left of the new line. The Seventeenth Pennsylvania Cavalry was placed in support of Calef's battery, while the carbineers of the division were hastened to the support of the First Corps in defeating the advance of the enemy to the Emmitsburg Pike."[134]

After the crisis of the evening passed and more reinforcements came up, Buford moved his division farther to the left and encamped near the Sherfy Peach Orchard.[135] Lieutenant Calef recalled that when his battery went into camp, Geary's division had already formed nearby and "The Third Corps was coming up."[136] As his artillerymen "lay around the guns, resting and awaiting instructions about camping," General Buford came up and told them, "Men, you have done splendidly. I never saw a battery served so well in my life." Calef noted that, "This recognition of their services by their general was ample compensation to these brave men for the hardships of the day and nerved them for the trials which the morrow's sun would surely bring."[137]

We return now to Cemetery Hill.

Once Hancock had assessed the initial situation there, he sent Major William T. Mitchell to Meade with an assessment of the situation and a verbal message that "he would hold on until dark." Hancock later explained to the Committee on the Conduct of the War that he intended to stay that long in order "to allow the commanding general time to decide the question of maintaining the position."[138]

By 1725 Hancock felt that the immediate crisis was passed, so he

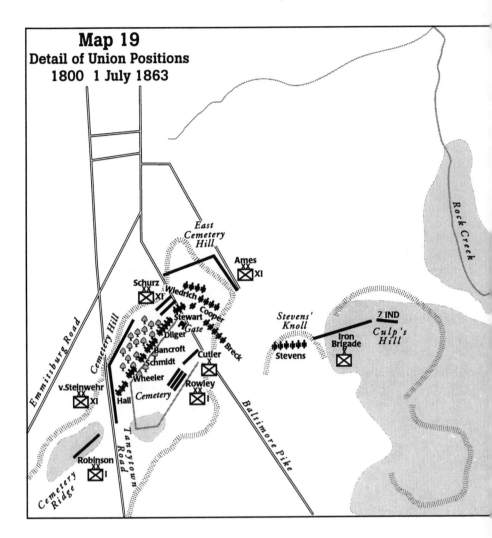

Map 19
Detail of Union Positions
1800 1 July 1863

sent the following concise description of the situation to Meade; carried by his aide Captain I.B. Parker:

5.25 [P.M., July 1, 1863.]

General: When I arrived here an hour since, I found that our troops had given up the front of Gettysburg and the town. We have now taken up a position in the cemetery, and cannot well be taken. It is a position, however, easily turned. Slocum is now coming on the ground, and is taking position on the right, which will protect the right. But we have, as yet, no troops on the left, the Third Corps not having yet reported; but I suppose that it is marching up. If so, its flank march will in a degree protect our left flank. In the meantime Gibbon had better march on so as to take position on our right or left, to our rear, as may be necessary, in some commanding position. General G. will see this dispatch. The battle is quiet now. I think we will be all right until night. I have sent all the trains back. When night comes, it can be told better what had best be done. I think we can retire; if not, we can fight here, as the ground appears not unfavorable with good troops. I will communicate in a few moments with General Slocum, and transfer the command to him.

Howard says that Doubleday's command gave way.

General Warren is here.

Your obedient servant,
Winf'd S. Hancock.
Major-General, Commanding Corps.[139]

Notice that Hancock's assessment is dry and non-committal: it lists the troops on the field, those expected to come up shortly, and the strengths and weaknesses of the position. Nowhere does he state that the position was an excellent one on which to fight; the exact phrase he uses is that "the ground appears not unfavorable with good troops." The decision whether to stay or fight was Meade's; the army could readily withdraw if Meade desired, since Hancock had sent all the trains back.

Hancock felt that his assignment was accomplished by about 1800, when Slocum at last arrived. Since Slocum was his senior, Hancock transferred command to him and prepared to leave the field, which he did not do until "about dark." He must have been pleased to see the advance elements of the III Corps coming up as he left the field.[140] He stopped to meet for some time with General Gibbon, acting commander of the II Corps, when he met him advancing up the Taneytown Road several miles south of Gettysburg, and then proceeded on to report to Meade in person.[141]

Meade's decision based on these reports was a difficult one to make. Two of his corps had been defeated (though he did not know the enormity of their losses), and he certainly could not have been faulted for ordering a withdrawal to his prearranged defensive line along Pipe Creek. This would have been militarily sound, but not a welcome political or popular one. He could also easily stay and fight. Though the I and XI Corps had been defeated, they were still near the field, and two more corps were close at hand (III and XII). Since II and V corps could reach the field early the next day, he could have most of his army concentrated, provided that Lee did not continue to press his advantage strongly.

Meade understood that he had half of his army at or near the field, and at 1800 announced his intention to stay and fight at Gettysburg. This decision was a key one, made before the arrival of Hancock's 1725 message. It must, though, have been formed on the basis of some other encouraging news from the field, probably Captain Mitchell's verbal message from Hancock.[142] The message, which is addressed to Hancock and Doubleday instead of Hancock and Howard, is as follows:

Headquarters Army of the Potomac
July 1, 1863-6 p.m.

Major-Generals Hancock and Doubleday:

If General Slocum is on the field, and I hope he is, of course he takes command. Say to him I thought it prudent to leave a division of the Third Corps at Emmitsburg, to hold in check any force attempting to come through there. It can be ordered up to-night, if necessary. Sedgwick is moving up here, and will be pushed forward in the night, if required. It seems to me we have so concentrated that a battle at Gettysburg is now forced on us, and that, if we get up all our people, and attack with our whole force to-morrow, we ought to defeat the force the enemy has.

Very respectfully, &c.
Geo. G. Meade,
Major-General, Commanding.[144]

It also appears that Meade's decision to stay and fight was influenced by a hope that only Hill and Ewell were on the field. If he could concentrate most of his army at Gettysburg before Longstreet came up, he might be able to win the general battle that was being thrust upon him. This is what he wrote to General Halleck in Washington at 1800:

Headquarters Army of the Potomac
July 1, 1863-6 p.m.
(Received 10.20 p.m., via Frederick City.)

Maj. Gen. H.W. Halleck,
General-in-Chief:

The First and Eleventh Corps have been engaged all day in front of

Gettysburg. The Twelfth, Third, and Fifth have been moving up, and all, I hope, by this time on the field. This leaves only the Sixth, which will move up to-night. General Reynolds was killed this morning early in the action. I immediately sent up General Hancock to assume command. A.P. Hill and Ewell are certainly concentrating; Longstreet's whereabouts I do not know. If he is not up to-morrow, I hope with the force I have concentrated to defeat Hill and Ewell. At any rate, I see no other course than to hazard a general battle. Circumstances during the night may alter this decision, of which I will try to advise you. I have telegraphed Couch that if he can threaten Ewell's rear from Harrisburg without endangering himself, to do so.

Geo. G. Meade,
Major-General.[144]

In a further flurry of activity, perhaps influenced by receipt of Hancock's 1725 message, Meade sent orders to hurry the rest of his corps forward. At 1900 he directed Sykes "to move up to Gettysburg at once upon receipt of this order, if not already ordered to do so by Slocum. The present prospect is that our general engagement must be there."[145] At 1930 he ordered Sedgwick to take his corps and force march directly to Gettysburg, since "a general battle seems to be impending tomorrow." Meade stressed that "it is of the utmost importance that your command should be up" because "we will probably be outnumbered without your presence."[146]

Meade spent the rest of the evening sending orders to his various commanders. At 1930 he sent directions for the troops at Emmitsburg to proceed to Gettysburg, and noted that "the whole army are there (Gettysburg) or under way for that point."[147] The II Corps, as previously noted, was already on its way from Taneytown to Gettysburg. Meade also had to make arrangements for the movement of the artillery reserve and supply trains. As a result he was not able to leave his headquarters in Taneytown until 2200. By that time he had not received Howard's brief message sent at 2200 that admitted to only 3000 losses in the XI Corps; Howard closed with the reassuring note, "This position is plenty good for a general battle unless you fear it being turned at considerable distance from Gettysburg."[148]

The Confederates Fail to Press Their Advantage

Unlike Meade, Lee was on the field for most of the afternoon's fighting, and was an active participant in the critical events that occurred just before dark. He probably witnessed Hill's final attacks on Doubleday's lines from a position near Pegram's artillery on Herr Ridge. He then rode forward on the Chambersburg Pike to the crest of Seminary Ridge, from where he was able to view the Union retreat and the enemy's rallying point on Cemetery Hill.[149] Tradition has it that Lee observed the Federal troops from the cupola on the Seminary, but this was specifically denied by his aide, Colonel W.H. Taylor.[150]

Lee's first reaction to the Union retreat was to order some of Hill's guns that had advanced to Seminary Ridge to begin firing on the Union troops and Cemetery Hill. The identity of these guns unfortunately has not been preserved.[151] He then suggested to Brigadier General William N. Pendleton, the army's chief of artillery, "Whether positions on the right could not be found to enfilade the valley between our position and the town and the enemy's batteries next the town." Pendleton succeeded at moving Marmaduke Johnson's battery of McIntosh's battalion forward to the point where Fairfield Road crosses McPherson's Ridge, but declined to advance it or open fire because of a lack of infantry support, and the number of Union troops occupying Schultz Woods.[152]

Once the Yankees had all retreated, Pendleton brought up two battalions of fresh artillery which had been held in reserve behind Herr Ridge. Garnett's battalion, which had fired a few shots in the closing stages of the fighting, was placed in the vale behind the Seminary. Poague's battalion was placed, under cover, on Garnett's right; his right extended past the Fairfield Road, and was between Johnson's guns and the town.[153]

Pendleton now sent some of his staff to reconnoiter the woods on his right (McMillan's); they may have explored as far south as the Millerstown Road leading to the Sherfy Peach Orchard.[154] Pendleton's immediate goal was to establish Garnett's and Poague's guns in a grand battery south of the Schultz house, since "the position was within range of the hill beyond the town, to which the enemy was retreating, and where he was massing his batteries." As he was doing so, General

Ramseur rode up from the town, which he had just occupied, and "requested that our batteries might not open, as they would draw a concentrated fire on his men, much exposed." Pendleton assented, and later reported, "unless as part of a combined assault, I at once saw it would be worse than useless to open fire there." He directed Captain Victor Maurin of Garnett's battalion to post his guns, keep his horses under cover, and not to fire until given orders.[155]

Pendleton's decision not to open fire was but the first in a series of poor decisions made that evening by a number of leading officers. Had Lee given him positive orders to do so, he surely would have, but such was not Lee's way. Pendleton used his discretion to hold fire and wait to see what everyone else was going to do; he was not aggressive enough to take on the responsibility of renewing the battle by himself. If he had opened fire, it is likely that the other Confederate commanders would have followed up on his initiative. As it was, Pendleton suspended operations and returned to report to Lee. He was more excited about a road to the right that seemed to outflank the Union lines than he was about trying to carry Cemetery Hill.[156]

Lee meanwhile was conferring with Hill about the possibility of sending the Third Corps troops to attack Cemetery Hill. Hill was usually up for a good fight, as he had shown during the Seven Days' Battles and at Antietam, but this day he was not feeling well. British observer Colonel Arthur Fremantle wrote that he joined Generals Lee and Hill on Seminary Ridge at 1630 and watched "the enemy retreating up one of the opposite ridges, pursued by Confederates with loud yells... General Hill now came up and told me he had been very unwell all day, and in fact he looks very delicate. He said he had two of his divisions engaged, and had driven the enemy four miles into his present position, capturing a great many prisoners, some cannon, and some colors. He said, however, that the Yankees had fought with a determination unusual to them."[157]

When Hill complained that his troops were exhausted and disorganized, and that he had captured prisoners from two different Union corps, Lee did not press the issue, and decided to look to other troops to push the enemy. Hill's reluctance to fight, regardless of his own physical condition, was the second Confederate mistake of the evening. Yes, most of Heth's division was pretty well used up, with the possible exception of Brockenbrough's brigade. Only two of Pender's brigades, Scales' and Perrin's had seen heavy action, and his other two, Lane's and Thomas', could at least have been used to support Pendleton's guns south of the

Fairfield Road. Hill did not have enough troops to make an attack here, but he certainly could have created a second front in support of an attack from the left, particularly in view of all the artillery he had available. Instead, he begged to stand down. He reported after the battle, "under the impression that the enemy were entirely routed, my own two divisions exhausted by some six hours' hard fighting, prudence led me to be content with what I had gained, and not push forward troops exhausted and necessarily disordered, probably to encounter fresh troops of the enemy. The two divisions were bivouacked in the positions won."[158]

The troops of Perrin's brigade were particularly upset at being recalled. As already noted, Perrin's 1st and 14th South Carolina regiments had earlier advanced deep into the town, only to be pulled back; they were eager to renew the fight despite their heavy casualties. Likewise the 12th and 13th regiments were recalled from their foray across the Schultz Woods and into the plain beyond, where they had begun pursuing Buford's cavalry. Perrin was anxious to consolidate his brigade once again, since its two wings had been fighting separate actions for about half an hour. After he received orders from Pender "to get the brigade together and let the men rest," Perrin reformed his regiments on Seminary Ridge near the Seminary. While they withdrew, they were fired upon by the Union guns on Cemetery Hill (probably Wheeler's). Perrin thought they were "the same artillery which we had driven from our left near Gettysburg," and severely regretted for the next two days that he had not captured these guns during their retreat or made an attempt to seize them on Cemetery Hill that evening.[159]

Brigadier General James H. Lane was also disappointed not to renew the attack on the last Federal line. His brigade had only been lightly engaged in skirmishing against Union cavalry that afternoon, and so was reasonably fresh in numbers, though not in energy. Lane had passed through the McMillan Woods and into the fields beyond when he was ordered by Pender "not to advance farther unless there was another general forward movement." Since he saw no prospects of one and was under fire from one of the Union batteries on Cemetery Hill, Lane pulled his brigade back in order to secure shelter from a stone wall at the edge of the woods. He then waited in vain for the general advance that never began.[160] Had he established communications with Pendleton, who was only a few hundred yards away, he could have moved to support Pendleton's guns, or had some of these guns move to join him.

Pender apparently forgot about his other fresh brigade, Thomas', and allowed it to remain behind Herr Ridge until near sunset, when he advanced it to support the artillery line being drawn up on Seminary Ridge.[161] As already noted, Pender could have used Thomas' men much more effectively by having them join in the division's 1600 attack, or by bringing them forward to support Lane's troops or Pendleton's guns before sunset. Thomas' command was certainly living a charmed life during this battle. It would also be held in reserve during Longstreet's grand assault on July 3, and would suffer only 264 casualties (20%) in the battle, while the other three brigades in its division suffered an average of 42% casualties.[162]

Pender's fourth brigade, Scales', was so battered by the Union artillery fire it met during the 1600 attack that it could not be depended on to do anything else that day. Colonel William L.J. Lowrence of the 34th North Carolina, who took charge of the brigade after Scales was wounded, reported that "at this time I found the brigade on the extreme left of the division, and numbering in all about 500 men, without any field officers, excepting Lieutenant Colonel Gordon and myself, and but few line officers, and many companies were without a single officer to lead them or to inquire after them. In this depressed, dilapidated and almost unorganized condition I took command of the brigade." He held the unit on Seminary Ridge until nightfall, when he moved to the far right of the division's line, from where he sent out a strong picket. The survivors of the brigade stacked guns and retired at 0100 for a few hours' sleep.[163]

By midnight Pender also shifted Perrin's and Thomas' brigades to the right, so that the division's left was now on the Fairfield Road.[164]

Heth's division, now commanded by Brigadier General J.J. Pettigrew, was so battered by its full day of fighting that it was allowed to go into bivouac in the woods at the eastern slope at Herr Ridge, from where Pettigrew and Brockenbrough had begun their attack at 1430. The bloodied regiments would be given 24 hours of much needed rest before they were moved to the right to take part in another even greater attack—Longstreet's assault on July 3.[165]

Surgeon S.G. Welch of Perrin's 13th South Carolina complained loudly after the war that Hill had not brought up his third division, R.H. Anderson's, to assault Cemetery Hill at dusk: "Then the strong position last occupied by the enemy could have been taken, and next day, when Ewell and Longstreet came up, the victory completely won. If 'Old Stonewall' had been alive and there, there is no doubt what would have been done. Hill was a good division commander, but is not a superior corps commander. He lacks the mind and sagacity of Jackson."[166] We can only wonder what Welch might have said had he learned that the decision not to employ Anderson was made by Lee, not Hill.

Anderson's five brigades had been peaceably encamped since June 27 at Fayetteville, six miles east of Chambersburg. Soon after daylight on 1 July, Hill directed Anderson to begin marching to Cashtown. Some of the troops were disappointed to learn of their destination, since they thought they were going to be headed to Harrisburg.[167] The column proceeded at a leisurely pace, and then came to a halt near Greenwood while Johnson's division and all its trains filed into the road on a side road from Scotland.[168] As noted earlier, had Johnson's division proceeded south on the eastern side of the mountains, it would have arrived on the field much earlier in the day, and the Chambersburg Pike would have been free for Anderson to use and so arrive more quickly on the field. If Johnson and Anderson had arrived at mid-afternoon instead of in the evening, they would have helped make the battle a complete victory for Lee; McLaws' and Hood's divisions, which were stacked up on the road behind Anderson, would also have arrived earlier.

Anderson allowed the rear of the division to rest for about an hour after they climbed through the gap at Cashtown. While resting they were doused by a heavy shower. About 1000 of the men heard the sound of artillery fire at Gettysburg, but most remained unconcerned. The column proceeded only a mile beyond Cashtown and then halted again for an hour. These halts and delays were certainly due to all the congested traffic on the roadway ahead of them.[169]

When the division finally renewed its march, the artillery fire from Gettysburg was still louder. Frank Foote of the 48th Mississippi wrote in his diary, "as we neared Gettysburg the sounds of battle went on increasing. The steady roll of musketry was heard, and the rapid fire of artillery told that 'something was up.' All thoughts that it was only a cavalry engagement were dispelled by that sullen roar. We had an intimate acquaintance with such sounds, and we knew that our old foe, the Army of the Potomac, was in the neighborhood."[170]

As the division neared Gettysburg, its men began to see the familiar sights of the lines behind a battle—streams of wounded, ambulances, ammunition wagons, and scattered prisoners heading to the rear. British Colonel Arthur Fremantle was traveling the same road and the same time, and wrote that: "At 3 p.m., we began to meet wounded men coming to the rear, and the number of these soon increased most rapidly, some hobbling alone, others on stretchers carried by the ambulance corps, and others in the ambulance wagons. Many of the latter were stripped nearly naked, and displayed very bad wounds. This spectacle so revolting to a person unaccustomed to such sights, produced no impression whatever upon the advancing troops, who certainly go under fire with the most perfect nonchalance. They show no enthusiasm or excitement, but the most complete indifference. This is the effect of two years' almost uninterrupted fighting. We now began to meet Yankee prisoners coming to the rear in considerable numbers. Many of them were wounded, but they seemed already to be on excellent terms with their captors, with whom they had commenced swapping canteens, tobacco, & c. Among them was a Pennsylvanian colonel, a miserable object from a wound in his face. In answer to a question, I heard one of them remark, with a laugh, 'We're pretty nigh whipped already.' We next came to a Confederate soldier carrying a Yankee color, belonging, I think, to a Pennsylvania regiment, which he told us he had just captured."[171]

Frank Riley of Company B, 16th Mississippi, of Posey's brigade, expected to go into battle at once, but instead the division was drawn up in battle line on Knoxlyn Ridge, at the position held earlier in the day by Pender's division. Hill directed Anderson to "place a brigade and a battery of artillery a mile or more on the right of the line, in a direction at a right angle with it and facing to the right," much as Pender had deployed Lane's brigade earlier in the day in order to watch out for Union cavalry. Anderson sent Wilcox's brigade and Ross' Georgia battery to do the job.[172]

Anderson's division arrived on Knoxlyn Ridge between 1600 and 1700, certainly in plenty of time to join the battle by dusk if Lee and Hill had chosen to commit it. Its 7100 men were certainly all ready to go, except perhaps Brigadier General A.R. Wright, who had been "compelled by severe indisposition to leave my command" about half way between Cashtown and Gettysburg.[173] Private Riley of the 16th Mississippi thought that the division was being held back because "our men didn't need help."[174]

The truth of the matter was that Lee did not wish to risk Anderson's men, who were his only fresh reserves after Johnson's division was forwarded to Ewell. After the war Anderson told Captain Louis G. Young that he had been hurrying his men to join the battle when he received a messenger from Lee to stop and go into bivouac. He was so surprised by the order that he rode to see Lee himself after he halted his men, to see if the order had been relayed correctly. "General Lee replied that there was no mistake made and explained that his army was not all up, that his (General Anderson's) alone of the troops present had not been engaged, and that a reserve in case of disaster was necessary."[175]

This was the third major mistake of the evening. Even if Lee were concerned about the appearance of even more Union troops on the field, he knew that McLaws' and Hoods' divisions were not far away. In addition, it was unlikely that the Yankees were going to mount a major counterattack this late in the day. Anderson should have been rushed forward to attack the western side of Cemetery Hill while Johnson attacked the northern side. This is probably what Jackson would have urged had he been present. It is also enlightening to note how quickly Meade was pushing his corps forward on several different roads, while Lee's divisions were all backed up on the Chambersburg Pike. This would enable Meade to concentrate his army quicker than Lee, and so ensure his victory.

Since Hill's men were not able to continue the battle, Ewell's would have to handle the job. Sometime between 1630 and 1700 Lee sent Colonel Walter M. Taylor of his staff to suggest to Ewell that he push the enemy and seize Cemetery Hill. Taylor's recollection of the order, which was verbal and not written, was as follows: "He then directed me to go to General Ewell and to say to him that, from the position which he occupied, he could see the enemy retreating over those hills, without organization and in great confusion; that it was only necessary to press 'those people' in order to secure possession of the heights, and that, if possible, he wished him to do this."[176]

Taylor's recollection of this key order, though, was challenged by others who were present at the battle. Most significant is the phrasing Lee used in his battle report, which indicates a significant qualifying clause to his request: "General Ewell was, therefore, instructed to carry the hill occupied by the enemy, if he found it practicable, but to avoid a general engagement until the arrival of the other divisions of the army, which were ordered to hasten forward."[177] Lee's thinking at this moment is unclear, since he at about the same time ordered Anderson to halt and go into camp. Perhaps he intended to halt offensive operations on Hill's wing, but to continue them on Ewell's wing. If so, he should have stated this more clearly to Ewell.

This was the fourth Confederate mistake of the evening. Lee was in the custom of giving his orders in the form of suggestions, or directing them to be carried out "if practicable." In this way he allowed his subordinates considerable discretion as to how, when or even if his commands should be carried out. This procedure had worked well with Jackson and Longstreet over the past year, but now he had a new set of lieutenants. Ewell was fighting his first major battle as corps commander under Lee, and there was no predicting how he would react to such discretionary orders. Lee should have been alert to this, and should have worded his order more strongly. His plan seems to have been for Early to make an attack on the enemy's position from the northwest, supported by Johnson's division as it came up from Cashtown. Details of the attack, though, would be left to his subordinate, as usual.

While Lee was waiting for a reply from Ewell, Lieutenant General James Longstreet, his senior corps commander, rode up to Lee's command post on Seminary Ridge. Lee and Longstreet had begun the day's march together from Chambersburg, as already has been noted, but Lee decided to ride on ahead when Johnson's division cut into the main road at Greenwood and so slowed down all the troops behind him. Longstreet stayed with his command, which was on the Pike behind Anderson's, until midafternoon, when he became so frustrated with its slow progress that he rode on ahead to see how the battle was going. He reached Lee's headquarters "on Seminary Ridge at the crossing of the Cashtown Road" at about 1700.[178]

Lee pointed out the enemy's position, and Longstreet studied the ground for awhile with his binoculars. He was a bit surprised to learn that Lee wanted to continue fighting an offensive battle. To him, the opportunity seemed perfect to slip around the Union army's left, now that their position had at last been located. After five or ten minutes at studying the situation, he told Lee that he thought an attack on the Union army's position on those heights was "at variance with the plan of the campaign that had been agreed upon before leaving Fredericksburg." Lee replied, "If the enemy is there tomorrow, we must attack him." To which Longstreet retorted, "If he is there, it will be because he is anxious that we should attack him, a good reason in my judgement, for not doing so."[179]

Longstreet then elaborated his strategy: "I urged that we should move around by our right to the left of Meade, and put our army between him and Washington, threatening his left and rear, and thus force him to attack us in such position as we might select. I said that it seemed to me that if, during our council at Fredericksburg, we had described the position in which we desired to get the two armies, we could not have expected to get the enemy in a better position for us than that he then occupied; that he was in strong position and would be awaiting us, which was evidence that he desired that we should attack him. I said, further, that his weak point seemed to be his left; hence, I thought that we should move around to his left, that we might threaten it if we intended to maneuver, or attack it if we determined upon a battle. I called his attention to the fact that the country was admirably adapted for a defensive battle, and that we should surely repulse Meade with crushing loss if we would take position so as to force him to attack us, and suggested that, even if we carried the heights in front of us, and drove Meade out, we should be so badly crippled that we could not reap the fruits of victory; and that the heights of Gettysburg were, in themselves, of no more importance to us than the ground we then occupied, and that the mere possession of the ground was not worth a hundred men to us. That Meade's army, not its position, was our objective."[180]

Lee, though, was not to be persuaded by Longstreet's argument. He had defeated a portion of the Union army, and wanted to continue attacking in order to defeat them in detail. Longstreet reminded him "that if the Federals were there in the morning, it would be proof that they had their forces well in hand, and that with Pickett in Chambersburg and Stuart out of reach, we should be somewhat in detail." Lee, however, did not want to give up the idea of attacking. Longstreet had seen him in this state of excitement before, and noted "he seemed under a subdued excitement, which occasionally took possession of him when 'the hunt was up' and threatened his superb equipoise. The sharp battle fought by Hill and Ewell on that day had given him a taste of victory."[181]

Since Lee's fighting blood was up, Longstreet decided not to push the matter, but determined "to renew the subject next morning."[182] We can only wonder how much Longstreet's assessment of the situation and disagreement with Lee's intentions may have affected Lee's plans and state of mind. The most significant result of this meeting, though, is the fact that Longstreet did not heartily endorse an immediate attack on Cemetery Hill. Anderson's division had until recently been in his corps, and he knew its officers and men. He could well have offered to lead it into action, but his fighting blood was not up at the moment.

While Longstreet was still with Lee, Colonel A.L. Long came up to report the results of a reconnaissance Lee had ordered him to make of the enemy's primary position on Cemetery Hill. He stated that he found the hill "occupied by a considerable force, a part strongly posted behind a stone fence near its crest, and the rest on the reverse slope." In his opinion, "an attack at that time, with the troops then at hand, would have been hazardous and very doubtful of success."[183]

Long's report was certainly far from encouraging, and he did not recall the question of an attack being discussed any more that evening.[184] This last statement may have been true, at least in so far as Hill's front was concerned. The nature of Long's report makes it clear that he had not surveyed the eastern side of Cemetery Hill, and that was where Lee was already focusing his attention.[185]

Lee's apparent intention, then, was for Ewell to press the battle on the eastern side of Cemetery Hill. Ewell had been on the field since noon, and was well aware of the activity and strength of his troops. He had travelled with Rodes' command that morning, and first saw the battlefield from Oak Hill. Soon after Rodes began his attack on Robinson's line, Ewell rode to the left to consult with Early. As he rode by the position of W. Carter's battery, a Union shell fragment killed his horse. Ewell was thrown to the ground and had to be helped up because of the wooden leg he had since the battle of Groveton (he usually had to be strapped to his horse in order to avoid falling off). He said he was not hurt as he mounted a fresh horse, but the incident surely must have been unnerving.[186]

Ewell reached Early's front after the advanced line of the XI Corps had been driven back, and stopped to confer with Brigadier General John B. Gordon, whose Georgia brigade had done such a magnificent job at breaking Barlow's line on Barlow's Knoll. While the two were conversing, Major Henry Kyd Douglas of Major General Ed Johnson's staff came up with the welcome news that Johnson's division was only three miles west of Gettysburg on the Chambersburg Pike, and ready for action.[187]

Johnson's division (formerly Jackson's own), had been recalled from Carlisle on June 29, and marched westward through Shippensburg to Scotland, where it encamped the night before the battle. The division broke camp by 0700 on 1 July, and marched southward toward Greenwood, located on the Chambersburg Pike, with its brigades in the following order: Nicholls', J.M. Jones', Steuart's, J.A Walker's.[188] Also accompanying the division was Latimer's battalion of artillery, plus the corps' reserve artillery (Dance's and Nelson's battalions) and the corps' wagons. The lengthy column reached the Chambersburg Pike at mid morning just ahead of Anderson's division, which was coming up from Fayetteville, and was given the right of way on the road. This, of course, greatly slowed down the progress of Anderson's troops and

Longstreet's men behind Anderson's, with the ramifications already discussed. Ironically, Johnson complained that his own progress was delayed "because of the obstructions caused by the wagons of Longstreet's [he must mean Hill's] corps." [189]

Johnson's men clearly heard the sound of the battle once they reached Cashtown, and pushed on as fast as they could to reach the field. Douglas thought that Johnson "seemed to be spoiling for a fight with his new division"; Johnson had just returned to the army after recovering from a bad wound received at McDowell over a year earlier, and had replaced Raleigh Colston as commander of Jackson's old division after Chancellorsville. When the division was about halfway between Cashtown and Gettysburg, Johnson directed Douglas "to ride rapidly to General Ewell and say to him that he was marching on Gettysburg rapidly, with his division in prime condition and was ready to put in as soon as he got there."[190]

When Douglas finished giving his message to Ewell, Gordon offered to join in an attack when Johnson arrived, and expressed confidence that he and Johnson could certainly "carry that hill" (Cemetery Hill) before dark. Ewell, though, did not seem to be excited by the prospect. He replied to both officers, "General Lee told me to come to Gettysburg and gave me no orders to go further. I do not feel like advancing and making an attack without orders from him, and he is back at Cashtown." He then directed Douglas to tell Johnson "when he got to the front, to halt and wait for orders."[191]

Ewell's reluctance to push on without orders amazed all the officers present, who were accustomed to Jackson's aggressiveness. All were silent for a moment. Then Sandie Pendleton, Ewell's Chief of Staff, said to Douglas "quietly and with much feeling," "Oh for the presence and inspiration of Old Jack for one hour."[192]

It was not long before Ewell received the contact with Lee that he had been looking for. He and Gordon had just ridden to the town square at about 1700, when Colonel Taylor of Lee's staff rode up and let him know that Lee was not at Cashtown, but on Seminary Ridge only about one mile away. Taylor then relayed Lee's request that Ewell press "those people" and take the heights "if practicable." Ewell acknowledged the message, and sent Taylor back to Lee with "some message for the commanding general in regard to the prisoners captured." Taylor remembered that "General Ewell did not express any objection, or indicate any objection, or indicate the existence of any impediment, to the execution of the order conveyed to him, but left the impression upon my mind that it would be executed."[193]

Lieutenant James P. Smith of Ewell's staff was with the general in the square at this time: "The square was filled with Confederate soldiers, and with them were mingled many prisoners, while scarcely a citizen was to be seen. As our corps commander sat in his saddle under the shade of a tree, a young officer brought from a cellar a bottle of wine, which the General pleasantly declined, while he chatted amiably with his men, and the Federal prisoners gathered about him."[194]

It was a critical moment, one that called for action. Ewell may well have been waiting for Johnson's division to arrive before attempting another advance, especially in view of Lee's precaution "to avoid a general engagement until the arrival of the other divisions of the army." At the least, though, he could have gone forward himself, or sent staff members forward to scout the Union position. Instead, he seemed to his staff to be basking in the glory of an unfinished victory. Smith and several of his fellows who had served with Jackson looked askance at each other, and one said sadly, "Jackson's not here." Smith later lamented that "our corps commander, General Ewell, as true a Confederate soldier as ever went into battle, was simply waiting for orders, when every moment of time could not be balanced with gold."[195]

While Ewell was at the town square, he was joined by his two principal lieutenants on the field, Rodes and Early. Rodes' whereabouts during the afternoon are not certain. He probably watched his division's attacks from Oak Hill, but it is not known what route he took to enter the town. At the time Rodes met Ewell, his brigades were much scattered. Doles and Ramseur were in the town,[196] and Daniel was at its northwestern outskirts.[197] Iverson was on his way into the town,[198] and O'Neal, if he is to be believed, was at the southern edge of the town, pressing to make an attack.[199]

Early's whereabouts are known with more certainty. He followed the axis of his division's advance, and ordered up Carrington's battery to shell the enemy's troops in the town and to the right of it. However, the advance of his own troops was so quick that the guns were not able to get off a clear shot. He was also concerned that the advance of his troops was being "considerably disturbed" by Rodes' rapid advance on the right.[200]

Early was anxious to have Smith's fresh brigade come forward to join the rest of the division near the town, and had sent Smith an order to come up and support Hays and Avery. When Smith did not appear,

Early followed his victorious troops into the town, and sent a second order for Smith to advance. After he briefly reconnoitered his front, he rode to his right in order to find either Ewell, Rodes or Hill "for the purpose of urging an immediate advance."[201]

While he rode forward behind his advance troops, Early received not one but two messages from Smith. As has been noted, Smith had originally been deployed in reserve, some ½ mile behind Jones' cannons, almost two miles northeast of Gettysburg on the Harrisburg Road. The first message he sent Rodes was that he had received a report "that a large force of the enemy was advancing on the York Pike on our then rear," for which reason "he thought proper to detain his brigade to watch that road." The second message was more desperate "that the enemy was advancing a large force of infantry, artillery and cavalry on the York road, menacing our left flank and rear."[202]

It has never been established what these troops were, or where exactly they were located. There were no Union troops near the York Pike, and in fact the closest Union command was Williams' division of the XII Corps, which was well over 1 ½ miles away, south of the Hanover Road. Perhaps one of Smith's skirmishers saw a detachment of Devin's cavalry that had not rejoined its brigade, or some advance skirmishers of Williams' command. It is also possible that Smith had received a report about Union troops advancing, from some of White's 35th Virginia cavalry troops, who were then operating on his flank;[203] if so, these might have seen Williams' troops approaching, but mistook what road he was on.[204]

The actual truth of the matter may lie in Smith's character. He was a leading politician in Virginia before the war, and had earned his colorful nickname "Extra Billy" while operating the postal service between Washington D.C. and Georgia in the 1830's. At the age of 66, he was by far the oldest general in Lee's army, but he certainly had fought well up to this point, having received no less than five wounds in the defense of his country. However, he was very close to the end of his campaigning days. Life in the field had worn him down, and he would resign his field command only nine days after the opening day of Gettysburg.[205] Lieutenant Cyrus B. Coiner of Smith's 52nd Virginia heard the General instructing his son Lieutenant Fred Smith, to tell Early that the enemy was advancing. Coiner could see no reason for the alarm "unless he mistook a fence with a growth of small trees for a line of troops."[206]

In later years Early defended his decision to send Smith off to the left by saying, "I had no faith in the report myself, but knowing the effect such a report must have on the men in Gettysburg and to the right and left of it, as if true, it would bring the enemy in their rear, I immediately ordered one of my staff officers to go and tell Gordon to take his brigade...and stop that 'stampeding.'" He added, in retrospect, that "it was by no means improbable" that there were Yankee cavalry and other troops to the left "as we knew Stuart had had a fight at or near Hanover the day before, and Colonel White, who moved on the York Road on the march back, had reported to me that a force of the enemy's infantry and cavalry had been on the road."[207]

Early, who should have known Smith's character and inclinations better, felt that he had no choice but to heed Extra Billy's report. Quite surprisingly, he sent Gordon's brigade to support Smith's, and directed Gordon (whom he certainly trusted more than Smith) to take charge of both brigades. This, Early trusted, would "stop all further alarms from that direction."[208] But this would be done at the cost of half of his division, troops that could have been much better employed against Cemetery Hill. Mistake number five of the evening.

Gordon moved back as ordered, and then took charge of Smith's command. The two units probably headed south on Shealer Road, and received some Union artillery fire after they crossed York Pike. They did not encounter any Union troops until they neared the Hanover Road, when Smith's 49th Virginia advanced as skirmishers and met some of Williams' skirmishers.[209] Smith did not even conduct this advance well. Captain Robert K. Funkhouser of Company D, 49th Virginia, recalled that his brigade was sent out to the division's left at 1700. His major did not deploy the regiment properly when it was sent forward as skirmishers, and as a result "it was a general jumble up and we danced like a set of rabbits." The regiment ran into a heavy skirmish line of the enemy and then encountered artillery fire that hit their flank.[210]

After dealing with Smith, Early proceeded to inspect the position held by his other two brigades, Hays' and Avery's. He found Hays' troops, especially on their left, being annoyed by the fire of Union troops posted in the houses and streets at the southern edge of the town. Any advance on his front had to be made "along the streets by flank or in columns so narrow as to have been subjected to a destructive fire from the batteries on the crest of the hill, which enfiladed the streets." Avery, who was on Hays' left in the southeastern edge of the town and beyond, faced a hill with a "very rugged" ascent that was "much obstructed by plank and stone fences on the side of it."[211]

These conditions persuaded Early that he would not be able to assault the Union lines on his front by himself without help. They may also have eased his decision to send Gordon to support Smith, if Smith's second message arrived after Early's tour of Hays' and Avery's positions. Even so, Early still garnished hopes of taking the hill, and requested one of Pender's aides that he met in the town "to go and inform General Hill that if he would send a division forward we could take the hill to which the enemy had retreated."[212]

It was now that Early joined Rodes and Ewell in the town square. Both division commanders described the positions of their troops "with great earnestness and animation," and asked Ewell to inform Lee "that they could go forward and take Cemetery Hill if they were supported on their right." They also noted "that to the south of the Cemetery there was a commanding height that ought to be taken at once."[213]

Lieutenant J.P. Smith was sent to carry this message to Lee. He found the commander "quite well to the right, in an open field, with General Longstreet, dismounted, and with glasses inspecting the position to the south of Cemetery Hill." When he had delivered his message, Lee gave him his "glasses" and said that some of "those people" were there on the elevated, commanding position evidently indicated by Early and Rodes; he regretted that he had "no force on the field with which to take that position."[214]

Lee now turned to Longstreet and asked "where his troops were, and expressed the wish that they might be brought immediately to the front." Longstreet bluntly replied that his lead division, McLaws', was some six miles away, "and then was indefinite and noncommittal."[215] "Old Pete," who does not mention this conversation in any of his three accounts of this period, clearly was not interested in participating in a frontal assault on Cemetery Hill. Because he had no troops available to make the attack that Rodes and Early requested, Lee told Lieutenant Smith to say to Ewell that "he regretted that his people were not up to support him on the right, but he wished him to take the Cemetery Hill if it were possible; and that he would ride over to and see him very soon."[216]

While Lieutenant Smith was with Lee, Generals Ewell, Rodes and Early rode down Baltimore Street in order to inspect the Union lines together. The body of officers provided an excellent target for Von Steinwehr's skirmishers posted in the houses at the base of the hill, who rose and let loose a volley. Major Daniel heard a thud, and thought that the officer next to him had been hit. Upon inquiry, he discovered that it was only the man's leather stirrups that had been struck.[217]

Gordon claimed in his autobiography that the incident occurred as follows: a body of Union soldiers that had been overrun suddenly opened a "brisk fire" from behind some buildings and fences on the outskirts of town. Gordon remembered that "a number of Confederates were killed or wounded, and I heard the ominous thud of a minié ball as it struck General Ewell at my side." He quickly asked, "Are you hurt, sir?" Ewell replied, "No, No. I'm not hurt. But suppose the ball had struck you. We would have had the trouble of carrying you off the field, sir. You see how much better fixed for a fight I am than you are. It don't hurt a bit to be shot in a wooden leg."[218] This episode, however, more probably occurred at about 1200 on 3 July.[219]

Ewell and his entourage turned left along High Street in order to view Howard's line, and Ewell directed his two division commanders to prepare to make an assault.[220] But when Lieutenant Smith returned from Lee, it was clear to all that any attack would have no support from the right. Ewell by now was also aware of the weakened condition of Rodes' brigades. He was further concerned by a lack of suitable artillery positions from which to support an attack. It was impossible to form any batteries in the town, and any guns set up to the left or right of Gettysburg would have no cover and so would be instantly blasted by all the Union guns on Cemetery Hill. As a result of these factors, Ewell directed Rodes and Early to hold their troops in place until Johnson's command could be brought up and advanced to seize "the wooded hill to my left" (Culp's Hill).[221]

Early, however, at one time claimed that it was he who directed Johnson to proceed to Culp's Hill. He said in an 1877 article that while he was in the town dealing with the staff officer from Pender's division and one of Smith's messengers, "Colonel Smead, of Ewell's staff, came to me and informed me that Johnson was coming up, and to ask me where I thought he ought to be put." As the two conversed, a Union artillery barrage started. Amidst the bursting shells, Early "designated to Colonel Smead Culp's Hill, the wooded hill east of the town and adjoining Cemetery Hill, as the position Johnson should take when he got up, as it evidently commanded the enemy's position." Early says he then rode in person, to Ewell, who again asked him where to post Johnson. Early says "I urged the propriety of pushing on and capturing Cemetery Hill."[222] It is not unlikely that Early was still desirous of attacking the Union line, but it seems odd that Ewell would have sent Smead to let Early make the decision on where Johnson should be posted.

The officers and men of Early's and Rodes' divisions, especially those deployed within sight of the enemy, were gravely disappointed when they received instructions to pull back to defensive positions instead of advancing to the attack. Hays, who claimed that he had "driven the enemy entirely out of the city," pulled his main line back to High Street. His losses for the day had been light—one officer and six men killed, four officers and 37 wounded, and 15 men missing—and he was ready and eager to continue the fight.[223] He reportedly told Longstreet long after the battle that he "could have seized the heights without the loss of ten men."[224] Hays insisted on making an attack on the hill, and was asked whether his men ever "got a bellyful of fighting." Hays curtly replied that he only wanted to avoid losing still more men if he had to attack the hill later.[225]

Avery's brigade, though, was unable to retire safely, and had to remain in an advanced position south of the railroad. Colonel A.C. Godwin of the 57th North Carolina reported that the brigade had just formed along the railroad line immediately east of the town when a Union battery (Stevens') began shelling them. The brigade moved some 400 yards to the left, under cover of the railroad embankment, and then moved forward. By now the enemy shells were so effective that "we were soon after halted in a depression on the hillside, and the men ordered to lie down." The unit then remained in this position, with skirmishers sent forward. Lieutenant Colonel H.C. Jones Jr. of the 57th later felt strongly that, "There was not an officer, not even a man, that did not expect that the war would be closed upon the hill that evening, for there was still two hours of daylight when the final charge was made, yet for reasons that have never been explained nor ever will be...someone made a blunder that lost the battle of Gettysburg, and humanly speaking, the Confederate cause."[226]

General Gordon was also very reluctant to halt his brigade when ordered, even though he had not yet come within range of the Union troops on Cemetery Hill. As already noted, his men had participated in the initial assault on Barlow's right, but then had been halted near the Almshouse in order to allow Hays and Avery to pass by and continue the battle. Gordon later wrote, "On the first day neither General Early nor General Ewell could possibly have been fully cognizant of the situation at the time I was ordered to halt. The whole of that portion of the Union army on my front was in inextricable confusion and in flight. They were necessarily in flight, for my troops were upon their flank and rapidly sweeping down the lines. The firing upon my men had almost ceased. Large bodies of Union troops were throwing down their arms and surrendering, because in disorganized and confused masses they were wholly powerless either to check the movement or return fire. As far down the lines as my eye could reach the Union troops were in retreat. Those at a distance were still resisting, but giving ground, and it was necessary for me to press forward in order to insure the same results which invariably follow such flank movements. In less than half an hour my troops would have swept up and over those hills, the possession of which was of such momentous consequence. It is not surprising, with a full realization of the consequences of a halt, that I should have refused to obey the order. Not until the third or fourth order of the most peremptory character reached me did I obey. I think I should have risked the consequences of disobedience even then but for the fact that the order to halt was accompanied with the explanation that General Lee, who was several miles away, did not wish to give battle at Gettysburg."[227] Gordon's command was then withdrawn to support Smith's brigade, as already noted.

Colonel O'Neal of Rodes' division was particularly incensed when Rodes pulled his units back on the western side of the town. He wrote in his battle report that "the greater portion of my brigade had passed through the town, and I had ordered up some pieces of artillery and had formed my brigade, and, in conjunction with General Doles, was in the act of charging the hill, when I was recalled." According to the account by Private C.D. Grace of Doles' Brigade, O'Neal was so angry at Rodes that he rode up to Brigadier General Doles and "requested him to take charge of the division and drive the Federals from the Cemetery Ridge." Doles refused to do anything without orders from Ewell or Rodes. Still O'Neal persisted, "saying that the Federals were demoralized, and we would have no trouble carrying the ridge." Doles agreed, but still refused to act without orders, and both units were soon pulled back.[228]

The Confederate troops who were most disappointed, even angry, to be pulled back, were those of Ramseur's brigade. As already noted, Ramseur's men had broken Paul's brigade and then advanced a mile to the south, driving the Yankees before them and capturing numerous prisoners. They halted in the southwest quarter of the town soon after Perrin withdrew the 1st and 14th South Carolina, and were very ready to continue the fight. Lieutenant William Calder felt that "it was here that the great mistake was made which lost us the advantage of so many gallant men. Our generals should have advanced immediately on that hill. It could have been taken then with comparatively little loss and would have deprived the enemy of that immense advantage of position which was afterward the cause of his success."[229]

T.M. Gorman of Ramseur's 2nd North Carolina felt a full range of emotions when the battle was not continued: "Instead of following the enemy up, and continuing the fight, (as "Old Jack" would have done), the pursuit was carried no further than the base of the enemy's new position, when our line was halted for the day, and new lines of battle were formed, and we rested in that position till the next day, waiting for Longstreet and Hill to come up. That delay was fatal to us. Our new line of battle extended through the streets of Gettysburg, and there we slept that night. It is the opinion of many that we lost the golden opportunity in not keeping up the attack that evening, and I concur in that opinion. The [enemy's] reinforcement had not come up. They had been badly whipped and demoralized, and it is believed that we could have taken their position that evening with the loss of less than 500. It afterwards cost us 10,000, and then we could not hold it. Had we taken it that evening it is hardly possible to say how great our victory could have been. Washington would have been evacuated, Baltimore would have been free, Maryland unfettered, the enemy discomfitted, and our victorious banners flaunting defiantly before the panic-stricken North."[230]

General Rodes carefully outlined his reasons for not pressing an attack on Cemetery Hill in his undated battle report. His analysis reflects the state of mind, and frustration, of each of the army's division commanders on the field at that moment: "The troops, being greatly exhausted by their march and somewhat disorganized by the hot engagement and rapid pursuit, were halted and prepared for further action. I did not change their position materially, nor order another attack, for the following reasons: 1st, in the midst of the engagement just described, the corps commander informed me, through one of his officers, that the general commanding did not wish a general engagement brought on...; 2d, before the completion of his defeat before the town, the enemy had begun to establish a line of battle on the heights back of the town, and by the time my line was in a condition to renew the attack, he displayed quite a formidable line of artillery immediately in my front....To have attacked this line with my division alone, diminished as it had been by a loss of 2500 men, would have been absurd. Seeing no Confederate troops at all on my right; finding that General Early, whom I encountered in the streets of the town within thirty minutes after its occupation by my forces, was awaiting further instructions, and, receiving no orders to advance, though my superiors were on the ground, I concluded that the order not to bring on a general engagement was still in force, and hence placed my lines and skirmishers in a defensive attitude, and determined to await orders or further movements either on the part of Early or of the troops on my right."[231]

As a result of the pullback by Pender's, Rodes' and Early's infantry, there was only a limited exchange of infantry and artillery fire between these Confederate troops and the Union forces reforming on Cemetery Hill. As already noted, the first artillery fired at the Confederate troops on Hill's front had been aimed at Perrin's regiments after they had been recalled from their advanced positions. Perrin was particularly annoyed that this "was the same artillery which we had driven from our left near Gettysburg. I saw it move off from my left, and file into position over the hill." On Ewell's front, the Confederates had met cannon fire from Stevens' battery on Stevens' knoll and sporadic shots from East Cemetery Hill, as already discussed.[232]

The Confederate artillery did not reply with any intensity to this intermittent Union fire from Cemetery Hill. As already noted, several battalions were drawn up on Seminary Ridge well before dark (which came at about 2000), but they did not all open fire as Lee hoped. Most of the few Confederate artillery shells that struck Cemetery Hill at this time were fired by guns of Jones' battalion of Early's division from positions east of the town. The effects of one of the early Confederate shots were recorded by Captain E.P. Halstead of Doubleday's staff: "An amusing incident occurred soon after our forces had concentrated on Cemetery hill. The enemy opened quite a brisk artillery fire upon our position, causing some confusion among our troops. About the first shell fired exploded directly under the kettle which the servant had on boiling our dinner and supper, for we had had neither that day. He had brought up 'old shave-tail,' our pack horse, and left him feeding a few feet east of the fire while he was busy about six feet north of it. The shell came from the west, and while it tore 'old shave-tail' all to pieces, the man did not receive a scratch, but was so badly frightened that he stood like a statue for some moments as if paralyzed and as white as a corpse. It was the most laughable sight I ever saw in battle. We dined and supped on hardtack that night as our provisions went up with the kettle."[233]

Shortly after this incident, Halstead noted, "what resembled a column of infantry, platoon in front, moving south along the stone fence east of the Cemetery." He rode over towards the column, and found them to be some "rabble from the Eleventh Corps," apparently being guided from the field by five cavalrymen "with swords at a carry." Halstead drew his revolver and ordered them all back: "A man in the vanguard who looked like a good runner said, 'We are musicians!' I told him it made no difference what he was, that he must go down the wall or I would shoot him. I then asked the cavalryman nearest me why they permitted those men to leave in that manner, and he replied, 'Captain, there are only five of us and more than a thousand of these men. What can we do with them?' I ordered them to halt, about face, and cut down every man that attempted to pass them. The order was promptly obeyed, and in less than five minutes over a thousand men were crouching behind that stone fence, a stampede ended, and subsequently the men were returned to their commands."[234]

There was for a brief period, perhaps from 1715 to 1830, some sharp skirmishing between the most advanced Confederate infantry and Hancock's forward skirmishers. Captain John Cook of the 76th New York reported that he had "a few men slightly wounded on the hill in the rear of the town" after his retreat. Contact between the opposing forces was closest at the extreme southern edge of the town, where skirmishers from both sides secured shelter in the buildings at the northern base of Cemetery Hill. The historian of the 14th Brooklyn recalled that "The Confederates were so near that a continual line of conversation was kept up between the two armies, orders to surrender being answered by shots and shouts of defiance all along the line."[235]

Sometime after dark a drummer boy from the 28th Pennsylvania of Candy's brigade of Williams' division, XII Corps, came up the Baltimore Pike from his division's encampment to visit a relative and some friends in the 11th Pennsylvania of the I Corps, then on Cemetery Hill. He wrote later, "I finally found fighting Dick Coulter's 11th regiment hugging up against a wall....I sat against a tree and I heard the exciting story of the 11th's important part the first day's fight. Next thing I knew, a ball struck the tree over my head....Bullets were flying all about us....my life was saved by a shoestring while I was on the knoll there. As I stooped to tie my shoe, a bullet whizzed by me and struck a man named Gillizin in the fleshly part of the thigh. He went over to a corner, had the wound tied up and went along as if nothing bothered him. He was grit, that fellow."[236]

There was also a limited amount of skirmishing near the base of East Cemetery Hill, where Smith's brigade anxiously watched the advance of Early's troops. While the men of the 33rd Massachusetts of Smith's brigade were on the skirmish line there, they anxiously watched the Confederates—probably Hays' men—forming on the edge of the town. A staff officer rode up to the regiment's commander, Colonel Adam B. Underwood, and asked him "if he could hold his men's fire until the rebels were in short range." Underwood thought that this looked like business and responded, "Yes, sir, if that is the order." He then watched the "butternut columns" closely, but they came no closer, so he had his men continue to hold their fire.[237]

Smith's 73rd Ohio lost several men skirmishing with Early's troops during the late afternoon and evening. The regiment had a few men wounded while it was supporting the batteries on the hill during the army's retreat. Once all the Union troops had cleared Gettysburg, the town was occupied by a number of Confederate sharpshooters. At this time "the 73rd Ohio, with a portion of its brigade, was again sent across the turnpike, and took position forward in the angle of our lines, and but a few yards from that part of the village nearest the hill. A few shots were exchanged with the rebel sharpshooters, two of our men being wounded." At about 2200 one regiment was relieved and withdrew to the hill, "where we lay down and slept heavily after the fatigue of the day. We lay on the grass, among the neatly trimmed graves, and some, with no irreverance, rested their heads on the green hillocks for pillows."[238]

While they waited for Johnson's division to arrive, Generals Ewell, Early and Rodes decided to ride to their left and see what the situation was to the east of the town, where Smith had been reporting the advance of a large Union force. Early later wrote that the three generals "rode out of the town a short distance to look out on the York Road, which was visible for nearly or quite two miles, to see if we could discover any indications of the enemy's advance. I placed no confidence in the rumor, but Rodes was inclined to believe it, while Ewell seemed at a loss as to what opinion to form, as the reports came mainly from straggling cavalrymen, some of whom I think were waifs from the battlefield at Hanover." Early continues: "While we were discussing the matter, a line of skirmishers was seen away out on our right of the York road, as we stood, apparently advancing towards us, when Rodes exclaimed: 'There they come now!' To this I replied in somewhat emphatic language, that it could not be the enemy; that Gordon was out there; and if the enemy was advancing he would certainly be firing on him. It must be recollected that it was very hard to distinguish between the blue and the gray at a distance, as both looked dark. To solve the doubt, Lieutenant T.T. Turner, of Ewell's staff, and Robert D. Early of mine, were sent to ascertain the fact. It turned out that the skirmishers were some General Smith had sent out, which Gordon was having moved back to post differently. All this consumed time, and Johnson had not yet arrived."[239]

This incident still did not allay Ewell's fear for the security of his left flank. In spite of his own reading of the situation, Early chose not to argue the point, and half of his division (Gordon's and Smith's brigades) would remain inactive on this front for another 24 hours, watching for Union cavalry that was nowhere nearby. Later on 2 July Smith would advance his 31st Virginia across the Hunterstown Road and link up with Stuart's cavalry, which had just reached the field and moved up on Ewell's far left, so allowing Smith and Gordon to at last rejoin their division.[240]

Ewell here made a great mistake not to make better use of the cavalry he had at his disposal to scout the roads east of Gettysburg. As previously noted, four companies of the 1st Maryland cavalry had reported to him for duty early in the afternoon after they arrived from Chambersburg. Ewell forwarded them from Oak Hill to Early's command, where they were held in reserve in support of Jones' artillery. Perhaps Ewell and Early could not locate this command at this time, due to the haste of Early's advance. It is also possible that both generals forgot about the 1st Maryland, since neither mention it in their reports or accounts.[241]

It is also clear that most if not all of the 35th Virginia Cavalry Battalion ("White's Comanches") was on the field available for scouting duty. Captain Frank M. Myers of Company A of this unit published in 1871 a history of his command that includes an imprecise account of its participation in the battle. The Comanches had been assigned to Ewell's Corps when the invasion started, and reached Ewell's advance troops at Greencastle. They were then put under Early's command, and as such participated in the skirmish near Gettysburg on 26 June. The Comanches then moved on to Hanover, and later to York. When Early withdrew on 29 June, he sent the Comanches "in advance, with orders to watch carefully the left flank." During the afternoon a detachment from Company A ran across some Union cavalry, and lost one man (Thomas Spates), who was caught while "picketing" in a cherry tree. This was the command's first indication that there were enemy regular troops, not just militia, in the area.[242]

Myers' company of the 35th, if not the whole command, arrived at Gettysburg on the afternoon of 1 July, apparently with Rodes' column.

Myers narrates that, "White's battalion, then the only body of cavalry with the A.N.V., was sent by General Ewell to the left of his Corps." As they reached "the high hills in that direction" (probably Benner's Hill), the Comanches had a clear view of Early's attack and rout of the XI Corps. Myers' account is not clear, but he appears to describe Gordon's attack on Ames' line at the Almshouse. He then saw "one of Ewell's brigades" (Avery's?) march "to the left of the town and into a large wheat field where lay a line of men in blue, who raised up when the gray jackets were in about fifty yards, and, throwing down their guns, surrendered in a body—in all over a thousand."[243]

As Myers' men pushed forward towards Rock Creek, they came under fire from the Union artillery on Cemetery Hill. So did the skirmishers of Gordon's brigade, which had marched "to the support of the cavalry." Myers relates, "About this time a battery, from the Cemetery Hill, was fiercely shelling White's men, and as Gordon's skirmishers appeared on the field a storm of shot and shell ploughed the ground along the line causing part of it to falter; but the Major who commanded was a splendid officer, and brought his people up to it handsomely; once, indeed, he displayed almost more than human coolness and daring—in reforming a part of his line that had broken under the fire, and just as the Major reached it a heavy shell exploded exactly under his horse, causing both it and the rider to roll over on the ground in a cloud of dirt and smoke, all who saw it thinking that they were surely both killed, but amid the cloud the beautiful bay sprang up, with the gallant Major still in the saddle exclaiming, 'Steady men, steady; no use to break; keep the line steady;' and the men were steady after that."[244]

Myers claims that before Gordon's men came up, "The battalion passed on, and soon met some of the Yankee skirmishers from a division of infantry on Rocky Creek, whom they captured and sent back."[245] These skirmishers were almost certainly the advance elements of Williams' division of the XII Corps, about which more will be discussed shortly. This contact was critical, but it is not clear to whom Myers reported his discovery. He simply states that they were "sent back," but none of the Confederate generals on the flank—Smith, Gordon, Early, or Ewell—specifically acknowledged receiving this critical intelligence. It is possible that Myers sent the prisoners back to Smith, and that their arrival, along with the news of the Union cavalry presence at Hanover, is what excited him so much in his appeals to Early for help. If so, this situation forces a totally new interpretation of Smith's reaction to the pressures on his front.

If Myers did send captured skirmishers from the XII Corps back to Smith, Smith clearly erred by not forwarding them to Early or Ewell. But Early and Ewell also erred by not making more aggressive use of the cavalrymen of the 35th Virginia to scout their left. Myers reports that his command encamped "at dark," and "in the morning the battalion was broken up into scouting parties for the Generals of the left wing." This statement shows that Ewell and his key subordinates were by then aware of the unit's availability on this flank. On 2 July several scouts from the Comanches succeeded in locating the right flank of Meade's army and even penetrated to the enemy's rear, where they found some lengthy wagon trains.[246] It is unfortunate for the Confederacy that the services of these scouts were not better employed on the afternoon, evening or night of 1 July.

Other sources show that Ewell had at least one more cavalry unit on hand that he did not fully employ on the afternoon and evening of 1 July. This was the 17th Virginia of Jenkins' brigade. This unit, commanded by Colonel William H. French, had been detached from its brigade on 22 June in order to serve with Early's advance through Pennsylvania. On the morning of 1 July it was encamped near Hunterstown, and then led Early's advance down the Heidlersburg Road towards Gettysburg. The advanced guard of the 17th pushed back a small Union cavalry outpost a few miles to the northeast of Gettysburg, and then yielded its post to a detachment of Early's infantry.[247]

When Early's troops approached Rock Creek and began forming up to attack the XI Corps, Early held French's command in reserve instead of sending it to scout his left flank. Private James C. Hodam of the 17th's Company C remembered that, "Heavy firing of artillery and musketry had been heard for some time in the direction of the town, and we realized that hot work was before us. Our regiment was halted near a strip of woods that intervened between us and the battlefield, while the infantry brigades and artillery hurried to the front and disappeared in the timber. Infantry of those days generally held the cavalry service in light esteem, and as we sat on our horses by the roadside, we were the subjects of many goodnatured remarks and much badinage from those gallant fellows, who, with quick step, were marching into the jaws of death. As Gordon's and Smith's brigades passed, a hearty cheer was given as we recognized our comrades in the march to the Susquehanna."[248]

Hodam and his comrades remained stationary for two hours as they supported Jones' artillery while Early's infantry finished forming up and then attacked Barlow's line, driving it from the field. Hodam continues: "Through the timber, across a small stream, and the battlefield was before us in all its horrors and excitement....In our front were open fields, and a little further, the town. Many pieces of artillery occupied the high ground to our right, but their thunder was silenced now, while heaps of dead and dying around them told how the boys in blue had bravely stood by their guns. A little beyond, to judge from the windrows of dead, a Union regiment had been blotted out. Along the road the blue and gray veterans lay thickly....Dashing forward we came up with our infantry, driving Howard's corps through the town. Confusion seemed to reign in the Federal ranks, and thousands were made prisoners in a short time."[249] Thus the 17th Virginia finished the day gathering up and guarding Union prisoners.

The remainder of Jenkins' brigade reached the battlefield towards evening, and it was not used to scout the enemy position, either. The brigade had left Carlisle on the evening of 30 June, serving now as Early's rearguard rather than his vanguard, since Early's infantry had already begun marching to the south and west. The 14th Virginia Cavalry led the way, while Lieutenant Colonel V.A. Witcher commanded the brigade's rear guard, consisting of his 34th Virginia Battalion, two companies of the 36th Virginia Battalion, and two pieces of artillery.[251] Witcher was at Mechanicsburg and did not receive his orders to head south until sunset. The column stopped at Petersburg (York Springs) at 0200 for a few hours' rest, and was off again at dawn on 1 July. During the forenoon Jenkins' men heard the sound of heavy cannonading at Gettysburg, but they did not reach the battle area until late afternoon.[252] At about 1700 Jenkins halted his command on a hill near the Heidlersburg Road some three miles northeast of Gettysburg while he or a staff orderly rode forward to report his arrival to Ewell.[253] The brigade then went into camp, except for six companies of the 16th Virginia that were detailed to help Colonel French guard prisoners.[254] Jenkins set up his headquarters at the farm of John Henry Majors, and during the night his troops did a fair amount of damage there and in neighboring farms as they looked for food, fodder, and other supplies.[255]

Late Arrival of the XII Corps

Indeed, had Ewell been aware of the approach of Major General Henry W. Slocum's fresh XII Corps of almost 10,000 men, he would have been much more concerned about the safety of his left flank than for the prospects of success for an attack on Cemetery Hill. Slocum's advance and arrival on the field are another of the great controversies of the battle, though they have not received as much attention as they are due. Slocum had encamped on 30 June one mile northeast of Littlestown, and on the morning of 1 July, marched about 7 miles to Two Taverns, pursuant to Meade's marching orders for the day. Slocum reached Two Taverns, which was only 4 ½ miles southwest of Gettysburg on an excellent road, the Baltimore Pike, at mid-morning, yet he and his men did not reach the battle area until late afternoon, after all the significant fighting for the day was completed. The story of how and why this happened is long and controversial. Had he arrived earlier in the day he clearly would have changed the course of the battle.

Some of Slocum's men had experienced a little excitement on the afternoon of 30 June when they were approaching Littlestown. The lead troops heard the noise of an engagement near the town between Kilpatrick's cavalry and a portion of Stuart's Confederate command, and were rushed forward to the town at the double quick in order to help. Brigadier General Thomas Ruger's 3rd Brigade of Williams' 1st Division led the way, and its men advanced at a rapid pace with skirmishers deployed in their front. Samuel Toombs of the 13th New Jersey recalled that his unit was stopped before reaching the town in order to allow Winegar's New York battery to pass by. The battery's horses were frothing at the mouth and had sweat streaming from every pore.[256] Lieutenant Colonel James C. Rogers of the 127th New York expressed disappointment that "the rebels had flown," and everyone began setting up camp.[257]

Ezra Carman noted that, "A good deal of amusement was afforded the troops by the actions of a crowd of citizens who fled from the town, on hearing of the approach of the enemy, and took up position on a rail fence along the road. They seemed to fear that the 'rebs' would prove too much for us, which accounted perhaps, for the celerity which actuated their movements. Our arrival in the town, however, was the cause of great rejoicing by the inhabitants, and from every house we received tokens of gratitude and delight in the shape of cooked provisions, biscuits, bread and butter, cakes, pies and other luxuries which were keenly relished."[258] The men of Colonel Charles Candy's 1st Brigade of Geary's 2nd Division did not get a chance to enjoy these delicacies because they were advanced on the right of the town, in the direction of Hanover, with instructions to throw forward skirmishers and put out pickets to the front and right.[259] They were not disturbed during the night by any Confederate cavalry, all of which was headed to the north.

Despite the cavalry clash on 30 June at Littlestown, nobody in the XII Corps was expecting to fight a battle on 1 July. After receiving his marching orders for the day, Slocum had his men on the road soon after dawn on 1 July.[260] Brigadier General Alpheus S. Williams' 1st Division of two brigades led the way. The march was an easy one, and Williams noted the wealth and fertility of the farmland along the road. He also saw crowds of civilians line the roadway and assemble at the crossings in their great curiosity to see his men.[261] E.R. Brown of the 27th Indiana, which led Williams' column, recalled that, "We pressed steadily along, through an open fertile country, though there was no evidence of haste in any quarter."[262]

There was still, however, a certain tension in the air. The column proceeded with skirmishers deployed, and soon the sounds of the battle at Gettysburg began to be heard. E.R. Brown of the 27th Indiana later wrote of this march, "To those not advised of the orders under which the army was acting, our movements soon became mysterious. The writer's impression is that when we started in the morning, or very soon afterwards, we heard rumblings of artillery. It is certain that artillery firing early became so distinct and rapid that many were apprehensive that the decisive battle, impending some days, might be on. This apprehension was increased by the fact of our keeping skirmishers out so carefully, when we could see so far ahead, as well as by the many rumors that always circulate at such a time. Still the pace was not increased and, slowly as we had been moving, when we reached the hamlet of Two Taverns, half way to Gettysburg, we filed leisurely into a field, under orders, and went into bivouac. This greatly increased our perplexity. The sounds of battle ahead of us had grown more and more fierce. There was no longer room for doubt that a large force on each side was engaged, and that musketry firing was mixed with that of the artillery. For some years most of the soldiers of the Twelfth Corps were greatly puzzled over our orders this morning. The Corps could easily have joined in the battle the first day. The distance from our starting point to the battlefield might have been traversed by noon."[263]

Geary's 2nd Division, which consisted of three brigades, followed Williams' and reached Two Taverns by 1100.[264] The column was accompanied by Lieutenant Edward D. Muhlenberg's artillery battalion of 20 guns in 4 batteries. Despite the noise of the fight at Gettysburg,

Slocum's troops routinely prepared lunch and began taking naps or attending to other routine business, such as completing inspection and muster reports from the previous day. One squad of soldiers sat down to enjoy some large cheese balls they had purchased from a farmer along the road. The cheese balls, however, smelled so bad when they were opened that they could not be eaten, and their purchasers ended up throwing them at each other for sport.[265]

Many of Slocum's men thought it was odd that they were allowed to sit and rest while the noise of artillery and musketry indicated that an engagement of some sort was going on only a few miles away. Some probably assumed this was only a heavy skirmish, or perhaps a cavalry skirmish such as they had encountered at Littlestown the day before. Slocum himself was aware of the firing, but considered it to be only a minor cavalry action, and continued to rest his men awaiting further orders.[266] One Slocum apologist claims that the General could not hear the sounds of the battle clearly because "The wind was blowing to the north, rendering the sound of the firing very indistinct." He also suggests that there was little battle noise to hear at this time, because "the main battle of the First Day had not commenced as yet."[267] The second explanation is not nearly as plausible as the first, since there is evidence of considerable artillery fire on the field at Gettysburg after 1130, and it increased as the day wore on.

Slocum's actions to this point are fully understandable, though it does seem a bit odd that he did not send an aide towards Gettysburg in an effort to find out what was going on there. He knew from Meade's orders for the day that the army's left wing under Reynolds was concentrating at and near Gettysburg, and probably judged that Reynolds had sufficient troops available to deal with whatever Confederate forces were at Gettysburg. Slocum had nominal command of the army's right wing, consisting of his own XII Corps and Major General George Sykes' V Corps, then at Hanover, and had a good deal of ground to guard as he watched for signs of a Confederate advance in his quarter. He certainly did not have a clear view of what enemy troops might be in his front, since he had no active cavalry scouting for him. Kilpatrick's cavalry command at that moment was more concerned with pursuing Stuart than with keeping Slocum advised of enemy movements. Buford's 1st Cavalry Division was assigned to work with Reynolds, and Buford was certainly not obligated to make reports to Slocum, if he indeed knew where the XII Corps was.

In addition, Slocum's orders from headquarters did not particularly encourage him to be aggressive that day. His marching orders for 1 July included a note that Meade wanted to "assume position for offensive or defensive, as occasion requires, or rest to the troops." They also noted that "It is not his desire to wear the troops out by excessive fatigue and marches."[268] More significantly, the Pipe Creek Circular, which he received late in the morning, made it appear that Meade was inclined to withdraw to a defensive line.[269] This impression was reinforced by a directive Slocum received with the Pipe Creek Circular that informed him that the Confederates were moving in force on Gettysburg. Slocum was to send his trains towards Westminster at once, and should be prepared to withdraw to Union Mills and Pipe Creek, "upon receipt of intelligence from General Reynolds that he has uncovered Two Taverns." The key final sentence of this order stated, "You will, if in good position for the purposes of the circular enclosed, halt your command where this order reaches you, and, in communicating to General Sykes, halt his advance in a similar manner, and give him instructions necessary for a proper compliance with the circular order enclosed in case intimations from General Reynolds render it necessary."[270]

Slocum, then, had orders from Meade to stop where he was (at Two Taverns) and await word from Reynolds, presumably to initiate a movement to the rear. But no word could come from Reynolds, who was shot at about 1030. As already discussed, Reynolds' successor, Howard, did not learn of Reynolds' death until 1230, and did not attempt to make contact with Slocum until 1300. His message then was brief and did not describe the full situation. It was relayed by the XI Corps Chief of Staff, T.A. Meysenburg, and read as follows: "The general commanding directs me to inform you that Ewell's Corps is advancing from York. The left wing of the Army of the Potomac is engaged with A.P. Hill's Corps."[271]

Slocum probably received this message at around 1400.[272] Howard certainly erred by not relating everything that had happened that morning, especially the death of Reynolds. Even had he done so, however, it is unlikely that he would have requested Slocum to hurry forward to Gettysburg, since Howard at that time felt he had the situation under control. Nevertheless, Howard's message seems odd, particularly because he did not explain his situation in full.

It was not until around 1500 that Howard found himself in a fix and sent to Slocum for help. In his battle report he states that "I now sent again to General Slocum, stating that my right flank was being attacked, and asking him if he was moving up, and stating that I was in danger of being turned and driven back."[273] Howard had no authority to order Slocum to come forward, but he did not urgently request him to march to Gettysburg, either. Nor did he make it clear that Reynolds was dead and he was commanding the army's left wing.

Captain Daniel Hall of Howard's staff carried this message to Slocum. Hall brought the message in haste, primarily because he falsely believed he was being pursued by Confederate cavalry all the way to Two Taverns. Hall doubtless informed Slocum of the escalating battle at Gettysburg, but he did not record Slocum's response except to say that he thought Slocum's "conduct on this occasion anything but honorable, soldierly or patriotic."[274]

Hall's harsh evaluation of Slocum's reaction to his message was presumably provoked by Slocum's refusal to move forward to Gettysburg as Howard desired. A more aggressive general such as Reynolds, Hancock, or Sedgwick would surely have "marched to the sound of the guns," as the Napoleonic maxim states. Instead, Slocum clung to Meade's directive to hold his position and await orders or the proper circumstance to withdraw. He did not even attempt a compromise by advancing some of his troops and holding the rest where they were, which is what III Corps commander Daniel E. Sickles decided to do under somewhat similar circumstances at exactly the same time.

The total situation was enigmatic to many of the officers and men of Slocum's command. They could plainly hear the increasing din of the battle at Gettysburg, but no orders came to form up and march out. All they saw was one, then two staff officers ride up to Slocum's headquarters on frothing mounts; then a bevy of officers met to discuss the missive; then they all dispersed to what they had been doing before.[275]

In retrospect, Slocum's reluctance to advance to Gettysburg is indeed difficult to explain. One critic intimated that he did not want to go forward and take command, as the senior of Howard, on a losing field. General Doubleday suggests that "Slocum declined, without orders from Meade. He probably thought if any one commander could assume the direction of the other corps, he might antagonize the plans of the General-in-Chief."[276]

Slocum was sensitive to all this criticism, particularly a statement by historian Samuel P. Bates that the XII Corps should have been prepared to move to the offensive if circumstances favored this. The army's 1 July marching orders called for all the corps commanders to be "ready to attack at any moment" and the Pipe Creek circular noted that "Developments may cause the commanding General to assume the offensive from his previous position."[277] Slocum pointed out that, "I was not summoned by General Howard or any other person," and then listed a number of his own subordinates who had not denounced him for not moving more promptly to Gettysburg.[278] In 1886, Slocum wrote to Sidney G. Cooke of the 147th New York that, "My orders were to march to Two Taverns, and await orders from General Meade. The Twelfth Corps was in that position when we heard of the engagement at Gettysburg. We received no word from General Howard, but started as soon as we heard of the battle."[279]

Slocum's arguments possess elements of truth, but do not address the issue directly. He was not in fact "summoned" by Howard, but a reading between the lines of Howard's message of 1500 or judicious interrogation of the bearer or the message, Captain Hall, would have revealed that things were not going well at Gettysburg. Slocum's listing of subordinates who had not criticized him is an indirect proof; besides, most would have been loyal enough to support him, or some might have done so in order to protect their own interests.[280] His note to Sidney Cooke, just quoted, appears to ignore Howard's message sent at 1500.

In the last analysis, Slocum was technically correct in not advancing to Gettysburg anytime before 1500, since he had not received any positive orders from Meade to do so, nor had he received a desperate and clear cry for help from Howard. But in a larger sense, he was not doing his job thoroughly because he did not make an effort to determine what was occurring a few miles up the road. Slocum could, and should, have sent at least part of his force forward to help Howard earlier in the day. Howard must bear a smaller portion of fault then Slocum in this situation, for not being more clear and detailed in his communications with Slocum. Meade should bear no fault at all in this situation. As soon as he learned of Reynolds' death, he sent Captain A.G. Mason of his staff to carry sealed orders to Slocum and Sykes reporting, "the fall of General Reynolds, and that General Hancock had been sent to take his place, and urging them to push forward with all possible dispatch." Captain Mason wrote to General Meade in 1864 that he delivered these orders to Lieutenant Colonel Hiram G. Rodgers, assistant adjutant general of the XII Corps, at Two Taverns between 1500 and 1600 on 1 July.[281]

It is interesting to speculate what might have happened if Slocum had acted more aggressively on 1 July. Had he advanced at least one of his divisions to the sound of the guns at 1100 instead of stopping his entire command at Two Taverns, it would have arrived on the field by

1300, in plenty of time to beef up Schurz's line north of the town. Another 4000 or 5000 men to help the XI Corps might have defeated Early's attack, or at least would have blunted it long enough to enable the XI Corps to retreat with significantly fewer losses. On the other hand, if Howard had been more detailed in his 1300 message, Slocum might have sent part or all of his men forward then. They would have reached the field by about 1600. They probably would not have had time to deploy and help hold the I or XI Corps' line, but certainly could have made local counterattacks or helped cover the withdrawal of Doubleday's and Schurz's exhausted troops, so avoiding many of their losses through capture. Another interesting "what if" scenario would posit Slocum making an attack on Early's left flank at midafternoon. Such an attack would probably have stymied Early, but still could not have saved the I Corps line. The first day's battle might well have ended in a draw if Slocum had arrived early enough (by 1400) and sent one division to support Doubleday and one division to support Schurz.

But such was not to be. As affairs developed, Slocum at last began moving his troops forward sometime after 1500.[282] His decision to advance—which he later rightly emphasized was made on his own judgment—was not based on any of Howard's messages, but on a reconnaissance conducted by Major Eugene W. Guindon of his staff. It seems that early in the afternoon a civilian reached Two Taverns with the news that "a great battle was being fought on the hills beyond Gettysburg." Slocum responded to this report by sending Major Guindon with a few orderlies to investigate the situation. Guindon rode forward until he was able to clearly discern the noise of a heavy engagement at Gettysburg, and then rode back to report to Slocum, who at once made the decision to move forward.[283]

One source claims that Slocum sent Major Guindon out at about 1300,[284] but this does not coincide with other evidence. Guindon was probably dispatched after 1400, and reported back at about 1530. He arrived after Howard's message of 1500, but before Meade's untimed order sent with Captain Mason. Mason, as already noted, delivered Meade's order to Lieutenant Colonel Rodgers of Slocum's staff between 1500 and 1600. When he arrived, Slocum had already departed for Gettysburg, and Rodgers forwarded the message to him on the march.[285] Slocum acknowledged receipt of the order by sending a note addressed to "General Hancock or General Howard" that read as follows: "I am moving the Twelfth Corps so as to come in about one mile to the right of Gettysburg."[286] The note was timed at 1535, but Slocum's watch must have been slow; the message was probably sent about half an hour later.

Slocum's intention to "come in about one mile to the right of Gettysburg" was an interesting decision, particularly if it was derived on his own. Slocum may simply have decided that this was the sector he could reach the quickest from his position at Two Taverns. If so, it was an awkward one, particularly as affairs finally developed, since he had no idea of the topography in that area. He might have done better to have simply reported his approach to Hancock, and asked where he could help the most. Historian Harry Pfanz puts forward an interesting suggestion that Slocum may have been responding to a suggestion from Howard, delivered verbally by Captain Hall, to come in on the right of Gettysburg so as to assist the advanced XI Corps line at Barlow's Knoll. Such a request would have been much more appropriate at 1500, when Howard sent Hall to Slocum, than at 1600, when the entire XI Corps line was in retreat and Slocum would have been needed more at Cemetery Hill.[287]

The anxious troops of the XII Corps were relieved to at last receive the command to march to the aid of their comrades. E.R. Brown of the 27th Indiana noted that, "any soldier will recall how a knot of aides and orderlies, gathered in a circle about their chief, would break apart and dissolve in many directions, after these fresh arrivals. So it was now more promptly almost than it can be told, we had received orders and were on the way. The baggage trains, and the sick and the disabled were sent to the rear, noncombatants and stretcher bearers were instructed to report to the surgeon and the column pressed forward on quick time. After this those not in good form for marching could not keep up."[288]

Slocum's troops probably left Two Taverns at around 1545. As they drew closer to Gettysburg, they could hear more and more clearly the increasing din of the climax of the battle, particularly Pender's decisive assault on Seminary Ridge at 1600. "Every rod towards the front brought the various noises of the struggle more distinctly to our ears....When we reached the point from which the ground begins to break off towards the valley of Rock Creek, the tremendous crash and din, though still three or four miles distant, seemed almost at our feet. As Culp's Hill and Cemetery Ridge loomed into view, we could scarcely believe that the scene of action was not on our side, rather than beyond, those heights. While rising above them higher and higher, and reaching far around the horizon, was a cloud of dust and smoke, of ever-increasing density."[289]

The afternoon was a warm one, and the XII Corps' troops soon were working up a good sweat, especially since they were ordered to move at the double quick much of the time.[290] Sergeant Henry H. Tallman of the 66th Ohio noted, "It was a hot day. The sun was hot. The ground was hot. The breezes that fanned our brows were hot, and the men panted like dogs on the chase and sweated and sweltered through clouds of dust."[291]

Samuel Toombs of the 13th New Jersey noted that the march to the battlefield was made in great haste under a broiling sun. There was scarcely a halt, and "men fell out of the ranks in squads by the roadside for a brief rest." "Everywhere along the road we received a grateful welcome, and in front of every house large buckets and tubs were kept constantly full of fresh water." At one point the column passed several women from Gettysburg who had been forced to flee their homes. They began to wave their bonnets and aprons in support of the troops, and the men began to wave their hands in reply, then their caps. Before long "the column broke into a hearty cheer. Tired and exhausted men rallied under the inspiring huzzas rejoined the column and moved briskly toward the enemy."[292]

The spirits of some of the men also lightened when the column began to meet fugitives from the XI Corps who were fleeing from the field. Some wags from the 66th Ohio called out, "Oh come back, we are going to have lots of fun;" "come back and we'll show you how to cock a cannon," and "What are you going away from the picnic for?" This levity quickly died when the column began to meet ambulances and walking wounded heading for the rear.[293]

The column had not gone far when Slocum received Meade's message about Reynolds' death, which had been forwarded to him by Captain Mason from Two Taverns. Since the message also directed him to hurry his troops to Gettysburg, Slocum decided to ride up to the head of his column. When he did so, he turned over temporary control of the corps to Brigadier General Alpheus Williams, his senior division commander.[294] His exact reason for doing so is unclear. He may have been preparing to take over command of the field as the senior officer present, despite his initial protestations to doing so. Alternatively, he could have been setting himself up in his role as right wing commander, though the other half of his wing, the V Corps, was nowhere near the field yet. Another possible explanation is that he may have intended to ride on ahead, and so wished Williams to take over for just an hour or two until the corps came up and formed.

Slocum's unwillingness to come to Cemetery Hill was motivated by two principal factors. A short while after receipt of Howard's message, he met Lieutenant Colonel Charles H. Morgan of Hancock's staff, and told him that he did not wish to supplant Hancock, who had been sent forward by Meade specifically for this purpose and already had a familiarity with the field. In other words, Slocum's arrival to the front would create a surfeit of generals there, since he would be obligated to take command by seniority. Slocum's second motivation was that he felt his presence would be more useful in the rear. Someone was needed to check and rally the numerous stragglers that were streaming down the Baltimore Pike, and he was in a good position to do so.[296]

Neither of Slocum's alleged reasons for declining to come to Cemetery Hill are very strong. He could readily have declined command of the field to Meade's emissary, Hancock, had he been inclined to do so, and should have been eager to hurry to Cemetery Hill to consult personally with Hancock about what needed to be done to save the army. His willingness to stay in the rear to direct his troops and gather in stragglers does not speak well of his sense of duty. The bottom line was clearly his reluctance, as he told Morgan, to come up and take charge of the field, "which might make him responsible for a condition of affairs over which he had no control."[296]

However, when Morgan told Slocum that Hancock had orders from Meade to turn over command to him upon his arrival, Slocum found himself in a corner and had no choice but to go forward to Cemetery Hill.[297] He could no longer avoid taking command on the field, and Morgan's reassurance assuaged his concern that there might be a disagreement with Hancock over who should hold command. Slocum arrived at Cemetery Hill at 1900, not long after Howard received Meade's written notification that Hancock was to direct the left wing. What might have been an awkward excess of generals was readily resolved when Hancock transferred his authority to Slocum and prepared to return to report to Meade. Howard readily accepted Slocum's seniority, as he stated in his report: "a formal order was at the same time put into my hands, placing Hancock in command of the left wing. But General Slocum being present and senior, I turned command over to him, and resumed the direct command of the Eleventh Corps; whereupon General Hancock repaired to the headquarters of General Meade."[298]

Slocum rode to the field in front of his column, and was about a mile from Gettysburg when he received a verbal message sent by General Howard a few minutes earlier at 1600. It was transmitted by Major

Charles Howard, who was told "to inform him of the state of affairs, requesting him to send one of his divisions to the left, the other to the right of Gettysburg, and that he would come in person to Cemetery Hill."[299] Slocum acknowledged the arrangements for his corps, but stated, "I'll be damned if I will take the responsibility of this fight."[300] It was in response to this statement that General Howard closed his 1700 message to Meade with the line, "Slocum is near, but will not come up to assume command."[301] Slocum at the same hour sent the following rather despondent note to Meade: "A portion of our troops have fallen back to Gettysburg. Matters do not appear well. My Second Division has gone up to the town, and the First on the right of the town. I hope the work for the day is nearly over."[302]

By this time the immediate battle crisis had passed, since Hancock, Howard, Doubleday, and Warren had already formed all the troops available and resupplied them as best they could, and the Confederates were not pressing to make an immediate attack. There was not really much for Slocum to do except await the arrival of Meade, who was expected at any time. There is no record of Slocum making any major decisions during the few hours that he held overall command of all the troops on the field. His only recorded communication to Meade was a brief note sent at 2120 to acknowledge receipt of Meade's 1800 message to Hancock. In it Slocum advised, "If you conclude to make a fight here, the most of the artillery reserve can be used to advantage; and in that case the Fifth and Sixth Corps can be used to extend our right."[303]

In later years a number of battle participants, particularly Major Charles Howard, bore ill will towards Slocum for his late arrival on the field and reluctance to come to the aid of the XI Corps in its hour of greatest need. Major Howard expressed the feelings of a great many when he wrote a friend later that month that the XII Corps commander had lived up to his name, "Slow-Come."[304]

General Howard also was disappointed in Slocum, but apparently bore him no long lasting enmity. He wrote later that Slocum "declined to come up to Gettysburg to participate in the action, and only sent his troops late in the afternoon at my request. He explained the course he took by showing that it was contrary to the plan and purpose of General Meade to bring on the battle at Gettysburg, he having arranged for another defensive position at Pipe Clay Creek. I think he did wrong to delay, and was hardly justified under the circumstances, even by the written orders of General Meade; still in all his previous history and subsequent lengthy service by my side in the West and South he showed himself a patriot in spirit, a brave man, and an able commander."[305]

General Doubleday also had strong feelings on the subject. He rightly pointed out that if Slocum were unsure of leading his troops to the field earlier than he did, he should have sent a "swift courier" to Meade at Taneytown, about 12 miles away, to explain the situation and request instructions. He also felt that Slocum would have been correct to move forward, despite his interpretation of Meade's orders, since "the safety of his own corps might be seriously endangered by inaction. This and a regard to the general interest of the army would have justified him in interfering to cover the retreat."[306]

Slocum's delay in reaching the field could have become a major cause of controversy after the battle, but did not for several reasons. Firstly, the battle was a Union victory, and a victory does not need scapegoats. Secondly, Slocum did not clearly violate any orders, he simply failed to read the situation properly. His was an error of omission, not commission. Thirdly, Slocum was a strong general with a solid service record before and after the battle, and also handled the fighting on Culp's Hill very well on 2-3 July. He had no strong personal or political enemies against him, such as Dan Sickles did when he became embroiled in controversy for his handling of the III Corps on 2 July. Lastly, as historian Harry Pfanz points out, neither Meade nor Howard chose to press the matter, and quietly let it drop.[307]

But there was still more controversy concerning the XII Corps to be encountered on this evening. It concerns the ineffective use of Williams' division to meet the crisis at hand. As already noted, Slocum during his march from Two Taverns had decided to put his lead division (Williams') in position a mile to the right of Gettysburg, perhaps at Howard's suggestion. Soon after he rode to the head of the corps' column at about 1600, he sent Williams, now the acting corps commander, an order to turn the 1st Division to the right, taking a cross road to the Hanover Road, and to send Geary's division on towards Gettysburg.[308]

Slocum's order reached Williams before the head of the XII Corps reached Rock Creek. Williams quickly sent some staff officers to locate a route to the Hanover Road, and soon had his men moving on a zigzag lane that went north on the eastern side of Wolf Hill.[309] The division's 1st Brigade, now under command of Colonel Silas Colgrove of the 27th Indiana, led the way, followed by Colonel Archibald L. McDougall's 3rd Brigade.[310] Williams described the road as narrow, winding, muddy and slippery, and his men consumed a great deal of energy to keep up, sometimes at the double-quick.[311] Some of the troops of the 2nd Massachusetts found time to shake hands with a "hard featured" woman who came down from an old farmhouse with her children to greet them. She seemed excited to see them until she saw their national flag, whereupon she growled, "Why, I thought you were Rebs!" and scurried her children back to her house.[312]

Williams wanted to post his men on a high, bald hill (Benner's Hill) that his staff officers had found to the east of the town, "on which a good position could be had in sight and rear of the town." However, when he reached the "woody screen" at the northern end of Wolf Hill, he received a report that the enemy had occupied Benner's Hill with artillery. Williams decided to halt his column, and rode forward to reconnoiter for himself: "I rode into the woods, and, dismounting, went forward to the foot of the hill, where I had a good view of the sides and crest. I could see on the top, mounted rebel officers, evidently reconnoitering, but no signs of artillery or large forces."[313]

Since there was no evidence of a large Confederate force on Benner's Hill, Williams determined to move his command forward and take it. He rode back to the woods where he had halted his column, and began leading them westward across the northern slope of Wolf's Hill, probably on the lane leading to the Rosenstiel House.[314] Since the line of heavy woods ran continuously to the north-northeast from Wolf Hill onto Brinkerhoff's Ridge, Williams formed Ruger's brigade in the eastern part of the woods, with its right on the Hanover Road, about ½ mile east of his goal of Benner's Hill. Once Ruger's men were formed under the cover of the woods, they were to charge Benner's Hill, supported by McDougall's brigade, which was being drawn up in column behind Ruger. In addition, Williams stationed the two batteries he had with him (Winegar's and Rugg's) on the road, with directions "to follow the assault, come into battery on the crest of the hill, and open on the enemy's masses."[315]

As the troops were being formed, each of Ruger's regiments sent forward a company as skirmishers. Before long the skirmishers of Company G, 27 Indiana, and Company F of the 2nd Massachusetts reported that Benner's Hill was occupied by enemy mounted cavalry and skirmishers.[316] Colonel Colgrove of the 27th Indiana relayed this information to Ruger, and at once received orders to advance with the rest of the brigade and seize the hill: "I advanced my regiment in line, keeping skirmishers well to the front. By the time the regiment had reached a ravine or small creek, thickly skirted with undergrowth, at

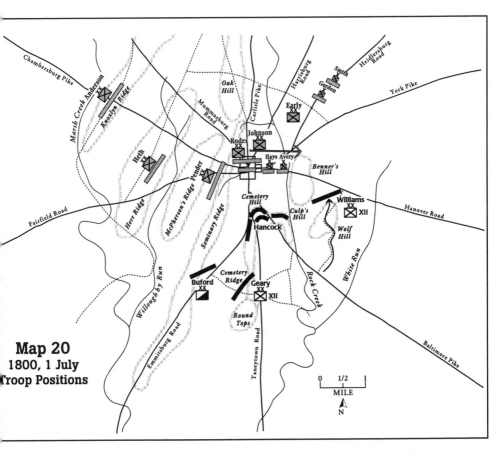

Map 20
1800, 1 July
Troop Positions

0 1/2 1
MILE

N

the foot of the hill, my skirmishers had nearly reached the crest of the hill occupied by the enemy, who had retired as my skirmishers advanced."[317]

The brigade's skirmish line was only 300 yards from the crest of the hill when Colgrove and his fellow regimental commanders received unexpected orders to fall back. It seems that at the height of the advance, Williams received a message from Slocum to withdraw, "as the Rebels had already driven back our troops in front of Gettysburg, and occupied the town, and we were in danger of being cut off from our line towards the main road."[318]

Williams obediently cancelled his attack, and withdrew his skirmishers to the stream at the base of Benner's Hill. After delaying there for about half an hour[319]—perhaps to ensure that the enemy would not attack him as he withdrew—Williams withdrew his entire division back the way it had come, and put it into bivouac on the north side of the road "within half a mile of the Pike, facing north westerly with open fields in front."[320] Because of the closeness of the enemy, the troops were directed to lay on their arms all night.[321]

It is understandable why Slocum was anxious for the safety of Williams' command. If Cemetery Hill were indeed attacked and captured by the Confederates, Williams might not have been able to return safely to the Baltimore Pike, though he probably would have been able to retire eastward on the Hanover Road. It is more interesting to conjecture what might have happened had Williams completed his attack and occupied Benner's Hill between 1800 and 1900. The hill was so open that his presence would have been clearly noticed by Ewell (who was then in fact observing his left flank). This probably would have drawn Ewell's attention away from an attack on Cemetery Hill and Culp's Hill, so ensuring the safety of those positions. But it is not likely that Williams could have held on without support against an attack, or even a confrontation, with half of Early's division (Smith's and Gordon's brigades), plus Johnson's as it came up.

Thus Slocum was justified in recalling Williams' command from Wolf Hill. The question remains, though, why he even permitted Williams to go there in the first place. If Williams were being sent in response to a request Howard made at 1500, this situation was certainly markedly different by 1700 or 1800, as Slocum should have understood. All available forces at that time were greatly needed at Cemetery Hill, and the proper station for Williams' division should have been on Culp's Hill, the status of which was still uncertain until past midnight. By the time Williams' men returned to the Baltimore Pike, it was dark, and Slocum decided not to bring them up to the unreconnoitered, forested and rocky ground on his immediate right at lower Culp's Hill.

For these reasons, Williams' division of 3400 men, by arriving late and marching to the foot of Benner's Hill and back, did very little to help the Union cause on 1 July. The historian of the 27th Indiana noted as much when he observed, "apparently we had accomplished nothing this first day at Gettysburg."[322] Had Williams at least succeeded at making his presence a little better known to Ewell, beyond losing a few skirmishers to White's Comanches, he might have drawn more of the Confederate troops away from Cemetery Hill. As it was, no Confederates except a few cavalrymen and perhaps "Extra Billy" Smith were aware of Williams' presence in the heavy woods on Wolf Hill. Some of Williams' men later tried to console themselves for their day's effort by claiming that it was their presence that detained Smith and Gordon, and so delayed Ewell's intended attack on Cemetery Hill.[323] This indeed may actually have been the case, though it has not been previously recognized as such.

Williams was quite uneasy when he returned his command to the Baltimore Pike area—by then it was dark, and all he knew of the terrain was what he had seen from the roadway and his march to and from Culp's Hill. He knew that the main army's position was ahead of him, and to the left, but all he could see in that direction was heavy woods and the waters of Rock Creek. Williams was also concerned about the whereabouts of Geary's division. Due to Slocum's increased responsibilities, Williams was now acting commander of the XII Corps, but he had no idea where more than half his men were.[324]

After Williams began his trek to Wolf Hill, Geary had continued on towards Gettysburg along the Baltimore Pike, as ordered. He had not gone far when he received instructions from Slocum to leave a brigade with two cannons as a reserve "and with the balance of my command to report to Major General Howard, whom I should have found at a point some mile and a half east of the town, where an engagement with the right wing of the enemy's forces was then in progress."[325] Geary accordingly left his smallest brigade, Brigadier General Thomas L. Kane's three Pennsylvania regiments, and two guns of Battery K 5th U.S. artillery, "on the immediate left of the turnpike, about 2 miles from Gettysburg." These troops rested on their arms all night without incident.[326] It is not clear what Slocum intended these troops to accomplish, other than to serve as general reserve if needed. Kane's troops could have been much better employed to help gather and turn back the numerous stragglers that were still moving down the Pike towards Two Taverns. But there is no evidence he was ordered to do so, or took the initiative to. This task was mostly taken up by the corps' provost guard, a battalion of the 10th Maine Infantry, and other units.[327]

After detaching Kane's brigade, Geary continued on with his two remaining brigades (Colonel Charles Candy's Ohio and Pennsylvania command, and Brigadier General George S. Greene's New York brigade) towards Cemetery Hill, as ordered. For some reason, he was unable to locate General Howard, so he reported instead to Hancock. Hancock told him "that the right could defend itself, and the immediate need of a division on the left was imperative." Geary did not stop to consider what the command situation was, and accepted Hancock's directive: "By his direction, upon this threatening emergency, I took up a position on the extreme left of the line of battle, as the enemy was reported to be attempting to flank it, and cavalry were already skirmishing in front of that position."[328] Slocum, once he learned of Hancock's command, did not cancel it, even though it directed his own troops; he must have agreed with Hancock's assessment that something needed to be done at once to strengthen the position's left flank.

Geary did not form his men in immediate support of Robinson's division, which was on the extreme northern end of Cemetery Ridge, but instead moved southward to within half a mile of "Sugar Loaf Mountain" (the Round Tops).[329] Once he neared his intended position, he formed his regiments in column of division, and sent skirmishers to the front. They then advanced in this formation until they reached the neighborhood of Little Round Top. Greene's brigade formed on the right, on "the brow of a hill," probably Swisher's Hill, the next eminence north of Little Round Top.[330] His regiments did not reform into line formation, but remained in line of double columns, prepared to move forward wherever needed.[331] A strong line of skirmishers was sent forward, and Captain L.R. Stegman reported a brief engagement with those of the enemy, perhaps some of Lane's men.[332]

Geary's remaining brigade, Candy's, formed on Greene's left. It is not clear if this was on the east or west side of Swisher's Hill. Captain Wilbur F. Stevens of the 29th Ohio reported that his command encamped "in the wheatfield on the left of the road approaching Gettysburg."[333] These dispositions were completed between 1800 and 1900.[334]

Towards sunset Geary directed Candy to send two regiments to occupy the Round Tops, which he "regarded as of the utmost importance, since their possession by the enemy would give him an opportunity of enfilading our entire left wing and center with a fire which could not fail to dislodge us from our position."[335] Candy dispatched the 147th Pennsylvania and 5th Ohio for this purpose, under command of Colonel John H. Patrick of the 5th Ohio. These two units apparently did not occupy Little Round Top proper, as the 147th's monument and flank markers on northern Little Round Top might seem to indicate. Colonel Patrick reported that "we deployed as skirmishers in our front across an open valley to a light strip of woods, and in front of that timber facing an open field, for the purpose of guarding against a flank movement of the enemy."[336] It would thus appear that Patrick's men formed in the woods on Houck's Ridge and in the famous Wheatfield, rather than in the woods and fields of the J. Weikert farm slightly to the north.

Geary apparently did not make any effort to notify Williams of his position, though he was no doubt aware that Williams was serving as acting corps commander. He probably thought it was sufficient that Slocum knew where he was. Nor did Slocum take the time to tell Williams where Geary was. Williams actually went to sleep that night under the false impression that Geary's division was nearby on Cemetery Hill, since a staff officer had come up after dark "with information that it had been ordered to the vicinity of Gettysburg to support the right of Wadsworth's division, 1st Corps."[337]

It is thus clear that Slocum did not maintain very close control of his XII Corps once it finally did reach the field. By sunset his command was spread out all across the field in three separate, disjointed and unsupported locations: Williams' two brigades east of Rock Creek, Kane's brigade on the Baltimore Pike, and Geary's other two brigades near Little Round Top. None were in direct contact with the enemy, and all might have been more effectively employed closer to the army's main position on Cemetery Hill. The best that can be said of the XII Corps' position that night was that it was at last on (or at least near) the field, and was preventing the enemy from occupying the positions held by it.

Arrival of III Corps

The lead element of Major General Daniel E. Sickles' III Corps also began to reach the southern edge of the battlefield area at about 1800, at the same time that Geary's division was approaching Little Round Top. As previously noted, the III Corps had encamped between Bridgeport and Emmitsburg on the night of 30 June. When the XI Corps moved north to support Reynolds at Gettysburg, Sickles moved his troops forward to shield the town. Most of Major General David B. Birney's 1st Division moved to a position north of the town in order to watch the road to Fairfield and Gettysburg, and Major General H.H. Humphreys' 2nd Division marched just past the town to guard its western approaches.[338]

Sickles spent the morning and early afternoon near Emmitsburg, guarding the town as directed by Meade and waiting for any further directions from Reynolds, his wing commander. Since he had been criticized by Meade twice for his slow march rate the last few days,[339] he was extra alert that morning, and sent his senior aide, Major Henry Tremain, to Reynolds to see what his directions were for the day. Tremain met Reynolds on the battlefield, near the Seminary, and received the verbal message, "Tell General Sickles I think he had better come up."[340] Tremain then headed back to Emmitsburg, just minutes before Reynolds was killed.

Reynolds' message, which should have reached Sickles by noon, placed the III Corps commander in a quandary. His marching orders from Meade directed him to hold Emmitsburg, but Reynolds was now directing him to come up to Gettysburg. Uncertain what he should do, he sent another messenger to Reynolds, and anxiously awaited his reply.[341]

Sickles did not hear anything from Gettysburg until 1515, when he received Howard's curt dispatch, sent at 1330, "General Reynolds is killed, for God's sake come up."[342] Sickles understood that the situation at Gettysburg was desperate, but he still had no answer to his dilemma about what to do concerning Meade's orders to hold Emmitsburg. Had he been of the same mind as Slocum, he would have remained at Emmitsburg until he received definite orders to move from either Hancock or Meade. But Sickles was more impetuous than Slocum, and being a political general rather than a West Pointer, did not stick as much as Slocum to the exact letter of his orders from Meade. He promptly decided to leave two brigades and a battery at or near Emmitsburg—enough to secure the town and watch its western approaches—and advance the rest of his corps to Gettysburg by two parallel roads. Sickles replied to Howard that he would move to Gettysburg immediately.[343] He also forwarded Sickles' dispatch to Meade as requested, and sent Meade two dispatches to outline his movements and intentions.[344] Slocum would have done well to be equally as responsive and responsible.

Sickles decided to leave one brigade behind from each of his two divisions, and take the rest of his troops to Gettysburg.[345] Birney's division, which was stationed farther north of Emmitsburg than Humphreys', began the march first, soon after 1530.[346] Birney took with him Brigadier General Charles K. Graham's 1st Brigade and Brigadier General J.H.H. Ward's large 2nd Brigade, as well as Randolph's and Clark's batteries.[347] He left Colonel Regis DeTrobriand's 3rd Brigade and Winslow's New York battery at Emmitsburg.[348] Humphreys' 2nd Division, which had just reached Emmitsburg at noon, marched out at the same time as Birney. Humphreys brought with him Brigadier General Joseph Carr's 1st Brigade and Colonel William Brewster's 2nd Brigade, along with Seeley's regular battery.[349] Colonel George C. Burling's 3rd

Brigade and Smith's New York battery were left behind at Emmitsburg to guard the road to Fairfield.[350] Altogether Sickles left about 2900 of his men at Emmitsburg, and took about 6400 with him to Gettysburg.[351]

Several sources note how muddy and terrible the road between Emmitsburg and Gettysburg was by the end of the day.[352] It is no wonder, since three full infantry divisions, over 9,000 men, had already passed over it, along with six batteries and all the I Corps trains. In addition, there had been off and on showers during the day that kept the mud sticky and fresh. In spite of the deteriorated condition of the road, Birney's men covered their nine mile march in about four hours,[353] with minimal straggling. Colonel Calvin A. Craig of the 105th Pennsylvania was pleased to report that only three of his men straggled during his command's hurried march to Gettysburg.[354]

Sickles rode on ahead of his troops in order to confer with Slocum and Howard on Cemetery Hill. The exact time of his arrival there was not recorded, but it must have been before dark. He was anxious to justify his march to the front, particularly since he had received while en route a strong message that Meade had sent at 1645 directing him not to leave Emmitsburg unguarded, since "it is a point not to be abandoned excepting in an extremity." Sickles was supposed to hold on there until he heard from Hancock, and in any event was supposed to leave a division there to cover the army's left and rear.[355]

After conferring with Slocum and Howard, Sickles drafted the following lengthy and apologetic note to Meade, which was sent at 2130:

Headquarters Third Army Corps
July 1, 1863-9:30p.m.

Major-General Butterfield, Chief of Staff

General: Before the receipt of your dispatch (dated 4.45 p.m.), four brigades and three batteries of my corps had advanced to the support of General Howard, and reached Gettysburg.

I left two brigades and two batteries at Emmitsburg, assuming that the approaches through Emmitsburg toward our left and rear must not be uncovered.

General Hancock is not in command-General Howard commands.

My impression is, if I may be allowed to make a suggestion, that our left and rear are not sufficiently guarded. Nothing less than the earnest and frequent appeals of General Howard, and his supposed danger, could have induced me to move from the position assigned to me in general orders; but I believed the emergency justified my movement.

Shall I return to my position at Emmitsburg, or shall I remain and report to Howard?

If my corps is to remain in position here, I hope my brigades at Emmitsburg (and batteries) may be relieved and ordered to join me.

This is a good battle-field.
Very respectfully,
D.E. Sickles,
Major-General, Commanding[356]

Sickles must have been greatly relieved to learn that Meade implicitly approved his march to Gettysburg when he sent a note at 1930 to the "commanding officer at Emmitsburg" to "move up to join their corps at the field in the vicinity of Gettysburg with the greatest dispatch." Meade was particularly concerned that these last III Corps troops would not march straight up the Emmitsburg Road into the Confederate lines, and directed that they should cross over to the Taneytown Road after passing Marsh Creek, by the road through Horner's Hills. He then repeated that "you take care that you do not come in collision with any force of the enemy in moving up."[357]

After sending off his message to Meade, Sickles sat down with Howard and Slocum for a light supper at Howard's headquarters in the cemetery gate house. Their hostess was Mrs. Catherine Thorn, wife of Peter Thorn, the cemetery's caretaker who was then a soldier stationed at Harpers Ferry. Mrs. Thorn had already had a busy and tiring day as the war literally came to her doorstep. During the afternoon she had pumped water and baked bread for the soldiers, and had even given one officer a brief topographical tour of what could be seen from the hill. After the tour she went to her upstairs bedroom, and was scared to death by a Confederate shell that came flying in through the window and crashed into the ceiling. She promptly headed downstairs for safety.[358]

During the evening Mrs. Thorn was asked to prepare dinner for General Howard. She objected that she had no more bread and could only make "cakes," but that was thought to be sufficient. Mrs. Thorn, though, wanted to serve more than this, and went to a neighbor's house, the Myers', on Baltimore Street, to ask to borrow some meat. They had none, and their house was full of wounded. By the time she returned, empty handed, to her own house, it too, was being filled with wounded, even in the kitchen. In spite of this, Mrs. Thorn somehow managed to prepare a dinner of "two good sized dough cakes", three pieces of meat, and some coffee, for Howard and his two guests, Generals Slocum and Sickles.[359] Howard was particularly pleased with the meal and never forgot it, since he "had been all day from breakfast at sunrise without food and was nearly famished."[360]

After supper, Mrs. Thorn asked if she should leave her house, since the generals were using part for a headquarters and most of the rest was filled with wounded soldiers. Howard told her that she could stay, but told her that she should go to the cellar, since he expected that the battle would be renewed at dawn. He suggested that she should pack up her valuables, and in two hours he would send someone to help her carry them to the cellar. She did so, and when a soldier came to help her, he bore a message from Howard, "When I give you the order to leave the house, don't study about it but go right away." By the time Mrs. Thorn prepared her things and actually went to her cellar, it was 0400, less than an hour from sunrise. She would not be lonesome during the day, since she found 17 other people already enjoying the shelter of her cellar when she finally got there.[361]

Among the officers who spent the night in Mrs. Thorn's home were Brigadier General Adelbert Ames of the XI Corps and Colonel Charles Wainwright of the I Corps. Wainright recalled that after dark he secured some coffee and hardtack from his men; none of the supply wagons had yet come up, so "consequently generals and staff were in a bad way." He went to bed at about 2300 along with General Ames "in one of the rooms of the gate house."[362]

General Schurz also retained a vivid memory of the time he spent at Mrs. Thorn's that evening: "I remember a picturesque scene that happened that night in a lower room of the gate house of the Gettysburg Cemetery. In the center of the room a barrel set upright, with a burning tallow candle stuck in the neck of a bottle on top ot it; around the walls six or seven generals accidentally gathered together, sitting some on boxes but most on the floor, listening to the accounts of those who had been in the battle of the day, then making critical comments and discussing what might have been and finally all agreeing in the hope that General Meade had decided or would decide to fight the battle of the morrow on the ground on which we then were. There was nothing of extraordinary solemnity in the 'good night' we gave one another when we parted. It was rather a commonplace, business-like 'good-night,' as that of an ordinary occasion. We of the Eleventh Corps, occupying the cemetery, lay down, wrapt in cloaks, with the troops among the grave stones. There was profound stillness in the graveyard, broken by no sound but the breathing of the men and here and there the tramp of a horse's foot; and sullen rumblings mysteriously floating on the air from a distance all around."[363]

After dining with Howard and Slocum, Sickles rode southward about ¾ of a mile to where Birney's troops were encamped on central Cemetery Ridge, about midway between Geary's troops near Little Round Top and Robinson's on the northern end of the ridge. As already noted, Birney's two brigades had arrived on the field around 1930. It is not clear at what point they crossed over to the Taneytown Road from the Emmitsburg Road. Birney must have received instructions from Sickles or Slocum as to where to encamp, since he marched past Geary's troops and formed his men in column by regiments along the middle of the ridge.[364] Ward's brigade, which had led the march, formed on the right, and Graham's on the left. Major John W. Moore of the 99th Pennsylvania reported that his command went into camp "in a field on the right of the road, distant about one mile from the town, a short time after sunset."[365] Ward sent two of his regiments out to picket his front. The 4th Maine was pushed forward to the right to link up with the skirmishers of Robinson's division, and had a detachment of the 99th Pennsylvania on his left.[366] Farther to the left, Graham had at least one of his regiments, the 63rd Pennsylvania, on picket duty along the Emmitsburg Road.[367] Sickles set up his headquarters in a tent pitched in the woods on the east side of the Taneytown Road, about ⅜ miles south of the Leister house.[368] Here he at last went to sleep sometime after midnight.

Sickles had stayed up to await the arrival of Humphreys' division, which did not come in until about 2000, after experiencing a long and dangerous march to the field. Humphreys had not been with his troops when Sickles' original marching orders were issued at about 1530 because Meade had directed him to examine the ground around Emmitsburg "for a position for fighting if necessary."[369] For this reason it was his senior brigade commander, Brigadier General Joseph Carr, who marshalled the division and got it underway. Humphreys soon heard of the movement and joined his troops about a mile north of the town, where they had been forced to halt because they caught up to the rear of Birney's column.[370]

At this point Humphreys received orders from Lieutenant Colonel Julius Hayden, III Corps Assistant Adjutant General, to move off to the left and take a side road to Gettysburg that ran parallel to and about

2 miles west of the Emmitsburg Road. A local doctor named Ana would serve as a guide, and Hayden would also accompany the column.[371] It is not clear if this alternate route was arranged by Sickles alone, or was ordered by one of Sickles' superiors. In the absence of other evidence, it was probably Sickles. His motives might have been two. One was to speed up his corps' advance by having Humphreys slide over to a parallel road and march at his own rate, rather than be slowed by Birney's troops and wagons ahead of him on the by now abused Emmitsburg Road. Sickles might also have ordered Humphreys to take this route in order to screen Birney and keep a lookout for Confederate troops in the direction of Fairfield, thereby continuing to carry out, at least partially, the orders he had received from Meade during the afternoon. Whatever were the reasons for Humphreys being assigned this route, they did not turn out to be good enough, because they ended up delaying his arrival by 4-6 hours, and caused great danger to the column when it unknowingly began to approach the Confederate right rear after dark.

Sickles himself became concerned about this latter possibility, and soon after Humphreys moved to the west, sent Captain John G. McBlair of his staff with a warning for Humphreys "to look out for his left while coming up to Gettysburg." Humphreys received the message when he was about halfway to his destination, probably somewhere west of Greenmount. At the same time he learned from a citizen who had helped guide Reynolds' troops that morning, "that our troops occupied no ground near Gettysburg west of the road from that town to Emmitsburg."[372]

Humphreys clearly needed to be alert and careful in his final approach to the Gettysburg area, especially since sunset was near. As he was approaching Marsh Run he received a directive from Sickles "to take a position on the left of Gettysburg as soon as I came up." Humphreys interpreted the situation correctly and prepared to turn the column to the right when it reached Marsh Creek; he could then reach the Emmitsburg Road by the road past the Pitzer School House (Millerstown Road) or by a local crossroad farther to the south. Lieutenant Colonel Hayden, however, "was positive that General Sickles had instructed him to guide the division by way of the Black Horse Tavern, on the road from Fairfield to Gettysburg." Against his better judgement, Humphreys gave in to Hayden and turned his troops to the left when they reached the creek.[373]

It did not take Humphreys long to find out that he had made a mistake and was headed into the Confederate lines. He halted his command in order to close up after wading "Marsh Run, a considerable stream," and rode on ahead with three staff officers, Lieutenant Colonel Hayden and the guide to find the Black Horse Tavern. He later admitted that he had misread his map, and thought "we were half a mile from it instead of 100 or 200 yards." When he reached the tavern, he was astonished to learn from its proprietor that Confederate pickets were posted only 100 yards away. In addition, there was a hill "not over four hundred yards distant upon which he said were seen just before sundown thirty-six pieces of artillery."[374]

Humphreys at once realized the seriousness of the situation and directed his troops to face about and turn back. They were lucky to get away without being detected. The only actual contact they had with the enemy came when a trumpeter of Seeley's battery sounded the call to halt while Humphreys was talking to the tavern keeper. A Confederate artillery man who was nearby recognized the call and came forward, believing that Humphreys' troops were another Confederate column coming up. He was quickly taken prisoner before he could spread an alarm.[375]

Humphreys' troops were indeed lucky to be able to sneak away without loss. His artillery and ambulance wagons made a considerable noise, but those few Confederates who heard it must have thought that more friendly troops were coming up, just as the single captured artilleryman did. Humphreys' escape was also aided greatly by the darkness, which concealed the size and even the identity of his command. Quite amazingly, Humphreys in his battle report noted that he briefly considered staying near the Tavern in order to conduct a surprise attack on the enemy at dawn: "He was not aware of my presence, and I might have attacked him at daylight with the certainty of at least temporary success." However, he wisely thought better of the idea, especially because he was at least three miles distant from any support. He also felt "such a course would have been inconsistent with the general plan of operations of the commanding general."[376]

After the war Humphreys went to see the tavern keeper and his house during one of his visits to the battlefield, and was astonished to learn how close he had come to being personally captured or shot during his brief stop at the tavern that night: "They told me that a few minutes after I had left, less than 10 minutes, some twenty or thirty of the enemy, armed of course, came there and remained all night, and that early the next day Longstreet's corps passed there."[377]

This information caused Humphreys to reflect upon how vulnerable he and his small party of six mounted men had been that night: "Now when you call to mind what I had been doing all the day; where I had marched from and the roads I had followed, and how many little things might have made me ten minutes later reaching the Black Horse Tavern; two or three minutes more at the various halts I made, which I was sorely tempted to give, for the troops were fatigued, would have made me not only ten but fifteen or twenty minutes later in reaching the Black Horse Tavern. There were a thousand chances that I might have been that much later, but few that I might have been shot much earlier. Now for certain good reasons connected with the effect of what I did upon the spirit of the men and from an invincible repugnance to ride anywhere else, I always rode at the head of my troops, with no advance guard in front of me. Now imagine me ten or fifteen minutes later: the party of Confederates hearing a few horsemen would have got behind the stone fence or barn within twenty feet of us unseen; and would at once have recognized an officer of high rank; the ground is hilly and broken. From behind the stone fence within twenty feet of us, the men would have deliberately fired a volley at us, and have escaped before my troops could have got up there. It was one more of my many good fortunes, almost a thousand. You will call it a Special Providence."[378]

Humphreys' men, though, still had a dangerous march to make in order to reach their own lines, wherever those might be. The column recrossed Marsh Run and then headed east towards the Pitzer School as Humphreys had originally wanted to do. Before long they reached the top of a hill (Warfield Ridge) and "in front of the division were seen the extensive smouldering fires of some troops." Chastened by his close call at the tavern, Humphreys took special care to identify the troops ahead of him before approaching. He called for an experienced officer and gave him instructions "how to proceed in this matter, which was exceedingly delicate."[378]

The officer went forward with a company of infantry to reconnoiter. After some time he returned and reported that the troops ahead were friends. He had experienced "some difficulty in convincing the outposts that he was of the Army of the Potomac." Fortunately, Colonel O.H. Hart, III Corps adjutant general, heard the commotion and came forward to investigate. Sickles had sent Hart "to find out what had become of the Division" since "there was much uneasiness expressed about it because of its non-arrival." Humphreys' weary troops then "passed through the outposts, halted some distance beyond it, sank into slumber at once at the foot of a range of hills which was ascertained the next morning to be Round Top Ridge."[379] By then it was well after midnight; Lieutenant Colonel Clark Baldwin of the 1st Massachusetts reported that his command did not go into bivouac until 0230.[380]

During the evening a number of additional fresh troops also arrived on the field to reinforce the battered Union regiments on Cemetery Hill. The largest of these detachments was composed of about 2000 men of Brigadier General George J. Stannard's brigade of nine-months regiments from Vermont. Stannard's command had been attached to the defenses of Washington and until 24 June was picketing the Occoquan River in northern Virginia. On that date it was directed to march north to reinforce Meade's army, and would soon be assigned to the I Corps as the 3rd Brigade of Doubleday's division. The brigade marched north from Centreville on 25 June and had to undergo a series of exhausting marches that averaged 18 miles a day in order to catch up with the I Corps. En route, Stannard was directed by Reynolds to leave two of his regiments (the 12th and 15th) with the corps train as a guard. Thus Stannard had only three of his regiments (13th, 14th and 16th) with him when he reached the field on the evening of 1 July.[381] They were "placed in position in column by regiment on the front line," on Cemetery Ridge between Robinson's and Birney's divisions. When Colonel Dick Coulter of the 11th Pennsylvania, now commanding Paul's brigade because of that unit's heavy officer casualties, heard Stannard's men approaching, he commented, "If these fellows will fight as we do, we will give the Johnnies hell tomorrow."[382]

After the day's fighting ended a number of detached units of the XI Corps arrived on the field to augment their depleted commands. The previous night Captain George B. Fox had been sent with 100 men of the 75th Ohio of Ames' brigade to conduct a reconnaissance from Emmitsburg towards Monterey Springs. At 0900 on 1 July he received orders "to proceed via quickest manner to Gettysburg and there join the corps." The detachment reached Cemetery Hill at 1700 and was dismayed to learn that the 75th had "suffered greatly" during the day's severe engagement. Due to the unit's heavy loss in officers, Captain Fox was now the senior commander present and assumed command of the unit, "which was stationed at the base of the hill on the right of the Baltimore Pike and just on the eastern edge of the town, behind a stone wall."[383]

The 41st New York of Von Gilsa's brigade did not reach the field until 2200. As already noted, Captain Clemens Knipschild of the 41st had been detached at 0200 on 1 July to arrest and detain all the farmers and civilians in the neighborhood of Emmitsburg. Since he had not returned by 0800, when Von Gilsa's brigade was ordered to advance to Gettysburg, the remainder of the regiment was ordered to stay behind and wait for it, and then escort an ammunition train to Gettysburg. Apparently Knipschild's detachment did not return during the day, even though Lieutenant Colonel Von Einsiedel waited for it until late in the afternoon. At last he gave up waiting and departed for the battlefield, where he arrived at 2200 with 14 officers, 187 men, and 17 musicians.[384]

A detachment of 200 men from Coster's brigade (50 from each of his four regiments) had not marched to the battlefield with their corps because they had been sent out at 0500 on 1 July under the command of Major Lewis Warner of the 154th New York to conduct a reconnaissance from Emmitsburg to Sabillasville, Maryland.[385] The expedition reached its objective and retuned to Emmitsburg, having accomplished "nothing of importance" during the foray. When Major Warner heard the low thud of cannons from the direction of Gettysburg, he headed his command north. After proceeding a few miles, Warner let his men encamp near a stone barn while he hurried on to Gettysburg. When he located Colonel Coster, Warner was ordered to return to his command and bring it up as soon as possible.[386] He arrived back at the stone barn at 0300 bearing "the sad news that there was a terrible battle in progress and that [nearly] every man had been killed, wounded or captured." Warner's command did not reach Cemetery Hill until 1000 on 2 July.[387]

As already noted, Hancock's II Corps, under the temporary command of Brigadier General John Gibbon of the 2nd Division, had been ordered to proceed northward from Taneytown in order to cover the army's center in case Reynolds withdrew or was driven back towards Emmitsburg. The corps broke camp at 1330 and encamped for the night about three miles south of Gettysburg. The corps was joined there at about 2230 by Brigadier General Robert Tyler, commander of the army's artillery reserve, who had been ordered at dusk to take eight of his batteries and report to General Hancock at Gettysburg. Since Tyler could not locate Hancock, who was just returning from his final conference with Meade at Taneytown, Tyler instead reported to Gibbon and went into camp near the II Corps' encampment, about a mile south of Big Round Top.[388]

The 7th Indiana Saves Culp's Hill

Another significant reinforcement that reached the field after the day's fighting was over was the 7th Indiana of Cutler's brigade. This regiment, well over 400 strong, had been left behind that morning as a guard for the corps trains at Emmitsburg, with orders to wait there until relieved by one of Stannard's regiments. After waiting in vain until 1000, the 7th's commander, Colonel Ira Grover, decided to leave for the front anyway. Grover was later brought before a court martial for abandoning his post, but was exonerated.

Since he had no news about the battle that was already underway, Grover did not push his troops, and halted them at 1400 to cook dinner. They had scarcely started their fires when a sudden thunderstorm drowned them out. During the shower Quartermaster Burlingame arrived with long awaited news and orders from the front—there was a battle on and the regiment was to hurry forward to Gettysburg.[389]

Grover hurried his men forward in the rain, and reached the southern edge of the battlefield at evening. He then halted the column in order to allow his men to catch their breath, and sent Major Merit C. Welsh forward to report and get instructions on where to deploy. Welsh saw a body of men off to the left, "and in the darkness mistaking them for ours, he had a narrow escape from capture."[390] These were probably some of Lane's North Carolinians on Seminary Ridge.

Welsh hastily returned to the Emmitsburg Road, and soon found the I Corps after he rode northwards towards the town. He reported the 7th's arrival to General Wadsworth, and was directed to bring the "regiment up to Cemetery Ridge." Welsh carried the command back to Grover, who brought his regiment up on side roads (apparently in order to avoid any more contact with the enemy) and ended up reaching the Cemetery area via the Baltimore Pike.[391]

As Colonel Grover reached the hill, he and his men had an interesting but disturbing reunion with Generals Wadsworth and Cutler: "Reaching there, we found General Wadsworth sitting on a stone fence by the roadside, his head bowed in grief, the most dejected woe-begone person one would likely find on a world-around voyage-a live picture of Despair: General Reynolds killed, the first corps decimated a full half, and its first division almost wiped out of existence. The General greeted us warmly, adding, 'I am glad you were not with us this afternoon;' and, in response to a remark of General Cutler, 'If the Seventh had been with us we could have held our position,' said, 'Yes, and all would now be dead or prisoners.'"[392]

The exact time of the 7th's arrival is not certain. The anecdote concerning Welsh's encounter with Confederate troops on Cemetery Ridge suggests that the regiment reached Cemetery Hill at about dark (1930-2000). However, Coddington and other sources favor an arrival time between 1700 and 1800.[393] The earlier time range appears to be preferable based on other source information, which relates how the regiment witnessed the arrival of Howard's retreating troops and even served as a rallying point.[394] The source of the Welsh anecdote may not have remembered the incident clearly, or may have added the factor of darkness in order to make the story more exciting.

The 7th had not been on Cemetery Hill long when Wadsworth directed Grover to move to the right to the summit of Culp's Hill.[395] The remains of the Iron Brigade had already formed on the Hill's western slope, and Grover moved his men to the crest of the hill, on the right of the 6th Wisconsin.[396] The Hoosiers found the hill to be "somewhat on the order of our Ohio River hills— its sides pretty heavily timbered, and strewn with rocks varying in size from a chicken coop to a pioneer's cabin." The men quickly set to work felling trees and building breast-works, for which there was plenty of building material handy.[397]

The 7th was a good choice to anchor the far right of the Union position, since it was a large and fresh unit. Due to the configuration of the hill and the position of the Iron Brigade, Grover needed most of his command to cover the northern face of the hill's crest and extend to the left to connect with the Iron Brigade. This left him only one company, B, to picket the eastern face of the hill. Sometime later Grover found it necessary to contract even this thin picket line.[398] As a result, there were no Union pickets at all patrolling the gap of almost a mile in the Federal line between the peak of Culp's Hill and Williams' camp on the eastern side of Rock Creek.

Thus the Union line at nightfall was fairly well secure. Over 12,000 survivors of the first day's fight, supported by 50 cannons, occupied the principal position on Culp's, Cemetery, and East Cemetery Hills. Over 1200 fresh troops in the 7th Indiana, Kane's brigade, and other recent arrivals buttressed or supported this line. Williams' 3500 men guarded the extreme right of the position, and almost 13,000 new but tired troops in the III Corps, Geary's division and Stannard's brigade held Cemetery Ridge all the way to Little Round Top. In addition, Buford's well used cavalry division was encamped somewhere near the Peach Orchard, with pickets extending almost to Fairfield.

Most of the Union batteries had begun constructing lunettes as soon as they reformed on Cemetery Hill, and by sunset many of the infantry units began building defensive ramparts also.[399] These lines were made particularly strong on Culp's Hill, whose numerous rocks and trees furnished readymade building material. Wadsworth's line there was begun by a civil engineer from the 7th Indiana.[400] It should also be noted that before dark all the Union units had been resupplied with ammunition, but not with food. Lieutenant Colonel Adolphus Dobke of the 45th New York reported that his men were resupplied with cartridges that evening,[401] and the men of the 121st Pennsylvania were grateful to receive a fresh ammunition supply from wagons belonging to the XI Corps.[402] Not all the Federal ammunition wagons remained on the field during this critical time, however. Andrew J. Boies of the 33rd Massachusetts, who was serving this day as a wagoneer for the ordnance department, later admitted that he "went as far as the foot of Cemetery Hill and 'scooted' back" when he was "ordered to the front with my load of ammunition, to supply the boys."[403]

The only weakness in the Union line was the gap already mentioned to the right (south) of the crest of Culp's Hill. By some coincidence, this was exactly the portion of the Union line that Ewell was looking to attack. While he was waiting for Johnson's division to come up, Ewell sent Robert D. Early and Lieutenant Thomas T. Turner to reconnoiter Culp's Hill. The two officers went to the "very summit of the knoll without meeting a Federal and there saw stretched out before us the enemy's line of battle." They thought that the hill would be a fine position to occupy and turn the enemy's position, and hurried back to report this to Ewell.[404]

It is difficult today to understand how Turner and Early managed to reach the summit of the hill without encountering any Union troops. We do not know exactly when they conducted their reconnaissance, but it was clearly made after the Iron Brigade had formed on the western side of Culp's Hill. The two scouts must have reached the summit of Culp's Hill just before the 7th Indiana arrived there, and for some reason did not see the men of the 6th Wisconsin or the rest of the Iron Brigade because of the thick woods. They probably approached the hill's summit from the east, after passing around the northern edge of the hill in order to avoid the Iron Brigade's skirmishers.[405]

Turner and Early reported to General Ewell while he was still on the left of his position with General Rodes and Early. Ewell asked Rodes what he thought about sending Johnson to try to occupy Culp's Hill (rather than to help attack Cemetery Hill). By now Rodes was weary from all the day's activity, and all he could advise was that Johnson's men were probably worn out from marching almost 25 miles that day. He added that he did not think "it would result in anything one way or the other." Early, on the other hand, urged Ewell to occupy the hill, stating, "If you do not go up there tonight, it will cost you ten thousand men to get there tomorrow." Ewell agreed with Early, and sent an order for Johnson to move towards Culp's Hill and occupy it, if he found no enemy troops there.[406]

Early's suggestion to try to take Culp's Hill was not the first prodding Ewell had received on that subject this day. Major General Isaac R. Trimble, who was accompanying his headquarters because he as yet had no re-assignment after recovering from a wound, was full of advice that day. After the retreat of the XI Corps, Trimble approached Ewell at the Almshouse and asked him, "General, don't you intend to pursue our sweep and push the enemy vigorously?" Trimble claims that Ewell replied in the negative, citing Lee's orders not to bring on a general engagement. Trimble replied to this, "But General, that order cannot have reference to the present situation, for we have had a general engagement and gained a great victory and by all military rules we ought to follow up our success, and we are losing golden moments." Ewell did not reply to this, but only paced about and looked confused.[407]

Trimble then left the Almshouse, presumably to look at the Union positions, and returned half an hour later with still more unsolicited advice: "General, if you have decided not to advance against the enemy and we are only to hold our ground, I advise you to send a brigade with artillery to take possession of that hill (Culp's), it commands Gettysburg and Cemetery Hill." Ewell asked how he knew this, and Trimble replied, "I have been round there, and you know I am not often mistaken in judging of topography - and if we don't hold that hill, the enemy will certainly occupy it, as it is, the key to the whole position about here, and I beg you to send a force at once to secure it." Ewell, who was by now thoroughly irritated, snapped back, "when I need advice from a junior officer, I generally ask it." Trimble shot back as he left, "General Ewell, I am sorry you don't appreciate my suggestions, you will regret it."[408]

Lt. Randolph McKim gives a slightly different, and more familiar, version of Trimble's last word to Ewell at this stormy meeting. He relates that, "Trimble was most urgent. 'Give me a division' said he, 'and I will engage to take that hill.' When this was declined he said, 'Give me a brigade and I will do it.' When this, too, was declined, he said, 'Give me a good regiment and I will engage to take that hill.' When this was declined the gallant Trimble threw down his sword and left General Ewell's headquarters, saying that he would no longer serve under such an officer!"[409]

Johnson's weary men were on the Chambersburg Pike near Gettysburg at about 1900 when their commander received Ewell's order to proceed east of the town along the railroad line. As they neared the battlefield, they heard the steady sound of artillery booming; but soon this din all but ceased as the day's battle came to a close.[410] Nicholls' brigade, led by Colonel J.M. Williams' 2nd Louisiana, led the way, and marched across the debris of the battlefield.[411] The shocking sights they passed were gruesomely familiar to all of Johnson's veterans, but not to many of the Marylanders of Steuart's brigade, whose faces turned pale as they entered their first battle.[412]

Johnson rode on ahead of his men and sought out Ewell for more specific instructions. Ironically, Ewell, accompanied by Early, was also riding to find Johnson. The three generals accidentally ran into each other at about 1815 on the Chambersburg Pike just west of the town.[413] Johnson probably complained something about being delayed by Longstreet's trains,[414] and then reported that his troops were about a mile away and would be up in less than an hour. According to Major J.W. Bruce of General John Jones' staff, who was a witness to the meeting, Ewell became concerned about the lateness of the hour and ordered Early "to take position on the heights beyond the town." Early became annoyed and muttered that "his command had been doing all the hard marching and fighting and was not in condition to make the move." When Johnson replied in kind, the two generals began arguing with "a few oaths" and language "more forceful than elegant." According to Bruce, Ewell got so flustered by the situation that he rescinded Early's order to take Cemetery Hill.[415]

Johnson, then, was probably not in a very good mood when he returned to his division. By then his leading brigade, Nicholls', was at the railroad station on the northern edge of town, waiting for the rest of the division to catch up.[416] Once his troops were in hand, Johnson led them eastward along the railroad line towards Benner's Hill. By now it was twilight, still light enough for Lieutenant R.M. McKim of Stewart's staff to read a dispatch brought up by Major Douglas, but gloomy enough to promise that Johnson's men would soon be marching in the dark.[417]

When they reached Rock Creek, Johnson's men had to wade across because Early had destroyed the railroad bridge there the week before the battle. About ⅜ mile east of the Creek, Johnson sent Nicholls' lead brigade off to the right down the lane leading to the George Wolf farmhouse. Nicholls formed here about 600 yards south of the York Pike, and at right angles to it along the farm lane. The rest of the division then formed in the reverse order to which it had been marching. Jones formed on Nicholls' left on a line running roughly parallel to the Hanover Road ½ mile to the south, and Steuart formed on Jones' left. Lastly, the Stonewall Brigade formed on the left of the division line, in the edge of the heavy woods that ran up Brinkerhoff's Ridge.[418] All four brigades at once sent skirmishers to their front.[419] Johnson's divisional artillery battalion, 16 guns under Major J.W. Latimer, came up after dark because it had made a detour around the town in order "to prevent the enemy from finding out his movements." It then encamped for the night on the south side of the York Pike, in the rear of the division.[420] Johnson did not have his divisional train with him, but reportedly left it parked at Cashtown.[421]

Johnson's position was indeed a strange one if he intended to make a movement against Culp's Hill as Ewell had originally directed. Culp's Hill was almost a mile distant, and the whole open crest of Benner's Hill rose up in the interval. It is not at all clear why he did not simply occupy Benner's Hill. Perhaps he adhered too closely to Ewell's instructions to proceed east of town along the railroad line. It is also possible that Ewell directed him to form there in order to give still more support to Smith and Gordon against the large force of the enemy reported to be in that quarter.[422]

Despite the awkward posting of his division, Johnson continued to carry out Ewell's instructions as ordered. While his brigades were forming, he sent a reconnoitering party to Culp's Hill "with orders to report as to the position of the enemy in reference to it."[423] This party, the size of which is not known, probably followed much the same route as Lieutenant Turner and Robert Early had done in their earlier reconnaissance before dark. As these Confederate scouts clambered up the rocky, wooded eastern crest of Culp's Hill, their advance was heard by the 7th Indiana's extreme right picket post, which was manned by Sergeant William Hussey and Privates Harshberger and Odell of Company B. One account relates that the Union pickets heard a noise "as of men moving cautiously in the timber some distance to their right. As they advanced to investigate, before the enemy discovered them, they got behind some boulders, permitting the officer leading to pass them, when Sergeant Hussey dashed out and seized the officer, while Harshberger and Odell fired on the advancing body of troops. Other members of the company running up, poured in such a rapid fire that the enemy turned and fled in the direction of Rock Creek, where Johnson's division lay. Some prisoners were captured in that night's encounter."[424]

The surprised Confederate scouts quickly returned and reported to Johnson that "This party, on nearing the summit, was met by a superior force of the enemy, which succeeded in capturing a portion of the reconnoitering party, the rest of it making its escape."[425] Since Johnson had orders from Ewell to seize the hill only if it were unoccupied, he held his division where it was. Thus the Confederates lost their last opportunity to advance and follow up the day's victory.

It is interesting to speculate what might have happened if Johnson's reconnoitering party had climbed Culp's Hill a bit farther to the south and so avoided contact with the 7th Indiana's last picket post. They would not have seen any other Union troops until they passed over the crest of Culp's Hill and by chance stumbled upon the rear of the Iron Brigade, or emerged from the woods on the edge of the hill and seen the campfires of all the Union troops on or near Cemetery Hill. This information might well have been enough for Johnson to move forward and make a rare night attack to seize the hill. If he did do so, the whole nature of the battle would have been changed—Johnson would have enjoyed an initial advantage, but would have been counterattacked in the morning by Williams and the V Corps when it came up, and this in turn would have led Lee to commit Longstreet's Corps on the army's left rather than the right, if he did not withdraw from the field altogether. Thus the course of the battle was changed by the alertness of only three men of the 7th Indiana regiment.

Despite the report that Culp's Hill was now occupied by the enemy, Johnson could still have advanced, or at least moved closer to the hill and sought advice from Ewell. Whatever inclination he might have had to do this was extinguished by a dispatch his scouts intercepted as they returned from Culp's Hill at about 0100. The message, which had been sent to Slocum by Major General George Sykes at 2400 states that the V Corps was encamped at Bonnaughton (Bonneville) and would resume its march at 0400.[426] This town was located on the Hanover Road a scant four miles east of Johnson's position. The general would do well just to stay put and defend the army's left flank.

The sudden appearance and repulse of Johnson's scouting party on Culp's Hill caused the Union troops there to be nervously alert for the rest of the night. Their anxiety was triggered at about 0100 when a member of Company K, 7th Indiana, had a nightmare and began screaming with horrible yells. His cries aroused all the troops in the vicinity including Colonel Rufus Dawes of the 6th Wisconsin. Dawes groggily jumped up and ordered his command to "fall in!" Before long "a heavy fire of musketry broke out from along the whole line of men."[427] The historian of the 7th Indiana wrote that, "a comrade of Company K was seized by a violent attack of nightmare, followed by yells that would have made a wild Comanche ashamed of himself. The sleepers along the line to our left, extending to several regiments, were roused by it, and in their half-waked condition taking it to be a charge by the enemy, sprang for their guns—many leaping over the breastworks and charging down the hill; others, but few, however, charging as vigorously to the rear. Order was soon restored, and quiet again reigned supreme."[428]

While Johnson's division was still moving into position east of Rock Creek, and before Johnson sent out the reconnoitering party just described, Ewell had a surprise visitor at his headquarters[429]—none other than Robert E. Lee himself, whom Ewell had not seen face to face since before the campaign had started. As historian Harry Pfanz so succinctly put it, "They had much to discuss.[430]

Rodes and Early were both present at the meeting and Early later wrote a detailed account of it: "I found General Lee, himself and Rodes in the porch, or, rather, I should say arbor, attached to the house already mentioned. No one else was there, and at that time all idea of advancing that night against the heights beyond Gettysburg for the purpose of attack had been abandoned, as it was then after sunset. I was soon given to understand that General Lee's purpose was to ascertain our condition, what we knew of the enemy and his position, and what we could probably do next day. It was evident from the first that it was his purpose to attack the enemy as early as possible next day—at daylight, if practicable. This was a proposition the propriety of which was so apparent that there was not the slightest discussion or difference of opinion upon it. It was a point taken for granted."[431]

After the three Second Corps generals described the conditions on their front, Lee asked, "Can't you, with your Corps, attack on this flank at daylight tomorrow?" Early replied first, and argued at length that an attack would be easier to make on the other end of the Union line: "The purport of what I said was, that the ground over which we would have to advance on our flank was very rugged and steep; that the enemy was then evidently concentrating and fortifying in our immediate front, and by morning would probably have the greater part of his force concentrated on that flank and the position strongly fortified, as ours were the only troops then confronting him in close proximity; that we could not move through the town in line of battle, and would therefore have to go on the left of the town right up against Cemetery Hill and the rugged hills on the left of it; and that the result of an attack there might be doubtful, but if successful it would inevitably be at very great loss. I then called General Lee's attention to the Round Tops, the outline of which we could see, though dusk was approaching, and suggested that those heights must evidently command the enemy's position and render it untenable; and I also called his attention to the more practicable nature of the ascents on that side of the town, adding the suggestion that the attack could be made on that side, and from our right flank, with better chances of success."[432]

When Ewell and Rodes both agreed with Early, Lee posed the suggestion that, "Then perhaps I had better draw you around towards my right, as the line will be very long and thin if you remain here, and the enemy may come down and break through it?" Early again replied first, and stated that his men were very much elated by their victory: "I knew what a damper it would be to their enthusiasm to be withdrawn from the position they had gained by fighting, as it might appear to them as if a reverse had occurred somewhere and we had not gained much of a victory after all." He was also concerned about leaving his wounded men behind. Lastly, he argued that his position on the left of the town was not a bad one defensively: "On that part of the line it was more difficult for the enemy to come down from the heights to attack him, as difficult as the latter would have been." On these points Ewell and Rodes disagreed, and each put forward arguments of his own.[433]

Lee was persuaded by the arguments of the three Second Corps generals and let the corps remain in its advanced position on the left of the town, at least for the moment. He would have been better advised, though, to have withdrawn it in order to consolidate his line on Seminary Ridge. The Second Corps as posted was simply too far forward, and liable to counterattack by the enemy, who clearly had the advantage of interior lines in his famous "fishhook" position. Nor did Early actually have that many wounded who needed to be moved. In addition, all his prisoners had already been moved towards Cashtown, and most of his trains had not been moved east of Seminary Ridge.

Lee's earlier discussion with Longstreet makes it clear that he, too, had his fighting blood up, and he was not about to abandon the field by withdrawing to Cashtown or any other location. The foremost question on his mind was where best to attack on the next day. Ewell and his subordinates argued strongly that this should not be done on the left. Lee's only other option was on the right, since Cemetery Hill with all its artillery looked very uninviting. At one point he was heard to say, "Well, if I attack from my right, Longstreet will have to make the attack. Longstreet is a very good fighter when he gets into position and gets everything ready, but he is so slow."[434]

Lee apparently left this meeting still undecided as to where he should attack the next day. He was concerned that Ewell and his generals preferred that Longstreet make the next day's attack on the right, but Longstreet had already stated his opinion that it was better to make a turning movement than another attack. At length he decided that he would need to withdraw the Second Corps from the left, unless Ewell felt that he could carry the Union line opposite him. An hour or two after dark he sent his aide Major Charles Marshall to tell Ewell that "he intended to move Longstreet around the enemy's left and draw Hill after him, directing General Ewell to prepare to follow the latter, "unless Ewell could persuade him otherwise." Marshall had difficulty locating Ewell's headquarters in the dark, and was lost for awhile until he by chance ran into Major Harry Gilmor, who was serving as Ewell's acting provost marshall. Marshall delivered his message, and had to wait for quite awhile for a reply. Ewell sent for Early to discuss the situation, and the two rode forward to survey Cemetery Hill, despite the darkness. At length Marshall stated that he needed to return Ewell's reply to Lee; Ewell decided to accompany the Colonel back to Lee's headquarters and consult with the commander himself.[435]

The two officers rode back together to Lee's headquarters, which were then set up near the Seminary. Ewell met privately with Lee, and neither officer recorded their conversation, so it is difficult to determine what the course of the discussion was. Ewell probably continued his plea to maintain his corps on the ground he had won. He also probably brought up the intelligence that Lieutenant Turner and Robert Early had brought in, that Culp's Hill was not occupied by the enemy. If Johnson had by then occupied Culp's Hill as Ewell hoped, his division and Early's should be able to force the Yankees to abandon Cemetery Hill. His arguments won out, and Lee permitted him to hold his troops where they were. Ewell left the meeting under the impression that "General Lee had determined to suspend all offensive operations until General Longstreet's arrival, which was momentarily expected." On which wing the army would attack, would be decided in the morning.[436]

As soon as Ewell returned to his headquarters, he sent orders for Hays "to make a reconnaissance of the ground between my situation and that of the enemy." Hays, who then had his regiments drawn up in the town, received his instructions at midnight and carried out his reconnaissance without much opposition. As a result of it, he moved his brigade forward at 0200 to an open field southeast of the city (now the site of the Gettysburg Middle School).[437]

Ewell also at once sent Lieutenant Turner to Johnson with a direct order to occupy Culp's Hill if he had not already done so. Turner was surprised to find Johnson's command still posted north of the Hanover Road. Johnson had not taken Culp's Hill or even attempted to do so, nor had he reported his actions to Ewell. All Johnson could do for the moment was ready his troops to move on Culp's Hill at daylight. He did, though, send Turner back to Ewell with the message his scouts had intercepted from General Sykes.[438]

Thus, Lieutenant Turner was given the awkward task of telling Ewell that Johnson had not carried out his mission, and that the enemy's lines on his front were going to be heavily reinforced in the morning. Johnson also stated that he would refrain from attacking the position "until he had received notice of the fact that the enemy were in possession of the hill" and Ewell sent him further orders. Ewell's reaction to this situation is not recorded. All he wrote in his battle report was "Day was now breaking, and it was too late for any change of plans." At about that time he also received a directive from Lee "to delay my attack until I heard General Longstreet's guns open on the right."[439] The action of the first day was now over.

Ewell has been roundly criticized by a number of historians in both the last century and this for being indecisive about ordering a final attack on Cemetery Hill to complete the Confederate victory of the first day at Gettysburg. However, close enough analysis of the situation, as presented in this study, shows that Ewell did not hesitate, but made a clear decision not to attack, based on Lee's discretionary orders and the facts of the situation as it developed—he was promised no cooperation from Hill, two of Early's brigades had to be detailed to watch his left flank, and Johnson arrived too late to be of use. Had Johnson come up about two hours sooner, Ewell would probably have put him into action at Culp's Hill. But as the situation developed, Ewell acted decisively by not attacking. Several historians have correctly pointed out that the Confederates needed to have pushed their attack on Cemetery Hill by 1730 or 1800 in order to have any chance of success. After that hour the Union troops were reformed there, and there were too many new Union troops on the field to allow a Confederate success after 1800. The general who failed to drive the Confederates forward at the opportune hour was not Ewell, or even Hill, but Lee himself, as historians Edwin B. Coddington and Alan T. Nolan have rightly observed.[440]

If Jackson Had Been Present

Much has been made of the belief that the course of the battle would have gone differently had Stonewall Jackson been present on the field. Numerous Lee partisans who sought to blame Ewell or Longstreet or Stuart for the loss of the battle rather than Lee himself, felt this way. So apparently did Lee himself. After the war he held several conversations about the battle with William Allan, one time ordnance officer for the Second Corps. In one of these discussions he told Allan that he felt "if Jackson had been there he [Lee] would have succeeded."[441] On another occasion Lee told Rev. J. William Jones and Professor James J. White in his Lexington office, "using an emphasis I cannot forget, and bringing his hand down on the table with a force that made things rattle, 'If I had had Stonewall Jackson at Gettysburg, I would have won that fight, and a complete victory there would have given us Washington and Baltimore, if not Philadelphia, and would have established the independence of the Confederacy.'"[442]

There is no question that Jackson's absence was severely felt by many of the men on the field, especially in view of Ewell's reluctance to move against Cemetery Hill late in the day. The feelings of Private Gorman of the 2nd North Carolina on this issue have already been cited.[443] J.A. Stikeleather of the 4th North Carolina of the same brigade wrote soon after the battle, "The simplest soldier in the ranks felt it. But, timidity in the commander that stepped into the shoes of the fearless Jackson prompted delay, and all night long the busy axes from tens of thousands of busy hands on that crest rang out clearly on the night air, and bespoke the preparation the enemy were making for the morrow."[444]

Jackson's absence was even more keenly felt by his former officers. The feelings of Captain J.P. Smith and Major Henry Kyd Douglas have already been cited in this chapter.[445] Late on 1 July Brigadier General Harry Hays urged Jubal Early to move against Culp's Hill, and Early even agreed that this objective "should be occupied on the spot." Nevertheless, he decined to move because Early had ordered him not to move beyond the town. Early reportedly turned away from Hays and muttered, "If Jackson were on the field, I could act on the spot."[446] After the battle Brigadier General John B. Gordon wrote, "No soldier in a great crisis ever wished more ardently for a deliverer's hand than I wished for one hour of Jackson when I was ordered to halt. Had he been there, his quick eye would have caught at a glance the entire situation, and instead of halting me he would have urged me forward and have pressed the advantage to the utmost, simply notifying General Lee that the battle was on and he had decided to occupy the heights."[447]

If Jackson had been in command of the Second Corps during the campaign, there is certainly no guarantee the course of the invasion would have gone the same way that it did. Assuming the course of the campaign and the opening of the battle went the same, how might Jackson's presence have altered the course of the battle? It is possible that he might have assisted Rodes to control his division more effectively. The greatest effect of his presence, though, would have been that Hill would have retained command of the Light Division. As such Hill would have opened the battle with more troops than Heth had available, and Jackson certainly would not have held the troops that constituted Pender's division out of action all morning. Jackson's presence on the field during the morning, though, would not necessarily have guaranteed a quicker or more decisive Confederate victory at that time. Jackson was often at his worst when conducting a meeting engagement, as he showed at Kernstown and the early stages of Cedar Mountain. He could also be impetuous in his attacks as he demonstrated at Port Republic. He was more often at his best when he had time to analyze the enemy's position and strike it at its weak point, as he did at Winchester and Chancellorsville. In this regard he would probably have made more of an effort to break Doubleday's right flank than Ewell did.

The ultimate question is whether or not Jackson would have taken Cemetery Hill at the end of the day's fighting. Every indication is that he was aggressive enough to at least make the attempt—witness his rapid maneuvers during the Valley and 2nd Bull Run Campaigns, and his suggestions to counterattack McClellan after Antietam and Burnside after Fredericksburg. Jackson would probably have disregarded Smith's concerns about the approach of more Union troops from the left, or at least left only a regiment with some cavalry to watch that front. He then could have used almost all of Early's command to move promptly against Culp's Hill and/or East Cemetery Hill. This rapid a movement would have brought support from Pendleton, Perrin and Lane on the right, and O'Neal and Ramseur in the center, all of whom were waiting for someone else to make the first move.

Jackson would probably have made an attempt to capture Cemetery or Culp's Hill, but if he would have succeeded is another question. As already noted, such an attack would have had to be made as a continuation of the afternoon's success, so as not to lose any forward momentum or allow the defenders time to reform. Wargaming and the example of Hays' attack on East Cemetery Hill on 2 July shows that the best way for the Confederates to attack in this quarter was southeastward towards Stevens' Knoll, along the western fringe of the woods on northern Culp's Hill, which was not held at this time. Whether Jackson would have instinctively or accidentally discovered this approach will never be known. If he would have made an attempt to seize Culp's Hill, which he surely would have, he certainly would have taken a large step in the right direction.

General Ewell was roundly criticized, particularly in the years immediately following the battle, for not pushing on to attack Cemetery Hill on the evening of 1 July.[448] More recent scholarship has been more kind to him. It is agreed that Ewell was not as aggressive as Jackson, but he was by no means "indecisive" at Gettysburg on 1 July. Lee gave him discretionary orders to attack Cemetery and/or Culp's Hill, and Ewell responded by reading the situation as best he could and not pushing the attack. If anyone was guilty of not acting decisively on the evening of 1 July, it was Lee for not being more forceful in his commands to Pendleton, Hill and Ewell.[449] Lee himself perhaps recognized this when he told his cousin Cassius Lee after the war, "Ewell was a fine officer, but would never take the responsibility of exceeding his orders, and having been ordered to Gettysburg, he would not go farther and hold the heights beyond the town."[450]

Most historians are in agreement that a Confederate attack on Cemetery Hill before 1700 or 1730 (about the time that Hancock arrived) would have had the best chance for success. John B. Bachelder, the first great historian of the battle, wrote, "There is no question but what a combined attack on Cemetery Hill made within one hour would have been successful."[451] General Winfield Hancock felt the same way, and wrote in 1878, "In my opinion, if the Confederates had continued the pursuit of General Howard on the afternoon of the 1st July at Gettysburg, they would have driven him over and beyond Cemetery Hill."[452]

However, Federal artillery commander Henry J. Hunt in the 1880s wrote succinctly that, "In fact an assault by the Confederates was not practicable before 5:30 p.m. and after that the position was perfectly secure. For the first time that day the Federals had the advantage of position, and sufficient troops and artillery to occupy it, and Ewell would not have been justified in attacking without the positive orders of Lee, who was present, and wisely abstained from giving them."[453] Confederate artillery commander Colonel E.P. Alexander was in basic agreement with Hunt when he wrote, "I think any attack we could have made that afternoon would have failed."[454] The Confederate troops were simply too disorganized in their victory to push on immediately against Cemetery Hill at the moment of its greatest vulnerability. What may have saved the Union position there was perhaps the same factor that caused the loss of so many captured troops—the town of Gettysburg. The town certainly caused many Union troops to be lost because of its confusing maze of streets and byways, but it was this same factor that slowed down and hindered the Confederate advance. Once the Southern regiments finished their mopping up operations in the town and began to form to assault Cemetery Hill, their moment of advantage had passed—it was too late in the day, the Union forces had rallied on the hill, and numerous Federal reinforcements were now on hand.

Lee's decision not to follow up his day's victory with a determined advance against Cemetery Hill may not have been as wise as Alexander suggests. The consensus of several historians and generals, just cited, was that the hill was vulnerable if Lee had pushed an attack by 1730 or so. Lee, however, failed to push this attack, and he left it up to his corps commanders to determine if their troops were in condition to make the assault. He, like them, was overly concerned with the high level of losses in many units, and no one seemed to have been fully aware of the full extent of the day's victory. In addition, the determined defense put up by the I Corps had sapped all the vigor from Hill's and Rodes' troops, and probably even Lee himself, for that day. As a Confederate officer of Rodes' division told Lieutenant Francis Wiggin of the 16th Maine in 1864, "The First Corps put up such a hell of a fight before Cemetery Ridge was reached that Ewell [Hill?] had got quite enough of it for the day."[455]

Numerous historians have also blamed General Stuart for causing Lee to head blindly into the battle without the benefit of sufficient cavalry screening or reconnaissance.[456] Lee himself felt that "Stuart's failure to carry out his instructions forced the battle of Gettysburg."[457] There is no question that Stuart's absence from the 1 July battle with the army's three best cavalry brigades severely affected the course of the battle; indeed, had Stuart and these troops been with Lee on 30 June, the decisive battle might not have even been fought at Gettysburg. But in recent years scholarship has tended to favor Stuart by arguing that he followed Lee's discretionary orders about his route into Pennsylvania as best he could, given the situation that he faced when he was about to cross the Potomac. If anyone was at fault for Stuart not being at Gettysburg on 1 July, it was Lee.[458] It has also been pointed out that Lee and Ewell both had sufficient cavalry available to use for scouting and screening purposes, but did not use it properly.[459]

Nor may it have been in Lee's best interest to drive the Yankees completely from the field. If this had happened, Meade would have enacted his prearranged Pipe Creek plan, and Lee would have been faced with the one prospect he did not want - Union troops occupying a strong and prepared defensive line. What Lee really wanted was to meet and defeat the Union army piecemeal in a series of meeting engagements, or to force the Yankees to attack him on a line of his own choice. In this regard Lee failed to follow his own campaign strategy when he stayed to fight Meade on 2 and 3 July. Such a battle was not one he was likely to win, especially if Meade had all his troops up, as he did by the afternoon of the 2nd.

Lee tried to rationalize his reasons for staying on the field after 1 July when he wrote the following in his campaign report, dated January 1864: "It had not been intended to deliver a general battle so far from our base unless attacked, but coming unexpectedly upon the whole Federal Army, to withdraw through the mountains with our extensive trains would have been difficult and dangerous. At the same time we were unable to await an attack, as the country was unfavorable for collecting supplies in the presence of the enemy, who could restrain our foraging parties by holding the mountain passes with local and other troops. A battle had, therefore, become in a measure unavoidable, and the success already gained gave hope of a favorable issue."[460]

Lee's arguments, though, are unconvincing. He had enough strength to cover the withdrawal of his trains past South Mountain, and would have been better advised to follow Longstreet's advice and shift to the south of Meade's position, or at least to pull Ewell back to northern Seminary Ridge that night. In the last analysis, Lee stayed to fight the next day for two reasons—it was simply too difficult for him to withdraw from a successful field, and he did not believe that Meade could concentrate his army as quickly as he did.[461]

It is not very often that an army loses the first day of a multi-day battle as badly as the Army of the Potomac did at Gettysburg on 1 July 1863, and then recovers to win the battle. The only other instance this happened during the Civil War was at Shiloh, and that was because Grant was heavily reinforced on 7 April 1862 by a fresh army under Buell. Meade's I and XI Corps fought their hearts out on 1 July, so much so that they were permanently wrecked, but the strategic decisions made by Buford, Reynolds, Howard and Hancock enabled their survivors to barely hold a corner of the field long enough for Meade to bring up the rest of his army faster than Lee ever anticipated.

Meade was no McClellan, and when he at last left his headquarters at Taneytown at 2200 on 1 July, he knew well that he had done his best to concentrate his army quickly and effectively on the field of battle that was recommended as a good one by several of his ablest subordinates. Well over half of his army was already at Gettysburg at nightfall, and another 2 ½ corps, plus the artillery reserve, would arrive first thing in the morning. The only significant unit not yet near the field was Sedgwick's large VI Corps, which was already in motion in one of the longest forced marches of the war, during which its men would cover from 32 to 35 miles in about 20 hours in order to reach the field late on the afternoon of 2 July.[462] Despite his army's severe loss on 1 July, Meade would eventually emerge victorious from the battle for two reasons—he had the guts not to order the abandonment of the good defensive position on Cemetery Hill, and he had confidence in the ability of his men to stay and fight, particularly since he knew he would have all his troops on the field, and that he would use them.

Meade, of course, did not know who would win the next day's battle, if there would even be one, when he approached the field just before midnight on 1 July.[463] He and his small party (two aides, an orderly, and the army's chief of artillery, Brigadier General Henry J. Hunt) rode forward so fast that they outstripped their civilian guide and several staff members. This quick ride was made in spite of all the II Corps infantry and artillery reserve cannons that clogged the road. It took only 57 minutes for the party to reach the II Corps headquarters a short distance south of Big Round Top.[464]

Meade then continued north on the Taneytown Road to Cemetery Hill, where he found General Howard at the gate house. Howard was concerned about being censured for the day's defeat, and was relieved to hear Meade say that he bore him no fault: "The first words he spoke to me were very kind. I believed that I had done my work well the preceding day; I desired his approval and so I frankly stated my earnest wish. Meade at once assured me that he imparted no blame; and I was as well satisfied as I would have been with positive praise from some other commanders."[465]

Soon Sickles and Slocum came up, and the generals began talking about the position of their troops and their prospects for success. Howard told Meade, "I am confident we can hold this position." Slocum supported him by saying, "It is good for defense." When Sickles agreed, "It is a good place to fight from, general!" Meade replied, "I am glad to hear you say so, gentlemen, for it is too late to leave it."[466]

The other generals soon parted to their own troops, and Meade walked across the road to East Cemetery Hill to view the position there. He then returned to the gate house and rode off with Generals Howard and Hunt and one aide to examine the line of Cemetery Ridge as far south as Little Round Top. When this was done, the party returned to Cemetery Hill and then rode out to Culp's Hill and Rock Creek.[467] The commanding general of the Army of the Potomac was now personally familiar with his chosen battlefield, and he was not displeased with what he saw.

Appendix I
Order of Battle

ARMY OF THE POTOMAC
Maj. Gen. GEORGE G. MEADE
Escort
Oneida (NY) Cavalry—Capt. Daniel P. Mann

ADVANCE (LEFT) WING
Maj. Gen. JOHN F. REYNOLDS

FIRST ARMY CORPS
Maj. Gen. ABNER DOUBLEDAY

GENERAL HEADQUARTERS
1st Maine Cavalry, Company L, Capt. Constantine Taylor

FIRST DIVISION
Brig. Gen. JAMES S. WADSWORTH

First Brigade
Brig. Gen. SOLOMON MEREDITH
Col. WILLIAM W. ROBINSON
 19th Indiana, Col. Samuel J. Williams
 24th Michigan:
  Col. Henry A. Morrow
  Capt. Albert M. Edwards
 2d Wisconsin:
  Col. Lucius Fairchild
  Maj. John Mansfield
  Capt. George H. Otis
 6th Wisconsin, Lieut. Col. Rufus R. Dawes.
 7th Wisconsin:
  Col. William W. Robinson
  Maj. Mark Finnicum

Second Brigade
Brig. Gen. LYSANDER CUTLER
 7th Indiana, Col. Ira G. Grover
 76th New York:
  Mai. Andrew J. Grover
  Capt. John E. Cook
 14th Brooklyn (84th New York), Col. Edward B. Fowler
 95th New York:

Col. George H. Biddle
Maj. Edward Pye
147th New York:
   Lieut. Col. Francis C. Miller
   Maj. George Harney
56th Pennsylvania (nine companies),
   Col. J. William Hofmann

SECOND DIVISION
Brig. Gen. JOHN C. ROBINSON
First Brigade
   Brig. Gen. GABRIEL R. PAUL
   Col. SAMUEL H. LEONARD
   Col. ADRIAN R. ROOT
   Col. RICHARD COULTER
   Col. PETER LYLE
16th Maine:
   Col. Charles W. Tilden
   Maj. Archibald D. Leavitt
13th Massachusetts:
   Col. Samuel H. Leonard
   Lieut. Col. N. Walter Batchelder
94th New York:
   Col. Adrian R. Root
   Maj. Samuel A. Moffett
104th New York, Col. Gilbert G. Prey
107th Pennsylvania:
   Lieut. Col. James MacThomson
   Capt. Emanuel D. Roath

Second Brigade
Brig. Gen. HENRY BAXTER
12th Massachusetts:
   Col. James L. Bates
   Lieut. Col. David Allen, Jr
83d New York (9th Militia), Lieut. Col. Joseph A. Moesch
97th New York:
   Col. Charles Wheelock
   Maj. Charles Northrup
11th Pennsylvania:
   Col. Richard Coulter
   Capt. Benjamin F. Haines
   Capt. John B. Overmyer
88th Pennsylvania:
   Maj. Benezet F. Foust
   Capt. Henry Whiteside
90th Pennsylvania:
   Col. Peter Lyle

Maj. Alfred J. Sellers
Col. Peter Lyle

THIRD DIVISION
Brig. Gen. THOMAS A. ROWLEY

Provost Guard
149th Pennsylvania Infantry, Company D:
    Capt. James Glenn

First Brigade
Col. CHAPMAN BIDDLE
    80th New York (20th Militia), Col. Theodore B. Gates
    121st Pennsylvania:
        Maj. Alexander Biddle
    142d Pennsylvania:
        Col. Robert P. Cummins
        Lieut. Col. A.B. McCalmont
    151st Pennsylvania:
        Lieut. Col. George F. McFarland
        Capt. Walter L. Owens
        Col. Harrison Allen

Second Brigade
Col. ROY STONE
Col. LANGHORNE WISTER
Col. EDMUND L. DANA
    143d Pennsylvania:
        Col. Edmund L. Dana
        Lieut. Col. John D. Musser
    149th Pennsylvania (nine companies):
        Lieut. Col. Walton Dwight
        Capt. James Glenn
    150th Pennsylvania:
        Col. Langhorne Wister
        Lieut. Col. H.S. Huidekoper
        Capt. Cornelius C. Widdis

ARTILLERY BRIGADE
Col. CHARLES S. WAINWRIGHT
    Maine Light, 2d Battery (B), Capt. James A. Hall
    Maine Light, 5th Battery (E):
        Capt. Greenleaf T. Stevens
        Lieut. Edward N. Whittier
    1st New York Light, Battery L: (Battery L 1st New York Light Attached):
        Capt. Gilbert H. Reynolds
        Lieut. George Breck
    1st Pennsylvania Light, Battery B, Capt. James H. Cooper
    4th United States, Battery B, Lieut. James Stewart

ELEVENTH ARMY CORPS
Maj. Gen. OLIVER O. HOWARD
Maj. Gen. CARL SCHURZ

GENERAL HEADQUARTERS
1st Indiana Cavalry, Companies I and K, Capt. Abram Sharra
17th Pennsylvania Cavalry, Company K
8th New York Infantry (one company), Lieut. Hermann Foerster

FIRST DIVISION
Brig. Gen. FRANCIS C. BARLOW
Brig. Gen. ADELBERT AMES

First Brigade
Col. LEOPOLD VON GILSA
41st New York (nine companies), Lieut. Col. Detleo von Einsiedel
54th New York:
  Maj. Stephen Kovacs
  Lieut. Ernst Both [?]
68th New York, Col. Gotthilf Bourry
153d Pennsylvania, Maj. John F. Frueauff

Second Brigade
Brig Gen. ADELBERT AMES
Col. ANDREW L. HARRIS
  17th Connecticut:
    Lieut. Col. Douglas Fowler
    Maj. Allen G. Brady
  25th Ohio:
    Lieut. Col. Jeremiah Williams
    Capt. Nathaniel J. Manning
    Lieut. William Maloney
    Lieut. Israel White
  75th Ohio:
    Col. Andrew L. Harris
    Capt. George B. Fox
  107th Ohio:
    Col. Seraphim Meyer
    Capt. John M. Lutz

SECOND DIVISION
Brig. Gen. ADOLPH VON STEINWEHR

Provost Guard
29th New York Infantry (one company)

First Brigade
Col. CHARLES R. COSTER

134th New York, Lieut. Col. Allan H. Jackson
154th New York, Lieut. Col. D.B. Allen
27th Pennsylvania (nine companies), Lieut. Col. Lorenz Cantador
73d Pennsylvania, Capt. D.F. Kelley

Second Brigade
Col. ORLAND SMITH
33d Massachusetts, Col. Adin B. Underwood
136th New York, Col. James Wood, Jr
55th Ohio, Col. Charles B. Gambee
78d Ohio, Lieut. Col. Richard Long

THIRD DIVISION
Maj. Gen. CARL SCHURZ
Brig. Gen. ALEXANDER SCHIMMELFENNIG

First Brigade
Brig. Gen. ALEXANDER SCHIMMELFENNIG
Col. GEORGE VON AMSBERG
82d Illinois, Lieut. Col. Edward S. Salomon
45th New York:
  Col. George von Amsberg
  Lieut. Col. Adolphus Dobke
157th New York, Col. Philip P. Brown, Jr.
61st Ohio, Col. Stephen J. McGroarty
74th Pennsylvania: (nine companies)
  Col. Adolph von Hartung
  Lieut. Col. Alexander von Mitzel
  Capt. Gustav Schleiter
  Capt. Henry Krauseneck

Second Brigade
Col. WLADIMIR KRZYZANOWSKI
58th New York:
  Lieut. Col. August Otto
  Capt. Emil Koenig
119th New York:
  Col. John T. Lockman,
  Lieut. Col. Edward F. Lloyd
82d Ohio:
  Col. James S. Robinson
  Lieut. Col. David Thomson
75th Pennsylvania (nine companies):
  Col. Francis Mahler
  Maj. August Ledig
26th Wisconsin:
  Lieut. Col. Hans Boebel
  Capt. John W. Fuchs

ARTILLERY BRIGADE
Maj. THOMAS W. OSBORN
  1st New York Light, Battery I, Capt. Michael Wiedrich
  New York Light, 13th Battery, Lieut. William Wheeler
  1st Ohio Light, Battery I, Capt. Hubert Dilger
  1st Ohio Light, Battery K, Capt. Lewis Heckman
  4th United States, Battery G:
    Lieut. Bayard Wilkeson
    Lieut. Eugene A. Bancroft

FIRST CAVALRY DIVISION
Brig. Gen. JOHN BUFORD
First Brigade
Col. WILLIAM GAMBLE
  8th Illinois, Maj. John L. Beveridge
  12th Illinois (four cos.), Col. George H. Chapman
  3d Indiana (six cos.), Col. George H. Chapman
  8th New York, Lieut. Col. William L. Markell

Second Brigade
Col. THOMAS C. DEVIN
  Headquarters Guard 6th New York Cavalry, Co. L
  6th New York, (six companies) Maj. Wm. E. Beardsley
  9th New York: Col. William Sackett
  17th Pennsylvania (nine companies), Col. J. H. Kellogg
  3d West Virginia (two companies): Capt Seymour B. Conger,

Horse Artillery
  2d United States Battery A, Lieut. John H. Calef

ARMY OF NORTHERN VIRGINIA
General ROBERT E. LEE

Escort
39th Virginia Cavalry Battalion, Companies A and C

SECOND ARMY CORPS
Lieut. Gen. RICHARD S. EWELL

Escort
39th Virginia Cavarly Battalion, Co. B

EARLY'S DIVISION
Maj. Gen. JUBAL A. EARLY
Hays' Brigade
Brig. Gen. HARRY T. HAYS

5th Louisiana:
  Maj. Alexander Hart
  Capt. T.H. Biscoe
6th Louisiana, Lieut. Col. Joseph Hanlon
7th Louisiana, Col. D.B. Penn
8th Louisiana:
  Col. T.D. Lewis
  Lieut. Col. A. de Blanc
  Maj. G.A. Lester
9th Louisiana (nine companies), Col. Leroy A. Stafford

Smith's Brigade
Brig. Gen. WILLIAM SMITH
  31st Virginia, Col. John S. Hoffman
  49th Virginia, Lieut. Col. J. Catlett Gibson
  52d Virginia, Lieut. Col. James H. Skinner

Hoke's Brigade
Col. ISAAC E. AVERY
  6th North Carolina, Maj. S. McD. Tate
  21st North Carolina, Col. W.W. Kirkland
  57th North Carolina, Col. A.C. Godwin

Gordon's Brigade
Brig. Gen. J.B. GORDON
  13th Georgia, Col. James M. Smith
  26th Georgia, Col. E.N. Atkinson
  31st Georgia, Col. Clement A. Evans
  38th Georgia, Capt. William L. McLeod
  60th Georgia, Capt. W.B. Jones
  61st Georgia, Col. John H. Lamar

Artillery
Lieut. Col. H.P. Jones
  Charlottesville (Virginia) Artillery, Capt. James McD. Carrington
  Courtney (Virginia) Artillery Capt. W.A. Tanner
  Louisiana Guard Artillery, Capt. C.A. Green
  Staunton (Virginia) Artillery, Capt. A.W. Garber

RODES' DIVISION
Maj. Gen. R.E. RODES

Daniel's Brigade
Brig. Gen. JUNIUS DANIEL
  32d North Carolina (nine companies), Col. E.C. Brabble
  43rd North Carolina:
    Col. T.S. Kenan
    Lieut. Col. W.G. Lewis
  45th North Carolina (eight companies):
    Lieut. Col. S.H. Boyd
    Maj. John R. Winston

Capt. A.H. Gallaway
Capt. J.A. Hopkins
53d North Carolina, (nine companies) Col. W.A. Owens
2d North Carolina Battalion (seven companies):
Lieut. Col. H.L. Andrews
Capt. Van Brown

Doles' Brigade

Brig. Gen. GEORGE DOLES
4th Georgia:
Lieut. Col. D.R.E. Winn
Maj. W.H. Willis
12th Georgia, Col. Edward Willis
21st Georgia, (nine companies) Col. John T. Mercer
44th Georgia:
Col. S.P. Lumpkin
Maj. W.H. Peebles

Iverson's Brigade

Brig. Gen. ALFRED IVERSON
5th North Carolina:
Capt. Speight B. West
Capt. Benjamin Robinson
12th North Carolina, Lieut. Col. W.S. Davis
20th North Carolina:
Lieut. Col. Nelson Slough
Capt. Lewis T. Hicks
23d North Carolina:
Col. D.H. Christie
Capt. William, H. Johnston

Ramseur's Brigade

Brig. Gen. S.D. RAMSEUR
2d North Carolina:
Maj. D.W. Hurtt
Capt. James T. Scales
4th North Carolina, Col. Bryan Grimes
14th North Carolina:
Col. R. Tyler Bennett
Maj. Joseph H. Lambeth
30th North Carolina:
Col. Francis M. Parker
Maj. W.W. Sillers,

O'Neal's Brigade

Col. E.A. O'NEAL
3d Alabama (eleven companies), Col. C.A. Battle
5th Alabama, Col. J.M. Hall
6th Alabama (twelve companies):
Col. J.N. Lightfoot

Capt. M.L. Bowie
12th Alabama. Col. S.B. Pickens
26th Alabama, Lieut. Col. John C. Goodgame

Artillery
Lieut. Col. THOMAS H. CARTER
Jeff Davis (Alabama) Artillery, Capt. W.J. Reese
King William (Virginia) Artillery, Capt. W.P. Carter
Morris (Virginia) Artillery, Capt. R.C.M. Page
Orange (Virginia) Artillery, Capt. C.W. Fry

THIRD ARMY CORPS
Lieut. Gen. AMBROSE P. HILL

HETH'S DIVISION
Maj. Gen. HENRY HETH
Brig. Gen. J.J. PETTIGREW

First Brigade
Brig. Gen. J.J. PETTIGREW
Col. J.K. MARSHALL
11th North Carolina, Col, Collett Leventhorpe
26th North Carolina:
    Col. Henry K. Burgwyn, Jr.
    Capt. H.C. Albright
47th North Carolina, Col. G.H. Faribault
52d North Carolina:
    Col. J.K. Marshall
    Lieut. Col. Marcus A. Parks

Second Brigade
Col. J.M. BROCKENBROUGH
40th Virginia:
    Capt. T.E. Betts
    Capt, R.B. Davis
47th Virginia (nine companies), Col. Robert M. Mayo
55th Virginia (eleven companies), Col. W.S. Christian
22d Virginia Battalion (six companies), Maj. John S. Bowles

Third Brigade
Brig. Gen. JAMES J. ARCHER
Col. B.D. FRY
13th Alabama, Col. B.D. Fry
5th Alabama Battalion (four companies), Maj. A.S. Van de Graaff
1st Tennessee (Provisional Army), Maj. Felix G. Buchanan
7th Tennessee, Lieut. Col. S.G. Shepard
14th Tennessee, Capt. B.L. Phillips

Fourth Brigade
Brig. Gen. Joseph R. Davis

2d Mississippi (eleven companies), Col. J.M. Stone
11th Mississippi, Col. F.M. Green
42d Mississippi, Col. H.R. Miller
55th North Carolina, Col. J.K. Connally

Artillery

Lieut, Col. John J. Garnett
Donaldsonville (Louisiana) Artillery, Capt. V. Maurin
Huger (Virginia) Artillery, Capt. Joseph D. Moore
Lewis (Virginia) Artillery, Capt. John W. Lewis
Norfolk Light Artillery Blues, Capt. C.R. Grandy

PENDER'S DIVISION

Maj. Gen. WILLIAM D. PENDER

First Brigade

Col. ABNER PERRIN
  1st South Carolina (Provisional Army)
    Maj. C.W. McCreary
  1st South Carolina Rifles, Capt. William M. Hadden (Not Present 1 July)
  12th South Carolina, Col. John L. Miller
  13th South Carolina, Lieut. Col. B.T. Brockman
  14th South Carolina, Lieut. Col. Joseph N. Brown

Second Brigade

Brig. Gen. JAMES H. LANE
  7th North Carolina:
    Capt. J. McLeod Turner
    Capt. James G. Harris
  18th North Carolina, Col. D. Barry
  28th North Carolina
    Col. S.D. Lowe
    Lieut. Col. W.H.A. Speer
  33rd North Carolina Col. C.M. Avery
  37th North Carolina, Col. W.M. Barbour

Third Brigade

Brig. Gen. EDWARD L. THOMAS
  14th Georgia
  35th Georgia
  45th Georgia
  49th Georgia, Col. S.T. Player

Fourth Brigade

Brig. Gen. A.M. SCALES
Lieut. Col. G.T. GORDON
Col. W. LEE J. LOWRANCE
  13th North Carolina:
    Col. J.H. Hyman
    Lieut. Col. H.A. Rogers

16th North Carolina, Capt. L.W. Stowe
22d North Carolina, Col. James Conner
34th North Carolina:
  Col. William Lee J. Lowrance
  Lieut. Col. G.T. Gordon
38th North Carolina:
  Col. W.J. Hoke
  Lieut. Col. John Ashford

Artillery
Maj. WILLIAM T. POAGUE
  Albemarle (Virginia) Artillery, Capt. James W. Wyatt
  Charlotte (North Carolina) Artillery, Capt. Joseph Graham
  Madison (Mississippi) Light Artillery, Capt. George Ward
  Virginia Battery, Capt. J.V. Brooke

ARTILLERY RESERVE
Col. R. LINDSAY WALKER

McIntosh's Battalion
Maj. D.G. McINTOSH
  Danville (Virginia) Artillery, Capt. R.S. Rice
  Hardaway (Alabama) Artillery, Capt. W.B. Hurt
  2d Rockbridge (Virginia) Artillery, Lieut. Samuel Wallace
  Virginia Battery, Capt. M. Johnson

Pegram's Battalion
Maj. W.J. PEGRAM
Capt. E.B. BRUNSON
  Crenshaw (Virginia) Battery
  Fredericksburg (Virginia) Artillery, Capt. E.A. Marye
  Letcher (Virginia) Artillery, Capt. T.A. Brander
  Pee Dee (South Carolina) Artillery, Lieut. William E. Zimmerman
  Purcell (Virginia) Artillery, Capt. Joseph McGraw

CAVALRY DETACHMENTS
1st Maryland Battalion:
  Maj. Harry Gilmor
  Maj. Ridgely Brown
17th Virginia, Col. W.H. French
35th Virginia Battalion, Lt. Col. E.V. White

Appendix II[1]

Unit	Number of Companies	Engaged Strength	Killed	Wounded	Missing	Total
Army of the Potomac		23,538				8955
I Corps	343	12,222	619	2950	2127	5798
1st Division (Wadsworth's)	109	3857	297	1224	624	2145[2]
2nd Division (Robinson's)	110	3248	91	616	983	1690
3rd Division (Rowley's)	119	4701	220	1023	509	1752
XI Corps	276	9439	203	1588	1493	3195[3]
1st Division (Barlow's)	89	2477	107	619	505	1231
2nd Division (VonSteinwehr's)	80	2894	56	231	317	604
3rd Division (Schurz's)	98	3109	133	684	659	1476
Army of Northern Virginia		28,348				6037
Second Corps (Ewell's)	615	13,475				
Rodes' Division	219	7873	598	1684	810	3092[4]
Early's Division	172	5460				710
Third Corps (Hill's)	575	14,524				
Heth's Division	165	7458	779	1930	627	3336[5]
Pender's Division	184	6315				1087

[1] The strength data is derived from *Regimental Strengths and Losses at Gettysburg* by John Busey and David G. Martin. Loss figures are based on OR 27.1.173-187 for Union forces and *The Gettysburg Death Roster* by Robert Krick, with some input on 1 July proportional losses from *Gettysburg Then and Now* by John Vanderslice. Division totals do not add up to stated corps totals because corps artillery units are not included in subtotals.

[2] 95% 1 July

[3] 94% 1 July

[4] 80% 1 July

[5] 50% 1 July

Note: Corps composite engaged strength and casualty figures also include artillery and headquarters units not individually listed.

Appendix III

Topographical

The primary reason a great battle arose at Gettysburg was the great road net—eleven in all—that radiated from the town and drew the troops of the two opposing sides to it. Buford was sent to hold the town precisely because it was such an important road hub, and the roads played a key part in the battle by allowing Ewell to bring in Early's division on Howard's flank, and by aiding Meade to concentrate his army there quickly at the end of the day and early next morning. The only negative effect of the road network was the fact that only one roadway extended to Cashtown and Chambersburg. About ¾ of Lee's army had to travel over it. Invariably a traffic jam developed, which was at its height on the afternoon of 1 July and delayed much-needed Confederate reinforcements from arriving on the field.

The roads that approached Gettysburg were as follows, going clockwise from the north:

The Carlisle Road, from the north, also called the Carlisle Pike. It forked a mile north of the town (all distances are given from the town square, or "diamond"). The Carlisle Pike swung slightly to the east from north, while the Newville Road headed on a north-northwest course.

The Harrisburg Road, from the northeast, had a juncture with the Carlisle Pike three blocks north of the town square.

The Hunterstown Road, also from the northeast, ran parallel to and about 3/4 mile east of the Harrisburg Road until it met the York Pike 1/4 mile east of Rock Creek (3/4 mile east of the town).

The York Pike, from the east northeast. It united with the Hanover Road on the eastern outskirts of the town.

The Hanover Road, from the east southeast, ran on an east-west course for its final 3/4 mile stretch between Rock Creek and the town.

The Baltimore Pike, from the southeast, united with the Emmitsburg Road near Cemetery Hill, 1/2 mile south of the town, and ran on a north-south course from there to the town square.

The Taneytown Road, from the south, became Washington Street when it entered the town.

The Emmitsburg Road, from the southwest, joined the Baltimore Pike 1/2 mile south of the town square, as already noted.

The Hagerstown Road, from the west southwest, joined the Chambersburg Pike at the western edge of town. It was also known as the Fairfield or Millerstown Road.

The Chambersburg Pike, from the northwest, joined the Fairfield Road at the western edge of town, as noted. It is also known as the Cashtown Road.

The Mummasburg Road, from the northwest, met the Carlisle Pike at its intersection with the Harrisburg Road, three blocks north of the town square.

At the time of the battle there was a railroad spur that ran to Gettysburg from Hanover. It did not play any role in the battle other than its physical effect on the terrain. It was not until after the battle that the railroad became important for bringing in supplies and helping to remove the dead and wounded. The line approached the town from the northeast, on the north side of the York Pike, but did not run on as straight a course as the roadway. The railroad line ended in the northern section of the town, two blocks west of the passenger railroad station, which was located on Carlisle Street. The railroad line west of the town had been laid out and graded before the war, but no rails were laid there before the battle. The line ran on the north side of the Chambersburg Pike at a distance varying from 150 to 300 yards, and averaged 200 yards.

Both the finished and unfinished portions of the railroad were used as roadways by the troops of both sides during the course of the battle. The greatest effect of the railroad line on the fighting was the fact that extended cuts had been made through the ridges west of town in order to keep the rail line level. The cuts were about 20 to 30 feet in width, and varied in length and height depending on the nature of the ridges through which they passed. The greatest of the cuts was that in Seminary Ridge (called the eastern cut in the text). It ran for some 200 yards and had steep sides running to a height of about 30 feet on its northern face. It was at the western entrance of this cut that Stewart's Union battery was posted during most of the afternoon.[1] A second railroad cut (called the middle cut in the text) was one quarter mile east of Seminary Ridge, through what will be called Eastern McPherson's Ridge in the text. It was about 100 yards long and about 15 feet in height.[2] It was in this cut that a large portion of Davis' brigade was captured at about 1100. About 300 yards west of this cut is a third cut (called the western cut in the text) through the main section of McPherson's Ridge. This cut is slightly shorter and lower than the middle cut. It was in here that Daniel's troops engaged Stone's during much of the afternoon. In addition, the 147th New York defended the rise on the northern side of the western cut during the morning's fighting.

The land around Gettysburg is basically slightly rolling farmland, with numerous ridges and a few high rocky hills. The highest two hills on the field, Big Round Top (close to 800 feet), and Wolf Hill (close to 700 feet) were on the periphery of the first day's field and so did not figure in the fighting. Four hills were well over 600 feet high. Cemetery Hill, which was almost totally devoid of trees, dominated the landscape immediately south of town and was perhaps the single most key point of the battle, since it provided a rallying point for the defeated Union troops at the close of the battle. Its highest point, just over 630 feet, was at the rear of the local cemetery. In general, Cemetery Hill is about 100 feet higher than the ground at its base. A section of the hill extends northeastward across the Baltimore Pike, and is called East Cemetery Hill. The

---

1 This is the railroad cut that was drastically altered by Gettysburg College in December 1991 following a controversial land trade with the battlefield park.
2 The depth of the middle railroad cut varied from 2 feet deep at the ends to 10-20 feet in the middle, Coddington, p. 267. Even so, the cut could not be seen from the fields directly to the south, Dawes, *Service with the Sixth Wisconsin Volunteers*, p. 167.

fields on the slopes of both walls were lined with stone walls, which added to their defensive value.

Culp's Hill, 1/2 mile to the east of Cemetery Hill, was about the same height but of quite different character, being covered with heavy woods and several large rock formations. It did not figure in the battle until late in the day when it was occupied by Wadsworth's division and a detachment of the 7th Indiana drove back scouts from Johnson's division.

Oak Hill, which was actually an extension of Seminary Ridge, will be discussed in a moment. The fourth hill over 600 feet, Little Round Top, was 2 1/2 miles south of town and did not figure in the day's fighting, except to be occupied by two regiments of Geary's division very late in the day.

There were a number of ridges on the field, all running in a north south direction, that played key roles in the day's fighting. West of Gettysburg there were four lines of ridges, each of slightly different character. All ran perpendicular to the Confederates' primary approach road, the Chambersburg Pike, and so gave the Union troops a "defense in depth" that appealed so much to Buford and Reynolds.

The closest ridge to the town was Seminary Ridge, named for the Lutheran Seminary that was located 3/4 due west of the town square. This ridge rose to a height of 500 feet in places, with a much steeper slope on its eastern side - which is not the direction the Confederates were attacking from. Its western slope, which did face the Confederate advance, was much less pronounced. Oak Hill, which was actually a northern extension of Seminary Ridge, rose to over 600 feet. Since it totally dominated the plain to the east, and also the fields to the southwest, it provided an excellent position for Rodes' artillery.

Seminary Ridge was covered by woods at several key locations. The extensive woods on northern Seminary Ridge (Oak Ridge) provided cover for Rodes' troops before they began their attack on Robinson's division. A large nameless woods that ran for 1/2 mile north of the eastern railroad cut gave considerable protection to Doubleday's right wing. It is called the Wills Woods in the text after the local farmer, James J. Wills, who owned most of it. The stretch of ridge near the Seminary had a more open woods, particularly opposite the Seminary building and the Schmucker House. The Seminary woods provided good defensive cover for the I Corps' final line of the day. Immediately south of the Fairfield Road was the Schultz Woods, where Gamble's dismounted troops fought Perrin's infantry at 1615. The McMillan Woods was another 1/2 mile to the south. It was occupied by Lane's brigade and Pendleton's artillery at the close of the day's action. During the battle Seminary Ridge saw extensive fighting all the way from Oak Hill to the Schultz Woods.

McPherson's Ridge was lower and more open than Seminary Ridge. It ran along the eastern side of Willoughby Run, and was about 1/2 mile to the west of Seminary Ridge, though it ran at a slight angle and joined Seminary Ridge at Oak Hill. The central portion of the ridge actually had two crests, a higher western crest, on which the McPherson farm was located (today all its buildings are gone except the barn), and a slightly lower eastern crest some 400 yards closer to town. For purposes of the text, the eastern crest will be called Eastern McPherson's Ridge, and the western or primary crest (as well as the solitary crest farther to the south) will be called McPherson's Ridge. There was a slight dip or swale between McPherson's Ridge and Eastern McPherson's Ridge, and a more pronounced swale between Eastern McPherson's Ridge and Seminary Ridge.

The key to the Union defensive position for most of the day was the woods south of the McPherson farm. Known popularly as McPherson's Woods, it actually belonged to John Herbst, and for this reason is called Herbst Woods in the text. (The only woods Edward McPherson[1] owned were north of the eastern railroad cut adjacent to James Wills' Woods). Herbst Woods was about 1/4 mile long (running from Willoughby Run to Eastern McPherson's Ridge) and 1/8 mile wide. Altogether it covered some five acres, and was much more open than today; it had little or no underbrush because of its use for pasturing. The ground within the woods was quite undulating, as the numerous troops who fought there came to find out. It had one high point in the middle of its northern side, and another at its southeastern corner, with a noticeable ravine in between.[2]

Herr Ridge ran about a mile to the west of McPherson's Ridge, but on a general more southwesterly course. It was named after the Tavern located on the northern end of the ridge at Chambersburg Pike. This ridge, which topped off at over 600 feet, dominated all the land to its east and west except for Oak Hill, 1 1/4 miles to the northeast of the tavern. Most of the ridge, particularly its crest, was open, and offered a superb position for the Confederate artillery; over 40 guns of which were positioned here for most of the day. There was an extensive woods a mile long and 1/6 mile wide on the ridge's eastern face, south of the Chambersburg Pike, that provided excellent cover for Heth's troops from 1130 to 1430.

The fourth ridge west of town, Knoxlyn Ridge, was 1 1/4 miles west of Herr Ridge (three miles west of the town square via the Chambersburg Pike). It was about 600 feet in height, with gentle and open slopes. It was located on the eastern side of Marsh Creek, and formed Buford's forward picket line at the beginning of the battle.

The most important ridge south of town was Cemetery Ridge, which ran southwards for two miles from Cemetery Hill to Little Round Top. It did not figure in the first day's battle except to be occupied by troops of the I, III and XII corps late in the day.

A long and open ridge ran northeastward from Benner's Hill, which was located 1/2 mile northeast of Culp's Hill. Johnson's division formed on this ridge at sunset. There were a number of other ridges in the battle area which will not be mentioned because they did not figure in the day's action.

The ground north of Gettysburg, where the XI Corps fought, featured open fields and flat or slightly undulating terrain. Its only high point was a small knoll a mile northeast of town, called Blocher's Knoll then but Barlow's Knoll now. It rose to a height of 540 feet, some 70 or so feet above the course of nearby Rock Creek.

The Gettysburg area was well watered by numerous creeks and their tributaries, but none were large enough to form significant military obstacles in the battlefield area. Rock Creek ran on a north-south course 1/2 mile to the east of Gettysburg, passing by the eastern base of Barlow's Knoll to the north of town and Culp's Hill to the south. None of its several east-west small tributaries were important militarily. The area to the

---

1 McPherson was a former editor of the *Pittsburgh Daily Times,* as well as a local politician of note. He was serving as the Congressman from the Gettysburg district at the time of the battle, see Tucker, *High Tide at Gettysburg,* p. 105.

2 See Tucker, *Hide Tide at Gettysburg,* p. 146, and Hadden, "The Deadly Embrace," *Gettysburg Magazine,* No. 5, p. 22, especially note 22.

west of Gettysburg was drained by Marsh Creek and its tributaries. Marsh Creek itself was some three miles west of town, and did not figure in the fighting except to witness some of the battle's opening shots. The stream that saw by far the most fighting during the day was Willoughby Run, which ran along the western base of McPherson's Ridge. Its banks were wooded in the area of Herbst Woods, and reasonably steep in some sections.[1]

The principal wooded areas on the field have already been mentioned. As noted, woods located on ridges usually helped strengthen defensive positions (Herbst, Schultz, Seminary, and Wills Woods) or offered cover for attacking forces[2] (woods on Herr Ridge and Oak Hill). The woods on the northern edge of Barlow's Knoll apparently did both at the same time, as they gave cover to both Gordon's attackers and Barlow's defenders. There were also a number of orchards in the battle area—significantly Blocher's (near Barlow's Knoll), Hagy's, McLean's, and Forney's (all near the Mummasburg Road), Spangler's (near the northern end of Willoughby Run), McPherson's (north of Herbst Woods), Herbst's and Harman's (southwest of Herbst Woods) and one north of the Seminary. These orchards did not offer any special advantage to defensive troops, though they are often mentioned in battle accounts and thus help locate troop positions and movements.

The countryside around Gettysburg was much more open than the terrain in Virginia where the two opposing armies had been fighting for the previous two years. This gave both sides greater fields of fire, a situation that caused special problems for the Union defense, which had only 11 batteries on the field against twice that many Confederate. The Union troops suffered from converging fire on both fronts during the day. Doubleday's guns were overwhelmed by Hill's on Herr Ridge and Rodes' on Oak Hill, and the XI Corps troops suffered from Rodes' guns on Oak Hill and Ewell's along the Harrisburg Road. The open fields of fire, though, also greatly aided the defensive lines, particularly Doubleday's last line on Seminary Ridge.

All this open farmland, then, gave an advantage to defensive troops by giving them a greater field of fire. In addition, attacking as well as retreating troops were often hindered by the many fences that lined the fields. There were some stone fences on Cemetery Hill and south of the Seminary that gave good cover to defensive troops, but most of the fences were wooden. These came in two varieties. Virginia worm (zigzag) fences could readily be knocked down by a band of pioneers, but post and slat fences (such as ran along the southside of the Chambersburg Pike) caused a serious hindrance to moving troops, as the 6th Wisconsin discovered in its charge against Davis' troops in the middle railroad cut.

The battlefield, of course, has suffered significant alterations since 1863. Most notable is the expansion of the town of Gettysburg, which today covers four times as much area as it did at the time of the battle. The northern, eastern and western approaches of the town were open except for scattered houses, and the area southwest of town (now a development) was all fields. There are also modern housing developments along the Harrisburg Road (where Early's artillery first formed) and south of Fairfield Road (where

1 See Hadden, "The Deadly Embrace," *Gettysburg Magazine*, No. 5, p. 27, note 41.
2 See Herdegun and Beaudet, *In the Bloody Railroad Cut at Gettysburg*, pp. 183-190

Lane advanced), not to mention extended commercial development, near the forks of
the Carlisle Pike, along the York Pike, and at spots (such as General Lee's Restaurant)
along the Chambersburg Pike. In addition, Pennsylvania (Gettysburg) College, located
at the northwest corner of the town, had only three buildings at the time of the battle,
and has greatly expanded since the war.[1] The Seminary has also added numerous
buildings. The battlefield park owns a small parcel of land where Coster's brigade fought
where there is a beautiful mural well worth seeing; however, this is not the entire Union
line here, and the town's expansion has covered the ground over which Early's men
attacked. But the most intensive development has been the extensive commercial building
south of the town (ironically, most of it intended to serve the tourists who come to visit
the battlefield). This makes it very difficult to study and appreciate the natural strength
of Cemetery Hill as the Union Army's final defensive position on 1 July. Another
significant alteration to the first day's battlefield is the recent and unforgivable drastic
alteration of the northern face of the eastern railroad cut carried out by Gettysburg
College.

A number of minor changes need to be mentioned for those who wish to visit and
study the field. At the time of the battle, the northwest crest of Barlow's Knoll was
totally wooded all the way to the creek. The Almshouse complex, where Barlow's men
attempted to rally 3/8 mile south of Barlow's Knoll, is no longer standing. Herbst Woods
was more open than today, and would have extended farther to the east. Today only the
McPherson barn remains to the north of Herbst Woods; McPherson's house, outbuilding
and apple orchard, all gone today, would have given a much different view of this part
of the Union line. Northern Doubleday Avenue has more trees lining it than would
have been there during the battle. The northern part of Baxter's line actually ran along
a stone wall (no longer extant) that angled towards the Mummasburg Road farther to
the west of Doubleday Avenue.

Despite all these changes and alterations to the battlefield scene, much of the battle
area still remains basically like it was in 1863. The National Battlefield Park owns and
protects most of the ground on which the heaviest fighting occurred; the significant
exceptions are at the Seminary (where most of the ground is fortunately preserved in
park like condition) and the final XI Corps line on the northern edge of town (now
lost to housing). But the Park does not by any means own all the ground on which the
troops of both sides marched and fought on 1 July. Most significant is its very limited
holdings on Herr Ridge (where most of Hill's Confederates formed prior to their attacks),
the ground east of Rock Creek (over which Early attacked), and the area to the left and
right of the Almshouse (over which the XI Corps fought and retreated). Hopefully much
of this line can be acquired by the Park under expanded boundary goals, before it suffers
further loss and development.

These somewhat limited Park holdings on the 1st day's field have noticeably affected
the location and placement of battlefield markers. The I Corps' forward line on
McPherson's and northern Seminary Ridges is well marked, but little note (besides a
few markers, mostly of batteries) is made of positions on the final I Corps line near the
Seminary. The positions of the attacking Confederate troops are very poorly marked,

1 Frassanito, *Gettysburg: A Journey in Time*, pp. 82-83.

primarily because the park does not own their jump off positions on Herr Ridge.[1] The pre-attack positions of Early's troops are also unmarked for the same reason. On the XI Corps' line, the forward position of Barlow's troops on Barlow's Knoll are well marked, but their secondary position near the Almshouse is not. The position of the monuments of Schimmelfennig's division along western Howard Avenue (between the Mummasburg Road and Carlisle Pike) is very deceptive and gives the impression that Howard had a continuous line here. Most of these troops were actually positioned farther to the south, on land not yet owned by the park. Since these regiments could not erect their markers on private land, they had to place them here on Howard Avenue on the edge of the Park's property. Thus it is very difficult today to get a true picture of the position of much of the XI Corps during the afternoon solely from the location of its regimental monuments.

---

1 See Martin, *Confederate Monuments at Gettysburg*, pp. 218-221, for suggested text and placing of missing Confederate markers on the first day's field. See pp.10-15 of the same work for a discussion of why there are so few Confederate regimental markers on the field.

Appendix IV

Chronological and Meteorological

One of the most frustrating aspects of attempting to study the battle is giving absolute times to events. Soldiers often lose track of time during the heat of battle, and an activity that seemed like a few minutes to one man may have seemed like an hour or more to another. Not everyone carried watches, and those who did, did not always keep them wound or accurate. To make matters worse, there was no such thing as standardized time; this was not initiated until after the war when the railroads found it necessary in order to keep to their schedules. In short, those who had watches were not necessarily in synchronization with anyone else.[1]

All we can be sure of, then, was that, by modern computation the sun rose on 1 July at 0436 and set at 1929.[2] Even this figure is compounded by the concept of actual "nautical twilight," the time at which an object can be seen at a distance of 400 yards. The beginning of Morning Nautical Twilight occurred at 0323 and the end of Evening Nautical Twilight was at 2003. The moon rose at 2008.[3]

It would be very convenient if everyone at the battle adjusted their time to that shown on the clock on the tower of the Adams County Courthouse in Gettysburg. This, however, did not happen, and perhaps fortunately so. One soldier of the 45th NY of the XI Corps, reported that the Courthouse clock said it was 1115 when his regiment arrived in town, but all other evidence is clear that this unit did not reach Gettysburg until about 1230.[4] Either the soldier's memory was wrong, or the courthouse clock was running over an hour slow.[5]

---

1 For an early discussion of this problem in general, see Beale, *The Statements of Time on July 1 at Gettysburg, Pa*, (Philadelphia: James Beale, 1897), reprinted in McLean, *Gettysburg Sources*, Vol. 3, pp. 38-72. See also Coddington, p. 692, n. 97.

2 Times are taken from the chart in Boatner, *The Civil War Dictionary*, p. 820, which in turn is drawn from the *American Nautical Almanac* for 1959; Boatner claims these times "are within a minute or two of what they were a century ago." Beale, "The Statements of Time on July 1 at Gettysburg," in *Gettysburg Sources*, Vol. 3, p. 41, gives sunrise on 1 July at 0425. The sun set on 2 July at 1923, according to John Day Smith, *The History of the Nineteenth Regiment of Maine Volunteer Infantry*, p. 73.

3 See a discussion of this issue in Boatner, *The Civil War Dictionary*, p. 821

4 *NYG*, p. 378.

5 See Chapter 7, Note 2.

It would also be useful to locate an account by someone who possessed a reasonably accurate watch and kept a chronolog of events. Unfortunately none readily exists, though it is sometimes possible to time the length of events by the reports of certain individual's watches. The longest chronolog apparently kept of the battle was by Ewell's topographical engineer, Jed Hotchkiss. However, not all of Hotchkiss' events can be identified, nor do historians all agree with those of other accounts. It can, though, be used to construct a relative order of events.[1]

1100	Firing of artillery by Hill
1130	Infantry firing by Hill
1200	Hill advances, enemy driven back
1220	Hill's artillery brisk on the right
1430	Early's artillery opens on the left
1515	Early's infantry attacks
1600	Early reforms
1630	Lee came up
1700	Early moved into the town

The best that can be done, then, is to establish set times for several key events during the day, and then relate everything else to them. The reader is advised not to take at face value a time given by any individual primary source, without first checking it against other known events for both relative and absolute time.

Buford deployed the main body of his command at 0800 in response to Major John Beveridge's report of Heth's advance.[2]

Heth stopped advancing his skirmishers at 0900 in order to form his line, and resumed his attack at 0930.[3]

The lead elements of the I Corps reached the Seminary area at or shortly after 1000,[4] and Reynolds was killed about 1030. The time of Reynolds' death is one of the key points of the day, and was placed as late as 1115 by some sources.[5]

The exact and even relative chronology of events during the "noontime lull" from 1130 to about 1330 is difficult to evaluate. The relative order of the arrival and deployment of the Union reinforcements at this time, as well as the timing of the artillery actions on McPherson's Ridge, is not at all clear. Nor is the time of Rodes' arrival, deployment and organization of his first attack clear. For purposes of the text Iverson's attack is placed at 1400; some place it up to an hour earlier.[6]

---

1 Hotchkiss, *Make Me a Map of the Valley*, pp. 156-157

2 *OR* 27.1.934 and Beveridge, "The First Gun at Gettysburg," in *Gettysburg Papers*, Vol. I, p. 173 (Illinois MOLUS, Vol. 2, p.91).

3 *OR* 27.2.637, see chapter 3, pages 82-83.

4 McLean, *Cutler's Brigade*, p. 57.

5 On the time of Reynolds' death see Coddington, p. 692, note 94. O.O. Howard placed Reynolds' death at 1115, *OR* 27.1.696. The account given in, Chapter 4, favors a time almost an hour earlier. Marshall Krolick favors a time shortly before 1100, "Gettysburg, the First Day," *Blue & Gray Magazine*, Vol. 5, No. 2 (Nov. 1987), p.16. Richard Shue estimates Reynolds was shot between 1035 and 1045, *Morning at Willoughby Run*, p. 221.

6 See Chapter VI, note 83; see also Coddington, p.286 and p. 694, note 1.

The same is true of the time of Early's arrival and attack. The text presents these as 1400 and 1500 respectively.[1]

The beginning of Heth's final attack is placed at 1430.[2] A number of sources are surprisingly in agreement that Pender's final attack occurred at 1600, and that the I Corps held out for about half an hour before withdrawing.[3]

The Union retreat to Cemetery was at its height, then, between 1630 and 1730. It is not clear when Hancock arrived to take charge there. He states in his own report that he arrived at 1500, but this was probably too early.[4] Other events and accounts place him on Cemetery Hill between 1700 and 1800.[5]

The weather on Tuesday, 30 June 1863, was overcast, with rain nearly all day at Chambersburg.[6] Wednesday, 1 July 1863 was cloudy with Cumulo-stratus clouds in the forenoon and cirro-stratus clouds in the afternoon. Professor Michael Jacobs of Gettysburg College noted that there was a gentle southern breeze of about 2 miles per hour, and recorded the following temperatures during the day: 72F at 0700, 76F at 1400, and 74F at 1900.[7] Dawn was clear, moist and warm.[8] Though there was no rain on the battlefield area itself, frequent showers to the south of Gettysburg, particularly in the morning, kept the roads there muddy.[9] The weather was also muggy that night with continuing local showers nearby. The full moon, which rose at 2008 as noted above, aided the placement of troops when it was able to break through the clouds.

---

1 See Chapter VII, pages 313-314. Lee places Early's arrival at 1430, *OR* 27.2.317.

2 See above Chapter VIII, p. 382.

3 See Chapter VIII, note 251.

4 *OR* 27.1.368.

5 Pfanz, *Gettysburg—Cemetery Hill and Culp's Hill,* p. 700, favors a time between 1600 and 1630, but see above, Chapter IX, note 83.

6 Lineback, "Extracts from a Civil War Diary," *Winston-Salem Sentinel,* 13 June 1914-3 April 1915, p. 55, quoted in Davis, *Boy Colonel of the Confederacy,* p. 296.

7 Professor Jacobs' notes, GNMP Collections; see also "Gettysburg Weather Reports," *Blue & Gray Magazine,* Vol. 5, No. 2 (Nov., 1987), p. 23; on the wind direction see *NYG,* p.29.

8 Vautier, *History of the Eighty-Eighth Pennsylvania Volunteers,* p. 105.

9 *OR* 27.1.482; Craft, *History of the One Hundred and Forty-First Regiment Pennsylvania Volunteers,* p. 115.

Appendix V

Medal of Honor Winners

A total of 59 Medals of Honor were awarded for bravery at the battle of Gettysburg. There were eight awarded for action on 1 July, twenty-four for 2 July, and twenty-seven for 3 July. The Medal of Honor winners for 1 July were as follows:

Name	Company/Regiment Brigade/Corps	Issued	Place of Birth
Sgt. Jefferson Coates	Co. H, 7th Wisconsin Infy. Meredith/ I	6/29/66	Grant Co.,WI
Sgt. Edward L. Gilligan*	Co. E, 88th Pennsylvania Infy. Baxter /I	4/30/92	Philadelphia, PA
Lt. Col. Henry S. Huidekoper	150th Pennsylvania Infy. Stone/XI	5/27/05	Meadville, PA
Capt. Francis Irsch	Co. D, 45th New York Infy. Schimmelfinnig /XI	5/27/92	Unknown
Corp. J. Monroe Reisinger	Co. H, 150th Pennsylvania Infy. Stone/I	Unknown	Beaver Co., PA
Sgt. James M. Rutter	Co. C, 143rd Pennsylvania Infy. Stone /I	10/30/96	Wilkes-Barre, PA
Maj. Alfred J. Sellers	90th Pennsylvania Infy. Baxter/I	7/21/94	Plumsteadville, PA
Corp. Francis A. Waller*	Co. I, 6th Wisconsin Infy. Meredith/I	12/1/64	Gurney, OH
* Awarded for capturing an enemy flag			
Drawn from *The Congressional Medal of Honor, The Names, The Deeds*			

Appendix VI

Battery Armaments

USA	12 pdr Howitzer	12 pdr Napoleon	10 pdr Parrott	3-inch Rifles	Other
I Corps					
Hall's				6	
Stevens'		6			
G. Reynolds'				6	
Cooper's				4	
Stewart's		6			
III Corps					
Clark's			6		
Winslow's		6			
J. Smith's			6		
Bucklyn's		6			
Sully's		6			
XI Corps					
Wheeler's				4	
Wiedrich's				6	
Dilger's		6			
Heckman's		4			
Wilkeson's		6			
XII Corps					
Winegar's			4		
Atwell's			6		
Rugg's		6			
Kinzie's		4			
Cavalry					
Calef's				6	
CSA	12 pdr Howitzer	12 pdr Napoleon	10 pdr Parrott	3-inch Rifles	Other
Latimer's Battalion					
Derment's		4			
J. Carpenter's		2		2	
W. Brown's			4		
Raine's			1	1	2[1]

H. Jones' Battalion					
Carrington's		4			
Tanner's				4	
Green's			2	2	
Garber's		4			
T. Carter's Battalion					
Reese's				4	
W. Carter's		2	2		
Page's		4			
Fry's			2	2	
Garnett's Battalion					
Maurin's			1	2	
Moore's		2	1	1	
Lewis'		2		2	
Grandy's	2			2	
Poague's Battalion					
Wyatt's	1		1	2	
Graham's	2	2			
Ward's	1	3			
Brooke's	2	2			
J. Lane's Battalion					
Ross'	1	1	3	1	
Patterson's	4	2			
Wingfield's		2		3	
McIntosh's Battalion					
Hurt's				2	2[2]
Rice's		4			
Wallace's		2		2	
M. Johnson's				4	
Pegram's Battalion					
Zimmerman's				4	
Johnston's	2	2			
Marye's		2		2	
Brander's		2	2		
McGraw's		4			

For sources see Busey and Martin, *Regimental Strengths and Losses* at Gettysburg, pp. 30, 55, 87, 97, 110, 156, 162, 169, 178, 184, 191, 193.

[1] 20 pounder Parrotts

[2] Whitworth rifles

Notes

I. The Confederate Tide Crests

1. Ewell received orders from Lee on 21 June "to take Harrisburg," *OR* 27.2.443.
2. See Nye, *Here Come the Rebels!*, Chapters 17 and 20. Ewell wanted the Wrightsville bridge to be burned in order to partially cut the communications between Harrisburg and Baltimore. Early misunderstood Ewell's wishes and directed Gordon to seize the bridge. It was set afire by Union militia and Gordon's men were unable to save it. See Coddington, *The Gettysburg Campaign*, pp. 169-170 and *OR* 27.2.492.
3. *OR* 27.2.466.
4. *OR* 27.2.443.
5. *OR* 27.2.464-465.
6. *OR* 27.2.465.
7. *OR* 27.3.912-913. See also Coddington, p. 16 and p. 646 n.40.
8. Thaddeus Stevens Papers, Manuscript Division, Library of Congress.
9. Early, *War Memoirs*, p. 256.
10. See a summary of this action in Nye, *Here Come the Rebels!*, pp. 271-273.
11. Myers, *The Comanches*, pp. 192-193.
12. Myers, *The Comanches*, p. 193.
13. For a detailed account of Confederate activity in the town of Gettysburg on 26 June, and reactions of the townspeople to the Confederate troops, see Black, "Gettysburg's Preview of War: Early's June 26, 1863, Raid," *Gettysburg Magazine*, No. 3, pp. 3-8.
14. Jacobs, *Notes on the Rebel Invasion*, p. 15.

15. Myers, *The Comanches*, p. 193.
16. Myers, *The Comanches*, p. 193.
17. Nye, *Here Come the Rebels!*, pp. 275-276.
18. Early, *War Memoirs*, pp. 257-258.
19. Nye, *Here Come the Rebels!*, p. 277.
20. Jacobs, *Notes on the Rebel Invasion*, pp. 16-18.
21. Early, *War Memoirs*, p. 258.
22. *OR* 27.2.465.
23. Jacobs, *Notes on the Rebel Invasion*, p. 17.
24. *OR* 27.2.466.
25. Isaac R. Trimble to John B. Bachelder, 8 February 1883, NHHS, where the conversation is dated to the afternoon of 25 June. Trimble gave the conversation in a different form in "The Battle and Campaign of Gettysburg," *SHSP* 26 (1898), p. 121, where it is placed on 27 June, and again in "The Campaign and Battle of Gettysburg," *CV* 25 (1917), p. 210, where it is placed on 26 June. Some of Trimble's later claims to have had a firm understanding of the proper strategy during the campaign, appear to have been augmented by hindsight.
26. *OR* 27.2.318.
27. Maurice, *An Aide de Camp of Lee*, p. 250.
28. *OR* 27.2.313.
29. Maurice, *An Aide de Camp of Lee*, pp. 250-251.
30. Longstreet, "Lee in Pennsylvania", in *The Annals of the War*, p. 417.
31. Longstreet to McLaws, 25 July 1873, McLaws Papers, Southern Historical Collection, University of North Carolina, Chapel Hill.
32. Alan T. Nolan, however, interprets that Lee possessed an "offensive grand strategy," and as such the entire Gettysburg campaign "was a strategic mistake because of the inevitable casualties that the Army of Northern Virginia could not avoid." See Nolan, "R.E.Lee and July 1 at Gettysburg," in *The First Day at Gettysburg*, pp. 1-29, especially pp. 4-5 and 12.
33. Isaac R. Trimble to John B. Bachelder, 8 February 1883, NHHS.
34. *OR* 27.3.931. Coddington, pp. 186-187, accurately points out that Lee's intended abandonment of his communications was not as critical as it would seem. All he really needed a supply for was to bring up ammunition. The army could certainly live off the land in Pennsylvania, and, if necessary, it could fight its way out of the Cumberland Valley to any of the several Potomac River fords that were useable at the height of the summer.
35. Marshall, "Events Leading up to the Battle of Gettysburg," *SHSP* 23(1895), pp. 225-226.
36. Longstreet, "Lee in Pennsylvania," in *The Annals of War*, p. 419. For many years this scout was simply known to history as "Harrison." He has been identified as Lt. Thomas Harrison by James O. Hall in "Hunting the Spy Harrison," *CWTI*, Vol. 24, No. 10 (Feb. 1986), pp. 19-25.
37. Maurice, *An Aide de Camp of Lee*, p. 219. Marshall claims here that Lee learned from Harrison at this time that Hooker had been replaced

by Meade. It seems more likely, though, that Lee did not learn of the Union change of command until 30 June. See Fremantle, *The Fremantle Diary*, p. 199.

38. *OR* 27.2.316.
39. *OR* 27.3.913, 915, 923.
40. *OR* 27.3.913,923.
41. A good survey of this controversy can be found in Coddington, pp. 198-208, and McIntosh, "Review of the Gettysburg Campaign," *SHSP* 37(1909). pp. 74-143.
42. *OR* 27.2.307,316,321.
43. Coddington, pp. 183-186, gives a good summary of Lee's misuse of the cavalry that Stuart did not take with him.
44. *OR* 27.2.296.
45. Longstreet, *From Manassas to Appomattox*, p. 348.
46. This order is not preserved but is mentioned in *OR* 27.2.467 and 27.3.943.
47. McKim, *A Soldier' Recollections*, pp. 167, 288.
48. Hotchkiss, *Make Me a Map of the Valley*, p. 156. Hotchkiss notes on p. 155 that he had just finished making a map of Adams County that morning.
49. Turner, *The War Letters of W.B. Pettit*, Vol. 1, p. 128, and *OR* 27.2.456.
50. Goldsborough, *The Maryland Line in the Confederate Army*, p. 101. Goldsborough says that his command did not move out until "late in the afternoon."
51. *OR* 27.2.467.
52. *OR* 27.2.552.
53. Maurice, *An Aide de Camp of Lee*, p. 220.
54. The wording of the order as preserved in *OR* 27.3.943 says "move in the direction of Gettysburg, via Heidlersburg," but this phrasing was worded from memory, as a footnote on p. 944 attests. It is more likely that Ewell was ordered to march to "Cashtown, near Gettysburg," which is the phrase that Ewell uses in *OR* 27.2.443. See discussion of this question in Nye, *Here Come the Rebels!*, p. 345, and Haines, "R.S. Ewell's Command," *Gettysburg Magazine*, No.9, p. 20.
55. *OR* 27.2.503.
56. Coddington, p. 191.
57. See Nye, *Here Come the Rebels!*, p. 348, and Haines, "R.S. Ewell's Command," *Gettysburg Magazine*, No. 9, p. 20.
58. Schuricht, "Jenkins' Brigade in the Gettysburg Campaign, *SHSP* 24(1896), pp. 343-344; see also Shevchuk, "The Wounding of Albert Jenkins," *Gettysburg Magazine*, No. 3, pp. 56-57. Jenkins' 17th Virginia was detached from its brigade and led Early's advance to Gettysburg.
59. *OR* 27.2.606-607.
60. *OR* 27.2.607.
61. *OR* 27.2.444.
62. *OR* 27.2.468.
63. *OR* 27.2.526.

64. *OR* 27.1.926
65. *OR* 27.2.637.
66. Heth, *The Memoirs of Henry Heth*, p. 173.
67. See Jacobs, *Notes on the Rebel Invasion*, p. 21, and Edward Everett's speech at the National Cemetery dedication as cited in Coddington, p. 657 n. 64.
68. Nye, *Here Come the Rebels!* p. 275.
69. For Heth's impulsive nature, see James L. Morrison's introduction to Heth, *The Memoirs of Henry Heth*, pp. lvii-lviii. Heth graduated last in his class at West Point (1847), mostly due to his excessive number of demerits.
70. Young, "Pettigrew's Brigade at Gettysburg", *NC Regts*, Vol. 5, p. 115.
71. Young, "Pettigrew's Brigade at Gettysburg," *NC Regts*, Vol. 5, p. 115. Jacobs, *Notes on the Rebel Invasion*, p. 15, says that Pettigrew brought 15 wagons.
72. Young, "Pettigrew's Brigade at Gettysburg," *NC Regts*, Vol. 5, pp. 235-236.
73. Robinson, "Fifty-Second Regiment," *NC Regts*, Vol. 3, p. 236. See also Cross, *The War. Battle of Gettysburg and the Christian Commission*, pp. 26-27.
74. Busey and Martin, *RSLG*, pp. 174.
75. Busey and Martin, *RSLG*, pp. 175-177.
76. Lineback, "Extracts From a Civil War Diary," *Winston-Salem Sentinel*, 13 June 1914-3 April 1915, p.49.
77. W.S. Christian to John W. Daniel, 24 October 1903, Daniel Papers, Alderman Library, University of Virginia.
78. W.S. Christian to John W. Daniel, 24 October 1903, Daniel Papers, Alderman Library, University of Virginia.
79. Young, "Pettigrew's Brigade at Gettysburg," *NC Regts*, Vol. 5, p. 115. The spy's information was inaccurate, since Buford's cavalry had not yet entered Gettysburg.
80. Thorp, "Forty-Seventh Regiment," *NC Regts*, Vol. 3, p. 89.
81. Jacobs, *Notes on the Rebel Invasion*, p. 21, gives the time as 0930. The author of *NYG*, p. 7, says 1000.
82. *NYG*, p. 7. A similar description is in Jacobs, *Notes on the Rebel Invasion*, p. 21; Sarah M. Broadhead Diary, entry for 30 June 1863, GNMP Collections.
83. Jacobs, *Notes on the Rebel Invasion*, p. 22.
84. Heth, *Memoirs of Henry Heth*, p. 173. The source of the drumming is unknown. There was no infantry with Buford.
85. Young, "Pettigrew's Brigade at Gettysburg," *NC Regts*, Vol. 5, pp. 115-116.
86. W.S. Christian to John W. Daniel, 24 Oct 1903, Daniel Papers, Alderman Library, University of Virginia.
87. Moyer, *History of the Seventeenth Regiment Pennsylvania Volunteer Cavalry*, p. 49.
88. A detachment of Company C, 3rd Indiana Cavalry picked up some

Confederates who "seemed to be straggling through the streets and mingling with the citizens," *Indiana at the Fiftieth Anniversary of Gettysburg*, p. 42. Tucker in *High Tide at Gettysburg*, p. 99, suggests that these Confederates may have been stragglers from Early's division.

89. Young, "Pettigrew's Brigade at Gettysburg," *NC Regts*, Vol. 5, p. 116.

90. Jacobs, *Notes on the Rebel Invasion*, p. 22. This incident is not accepted by Shue, *Morning at Willoughby Run*, p. 257, note 76.

91. Underwood, "Twenty-Sixth Regiment," *NC Regts*, Vol. 2, p. 342. Since Underwood does not mention that the 26th North Carolina marched with Pettigrew's vanguard towards Gettysburg, it is possible that this unit was at the rear of the column and never crossed Marsh Creek on 30 June.

92. Lineback, "Extracts from a Civil War Diary," p. 55.

93. Underwood, "Twenty-Sixth Regiment," *NC Regts*, Vol. 2, p. 342.

94. *OR* 27.2.642. See also W.B. Taylor letter to his mother, 29 July 1863, collection of William B. Floyd, GNMP Collections, and Alexander, *Military Memoirs of a Confederate*, p. 380. Underwood in "Twenty-Sixth Regiment," *NC Regts*, Vol. 2, p. 343, mistakenly places Heth's entire division at the 26th's forward picket post.

95. Col. Christian of the 55th Virginia wrote, "We all moved back to Cashtown," W.S. Christian to John W. Daniel, 24 Oct. 1903, Daniel Papers, Alderman Library, University of Virginia.

96. Robinson, "Fifty-Second Regiment," *NC Regts*, Vol. 3, p. 236. Capt. B.F. Little of Company F, 52nd North Carolina, in a partly garbled account seems to say that the entire regiment was engaged against Union Cavalry at Millerstown on 30 June, and then was recalled by Pettigrew when he saw Buford's cavalry at Gettysburg. See Cross, *The War. Battle of Gettysburg and the Christian Commission*, p. 27.

97. Rogers, "Additional Sketch, Forty-Seventh Regiment," *NC Regts*, Vol. 3, p. 103.

98. Lineback, "Extracts from a Civil War Diary," p. 55. Tucker in *High Tide at Gettysburg*, p. 98, says the 11th North Carolina led the march, with skirmishers deployed, but gives no source.

99. Heth, *Memoirs of Henry Heth*, p. 173. Heth wrote a condensed version of this episode twenty years before his memoirs were published in "Letter from Major General Henry Heth of A.P. Hill's Corps, A.N.V." *SHSP* 4(1877), p. 157.

100. Heth, "Letter from Major General Henry Heth of A.P. Hill's Corps, A.N.V.," *SHSP* 4(1877), p. 157.

101. Young, "Pettigrew's Brigade at Gettysburg," *NC Regts*. Vol 5., pp. 116-117.

102. Heth, "Letter from Major General Henry Heth of A.P. Hill's Corps, A.N.V.," *SHSP* 4(1877), p. 157.

103. *OR* 27.2.607.

104. *OR* 27.2.607.

105. *OR* 27.2.126.

106. Maurice, *An Aide de Camp of Lee*, p. 250.

107. Heth, "Letter from Major General Henry Heth of A.P. Hill's Corps, A.N.V.," *SHSP* 4(1877), p. 157, and Taylor, *Four Years with General Lee*, pp. 92-93.
108. *OR* 27.2.126.
109. Young, "Pettigrew's Brigade at Gettysburg," *NC Regts*, Vol. 5, p. 117. It is uncertain which ridge near Gettysburg was meant by Pettigrew.

II. The Army of the Potomac Moves North

1. Benjamin, "Hooker's Appointment and Removal," *B & L*, Vol. 3, p. 241.
2. Couch would be named commander of the newly formed Department of the Susquehanna on 11 June and as such directed most of the militia units that opposed Lee's invasion of Pensylvania.
3. Benjamin, "Hooker's Appointment and Removal," *B & L*, Vol. 3, p. 241 note.
4. Benjamin, "Hooker's Appointment and Removal," *B & L*, Vol. 3, p. 241.
5. See Coddington, pp. 121-125.
6. Benjamin, "Hooker's Appointment and Removal," *B & L*, Vol. 3, p. 241.
7. *OR* 27.1.60. Coddington, pp. 130-133, gives a good analysis of the situation.
8. *OR* 27.1.60.
9. Hebert, *Fighting Joe Hooker*, p. 245.
10. Nichols, *Toward Gettysburg*, pp. 182-184 and 192-193.
11. Cleaves, *Meade of Gettysburg*, p. 123.
12. Benjamin, "Hooker's Appointment and Removal," *B & L*, Vol. 3, p. 242.
13. Benjamin, "Hooker's Appointment and Removal," *B & L*, Vol. 3, p. 243.
14. Benjamin, "Hooker's Appointment and Removal," *B & L*, Vol. 3, p. 243.
15. Benjamin, "Hooker's Appointment and Removal," *B & L*, Vol. 3, p. 243.
16. James A. Bell Letter, 1 July 1863, Huntington Library.
17. Long, *Memoirs of Robert E. Lee*, p. 274.
18. Eggleston, *A Rebel's Recollection*, p. 130.
19. Long, *Memoirs of Robert E. Lee*, p. 274.
20. *OR* 27.1.61.
21. *OR* 27.1.61.
22. *OR* 27.1.62.
23. *OR* 27.3.373,376.
24. *OR* 27.1.67.
25. *OR* 27.3.402.
26. *OR* 27.3.400.
27. Busey and Martin, *RSLG*, pp. 99, 110.
28. *OR* 27.1.943, 27.3.400; Busey and Martin, *RSLG*, pp. 98,103.
29. Morton, *Deeds of Daring (Eighth New York Cavalry)*, p. 68.

30. *Pa at G*, p. 883. Abner B. Frank Diary, Entry for 30 June 1863, GNMP Collections.
31. *OR* 27.1.926, 938. Abner B. Frank Diary, Entry for 30 June 1863, GNMP Collections.
32. *Pa at G*, p. 882.
33. *Pa at G*, p. 883; Moyer, *History of the Seventeenth Regiment Pennsylvania Volunteer Cavalry*, p. 48.
34. Norton, *Deeds of Daring (Eighth New York Cavalry)*, p. 68; Cheney, *History of the Ninth Regiment New York Volunteer Cavalry*, p. 101; Abner B. Frank Diary, Entry for 30 June 1863, GNMP Collections.
35. Moyer, *History of the Seventeenth Regiment Pennsylvania Volunteer Cavalry*, p. 49.
36. Norton, *Deeds of Daring (Eighth New York Cavalry)*, p. 68; Daniel Pulis to his Parents, 6 July 1863, Rochester (NY) Public Library.
37. Robinson, "Fifty-Second Regiment," *NC Regts*, Vol. 3, p. 236, and Cross, *The War. Battle of Gettysburg and the Christian Commission*, pp. 26-27. Buford believed that the Confederate force consisted of two Mississippi regiments and two cannons, *OR* 27.1.926.
38. *OR* 27.1.926.
39. *OR* 27.1.926.
40. Hard, *History of the Eighth Cavalry Regiment Illinois Volunteers*, pp. 255-256.
41. Hard, *History of the Eighth Cavalry Regiment Illinois Volunteers*, p. 256, mistakenly puts their arrival at "about noon."
42. *OR* 27.1.926. Pleasonton's orders on 29 June directed Custer to move his brigade to Emmitsburg and then to join Farnsworth's brigade at Littlestown, *OR* 27.3.400.
43. Fox gives Buford's arrival in Gettysburg as about 1000 (*NYG*, p. 7), while Cheney gives it as 110 (*History of the Ninth Regiment New York Volunteer Cavalry*, p. 102) and Jacobs says 1130 (*Notes on the Rebel Invasion*, p. 22). Colonel George H. Chapman of the 3rd Indiana cavalry (Chapman to John B. Bachelder, 30 March 1864, NHHS) and Tillie Pierce Alleman of Gettysburg (*At Gettysburg*, p. 28) place Buford's arrival as "about noon." Buford reported in a dispatch to Pleasonton that he arrived at 1100 (*OR* 27.1.923), though he states his arrival was "in the afternoon" in his battle report (*OR* 27.1.926).
44. Marcellus E. Jones' Recollections, 30 June 1863 entry in "The Marcellus E. Jones House."
45. Jacobs, *Notes on the Rebel Invasion*, p. 22.
46. *Indiana at the Fiftieth Anniversary of Gettysburg*, p. 42. Aaron B. Jerome says that Buford's advance troops "entered Gettysburg driving the few pickets of the enemy before them," Jerome to W.S. Hancock, 18 Oct.1865, NHHS.
47. Tucker, *High Tide at Gettysburg*, p. 99.
48. All four mentioned regiments claimed to be at the head of Buford's column. The evidence seems to suggest that Gamble's brigade came first, then Devin's. W.M. Redman of the 12th Illinois claimed that "I was one

of the first to charge into this place," Redman to his mother, 1 July 1863, Alderman Library, University of Virginia. See also: William Gamble to William L. Church, 10 March 1864, Gamble Collection, Chicago Historical Society; *NYG*, p. 1145; Cheney, *History of the Ninth Regiment New York Volunteer Cavalry*, p. 102; Beveridge, "The First Gun at Gettysburg," *Gettysburg Papers*, Vol. 1, p. 171 (*Ill. MOLLUS*, Vol. 2, p. 89); Beveridge, "Illinois Monuments at Gettysburg," *Gettysburg Sources*, Vol. 3, p. 17.

49. Alleman, *At Gettysburg*, p. 28. Longacre (*The Cavalry at Gettysburg*, p. 180) claims that the cavalry first went to the Gettyburg "Diamond" (Square), but gives no evidence.

50. Moyer, *History of the Seventeenth Regiment Pennsylvania Volunteer Cavalry*, p. 49; Daniel Pulis to his parents, 6 July 1863, Pulis Collection, Rochester (NY) Public Library; Longacre, *The Cavalry at Gettysburg*, p. 180.

51. Cheney, *History of the Ninth Regiment New York Volunteer Cavalry*, p. 102; Daniel Pulis to his parents, 6 July 1863, Pulis collection, Rochester (NY) Public Library; Hall, *History of the Sixth New York Cavalry*, p. 133; and James A. Bell letter, 1 July 1863, Huntington Library; Calef, "Gettysburg Notes: The Opening Gun," *JMSIUS*, Vol. 40 (1907), p. 47.

52. Alleman, *At Gettysburg*, pp. 28-29.

53. Gamble to W.L. Church, 10 March 1864, Gamble Collection, Chicago Historical Society.

54. Beveridge, "Illinois Monuments at Gettysburg," *Gettysburg Sources*, Vol. 3, p. 17.

55. Calef, "Gettysburg Notes: The Opening Gun," *JMSIUS*, Vol. 40 (1907), p. 47. Calef in *OR* 27.1.1030 mistakenly calls the Chambersburg Pike the "Carlisle Pike."

56. Marcellus E. Jones' Recollections, 30 June 1863 entry, in "The Marcellus E. Jones House," and Beveridge, "The First Gun at Gettysburg," *Gettysburg Papers*, Vol 1, p. 172 (*Ill. MOLLUS*, Vol. 2, p. 90).

57. Beveridge, "Illinois Monuments at Gettysburg," *Gettysburg Sources*, Vol. 1, p. 17. Marcellus E. Jones (Recollections, 30 June 1863 entry, in "The Marcellus E. Jones House") claims that his own detachment picketed all the way to the left to the Fairfield Road, but the distance seems excessive. Kross suggests that these vedettes were posted at 120-200 yard intervals, "much closer to one another than those elsewhere along the line," "Fight like the Devil to Hold your Own," *Blue and Gray Magazine*, Vol. 12, No. 3 (Feb. 1995), p. 13.

58. Beveridge says that the 8th New York "sent a picket force down through McPherson's Woods to the southwest," The First Gun at Gettysburg," *Gettysburg Papers*, Vol. 1, p. 172 (*Ill. MOLLUS*, Vol. 2, p. 90). The far left of Gamble's picket line extended as far south as the confluence of Willoughby Run and Marsh Creek, see *Pa at G*, p. 884. See also Cheney, *History of the Ninth Regiment New York Volunteer Cavalry*, p. 103. Kross believes that the far left of Gamble's picket line was held by

company D of the 9th NY, "Fight Like the Devil to Hold Your Own," *Blue and Gray Magazine*, Vol. 12, No. 3 (Feb 1995), p. 13.

59. Beveridge (*Ill. MOLLUS*, Vol. 2, p. 90),"The First Gun at Gettysburg," *Gettysburg Papers*, Vol.1, p. 172 and "Illinois Monuments at Gettysburg," *Gettysburg Sources*, Vol. 1, p. 17. See also Hoffman Diary, 1 July 1863, Brake Collection, USAMHI. Marcellus E. Jones (Recollections, 30 June 1863 entry, in "The Marcellus E. Jones House") says that the right of his picket line connected with Devin's left, but this claim contradicts Beveridge's account, which says that Devin's line was to the east of Willoughby Run. Kross states that the vedettes of the 3rd Indiana were from Company A, "Fight Like the Devil to Hold Your Own," *Blue and Gray Magazine*, Vol. 12, No 3 (Feb 1995), p. 13. Kross also suggests that the picket reserve for the right of Gamble's vedette line was behind Black's Graveyard in the Belmont Road.

60. Cheney, *History of the Ninth Regiment New York Volunteer Cavalry*, pp. 102-103

61. James Bell Letter, 1 July 1863, Huntington Library.

62. Moyer, *History of the Seventeenth Regiment Pennsylvania Volunteer Cavalry*, p. 49.

63. *NYG*, p. 9. Several sources from Gamble's brigade state that the right of Gamble's picket line along Knoxlyn Ridge connected with the left of Devin's pickets. Sources for Devin's regiments, however, clearly state that the left of their picket line was where Chambersburg Pike crosses Willoughby Run. See *B & L*, Vol. 3, p. 274 note; McLean, "The First Union Shot at Gettysburg," *Lincoln Herald*, Vol. 82, No. 1 (Spring 1980), p. 38; and the sources cited in note 56 above. Kross suggests that Devin's pickets extended as far north as Keckler's Hill, "Fight like the Devil to Hold Your Own," *Blue and Gray Magazine*, Vol. 12, No. 3, (Feb. 1995), p. 13.

64. *NYG*, p. 1153 and Cheney, *History of the Ninth Regiment New York Volunteer Cavalry*, p. 103. Cheney in *B & L*, Vol. 3, p. 274 note, states that the left of Devin's picket line was south of the Chambersburg Pike.

65. *Pa at G*, p. 885; *NYG*, p. 1153, and Cheney, *History of the Ninth Regiment New York Volunteer Cavalry*, p. 103. Kross, "Fight Like the Devil to Hold Your Own," *Blue and Gray Magazine*, Vol. 12, No. 3, (Feb. 1995), pp. 13-14.

66. James A. Bell letter, 1 July 1863, Huntington Library.

67. Hard, *History of the Eighth Cavalry Regiment Illinois Volunteers*, p. 255.

68. *OR* 27.1.923.

69. Cheney, *History of the Ninth Regiment New York Volunteer Cavalry*, pp. 104-105; *OR* 27.1 938, 27.3. 414.

70. Beecham, *Gettysburg, The Pivotal Battle of the War*, p. 44.

71. Quoted in Bates, *The Battle of Gettysburg*, p. 55, from DePeyster, *Decisive Conflicts*. Some elements of Jerome's story sound apocryphal.

72. *OR* 27.1.923,924.

73. *OR* 27.1.923,924,987-988.

74. Coddington, p. 228.

75. *OR* 27.3.417; Busey and Martin, *RSLG,* p. 16.

76. Buford in *OR* 27.1.926-927 makes no reference to a regiment on picket duty in Fairfield after he left there on 30 June. Meade thought that Buford had a regiment between Fairfield and Emmitsburg, *OR* 27.3.420.

77. *OR* 27.1.402.

78. *OR* 27.3.417-418, *OR* 27.1.243-24.

79. *OR* 27.3.418.

80. *OR* 27.3.419; *OR* 27.1.715,727.

81. *OR* 27.3.419; *OR* 27.1 707-708.

82. *OR* 27.1.244.

83. *OR* 27.3. 418-419.

84. *OR* 27.3. 414-415, 419,422.

85. *OR* 27.3.422,424.

86. *OR* 27.3.425.

87. Coddington, p. 232.

88. *OR* 27.3. 418, 419.

89. *OR* 27.3. 417-419.

90. Nichols, *Towards Gettysburg,* p. 195; Carpenter, *Sword and Olive Branch,* p. 51; *OR* 27.1.701.

91. O.O. Howard to Professor Jacobs, 23 March 1864, Howard Papers, Bowdoin College.

92. *OR* 27.3.421.

93. Coddington, p. 235.

94. *OR* 27.3.419-420.

95. *OR* 27.3.417.

96. *OR* 27.1.68-69.

97. *OR* 27.3.416.

98. *OR* 27.3.416-417.

99. *OR* 27.3.415.

100. *OR* 27.3.416.

101. *OR* 27.3.421.

102. *OR* 27.1. 923-924; *Report of the Joint Committee of the Conduct of the War,* Vol. 1 (1865), p. 347.

103. *OR* 27.1.69-70; 27.3.434,460. See also Coddington, p. 670 n. 129.

104. *OR* 27.3.460-461.

105. *OR* 27.3.458-459. There is a good analysis of the plan's strengths and weaknesses in Coddington, pp. 238-239. Coddington rightly argues that a rapid withdrawal to Pipe Creek would probably have demoralized the Union troops, and would certainly have surrendered the initiative to Lee, who could have attacked wherever he saw a weak point.

106. *OR* 27.3.458.

107. See Coddington, p. 240, and Sauers, *A Caspian Sea of Ink,* passim.

108. Williams, *Lincoln Finds a General,* Vol.2, p. 675.

109. Alexander, *Military Memoirs of a Confederate,* p. 282.

110. *OR* 27.3.459.

111. *OR* 27.1.701.

112. William Riddle to LeBouvier, 4 August 1863, Reynolds Family Papers, Franklin and Marshall Library.
113. *Pa at G,* p. 343; Coddington, p. 670 n. 129 and p. 671 n. 130; and Nichols, *Towards Gettysburg,* p. 251 n.2.

III. Opening Shots

1. Beale, "The Statements of Time on July 1," *Gettysburg Sources,* Vol. 1, p.41 (p. 4 in original 1897 edition), says 0425; see Appendix IV.
2. *OR* 27.2.657; Heth, *The Memoirs of Henry Heth,* p. 173; Fulton, *The War Reminiscences of William Frierson Fulton II,* p. 76.
3. "Memoir of Colonel John A. Fite," from Tennessee State Library and Archives, as cited in Storch and Storch, "What a Deadly Trap We Were In," *Gettysburg Magazine,* No. 6, p. 16.
4. W. H. Bird, *Stories of the Civil War,* p. 6.
5. Moore, "Heth's Division at Gettysburg," *Southern Bivouac,* Vol. 3, p. 384. It is difficult to determine which troops it was that Moore saw. They may have been one of Gamble's patrols coming from the direction of Knoxlyn or Ortanna; it is unlikely that any Union cavalry could have passed by Pettigrew's brigade encamped on the Chambersburg Pike west of Marsh Creek. Buford says that he was aware as early as 0300 that the enemy was stirring at Cashtown and coming down from Gettysburg in force." See Bean, "Who Fired the Opening Shots!", *Philadelphia Weekly Times,* 2 Feb. 1878.
6. *OR* 27.2.648-649.
7. Compare *OR* 27.2.649.
8. *OR* 27.2.649.
9. Marye, "The First Gun at Gettysburg," *Civil War Regiments,* Vol. 1, No. 1, p. 30; Boland, "Beginning of the Battle of Gettysburg," *CV* 14(1906), p. 308.
10. Robinson ("Fifty-Second Regiment," *NC Regts,* Vol. 3, pp. 235-236) states that the 52nd N.C. arrived at Cashtown on 29 June and rested there until the morning of 1 July, except for a detachment sent to Millerstown.
11. Heth apparently gives his order of march when he discusses the order of the deployment of his brigades, *OR* 27.2.637; see Hassler, *Crisis at the Crossroads,* p. 29. However, Col. W.S. Christian of the 55th Virginia (Christian to Bachelder, 24 Oct. 1903, NHHS) says Pettigrew's brigade was last in the division's column.
12. *OR* 27.2.607,652.
13. *OR* 27.2.656, 661, 673. It is unusual that Heth and Pender took along the corps' reserve battalions rather than their own divisional artillery battalions. This may have been because McIntosh's and Pegram's battalions were better armed. Wise, *The Long Arm of Lee,* p. 616, offers no explanation.

14. For a candid evaluation of Heth's abilities, see James L. Morrison in *The Memoirs of Henry Heth*, pp. lv-lviii.

15. Heernance, "The Cavalry at Gettysburg," *Gettysburg Papers*, Vol. 1, p. 432 (*N.Y. MOLLUS*, Vol. 3, p. 402). See also Heth's comments in *OR* 27.2.637.

16. Busey and Martin, *RSLG*, p. 177.

17. For a brief history of the background of Davis' regiments, see McLean, *Cutler's Brigade*, pp. 36-37, and Winschel, "Heavy Was Their Loss," *Gettysburg Magazine*, Vol. 2, pp. 6, 8.

18. William C. Davis, *The Confederate General*, Vol. 2, p. 51.

19. Marye, "The First Gun at Gettysburg," *Civil War Regiments*, Vol. 1, No. 1, p. 30.

20. Boland, "Beginning of the Battle of Gettysburg," *CV* 14(1906), p. 308. This detachment from the 13th Alabama was commanded by Lt. Will Crawford, see Moon, "Beginning of the Battle of Gettysburg," *CV* 33(1925), p. 448.

21. Belo and Robbins, *The Battle of Gettysburg*, *CV* 8(1900), p. 165; Love, "Mississippi at Gettysburg," *Gettysburg Sources*, Vol. 1, p. 127.

22. Boland, "Beginning of the Battle of Gettysburg," *CV* 14 (1906), p. 308. Also see Fulton, *The War Reminiscences of William Frierson Fulton*. II, p. 76.

23. Marye, "The First Gun at Gettysburg," *Civil War Regiments*, Vol. 1, No. 1, pp. 30-31.

24. Unattributed manuscript entitled "First Shot," GNMP Collections.

25. Unattributed manuscript entitled "First Shot," GNMP Collections.

26. Marcellus Jones Journal, 1 July 1863 entry, in "The Marcellus E. Jones House;" unattributed manuscript, "The First Shot," GNMP Collections.

27. Bean, "Who Fired the Opening Shots!" *Philadelphia Weekly Times*, 2 Feb. 1878; unattributed manuscript, "The First Shot," GNMP collections; Marcellus E. Jones Journal, 1 July 1863 entry, in "The Marcellus E. Jones House." Jones was born in Poultney, VT, on 5 June 1830 and died in Wheaton, Illinois, on 8 October 1900. For his full biography, see Krolik, "Marcellus Jones' Proudest Moment," *Blue and Gray Magazine*, Vol. 5, No. 2 (Nov. 1987), pp. 27-29. The unattributed manuscript, "The First Shot," in the GNMP collections, claims that the Confederate officer at whom Jones fired was Col. W. Marion McCarty of the 1st Texas Legion. McCarty's service record is not known, and his unit was not even at Gettysburg. He was living at Hagerstown, Md., after the war and came to Gettysburg to have his photograph taken at the dedication of the 8th Illinois Cavalry's movement on 1 July 1891; See also Shue, *Morning at Willoughby Run*, p. 59. For another account that mentions McCarty (McCarthy), see Dodge, "Opening the Battle," *National Tribune*, 24 September 1891. For other accounts of the first shot by Jones, see Beveridge, "The First Gun at Gettysburg," *Gettysburg Papers*, Vol.1, pp. 173-174 (*Ill. MOLLUS*, Vol. 2, pp. 91-92), and Beveridge, "Illinois Monuments at Gettysburg," *Gettysburg Sources*, Vol. 3, p. 18.

28. Boland, "Beginning of the Battle of Gettysburg," *CV 14*(1906), p. 308.
29. Beveridge, "The First Gun at Gettysburg," *Gettysburg Papers*, Vol. 1, p. 174 (*Ill. MOLLUS*, Vol. 2, p. 92).
30. For a summary of the controversies connected with the first Union shot, see Beveridge, "Illinois Monuments at Gettysburg," *Gettysburg Sources*, Vol.3, p. 18, and McLean, "The First Union Shot at Gettysburg," *Lincoln Herald*, Vol. 82, No. 1 (Spring 1980), pp. 318-323.
31. *Pa at G*, p. 885. Beveridge ("Illinois Monuments at Gettysburg," *Gettysburg Sources*, Vol. 3, p. 18) rejects this incident because he mistakenly locates it as occurring at the Chambersburg Pike bridge over Marsh Creek; see also Shue, *Morning at Willoughby Run*, pp. 31, 211.
32. *NYG*, p. 1153 and Cheney, *History of the Ninth Regiment New York Volunteer Cavalry*, pp. 105-106.
33. Cheney, *History of the Ninth Regiment New York Volunteer Cavalry*, p.106. A slightly different version can be found in *B & L*, Vol. 3, p. 275 note. See also *NYG*, p. 1153.
34. Cheney, *History of the Ninth Regiment New York Volunteer Cavalry*, pp. 106-107. See also Shue, *Morning at Willoughby Run*, p. 212.
35. "Illinois Monuments at Gettysburg," *Gettysburg Sources*, Vol. 1, p. 18; McLean, "The First Union Shot at Gettysburg," *Lincoln Herald*, Vol. 82, No. 1, pp. 319, 322; Shue, *Morning at Willoughby Run*, p. 212.
36. "Illinois Monuments at Gettysburg," Gettysburg Sources, Vol. 1, p. 18; McLean, "The First Union Shot at Gettysburg," *Lincoln Herald*, Vol. 82., No. 1, pp. 318, 322.
37. Marye, "The First Gun at Gettysburg," *Civil War Regiments*, Vol. 1, No. 1, p. 31; Boland, "Beginning of the Battle of Gettysburg," *CV 14* (1900), p. 535.
38. Norton, *Deeds of Daring*, p. 147; Shue, *Morning at Willoughby Run*, p. 56.
39. Turney, "The 1st Tennessee at Gettysburg," *CV* 8(1900), p. 535.
40. *OR* 27.1.934, and Belo and Robbins, "The Battle of Gettysburg," *CV* 8(1900), p. 165. See Beveridge, "The First Shot at Gettysburg," *Gettysburg Papers*, Vol. 1, p. 174 (*Ill MOLLUS*, Vol. 2, p. 92); Beveridge, "Illinois Monuments at Gettysburg," *Gettysburg Sources*, Vol. 1, p. 19.
41. Bean, "Who Fired the Opening Shots," *Philadelphia Weekly Times*, 2 Feb 1878. Captain Dana mistakenly placed this sequence of events at "about sunrise." He also erred by stating that he saw the Confederates already forming battle lines at this time. Heth's men were still in column formation on the road, with the exception of the specific skirmish units mentioned. See Moon, "Beginning of the Battle of Gettysburg," *CV* 33(1925), p. 448.
42. Bean, "Who Fired the Opening Shots," *Philadelphia Weekly Times*, 2 Feb 1878. See also Kelly, "Gettysburg, An Account of Who Opened the Battle by One Who Was There," *National Tribune*, 31 December 1891.
43. Bean, "Who Fired the Opening shots," *Philadelphia Weekly Times* 2 Feb 1878. One of Pegram's shells struck near Ephraim Whisler's home and Blacksmith shop near the 8th Illinois' advance picket line, just as Whis-

ler was stopping outside to see what was going on. Whisler was so shocked that he lashed back to his bed for the rest of the day, "Some Stories of the Great Battle," *Gettysburg Compiler*, 14 Jan 1903.

44. Bean, "Who Fired the Opening shots," *Philadelphia Weekly Times*, 2 Feb 1878.
45. Fulton, *The War Reminiscences of William Frierson Fulton II*, pp. 79-80.
46. Fulton, *The War Reminiscences of William Frierson Fulton II*, p. 79.
47. Bird, *Stories of the Civil War*, p. 7.
48. Bean, "Who Fired the Opening Shots," *Philadelphia Weekly Times*, 2 Feb 1878, and Marcellus E. Jones Journal, entry for 1 July 1863, in "The Marcellus E. Jones House."
49. *OR* 27.1.934 and *NYG*, p. 1145.
50. Gamble's squadrons averaged about 98 men each, see Busey and Martin, *RSLG*, pp. 99, 101-102.
51. *OR* 27.2.677.
52. Ivry, "At Gettysburg - Who Was the Lone Cavalryman Killed Between the Lines?" *National Tribune*, 11 July 1901. This man might have been private David Diffenbaugh of Co. G, 8th Ill. Cavalry.
53. *OR* 27.1.934.
54. Weaver, *Third Indiana Cavalry*, pp. 4-5; Busey, *These Honored Dead*, p. 31. Kross believes that Major Charles Lemon of the 3rd Indiana was wounded at this time, "Fight Like the Devil to Hold Your Own," *Blue and Gray Magazine*, Vol. 12, No. 3 (Feb 1995), p. 16. Members of the 12th Illinois believed that their Sergeant Gabriel B. Durham was the first Union soldier killed in the battle, see Shue, *Morning at Willoughby Run*, p. 214.
55. Fulton, *The War Reminiscences of William Frierson Fulton II*, pp. 79-80; Storch and Storch, "What a Deadly Trap We Were In," *Gettysburg Magazine*, No. 6, p. 18.
56. *NYG*, p. 1145.
57. Heth, *The Memoirs of Henry Heth*, p. 173.
58. *OR* 27.2.677-678.
59. Kempster, "The Cavalry at Gettysburg," *Gettysburg Papers*, Vol. 1, p. 432 (*Wis. MOLLUS*, Vol. 4, p. 402).
60. See Chapter 1, Note 107.
61. Kempster, "The Cavalry at Gettysburg," *Gettysburg Papers*, Vol.1, pp. 432-433 (*Wis. MOLLUS*, Vol. 4, p. 402-403).
62. Storch and Storch, "What a Deadly Trap We Were In," *Gettysburg Magazine*, No. 6, p. 18.
63. Col. B.D. Fry to John B. Bachelder, 10 Feb. 1878, Bachelder Papers, collection of Francis C. Carleton (see Coddington, p. 689 n.76).
64. Moon, "Beginning of the Battle of Gettysburg," *CV* 33(1925), p. 450.
65. Moon, "Beginning of the Battle of Gettysburg," *CV* 33(1925), p. 449.
66. *OR* 27.2.649.
67. Bachelder Map, 1 July 1863.
68. Belo and Robbins, "The Battle of Gettysburg," *CV* 8(1900), p. 165.; Bachelder Map, 1 July 1863.

69. Rogers, "Additional Sketch, Forty-Seventh Regiment." *NC Regts*, Vol. 3, pp. 103-105.
70. Beveridge, "The First Gun at Gettysburg," *Gettysburg Papers*, Vol. 1, pp. 172-173 (*Ill MOLLUS*, Vol. 2, pp. 90, 91). Mix, "Experiences at Gettysburg," *National Tribune*, 27 February 1934; Calef, "Gettysburg Notes: The Opening Gun," *JMSIUS* 40(1907), p. 47.
71. Warren, "Recollections of the Battle of Gettysburg," p. 4.
72. Cheney, *History of the Ninth Regiment New York Volunteer Cavalry*, p. 107.
73. Jerome to W. S. Hancock, 18 Oct. 1865, Bachelder Papers, NHHS.
74. Doubleday, *Chancellorsville and Gettysburg*, p. 126 note.
75. Beveridge, "The First Gun at Gettysburg", Gettysburg Papers, Vol. 1, p. 173 (*Ill. MOLLUS*, Vol.2, p. 91).
76. Scott, *The Story of the Battles at Gettysburg, Book 1*, p. 276.
77. Gamble to M.L. Church, 10 March 1864, Gamble Collection, Chicago Historical Society; Stine, (*History of the Army of the Potomac*, p. 453) says Buford deployed all of Chapman's command (8th Ill. and 3rd Ind.) plus half of the 8th N.Y.
78. Busey and Martin, *RSLG*, pp. 99, 101-102.
79. For example, Gamble states that Merritt's brigade was on his left on the morning of 1 July, when Merritt was actually nowhere near the battlefield. Gamble to M.L. Church, Gamble Collection, Chicago Historical Society.
80. Hardman, "As a Union Prisoner Saw the Battle of Gettysburg", *CWTI* Vol. 1, No. 4 (July 1962) p. 47.
81. Calef, "Gettysburg Notes: The Opening Gun," *JMSIUS* 40(1907), p. 47.
82. Calef, "Gettysburg Notes: The Opening Gun," *JMSIUS* 40(1907), p. 47.
83. *OR* 27.1.1030; Calef, "Gettysburg Notes: The Opening Gun," *JMSIUS* 40(1907), pp. 47-48.
84. Calef, "Gettysburg Notes: The Opening Gun," *JMSIUS* 4(1907), p. 47.
85. *OR* 27.1.1030.
86. It is possible that some of Jenkins' cavalry accompanied Hill's advance on 1 July. E.E. Bouldin of Jenkins' command states that "Some of Jenkins' brigade were in the extreme advance, the 1st day, and brought on the first [fighting?] at Gettysburg," Bouldin to B.F. Eakle, 31 March 1886, Bachelder Papers, NHHS. See also Dickinson, *16th Virginia Cavalry*, p. 26, and Coddington, p. 684 n. 34.
87. In June 1864 Calef's battery was rearmed, and Calef had to turn in "four of the rifled three inch wrought-iron guns which had formed a part of it since it was organized as a horse battery, at the beginning of the Civil War." Calef continues, "The four guns to be turned in being parked, something impelled me—probably the sentiment of parting with old friends—to make a record of the identifying marks on those pieces, their weight, numbers, initials of inspector, etc., not dreaming that thirty-one years after my memoranda would come into use." Calef for-

got about this diary entry until 1894, when he was discussing the proposed Buford statue on the battlefield and "suggested that the very guns that opened the battle might appropriately be incorporated in the memorial." He then located his diary, now "yellow with age," and tracked down the four guns by their serial numbers; two of them had "wandered" as far as the Pacific Coast. "Four of them now repose at the foot of the Buford monument, their muzzles in the direction of the cardinal points, the 'opening gun', number 233, pointing up the Chambersburg Pike in almost the same spot it occupied July 1, 1863, when it notified the Confederates they reached the limit of their northern invasion, and signaled the beginning of a battle which sealed the fate of a southern Confederacy," Calef, "Gettysburg Notes: The Opening Gun", *JMSIUS* 40(1907), pp. 53-54. The four guns are numbered 233(1862), 244(1862), 632(1863) and 756(1864). Clearly, the 1864 gun could not have been at the battle.

88. Harman Manuscript, Human Interest File, GNMP Collections.
89. *OR* 2.1.1030.
90. Calef, "Gettysburg Notes: The Opening Gun," *JMSIUS* 40(1907), p. 48.
91. *OR* 27.1.938.
92. Cheney, *History of the Ninth Regiment New York Volunteer Cavalry*, p. 107. Cheney certainly does not mean the main channel of Rock Creek, which flows on the east side of Gettysburg. Perhaps he meant the tributary of Rock Creek that flows from west to east from near Oak Hill past Barlow Knoll. Stine, (*History of the Army of the Potomac*, p. 453) says Devin initially held the 9th New York in reserve.
93. Cheney, *History of the Ninth Regiment New York Volunteer Cavalry*, p. 107, Shue, *Morning at Willoughby Run*, p. 56, places this incident earlier in the day.
94. Scott, *The Story of the Battles at Gettysburg, Book 1*, p.277. Both the 9th N.Y.(*NYG*, p. 73) and 6th N.Y. (*NYG*, p. 1138) also claimed to have held the brigade's right at this time.
95. The battle monuments of Devin's regiments show his brigade's general line before this withdrawal.
96. *Pa at G*, p. 885 note. Bean ("Who Fired the Opening Shots!," *Philadelphia Weekly Times*, 2 Feb 1878) mistakes these two companies as two squadrons.
97. *OR* 27.1.939.
98. Moyer, *History of the Seventeenth Regiment Pennsylvania Volunteer Cavalry*, p. 50.
99. Cheney, *History of the Ninth Regiment New York Volunteer Cavalry*, pp. 107-108.
100. *OR* 27.1.939.
101. Cheney, *History of the Ninth Regiment New York Volunteer Cavalry*, p. 108. See also Moyer, *History of the Seventeenth Regiment Pennsylvania Volunteer Cavalry*, p. 50.

102. Cheney, *History of the Ninth Regiment New York Volunteer Cavalry*, p. 108.

103. *NYG*, p. 1153.

104. Heermance, "The Cavalry at Gettysburg," *Gettysburg Papers*, Vol. 1, p. 418 (*NY MOLLUS*, Vol. 3, p. 200).

105. *B & L*, Vol. 3, p. 275 note.

106. Cheney, *History of the Ninth Regiment New York Volunteer Cavalry*, p. 108.

107. *OR* 27.1.934.

108. Beveridge, "Illinois Monuments at Gettysburg," *Gettysburg Sources*, Vol. 3, p. 19.

109. Marcellus E. Jones Journal, entry for 1 July 1863, in "The Marcellus E. Jones House".

110. See, for example, *NYG*, p. 1134, and Starr, *The Union Cavalry in the Civil War*. Vol.1, pp. 426-427.

111. A.S. van de Graaff, letter to his wife, 8 July 1863, Patricia Hanson Collection, GNMP Collections; B.D. Fry to John B. Bachelder, 26 Jan 1878, Bachelder Papers, NHHS.

112. Gamble claimed that he had 800 men—almost half his command— on the skirmish line at this time, Gamble to M.L. Church, 10 March 1864, Gamble Collection, Chicago Historical Society.

113. Busey and Martin, *RSLG*, p. 206. For the charactersitics of these carbines, see Bilby, "Carbines - Yesterday." *Civil War News*, Dec. 1992, pp. 50-52.

114. Conversation with Joseph G. Bilby.

115. Bilby, "The Spencer - Then", *Civil War News*, May 1992, p. 44; McHaffy, "And, Finally, about Spencer Carbines at Gettysburg," *The Banner*, Vol. 97, No. 5, (Spring 1994), p. 20; Wittenburg, "John Buford and the Gettysburg Campaign, *Gettysburg Magazine*, No. 11, p. 33, No. 84. See p. 213 New evidence, however, does show that one of Buford's companies, A of the 17th Pennsylvania, was equipped with Spencer rifles, see Shue, *Morning at Willoughby Run*, pp. 213-214.

116. Scott, *The Story of the Battles at Gettysburg, Book 1*, p. 135.

117. *OR* 27.2.637. See also Heth, *The Memoirs of Henry Heth*, pp. 173-174. Moon, in "Beginning of the Battle at Gettysburg," *CV* 33 (1935), p. 449, states that Heth sent to Lee for instructions as soon as he encountered the Federal cavalry, and received the reply, "Develop the infantry, but don't bring on a battle if it can be avoided."

118. Marcellus E. Jones Journal, entry for 1 July 1863, in "The Marcellus E. Jones House."

119. Beveridge, "Illinois Monuments at Gettysburg," *Gettysburg Sources*, Vol. 3, p. 19; Marcellus E. Jones Journal, entry for 1 July 1863, in "The Marcellus E. Jones House."

120. Calef, "Gettysburg Notes: The Opening Gun", *JMSIUS* 40(1907), p. 48.

121. Calef, "Gettysburg Notes: The Opening Gun," *JMSIUS* 40(1907), p. 48.

122. Boland, "Beginning of the Battle of Gettysburg," *CV* 14(1906), p. 308.

123. Boland, "Death of General Reynolds," *National Tribune*, 20 May 1915.

124. A.S. van de Graaf to his wife, 8 July 1863, Patricia Hanson Collection, GNMP Collections.

125. Moon, "Beginning of the Battle of Gettysburg," CV 33(1925), p. 449.

126. Moon, "Beginning of the Battle of Gettysburg," *CV* 33(1925), p. 449.

127. Fulton, *The War Reminiscences of William Frierson Fulton II*, p. 76.

128. Moon, "Beginning of the Battle of Gettysburg," *CV* 33(1925), p. 449; Boland, "Beginning of the Battle of Gettysburg," *CV* 14 (1906), p. 308; Turney, "The First Tennessee at Gettysburg," *CV* 8(1900) p. 535.

129. Moon, "Beginning of the Battle of Gettysburg," *CV* 33(1925), p. 449. Storch and Storch ("What a Deadly Trap We Were In," *Gettysburg Magazine*, No. 6, p. 20) give a good description of the bluff on the eastern side of Willoughby Run where the two Confederate regiments halted.

130. See Storch and Storch, "What a Deadly Trap We Were In," *Gettysburg Magazine*, No. 6, p. 22. Kross states that the 13th Alabama had to detach a company (C) to its left to watch two companies of the 8th New York Cavalry that had taken a position in Meals' orchard (west of Willoughby Run and south of the Fairfield Road), "Fight Like the Devil to Hold Your Own," *Blue and Gray Magazine*, Vol. 12, No. 3, (Feb 1995), p. 16.

131. Moon, "Beginning of the Battle of Gettysburg," *CV* 33(1925), p. 449.

132. Turney, "The First Tennessee at Gettysburg," *CV* 8(1900), p. 535.

133. Boland, "Beginning of the Battle of Gettysburg," *CV* 14(1906), p. 308; Turney, "The First Tennessee at Gettysburg," *CV* 8(1900), p. 535; Bird, *Stories of the Civil War*, p.7.

134. *OR* 27.1.1031. See also Calef, "Gettysburg Notes" The Opening Gun," *JMSIUS* 40(1907), p. 48.

135. *The Tennessee Civil War Veteran's Questionnaire*, p. 449.

136. For example, Vautier, *History of the Eighty-eighth Pennsylvania Volunteers*, p. 117, and Swallow, "The First Day at Gettysburg," *Southern Bivouac*, Vol.4 (1885), p. 437. See also Shue, *Morning at Willoughby Run*, pp. 214-215, and Moore," Heth's Division at Gettysburg," *Southern Bivouac*, Vol. 3 (May 1885) p. 385.

137. Rison originally enlisted in Nashville on 20 May 1861. His age when he died is not known. I am grateful to Jim Clouse for helping to research Henry Rison's military service record in the National Archives.

138. Hard, *History of the Eighth Cavalry Regiment Illinois Volunteers*, p. 257.

139. W.H. Redman Letter to Catherine Redman, 1 July 1863, Manuscripts Dept., University of Virginia Library; Busey, *These Honored Dead*, p. 23.

140. R.T. Mockbee, "Historical Sketch of the 14th Tennessee," p. 41.

141. See map in Storch and Storch, "What a Deadly Trap We Were In," *Gettysburg Magazine*, No. 6, p. 15. Scott (*The Story of the Battles at Gettysburg*, Book 1, p. 278) and Bachelder (1 July Map) show the entire 7th Tenn. as being positioned north of the woods. However, had the entire

regiment been there, it would have run into the 84th N.Y. of the I
Corps, which had just come up (see next Chapter).

142. Moon, "Beginning of the Battle of Gettysburg," *CV* 33(1925), p. 449.
143. Bachelder, 1 July Map; Busey and Martin, *RSLG*, p. 175.
144. He gives the time as 1030 in his battle report, *OR* 27.2.649.
145. John M. Stone to Joseph R. Davis, undated letter, Bachelder Papers, GNMP Collections.
146. Woollard, Journal of Events.
147. Belo and Robbins, "The Battle of Gettysburg," *CV* 8(1900), p. 165, and Krick, "Three Confederate Disasters on Oak Ridge," in Gallagher, *The First Day at Gettysburg*, p. 104.
148. Cheney mistakenly believed that these skirmishers were part of Early's command (*History of the Ninth Regiment New York Volunteer Cavalry*, p. 109).
149. *NYG*, p. 1134; Heermance, "The Cavalry at Gettysburg," *Gettysburg Papers*, Vol. 1, p. 418 (*NY MOLLUS*, Vol. 3, p. 200).
150. *OR* 27.1.1031.
151. *OR* 27.1.924.
152. Kempster, "The Cavalry at Gettysburg," *Gettysburg Papers*, Vol. 1, p. 432 (*Wis. MOLLUS*, Vol. 4, p. 402); Shue, *Morning at Willoughby Run*, pp. 215-216, shows that this message was probably sent at about 0900.
153. *OR* 27.1.924.

IV. Reynolds to the Rescue

1. *OR* 27.3.417-418.
2. *OR* 27.1.923-924.
3. *OR* 27.3.419-420.
4. William Riddle to Lebouvier, 4 August 1863, Reynolds Papers, Fackenthal Library, Franklin and Marshall College. An exhibit in the lower level of the main museum at the Gettysburg National Military Park claims that Reynolds spent his last night sleeping on some kitchen chairs that are on display at the museum.
5. *OR* 27.1.416.
6. William Riddle to Lebouvier, 4 August 1863, Reynolds Papers, Fackenthal Library, Franklin and Marshall College.
7. Vautier, *History of the Eighty-Eighth Pennsylvania Volunteers*, p. 105; Tevis, *The History of the Fighting Fourteenth*, p. 81. Sunrise was at 0436. See appendix 4, note 2.
8. James P. Sullivan, "The Old Iron Brigade at Gettysburg," *Milwaukee Sunday Telegraph*, 20 Dec 1884.
9. M.C. Barnes to W.W. Dudley 28 March 1883, Bachelder Papers, NHHS.
10. Chamberlin, *History of the One Hundred and Fiftieth Regiment*, p. 117.
11. *NYG*, p. 990
12. *OR* 27. 3. 416-417.
13. Curtis, *History of the Twenty-Forth Michigan*, p. 155.

14. Smith, *History of the Seventy-Sixth Regiment New York Volunteers*, p. 235.

15. *OR* 27.3.416.

16. *OR* 51.1.1066.

17. *OR* 27.3.457.

18. *OR* 27.3.416,457.

19. *OR* 51.1.1066.

20. Pearson, *James S. Wadsworth of Geneseo*, p. 204.

21 Nichols, *Towards Gettysburg*, p. 199; McLean, *Cutler's Brigade*, p.55.

22. Doubleday in *Chancellorsville and Gettysburg*, p. 124, says that the hour was 0600, but in his battle report (OR 27.1.244) he says that their meeting was "between 7 and 8 o'clock."

23. *OR* 27.1.244; Doubleday, *Chancellorsville and Gettysburg*, p. 124.

24. Nevins, *A Diary of Battle*, p. 232.

25. Tevis, *History of the Fighting 14th*, p.81.

26. *NYG*, p. 736; Todd, *History of the Ninth Regiment N.Y.S.M. (83rd New York)*, p. 268; McLean, *Cutler's Brigade*, p.52; Tevis, *History of the Fighting Fourteenth*, p. 132.

27. McLean, *Cutler's Brigade*, p. 52.

28. Buell, *The Cannoneer*, p. 64.

29. *Pa at G*, p. 343; *NYG*, p. 990; Tevis, *History of the Fighting 14th*, p. 132.

30. Hall in *OR* 27.1.359 says that he left camp at 0900.

31. Thomson, *From Philippi to Appomattox*, p. 161.

32. Dawes, *Service With the Sixth Wisconsin Volunteers*, p. 158.

33. Goff, "Here was Made Out Our Last and Hopeless Stand," *Gettysburg Magazine*, Vol.2, p. 29.

34. Herdegen and Beaudot, *In the Bloody Railroad Cut at Gettysburg*, p. 162. See also McLean, *Cutler's Brigade*, p. 65, n.9. E.R. Reed says that the road ahead of the 2nd Wisconsin was clear for a mile or more ("The Second Wisconsin Stakes its Claim", *National Tribune*, 20 March 1884), and Earl M. Rogers says the gap was "one mile" ("A Brave Deed at Gettysburg," *National Tribune*, 28 May 1885).

35. Earl M. Rogers, "The Second, or Fifty-Sixth—Which?", *Milwaukee Sunday Telegraph*, 22 June 1884.

36. Curtis, *History of the Twenty-Fourth Michigan of the Iron Brigade*, p. 156; Dudley, *The Iron Brigade At Gettysburg*, p.5.

37. Dawes, *Service with the Sixth Wisconsin Volunteers*, p. 165; Dudley, *The Iron Brigade at Gettysburg*, p.5.

38. Buell, *The Cannoneer*, pp. 63-64.

39. James P. Sullivan, "The Old Iron Brigade at Gettysburg," *Milwaukee Sunday Telegraph*, 20 December 1864.

40. Smith, *History of the Seventy-Sixth Regiment, New York Volunteers*, p. 237; Herdegen and Beaudot, *In the Bloody Railroad Cut*, p. 236. McLean (*Cutler's Brigade*, p. 52) places the halt 1 1/2 miles north of Marsh Creek and estimates that it lasted about ten minutes.

41. Smith, *History of the Seventy-sixth Regiment, New York Volunteers*, pp.

236-237. The men felt no guilt about stealing the cherries when they learned the orchard belonged to a pro-secessionist farmer.

42. Smith, *History of the Seventy-Sixth Regiment, New York Volunteers,* p. 236.

43. Smith, *History of the Seventy-Sixth Regiment, New York Volunteers,* p. 236.

44. Bates, *Martial Deeds of Pennsylvania,* p. 204. See also Nichols, *Towards Gettysburg,* pp. 199-200.

45. Charles H. Veil to D. McConaughy, 7 April 1864, Peter F. Rothermel Papers, Pennsylvania Division of Public Records.

46. Weld, *War Diary and Letters,* pp. 229-231.

47. *OR* 27.1.924.

48. Charles H. Veil to D. McConaughy, 7 April 1864, Peter F. Rothermel Papers, Pennsylvania Division of Public Records. The house was owned by George George and is still standing near the intersection of South Washington Street and the Emmitsburg Road.

49. Charles H. Veil to D. Mcconaughy, 7 April 1864, Peter F. Rothermel Collection, Pennsylvania Division of Public Records.

50. Stine, *History of the Army of the Potomac,* p. 453.

51. A.B. Jerome to W.S. Hancock, 18 October 1865, Bachelder Papers, NHHS.

52. Jerome's account in DePeyster, *Decisive Conflicts of the Late Civil War,* pp. 152-153.

53. DePeyster, *Decisive Conflicts of the Late Civil War,* p. 153. Jerome says that Reynolds arrived about one half hour after he first saw the I Corps approaching, A.B. Jerome to W.S. Hancock, 18 Oct. 1865, Bachelder Papers, NHHS. Shue, *Morning at Willoughby Run,* p. 94, places this meeting at 0930.

54. Comte de Paris, *The Battle of Gettysburg,* p. 100.

55. A.B. Jerome to W.S. Hancock, 18 Oct. 1865, Bachelder Papers, NHHS.

56. DePeyster, *Decisive Conflicts of the Late Civil War,* p. 153. See also Nichols, *Towards Gettysburg,* p. 202.

57. Jerome in DePeyster, *Decisive Conflicts of the Late Civil War,* p. 153.

58. Doubleday, *Chancellorsville and Gettysburg,* p. 126.

59. Coddington, p. 682 n. 14. See also Sauers, "Gettysburg Controversies," *Gettysburg Magazine,* No. 4, p. 113.

60. Charles H. Veil to D. McConaughy, 7 April 1864. Peter F. Rothermel Collection, Pennsylvania Division of Public Records.

61. Lt. Jerome's account in DePeyster (*Decisive Conflicts of the Late Civil War,* p. 153) is fuller than his comments in his 18 Oct. 1865 letter to W.S. Hancock (Bachelder Papers, NHHS). Wittenberg in a footnote cites unpublished evidence that the meeting between Buford and Reynolds took place at the "Blue Eagle Hotel" in town, but this seems unlikely in view of all the other evidence ("John Buford and the Gettysburg Campaign", *Gettysburg Magazine,* No. 4, p. 42, n. 141). Stine accepts the meeting in the cupola, though the account he cites by Captain Weld does not specifically mention it (*History of the Army of the Poto-*

mac, p. 454). Shue, *Morning at Willoughby Run*, pp. 94, 216-217, rejects the meeting in the cupola.

62. Jerome in DePeyster, *Decisive Conflicts of the Late Civil War*, p. 153, quotes Reynolds as saying, "Let's ride out and see all about it." Stine in *History of the Army of the Potomac*, p. 454, says that the two walked towards the front lines, which were nearby. Rosengarten says that "Reynolds himself with his staff went through the town and out on the Chambersburg Pike, where he met General Buford, and with him made an examination of the ground in front of the town" (Rosengarten to Prof. Jacobs, 15 Oct. 1863, Reynolds Papers, Franklin and Marshall College). Calef remembered that he saw Buford and Reynolds "on the Cashtown Pike, near my position," "Gettysburg Notes: The Opening Gun," *JMSIUS* 40(1907), p. 47.

63. Dudley, *The Iron Brigade at Gettysburg*, p.5.

64. Veil, "On the Death of General Reynolds," p. 22.

65. Charles H. Veil to D. McConaughy, 7 April 1864. Peter F. Rothermel Collection, Pennsylvania Division of Public Records.

66. For example, see O.O.Howard's evaluation in *OR* 27.1.702.

67. Rosengarten to Prof. Jacobs, 15 Oct. 1863, Reynolds Papers, Franklin and Marshall College.

68. Weld, *War Diary and Letters of Stephen Minot Weld*, p. 230; Meade, *With Meade at Gettysburg*, pp. 62-63; Stine, *History of the Army of the Potomac*, p. 454.

69. Cleaves, *Meade of Gettysburg*, p. 135. Meade's orders to Sedgwick are discussed in Meade, *With Meade at Gettysburg*, pp. 56-57.

70. New York Monuments Commission, *In Memoriam, James Samuel Wadsworth*, p. 37.

71. Charles H. Veil to D. McConaughy, 7 April, 1864, Peter F. Rothermel Collection, Pennsylvania Division of Public Records. Sickles claimed he never received this order.

72. Doubleday, *Chancellorsville and Gettysburg*, p. 126. Rosengarten says he heard Reynolds give the order, but Howard says he was mistaken, see Tucker, *High Tide at Gettysburg*, p. 124. Howard wished to claim the credit for himself for selecting Cemetery Hill as the army's reserve position. On 28 January 1864 he was voted the official Thanks of Congress for being "The man who selected the position where the battle of Gettysburg was fought," see Carpenter, *Sword and Olive Branch*, p. 63.

73. Charles H. Veil to D. McConaughy, 7 April 1864, Peter F. Rothermel Collection, Pennsylvania Division of Public Records.

74. Halstead, "The First Day of the Battle of Gettysburg," *Gettysburg Papers*, Vol. 1, p. 152 (*D.C. MOLLUS*, 2 March 1887, p. 4).

75. Beecham, *Gettysburg*, p. 61.

76. Charles H. Veil to D. McConaughy, 7 April 1864, Peter F. Rothermel Collection, Pennsylvania Division of Public Records.

77. Tevis, *History of the Fighting 14th*, p. 82.

78. *NYG*, p. 990.

79. "A Chaplain at Gettysburg", Gettysburg Newspaper Clippings Relating to the Battle, GNMP Collections.

80. Smith, *History of the Seventy-Sixth Regiment New York Volunteers*, p. 237; Gates, *The Ulster Guard and the War of the Rebellio*n, p. 425.

81. *NYG*, p. 990.

82. Tevis, *History of the Fighting 14th*, p. 82.

83. J.V. Pierce to John Bachelder, 1 November 1882, Bachelder Papers, NHHS.

84. McLean, *Cutler's Brigade*, p. 57.

85. *NYG*, p. 991.

86. Gates, *The Ulster Guard and the War of The Rebellion*, p. 425.

87. Otis, *The Second Wisconsin Infantry*, p. 168, n. 167.

88. Dawes, *Service with the Sixth Wisconsin Volunteers*, p. 164.

89. Dawes, *Service with the Sixth Wisconsin Volunteers*, p. 164.

90. Harris, "With the Iron Brigade Guard at Gettysburg," *Gettysburg Magazine*, No. 1, p. 31.

91. Sullivan, "The Old Iron Brigade at Gettysburg," *Milwaukee Sunday Telegraph*, 20 December 1884.

92. Dawes, *Service with the Sixth Wisconsin Volunteers*, p. 164.

93. James P. Sullivan, *Mauston Star*, 13 February 1883, as quoted in Herdegen and Beaudot, *In the Bloody Railroad Cut at Gettysburg*, p. 167 n. 61.

94. Otis, *The Second Wisconsin Infantry*, p. 83.

95. Cheek and Pointon, *History of the Sauk County Riflemen*, p. 70.

96. Sullivan, "The Old Iron Brigade at Gettysburg," *Milwaukee Sunday Telegraph*, 20 Dec. 1884.

97. Dudley, *The Iron Brigade at Gettysburg*, p. 5; M.C. Barnes to W.W. Dudley, 28 March 1883, Bachelder Papers, NHHS.

98. Beecham, "Adventures of an Iron Brigade Man," *National Tribune*, 1902.

99. Huntington, *8th New York Cavalry*, p. 14.

100. James A. Hall to John Bachelder, 29 Dec. 1869, Bachelder Papers, NHHS.

101. James A. Hall to John Bachelder, 27 Feb. 1867, Bachelder Papers, NHHS.

102. James A. Hall to Bachelder, 29 Dec. 1869, Bachelder Papers, NHHS.

103. Mockbee, *Historical Sketch of the 14th Tennessee*, p. 41.

104. *OR* 27.1.266; McLean, *Cutler's Brigade*, p. 61.

105. *OR* 27.1.281; McLean, *Cutler's Brigade*, p. 61.

106. Doubleday, *Chancellorsville and Gettysburg*, p. 129; on the time, see Shue, *Morning at Willoughby Run*, p. 108.

107. *OR* 27.1.281; McLean, *Cutler's Brigade*, p. 61

108. Tevis, *History of the Fighting 14th*, p. 82; *NYG*, p. 733.

109. Beveridge, "The First Gun at Gettysburg," *Gettysburg Papers*, Vol. 1, p. 175 (*Illinois MOLLUS*, Vol. 2, p. 93).

110. Busey and Martin, *RSLG*, p. 24; *NYG*, p. 733; *OR* 27.1.286.

111. *NYG*, p. 736.

112. Tevis, *History of the Fighting 14th*, pp. 132-133.

113. George Harvey (letter to John Bachelder, 18 Aug. 1865, Bachelder Papers, NHHS), insists that the 147th N.Y. did not become detached from the 56th Pa. and 76th N.Y. until after these two regiments were defeated by Davis' attack. The movements of the 147th are still not clear to some historians; see map on page 103 of Gallagher, *The First Day at Gettysburg*. The account given in my text follows that of J.V. Pierce in *NYG*, pp. 989-1010 and McLean, *Cutler's Brigade*, pp. 59-61, 79-96.

114. McLean, *Cutler's Brigade*, p. 61.

115. *NYG*, p. 991.

116. J.V. Pierce to John Bachelder, 1 Nov. 1882, Bachelder Papers, NHHS.

117. J.V. Pierce to John Bachelder, 1 Nov. 1882, Bachelder Papers, NHHS.

118. *NYG*, p. 991.

119. H.H. Lyman to John Bachelder, n.d. Bachelder Papers, NHHS.

120. Bartlett letter, 23 Nov. 1889, in 147th New York File, GNMP Collections.

121. H.H. Lyman to John Bachelder, n.d., Bachelder Papers, NHHS.

122. See McLean, *Cutler's Brigade*, p. 62-63.

123. J.V. Pierce to John Bachelder, 1 Nov. 1882, Bachelder Papers, NHHS; Bartlett letter 23 Nov. 1889, in 147th New York File, GNMP collections. See analysis of the situation in McLean, *Cutler's Brigade*, pp. 62-64.

124. Bachelder, 1 July Map, and maps in McLean, *Cutler's Brigade*, pp. 60, 63, 67, 71.

125. Hall to Bachelder, 29 Dec. 1869, Bachelder Papers NHHS.

126. Actually owned by James Wills.

127. *OR* 27.2.649.

128. *NYG*, p. 616.

129. Map in McLean, *Cutler's Brigade*, p. 63.

130. *Pa at G*, p. 344.

131. McLean, *Cutler's Brigade*, p. 68.

132. There has been an intense controversy through the years over which unit fired the first infantry shots of the battle. For a summary of the literature, see Sauers, "Gettysburg Controversies" *Gettysburg Magazine*, No. 4, pp. 113-114 and Herdegen, "Old Soldiers and War talk - The Controversy over the Opening Infantry Fight at Gettysburg," *Gettysburg Magazine*, No. 2, pp. 15-24. Present consensus is that the 56th Pa.'s first volley was before the Iron Brigade entered the fight south of the Chambersburg Pike, but not by much. See Shue, *Morning at Willoughby Run*, pp. 222-224.

133. Bates, *History of Pennsylvania Volunteers*, Vol. 2, p. 220.

134. McLean, *Cutler's Brigade*, p. 68, sets the time as 1015.

135. Cooke, "Fifty-Fifth Regiment", *NC Regts*, Vol 3, p. 297.

136. Busey and Martin, *RSLG*, pp. 175, 527.

137. Bates, *History of Pennsylvania Volnteers*, Vol. 2, p. 220.

138. *OR* 27.1.288; McLean, *Cutler's Brigade*, p. 70.

139. Smith, *History of the Seventy-Sixth Regiment New York Volunteers*, p. 372.

140. Cooke, "Fifty-Fifth Regiment", *NC Regts,* Vol 3., p.297; Belo and Robbins, "The Battle of Gettysburg," *CV,* Vol. 8, p. 165.

141. Jordan, *North Carolina Troops,* Vol. 13, p. 430.

142. J.M. Stone to Joseph Davis, n.d., Bachelder Papers, NHHS.

143. *OR* 27.2.650.

144. *OR* 27.1.245.

145. *OR* 27.2.650. Krick, "Three Confederate Disasters on the First Day at Gettysburg," in Gallagher, *The First Day at Gettysburg,* p. 106.

146. Smith, *History of the Seventy-Sixth Regiment New York Volunteers,* p. 244.

147. *OR* 27.2.649.

148. *OR* 27.1.285; J.V. Pierce to John B. Bachelder, Nov. 1882, Bachelder Papers, NHHS.

149. W.B. Murphy to F.A. Dearborn, 29 June 1900, State Historical Society of Wisconsin.

150. *OR* 27.1.285; Dawes, "With the Sixth Wisconsin at Gettysburg," *Gettysburg Papers,* Vol. 1, p. 217 (*Ohio MOLLUS,* Vol. 3, p. 367).

151. *OR* 27.1.282.

152. John A. Kellogg to John B. Bachelder, 1 Nov. 1865, Bachelder Papers, NHHS.

153. J.V. Pierce to John Bachelder, 1 Nov. 1882, Bachelder Papers, NHHS.

154. McLean, *Cutler's Brigade,* p. 79.

155. J.V. Pierce to John Bachelder, 1 Nov. 1882, Bachelder Papers, NHHS.

156. *NYG,* p. 991.

157. *NYG,* p. 991.

158. Woollard, "Journal of Events".

159. Coey, "Cutler's Brigade," *National Tribune,* 17 July 1915.

160. Woollard, "Journal of Events".

161. *NYG,* p. 991; McLean, *Cutler's Brigade,* p. 81-82.

162. *NYG,* p. 991.

163. *NYG,* p. 991.

164. *OR* 27.1.359.

165. James A. Hall to John B. Bachelder, 29 Dec. 1869, Bachelder Papers, NHHS.

166. *NYG,* p. 991.

167. *OR* 27.1.359.

168. *NYG,* p. 991.

169. *NYG,* p. 992.

170. *NYG,* p. 991.

171. *NYG,* p. 1001.

172. *NYG,* p. 992; J.V. Pierce to John B. Bachelder, 1 Nov. 1882, Bachelder Papers, NHHS.

173. *OR* 27.1.359.

174. James A. Hall to John B. Bachelder, 27 Feb. 1867, Bachelder Papers, NHHS.

175. *Maine at Gettysburg,* p. 18; James A. Hall to John B. Bachelder, 29 Dec. 1869, Bachelder Papers, NHHS.

176. James A. Hall to John B. Bachelder, 29 Dec. 1869, Bachelder Papers, NHHS.

177. W.B. Murphy to F.A. Dearborn, 29 June 1900, State Historical Society of Wisconsin.

178. James A. Hall to John B. Bachelder, 29 Dec. 1869, Bachelder Papers, NHHS.

179. Smith, *History of the Seventy-Sixth Regiment, New York Volunteers*, pp. 241-242.

180. James A. Hall to John B. Bachelder, 29 Dec. 1869, Bachelder Papers, NHHS.

181. James A. Hall to John B. Bachelder, 29 Dec. 1869, Bachelder Papers, NHHS; *OR* 27.1.359.

182. *Maine at Gettysburg*, p. 19; James A. Hall to John B. Bachelder, 29 Dec. 1869, Bachelder Papers, NHHS; *OR* 27.1.274. Busey, *These Honored Dead*, p. 44, however, lists no men of Hall's battery as killed.

183. *NYG*, p. 992.

184. *NYG*, p. 992.

185. Woollard, "Journal of Events".

186. *NYG*, p. 1005.

187. *NYG*, p. 1005.

188. Cooey, "Cutler's Brigade", *National Tribune*, 17 July 1915.

189. *NYG* p. 993; Cooey, "Cutler's Brigade", *National Tribune*, 17 July 1915.

190. Snyder, *Oswego County New York, In the Civil War*, p. 63.

191. *NYG*, p. 992. Aylesworth was captured by the Confederates and had his leg amputated on 3 July. He died at the Seminary Hospital on 10 July (Busey, *These Honored Dead*, p. 164).

192. Belo and Robbins, "The Battle of Gettysburg," *CV*, Vol. 8, p. 165.

193. Rufus R. Dawes to John Kranth, 29 April 1885, as cited in Herdegen and Beaudot, *In the Bloody Railroad Cut at Gettysburg*, p. 171, n. 169.

194. Cooey, "Cutler's Brigade", *National Tribune*, 17 July 1915.

195. J.V. Pierce to John B. Bachelder, 1 Nov. 1882, Bachelder Papers, NHHS.

196. *NYG*, pp. 992-993; J.V. Pierce to John B. Bachelder, 1 Nov. 1882, Bachelder Papers, NHHS.

197. Snyder, *Oswego County, New York, in the Civil War*, p. 63.

198. McLean, *Cutler's Brigade*, p. 95.

199. See, for example, Vanderslice, *Gettysburg, Then and Now*, p. 76, and more recently, Symonds, *Gettysburg: A Battlefield Atlas*, p. 32.

200. See *NYG*, pp. 1003-1008. The 147th's monument is located east of North Reynolds Avenue, 200 feet north of the middle railroad cut.

201. *NYG*, p. 1006.

202. McLean, *Cutler's Brigade*, p. 109.

203. *NYG*, p. 1006.

204. See map in McLean, *Cutler's Brigade*, p. 98.

205. Tevis, *History of the Fighting Fourteenth*, p. 133.

206. Tevis, *History of the Fighting Fourteenth*, p. 133.

207. Tevis, *History of the Fighting Fourteenth*, p. 83.

208. Tevis, *History of the Fighting Fourteenth*, p. 83.

209. *OR* 27.1.275; Dawes, *Service with the Sixth Wisconsin Volunteers*, p. 164.

210. Harris, "With the Iron Brigade Guard at Gettysburg," *Gettysburg Magazine*, No. 1, p. 31.

211. Harris, "With the Iron Brigade Guard at Gettysburg," *Gettysburg Magazine*, No. 1, p. 32.

212. Harris, "With the Iron Brigade Guard at Gettysburg," *Gettysburg Magazine*, No. 1, p. 32.

213. *OR* 27.1.275; Doubleday, *Chancellorsville and Gettysburg*, pp. 131-133. See map Herdegen and Beaudot, *In the Bloody Railroad Cut at Gettysburg*, p. 170.

214. Rufus R. Dawes to John Kranth, 20 April 1885, as cited in Herdegen and Beaudot, *In the Bloody Railroad Cut at Gettysburg*, p. 171.

215. Dawes, *Service with the Sixth Wisconsin Volunteers*, p. 165; *OR* 27.1.275.

216. Young, "A Pilgrimage", *Milwaukee Sunday Telegraph*, 22 April 1888.

217. Watrous, "Some Premonitions," *Milwaukee Sunday Telegraph*, 27 July 1895.

218. Dawes, *Service with the Sixth Wisconsin Volunteers*, p. 166; *OR* 27.1.275; Dudley, *The Iron Brigade at Gettysburg*, p. 7; Rufus Dawes to John Bachelder, 18 March 1868, Bachelder Papers, NHHS.

219. Herdegen and Beaudot, *In the Bloody Railroad Cut at Gettysburg*, p. 179. Rogers had been especially eager to reach the battlefield because he was "Greatly excited at the prospect of seeing a cavalry fight, having been two years in the service without seeing one," Rogers, "Gettysburg Scenes", *Milwaukee Sunday Telegraph*, 13 May 1887.

220. Dawes, *Service with the Sixth Wisconsin Volunteers*, p. 166; Rufus Dawes to John Bachelder, 18 March 1868, Bachelder Papers, NHHS.

221. George Fairfield Diary, 1 July 1863, State Historical Society of Wisconsin.

222. George Fairfield to Jerome A. Watrous, undated letter, State Historical Society of Wisconsin.

223. J.V. Pierce to John B. Bachelder, 1 Nov. 1882, Bachelder Papers, NHHS.

224. Dawes, *Service with the Sixth Wisconsin Volunteers*, p. 166.

225. Rufus Dawes to John B. Bachelder, 18 March 1868, Bachelder Papers, NHHS; Dawes, "Align on the Colors," *Milwaukee Sunday Telegraph*, 27 April 1890.

226. Rufus Dawes to John B. Bachelder, 18 March 1868, Bachelder Papers, NHHS.

227. Dawes, *Service with the Sixth Wisconsin Volunteers*, p. 167.

228. Dawes, "Align on the Colors," *Milwaukee Sunday Telegraph*, 27 April 1890.

229. Dawes, *Service with the Sixth Wisconsin Volunteers*, p. 167.

230. Dawes, *Service with the Sixth Wisconsin Volunteers*, p. 167.

231. Dawes, "Align on the Colors," *Milwaukee Sunday Telegraph*, 27 April 1890.
232. Watrous, "Gettysburg," *Milwaukee Sunday Telegraph*, 26 Nov. 1879. However, J.V. Pierce (*NYG*, p. 95) rejects the notion of the 6th Wis. being the 147th New York's savior.
233. Belo and Robbins, "The Battle of Gettysburg," *CV*, Vol. 8 (1900), p. 165.
234. Corporal W.B. Murphy of the 2nd Miss. wrote that, "John A. Blair commanded our regiment to right wheel into line and charge the enemy. They made a charge to the south of about 200 yards to the railroad cut," W.B. Murphy to F.A. Dearborn, 29 June 1900, E.S. Bragg Papers, State Historical Society of Wisconsin.
235. W.B. Murphy to F.A. Dearborn, 20 June 1900, E.S. Bragg Papers, State Historical Society of Wisconsin.
236. Vairin Diary, 1 July 1863, as cited in Jordan, *North Carolina Troops*, Vol. 13, pp. 377-378.
237. *NYG*, p. 1006.
238. W.B. Murphy to F.A. Dearborn, 29 June 1900, E.S. Bragg Papers, State Historical Society of Wisconsin.
239. Woollard Diary, as quoted in Long, "A Mississippian in the Railroad Cut", *Gettysburg Magazine*, No. 4, p. 23.
240. Cooke, "Fifty-Fifth Regiment," *NC Regts*, Vol. 3, p. 298. A stake placed after the war located the left (eastern) end of the 55th North Carolina's line 109 yards east of the center of the bridge over the middle railroad cut, Cope Survey Notes, p. 18, GNMP Collections. It is possible a portion of the right wing of the 55th was on the berm north of the railroad cut and not in the cut itself, see Tucker, *High Tide at Gettysburg*, p. 115, and Shue, *Morning at Willoughby Run*, p. 158.
241. W.B. Murphy to F.A. Dearborn, 29 June 1900, E.S. Bragg Papers, State Historical Society of Wisconsin.
242. Cheek and Pointon, *History of the Sauk County Riflemen*, p. 74.
243. McLean, *Cutler's Brigade*, p. 109.
244. Dawes, *Service with the Sixth Wisconsin Volunteers*, p. 167.
245. Harris, "With the Iron Brigade Guard at Gettysburg," *Gettysburg Magazine*, No. 1, p. 32.
246. Sullivan, "The Old Iron Brigade at Gettysburg", *Milwaukee Sunday Telegraph*, 20 Dec. 1884.
247. Nolan, *The Iron Brigade*, p. 239.
248. McLean, *Cutler's Brigade*, pp. 109,111.
249. *OR* 27.2.649.
250. Cooke, "Fifty-Fifth Regiment," *NC Regts*, Vol. 3, p. 298.
251. *NYG*, p. 1006.
252. *OR* 27.2.649.
253. Rufus R. Dawes to John B. Bachelder, 18 March 1868, Bachelder Papers, NHHS; Herdegen and Beaudot, *In the Bloody Railroad Cut at Gettysburg*, p. 185.

254. Sullivan, "The Old Iron Brigade at Gettysburg", *Milwaukee Sunday Telegraph*, 20 Dec. 1884.

255. Dawes, *Service with the Sixth Wisconsin Volunteers*, p. 167; Rufus R. Dawes to John B. Bachelder, 18 March 1868, Bachelder Papers, NHHS; Young, "A Pilgrimage", *Milwaukee Sunday Telegraph*, 22 April 1888.

256. Dawes, *Service With the Sixth Wisconsin Volunteers*, p. 167.

257. Dawes, *Service with the Sixth Wisconsin Volunteers*, pp. 167-168; *OR* 27.1.276. Dawes' account is slightly different in his 18 March 1868 letter to Bachelder (Bachelder Papers, NHHS). Here he states that he had already ordered the 6th Wisconsin to charge when Major Pye came up to him, and Dawes said, "Let's go for them, Major."

258. Dawes, *Service with the Sixth Wisconsin Volunteers*, p. 167; Rufus Dawes to John B. Bachelder, 18 March 1868, Bachelder Papers, NHHS.

259. Dawes, *Service with the Sixth Wisconsin Volunteers*, p. 167n.

260. *OR* 27.1.287.

261. Dawes, *Service with the Sixth Wisconsin Volunteers*, p.167n.

262. Okey, "Echoes of Gettysburg", *Milwaukee Sunday Telegraph*, 29 April 1883.

263. Dawes, *Service with the Sixth Wisconsin Volunteers*, p. 168.

264. See sketch map in Herdegen and Beaudot, *In the Bloody Railroad Cut at Gettysburg*, p. 191.

265. Dawes, "Align on the Colors", *Milwaukee Sunday Tribune*, 27 April 1890.

266. Quoted in Herdegen and Beaudot, *In the Bloody Railroad Cut at Gettysburg*, p. 192. This account (pp. 187 ff.), describes in graphic detail when and where numerous members of the 6th Wisconsin fell during this charge. Levi Steadman, who was the tallest man in the regiment, was not killed, but was mortally wounded. He died at the Seminary Hospital on 19 July (Busey, *These Honored Dead*, p. 279).

267. Sullivan, "The Old Iron Brigade at Gettysburg" *Milwaukee Sunday Telegraph*, 20 Dec. 1884.

268. Dawes, *Service with the Sixth Wisconsin Volunteers*, p. 168; Herdegen and Beaudot, *In the Bloody Railroad Cut at Gettysburg*, p. 190.

269. Herdegen and Beaudot, *In the Bloody Railroad Cut at Gettysburg*, pp. 193-194.

270. Remington, "Wm. N. Remington's Story," *Milwaukee Sunday Telegraph*, 29 April 1883.

271. Herdegen and Beaudot, *In the Bloody Railroad Cut at Gettysburg*, pp. 194-196.

272. W.B. Murphy to F.A. Dearborn, 29 June 1900, E.S. Bragg Papers, State Historical Society of Wisconsin.

273. Dawes, *Service with the Sixth Wisconsin Volunteers*, p. 169.

274. Dawes, *Service with the Sixth Wisconsin Volunteers*, p. 169; *OR* 27.1.276.

275. Harris, "With the Iron Brigade Guard at Gettysburg", *Gettysburg Magazine*, No. 1, p. 32; Herdegen and Beaudot, *In the Bloody Railroad*

Cut at Gettysburg, p. 198; W.B. Murphy to Rufus R. Dawes, 20 June 1892, Dawes Collection, State Historical Society of Wisconsin.

276. Dawes, *Service with the Sixth Wisconsin Volunteers*, p. 169.

277. Dawes, *Service with the Sixth Wisconsin Volunteers*, p. 169.

278. Isaiah Kelly to Rufus R. Dawes, 2 August 1892, Dawes Papers, State Historical Society of Wisconsin.

279. W.B. Murphy to F.A. Dearborn, 29 June 1900, E.S. Bragg Papers, State Historical Society of Wisconsin.

280. Cheek and Pointon, *History of the Sauk County Riflemen*, p. 74; Dawes, *Service with the Sixth Wisconsin Volunteers*, pp. 168-169.

281. Earl M. Rogers to Jerome A. Watrous, undated letter, as quoted in Herdegen and Beaudot, *In the Bloody Railroad Cut*, p. 200.

282. Awarded 1 Dec. 1864.

283. Wallar "A Settled Question", *Milwaukee Sunday Telegraph*, 29 July 1883. For a full biography of Wallar, see Beaudot, "Francis Ashbury Wallar: A Medal of Honor at Gettysburg," *Gettysburg Magazine*, No. 4, pp. 16-21. He died in South Carolina on 30 April 1911.

284. W.B. Murphy to Rufus R. Dawes, 20 June 1892, Dawes Papers, State Historical Society of Wisconsin.

285. Dawes, *Service with the Sixth Wisconsin Volunteers*, p. 169.

286. Joseph Marston, *Milwaukee Sunday Telegraph*, 24 April 1881.

287. Isaiah Kelly to Rufus R. Dawes, 2 August 1892, Dawes Papers, State Historical Society of Wisconsin.

288. Sullivan, "The Old Iron Brigade at Gettysburg," *Milwaukee Sunday Telegraph*, 20 Dec. 1884.

289. Harris, "The Second Mississippi at Gettysburg," *CV* 25 (1917), p. 527.

290. O.J. Hill to Rufus Dawes, 12 Sept. 1893, Dawes Papers, State Historical Society of Wisconsin.

291. Belo and Robbins, "The Battle of Gettysburg," *CV* 8 (1900) p. 165.

292. Sullivan, "The Old Iron Brigade at Gettysburg,." *Milwaukee Sunday Telegraph*, 20 Dec. 1884.

293. Isaiah Kelly to Rufus R. Dawes, 2 August 1892, Dawes Papers, State Historical Society of Wisconsin.

294. Dawes, *Service with the Sixth Wisconsin Volunteers*, pp. 169-170.

295. Harris, "The Iron Brigade Guard at Gettysburg", *Milwaukee Sunday Telegraph*, 22 March 1885.

296. W.B. Murphy to F.A. Dearborn, 29 June 1900, E.S. Bragg Papers, State Historical Society of Wisconsin.

297. John A. Kellogg to John B. Bachelder, 1 Nov. 1865, Bachelder Papers, NHHS.

298. Herdegen and Beaudot, *In the Bloody Railroad Cut at Gettysburg*, pp. 205-206.

299. Tevis, *History of the Fighting Fourteenth*, pp. 83-84, 133; Hartwig, "Guts and Good Leadership," *Gettysburg Magazine*, No. 1, p. 13.

300. Tevis, *History of the Fighting Fourteenth*, pp. 83-84.

301. Dudley, *The Iron Brigade at Gettysburg*, p. 8.

302. Tevis, *History of the Fighting Fourteenth*, p. 84; *OR* 27.1.287.

303. For a summary of this controversy, see Herdegen and Beaudot, *In the Bloody Railroad Cut at Gettysburg*, pp. 206 and 287-299.

304. Dudley, *The Iron Brigade at Gettysburg*, p.8.

305. Wallar, "A Settled Question", *Milwaukee Sunday Telegraph*, 29 July 1883.

306. *OR* 27.1.1031; Calef, "Gettysburg Notes: The Opening Gun", *JMSIUS* 40(1907), p. 49.

307. Tevis, *History of the Fighting Fourteenth*, p. 134.

308. W.B. Murphy to F.A. Dearborn, 29 June 1900, E.S. Bragg Papers, State Historical Society of Wisconsin.

309. Earl M. Rogers to Jerome A. Watrous, undated letter, as quoted in Herdegen and Beaudot, *In the Bloody Railroad Cut*, p. 200.

310. Tevis, *History of the Fighting Fourteenth*, pp. 84; *OR* 27.1.276.

311. Busey, *These Honored Dead*, p. 133; Tevis, *History of the Fighting Fourteenth*, p. 85, says that Forester was killed by the shell that felled his rescuers.

312. *OR* 27.1.266; Herdegen and Beaudot, *In the Bloody Railroad Cut at Gettysburg*, p. 207.

313. Tevis, *History of the Fighting Fourteenth*, p. 134; *OR* 27.1.359.

314. Dawes, *Service with the Sixth Wisconsin Volunteers*, p. 173. W.B. Murphy claimed in 1900 that he had a list of all the men of his 2nd Mississippi who were captured on 1 July, and this included only one officer, Major Blair (letter to F.A. Dearborn, 29 June 1900, E.S. Bragg Papers, State Historical Society of Wisconsin).

315. Isaiah Kelly to Rufus R. Dawes, 2 August 1892, Dawes Papers, State Historical Society of Wisconsin.

316. W.B. Murphy to F.A. Dearborn, 29 June 1900, E.S. Bragg Papers, State Historical Society of Wisconsin. Murphy erroneously mentions the 11th Mississippi in place of the 55th N.C.; the 11th was not present on 1 July. See H.H. Lyman to John Bachelder, 15 April 1889, Bachelder Papers, NHHS.

317. Joseph R. Davis to Jubal A. Early, 12 March 1878, Early Papers, Library of Congress. Shue, *Morning at Willoughby Run*, pp. 229-231, estimated that Davis' prisoners numbered 300.

318. Woollard Diary, as quoted in Long, "A Mississippian in the Railroad Cut", *Gettysburg Magazine*, No. 4, p. 23.

319. W.B. Murphy to F.A. Dearborn, 29 June 1900, E.S. Bragg Papers, State Historical Society of Wisconsin.

320. Dawes, *Service With the Sixth Wisconsin Volunteers*, p. 178.

321. Herdegen and Beaudot, *In the Bloody Railroad Cut at Gettysburg*, p. 211 n. 78.

322. McLean, *Cutler's Brigade*, p. 116.

323. Busey and Martin, *RSLG*, pp. 23, 34.

324. McLean, *Cutler's Brigade*, p. 116.

325. Doubleday in *OR* 27.1.244 says that this aide was Lt. Benjamin T. Marten, but in *Chancellorsville and Gettysburg*, p. 130, he says he sent

Major E.P. Halstead and his acting aide, Lt. Meredith L. Jones, to carry the message.

326. *OR* 27.1.244; *Chancellorsville and Gettysburg,* p. 130. Coddington (p. 194) expresses a strong doubt that Doubleday was on the field as early as he claimed.

327. Charles H. Veil to D. McConaughy, 7 April 1864, Peter F. Rothermel Papers, Pennsylvania Division of Public Records.

328. Charles H. Veil to D. McConaughy, 7 April 1864, Peter F. Rothermel Papers, Pennsylvania Division of Public Records. Major John Mansfield of the 2nd Wis. states in his battle report (*OR* 2.1.273) that this order was brought by Lt. Col. John A. Kress from General Wadsworth.

329. *OR* 27.1.273.

330. *OR* 27.1.23; Otis, *The Second Wisconsin Infantry,* p. 84; Busey, *These Honored Dead,* p. 276. Lt. Col. Stevens is the highest ranking Union casualty from the battle to be buried in the Gettysburg National Cemetery (Wis. D-10).

331. See above, note 132.

332. Charles H. Veil to D. McConaughy, 7 April 1864, Peter F. Rothermel Papers, Pennsylvania Division of Public Records. See also Jennie Reynolds to her brother, 5 July 1863, Reynolds Family Papers, Franklin and Marshall College.

333. *OR* 27.1.273.

334. George H. Otis in *The Second Wisconsin Infantry,* pp. 289-290.

335. Charles H. Veil to D. McConaughy, 7 April 1864, Peter F. Rothermel Papers, Pennsylvania Division of Public Records.

336. Charles H. Veil, "On the Death of General Reynolds", *CWTI,* Vol. 21, No. 4 (June 1982), p. 22.

337. Charles H. Veil to D. McConaughy, 7 April 1864, Peter F. Rothermel Papers, Pennsylvania Division of Public Records.

338. Joseph G. Rosengarten to Samuel P. Bates, 13 Jan. 1876, Pennsylvania Division of Archives and Manuscripts. Rosengarten, however, was not present at the moment Reynolds was shot.

339. *OR* 27.1.266. Veil also carved an "R" on another smaller oak tree nearby; see Veil to McConaughy, 7 April 1864, Peter F. Rothermel Papers, Pennsylvania Division of Public Records. Numerous accounts place Reynolds' fall at 1015. Shue believes Reynolds was shot between 1035 and 1045, see *Morning at Willoughby Run,* pp. 113, 221.

340. Otis, *The Second Wisconsin Infantry,* pp. 290-291. Captain Stephen Weld understood from those who were present at the time that Reynolds was shot no more than 100 yards from the enemy, *Letters of Stephen Minot Weld,* p. 233.

341. Charles H. Veil to D. McConaughy, 7 April 1864, Peter F. Rothermel Papers, Pennsylvania Division of Public Records; Joseph G. Rosengarten (Letter to Samuel P. Bates, 13 Jan. 1871, Pennsylvania Division of Archives and Manuscripts), says several of the general's orderlies were hit, at the same time as the general, but does not name them.

342. Charles H. Veil to D. McConaughy, 7 April 1864, Peter F. Rothermel Papers, Pennsylvania Division of Public Records.

343. Charles H. Veil, "On the Death of General Reynolds", *CWTI*, Vol. 21, No. 4 (June 1982), p. 23.

344. Charles H. Veil, "On the Death of General Reynolds", *CWTI* Vol. 21, No. 4 (June 1982), p. 23. Stine in *History of the Army of the Potomac*, p. 455, names four members of the 76th New York who were supposed to have carried Reynolds' body from the field (Mike Morgan, France Brace, Melvin Reed, and B.F. Taylor). Another source (*NYG*, p. 688) says that some men of the 14th Brooklyn carried Reynolds' body away.

345. Dawes, *Service with the Sixth Wisconsin Volunteers*, p. 166. Capt. Joseph Rosengarten makes mention of a "hastily contrived litter" (Joseph G. Rosengarten to Samuel P. Bates, 13 Jan. 1876, Pennsylvania Division of Archives and Manuscripts).

346. Charles H. Veil to D. McConaughy, 7 April 1864, Peter F. Rothermel Papers, Pennsylvania Division of Public Records.

347. Charles H. Veil to D. McConaughy, 7 April 1864, Peter F. Rothermel Papers, Pennsylvania Divison of Public Records.

348. Veil, "On the Death of Reynolds", *CWTI* Vol. 21 No. 4 (June 1982), p. 23, says that he first realized that Reynolds was dead when he stopped with the body near the Seminary. A note by Lt. H.H.Lyman of the 147th New York claims that "Dr. J.T. Stillman, 1st Surgeon, called to see General Reynolds, examined him at railfence to right of our first position, 1st morning, and pronounced him dead within 15 monutes of being hit," H.H. Lyman to John B. Bachelder, n.d., Bachelder Papers, NHHS. This incident seems plausible, though it is not mentioned by Veil or any other source.

349. Charles H. Veil to D. McConaughy, 7 April 1864, Peter F. Rothermel Papers, Pennsylvania Division of Public Records; Veil, "On the Death of Reynolds", *CWTI*, Vol. 21, No. 4 (June 1982), p. 23; Joseph G. Rosengarten to Samuel P. Bates, 13 January 1876, Pennsylvania Division of Archives and Manuscripts.

350. Sgt. Veil says that they left at 1300 (Veil to D. McConaughy, 7 April 1864, Peter F. Rothermel Papers, Pennsylvania Division of Public Records). Capt. Rosengarten places their departure at about 1500-1530 ("When the First Corps were just falling back to their second position on Seminary Ridge," see Rosengarten to Samuel P. Bates, 13 Jan. 1876, Pennsylvania Division of Archives and Manuscripts.)

351. Veil, "On the Death of Reynolds" *CWTI*, Vol. 21, No. 4, (June 1862), p. 23. Some men of the 2nd Pennsylvania Cavalry later claimed that they escorted Reynolds' body on its trip to Maryland (*Pa at G*, pp. 806, 812); see also Nichols, *Towards Gettysburg*, p. 254 n. 51.

352. Veil, "On the Death of Reynolds," *CWTI*, Vol. 21 No. 4 (June 1862), p. 23; Charles H. Veil to D. McConaughly, 7 April 1864, Peter F. Rothermel Papers, Pennsylvania Division of Public Records; Joseph G. Rosengarten to Samuel P. Bates, 13 Jan. 1876, Pennsylvania Division of Archives and Manuscripts; Nichols, *Towards Gettysburg*, p. 207; William

Riddle to Lebouvier, 4 Aug. 1863, Fackenthal Library, Franklin and Marshall College.

353. William Riddle to Lebouvier, 4 Aug 1863, Fackenthal Library, Franklin and Marshall College. The General's cap and "equipment" were picked up by some soldiers from the 14th Brooklyn, Tevis, *The Fighting 14th*, p. 82.

354. See Nichols, *Towards Gettysburg*, pp. 211-212, 255 n.78. Riddle says that Reynolds had a small gold ring on his finger with the legend, "Dear Kate," "which he valued very highly" (William Riddle to he Lebouvier, 4 Aug 1863, Fackenthal Library, Franklin & Marshall College).

355. Nichols, *Towards Gettysburg*, pp. 211-212, 255 n.78.

356. Nichols, *Towards Gettysburg*, pp. 210-211.

357. Doubleday, *Chancellorsville and Gettysburg*, p. 132.

358. See, for example, Col. Wainwright in Nevins, *A Diary of Battle*, p. 239.

359. *OR* 27.2.637,677.

360. Krick, *The Fredericksburg Artillery*, p. 59.

361. For example, *New York Times*, 4 July 1863 and Stine, *History of the Army of the Potomac*, pp. 454-455. See also sources listed in Nichols, *Towards Gettysburg*, p. 253 n. 48.

362. Account in the GNMP files, forwarded by the Surry (N.C.) County Historical Society in 1986.

363. Jordan, *North Carolina Troops, 1861-1865, A Roster*, Vol. 13.

364. This story was first published in a November 1902 issue of the *Lancaster Intelligencer*. It gained widespread attention when it was retold in the 23 November 1952 issue of the Lancaster *Sunday News*.

365. *The (Lancaster) Sunday News* 23 Nov. 1952; Jordan, *North Carolina Troops, 1861-1865, A. Roster*, Vol. 13, p. 531.

366. See also Nichols, *Towards Gettysburg*, p. 253 n.28.

367. Nichols, *Towards Gettysburg*, p. 253 n. 48.

368. First printed in the *Philadelphia Weekly Times*, now reprinted in *The Annals of the War*, p. 63.

369. Coddington, p. 686 n. 52.

370. Jennie Reynolds to her brother, 5 July 1863, Reynolds Papers, Franklin and Marshall College. Other accounts state that the bullet entered at the base of his neck and travelled upward; see Coddington, p. 686 n. 52.

371. Joseph G. Rosengarten to Samuel P. Bates, 13 Jan. 1876, Pennsylvania Division of Archives and Manuscripts; Veil, "On the Death of General Reynolds," *CWTI* Vol. 21, No. 4 (June 1982), p. 23. Dudley in *The Iron Brigade at Gettysburg*, p. 9, claims that it was one of Archer's skirmishers who shot Reynolds. However, it is clear from two accounts that Archer halted his skirmish line west of Willoughby Run and advanced his brigade "over and beyond the skirmish line"; see Fulton, *The War Reminiscences of William Frierson Fulton II*, p. 76, and Boland, "Beginning of the Battle of Gettysburg", *CV* vol. 13 (1906), p. 308. In addition, two of Reynolds' staff members lost their horses shot from under

them shortly before Reynolds was shot, Hopkins, "Death of Reynolds," *National Tribune,* 14 April 1910.

372. See Storch and Storch, "What a Deadly Trap We Were In, *Gettysburg Magazine,* No. 6, p. 24, and Boland, "Death of General Reynolds," *National Tribune,* 20 May 1915.

373. Moon, "Beginning of the Battle of Gettysburg," *CV* 33 (1925), pp. 449-450; John R. Callis to John B. Bachelder, undated letter, Bachelder Papers, NHHS.

374. Otis, *The Second Wisconsin Infantry,* p. 274.

375. W.B. Murphy to R.R. Dawes, 20 June 892, Rufus R. Dawes Papers, State Historical Society of Wisconsin.

376. Shue, *Morning at Willoughby Run,* pp. 218-221, discusses all the evidence and comes to the conclusion "that some Johny Reb drew a bead on General Reynolds and squeezed the trigger."

377. *OR* 27.1.278-279.

378. *OR* 27.1.279.

379. Stine, *History of the Army of the Potomac,* p. 457.

380. John R. Callis to John B. Bachelder, n.d., Bachelder Papers, NHHS.

381. M.C. Barnes to W.W. Dudley, 28 March 1883, Bachelder Papers, NHHS.

382. Goff, "Here was Made Out Our Last and Hopeless Stand", *Gettysburg Magazine,* No. 2, p. 29.

383. "The 19th Indiana at Gettysburg," manuscript at Indiana State Library.

384. M.C. Barnes to W.W. Dudley, 28 March 1883, Bachelder Papers, NHHS.

385. Goff, "Here was Made Out Our Last and Hopeless Stand", *Gettysburg Magazine,* No. 2, p. 29.

386. *OR* 27.1.267.

387. Curtis, *History of the Twenty-Fourth Michigan,* pp. 164, 181.

388. Doubleday, *Chancellorsville and Gettysburg,* p. 130. Coddington (pp. 275-277) doubts that Doubleday was on the field this early, and refuses to accept Doubleday's account of his arrival as stated in his battle report, *OR* 27.1.244-245. In *OR* 27.1.244 Doubleday says it was Lt. Benjamin Marten, not Capt. Halstead and Lt. Jones, whom he sent to Reynolds for instructions.

389. *OR* 27.1.244.

390. Doubleday, *Chancellorsville and Gettysburg,* p. 130.

391. Flavius J. Bellamy to his parents, 3 July 1863, Indiana State Library.

392. Beveridge, "The First Gun at Gettysburg", in *Gettysburg Papers,* Vol. 1, p. 176 (*Illinois MOLLUS,* Vol. 2., p. 94).

393. *OR* 27.1.273,278.

394. The 8th New York cavalry regiment's monument is located on South Reynolds Avenue (eastern McPherson's Ridge) "on the spot occupied by the main line of the regiment when relieved by the First Corps," *NYG,* p. 1145.

395. Hard, *History of the Eighth Cavalry Regiment Illinois Volunteers,* p. 257.

396. *OR* 27.1.927; Day, "Veteran of 3rd Indiana Cavalry," *National Tribune*, 30 July 1903.

397. Flavius J. Bellamy Diary, entry for 1 July 1863, Indiana State Library.

398. William H. Redman to his sisters, 3 July 1863, University of Virginia Library.

399. *OR* 27.1.185; these losses, however, include those suffered later in the afternoon.

400. M.C. Barnes of the 19th Indiana heard some of Archer's men say that "What puzzled them most was where we came from so quickly," Barnes to W.W. Dudley, 28 March 1883, Bachelder Papers, NHHS.

401. Compare McLean, *Cutler's Brigade*, p. 101, and Storch and Storch, "What a Deadly Trap We Were In," *Gettysburg Magazine*, Vol. 6, p. 15.

402. *OR* 27.2.646.

403. *OR* 27.1.274.

404. This quote is cited, for example, in Doubleday, *Chancellorsville and Gettysburg*, p. 132.

405. Storch and Storch, "What a Deadly Trap We Were In," *Gettysburg Magazine*, No. 6, p. 24.

406. Moon, "Beginning of the Battle of Gettysburg", *CV* 33(1925), p. 449.

407. See above, notes 372 and 373.

408. Moon, "Beginning of the Battle of Gettysburg", *CV* 33(1925), p. 449.

409. Bird, *Stories of the Civil War*, p. 7.

410. Bird, *Stories of the Civil War*, p. 7; Goff, "Here Was Made Out Our Last and Hopeless Stand," *Gettysburg Magazine*, No. 2, p. 29.

411. Moon, "Beginning of the Battle of Gettysburg", *CV* 33(1925), p. 449.

412. Boland, "Beginning of the Battle of Gettysburg", *CV* 14(1906), p. 308.

413. Norton, *History of the Eighth New York Volunteer Cavalry*, p. 69, records that Capt. Follett of Company D and one man of Company M were killed "in a charge in which the rebels were severely repulsed and a large number taken prisoners."

414. Moon, "Beginning of the Battle of Gettysburg", *CV* 33(1925), p. 450.

415. Smith, *The Twenty-Fourth Michigan*, p. 126; *OR* 27.1.267.

416. Bird, *Stories of the Civil War*, pp. 7-8.

417. Moon, "Beginning of the Battle of Gettysburg", *CV* 33 (1925), p. 449.

418. Turney, "The First Tennessee at Gettysburg", *CV* 8(1900), p. 535.

419. *OR* 27.1.279.

420. Moon, "Beginning of the Battle of Gettysburg", *CV* 8(1900), p. 450.

421. McCullough, "Fourteenth Tennessee Infantry," *Military Annals of Tennessee*, p. 327.

422. John B. Callis to John B. Bachelder, undated letter, Bachelder Papers, NHHS.

423. *OR* 27.1.274; Otis, *The Second Wisconsin Infantry*, p. 274.

424. *OR* 27.1.274.

425. *OR* 27.2.646.

426. *OR* 27.1.245,274; George W. Mew to Abner Doubleday, 24 March 1896, Bachelder Papers, NHHS.

427. D.B. Bailey to Abner Doubleday, 24 March 1890, Bachelder Papers, NHHS.

428. *OR* 27.1.274.

429. D.B. Bailey to Abner Doubleday, 24 March 1890, Bachelder Papers, NHHS. Lt. W.H. Harries of Co. B of the 2nd Wisconsin substantially supports Dailey's account. He says that he was taking Archer to the rear when Lt. Dailey stepped up to Archer and said, "I will relieve you of that sword," and did so; see Harries, "The Sword of General James J. Archer," *CV* 19(1911), pp. 419-420. For more on Archer's sword, see pages 457-458.

430. Castleberry, "Thirteenth Alabama - Archer's Brigade", *CV* 19 (1911), p. 338.

431. Halstead, "The First Day of the Battle of Gettysburg", in *Gettysburg Papers*, Vol. 1, p. 153 (*D.C. MOLLUS*, 2 March 1887, p.5). See also *B & L*, Vol. 3, p. 285.

432. See Doubleday, *Chancellorsville and Gettysburg*, p. 132.

433. Long, "The Confederate Prisoners of Gettysburg", *Gettysburg Magazine*, No.2, p. 92 n. Another apocryphal Archer capture story relates that Maloney told Archer to "Right about face, Gineral, March", after he was captured, and then took him to General Wadsworth and said, "Gineral Wadsworth, I make you acquainted with Gineral Archer." See Tucker, *High Tide at Gettysburg*, p. 113.

434. *OR* 27.1.274,279; Gaff, "Here Was Made Out Our Last and Hopeless Stand," *Gettysburg Magazine*, No. 2, p. 29.

435. *OR* 27.1.266. Curtis, *(History of the Twenty-Fourth Michigan*, p. 157) says that the 24th "drove the uncaptured foe over the crest and a hundred yards beyond."

436. *OR* 27.1.279.

437. *OR* 27.1.268.

438. *OR* 27.1.268; Curtis, *History of the Twenty-Fourth Michigan*, p. 157.

439. Gaff, "Here We Made Out Our Last and Hopeless Stand", *Gettysburg Magazine*, No.2, p. 29.

440. Busey and Martin, *RSLG*, pp. 23, 177.

441. Storch and Storch, "What a Deadly Trap We Were In", *Gettysburg Magazine*, No. 4, pp. 25-27. The 5th Alabama Battalion was on the brigade's skirmish line during the initial part of the day's fighting. It may have been held in reserve after Archer's main battle line passed over the skirmishers on the west side of the Willoughby Run. The Archer's brigade tablet on the battlefield says that the 5th Battalion was later sent to the right to watch Gamble's cavalry.

442. Storch and Storch, "What a Deadly Trap We Were In", *Gettysburg Magazine*, No. 4, pp. 26-27; Busey and Martin. *RSLG*, p. 177.

443. *OR* 27.1.243, *OR* 27.2.646. See also Coddington, p 687 n. 61.

444. Krick, *The Gettysburg Death Roster*, p. 14; Storch and Storch, "What a Deadly Trap We Were In", *Gettysburg Magazine*, No. 4, p. 26. Shue, *Morning at Willoughby Run*, pp. 225-227, accepts the number of Archer's prisoners as 200.

445. Moon, "Beginning of the Battle of Gettysburg", *CV* 33(1925), p. 450.
446. See Long, "The Confederate Prisoners of Gettysburg", *Gettysburg Magazine*, No. 2, pp. 92-96, and the sources cited there.
447. Castleberry, "Thirteenth Alabama - Archer's Brigade", *CV* 19(1911), p. 338.
448. Castleberry, "Thirteenth Alabama - Archer's Brigade", *CV* 19(1911), p. 338.
449. *OR* 27.2.637.
450. Undated Mosby letter, Coles Collection, University of Virginia Library, as cited in Coddington, p. 689 n. 76.
451. See strength figures in Busey and Martin, *RSLG*, pp. 23, 24, 175, 177.

V. Noontime Lull

1. *OR* 27.1.246. Doubleday went on in his report (*OR* 27.1.246-247) to give a longer explanation of why he did not withdraw after he learned of Reynolds' death. Among his reasons were the demoralizing effects of abandoning a victorious field, and the impropriety of withdrawing without orders from a superior officer. In 1882 he wrote in *Chancellorsville and Gettysburg* (p. 133) that he simply "awaited a fresh attack or orders from Gen. Meade."
2. Nevins, *A Diary of Battle*, pp. 233-234.
3. Nevins, *A Diary of Battle*, p. 233.
4. *OR* 27.1.245, 268.
5. *OR* 27.1.267-268, 274-275, 279; Gaff, "Here Was Made Out Our Last and Hopeless Stand," *Gettysburg Magazine*, No. 2, p. 29.
6. *OR* 27.1.176.
7. *OR* 27.1.167.268, 274-275, 279; Gaff, "Here Was Made Out Our Last and Hopeless Stand," *Gettysburg Magazine*, No. 2, p. 29. The 24th Michigan's skirmish line was manned by its Co. B, Curtis, *History of the Twenty-Fourth Michigan*, p. 159.
8. Curtis, *History of the Twenty-Fourth Michigan*, p. 159; Smith, *The Twenty-Fourth Michigan*, p. 129.
9. *OR* 27.1.279.
10. A.S. Barnes to W.W. Dudley, 28 March 1883, Bachelder Papers, NHHS.
11. *OR* 27.1.282.285; *Pa at G*, p. 344.
12. Hartwig, "Guts and Good Leadership," *Gettysburg Magazine*, No. 1, p. 11; see also OR. 27.1.283-284.
13. *OR* 27.1.287; Tevis, *History of the Fighting Fourteenth*, p. 134.
14. Lt. A.B. Jerome, Buford's signal officer, relates that soon after Reynolds was killed, Buford asked for a sheet from Jerome's notebook and wrote a note to General Meade, "For God's sake send up Hancock, everything is going at odds and we neeed a controlling spirit," A.B. Jerome to W.S. Hancock, 18 October 1865, Bachelder Papers, NHHS.
15. George Chapman to John B. Bachelder, 30 March 1864, Bachelder Pa-

pers, NHHS; Marcellus E. Jones diary, entry for 1 July 1863, in "The Marcellus E. Jones House."

16. *Pa at G*, p. 885; Cheney, *History of the Ninth Regiment New York Volunteer Cavalry*, p. 109. *NYG*, p. 1139; Cheney, *History of the Ninth Regiment New York Volunteer Cavalry*, p. 109; *History of the Seventeenth Regiment Pennsylvania Volunteer Cavalry*, p.50.

17. Hopkins, "Death of General Reynolds," *National Tribune*, 14 April 1910. See also Shue, *Morning at Willoughby Run*, pp. 114, 147.

18. Nevins, *A Diary of Battle*, p.232; *OR* 27.1.354.

19. Nevins, *A Diary of Battle*, p. 232.

20. Nevins, *A Diary of Battle*, p. 233. Coddington, p. 276, uses this sequence to discredit Doubleday's claim that he reached the field soon after 1000 (Doubleday, *Chancellorsville and Gettysburg*, p. 130). However, Wainwright's estimates of time and distance may not be accurate. The account Wainwright gives in his journal does not agree in several details with his 17 July 1863 battle report (*OR* 27.1.354). It is possible that Wainwright reworked his journal after the war.

21. *OR* 27.1.354.

22. Nevins, *A Diary of Battle*, pp. 233-234.

23. Buell, *The Cannoneer*, p. 65.

24. Buell, *The Cannoneer*, p.65.

25. It is not clear what Lt. Breck means when he refers to the nearby hillsides that "hid the village of Gettysburg from our view," *NYG*, p. 1256. He may have been thinking of one of his unit's later positions.

26. *OR* 27.1.354.

27. Nevins, *Diary of Battle*, p. 233.

28. Nevins, *Diary of Battle*, p. 233.

29. Chamberlin, *History of the One Hundred and Fiftieth Regiment*, p. 117, gives the departure time as 0900; *OR* 27.1.331 gives the time as 0930; see also Matthews, *The 149th Pennsylvania Volunteer Infantry*, pp. 76, 78.

30. Chamberlin, *History of the One Hundred and Fiftieth Regiment*, pp. 117.

31. Chamberlin, *History of the One Hundred and Fiftieth Regiment*, pp. 118.

32. Chamberlin, *History of the One Hundred and Fiftieth Regiment*, pp. 117-118, Matthews, The *149th Pennsylvania Volunteer Ingantry*, pp. 28-29.

33. Chamberlin, *History of the One Hundred and Fiftieth Regiment*, p. 118.

34. *Pa at G*, p. 745.

35. *OR* 27.1.332, 334; Matthews places these orders at "between 11:00 and 11:30 AM," *The 149th Pennsylvania Volunteer Infantry*, p. 79.

36. Chamberlin, *History of the One Hundred and Fiftieth Regiment*, p. 119; *Pa at G*, p. 752.

37. *OR* 27.1.333. Col. Dana in *OR* 27.1.335 states that the right of the 149th Pa. extended as far as the eastern railroad cut.

38. *Pa at G*, p. 745. The 149th's Company K was the first portion of the regiment to come under fire, Matthews, *The 149th Pennsylvania Volunteer Infantry*, p. 80

39. Chamberlin, *History of the One Hundred and Fiftieth Regiment*, p. 119; *OR* 27.1.329, 335, 341.

40. *OR* 27.1.335.
41. *Pa at G*, p. 752.
42. *OR* 27.1.329, 341.
43. Chamberlin, *History of the One Hundred and Fiftieth Regiment*, p. 119.
44. *OR* 27.1.341.
45. *OR* 27.1.344. The men of the 149th took advantage of a sunken farm lane that ran along the south edge of the Chambersburg Pike next to the McPherson farm; see Matthews, *The 149th Pennsylvania Volunteer Infantry*, p. 81.
46. Hartwig, "The Defense of McPherson's Ridge," *Gettysburg Magazine*, No. 1, p. 17.
47. Chamberlin, *History of the One Hundred and Fiftieth Regiment*, p. 120.
48. Less properly called the 80th New York Infantry; the men of the unit preferred to keep their pre-war designation, and carried it through the entire war.
49. Osborne, *The Civil War Diaries of Col. Theodore B. Gates*, pp. 88-91.
50. Osborne, *The Civil War Diaries of Col. Theodore B. Gates*, p. 91, *History of the 121st Regiment Pensylvania Volunteers*, p. 51.
51. Osborne, *Holding the Left at Gettysburg*, pp. 3-4; Vail, *Reminiscences of a Boy in the Civil War*, p. 117.
52. Osborne, *The Civil War Diaries of Col. Theodore B. Gates*, p. 91; Osborne, *Holding the Left at Gettysburg*, p.4.
53. Cook, "Personal Reminiscences of Gettysburg," in *Gettysburg Sources*, Vol. 2, p. 124.
54. Vail, *Reminiscences of a Boy in the Civil War*, p. 117.
55. Osborne, *The Civil War Diaries of Col. Theodore B. Gates*, p. 91; *OR* 27.1.326.
56. *History of the 12st Regiment Pennsylvania Volunteers*, p. 51.
57. *History of the 121st Regiment Pennsylvania Volunteers*, p. 119.
58. Cook, "Personal Reminiscences of Gettysburg," in *Gettysburg Sources*, Vol. 2, p. 125.
59. Cook, "Personal Reminiscences of Gettysburg, in *Gettysburg Sources*, Vol. 2, pp. 125-126.
60. *OR* 27.1.326; Osborne, *Holding the Left at Gettysburg*, p.6.
61. *History of the 121st Regiment Pennsylvania Volunteers*, p. 51; *OR* 27.1.327; Cook, "Personal Reminiscences of a Boy in the Civil War," in *Gettysburg Sources*, Vol. 2, p. 126.
62. *OR* 27.1.317, 319-320.
63. Cook, "Personal Reminiscences of Gettysburg," in *Gettysburg Sources*, Vol. 2, p. 126.
64. Cook, "Personal Reminiscences of Gettysburg," in *Gettysburg Sources*, Vol. 2, p. 126; Gates, *The Ulster Guard and the War of the Rebellion*, p. 432.
65. *OR* 27.1.317, where Biddle, oddly, does not mention this portion of the march.
66. Cook, "Personal Reminiscences of Gettysburg, in *Gettysburg Sources*, Vol. 2, p. 127. Cook's narrative is not completely clear, and this incident

may have occurred at the regiment's next position. Osborne places it here on the Fairfield Road (*Holding the Left at Gettysburg*, p. 6).

67. *OR* 27.1.320; Osborne, *Holding the Left at Gettysburg*, pp. 6-7; Gates, *The Ulster Guard and the War of the Rebellion*, p. 432.

68. *OR* 27.1.320; *Pa at G*, p. 665.

69. *OR* 27.1.247, 315, 320; Cook, "Personal Reminiscences of Gettysburg," in *Gettysburg Sources*, Vol. 2, p. 126.

70. *OR* 27.1.320.

71. Cook, "Personal Reminiscences of Gettysburg," in *Gettysburg Sources*, Vol. 2, p. 127.

72. Nevins, *A Diary of Battle*, p. 234.

73. Cook, "Personal Reminiscences of Gettysburg," in *Gettysburg Sources*, Vol. 2, p. 127.

74. *OR* 27.1.365.

75. *History of the 121st Regiment Pennsylvania Volunteers*, p. 51; see also *OR* 27.1.327. Most of the troops were not able to recover their knapsacks later.

76. Gates, *The Ulster Guard and the War of the Rebellion*, p. 432.

77. Gates, *The Ulster Guard and the War of the Rebellion*, p. 433.

78. *OR* 27.1.247.

79. Warner, *Generals in Blue*, p. 414.

80. Nevins, *A Diary of Battle*, p. 237; *OR* 36.2.270.

81. Nevins, *A Diary of Battle*, p. 237.

82. Theodore Gates to Abner Doubleday, 4 Feb. 1864, as cited in Osborne, *Holding the Left*, p. 22, 7.44.

83. See Chapter IX, notes 28-31.

84. Gates, *The Ulster Guard and the War of the Rebellion*, p. 433.

85. Hartwig, "The Defense of McPherson's Ridge," *Gettysburg Magazine*, No. 1, p. 18 (map).

86. Cook, "Personal Reminiscences of Gettysburg," in *Gettysburg Sources*, Vol. 2, p. 127.

87. Cook, "Personal Reminiscences of Gettysburg," in *Gettysburg Sources*, Vol. 2, p. 127.

88. See Osborne, *Holding the Left at Gettysburg*, pp. 7-8.

89. Vail, *Reminiscences of a Boy in the Civil War*, p. 127. According to Jacob Sheads, the Harman house was originally built by Reverend McLean, who was married to Helen Miller, an aunt of Stonewall Jackson's first wife, Eleanor Junkin. See Osborne, *Holding the Left at Gettysburg*, p. 27, n. 36.

90. Gates, *The Ulster Guard and the War of the Rebellion*, p. 433.

91. Vail, *Reminiscences of a Boy in the Civil War*, p. 127.

92. Osborne, *Holding the Left at Gettysburg*, pp. 8, 10.

93. Cook, "Personal Reminiscences of Gettysburg," in *Gettysburg Sources*, Vol. 2, p. 128.

94. Gates, *The Ulster Guard and the War of the Rebellion*, p. 433.

95. Col. Theodore Gates to Editor W. Romeyn of the *Kingston Democratic*

Journal, 23 Dec. 1863. See also Osborne, *The Civil War Diaries of Col. Theodore B. Gates*, p. 118 (entry for 23 Dec. 1863).

96. Cook, *History of the Twelfth Massachusetts*, p. 100; *OR* 27.1.807.

97. The 13th Mass. left at 0600 (OR 27.1.297); the 97th NY at 0630 (Hall, *History of the Ninety-Seventh New York*, p. 134, or 700 (*NYG*, p. 723); the 97th NY left at 0700 (OR 27.1.309); and the 83rd NY, soon after 0800 (Hussey, *History of the 9th Regiment NYSM-NGSNY*, p. 268).

98. Small, *The Sixteenth Maine*, p. 98. Vautier in "At Gettysburg," says that the division delayed quite a while before marching out.

99. *OR* 27.1.311; Vautier, "At Gettysburg;" Vautier, *History of the Eighty-Eighth Pennsylvania Volunteers*, p. 105; *Pa at G*, p. 177.

100. Vautier, *History of the Eighty-Eighth Pennsylvania Volunteers*, p. 105.

101. Small, *The Sixteenth Maine*, p. 98.

102. Grant, "The First Army Corps on the First Day at Gettysburg," in *Gettysburg Papers*, Vol. 1, p. 260 (*Minnesota MOLLUS*, Vol. 5, p. 48); Vautier, "At Gettysburg."

103. Hall, *History of the Ninety-Seventh Regiment New York Volunteers*, p. 134.

104. Northrop, "Going into Gettysburg," *National Tribune*, 11 October 1906.

105. Hall, *History of the Ninety-Seventh Regiment New York Volunteers*, p. 154; Hussey, *A History of the Ninth Regiment NYSM-NGSNY*, p. 268.

106. Vautier, *History of the Eighty-Eighth Pennsylvania*, p. 105.

107. Vautier, "At Gettysburg."

108. Wiggin, "Sixteenth Maine Regiment at Gettysburg," in *Gettysburg Papers*, Vol. 1, p. 294 (*Maine MOLLUS*, Vol. 4, p. 156). See also Locke, *The Story of the Regiment*, p. 19.

109. *OR* 27.1.247; Davis, *Three Years in the Army*, p. 226.

110. Davis, *Three Years in the Army*, p. 226.

111. Grant, "The First Army Corps on the First Day at Gettysburg," in *Gettysburg Papers*, Vol. 1, p. 259 (*Minnesota MOLLUS*, Vol. 5, p. 47).

112. Hussey, *A History of the Ninth Regiment NYSM-NGSNY*, p. 269.

113. *OR* 27.2.642.

114. R.M. Mayo, "Report of Part Taken by Heth's (Old) Brigade in the Battles of Maryland and Pennsylvania," 13 August 1863, Henry Heth Collection, Museum of the Confederacy, Richmond.

115. *OR* 27.2.642-643.

116. *OR* 27.2.638, 646; Bachelder, 1 July 1863 map; "Fifty-Second Regiment," *NC Regts*, Vol. 3, pp. 236-237.

117. *OR* 27.2.656, 661; Caldwell, *The History of a Brigade of South Carolinians*, p. 137; Busey and Martin, *RSLG*, p. 179.

118. Caldwell, *The History of a Brigade of South Carolinians*, p. 137.

119. Perrin, "A Little More Light on Gettysburg," *Mississippi Valley Historical Review*, 24 (1938), p. 523.

120. Littlejohn, "Recollections of a Confederate Soldiers." p. 6; *OR* 27.2.661.

121. *OR* 27.2.661

122. *OR* 27.2.673, 674. Both battalions had 16 guns, but Poague's had only 3 long range rifled guns while McIntosh's had 10; see Busey and Martin, *RSLG*, pp. 184, 192.

123. Littlejohn, "Recollections of a Confederate Soldier," p. 5; Perrin, "A Little More Light on Gettysburg," *Mississippi Valley Historical Review*, 24 (1938), p. 523.

124. Littlejohn, "Recollections of a Confederate Soldier," p. 5.

125. Caldwell, *The History of a Brigade of South Carolinians*, p. 137; Littlejohn, "Recollections of a Confederate Soldier," p. 6.

126. *OR* 27.2.656, 661; Bachelder, 1 July 1863 map.

127. Caldwell, *The History of a Brigade of South Carolinians*, p. 138.

128. Caldwell, *The History of a Brigade of South Carolinians*, p. 138.

129. *OR* 27.2.656, 661, 665.

130. *OR* 27.2.665.

131. Johnston's 2 howitzers were not deployed on 1 July, and one of Zimmerman's rifled guns had been disabled while being brought into position, *OR* 27.2.678.

132. *OR* 27.2.674; Bachelder, 1 July 1863 map.

133. *OR* 27.2.674-675, 678; Krick, *The Fredericksburg Artillery*, p. 59.

134. Matthews, *The 149th Pennsylvania Volunteer Infantry*, pp. 80-81.

135. *OR* 27.1.355.

136. Lt. Breck says that "several positions were taken and abandoned without opening fire" at around noon time, *OR* 27.1.362, *NYG*, p. 1256.

137. *OR* 27.1.355-356; Nevins, *A Diary of Battle*, p. 234.

138. *OR* 27.1.364. As already noted in note 74, one of Cooper's four guns was disabled soon after the battery first opened fire.

139. Conversely, Wainwright in his memoirs complained how Wadsworth was interfering with the placement of his guns, Nevins, *A Diary of Battle*, p. 234 note.

140. Wainwright Journal, page 213; this section was omitted from Nevins, *A Diary of Battle*, p. 234.

141. *OR* 27.1.1031.

142. Calef, "Gettysburg Notes: The Opening Gun," *JMSIUS* 40 (1907), p. 50.

143. Calef, "Gettysburg Notes: The Opening Gun," *JMSIUS* 40 (1907), p. 51.

144. *OR* 27.1.276.

145. Dawes, *Service with the Sixth Wisconsin Volunteers*, pp. 173-174; Tevis, *The History of the Fighting Fourteenth*, p. 134.

146. *OR* 27.1.1032.

147. Calef, "Gettysburg Notes: The Opening Gun," *JMSIUS* 40 (1907), p. 51.

148. *OR* 27.1.1032.

149. Nevins, *A Diary of Battle*, p. 134; Wainwright Journal, pp. 113-114; *NYG*, p. 1256; *OR* 27.1.1032.

150. Capt. Reynolds was taken to a hospital in town, where he was captured by the Confederates, but was left behind by them when they

evacuated the town on the night of 3/4 July (*NYG*, p. 1258). He was discharged for disability on 3 May 1864, and survived until 1913 (Raus, *A Generation on the March*, p. 88).

151. McLean (*Cutler's Brigade*, p. 126) argues that Cutler's advance occurred at 1300, but Calef's battery was not holding its forward position at that time.

152. McLean, *Cutler's Brigade*, pp. 126, 128; *NYG*, p. 993: J.V. Pierce to John B. Bachelder, 1 Nov. 1882, Bachelder Papers, NHHS; George Harvey to Col. Hofman, 16 Aug. 1865, Bachelder Papers, NHHS; H.H. Lyman to John B. Bachelder, undated, Bachelder Papers, NHHS.

153. Tevis, *History of the Fighting 14th*, p. 134.

154. *OR* 27.1.282.

155. *OR* 27.1.701; Howard, *Autobiography of Oliver Otis Howard*, Vol. 1, p. 404. Howard claims that it was customary to read dispatches addressed to other generals, "to forestall the possibility of their loss" in transit (Howard, *Autobiography of Oliver Otis Howard*, Vol. 1, p. 404).

156. *OR* 27.1.701; Howard, *Autobiography of Oliver Otis Howard*, Vol. 1, p. 408.

157. *OR* 27.3.457.

158. Howard, *Autobiography of Oliver Otis Howard*, Vol. 1, p. 409.

159. Howard, *Autobiography of Oliver Otis Howard*, Vol. 1, pp. 409-410.

160. *OR* 27.1.701.

161. Howard, *Autobiography of Oliver Otis Howard*, Vol. 1, p. 409.

162. Howard, *Autobiography of Oliver Otis Howard*, Vol. 1, p. 412. This sequence of events would place the time at 1115-1130, which agrees with the time that Howard suggests for these events in *OR* 27.1.701-703.

163. *OR* 27.1.701-702; Howard, *Autobiography of Oliver Otis Howard*, Vol. 1, p. 413. Howard originally thought that the news of Reynolds' death was brought to him by Major William Riddle of Reynolds' staff, but he later learned that the officer was Captain Hall. For the identity of Sgt. Guinn (Quinn), see Pfanz, *Gettysburg—Culp's Hill and Cemetery Hill*, p. 411, n. 20.

164. *OR* 27.1.702; Howard, *Autobiography of Oliver Otis Howard*, Vol. 1, p. 413.

165. *OR* 27.1.702.

166. *OR* 27.1.701

167. *OR* 27.1.727.

168. *OR* 27.1.702

169. Schurz, *The Reminiscences of Carl Schurz*, Vol. 3, p.1.

170. Schurz, *The Reminiscences of Carl Schurz*, Vol. 3, p. 4.

171. Schurz (*The Remininscences of Carl Schurz*, Vol. 3, p.4, and *OR* 27.1.727) says that he left camp at 700, but Howard's report (*OR* 27.1.701) states that the XI Corps did not march out until at least an hour later.

172. *NYG*, p. 430; *OR* 27.1.739-740.

173. Schurz, *The Reminiscences of Carl Schurz*, Vol. 3, pp. 4-5.

174. *OR* 27.1.742. Domschke quote from Pula, *The History of a German-Polish Civil War Brigade*, p. 74.
175. Schurz, *The Reminiscences of Carl Schurz*, Vol. 3, pp. 5-6.
176. Schurz, *The Reminiscences of Carl Schurz*, Vol. 3, p. 5; *OR* 27.1.727; *OR* 27.3.463.
177. Schurz, *The Reminiscences of Carl Schurz*, Vol. 3, p. 7, gives the time as 1230. A member of the 45th NY says that the unit reached Gettysburg at 1115 "by the town clock in the town," *NYG*, p. 378. This statement does not agree with the time reported in other accounts; see Appendix IV.
178. *OR* 27.1.748, 751.
179. Ward, *Sketch of Battery "I,"* p. 40; Kepf, "Dilger's Battery at Gettysburg," *Gettysburg Magazine*, No. 4, p. 52.
180. Howard, *Autobiography of Oliver O. Howard*, Vol. 1, p. 414.
181. Schurz, *The Reminiscences of Carl Schurz*, Vol. 3, p. 7; *OR* 27.1.727.
182. Busey and Martin, *RSLG*, p. 86.
183. *OR* 27.1.715; Andrew Harris to John B. Bachelder, 14 March 1881, Bachelder Papers, NHHS.
184. *OR* 27.1.715; *NYG*, p. 308; Martin, *Carl Bornemann's Regiment*, pp. 147-148.
185. *OR* 27.1.747, 752.
186. *OR* 27.1.748, 751.
187. *OR* 27.1.723.
188. *OR* 27.1.721, 724.

VI. The Fight on Oak Hill

1. *OR* 27.2.638
2. *OR* 27.2.444, 468
3. *OR* 27.2.444
4. Trimble, "The Battle and Campaign of Gettysburg," *SHSP* 26 (1898), p. 122
5. *OR* 27.2.444, 468, 552
6. *OR* 27.2.444, 468; Early, *Autobiographical Sketch*, p. 266
7. *OR* 27.2.589
8. *OR* 27.2.444; Brown, "Reminiscences."
9. *OR* 27.2.444; Brown, "Reminiscences." Campbell Brown was Ewell's stepson.
10. *OR* 27.2.552
11. Kross, "Fight Like the Devil to Hold Your Own," *Blue and Gray Magazine*, Vol. 12, No. 3 (Feb 1995), pp. 17,19; *OR* 27.2.597.
12. Hotchkiss, *Make Me a Map of the Valley*, p. 156.
13. *OR* 27.2.552. Rodes may have ridden on ahead of his troops in order to scout the Union positions from Oak Hill. If he did so, he would have run a risk of being shot or captured by Devin's active cavalrymen, see

Coddington, p. 695, p. 2. See also Kross, "Fight Like the Devil to Hold Your Own," *Blue and Gray Magazine*, Vol. 12, No. 3, (Feb 1995), p. 19.

14. OR 27.2.602; Bachelder, 1 July, 1863 map. These batteries were located on the southern edge of a woods (no longer extant at this point) in the area of the present Peace Light Memorial.

15. The timing of Carter's first shots is estimated from Hotchkiss, *Make Me a Map of the Valley*, p. 156, and the Union response to this fire. Krick places Carter's first shots at "about 1:00 P.M.," "Three Confederate Disasters on Oak Ridge," in *The First Day at Gettysburg*, p. 118.

16. OR 27.1.356, 362; Calef, "Gettysburg Notes: The Opening Gun," *JMSIUS* 40 (1907), p. 56.

17. OR 27.1.356, 362, 364

18. Buell, *The Cannoneer*, pp. 65-66; Tevis, *History of the Fighting 14th*, p. 364

19. Chamberlin, *History of the One Hundred and Fiftieth Regiment Pennsylvania Volunteers*, p. 122; OR 27.1.332; Bassler, "The Color Episode of the 149th Regiment," *SHSP* 37 (1909), p. 268.

20. OR 27.1.329; Chamberlin, *History of the One Hundred and Fiftieth Regiment Pennsylvania Volunteers*, p. 122.

21. Chronicles of Francis D. Jones, GNMP Collections.

22. Bassler, "The Color Episode of the 149th Regiment," *SHSP*, 37 (1909), pp. 268-269

23. OR 27.1.356, 362; Wainwright, Journal, p. 214.

24. OR 27.2.602

25. Hotchkiss, *Make Me a Map of the Valley*, p. 156; Haines, "R.S. Ewell's Command," *Gettysburg Magazine*, No. 9, p. 24; John W. Daniel account, Daniel Papers, University of Virginia.

26. Wharton J. Green, "Second Battalion," *NC Regts*, Vol. 4, p. 255.

27. OR 27.2.552

28. Brown, "Reminiscences."

29. Brown ("Reminiscences") says that Lee stated "very strongly that a general engagement was to be avoided with the arrival of the rest of the army." Ewell (OR 27.2.444) says that he "was informed that, in case we found the enemy's force very large, he did not want a general engagement brought on until the rest of the army came up."

30. OR 27.2.444

31. Brown, "Reminiscences," p. 29; Brown, "Personal Narrative," Hunt Papers, LC. Ewell usually sent two couriers to deliver important dispatches in order to ensure delivery. At First Bull Run he had not received an important message from General Beauregard because the messenger got lost, Pfanz, *Gettysburg—Culp's Hill and Cemetery Hill*, p. 414, n. 14.

32. OR 27.2.696; Brown, "Reminiscences;" Brown, "Personal Narrative," Hunt Papers, LC.

33. OR 27.2.443, 696-697

34. OR 27.2.696-697

35. Nye, *Here Come the Rebels!*, p. 348.

36. Shevchuk, "The Wounding of Albert Jenkins," *Gettysburg Magazine*, No. 3, p. 57.
37. Goldsborough, *The Maryland Line in the Confederate Army*, pp. 176-177.
38. *Pa. at G*, p. 885
39. Busey and Martin, *RSLG*, pp. 194-201
40. See a good discussion of this issue in Coddington, pp. 183-186, 197-198.
41. *OR* 27.2.552; Kross, "That One Error Fills Him with Faults," *Blue and Gray Magazine*, Vol 12, No. 3 (Feb 1995), p. 48.
42. *OR* 27.2.247, 927; Kross, "That One Error Fills Him with Faults," *Blue and Gray Magazine*, Vol 12., No. 3, (Feb 1995), p. 48.
43. Tevis, *History of the Fighting 14th*, p. 134.
44. *OR* 27.1.282
45. McLean, *Cutler's Brigade*, pp. 129-132.
46. Tevis, *History of the Fighting 14th*, p. 135; H.H. Lyman to John B. Bachelder, undated, Bachelder Papers, NHHS.
47. Tevis, *History of the Fighting 14th*, p. 134.
48. Tevis, *History of the Fighting 14th*, p. 135.
49. Dawes, *Service with the Sixth Wisconsin Volunteers*, pp. 173-174.
50. Doubleday says in *Chancellorsville and Gettysburg*, pp. 142-143, that he was reacting to a report by Lt. Col. Henry C. Bankhead of his staff that there was a "wide interval" between the I and XI Corps.
51. *OR* 27.1.248, 289, 307
52. Hall, *History of the Ninety-Seventh Regiment New York Volunteers*, p. 135
53. *OR* 27.1.309
54. *OR* 27.1.292; Hall, *History of the Ninety-Seventh Regiment New York Volunteers*, p. 135.
55. Thomas, *Boys in Blue from the Adirondack Foothills*, p. 148
56. Hall, *History of the Ninety-Seventh New York Volunteers*, p. 135
57. Cook, *History of the Twelfth Massachusetts Volunteers*, p. 100.
58. C.C. Wehrum to John B. Bachelder, 21 Jan. 1884. Bachelder Papers, NHHS; Busey, *These Honored Dead*, p. 56
59. Hall, *History of the Ninety-Seventh New York Infantry*, pp. 135-137
60. Hussey, *History of the 9th Regiment, NYSM-NGSNY*, p. 269
61. Grant, "The First Army Corps on the First Day at Gettysburg," in *Gettysburg Papers*, Vol. 1, p. 260 (*Minnesota MOLLUS*, Vol 5, p. 48); Vautier, *History of the 88th Pennsylvania Volunteers*, p. 105
62. Bachelder, 1 July 1863 Map.
63. *OR* 27.1.289
64. *OR* 27.1.702
65. Griffin, "Rodes on Oak Hill," *Gettysburg Magazine*, No. 4, p. 36, believes that Rodes' division was deployed "by 1:00P.M."
66. *OR* 27.2.552-553, 566
67. *OR* 27.2.587
68. *OR* 2.2.696
69. *OR* 27.2.602-603

70. *OR* 27.2.444, 552
71. *OR* 27.2.553
72. Park, "War Diary of Capt. Robert Emory Park," *SHSP* 26 (1898), pp. 12-13.
73. *OR* 27.2.592.
74. *OR* 27.2.592, 600
75. *OR* 27.2.553
76. *OR* 27.2.553
77. Krick, "Three Confederate Disasters on Oak Ridge," in *The First Day at Gettysburg*, pp. 121-123.
78. Griffin, "Rodes on Oak Hill," *Gettysburg Magazine*, No.4, pp. 36-37.
79. Vautier, *History of the 88th Pennsylvania Volunteers*, pp. 139-140.
80. Vautier, *History of the 88th Pennsylvania Volunteers*, p. 106; Hassler, *Crisis at the Crossroads*, pp. 90-91; Lash, "Brigadier General Henry Baxter's Brigade at Gettysburg," *Gettysburg Magazine*, No. 10, pp. 14-22.
81. *OR* 27.1.307. Historian Gary Kross argues strongly that O'Neal's attack was so slow to develop that it did not get mounted until after Iverson was repulsed, "That One Error Fills Him with Faults," *Blue and Gray Magazine*, No. 12, Vol. 3, (Feb 1995) pp. 49-50.
82. *OR* 27.2.592, 601
83. Krick, "Three Confederate Disasters on Oak Ridge," in *The First Day at Gettysburg*, p. 126, gives the time as 1415; Gallagher, "Confederate Corps Leadership on the First Day at Gettysburg," in *The First Day at Gettysburg*, p. 49, places the attack at 1430.
84. *OR* 27.2.553
85. *OR* 27.2.553, 596
86. *OR* 27.2.592; May, "First Confederates to Enter Gettysburg," *CV* 5 (1897), p. 620
87. *OR* 27.2.592. Rodes may have been influenced to interfere with O'Neal's regiments directly, because he knew their commanders well from his long tenure as their brigade commander earlier in the war. It is interesting to conjecture if he would have bypassed the brigade commander as readily if some other unit had been in O'Neal's position.
88. Busey and Martin, *RSLG*, p. 166
89. Busey and Martin, *RSLG*, p. 26. The exact order of Baxter's regiments is not agreed on. The lineup presented here is that which agrees best with the various regimental accounts; see Lash, "Brig. Gen. Henry Baxter's Brigade at Gettysburg," *Gettysburg Magazine*, No. 10, pp. 13-15
90. *OR* 27.2.553
91. *OR* 27.2.553
92. Griffin in "Rodes on Oak Hill," *Gettysburg Magazine*, No. 4, p. 40, suggests that Rodes wanted O'Neal to strike Baxter's left. Such an attack however, would have required a wheel across Iverson's front. It is more likely that Rodes wanted O'Neal to attack Baxter's center.
93. Vautier, *History of the 88th Pennsylvania Volunteers*, p. 105.
94. Vautier, "At Gettysburg,"

95. Grant, "The First Army Corps on the First Day at Gettysburg," in *Gettysburg Papers*, Vol 1, p. 260 (*Minnesota MOLLUS*, Vol. 5, p. 48).
96. Park, "War Diary of Captain Robert Emory Park," *SHSP*, 26 (1898), p. 15.
97. C.C. Wehrum to John B. Bachelder, 21 Jan 1884, Bachelder Papers, NHHS.
98. *OR* 27.1.734
99. *OR* 27.2.596
100. *OR* 27.2.593
101. *OR* 27.2.601
102. Park, "War Diary of Capt. Robert E. Park," *SHSP* 26 (1898), p. 113.
103. *OR* 27.2.596
104. *OR* 27.2.595
105. *OR* 27.2.553-554
106. *OR* 27.2.579
107. *OR* 27.2.579. Some sources believe that Iverson delayed his advance because of the firing of Carter's artillery across his front; see Vautier, *History of the 88th Pennsylvania Infantry*, p. 135 and Griffin, "Rodes on Oak Hill," *Gettysburg Magazine*, No. 4, p. 40.
108. Turner, "Twenty-Third Regiment," *NC Regts*, Vol. 2, p. 235.
109. Griffin, "Rodes on Oak Hill," *Gettysburg Magazine*, No. 4, p. 40.
110. Montgomery, "Twelfth Regiment," *NC Regts*, Vol. 1, pp. 634-635.
111. Montgomery, "Twelfth Regiment," *NC Regts*, Vol. 1, p. 635.
112. Isaac Hall to John B. Bachelder, 15 Aug. 1885, Bachelder Papers, NHHS.
113. Bachelder, 1 July 1863 Map, and Hall, *Ninety-Seventh New York Volunteers*, p. 136. See also Thomas L. Elmore, "Attack and Counter Attack," *Gettysburg Magazine*, No. 5, p. 128.
114. Montgomery, "Twelfth Regiment," *NC Regts*, Vol. 1, p. 235.
115. Hufham, "Gettysburg," *Wake Forest Student*, 16 (1897), p. 454.
116. Montgomery, "Twelfth Regiment," *NC Regts*, Vol. 1., p. 635
117. Hall, *History of the Ninety-Seventh Regiment*, p. 134 n., suggests that Iverson's attack was channeled to the southeast by two fences in the Forney farm.
118. *OR* 27.2.579
119. *OR* 27.1.289
120. *OR* 27.1.292
121. Isaac Hall to John B. Bachelder, 15 Aug. 1885, Bachelder Papers NHHS.
122. Hall, *History of the Ninety-Seventh Regiment*, p. 139 n.
123. *OR* 27.1.311
124. *OR* 27.1.311
125. Vautier, *History of the Eighty-Eight Pennsylvania Infantry*, p. 106
126. Vautier, "At Gettysburg"
127. Hall, *History of the Ninety-Seventy Regiment*, p. 136.
128. Vautier, *History of the Eighty-Eighth Pennsylvania*, p. 135.
129. Hussey, *History of the Ninth Regiment, NYSM-NGSNY*, p. 270.

130. *OR* 27.1.307

131. *OR* 27.248, 289; Stine, *History of the Army of the Potomac*, p. 473.

132. Turner, "Twenty-Third Regiment, *NC Regts*, Vol. 2, p. 235.

133. Grant, "The First Army Corps on the First Day at Gettysburg," in *Gettysburg Papers*, Vol. 1, p. 261 (*Minnesota MOLLUS*, Vol. 5, p. 49).

134. Vautier, "At Gettysburg;" Vautier, *History of the Eighty-Eighth Pennsylvania*, p. 106

135. Vautier in *History of the Eighty-Eighth Pennsylvania*, p. 135, gives the distance as "about 100 paces," which would be about 170 yards; in "At Gettysburg," he gives the distance as 50 yards, a number also given by Grant, "The First Army Corps on the First Day at Gettysburg," in *Gettysburg Papers*, Vol. 1, p. 261 (*Minnesota MOLLUS*, Vol. 5, p. 49.) Iverson's left would have been much closer to the Yankee line than his right because the Confederate line approached Baxter's at an angle.

136. Vautier, *History of the Eighty-Eighth Pennsylvania*, p. 106.

137. Turner, "Twenty-Third Regiment," *NC Regts*, Vol. 2, p. 235.

138. Montgomery, "Twelfth Regiment," *NC Regts*, Vol. 1, p. 635.

139. *OR* 27.2.554

140. *OR* 27.2.562-563; MacRae and Busby, "Fifth Regiment," *NC Regts*, Vol 1, p. 287; Toon, "Twentieth Regiment," *NC Regts*, Vol. 1, p. 635.

141. Turner, "Twenty-Third Regiment," *NC Regts* Vol. 2, p. 236.

142. Montgomery, "Twelfth Regiment," *NC Regts*, Vol. 1, p. 635.

143. *OR* 27.1.282, 286; see also Doubleday, *Chancellorsville and Gettysburg*, p. 143, and Stine, *History of the Army of the Potomac*, p. 472.

144. Montgomery, "Twelfth Regiment," *NC Regts*, Vol. 2, p. 637.

145. Vautier, *History of the Eighty-Eighth Pennsylvania*, p. 106; Grant, "The First Army Corps on the First Day at Gettysburg," in *Gettysburg Papers*, Vol. 1, p. 262 (*Minnesota MOLLUS*, Vol. 5 p. 49).

146. Grant, "The First Army Corps on the First Day at Gettysburg," in *Gettysburg Papers*, Vol. 1 pp. 261-262 (*Minnesota MOLLUS*, Vol. 5, pp. 49-50).

147. Samuel G. Boone Memoirs, 1 July 1863, USAMHI.

148. Jacob R. Menges, Corporal's Memoirs, 18 Aug. 1861- 9 June 1865, USAMHI.

149. Vautier, *History of the Eighty-Eighth Pennsylvania*, pp. 106-107

150. Grant, "The First Army Corps on the First Day at Gettysburg," in *Gettysburg Papers*, Vol. 1, p. 262 (*Minnesota MOLLUS*, Vol. 5, p. 50); Vautier, *History of the Eighty-Eighth Pennsylvania*, p. 107; Vautier, "At Gettysburg."

151. Grant, "The First Army Corps on the First Day at Gettysburg," in *Gettysburg Papers*, Vol. 1, p. 262 (*Minnesota MOLLUS*, Vol. 5, p. 50).

152. Vautier, *History of the Eighty-Eighth Pennsylvania*, p. 107; *OR* 27.1.311

153. Vautier, "At Gettysburg"

154. *OR* 27.1.292, 307; Stine, *History of the Army of the Potomac*, p. 472; Vautier, *History of the Eighty-eighth Pennsylvania*, p. 135; Grant, "The First Army Corps on the First Day at Gettysburg," in *Gettysburg Papers*, Vol. 1, p. 262 (*Minnesota MOLLUS*, Vol. 5, p. 50).

155. Hall, *History of the Ninety Seventh Regiment*, p. 138. Hall mistakenly believed that the 12th Mass. was on his right instead of the 83rd N.Y.

156. C.C. Wehrum to John B. Bachelder, 21 Jan. 1884, Bachelder Papers, NHHS.

157. C.C. Wehrum, to John B. Bachelder, 21 Jan 1884, Bachelder Papers, NHHS.

158. It is also possible that the 12th Mass. did not counter attack because of a fence that ran between their position and most of Iverson's men; see Elmore, "Attack and Counter Attack," *Gettysburg Magazine*, No. 5, p. 128.

159. Hall, *History of the Ninety-Seventh Regiment*, p. 138

160. C.C. Wehrum to John B. Bachelder, 21 Jan. 1884, Bachelder Papers, NHHS; *OR* 27.1.307. Bates thought that he was hit by a sharpshooter from O'Neal's brigade posted at the McLean "red barn," undated statement by Bates in Bachelder Papers, NHHS.

161. *OR* 27.1.307; see also Vautier, "At Gettysburg."

162. Grant, "The First Army Corps on the First Day at Gettysburg," in *Gettysburg Papers*, Vol. 1, p. 262 (*Minnesota MOLLUS*, Vol. 5, p. 50); see also *NYG*, p. 736.

163. Vautier, "At Gettysburg;" see also Beyer and Keydel, *Deeds of Valor*, p. 223.

164. Grant, "The First Army Corps on the First Day at Gettysburg," in *Gettysburg Papers*, Vol. 1, p. 262. (*Minnesota MOLLUS*, Vol. 5, p. 50); see also Vautier, *History of the Eighty-Eighth Pennsylvania*, p. 107.

165. *OR* 27.1.311

166. Griffin, "Rodes on Oak Hill," *Gettysburg Magazine*, No. 4, p. 42; see also Stine, *History of the Army of the Potomac*, p. 484.

167. Hall, *History of the Ninety-Seventh Regiment*, p. 141 note; *OR* 27.1.310. The flag of the 20th NC was recaptured by Daniel's 45th NC later in the afternoon, Vautier, *History of the 88th Pennsylvania Volunteers*, p. 135.

168. Kross, "That One Error Fills Him with Faults," *Blue and Gray Magazine*, Vol. 12, No. 3 (Feb 1995), p. 51.

169. *OR* 27.1.286.

170. *OR* 27.1.286, 299.

171. Hussey, *History of the Ninth Regiment, NYSM-NGSNY*, p. 271.

172. Samuel G. Boone Memoirs, USAMHI.

173. Boone, "Captured at Gettysburg," *National Tribune*, 9 May 1912.

174. Vautier, *History of the Eighty-Eighth Pennsylvania Volunteers*, p. 107.

175. Vautier, "At Gettysburg;" Vautier, *History of the Eighty-Eighth Pennsylvania Volunteers*, p. 107.

176. Hall, *History of the Ninety-Seventh Regiment*, p. 138.

177. Turner, "Twenty-third Regiment," *NC Regts*, Vol. 2, pp. 236-237.

178. *OR* 27.2.579

179. *OR* 27.2.580

180. H.H. Lyman of the 147th N.Y. says that this fight lasted "about one half hour," letter to John Bachelder, Bachelder Papers, NHHS.

181. *OR* 27.2.444
182. *OR* 27.2.579
183. Busey and Martin, *RSLG*, p. 288
184. Busey and Martin, *RSLG*, p. 165; Vautier, *History of the Eighty-Eighth Pennsylvania*, p. 136; Comte de Paris, *History of the Civil War in America*, Vol. 3, p. 563.
185. Montgomery, "Twelfth Regiment," *NC Regts*, Vol. 1, p. 636. The historian of the 23rd N.C. estimate the brigade's losses were at least 750 men, Turner "Twenty-Third Regiment," *NC Regts*, Vol. 2, p. 237.
186. Turner, "Twenty-third Regiment," *NC Regts*, Vol. 2, p. 237.
187. Berkeley, *Four Years in the Confederacy Artillery*, p. 50; see also *OR* 27.2.554.
188. Vautier, *History of the Eighty-Eighth Pennsylvania Volunteers*, p. 135.
189. Turner, "Twenty-Third Regiment," *NC Regts*, Vol. 2, p. 238.
190. Montgomery, "Twelfth Regiment," *NC Regts*, Vol. 1, p. 637; Turner, "Twenty-third Regiment," *NC Regts*, Vol. 2, p. 238; see also Nesbitt, *Ghosts of Gettysburg*, pp. 23-26 and *More Ghosts of Gettysburg*, pp. 77-78.
191. Quoted in Krick, "Three Confederate Disasters on Oak Ridge," in *The First Day at Gettysburg*, p. 136.
192. Hufham, J.D. Jr., "Gettysburg," *The Wake Forest Student*, Vol. 16 (1897), p. 454.
193. Turner, "Twenty-third Regiment," *NC Regts*, Vol. 2, p. 237.
194. Toon, "Twentieth Regiment," *NC Regts*, Vol. 2, p. 111.
195. Turner, "Twenty-Third Regiment," *NC Regts*, Vol. 2, p. 235.
196. See a favorable evaluation of Iverson's pre-Gettysburg service in Patterson, "The Death of Iverson's Brigade," *Gettysburg Magazine*, No. 5, p. 15.
197. Davis, *The Confederate General*, Vol. 3, p. 143.
198. Turner, "Twenty-third Regiment," *NC Regts*, Vol. 2, p. 236.
199. Montgomery, "Twelfth Regiment," *NC Regts*, Vol. 1, pp. 637-638.
200. *OR* 27.2.580
201. *OR* 27.2.574
202. *OR* 27.2.566. Daniel claims he sent three regiments (53rd, 43th, and 2nd N.C. Battalion to support Iverson), but the 32nd stayed with the right wing of the brigade.
203. *OR* 27.2.579. It is odd that Daniel sent the 53rd from his right center rather than a unit farther to the left.
204. *OR* 27.2.576
205. *OR* 27.1.282
206. H.H. Lyman to John Bachelder, undated, Bachelder Papers, NHHS.
207. *OR* 27.2.573
208. *OR* 27.2.573
209. 27.2.576
210. *OR* 27.2.574, 578
211. *OR* 27.2.566
212. Green, "Second Battalion," *NC Regts*, Vol. 4, p. 255
213. *OR* 27.2.341

214. *OR* 27.1.329, 332, 335

215. *OR* 27.1.330

216. *OR* 27.1.342

217. Chronicles of Francis P. Jones, GNMP Collections

218. Watson, "Forty-Fifth Regiment," *NC Regts*, Vol. 3, p. 42

219. Green, "Second Battalion," *NC Regts*, Vol. 4, p. 256

220. *OR* 27.1.332, 345. Dwight mistakenly placed his advance before the repulse of Daniel's first attack; see Hartwig, "The Defense of McPherson's Ridge," *Gettysburg Magazine*, No. 1, p. 21, n. 34.

221. *Pa. at G*, p. 745.

222. John Bassler to John B. Bachelder, Feb. 1882, Bachelder Papers, NHHS; Chamberlin, *History of the One Hundred and Fiftieth Regiment*, p. 124.

223. Doubleday, *Chancellorsville and Gettysburg*, p. 144.

224. *OR* 27.1.342, 345

225. *OR* 27.1.342. Stone's account confuses elements of Daniel's first and second attacks.

226. Green, "Second Battalion," *NC Regts*, Vol. 4, pp. 255-256.

227. *OR* 27.2.566

228. *OR* 27.2.572

229. *OR* 27.2.567

230. *OR* 27.1.342

231. *OR* 27.1.342

232. Chamberlin, *History of the One Hundred and Fiftieth Regiment*, p. 124.

233. John Bassler to John B. Bachelder, Feb. 1882, Bachelder Papers, NHHS; for detailed losses of the 149th Pa. during this retreat, see Matthews, *The 149th Pennsylania Volunteers Infantry*, pp. 88-89.

234. *OR* 27.1. 342

235. *OR* 27.2.574-575

236. Musser to D. Ribu, 10 Dec. 1863, Musser Papers, USAMHI.

237. Green, "Second Battalion," *NC Regts*, Vol. 4, p. 256.

238. *OR* 27.2.567

239. *OR* 27.1.332

240. *OR* 27.2.572

241. *OR* 27.1.332; Chamberlin, *History of the One Hundred and Fiftieth Regiment*, p. 124.

242. *OR* 27.1.343-344

243. W.H. Bassler to John B. Bachelder, Feb. 1882, Bachelder Papers, NHHS. Bassler also noted that the regiment was not properly reformed when it attacked. Nevertheless, he felt that "after the previous blunder," the attack was the best thing Dwight could do in order to "preserve the prestige of the Regt."

244. OR 27.1.345

245. *OR* 27.1.346

246. Chamberlin, *History of the One Hundred and Fiftieth Regiment*, p. 126.

247. Chamberlin, *History of the One Hundred and Fiftieth Regiment*, p. 127.

248. Chamberlin, *History of the One Hundred and Fiftieth Regiment*, p. 125; see also Scott, *The Story of the Battles of Gettysburg*, p. 202

249. Chamberlin, *History of the One Hundred and Fiftieth Regiment*, pp. 125-127, which also lists the names of the unit's individual casualties during this attack.

250. *OR* 27.1.336

251. *NYG*, p. 753

252. For example, Private Harry Hunterston of Co. B, 88th Pa., was directed to escort a wounded Confederate prisoner into Gettysburg. As he was passing near the Lutheran Church on Chambersburg St., he was fired on by one of Ewell's men who had entered the north edge of the town on the heels of the retreating XI Corps. Hunterston used his prisoner as a human shield and withdrew to safety. Chaplain H.S. Howell of the 90th Pa. was killed in front of the church at the same time perhaps by the same soldier who shot at Hunterston. See Hunterston, "Escaped Capture," *National Tribune*, 23 March 1911.

253. Grant, "The First Army Corps on the First Day at Gettysburg," in *Gettysburg Papers*, Vol. 1, p. 262 (*Minnesota MOLLUS*, Vol. 5, p. 50); Hussey *History of the Ninth Regiment, NYSM-NGSNY*, p. 271.

254. Busey and Martin, *RSLG*, pp. 25-26

255. *OR* 27.1.301

256. *OR* 27.1.301; Small, *The Road to Richmond*, p. 99. Lt. Francis Wiggin of the 16th claims that his regiment advanced on the western side of Seminary Ridge, but the remainder of his account makes it clear he meant the eastern side, Wiggin, "Sixteenth Maine Regiment at Gettysburg," *Gettysburg Papers*, Vol. 1, p. 294, (*Maine MOLLUS*, Vol. 4, p. 156). See also *Maine at Gettysburg*, p. 40.

257. *OR* 27.1. 297-298, 301.

258. Stearns, *Three Years with Company K*, p. 189; Busey, *These Honored Dead*, p. 56.

259. *NYG*, p. 756

260. *OR* 27.1.301.

261. Small, *The Road to Richmond*, pp. 99-100; *Maine at Gettysburg*, pp. 40-41.

262. Stine, *History of the Army of the Potomac*, p. 474 note.

263. Stine, *History of the Army of the Potomac*, p. 474 note.

264. *OR* 27.1.299

265. Stine, *History of the Army of the Potomac*, p. 474 note; Vautier, *History of the Eighty-Eighth Pennsylvania Volunteers*, p. 135.

266. Hall, *History of the Ninety-Seventh Regiment*, pp. 138-139.

267. Hall, *History of the Ninety-Seventh Regiment*, p. 140.

268. Grant, "The First Army Corps on the First Day at Gettysburg," in *Gettysburg Papers*, Vol. 1, p. 263 (*Minnesota MOLLUS*, Vol. 5, p. 51)

269. Vautier, "At Gettysburg"

270. Locke, *The Story of the Regiment*, p. 230

271. Grant, "The First Army Corps on the First Day at Gettysburg," in *Gettysburg Papers*, Vol. 1, p. 263 (*Minnesota MOLLUS*, Vol. 5, p. 51.

272. Grant, "The First Army Corps on the First Day at Gettysburg," in *Gettysburg Papers*, Vol. 1, p. 263 (*Minnesota MOLLUS*, Vol. 5, p. 51). The flag of the 20th NC was recaptured a short while later by one of Daniel's regiments, Vautier, *History of the Eighty-Eighth Pennsylvania Volunteers*, p. 135.
273. Vautier, "At Gettysburg"
274. Beyer and Keydel, *Deeds of Valor*, p. 221.; Small, *The Road to Richmond*, p. 100.
275. *OR* 27.2.587, 595
276. *NYG*, p. 756
277. *NYG*, p. 756
278. *OR* 27.1.290, 293-294; See also Hassler, *Crisis at the Crossroads*, p. 95. It is interesting to note that Captain Abner Small of the 16th Maine was also uncertain who was in charge of Paul's brigade after Paul was wounded. Small stated that his regiment was then "under the direct orders of the division commander," Small, *The Road to Richmond*, p. 100.
279. *NYG*, p. 757
280. *OR* 27.1.298; Davis, *Three Years in the Army*, p. 227. Col. Prey of the 104th NY says that Bachelder included in his count the prisoners captured by the 104th and sent to the rear, *NYG*, p. 757.
281. Stearns, *Three Years with Company K*, pp. 179-180.
282. Vautier, *History of the Eighty-Eighth Pennsylvania Volunteers*, p. 144
283. *OR* 27.1.589; Osborne, "Fourth Regiment," *NC Regts*, Vol. 1, p. 253.
284. *OR* 27.1.589
285. *NYG*, p. 17
286. Hall, *History of the Ninety Seventh Regiment*, p. 141
287. Vautier, *History of the Eighty-Eighth Pennsylvania Volunteers*, p. 108; Vautier, "At Gettysburg,"
288. Battle report of B.F. Look, Dec. 1863, Bachelder Papers, NHHS.
289. Grant, "The First Army Corps on the First Day at Gettysburg," in Gettysburg Papers, Vol. 1, p. 264 (*Minnesota MOLLUS*, Vol. 5, p. 52); Vautier, *History of the Eighty-Eighth Pennsylvania Volunteers*, p. 108
290. *OR* 27.1.276, 282
291. *OR* 27.1.282-283
292. Tevis, *History of the Fighting 14th*, p. 85.

VII. Collapse of the XI Corps

1. *OR* 27.1.727; Schurz, *The Reminiscences of Carl Schurz*, Vol. 2, p. 7. See also *OR* 27.1.702, where Howard plainly states that it was about noon when he ordered Schurz to advance to Oak Hill in response to a message from Doubleday that his right was being hard pressed. Howard in *Autobiography of Oliver Otis Howard*, Vol. 1, p. 414, however, states that his advance was ordered after his meeting with Doubleday at 1400, because he was concerned with the weakness of Doubleday's left and wished to draw the enemy's attention away from that quarter. The time

given by Howard's battle report is more acceptable because it is closer to the event and more in tune with other accounts.

2. *NYG*, p. 375. The account given in *OR* 27.1.734 places the regiment's arrival at 1100 and deployment at 1130. The 45th's regimental account in *NYG* p. 378, says that the regiment arrived "at 1115 A.M. by the town-clock in the town." Either this soldier's recollection was wrong or the clock was off, since this early an arrival does not agree with other events and accounts of this time period. (See Appendix IV).

3. *NYG*, p. 378.

4. *NYG*, p. 378.

5. *OR* 27.2.597

6. *NYG*, p. 378

7. *OR* 27.2.581, 597

8. *OR* 27.2.552-553, 581, 584; Thomas, *History of the Doles-Cook Brigade*, p. 359; see also Bachelder, 1 July 1863 map.

9. *OR* 27.1.734; *NYG*, p. 378

10. Busey and Martin, *RSLG*, p. 85

11. Lt. Col. Brown of the 61st claimed in his battle report that his unit had "the honor to be the advance regiment of the Third Division," *OR* 27.1.738. However, all other accounts are clear that the 45th NY arrived ahead of Brown's regiment.

12. *OR* 27.1.738

13. This unit was also understrength, see Hartwig, "The 11th Army Corps on July 1, 1863," *Gettysburg Magazine*, No. 2, p. 37, and Busey and Martin, *RSLG*, p. 85.

14. Bates, *History of Pennsylvania Volunteers*, Vol. 2, p. 896.

15. Vautier, *History of the Eighty-Eighth Pennsylvania Volunteers*, p. 139, claims that the 74th Pa. was in Von Amsberg's reserve line, but Bachelder's 1 July 1863 map places the 74th in the brigade's front line between the 45th NY and the 61st Ohio.

16. Schurz, *The Reminiscences of Carl Schurz*, Vol. 2, p. 7.

17. *OR* 27.1.754

18. *OR* 27.1.754

19. *OR* 27.3.603; Bachelder, 1 July 1863 map.

20. *OR* 27.1.754; Applegate, *Reminiscences and Letters of George Arrowsmith of New Jersey*, p. 211.

21. Applegate, *Reminiscences and Letters of George Arrowsmith of New Jersey*, pp. 211-212; Marcus, *A New Canaan Private in the Civil War*, p. 42.

22. Applegate, *Reminiscences and Letters of George Arrowsmith of New Jersey*, pp. 211, 212; Philip Brown to John B. Bachelder, 8 April 1864, Bachelder Papers, NHHS.

23. Busey and Martin, *RSLG*, p. 305; *OR* 27.1.754; *OR* 27.2.603

24. Ward, *Sketch of Battery I*, pp. 45, 46.

25. *OR* 27.1.755; Howard, "The First Day at Gettysburg," in *Gettysburg Papers*, Vol. 1, pp. 326-327 (*Illinois MOLLUS*, Vol. 4, pp. 254-255); Ohio Gettysburg Monument Commission, *Report of the Gettysburg Memorial Commission*, pp. 20, 23.

26. *OR* 27.1.752, 754; *In Memoriam, Letters of William Wheeler*, pp. 409-411.
27. *OR* 27.2.592.
28. *OR* 27.1.596, 601
29. *NYG*, pp. 378-379
30. *OR* 27.2.601-602; *OR* 27.1.734; *NYG*, p. 378-379; *NYG*, photo caption facing p. 16, suggests that some of the prisoners taken by the 45th NY came from the 5th and 6th Alabama.
31. *NYG*, p. 379
32. Busey and Martin, *RSLG*, p. 288
33. The brigade came up and formed between 1330 (*OR* 27.1.745) and 1400 (*OR* 27.1.746).
34. Busey and Martin, *RSLG*, p. 86.
35. Hartwig, "The Eleventh Army Corps on July 1, 1863," *Gettysburg Magazine*, No. 2, p. 39. However, Major August Ledig of the 75th Pa. says that the brigade was formed "in line of battle," *OR* 27.1.745.
36. *OR* 27.1.745-746
37. *OR* 27.1.742
38. Lee, "Reminiscences of the Gettysburg Battle," *Lippincott Magazine*, Vol. 6 (1883), p. 55.
39. *OR* 27.1.745; *Pa at G*, p. 438
40. *OR* 27.1.702; Howard, *Autobiography of Oliver Otis Howard*, Vol. 1, p. 416
41. *OR* 27.1.702
42. *OR* 27.1.727-728
43. Schurz, *Reminiscences of Carl Schurz*, Vol. 2, p. 8; Keifer, *History of the One Hundred and Fifty-Third Regiment Pennsylvania Infantry*, p. 23; Hartwig, "The Eleventh Army Corps on July 1, 1863," *Gettysburg Magazine*, No. 2, p. 39, n. 23.
44. *OR* 27.1.728. One source claims that Schurz at this time asked for Von Steinwehr's entire division to be sent to him. Charles Howard, "First Day at Gettysburg," in *Gettysburg Papers*, Vol. 1, pp. 327-328 (*Illinois MOLLUS*, Vol. 4, pp. 255-256).
45. *OR* 27.1.728
46. For more arguments for and against Howard's decision to stand and fight, see Greene, "From Chancellorsville to Cemetery Hill," in *The First Day at Gettysburg*, pp. 73-74, and Coddington, pp. 301-302.
47. *OR* 27.3.463
48. *OR* 27.3.465
49. *OR* 27.3.463
50. *OR* 27.1.702; *OR* 27.3.464
51. *OR* 27.3.465
52. *OR* 27.3.457-458
53. Howard in *The Autobiography of Oliver Otis Howard*, Vol. 1, p. 414, claims that he rode with Barlow all the way out to Barlow's Knoll. This statement is not accurate, because Barlow did not deploy at this time on the knoll, which was then occupied by Confederate sharpshooters.

54. Howard, "The Campaign and Battle of Gettysburg," *Atlantic Monthly*, 38 (1876), p. 55; Biddle, *The First Day of the Battle of Gettysburg*, p. 39 (in *Gettysburg Sources*, Vol. 3, p. 118); Howard, *The Autobiography of Oliver Otis Howard*, Vol. 1, p. 414.

55. Hartwig, "The Eleventh Army Corps on July 1, 1863," *Gettysburg Magazine*, No. 2, pp. 39-40.

56. Howard, *The Autobiography of Oliver Otis Howard*, Vol. 1, p. 414.

57. Howard, *The Autobiography of Oliver Otis Howard*, Vol. 1, p. 414

58. *OR* 27.1.266

59. Howard, *The Autobiography of Oliver Otis Howard*, Vol. 1, p. 414.

60. *OR* 27.1.702

61. Doubleday, *Chancellorsville and Gettysburg*, p. 141. Doubleday adds here that "I think this was the first and only order I received from him all day." This statement, however, does not agree with Howard's recollections; see, for example, Howard, *The Autobiography of Oliver Otis Howard*, Vol. 1, pp. 414, 417, and *OR* 27.1.704

62. *OR* 27.1.703

63. *OR* 27.1.248

64. Doubleday, *Chancellorsville and Gettysburg*, pp. 140-141.

65. *OR* 27.1.715

66. Howard, *The Autobiography of Oliver Otis Howard*, Vol. 1, pp. 408-409.

67. James Brown to John B. Bachelder, 8 April 1864, Bachelder Papers, NHHS.

68. James Brown to John B. Bachelder, 8 April 1864, Bachelder Papers, NHHS; William H. Warren Diary, Sterling Library, Yale University, New Haven, p. 84.

69. *OR* 27.1.701. Major Thomas W. Osborn, commander of the XI Corps artillery battalion, says that Wilkeson was not ordered to report to Barlow until after he reached the field, *OR* 27.1.748.

70. Keifer, *History of the One Hundred and Fifty-Third Regiment Pennsylvania Volunteer Infantry*, p. 210.

71. Coddington, p. 301, believes that Barlow may have advanced to the knoll on direct orders from Howard. Wilson Greene argues more persuasively that Barlow advanced on his own initiative, "From Chancellorsville to Cemetery Hill," in *The First Day at Gettysburg*, pp. 77-78.

72. *OR* 27.1.727

73. See Greene, "From Chancellorsville to Cemetery Hill," in *The First Day at Gettysburg*, p. 78

74. *NYG*, p. 308; Martin, *Carl Bornemann's Regiment*, pp. 147, 149.

75. J. Clyde Miller to John B. Bachelder, 2 March 1884, Bachelder Papers, NHHS

76. Keifer, *History of the One Hundred and Fifty Third Regiment Pennsylvania Volunteers*, p. 210

77. J. Clyde Miller to John B. Bachelder, 2 March 1884, Bachelder Papers, NHHS

78. J. Clyde Miller to John B. Bachelder, 2 March 1884, Bachelder Papers, NHHS

79. Keifer, *History of the One Hundred and Fifty-third Regiment Pennsylvania Volunteers,* pp. 140, 182.

80. Keifer, *History of the One Hundred and Fifty Third Regiment Pennsylvania Volunteers,* pp. 210-211.

81. *NYG,* p. 404; Keifer, *History of the One Hundred and Fifty-Third Regiment Pennsylvania Volunteers,* p. 211; J. Clyde Miller to John B. Bachelder, 2 March 1884, Bachelder Papers, NHHS; see also Hartwig, "The 11th Army Corps on July 1, 1863," *Gettysburg Magazine,* No. 2, pp. 36, 41.

82. Keifer, *History of the One Hundred and Fifty-Third Regiment Pennsylvania Volunteers,* p. 211

83. Andrew L. Harris to John B. Bachelder, 14 March 1881, Bachelder Papers, NHHS.

84. *OR* 27.1.756

85. *OR* 27.1.727

86. *OR* 27.1.717

87. *OR* 27.1.717

88. *OR* 27.1.728

89. Schurz, *The Reminiscences of Carl Schurz,* Vol. 3, p. 9.

90. Barlow wrote to his mother soon after the battle that he simply "formed as directed," Francis C. Barlow to his mother, 7 July 1863, copy in GNMP Collections.

91. Schurz, *The Reminiscences of Carl Schurz,* Vol. 3, p. 9.

92. *OR* 27.1.728

93. *OR* 27.1.756

94. *OR* 27.1.712, 715; Francis C. Barlow to his mother, 7 July 1863, copy in GNMP Collections.

95. *OR* 27.1.717; Hamblen, *Connecticut Yankees at Gettysburg,* p. 136 n. 25.

96. Francis C. Barlow to his mother, 7 July 1863, copy in GNMP Collections.

97. Pfanz, *Gettysburg: Culp's Hill and Cemetery Hill,* p. 38.

98. Cheney, *History of the Ninth Regiment New York Volunteer Cavalry,* p. 109.

99. Cheney, *History of the Ninth Regiment New York Volunteer Cavalry,* p. 109; *OR* 27.1.939

100. Cheney in *History of the Ninth Regiment New York Volunteer Cavalry,* p. 110, says this episode happened at 1100, but it probably occurred about two hours later.

101. Cheney, *History of the Ninth Regiment New York Volunteer Cavalry,* p. 110.

102. Cheney, *History of the Ninth Regiment New York Volunteer Cavalry,* p. 11.

103. *OR* 27.1.939.

104. *OR* 27.1.939. See also Moyer, *History of the Seventeenth Regiment Pennsylvania Volunteer Cavalry,* p. 50

105. *NYG,* p. 1247

106. *OR* 27.1.751; Cheney, *History of the Ninth Regiment New York Volunteer Cavalry*, p. 111.

107. Early, *Autobiographical Sketch and Narrative of the War Between the States*, pp. 266-267; Pfanz, *Gettysburg—Culp's Hill and Cemetery Hill*, p. 39; J.W. Daniel, "Memoir of the Battle of Gettysburg," pp. 23, Virginia Historical Society; *OR* 27.2.468; Tucker, *High Tide at Gettysburg*, p. 155.

108. Bachelder, 1 July 1863 Map

109. *OR* 27.2.495

110. Stiles, *Four Years Under Marse Robert*, p. 109.

111. *OR* 27.1.756; Busey, *Those Honored Dead*, p. 263; *B & L*, Vol. 3, p. 281.

112. Hamblen, *Connecticut Yankees at Gettysburg*, p. 19.

113. *OR* 27.1.757; Francis C. Barlow to his mother, 7 July 1863, GNMP Collections.

114. Campbell Brown Journal, Southern Historical Collection, University of North Carolina, Chapel Hill.

115. *B & L*, Vol. 3, p. 281, note. There is a sketch of Wilkeson in action just before he was felled, *ibid* p. 280. See also Boyle, *Soldiers True*, p. 116.

116. *OR* 27.2.495. The disabled gun was replaced by a Union Napoleon captured later in the afternoon, *OR* 27.2.458; see also Driver, *The Staunton Artillery*, pp. 31-32

117. *OR* 27.2.497

118. *OR* 27.2.495

119. *OR* 27.2.495-497

120. *OR* 27.1.756

121. Bachelder, 1 July 1863 Map.

122. Stiles, *Four Years Under Marse Robert*, p. 210.

123. Busey and Martin, *RSLG*, p. 159.

124. *OR* 27.2.429

125. Busey and Martin, *RSLG*, p. 161.

126. *OR* 27.1.581-582. C. D. Grace in "Rodes' Division at Gettysburg," *CV* 5 (1897), p. 614, says that Rodes' sharpshooters had advanced on the left all the way to the York Pike.

127. *OR* 27.2.492

128. Early, *Autobiographical Sketch and Narrative of the War Between the States*, p. 267

129. Gordon, *Reminiscences of the Civil War*, pp. 150-151.

130. Doubleday, however, thought that Barlow's chances of success were good if he did attack, *Chancellorsville and Gettysburg*, p. 142

131. Gordon gives the time of his attack as 1500 in *OR* 27.2.492; other sources place the attack a bit later.

132. Bachelder, 1 July 1863 Map.

133. *OR* 27.2.492

134. J. Clyde Miller to John B. Bachelder, 2 March 1884, Bachelder Papers, NHHS.

135. *OR* 27.1.756, 757

136. *OR* 27.2.492
137. Nichols, *A Soldier's Story of His Regiment*, p. 116.
138. Keifer, *History of the One Hundred and Fifty-third Regiment Pennsylvania Volunteers*, pp. 211-212
139. J. Clyde Miller to John B. Bachelder, 2 March 1884, Bachelder Papers, NHHS.
140. Keifer, *History of the One Hundred and Fifty-third Regiment Pennsylvania Volunteers*, p. 212.
141. Keifer, *History of the One Hundred and Fifty-third Regiment Pennsylvania Volunteers*, pp. 178, 214, 252.
142. *OR* 27.1.756
143. *OR* 27.1.757
144. Grace, "Rodes' Division at Gettysburg," *CV* 5 (1897), p. 614, Doles' skirmishers had advanced almost as far as the Almshouse before the XI Corps arrived, *OR* 27.1.742.
145. *OR* 27.2.582
146. *OR* 27.2.585; Thomas, *History of the Doles-Cook Brigade*, p. 474
147. *OR* 27.2.562, 584
148. Grace, "Rodes' Division at Gettysburg," *CV* 5 (1897), p. 614.
149. *OR* 27.1.719-720
150. Andrew L. Harris to John B. Bachelder, 14 March 1881, Bachelder Papers, NHHS.
151. Andrew L. Harris to John B. Bachelder, 14 March 1881, Bachelder papers, NHHS.
152. Hamblen, *Connecticut Yankees at Gettysburg*, pp. 23-24.
153. *OR* 27.1.717; William H. Warren Diary, Sterling Library, Yale University, New Haven, p. 87.
154. J. Henry Blakeman to his mother, 4 July 1863, Lewis Leigh Collection, USAMHI, Carlisle Barracks, Carlisle Pa.
155. Jeremiah Williams to John B. Bachelder, 18 June 1880, Bachelder Papers, NHHS.
156. C. Frederick Betts to Henry Allen, as quoted in William H. Allen Scrapbooks, Bridgeport Public Library, Bridgeport.
157. Hamblen, *Connecticut Yankees at Gettysburg*, p. 137, p. 33; *17th Connecticut Volunteers at Gettysburg*, p. 12.
158. William H. Warren Diary, Civil War Manuscripts Collection, Manuscripts and Archives, Yale University Library, p. 87.
159. Francis C. Barlow letter to his mother, 7 July 1863, copy in GNMP Collections.
160. Francis C. Barlow letter to his mother, 7 July 1863, copy in GNMP Collections.
161. Francis C. Barlow letter to his mother, 7 July 1863, copy in GNMP Collections.
162. Boatner, *Civil War Dictionary*, *s.v.* "Barlow"
163. Hanna, "A Gettysburg Myth Exploded," *CWTI*, Vol. 24, No. 3, (May 1985), pp. 45-47; the author unfortunately does not cite his primary sources.

164. Gordon, *Reminiscences of the Civil War*, p. 151.
165. Gordon, *Reminiscences of the Civil War*, p. 151.
166. Gordon, *Reminiscences of the Civil War*, pp. 152-153.
167. See particularly Hanna, "A Gettysburg Myth Exploded," *CWTI*, Vol. 24, No. 3 (May 1985), pp. 42-47.
168. Francis C. Barlow letter to his mother, 7 July 1863, copy in GNMP Collections.
169. Pullen, "The Gordon-Barlow Story, with Sequel," *Gettysburg Magazine*, No. 8, p. 6.
170. Pullen, "The Gordon-Barlow Story, with Sequel," *Gettysburg Magazine*, No. 8, p. 7.
171. A 1901 version of the speech, given in Brooklyn, is printed in Pullen, "The Gordon-Barlow Incident, with Sequel," *Gettysburg Magazine*, No. 8, pp. 5-7. Peter S. Carmichael in *The Confederate General*, Vol. 3, p. 12, says that "Dripping with romanticism and full of half truths, Gordon's recollections reflect his desire to foster harmonious relations between the two sections."
172. *OR* 27.1.493
173. Nichols, *A Soldier's Story of His Regiment*, p. 116.
174. *OR* 27.1.745; Lee, "Reminiscences of the Gettysburg Battle," *Lippincott Magazine*, Vol. 6 (1883) p. 56.
175. *OR* 27.1.584-585
176. Lee, "Reminiscences of the Gettysburg Battle," *Lippincott Magazine*, Vol. 6 (1883), p. 56.
177. *OR* 27.2.585
178. *OR* 27.1.745
179. *OR* 27.1.745, *OR* 27.2.585
180. *OR* 27.2.585; Thomas, *History of the Doles-Cook Brigade*, p. 475.
181. Grace, "Rodes' Division at Gettysburg," *CV* 5 (1897) p. 615.
182. Grace, "Rodes' Division at Gettysburg," *CV* 5 (1897) p. 615.
183. *OR* 27.1.742.
184. Pula, *The History of a German-Polish Civil War Brigade*, p. 79, and the sources cited there.
185. *OR* 27.1.746
186. Busey and Martin, *RSLG*, p. 86.
187. Pula, *The History of a German-Polish Civil War Brigade*, p. 78, and the sources cited there.
188. Pula, *The History of a German-Polish Civil War Brigade*, p. 78, with name spellings corrected by Busey, *These Honored Dead*, pp. 183-184; *OR* 27.1.745.
189. Lee, "Reminiscences of the Gettysburg Battle," *Lippincott Magazine*, Vol. 6 (1883) p. 56; Hartwig, "The Eleventh Corps on July 1, 1863," *Gettysburg Magazine*, No. 2, pp. 45, 47.
190. Pula, *The History of a German-Polish Civil War Brigade*, pp. 78-79.
191. *OR* 27.1.745.
192. Pula, *The History of a German-Polish Civil War Brigade*, p. 79.
193. Krzyzanowski, *Memoirs*, p. 79.

194. Pula, *The History of a German-Polish Civil War Brigade*, p. 79.
195. *OR* 27.1.195; Busey and Martin, *RSLG*, pp. 86, 158, 167.
196. Pula, *The History of a German-Polish Civil War Brigade*, pp. 79-83, argues that the brigade fought more valiantly than just described.
197. Philip Brown to John B. Bachelder, 4 April 1864, Bachelder Papers, NHHS
198. *OR* 27.2.586
199. Thomas, *History of the Doles-Cook Brigade*, pp. 475-476.
200. *OR* 27.2.585-586; Applegate, *Reminiscences and Letters of George Arrowsmith of New Jersey*, p. 217.
201. *OR* 27.1.254, 262; Busey and Martin, *RSLG*, p. 262.
202. *NYG*, pp. 1060-1061.
203. *OR* 27.1.745; *NYG*, p. 808.
204. *NYG*, p. 1320; *OR* 27.1.753.
205. *OR* 27.1.753.
206. *OR* 27.1.754.
207. *OR* 27.1.754; Ward, *Sketch of Battery I First Ohio Artillery*, p. 46.
208. *OR* 27.1.756, 757.
209. *OR* 27.1.712-713.
210. Andrew L. Harris to John B. Bachelder, 14 March 1881, Bachelder Papers, NHHS.
211. Nichols, *A Soldier's Story of his Regiment*, p. 116.
212. Keifer, *History of the One Hundred and Fifty-third Pennsylvania Volunteers*, p. 215.
213. Nichols, *A Soldier's Story of his Regiment*, p. 116.
214. *OR* 27.2.492.
215. *OR* 27.1.713.
216. Busey and Martin, *RSLG*, p. 286.
217. Stiles, *Four Years Under Marse Robert*, p. 211
218. Busey and Martin, *RSLG*, p. 286.
219. Stiles, *Four Years Under Marse Robert*, p. 211
220. Dunkelman and Winey, *The Hardtack Regiment*, p. 71.
221. Dunkelman and Winey, "The Hardtack Regiment in the Brickyard Fight," *Gettysburg Magazine*, No. 8, p. 19.
222. *OR* 27.1.721.
223. *OR* 27.1.721.
224. Dunkelman and Winey, "The Hardtack Regiment in the Brickyard Fight,' *Gettysburg Magazine*, No. 8, p. 19; *NYG*, p. 1055.
225. *OR* 27.1.721; Hirz, *The Letters of Frederick C. Winkler*, pp. 69-70.
226. Dunkelman and Winey, *The Hardtack Regiment*, p. 71.
227. Dunkelman and Winey, "The Hardtack Regiment in the Brickyard Fight," *Gettysburg Magazine*, No. 8, p. 19.
228. McKay, "Three Years *or* During the War with the Crescent and Star," *The National Tribune Scrap Book*, p. 131; John F. Wellman letter to "Dear Comrades of the 154 Regiment," 10 August 1888, in *Ellicottville (NY) Post*, 5 Sept. 1888.
229. *OR* 27.1.755

230. *The Seventy-Third Regiment Pennsylvania Volunteers at Gettysburg*, p. 12.

231. It is possible that Schurz ordered the 73rd to be detached, as suggested by Dunkelman and Winey in *The Hardtack Regiment*, p. 73.

232. Hirz, *The Letters of Frederick C. Winkler*, p. 71.

233. *OR* 27.1.729; Schurz, *The Reminiscences of Carl Schurz*, Vol. 3, p. 11.

234. John F. Wellman letter to "Dear Comrades of the 154 Regiment," 10 August 1888, in *Ellicottville (NY) Post*, 5 Sept. 1888.

235. McKay, "Three Years or During the War with the Crescent and Star," *The National Tribune Scrap Book*, p. 131.

236. McKay, "Three Years or During the War with the Crescent and Star," *The National Tribune Scrap Book*, p. 131.

237. *NYG*, p. 1051

238. Stiles, *Four Years With Marse Robert*, p. 210.

239. *OR* 27.2.479; Bachelder, 1 July 1863 Map.

240. Busey and Martin, *RSLG*, p. 286; *OR* 27.1.717.

241. *OR* 27.2.479

242. *OR* 27.1.717

243. Early, *Autobiographical Sketch and Narrative of the War Between the States*, p. 268.

244. *OR* 27.2.484.

245. McKay, "Three Years or During the War with the Crescent and Star," *The National Tribune Scrap Book*, p. 131.

246. *OR* 27.2.486.

247. *NYG*, pp. 918, 1051.

248. Bates, *History of Pennsylvania Volunteers*, Vol. 2, p. 391.

249. Alonson Crosby to Samuel G. Love, 28 February 1864, published in *Jamestown Journal*, 18 March 1864.

250. *NYG*, p. 1055.

251. James D. Quilliam to William Quilliam, 23 August 1863, as cited in Dunkelman and Winey, "The Hardtack Regiment in the Brickyard Fight," *Gettysburg Magazine*, No. 8, p. 21.

252. *NYG*, p. 1051.

253. Alonson Crosby to Manley Crosby, 17 July 1863, published in *Cattaraugus Freeman*, 30 July 1863.

254. See Dunkelman and Winey, "The Hardtack Regiment in the Brickyard Fight," *Gettysburg Magazine*, No. 8, pp. 21-22.

255. William Charles to Dear Ann, 12 July 1863, as cited in Dunkelman and Winey, "The Hardtack Regiment in the Brickyard Fight," *Gettysburg Magazine*, No. 8, p. 21.

256. Imholte, "Civil War Diary and Related Sources of Corporel Newell Burch," Minnesota Historical Society.

257. Hartwig, "The 11th Army Corps on July 1, 1863," *Gettysburg Magazine*, Vol. 2, pp. 48-49.

258. McKay, "Three Years or During the War With the Crescent and Star," *The National Tribune Scrap Book*, p. 131.

259. Alex Bird, "At Gettysburg," *Ellicottville Post*, 16 September 1898.

260. *NYG*, p. 1055 note.

261. *NYG*, p. 1055.

262. *History of the 134th Regiment*, p. 29.

263. Busey and Martin, *RSLG*, pp. 254, 262, 1055

264. McKay, "Three Years or During the War with the Crescent and Star," *The National Tribune Scrap Book*, p. 131.

265. The mural which was designed by Mark Dunkelman was dedicated on 1 July 1988. See Dunkelman and Winey, "The Hardtack Regiment in the Brickyard Fight," *Gettysburg Magazine*, No. 8, pp. 28-30, and Dunkelman, *The Coster Avenue Mural in Gettysburg*.

266. John F. Wellman to "Dear Comrades of the 154 Regiment," 10 August 1888, published in the *Ellicottville (NY) Post*, 5 September 1888.

267. Unidentified, undated newspaper clipping from the *Rochester Press*, cited in Dunkelman and Winey, "The Hardtack Regiment in the Brickyard Fight," *Gettysburg Magazine*, No. 8, p. 23.

268. Dunkelman and Winey, "The Hardtack Regiment in the Brickyard Fight," *Gettysburg Magazine*, No. 8, pp. 26-27.

269. Dunkelman and Winey, "The Hunt for Sergeant Humiston," *CWTI*, Vol. 21, No. 1 (March 1982), pp. 28-31.

270. *OR* 27.1.755, 27.2.486

271. Hirz, *The Letters of Frederick C. Winkler*, pp. 70-71.

272. Vautier, *History of the Eighty-Eighth Pennsylvania Volunteers*, p. 141.

273. *OR* 27.1.754

274. *OR* 27.1.756, 757; Ward, *Sketch of Battery I, First Ohio Light Artillery*, p. 46.

275. Vautier, *History of the Eighty-Eighth Pennsylvania Volunteers*, p. 149.

276. *OR* 27.1.718.

277. Schurz, *The Reminiscences of Carl Schurz*, Vol. 3, pp. 11-12.

278. *NYG*, p. 379, Busey and Martin, *RSLG*, p. 254.

279. *NYG*, p. 379.

280. Busey and Martin, *RSLG*, P. 254. Unfortunately, no battle reports were filed by the 61st Ohio, or 74th Pa., and that of the 82nd Illinios was lost (OR 27.1.733).

281. *OR* 27.2.586.

282. Grace, "Rodes' Division at Gettysburg," *CV* 5 (1897), p. 615.

283. *OR* 27.2.583.

284. Grace, "Rodes' Division at Gettysburg," *CV* 5 (1897), p. 615.

285. Thomas, *History of the Doles-Cook Brigade*, p. 9.

286. *NYG*, p. 380

287. *NYG*, p. 376

288. *NYG*, p. 380

289. *NYG*, pp. 380-381; *OR* 27.1.735

290. *OR* 27.1.735.

291. *NYG*, p. 380.

292. *NYG*, p. 380.

293. *NYG*, pp. 380-381; See also Busey, *These Honored Dead*, p. 11.

294. Carrington, "First Day on the Left at Gettysburg," *SHSP* 37 (1909), p. 330.
295. Carrington, "First Day on the Left at Gettysburg," *SHSP* 37 (1909), pp. 330-331.
296. Carrington, "First Day on Left at Gettysburg," *SHSP* 37 (1909) pp. 331-332.
297. Carrington, "First Day on Left at Gettysburg," *SHSP* 37 (1909), p. 332.
298. Battery tablets on the battlefield for these units, Martin, *Confederate Monuments at Gettysburg*, pp. 10, 70, 95, 117.
299. *OR* 27.2.495.
300. Stiles, *Four Years With Marse Robert*, p. 212.
301. Stiles, *Four Years With Marse Robert*, p. 212.
302. Stiles, *Four Years With Marse Robert*, p. 214.
303. Stiles, *Four Years With Marse Robert*, p. 214. Carrington in "First Day on Left at Gettysburg," *SHSP*, 37 (1909), p. 333, says that he did not move his command out of the town until daylight on 2 July, but he does not appear to be completely certain about the fact.
304. *OR* 27.2.498
305. Goldsborough, *The Maryland Line in the Confederate Army*, p. 178.
306. Gilmor, *Four Years in the Saddle*, pp. 95-96. Goldsborough, *The Maryland Line in the Confederate Army*, p. 178, is inaccurate by stating that Gilmor's command was posted in a ravine in support of Poague's and Carter's batteries.
307. Gilmor, *Four Years in the Saddle*, pp. 95-96.
308. Pfanz, *Gettysburg—Culp's Hill and Cemetery Hill*, p. 417, n. 4.
309. Cheney, *History of the Ninth Regiment New York Volunteer Cavalry*, p. 113.
310. Cheney, *History of the Ninth Regiment New York Volunteer Cavalry*, pp. 112-113.
311. *OR* 27.1.939.
312. *OR* 27.2.484.
313. *OR* 27.2.429. These were the same two guns of Heckman's Ohio battery that Avery's men claimed to have captured.
314. *OR* 27.2.479.
315. *OR* 27.2.479.
316. *OR* 27.2.479.
317. Jackson to Boyd, 20 July 1863, as quoted in Jones, *Lee's Tigers*, p. 168.
318. *OR* 27.2.480.
319. General Howard noted that "the time of greatest confusion" was from 1600-1700, *The Autobiography of Oliver Otis Howard*, Vol. 1, p. 418.
320. For the unhurried aspect of the Union retreat, see E.A. Culp, "Gettysburg," *National Tribune*, 19 March 1885.
321. Schurz, *The Reminiscences of Carl Schurz*, Vol. 3, pp. 11-12.
322. Butts, *A Gallant Captain*, pp. 76-77.
323. E.A. Culp, "At Gettysburg," *National Tribune*, 19 March 1885.

324. Anna Garlach account, GNMP Collections, based on 9 Aug. 1905 article in the *Gettysburg Compiler.*
325. Schurz, *The Reminiscences of Carl Schurz,* Vol. 3, pp. 34-37.
326. Busey and Martin, *RSLG,* pp. 253-255, after deducting approximate losses on 2 and 3 July.
327. Hassler, *Crisis at the Crossroads,* p. 149.
328. See Martin, *Carl Bornemann's Regiment,* pp. 132-135.

VIII. Climax on Seminary Ridge

1. *OR* 27.2.444.
2. Smith, "With Stonewall Jackson," *SHSP* 43 (1920) pp. 55-56.
3. Longstreet, *From Manassas to Appomattox,* p. 351.
4. *OR* 27.2.358.
5. Freeman, *R.E. Lee,* Vol. 3, p. 66.
6. Alexander, *Military Memoirs of a Confederate,* p. 381; Longstreet, *From Manassas to Appomattox,* p. 357; *OR* 27.2.358; Fremantle, *The Fremantle Diary,* p. 201.
7. Long, *Memoirs of Robert E. Lee,* p. 275.
8. Fremantle, *The Fremantle Diary,* p. 203.
9. Taylor, *Four Years with General Lee,* pp. 92-93.
10. Long, *Memoirs of Robert E. Lee,* p. 357.
11. Long, *Memoirs of Robert E. Lee,* p. 276.
12. See Chapter 6, note 29.
13. Smith, "With Stonewall Jackson," *SHSP* 43 (1920), p. 55.
14. Haines, "A.P. Hill's Advance to Gettysburg," *Gettysburg Magazine,* No. 5, p. 10.
15. Heth, "Letter From Major General Henry Heth," *SHSP* 4 (1877), p. 158; Heth, *The Memoirs of Henry Heth,* p. 175.
16. *OR* 27.2.317.
17. Heth, *The Memoirs of Henry Heth,* p. 175 Heth, "Letter from Major General Henry Heth," *SHSP* (1877), p. 126. It is odd that Heth was reporting to Lee for instructions rather than to Hill, who was nearby.
18. *OR* 27.2.638.
19. That is where Howard found him during his inspection tour that began about 1400, Howard, *The Autobiography of O.O. Howard,* Vol. 1, p. 414.
20. See, for example, Nevins, *A Diary of Battle,* p. 237.
21. Howard found Doubleday on this portion of the I Corps line during his inspection tour mentioned in note 19.
22. *OR* 27.1.327.
23. *OR* 27.1.247.
24. Doubleday, *Chancellorsville and Gettysburg,* p. 146.
25. Civil War Generals Report of Civil War Service, NA, Vol. 13, p. 584; Doubleday, *Chancellorsville and Gettysburg,* p. 146.
26. *OR* 27.1.246.
27. *Pa at G,* p. 752.

28. *Pa at G,* p. 754.
29. Chamberlin, *History of the One Hundred and Fiftieth Regiment,* p. 154.
30. Underwood, "Twenty-Sixth Regiment," *NC Regts,* Vol. 2, p. 350.
31. Both Garnett and Poague had been ordered forward from Cashtown at 1100, *OR* 27.2.652, 673.
32. *OR* 27.2.678.
33. *OR* 27.2.602-603.
34. *OR* 27.1.1032; Calef, "Gettysburg Notes: The Opening Gun," *JMSIUS* 40 (1907), p. 51.
35. *OR* 27.1.248, 372.
36. *Pa at G,* p. 908.
37. *Pa at G,* p. 908.
38. *OR* 27.1.356; Nevins, *Diary of Battle,* p. 235.
39. *OR* 27.1.268.
40. Young, "Pettigrew's Brigade at Gettysburg," *NC Regts,* Vol. 1, pp. 118-120.
41. Underwood, "Twenty-Sixth Regiment," *NC Regts,* Vol. 2, p. 348; strength figures from Busey and Martin, *RSLG,* p. 174.
42. Underwood, "Twenty-Sixth Regiment," *NC Regts,* Vol. 2, p. 351.
43. *OR* 27.2.643.
44. *OR* 27.1.268.
45. Underwood, "Twenty-Sixth Regiment," *NC Regts,* Vol. 2, p. 351.
46. Curtis, *History of the Twenty-Fourth Michigan,* p. 160. R. Lee Hadden, "The Deadly Embrace," *Gettysburg Magazine,* No. 5, p. 28, suggests that this officer may have been Gen. Pettigrew, who rode a dappled mare into the battle.
47. *OR* 27.1.268.
48. Underwood, "Twenty-Sixth Regiment," *NC Regts,* Vol. 2, p. 351.
49. Louis G. Young to Major William Baker, 10 February 1864, Francis B. Winston Papers, N.C. State Archives.
50. Underwood, "Twenty-Sixth Regiment," *NC Regts,* Vol. 2, p. 351.
51. *OR* 27.1.268.
52. *OR* 27.2.639.
53. Curtis, *History of the Twenty-Fourth Michigan,* p. 160. This anecdote is usually told in connection with Archer's fight with the 24th that morning; see for example, Hassler, *Crisis at the Crossroads,* p. 52. The Curtis account is inaccurate by intimating that Pettigrew's troops had previously encountered the Iron Brigade; Pettigrew's brigade had not been in combat before as a unit and only the 26th N.C. had seen action before, a year earlier at Seven Pines.
54. Emerson, "The Most Famous Regiment," *CV* 25 (1917), pp. 353-354.
55. Underwood, "Twenty-Sixth Regiment," *NC Regts,* Vol. 2, p. 352.
56. Underwood, "Twenty-Sixth Regiment," *NC Regts,* Vol. 2, p. 352.
57. Curtis, *History of the Twenty-Fourth Michigan,* p. 164; *OR* 27.1.268.
58. Underwood, "Twenty-Sixth Regiment," *NC Regts,* Vol. 2, p. 352.
59. Underwood, "Twenty-Sixth Regiment," *NC Regts,* Vol. 2, pp. 352-353.
60. *OR* 27.1.268; Curtis, *History of the Twenty-Fourth Regiment,* p. 162.

61. Brig. Gen. Solomon Meredith had been disabled early in the morning's fighting, when his horse was shot dead and fell on him, Nolan, *The Iron Brigade*, p. 243, and Dudley, *The Iron Brigade at Gettysburg*, p. 13.
62. Gaff, "Here Was Made out our Last and Hopeless Stand," *Gettysburg Magazine*, No. 2, pp. 29-30; M.C. Barnes to W.W. Dudley, 28 March 1883, Bachelder Papers, NHHS.
63. Gaff, "Here Was Made out our Last and Hopeless Stand," *Gettysburg Magazine*, No. 2, p. 29.
64. Gaff, "Here Was Made out our Last and Hopeless Stand," *Gettysburg Magazine*, No. 2, p. 30; Hawkins, "Sergeant Major Blanchard at Gettysburg," *Indiana Magazine of History*, Vol. 34, No. 2 (June 1938), pp. 215-216.
65. Gaff, "Here was Made out our Last and Hopeless Stand," *Gettysburg Magazine*, No. 2, p. 30; Hawkins, "Sergeant Major Blanchard at Gettysburg," *Indiana Magazine of History*, Vol. 34, No. 2 (June 1938), pp. 215-216.
66. Gaff, "Here Was Made out our Last and Hopeless Stand," *Gettysburg Magazine*, No. 2, p. 30; Hartwig, "The Defense of McPherson's Ridge," *Gettysburg Magazine*, No. 1, p. 23.
67. Gaff, "Here was Made our Last and Hopeless Stand," *Gettysburg Magazine*, No. 2, p. 30.
68. Martin and Outlaw, "Eleventh Regiment," *NC Regts*, Vol. 1, p. 589; Vanderslice, *Gettysburg Then and Now*, p. 120.
69. *OR* 27.1.313, 315, 317.
70. Busey and Martin, *RSLG*, p. 174.
71. *OR* 27.1.317.
72. Nevins, *Diary of Battle*, p. 235.
73. Gates, *The Ulster Guard and the War of the Rebellion*, pp. 433-434; Osborne, *Holding the Left*, pp. 11-12.
74. Kross, "Fighting Like the Devil to Hold Your Own," *Blue and Gray Magazine*, Vol 12., No. 3, (Feb 1995), p. 20.
75. Rogers, "Additional Sketch Forty-Seventh Regiment," *NC Regts*, Vol. 3, p. 105.
76. Osborne, *Holding the Left*, p. 12.
77. *History of the 121st Regiment Pennsylvania Volunteers*, p. 52.
78. *OR* 27.1.323.
79. *Pa at G*, p. 665.
80. Rogers, "Additional Sketch Forty-Seventh Regiment," *N.C. Regts*, Vol. 2, p. 106; Thorp, "Forty-Seventh Regiment," *N.C. Regts*, Vol. 3, p. 89.
81. Osborne, *Holding the Left*, p. 12.
82. Osborne, *Holding the Left*, p. 13.
83. *Roundout (N.Y.) Courier*, 17 July 1863.
84. Osborne, *Holding the Left*, p. 13.
85. *OR* 27.1.323.
86. *History of the 121st Regiment Pennsylvania Volunteers*, p. 53.
87. *History of the 121st Regiment Pennsylvania Volunteers*, p. 53.
88. Thorp, "Forty-Seventh Regiment," *NC Regts*, Vol. 3, p. 90.

89. *History of the 121st Regiment Pennsylvania Volunteers*, pp. 53, 55.

90. Breck, *OR* 27.1.362, claims that he fired no shots before retiring, but see Gates' account in *OR* 27.1.320. For Wainwright's decision to withdraw the battery, see *OR* 27.1.356 and Nevins, *A Diary of Battle*, p. 235. Gates, *The Ulster Guard and the War of the Rebellion*, p. 441, and others mistakenly say that this was Cooper's battery.

91. Gates, *The Ulster Guard and the War of the Rebellion*, p. 442.

92. Rogers, "Additional Sketch Forty-Seventh Regiment," *NC Regts*, Vol. 3, p. 106.

93. *OR* 27.2.639.

94. *Pa at G*, p. 696.

95. George McFarland to John B. Bachelder, n.d., Bachelder Papers, NHHS.

96. Warren, *Two Reunions of the 142'd Regiment*, p. 10. Busey, *These Honored Dead*, p. 227, says that Col. Cummins was mortally wounded and died on 2 July.

97. Rogers, "Additional Sketch Forty-Seventh Regiment," *NC Regts*, Vol. 3, p. 107.

98. The 151st included a large number of students and over a hundred school teachers. One company was composed entirely of students from an academy in Juniata County, of which Colonel McFarland was the principal; Vanderslice, *Gettysburg Then and Now*, p. 115.

99. *OR* 27.1.327.

100. *OR* 27.2.639.

101. *OR* 27.1.328.

102. Busey and Martin, *RSLG*, p. 262.

103. Scott, *The Story of the Battles at Gettysburg*, p. 229; Young, *The Battle of Gettysburg*, p. 389.

104. McFarland believed that "The Iron Brigade considered the 151st Pennsylvania a relief and immediately fell back to the hollow and reformed," "Notes in a Conversation with Col. George F. McFarland," undated, Bachelder Papers, NHHS.

105. Gaff, "There Was Made Out Our Last and Hopeless Stand," *Gettysburg Magazine*, No. 2, p. 30.

106. Curtis, *History of the Twenty-Fourth Michigan*, pp. 162, 163, 165, 182.

107. Curtis, *History of the Twenty-Fourth Michigan*, pp. 181-182. Harrison is buried in grave A-2 of the Michigan plot of the Gettysburg National Cemetery. Welch's burial place is not recorded; see Busey, *These Honored Dead*, pp. 78, 80.

108. Curtis, *History of the Twenty-Fourth Michigan*, p. 182.

109. Underwood, "The Twenty-Sixth Regiment," *NC Regts* Vol. 2, p. 353.

110. Curtis, *History of the Twenty-Fourth Michigan*, p. 165.

111. Curtis, *History of the Twenty-Fourth Michigan*, pp. 187-189.

112. Curtis, *History of the Twenty-Fourth Michigan*, pp. 189-191.

113. Smith, *The Twenty-fourth Michigan of the Iron Brigade*, p. 264.

114. John Callis to John B. Bachelder, Undated, Bachelder Papers, NHHS.

115. Heth, *The Memoirs of Henry Heth*, p. 174-176, Davis, *The Confederate*

General, Vol. 3, p. 90, Col. J.K. Marshall of the 52nd N.C. took command of Pettigrew's brigade when Pettigrew took Heth's post.

116. *OR* 27.2.643; see also Flowers, "Thirty-Eighth Regiment," *N.C. Regts,* Vol. 2, p. 691.
117. Olds, "Brave Carolinian who fell at Gettysburg," *SHSP,* 36 (1908), pp. 245-247.
118. Busey and Martin, *RSLG,* p. 176.
119. Bachelder, 1 July 1863 map.
120. Scott, *The Story of the Battles at Gettysburg,* pp. 198-199.
121. *Pa at G,* pp. 755-756.
122. *OR* 27.1.347; see also Chamberlin, *History of the One Hundred and Fiftieth Regiment,* pp. 119-120.
123. *Pa at G,* p. 756.
124. *Pa at G,* p. 756.
125. *Pa at G,* p. 756.
126. *OR* 27.1.274.
127. Scott, *The Story of the Battles at Gettysburg,* p. 204.
128. Bachelder, 1 July 1863 Map.
129. *OR* 27.1.274.
130. *OR* 27.1.279.
131. *OR* 27.1.347.
132. Vautier, *History of the Eighty-Eighth Pennsylvania Volunteers,* p. 130.
133. Some reports list Col. Morrow of the 24th Michigan as brigade commander after Gen. Meredith was disabled, but Morrow emphatically denied assuming the post, Curtis, *History of the Twenty-fourth Michigan,* pp. 159-160.
134. *OR* 27.1.279.
135. *OR* 27.1.274.
136. *OR* 27.1.280.
137. *OR* 27.1.280.
138. *OR* 27.1.274.
139. *OR* 27.1.280.
140. Busey, *These Honored Dead,* p. 276.
141. Cheney, *History of the Ninth Regiment New York Volunteer Cavalry,* p. 112.
142. Halstead, "The First Day of the Battle of Gettysburg," in *Gettysburg Papers,* Vol. 1, p. 152 (*D.C. MOLLUS,* p. 4).
143. *Pa at G,* pp. 752-753. John J. Kensill of the 149th Pa. mentions that his unit gave "brave John Burns" a chorus of "three rousing cheers" after he finished talking with Col. Wister, Kensill to John B. Bachelder, 11 Feb. 1882, Bachelder Papers, NHHS.
144. *Pa at G,* pp. 943-944. Another version of the story states that Lt. A.D. Rood of Co. K, 7th Wisconsin, took Burns to Col. Callis, who swore Burns in as a "Volunteer soldier" so that he could not be executed as a "bushwacker" if he were captured by the enemy. See Johnston, *The True Story of John Burns,* p. 11.
145. *B & L,* Vol. 3, p. 276 note.

146. *OR* 27.1.255.
147. Curtis, *History of the Twenty-Fourth Michigan*, pp. 182-183; *B & L*, Vol. 3, p. 276. Bret Harte wrote a noted poem called, "John Burns at Gettysburg," Stine, *History of the Army of the Potomac*, p. 477.
148. Cheney, *History of the Ninth Regiment New York Volunteer Cavalry*, pp. 111-112.
149. Beale, "Gettysburg," p. 17; Coco, "On the Bloodstained Field," p. 9.
150. *OR* 27.1.332-333.
151. *OR* 27.1.156.
152. *Pa at G*, p. 756.
153. *Pa at G*, p. 757.
154. *Pa at G*, p. 757.
155. *Pa at G*, p. 757.
156. *OR* 27.1.347. Lt. Col. Huidekoper in an undated memorandum in the Bachelder Papers, NHHS, says that "The Iron Brigade in the woods gave way before our men did and were slowly retreating when a battery or section galloped up to help stem the tide of men pouring into our lines; seeing that the rebels in the woods had advanced to a line parallel to the position of the battery, I sent word to the commander to retire, which he did without having time to fire a shot."
157. *OR* 27.2.567.
158. *OR* 27.2.567. The exact time of this attack is not clear. Bachelder's 1 July 1863 map suggests that it was at 1530, but by then the Union troops had all been driven from Herbst Woods. The attack was probably a little bit earlier than that.
159. *OR* 27.2.572.
160. Vautier, *History of the Eighty-Eighth Pennsylvania Volunteers*, p. 132.
161. *OR* 27.1.335.
162. *OR* 27.1.343.
163. *OR* 27.1.333.
164. Undated Memorandum by Lt. Col. Huidekoper, Bachelder Papers, NHHS.
165. Sharp, *The Congressional Medal of Honor*, p. 813.
166. *Pa at G*, p. 757.
167. Chamberlin, *History of the One Hundred and Fiftieth Regiment*, p. 134; *Pa at G*, p. 757-758.
168. Kross, "That One Error Fills Him with Faults," *Blue and Gray Magazine*, Vol 12., No. 3, (Feb 1995), p. 51.
169. Bassler, "The Color Episode," *SHSP* Vol. 37 (1909), pp. 268-269.
170. *Pa at G*, p. 755.
171. Bassler, "The Color Episode," *SHSP* Vol. 37 (1909), p. 278; Vautier, *History of the Eighty-Eighth Pennsylvania*, p. 132; Frank D. Price to Col. Bond, 27 Jan. 1878, Bachelder Papers, NHHS.
172. Bassler, "The Color Episode," *SHSP*, Vol. 37 (1909), p. 275.
173. Bassler, "The Color Episode," *SHSP*, Vol. 37 (1909), pp. 272-273.
174. Bassler, "The Color Episode," *SHSP*, Vol. 37 (1909), p. 274.
175. Frank D. Price to Col. Bond, 27 Jan 1878, Bachelder Papers, NHHS;

see also B. Jones to John B. Bachelder, 19 May 1878, Bachelder Papers, NHHS.

176. Bassler, "The Color Episode," *SHSP,* Vol. 37 (1909), p. 279.

177. Bassler, "The Color Episode," *SHSP,* Vol. 37 (1909), pp. 276, 283.

178. Bassler, "The Color Episode," *SHSP,* Vol. 37 (1909), pp. 271, 282; Busey, *These Honored Dead,* p. 233.

179. The colors of the 149th were not recaptured by members of the 150th Pa., as some sources claim. See for example, Hassler, *Crisis at the Crossroads,* p. 105, and Scott, *The Story of the Battles at Gettysburg,* p. 202.

180. *Pa at G,* p. 758.

181. W.S. Christian to John W. Daniel, 24 Oct. 1903, Daniel Papers, (#158) Manuscripts Division, Special Collections Department, University of Virginia Library.

182. *Pa at G,* p. 758.

183. *Pa at G,* pp. 758-759.

184. Fremantle, *The Fremantle Diary,* p. 204.

185. *Pa at G,* p. 702.

186. Lash, "Brig. Gen. Henry Baxter's Brigade at Gettysburg," *Gettysburg Magazine,* No. 10, p. 25.

187. *Pa at G,* p. 566.

188. *OR* 27.2.554.

189. *OR* 27.2.587.

190. *NYG,* p. 757.

191. Griffin, "Rodes on Oak Hill," *Gettysburg Magazine,* No. 4, p. 47. Fred Philips, letter to David Schenck, 27 October 1891, North Carolina State Archives, says the sharpshooters in front of Ramseur's brigade were from Iverson's command.

192. R.T. Bennett to Fred Philips, 28 May 1891, North Carolina State Archives; Fred Philips to David Schenck, 27 Oct. 1891, North Carolina State Archives.

193. Fred Philips to David Schenck, 27 Oct 1891, North Carolina State Archives.

194. Fred Philips to David Schenck, 27 Oct 1891, North Carolina State Archives. A.M. Parker letter, 29 May 1891, N.C. State Archives.

195. Fred Philips to David Schenck, 27 Oct. 1891, North Carolina State Archives.

196. Griffin, "Rodes on Oak Hill," *Gettysburg Magazine,* No. 4, p. 47.

197. *OR* 27.2.554.

198. *OR* 27.2.566.

199. R.T. Bennett to Fred Philips, 28 May 1891, North Carolina State Archives.

200. Small, *The Road to Richmond,* p. 101. Lt. Col. Farnham of the 16th reported in *OR* 27.1.295 that "we were ordered, alone, by General Robinson, to take possession of a hill which commanded the road, and hold the same as long as there was a man left."

201. Small, *The Road to Richmond,* pp 101-102.

202. *OR* 27.2.582, 287.

203. Davis, *Three Years in the Army*, pp. 227-228.
204. *OR* 27.1.298; Busey and Martin, *RSLG*, p. 240; Vautier, *History of the Eighty-Eighth Pennsylvania*, p. 108.
205. *OR* 27.1.299; *NYG*, p. 372; Busey and Martin, *RSLG*, pp. 240, 267; Stine, *History of the Army of the Potomac*, p. 475.
206. *OR* 27.1.299.
207. Regimental survivors later erected a marker to show the location of their stand near the Mummasburg Road, *Maine at Gettysburg*, p.42.
208. Small, *The Road to Richmond*, p. 102; *OR* 27.1.295.
209. *Maine at Gettysburg*, p. 45.
210. Small, *The Road to Richmond*, p. 102; *Maine at Gettysburg*, p. 44.
211. *Maine at Gettysburg*, p 44.
212. Busey and Martin, *RSLG*, pp. 240, 262.
213. Fred Philips to David Schenck, 27 Oct. 1891, North Carolina State Archives.
214. Raleigh, N.C., *Semi-Weekly Standard*, 4 August 1863.
215. *OR* 27.2.589.
216. Osborne, "Fourth Regiment," *NC Regts*, Vol. 1, p. 254.
217. Bennett, "Fourteenth Regiment," *NC Regts*, Vol. 1, p. 715.
218. *OR* 27.2.590; Osborne, "Fourth Regiment," *NC Regts*, Vol. 1, p. 254.
219. Raleigh, N.C., *Semi-Weekly Standard*, 4 August 1863.
220. T.M. Gorman, undated letter in *Pierce's Memorandum Account Book*, n.d., North Carolina State Archives.
221. Manly, "Second Regiment," *NC Regts*, Vol. 1, p. 171.
222. *OR* 27.2.587, 590.
223. *OR* 27.2.573.
224. *OR* 27.1.573, 578.
225. Busey and Martin, *RSLG*, p. 179.
226. *OR* 27.2.656.
227. *OR* 27.2.656.
228. *OR* 27.2.656, 668.
229. Busey and Martin, *RSLG*, p. 179.
230. The exact location and length of this barricade of fence rails has not been established. It was said to be crescent shaped (Hussey, *History of the Ninth Regiment, NYSM-NGSNY*, p. 287), and a portion of it was 50 yards west of the position held by Cooper's battery (Nevins, *A Diary of Battle*, p. 236). See also the rough sketch map in George McFarland's 13 Aug 1884 letter to John B. Bachelder, Bachelder Papers, NHHS. The barricade apparently ran much farther to the north of the Seminary than to the south.
231. *Maine at Gettysburg*, p. 384.
232. *OR* 27.1.356, 360, 363; Nevins, *A Diary of Battle*, p. 235; *Pa at G*, p. 908.
233. *OR* 27.1.361; *Maine at Gettysburg*, pp. 84-85.
234. *Pa at G*, p. 909.
235. *OR* 27.1.323.
236. *Pa at G*, p. 665.

237. Gates, *The Ulster Guard and the War of the Rebellion*, p. 442; *OR* 27.1.328.
238. Gates, *The Ulster Guard and the War of the Rebellion*, p. 442; Osborne, *Holding the Left*, p. 14.
239. *OR* 27.1.328.
240. *OR* 27.1.328; see also Gates, *Holding the Left*, p. 23, n. 52.
241. Stine, *History of the Army of the Potomac*, pp. 480, 485.
242. Curtis, *History of the Twenty-Fourth Michigan*, p. 163.
243. Gaff, "Here was Made out our Last and Hopeless Stand," *Gettysburg Magazine*, No. 2, p. 30.
244. *OR* 27.1.280.
245. *OR* 27.1.274.
246. Brown, *A Colonel at Gettysburg and Spotsylvania*, p. 80.
247. *OR* 27.1.274; Stine, *History of the Army of the Potomac*, p. 485.
248. John Callis to John B. Bachelder, undated, Bachelder Papers, NHHS.
249. Dawes, *Service with the Sixth Wisconsin Volunteers*, p. 175.
250. *Maine at Gettysburg*, p. 85.
251. For example, *OR* 27.2.656 and Harris, "Seventh Regiment," *NC Regts*, Vol. 1, p. 579.
252. *OR* 27.2.657.
253. *OR* 27.2.657; Underwood, "Twenty-Sixth Regiment," *NC Regts*, Vol. 2, p. 353.
254. See Bachelder map, 1 July 1863.
255. *OR* 27.2.669.
256. *OR* 27.2.670.
257. *OR* 27.2.670.
258. *OR* 27.2.670.
259. *Maine at Gettysburg*, p. 85.
260. Brown, *A Colonel at Gettysburg and Spotsylvania*, p. 211.
261. Lattimore, "Thirty-fourth Regiment," *NC Regts*, Vol. 2, p. 587.
262. Flowers, "Thirty-Eighth Regiment," *NC Regts*, Vol. 2, p. 692; "North Carolina at Gettysburg," *Releigh Observer*, 30 Nov 1877.
263. Vautier, *History of the Eighty-Eighth Pennsylvania*, p. 146.
264. Gordon, *Reminiscences of the Civil War*, p. 114.
265. The order of Perrin's regiments has been much debated. Bachelder, 1 July 1863 map, places the 12th and 13th regiments on the brigade's left, while Caldwell, *The History of a Brigade of South Carolinians*, p. 138, places the 1st and 12th on the left. A map in the Bachelder Papers, NHHS, by John A. Leach, places the 13th and 14th regiments on the brigade's left. Brown, *A Colonel at Gettysburg and Spotsylvania*, map facing p. 201, places the 1st and 14th on the left. This positioning is accepted as most likely in view of the following statement by U.R. Brooks in *Stories of the Confederacy*, p. 37: "McGowan's Brigade was at the right of the division and the Thirteenth Regiment at the right of the brigade." Compare also the note by Thomas M. Littlejohn in "Recollections of a Confederate Soldier," p. 6:"The 12th South Carolina regiment was in front on the march that day [30 June] and the 13th the next [1 July],

which placed the 12th on our right when facing to the front in a battle line." These two statements show that the 12th and 13th were on the brigade's right, not the left.

266. *OR* 27.2.661.
267. Brown, *A Colonel at Gettysburg and Spotsylvania*, p. 77.
268. Caldwell, *The History of a Brigade of South Carolinians*, p. 138.
269. *OR* 27.2.661.
270. Brown, *A Colonel at Gettysburg and Spotsylvania*, p. 79; Caldwell, *The History of a Brigade of South Carolinians*, p.138.
271. Littlejohn, "Recollections of a Confederate Soldier," p.5.
272. Brown, *A Colonel at Gettysburg and Spotsylvania*, p. 79.
273. Perrin, "A Little More Light on Gettysburg;" see also *OR* 27.2.268.
274. *OR* 27.2.661.
275. Caldwell, *The History of a Brigade of South Carolinians*, p. 138.
276. Perrin, "A Little More Light on Gettysburg."
277. Littlejohn, "Recollections of a Confederate Soldier," p.6.
278. Caldwell, *The Story of a Brigade of South Carolinians*, pp. 138-139.
279. Littlejohn, "Recollections of a Confederate Soldier," p.6.
280. J.A. Leach to John B. Bachelder, 2 June 1884, Bachelder Papers, NHHS.
281. *OR* 27.2.661.
282. *OR* 27.2.661.
283. *OR* 27.2.661; Caldwell, *The History of a Brigade of South Carolinians*, p. 139.
284. Perrin, "A Little More Light on Gettysburg."
285. Caldwell, *The History of a Brigade of South Carolinians*, p. 139.
286. Brown, *A Colonel at Gettysburg and Spotsylvania*, p. 80.
287. *OR* 27.2.661.
288. *Pa at G*, p. 909.
289. Brown, *A Colonel at Gettysburg and Spotsylvania*, p. 85.
290. *OR* 27.2.661.
291. Caldwell, *The History of a Brigade of South Carolinians*, p. 139.
292. Brown, *A Colonel at Gettysburg and Spotsylvania*, pp. 206-207.
293. *OR* 27.2.658, 662.
294. *OR* 27.2.662.
295. J.A. Leach to John B. Bachelder, 2 June 1884, Bachelder Papers, NHHS.
296. Gates, *The Ulster Guard and the War of the Rebellion*, p. 443.
297. Halstead, "The First Day of the Battle of Gettysburg," in *Gettysburg Papers*, Vol. 1, pp. 154-155 (*D.C. MOLLUS*, 2 March 1887, pp. 6-7).
298. Gates, *The Ulster Guard and the War of the Rebellion*, p. 443; *Roundout Courier*, 17 July 1863.
299. *OR* 27.1.323.
300. *History of the 121st Regiment Pennsylvania Volunteers*, pp. 55-56.
301. *OR* 27.1.323.
302. *History of the 121st Regiment Pennsylvania Volunteers*, p. 56.
303. Gates, *The Ulster Guard and the War of the Rebellion*, p. 444.

304. *OR* 27.1.318, 321.
305. Cook, "Personal Reminiscences of Gettysburg," in *Gettysburg Sources*, Vol. 2, p. 30.
306. Osborne, *Holding the Left*, p. 16.
307. Osborne, *Holding the Left*, p. 17; Oates, *The Ulster Guard and the War of the Rebellion*, p. 444.
308. *OR* 27.1.328.
309. *OR* 27.1.328.
310. George F. McFarland to John B. Bachelder, 13 August 1884, Bachelder Papers, NHHS.
311. *OR* 27.1.328.
312. *OR* 27.1.328.
313. Curtis, *History of the Twenty-Fourth Michigan*, pp. 165-166.
314. Curtis, *History of the Twenty-Fourth Michigan*, p. 158; Brown, *A Colonel at Gettysburg and Spotsylvania*, p. 216.
315. Smith, *The Twenty-Fourth Michigan of the Iron Brigade*, p. 298.
316. Curtis, *History of the Twenty-Fourth Michigan*, pp. 165-166.
317. Gaff, "Here Was Made out our Last and Hopeless Stand," *Gettysburg Magazine*, No. 2, pp. 30-31.
318. *OR* 27.1.280.
319. *OR* 27.1.280. At some point during this stand on Seminary Ridge, Capt. Richardson, who was serving as Meredith's assistant inspector general, "rode up and down the line, waving a regimental flag and encouraging the men to do their duty," *OR* 27.1.250. This may have been the flag of the 7th Wisconsin, which Col. Rufus Dawes saw him "carrying on his horse and waving aloft" during the brigade's retreat from McPherson's to Seminary Ridge, Dawes, *Service with the Sixth Wisconsin Volunteers*, p. 174.
320. *OR* 27.1.281.
321. John R. Callis to John B. Bachelder, undated, Bachelder Papers, NHHS.
322. Brown, *A Confederate Colonel at Gettysburg and Spotsylvania*, p. 211.
323. Brown, *A Confederate Colonel at Gettysburg and Spotsylvania*, p. 212.
324. *OR* 27.1.274.
325. Brown, *A Confederate Colonel at Gettysburg and Spotsylvania*, p. 212; p. 81 of the same source adds that the Union artillery pulled out before all the Federal infantry was driven back.
326. Caldwell, *The History of a Brigade of South Carolinians*, p. 138.
327. Halstead, "The First Day of the Battle of Gettysburg," in *Gettysburg Papers*, Vol. 1, p. 156 (*D.C. MOLLUS*, 2 March 1887, p. 8).
328. *OR* 27.1.357.
329 *OR* 27.1.363.
330. *Pa at G*, p. 909; *OR* 27.1.365.
331. *OR* 27.1.365.
332. Brown, *A Colonel at Gettysburg and Spotsylvania*, p. 81.
333. *OR* 27.1.357. There is a more colorful account of this incident in Nevins, *A Diary of Battle*. pp. 236-237. The gun lost by Wilber's section

was serial No. 1, the first three-inch rifled gun accepted by the Ordnance Department, Nevins, *A Diary of Battle*, p. 237.

334. *Maine at Gettysburg*, p. 86.

335. *OR* 27.1.336.

336. *OR* 27.1.336. *OR* 27.2.658.

337. *OR* 27.1.338.

338. *OR* 27.1.336.

339. Chamberlin, *History of the One Hundred and Fiftieth Regiment Pennsylvania Volunteers*, p. 136.

340. Chamberlin, *History of the One Hundred and Fiftieth Regiment Pennsylvania Volunteers*, p. 137.

341. Chamberlin, *History of the One Hundred and Fiftieth Regiment Pennsylvania Volunteers*, p. 136.

342. Chamberlin, *History of the One Hundred and Fiftieth Regiment Pennsylvania Volunteers*, pp. 136-139.

343. Brown, *A Colonel at Gettysburg and Spotsylvania*, p. 81.

344. Caldwell, *The History of a Brigade of South Carolinians*, p. 140.

345. J.A. Leach to John B. Bachelder, 2 June 1884, Bachelder Papers, NHHS.

346. Brown, *A Colonel at Gettysburg and Spotsylvania*, pp. 82, 226.

347. Brown, *A Colonel at Gettysburg and Spotsylvania*, pp. 226; *OR* 27.1.662-663.

348. Caldwell, *The History of a Brigade of South Carolinians*, p. 140.

349. Brown, *A Colonel at Gettysburg and Spotsylvania*, p. 83, which falsely claims that the Union cavalrymen had repeating guns..

350. *OR* 27.1.927, 934. Col George H. Chapman, letter to John B. Bachelder, 30 march 1864, Bachelder Papers, NHHS, says that the 8th New York, and 3rd Indiana were deployed late in the afternoon "dismounted, along an old stone wall to the left of the Theological Seminary, along which is a thin skirt of timbers." See also Howard, "First Day at Gettysburg," in *Gettysburg Papers*, Vol. 1, p. 333 (*Illinois MOLLUS*, Vol. 4, p. 261). On Calef's battery, see Calef "Gettysburg Notes: The Opening Gun," *JMSIUS* 40 (1907), p. 51 and *OR* 27.1.1032, where he speaks of opening fire "on a heavy column of rebel infantry advancing down the Carlisle Pike [SIC]."

351. *OR* 27. 1.662. J.A. Leach of the 1st South Carolina, on Perrin's left, apparently saw only a few of the cavalry skirmishers, "who gave us a Volley and then they went down the hill in rear of a house that was south of the college," letter to John B. Bachelder, 12 Sept. 1882, Bachelder Papers, NHHS. He uses similar language in his 2 June 1884 letter to Bachelder, Bachelder Papers, NHHS.

352. Brooks, *Stories of the Confederacy*, p. 37.

353. Pulis says that he was a 'Number 3' and so got to fight when every fourth man (the horseholders) took their mounts to the rear, Daniel Pulis to his parents, 6 July 1863, Rochester Public Library.

354. Daniel Pulis to his parents, 6 July 1863, Rochester Public Library.

355. *OR* 27.1.934. See also *NYG*, p. 1145.

356. Col. George M. Chapman to John B. Bachelder, 30 March 1864, Bachelder Papers, NHHS.

357. *OR* 27.1.935. Col. Gamble notes that this occurred "with the loss of some of our best officers and men," and lamented that nothing of this action was "mentioned in newspapers or despatches," Gamble to M.L. Church, 10 March 1864, Chicago Historical Society. Lt. Calef felt much the same, see "Gettysburg Notes: The Opening Gun," *JMSIUS* 40 (1907), p. 51.

358. Busey and Martin, *RSLG*, p. 180.

359. Brown, *A Colonel at Gettysburg and Spotsylvania*, p. 82.

360. Brown, *A Colonel at Gettysburg and Spotsylvania*, p. 82.

361. Busey and Martin, *RSLG*, p. 21; Matthews, *The 149th Pennsylvania Volunteer Infantry*, pp. 76, 91.

362. *Pa at G*, p. 747. Matthews suggests that Glenn's company may also have been joined by Company K of the 149th, which had been on skirmish duty all afternoon, *The 149th Pennsylvania Volunteer Infantry*, p. 95.

363. *Pa at G*, p. 747.

364. Nesbit, *General History of Co. D, 149th Pa. Volunteers*, pp. 15-16. Doubleday, however, reported that Capt. Glenn and his Company (which Doubleday calls his "Headquarters Guard") defended the Seminary building for fully twenty minutes against a whole brigade of the enemy, enabling the few remaining troops, the ambulances, artillery, etc., to flee to safety, *OR* 27.1.251 (see also Doubleday, *Chancellorsville and Gettysburg*, p. 149.) Brown, *A Colonel at Gettysburg and Spotsylvania*, p. 210 note 1, doubts that Company D held out that long ("perhaps a few minutes seemed like twenty.")

365. Nesbit, *General History of Co. D. 149th Pa. Volunteers*, p. 16. The company's losses during its brief stand are commemorated by a marker set up near the intersection of Fairfield Road and West Confederate Avenue. For more on Captain Glenn, see Sword, "Captain Glenn's Sword and Pvt. J. Marshal's Enfield in the Fight for the Lutheran Seminary," *Gettysburg Magazine*, No. 8, p. 11.

366. Perrin, "A Little More Light on Gettysburg."

367. Brown, *A Colonel at Gettysburg and Spotsylvania*, p. 85.

368. Perrin, "A Little More Light on Gettysburg."

369. Busey and Martin, *RSLG*, p. 292.

370. *OR* 27.2.663.

371. Brown, *A Colonel at Gettysburg and Spotsylvania*, p. 85.

372. Perrin, "A Little More Light on Gettysburg."

373. Brown, *A Colonel at Gettysburg and Spotsylvania*, pp. 83-84.

374. Perrin, "A Little More Light on Gettysburg."

375. *OR* 27.1.643, *Pa at G*, p. 909.

376. *Pa at G*, pp. 908-909.

377. Lt. W.B. Taylor to his mother, Collection of William B. Floyd, GNMP Collections.

378. Brown, *A Colonel at Gettysburg and Spotsylvania*, p. 216, note.

379. Perrin, "A Little More Light on Gettysburg."
380. *OR* 27.2.665.
381. Col. George H. Chapman to John B. Bachelder, 30 March 1864, Bachelder Papers, NHHS.
382. Beveridge, "The First Gun at Gettysburg," in *Gettysburg Papers*, Vol. 1, p. 177. (*Illinois MOLLUS*, Vol. 2, p. 95); Kross, "Fight Like to Devil to Hold Your Own." *Blue and Gray Magazine*, Vol. 12, No. 3 (Feb 1995), p. 20; Busey and Martin, *RSLG*, p. 101.
383. *OR* 27.2.667; Wiggins, "Thirty-Seventh Regiment," *NC Regts*, Vol. 2, p. 660.
384. *OR* 27.2.665; Kross, "Fight Like to Devil to Hold Your Own." *Blue and Gray Magazine*, Vol. 12, No. 3 (Feb 1995), p. 20, gives a different interpretation of this sequence of events.
385. Beveridge, "The First Gun at Gettysburg," *Gettysburg Papers*, Vol. 1, p. 179 (*Ill. MOLLUS*, Vol. 2, p. 97). See also note 384 previous. James Bell of the 8th Illinois Cavalry (2 July 1863 letter, Henry E. Huntington Library, San Marino, California) says that Lane's troops at this time "moved down us in solid line, regiment after regiment, in the form of a crescent." This is not a reference to the forming of squares, as is sometimes thought; see, for example, Longacre, *The Cavalry at Gettysburg*, p. 302, note 41.
386. *OR* 27. 2.657, 665.
387. *OR* 27.2.665.
388. *OR* 27.2.665. Adjutant William H. McLaurin of the 18th North Carolina offers the plain explanation that Lane's advance simply diverged from Perrin's during the attack, McLaurin, "Eighteenth Regiment," *NC Regts*, Vol. 2, p. 42.
389. Harris, "Seventh Regiment," *NC Regts*, Vol. 1, p. 329.
390. Stine, *History of the Army of the Potomac*, p. 481.
391. Doubleday, *Chancellorsville and Gettysburg*, p. 149. The authors of one history of the 45th New York claimed that, "We also saw some of the enemy forming square against some of our cavalry to the left" while the 45th was formed at Pennsylvania College at around 1600 (*NYG* p. 380). It is doubtful, however, that the men of the 45th could have had a clear line of sight all the way to Lane's position on the western side of Seminary Ridge below the Seminary.
392. On the earlier episode, see Robinson, "Fifty-SecondRegiment," *NC Regts*, Vol. 3, pp. 236-237. On the episode described by Halstead, see Chapter IX, note 127, and *B&L*, Vol. 3, p. 285.
393. Buell, *The Cannoneer*, pp. 65-66.
394. The following long quotes are from *The Cannoneer* by Augustus Buell. He was not actually at the battle, but, from the detail of his narrative, he clearly talked to others who were. See Felton, "Chasing the Elusive 'Cannoneer,'" *Gettysburg Magazine*, No. 9, pp. 33-39.
395. Buell, *The Cannoneer*, pp. 65-66.

396. The Wills Woods extended to the west of the battery's position on the north side of the railroad line.

397. *OR* 27.1.566.

398. Buell, *The Cannoneer*, p.66.

399. Buell, *The Cannoneer*, p. 66.

400. See Felton, "The Iron Brigade Battery at Gettysburg," *Gettysburg Magazine*, No. 11, n. 17, for the placement of Scales' left flank.

401. Buell, *The Cannoneer*, p. 66.

402. Buell, *The Cannoneer*, p. 68.

403. Stewart in "Battery B Fourth United States Artillery at Gettysburg," *Gettysburg Papers*, Vol. 1, p. 369 (*Ohio MOLLUS*, Vol. 4, p. 185), says that he ordered the move himself.

404. Buell, *The Cannoneer*, p. 68.

405. Buell, *The Cannoneer*, p. 68.

406. Dawes, *Service with the Sixth Wisconsin Volunteers*, p. 175.

407. Buell, *The Cannoneer*, p. 73.

408. *OR* 27.1.307.

409. Hall, *History of the Ninety-Seventh Regiment New York Volunteers*, p. 141.

410. *NYG*, p. 678.

411. *OR* 27.1.282-283.

412. Dawes, *Service with the Sixth Wisconsin Volunteers*, p. 174.

413. Dawes, *Service with the Sixth Wisconsin Volunteers*, p. 175.

414. Dawes, *Service with the Sixth Wisconsin Volunteers*, p. 176.

415. Dawes, *Service with the Sixth Wisconsin Volunteers*, p. 176.

416. Dawes, *Service with the Sixth Wisconsin Volunteers*, pp. 176-179.

417. *OR* 27.1.290.

418. *OR* 27.1.307.

419. *OR* 27.1.290.

420. Vautier, *History of the Eighty-Eighth Pennsylvania Volunteers*, p. 108.

421. *OR* 27.1331; Lash, "Brigadier General Henry Baxter's Brigade at Gettysburg, July1, " *Gettysburg Magazine*, No. 10, p. 26.

422. Vautier, "At Gettysburg;" Lash, "Brigadier General Henry Baxter's Brigade at Gettysburg, July 1," *Gettysburg Magazine*, No. 10, p. 26.

423. Vautier, "At Gettysburg."

424. Vautier, "At Gettysburg."

425. Vautier, "At Gettysburg."

426. Vautier, *History of the Eighty-Eighth Pennsylvania Volunteers*, p. 109.

427. Samuel G. Boone Memoirs, 1 July 1863, USAMHI.

428. Hussey, *History of the Ninth Regiment, NYSM-NGSNY*, p. 272.

429. Hall, *History of the Ninety-Seventh Regiment New York Volunteers*, pp. 141-142; Vautier, *History of the Eighty-Eighth Pennsylvania Volunteers*, pp. 135-136. The 20th N.C.'s flag was recaptured by Capt. A.H. Galloway's Company F of the 45th NC, Kross, "Fight Like to Devil to Hold Your Own." *Blue and Gray Magazine*, Vol. 12, No. 3 (Feb 1995), p. 51.

430. Hall, *History of the Ninety-Seventh Regiment New York Volunteers*, pp. 142-143.

431. Howard, *Boys in Blue*, pp. 149-150.
432. Howard, *Boys in Blue*, pp. 151.
433. Grant, "The First Army Corps on the First Day at Gettysburg," in *Gettysburg Papers*, Vol. 1, pp. 264-265 (*Minnesota MOLLUS*, Vol. 5, pp. 52-53).
434. Tevis, *The History of the Fighting Fourteenth*, p. 87.
435. Locke, *The Story of the Regiment*, pp. 230-232.
436. Lippy, *The War Dog*, p. 19.
437. Lippy, *The War Dog*, p. 38.
438. *OR* 27.1.286.
439. *OR* 27.1.283.
440. Tevis, *History of the Fighting Fourteenth*, p. 136.
441. Tevis, *History of the Fighting Fourteenth*, p. 86.
442. Tevis, *History of the Fighting Fourteenth*, pp. 86-87.
443. Tevis, *History of the Fighting Fourteenth*, p. 136.
444. Tevis, *History of the Fighting Fourteenth*, p. 136.
445. *OR* 27.1.286.
446. Tevis, *History of the Fighting Fourteenth*, p. 136.
447. Stewart, "Battery B Fourth United States Artillery at Gettysburg," *Gettysburg Papers*, Vol. 1, p. 370 (*Ohio MOLLUS*, Vol. 4, p. 186).
448. Buell, *The Cannoneer*, p. 73.
449. Grant, "The First Army Corps on the First Day at Gettysburg," in *Gettysburg Papers*, Vol. 1, p. 264 (*Minnesota MOLLUS*, Vol. 5, p. 52).
450. Buell, *The Cannoneer*, p. 73.
451. Stewart, "Battery B Fourth United States Artillery at Gettysburg," *Gettysburg Papers*, Vol. 1, p. 371 (*Ohio MOLLUS*, Vol. 4, p. 187).
452. Stewart, "Battery B Fourth United States Artillery at Gettysburg," *Gettysburg Papers*, Vol. 1, p. 371 (*Ohio MOLLUS*, Vol. 4, p. 187).
453. Stewart, "Battery B Fourth United States Artillery at Gettysburg," *Gettysburg Papers*, Vol. 1, p. 371 (*Ohio MOLLUS*, Vol. 4, p. 187).
454. Stewart, "Battery B Fourth United States Artillery at Gettysburg," *Gettysburg Papers*, Vol. 1, p. 372 (*Ohio MOLLUS*, Vol. 4, p. 188).
455. Buell, *The Cannoneer*, p. 75.
456. Stewart, "Battery B Fourth United States Artillery at Gettysburg," *Gettysburg Papers*, Vol. 1, pp. 372-373 (*Ohio MOLLUS*, Vol. 4, pp. 188-189).
457. Buell, *The Cannoneer*, p. 73. Stewart's retiring guns received some covering fire from Stevens' battery, which was for a time posted near the edge of the town, see Felton, "The Iron Brigade Battery at Gettysburg," *Gettysburg Magazine*, No. 11, p. 63.
458. Buell, *The Cannoneer*, p. 74.
459. Buell, *The Cannoneer*, p. 74; Stewart, "Battery B Fourth United States Artillery at Gettysburg," *Gettysburg Papers*, Vol. 1, p. 373 (*Ohio MOLLUS*, Vol. 4, p. 189).
460. *OR* 27.1.357; Felton, "The Iron Brigade Battery at Gettysburg," *Gettysburg Magazine*, Vol. 11, p. 63, and name listing of casualties, pp. 68-70.

461. Tevis, *History of the Fighting Fourteenth*, p. 87.

462. Buell, *The Cannoneer*, p. 75.

463. Nevins, *A Diary of Battle*, p. 236.

464. Nevins, *A Diary of Battle*, pp. 236-237. During the initial part of the withdrawal, the guns of Cooper's and Stevens' batteries became intermingled; they were not sorted out until they reached Cemetery Hill and were able to reform, *Maine at Gettysburg*, pp. 88-89.

465. *OR* 27.1.251.

466. Doubleday, *Chancellorsville and Gettysburg*, p. 146.

467. *OR* 27.1.251; Doubleday, *Chancellorsville and Gettysburg*, p 148.

468. Smith, *History of the Seventy-Sixth Regiment New York Volunteers*, p. 240.

469. *OR* 27.1.251.

470. Smith, *History of the Seventy-Sixth Regiment New York Volunteers*, p.241.

471. *OR* 27.1.251.

472. Dawes, *Service with the Sixth Wisconsin Volunteers*, p. 178.

473. Smith, *History of the Seventy-Sixth Regiment New York Volunteers*, pp. 242-243. The name of this "heroine" is not otherwise known. This incident may be confused with the memory of Jennie Wade's death on the morning of 3 July.

474. Hufham, "Gettysburg," *The Wake Forest Student*, Vol. 16, No. 7 (April 1897), pp. 455-456.

475. *OR* 27.2.603.

476. Stewart, "Battery B Fourth United States Artillery at Gettysburg," *Gettysburg Papers*, Vol.1, pp. 372-372 (Ohio MOLLUS, Vol.4 pp. 188-189).

477. Hufham, "Gettysburg," *The Wake Forest Student*, Vol. 16, No. 7 (April 1897), pp. 454-456.

478. Doubleday, *Chancellorsville and Gettysburg*, p. 149.

479. *NYG*, p. 380.

480. *OR* 27.1.730; see also Schurz, *The Reminiscences of Carl Schurz*, Vol. 3, p. 12.

481. Dawes, *Service with the Sixth Wisconsin Volunteers*, p. 176.

482. *OR* 27.2.582.

483. See, for example, Dawes, *Service with the Sixth Wisconsin Volunteers*, p. 176 note.

484. Pfanz, *Gettysburg—Culp's Hill and Cemetery Hill*, p. 47.

485. Doubleday, *Testimony, Report of the Joint Committee on the Conduct of the War*, p. 308.

486. See, for example, Dawes, *Service with the Sixth Wisconsin Volunteers*, p. 178.

487. Garlach, "The Story of Mrs. Jacob Kitzmiller," Adams County Historical Society.

488. *OR* 27.2.479.

489. *OR* 27.2.662-663.

490. *OR* 27.2.582, 587.

491. See Pfanz, *Gettysburg—Culp's Hill and Cemetery Hill*, pp. 60-64.

492. *NYG,* p. 380; Busey and Martin, *RSLG,* p. 254.
493. Dunkelman and Winey, "The Hardtack Regiment in the Vineyard Fight," *Gettysburg Magazine,* No. 8, pp. 22-26.
494. Fahnestock, "Recollections of the Battle of Gettysburg," p. 2, Adams County Historical Society.
495. Jacobs, "How an Eyewitness Watched the Battle," GNMP Collections.
496. Pfanz, *Gettysburg—Culp's Hill and Cemetery Hill,* p. 418, n. 10.
497. McCreary, "Gettysburg: A Boy's Experience of the Battle, " pp. 5-6, GNMP Collections.
498. Coco, *A Vast Sea of Misery,* p. 3; United States Christian Commission Report.
499. Hard, *History of the Eighth Cavalry Regiment, Illinois Volunteers,* p. 257.
500. Hard, *History of the Eighth Cavalry Regiment, Illinois Volunteers,* pp. 257-258.
501. Coco, *A Vast Sea of Misery,* pp. 3-4; Ebersole, "Incidents of Field Hospital Life with the Army of the Potomac," *Ohio MOLLUS,* Vol. 4.
502. George New to John B. Bachelder, 8 September 1865, Bachelder Papers, NHHS.
503. Coco, *A Vast Sea of Misery,* pp. 5-6.
504. McAllister, *Philadelphia Inquirer,* 26-27 June 1938.
505. McCurdy, *Gettysburg, A Memoir.*
506. Croll, "Memoir of Mary A. Horner," *Philadelphia Weekly Press,* 16 November 1887.
507. Walker, "A Captive of Lee's Army at Gettysburg," *National Tribune,* 22 October 1925.
508. *NYG,* p. 24.
509. Hunterston, "Escaped Capture," *National Tribune,* 23 March 1911.
510. Huidekoper, *Historic Church and Hospital on the Battlefield of Gettysburg.*
511. Croll, "Memoir of Mary A. Horner," *Philadelphia Weekly Press,* 16 November 1887.
512. Jennie McCreary, letter published in *Philadelphia Evening Bulletin,* 2 July 1938.
513. McAllister, *Philadelphia Inquirer,* 26-29 June 1938; Harries, "The Sword of Gen. James J. Archer, *CV* 19 (1911), pp. 419-420.
514. Dennis B. Dailey to Abner Doubleday, 24 March 1890, Bachelder Papers, NHHS.
515. Dennis B. Dailey to Abner Doubleday, 24 March 1890, Bachelder Papers, NHHS. Dailey was not aware that Archer had died in 1864.
516. Dawes, *Service with the Sixth Wisconsin Volunteers,* pp. 170-172.
517. *OR* 27.1.278; Dawes, *Service with the Sixth Wisconsin Volunteers,* p. 171.
518. Dawes, *Service with the Sixth Wisconsin Volunteers,* p. 170.
519. Coco, *A Vast Sea of Misery,* pp. 5, 40.
520. Coco, *A Vast Sea of Misery,* p.35, Jennie McCreary letter, *Philadelphia Evening Bulletin,* 2 July 1938; Warner, *Generals in Blue,* p. 364.

521. Coco, *A Vast Sea of Misery*, p. 86; Stine, *History of the Army of the Potomac*, p. 477; Dudley, *The Iron Brigade at Gettysburg*, p. 13.

522. Smith, *History of the Seventy-Sixth Regiment New York Volunteers*, p. 244.

523. John R. Callis to John B. Bachelder, undated, Bachelder Papers, NHHS; Long, "A Gettysburg Encounter," *Gettysburg Magazine*, No. 7, pp. 114-115.

524. John R. Callis to John B. Bachelder, undated, Bachelder Papers, NHHS; Long, "A Gettysburg Encounter," *Gettysburg Magazine*, No. 7, pp. 115-116.

525. John R. Callis to John B. Bachelder, undated, Bachelder Papers, NHHS. The details of Callis' wound and treatment are given in Long, "A Gettysburg Encounter," *Gettysburg Magazine*, No. 7, pp. 116-117. For the correspondence between Callis and Kenan, see Kenan and Callis, "An Incident at Gettysburg," *NC Regts*, Vol. 5, pp. 611-616 and Long, "A Gettysburg Encounter," *Gettysburg Magazine*, No. 7, pp. 117-118.

526. Coco, *A Vast Sea of Misery*, pp. 44-45.

527. Dodge, "Left Wounded on the Field," *Putnam's Monthly Magazine*, Vol. 4 (Sept. 1869), pp. 317-326.

528. Coco, *A Vast Sea of Misery*, p. 124; Francis C. Barlow letter to his mother, 7 July 1863, GNMP Collection.

529. Coco, *A Vast Sea of Misery*, p. 133

530. Johnson, *Battleground Adventures*, as cited in Coco, *a Vast Sea of Misery*, p. 134.

531. Merrill, *The Soldier of Indiana in the War for the Union*, Vol. 2, as cited in Coco, *A Vast Sea of Misery*, p. 123.

532. Mrs. Hugh McIlhenny Sr.'s memoir, GNMP Collections.

533. Caldwell, *The History of a Brigade of South Carolinians*, pp. 140-141.

534. Auginbaugh, *Personal Experience of a Young Girl During the Battle of Gettysburg*.

535. J.W. Daniel, "Memoir of the Battle of Gettysburg," pp. 5-6, Virginia Historial Society.

536. Busey and Martin, *RSLG*, p. 270.

537. Busey and Martin, *RSLG*, p. 272. Rowley's command, however, suffered a number of losses on 3 July.

538. Busey and Martin, *RSLG*, pp. 273-274.

539. Busey and Martin, *RSLG*, pp. 262-267.

540. Busey and Martin, *RSLG*, pp. 239, 262, 264, 265, 266.

541. Busey and Martin, *RSLG*, pp. 241, 262 264, 265.

542. Busey and Martin, *RSLG*, pp. 241, 264, 265.

543. Busey and Martin, *RSLG*, pp. 239, 240, 262.

544. Busey and Martin, *RSLG*, p. 309.

545. Busey and Martin, *RSLG*, p. 290, 298-301.

546. Underwood, "The Twenty-Sixth Regiment," *NC Regts*, Vol. 2, pp. 358-359.

547. Coco, *War Stories*, p. 15.

548. Underwood, "The Twenty-Sixth Regiment," *NC Regts*, Vol. 2, p. 369.
549. *OR* 27.1.2155-256.
550. See Vanderslice, *Gettysburg Then and Now*, pp. 123, 127, and Appendix II below.
551. See Vanderslice, *Gettysburg Then and Now*, p. 132, and Appendix II below.

IX. Cemetery Hill

1. *OR* 27.1.721.
2. *OR* 27.1.703. Howard places the time at 1545, but it was probably a little bit earlier.
3. *OR* 27.1.703-704.
4. *OR* 27.1.703, 939.
5. *OR* 27.1.939.
6. *OR* 27.1.721, 723-724.
7. *OR* 27.1.704; Howard, *The Autobiography of Oliver Otis Howard*, Vol. 1, p. 417.
8. *B & L*, Vol. 3, p. 285; Halstead, "The First Day of the Battle of Gettysburg," in *Gettysburg Papers*, Vol. 1, pp. 153-154, (*DC MOLLUS*, March 1887, pp. 5-6), Howard thought that Buford was with Devin, but Buford appears instead to have been with Gamble, to the west of Cemetery Hill.
9. *OR* 27.1.704.
10. Doubleday, *Chancellorsville and Gettysburg*, p. 149.
11. Greene, "O.O. Howard and Eleventh Corps Leadership," in *The First Day at Gettysburg*, p. 84; Howard, "The Campaign and Battle of Gettysburg," *Atlantic Monthly*, No. 38 (1876), p. 58; Culp, *The Twenty-Fifth Veteran Volunteer Infantry*, p.77; Busey and Martin, *RSLG*, p. 82. On the number of stragglers and battle refugees picked up by the XII Corps, see note 327 below.
12. Smith, *Camps and Campaigns of the 107th Regiment Ohio Volunteer Infantry*, p. 88.
13. Culp, "Gettysburg," *National Tribune*, 19 March 1885.
14. Howard, *The Autobiography of Oliver Otis Howard*, Vol. 1, p. 419. Howard in "Campaign and Battle of Gettysburg," *Atlantic Monthly*, Vol. 38, p. 58, claims that this German officer was Col. George Von Amsberg of the 45th New York, but this is not likely because he was serving as a brigade commander at the time; see Pfanz, *Gettysburg—Culp's Hill and Cemetery Hill*, p. 416, n.26.
15. *OR* 27.1.718.
16. *OR* 27.1.925.
17. At 1520 Buford wrote Pleasonton, "General Reynolds was killed early this morning. In my opinion, there seems to be no directing person. P.S. We need help now," *OR* 27.1.924-925. See also Lt. Aaron B. Jones to Winfield Hancock, 18 October 1865, Bachelder Papers, NHHS where

Jerome quotes Buford as writing to Meade, "For God's sake send up
Hancock, everything is going at odds and we need a controlling spirit."
Jerome, however, places this message "a few minutes after the death of
Major General Reynolds."

18. Doubleday, *Chancellorsville and Gettysburg*, p. 150.
19. *OR* 27.1.713, 721, 730; see also Pfanz, *Gettysburg—Culp's Hill and Cemetery Hill*, p. 54.
20. Doubleday, *Chancellorsville and Gettysburg*, p. 150.
21. Otis, *The Second Wisconsin Infantry*, p. 286; Curtis, *History of the Twenty-Fourth Michigan*, pp. 163, 165.
22. Walter L. Owens to George F. McFarland, 6 August 1866, Bachelder Papers, NHHS. *Pa at G*, pp. 665-666. The reason the 151st was out of ammunition was because Lt. Col. Huidekoper of the 150th Pennsylvania had sent the division's ammunition train (commanded by Capt. Shaw) to the rear when he met it near the town during his retreat from Seminary Ridge, Huidekoper memoranda concerning the 150th Pennsylvania on July 1, Bachelder Papers, NHHS.
23. Davis, *Three Years in the Army*, pp. 228-229.
24. *OR* 27.1.290, 308.
25. *OR* 27.1.321.
26. Pfanz, *Gettysburg—Culp's Hill and Cemetery Hill*, pp. 74-75.
27. Dawes, *Service with the Sixth Wisconsin Volunteers*, pp. 178-179.
28. Herdegen, "The Lieutenant who Arrested a General," *Gettysburg Magazine*, No. 4, p. 26.
29. Nevins, *A Diary of Battle*, p. 237.
30. Rogers, "Gettysburg Sources," *Milwaukee Sunday Telegraph*, 13 May 1887; Dawes, "A Gallant Officer", *Milwaukee Sunday Telegraph*, 3 February 1884.
31. For a summary of Rowley's trial and the evidence given there, see Herdegen, "The Lieutenant who Arrested a General," *Gettysburg Magazine*, No. 4, p. 29-30. Rowley's life is summarized in Warner, *Generals in Blue*, pp. 413-414.
32. Nevins, *A Diary of Battle*, pp. 237-238.
33. *OR* 27.1.748.
34. Osborn, *The Eleventh Corps Artillery at Gettysburg*, p. 15.
35. Osborn, *The Eleventh Corps Artillery at Gettysburg*, p. 15; one of Cooper's four rifled guns had been disabled earlier in the day, *OR* 27.1.365.
36. *Pa at G*, p. 909.
37. Nevins, *A Diary of Battle*, p. 238.
38. Stewart, "Battery B Fourth U.S. Artillery at Gettysburg," in *Gettysburg Papers*, Vol. 1, pp. 373-374 (Ohio MOLLUS, Vol. 4, pp. 189-190). These three guns were actually placed by Hancock as will be seen shortly. Wainwright in Nevins, *A Diary of Battle*, p. 238, errs in stating that he put two of Stewart's guns next to Breck's and four on the roadway. Stewart only had four operating guns since two had broken down during the retreat. Stewart, as cited, properly states that there were three guns in the road and one gun at right angles to them.

39. Nevins, *A Diary of Battle*, p. 238.
40. McKelvey, "George Breck's Civil War Letters," p. 199.
41. *OR* 27.1.357. These lunettes still survive on the field, making East Cemetery Hill one of the most picturesque spots in the battlefield park.
42. Nevins, *A Diary of Battle*, p. 238.
43. *OR* 27.1.361.
44. McKelvey, "George Breck's Civil War Letters," pp. 131-132.
45. Osborn, *Trials and Triumphs*, p. 96.
46. Frassanito, *Gettysburg: A Journey in Time*, pp. 118-119; Wheeler, *Witness to Gettysburg*, p. 156.
47. Osborn, *The Eleventh Corps Artillery at Gettysburg*, p. 15.
48. *OR* 27.1.7.53.
49. Nevins, *A Diary of Battle*, p. 238; Remington, *A Record of Battery I*, p. 21.
50. *OR* 27.1.748.755.
51. Pfanz, *Gettysburg— Culp's Hill and Cemetery Hill*, p. 54.
52. Osborn, *The Eleventh Corps Artillery at Gettysburg*, p. 15.
53. Osborn, *The Eleventh Corps Artillery at Gettysburg*, p. 18.
54. This point is difficult to appreciate now because of all the motels, etc., that have been built along the northern and western slopes of the hill.
55. Dawes. *Service with the Sixth Wisconsin Volunteers*, p. 179.
56. Osborn, *The Eleventh Corps Artillery at Gettysburg*, p. 16.
57. *OR* 27.1.356; Tucker, *Hancock the Superb*, p. 129.
58. *OR* 27.3.462. This and the following dispatch to Slocum were probably written late in the morning, since Slocum's message was sent out with a copy of the Pipe Creek circular, which was issued at that time.
59. *OR* 27.3.462.
60. Meade, *The Life and Letters of George Gordon Meade* , Vol. 2, pp. 35-36.
61. *OR* 27.1.70-71. Shue, *Morning at Willoughby Run*, pp. 215-6, argues that Buford sent this dispatch at 0900.
62. Meade, *The Life and Letters of George Gordon Meade*, Vol. 2, p. 36; Weld, *War Diaries and Letters of Stephen Minot Weld*, pp. 231-232.
63. *OR* 27.1.70-71.
64. *OR* 27.3.458-459.
65. *OR* 27.3.461.
66. The II Corps began marching at 1330 and encamped three miles south of Gettysburg. It resumed its march at daylight on 2 July and was on the field by 0700, *OR* 27.1.369.
67. *OR* 27.3.458.
68. *OR* 27.1.71.
69. Comte de Paris, *The Battle of Gettysburg*, pp. 238-239.
70. Coddington, p. 323.
71. For Meade's relationship with Reynolds and Hancock, see Coddington, p. 694, notes 115 and 116.
72. Lt. Col. C.H. Morgan's account, Bachelder Papers, NHHS.
73. The only other officer Meade might have trusted with this mission was

probably Maj. Gen. John Sedgwick of VI Corps, see Tucker, *Hancock the Superb*, p. 130.

74. *OR* 27.3.461.

75. Hancock in *OR* 27.1.368 states that he left Meade at 1310 and arrived at Gettysburg at 1500, but his watch must have been a little fast.

76. *OR* 27.3.465.

77. *OR* 27.3.466 Sickles had already anticipated this order, and left two brigades at Emmitsburg when he marched the rest of his corps to Gettysburg at midafternoon, *OR* 27.1.482, 531; *OR* 27.3.464.

78. *OR* 27.3.465; *OR* 51.1.1066.

79 Doubleday, *Chancellorsville and Gettysburg*, p. 135, suggests that Howard had seen Cutler's retreat to northern Seminary Ridge at about 1015, but Howard was not yet on the field at that time. Hassler, *Crisis at the Crossroads*, p. 65, suggests that Howard "evidently saw a temporary retrograde movement of several regiments of Cutler's brigade" when he was viewing the battlefield from the roof of the Fahnestock building at about 1130.

80. *OR* 27.1.368.

81. Hancock, *Reminiscences of Winfield Scott Hancock*, pp. 188-189; Tucker, *Hancock the Superb*, p. 131.

82. Hancock, "Gettysburg Reply to General Howard," *Galaxy*, No. 22 (1876), p. 822.

83. Hancock says that he arrived at 1500 (*OR* 27.1.368), but this is too early. See Coddington, *The Gettysburg Campaign*, p. 700; Pfanz, *Gettysburg—Culp's Hill and Cemetery Hill*, pp. 379-381, and Tucker, *Hancock the Superb*, p. 132.

84. Hancock, "Gettysburg, Reply to General Howard," *Galaxy*, No. 22, (1876), P. 822.

85. Osborn, *Trials and Triumphs*, p. 98.

86. Osborn, *Trials and Triumphs*, p. 98.

87. This aide was Major William G. Mitchell, see Tucker, *Hancock the Superb*, p. 132.

88. Halstead, "The First Day of the Battle of Gettysburg," in *Gettysburg Papers*, Vol. 1, pp. 154-155 (*DC MOLLUS*, 2 March 1887, pp. 6-7).

89. See a good discussion of these issues in Pfanz, *Gettysburg—Culp's Hill and Cemetery Hill*, p. 424, n. 40.

90. James W. Wadsworth Jr., "Battle of July 1st," Wadsworth Family Papers, Library of Congress.

91. See Pfanz, *Gettysburg—Culp's Hill and Cemetery Hill*, p. 424, n. 40.

92. Lt. Col C.H. Morgan's account, p. 320, Bachelder Papers, NHHS.

93. Hancock's written commission from Meade did not direct him to do so. Meade clarified this unclear situation when he wrote to Hancock and Doubleday at 1800 that Slocum was to assume command of the field when he arrived, *OR* 27.3.466.

94. Halstead, however, claimed that his account was endorsed by Hancock, "The First Day of the Battle of Gettysburg," in *Gettysburg Papers*, Vol. 1, pp. 155-156 (*DC MOLLUS*, 2 March 1887, pp. 7-9).

95. Hancock to Howard, 14 March 1864, responding to Howard's letter to Hancock, 25 February 1864, both in O.O. Howard Papers, Library of Congress.

96. Howard, "The Campaign and Battle of Gettysburg," *Atlantic Monthly*, No. 38 (1876), p. 58.

97. Howard, *The Autobiography of Oliver Otis Howard*, Vol. 1, p. 418.

98. Hancock, "Gettysburg, Reply to General Howard," *Galaxy*, No. 22 (1876), pp. 821-831; Hancock's battle report reference is *OR* 27.1.368.

99. Howard, "The Campaign and Battle of Gettysburg," *Atlantic Monthly*, No. 38 (1876), p. 58; *OR* 27.3.466.

100. *OR* 27.1.696.

101. *OR* 27.1.696.

102. *Maine at Gettysburg*, p. 89.

103. *Maine at Gettysburg*, p. 89.

104. *Maine at Gettysburg*, p. 89-90; this anecdote may not belong at this time, since other sources show that Hunt did not reach the field until almost midnight, see *B & L*, Vol. 3, p. 291.

105. Doubleday, *Chancellorsville and Gettysburg*, p. 151, *OR* 27.1.252. Doubleday later claimed that he sent Wadsworth's entire division to the right at this time, but Cutler's brigade did not move to Culp's Hill until the morning of 2 July, when it formed between the Iron Brigade and Greene's division, on the right of the hill top, *OR* 27.1.283.

106. McLean, *Cutler's Brigade*, pp. 141, 143.

107. Howard, "The Campaign and Battle of Gettysburg," *Atlantic Monthly*, No. 38 (1876), p. 58.

108. *OR* 27.1.252, Hancock and Howard had both been appointed major general on the same date, 29 November 1862. Howard was senior to Hancock because he became a brigadier general on 3 September 1861, twenty days before Hancock did. Warner, *Generals in Blue*, pp. 203, 237-238.

109. *Maine at Gettysburg*, p. 90.

110. Dawes, *Service with the Sixth Wisconsin Volunteers*, p. 179.

111. *Maine at Gettysburg*, p. 91.

112. Stewart, "Battery F Fourth U.S. Artillery at Gettysburg," in *Gettysburg Papers*, pp. 373-374 (*Ohio MOLLUS*, Vol. 4, pp. 189-190).

113. *Pa at G*, p. 909.

114. Nevins, *A Diary of Battle*, p. 237.

115. Wiedrich to John B. Bachelder, 30 January 1886, Bachelder Papers, NHHS.

116. Warren had left Taneytown for Gettysburg before Hancock did, but he got lost on the way and ended up coming via Emmitsburg, see Tucker, *Hancock the Superb*, p. 138.

117. Warren Testimony, *Report of the Joint Committee of the Conduct of the War at the Second Session, Thirty-Eighth Congress (1865)*, p. 377.

118. *OR* 27.1.825.

119. *OR* 27.1.825, 836.

120. Schurz, *The Reminiscences of Carl Schurz*, Vol. 2, pp. 15-16.

121. *OR* 27.1.368.
122. Comte de Paris, *The Battle of Gettysburg*, p. 16.
123. Schurz, *The Reminiscences of Carl Schurz*, Vol. 3, pp. 14-15.
124. Halstead, "The First Day of the Battle of Gettysburg," in *Gettysburg Papers*, Vol. 1, pp. 155-156 (*DC MOLLUS*. 2 March 1887, pp. 7-8).
125. *OR* 27.1.927.
126. Halstead, "The First Day of the Battle of Gettysburg," in *Gettysburg Papers*, Vol. 1, p. 156 (*DC MOLLUS* 2 March 1887, p. 8).
127. *Ibid.* See also Kross, "Fight Like the Devil to Hold Your Own," *Blue and Gray Magazine*, Vol. 12, No. 3 (Feb. 1995), p. 21.
128. It should be noted that we do not have battle reports from all of Buford's regiments.
129. Robinson, "Fifty-Second Regiment," *North Carolina Regiments*, Vol. 3, p. 236.
130. Doubleday, *Chancellorsville and Gettysburg*, p. 149. See Chapter VIII, note 391.
131. *OR* 27.1.368; Calef, "Gettysburg Notes: The Opening Gun," *JMSIUS*, Vol. 40 (1907), p. 51.
132. *OR* 27.1.927.
133. Wittenberg, "John Buford and the Gettysburg Campaign," *Gettysburg Magazine*, No. 11, p. 43; some of the sources he cites, however, may refer to episodes earlier in the day.
134. *Pa at G*, p. 886. The brigade's location was probably "on Cemetery Ridge" or "near Cemetery Hill."
135. Bachelder, 2 July 1863 map. Buford unfortunately does not state at what time he went into camp, or exactly where the camp was.
136. Calef, "Gettysburg Notes: The Opening Gun," *JMSIUS*, Vol. 40 (1907), p. 51-52.
137. Calef, "Gettysburg Notes: The Opening Gun," *JMSIUS*, Vol. 40 (1907), p. 52.
138. Meade, *The Life and Letters of General George Gordon Meade*, Vol. 2, p. 38.
139. *OR* 27.1.366.
140. *OR* 27.1.368-369.
141. *OR* 27.1.369.
142. The distance from Taneytown to Gettysburg is about 15 miles. A determined horseman could have covered this in about an hour.
143. *OR* 27.3.466.
144. *OR* 27.1.71-72.
145. *OR* 27.3.467.
146. *OR* 27.3.467.
147. *OR* 27.3.467.
148. *OR* 27.1.115; *OR* 57.1.1067.
149. Maurice, *An Aide de Camp of Lee*, pp. 227-228.
150. Freeman. *R.E. Lee*, Vol.3, p. 71. Freeman suggests that this story originated from Lee's ascent to the cupola of the Almshouse on 2 July.
151. Freeman, *R.E.Lee*, Vol. 3, p. 71; Wise, *The Long Arm of Lee*, p. 622.

152. *OR* 27.2.349.
153. *OR* 27.2.349.
154. Wise, *The Long Arm of Lee*, p. 623.
155. *OR* 27.2.349.
156. *OR* 27.2.349. Lee's concern to find a route to attack the Federal left is also shown by the fact that when he was at the "observatory of the college building" at sunset, he asked Maj. Gen. I.R. Trimble "to find a practicable road to carry the artillery around to the right, to which he proposed transferring Ewell's corps during the night." Trimble after the war told Col. William C. Oates of the 48th Alabama "that it was so late at night before a practicable way was found that General Lee deemed it impracticable." Oates, *The War Between the Union and the Confederacy*, p. 204.
157. Fremantle, *The Fremantle Diary*, pp. 203-204.
158. *OR* 27.2.607.
159. *OR* 27. 2.663. Pender would be mortally wounded by a shell fired from one of the guns on Cemetery Hill on the evening of 2 July, *OR* 27.2.658.
160. OR27.2.665.
161. *OR* 27.2.668.
162. Busey and Martin, *RSLG*, pp. 292-293.
163. *OR* 27.2.671.
164. *OR* 27.2.658.
165. *OR* 27.2.643. Col J.K. Marshall of the 52nd North Carolina succeeded Pettigrew as commander of Pettigrew's brigade.
166. Brooks, *Stories of the Confederacy*, p. 38. Col. Perrin also wondered why Anderson "was out of the way at so critical a juncture." Perrin strongly felt that "his failure to come up was the cause of the failure of the campaign;" Perrin, "A Little More Light on Gettysburg," *Mississippi Valley Historical Review*, Vol. 24 (1937-38), p. 519.
167. Dobbins, *Grandfather's Journal*, p. 148.
168. *OR* 27.2.613.
169. On the traffic jam caused by the arrival of Johnson's division on this road, see Coddington, p. 709, n. 160.
170. Foote, "Marching in Clover," *Philadelphia Weekly Times*, 8 October 1881.
171. Fremantle, *The Fremantle Diary*, pp. 202-203. See also Dobbins, *Grandfather's Journal*, p. 148. Terence Winschel suggests that the flag seen by Fremantle belonged to the 149th Pennsylvania, "Posey's Brigade at Gettysburg, Part I," *Gettysburg Magazine*, No. 4, p. 15, n. 49.
172. *OR* 27.2.613; Dobbins, *Grandfather's Journal*, p. 148.
173. *OR* 27.2.622.
174. Dobbins, *Grandfather's Journal*, p. 148.
175. Young, "Pettigrew's Brigade at Gettysburg," *NC Regts*, Vol. 5, p. 121 note.
176. Taylor, *General Lee, His Campaigns in Virginia*, p. 190.
177. *OR* 27.2.308.

178. Longstreet, *From Manassas to Appomattox*, pp. 357-358; *B & L*, Vol. 3, p. 340.

179. Longstreet, "Lee in Pennsylvania," in *The Annals of the War*, pp. 420-421. Slightly different versions appear in *B & L*, Vol. 3, pp. 339-340, and Longstreet, *From Manassas to Appomattox*, pp. 357-358.

180. Longstreet, "Lee in Pennsylvania," in *The Annals of the War*, p. 421.

181. Longstreet, "Lee in Pennsylvania." in *The Annals of the War*, p. 421.

182. *B & L*, Vol. 3, p. 340.

183. A.L. Long to J.A. Early, 5 April 1876, *SHSP* 4 (1877), pp. 66-67.

184. A.L. Long to J.A. Early, 5 April 1876, *SHSP* 4 (1877), p. 67.

185. Had Long been on the other side of Cemetery Hill, he would have mentioned the weakness of the Union line in the direction of Culp's Hill.

186. James P. Smith to J.W. Daniel, 15 July 1903, Daniel Papers, University of Virginia; W.P. Carter statement, Jubal Early material, Daniel Papers, University of Virginia.

187. Douglas, *I Rode with Stonewall*, p. 238.

188. *OR* 27.2.513, 531. Stewart's and Walker's brigades may have been reversed.

189. *OR* 27.2.504.

190. Douglas, *I Rode with Stonewall*, p. 238.

191. Douglas, *I Rode with Stonewall*, p. 239.

192. Douglas, *I Rode with Stonewall*, p. 239.

193. Taylor, *General Lee, His Campaigns in Virginia*, p. 190; Taylor, *Four Years with General Lee*, p. 95; on the time, see Smith, "General Lee at Gettysburg," *SHSP* 33 (1905), p. 144. Captain Francis Irsch of the 45th New York gives a quite different impression of Ewell's reaction to Lee's order. Irsch and a large number of his men had just been captured a couple blocks west of the town square, and he had been offered a "safe conduct" by his captors "if he would look out for himself." He wandered into the square, where he saw Ewell receive Lee's message and was close enough to hear Ewell mutter afterwards, "If he [Lee] knew the condition of his [Ewell's] troops, he would not think of such an order, and that the attack should not be risked," Schurz, *The Reminiscences of Carl Schurz*, Vol. 3, pp. 18-19. For Ewell's actual feelings on this order, see note 195 below.

194. Smith, "General Lee at Gettysburg." *SHSP* 33 (1905 p. 144.

195. Ewell himself wrote in his battle report, "On entering the town, I received a message from the commanding general to attack this hill, if I could do so to advantage. I could not bring artillery to bear on it, and all the troops with me were jaded by twelve hours' marching and fighting." Since Johnson's fresh division was at hand, and Cemetery Hill did not seem assailable, he decided "with Johnson's division, to take possession of a wooded hill to my left (Culp's Hill)," *OR* 27.2.445.

196. *OR* 27.2.555.

197. *OR* 27.7.567.

198. *OR* 27.2.580.

199. *OR* 27.2.593.

200. Early, *Autobiographical Sketch*, p. 269.
201. Early, *Autobiographical Sketch*, p. 269.
202. Early, *Autobiographical Sketch*, pp. 269-270.
203. Pfanz, *Gettysburg—Culp's Hill and Cemetery Hill*, p. 420; White, *The Comanches*, p. 98; see below, note 245.
204. See below, notes 245 and 309.
205. Warner, *Generals in Gray*, p. 285.
206. Statement of C.B. Coiner, Finley Papers, University of Virginia; Driver, *52nd Virginia Infantry*, p. 40.
207. Early, "Leading Confederates in the Battle of Gettysburg." *SHSP* Vol. 4 (1877), pp. 255-256.
208. Early, *Autobiographical Sketch*, p. 270.
209. *OR* 27.2.489; statement of C.B. Coiner, Finley Papers, University of Virginia; see also Pfanz, *Gettysburg—Culp's Hill and Cemetery Hill*, p. 418, n. 22.
210. Hale and Phillips, *History of the Forty-Ninth Virginia Infantry*, pp. 77-78.
211. Early, *Autobiographical Sketch*, pp. 269-270.
212. Early, *Autobiographical Sketch*, p. 270.
213. Smith, "General Lee at Gettysburg," *SHSP* 33 (1905), p. 144. The officers probably meant northern Cemetery Ridge, not Little Round Top, as the "commanding height."
214. Smith, "General Lee at Gettysburg," *SHSP* 33 (1905), p. 145.
215. Smith, "General Lee at Gettysburg," *SHSP* 33 (1905), p. 145.
216. Smith, "General Lee at Gettysburg," *SHSP* 33 (1905), p. 145.
217. J.W. Daniel, "Commentary on John B. Gordon's *Reminiscences of the Civil War*," Gettysburg material, J. Daniel Papers, University of Virginia. Daniel thought that the man who was shot was named Williamson, but there was no staff officer present with that name. See Pfanz, *Gettysburg—Culp's Hill and Cemetery Hill*, p. 419, n. 7.
218. Gordon, *Reminiscences of the Civil War*, p. 157.
219. Pfanz, *Gettysburg—Culp's Hill and Cemetery Hill*, p. 357, and 465 note 12.
220. G.C. Brown, "Reminiscences," Brown-Ewell Papers, Tennessee State Library and Archives, Nashville.
221. *OR* 27.2.445. Campbell Brown of Ewell's staff wrote later, "It was, as I have always understood, with the express concurrence of both Rodes and Early and largely in consequence of the inactivity of the troops under General Lee's own eye...that General Ewell finally decided to make no direct attack, but to wait for Johnson's coming up and with his fresh troops seize and hold the high peak [Culp's Hill] to our left of Cemetery Hill," G.C. Brown Memoir, Brown-Ewell Papers, Tennessee State Archives.
222. Early, "Leading Confederates in the Battle of Gettysburg." *SHSP* 4 (1877), pp. 255-256.
223. *OR* 27.2.480.

224. Early, "Leading Confederates in the Battle of Gettysburg." *SHSP* 4 (1877), pp. 296-297.

225. Jones, *Lee's Tigers*, p. 168; Martin, *The Road to Glory*, p. 215.

226. OR 27.2.484; Jones, "Fifty-Seventh Regiment," *NC Regts*, Vol. 3, p. 414.

227. Gordon, *Reminiscences of the Civil War*, pp. 153-154.

228. *OR* 27.2.593; Grace, "Rodes' Division at Gettysburg," *CV* 5 (1897), p. 615.

229. William Calder to his mother, Brake Collection, USAMHI.

230. Gorman, undated letter to "Friend Gorman" on "Battles of Gettysburg," in "Pierce's Memorandum Account Book," North Carolina State Archives.

231. *OR* 27.2.555.

232. *OR* 27.2.663; see also Early, "Leading Confederates in the Battle of Gettysburg," *SHSP* 4 (1877), p. 254.

233. Halstead, "The First Day of the Battle of Gettysburg," in *Gettysburg Papers*, Vol. 1, p. 157 (*DC MOLLUS*, 2 March 1887, p. 9).

234. Halstead, "The First Day of the Battle of Gettysburg," in *Gettysburg Papers*, Vol. 1, pp. 157-158 (*DC MOLLUS*, 2 March 1887, pp. 9-10). Halstead doubtlessly exaggerates the number of men he helped rally.

235. *OR* 27.1.286; Tevis, *History of the Fighting Fourteenth*, pp. 87-88.

236. Simpson, "The Drummer Boys of Gettysburg, " *Philadelphia North American*, 29 June 1913, p. 2.

237. Underwood, *Three Years' Service in the Thirty-Third Massachusetts*, p. 119.

238. Hurst, *Journal-History of the Seventy-Third Ohio Volunteer Infantry*, p. 67.

239. Early, "Leading Confederates in the Battle of Gettysburg," *SHSP* 4 (1877), p. 256.

240. *OR* 27.2.489.

241. Goldsborough, *The Maryland Line in the Confederate Army*, p. 178.

242. White, *The Comanches*, pp. 192-195.

243. White, *The Comanches*, pp. 197-198.

244. White, *The Comanches*, p. 198.

245. White, *The Comanches*, p. 198.

246. White, *The Comanches*, p. 199.

247. Shevchuk, "The Wounding of Albert Jenkins," *Gettysburg Magazine*, No. 3, p. 57.

248. Vickers, *Under Both Flags*, p. 80.

249. Vickers, *Under Both Flags*, p. 80.

250. Schuricht, "Jenkins' Brigade in the Gettysburg Campaign," *SHSP* 24 (1896), p. 344.

251. V.A. Witcher to John W. Daniel, 1 March 1906, Daniel Papers, University of Virginia.

252. Schuricht, "Jenkins' Brigade in the Gettysburg Campaign," *SHSP* 24 (1896), p. 344; Witcher to John W. Daniel, 1 March 1906, Daniel Papers, University of Virginia.

253. Witcher to John W. Daniel, 1 March 1906, Daniel Papers, University of Virginia; Sevchuk, "The Wounding of Albert Jenkins," *Gettysburg Magazine*, No. 3, p. 58.
254. Witcher to John B. Bachelder, 19 March 1886, Bachelder Papers, NHHS.
255. Serchuk, "The Wounding of Albert Jenkins," *Gettysburg Magazine*, No. 3, p. 58.
256. Toombs, *Reminiscences of the War*, pp. 71-72.
257. *OR* 27.1.798.
258. Toombs, *Reminiscences of the War*, p. 72.
259. *OR* 27.1.836.
260. *OR* 27.1.796 and 825 say that the camp was broken at 0500. The historian of the 27th Indiana, which led the column, says that it began marching at 0700, Brown, *The Twenty-Seventh Indiana Volunteer Infantry*, p. 365; Bates, *The Battle of Gettysburg*, p. 92, cites an officer of Kane's brigade who gives the time as 0600.
261. Quaife, *From the Cannon's Mouth*, p. 224.
262. Brown, *The Twenty-Seventh Indiana Volunteer Infantry*, p. 365.
263. Brown, *The Twenty-Seventh Indiana Volunteer Infantry*, p. 365.
264. OR. 27.1.825; Quaife, *From the Cannon's Mouth*, p. 224.
265. Pfanz, *Gettysburg—Culp's Hill and Cemetery Hill*, p. 92.
266. Henry W. Slocum to T.M. Davis, Samuel P. Bates Papers, Pennsylvania State Archives, Harrisburg.
267. New York Monuments Commission, *In Memoriam, Henry Warner Slocum*, p. 175.
268. *OR* 27.3.416.
269. *OR* 27.3.458-459.
270. *OR* 27.3.458.
271. *OR* 27.3.463.
272. New York Monuments Commission, *In Memoriam: Henry Warner Slocum*, p. 175; Pfanz, *Gettysburg—Culp's Hill and Cemetery Hill*, pp. 92-93.
273. *OR* 27.1.703; compare Howard, *The Autobiography of Oliver Otis Howard*, Vol. 1, p. 416.
274. Daniel Hall to O.O. Howard, 19 February 1877, O.O. Howard Papers, Bowdoin College Library.
275. See Brown, *The Twenty-Seventh Indiana Volunteer Infantry*, p. 366.
276. Doubleday, *Chancellorsville and Gettysburg*, p. 137.
277. Bates, *The Battle of Gettysburg*, pp. 92-93.
278. Henry W. Slocum to T.M. Davis, 8 September 1875, Samuel P. Bates Papers, Pennsylvania State Archives.
279. Cooke, "The First Day at Gettysburg," in *Gettysburg Papers*, Vol. 1, p. 250 (*Kansas MOLLUS*, 4 November 1897, p. 286).
280. Pfanz, *Gettysburg—Culp's Hill and Cemetery Hill*, p. 94, suggests that Slocum's subordinates did not have enough information to evaluate the strategic situation.
281. *OR* 27.1.126.
282. Coddington, pp. 312-313.

283. Henry W. Slocum to T.M. Davis, 8 September 1875, Samuel P. Bates Papers, Pennsylvania State Archves.

284. New York Monuments Commission, *In Memoriam, Henry Warner Slocum*, p. 175.

285. *OR* 27.1.126.

286. *OR* 27.3.465.

287. Pfanz, *Gettysburg— Culp's Hill and Cemetery Hill*, pp. 94-95.

288. Brown, *The Twenty-Seventh Indiana Volunteer Infantry*, pp. 367-368.

289. Brown, *The Twenty-Seventh Indiana Volunteer Infantry*, p. 367.

290. A.S. Williams to John B. Bachelder, 10 November 1865, Bachelder Papers, NHHS.

291. Tallman, "The War of the Rebellion" (66th Ohio), GNMP Collections.

292. Toombs, *New Jersey Troops in the Gettysburg Campaign*, p. 187; Toombs, *Reminiscences of the War*, pp. 74-75.

293. Tallman, "The War of the Rebellion," (66th Ohio), GNMP Collections.

294. A.S. Williams to John B. Bachelder, 10 November 1865, Bachelder Papers, NHHS.

295. "Col. C.H. Morgan's Statement," p. 323, Bachelder Papers, NHHS.

296. "Col. C.H. Morgan's Statement," p. 323, Bachelder Papers, NHHS.

297. "Col. C.H. Morgan's Statement," p. 323, Bachelder Papers, NHHS.

298. *OR* 27.1.704.

299. *OR* 27.1.704.

300. C.H. Howard, "The First Day at Gettysburg," in *Gettysburg Papers*, Vol. 1, p. 330 (Illinois *MOLLUS*, Vol. 4, p. 238).

301. *OR* 27.1.696.

302. *OR* 27.3.466.

303. *OR* 27.3.468.

304. C.H. Howard to E. Whittlesday, 9 July 1863, C.H. Howard Papers, Bowdoin College Library.

305. O.O. Howard, "Campaign and Battle of Gettysburg," *Atlantic Monthly*, Vol. 38 (July 1876), p. 60.

306. Abner Doubleday to Samuel P. Bates, 24 April 1874, Bates Papers, Pennsylvania State Archives.

307. Pfanz, *Gettysburg—Culp's Hill and Cemetery Hill*, p. 98.

308. A.S. Williams to John B. Bachelder, 10 November 1865, Bachelder Papers, NHHS.

309. A.S. Williams to John B. Bachelder, 10 November 1865, Bachelder Papers, NHHS. This roadway meets the Baltimore Pike about one-half mile east of Rock Creek, immediately west of the present Route 15 interchange. For a description of it, see Pfanz, *Gettysburg—Culp's Hill and Cemetery Hill*, p. 423, note 23.

310. Williams' division had no 2nd brigade at the moment. A provisional command under Brig. Gen. Henry Lockwood, whose components had not yet reached the field, would be assigned as Williams' second brigade.

See Pfanz, *Gettysburg—Culp's Hill and Cemetery Hill*, p. 191; *OR* 27.1.165; *OR* 27.3.375; and Quaife, *From the Cannon's Mouth*, p. 228.

311. A.S. Williams to John B. Bachelder, 10 November 1865, Bachelder Papers, NHHS.

312. Morse, *History of the Second Massachusetts Regiment of Infantry*, p. 6.

313. Quaife, *From the Cannon's Mouth*, p. 224; A.S. Williams to John B. Bachelder, 10 November 1865, Bachelder Papers, NHHS.

314. Pfanz, *Gettysburg—Culp's Hill and Cemetery Hill*, p. 96.

315. A.S. Williams to John B. Bachelder, 10 November 1865, Bachelder Papers, NHHS.

316. *OR* 27.1.811, 816.

317. *OR* 27.1.811.

318. Quaife, *From the Cannon's Mouth*, p. 225.

319. *OR* 27.1.816.

320. A.S. Williams to John B. Bachelder, 10 November 1865, Bachelder Papers, NHHS; *OR* 27.1.811.

321. *OR* 27.1.782, 816.

322. Brown, *The Twenty-Seventh Indiana Volunteer Infantry*, p. 368.

323. Brown, *The Twenty-Seventh Indiana Volunteer Infantry*, p.368

324. Quaife, *From the Cannon's Mouth*, p. 225.

325. *OR* 27.1.825.

326. *OR* 27.1.825, 848, 851.

327. Upon reaching the field, the 10th Maine Battalion "was at once put to the task of arresting the stream of stragglers and skulks which is always flowing out of the fighting line." Their line ran across the Baltimore Pike, with its center at the stone bridge over McAllister's Run; its left extended towards, but did not reach, the Taneytown Road, see *Maine at Gettysburg*, p. 520. Altogether the XII Corps Provost Guard picked up about 1200 fugitives that night on the Baltimore Pike southeast of Gettysburg; see Hancock, *Reminiscences of Winfield Scott Hancock*, p. 189. On 2 July, Company C of the 110th Pennsylvania was on the provost guard duty for the III Corps and found a large number of stragglers from the first day's fight, to the south of Gettysburg; see Hamilton, "The 110th Regiment in the Gettysburg Campaign," *Philadelphia Weekly Press*, 24 February 1886.

328. *OR* 27.1.825.

329. *OR* 27.1.855.

330. *OR* 27.1.866.

331. *OR* 27.1.868.

332. *OR* 27.1.864.

333. *OR* 27.1.842.

334. Col. M.A. Barnum of the 149th New York says he sent out his skirmishers at 1800, *OR* 27.1.868. General Geary says the movement was completed at 1700, but that is too early, *OR* 27.1.825.

335. *OR* 27.1.825, 836.

336. *OR* 27.1.839.

337. Quaife, *From the Cannon's Mouth*, p. 225.

338. *OR* 27.1.482, 530.
339. *OR* 27.2.399, 420.
340. Tremain, *Two Days of War*, p. 14.
341. Tremain, *Two Days of War*, p. 19.
342. Tremain, *Two Days of War*, p. 19.
343. *OR* 27.3.463.
344. *OR* 27.3.464.
345. Sickles sent an order at 1515 for Humphreys to move (OR 51.1.1066) and at 1530 for Birney (OR 27.1.465).
346. Birney could not have left until after he received Sickles' orders sent at 1530 (OR 27.1.465). However, various reports place his departure time at 1400 (OR 27.1.482, 497, 502) and at 1500 (OR 27.1.493).
347. *OR* 27.1.482, 581.
348. *OR* 27.1.519.
349. *OR* 27.1.530.
350. *OR* 27.1.570.
351. Busey and Martin, *RSLG*, p. 47.
352. *OR* 27.1.482, 493.
353. Birney's report (OR 27.1.482) gives a 3 1/2 hour march time, while the commander of the 114th Pennsylvania says he marched for 5 hours (OR 27.1.502).
354. *OR* 27.1.500.
355. *OR* 27.3.466.
356. *OR* 27.3.468.
357. *OR* 27.3.467.
358. "Mrs. Thorn's War Story," *Gettysburg Times*, 2 July 1938.
359. "Wife of Cemetery Caretaker Relates Horrors of Battle of Gettysburg," *Hundredth Anniversary of the Battle of Gettysburg*.
360. Howard, *Autobiography of Oliver Otis Howard*, Vol. 3, p. 419.
361. "Mrs. Thorn's War Story, " *Gettysburg Times*, 2 July 1938.
362. Nevins, *A Diary of Battle*, pp. 238-239.
363. Schurz, *The Reminiscences of Carl Schurz*, Vol. 3, pp. 19-20.
364. *OR* 27.1.497.
365. *OR* 27.1.513.
366. *OR* 27.1.509.
367. *OR* 27.1.498.
368. Meade. *Life and Letters of General George Gordon Meade*, Vol. 2, p. 66.
369. Humphreys, *Andrew Atkinson Humphreys*, p. 187.
370. *OR* 27.1.531, 543.
371. *OR* 27.1.531, 543.
372. *OR* 27.1.531.
373. *OR* 27.1.382.
374. Humphreys, *Andrew Atkinson Humphreys*, pp. 188-190.
375. *OR* 27.1.531; Humphreys, *Andrew Atkinson Humphreys*, pp. 188-189.
376. *OR* 27.1.531.
377. Humphreys, *Andrew Atkinson Humphreys*, pp. 189-190.
378. Humphreys, *Andrew Atkinson Humphreys*, pp. 191.

379. Humphreys, *Andrew Atkinson Humphreys*, pp. 191-192.

380. *OR* 27.1.547. Two officers in Brewster's brigade recorded their arrival time as midnight (OR 27.1.558, 563), and two others gave the time of their arrival as 0200 (OR 27.1.565, 568). Lt. Col. Baldwin of the 1st Massachusetts blamed the column's difficulties during the march on Lt. Col. Hayden; after the battle he wrote that the column was "led by a staff officer who was more noted for froth and foam than for common sense, although a West Pointer and on a major general's staff; got on the wrong road and got lost," Baldwin to John B. Bachelder, 20 May 1865, Bachelder Papers, NHHS.

381. *OR* 27.1.351. Col. Randall of the 13th Vermont gives his arrival time as 1700, but Stannard's report makes it clear that Birney's division was already on the field when the Vermonters arrived, so Stannard must have come up an hour or more later than Randall stated. See Scott, "Vermont at Gettysburg," p. 5 (McLean, *Gettysburg Sources*, Vol. 1, p. 60).

382. *OR* 27.1.349; Davis, *Three Years in the Army*, p. 229. Coulter's 11th Pennsylvania was transferred from Baxter's brigade to Paul's at 1700 in order to enable Coulter to take over command of Paul's brigade, *OR* 27.1.293.

383. George B. Fox to A.L. Harris, 14 November 1885, Bachelder Papers, NHHS.

384. *OR* 27.1.713; Martin, *Carl Bornemann's Regiment*, pp. 147, 149, 254; however, Bornemann in *NYG*, p. 308, gives the unit's arrival time as midnight.

385. Dunkelman and Winey, "The Hardtack Regiment in the Brickyard Fight." *Gettysburg Magazine*, No. 8, p. 19; Dunkelman and Winey, *The Hardtack Regiment*, p. 71.

386. Lewis D. Warner Diary, 1 July 1863, as cited in Dunkelman and Winey, "The Hardtack Regiment in the Brickyard Fight," *Gettysburg Magazine*, No. 8, p. 24.

387. Account by William D. Harper of the 154th New York, as cited in Dunkelman and Winey, "The Hardtack Regiment in the Brickyard Fight," *Gettysburg Magazine*, No. 8, p. 24.

387. Account by William D. Harper of the 154th New York, as cited in Dunkelman and Winey, "The Hardtack Regiment in the Brickyard Fight," *Gettysburg Magazine*, No. 8, p. 24.

388. *OR* 27.1.369, 872.

389. McLean, *Cutler's Brigade*, p. 142; Thomson, *From Philippi to Appomattox*, pp. 161-162.

390. Thomson, *From Philippi to Appomattox*, p. 162.

391. McLean, *Cutler's Brigade*, p. 145.

392. Thomson, *From Philippi to Appomattox*, pp. 162-163.

393. See Coddington, p. 712, n. 182.

394. McLean, *Cutler's Brigade*, p. 145.

395. *OR* 27.1.283; Stine, *History of the Army of the Potomac*, p. 492.

396. *OR* 27.1.284; Dawes, *Service with the Sixth Wisconsin Volunteers*, p. 180.

397. Thomson, *From Philippi to Appomattox*, p. 163.
398. "At Gettysburg, How a Proposed Night Attack by the Enemy Was Foiled," *National Tribune*, 11 February 1886.
399. *OR* 27.1.357.
400. H.J Hunt to Gantt, 20 March 1886, Hunt Papers, Library of Congress.
401. *OR* 27.1.735.
402. *Pa at G*, pp. 665-666.
403. Boies, *Record of the Thirty-Third Massachusetts Volunteer Infantry*, p. 32.
404. "Gettysburg, Captain Turner," manuscript in J.A. Early Papers, Earl Gregg Swem Library, College of William and Mary; see also Pfanz, *Gettysburg—Culp's Hill and Cemetery Hill*, p. 421, note 20.
405. The route and timing of this reconnaissance is as enigmatic as the more famous reconnaissance of Little Round Top made by Capt. Samuel R. Johnston on the morning of 2 July (see Pfanz, *Gettysburg—The Second Day*, pp. 166-167). For a discussion of this problem, see Pfanz, *Gettysburg—Culp's Hill and Cemetery Hill*, p. 80 and p. 421, note 21.
406. "Gettysburg, Captain Turner" manuscript in J.A. Early Papers, Earl Gregg Swem Library, College of William and Mary; see also Pfanz, *Gettysburg—Culp's Hill and Cemetery Hill*, p. 421, note 20.
407. J.R. Trimble to John B. Bachelder, 8 February 1883, Bachelder Papers, NHHS; See also Trimble, The Battle of Gettysburg, *SHSP* 26 (1898), pp. 123.
408. J.R. Trimble to John B. Bachelder, 8 February 1883, Bachelder Papers, NHHS; See also Trimble, "The Battle of Gettysburg," *SHSP* 26 (1898), pp. 123-124.
409. McKim, "The Gettysburg Campaign" *SHSP* 40 (1915), p. 273.
410. *OR* 27.1.513; Goldsborough, *The Maryland Line*, p. 102.
411. *OR* 27.1.513
412. Goldsborough, *The Maryland Line*, p. 102
413. J.W. Bruce to John W. Daniel, 8 April 1904, Daniel Papers, University of Virginia Library.
414. *OR* 27.2.504
415. Bruce, "Would Have Saved Officers," *Charlottesville Daily Progress*, 22 March 1904; Bruce to John W. Daniel, 8 April 1904, Daniel Papers, University of Virginia Library. Bruce in the two sources cited says that he heard Ewell order Early to go into camp and Johnson to "go into camp in a wood." Since neither general proceeded to go into camp, it is possible that Bruce misheard Ewell. For an evaluation of this episode, see Pfanz, *Gettysburg—Culp's Hill and Cemetery Hill*, p. 420 note 19.
416. Pfanz, *Gettysburg—Culp's Hill and Cemetery Hill*, p. 79.
417. McKim, "Steuart's Brigade at the Battle of Gettysburg," *SHSP* 5 (1878), p. 292.
418. See map in *B & L*, Vol. 3, p. 282.
419. *OR* 27.2.504, 509, 513, 521, 531.
420. *OR* 27.2.523.
421. Pfanz, *Gettysburg—Culp's Hill and Cemetery Hill*, p. 420, note 17.

422. Ewell in *OR* 27.2.470 says that Johnson's advance was "delayed by the report of the advance along the York Road."

423. *OR* 27.2.446

424. Stine, *History of the Army of the Potomac*, p. 493.

425. *OR* 27.2.446.

426. *OR* 27.2.446.

427. Dawes, *Service with the Sixth Wisconsin Volunteers*, p. 180.

428. Thomson, *From Philippi to Appomattox*, p. 164.

429. There has been much discussion of the location of Ewell's headquarters at this time. D.S. Freeman believed it was at the Blocher house, near the junction of Carlisle and Table Rock Roads about .8 mile north of the town square, *Lee's Lieutenants*, Vol. 3, pp. 94,101. Douglas C. Haines believes it was at the Spangler house located near the intersection of the Carlisle, Mummasburg and Harrisburg Roads, about two blocks north of the town square, "R.S. Ewell's Command," *Gettysburg Magazine*, No. 9, p. 30. Harry Pfanz gives the most persuasive argument to place Ewell's headquarters somewhere near the Almshouse or the J. Crawford about .6 miles northeast of the town square, near the Harrisburg Road, *Gettysburg—Culp's Hill and Cemetery Hill*, p. 421, note. 27. Ewell's headquarters later in the battle was on the Hanover Road, some 150 yards west of Rock Creek, as is now marked by an upturned cannon and plaque.

430. Pfanz, *Gettysburg—Culp's Hill and Cemetery Hill*, p. 81. While on the way to see Ewell, Lee stopped at the observatory of the "college building" to survey the town at sunset. While at the college he ran into General Trimble and asked him to locate a road to move artillery and troops to the right, see note 156 above.

431. Early, "Leading Confederates of the Battle of Gettysburg," *SHSP* 4 (1877), p. 271.

432. Early, "Leading Confederates of the Battle of Gettysburg," *SHSP* 4 (1877), p. 272.

433. Early, "Leading Confederates of the Battle of Gettysburg," *SHSP* 4 (1877), p. 272-273.

434. Early, "Leading Confederates of the Battle of Gettysburg," *SHSP* 4 (1877), p. 272-274.

435. Charles Marshall to Jubal Early, 23 March 1870 and 13 March 1878, Early Papers, Library of Congress.

436. Charles Marshall to Jubal Early, 23 March 1870 and 13 March 1878, Early Papers, Library of Congress; "Gettysburg, Captain Turner," manuscript in Early Papers, Virginia Historical Society.

437. *OR* 27.2.480.

438. *OR* 27.2.446.

439. *OR* 27.2.446.

440. Nolan, "R.E. Lee and July 1 at Gettysburg," in *The First Day at Gettysburg*, p. 29; Coddington, p. 320.

441. Transcript of conversation between Lee and Allan, 19 February 1870,

William Allan Papers, Southern Historical Collection, Wilson Library, University of North Carolina.

442. J. William Jones, as quoted by Gordon, *Reminicences of the Civil War*, p. 154.

443. Gorman, undated letter to "Friend Gorman" on "Battles of Gettysburg," in "Pierce's Memorandum Account Book," North Carolina State Archives.

444. Stikeleather in the *Raleigh Semi-weekly Standard*, 4 August 1863, as quoted in Tucker, High Tide at Gettysburg, p. 186.

445. Smith, "General Lee at Gettysburg," *SHSP* 33 (1905), p. 144; Douglas, *I Rode with Stonewall*, p. 247.

446. W.H. Swallow, "The First Day at Gettysburg," *Southern Bivouac* N.S.1 (December 1885), pp. 441-442.

447. Gordon, *Reminiscences of the Civil War*, pp. 154-155.

448. See, for example, *Wise, The Long Arm of Lee*, pp. 625-628.

449. See the persuasive arguments by Gary Gallagher "Confederate Corps Leadership on the First Day at Gettysburg: AP Hill and Richard S. Ewell in a Difficult Debut," *The First Day at Gettysburg*, pp. 30-56. On Ewell's alleged indecisiveness see Haines, "R.S. Ewell's Command," *Gettysburg Magazine*, No. 9, p. 32.

450. Robert E. Lee Jr. *Recollections and Letters of R.E. Lee*, pp. 415-416 Ewell was well aware of his own shortcomings. After the war he told Col. Eppa Hunton of the 8th Virginia that "It took a dozen blunders to lose Gettysburg, and he had committed a good many of them," Hunton, *Autobiography*, p. 98.

451. John B. Bachelder to Fitzhugh Lee, 18 January 1875, Bachelder Papers, NHHS.

452. "Letter from General Winfield Scott Hancock, *SHSP* 5 (1878), p. 168.

453. *B & L*, Vol. 3, p. 284.

454. Alexander, *Fighting for the Confederacy*, p. 233.

455. Wiggin, "Sixteenth Maine Regiment at Gettysburg," in *Gettysburg Papers*, Vol. 1. p. 299 (*Maine MOLLUS*, Vol.4, p. 161).

456. See, for example, D.S. Freeman, *Lee's Lieutenants*, Vol. 3, pp. 170-171.

457. Transcript of conversation between Lee and William Allan, 15 April 1868, William Allan Papers, Southern Historical Collection, Wilson Library, University of North Carolina, Chapel Hill.

458. See the most recent defense of Stuart by Marc Nesbitt, *Saber and Scapegoat: J.E.B. Stuart and the Gettysburg Controversy*, Mechanicsburg Pa: Stackpole Books, 1994.

459. See for example, Mosby, "The Confederate Cavalry in the Gettysburg Campaign," *B & L*, Vol. 3, pp. 251-252.

460. *OR* 27.2. 318.

461. It is difficult to believe that Lee would have attempted Longstreet's assault on 3 July if he had known that Meade's VI Corps was on the field, as well as all the additional troops that had been called up from Washington and Maryland. Lee simply did not believe that Meade's army was as strong as it was, particularly after so many of its two years' troops had

gone home after the battle of Chancellorsville (see Coddington, p. 673, note 2).

462. See Coddington, p. 357.

463. For the time of his arrival, see Pfanz, *Gettysburg—Culp's Hill and Cemetery Hill,* p. 426, note 2.

464. Meade, *With Meade at Gettysburg,* p. 69

465. Howard, *Autobiography of Oliver Otis Howard,* Vol. 1 p. 423.

466. Howard, *Autobiography of Oliver Otis Howard,* Vol. 1 p. 423.

467. Meade, *The Life and Letters of General George Gordon Meade,* Vol. 2, pp. 61-62.

Abbreviations Used in Footnotes and Bibliography

B & L	*Battles and Leaders of the Civil War*, edited by Robert U. Johnson and Clarence C. Buel
CV	*Confederate Veteran Magazine*
CWTI	*Civil War Times Illustrated*
Gettysburg Papers, edited by Ken Bandy & Florence Freeland	
Gettysburg Sources, edited by James & Judy McLean	
GNMP	Gettysburg National Military Park
JMSIUS	*Journal of the Military Service Institution of the United States*
LC	Library of Congress
MOLLUS	Military Order of the Loyal Legion of the United States
NC Regts	*History of the Several Regiments and Battalions from North Carolina in the Great War, 1861-65*, edited by Walter Clark
NHHS	New Hampshire Historical Society
NYG	New York Monuments Commision for the Battlefields of Gettysburg and Chattanooga. *Final Report on the Battlefield of Gettysburg*
OR	*War of the Rebellion: A Compilation of the Official Records of the Union and Confederate Armies*
Pa at G	*Pennsylvania at Gettysburg*, edited by John P. Nicholson
RSLG	*Regimental Strengths and Losses at Gettysburg*, by John W. Busey and David G. Martin
SHSP	Southern Historical Society Papers
USAMHI	United States Army Military History Institute

Bibliography

Alexander, Edward Porter. *Fighting for the Confederacy*. Chapel Hill: Univ. of NC Press, 1989.

Alexander, Edward Porter. *Military Memoirs of a Confederate*. New York: Charles Scribner's Sons, 1907. Reprinted 1962 by Indiana University Press.

Alleman, Mrs. Tillie Pierce. *At Gettysburg, or What a Girl Saw and Heard of the Battle*. New York: W. Lake Borland, 1889. Reprinted 1987 by Butternut and Blue.

The Annals of the War Written by Leading Participants, North and South, originally published in the *Philadelphia Weekly Times*. Dayton, Ohio: Morningside Press, 1988.

Applegate, John S. *Reminiscences and Letters of George Arrowsmith of New Jersey*. Red Bank, NJ: John H. Cook, 1893.

"At Gettysburg, How a Proposed Night Attack by the Enemy was Foiled." *National Tribune*, 11 February 1886.

Auginbaugh, Nellie E. *Personal Experience of a Young Girl During the Battle of Gettysburg*. Washington DC: Louisdale Leeds, n.d.

Bachelder, John B. 1 July 1863 Map.

Bandy, Ken and Florence Freeland (Editors). *The Gettysburg Papers*. 2 Vols. Dayton, Ohio: Morningside Press, 1978.

Bassler, J.H. "The Color Episode of the 149th Regiment, Pennsylvania Volunteers, in the Civil War." *SHSP* 37 (1909): 266-301.

Bates, Samuel P. *The Battle of Gettysburg*. Philadelphia: T.H. Davis & Co., 1875. Reprinted 1987 by Van Sickle Military Books.

Bates, Samuel P. *History of Pennsylvania Volunteers, 1861-5*. 5 Vols. Harrisburg: B. Singerly, 1869.

Bates, Samuel P. *Martial Deeds of Pennsylvania*. Philadelphia: T.H. Davis & Co., 1875.

Beale, George W. "Gettysburg, A Paper Read Before the United Service Club, Philadelphia, Penna., January 5, 1887." Philadelphia: privately published, 1887.

Beale, James. "The Statement of Time on July 1 at Gettysburg PA 1863" in *Gettysburg Sources*, Vol. 3: 38-72.

Bean, Theodore W. "Who fired the opening Shots! General Buford at Gettysburg—The Cavalry Ride into Pennsylvania and the Choice of the Field of Battle—The First Day on the Outposts Before the Arrival of the Infantry." *Philadelphia Weekly Times*, 2 February 1878. In *Gettysburg Sources*, Vol. 3: 73-80.

Beaudot, William J.K. "Francis Asbury Wallar: A Medal of Honor at Gettysburg" in *Gettysburg Magazine*, No. 4, July 1990: 16-21.

Beecham, R.K. "Adventures of an Iron Brigade Man," *National Tribune*, 1902.

Beecham, Robert K., *Gettysburg, The Pivotal Battle of the War*. Chicago: A.C. McClurg & Co, 1911.

Belo, A.H. and William Robbins. "The Battle of Gettysburg." *CV* 8 (1900): 165-168.

Benjamin, Charles F. "Hooker's Appointment and Removal" *B & L*, Vol. 3: 239-243.

Bennet, R.T. "Fourteenth Regiment" *NC Regts*, Vol. 1: 704-732.

Berkeley, Henry R. *Four Years in the Confederate Artillery: The Diary of Private Henry Robinson Berkeley*. Chapel Hill: University of North Carolina Press, 1961.

Beveridge, John L. "The First Gun at Gettysburg" in *The Gettysburg Papers*, Vol I: 159-180.

Beveridge, John L. "Illinois Monuments at Gettysburg" in *Gettysburg Sources*, Vol 3: 1-37.

Beyer, W.F., and O.F. Keydel, editors. *Deeds of Valor: How America's Civil War Heroes Won the Medal of Honor*. Detroit: The Perrien-Keydel Co., 1905.

Biddle, Chapman. *The First Day of the Battle of Gettysburg*. Philadelphia: J.B. Lippincott, 1880.

Bilby, Joseph G. "Carbines-Yesterday." *Civil War News*, Dec. 1992: 50-52.

Bilby, Joseph G. "The Spencer-Then." *Civil War News*, May 1992: 44-45.

Bird, Alex. "At Gettysburg" *Ellicottville (NY) Post*, 16 Sept 1898.

Bird, W.H. *Stories of the Civil War, Company C, 13th Regiment of Alabama Volunteers*. Columbia, Ala: Advocate Print, n.d.

Black, Linda G. "Gettysburg's Preview of War: Early's June 26, 1863 Raid," *The Gettysburg Magazine*, No 2: 3-8.

Boatner, Mark M. III. *The Civil War Dictionary* New York: David Mackay Co., 1959.

Boies, Andrew J. *Record of the Thirty-third Massachusetts Volunteer Infantry, From August 1862 to August 1865*. Fitchburg: Sentinel Printing Company, 1880.

Boland, E.T. "Beginning of the Battle of Gettysburg" *CV* 14 (1906): 308-309.

Boland, E.T. "Death of Gen. Reynolds. An Ex-Confederate who was a witness describes the Event." *National Tribune*, 20 May 1915.

Boone, Samuel G. "Captured at Gettysburg." *National Tribune*, 9 May 1912.

Boyle, John Richards. *Soldiers True: The Story of the One Hundred and Eleventh Regiment Pennsylvania Veteran Volunteers and of Its Campaigns in the War for the Union. 1861-1865*. New York: Eaton & Wains, 1903.

Brooks, O.R. *Stories of the Confederacy* Camden, S.C. J.J. Fox, ca. 1990.

Brown, Edmund R. *The Twenty-Seventh Indiana Volunteer Infantry in the War of the Rebellion*. Monticello: 1899.

Brown, Varina D. *A Colonel at Gettysburg and Spotsylvania*. Columbia, S.C.: The State Company, 1931.

Buell, Augustus. *The Cannoneer: Recollections of Service in the Army of the Potomac by "A Detached Volunteer" in the Regular Artillery*. Washington DC: The National Tribune, 1890. Reprinted 1988.

Busey, John W. *These Honored Dead: The Union Casualties at Gettysburg*. Hightstown, NJ: Longstreet House, 1988.

Busey, John W. *The Last Full Measure: Burials in the Soldiers' National Cemetery at Gettysburg*. Hightstown, NJ: Longstreet House, 1988.

Busey, John W. and David G. Martin. *Regimental Strengths and Losses at Gettysburg*. Third Edition. Hightstown, NJ: Longstreet House, 1994.

Butts, John T. (Editor). *A Gallant Captain of the Civil War: From the Record of the Extraordinary Adventures of Friedrich Otto Baron Von Fritsch*. New York: F. Tennyson Neely, 1902.

Caldwell, J.F.J. *The History of a Brigade of South Carolinians First Known as "Gregg's" and Subsequently as "McGowan's".* Philadelphia: King & Baird, 1866.

Calef, John H. "Gettysburg Notes: The Opening Gun." *Journal of the Military Service Institution of the United States,* Vol. 40 (1907): 40-58.

Cameron, Bill. "The Signal Corps at Gettysburg." *The Gettysburg Magazine,* No. 3: 9-15.

Carpenter, John A. *Sword and Olive Branch: Oliver Otis Howard.* Pittsburgh: University of Pittsburgh Press, 1964.

Carrington, James M. "First Day on Left at Gettysburg." *SHSP* 37 (1969): 326-337.

Castleberry, W.A. "Thirteeth Alabama—Archer's Brigade." *CV,* 19 (1911): 338.

Chamberlin, Thomas. *History of the One Hundred and Fiftieth Regiment Pennsylvania Volunteers, Second Regiment, Bucktail Brigade.* Philadelphia: J.B. Lippincott Co., 1895.

Cheek, Philip, and Max Pointon. *History of the Sauk County Riflemen Known as Company "A," Sixth Wisconsin Veteran Volunteer Infantry, 1861-1865.* Madison: Democrat Printing Company, 1909. Reprinted 1984 by Butternut Press.

Cheney, Newel. *History of the Ninth Regiment New York Volunteer Cavalry.* Jamestown, NY: Poland Center, 1901.

Clark, Walter (Editor). *Histories of the Several Regiments and Battalions from North Carolina in The Great War 1861-65.* Goldsboro: Nash Brothers, 1901. Reprinted 1982 by Broadfoot's Bookmark.

Cleaves, Freeman. *Meade of Gettysburg.* Norman, Okla: University of Oklahoma Press, 1960. Reprinted 1980 by Morningside Press.

Coco, Gregory A. *Killed in Action.* Gettysburg: Thomas Publications, 1992.

Coco, Gregory A. *On the Blood Stained Field. 130 Human Interest Stories From the Campaign and Battle of Gettysburg.* Hollidaysburg, PA: Robert B. Moore, 1987.

Coco, Gregory A. *A Vast Sea of Misery: A History and Guide to the Union and Confederate Field Hospitals at Gettysburg, July 1-November 20, 1863.* Gettysburg: Thomas Publications, 1988.

Coco, Gregory A. *War Stories, A Collection of 150 Little Known Human Interest Accounts of the Campaign and Battle of Gettysburg.* Gettysburg: Thomas Publications 1992.

Coddington, Edwin B. *The Gettysburg Campaign: A Study in Command.* New York: Charles Scribner's Sons, 1968. Reprinted 1979 by Morningside House.

Coey, James. "Cutler's Brigade. The 147th New York's Magnificent Fight on the First Day at Gettysburg." *National Tribune,* 17 July 1915.

Confederate Veteran Magazine, 40 Vols. (1893-1932).

The Congressional Medal of Honor: The Names, The Deeds. Forest Ranch, Cal: Sharp & Dunnigan, 1984.

Cook, Benjamin F. *History of the Twelfth Massachusetts. Volunteers, Webster Regiment* Boston: Twelfth Regiment Assoc., 1882.

Cook, John D.S. *Personal Glimpses of Gettysburg,* in *Gettysburg Sources,* Vol. 2:122-144. (*Kansas MOLLUS,* 12 Dec 1903).

Cooke, Charles M. "Fifty-Fifth Regiment," *NC Regts,* Vol 3, 286-312.

Cooke, Sidney G. "The First Day at Gettysburg" in *Gettysburg Papers,* Vol. I: 239-253. (*Kansas MOLLUS,* 4 November 1897, 275-289.

Craft, David. *History of the One Hundred Forty-First Regiment, Pennsylvania Volunteers, 1862-1865.* Towanda, Pa: Reporter-Journal Printing Co, 1885.

Croll, Jennie C. "Memoir of Mary A. Horner." *Philadelphia Weekly Press,* 16 November 1887.

Cross, Andrew. *The War. Battle of Gettysburg and the Christian Commission.* Baltimore, 1865.

Culp, E.A. "Gettysburg." *National Tribune,* 19 March 1885.

Curtis, O.B. *History of the Twenty-Fourth Michigan of the Iron Brigade, Known as the Detroit and Wayne County Regiment.* Detroit: Winn & Hammond, 1891. Reprinted 1984 by Butternut Press.

Davis, Archie K. *Boy Colonel of the Confederacy: The Life and Times of Henry King Burgwyn, Jr.* Chapel Hill: University of North Carolina Press, 1985.

Davis, Charles E. Jr. *Three Years in the Army: The Story of the Thirteenth Massachusetts Volunteers From July 16, 1861 to August 1, 1864.* Boston: Estes & Lownat, 1864.

Davis, William C. (Editor). *The Confederate General.* 6 Vols. National Historical Society, 1991.

Dawes, Rufus R. "A Gallant Officer." *Milwaukee Sunday Telegraph,* 3 February 1884.

Dawes, Rufus R. "Align on the Colors." *Milwaukee Sunday Telegraph,* 27 April 1890.

Dawes, Rufus R. *Service with the Sixth Wisconsin Volunteers.* Marietta, Ohio: E.R. Alderman & Sons, 1890. Reprinted 1984 by Morningside Press.

Dawes, Rufus. "With the Sixth Wisconsin at Gettysburg" in *Gettysburg Papers,* Vol. I: 213-238.

Day, Thomas G. "Veteran of 3rd Indiana Cavalry Describes the First Day's Fight at Gettysburg." *National Tribune,* 3 July 1903.

De Peyster, John W. *Decisive Conflicts of the Late Civil War.* New York: MacDonald & Co. 1867.

Dickinson, Jack L. *16th Virginia Cavalry.* Lynchburg, Va: H.E. Howard, Inc., 1989.

Dobbins, Austin C. *Grandfather's Journal, Company B, Sixteenth Mississippi Infantry Volunteers, Harris' Brigade, Mahone's Division, Hill's Corps, ANV, May 27, 1861-July 15, 1865.* Dayton, Ohio: Morningside House, 1988.

Dodge, H.O. "Opening The Battle. Lieutenant Jones, The 8th Illinois Cavalryman Fired the First Shot at Gettysburg." *National Tribune,* 24 Sept. 1891.

Dodge, Theodore A. "Left Wounded on the Field." *Putnam's Monthly Magazine,* 4 (1869). 317-326.

Doubleday, Abner. *Chancellorsville and Gettysburg.* New York: Charles Scribner's Sons, 1882. Reprinted 1989 by Broadfoot Publishing Co.

Douglas, Henry Kyd. *I Rode with Stonewall.* Chapel Hill: University of North Carolina Press, 1940.

Downey, Fairfax. *The Guns at Gettysburg.* New York: David Mackay Co. 1958.

Driver, Robert J. Jr. *52nd Virginia Infantry.* Lynchburg, Va: H.E. Howard, NC, 1986.

Driver, Robert J. Jr. *The Staunton Artillery-McClanahan's Battery.* Lynchburg VA: H.E. Howard Inc., 1988.

Dudley, William W. *The Iron Brigade at Gettysburg, Official Report of the Part Borne by the First Brigade, First Division, First Army Corps, Army of the Potomac, in Action at Gettysburg, Pennsylvania. July 1st, 2d and 3d, 1863.* Cincinnati: Peter G. Thompson, 1879.

Dunkelman, Mark H. *The Coster Avenue Mural in Gettysburg.* Privately printed, 1989.

Dunkelman, Mark H. and Michael J. Winey. "The Hardtack Resiment in the Brickyard Fight." *The Gettysburg Magazine,* No. 8: 16-30.

Dunkelman, Mark H. and Michael J. Winey. *The Hardtack Regiment: An Illustrated History of the 154th Regiment New York State Infantry Volunteers.* Rutherford NJ: Farleigh Dickerson University Press, 1981.

Dunkelman, Mark H. and Michael Winey. "The Hunt for Sergeant Humiston." *CWTI*, Vol. 21, No.1 (March 1982): pp. 28-31.

Dyer, Frederick H. *A Compendium of the War of the Rebellion.* New York: Thomas Yoseloff, 1959.

Early, Jubal A. *War Memoirs: Autobiographical Sketch and Narrative of the War between The States.* Philadelphia: J.B. Lippincott Co., 1912. Reprinted 1960 by Indiana University Press.

Early, Jubal A. "Leading Confederates on the Battle of Gettysburg." *SHSP* 4, 1877: 241-302.

Eggleston, Cary E. *A Rebel's Recollection.* Bloomington: Indiana University Press, 1959.

Elmore, Thomas L. "Attack and Counterattack." *Gettysburg Magazine,* No. 5: 128.

Elmore, Thomas L. "The Effects of Artillery Fire on Infantry at Gettysburg." *The Gettysburg Magazine,* No.5: 117-122.

Elmore, Thomas L. "Skirmishers." *The Gettysburg Magazine,* No. 6: 6-12.

Emerson, Mrs. B.A.C. "The Most Famous Regiment." *CV* 25 (1917): 352-355.

Esposito, Col. Vincent. *The West Point Atlas of the Civil War.* Frederick A. New York: Frederick Praeger, 1962.

Eversole, Jacob. "Incidents of Field Hospital Life with the Army of The Potamac," *Ohio MOLLUS,* Vol. 4.

Fahnestock, Gates D. "Recollections of the Battle of Gettysburg." Adams County Historical Society, Gettysburg.

Fairfield, George. Diaries. State Historical Society of Wisconsin.

Felton, Silas. "The Iron Brigade Battery at Gettysburg," *Gettysburg Magazine* No. 11: 56-70.

Felton, Silas. "Pursuing the Elusive 'Cannoneer.'" *The Gettysburg Magazine,* No. 9: 33-39.

Flowers, George W. "Thirty-Eighth Regiment." *NC Regts,* Vol. 2: 674-697.

Foote, Frank H. "Marching in Clover." *Philadelphia Weekly Times,* 8 October 1881.

Frampton, Roy E. *One Country, One Flag: The Strife of Brothers is Past. Inscriptions and Locations of the Memorials of the Gettysburg Battlefield..* 3 Vols. Gettysburg: Roy E., Frampton, 1987.

Frassanito, William A. *Gettysburg: A Journey In Time.* New York: Charles Scribner's Sons, 1975.

Freeman, Douglas S. *Lee's Lieutenants: A Study In Command.* 3 Volumes. New York: Charles Scribner's Sons, 1942-1944.

Freeman, Douglas S. *R.E. Lee: A Biography* 4 Volumes. New York: Charles Scribner's Sons, 1934-1935.

Fremantle, James Arthur Lyon. *The Fremantle Diary.* Boston: Little, Brown & Co., 1954.

Fulton, W.F. "The Fifth Alabama Battalion at Gettysburg," *CV* 31 (1923): 379-380.

Fulton, William F. II. *The War Reminiscences of William Frierson Fulton II, 5th Alabama Battalion, Archer's Brigade. A.P. Hill's Light Division, A.N.V.* n.p., n.d. Reprinted 1986 by Butternut Press.

Gaff, Alan D. "'Here Was Made Out Our Last and Hopeless Stand': The (Lost)

Gettysburg Reports of the Nineteenth Indiana." *The Gettysburg Magazine*, No. 2: 25-31.

Gallagher, Gary W. "Confederate Corps Leadership on the First Day at Gettysburg. A.P. Hill and Richard S. Ewell in a Difficult Debut" in Gallagher, *The First Day at Gettysburg*, 30-56.

Gary W. Gallagher (Editor), *The First Day at Gettysburg*. Kent, Ohio: Kent State Univ. Press, 1992.

Gallagher, Gary W., "Three Confederate Disasters on Oak Ridge," in Gallagher, *The First Day at Gettysburg*: 92-139.

Garlach, Anna. "The Story of Mrs. Jacob Kitzmiller." Adams County Historical Society.

Gates, Theodore B. *The "Ulster Guard" [20th NY State Militia] and the War on the Rebellion*. New York: Benjamin H. Tyrrel, 1879.

Gilmor, Harry. *Four Years in the Saddle*. New York: Harper and Brothers, 1866.

Goldsborough, W.W. *The Maryland Line in the Confederate Army, 1861-1865*. Baltimore: Guggenheimer, Weil & Co, 1900. Reprinted 1983 by Butternut Press.

Gordon, John B. *Reminiscences of the Civil War*. New York: C. Scribner's Sons, 1903.

Grace, C.D. "Rode's Division at Gettysburg" *CV*, 5 (1897): 614-615.

Grant, George W. "The First Army Corps on the First Day at Gettysburg" in *Gettysburg Papers*, Vol. 1: 255-270 (*Minnesota MOLLUS*, Vol. 5: 43-58.)

Green, Wharton J. "Second Battalion." *NC Regts*, Vol. 4: 243-260.

Greene, A. Wilson. "From Chancellorsville to Cemetery Hill: O.O. Howard and Eleventh Corps Leadership" in Gallagher, *The First Day at Gettysburg*: 57-91.

Griffin, D. Massy. "Rodes on Oak Hill: A Study of Rodes' Division on the First Day at Gettysburg." *Gettysburg Magazine*, No. 4: 33-48.

Hadden, Lee R. "The Deadly Embrace: The Meeting of the Twenty-Fourth Regiment, Michigan Infantry, and the Twenty-sixth Regiment of North Carolina Troops at McPherson's Woods, Gettysburg, Pennsylvania, July 1, 1863." *The Gettysburg Magazine*. No. 5: 19-33.

Haines, Douglas Craig. "A.P. Hill's Advance to Gettysburg." *The Gettysburg Magazine*. No. 5: 4-11.

Haines, Douglas C. "R.S. Ewell's Command, June 29-July 1, 1863." *The Gettysburg Magazine*, No. 9: 7-32.

Hale, Laura V. and Stanley S. Phillips. *History of the Forty-ninth Virginia Infantry CSA,. "Extra Billy Smith's Boys."* Lanham, MD: S.S. Phillips & Assoc, 1981.

Hall, Hillman and W.B. Besley. *History of the Sixth New York Cavalry, Second Ira Harris Guard Second Brigade, First Division, Cavalry Corps, Army of the Potomac, 1861-1865*. Worcester: The Blanchard Press, 1908.

Hall, Isaac. *History of the Ninety-Seventh Regiment New York Volunteers*. Utica: Press of L.C. Childs & Son, 1890.

Hall, James O. "Hunting the Spy Harrison" *CWTI* 24 (Feb 1986): 19-25.

Halstead, E.P. "The First Day at the Battle of Gettysburg" in *The Gettysburg Papers*, Vol. 1: 149-158. (*D.C. MOLLUS*, 2 March 1887: 1-10).

Hamblen, Charles P. *Connecticut Yankees at Gettysburg*. Kent, OH: Kent State University Press, 1993.

Hamilton, James C.M. "The 110th Regiment in the Gettysburg Campaign." *Philadelphia Weekly Press*, 24 Feb 1886.

Hancock, Almira R. *Reminiscences of Winfield Scott Hancock.* New York: Charles L. Webster & Co., 1887.

Hancock, Winfield S. "Gettysburg. Reply to General Howard." *Galaxy,* 22 (1876): 821-831.

Hancock, Winfield S. "Letter from General Winfield Scott Hancock." *SHSP* 5 (1878): 168-172.

Hanna, William. "A Gettysburg Myth Exploded" *CWTI,* Vol. 24, No. 3 (July 1985): 42-47.

Hard, Abner. *History of the Eighth Cavalry Regiment Illinois Volunteers During the Great Rebellion.* Aurora, Ill, 1868. Reprinted 1984 by Morningside Press.

Hardman, Asa S. "As a Union Prisoner Saw the Battle of Gettysburg." *CWTI,* Vol. I, No. 4: 46-50.

Harries, W.H. "The Sword of Gen. James J. Archer" *CV* 19 (1911): 419-420.

Harris, J.S. "Seventh Regiment" *NC Regts,* Vol. 1: 360-386.

Harris, Loyd G. "With the Iron Brigade Guard at Gettysburg." *The Gettysburg Magazine* No. 1: 29-34.

Harris, T.C. "The Second Mississippi at Gettysburg." *CV* 25 (1917): 527.

Hartwig, D. Scott. "The Defense of McPherson's Ridge" *The Gettysburg Magazine,* No. 1: 15-24.

Hartwig, D. Scott. "The 11th Army Corps on July 1, 1863, - The Unlucky 11th," *Gettysburg Magazine,* No. 2: 33-50.

Hartwig, D. Scott. "Guts and Good Leadership: The Action at the Railroad Cut, July 1, 1865." *The Gettysburg Magazine,* No. 1: 5-14.

Hassler, Warren W. Jr. *Crisis at the Crossroads The First Day at Gettysburg.* Univ. of Alabama Press, 1970.

Hawkins, Norma F. "Sergeant Major Blanchard at Gettysburg." *Indiana Magazine of History* 34 (1938): 212-216.

Hebert, Walter M. *Fighting Joe Hooker.* Indianapolis: Bobbs-Merrill, 1944.

Heermance, William L. "The Cavalry at Gettysburg" in *Gettysburg Papers,* Vol 1: 414-424.

Herdegen, Lance J. "The Lieutenant who Arrested a General." *The Gettysburg Magazine.* No. 4: 24-32.

Herdegen, Lance J. "Old Soldiers and War Talk: The Controversy Over the Opening Infantry Fight at Gettysburg." *The Gettysburg Magazine,* No 2: 15-24.

Herdegen, Lance J., and William J.K. Beaudot. *In the Bloody Railroad Cut at Gettysburg.* Dayton, Ohio: Morningside Press, 1990.

Heth, Henry. "Letter From Major General Henry Heth of A.P. Hill's Corps, A.N.V." *SHSP,* Vol. 4 (1877): 151-160.

Heth, Henry. *The Memoirs of Henry Heth.* Westport, CT: Greenwood Press, 1974.

Hirz, Louise W. (Editor). *The Letters of Frederick C. Winkler.* Privately Printed, 1963.

History of the 121st Regiment Pennsylvania Volunteers. Revised Edition. Philadelphia: Press of Catholic Standard and Times, 1906.

History of the 134th Regiment, N.Y.S. Vol. Schenectady: J.J. Marlett, n.d.

Hoffsommer, Robert D. (Editor). "Sergeant Charles Veil's Memoir on the Death of Reynolds" *CWTI,* Vol. 21 No. 4 (June 1982): 16-25.

Hopkins, Thomas S. "Death of Reynolds." *National Tribune,* 14 April 1910.

Hotchkiss, Jeaediah. *Make Me a Map of the Valley*. Dallas: Southern Methodist University Press, 1973.

Howard, Charles H. "The First Day at Gettysburg." *Gettysburg Papers*. Vol. 1: 306-336. (*Illinois MOLLUS*, Vol. 4: 236-264).

Howard, Oliver O. *Autobiography of Oliver Otis Howard*. 2 Volumes. New York: Baker & Taylor, 1908.

Howard, Oliver O. "The Campaign and Battle of Gettysburg." *Atlantic Monthly* 38 (1876) 48-71.

Howard, Oliver O. "O.O. Howard's Commencement Address to Syracuse University." *The Gettysburg Magazine*, No. 11: 71-79.

Hufham, J.D. Jr. "Gettysburg." *Wake Forest Student* 16 (1897): 454.

Huidekoper, Henry S. "Historic Church and Hospital on the Battlefield of Gettysburg." Pamphlet in GNMP Collections.

Humphreys, Henry H., *Andrew Atkinson Humphreys, A Biography*. Philadelphia: John C. Winston Co., 1924. Reprinted 1988.

Hunt, Henry J. "The First Day at Gettysburg. *B & L*, Vol. 3: 255-284.

Hunt, Henry J. "The Second Day at Gettysburg." *B & L*, Vol 3, 290-313.

Hunterston, Harry. "Escaped Capture." *National Tribune*, 23 March 1911.

Huntington, Albert. *8th New York Cavalry: Hisorical Papers*. Palmyra, NY, 1902.

Hunton, Eppa. *Autobiography of Eppa Hunton*. Richmond: William Byrd Press, 1933.

Hurst, Samuel H. *Journal-History of the Seventy-Third Ohio Volunteer Infantry*. Chillicothe: 1866.

Hussey, George A. *History of the Ninth Regiment, N.Y.S.M.-N.G.S.N.Y. (Eighty-Third N.Y. Volunteers)*. New York: Regimental Veterans Association, 1889.

Imholte, John Q. (Editor) "Civil War Diary and Related Sources of Corporal Newel Burch." Minnesota Historical Society.

In Memoriam, Letters of William Wheeler of the Class of 1855, Yale College. Cambridge, 1875.

Indiana at the Fiftieth Anniversary of the Battle of Gettysburg. Indianapolis, ca. 1913.

Ivry, William T. "At Gettysburg—Who was the Lone Cavalryman Killed Between the Lines?" *National Tribune*, 11 July 1901.

Jacobs, M. *Notes on the Rebel Invasion and the Battle of Gettysburg*. Philadelphia: J.B. Lippincott, Co., 1864.

Johnson, Clifton. *Battleground Adventures*. Boston: Houghton Mifflin, 1915.

Johnson, Robert U. and Clarence C. Buel (Editors). *Battles and Leaders of the Civil War*. 4 Vols. New York: The Century Co., 1887. Reprinted 1956 by Thomas Yoseloff Inc.

Johnston, John W. *The True Story of John Burns*. Philadelphia: William, Brown & Earle, 1916.

Jones, Hamilton C., Jr. "Fifty-Seventh Regiment." *NC Regts*, Vol. III: 404-429.

Jones, Terry L. *Lee's Tigers: The Louisiana Infantry in the Army of Northern Virginia* Baton Rouge: Louisiana State University Press, 1987.

Jordan, Weymouth T. Editor. *North Carolina Troops, 1861-1865, A Roster*. Vol. 13. Raleigh: North Carolina Division of Archives and History, 1993.

Keifer, William R. *History of the One Hundred and Fifty-Third Regiment Pennsylvania Volunteer Infantry*. Easton: Press of the Chemical Publishing Company, 1909.

Kelly, T.B. "Gettysburg—An Account of Who Opened the Battle by One Who Was There." *National Tribune*, 31 December 1891.

Kempster, Walter. *The Cavalry at Gettysburg.* In *Gettysburg Papers,* Vol. 1: 425-462. (*Wisconsin MOLLUS,* Vol. 4: 395-432.

Kenan, Tom and John R. Callis. "An Incident at Gettysburg." *NC Regts,* Vol. 5: 611-616.

Kepf, Kenneth M. "Dilger's Battery at Gettysburg." *The Gettysburg Magazine,* No.4: 49-64.

Krick, Robert K. *The Fredericksburg Artillery.* Lynchburg: H.E. Howard Inc. 1986.

Krick, Robert K. "From Eacho's Farm to Appomattox: The Fredericksburg Artillery." *Civil War Regiments,* Vol. 1, No. 1: 1-25.

Krick, Robert K. *The Gettysburg Death Roster: The Confederate Dead at Gettysburg.* 3rd Edition, Revised. Dayton, Ohio: Morningside Bookshop, 1993.

Krick, Robert K. *Lee's Colonels: A Biographical Register of the Field Officers of the Army of Northern Virginia.* 2nd Edition, Revised. Dayton: Morningside Bookshop, 1984.

Krick, Robert K. "Three Confederate Disasters on Oak Ridge, Failures of Brigade Leadership on the First Day at Gettysburg," in Gallagher, *The First Day at Gettysburg:* 92-139.

Krolick, Marshall D., "Marcellus Jones' Proudest Moment." *Blue & Gray Magazine,* Vol. 5, No. 2 (Nov. 1987): 27-29.

Kross, Gary. "At the Time 'Impracticable: Dick Ewell's Decision on the First Day at Gettysburg with Excerpts from Campbell Brown's Journal." *Blue & Gray Magazine,* Vol. 12, No. 3 (Feb. 1995): 53-58.

Kross, Gary. "Fight Like the Devil to hold your own: General John Buford's Cavalry at Gettysburg on July 1, 1863." *Blue & Gray Magazine,* Vol. 12, No. 3 (Feb. 1995): 9-22.

Kross, Gary. "That one Error Fills him with Faults: Gen. Alfred Iverson and his Brigade at Gettysburg." *Blue & Gray Magazine.* Vol. 12, No. 3 (Feb. 1995): 22-24, 48-53.

Krzyzanowski, Wladimir. *The Memoirs of Wladimir Krzyzanowski.* Edited by James S. Pula. Reprint of 1883 Warsaw Edition. San Francisco: Rande Research Associates, 1978.

Ladd, David L and Audrey J. Ladd. *The Bachelder Papers: Gettysburg in Their Own Words.* 3 Vols. Dayton, Ohio: Morningside Press, 1993-1995.

Lang, Theodore F. *Loyal West Virginia From 1861 to 1865.* Baltimore: Deutsch Publishing Company, 1895.

Lash, Gary G. "Brig. Gen. Henry Baxter's Brigade at Gettysburg, July 1." *The Gettysburg Magazine.* No 10: 6-27.

Lattimore, T.D. "Thirty-Fourth Regiment," *NC Regts,* Vol. 2: 580-590.

Lee, Alfred. "Reminiscences of the Gettysburg Battle." *Lippincott Magazine,* Vol. 6 (1883): 55 ff.

Lee, Robert E. Jr. *Recollections and Letters of Robert E. Lee.* Garden City: Garden City Publishing Co., 1904.

Lineback, Julius A. "Extracts From a Civil War Diary." *Winston-Salem Sentinel,* 13 June 1914-3 April 1915: 49.

Lippy, John D. *The War Dog.* Harrisburg: The Telegraph Press, 1962.

Littlejohn, Thomas M. "Recollections of a Confederate Soldier." Collection of Manassas National Battlefield Park.

Livermore, Thomas L. *Numbers & Losses in the Civil War in America, 1861-65.* Boston: Houghton Mifflin Co., 1900. Reprinted 1957 by Indiana University Press.

Locke, William Henry. *The Story of the Regiment.* Philadelphia: J.B. Lippincott & Co., 1872.

Long, A.L. *Memoirs of Robert E. Lee: His Military and Personal History, Embracing a Large Amount of Information Hitherto Unpublished.* New York: J.M. Stoddart & Co., 1886. Reprinted 1983 by Blue and Grey Press.

Long, Roger. "The Confederate Prisoners of Gettysburg," *The Gettysburg Magazine,* No. 2: 91-112.

Long, Roger. "A Gettysburg Encounter." *The Gettysburg Magazine.* No. 7: 114-118.

Long, Roger. "A Mississippian in the Railroad Cut," *The Gettysburg Magazine.* No. 4: 22-23.

Longacre, Edward G. *The Cavalry at Gettysburg: A Tactical Study of Mounted Operations During the Civil War's Pivotal Campaign, 9 June-14 July 1863.* Rutherford, NJ: Associated University Press, 1986.

Longstreet, James. "The Campaign of Gettysburg." *Philadelphia Weekly Times,* 3 Nov. 1877. (Reprinted as "Lee in Pennsylvania" in *The Annals of the War.* 414-446).

Longstreet, James. *From Manassas to Appomattox, Memoirs of the Civil War in America.* Reprinted 1960 by Indiana University Press. Philadelphia: J.B. Lippincott, 1895.

Longstreet, James. "Lee in Pennsylvania" *The Annals of the War,* pp. 414-446. (originally published as "The Campaign of Gettysburg," *Philadelphia Weekly Times,* 3 Nov. 1877).

Love, William A. "Mississippi at Gettysburg" in *Gettysburg Sources,* Vol. 1: 122-149.

MaCrae, James and C.M. Busbee. "Fifth Regiment," *NC Regts,* Vol 1: 280-292.

Maine at Gettysburg: Report of the Maine Commissioners Prepared by the Executive Committee. Portland: Lakeside Press, 1898.

Manly, Matt. "Second Regiment." *NC Regts,* Vol. 1:156-176.

"The Marcellus E. Jones House." Wheaton, Ill. (?). Undated Pamphlet.

Marcus, Edward. *A New Canaan Private in the Civil War: Letters of Justus M. Sullivan, 17th Connecticut Volunteers.* New Canaan: New Canaan Historical Society, 1984.

Marshall, Charles. "Events Leading up to the Battle of Gettysburg." *SHSP.* 23 (1895): 205-229.

Martin, David G. *Carl Bornemann's Regiment: The Forty-First New York Infantry (Dekalb Regt.) in the Civil War.* Hightstown, NJ: Longstreet House, 1989.

Martin, David G. *Confederate Monuments at Gettysburg, The Gettysburg Battle Monuments,* Vol. I. Hightstown, NJ: Longstreet House, 1986.

Martin, Samuel J. *The Road to Glory: Confederate General Richard S. Ewell.* Indianapolis: Guild Press of Indiana, 1991.

Martin, W.J. and E.R. Outlaw. "Eleventh Regiment." *NC Regts,* Vol. 1: 582-604.

Marye, John L. "The First Gun at Gettysburg." *Civil War Regiments,* Vol. 1, No. 1: 26-34.

Matthews, Richard E. *The 149th Pennsylvania Volunteer Infantry Unit in the Civil War.* Jefferson, N.C.: McFarland & Co., 1994.

Maurice, Frederick (Editor). *An Aide De Camp of Lee, Being the Papers of Colonel Charles Marshall.* Boston: Little Brown, 1927.

May, W.H. "First Confederates to Enter Gettysburg. *CV* 5 (1897): 620.

Mayo, R.M. "Report of Part Taken by Heth's (Old) Brigade in the Battles of Maryland and Pennsylvania," 13 Aug 1863. Henry Heth Collection, Museum of the Confederacy, Richmond.

McAllister, Mary. Memoirs Published in *Philadelphia Inquirer,* 26-29 June 1938.

McCreary, Albertus. "Gettysburg: A Boy's Experience of the Battle." GNMP Collections.

McCullough, R.E. "Fourteenth Tennessee Infantry." *Military Annals of Tennessee.*

McCurdy, Charles M. *Gettysburg, A Memoir.* Pittsburgh: Reed and Whitting Co., 1929.

McIntosh, David G. "Review of the Gettysburg Campaign, By One Who Participated Therein." *SHSP* 37 (1907): 74-143.

McKay, Charles W. "Three Years or During the War With the Crescent and Star." *The National Tribune Scrap Book.* Washington DC, n.d.

McKelvey, Blake (Editor). "George Breck's Civil War Letters form Reynolds' Battery." *Rochester Historical Society Publications.* 22 (1944): 91-149.

McKim, Randolph H. *A Soldier's Recollections.* New York: Longman's, Green and Company, 1910. Reprinted 1983 by Zenger Publishing Co.

McKim, Randolph H. "The Gettysburg Campaign." *SHSP* 40 (1915): 253-295.

McKim, Randolph. "Steuart's Brigade at the Battle of Gettysburg" *SHSP* 5 (1878): 291-300.

McLaurin, William H. "Eighteenth Regiment," *NC Regts,* Vol 2: 14-78.

McLean, James L. Jr. *Cutler's Brigade at Gettysburg.* Revised, Second Edition. Baltimore: Butternut and Blue, 1994.

McLean, James L. Jr. and Judy W. McLean. *Gettysburg Sources.* Vol I. Baltimore: Butternut and Blue, 1986.

McLean, James L. Jr. and Judy W. McLean. *Gettysburg Sources.* Vol II. Baltimore: Butternut and Blue, 1987.

McLean, James L. Jr. and Judy W. McLean. *Gettysburg Sources.* Vol III. Baltimore: Butternut and Blue, 1990.

McLean, James L. Jr. "The First Union Shot at Gettysburg" *Lincoln Herald,* Vol. 82, No. 1 (Spring 1980): 318-323.

Meade, George G. *The Life and Letters of General George Gordon Meade.* 2 Vols. New York: Charles Scribner's Sons, 1913.

Meade, George G. *With Meade at Gettysburg.* Philadelphia: John C. Winston Co., 1930.

Mehaffey, William. "And, Finally, about Spencer Carbines at Gettysburg." *The Banner,* Vol. 97, No. 5 (Spring 1994): 20.

Merrill, Catherine. *The Soldier of Indiana in the War for the Union.* Vol. 2. Indianapolis. 1866.

Mix, A.R. "Experience at Gettysburg." *National Tribune,* 22 February 1934.

Mockbee, R.T. "Historical Sketch of the 14th Tennessee." Manuscript at the Brockenbrough Library, Museum of the Confederacy, Richmond.

Montgomery, Walter A. "Twelfth Regiment." *NC Regts,* Vol. 1: 604-652.

Moon, W.H. "Beginning of the Battle of Gettysburg." *CV* 33 (1925), 449-450.

Moore, James H. "Heth's Division at Gettysburg." *The Southern Bivouac,* Vol. 3, No. 9 (May 1885): 383-395.

Morse, Charles F. *History of the Second Massachusetts Regiment of Infantry.* Boston: George H. Ellis, 1882.

Moyer, Henry P. *History of the Seventeenth Regiment Pennsylvania Volunteer Cavalry.* Lebanon, Pa: Sowers Printing Co., 1911.

"Mrs. Thorn's War Story." *Gettysburg Times,* 2 July 1938.

Myers, Frank M. *The Comanches: A History of White's Battalion, Virginia Cavalry, Laurel*

Brig., Hampton Div., A.N.V., C.S.A. Baltimore: Kelly, Pieta & Co., 1871: Kelly, Piet & Co, 1871 Reprinted 1987 by Butternut Press.

Naisawald, L. Van Loan. *Grape and Canister: The Story of the Field Artillery in the Army of the Potomac.* New York: Oxford Univ. Press. 1960.

Nesbit, John W. *General History of Company D, One Hundred and Forty-Ninth Pennsylvania Volunteers.* Oakdale, Cal: Oakdale Printing & Publishing Co., 1908.

Nesbit, Mark. *Ghosts of Gettysburg.* Gettysburg: Thomas Publications, 1991.

Nesbitt, Mark. *More Ghosts of Gettysburg.* Gettysburg: Thomas Publications, 1992.

Nesbitt, Mark. *Saber and Scapegoat: J.E.B. Stuart and the Gettysburg Controversy,* Mechanicsburg, Pa: Stackpole Books, 1994.

Nevins, Allan (Editor). *A Diary of Battle: The Personal Journals of Colonel Charles S. Wainwright, 1861-1865.* New York: Harcourt, Brace & World, 1962.

New York Monuments Commission for the Battlefields of Gettysburg and Chattanooga. *Final Report on the Battle of Gettysburg.* 3 Vols. Albany: J.B. Lyon Co., 1902.

New York Monuments Commission for the Battlefields of Gettysburg and Chattanooga. *In Memoriam, Henry Warner Slocum, 1826-1894.* Albany: J.B. Lyon Company, 1904.

New York Monuments Commission for the Battlefields of Gettysburg and Chattanooga. *In Memoriam, James Samuel Wadsworth, 1807-1864: Major General James S. Wadsworth at Gettysburg and Other Fields.* Albany: J.B. Lyon Co., 1916.

Nichols, Edward J. *Toward Gettysburg: A Biography of General John F. Reynolds.* University Park, Pa: Pennsylvania State University Press, 1958.

Nichols, G.W. *A Soldier's Story of His Regiment (61st Georgia).* Jessup, Ga., 1898.

Nicholson, John P. (Editor). *Pennsylvania at Gettysburg.* 2 Vols. Harrisburg: William Stanley Ray, 1914.

Nolan, Alan T. *The Iron Brigade: A Military History.* New York: The Macmillan Company, 1961.

Nolan, Alan T. "R.E. Lee and July 1 at Getttysburg" in Gallagher (Editor), *The First Day at Gettysburg:* 1-29.

Nolan, Alan T. "Three Flags at Gettysburg," *The Gettysburg Magazine.* No. 1: 25-28.

Northrop, Winthrop P. L. "Going into Gettysburg," *National Tribune,* 11 October 1906.

Norton, Henry. *Deeds of Daring, or, History of the Eighth New York Volunteer Cavalry.* Norwich, NY: Chenango Telegraph Printing House, 1889.

Nye, Wilbur S. *Here Come the Rebels!* Baton Rouge: Louisiana State University Press, 1965. Reprinted 1988 by Morningside House.

Oates, William C. *The War Between the Union and the Confederacy and its Lost Opportunities.* New York: Neale Publishing Co., 1905. Reprinted 1974 by Morningside House.

Official Army Register of the Volunteer Force of the United States Army for the Years 1861, 62, 63, 64, 65. Washington DC: Secretary of War, 1865.

Ohio Gettysburg Memorial Commission. *Report of the Gettysburg Memorial Commission.* Columbus: Press of the Nitschike Brothers, 1887.

Okey, C.W. "Echoes of Gettysburg," *Milwaukee Sunday Telegragh,* 29 April 1883.

Olds, Fred A. "Brave Carolinian Who Fell at Gettysburg. How Colonel Henry King Burgwyn Lost His Life." *SHSP* 36 (1908): 245-247.

Osborn Hartwell. *Trials and Triumphs, the Record of the Fifty-Fifth Ohio Volunteer Infantry.* Chicago: A.C. McClurg & Co., 1904.

Osborn, Thomas W. *The Eleventh Corps Artillery at Gettysburg: The Papers of Major*

Thomas Ward Osborn, Chief of Artillery. Edited by Hobb S. Ozurus. Hamilton, NY: Edmonton Publishing Co., 1991.

Osborne, E.A. "Forth Regiment." *NC Regts,* Vol 1: 228-280.

Osborne, Seward (Editor) *The Civil War Diaries of Col. Theodore B. Gates, 20th New York State Militia.* Hightstown NJ: Longstreet House, 1991.

Osborne, Seward R. *Holding the Left at Gettysburg: The 20th New Yok State Militia on July 1, 1863.* Hightstown, NJ: Longstreet House, 1990.

Otis, George H. *The Second Wisconsin Infantry.* Dayton, Ohio: Morningside House, 1984.

Paris, Comte De. *History of the Civil War in America.* 4 Vols. Philadelphia: Porter & Coates, 1883.

Park, Robert E. "War Diary of Capt. Robert Emory Park," *SHSP* 26 (1898): 1-31.

Patterson, Gerard A. "The Death of Iverson's Brigade." *The Gettysburg Magazine.* No. 5: 13-18.

Pearson, Henry G. *James S. Wadworth of Geneseo, Brevet Major General of United States Volunteers.* New York: Charles Scribner's Sons, 1913.

Perrin, Abner. "A Little More Light on Gettysburg." *Mississippi Valley Historical Review.* 24 (1938): 519-525.

Pfanz, Harry W. *Gettysburg—Culp's Hill and Cemetery Hill.* Chapel Hill: University of North Carolina Press, 1993.

Pfanz, Harry W. *Gettysburg, the Second Day.* Chapel Hill: University of North Carolina Press, 1987.

Phisterer, Frederick. *New York in the War of the Rebellion, 1861-1865.* Albany: J.B. Lyon and Company, 1912.

Pickerill, William N. *History of the Third Indiana Cavalry.* Indianapolis: Aëtna Printing Co., 1906.

Pula, James S. *The History of a German-Polish Civil War Brigade.* San Francisco: R and E Research Associates, 1976.

Pullen, John J. "The Gordon-Barlow Story, with Sequel," *Gettysburg Magazine,* No. 8: 5-7.

Quaife, Milo M. (Editor). *From the Cannon's Mouth, the Civil War Letters of General Alpheus S. Williams.* Detroit: Wayne State University Press, 1959.

Raus, Edmund J. Jr. *A Generation on the March, the Union Army at Gettysburg.* Lynchburg, VA: H.E. Howard Inc., 1987.

Reed, E.R. "The Second Wisconsin Stakes its Claim." *National Tribune,* 20 March 1884.

Remington, Cyrus K. *A Record of Battery I, First New York Rgmt Artillery.* Buffalo: Courier Publishing Co., 1891.

Remmington, William N. "Wm. N. Remmington's Story," *Milwaukee Sunday Telegraph,* 24 April 1883.

Robinson, John H. "Fifty-second Regiment." *NC Regts,* Vol. 3: 223-253.

Rogers, Clayton E. "Gettysburg Scenes." *Milwaukee Sunday Telegraph,* 13 May 1887.

Rogers, Earl M. "A Brave Deed at Gettysburg." *National Tribune,* 28 May 1885.

Rogers, Earl M. "The Second, or Fifty-Sixth—Which?" *Milwaukee Sunday Telegraph,* 22 June 1884.

Rogers, J. Rowan. "Additional Sketch, Forty-Seventh Regiment." *NC Regts.* Vol. 3: 103-112.

Sauers, Richard A. *A Caspian Sea of Ink: The Meade-Sickles Controversy.* Baltimore: Butternut and Blue, 1989.

Sauers, Richard A. *The Gettysburg Campaign, June 3-August 1, 1863, A Comprehensive Selectively Annotated Bibliography.* Westport, Conn: Greenwood Press, 1982.

Sauers, Richard A. "Gettysburg Controversies." *The Gettysburg Magazine.* No. 4: 113-125.

Schildt, John W. *Roads to Gettysburg.* Parsons, WVA: McLain Printing Co., 1978.

Schuricht, Herman. "Jenkins' Brigade in the Gettysburg Campaign: Extracts from the Diary of Lieutenant Hermann Schuricht of the Fourteenth Virginia Cavalry." *SHSP* 24 (1896): 339-351.

Schurz, Carl. *The Reminiscences of Carl Schurz.* 3 Vols. New York: The McClure Co., 1908.

Scott, George H. "Vermont at Gettysburg." *Proceedings of the Vermont Historical Society.* Vol. 1, No. 2 (1930), in McLean, *Gettysburg Sources,* Vol. 1: 57-81.

Scott, James K.P. *The Story of the Battles at Gettysburg, Book I..* Harrisburg: Telegraph Press, 1927.

The Seventy-third Regiment Pennsylvania Volunteers at Gettysburg, n.p., n.d.

17th Connecticut Volunteers at Gettysburg, June 30th and July 1st, 2d, and 3d, 1884. Bridgeport: Standard Association, 1884.

Shevchuk, Paul M. "The Wounding of Albert Jenkins, July 2, 1863." *Gettysburg Magazine,* No. 3: 51-64.

Shue, Richard S. *The Morning at Willoughby Run, July 1, 1863.* Gettysburg, Pa: Thomas Publications, 1995.

Simpson, William T. "The Drummer Boys of Gettysburg." *Philadelphia North American,* 29 June 1913.

Small, Abner R. *The Sixteenth Maine Regiment in the War of the Rebellion, 1861-1865.* Portland, Me: B. Thurston & Co., 1886.

Smith, Abram P. *History of the Seventy-sixth Regiment, New York Volunteers.* Syracuse: Truair, Smith & Miles, 1867.

Smith, Donald L. *The Twenty-Fourth Michigan of the Iron Brigade.* Harrisburg: The Stackpole Company, 1962.

Smith, Jacob. *Camps and Campaigns of the 107th Regiment Ohio Volunteer Infantry* n.p., n.d.

Smith, James P. "General Lee at Gettysburg." *SHSP* 33 (1905): 135-160.

Smith, James P. "With Stonewall Jackson." *SHSP* 43 (1920): 1-110.

Smith, John Day. *The History of the Nineteenth Regiment of Maine Volunteer Infantry, 1862-1865.* Minneapolis: The Great Western Printing Co., 1908.

Snyder, Charles. *Oswego County, New York in the Civil War.* Oswego County Historical Society, 1962.

"Some Stories of the Great Battle," *Gettysburg Compiler,* 14 Jan. 1903.

Southern Historical Society Papers. 52 Vols. (1876-1927).

Starr, Steven Z. *The Union Cavalry in the Civil War.* Baton Rouge: Louisiana State University Press, 1979.

Stearns, Austin C. *Three Years with Company K.* Cranbury NJ: Fairleigh Dickinson University Press, 1976.

Stewart, James. "Battery B Fourth U.S. Artillery at Gettysburg" in *Gettysburg Papers* Vol. 1: 363-377. (*Ohio MOLLUS,* Vol. 4: 179-193.)

Stiles, Robert. *Four Years Under Marse Robert.* New York: Neale Publishing Co. 1904.

Stine, James H. *History of the Army of the Potomac.* Philadelphia: J.B. Rodgers Printing Co., 1892.

Storch, Marc and Beth "'What a Deadly Trap We Were In': Archer's Brigade on July 1, 1863." *The Gettysburg Magazine.* No. 6: 13-28.

Sullivan, James P. "The Old Iron Brigade at Gettysburg." *Milwaukee Sunday Telegraph,* 20 December 1864.

Swallows, W.M. "The First Day at Gettysburg." *Southern Bivouac.* 4 (1885): 436-444.

Swanberg, W.A. *Sickles the Incredible.* New York: Charles Scribner's Sons, 1956.

Sword, Wiley. "Capt. James Glenn's Sword and Pvt. J. Marshall Hill's Enfield in the Fight for the Lutheran Seminary." *The Gettysburg Magazine.* No. 8: 9-15.

Symonds, Craig L. *Gettysburg: A Battlefield: A Battlefield Atlas.* Baltimore: Nautical and Aviation Publishing Co., 1992.

Tallman, William Henry. "The War of the Rebellion." (66th Ohio). GNMP Collections.

Taylor, Michael W. *The Cry is War, War, War. The Civil War Correspondence of Lts. Burwell Thomas Cotton and George Job Huntley, 34th Regiment North Carolina Troops.* Dayton, Ohio: Morningside Press, 1994.

Taylor, Walter H. "Causes of Lee's Defeat at Gettysburg" *SHSP* 4 (1877): 124-139.

Taylor, Walter H. *Four Years with General Lee.* New York: D. Appleton & Co., 1877.

Taylor, Walter H. *General Lee, His Campaigns in Virginia, 1861-1865, with Personal Reminiscences.* Brooklyn: Press of Braunworth & Co. 1906.

The Tennessee Civil War Veteran's Questionnaire. Easley, S.C.: Southern Historical Press, 1985.

Tevis, C.V. *The History of the Fighting Fourteenth.* New York: Brooklyn Eagle Press, 1911. Reprinted 1994 by Butternut and Blue.

Thomas, Henry W. *History of the Doles-Cook Brigade, Army of Northern Virginia.* Atlanta: Franklin Publishing Co., 1903.

Thomas, Howard. *Boys in Blue From the Adirondack Foothills.* Prospect, NY: Prospect Books, 1960.

Thomson, Orville. *From Philippi to Appomattox, Narrative of the Service of the Seventh Indiana Infantry in the War for the Union.* n.p.,n.d.

Thorp, John H. "Forty-Seventh Regiment." in *NC Regts,* Vol. 3: 83-101.

Todd, William (Editor). *History of the Ninth Regiment, N.Y.S.M, N.G.S.N.Y. (83rd New York Volunteers), 1845-1888.* New York: George Hussey, 1889.

Toombs, Samuel. *New Jersey Troops in the Gettysburg Campaign, from June 5 to July 31, 1863.* Orange: The Evening Hall Publishing House, 1888. Reprinted 1988 by Longstreet House.

Toombs, Samuel. *Reminiscences of the War, Comprising a Detailed Account of the Experiences of the 13th Regiment New Jersey Volunteers in Camp on the March, and in Battle.* Orange: Journal Office, 1878. Reprinted 1994 by Longstreet House.

Toon, Thomas F. "Twentieth Regiment." *NC Regts,* Vol 2: 110-127.

Tremain, Henry E. *Two Days of War: A Gettysburg Narrative and Other Excursions.* New York: Bonnell, Silver & Bowers, 1905.

Trimble, Isaac R. "The Battle and Campaign of Gettysburg." *SHSP* 26 (1898): 116-128.

Trimble, Isaac R. "The Campaign and Battle of Gettysburg." *CV,* 25 (1917): 209-213.

Tucker, Glenn. *Hancock the Superb.* Indianapolis: Bobbs-Merrill, 1960.

Tucker, Glenn. *High Tide at Gettysburg, The Campaign in Pennsylvania.* New York: Bobbs Merrill, 1958.

Turner, Charles W. (Editor). *Civil War Letters of Arabella Spears and William Beverly Pettit of Fluvanna County, Virginia, March 1862-March 1865.* 2 Volumes. Roanoke, VA: Virginia Lithography & Graphics Company, 1988, 1989.

Turner, V.E. "Twenty-third Regiment." *NC Regts,* Vol 2: 180-268.

Turney, J.B. "The First Tennessee at Gettysburg." *CV* 8 (1900): 535-537.

Underwood, A.B. *Three Years' Service in the Thirty-third Massachusetts Infantry Regiment, 1862-1865.* Boston: A. Williams & Co., 1881.

Underwood, George C. "Twenty-Sixth Regiment." *NC Regts,* Vol. 2: 303-423.

United States Christian Commission for the Army and Navy, Work and Incidents, First Annual Report. Philadelphia: 1863.

U.S. Congress. *Report of the Joint Committee on the Conduct of the War at the Second Session, Thirty-Eighth Congress.* Vol. 1. Washington: Government Printing Office, 1865.

Vail, Enos B. *Reminiscences of a Boy in the Civil War.* Brooklyn: 1915.

Vautier, John. "At Gettysburg: The Eighty-Eighth Pennsylvania in the Battle." *Philadelphia Weekly Press,* 10 November 1886.

Veil, Charles H. "Sergeant Veil's Memoir on the Death of Reynolds," *CWTI,* Vol. 21 No. 4 (June 1982): 16-25.

Vanderslice, John M. *Gettysburg Then and Now. The Field of American Valor, Where and How the Regiments Fought and the Troops They Encountered.* New York: G.W. Dillingham Co., 1899. Reprinted 1983 by Morningside Press.

Vautier, John D. *History of the Eighty-Eighth Pennsylvania Volunteers in the War for the Union, 1861-1865.* Philadelphia: J.B. Lippincott Co., 1894.

Vickers, George M.B. *Under Both Flags...A Panorama of the Great Civil War.* Philadelphia: People's Publishing Co, 1896.

Walker, Melvin H. "A Captive of Lee's Army at Gettysburg." *National Tribune.* 22 October 1925.

Wallar, Frank A. "A Settled Question." *Milwaukee Sunday Tribune.* 29 July 1883.

War of the Rebellion: A Compilation of the Official Records of the Union and Confederate Armies. 128 Vols. Washington: Government Printing Office, 1880-1901.

Ward, Fanny B. *Sketch of Battery "I" First Ohio Artillery.* n.p.,n.d.

Warner, Ezra J. *Generals in Blue.* Baton Rouge: Louisiana State University Press, 1964.

Warner, Ezra J. *Generals in Gray.* Baton Rouge: LSU Press, 1959.

Warren, Horatio N. *Two Reunions of the 142d Regiment Pennsylvania Volunteers.* Buffalo: The Courier Co. 1890.

Warren, Leander H. "Recollections of the Battle of Gettysburg." Adams County Historical Society, Gettysburg.

Watrous, Jerome A. "Gettysburg." *Milwaukee Sunday Telegraph,* 26 Nov. 1879.

Watrous, Jerome A. "Some Premonitions." *Milwaukee Sunday Telegraph,* 27 July 1895.

Watson, Cyrus B. "Forty-Fifth Regiment." *NC Regts,* Vol. 3: 4-61.

Weaver, Augustus C. *Third Indiana Cavalry.* Greenwood, 1919.

Weld, Stephen M. *War Diary and Letters of Stephen Minot Weld, 1861-1865.* Cambridge: Riverside Press, 1912 Reprinted 1979 by the Massachusetts Historical Society.

Wheeler, Richard. *Witness to Gettysburg.* New York: Harper & Row, 1987.

"Wife of Cemetery Caretaker Relates Horrors of Battle of Gettysburg." in *Hundredth Anniversary of the Battle of Gettysburg.* Gettysburg: Gettysburg Times, 1963.

Wiggin, Frances. "Sixteenth Maine Regiment at Gettysburg." in *Gettysburg Papers,* Vol. 1: 287-308. (*Maine MOLLUS*, Vol. 4: 149-170.

Wiggins, Octavius A. "Thirty-Seventh Regiment, *NC Regts,* Vol. 2: 652-674.

Williams, Kenneth P. *Lincoln Finds a General: A Military Study of the Civil War.* 5 Vols. New York: Macmillan, 1949-1959.

Winschel, Terrence J. "The Colors are Shrowded in Mystery." *The Gettysburg Magazine.* No. 6: 76-86.

Winschel, Terrence J. "Heavy Was Their Loss: Joe Davis' Brigade at Gettysburg, Part II." *The Gettysburg Magazine,* No. 3: 76-85.

Winschel, Terrence J. "Posey's Brigade at Gettysburg, Part I." *The Gettysburg Magazine,* No. 4: 7-15.

Wise, Jennings C. *The Long Arm of Lee: The History of the Army of Northern Virginia.* Lynchburg: J.P. Bell, 1915. Reprinted 1959 by Oxford University Press.

Wittenberg, Eric J. "John Buford and the Gettysburg Campaign" *The Gettysburg Magazine,* No. 11: 19-55.

Woollard, Leander G. "Journals of Events and Incidents as they came to the Observation of the 'Senatobia Invincibles.'" Unpublished Diary in Library of Memphis State University.

Young, Albert V. "A Pilgrimage." *Milwaukee Sunday Telegraph,* 22 April 1888.

Young, Jesse Bowman. *The Battle of Gettysburg: A Comprehensive Narrative.* New York: Harper & Bros. 1913.

Young, Louis G. "Pettigrew's Brigade at Gettysburg, 1-3 July 1863." *NC Regts,* Vol. 5: 113-135.

Manuscript Sources

Adams County Historical Society, Gettysburg, PA
    "The Story of Mrs. Jacob Kitzmiller"
Bowdoin College Library, Brunswick, ME
    Charles H. Howard Papers
    Oliver O. Howard Papers
Bridgeport Public Library, Bridgeport, CT
    William H. Warren Scrapbooks
Chicago Historical Society, Chicago, IL
    William Gamble Collection
Franklin and Marshall College, Fackenthal Library Lancaster, PA
    Reynolds Family Papers
Gettysburg National Military Park, Gettysburg PA
    John B. Bachelder Papers
    William B. Floyd Collection
    Abner B. Frank Diary
    Henry Jacobs, "How an Eyewitness Watched the Battle"
    Henry H. Lyman Diary
    Albertus McCreary, "Gettysburg: A Boy's Experience of the Battle."
Henry E. Huntington Library, San Marino, CA
    James A. Bell Letters
Indiana Historical Society, Indianapolis IN
    George H. Chapman Diary
Indiana State Library, Indianapolis, IN
    Flavius J. Bellamy Papers
    Manuscript, "The 19th Indiana at Gettysburg"
Library of Congress, Washington DC
    Jubal A. Early Papers
    Richard S. Ewell Papers
    Thaddeus Stevens Papers
National Archives, Washington DC
    Civil War Generals, Report of Civil War Service
New Hampshire Historical Society, Concord, NH
    John B. Bachelder Papers
Pennsylvania Historical and Museum Commision, Pennsylvania State Archives, Harrisburg, PA
    Peter F. Rothermel Papers
Rochester Public Library, Rochester, NY
    Daniel Pulis Papers

University of North Carolina, Wilson Library, Southern Historical Collection, Chapel Hill, NC
  Lafayette McLaws Papers
University of Virginia, Alderman Library, Charlottesville, VA
  John W. Daniel Papers
  William H. Redman Letters
U.S. Army Military History Institute, Carlisle, PA
  Robert L. Brake Collection
  Jacob R. Menges, "Corporal's Memoirs, 1861-1865"
Virginia Historical Society, Richmond, VA
  John W. Daniel, "Memoir of the Battle of Gettysburg"
State Historical Society of Wisconsin, Madison, WI
  Rufus R. Dawes Papers
  George Fairfield Diaries
  W.B. Murphy Letters
  Jerome A. Watrous Papers
Yale University, Sterling Library, New Haven, CT
  William H. Warren Diary and Scrapbooks

Index

Aikin, Lt. Col. James, 156, 162
ALABAMA TROOPS: Jeff Davis Art.—
see Reese's battery. Hardaway Art.—*see*
Hurt's battery. 3rd Inf., 221, 223, 228,
234, 235, 239, 240, 251, 263, 387,
432, 577.; 5th Inf., 205, 206, 218,
221, 223, 224, 258, 263, 267, 284,
577, 650 n. 30.; 5th Inf. Batn., 62, 66,
68-70, 83, 162, 178, 578, 631 n. 441.;
6th Inf., 219, 223, 263, 577, 630 n.
30.; 12th Inf., 219, 222, 223, 263,
578.; 13th Inf., 59, 62, 64, 68, 70, 71,
81-86, 148, 149, 156-160, 162, 163,
187, 342, 578, 606 n. 20, 612 n. 130.;
16th Inf., 233.; 26th Inf., 233, 263,
264, 578.; 48th Inf., 686 n. 156
Alexander, Col. E.P., 56, 566
Allan, Col. William, 17, 563.
Allen, Lt. Col. D.B., 306, 309, 313,
315, 574.
Almshouse, 265, 267, 271, 272, 273,
274, 275, 281, 282, 297 298, 303,
305, 311, 328, 460, 521, 555, 587,
655 n. 144, 685 n. 150, 696 n. 429.
Ames, Brig. Gen. Adelbert, 304, 305,
310, 333, 489, 545, 573.
Ames' Brigade, 271, 274, 275, 289, 303,
305, 306, 318, 328, 329, 470, 471,
521, 550.
Anderson, Maj. John, 45
Anderson, Maj. Gen. R.H., 340, 503,
686 n. 166.
Anderson's Division, 23, 31, 52, 60, 62,
338, 395, 501–508.
Andersonville Prison, 316.
Andrews, Lt. Col. H.L., 244, 577.
Antietam, Md., 16, 20, 237, 292, 499,
565.
Archer, Brig. Gen. James J., 31, 62, 84,
85, 88, 158-163, 371, 456, 457, 578,
630 n. 429, 631 n. 433.
Archer's Brigade, 25, 59-61, 66, 70, 80,

82-88, 102, 104, 105, 120, 121, 127,
140, 142, 148, 149, 152-167, 178,
181, 183, 186-191, 242, 361, 374,
377, 396, 397, 426, 463, 628 n. 371,
630 n. 400, 631 n. 441, 631 n. 444.
Ashford, Lt. Col. John, 403.
Ashurst, Adj. Richard, 247, 417, 418.
Auginbaugh, Nellie, 462.
Avery, Col. Isaac, 283, 576.
Avery's Brigade, 283, 305, 310-313, 317,
320, 324, 327, 328, 373, 465, 509,
511, 512, 514, 521.

Bachelder, John, 81, 127, 324, 492, 565,
566.
Bailey's Hill, Pa., 13, 14.
Baldwin, Lt. Col. Clark, 550.
Baltimore, Md., 12, 16, 17, 22, 37, 38,
52, 53, 55, 56, 139, 144, 163, 211,
346, 516, 595 n. 2.
Bancroft, Lt. Eugene, 287, 317, 318,
575.
Bancroft's U.S. Battery, 286, 314, 318,
319, 476.
Bankhead, Col. Henry C., 254.
Barbour, Col. William, 427.
Barlow, Arabella, 292-294.
Barlow, Brig. Gen. Francis C., 196-198,
267, 271-277, 282, 284, 288, 291-
296, 304, 333, 334, 460, 466, 573,
651 n. 53, 652 n. 71, 654 n. 130.
Barlow's Division, 91, 195, 200, 201,
217, 251, 257, 266-272, 276, 278,
281, 288, 296-298, 303, 327, 448,
468, 502, 514, 523, 573, 581, 587,
588.
Bassler, J.M., 209, 245, 246, 381-383.
Batchelder, Lt. Col. N.W., 248, 252, 571.
Bates, Col. James, 216, 233, 376.
Battle, Col. Cullen, 223, 251, 577.
Baxter, Brig. Gen. Henry, 215, 229, 231,
233, 242, 250, 251, 435, 571.

Baxter's Brigade, 214, 216-218, 222, 223, 226-234, 238-240, 252, 263, 343, 344, 376, 432, 571.

Beecham, Capt. Robert, 403, 414.

Belo, Maj. A.H., 109, 118, 124, 125, 133.

Bender farm, 87, 107, 190, 347.

Benjamin, Charles, 34.

Benner house, 275, 277, 281, 460.

Benner's Hill, 46, 521, 536-538, 556, 557, 585.

Bennett, Col. Robert, 389, 392, 577.

Bentley, Col. W.G., 88

Berlin, Pa., 48, 52, 204.

Beveridge, Maj. John, 43, 63, 65, 73, 74, 79, 80, 154, 426, 575, 590.

Biddle, Maj. Alexander, 358-360, 397, 409, 572.

Biddle, Col. Chapman, 91, 170, 176-180, 183, 343, 358, 360, 361, 398, 409, 410, 572.

Biddle's Brigade, 91, 173, 175, 180, 181, 183, 191, 341, 343, 347, 350, 354-357, 360-363, 368, 396-398, 412, 419, 469, 473, 572.

Biddle, Col. George, 105, 571.

Bird, Pvt. W.H., 59, 68, 157, 158.

Birney's Division, 541, 542, 546, 547, 550, 694 n. 381.

Blackford, Maj. Eugene, 201, 206, 250, 258-260, 266, 274, 284.

Black Horse Tavern, 173, 547.

Blackwell, Maj. C.C., 230.

Blair, Maj. J.A., 109, 114, 118-120, 124, 125, 127, 131-133.

Blanchard, Sgt. Asa, 354

Blocher farm, 274, 292, 297.

Boebel, Lt. Col. Hans, 298, 514

Boland, Pvt. E.T., 48, 62, 64, 157.

Boone, Sgt. Samuel, 231, 234, 436, 437.

Bower, Lt. William, 347, 350.

Boyd, Lt. Col. S.H., 244, 576.

Brabble, Col. E.C., 241, 246, 379, 576.

Brady, Maj. Alan, 275, 310, 318, 471, 573.

Brander's Va. Battery, 189, 190, 193, 243, 346, 347, 580, 594.

Breck, Lt. George, 172, 194, 209, 415, 423, 424, 475, 476, 572, 633 n. 25.

Breck's NY Battery, 343, 347, 349, 350, 361, 378, 396, 415, 419, 572, 663 n. 90, 681 n. 38.

Brehm, Sgt. Henry, 208, 381-383.

Broadhead, Sarah, 27.

Brockenbrough, Col. J.M., 26, 186, 578.

Brockenbrough's Brigade, 25, 60, 71, 81, 164, 178, 186, 342, 350, 368-370, 377, 378, 385, 395, 401, 402, 499, 501, 578.

Brooks, Edward, 131.

Brooks, Maj. J.S., 230.

Brown, Maj. Campbell, 205, 209, 210, 244, 282, 340.

Brown, Lt. Col. H.H., 260.

Brown, Lt. Col. Joseph N., 416, 420, 423, 425, 579.

Brown, Col. Philip, 262, 301, 574

Brown, Maj. Ridgely, 327, 580

Buchanan, Maj. Felix, 66, 578.

Buck, Capt. Daniel, 44-46, 73, 74.

Buell, Augustus, 172.

Buford, Brig. Gen. John, 26, 39, 40, 43, 46-49, 53, 69, 72-83, 88, 89, 92, 95-101, 136, 137, 155, 170, 193, 196, 213, 267, 270, 409, 420, 428, 452, 471, 478, 491 493, 568, 575, 584, 590, 601 n. 37. 601 n. 43, 604 n. 76, 610 n. 87, 615 n. 61, 616 n. 62, 632 n. 14, 680 n. 1, 680 n. 17.

Buford's Division, 27, 38-48, 72, 75, 76, 80, 96, 102, 104, 141, 157, 162, 164, 197, 208, 426, 427, 448, 452, 464, 465, 468, 469, 480, 484, 490-492, 500, 553, 554, 575, 585, 599 n. 96.

Burgwyn, Col. Henry, 28, 349-353, 367, 368, 578.

Burns, John, 99, 371-377, 665 n. 144, 665 n. 143, 665 n. 147.

Butterfield, Maj. Gen. Dan, 37, 479, 482, 543.

Caldwell, J.F.J., 188, 405, 406, 414, 420, 461,

Caldwell, Gen. John C., 481.

Calef, Lt. John, 42, 72, 74, 75, 83, 85, 88, 127, 137, 191-194, 493, 575, 609 n. 87,

Calef's U.S. Battery, 39, 43, 77, 79, 83,

85-87, 102, 104, 106, 136, 167, 170, 190-194, 207, 208, 343, 347, 420, 493, 593, 609 n. 87. 637 n. 151.

Callis, Lt. Col. John R., 148-151, 159, 366, 373, 374, 413, 414, 459, 460, 665 n. 144, 679 n. 525.

Candy's Brigade, 490, 524, 539, 540.

Cantador, Col. Lorenzo, 309, 317, 574.

Carlisle, Pa., 11, 12, 15, 16, 21, 22, 24, 34, 38, 47, 52, 54, 72, 98, 203, 211, 327, 507, 523

Carrington, Capt. James, 323, 324.

Carrington's Va. Battery, 283, 305, 323, 509, 576, 594.

Carr's Brigade, 542, 546.

Carter's (Thomas) Battalion, 207-214, 226, 258, 259, 296, 320, 334, 343, 356, 430, 437, 448, 473, 511, 578, 639 n. 15, 643 n. 107.

Carter's (William) Va. Battery, 207, 209, 218, 224, 263, 347, 387, 507, 578, 594.

Cashtown, Pa., 13, 22, 23, 25, 27-31, 40, 43, 46-49, 52-54, 59, 60, 71, 72, 86, 89, 99, 109, 164, 187, 203-205, 210, 211, 277, 338, 340, 366, 479, 502, 505, 508, 557, 560, 582, 597 n. 54, 661 n. 31.

Castleberry, W.A., 160, 163, 164.

Cemetery Hill, 48, 96-99, 116, 139, 167-170, 191, 196, 198-202, 252, 257, 262, 267. 270, 278, 280, 281, 282, 306, 308, 315-318, 321, 322, 328-330. 344, 346, 364, 374, 393, 393, 397 412, 415, 417, 424, 427, 428, 434, 435, 440, 442, 445, 446, 449, 450, 459, 467-477, 485-487, 490, 491, 493, 499, 500, 501, 504, 506-508, 511-518, 520, 521, 524, 531, 533, 534, 538, 539, 541, 543, 550, 553, 554, 558, 561-566, 569, 582-587, 616 n. 72, 687 n. 185, 687 n. 195, 688 n. 221.

Cemetery Ridge, 196, 278, 375, 410, 450, 531, 540, 546, 551-556, 568, 585.

Chamberlin, Maj. Thomas, 245, 247, 369, 372, 373, 380.

Chambersburg, Pa., 11, 12, 16, 18, 21-24, 34, 38, 48, 50, 54, 63, 70, 212,

213, 281, 327, 337-339, 340, 502, 505, 506, 582.

Chancellorsville, Va., 33, 60, 163, 173, 175, 220, 237, 268, 283, 333, 345, 470, 472, 508, 564, 698 n. 461.

Chapman, Col. George, 74, 422, 423, 575, 601 n. 43.

Christian, Col. W.S., 25-27, 384, 578, 599 n. 95, 605 n. 11.

Christie, Col. D.H., 230, 577.

Clark's NJ Battery, 542

Cliff, Sgt. Henry, 109-110.

Coates, Sgt. Jefferson, 592.

Cobean, Samuel, 265, 462.

Coddington, Edwin B., 22, 50-52, 97, 148, 563.

Codori farm, 99-102, 171-174, 185.

Coey, Capt. James, 111, 117, 118.

Colgrove, Col. Silas, 535-537.

Connally, Col. J.K., 107-109, 119, 579.

CONNECTICUT TROOPS: 17th Inf., 39, 42, 45, 64, 65, 76, 77, 170, 262, 275, 277, 281, 288-290, 310, 311, 318, 333, 471, 573.

Cook, Capt. John, 110, 176-178, 181, 410, 440, 442, 518.

Cooper's Pa. Battery, 49, 171, 175, 180-182, 191, 207, 240, 344, 347, 396-399, 403, 406, 407, 415, 489, 572, 593, 677 n. 464.

Coster, Col. Charles, 308, 309, 473.

Coster's Brigade, 202, 307-312, 316-319, 324, 328, 329, 334, 470-472, 551, 573, 574, 587.

Couch, Maj. Gen. Darius, 22, 33, 35, 38, 54, 98, 480, 600 n. 1.

Coulter, Col. Richard, 214-216, 252, 440, 550, 571, 694 n. 382.

Craig, Col. Calvin, 543.

Crawford farm, 271, 276, 305, 328, 696 n. 429.

Crippen, Sgt. Ben, 385, 386.

Croft, Maj. Edward, 416, 419.

Croll, Jennie, 453.

Crosby, Alanson, 316.

Culp, Peter, 96.

Culp's Hill, 48, 460, 464, 473, 475, 484, 487-489, 513, 531, 535, 538, 539,

553-565, 569, 584, 585, 684 n. 105, 687 n. 195, 688 n. 221.
Cummins, Col. Robert, 361, 362, 398, 572.
Curtin, Gov. Andrew, 107.
Custer, Brig. Gen. George A., 38, 481, 601 n. 42.
Cutler, Brig Gen. Lysander, 93, 95, 104, 107-110, 127, 153, 167, 169, 214, 230, 441, 552, 553, 570.
Cutler's Brigade, 87, 93-95, 101-107, 114, 120-126, 137, 140, 141, 145, 154, 162-165, 168, 169, 190, 194, 207, 208, 213-217, 226, 227, 230-234, 238-240, 254, 264, 343, 386, 391, 437, 440, 552, 570, 571, 637 n. 151, 683 n. 79, 684 n. 105.

Dailey, Lt. Dennis, 160, 456, 457, 630 n. 429.
Dana, Capt. A.E., 67-69, 607 n. 41.
Dana, Col. Edmund L., 174, 247, 377, 417, 473, 572.
Daniel, Maj. John, 462, 512.
Daniel, Brig. Gen. Junius, 209, 221, 223, 224, 227, 235, 239, 240, 242, 244, 379, 576.
Daniel's Brigade, 207, 209, 217, 219, 220, 223, 224, 234, 238-247, 259, 263, 269, 341, 342, 386, 389, 396, 397, 429, 433, 437, 447, 463, 509, 576, 577, 583, 647 n. 225.
Davis, Jefferson, 18, 61, 418, 419.
Davis, Brig. Gen. Joseph, 61, 62, 66, 70, 87, 107, 109, 110, 119, 125, 127, 133, 138, 158, 165, 578.
Davis' Brigade, 25, 40, 60, 61, 71, 76-81, 86, 87, 102, 104-107, 111-113, 116-127, 130, 131, 134-137, 140, 146, 149, 153, 164, 167, 183, 186-192, 246, 258, 342, 378, 380, 381, 394, 401, 433, 463, 465, 578, 579, 583, 606 n. 17, 625 n. 317.
Davis, Lt. Col. W.S., 230, 238, 577.
Dawes, Col. Rufus, 93, 101, 110, 121-139, 143, 192, 399, 401, 433-435, 447, 458, 474, 477, 488, 559, 570, 623 n. 257, 671 n. 319.

Devin, Col. Thomas, 39, 46, 47, 70, 76, 77, 79, 278-280, 575.
Devin's Brigade, 42, 45, 46, 65, 71, 72, 75, 77, 81, 87, 102, 110, 170, 205, 212, 215, 259, 276-280, 284, 328, 467, 468, 493, 510, 575, 601 n. 48, 603 n. 59, 603 n. 64.
Dilger, Capt. Hubert, 261-263, 304, 317, 318, 333, 575.
Dilger's Ohio Battery. 91, 218, 261, 263-266. 269, 272, 279, 301-304, 319, 476, 593.
Dillsburg, Pa., 12, 211
Dobke, Col. Adolphus, 222, 258, 259, 321, 554, 575, 577.
Doles, Brig. Gen. George, 297, 298, 577.
Doles' Brigade, 259, 263, 266, 274, 277, 281, 287-291, 296-298, 301-303, 309, 310, 319, 320, 328, 387, 390, 451, 465, 515, 577, 655 n. 144.
Dorr, Capt. William, 472
Doubleday, Maj. Gen. Abner, 49, 73, 91-93, 95, 97, 122, 145, 153, 153, 160-162, 168, 170-174, 176, 178, 180, 181, 185, 190-193, 196-198, 200, 203, 209, 213, 213, 217, 242, 255, 270, 271, 342-345, 347, 349, 371, 375, 396, 408, 409, 414, 415, 427, 428, 431, 446-449, 468, 469, 471, 472-475, 478, 482, 483, 488, 491, 495, 496, 528, 534, 535. 570, 625 n. 326, 629 n. 388, 632 n. 1., 633 n. 20, 641 n. 50, 649 n. 1, 652 n. 61, 654 n. 130, 666 n. 21, 673 n. 364, 683 n. 93.
Doubleday's Corps, 38, 41, 49, 50, 53, 88-92, 172, 175, 176, 195, 196, 197-200, 213, 220, 250, 261, 267, 269, 270, 320-322, 329, 341-345, 359, 393, 408, 420, 423, 428, 434, 435, 445, 449, 450, 462-469, 471-475, 482, 483, 486, 487, 491, 492, 496, 530, 543, 547, 552, 566, 570-572, 581, 585, 587, 590.
Douglas, Maj. Henry K., 507, 507, 556, 564.
Dover, Pa., 210, 211.
Dow, Capt. Charles, 160.
Drummer boy, 518.

Dudley, Lt. Col. W.W., 136, 354, 355, 398, 457.
Dwight, Lt. Col. Walton, 174, 175, 190, 241-243, 379, 381, 384, 572, 646 n. 220.

Eagle Hotel, 46, 96, 321, 322, 451, 615 n. 61.
Early, Maj. Gen Jubal, 12-15, 21, 24, 46, 70, 204, 205, 210, 220, 278, 281, 284, 305, 306, 309-311, 323, 325, 327, 460, 461, 509-514, 516, 517, 519-522, 555-561, 564, 575, 582, 688 n. 221, 695 n. 415.
Early's Division, 11, 12, 15, 16, 22, 24, 42, 46, 77, 88, 210, 217, 218, 220, 252, 258, 259, 267, 268, 275, 284, 288, 289, 296, 310. 318, 334, 341, 449, 450, 468, 475, 493, 507, 514, 517, 518, 520, 523, 529, 538, 562, 576, 577, 581, 587, 591, 613 n. 148.
Early, Robert D., 520, 554, 557, 558, 561.
East Cemetery Hill, 307, 471-472, 474, 475, 487, 489, 518, 565, 569, 583, 682 n. 41.
Emmitsburg, Md., 38-41, 49-53, 56, 89, 91, 145, 152, 168, 171-175, 184, 195-200, 213, 269, 271, 306, 376, 467, 480, 482, 497, 541-544, 546, 551, 552, 559-561, 601 n. 42, 604 n. 76, 683 n. 77, 684 n. 116, 685 n. 142.
Englehard, Maj. Joseph, 395, 401.
Eustice, Sgt., George, 374, 375.
Ewell, Lt. Gen. Richard, 11, 12, 18, 21-23, 46, 203, 205, 209-212, 218, 257, 278, 297, 306, 326, 327, 340, 461, 504-510, 512-514, 519-523, 538, 554-557, 562-568, 575, 595 n. 1, 595 n. 2, 597 n. 54, 640 n. 29, 640 n. 31, 687 n. 193, 687 n. 195, 688 n. 221, 695 n. 415, 696 n.429, 696 n. 430.
Ewell's Corps, 16, 18-25, 30, 31, 34, 47, 52, 54, 88, 98, 99, 170, 185, 203, 210, 211, 268, 280, 307, 338, 434, 478, 480, 493, 496, 497, 504, 517, 520, 539, 575-578, 581, 587.

Fairchild, Col. Lucius, 141, 445, 458, 570.
Fairfield, Pa., 24, 25, 28, 39-41, 46, 48-50, 54, 91, 173, 176, 541, 543, 547, 554, 599 n.76, 604 n. 76, 605 n. 10.
Faribault, Col. G.H., 26, 71, 578.
Faust, Maj. Benezet, 216.
Fayetteville, Pa., 23, 29, 502, 508.
Finnefrock farm, 178, 187.
First casualties, 69, 151, 608 n. 54.
First shots of the battle, 63-66, 75, 141.
Fite, Col. John, 59,
Flags captured, 130, 132, 136, 233, 234, 383, 418, 419, 424, 457, 458, 597, 645 n. 167, 648 n. 272, 667 n. 179.
Flags destroyed, 391, 392, 436, 437.
Flags in action, 62, 108, 116, 117, 126, 129, 152, 159, 163, 169, 170, 208, 209, 231, 244, 250, 298, 314, 315, 351-353, 356, 360, 364, 378, 380-385, 398, 399, 413, 470, 470, 471, 571 n. 319.
Flags recaptured, 438, 645 n. 167, 648 n. 272.
Flannigan, Lt. Col. Mark, 161.
Forney farm, 45, 76, 87, 107, 216, 218, 226, 235, 237-239, 643 n. 117.
Fort Delaware, 139, 163.
Fort McHenry, 139, 163.
Fowler, Col. Edward, 93, 105, 120, 121, 125, 128, 135 137, 169, 214, 275, 281, 282, 289, 290, 291, 441, 442, 570, 573.
Frederick, Md., 19-22, 34, 35, 38, 50, 52, 203, 213, 237.
Fredericksburg, Va., 11, 33, 55, 173, 175, 252, 365, 505, 565.
Fremantle, Lt. Col. Arthur J., 385, 499, 502, 503, 686 n. 171.
French, Col. W.H., 13-15, 46, 523, 580.
Friendly fire, 280, 285, 320, 327, 493.
Frueauff, Maj. John F., 273, 577.
Fry, Col. B.D., 62, 81, 187, 342, 361, 427, 578.
Fry's Va. Battery, 207, 218, 347, 389, 397, 578, 594.
Fulton, Pvt. W.F., 68.

Gamble, Col. William, 39, 41, 63, 67,

73, 79, 102, 154, 155, 420, 422, 575, 609 n. 79, 673 n. 357.

Gamble's Brigade, 40, 42, 43, 65-71, 74-77, 80, 81, 102, 105, 150, 153-155, 170-172, 207, 343, 347, 357, 395, 396, 420-428, 467, 492, 493, 575, 601 n. 48, 602 n. 58, 603 n. 63, 605 n. 5.

Garber's Va. Battery, 282, 283, 324, 576, 594.

Garlach, Anna, 331, 332, 450.

Garnett's Battalion, 346, 498, 499, 661 n. 21.

Gates, Col. Theodore, 180, 182, 183, 356, 360, 361, 398, 408-410, 572.

Geary, Brig. Gen. John, 490, 493, 540, 541.

Geary's Division, 525, 535, 539, 541, 546, 553, 584.

George, George, 96, 143, 144, 615 n. 48.

George, Lt. Col. Newton, 156.

GEORGIA TROOPS: 4th Inf., 259, 288, 301, 302, 577.; 12th Inf., 259, 301, 577.; 13th Inf., 285, 305, 576. 14th Inf., 579.; 21st Inf. 259, 297, 298, 301, 302, 577.; 26th Inf., 384, 576.; 31st Inf., 285, 298, 301, 576.; 35th Inf., 579.; 38th Inf., 285, 305, 576. 44thInf., 259, 298-302, 320, 577.; 45th Inf., 579.; 49th Inf. 579.; 60th Inf., 285, 298, 301, 576.; 61st Inf., 285, 286, 295, 304, 305, 308, 576.

GETTYSBURG: skirmish near on 26 June, 12-14. Confederates occupy on 26 June, 15-16. Pettigrew's expedition to on 30 June, 26-29. Occupied by Buford, 41-43. Union retreat through, 317-333, 434-452.

Gettysburg Churches: Lutheran, 321, 359, 453-456. Presbyterian, 452. St. Francis Catholic, 455, 456.

Gettysburg College—see Pennsylvania College.

Gettysburg National Cemetery, 316, 372.

Gettysburg National Military Park, 64, 587, 588.

Gettysburg Town Cemetery, 472-476, 488, 518, 544-546, 591.

Gibbon, Gen. John, 481, 495, 551.

Gilligan. Sgt. Edward, 592.

Gilmor, Maj. Henry, 326, 327, 561, 580.

Glenn, Capt. James, 245, 377, 423, 424, 572, 673 n. 364, 673 n. 365.

Godwin, Col. A.C., 311, 312, 514.

Goldsborough, Maj. W.W., 21.

Gordon, Col. G.T., 417.

Gordon, Brig. Gen. John, 283-286, 293-296, 305, 365, 404, 507, 508, 512-515, 521, 564, 595 n. 2, 656 n. 171.

Gordon's Brigade, 11, 13, 15, 21, 283-291, 296, 297, 303-306, 309-311, 323, 324, 333, 465, 511, 512, 515, 519-522, 538, 539, 557, 576, 586.

Gorman, Pvt. T.M., 393, 516, 563.

Graham's NC Battery, 580, 594.

Graham's Brigade, 490, 540, 542, 546.

Grant, Lt. George, 222, 231, 233, 247, 250, 254, 439, 442.

Grant, Gen. U.S., 292, 568.

Graves, Lt. Col. John, 358.

Green, Lt. Col. Wharton, 241, 242.

Green's La. Battery, 282, 283, 324, 576, 593.

Greencastle, Pa., 49, 50.

Greene's Brigade, 490, 539, 540.

Greenwood, Pa., 12, 22, 23, 339, 505, 507, 562.

Gregg, Brig. Gen. D.M., 37, 48, 52.

Grimes, Col. Bryan, 253, 577.

Grover, Maj. Andrew, 95, 108.

Grover, Col. Ira, 552, 553, 570.

Guindon, Maj. Eugene, 530.

Guinn, Sgt. George, 197.

Hagerstown, Md., 38, 53, 462.

Hagy farm, 259-261, 266, 267, 270.

Hall, Capt. Daniel, 196-198, 528, 529, 531.

Hall, Capt. Delos, 25.

Hall, Capt. James, 102, 104, 112-115, 192, 483, 572, 638 n. 163.

Hall, Col. J.M., 221, 223, 577.

Hall's Me. Battery, 49, 92-94, 100, 102, 105, 106, 111- 116, 119, 120, 123, 135, 137, 138, 145, 156, 163, 170, 171, 190-194, 347, 397, 429, 445, 463, 469. 476, 572, 593, 620 n. 182.

Halleck, Maj. Gen. Henry W., 34, 35, 37, 52, 54, 479- 481, 485.

Halstead, Capt. E.P., 99, 344, 372, 408, 409, 428, 469, 484, 491, 492, 517, 518, 625 n. 325, 629 n. 388, 689 n. 234.

Hampton, Brig. Gen. Wade, 211.

Hancock, Maj. John, 244.

Hancock, Maj. Gen. Winfield S., 144, 337, 480-482, 529-534, 539, 540, 543, 551, 565-568, 591, 632 n. 14, 681 n.38, 682 n. 71, 683 n. 75, 683 n. 93, 684 n. 108, 684 n. 116. Arrives at Gettysburg, 483-491. Encounters Howard, 484-487. Rallies troops, 493-497.

Hanover, Pa., 13-15, 52-56, 211, 212, 479, 519, 520, 524, 526.

Hardee hats, 155, 156, 351.

Hardie, James A., 35, 36.

Harman, Amelia, 75, 182, 357.

Harman farm, 161, 181-183, 187, 189, 343, 346, 347, 395, 405, 635 n. 89.

Harney, Maj. George, 112, 113, 116-118, 169, 239, 571.

Harpers Ferry, W.Va., 34, 37, 595 n. 1, 595 n-2.

Harris, Col. Andrew, 289, 304, 573.

Harris, Lt. Lloyd, 94, 457, 458.

Harrisburg, Pa., 11, 12, 16, 18, 21, 22, 48, 52, 54, 55, 98, 101, 203, 212, 480, 502.

Harrison, Thomas, 19, 26, 596 n. 36, 506 n. 37.

Hauser, Maj. John, 130, 133, 138.

Hauschild, Lt. Henry, 265.

Hawks, Maj,. C.S., 12.

Hayden, Lt. Col. Julius, 546-548, 694 n. 380.

Hays, Brig. Gen. Harry, 311, 329, 518, 564, 565, 575.

Hays' Brigade, 14, 15, 283, 305, 310, 311, 317, 318, 320, 324, 325, 327-329, 333, 393, 437, 450, 451, 462, 465, 468, 509, 511-514, 575, 576.

Heckman's Ohio Battery, 189, 201, 307, 308, 311, 317, 318, 329, 476, 477, 575, 593, 660 n. 313.

Heermance, Col. William, 87.

Heidlersburg, Pa., 22, 23, 46, 88, 89, 203, 204, 479.

Hendrix, Pvt. John, 148, 156.

Herbst Woods, 70, 74, 75, 79, 83-86, 99, 102-105, 120-122, 140, 141, 146-149, 151-157, 162, 169, 170, 174, 180-183, 187-190, 193, 194, 207-209, 270, 342, 344, 356, 363-369, 376, 377, 385, 394-398, 426, 460, 461, 585, 587.

Herr Ridge, 67-72, 79-84, 101, 104-106, 112, 120, 137, 161, 167, 178, 185-189, 193, 194, 207-209, 240, 341, 342, 346, 347. 356, 368, 369, 378, 394, 395, 404, 426, 429, 430, 498, 501, 584-588.

Herr Tavern, 44, 71, 461, 585.

Heth, Maj. Gen. Henry, 24-26, 29-31, 60-62, 70, 80-82, 85, 145, 164, 186-188, 196, 340-342, 363, 366, 394, 395, 445, 578, 590, 598 n. 69, 599 n. 99, 605 n.11, 605 n. 13, 606 n. 14, 611 n. 117.

Heth's Division, 23, 59-75, 79-82, 85, 88, 154, 161, 178, 181, 183, 186, 187, 190, 196, 203, 213, 345, 357, 368, 369, 379, 395, 395, 401, 404, 405, 425, 426, 430, 433, 447, 465, 499, 501, 578, 579, 581, 591, 599 n. 94, 607 n. 41.

Hewitt, Kate, 144, 627 n. 354.

Hill, Lt. Gen. A.P., 23, 29-31, 60, 61, 64, 189, 203, 205, 210, 213, 218, 337-341, 385, 394, 395, 499-505, 510, 563, 564, 578, 661 n. 17.

Hill's Corps, 22, 30, 47, 54, 61, 88, 98, 185, 205, 206, 212, 337, 338, 341, 345, 450, 461, 465, 477, 478, 486, 496, 497, 499, 504, 507, 508, 516, 517, 527, 561, 562, 566, 578-581.

Hodges, Corp. Alphonse, 45, 63.

Hoffman farm, 76, 77.

Hoffman, Col. J.W., 107, 108, 571.

Hood's Division, 23, 338, 339, 502, 504.

Hooker, Maj. Gen. Joseph, 16, 18, 20, 22, 29, 33-38, 118, 213, 596 n. 37.

Horner's Mill, 91, 195, 199, 201, 306, 544.

Hospitals, 452-460.

Hotchkiss, Maj. Jed, 21, 590, 597 n. 48.

Hotopp, Capt., 41, 43

Howard, Maj. Charles, 51, 197, 266, 270, 534.

Howard, Maj. Gen. Oliver 0., 49, 51, 56, 57, 91, 95, 97-99, 168, 195-203, 217, 257, 258, 261, 266-271, 275, 276, 280, 292, 306, 307, 319, 333, 334, 344, 345, 409, 446, 466, 472, 465-483, 488-491, 496, 527-535, 539, 542-546, 568, 569, 573, 616 n. 72, 638 n. 55, 649 n. 1, 651 n. 46, 651 n. 53, 652 n. 61, 652 n. 71, 661 n. 19, 680 n. 1, 683 n. 79, 684 n. 108. Rallies troops on Cemetery Hill, 467-471. Encounters Hancock, 484-487.

Howard's Corps, 38, 48-53, 91, 97, 98, 195, 197-206, 212, 217, 220, 222, 259-261, 268-271, 279, 281, 284, 319, 322, 327, 329-335, 341, 344, 359, 386, 387, 391, 413, 417, 420, 424, 428, 433, 437, 439, 446-452, 458, 462, 465-469, 471-477, 482, 483, 486-487, 490, 496, 497, 507,518, 521, 530-531, 432. 541, 550, 573-575, 581, 582, 587, 588.

Howell, Horatio, 454, 455, 648 n. 252.

Huidekoper, Lt. Col. Henry, 245, 246, 378, 383, 455, 572, 592, 666 n. 156.

Humiston, Sgt. Amos, 316-317.

Humphreys, Gen. H.H., 546-549, 693 n. 345.

Hunt, Brig. Gen. Henry, 488, 566, 568, 569, 684 n. 104.

Hunterstown, Pa., 46, 72, 204.

Hurt's Ala. Battery, 189, 580, 594.

Hurtt, Maj. D.W., 253, 577.

Hussey, George, 437.

ILLINOIS TROOPS: 8th Cav., 38, 40-44, 63, 64, 67, 69, 73, 74, 79, 85, 154, 155, 170, 178, 187, 343, 420, 422, 426, 427, 452, 492, 575, 606 n. 27, 607 n. 43, 607 n. 52, 674 n. 385.; 12th Cav., 43, 45, 74, 86, 105, 154, 155, 420, 575, 601 n. 48, 608 n. 54, 609 n.77 ; 82nd Inf., 260, 301, 319, 574, 659 n. 280.

Imboden's Brigade 23, 213.

INDIANA UNITS—1st Cav., 573.; 3rd Cav., 41-45, 69, 74, 76, 85, 105, 154, 155, 420, 575, 598 n. 88, 601 n. 54, 609 n. 77, 672 n. 350.; 7th Inf., 93, 552-554, 557-559, 570, 584.; 19th Inf., 90, 93, 94, 136, 151, 152, 157, 158, 161, 167, 169, 342, 343, 350, 353, 354, 356, 363, 368, 370, 398, 399, 412, 452, 570, 630 n. 400.; 27th Inf., 525, 531, 535, 536, 538, 690 n. 260.

Irsch, Capt. Francis, 258, 259, 263, 264, 321-323, 592, 687 n. 193.

Iverson, Brig. Gen. Alfred, 221, 224, 226, 227, 235-238, 577, 642 n. 81, 643 n. 107, 646 n. 196.

Iverson's Brigade, 205, 217, 219, 220, 226-229, 235-241, 247, 249, 251, 259, 264, 265, 334, 349, 386, 389, 463, 509, 577, 643 n. 117, 644 n. 158.

Jackson, Lt. Col. Allan, 309, 574.

Jackson, Lt. Gen. Thomas J., 61, 333, 338, 501-509, 563-565, 635 n. 89.

Jacobs, Prof. Michael, 14, 451, 591.

Jacobs, Col. William K., 298.

James, Corp. Cyrus, 79.

Jenkins, Brig. Gen. Albert, 11, 23.

Jenkins' Brigade, 20, 22, 212, 522, 523.

Jennings, Col. William C., 13, 15.

Jerome, Lt. Aaron B., 46, 47, 73, 96, 97, 601 n. 46, 603 n. 71, 632 n. 14, 680 n. 117.

Johnson. Maj. Gen. Edward, 508, 556, 558, 559, 562, 581, 595 n. 415.

Johnson's Division, 11, 21-23, 327, 339, 395, 502-507, 513, 516, 519, 520, 538, 554-559, 562, 563, 584.

Johnson's Va. Battery, 189, 580, 594.

Johnston's Va. Battery, 637 n. 131, 594.

Jones, Lt. Col. H.P., 514.

Jones' Battalion, 277, 281, 283, 298, 301, 304, 308, 324, 325, 327, 334, 510, 517, 520, 522, 576.

Jones, Brig. Gen. John, 556.

Jones' Brigade, 507, 557.

Jones' (William) Brigade, 20, 21, 212.

Jones, Lt. Marcellus, 44, 63, 64, 67, 68, 80, 82, 606 n. 27.

Kane's Brigade, 490, 539, 541, 553.
Keckler's Hill, 205, 206, 213, 259, 603 n. 63.
Kellogg, Capt. John, 110.
Kellogg, Col. Josiah, 39, 575.
Kenan, Col. Tom, 459, 460, 576.
Kilpatrick, Brig. Gen. Judson, 37, 38, 41, 48, 524, 526.
Kinzie's U.S. Battery, 490, 539, 593.
Koch, Maj. Charles, 321.
Koenig, Capt. Emil, 199, 574.
Kress, Lt. Col. John, 73, 626 n. 328.
Krzyzanowski, Col. Wladimir, 199, 265, 300, 305, 470, 574.
Kyzyzanowski's Brigade, 263, 267, 271, 277, 296-306, 318-320, 334.
Kuhn Brickyard, 309, 316.

Lambeth, Maj. J.M., 393.
Lancaster, Pa., 15, 144.
Lane, Gen. James, 426, 428, 579.
Lane's Brigade, 61, 187-189, 394, 396, 407, 426-428, 499-501, 503, 552, 585, 579, 587.
Lane, Lt. Col. J.R., 28, 350, 352, 353, 364.
Latimer's Battalion, 507, 557.
Law's Brigade, 23, 338.
Lawson, Maj. Charles, 384, 385.
Ledig, Maj. August, 297, 299, 303.
Lee, Capt. Alfred, 296, 299.
Lee, Gen. Robert E., 11, 12 16, 19, 23, 25, 29, 31, 34, 36-38, 48-52, 54, 60, 70, 89, 164, 189, 203-205, 209, 211-213, 220, 238, 316, 444, 477, 479, 498-505, 515, 517, 558, 562-565, 575, 595 n. 1, 596 n. 37, 611 n. 117, 640 n. 29, 666 n. 17, 682 n. 156, 687 n. 193, 688 n. 221, 696 n. 430, 697 n. 461. Campaign plans, 16-17. Anxious about Stuart, 18-21, 338-340, 506, 507. Changes plan on 28 June, 21-22. Opinion of Meade, 36-37. Use of cavalry, 211-213. Arrives at Gettysburg, 337-341, 590. Meets with Longstreet, 505-506. Meets with Ewell, 559-560.

Fails to press victory, 498-523, 565-567. Critique of campaign, 567-568.
Lehman, Franklin W., 381, 382.
Lemon, Maj. Charles, 155, 608 n. 54.
Leonard, Col. Samuel, 248, 251, 252, 456, 458, 571.
Leventhorpe, Col. Collett, 345, 578.
Libby Prison, 392, 410, 411.
Lightfoot, Col. J.N., 219, 577.
Lincoln, Abraham, 33-35, 372.
Little Round Top, 490, 540, 541, 546, 553.
Littlestown, Md., 53, 524-526, 601 n. 42.
Livingston, Lt. Col. Charles, 448, 492.
Lloyd, Lt. Col. Edward, 299.
Lockman, Col. John, 298, 574.
Long, Col. E.B., 340, 506-507, 687 n. 185.
Longstreet, Lt. Gen. James, 18, 19, 23, 338, 339, 341, 505, 514, 561, 562. Views on campaign, 17, 18. Views on evening of I July, 505, 506, 512.
Longstreet's Corps, 22, 23, 62, 212, 338, 341, 496, 497, 508, 516, 558, 568.
LOUISIANA TROOPS: Donaldsonville Art.—*see* Maurin's Battery. Louisiana Guard Art.—*see* Green's Battery.; 2nd Inf., 556.; 5th Inf., 310, 329,575.; 6th Inf., 310, 329, 575.; 7th Inf. 310, 575.; 8th Inf., 310, 575.; 9th Inf., 310, 325, 329, 575.
Lowrance, Col. W.L.J., 403, 501, 579.
Lumpkin, Col. S.P., 302, 577.
Lyle, Col. Peter, 252, 571.

Mahler, Col. Francis, 265, 299, 300, 318, 574.
MAINE TROOPS: 2nd Bat.—*see* Hall's Battery. 5th Bat. *see* Stevens' Battery.; 1st Cav., 570.; 4th Inf., 546,; 10th Inf., 539, 692 n. 327.; 16th Inf., 186, 390-392, 463, 567, 571, 648 n. 256, 649 n. 256, 667 n. 200, 667 n. 207.
Maloney, Pvt. Patrick, 160, 371, 631 n. 433.
Manchester, Md., 53, 55, 479.
Mansfield, Maj. John, 141, 154, 159,

160, 369, 370, 399, 414, 570, 626 n. 328.

Marsh Creek, 13, 28, 43-45, 48-51, 60, 62, 63, 66, 80, 81, 89, 93, 94, 172, 173, 176, 177, 188, 339, 544, 547, 548, 585, 599 n. 91, 602 n. 58, 605 n. 5, 607 n. 31, 614 n. 40.

Marshall, Col. Charles, 561, 596 n. 37

Marshall, Col. J.K., 71, 361, 492, 578, 664 n. 115, 686 n. 165.

Marshall, Col. William, 187.

Marye's Va. Battery, 60-63, 69, 145, 189, 580, 594.

MARYLAND TROOPS (CS): 1st Cav., 20, 64, 212, 326, 520, 580.; 1st Inf., 21.

MARYLAND TROOPS (US): Cole's Cav. Batn., 197.

MASSACHUSETTS TROOPS: 1st Inf., 550, 694 n. 380.; 2nd Inf., 536.; 12th Inf., 183, 215-217, 221, 228, 229, 232-234, 253, 254, 376, 440, 571, 644 n. 155, 644 n. 158.; 13th Inf., 185, 248, 251-253, 386, 391, 453, 456, 472, 473, 571, 635 n. 97.; 33rd Inf., 469, 519, 554, 574.

Maurin's La. Battery, 24, 342, 399, 574.

Mayo, Col. R.M., 186, 578.

McAllister, Mary. 453, 456, 457.

McCalmont, Lt. Col. Alfred, 415, 571.

McClellan, Maj. Gen. George B., 16, 36, 101, 184, 568.

McCreary, Albertus, 451, 452.

McCreary, Maj, C.W., 408, 579.

McCreary, Jennie, 457.

McCurdy, Charles, 453.

McDougal's Brigade, 536

McGraw's Va, Battery, 580, 594.

McIntosh's Battalion, 60, 187, 189, 190, 207, 342, 346, 347, 498, 580. 605 n. 13.

McKim, Lt. Randolph, 555, 556.

McLaws' Division, 17, 338, 339, 504, 512.

McLean farm, 217, 222, 258, 260, 263, 264, 266, 278, 284, 323, 386, 387.

McMillan Woods, 427, 428, 498, 500, 584.

McPherson farm, 102, 105, 106, 120,

137, 140, 169, 174, 208, 245-247, 342, 347, 377-385, 396, 453, 455, 458, 585.

McPherson's Ridge, 43, 47, 72, 74, 76, 79, 81, 85, 88, 97, 104, 106, 116, 122, 141, 145, 150, 152-143, 168, 172, 178, 181, 184-186, 191, 192, 200, 207, 209, 213, 214, 221, 224, 245, 342, 343, 349, 356, 363, 365, 394402, 405, 406, 417, 418, 423, 427, 429, 430, 433, 450, 459, 464, 468, 498, 583-587, 590.

McThompson, Lt. Col. James, 249.

Meade, Maj. Gen. George G., 29, 37, 38, 49-52, 56, 88-92, 95-98, 144, 168, 171, 195, 198, 211, 213, 269, 292, 337, 344, 345, 478-480, 484-487, 490, 493, 494, 498, 504-506, 526-535, 541, 543-547, 551, 567, 568, 570, 582, 604 n. 76, 632 n. 1, 632 n. 14, 682 n. 73, 683 n. 93. Assumes command, 35-37. Plans on 28 June, 38. Plans for 1 July, 52-54. Pipe Creek Plan, 55-56. Appoints Hancock, 481-482. Opinion of Doubleday, 484-483. Decides to stay and fight, 496. Arrives on the field, 568, 569.

Medal of Honor, 132, 233, 251, 322, 380, 592.

Mercer, Col. John, 296, 297, 577.

Meredith, Brig. Gen. Solomon, 93, 161, 169, 342, 366, 457, 458, 570, 662 n. 61, 665 n. 133.

Meredith's Brigade, 93-95, 101, 102, 119-122, 136, 140, 141, 149, 153, 154, 159-164, 167-170, 174, 175, 178, 180-187, 342-344, 350, 356, 362, 363, 368-377, 394, 398-401, 412-414, 428, 434, 463, 489, 553, 554, 558, 570.

Merkle, Lt. C.F., 277, 282, 287, 318.

Merritt, Brig. Gen. Wesley, 38, 39, 481.

Meyer, Col. Seraphim, 289, 573.

Meysenberg, Capt. T.A., 196, 527.

MICHIGAN TROOPS: 6th Cav., 464.; 24th Inf., 90, 94, 152, 153, 157, 161, 167-169, 342, 350-353, 358, 363, 364, 369, 370, 376, 399, 412, 463,

464, 472, 570, 632 n.7, 662 n. 53, 665 n. 133.

Middleburg, Md., 38, 39, 51, 53, 55, 479.

Middletown, Md., 34, 39

Middletown, Pa., 204, 205, 209, 213, 340.

Militia, 13-14, 61, 62, 118, 156, 211, 595 n.2.

Miller, Lt. Col. Francis, 105, 106, 111, 112, 571.

Miller, Col. H.R., 87, 119, 579.

Millerstown—*see* Fairfield.

MISSISSIPPI TROOPS: 2nd Inf., 60, 61, 70, 86, 107-114, 119, 120, 124-127, 130-139, 149, 382, 457, 458, 463, 578, 625 n. 314.; 11th Inf., 60, 61, 71, 138, 579, 625 n. 316.; 16th Inf., 503.; 42nd Inf., 40, 61, 70, 82, 86, 87, 107, 109, 111, 112, 116, 117, 119, 125, 127, 138, 381, 382, 579.; 48th Inf., 503.

Mitchell, Capt. Robert W., 142, 489, 496.

Mitchell, Maj. William, 490, 493.

Montgomery, Walter, 226, 236.

Monuments, 146, 228, 235, 254, 291, 315, 385, 386, 440, 454, 475, 476, 540, 587, 588, 610 n. 87, 610 n. 95, 629 n. 394, 673 n. 365.

Moon, W.H., 70, 83-86, 156-158.

Moore, Maj. John, 546.

Morgan, Lt. Col. Charles, 483, 485, 533.

Moritz Tavern, Md., 51, 89, 175, 176, 195, 199.

Morrow, Col. Henry, 152, 157, 161, 350, 351, 364-366, 399, 510, 665 n. 115.

Mosby, Col. John S., 164.

Mummasburg, Pa., 13, 14, 46, 58, 88, 204, 205, 261.

Murphy, W.B., 110, 114, 125-127, 130, 132, 134, 137, 139, 149, 625 n. 314, Myers, Capt. Frank, 113, 520, 521, 527.

New Guilford, Pa., 23, 338.

NEW JERSEY TROOPS: 13th Inf., 524, 532.

Newman, Sgt. Joseph, 75, 88.

Newton, Maj. Gen. John, 144, 482.

NEW YORK TROOPS: Bat. I, 1st Art.—*see* Wiedrich's Battery. Bat. L, 1st Art.—*see* Reynolds' Battery and Breck's Battery. Bat. M, 1st Art.—*see* Winegar's Battery. 13th Bat.—*see* Wheeler's Battery. 6th Cav., 65, 66, 76, 87, 170, 575, 610 n. 94.; 8th Cav., 42-66, 69, 74, 75, 85, 102, 154, 155, 157, 357, 420, 575, 662 n. 58, 609 n. 77, 612 n. 130, 629 n. 394, 672 n. 350.; 9th Cav., 42, 45, 46, 64, 65, 72, 73, 76, 77, 79, 88, 170, 207, 213, 278-280, 327, 328, 376, 575, 603 n. 58, 610 n. 92, 610 n. 94 ; 8th Inf., 573.; 14th Brooklyn, 93, 100, 104, 105, 120, 121, 135-138, 140, 149, 167, 169, 170, 192, 194, 208, 213, 254, 433, 440-442, 518, 627 n. 344, 627 n. 353 ; 20th Militia, 175- 178, 181-183, 343, 346, 356, 357, 359-361, 395, 398, 408-411, 572.; 29th Inf., 573 ; 41st Inf., 201, 272, 550, 551, 573 ; 45th Inf., 200, 222, 223, 258-261, 263, 264, 266, 301, 319-323, 329, 449, 451, 454, 574, 584, 589, 638 n. 177, 649 n. 2, 650 n. 11, 650 n. 15, 650 n. 30, 674 n. 391, 680 n. 14, 687 n. 193.; 54th Inf., 272, 274, 285, 286, 573.; 58th Inf., 199, 265, 296, 300, 574.; 68th Inf., 272, 274, 285, 286, 288, 573.; 76th Inf., 90, 93, 95, 100, 104-110, 112, 113, 115, 118, 119, 126, 140, 153, 169, 194, 214, 234, 254, 433, 440, 442, 447, 458, 459, 518, 570, 618 n. 113, 627 n. 344.; 83rd Inf., 186, 216, 221, 231, 234, 247, 432, 437, 571, 635 n. 97, 644 n. 155.; 14th Brooklyn (84th New York), 570, 613 n. 141.; 94th Inf., 234, 249, 252, 386, 391, 417, 571 ; 95th Inf., 93, 104, 105, 120, 121, 128, 134, 136, 140, 167, 169, 170, 194, 214, 570.; 97th Inf., 184, 214-219, 226, 227, 231, 232, 233, 235, 249, 250, 253, 432, 437-439, 454, 571, 635 n. 97.; 104th Inf., 248, 251-253, 386, 387, 391, 424, 571, 649 n. 280.; 119th Inf., 265, 296, 298, 303, 318,

446, 574.; 127th Inf., 524.; 134th Inf., 307, 309, 313-315, 574.; 136th Inf., 469, 574.; 147th Inf., 90, 93, 100, 104-106, 111-119, 123-126, 136, 153, 167, 169, 194, 214, 215, 239, 241, 242, 254, 433, 440, 463, 529, 571, 583, 617 n. 113, 622 n. 232, 627 n. 348.; 149th Inf., 692 n. 334.; 154th Inf., 396-309, 312, 316, 333, 551, 574.; 157th Inf., 260-262, 301-303, 319, 333, 334, 574.

Nicholls' Brigade, 556.

Nichols, G.W., 286, 295, 304, 305.

NORTH CAROLINA TROOPS: Charlotte Art.: see Graham's Battery. 2nd Inf., 251, 253, 387, 389, 392, 393, 516, 563, 577.; 2nd Inf. Batn., 238-245, 379, 393, 432, 576, 646 n. 202.; 4th Inf., 251, 253, 387, 389, 392, 393, 563, 577.; 5th Inf., 226, 229, 230, 234, 236, 463, 516.; 6th Inf., 310, 312, 317, 576, 599 n. 94.; 7th Inf., 189, 426, 428, 579.; 11th Inf., 25, 28, 72, 186, 350, 353-356, 362, 394, 401, 425, 463, 578, 599 n. 98.; 12th Inf., 213, 215, 226-230, 234, 235, 238-240, 247, 387, 389, 393, 439, 576.; 13th Inf., 401, 404, 579.; 14th Inf., 251, 387, 389, 392, 577.; 16th Inf., 401, 579.; 18th Inf., 426, 579, 674 n. 388.; 20th Inf., 226, 229, 230, 233-237, 250, 437, 463, 576, 645 n. 147, 648 n. 27, 675 n. 429.; 21st Inf., 310, 312, 327, 576.; 22nd Inf., 401, 580.; 23rd Inf., 205, 226, 229, 237, 436, 437, 463, 576, 645 n. 185.; 26th Inf., 25, 28, 45, 72, 186, 346, 349-353, 364, 367, 369, 394, 401, 425, 463, 464, 578, 599 n. 91, 662 n. 53.; 28th Inf., 426, 579.; 30th Inf., 251, 387, 389, 577.; 32nd Inf., 238, 242-246, 379, 393, 432, 576, 646 n. 202.; 33rd Inf., 426, 579.; 34th Inf., 401, 403, 501, 580.; 34th Inf., 401, 403, 501, 580.; 37th Inf., 426, 427, 579.; 38th Inf., 401, 403, 430, 431, 580.; 43rd Inf., 238, 242, 389, 393, 432, 459, 576, 646 n. 202.; 45th Inf., 238-246, 379, 432, 576, 645 n. 167, 675 n.

429.; 47th Inf., 25, 26, 28, 71, 72, 186, 350, 356-362, 578.; 52nd Inf., 25 28, 40, 60, 71, 72, 186-187, 350, 356-361, 492, 578, 599 n. 96, 605 n. 10, 664 n. 92, 664 m. 115, 686 n. 165.; 53rd Inf., 238-240, 432, 576, 646 n. 202, 646 n. 203.; 54th Inf., 283.; 55th Inf., 60, 61, 67, 71, 86, 87, 106-109, 113-119, 124, 125, 127, 133, 135, 146, 147, 389, 393, 579, 622 n. 240, 625 n. 316,; 57th Inf., 310, 311, 313, 317, 514, 576.

Northrop, Maj. Charles, 439, 571.

Oak Hill, 13, 206, 207, 209, 213, 227, 253, 254, 257-261, 263-267, 272, 297, 302, 303, 334, 343, 237, 349, 356, 372, 387, 395, 397, 430, 447, 507, 509, 520, 584-586, 610 n. 92, 639 n. 13, 649 n. 1.

Oak Ridge, 45, 107, 110, 170, 217, 218, 233, 247, 263.

OHIO TROOPS: Bat. I, 1st Art.—see Dilger's Battery. Bat. K, 1st Art.—see Heckman's Battery. 5th Cav., 139.; 5th Inf., 490, 540.; 25th Inf., 274, 277, 289, 331, 333, 470, 573.; 29th Inf., 540.; 55th Inf., 469, 471, 476, 574.; 61st Inf., 260, 262, 301, 319, 574, 650 n. 11, 650 n. 15, 659 n. 280.; 66th Inf., 532.; 73rd Inf., 277, 435, 469, 473, 519, 574.; 75th Inf., 49, 200, 275, 288, 289, 290, 304, 550, 573.; 82nd Inf., 265, 296, 297, 299, 574.; 107th Inf., 274, 277, 288, 289, 470, 573.

O'Neal, Col. Edward. 206, 219-224, 237, 387, 515, 565, 577.

O'Neal's Brigade, 217-228, 232-234, 247, 248, 251, 253, 259, 263, 264, 284, 289, 322, 334, 387, 389, 509, 577-578, 645 n. 160.

Osborn, Maj. Thomas W., 262, 282, 474-478, 652 n. 69.

Otis, Capt. George H., 101, 142, 149, 472.

Owens, Col. William, 239, 240, 393, 577.

Page's Va. Battery, 218, 258, 260-264, 594.

Parker, Col. Francis, 389, 577.
Paul, Brig. Gen. Gabriel R., 249, 251, 252, 571, 649 n. 278.
Paul's Brigade, 184, 185, 214, 215, 234, 247-250, 252, 254, 255, 270, 343, 344, 386, 387, 390, 391, 397, 432, 449, 463, 515, 550, 571, 694 n. 382.
Peach Orchard, 91, 171, 173, 184, 196, 197, 493, 498, 554.
Pearson, Capt. Edward, 198, 459.
Peck, Sgt. Abel, 152.
Peebles, Maj. W.M., 301, 302, 577.
Pegram, Maj. John, 62, 63, 66, 70, 190.
Pegram's Battalion, 60, 66, 70, 75, 77, 79-82, 104, 106, 113, 120, 137, 145, 154, 167, 180, 186-190, 207, 346, 349, 498, 580, 605 n. 13, 607 n. 43.
Pender, Maj. Gen. Dorsey, 23, 29, 61, 188, 189, 196, 394-396, 401, 405, 407, 419, 420, 423, 425, 426, 428, 500, 501, 503, 519, 605 n. 13.
Pender's Division, 31, 60, 183, 203, 341, 368, 379, 426, 430, 450, 501, 503, 513, 531, 579-581, 591.
Pendleton, Sandie, 508.
Pendleton, Brig. Gen. William N., 498-500, 565, 584.
Pennsylvania College, 14, 45, 261, 264, 320, 372, 434, 448, 460, 587, 674 n. 391, 696 n. 430.
PENNSYLVANIA TROOPS: Bat. B, 1st Art.—*see* Cooper's Battery. Adams County Cav., 13, 14.; 2nd Cav., 627 n. 351.; 17th Cav., 39, 42, 45, 64, 65, 76, 77, 170, 493, 573, 575, 611 n. 115.; 20th Militia, 15.; 26th Militia, 13, 70.; 10th Inf., 180.; 11th Inf., 184, 214-217, 227, 228, 231, 232, 250, 252, 432, 439, 440, 518, 550, 571,694 n. 382.; 27th Inf., 307, 309, 313, 314, 317, 574.; 28th Inf., 518.; 56th Inf., 93, 104-113, 118, 119, 126, 140, 141, 153, 167, 169, 194, 214, 440, 571, 618 n. 113, 618 n. 132.; 63rd Inf., 546.; 73rd Inf., 307, 308, 315, 472, 574, 657 n. 231.; 74th Inf., 260, 274, 301, 319, 574, 659 n. 280.; 75th Inf., 265, 297, 300, 303, 514, 650 n. 35.; 88th Inf., 184, 185, 216, 221, 222, 227, 228, 231, 233-236, 247-250, 251, 253, 254, 432, 435-439, 442, 454, 571, 592, 647 n. 252.; 90th Inf., 184, 216, 221, 229, 247, 251, 454, 571, 592, 648 n. 252.; 99th Inf., 546.; 105th Inf., 543.; 107th Inf., 249, 253, 386, 391, 571.; 110th Inf., 692n. 327.; 114th Inf., 693 n. 353.; 121st Inf., 91, 175, 176, 181, 356, 358, 360, 361, 397, 398, 409, 410, 472, 554, 572.; 142nd Inf., 175, 181, 356, 358, 360, 362, 398, 415, 572.; 143rd Inf., 173-175, 244-247, 368, 377-379, 385, 386, 399, 417, 572, 592.; 147th Inf., 490, 540.; 149th Inf., 173-175, 190, 208, 209, 240, 247, 368, 377-385, 399, 423, 424, 463, 572, 633 n. 37, 633 n. 38, 633 n. 45, 647 n. 233, 665 n. 143, 667 n. 179, 673 n. 362, 673 n. 364, 673 n. 365, 686 n. 171.; 150th Inf., 90, 173-175, 208, 240, 245-247, 345, 346, 368-372, 375, 377, 380, 381, 385, 399, 417, 418, 451, 464, 465, 572, 592, 667 n. 179, 681 n. 22.; 151st Inf., 175, 181, 344, 361-363, 370, 398, 411, 463, 464, 472, 572, 664 n. 98, 664 n. 104, 681 n. 22.; 153rd Inf., 272-274, 285-287, 305, 573.
Pergel, Sgt. Charles, 75, 83-85.
Perrin, Col. Abner, 187, 404-407, 419-426, 451, 565, 579, 686 n. 166.
Perrin's Brigade, 60, 188, 393, 396, 401, 404-412, 415-428, 436, 439, 451, 464, 469, 499, 500, 517, 579.
Pettigrew, Brig. Gen. J. Johnston, 24-29, 31, 41, 61, 62, 352, 366, 367, 386, 395, 396, 405, 501, 578, 662 n. 4 6 .
Pettigrew's Brigade, 24-28, 40-43, 48, 60-62, 71, 81, 164, 178, 186, 189, 342, 349-361, 363, 368, 377, 395, 401, 405, 408, 425, 450, 463, 492, 501, 578, 605 n. 5, 605 n. 11, 686 n. 165.
Pfanz, Harry, 327, 450, 531, 535.
Phifer, Sgt. Samuel, 378, 418.
Philadelphia, Pa., 12, 13, 16-18, 35, 52, 55, 144, 211, 316, 383.
Pickens, Col. S.B., 219, 223, 578.
Pickett, Maj. Gen. George E., 237.

Pickett's Charge, 365, 451, 501.
Pickett's Division, 23, 213, 236, 339, 463, 506.
Pierce, Lt. J.V., 90, 100, 105, 111-113, 116-118
Pierce, Margaret, 43.
Pipe Creek, Md., 55-57, 478-480, 484, 495, 527, 528, 534, 604 n. 105.
Pitzer, Lt. A.L., 291, 294
Pitzer School, 173, 547, 549.
Pleasonton, Brig. Gen. Alfred, 39, 46-48, 53, 471, 601 n. 42, 601 n. 43, 680 n. 17.
Poague, Maj. W.T., 60, 380.
Poague's Battalion, 60, 346, 498, 580, 636 n. 122, 660 n. 306, 661 n. 31.
Potomac River, 18-20, 34, 39, 52, 177, 210, 213, 338, 340, 567, 596 n. 34.
Prey, Lt. Col. Gilbert, 248, 251, 252, 387, 571, 649 n. 280.
Price, Sgt. Frank, 382, 383.
Pye, Maj. Edward, 105, 128, 136, 170, 623 n. 257.

RAILROAD CUTS: Eastern, 208, 241, 393, 399, 429, 431, 433, 583, 587. Middle, 107, 117, 119, 123, 125, 126, 131, 134-137, 433, 583, 622 n. 240.
Railroad line at Gettysburg, 308, 583.
Ramseur, Brig. Gen. Stephen, 220, 223, 224, 251, 387, 389, 390, 447, 499, 565, 577.
Ramseur's Brigade, 207, 217, 219, 224, 234, 247, 251, 253, 387, 389, 391-394, 429, 434, 436, 437, 447-451, 509, 515, 577, 667 n. 192.
Reese's Ala. Battery, 218, 261-263, 577, 594.
Reisinger, Corp. J.M., 592.
Reynolds, Capt. Gilbert, 572, 637 n. 150.
Reynolds' NY Battery, 172, 191, 193, 207, 209, 240, 347, 403, 429, 572, 593.
Reynolds, Jennie, 148.
Reynolds. Maj. Gen. John F., 35-38, 41, 47-57, 87-96, 99-102, 104, 105, 114, 123, 140-142, 152-156, 168, 171, 176, 181, 185, 195- 197, 200, 268,

337, 345, 372, 424, 460, 466, 467, 471, 473, 478-486, 497, 526-529, 532, 541, 542, 550-552, 568, 570, 584, 590, 613 n. 4, 615 n. 53, 627 n. 348, 627 n. 353, 627 n. 353, 627 n. 354, 628 n. 371, 629 n. 376, 693 n. 71. Meets Buford, 96-98. Killed in action, 142-149.
Rice's Va. Battery, 189, 580, 594.
Richardson, Capt. Hollon, 161, 371, 398, 413, 671 n. 319.
Richmond, Va., 16, 19, 20, 61, 292, 294, 316, 365, 391, 424.
Riddle, Maj. William, 89, 90, 144, 638 n. 163.
Rison, Corp. Henry, 85, 612 n. 137.
Robertson's Brigade, 20, 21, 212.
Robinson, Brig. Gen. John, 214, 227, 251-254, 386, 390, 391, 435, 442, 448, 571.
Robinson's Division, 49, 92, 171, 183, 185, 206, 213, 219, 239, 247, 248, 252, 257, 258, 260, 266, 270, 271, 344, 386, 387, 393, 396, 428, 429, 436, 446, 449, 465, 473, 507, 540, 546, 550, 571, 581, 584.
Robinson, Col. William, 150, 151, 154, 156, 158, 161, 370, 399, 570.
Rock Creek, 15, 45, 46, 73, 76, 170, 271, 274, 275, 278-280, 283, 285, 289, 298, 310, 311, 318, 323, 327, 437, 521, 523, 531, 535, 538, 539, 541, 553, 557, 559, 569, 582, 585, 610 n. 92, 691 n. 309.
Roder, Lt. John, 75, 137, 170, 192.
Rodes, Maj. Gen. Robert, 21, 23, 204-210, 213, 218-227, 235, 259-261, 263, 310, 320, 387, 389, 461, 509-512, 515-519, 555, 559, 560, 564, 576, 639 n. 13, 642 n. 87, 642 n. 92.
Rodes' Division, 11, 22, 46, 77, 88, 203-214, 217-220, 254, 255, 257, 259, 260, 267, 278, 281, 284, 296, 334, 341, 343, 420, 429, 433, 465, 407, 507, 512, 515, 517, 520, 576-578, 581, 584, 590.
Rodgers, Lt. Col. Hiram, 529, 530,
Rogers, Lt. Clayton, 94, 121, 122, 443, 474.

Rogers, Lt. Earl, 129, 488, 489.
Rogers, Lt. Col. James, 524.
Root, Col. Adrian R., 251, 252, 301, 571.
Rosengarten, Capt- Joseph, 98, 99, 142, 144, 148, 616 n. 62, 616 n. 72.
Ross' Ga. Battery, 503
Ross, Maj. E.A., 356.
Round Top, 48, 484, 540, 550, 551, 560, 569, 583-585.
Rowley, Brig. Gen. Thomas A., 91, 174, 176, 178, 180, 181, 343, 356, 362, 446, 473, 474, 572, 681 n. 31.
Rowley's Division, 91, 92, 171, 172, 173, 175, 183, 206, 449, 462, 473, 572, 581.
Ruger's Brigade, 524.
Rutter, Sgt. James, 592.

Sabillasville, Md., 307, 551.
Sackett, Col. William, 45, 575.
Sallie The War Dog, 440.
Sanderson, Col. James M., 102.
Scales, Brig. Gen. A.M., 401-405, 579.
Scales' Brigade, 61, 187-189, 394, 396, 401-407, 417, 425, 428-433, 463, 499, 501, 579-580.
Schaeffer, Maj. H.J., 249.
Schimmelfennig, Brig. Gen. Alexander, 198, 259, 265, 276, 296, 301, 330-334, 574.
Schimmelfennig's Brigade, 219, 257, 258, 259, 260, 265, 266,267, 269, 271, 276, 278, 296, 306, 318, 329, 339, 471, 574.
Schmucker House, 100, 191, 584.
Schultz Woods, 427, 492, 498, 499, 584.
Schurz, Maj. Gen. Carl, 197-201, 257, 259, 260, 266, 267, 272, 275-277, 284, 296, 300, 305-309, 318, 319, 330, 332-334, 448, 468, 469, 472, 490, 491, 545, 573, 649 n. 1, 651 n. 44, 657 n. 231.
Schurz's Division, 49, 198-201, 266, 267, 270-272, 275, 344, 465, 467, 471, 574-575, 581.
Scotland, Pa., 22, 502, 507.
Scripture, Lt. Clark, 261, 304, 318.

Sedgwick, Maj. Gen. John, 55, 478, 480, 482, 496, 497, 528, 682 n. 73.
Sedgwick's Corps, 38, 53, 478, 497, 534, 568.
Seeley's RI Battery, 542, 548.
Sellers, Maj. Alfred, 251, 592.
Seminary, 43, 46, 69, 72, 76, 77, 81, 88, 99-104, 110, 114, 121, 127, 141, 143, 145, 152, 153, 155, 157, 169-172, 178, 181, 185, 186, 192-197, 206, 208, 213-216, 247, 254, 269, 343, 344, 347, 349, 354, 347, 360, 362-367, 372, 376, 385, 396-399, 402, 403, 406, 408, 410-420. 423-432, 438, 439, 446-452, 465, 477, 498, 500, 542, 552, 560, 561, 584, 587, 590, 620 n. 191, 668 n. 230, 672 n. 350, 673 n. 364.
Seminary Hill, 349, 415, 446.
Seminary Ridge, 27, 41, 43, 45, 47, 69, 72, 76, 77, 81, 88, 96, 99, 105, 110, 114, 115, 118, 126, 127, 135, 137, 139, 141, 152-155, 167-172, 185, 186, 190-192, 196, 197, 207, 208, 213-215, 244, 247, 250, 254, 257, 258, 260, 263, 264, 270, 271, 278, 290, 320, 343, 344, 349, 361, 364, 366, 371, 372, 386, 390, 393-399, 403, 406, 414-419, 423, 425, 428, 430, 432-434, 440, 440, 446-449, 463, 467, 468, 473, 487, 492, 498, 499, 500, 501, 505, 508, 517, 531.
Seven Stars, Pa., 28, 62, 71.
Shafer, Sgt. Levi, 63, 64, 66, 188.
Sharpshooters, 66, 147, 148, 389.
Sheads house, 27, 438, 439.
Shepard, Col S.G., 156, 162, 578.
Shippensburg, Pa., 12, 22-24, 210, 327, 507.
Shoes in Gettysburg, 24, 29, 73.
Showalter, Lt. Levi, 94, 121, 130.
Sickles. Maj. Gen. Daniel, 50, 51, 91, 99, 198, 268, 269, 467, 468, 481, 486, 528, 549, 541-547, 569, 683 n. 77, 693 n. 345, 693 n. 346.
Sickles' Corps, 38, 50, 52, 53, 98, 198, 268, 466, 467, 482, 493-497, 535, 541, 544, 549, 553, 585.
Skelly, Daniel, 197, 292.

Slocum, Maj. Gen. Henry W., 55, 98, 268, 467, 468, 478-480, 486, 487, 490, 494-497, 528-549, 568, 569, 583, 682 n. 58, 693 n. 93.

Slocum's Corps, 38, 53, 55, 98, 268, 269, 327, 466, 467, 490, 491, 496, 497, 510, 521-523, 525, 526, 528, 530, 531, 532, 539, 541, 585.

Slough, Col. Nelson, 230, 577.

Small, Abner, 184, 649 n. 278.

Smith, James P., 338, 480, 509, 512.

Smith, Col. Orland, 201, 574.

Smith's Brigade (U.S.), 202, 307, 483, 518, 574.

Smith, Brig. Gen. William, 510, 511, 516, 521, 522, 538, 565, 575

Smith's Brigade (C.S.), 283, 327, 328, 468-471, 509-512, 520, 522, 538, 539, 576.

Smith's NY Battery, 543.

Songs and music, 42, 43, 94, 101, 102, 121, 155, 183, 184.

SOUTH CAROLINA TROOPS: Pee Dee Art.—*see* Zimmerman's Battery. 1st Rifles, 60, 187, 404, 579.; 1st Inf., 188, 393, 404-408, 414, 416, 419-423, 451, 464, 500, 515, 579, 669 n. 215, 672 n. 351.; 12th Inf., 187, 404, 420, 422, 423, 425, 427, 500, 579, 669 n. 215.; 13th Inf., 404, 420, 422, 423, 427, 500502, 579, 669 n. 215.; 14th Inf., 393, 404-407, 416, 419-425, 451, 464, 500, 515, 579, 669 n. 215.

South Mountain, 12, 16, 17, 21, 34, 38, 39, 50, 56, 187, 204, 213, 237, 339, 457.

Spencer rifles, 82.

Spofford, Lt. Col. John. 232.

Squares against cavalry, 187, 428-429, 448, 492, 674 n. 385, 684 n. 391, 684 n. 392.

Stannard's Brigade, 92, 93, 550-553.

Stanton, Edwin M., 34, 35, 474, 481.

Steadman, Pvt. Levi, 129, 623 n. 266.

Steuart's Brigade, 327, 507, 556, 557.

Stevens. Lt. Col. George, 141, 626 n. 330.

Stevens, Capt. Greenleaf, 397, 416, 572,

Stevens' Me. Battery, 194, 247, 344, 349, 396, 399, 401, 403, 415, 416, 474, 475, 487-489, 513, 572, 593, 676 n. 457, 677 n. 464.

Stevens' Knoll, 487, 488, 565.

Stevens' Run, 100, 271, 272, 312, 315.

Stevens, Thaddeus, 12, 13.

Stewart, Lt. James, 208, 430, 443-445, 489, 572.

Stewart's U.S. Battery, 208, 241, 244, 254, 342, 349, 386, 393, 397, 403, 428-435, 442-447, 450, 474, 487, 593, 676 n. 457, 676 n. 460, 681 n. 38.

Stiles, Lt. Robert, 283, 305, 306, 310, 324, 326.

Stone, Col. John M., 86, 109, 119, 578.

Stone, Col. Roy, 174, 175, 208, 209, 240-245, 377, 380, 381, 458, 572, 647 n. 225.

Stone's Brigade, 173, 175, 177, 180, 187, 190, 238-240, 254, 269, 342, 343, 368, 377-399, 385, 386, 396, 397, 399, 401, 417, 430, 463, 473, 572.

Sullivan, Pvt. Mickey, 129, 133.

Susquehanna River, 11, 12, 18, 37, 38, 52, 53, 56, 338, 480.

Sykes, Gen. George, 171, 527, 558, 562.

Sykes' Corps, 38, 53, 55, 171, 479, 496, 497, 526, 532, 534, 558.

Taneytown, Md., 38, 50, 51, 53, 90, 98, 144, 199, 480, 497, 533, 551, 578, 684 n. 116, 685 n. 142.

Tanner's Va. battery, 324, 326, 576, 593.

Taylor, Lt. Col. Walter M., 338, 498, 504, 508.

TENNESSEE TROOPS: 1st Inf., 66, 70, 82, 84, 85, 148, 156, 158, 162, 578.; 7th Inf., 59, 70, 84-86, 104, 120, 156-159, 162, 578, 612 n. 141.; 14th Inf., 70, 84-86, 104, 120, 141, 156, 158, 159, 162, 578.

Thomas, Brig. Gen. Edward, 579.

Thomas' Brigade, 61, 187-189, 394, 395, 499-501, 679.

Thompson house, 208, 429, 444.

Thorn, Catherine, 544, 545,

Thorp, Pvt. Benjamin, 146-147.

Tilden, Col. Charles W., 248, 249, 390, 392, 571.

Toombs, Samuel, 524, 532.

Tremain, Maj. Henry, 541, 542.

Trimble, Maj. Gen. Isaac, 16-18, 204, 555, 556, 596 n. 25, 686 n. 156, 696 n. 430.

Turner, Capt. Thomas, 210, 520.

Two Taverns, Pa., 53, 198, 268, 458, 567, 490, 524, 525, 527, 529-532, 535, 539.

Tyler, Brig. Gen. Robert, 551.

Ulmer, Lt. William, 114, 115.

Underwood, George, 28, 351.

Union Mills, Md., 52, 53, 55, 527.

Uniontown, Md., 55, 478.

UNITED STATES TROOPS: Bat. A, 2nd Art.—*see* Calef's Battery. Bat. B, 4th Art.—*see* Stewart's Battery. Bat. G, 4th Art.—*see* Wilkeson's Battery and Bancroft's Battery. 2nd Cav., 38.; 5th Cav., 38.

Van de Graaff, Maj, A.S., 83, 518.

Vautier, John, 184, 185, 228, 229, 235, 236, 253, 254, 435, 436.

Veil, Sgt. Charles, 97, 98, 141-144, 148, 149.

Venable, Maj. Andrew, 210, 211.

Vermont Troops, 550.

VIRGINIA TROOPS: Albemarle Art.— *see* Wyatt's Battery. Brooke Art.—*see* Brooke's Battery. Charlottesville Art.— *see* Carrington's Battery. Courtney Art.—*see* Tanner's Battery. Danville Art.—*see* Rice's Battery. Fredericksburg Art.—*see* Marye's Battery. King William Art.—*see* Carter's Battery. Letcher Art.—*see* Brander's Battery. Morris Art.—*see* Page's Battery. Orange Art.— *see* Fry's Battery. Purcell Art.—*see* McGraw's Battery. Staunton Art.—*see* Garber's Battery.; 14th Cav., 523.; 16th Cav., 523.; 17th Cav., 13, 15, 46, 64, 212, 522, 597 n. 58.; 34th Cav. Batn., 523.; 35th Cav. Batn., 13, 14, 20, 46, 212, 278, 510, 520-522, 538.; 36th Cav. Batn., 523.; 39th Cav. Batn.,

575.; 7th Inf., 457.; 13th Inf., 283.; 22nd Inf. Batn., 368, 578.; 31st Inf., 520, 576.; 40th Inf., 368, 578.; 47th Inf., 186, 368, 578.; 49th Inf., 511, 576.; 52nd Inf., 510, 576.; 55th Inf.,25, 27, 28, 368, 383, 384, 578, 599 n. 95, 605 n. 11.; 58th Inf., 283.

Vogelbach, Lt. Adolphus, 313-315.

Von Amsberg, Col. George, 258, 260, 261, 319, 321, 574, 686 n. 14.

Von Amsberg's Brigade, 218, 222, 258, 260, 263, 278, 284, 301. 303, 319, 320, 449, 470, 574.

Von Einsiedel, Lt. Col. Detleo, 20, 573.

Von Gilsa, Col. Leopold, 272, 273, 305, 573.

Von Gilsa's Brigade, 20, 271, 274-277, 281, 287, 289-291, 330, 386, 550, 551, 573.

Von Hartung, Col. Adolph, 260, 574.

Von Mitzel, Lt. Col. Alexander, 260, 574.

Von Steinwehr, Brig. Gen. Adolph, 306, 468, 573.

Von Steinwehr's Division, 201, 262, 278, 344, 467, 471, 472, 512, 573, 574, 581, 651 n. 44.

Wadsworth, Capt. Craig, 151, 171.

Wadsworth, Gen. James, 92-95, 99, 100, 104-106, 109, 112-116, 137, 138, 145, 181, 191, 192, 209, 270, 343, 344, 371, 378, 415, 424, 446, 468, 473, 474, 488, 552, 553, 631 n. 433. 637 n. 139.

Wadsworth's Division, 49, 91-93, 99, 102, 167, 171, 174, 182, 183, 186, 192, 198, 200, 270, 343, 417, 428, 449, 453. 462, 473, 488, 541, 554, 570, 571, 581, 584.

Wainwright, Col. Charles, 92, 93, 168, 171, 172, 180, 191, 193, 194, 209, 347, 349, 357, 366, 412, 414-416, 429, 446, 473, 474, 476, 477, 489, 489, 545, 572, 633 n. 20, 637 n. 139, 663 n. 90, 681 n. 38.

Walker's Brigade, 503.

Wallace's Va. Battery, 189, 580, 594.

Wallar, Corp. Francis, 132, 134, 136, 592, 624 n. 283.

Ward's Brigade, 542, 546.
Warren, Maj. Gen. G.K., 482, 490, 491, 495, 534.
Washington, D.C., 16, 17, 20, 22, 34, 35, 37, 52, 53, 55, 56, 294, 479, 480, 496, 505, 510, 516, 550, 563.
Way, W.C., 90, 376.
Wehrum, C.C., 216, 232, 233.
Weld, Capt Steven, M., 95, 98, 479.
Westminster, Md., 38, 48, 53, 55, 163, 479, 527.
West Point, 51, 101, 144.
WEST VIRGINIA TROOPS: 3rd Cav., 76, 575.
Wheeler, Lt. William, 303, 575.
Wheeler's NY Battery, 201, 218, 262, 263, 281, 301, 304, 476, 477, 500, 593.
Wheelock, Col. Charles, 216, 218, 232, 234, 250, 262, 263, 437-439, 571.
White, Col. Elijah, 511, 580.
White's Comanches—see 35th Va. Cav. Batn.
Widdis, Capt. Cornelius, 377-378, 418, 572.
Wiedrich, Capt. Michael, 280, 475, 574.
Wiedrich's NY Battery, 201 202, 280, 281, 307, 327, 416-419, 467, 468, 475, 489, 593.
Wilber, Lt. Benjamin, 209, 347, 396, 415-419, 671 n. 373.
Wilcox's Brigade, 503.
Wilkeson, Lt. Bayard, 282, 287, 222, 575, 652 n. 19, 654 n. 113.
Wilkeson's US Battery, 195, 200, 272, 275, 281, 282, 593.
Williams, Gen. Alpheus, 535, 537, 539-541.
Williams' Division, 490, 510, 511, 525, 535, 537, 538, 541, 553, 558.
Williams, Col. Jeremiah, 289, 573.
Williams, Kenneth, 56.
Williams,Col. Samuel, 93, 152, 161, 353-356, 363, 399, 412, 413, 570.
Willis, Maj. W.H., 288, 577.
Willoughby Run, 45, 65, 66, 70, 71, 74, 76, 79-87, 102, 104, 105, 152-159, 162, 164-169, 175, 177, 178, 180-182, 186-189, 192, 240, 246, 342,

343, 345, 350, 351, 357, 358, 366, 368, 370, 397, 405, 426, 427, 431, 461, 584, 586, 602 n. 58, 610 n. 129, 628 n. 371, 631 n. 441.
Wills Woods, 77, 110, 167, 169, 169, 239, 247, 254, 270, 386, 429, 432, 450, 554, 586, 675 n. 396.
Winchester, Va., 11, 16, 30, 283, 563.
Winegar's NY Battery, 524, 536.
Winkler, Capt. Fred, 307, 308.
Winn, Lt. Col. D.R.E., 288, 577.
WISCONSIN TROOPS: 2nd Inf., 94, 101, 121, 141, 142, 145, 148, 149, 151-156, 169-161, 167, 169, 172, 342, 350, 366, 368-371, 394, 399, 403, 413, 414, 456, 458, 472, 570, 626 n. 328, 630 n. 429.; 6th Inf., 90, 93, 94, 101, 110, 121, 121-126, 128-133, 135-140, 143, 153, 162, 167, 169, 192, 194, 214, 254, 342, 431, 433-435, 442, 444, 445, 447, 457, 458, 473, 474, 477, 488, 553, 559, 570, 586, 592, 614 n. 34, 622 n. 232, 623 n. 257, 623 n. 266.; 7th Inf., 94, 102, 148, 150-152, 154, 156, 158-161, 167n 169, 342, 350, 366, 368-371, 373, 375, 377, 385, 394, 399, 413, 459, 570, 592, 671 n. 319.; 26th Inf., 100 265, 286, 296, 298, 301, 317, 574, 665 n. 144.
Wister, Col. Langhorne, 173, 208, 245-247, 250, 373, 375, 377, 380, 384, 572, 665 n. 143.
Witcher, Lt. Col. W.A., 253.
Wolf Hill, 535-539, 583.
Wolf, Rev. E.J., 373-376.
Woollard, Capt. Leander, 111, 125, 138, 139.
Wright, Brig. Gen. A.R., 503.
Wrightsville, Pa., 11-13, 21, 595 n. 2.
Wybourn, Sgt. William A., 117, 118, 169, 170.

Young, Lt. Lewis, 24-31, 349.
York, Pa., 12-16, 21, 34, 38, 48, 50, 53, 54, 56, 101, 211, 268, 520, 527.

Zimmerman's S.C. Battery, 70, 580, 594 n. 131.